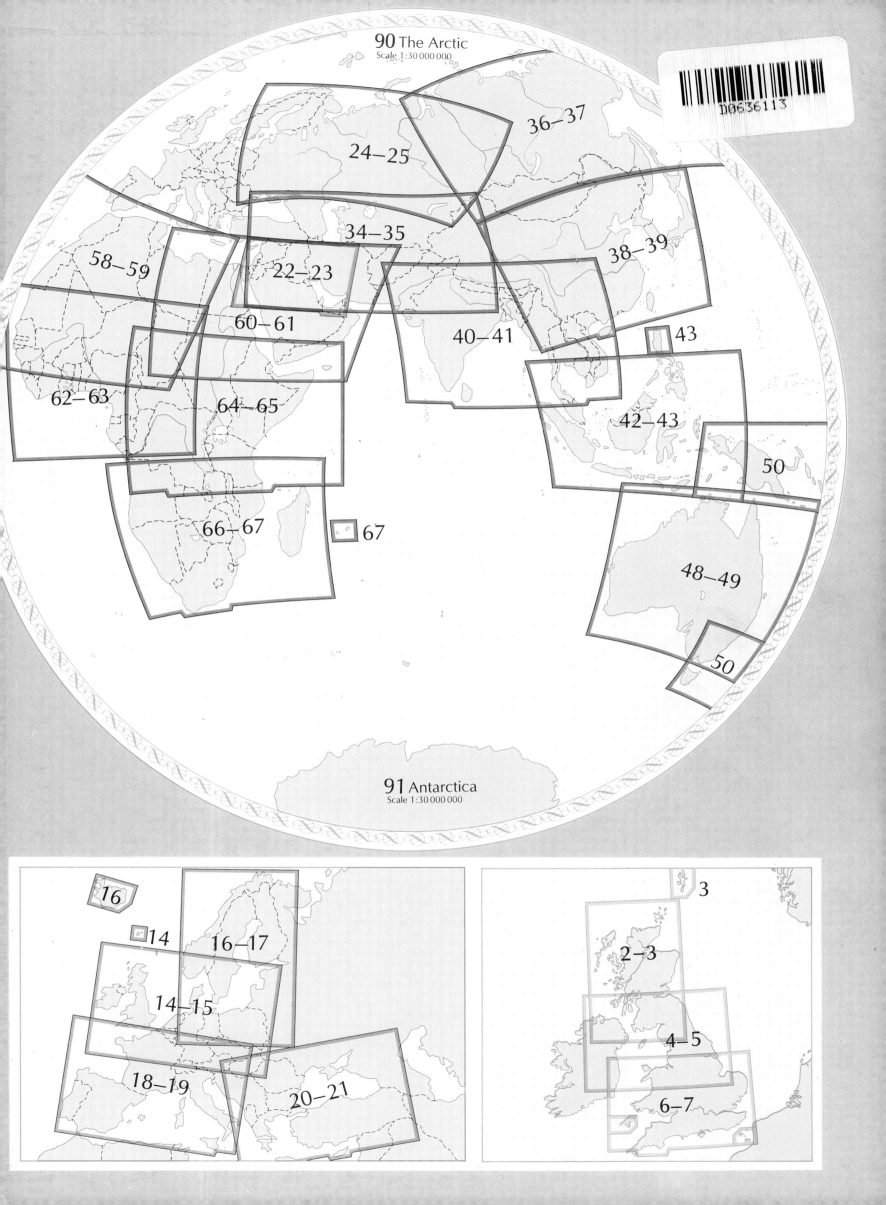

90 The Arctic
Scale 1:30 000 000

36–37

24–25

58–59

34–35

22–23

38–39

60–61

40–41

43

62–63

64–65

42–43

50

66–67

67

48–49

50

91 Antarctica
Scale 1:30 000 000

16

14

16–17

14–15

18–19

20–21

3

2–3

4–5

6–7

The Daily Telegraph

WORLD ATLAS

Published by Telegraph Publications,
Peterborough Court, At South Quay,
181 Marsh Wall, London E14 9SR

©Esselte Map Service AB, Stockholm, Sweden

First published 1988

Designed, edited, drawn and reproduced
by cartographers, geographers, artists
and technicians at ESSELTE MAP SERVICE.

British Library Cataloguing in Publication Data
The Daily Telegraph World Atlas.
  1. World Atlases
  912

ISBN 0-86367-241-8

Printed in Sweden

FOREWORD

In recent decades, the World appears to have become smaller and in many ways less mysterious. Air travel has brought different parts of the globe effectively closer. International telephone dialling provides instant long-distance communications, and television, radio and newspapers provide snapshots of events worldwide as they happen. An earthquake in Mexico, a drought in Ethiopia, a nuclear accident in Chernobyl – the day-to-day life of faraway places is brought vividly into our living rooms.

Our perception of the World is therefore conditioned largely by what we see. And it is in this context that a high-calibre atlas provides the essential overview, the framework on which a fuller understanding of the World around us can be based. We believe that by using a new, revolutionary approach to cartography, *The Daily Telegraph World Atlas* gives an insight into the life of the planet that today's readers require.

We have taken advantage of the great strides made in space technology and in particular the incredible detail supplied by satellite imagery and satellite photography to compile maps which relate the physical variations of the Earth's surface to the type of landscape and land-use found there. This exciting technique – often referred to as environmental mapping – surpasses traditional mapping by presenting more information at a glance with far greater clarity. One has only to compare this atlas with any other traditional physical atlas to see that we are now at the start of a new era in atlas publishing.

Christopher Milsome
Publishing Director

THE WORLD IN MAPS

UNITED KINGDOM

Scotland   2–3
Environment

Northern England and Northern Ireland   4–5
Environment

Wales, Central and Southern England   6–7
Environment

United Kingdom   8
Population

United Kingdom   9
Industrial employment and energy

EUROPE

Europe   10–11
Population, political divisions, environment

Europe   12–13
Organic and inorganic production, climate, soils

The British Isles and Central Europe   14–15
Belgium, Czechoslovakia, Federal Republic of Germany, German Democratic Republic, Luxembourg, The Netherlands, Poland

Northern Europe   16–17
Denmark, Finland, Iceland, Norway, Sweden

South-West Europe   18–19
Austria, France, Italy, Liechtenstein, Portugal, Spain, Switzerland, Yugoslavia

The Balkans   20–21
Bulgaria, Cyprus, Greece, Hungary, Romania, Turkey

Near East   22–23

Western Soviet Union   24–25
European USSR, Western Siberia

ASIA

Northern Asia   26–27
Environment

Southern Asia   28–29
Environment

Asia   30–31
Organic and inorganic production, climate, soils

Asia   32–33
Physical, precipitation, temperature, population, political divisions

The Middle East   34–35
Afghanistan, Iran, Pakistan

Eastern Soviet Union   36–37
Eastern Siberia, Mongolia

China and Japan   38–39
Incl. Mongolia, North Korea, South Korea, Taiwan

India and South-East Asia   40–41
Incl. Bangladesh, Bhutan, Burma, Kampuchea, Laos, Nepal, Sri Lanka, Thailand, Vietnam

The East Indies   42–43
Brunei, Indonesia, Malaysia, Philippines

AUSTRALIA

Australasia   44–45
Population, political divisions, environment

Australasia   46–47
Organic and inorganic production, climate, soils

Australia   48–49

New Guinea and New Zealand   50–51

Oceania   52–53
Melanesia, Micronesia, Polynesia

AFRICA

Africa   **54–55**
Population, political divisions, environment

Africa   **56–57**
Organic and inorganic production, climate, soils

North-West Africa   **58–59**
Algeria, Libya, Morocco, Mauretania, Niger, Tunisia

The Nile Valley and Arabia **60–61**
Bahrain, Egypt, Iraq, Israel, Jordan, Kuwait, Lebanon, Oman, Qatar, Saudi-Arabia, Southern Yemen, Sudan, Syria, United Arab Emirates, Yemen

West Africa   **62–63**
Benin, Burkina, Cameroon, Chad, Congo, Equatorial Guinea, Gabon, The Gambia, Ghana, Guinea, Guinea-Bissau, Ivory Coast, Liberia, Mali, Niger, Nigeria, Sao Tomé and Principe, Senegal, Sierra Leone, Togo

East Africa   **64–65**
Central Africa, Ethiopia, Kenya, Sudan, Tanzania, Uganda, Zaire

Central and Southern   **66–67**
Africa
Angola, Botswana, Comoros, Madagascar, Malawi, Mauritius, Mozambique, Namibia, Lesotho, South Africa, Swaziland, Zambia, Zimbabwe

NORTH AMERICA

North America   **68–69**
Population, political divisions, environment

North America   **70–71**
Organic and inorganic production, climate, soils

Alaska and Western   **72–73**
Canada
incl. the Aleutian Islands

Eastern Canada   **74–75**

The United States   **76–77**
incl. Mexico

Central America and   **78–79**
the West Indies
Belize, The Caribbean Archipelago, Costa Rica, Cuba, El Salvador, Guatemala, Honduras, Mexico, Nicaragua

SOUTH AMERICA

South America   **80–81**
Population, political divisions, environment

South America   **82–83**
Organic and inorganic production, climate, soils

South America, north   **84–85**
Brazil, Colombia, Ecuador, Guyana, Panama, Peru, Surinam, Venezuela

South America, central   **86–87**
Bolivia, Brazil, Chile, Peru

South America, south   **88–89**
Argentina, Bolivia, Brazil, Chile, Paraguay, Uruguay

THE ARCTIC AND ANTARCTIC

The Arctic   **90**
Environment

Antarctica   **91**
Environment

THE WORLD

The World   **92–93**
Environment

The World   **94–95**
Climate

The World   **96–97**
Geology

The World   **98–99**
Oceans and the ocean floor

The World   **100–101**
Population

The World   **102–103**
Political divisions

The World   **104–105**
Energy

The World   **106**
Languages, religions, time zones

Glossary, Index   **107–202**

Tundra

Coniferous forest

Mixed forest

Arable land

Grassland, pasture

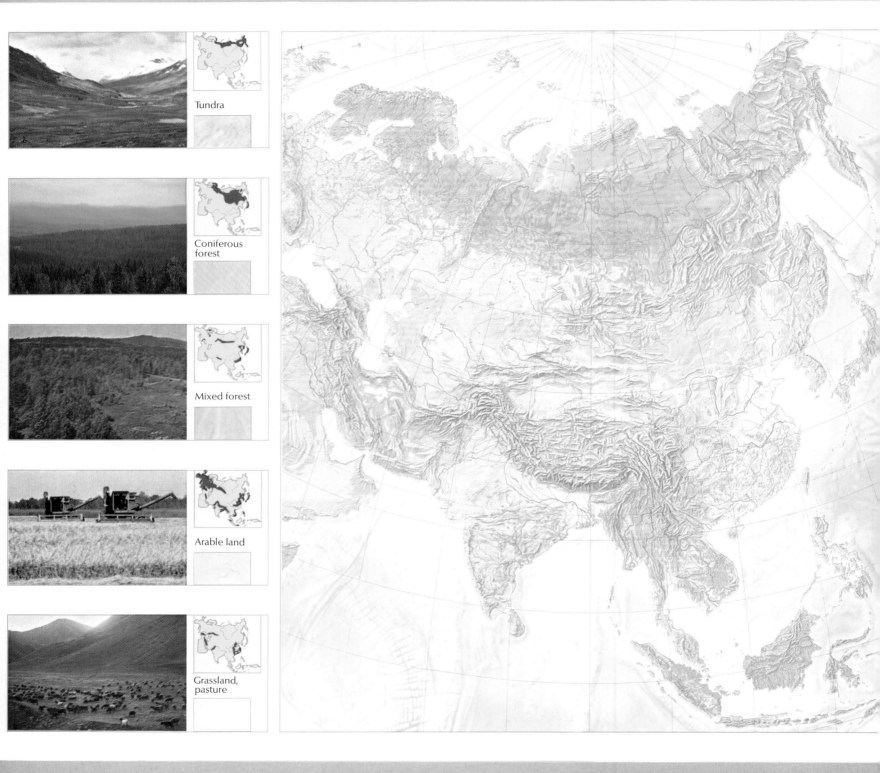

Semi-desert, Steppe

Other desert

Sand desert

Mountain

Tropical rain forest

THE WORLD
in maps

A map is a representation of the face of the Earth. It lacks, however, the realism of an aerial photograph: mountains, rivers, seas and cities are indicated by signs and colours. The Earth's surface, in all its endless variety, has to be sorted and arranged so that it may be presented in a form that is easily understood. In the past, cartography has perhaps been a little too abstract; most people will recall the traditional school atlas where the lowland Sahara was shown in lush green, while upland Africa's rich vegetation was represented in parched brown; the map gave no intimation of the specific characteristics of the landscape with its forests and grasslands, its deserts and cultivated plains.

Satellite imagery and photographs of the Earth taken from space have inspired a new era in cartography. Now the surface of the Earth can be shown as a series of interrelated environments. Each type of environment is represented by a particular colour which allows the reader to see land-use at a glance. Hill shading reveals the undulations of upland and mountainous areas. Settlement patterns, communications and administrative divisions are overprinted to give the user as clear a picture of our planet as is possible in two dimensions. The colour is superb – not only are these maps easy to read, they are also beautiful to behold.

The key on the left indicates the main classes into which different environments have been grouped. Certain specific environments not shown here have their own unique colour classification. A complete display of all the classes can be found inside the back cover. It should be noted that the British Isles has a separate series of colour classifications which is also displayed inside the back cover.

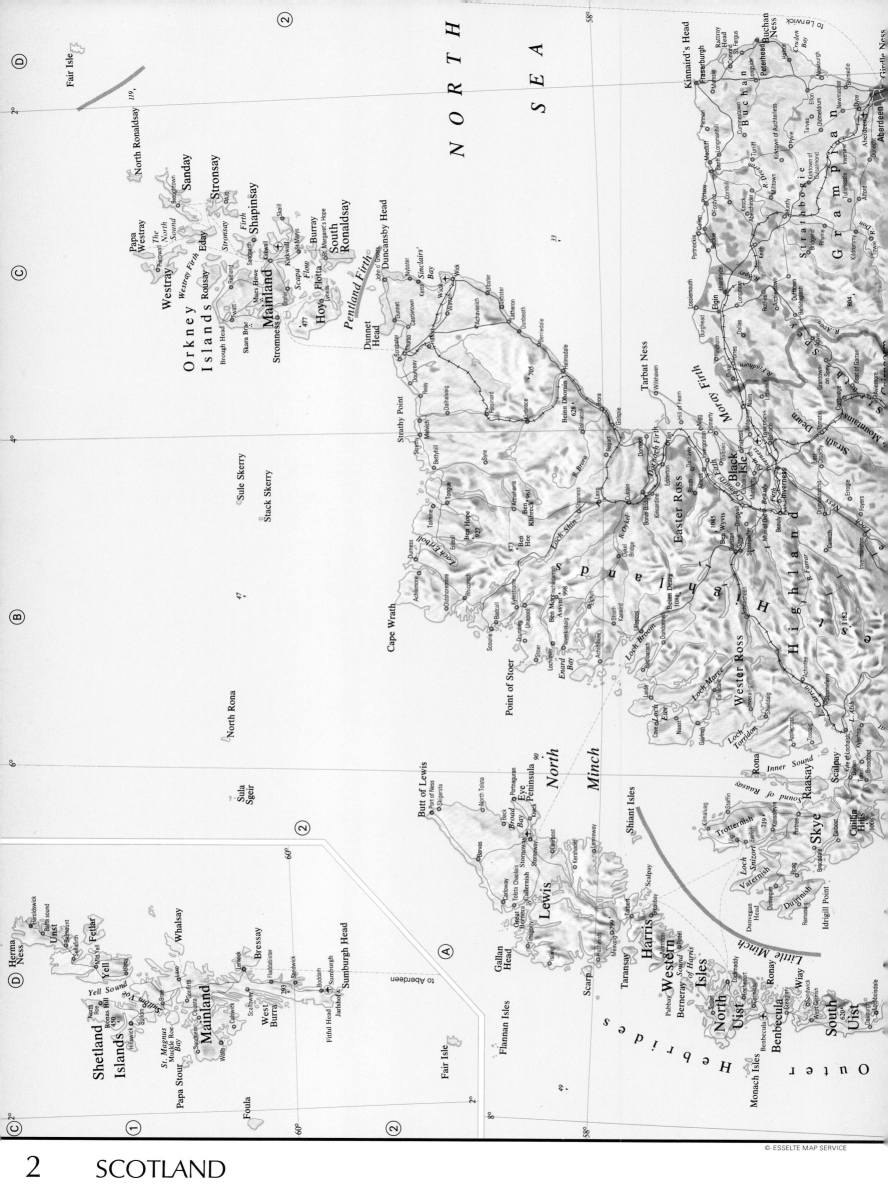

2   SCOTLAND

Scale 1:1 250 000

0 10 20 30 40 50 km
0   10   20   30 miles

3

Scale 1:1 250 000

0 10 20 30 50km
0   10   20   30 miles

5

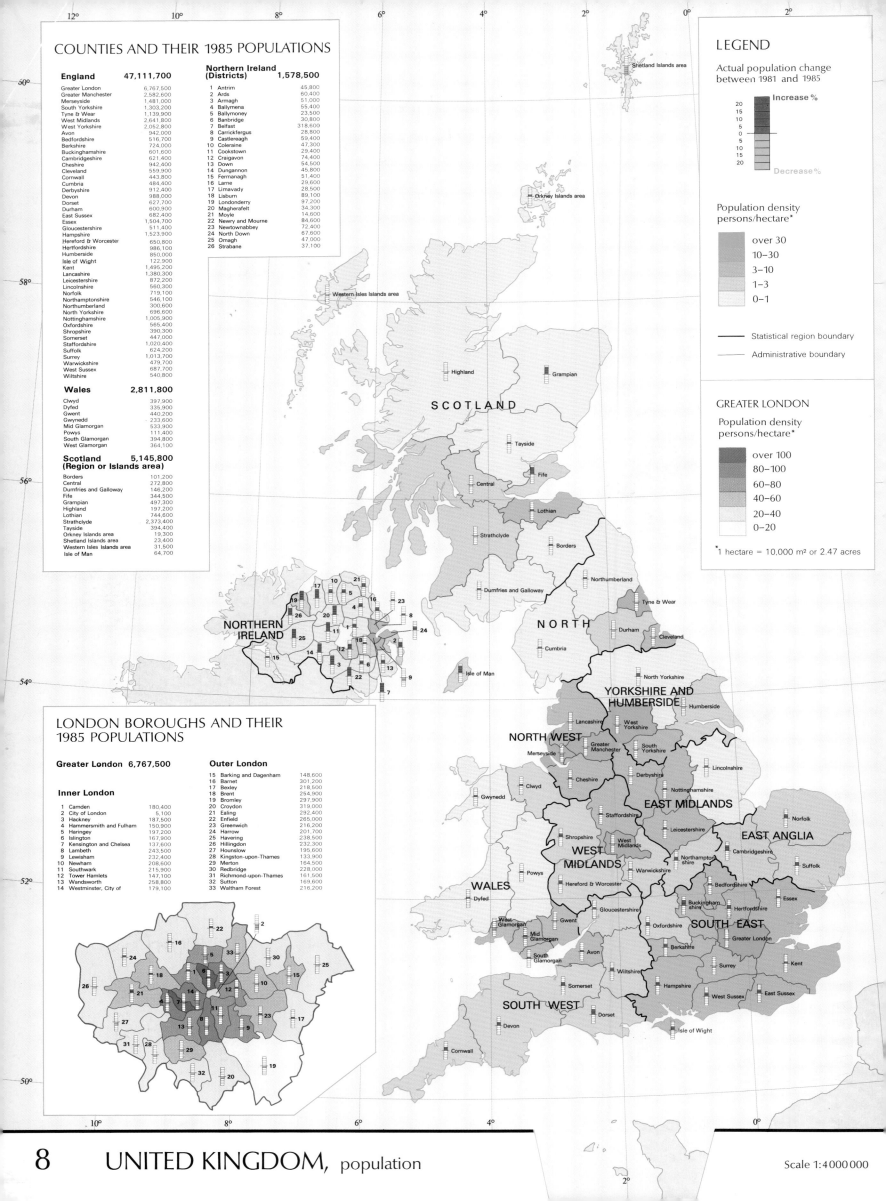

COUNTIES AND THEIR 1985 POPULATIONS

England	47,111,700
Greater London	6,767,500
Greater Manchester	2,582,600
Merseyside	1,481,000
South Yorkshire	1,303,200
Tyne & Wear	1,139,900
West Midlands	2,641,800
West Yorkshire	2,052,800
Avon	942,000
Bedfordshire	516,700
Berkshire	724,000
Buckinghamshire	601,600
Cambridgeshire	621,400
Cheshire	942,400
Cleveland	559,900
Cornwall	443,800
Cumbria	484,400
Derbyshire	912,400
Devon	988,000
Dorset	627,700
Durham	600,900
East Sussex	682,400
Essex	1,504,700
Gloucestershire	511,400
Hampshire	1,523,900
Hereford & Worcester	650,800
Hertfordshire	986,100
Humberside	850,000
Isle of Wight	122,900
Kent	1,495,200
Lancashire	1,380,300
Leicestershire	872,200
Lincolnshire	560,300
Norfolk	719,100
Northamptonshire	546,100
Northumberland	300,600
North Yorkshire	696,600
Nottinghamshire	1,005,900
Oxfordshire	565,400
Shropshire	390,300
Somerset	447,000
Staffordshire	1,020,400
Suffolk	624,200
Surrey	1,013,700
Warwickshire	479,700
West Sussex	687,700
Wiltshire	540,800

Northern Ireland (Districts)	1,578,500
1 Antrim	45,800
2 Ards	60,400
3 Armagh	51,000
4 Ballymena	55,400
5 Ballymoney	23,500
6 Banbridge	30,800
7 Belfast	318,600
8 Carrickfergus	28,800
9 Castlereagh	59,400
10 Coleraine	47,300
11 Cookstown	29,400
12 Craigavon	74,400
13 Down	54,500
14 Dungannon	45,800
15 Fermanagh	51,400
16 Larne	29,600
17 Limavady	28,500
18 Lisburn	89,100
19 Londonderry	97,200
20 Magherafelt	34,300
21 Moyle	14,600
22 Newry and Mourne	84,600
23 Newtownabbey	72,400
24 North Down	67,600
25 Omagh	47,000
26 Strabane	37,100

Wales	2,811,800
Clwyd	397,900
Dyfed	335,900
Gwent	440,200
Gwynedd	233,600
Mid Glamorgan	533,900
Powys	111,400
South Glamorgan	394,800
West Glamorgan	364,100

Scotland (Region or Islands area)	5,145,800
Borders	101,200
Central	272,800
Dumfries and Galloway	146,200
Fife	344,500
Grampian	497,300
Highland	197,200
Lothian	744,600
Strathclyde	2,373,400
Tayside	394,400
Orkney Islands area	19,300
Shetland Islands area	23,400
Western Isles Islands area	31,500
Isle of Man	64,700

LONDON BOROUGHS AND THEIR 1985 POPULATIONS

Greater London 6,767,500

Inner London

1 Camden	180,400
2 City of London	5,100
3 Hackney	187,500
4 Hammersmith and Fulham	150,900
5 Haringey	197,200
6 Islington	167,900
7 Kensington and Chelsea	137,600
8 Lambeth	243,500
9 Lewisham	232,400
10 Newham	208,600
11 Southwark	215,900
12 Tower Hamlets	147,100
13 Wandsworth	258,800
14 Westminster, City of	179,100

Outer London

15 Barking and Dagenham	148,600
16 Barnet	301,200
17 Bexley	218,500
18 Brent	254,900
19 Bromley	297,900
20 Croydon	319,000
21 Ealing	292,400
22 Enfield	265,000
23 Greenwich	216,200
24 Harrow	201,700
25 Havering	238,500
26 Hillingdon	232,300
27 Hounslow	195,600
28 Kingston-upon-Thames	133,900
29 Merton	164,500
30 Redbridge	228,000
31 Richmond-upon-Thames	161,500
32 Sutton	169,600
33 Waltham Forest	216,200

LEGEND

Actual population change between 1981 and 1985

20 / 15 / 10 / 5 / 0 — Increase %
5 / 10 / 15 / 20 — Decrease %

Population density persons/hectare*

- over 30
- 10–30
- 3–10
- 1–3
- 0–1

——— Statistical region boundary
——— Administrative boundary

GREATER LONDON

Population density persons/hectare*

- over 100
- 80–100
- 60–80
- 40–60
- 20–40
- 0–20

*1 hectare = 10,000 m² or 2.47 acres

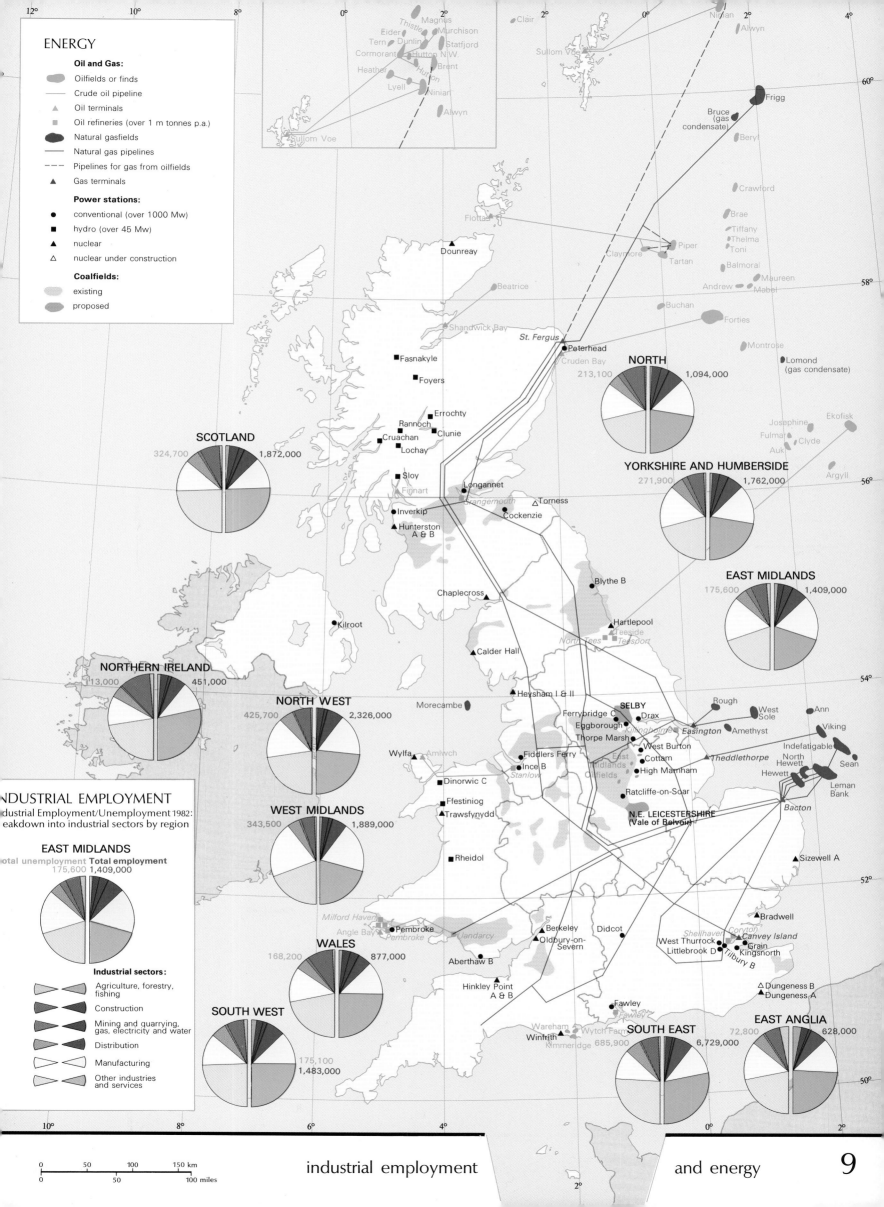

ENERGY

Oil and Gas:

- Oilfields or finds
- Crude oil pipeline
- ▲ Oil terminals
- ■ Oil refineries (over 1 m tonnes p.a.)
- Natural gasfields
- Natural gas pipelines
- Pipelines for gas from oilfields
- ▲ Gas terminals

Power stations:

- ● conventional (over 1000 Mw)
- ■ hydro (over 45 Mw)
- ▲ nuclear
- △ nuclear under construction

Coalfields:

- existing
- proposed

INDUSTRIAL EMPLOYMENT

Industrial Employment/Unemployment 1982:
breakdown into industrial sectors by region

EAST MIDLANDS

Total unemployment 175,600 Total employment 1,409,000

Industrial sectors:

- Agriculture, forestry, fishing
- Construction
- Mining and quarrying, gas, electricity and water
- Distribution
- Manufacturing
- Other industries and services

Map labels

Magnus, Murchison, Thistle, Eider, Dunlin, Statfjord, Tern, Hutton N.W., Cormorant, Heather, Hutton, Brent, Lyell, Ninian, Alwyn, Clair, Ninian, Alwyn, Frigg, Bruce (gas condensate), Beryl, Crawford, Brae, Tiffany, Thelma, Toni, Balmoral, Maureen, Andrew, Mabel, Sullom Voe, Flotta, Claymore, Piper, Tartan, Buchan, Forties, Montrose, Lomond (gas condensate), Josephine, Fulmar, Ekofisk, Auk, Clyde, Argyll

Dounreay, Beatrice, Shandwick Bay, St. Fergus, Peterhead, Cruden Bay, Fasnakyle, Foyers, Errochty, Rannoch, Clunie, Cruachan, Lochay, Sloy, Finnart, Longannet, Grangemouth, Torness, Cockenzie, Inverkip, Hunterston A & B

Chaplecross, Blythe B, Hartlepool, Teeside, Teesport, North Tees, Calder Hall, Kilroot, Heysham I & II, Morecambe, Ferrybridge C, Drax, Eggborough, Easington, West Sole, Ann, Amethyst, Viking, Thorpe Marsh, West Burton, Selby, Keadby, Indefatigable, North Hewett, Sean, Hewett, Leman Bank, Wylfa, Amlwch, Fiddlers Ferry, Ince B, Stanlow, Cottam, High Marnham, Dinorwic C, Ffestiniog, Trawsfynydd, Ratcliffe-on-Soar, N.E. Leicestershire (Vale of Belvoir), Bacton, Rheidol, Sizewell A

Milford Haven, Angle Bay, Pembroke, Llandarcy, Berkeley, Oldbury-on-Severn, Didcot, Shellhaven, Coryton, Canvey Island, West Thurrock, Grain, Littlebrook D, Tilbury B, Kingsnorth, Aberthaw B, Bradwell, Hinkley Point A & B, Fawley, Dungeness B, Dungeness A, Wareham, Wytch Farm, Winfrith, Kimmeridge

Region employment figures

- NORTH 213,100 / 1,094,000
- YORKSHIRE AND HUMBERSIDE 271,900 / 1,762,000
- EAST MIDLANDS 175,600 / 1,409,000
- SCOTLAND 324,700 / 1,872,000
- NORTHERN IRELAND 113,000 / 451,000
- NORTH WEST 425,700 / 2,326,000
- WEST MIDLANDS 343,500 / 1,889,000
- WALES 168,200 / 877,000
- SOUTH WEST 175,100 / 1,483,000
- SOUTH EAST 685,900 / 6,729,000
- EAST ANGLIA 72,800 / 628,000

Scale

0 50 100 150 km
0 50 100 miles

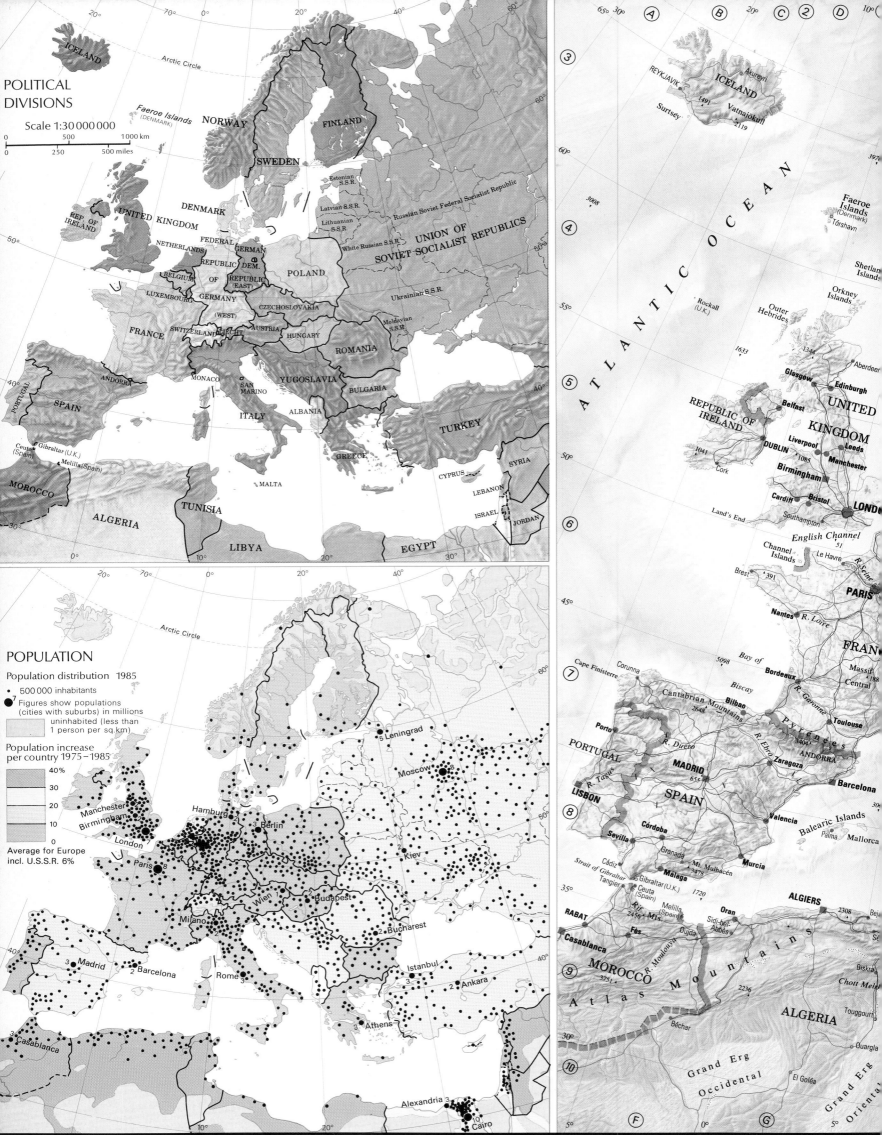

POLITICAL DIVISIONS

Scale 1:30 000 000

0   500   1000 km
0   250   500 miles

ICELAND

Arctic Circle

Faeroe Islands (DENMARK)

NORWAY

FINLAND

SWEDEN

Estonian S.S.R.

Latvian S.S.R.

Lithuanian S.S.R.

White Russian S.S.R.

Russian Soviet Federal Socialist Republic

UNION OF SOVIET SOCIALIST REPUBLICS

DENMARK

REP OF IRELAND

UNITED KINGDOM

NETHERLANDS

FEDERAL REPUBLIC OF GERMANY (WEST)

GERMAN DEM. REPUBLIC (EAST)

POLAND

Ukrainian S.S.R.

BELGIUM

LUXEMBOURG

CZECHOSLOVAKIA

Moldavian S.S.R.

FRANCE

SWITZERLAND

LIECHT.

AUSTRIA

HUNGARY

ROMANIA

ANDORRA

MONACO

SAN MARINO

YUGOSLAVIA

BULGARIA

PORTUGAL

SPAIN

ITALY

ALBANIA

TURKEY

GREECE

Ceuta (Spain)

Gibraltar (U.K.)

Melilla (Spain)

MALTA

CYPRUS

SYRIA

LEBANON

ISRAEL

JORDAN

MOROCCO

ALGERIA

TUNISIA

LIBYA

EGYPT

POPULATION

Population distribution 1985

•   500 000 inhabitants

• 7   Figures show populations (cities with suburbs) in millions

uninhabited (less than 1 person per sq. km)

Population increase per country 1975-1985

40%
30
20
10
0

Average for Europe incl. U.S.S.R. 6%

Arctic Circle

Manchester

Birmingham

London

Hamburg

Berlin

5 Leningrad

Moscow 8

Paris 8

Wien

Budapest

2 Kiev

Milano

Bucharest

3 Madrid

2 Barcelona

Rome 3

Istanbul

3

2 Ankara

3 Athens

3 Casablanca

Alexandria 3

Cairo 10

ATLANTIC OCEAN

REYKJAVIK

ICELAND

Akureyri

Surtsey

1491

Vatnajökull

2119

Faeroe Islands (Denmark)

Tórshavn

Rockall (U.K.)

Shetland Islands

Orkney Islands

Outer Hebrides

Aberdeen

Glasgow

Edinburgh

Belfast

UNITED KINGDOM

REPUBLIC OF IRELAND

DUBLIN

Liverpool

Leeds

Manchester

Cork

Birmingham

Cardiff

Bristol

LONDON

Land's End

Southampton

English Channel

51

Channel Islands

Le Havre

Brest

391

R. Seine

PARIS

Nantes

R. Loire

FRANCE

Cape Finisterre

Corunna

Bay of Biscay

5098

Massif Central

188

Bordeaux

R. Garonne

Cantabrian Mountains

Bilbao

2648

Pyrénées

Toulouse

Porto

R. Duero

3404

ANDORRA

PORTUGAL

MADRID

Zaragoza

R. Ebro

Barcelona

R. Tagus

SPAIN

LISBON

Valencia

Sevilla

Córdoba

Balearic Islands

Granada

Palma

Mallorca

Cádiz

Mt. Mulhacén

3478

Murcia

Strait of Gibraltar

Málaga

Gibraltar (U.K.)

Tangier

Ceuta (Spain)

1720

ALGIERS

RABAT

Rif Mts.

2456

Melilla (Spain)

Oran

Sidi-bel-Abbès

2308

Fès

Oujda

Casablanca

MOROCCO

R. Moulouya

3751

Atlas Mountains

2236

ALGERIA

Béchar

Biskra

Chott Mel

Touggourt

Grand Erg Occidental

El Goléa

Ouargla

Grand Erg Oriental

© ESSELTE MAP SERVICE

10   EUROPE, environment, political divisions, population

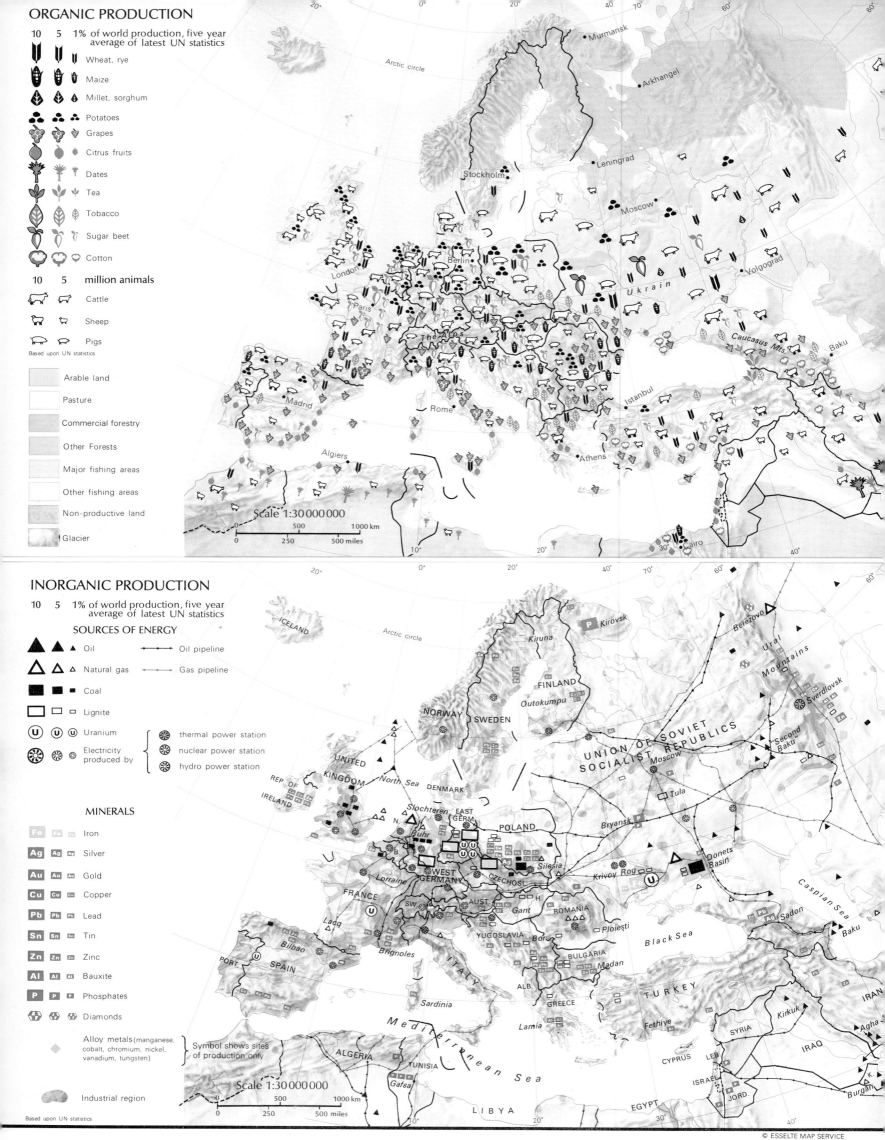

ORGANIC PRODUCTION

10 5 1% of world production, five year average of latest UN statistics

Wheat, rye
Maize
Millet, sorghum
Potatoes
Grapes
Citrus fruits
Dates
Tea
Tobacco
Sugar beet
Cotton

10 5 million animals

Cattle
Sheep
Pigs

Based upon UN statistics

Arable land
Pasture
Commercial forestry
Other Forests
Major fishing areas
Other fishing areas
Non-productive land
Glacier

Scale 1:30 000 000

| 0 | 500 | 1000 km |
| 0 | 250 | 500 miles |

INORGANIC PRODUCTION

10 5 1% of world production, five year average of latest UN statistics

SOURCES OF ENERGY

Oil   Oil pipeline
Natural gas   Gas pipeline
Coal
Lignite
U U U Uranium
Electricity produced by   thermal power station
                             nuclear power station
                             hydro power station

MINERALS

Fe Fe Fe Iron
Ag Ag Ag Silver
Au Au Au Gold
Cu Cu Cu Copper
Pb Pb Pb Lead
Sn Sn Sn Tin
Zn Zn Zn Zinc
Al Al Al Bauxite
P   P   P   Phosphates
Diamonds

Alloy metals (manganese, cobalt, chromium, nickel, vanadium, tungsten)

Symbol shows sites of production only

Industrial region

Based upon UN statistics

Scale 1:30 000 000

| 0 | 500 | 1000 km |
| 0 | 250 | 500 miles |

© ESSELTE MAP SERVICE

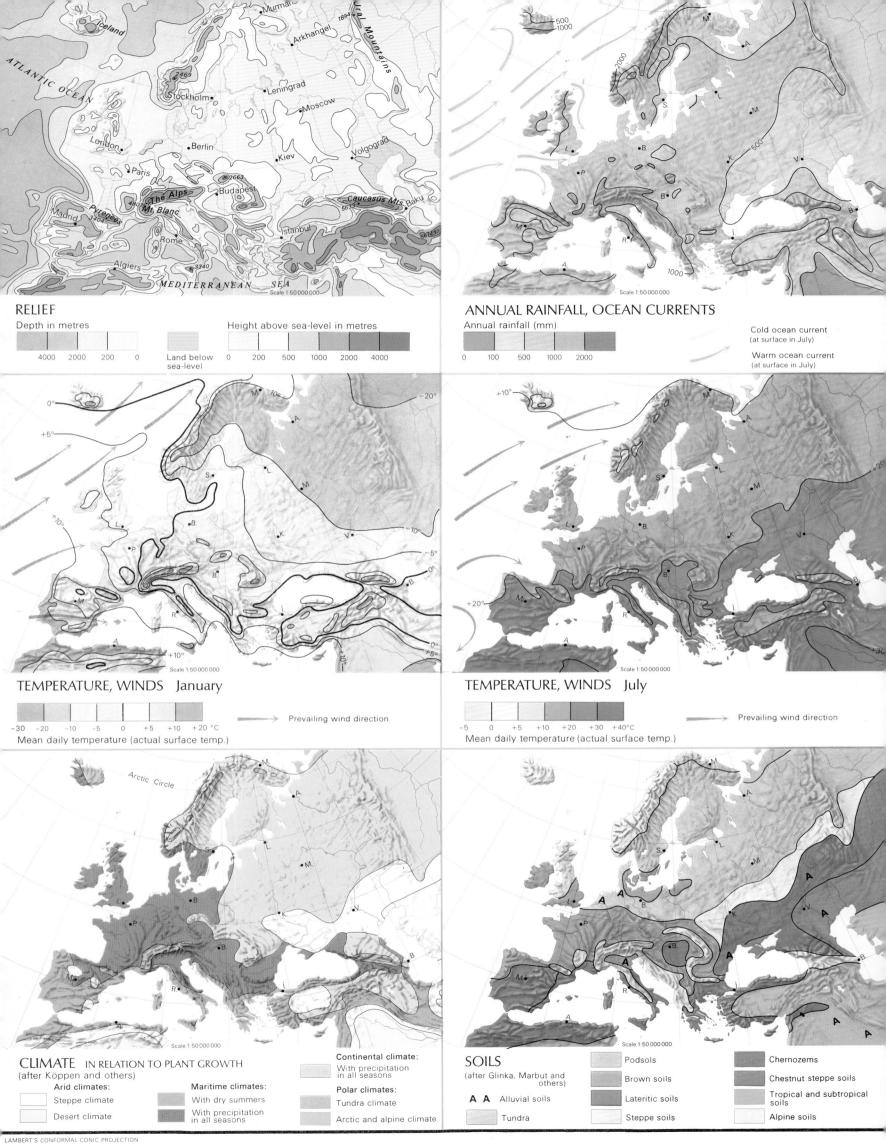

RELIEF

Depth in metres

4000 2000 200 0

Land below sea-level

Height above sea-level in metres

0 200 500 1000 2000 4000

Scale 1:50 000 000

ANNUAL RAINFALL, OCEAN CURRENTS

Annual rainfall (mm)

0 100 500 1000 2000

Cold ocean current
(at surface in July)

Warm ocean current
(at surface in July)

Scale 1:50 000 000

TEMPERATURE, WINDS   January

−30 −20 −10 −5 0 +5 +10 +20 °C

Mean daily temperature (actual surface temp.)

Prevailing wind direction

Scale 1:50 000 000

TEMPERATURE, WINDS   July

−5 0 +5 +10 +20 +30 +40°C

Mean daily temperature (actual surface temp.)

Prevailing wind direction

Scale 1:50 000 000

CLIMATE IN RELATION TO PLANT GROWTH
(after Köppen and others)

Arid climates:

Steppe climate

Desert climate

Maritime climates:

With dry summers

With precipitation in all seasons

Continental climate:

With precipitation in all seasons

Polar climates:

Tundra climate

Arctic and alpine climate

Scale 1:50 000 000

SOILS
(after Glinka, Marbut and others)

A A Alluvial soils

Tundra

Podsols

Brown soils

Lateritic soils

Steppe soils

Chernozems

Chestnut steppe soils

Tropical and subtropical soils

Alpine soils

© ESSELTE MAP SERVICE

Scale 1:5 000 000

0   100   200 km

0   50   100 miles

Scale 1:5 000 000

0   100   200 km

0   50   100 miles

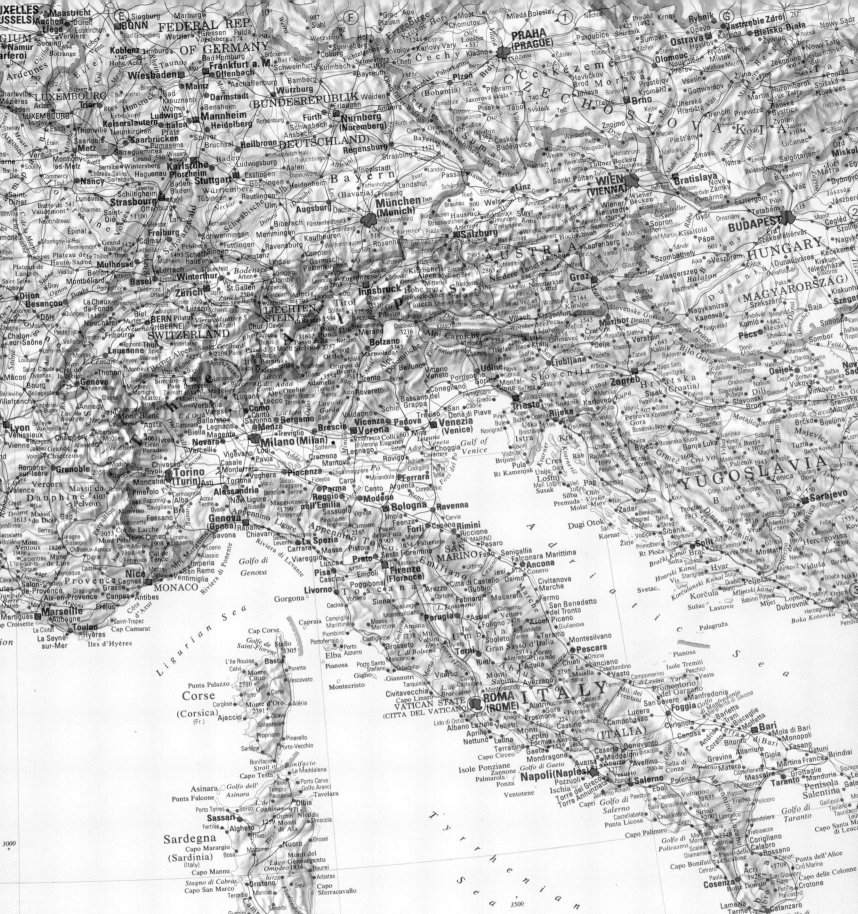

Scale 1:5 000 000

0   50   100 miles

0   100   200 km

21

© ESSELTE MAP SERVICE

© ESSELTE MAP SERVICE

LAMBERT'S AZIMUTHAL EQUAL-AREA PROJECTION

Scale 1:25 000 000

0	500	1000 km
0	200	400	600 miles

LAMBERT'S AZIMUTHAL EQUAL-AREA PROJECTION

Scale 1:25 000 000

0   500   1000 km

0   200   400   600 miles

29

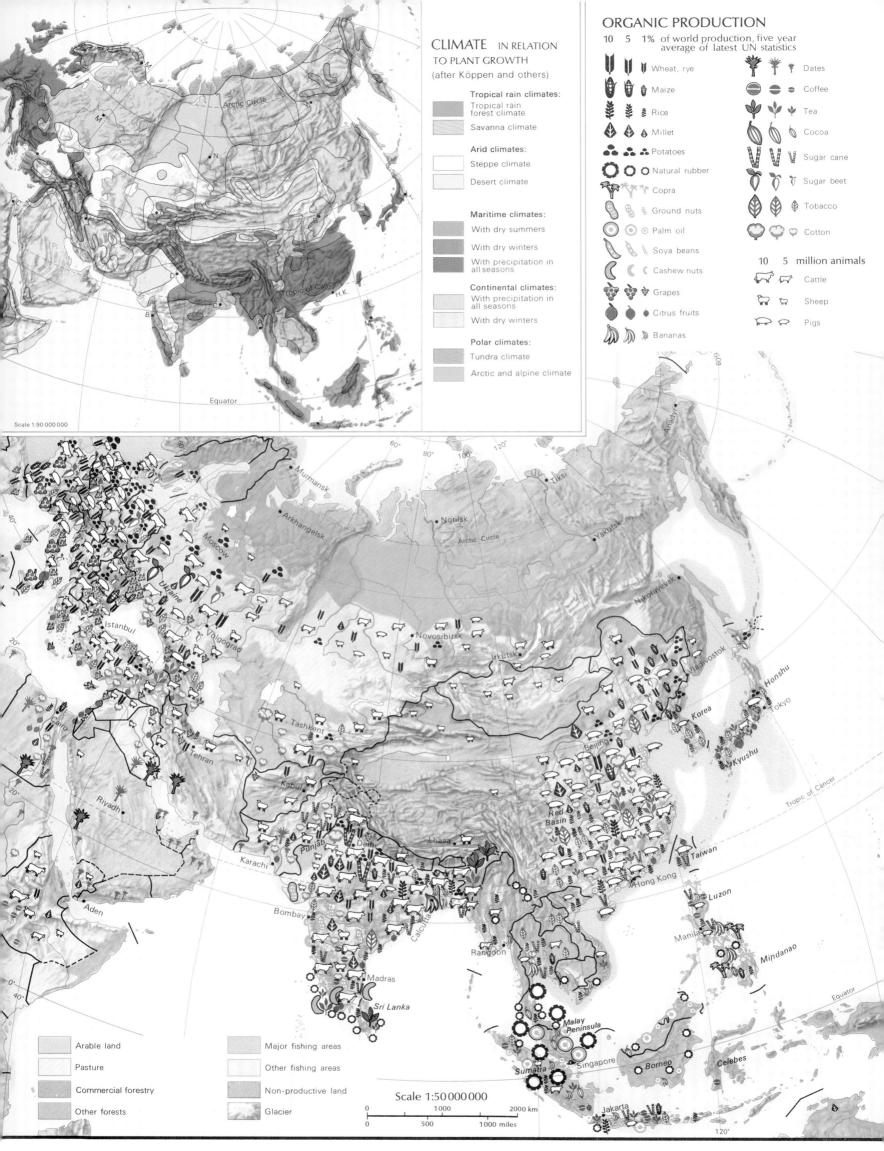

CLIMATE IN RELATION TO PLANT GROWTH
(after Köppen and others)

Tropical rain climates:
- Tropical rain forest climate
- Savanna climate

Arid climates:
- Steppe climate
- Desert climate

Maritime climates:
- With dry summers
- With dry winters
- With precipitation in all seasons

Continental climates:
- With precipitation in all seasons
- With dry winters

Polar climates:
- Tundra climate
- Arctic and alpine climate

Scale 1:90 000 000

ORGANIC PRODUCTION
10 5 1% of world production, five year average of latest UN statistics

- Wheat, rye
- Maize
- Rice
- Millet
- Potatoes
- Natural rubber
- Copra
- Ground nuts
- Palm oil
- Soya beans
- Cashew nuts
- Grapes
- Citrus fruits
- Bananas

- Dates
- Coffee
- Tea
- Cocoa
- Sugar cane
- Sugar beet
- Tobacco
- Cotton

10 5 million animals
- Cattle
- Sheep
- Pigs

Arable land
Pasture
Commercial forestry
Other forests

Major fishing areas
Other fishing areas
Non-productive land
Glacier

Scale 1:50 000 000

0 1000 2000 km
0 500 1000 miles

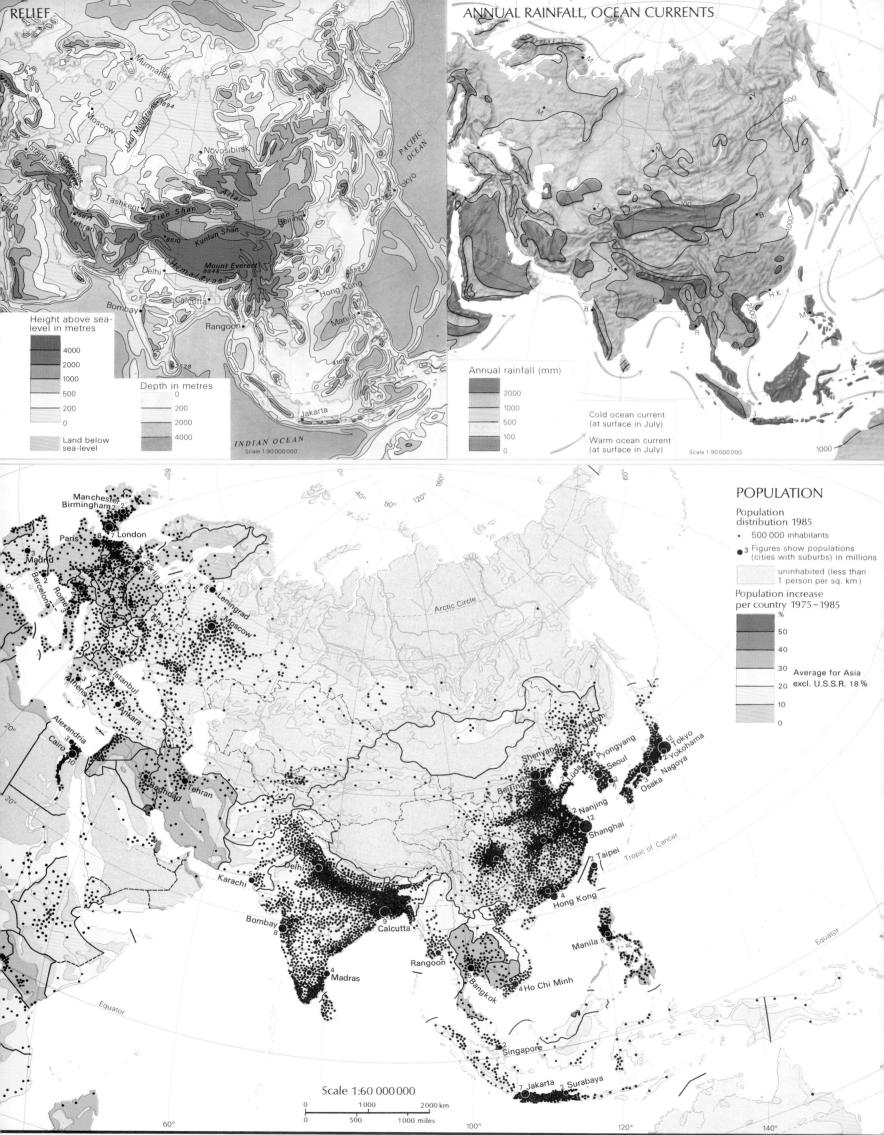

RELIEF

Murmansk

Moscow
Ural Mountains 1894

Novosibirsk

PACIFIC OCEAN

Istanbul
Cairo
Tehran 5671

Tashkent

Tien Shan
Altai

Beijing

Kunlun Shan
8610

Himalayas Mount Everest 8848

Tokyo

Delhi

Hong Kong

Bombay

Calcutta

Manila

Rangoon

8899

4101

2528

Jakarta

INDIAN OCEAN

Scale 1:90 000 000

Height above sea-level in metres

4000
2000
1000
500
200
0

Depth in metres

0
200
2000
4000

Land below sea-level

ANNUAL RAINFALL, OCEAN CURRENTS

M

M

Y

500

100

1000

B

D

C

B

H.K.

R

M

J

2000

1000

Annual rainfall (mm)

2000
1000
500
100
0

Cold ocean current (at surface in July)

Warm ocean current (at surface in July)

Scale 1:90 000 000

POPULATION

Population distribution 1985

• 500 000 inhabitants

● 3 Figures show populations (cities with suburbs) in millions

uninhabited (less than 1 person per sq. km)

Population increase per country 1975-1985

%
50
40
30
20
10
0

Average for Asia excl. U.S.S.R. 18%

Manchester
Birmingham 2
London 7
Paris 8
Madrid 3
Barcelona 2
Rome 3
Berlin
Leningrad 5
Kiev
Moscow
Athens 3
Istanbul
Ankara
Alexandria 3
Cairo 10
Baghdad 3
Tehran 6
Karachi 5
Delhi 5
Bombay 8
Calcutta 9
Madras 4
Rangoon 2
Bangkok 5
Ho Chi Minh 4
Singapore 2
Jakarta 7
Surabaya 2
Harbin
Shenyang
Beijing 4
Luda
Pyongyang
Seoul
Nanjing 2
Shanghai 12
Taipei 2
Hong Kong 4
Manila 6
Tokyo 12
Yokohama
Nagoya 2
Osaka 3

Arctic Circle

Tropic of Cancer

Equator

Equator

Scale 1:60 000 000

0   1000   2000 km
0   500   1000 miles

© ESSELTE MAP SERVICE

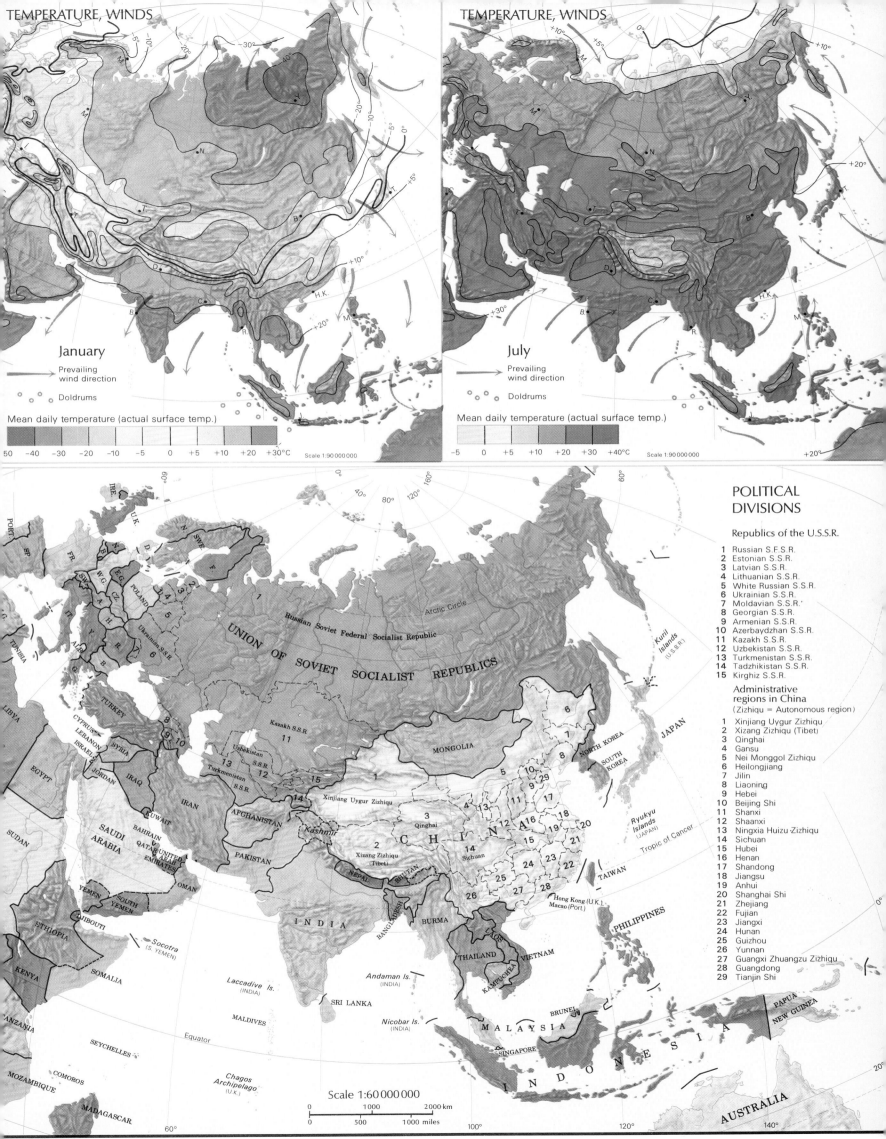

TEMPERATURE, WINDS

January

→ Prevailing wind direction
○ Doldrums

Mean daily temperature (actual surface temp.)

50 −40 −30 −20 −10 −5 0 +5 +10 +20 +30°C

Scale 1:90 000 000

TEMPERATURE, WINDS

July

→ Prevailing wind direction
○ Doldrums

Mean daily temperature (actual surface temp.)

−5 0 +5 +10 +20 +30 +40°C

Scale 1:90 000 000

POLITICAL DIVISIONS

Republics of the U.S.S.R.

1 Russian S.F.S.R.
2 Estonian S.S.R.
3 Latvian S.S.R.
4 Lithuanian S.S.R.
5 White Russian S.S.R.
6 Ukrainian S.S.R.
7 Moldavian S.S.R.
8 Georgian S.S.R.
9 Armenian S.S.R.
10 Azerbaydzhan S.S.R.
11 Kazakh S.S.R.
12 Uzbekistan S.S.R.
13 Turkmenistan S.S.R.
14 Tadzhikistan S.S.R.
15 Kirghiz S.S.R.

Administrative regions in China
(Zizhiqu = Autonomous region)

1 Xinjiang Uygur Zizhiqu
2 Xizang Zizhiqu (Tibet)
3 Qinghai
4 Gansu
5 Nei Monggol Zizhiqu
6 Heilongjiang
7 Jilin
8 Liaoning
9 Hebei
10 Beijing Shi
11 Shanxi
12 Shaanxi
13 Ningxia Huizu Zizhiqu
14 Sichuan
15 Hubei
16 Henan
17 Shandong
18 Jiangsu
19 Anhui
20 Shanghai Shi
21 Zhejiang
22 Fujian
23 Jiangxi
24 Hunan
25 Guizhou
26 Yunnan
27 Guangxi Zhuangzu Zizhiqu
28 Guangdong
29 Tianjin Shi

Scale 1:60 000 000

0 1000 2000 km
0 500 1000 miles

LAMBERT'S AZIMUTHAL EQUAL-AREA PROJECTION

THE MIDDLE EAST

© ESSELTE MAP SERVICE

Scale 1:10 000 000

0   100   200   300   400 km
0   100   200 miles

39

© ESSELTE MAP SERVICE

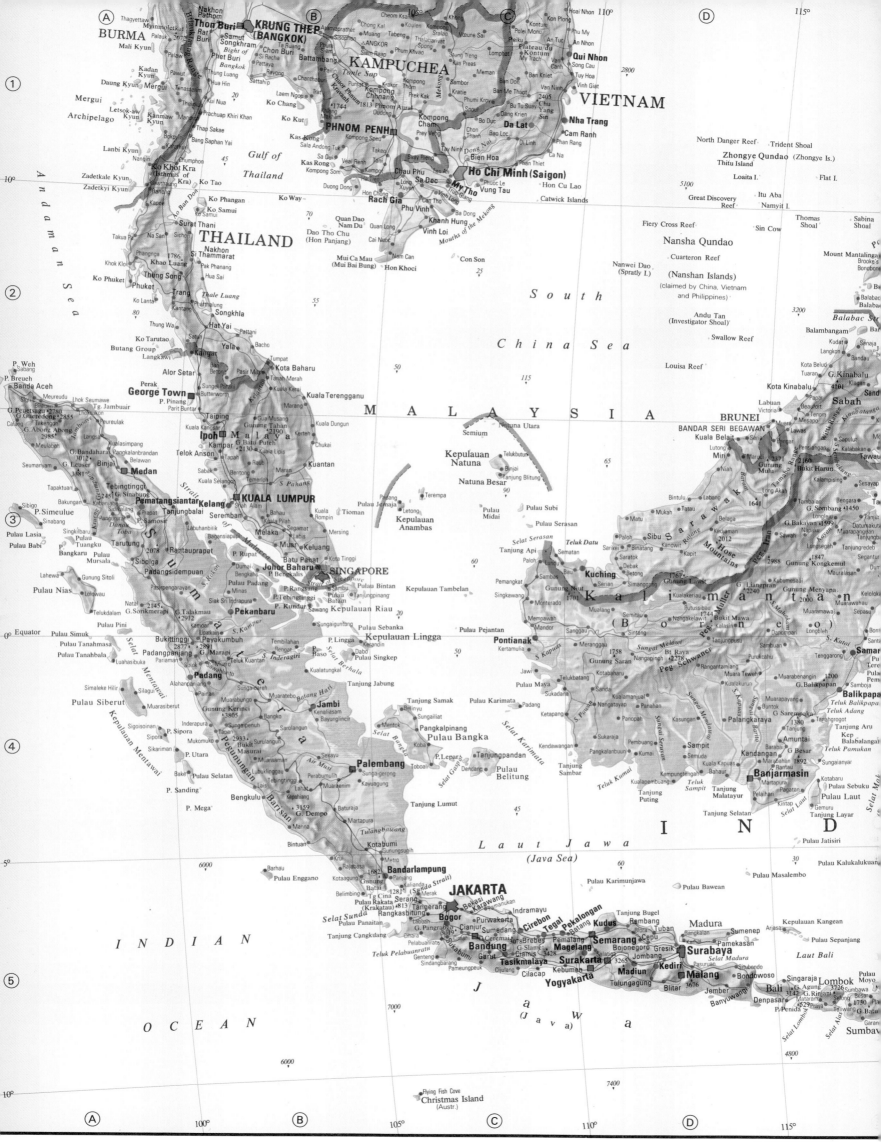

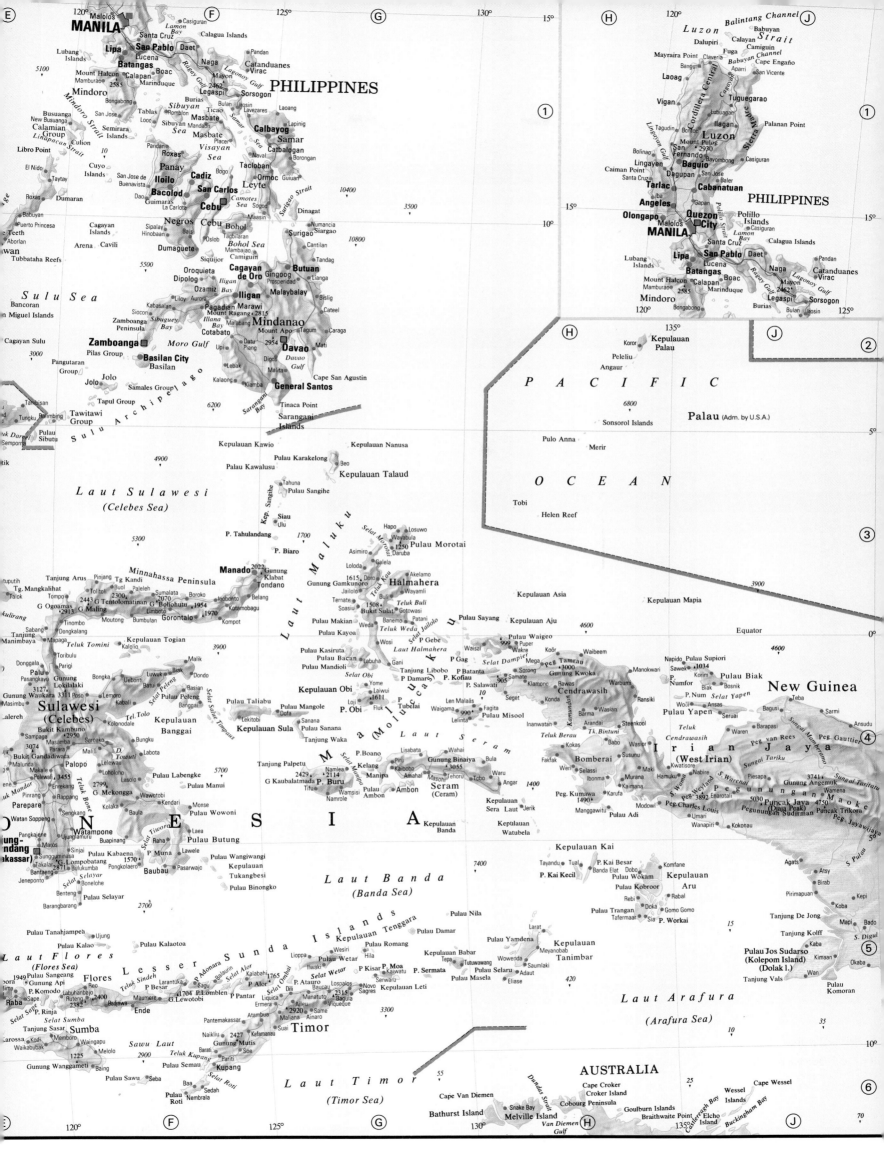

Scale 1:10 000 000

```
0    100   200   300   400 km
0         100        200 miles
```

43

POLITICAL DIVISIONS

Scale 1:60 000 000

POPULATION

Population distribution 1985

- 500 000 inhabitants
- Figures show populations (cities with suburbs) in millions
- uninhabited (less than 1 person per sq. km)

Population increase per country 1975–1985

0 10 20 30 40 50 % Average for Oceania 17%

44 AUSTRALASIA, environment, political divisions, population

LAMBERT'S AZIMUTHAL EQUAL-AREA PROJECTION

Scale 1:25 000 000

0 500 1000 km
0 200 400 600 miles

45

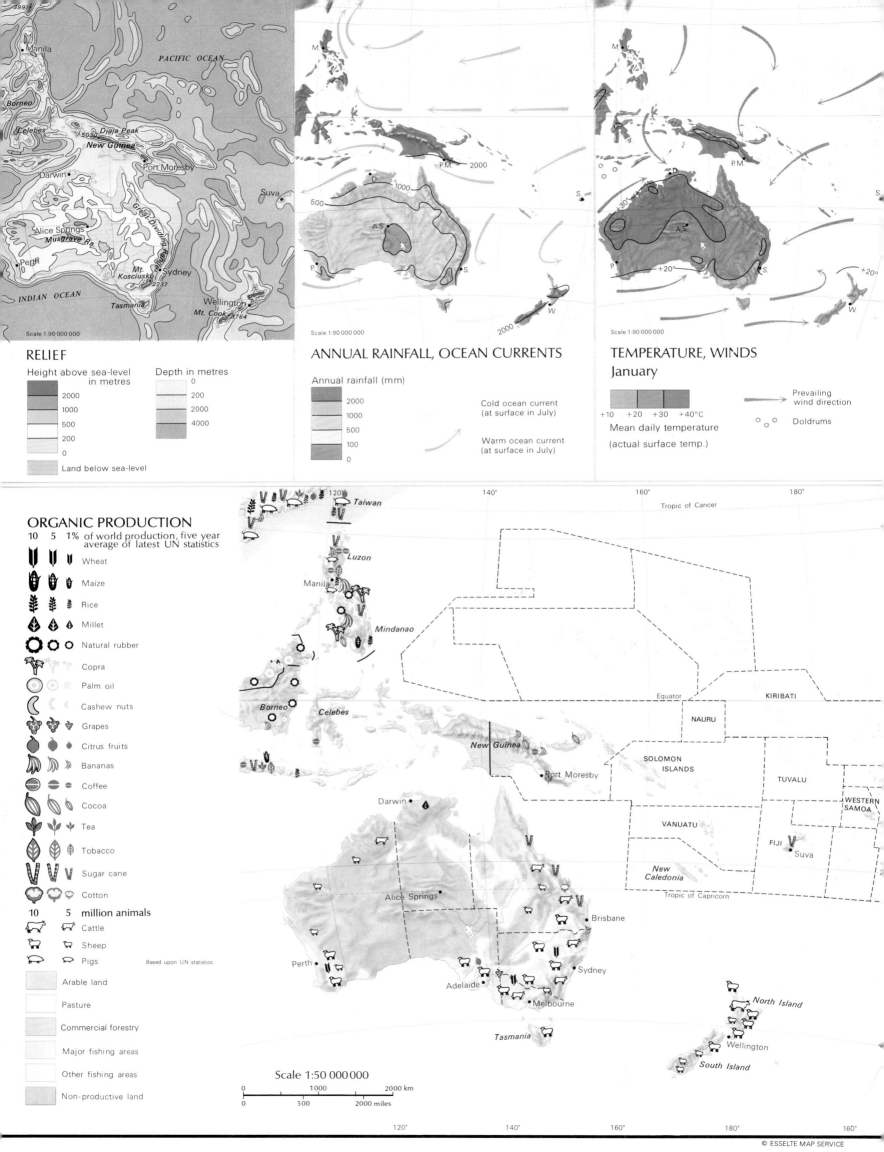

RELIEF

Height above sea-level
in metres

- 2000
- 1000
- 500
- 200
- 0

Land below sea-level

Depth in metres

- 0
- 200
- 2000
- 4000

Scale 1:90 000 000

ANNUAL RAINFALL, OCEAN CURRENTS

Annual rainfall (mm)

- 2000
- 1000
- 500
- 100
- 0

Cold ocean current
(at surface in July)

Warm ocean current
(at surface in July)

Scale 1:90 000 000

TEMPERATURE, WINDS
January

+10 +20 +30 +40°C

Mean daily temperature
(actual surface temp.)

Prevailing
wind direction

Doldrums

Scale 1:90 000 000

ORGANIC PRODUCTION

10 5 1% of world production, five year
average of latest UN statistics

- Wheat
- Maize
- Rice
- Millet
- Natural rubber
- Copra
- Palm oil
- Cashew nuts
- Grapes
- Citrus fruits
- Bananas
- Coffee
- Cocoa
- Tea
- Tobacco
- Sugar cane
- Cotton

10 5 million animals

- Cattle
- Sheep
- Pigs

Based upon UN statistics

- Arable land
- Pasture
- Commercial forestry
- Major fishing areas
- Other fishing areas
- Non-productive land

Scale 1:50 000 000

0   1000   2000 km
0   500   2000 miles

© ESSELTE MAP SERVICE

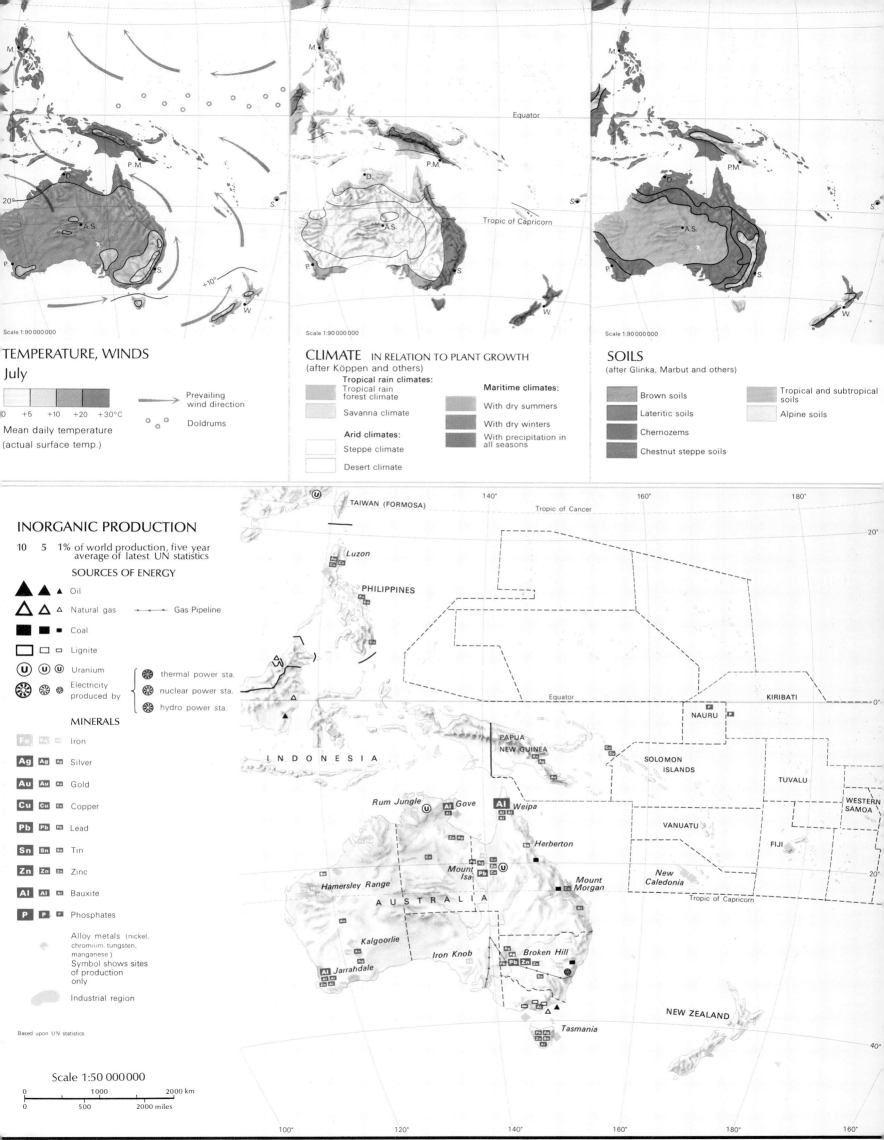

TEMPERATURE, WINDS
July

0	+5	+10	+20	+30°C

Mean daily temperature
(actual surface temp.)

→ Prevailing wind direction

∘ Doldrums

Scale 1:90 000 000

CLIMATE IN RELATION TO PLANT GROWTH
(after Köppen and others)

Tropical rain climates:
Tropical rain forest climate

Savanna climate

Arid climates:
Steppe climate

Desert climate

Maritime climates:
With dry summers

With dry winters

With precipitation in all seasons

Scale 1:90 000 000

SOILS
(after Glinka, Marbut and others)

Brown soils

Lateritic soils

Chernozems

Chestnut steppe soils

Tropical and subtropical soils

Alpine soils

Scale 1:90 000 000

INORGANIC PRODUCTION

10 5 1% of world production, five year average of latest UN statistics

SOURCES OF ENERGY

▲ ▲ ▲ Oil
△ △ △ Natural gas   ⊹ Gas Pipeline
■ ■ ▪ Coal
▭ ▭ ▭ Lignite
Ⓤ Ⓤ Ⓤ Uranium
✺ ✺ ✺ Electricity produced by

✺ thermal power sta.
✺ nuclear power sta.
✺ hydro power sta.

MINERALS

Fe Fe Fe Iron
Ag Ag Ag Silver
Au Au Au Gold
Cu Cu Cu Copper
Pb Pb Pb Lead
Sn Sn Sn Tin
Zn Zn Zn Zinc
Al Al Al Bauxite
P P P Phosphates

Alloy metals (nickel, chromium, tungsten, manganese)
Symbol shows sites of production only

Industrial region

Based upon UN statistics

Scale 1:50 000 000

0	1000	2000 km
0	500	2000 miles

LAMBERT'S AZIMUTHAL EQUAL-AREA PROJECTION

47

48 AUSTRALIA

Scale 1:10 000 000

© ESSELTE MAP SERVICE

© ESSELTE MAP SERVICE

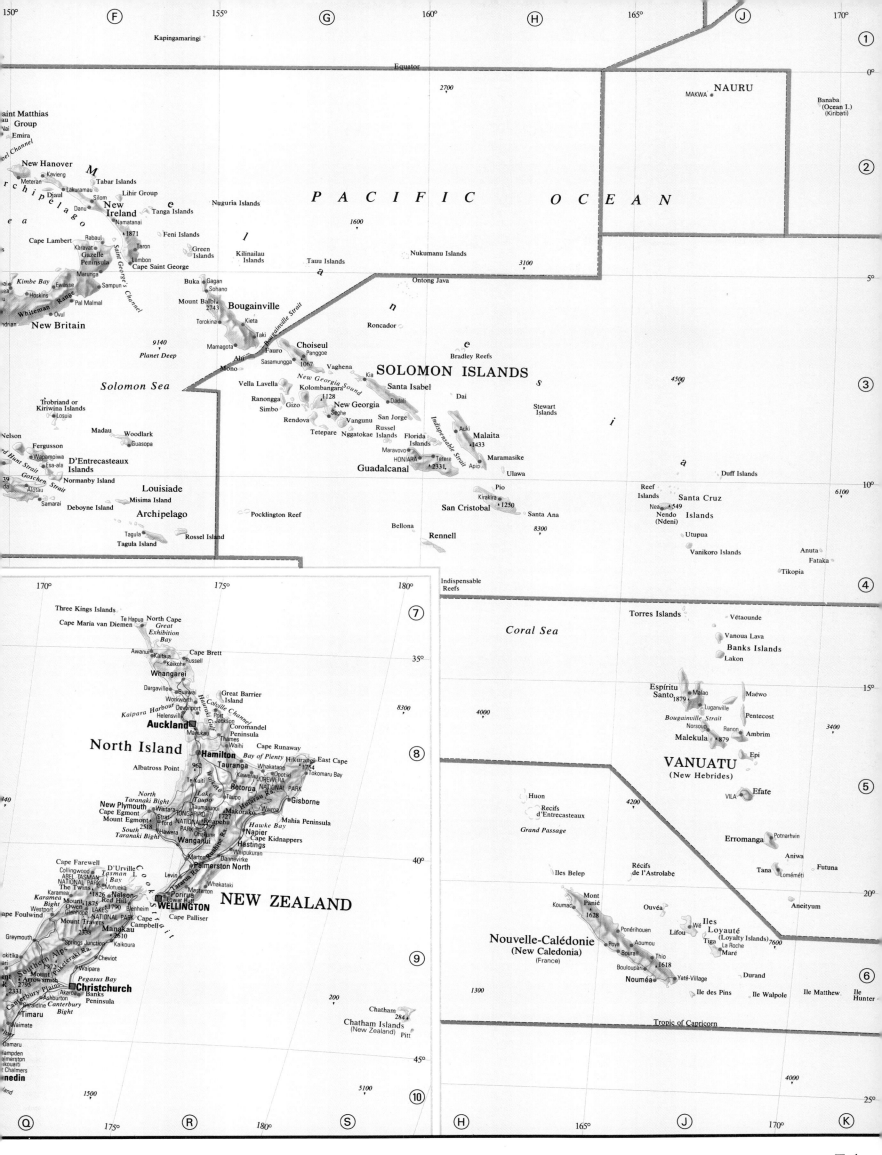

Kapingamarangi

P A C I F I C   O C E A N

NAURU

MAKWA

Banaba
(Ocean I.)
(Kiribati)

Saint Matthias
Group
Emira

New Hanover
Kavieng
Meteran
Djaul
Lakuramau
Silom
Danu
New Ireland
Namatanai
Tabar Islands
Lihir Group
Nuguria Islands

New Britain
Cape Lambert
Karavat
Rabaul
Gazelle Peninsula
Marunga
Cape Saint George
Feni Islands
Kilinailau Islands
Tauu Islands

Kimbe Bay
Ewasse
Hoskins
Pal Malmal
Ovul

Whiteman Range
1871
Taron
Lombon
Taga Islands
Green Islands

Buka
Gagan
Sohano
Mount Balbi
2743
Bougainville
Kieta
Torokina
Taki
Nukumanu Islands

Ontong Java

Roncador

Planet Deep
9140
Solomon Sea
Mamagota
Alu
Fauro
Mono
Choiseul
Panggoe
Sasamungga
1067
Vaghena

SOLOMON ISLANDS

Bradley Reefs

Stewart Islands

Trobriand or
Kiriwina Islands
Losuia

Vella Lavella
Kolombangara
Ranongga
1128
Simbo
Gizo
New Georgia
Rendova
Seghe
Vangunu
Dadali
Santa Isabel
Dai
New Georgia Sound
Kia

Madau
Guasopa
Woodlark

Nelson
Fergusson
Wapemoiwa
Esa-ala
D'Entrecasteaux Islands
Normanby Island
Tetepare
Ngatokae
Russel Islands
Florida Islands
San Jorge
Auki
Malaita
1433

Alotau
Samarai
Louisiade
Archipelago
Misima Island
Deboyne Island
Maravovo
HONIARA
Tetere
2331
Guadalcanal
Maramasike
Apia
Ulawa

Duff Islands

Pocklington Reef
Pio
San Cristobal
1250
Santa Ana
Reef Islands
Nea
549
Santa Cruz Islands

Tagula
Tagula Island
Rossel Island
Bellona
Rennell
8300
Nendo
(Ndeni)
Utupua

Vanikoro Islands
Anuta
Fataka
Tikopia

Indispensable Reefs

Coral Sea

Torres Islands
Vétaounde
Vanoua Lava
Banks Islands
Lakon

Espíritu Santo
1879
Malao
Luganville
Maéwo
Pentecost
Norsoup
Ranon
Ambrim

Bougainville Strait
Malekula
879
Epi

VANUATU
(New Hebrides)

Huon
Recifs d'Entrecasteaux
VILA
Efate

Grand Passage
Erromanga
Potnarhvin

Récifs de l'Astrolabe
Aniwa
Futuna
Iles Belep
Tana
Loméméti

Mont Panié
1628
Koumac
Aneityum

Ouvéa
Nouvelle-Calédonie
(New Caledonia)
(France)
Ponérihouen
Poya
Aoumou
Bourail
Thio
1618
Lifou
Wé
Tiga
Iles Loyauté
(Loyalty Islands)
La Roche
Maré

Nouméa
Bouloupari
Yaté-Village
Durand

Ile des Pins
Ile Walpole
Ile Matthew
Ile Hunter

Tropic of Capricorn

NEW ZEALAND

Three Kings Islands
Te Hapua
North Cape
Great Exhibition Bay
Cape Maria van Diemen
Awanui
Kaitaia
Cape Brett
Russell
Kaikohe
Whangarei

Dargaville
Ruawai
Workworth
Great Barrier Island
Kaipara Harbour
Helensville
Devonport
Port Jackson
Coromandel Peninsula
Manukau
Auckland
Thames
Waihi

North Island
Hamilton
Cape Runaway
962
Te Kuiti
Tauranga
Hikurangi
East Cape
Albatross Point
Kawerau
1754
Tokomaru Bay
TE UREWERA NATIONAL PARK
Opotiki
Rotorua
North Taranaki Bight
Waitara
Taumarunui
Lake Taupo
Taupo
Wairoa
Gisborne
New Plymouth
Cape Egmont
Mount Egmont
2518
TONGARIRO NATIONAL PARK
Ruapehu
2797
Makorako
Mahia Peninsula
South Taranaki Bight
Stratford
Hawera
Ohakune
Napier
Hawke Bay
Hastings
Cape Kidnappers
Wanganui
Marton
Waipukurau
Dannevirke

Cape Farewell
D'Urville Island
Collingwood
ABEL TASMAN NATIONAL PARK
Tasman Bay
Motueka
Levin
Masterton
Whakataki
Karamea
1826
The Twins
Nelson
Porirua
WELLINGTON
Cape Palliser
Karamea Bight
Mount Owen
1875
1790
Blenheim
Lower Hutt
Westport
Glenhope
NELSON LAKES NATIONAL PARK
Cape Campbell
Cape Foulwind
Mount Travers
2338
Mangakau
2610
Kaikoura
Greymouth
Springs Junction
Cheviot
Hokitika
1977
Waipara
Mount Arrowsmith
2795
Pegasus Bay
Christchurch
Banks Peninsula
2331
Akaroa
Canterbury Plains
Timaru
Ashburton
Geraldine
Canterbury Bight
Waimate

Oamaru
Palmerston
Waikouaiti
Port Chalmers
Dunedin

Chatham
284
Chatham Islands
(New Zealand)
Pitt

Scale 1:10 000 000

0 100 200 300 400 km
0 100 200 miles

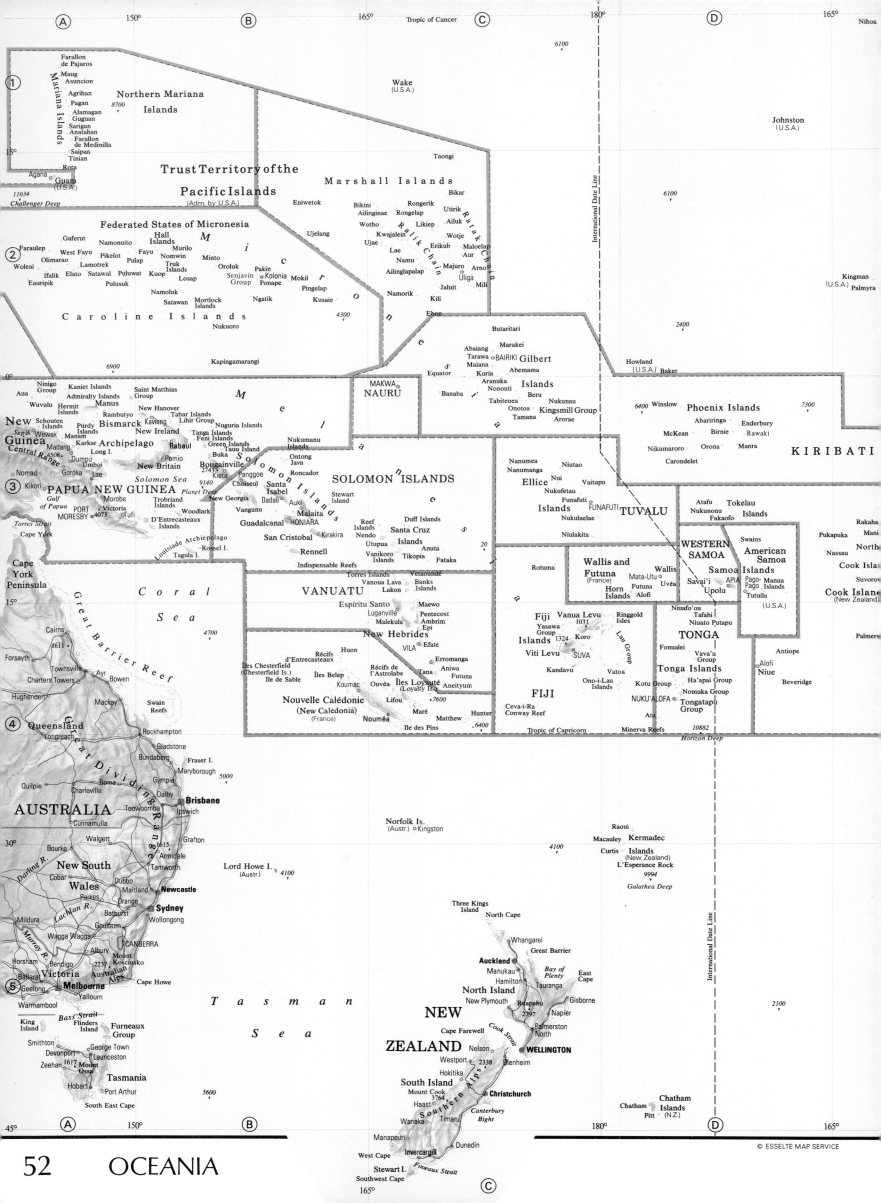

52 OCEANIA

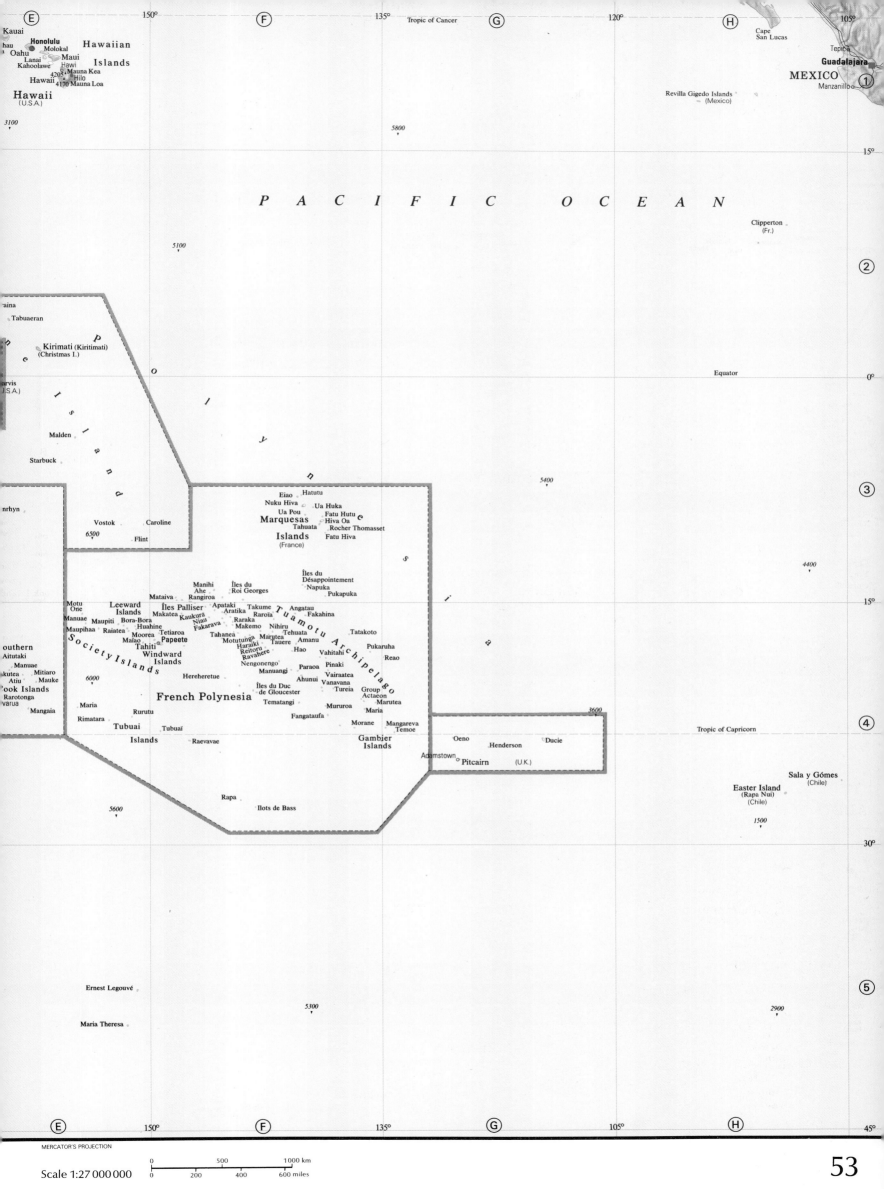

E　　150°　　F　　135°　Tropic of Cancer　G　120°　H　105°

Kauai
Niihau　Honolulu　Hawaiian
Oahu　Molokai　Maui
Lanai　Hawi
Kahoolawe　Mauna Kea
Hawaii　420　Hilo
Mauna Loa　4170
HAWAII
(U.S.A.)

Cape
San Lucas　Tepica
Guadalajara
MEXICO
Manzanillo

①

Revilla Gigedo Islands
(Mexico)

3100

5800

15°

P A C I F I C   O C E A N

Clipperton
(Fr.)

②

5100

5400

Equator

0°

raina
Tabuaeran

Kirimati (Kiritimati)
(Christmas I.)

③

Jarvis
(U.S.A.)

Malden

Starbuck

Eiao　Hatutu
Nuku Hiva　Ua Huka
Ua Pou　Fatu Hutu
Marquesas　Hiva Oa
Islands　Tahuata　Rocher Thomasset
(France)　Fatu Hiva

nrhyn

Vostok　Caroline
6500　Flint

4400

Îles du
Désappointement
Napuka
Pukapuka

15°

Manihi
Ahe　Îles du
Mataiva　Rangiroa　Roi Georges
Motu　Leeward　Îles Palliser　Apataki　Takume　Angatau
Orie　Islands　Makatea　Aratika　Takume　Fakahina
Manuae　Maupiti　Bora-Bora　Kaukura　Raraka　Raroia
Maupihaa　Raiatea　Huahine　Niau　Makemo　Nihiru
Maiao　Moorea　Tetiaroa　Fakarava　Tahanea　Tehuata
Tahiti　Papeete　Motutunga　Marutea　Amanu
Windward　Haraiki　Tauere
Reitoru　Hao　Vahitahi
Islands　Ravahere
Nengonengo　Pinaki
Manuangi　Paraoa　Vairaatea
Ahunui　Vanavana
Îles du Duc　Tureia
de Gloucester　Group
Tematangi　Actaeon
Maria　Morane　Marutea
Maria
Mururoa

Society Islands
French Polynesia

6000

Tatakoto

Pukaruha
Reao

Tuamotu Archipelago

southern
Aitutaki
Manuae
akutea　Mitiaro
Atiu　Mauke
ook Islands
Rarotonga
varua
Mangaia

Maria
Rimatara
Tubuai
Islands

Rururu
Tubuaï
Raevavae

Hereheretue

Fangataufa

Gambier
Islands

Mangareva
Temoe

3600

Oeno
Henderson
Adamstown
Pitcairn　(U.K.)

Ducie

Tropic of Capricorn

④

Sala y Gómes
(Chile)
Easter Island
(Rapa Nui)
(Chile)

Rapa

Ilots de Bass

5600

1500

30°

Ernest Legouvé

5300

2900

⑤

Maria Theresa

E　150°　F　135°　G　105°　H　45°

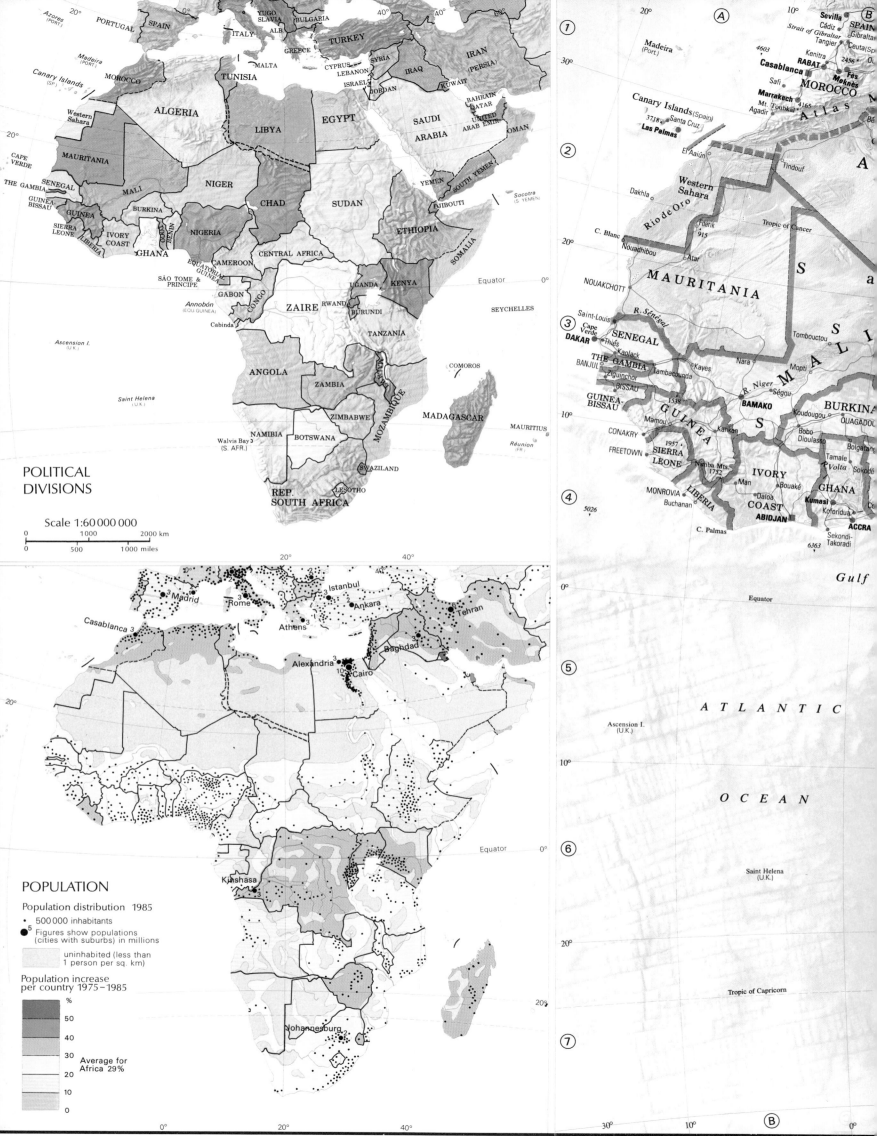

POLITICAL DIVISIONS

Scale 1:60 000 000

| 0 | 1000 | 2000 km |
| 0 | 500 | 1000 miles |

POPULATION

Population distribution 1985

- 500 000 inhabitants
- ⁵ Figures show populations (cities with suburbs) in millions

uninhabited (less than 1 person per sq. km)

Population increase per country 1975–1985

%
50
40
30 — Average for
20   Africa 29%
10
0

AFRICA, environment, political divisions, population

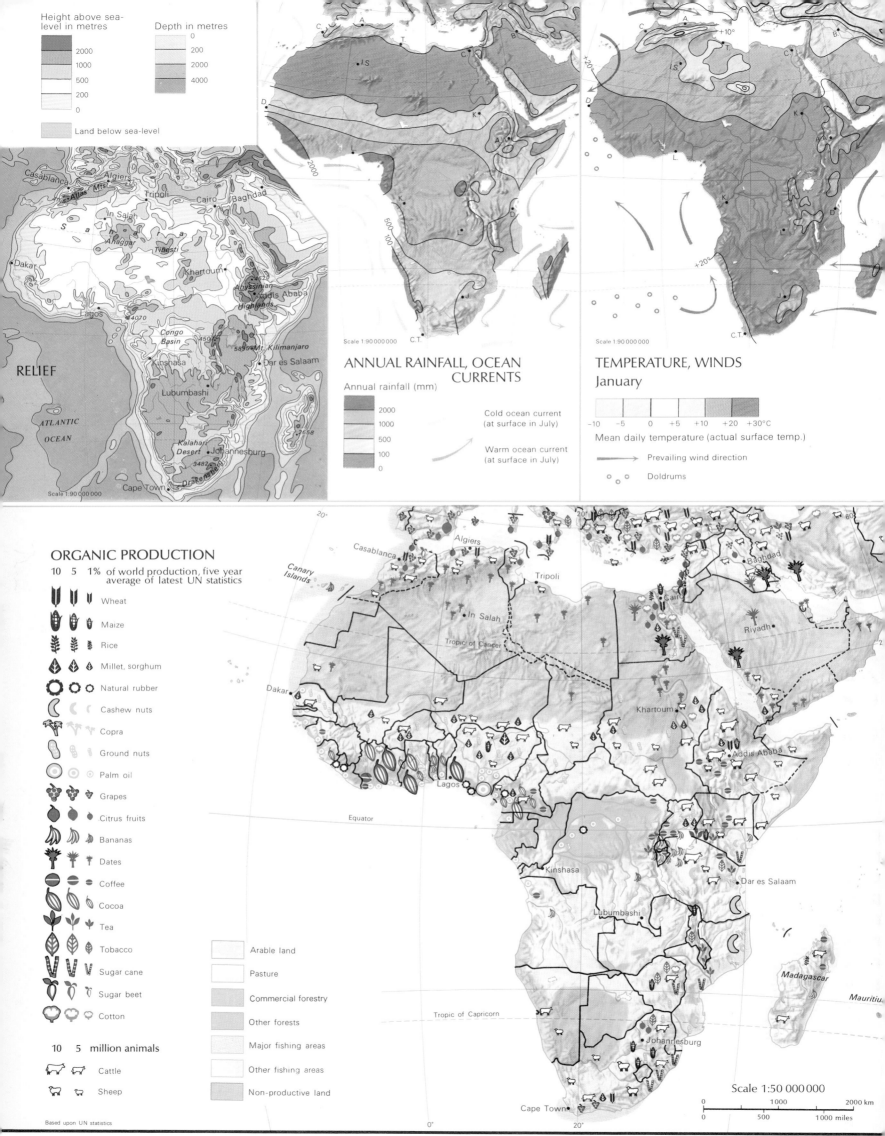

Height above sea-level in metres
2000
1000
500
200
0
Land below sea-level

Depth in metres
0
200
2000
4000

RELIEF

Casablanca · Algiers · Tripoli · Cairo · Baghdad
Atlas Mts.
In Salah
Ahaggar · Tibesti
Dakar
Khartoum
·4620
Abyssinian · Addis Ababa
Highlands
Lagos ·4070
Congo Basin ·450?
·5895 Mt. Kilimanjaro
Kinshasa · Dar es Salaam
Lubumbashi
ATLANTIC OCEAN
·2658
Kalahari Desert · Johannesburg
3482
Cape Town · Drakensberg

Scale 1:90 000 000

ANNUAL RAINFALL, OCEAN CURRENTS

Annual rainfall (mm)
2000
1000
500
100
0

Cold ocean current (at surface in July)
Warm ocean current (at surface in July)

Scale 1:90 000 000

TEMPERATURE, WINDS
January

−10 −5 0 +5 +10 +20 +30°C
Mean daily temperature (actual surface temp.)

Prevailing wind direction
Doldrums

Scale 1:90 000 000

ORGANIC PRODUCTION

10 5 1% of world production, five year average of latest UN statistics

Wheat
Maize
Rice
Millet, sorghum
Natural rubber
Cashew nuts
Copra
Ground nuts
Palm oil
Grapes
Citrus fruits
Bananas
Dates
Coffee
Cocoa
Tea
Tobacco
Sugar cane
Sugar beet
Cotton

10 5 million animals
Cattle
Sheep

Based upon UN statistics

Arable land
Pasture
Commercial forestry
Other forests
Major fishing areas
Other fishing areas
Non-productive land

Casablanca · Algiers · Tripoli
Canary Islands
In Salah
Dakar
Tropic of Cancer
Cairo
Riyadh
Baghdad
Khartoum
Addis Ababa
Lagos
Equator
Kinshasa
Dar es Salaam
Lubumbashi
Madagascar
Mauritius
Tropic of Capricorn
Johannesburg
Cape Town

Scale 1:50 000 000

0   1000   2000 km
0   500   1000 miles

© ESSELTE MAP SERVICE

56   AFRICA, physical, economic

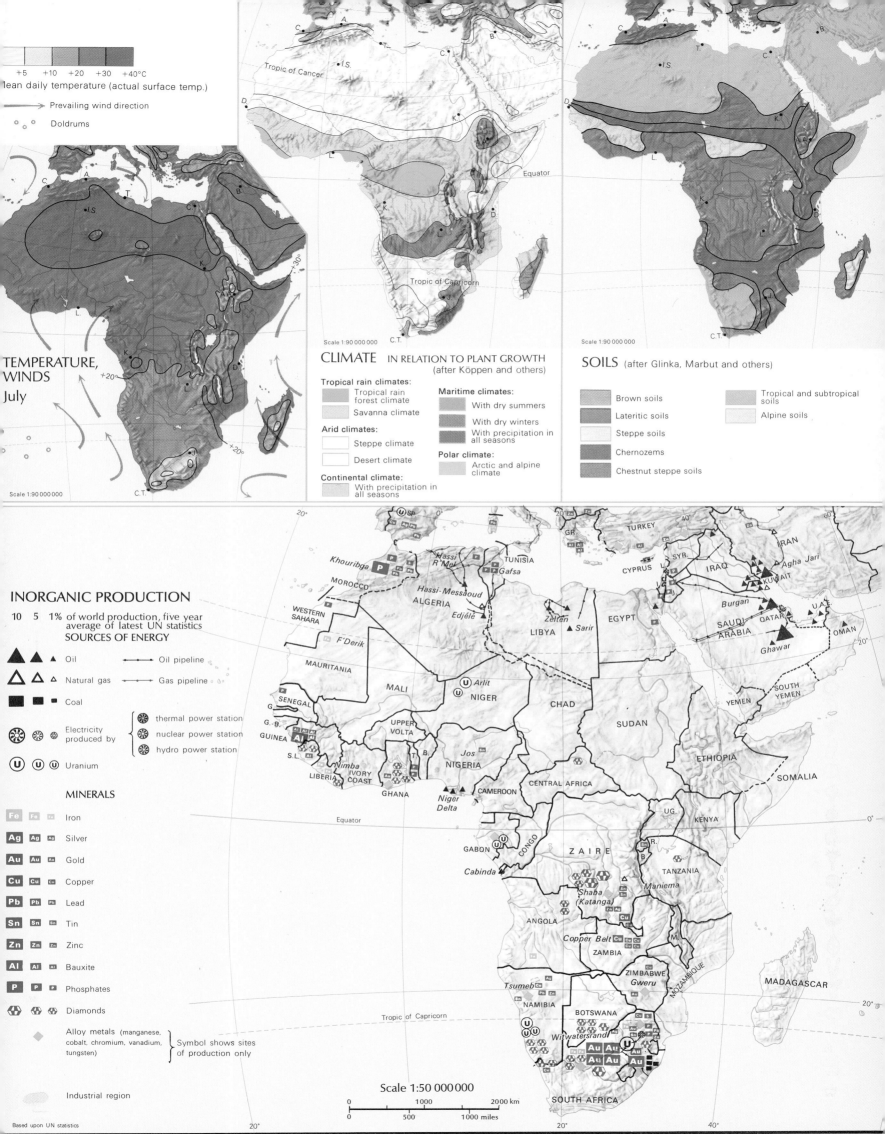

TEMPERATURE, WINDS
July

+5 +10 +20 +30 +40°C
Mean daily temperature (actual surface temp.)

→ Prevailing wind direction

○ ○ Doldrums

Scale 1:90 000 000

CLIMATE IN RELATION TO PLANT GROWTH
(after Köppen and others)

Scale 1:90 000 000

Tropical rain climates:
- Tropical rain forest climate
- Savanna climate

Arid climates:
- Steppe climate
- Desert climate

Continental climate:
- With precipitation in all seasons

Maritime climates:
- With dry summers
- With dry winters
- With precipitation in all seasons

Polar climates:
- Arctic and alpine climate

SOILS (after Glinka, Marbut and others)

Scale 1:90 000 000

- Brown soils
- Lateritic soils
- Steppe soils
- Chernozems
- Chestnut steppe soils
- Tropical and subtropical soils
- Alpine soils

INORGANIC PRODUCTION

10 5 1% of world production, five year average of latest UN statistics

SOURCES OF ENERGY

- ▲ ▲ ▲ Oil
- △ △ △ Natural gas
- ■ ■ ▪ Coal
- ⊛ ⊛ ⊛ Electricity produced by:
  - thermal power station
  - nuclear power station
  - hydro power station
- Ⓤ Ⓤ Ⓤ Uranium

- ←→ Oil pipeline
- ←→ Gas pipeline

MINERALS

- Fe Fe Fe Iron
- Ag Ag Ag Silver
- Au Au Au Gold
- Cu Cu Cu Copper
- Pb Pb Pb Lead
- Sn Sn Sn Tin
- Zn Zn Zn Zinc
- Al Al Al Bauxite
- P P P Phosphates
- ⬡ ⬡ ⬡ Diamonds

- ◆ Alloy metals (manganese, cobalt, chromium, vanadium, tungsten) Symbol shows sites of production only

- Industrial region

Based upon UN statistics

Scale 1:50 000 000

0   1000   2000 km
0   500   1000 miles

MILLER'S STEREOGRAPHIC PROJECTION

57

Scale 1:10 000 000

© ESSELTE MAP SERVICE

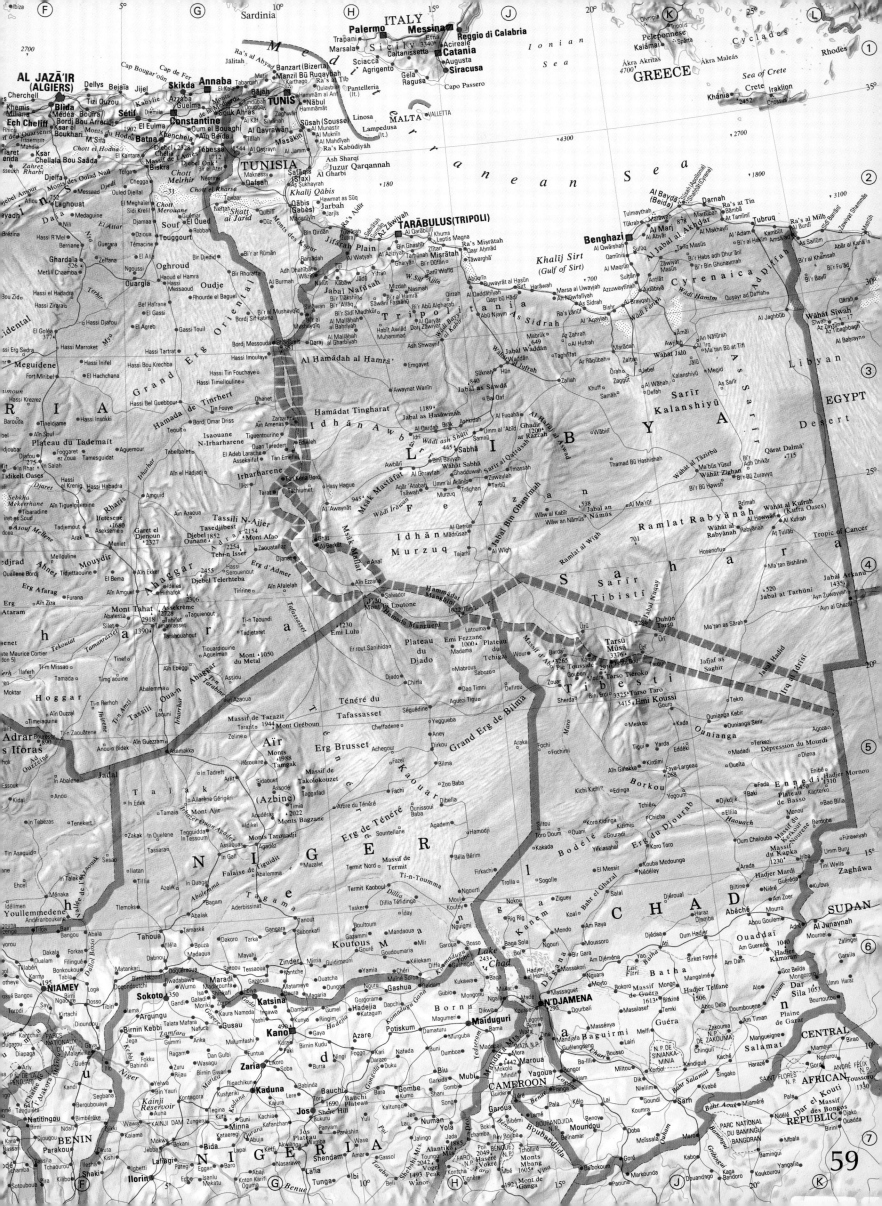

Scale 1:10 000 000

0 100 200 300 400 km
0   100   200 miles

© ESSELTE MAP SERVICE

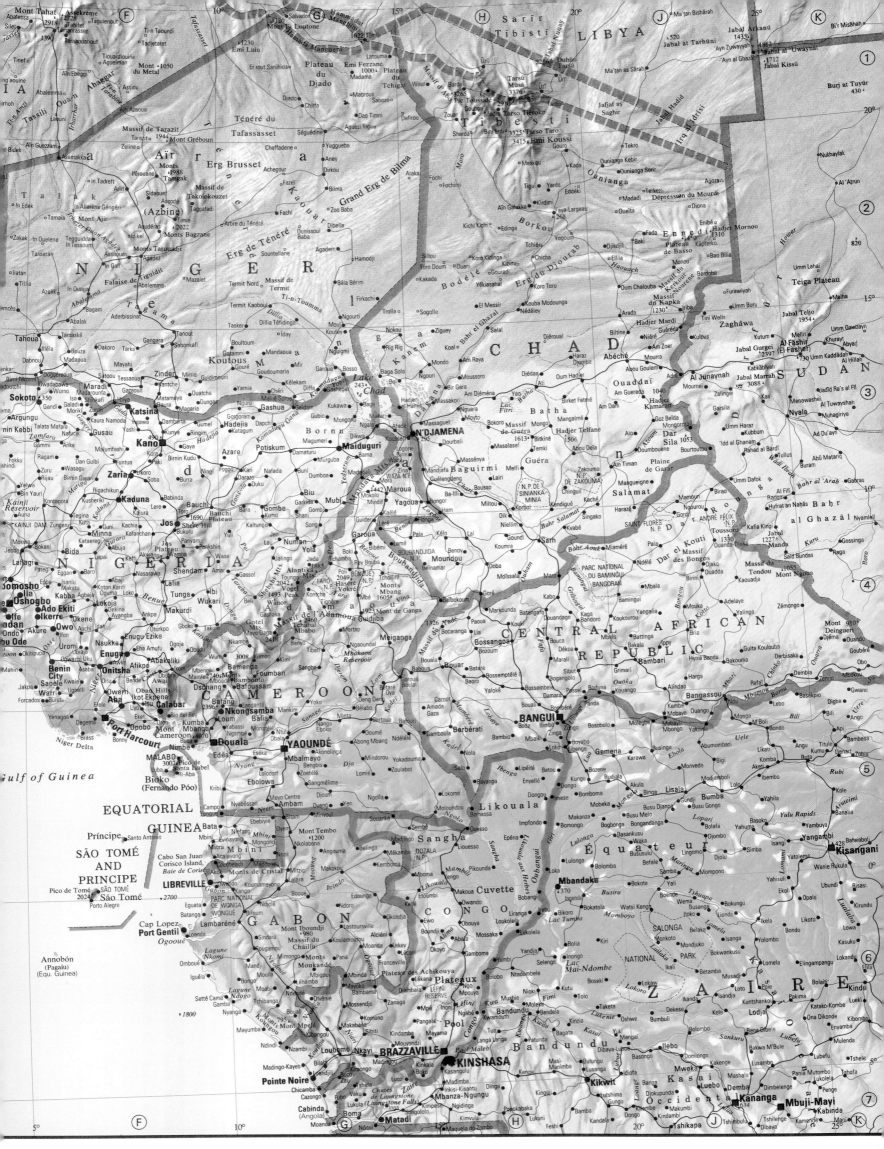

Scale 1:10 000 000

0   100   200   300   400 km

0   100   200 miles

© ESSELTE MAP SERVICE

65

SOUTHERN AFRICA

INDIAN OCEAN

SEYCHELLES

TANZANIA

MALAWI

MOZAMBIQUE

MADAGASCAR
(MALAGASY REPUBLIC)

Mozambique Channel

COMOROS

INDIAN
OCEAN

MAURITIUS

PORT-LOUIS

Saint-Denis

Saint-Paul
Saint-Pierre

Réunion
(France)

Mascarene Islands

Scale 1:10 000 000

0   100   200   300   400 km
0   100   200 miles

67

POLITICAL DIVISIONS

Names of the American states, with their standard abbreviations

AL.	Alabama
AK.	Alaska
AZ.	Arizona
AR.	Arkansas
CA.	California
CO.	Colorado
CT.	Connecticut
DE.	Delaware
FL.	Florida
GA.	Georgia
HI.	Hawaii
ID.	Idaho
IL.	Illinois
IN.	Indiana
IA.	Iowa
KS.	Kansas
KY.	Kentucky
LA.	Louisiana
ME.	Maine
MD.	Maryland
MA.	Massachusetts
MI.	Michigan
MN.	Minnesota
MS.	Mississippi
MO.	Missouri
MT.	Montana
NE.	Nebraska
NV.	Nevada
N.H.	New Hampshire
N.J.	New Jersey
N.M.	New Mexico
N.Y.	New York
N.C.	North Carolina
N.D.	North Dakota
OH.	Ohio
OK.	Oklahoma
OR.	Oregon

PA.	Pennsylvania
R.I.	Rhode Island
S.C.	South Carolina
S.D.	South Dakota
TN.	Tennessee
TX.	Texas
UT.	Utah
VT.	Vermont
VA.	Virginia
WA.	Washington
W.V.	West Virginia
WI.	Wisconsin
WY.	Wyoming
D.C.	District of Columbia (Federal)

POPULATION

Population distribution 1985

· 500 000 inhabitants

●3 Figures show populations (cities with suburbs) in millions

uninhabited (less than 1 person per sq.km)

Population increase per country 1975–1985

	50%
	40
	30
	20
	10
	0

Average for North and Central America 10%

Scale 1:60 000 000

0   1000   2000 km
0   500   1000 miles

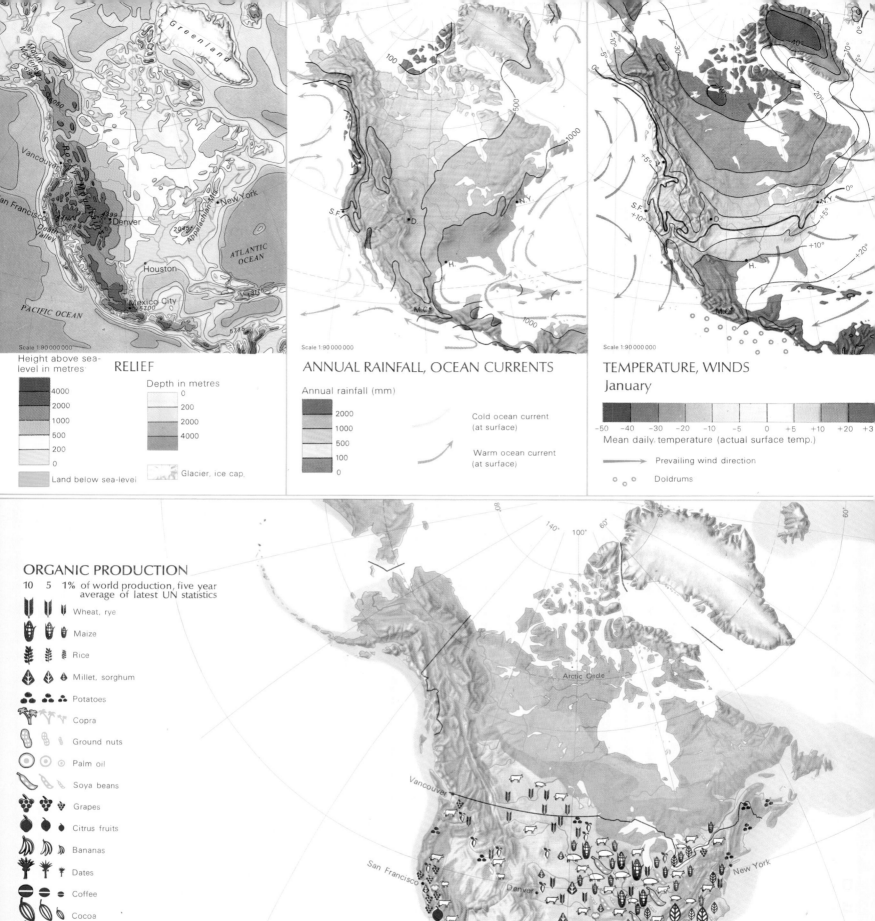

RELIEF

Height above sea-level in metres

- 4000
- 2000
- 1000
- 500
- 200
- 0

Land below sea-level

Depth in metres
- 0
- 200
- 2000
- 4000

Glacier, ice cap.

Scale 1:90 000 000

ANNUAL RAINFALL, OCEAN CURRENTS

Annual rainfall (mm)
- 2000
- 1000
- 500
- 100
- 0

→ Cold ocean current (at surface)

→ Warm ocean current (at surface)

Scale 1:90 000 000

TEMPERATURE, WINDS
January

-50 -40 -30 -20 -10 -5 0 +5 +10 +20 +3

Mean daily temperature (actual surface temp.)

→ Prevailing wind direction

o o o Doldrums

Scale 1:90 000 000

ORGANIC PRODUCTION

10 5 1% of world production, five year average of latest UN statistics

- Wheat, rye
- Maize
- Rice
- Millet, sorghum
- Potatoes
- Copra
- Ground nuts
- Palm oil
- Soya beans
- Grapes
- Citrus fruits
- Bananas
- Dates
- Coffee
- Cocoa
- Tea
- Tobacco
- Sugar cane
- Sugar beet
- Cotton

10 5 million animals

- Cattle
- Sheep
- Pigs

Based upon UN statistics

- Arable land
- Pasture
- Commercial forestry
- Other forests
- Major fishing areas
- Other fishing areas
- Non productive land
- Ice cap, glacier

Scale 1:50 000 000

0 ... 1000 ... 2000 km
0 ... 500 ... 1000 miles

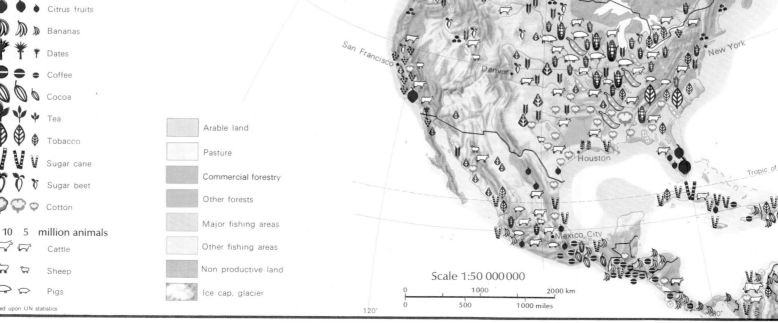

© ESSELTE MAP SERVICE

70 NORTH AMERICA, physical, economic

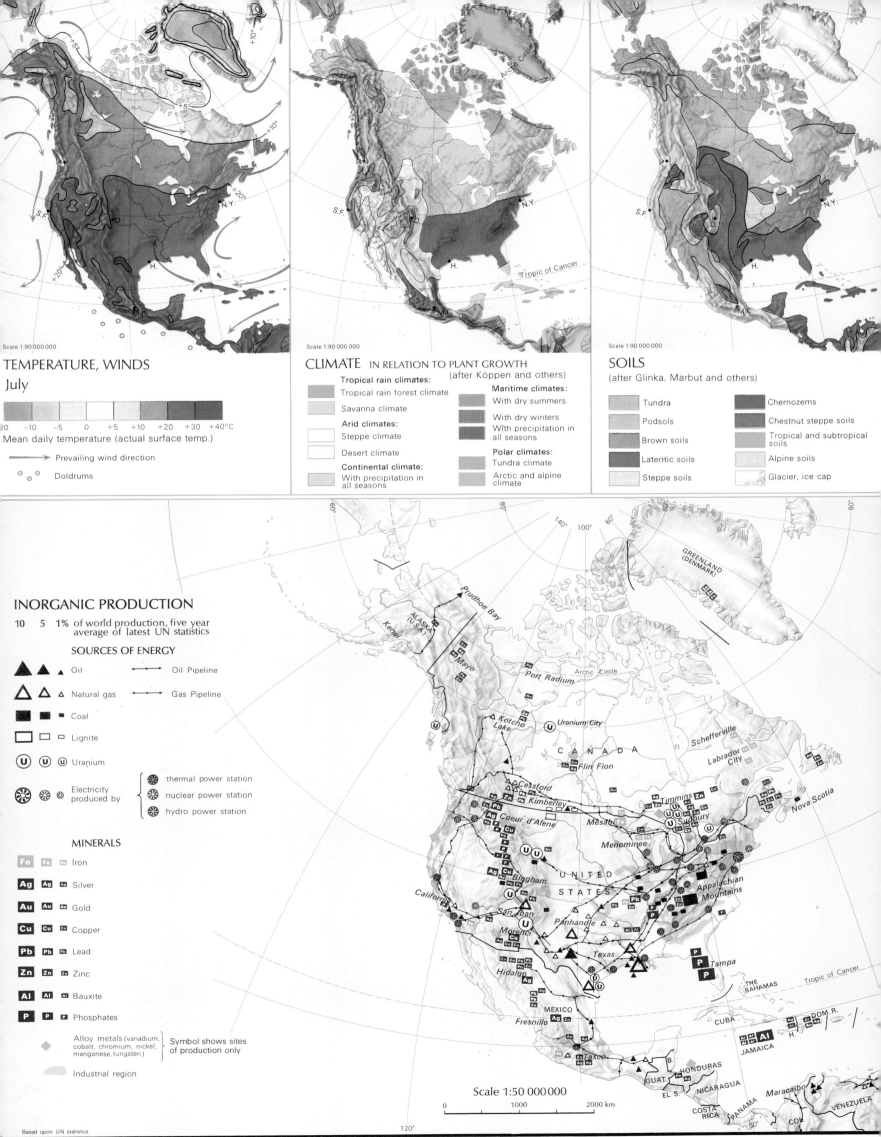

TEMPERATURE, WINDS
July

Scale 1:90 000 000

| -20 | -10 | -5 | 0 | +5 | +10 | +20 | +30 | +40°C |

Mean daily temperature (actual surface temp.)

→ Prevailing wind direction

○ ○ Doldrums

CLIMATE IN RELATION TO PLANT GROWTH
(after Köppen and others)

Scale 1:90 000 000

Tropical rain climates:
Tropical rain forest climate
Savanna climate

Arid climates:
Steppe climate
Desert climate

Continental climate:
With precipitation in all seasons

Maritime climates:
With dry summers
With dry winters
With precipitation in all seasons

Polar climates:
Tundra climate
Arctic and alpine climate

SOILS
(after Glinka, Marbut and others)

Scale 1:90 000 000

Tundra
Podsols
Brown soils
Lateritic soils
Steppe soils

Chernozems
Chestnut steppe soils
Tropical and subtropical soils
Alpine soils
Glacier, ice cap

INORGANIC PRODUCTION

10 5 1% of world production, five year
average of latest UN statistics

SOURCES OF ENERGY

▲ ▲ ▲ Oil ⟷ Oil Pipeline
△ △ △ Natural gas ⟷ Gas Pipeline
■ ■ ■ Coal
▭ ▭ ▭ Lignite
Ⓤ Ⓤ Ⓤ Uranium
⊛ ⊛ ⊛ Electricity produced by { thermal power station / nuclear power station / hydro power station }

MINERALS

Fe Fe Fe Iron
Ag Ag Ag Silver
Au Au Au Gold
Cu Cu Cu Copper
Pb Pb Pb Lead
Zn Zn Zn Zinc
Al Al Al Bauxite
P P P Phosphates

◆ Alloy metals (vanadium, cobalt, chromium, nickel, manganese, tungsten) } Symbol shows sites of production only

Industrial region

Scale 1:50 000 000

0   1000   2000 km

Based upon UN statistics

MILLER'S BIPOLAR PROJECTION

71

Scale 1:10 000 000

0   100   200   300   400 km
0   100   200 miles

73

© ESSELTE MAP SERVICE

© ESSELTE MAP SERVICE

© ESSELTE MAP SERVICE

Scale 1:10 000 000

79

80 SOUTH AMERICA, environment, political divisions, population

Scale 1:25 000

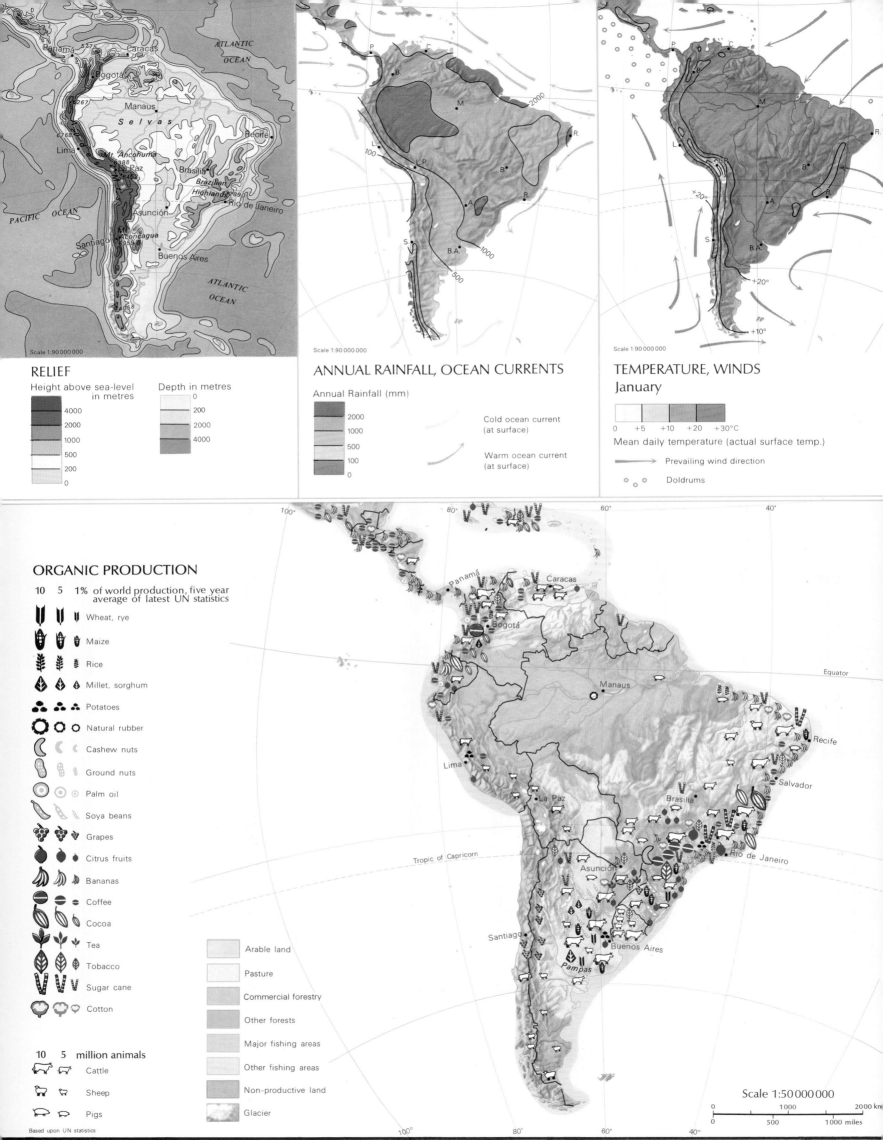

RELIEF

Height above sea-level in metres
- 4000
- 2000
- 1000
- 500
- 200
- 0

Depth in metres
- 0
- 200
- 2000
- 4000

Scale 1:90 000 000

ANNUAL RAINFALL, OCEAN CURRENTS

Annual Rainfall (mm)
- 2000
- 1000
- 500
- 100
- 0

→ Cold ocean current (at surface)

→ Warm ocean current (at surface)

Scale 1:90 000 000

TEMPERATURE, WINDS
January

0 +5 +10 +20 +30°C

Mean daily temperature (actual surface temp.)

→ Prevailing wind direction

o o o Doldrums

Scale 1:90 000 000

ORGANIC PRODUCTION

10 5 1% of world production, five year average of latest UN statistics

- Wheat, rye
- Maize
- Rice
- Millet, sorghum
- Potatoes
- Natural rubber
- Cashew nuts
- Ground nuts
- Palm oil
- Soya beans
- Grapes
- Citrus fruits
- Bananas
- Coffee
- Cocoa
- Tea
- Tobacco
- Sugar cane
- Cotton

10 5 million animals
- Cattle
- Sheep
- Pigs

- Arable land
- Pasture
- Commercial forestry
- Other forests
- Major fishing areas
- Other fishing areas
- Non-productive land
- Glacier

Based upon UN statistics

Scale 1:50 000 000

0   1000   2000 km
0   500   1000 miles

© ESSELTE MAP SERVICE

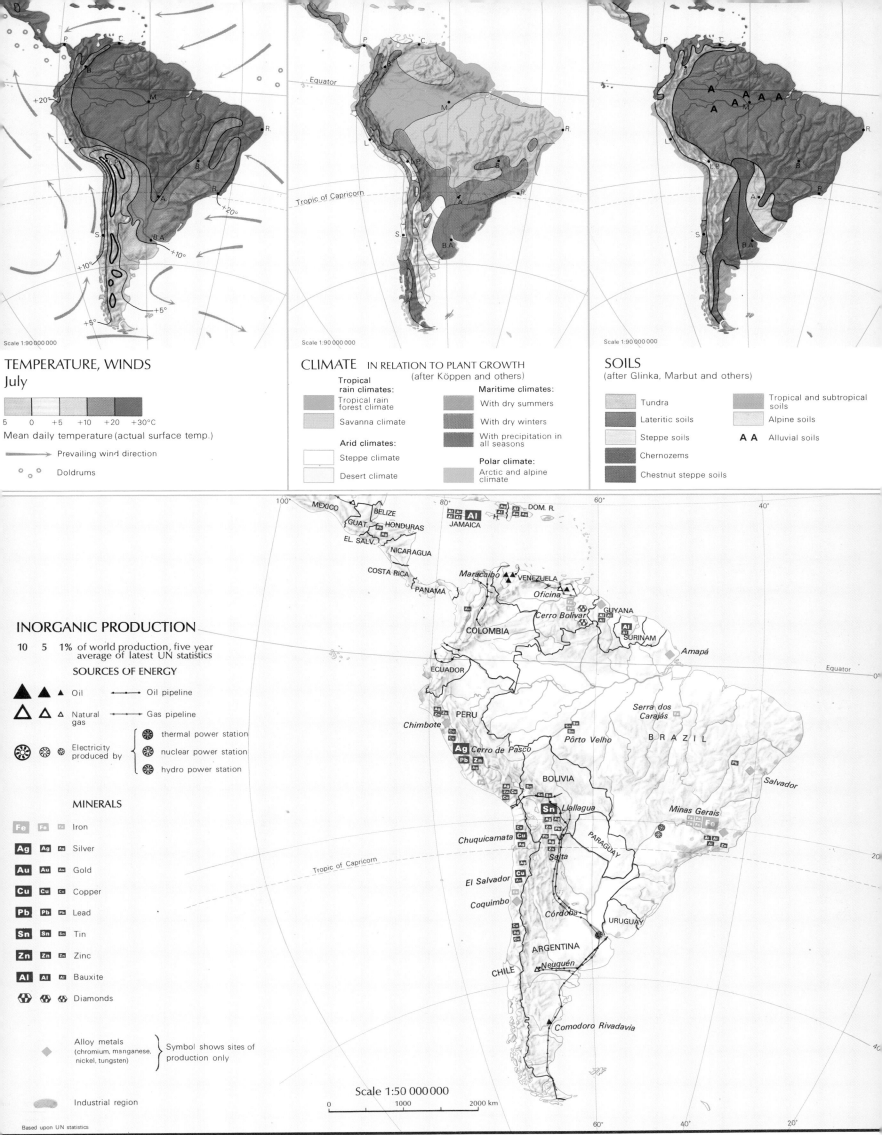

TEMPERATURE, WINDS
July

| −5 | 0 | +5 | +10 | +20 | +30°C |

Mean daily temperature (actual surface temp.)

→ Prevailing wind direction

∘ ∘ ∘ Doldrums

CLIMATE IN RELATION TO PLANT GROWTH
(after Köppen and others)

Tropical rain climates:
Tropical rain forest climate
Savanna climate

Arid climates:
Steppe climate
Desert climate

Maritime climates:
With dry summers
With dry winters
With precipitation in all seasons

Polar climate:
Arctic and alpine climate

SOILS (after Glinka, Marbut and others)

Tundra
Lateritic soils
Steppe soils
Chernozems
Chestnut steppe soils

Tropical and subtropical soils
Alpine soils
A A Alluvial soils

INORGANIC PRODUCTION

10 5 1% of world production, five year average of latest UN statistics

SOURCES OF ENERGY

▲ ▲ ▲ Oil
△ △ △ Natural gas

━━━ Oil pipeline
━━━ Gas pipeline

Electricity produced by:
⊛ thermal power station
⊛ nuclear power station
⊛ hydro power station

MINERALS

Fe Fe Fe Iron
Ag Ag Ag Silver
Au Au Au Gold
Cu Cu Cu Copper
Pb Pb Pb Lead
Sn Sn Sn Tin
Zn Zn Zn Zinc
Al Al Al Bauxite
⬡ ⬡ ⬡ Diamonds

◆ Alloy metals (chromium, manganese, nickel, tungsten) ⎱ Symbol shows sites of production only

Industrial region

Scale 1:50 000 000

0   1000   2000 km

© ESSELTE MAP SERVICE

85

SOUTH AMERICA, CENTRAL

© ESSELTE MAP SERVICE

SOUTH AMERICA, SOUTH

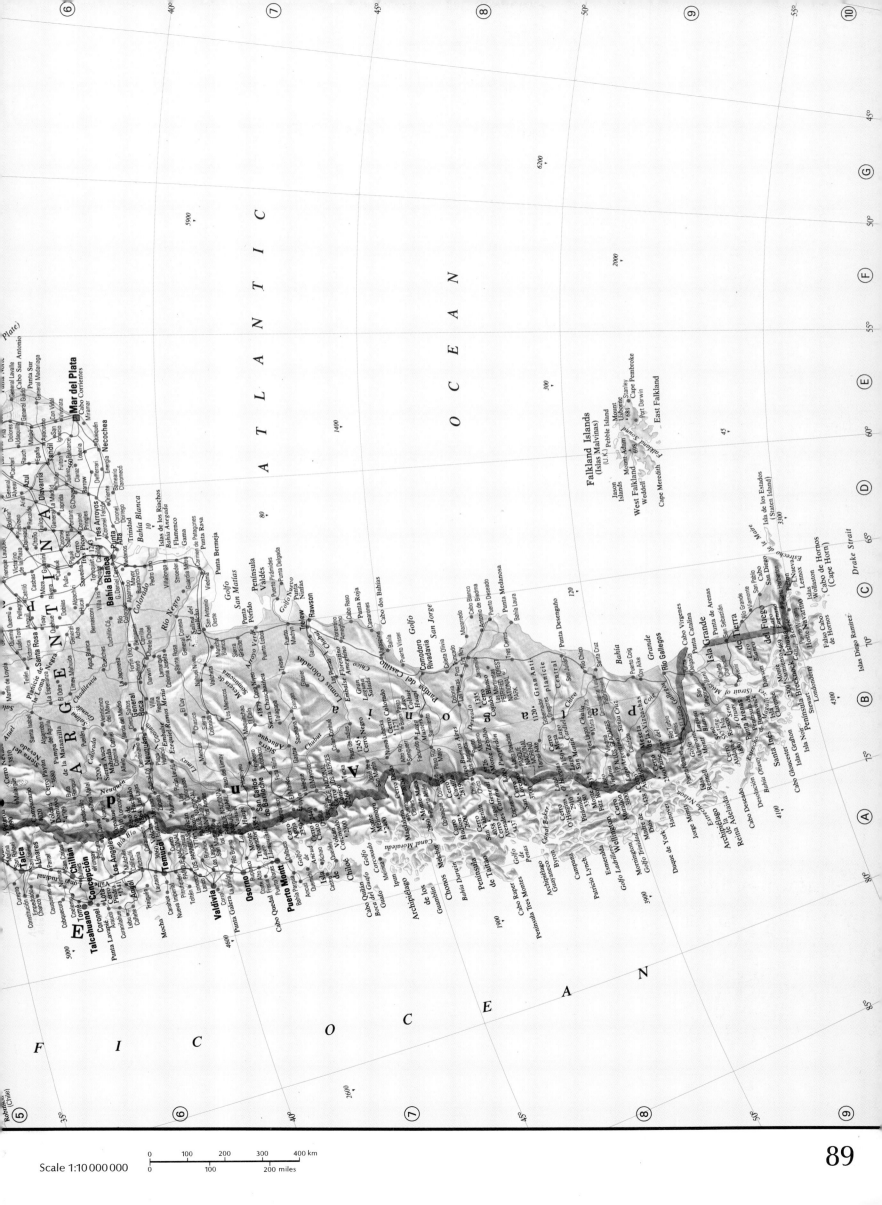

Scale 1:10 000 000

0 100 200 300 400 km
0 100 200 miles

89

Scale 1:30 000 000

© ESSELTE MAP SERVICE

0   500   1000 km
0   250   500 miles

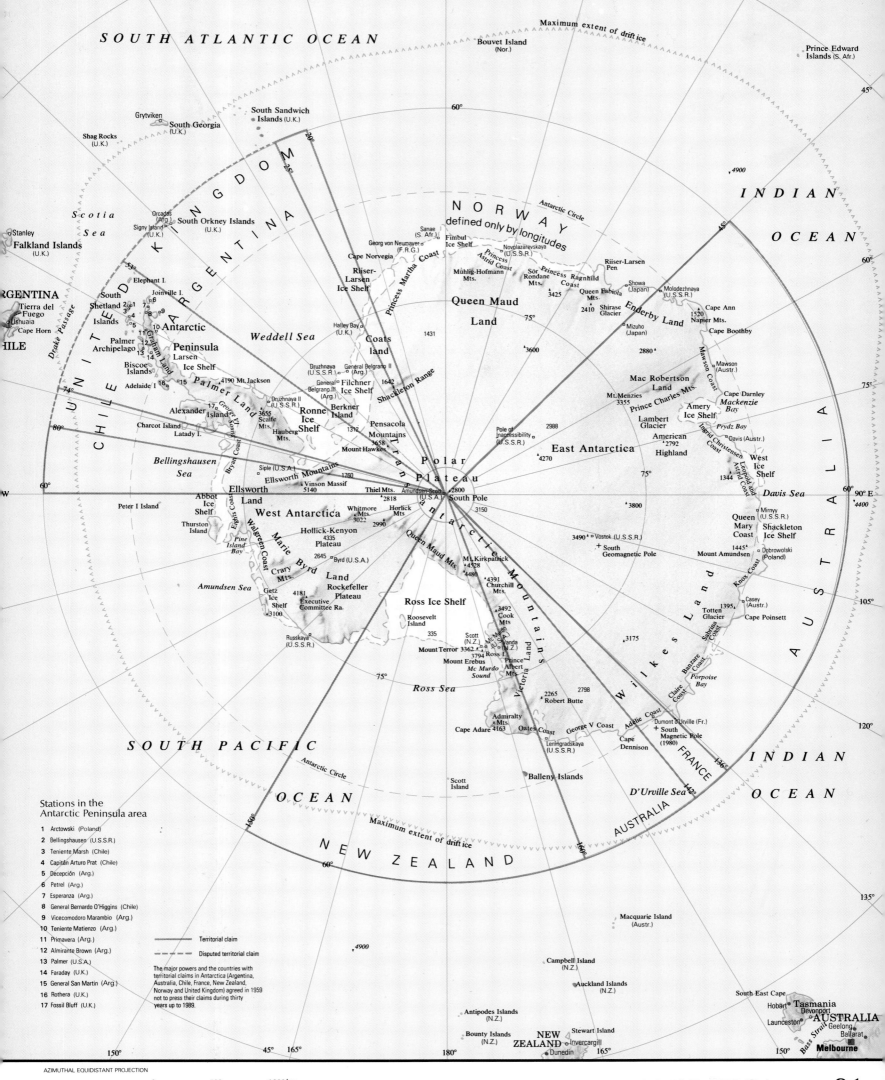

SOUTH ATLANTIC OCEAN

Maximum extent of drift ice

Bouvet Island (Nor.)

Prince Edward Islands (S. Afr.)

INDIAN OCEAN

Scotia Sea

Grytviken
South Georgia (U.K.)

Shag Rocks (U.K.)

South Sandwich Islands (U.K.)

NORWAY
defined only by longitudes

Antarctic Circle

Sanae (S. Afr.)   Fimbul Ice Shelf   Novolazarevskaya (U.S.S.R.)

Stanley
Falkland Islands (U.K.)

Georg von Neumayer (F.R.G.)   Cape Norvegia   Princess Astrid Coast   Princess Ragnhild Coast   Riiser-Larsen Pen.

Müehlig-Hofmann Mts.   Sör Rondane Mts.   Showa (Japan)   Molodezhnaya (U.S.S.R.)

ARGENTINA
Tierra del Fuego
Cape Horn
CHILE

Orcadas (Arg.)   South Orkney Islands (U.K.)
Signy Island (U.K.)

Elephant I.
South Shetland Islands
Joinville I.

UNITED KINGDOM   ARGENTINA   CHILE

Antarctic Peninsula
Palmer Archipelago
Graham Land
Biscoe Islands
Adelaide I.

Larsen Ice Shelf

Riiser-Larsen Ice Shelf

Princess Martha Coast

Queen Maud Land

3425   Queen Fabiola Mts.   2410   Shirase Glacier   Mizuho (Japan)

Enderby Land   1520   Napier Mts.   Cape Ann   Cape Boothby

Weddell Sea   Coats land   Halley Bay (U.K.)   1431   3600   2880   Mawson Coast   Mawson (Austr.)

Palmer Land   Mt. Jackson 4190   Druzhnaya (U.S.S.R.)   General Belgrano II (Arg.)   1642   Mac Robertson Land   Mt. Menzies 3355   Cape Darnley   Mackenzie Bay

Alexander Island   Scaife Mts. 3655   Ronne Ice Shelf   Berkner Island   Filchner Ice Shelf 1312   Shackleton Range   Prince Charles Mts.   Amery Ice Shelf   Prydz Bay   Davis (Austr.)

Charcot Island   Latady I.   Hauberg Mts. 3658   Pensacola Mountains   Mount Hawkes   Pole of Inaccessibility (U.S.S.R.) 2988   Lambert Glacier   American Highland 2792   West Ice Shelf

Bellingshausen Sea   Siple (U.S.A.)   Ellsworth Mountains 1760   Vinson Massif 5140   Thiel Mts. 2800   4270   East Antarctica   1344   Davis Sea

Peter I Island   Abbot Ice Shelf   Ellsworth Land   Whitmore Mts. 3022   Horlick Mts. 2990   Amundsen-Scott (U.S.A.) South Pole   3150   3800   Queen Mary Coast   Mirny (U.S.S.R.)   Shackleton Ice Shelf

Thurston Island   Eights Coast   West Antarctica   Hollick-Kenyon Plateau 4335   Queen Maud Mts.   3490   Vostok (U.S.S.R.)   South Geomagnetic Pole   Mount Amundsen   Dobrowolski (Poland)

Pine Island Bay   Walgreen Coast   Marie Byrd Land   2645   Byrd (U.S.A.)   Mt. Kirkpatrick 4528   4391   Churchill Mts.   1445   Mount Amundsen   Knox Coast   Casey (Austr.) 1395   Cape Poinsett

Amundsen Sea   Getz Ice Shelf 4181   3100   Executive Committee Ra.   Rockefeller Plateau   Ross Ice Shelf   3492   Cook Mts.   3175   Totten Glacier

Russkaya (U.S.S.R.)   Roosevelt Island   335   Scott (N.Z.)   Mt. Melbourne   Vanda (N.Z.)   Barzare Coast   Porpoise Bay

Mount Terror 3362   Ross I.   3794   Prince Albert Mts.   Claire Coast

Mount Erebus   Mc Murdo Sound   Victoria Land   Robert Butte 2798   2265   Wilkes Land   AUSTRALIA

Ross Sea   Admiralty Mts.   Cape Adare 4163   Oates Coast   George V Coast   Adélie Coast   Dumont d'Urville (Fr.)   South Magnetic Pole (1980)   FRANCE

SOUTH PACIFIC   Antarctic Circle   Cape Dennison   Leningradskaya (U.S.S.R.)   Balleny Islands   Cape Dennison   D'Urville Sea   INDIAN OCEAN

OCEAN   Scott Island

NEW ZEALAND   *Maximum extent of drift ice*

Macquarie Island (Austr.)

Campbell Island (N.Z.)

Auckland Islands (N.Z.)

South East Cape

Antipodes Islands (N.Z.)

Hobart   Tasmania   Devonport   AUSTRALIA   Launceston   Bass Strait   Geelong   Ballarat

Bounty Islands (N.Z.)   NEW ZEALAND   Stewart Island   Invercargill   Dunedin   Melbourne

Stations in the Antarctic Peninsula area

1   Arctowski (Poland)
2   Bellingshausen (U.S.S.R.)
3   Teniente Marsh (Chile)
4   Capitán Arturo Prat (Chile)
5   Decepción (Arg.)
6   Petrel (Arg.)
7   Esperanza (Arg.)
8   General Bernardo O'Higgins (Chile)
9   Vicecomodoro Marambio (Arg.)
10 Teniente Matienzo (Arg.)
11 Primavera (Arg.)
12 Almirante Brown (Arg.)
13 Palmer (U.S.A.)
14 Faraday (U.K.)
15 General San Martin (Arg.)
16 Rothera (U.K.)
17 Fossil Bluff (U.K.)

———— Territorial claim
- - - - Disputed territorial claim

The major powers and the countries with territorial claims in Antarctica (Argentina, Australia, Chile, France, New Zealand, Norway and United Kingdom) agreed in 1959 not to press their claims during thirty years up to 1989.

AZIMUTHAL EQUIDISTANT PROJECTION

Scale 1:30 000 000

0   500   1000 km
0   250   500 miles

ANTARCTICA   91

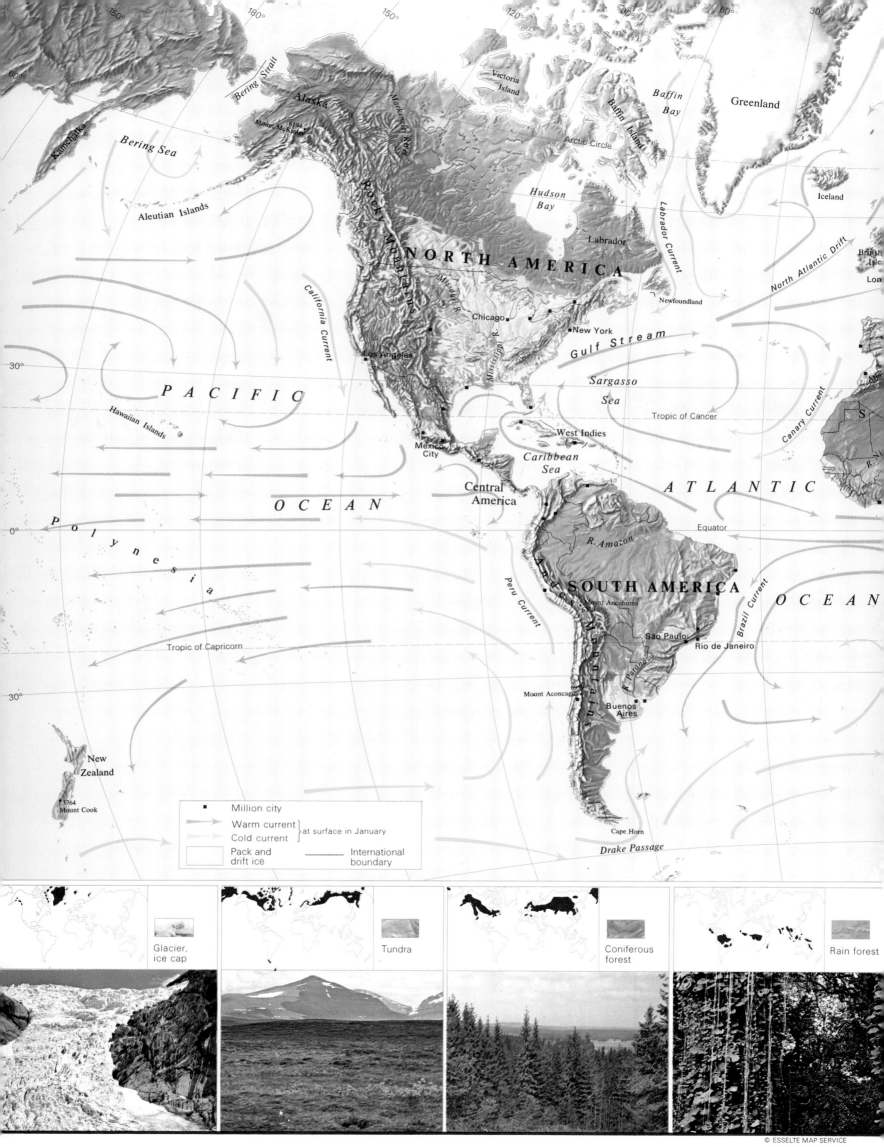

150° 180° 150° 120° 90° 60° 30°

60°

Kamchatka

Bering Sea

Bering Strait

Aleutian Islands

Alaska

Mount McKinley 6194

Mackenzie Rera

Rocky Mountains

Victoria Island

NORTH AMERICA

Arctic Circle

Baffin Island

Baffin Bay

Greenland

Iceland

Hudson Bay

Labrador

Labrador Current

Newfoundland

British Isle

Lon

North Atlantic Drift

California Current

Missouri R.

Chicago

New York

Gulf Stream

Sargasso Sea

30°

PACIFIC

Hawaiian Islands

Los Angeles

Mississippi R.

Tropic of Cancer

Canary Current

S

R. N

OCEAN

Mexico City

West Indies

Caribbean Sea

ATLANTIC

Equator

Polynesia

0°

Central America

R. Amazon

SOUTH AMERICA

OCEAN

Andes

Peru Current

Mount Ancohuma 6388

Brazil Current

Tropic of Capricorn

São Paulo

Rio de Janeiro

R. Paraná

Andes Mountains

New Zealand

30°

Mount Aconcagua 6959

Buenos Aires

3764 Mount Cook

■ Million city

Warm current

Cold current } at surface in January

Pack and drift ice

International boundary

Cape Horn

Drake Passage

Glacier, ice cap

Tundra

Coniferous forest

Rain forest

© ESSELTE MAP SERVICE

92   THE WORLD, environment

ARCTIC OCEAN

Svalbard

Barents Sea

North Cape

Norwegian Sea

Novaya Zemlya

Scandinavia

Taymyr Peninsula

S i b e r i a

R. Lena

Arctic Circle

Kamchatka

Bering Strait

Alaska

Mount McKinley
6194

Bering Sea

Aleutian Islands

R. Ob

Ural Mountains

Moscow

R. Volga

R. Yenisei

R. Ob

Sea of Okhotsk

Sakhalin

Oya Siwo

EUROPE

The Alps

Black Sea

Caspian Sea

Kirghiz Steppe

A S I A

Altai

Gobi

Manchuria

Honshu

Tokyo

Kuro Siwo

PACIFIC

Mediterranean Sea

Caucasus Mts.

Tien Shan

Takla Makan

Kunlun Shan

Tibet

Beijing

Seoul

Shanghai

R. Euphrates

Cairo

R. Nile

Red Sea

Rub al Khali

Himalayas

Kabul

Mount Everest
8848

R. Ganges

Calcutta

Hwang Ho

Yangtze Kiang

OCEAN

Sahara

AFRICA

Bombay

R. Mekong

Tropic of Cancer

30°

R. Zaire

R. Congo

Guinea

Arabian Sea

Sri Lanka

Equator

South China Sea

Philippine Islands

M i c r o n e s i a

M e l a n e s i a

0°

Mount Kilimanjaro
5895

INDIAN

Sumatra

Jakarta

Java

Borneo

Sunda Islands

New Guinea

R. Zambezi

Madagascar

OCEAN

Coral Sea

Kalahari Desert

Westralian Current

AUSTRALIA

Tropic of Capricorn

30°

Benguela Current

Cape Town
Cape of Good Hope

Sydney

Tasman Sea

Tasmania

Mount Cook
3764

New Zealand

30°

West Wind Drift

| Cultivated land | | Savanna | | Steppe | | Desert |

VAN DER GRINTEN'S PROJECTION

Scale 1:90 000 000
at the equator

0 400 800 km
200 600 1000 km
30°
60°

0 200 400 600 miles
100 300 500 miles
30°
60°

93

PRECIPITATION
PRESSURE
WINDS

January
Northern winter,
southern summer

Precipitation in mms.

■	400
▨	100
▨	25
□	0

L Low pressure

H High pressure

→ Prevailing wind direction
Short arrows = less constant winds
Long arrows = more constant winds
Thin arrows = light winds
Thick arrows = strong winds
∘ ∘ ∘ ∘ Doldrums

North East Trades
South East Trades
Westerlies
North East Monsoon
South East Trades
North West Monsoon

PRECIPITATION
PRESSURE
WINDS

July
Northern summer,
southern winter

Precipitation in mms.

■	400
▨	100
▨	25
□	0

L Low pressure

H High pressure

→ Prevailing wind direction
Short arrows = less constant winds
Long arrows = more constant winds
Thin arrows = light winds
Thick arrows = strong winds
∘ ∘ ∘ ∘ Doldrums

North East Trades
South East Trades
Westerlies
South West Monsoon
South East Trades
South East Monsoon

ANNUAL
PRECIPITATION

Precipitation in mms.

■	2000
▨	1000
▨	500
▨	100
□	0

Mean annual precipitation for
the following places in mms.

Cherrapunji	11 437		Rio de Janeiro	10
Douala	4 109		Perth	8
Cayenne	3 744		Chicago	8
Toamasina	3 530		Lisbon	7
Valdivia	2 396		Dakar	5
Bombay	2 078		Moscow	5
Bergen	1 958		Verkhoyansk	
San José	1 944		Barrow	
Jakarta	1 755		Las Vegas	
Tokyo	1 563		Kashgar	
Juneau	1 387		Walvis Bay	
New York	1 123		Aswân	
Brisbane	1 092		Arica	

compare: London 610

Arctic Circle
Tropic of Cancer
Equator
Tropic of Capricorn

Barrow · Juneau · Chicago · Las Vegas · New York · San José · Cayenne · Arica · Valdivia · Rio de Janeiro
Bergen · Moscow · Lisbon · Dakar · Douala · Walvis Bay · Aswân · Bombay · Cherrapunji · Kashgar · Verkhoyansk · Tokyo · Jakarta · Toamasina · Perth · Brisbane

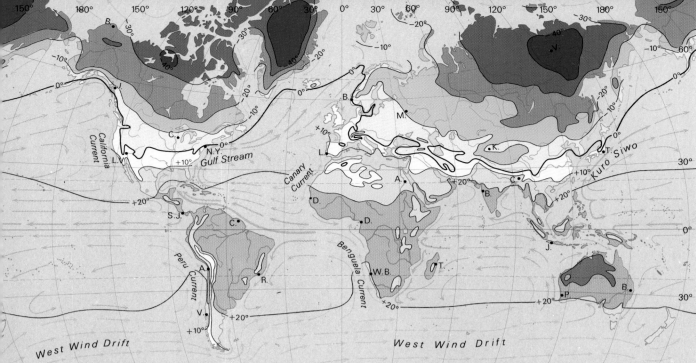

TEMPERATURE
OCEAN CURRENTS

January
Northern winter,
southern summer
Daily mean temperature
(actual surface temp.)

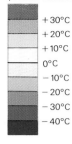

- +30°C
- +20°C
- +10°C
- 0°C
- −10°C
- −20°C
- −30°C
- −40°C

Cold ocean current
Warm ocean current

Short arrows = less constant currents
Long arrows = more constant currents
Thin arrows = slow currents
Thick arrows = fast currents

California Current · *Gulf Stream* · *Canary Current* · *Kuro Siwo* · *Peru Current* · *Benguela Current* · West Wind Drift

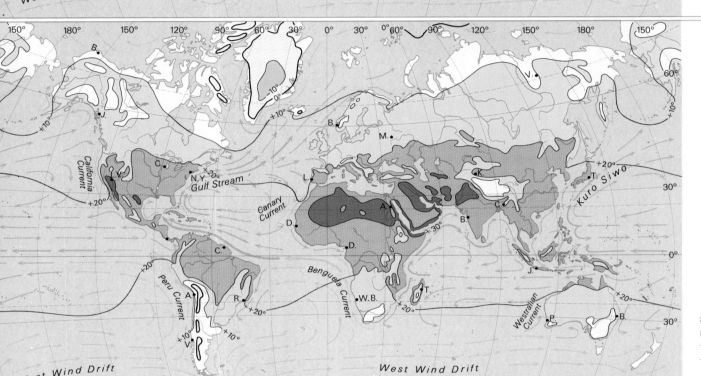

TEMPERATURE
OCEAN CURRENTS

July
Northern summer,
southern winter

Daily mean temperature
(actual surface temp.)

- +30°C
- +20°C
- +10°C
- 0°C
- −10°C

Cold ocean current
Warm ocean current

Short arrows = less constant currents
Long arrows = more constant currents
Thin arrows = slow currents
Thick arrows = fast currents

California Current · *Gulf Stream* · *Canary Current* · *Kuro Siwo* · *Peru Current* · *Benguela Current* · *Westralian Current* · West Wind Drift

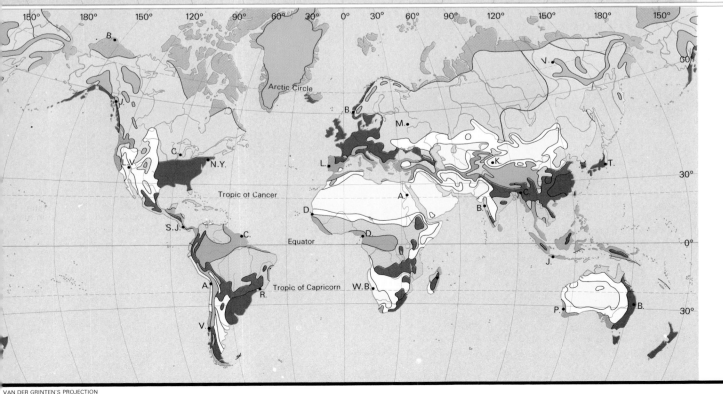

CLIMATE IN RELATION
TO PLANT GROWTH
(after Köppen and others)

Tropical rain climates:
- Tropical rain forest climate
- Savanna climate

Arid climates:
- Steppe climate
- Desert climate

Maritime climates:
- With dry summers
- With dry winters
- With precipitation in all seasons

Continental climates:
- With precipitation in all seasons
- With dry winters

Polar climates:
- Tundra climate
- Arctic and alpine climate

Arctic Circle · Tropic of Cancer · Equator · Tropic of Capricorn

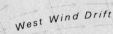

VAN DER GRINTEN'S PROJECTION

Scale 1:220 000 000
at the equator

95

The earth was formed several billion years ago – equivalent to more than four feet on the scale used here to show the last 600 million years.

PROTEROZOIC

PRE-CAMBRIAN | CAMBRIAN

The oldest rocks known date back 3.9 billion years

Worms
Jellyfish

Life in sea only
Trilobites

5000–4000 mill.years ago
Pre-Cambrian folding

600
Great extent of shallow

Ice cap

Continental shelf

CONTINENTAL DRIFT

PERMIAN/TRIASSIC
200 million years ago

Panthalassa

JURASSIC/CRETACEOUS
135 million years ago

LAURASIA

Panthalassa

Tethys Sea

GONDWANALAND

TERTIARY
65 million years ago

QUATERNARY
Present day

NORTH AMERICA

EURASIA

SOUTH AMERICA

AFRICA

AUSTRALIA

ANTARCTICA

Boundary between plates

PLATE TECTONICS

Canadian Shield

Baltic Shield

EURASIAN PLATE

PACIFIC PLATE

AMERICAN PLATE

AFRICAN PLATE

INDIAN PLATE

NAZCA PLATE

ANTARCTIC PLATE

Plate boundaries

Active ocean ridge

Ocean trench

Fracture zone

Direction of movement

Pre-Cambrian folding (later partly overlaid through sedimentation and younger folding)

THE WORLD, geology

MOUNTAIN BUILDING

- ⌇ Main trend lines
- ⌇ Main fault zones

- ░ Sediment overlaid plateau
- Pre-Cambrian folding (stable shields)

- Caledonian folding
- Hercynian folding
- Alpine folding

EARTHQUAKES AND VOLCANOES

- ■ Zone of strong seismic activity (frequent earthquakes)
- Zones of less frequent seismic activity (earthquakes can occasionally occur even in other areas)

- • Active volcano or zone of volcanic activity (several minor volcanoes)

VAN DER GRINTEN'S PROJECTION

97

FISHING

Density of animal plankton

Over 500 milligrams per cubic metre water
200–500 ›› ›› ›› ››
50–200 ›› ›› ›› ››
under 50 ›› ›› ›› ››

Important catch of:
whale
herring, cod and similar fish
tuna
crab, prawn and other shellfish

© EMS

Main Map (Pacific Ocean)

ⓒ 180° ⓓ 90° ⓔ

New Siberian Islands
ARCTIC OCEAN
Canada Basin
Baffin Bay
East Siberian Sea
Beaufort Sea
Victoria Island
Baffin Island
Arctic Circle
A
Alaska
Mt McKinley 6194
Rocky Mountains
Hudson Bay
NORTH AMERICA
Sea of Ochotsk
Kamchatka
Bering Sea
Aleutian Basin
Aleutian Trench
7822
Cascadia Basin
Kuril Trench
10542
Emperor Seamount Chain
PACIFIC OCEAN
North Pacific Basin
Patton Escarpment
Appalachians
Northwest Pacific Basin
Murray Fracture Zone
Sargasso Sea
Japan Trench
Mapmakers Seamounts
Hawaiian Ridge
Molokai Fracture Zone
Tropic of Cancer
Puerto Rico Trench 9219
Philippine Basin
Mariana Trench
Hawaii
Clarion Fracture Zone
Middle America Trench 6662
Antilles
11034
Challenger Deep
Central Pacific Basin
Clipperton Fracture Zone
Albatross Plateau
Borneo
Caroline Basin
Micronesia
Equator
Galapagos Islands
SOUTH AMERICA
New Guinea
Melanesia
East Pacific Basin
unda Islands
Sahul Shelf
Arafura Shelf
Polynesia
Peru Basin
Nazca Ridge
Andes Mountains
nch
Coral Sea
Tonga Trench
10882
East Pacific Ridge
Tropic of Capricorn
Easter Island
Chile Basin
7973
AUSTRALIA
Kermadec Trench
Peru-Chile Trench
Mt. Aconcagua 6959
South Australian Basin
Tasman Basin
PACIFIC OCEAN
Southwestern Pacific Basin
Australian-Antarctic Discordance
3764 Mt. Cook
New Zealand
Eltanin Fracture Zone System
Mornington Abyssal Plain
ralian-Antarctic Rise
South Tasman Rise
Campbell Plateau

Scale 1:96 000 000
at the equator
© HACHETTE/GUIDES BLEUS

180° 90°

Inset Map (Major Storm Areas)

Blizzard
Norther
Hurricane
Typhoon
Hurricane
Mauritius Cyclone

MAJOR STORM AREAS

Area subject to tropical storms

→ Storm track

Pack ice during northern winter

Drift ice limit

Coast subject to seismic surges (tsunamis)

Sea areas where fog often occurs

© EMS

MERCATOR'S PROJECTION

99

PACIFIC OCEAN

ATLANTIC

OCEAN

Arctic Circle

Alaska

Greenland

CANADA

NORTH AMERICA

UNITED

STATES

San Francisco 5

Los Angeles 12

Dallas 3

Houston 3

Minneapolis 2

Chicago

Saint Louis 2

Montreal

Toronto 3

Boston

18 New York

6 Philadelphia

2 Baltimore

Washington

Miami 3

Guadalajara 3

MEXICO

Mexico City 16

Havana 2

Caracas 3

VENEZUELA

Bogotá 4

SOUTH AMERICA

Lima 4

BRAZIL

Rio de Janeiro 9

São Paulo 12

Santiago 4

10 Buenos Aires

ARGENTINA

UNITED
KINGDOM

EUROPE

Londo

Madri

Casablanca 3

Tropic of Cancer

Equator

Tropic of Capricorn

30°

0°

30°

POPULATION INCREASE
1975–1985

In these cartograms each country's size is shown proportional to its population 1 sq.mm = 1,5 million inhabitants.

NORTH AMERICA

SOUTH AMERICA

EUROPE

AFRICA

ASIA

0	10	20	30	40	50%

CALORIE CONSUMPTION
daily consumption per head

Over 2900

2500–2900

2100–2500

Under 2100

1 calorie = 4.1868 joule

1	Canada	6	Argentina	15	China
2	U.S.A.	7	United Kingdom	16	India
3	Mexico	8	Sweden	17	Bangladesh
4	Venezuela	9	West Germany	18	Taiwan
5	Brazil	10	Italy	19	Japan
		11	Nigeria	20	Philippines
		12	Egypt	21	Indonesia
		13	South Africa	22	Australia
		14	U.S.S.R.	23	New Zealand

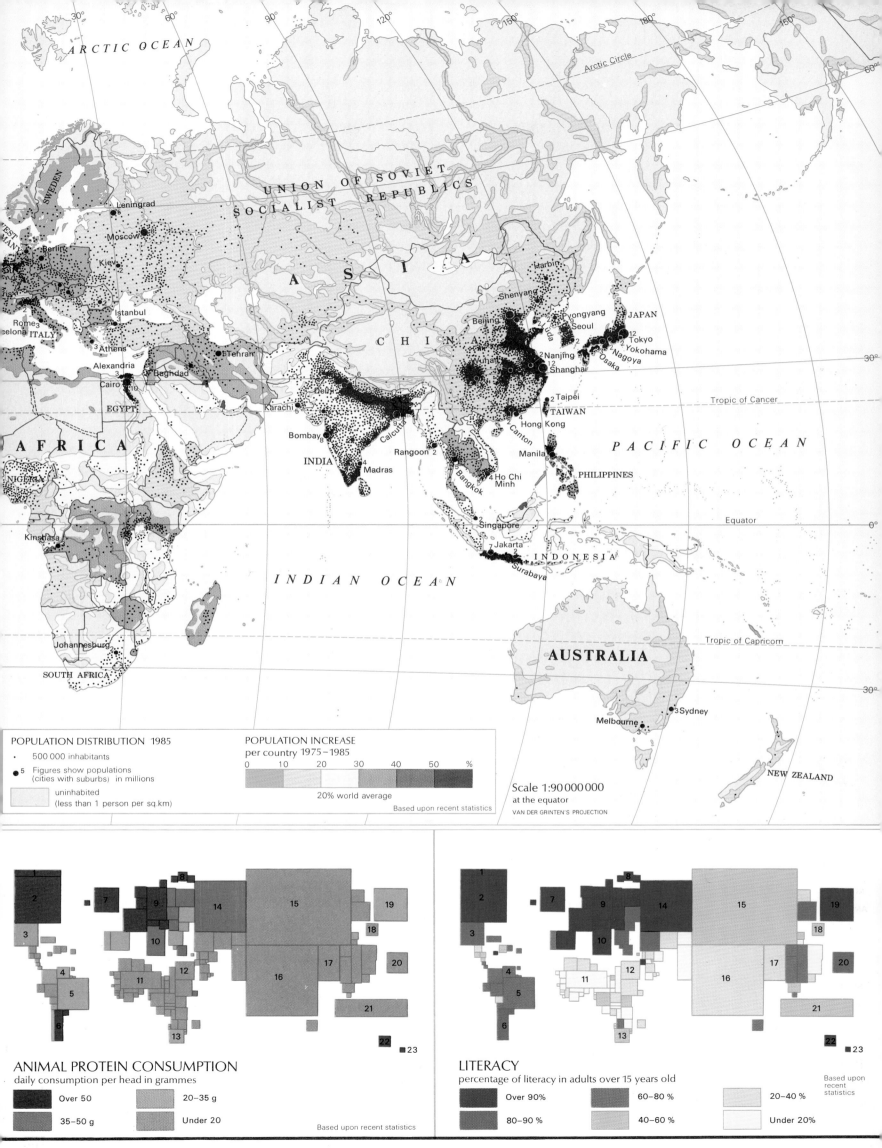

POPULATION DISTRIBUTION 1985
· 500 000 inhabitants
•5 Figures show populations
(cities with suburbs) in millions
uninhabited
(less than 1 person per sq.km)

POPULATION INCREASE
per country 1975–1985

0	10	20	30	40	50	%

20% world average
Based upon recent statistics

Scale 1:90 000 000
at the equator
VAN DER GRINTEN'S PROJECTION

ANIMAL PROTEIN CONSUMPTION
daily consumption per head in grammes

	Over 50		20–35 g
	35–50 g		Under 20

Based upon recent statistics

LITERACY
percentage of literacy in adults over 15 years old

Based upon recent statistics

	Over 90%		60–80 %		20–40 %
	80–90 %		40–60 %		Under 20%

MILITARY POLITICS

AMERICAN ASPECT

EUROPEAN ASPECT

EAST ASIATIC ASPECT

centre Chicago

centre London

centre Peking

| N.A.T.O., A.N.Z.U.S. | Warsaw Pact | Other communist states | Arab League | Other states | W. William-Olsson projection |

© ESSELTE MAP SERVICE

Scale 1:90 000 000

• National capital

———— International boundary

- - - - Disputed boundary

VAN DER GRINTEN'S PROJECTION

AMERICAN ASPECT

EUROPEAN ASPECT

EAST ASIATIC ASPECT

centre Chicago

centre London

centre Peking

TRADE POLITICS

E.E.C.	E.E.C. associated. Commonwealth	E.F.T.A.
L.A.I.A.	Comecon	Other countries

○ O.P.E.C.

103

PACIFIC

OCEAN

NORTH AMERICA

Prudhoe Bay
Beaufort Sea
Greenland
Baffin Bay
Baffin Island
Arctic Circle
Hudson Bay
Labrador
Newfoundland
Godthåb
Iceland
British Isles
Midlan

Kamchatka
Bering Sea
Bering Strait
Alaska
Aleutian Islands
Mackenzie River

Kemano
Alberta
Saskatchewan
Uranium City
Grand Coulee
North Dakota
Elliott Lake
Columbia River
Wyoming
Great Lakes
Montreal
St. Lawrence R.
Fremont Cr.
Utah
Kansas
Illinois
Pennsylvania
West Virginia
California
Hoover
Panhandle
Tennessee
Kentucky
Valencia
Texas
Louisiana
Gulf of Mexico
Tampico
Tropic of Cancer

Hawaiian Islands

West Indies
Caribbean Sea
Maracaibo

ATLANTIC

Equator
Orito
R. Amazon
S
R. Nil

SOUTH AMERICA

OCEAN

Santa Cruz
Minas Gerais
Tropic of Capricorn
Don Otto
R. Parana
Malargüe

New Zealand
Comodoro Rivadavia
Tierra del Fuego

CANADA
81
63
U.S.A.
615
422
WESTERN EUROPE
562
727
COMMUNIST COUNTRIES INCL. CHINA
687
JAPAN
196
133
MEXICO
115
95
NORTH AFRICA
132
115
17
REST OF ASIA
63
NORTHERN SOUTH AMERICA
129
31
MIDDLE EAST
779
50
71
11
101
SOUTH EAST ASIA
59
98
WEST AFRICA
19
27
20
OCEANIA
32
SOUTHERN SOUTH AMERICA
REST OF AFRICA

NORTH AMERICA
784
699
WESTERN EUROPE
496
583
1925
COMMUNIST COUNTRIES INCL. CHINA
2009
JAPAN
18
97
21
LATIN AMERICA 26
185
190
SOUTHERN ASIA
137
AFRICA
104
115
OCEANIA
68

OIL: production, consumption, sea transport (metric tons)

less than 20
20–100
100–200
200–400
400–800
over 800

139 production (million tons/year)
83 consumption (million tons/year)
transport of crude oil (million tons/year)

COAL: production, consumption (metric tons)

330 production (million tons/year)
394 consumption (million tons/year)
coal and lignite expressed in comparable values (coal equivalent)

© ESSELTE MAP SERVICE

LAND

sedimentary basin
(partly oil-bearing)

bedrock without
thick sediment cover

hydro electric
power > 500 Mw

deposits of:
— uranium
— crude oil
— tar sands or oil shales
— natural gas
— coal
— lignite

SEA

sedimentary basin
(partly oil-bearing)

shallow seabed
without thick
sediment cover

shallow sea
(continental shelf)

200 m

2000 m

deep sea

Scale 1:90 000 000
at the equator

PRODUCTION OF ENERGY

Total annual production of primary energy
(crude oil, natural gas, coal, lignite,
peat, hydro-electric and nuclear power)

primary energy expressed
in million tons coal

537 ← 1981
99 ← 1962
AFRICA

NORTH AMERICA 2359
1533

WESTERN
EUROPE 832
572

COMMUNIST
COUNTRIES
INCL. CHINA
1349
3089

CENTRAL AMERICA
(INCL. VENEZUELA
AND COLOMBIA)
285
428

AFRICA
500
99

MIDDLE
EAST
1193
408

REST OF ASIA
186
365

SOUTH AMERICA
133
145

OCEANIA
128
34

THE WORLD'S SOURCES OF ENERGY

Hydro-electric
& nuclear power
3,6%

Natural gas
21,4%

Coal,
lignite
29,4%

Crude oil
45,6%

CONSUMPTION OF ENERGY

Total annual consumption of primary
energy per person by country
(expressed in kilograms of coal)

100 1000 3000 6000 kilograms per person

VAN DER GRINTEN'S PROJECTION

105

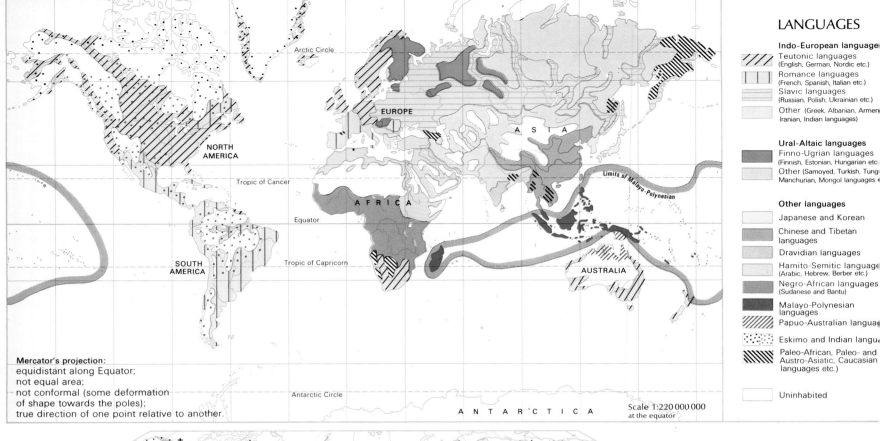

LANGUAGES

Indo-European language
- Teutonic languages (English, German, Nordic etc.)
- Romance languages (French, Spanish, Italian etc.)
- Slavic languages (Russian, Polish, Ukrainian etc.)
- Other (Greek, Albanian, Armeni Iranian, Indian languages)

Ural-Altaic languages
- Finno-Ugrian languages (Finnish, Estonian, Hungarian etc.)
- Other (Samoyed, Turkish, Tung Manchurian, Mongol languages

Other languages
- Japanese and Korean
- Chinese and Tibetan languages
- Dravidian languages
- Hamito-Semitic language (Arabic, Hebrew, Berber etc.)
- Negro-African languages (Sudanese and Bantu)
- Malayo-Polynesian languages
- Papuo-Australian langua
- Eskimo and Indian langu
- Paleo-African, Paleo- and Austro-Asiatic, Caucasian languages etc.)

- Uninhabited

Mercator's projection:
equidistant along Equator;
not equal area;
not conformal (some deformation of shape towards the poles);
true direction of one point relative to another.

Scale 1:220 000 000 at the equator

RELIGIONS

- Protestant
- Catholic } Christians
- Orthodox
- Sunnite } Moslems
- Shiite
- Jews
- Buddhists
- Shintoists and Buddhists
- Chinese religions (Confucians, Taoists etc).
- Hindus
- Animists (primitive religions)

Winkel's projection:
equidistant along Equator;
not equal area;
not conformal (considerable deformation of shape towards the poles).

Scale 1:220 000 000 at the equator

The world's population by religio

Others 23% · Christia 30% · Moslems 14% · Buddhists 7% · Chinese religions 13% · Hindus 13%

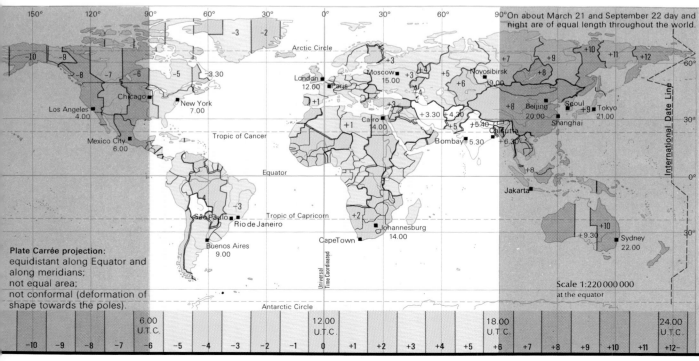

On about March 21 and September 22 day and night are of equal length throughout the world.

Plate Carrée projection:
equidistant along Equator and along meridians;
not equal area;
not conformal (deformation of shape towards the poles).

Scale 1:220 000 000 at the equator

TIME ZONES

About December 22 at 12.00 U.T.C.

Daylight:
north of Arctic Circle;
London (51°30'N.); 8
at the Equator 1

About June 21 at 12.00 U.T.C.

Daylight:
north of Arctic Circle;
London (51°30'N.); 1
at the Equator 1

→ direction of Earth's rotation.

The Earth rotates on its axis from west to east and completes one rotation in about 24 hours. The Earth has been divided into 24 Standard Time Zones. The lines separating these Zones on land mostly follow country or province boundaries. Many countries however use a different standard, eg. British Summer Time.

GLOSSARY and INDEX

The **GLOSSARY**, p. 107–109, provides an English translation of those geographical names and words which are presented on the maps in the langue of the area concerned. For languages using non-Latin alphabets, official transcriptions have been used throughout the entire atlas—in maps, glossary and index.

The words in the glossary are mostly single words, but some prefixes and suffixes are also translated into English. In some cases the name on the map is abbreviated, for instance **Khr**. for the Russian **Khrebet** (mountain chain or range). In the glossary both the full name and its abbreviation is given.

The **INDEX**, p. 111–202, contains about 47.000 names found in the map section. As a general rule each entry is referred to the map page where the place or feature is shown at the largest scale and where it is best seen in its national and environmental context. The oceans and some oceanic islands are referred to small-scale maps to show the extent of the oceans and, for the islands, their correct location.

Each name in the index is located by a map page number and an index square on that particular page. The locational reference is to the name and not, for instance, the extent of country or the position of the town. The squares are defined by letters and figures. For example the town Nyeri in Kenya is found in the index with the reference 65 F 5 which means that Nyeri is found on page 65 in index square F (marked at the top and at the bottom of the map spread) and 5 (marked at the sides of the spread).

Some names are given only a page number as reference. Some of these names appear on the maps of the Polar regions, where an index with letters and figures would be confusing. Other entries refer to names on the thematical maps of the continents which do not have index squares.

GLOSSARY

A
å *Dan., Nor., Swe.* — river
açude *Portugese* — reservoir
adrar *Berber* — mountains
ákra, akrotition *Greek* — cape
Alb, Alp *German* — mountains, peak
alpes *French* — mountains
alpi *Italian* — mountains
-älv, -älven *Swedish* — river
ao *Thai* — bay
archipiélago *Spanish* — archipelago
arquipélago *Portugese* — archipelago
arrecife *Spanish* — reef
arroyo *Spanish* — brook
-ås, -åsen *Swedish* — hills
atol *Portugese* — atoll
aïn *Arabic* — spring

B
bab *Arabic* — strait
bælt *Danish* — strait
bahia *Spanish* — bay
bahr, baḥr *Arabic* — river, sea
baia *Portugese* — bay
baie *French* — bay
ballon *French* — mountain
balta *Romanian* — marsh
bañados *Spanish* — marsh
-bandao *Chinese* — peninsula
barrage *French* — dam
baraji *Turkish* — reservoir
batang *Indonesian* — river
batu *Malay* — mountain
Becken *German* — basin
ben *Gaelic* — mountain
Berg *German* — mountain, hill
berg *Afrikaan, Dutch* — mountains
-berg *Swedish* — mountain, hill
Berge *German* — mountains
-bergen *Swedish* — mountains
-berget *Swedish* — mountain, hill
bi'r *Arabic* — well
birkat *Arabic* — lake
boca *Spanish* — river mouth
boğazi *Turkish* — strait
bogd *Mongolian* — range
bol'shoy *Russian* — big
bong *Korean* — mountain
-breen *Norwegian* — glacier
Bucht *German* — bay
bugt *Danish* — bay
buhayrah *Arabic* — lake
buḥayrat *Arabic* — lake, lagoon

bukit *Indon., Malay* — mountain
-bukten *Swedish* — bay
burnu, burun *Turkish* — cape

C
c., cabo *Spanish* — cape
c., cabo *Port.* — cape
cachoeira *Portugese* — waterfall
canal *Fr., Port., Sp.* — canal, channel
canale *Italian* — canal, channel, strait
cao nguyen *Vietnamese* — plateau
c., cap *French* — cape
capo *Italian* — cape
causse *French* — upland
c., co., cerro *Spanish* — mountain
c., co., cerros *Spanish* — mountains
chapada *Portugese* — hills
chott *Arabic* — intermittent lake, salt marsh
chuŏr phnum *Cambod.* — mountains
ciudad *Spanish* — city
co *Chinese* — lake
col *French* — pass
colina *Spanish* — hill
colinas *Spanish* — hills
colli *Italian* — hills
collines *French* — hills
con *Vietnamese* — islands
cord., cordillera *Sp.* — mountains
corno *Italian* — mountain
costa *Spanish* — coast
côte *French* — coast, hills
crêt *French* — peak
cuevas *Spanish* — caves

D
dağ, dağı *Turkish* — mountain
dāgh *Persian* — mountains
dağlar, dağlan *Turkish* — mountains
dahr *Arabic* — hill
-dal, -dalen *Nor., Swe.* — valley
danau *Indonesian* — lake
-dao *Chinese, Vietnam.* — island
daryācheh *Persian* — lake
dasht *Persian* — desert
deniz, denizi *Turkish* — sea
desierto *Spanish* — desert
détroit *French* — strait
dhar *Arabic* — escarpment
-dian *Chinese* — lake
dijk *Dutch* — dike
djebel *Arabic* — mountain, mountains
-djupet *Swedish* — deep

-do *Korean* — island
doi *Thai* — mountain
dolina *Russian* — valley
dolok *Indonesian* — mountain

E
-egga *Norwegian* — mountain
-elv, -elva *Nor.* — river
embalse *Spanish* — reservoir
erg *Arabic* — desert
espigão *Portugese* — highland
estero *Spanish* — estuary
estrecho *Spanish* — strait
étang *French* — pond
-ey *Icelandic* — island

F
falaise *French* — cliff
farsh *Arabic* — upland
-fell *Icelandic* — mountain
-feng *Chinese* — mountain
firth *Gaelic* — estuary, strait
-fjäll *Swedish* — hill, mountain
-fjällen *Swedish* — mountain, mountains
-fjället *Swedish* — mountain
-fjell, -fjellet *Norwegian* — mountain
-fjöll *Icelandic* — mountain
-fjord *Norwegian* — fjord
-fjorden *Nor., Swe.* — fjord, lake
-fjördur *Icelandic* — fjord, bay
-flói *Icelandic* — bay
foci *Italian* — river mouths
-fonni *Norwegian* — glacier
fontaine *French* — spring
-foss *Icelandic* — waterfall

G
g., gora *Russian* — mountain, hill
G., gunung *Malay* — mountain
G., gunung *Indonesian* — mountain
gebergte *Dutch* — mountains
Gebirge *German* — mountains
greçidi *Turkish* — pass
ghubbat *Arabic* — bay
Gipfel *German* — peak
gji *Albanian* — bay
gol *Mongol* — river
göl, gölü *Turkish* — lake
golfe *French* — gulf
golfo *It., Sp.* — gulf
gora *Serbo-Croathian* — mountains

107

góra Polish — mountain
gorje Serbo-Croatian — mountains, hills
gory Russian — mountains, hills
góry Polish — mountains
grotte French — grotto
gryada Russian — mountain
guba Russian — bay
guelb Arabic — mountain
-guntō Japanese — islands

H

Haff German — lagoon
-hai Chinese — sea, lake
-haixia Chinese — strait
-halvøya Norwegian — peninsula
-hama Japanese — beach
hamada Arabic — desert
hammādat Arabic — plateau
hāmūn Persian — lake, marsch
harrat Arabic — lava flow
-hav Swedish — sea, bay
havre French — harbor
hawr Arabic — lake
-he Chinese — river
Heide German — heath
hka Burmese — river
-holm Danish — island
horn German — cape, mountain
hory Czech., Slovenian — mountains
-hu Chinese — lake

I

i., isla Spanish — island
idhan Arabic — dunes
île French — island
îles French — islands
ilha Portugese — islands
Insel German — island
Inseln German — islands
Insulá Romanian — island
'irq Arabic — dunes
islas Spanish — islands
isola Italian — island
isole Italian — islands
istmo Spanish — isthmus

J

jabal Arabic — mountain, mountains
järv Estonian — lake
-järvi Finnish — lake
-jaur Lappish — lake
-javre Lappish — lake
jazā'ir Arabic — islands
jazīrat Arabic — island
jazīreh Persian — island
jebel Arabic — mountain
jezero Serbo-Croathian, Albanian — lake
jezioro Polish — lake, lagoon
-jiang Chinese — river
jibāl Arabic — mountains
-jima Japanese — island
-joki Finnish — river
-jøkulen Norwegian — glacier
-jökull Icelandic — glacier

K

kabīr Persian — mountains
-kaikuō Japanese — strait
-kaise Lappish — mountain
kalns Latvian — mountain
Kamm German — ridge
kanaal Dutch — canal
kanal Rus., S.C., Swe., Ger. — canal, channel
kanava Finnish — canal, channel
Kap German — cape
-kapp Norwegian — cape
kas Cambodian — island
kavīr Persian — desert
kep Albanian — cape
k., kep., kepulauan Indon. — islands
khalīj Arabic — gulf
khashm Arabic — mountain
Khr., Khrebet Russian — mountain range
ko Thai. — island
-ko Japanese — lake, lagoon
koh Afgan. — mountains
kólpos Greek — bay
körfezi Turkish — gulf, bay
Kórgustik Estonian — mountain
kosa Russian — spit
kotlina Polish — basin
-kou Chinese — bay, pass
krueng Indonesian — river
kryazh Russian — mountains
kuala Malay — bay
küh Persian — mountain

kūhha Persian — mountains
-kulle Swedish — hill
kyun Burmese — island

L

l., lac French — lake
la Tibethan — pass
lacs French — lakes
lacul Bulgarian — lake
lago It., Sp. Port. — lake
L., lagoa Portugese — lake, lagoon
lagos Port., Sp. — lakes
lag., laguna Spanish — lagoon, lake
l., laut Indonesian — sea
les Czechoslovakian — mountains, forest
liman Russian — estuary, bay
limni Greek — lake
-ling Chinese — peak
llano Spanish, Port. — plain
llanos Spanish, Port. — plains
loch Gaelic — lake, inlet
lough Gaelic — lake

M

m., munţii Romanian — mountains
mae Thai — river
-mak Turkish — river
-man Korean — bay
mar Spanish — sea
marais French — marsch
mare Italian — sea
massif French — mountain, mountains
Meer German — sea, lake
meer Afrikaans, Dutch — sea, lake
mer French — sea
mesa Spanish — mesa
meseta Spanish — plateau
mierzeja Polish — spit
-misaki Japanese — cape
mont French — mount
montagna Italian — mountain
montagne French — mountain
montagnes French — mountains
montaña Spanish — mountain
montañas Spanish — mountains
monte It., Port., Sp. — mount
montes Port., Sp. — mountains
monti Italian — mountains
monts French — mountains
more Russian — sea
morro Port., Sp. — hill, mountain
motu Polynesian — island, rock
mui Vietnamese — point
munkhafad Arabic — depression
munţii Romanian — mountains
mys Russian — cape

N

nafūd Arabic — desert
najor'ye Russian — plateau, mountains
namakzār Persian — salt flat
-näs Swedish — peninsula
nasjonal park Nor. — national park
neem Estonian — cape
-nes Ice., Nor. — peninsula, point
ness Gaelic — promontory
nev., nevado Spanish — mountain
ngoc Vietnamese — mountain
niso Greek — islands
nizmennost' Russian — plain
nunatakk Eskimoo — peak
nuruu Mongol — mountains
nuur Mongol — lake

O

-ö Swe., Dan., Nor. — island
o., ostrov Russian — island
-öarna Swedish — islands
-ön Swedish — island
óri Greek — mountains
óros Greek — mountain, mountains
ostrov Russian — island
ostrova Russian — islands
ostrovul Romanian — island
otok Serbo-croathian — island
-øy, -øya Norwegian — island
oz., ozero Russian — lake
ozera Russian — lakes

P

pahorkatina Czech. — hills
palla Italian — peak
pampa Spanish — plain
pantanal Port., Sp. — swamp
parc national French — national park
parq. nac., parque nacional Port., Sp. — national park
pas French — strait

paso Spanish — pass
Pass German — pass
passe French — passage
passo Italian — pass
pasul Romanian — pass
peg., pegunungan Indonesian — mountains
pélagos Greek — sea
peña Spanish — peak, rock
-pendi Chinese — basin
peninsula Spanish — peninsula
pereval Russian — pass
pertuis French — strait
peski Russian — desert
phnum Cambodian — mountain
pic French — peak
pico Port., Sp. — peak
picos Port., Sp. — peaks
-piggen Norwegian — mountains
pik Russian — peak
plaine French — plain
planalto Portugese — plateau
planina Serbo-Croathian — mountain
plato Bulgarian, Russian — plateau
playa Spanish — beach
ploskogorje Russian — plateau
pointe French — point
poluostrov Russian — peninsula
ponta Portugese — point
porog Russian — waterfall
presa Spanish — reservoir, dam
prohod Bulgarian — pass
proliv Russian — strait
promontorio It., Sp. — promonotyr
puerto Spanish — pass
puig Catalonian — peak
pulau Indon., Malay — island
puna Spanish — upland
punta It., Sp. — point, peak
puncak Indonesian — peak
puo Laotian, Thai — mountain
puy French — peak

Q

qanāt Arabic — canal
-quando Chinese — islands
qurnat Arabic — mountains

R

r. Port., Sp. — river
rags Latvian — cape
ramlat Arabic — dunes
räs, ra's Arabic — cape
räs Persian — cape
ravnina Russian — plain
récif French — reef
récifs French — reefs
R., reprêsa Portugese — dam, reservoir
-retto Japanese — islands
ria Spanish — estuary
rio Portugese — river
rio Spanish — river
riviera Italian — coast
rivière French — river
rt Serbo-Croathian — cape
Ruck German — mountain

S

sa. Portugese — mountains
saar Estonian — island
sabkhat Arabic — lagoon, salt marsh
sadd Arabic — dam
saguia Arabic — wadi
şsahrā' Arabic — desert
salar Spanish — salt flat
salina, salinas Spanish — salt marsh, salt flat
-sälkä Finnish — ridge
-sanmyaku Japanese — range
-san Jap., Korean — mountain
-sanchi Japanese — mountains
-sanmaek Korean — mountains
sarīr Arabic — desert
Sattel German — pass
saurums Latvian — strait
sebkha Arabic — salt flat
sebkra Arabic — intermittent lake
See German — lake
Seen German — lakes
selat Indonesian — strait
serra Portugese, Sp. — mountains, mountain
serania, serranias Sp. — mountains
shamo Chinese — desert
-shan Chinese — mountains, mountain, island
-shankou Chinese — pass
sharm Arabic — bay
-shima Japanese — island
-shotō Japanese — islands
-shuiku Chinese — reservoir
sierra Spanish — mountains

108

silsilesi *Turkish*   mountains
-sjö *Norwegian*   lake
-sjön *Swedish*   lake, bay
serrania *Spanish*   mountains
sopka *Russian*   mountain
Spitze *German*   peak
sierra *Spanish*   mountains
step' *Russian*   plain
štit *Slovenian*   peak
stretto *Italian*   strait
-suidō *Japanese*   channel
-sund *Swedish*   sound
s., sungai *Indonesian*   river

T

tg., tanjung *Indones.*   cape
-tangar-, tangi *Icelandic* point
tassili *Berber*   plateau
taung *Burmese*   mountain
teluk *Indonesian*   bay
ténéré *Berber*   desert
tepe, tepesi *Turkish*   peak, hill

thiu khao *Thai.*   mountains
-tind, -tindane *Nor.*   mountain
-tō *Japanese*   island
tónlé *Cambodian*   lake
-top *Dutch*   peak
-träsk *Swedish*   lake
-tunturi *Finnish*   mountain

U–V

uul *Mongol*   mountain, mountains
-vaara *Finnish*   hill
val *French, Italian*   valley
valle *Italian, Spanish*   valley
vallée *French*   valley
-vatn *Ice., Nor.*   lake
-vesi *Finnish*   lake
-vidda *Norwegian*   plateau
-viken *Swedish*   gulf
Virful *Romanian*   mountain
vodokhranilishche
    Russian   reservoir

vol., volcán *Spanish*   volcano
vozvyshennost *Russian* upland
vrh., vrchovina *Czech.,*
    Slo.   mountains
-väin *Estonian*   strait
-vötn *Icelandic*   lake

W–Z

wādi *Arabic*   wadi
wāhat *Arabic*   oasis
Wald *German*   forest, mountains
-wan *Ch., Jap.*   bay
-xan *Chinese*   strait
-yama *Japanese*   mountain
y., yarimadasi *Turkish* peninsula
yoma *Burmese*   mountains
-zaki *Japanese*   point
zalew *Polish*   lagoon
zaliv *Russian*   gulf, bay
zatoka *Polish*   gulf
zee *Dutch*   sea, lake

INDEX

A

Å 16 F 2
Aa Ṣumayh 64 D 3
Aachen 14 E 4
Aalen 15 F 5
Äänekoski 16 J 3
Aansluit 66 C 5
Aare 19 E 2
Aargub 58 B 4
Aba (China) 38 D 4
Aba (Nigeria) 63 F 4
Aba (Zaire) 64 E 4
Abā Ad Dūd (Saudi Arabia) 22 D 4
Abacaxis 85 G 5
Abadab, Jabal 60 F 5
Ābādān 34 D 4
Ābādān (Iran) 23 E 3
Ābādeh (Iran) 23 F 3
Ābādeh (Iran) 23 F 3
Abadla 58 E 2
Abaeté 87 G 4
Abaetetuba 85 J 4
Abagnar Qi 39 G 2
Abaí 88 E 4
Abaiang 52 C 2
Abaji 63 F 4
Abakaliki 63 F 4
Abakan 25 R 5
Abakan 36 F 5
Abakanskiy Khrebet 25 R 5
Abakanskiy Khrebet 25 S 5
Abakwasimbo 64 D 4
Abala (Congo) 64 H 6
Abala (Niger) 62 E 3
Abalak 63 F 2
Abalemma (Algeria) 59 G 4
Abalemma (Niger) 63 F 2
Abalemma (Niger) 63 F 2
Abalessa 59 F 4
Aban 36 G 4
Abancay 86 B 3
Abant Silsilesi 20 D 2
Abār al Kanā'is 60 D 2
Abariringa 52 D 3
Abarqu (Iran) 23 F 3
Abarqu, Kavir-e (Iran) 23 F 3
Abashiri 39 M 2
Abatskoye 25 O 4
Abau 50 E 4
Abava 17 H 4
Abay 25 O 6
Abaya, Lake 65 F 3
Abaza 36 F 5
Abbai 64 F 2
Abbāsābād 34 F 3
Abbāsābād (Iran) 23 G 1
Abbe, Lake 65 G 2
Abbeville (France) 18 D 1
Abbeville (LA, U.S.A.) 77 H 6
Abbeyleix 4 B 3
Abbeytown 5 D 2
Abborrträsk 16 GH 2
Abbot Ice Shelf 91
Abbots Bromley 7 D 1
Abbottabad 35 J 4
'Abd al Azīz, Jabal 61 F 1
'Abd al Kūrī 65 J 2
Ābdānān (Iran) 23 E 2
Abdul Ghadir 65 G 2
Abdulino 24 K 5
Abéché 63 J 3
Abel Tasman National Park 51 Q 9
Abelvær 16 F 3
Abemama 52 C 2
Abenab 66 B 3
Abengourou 62 D 4
Åbenrå 17 E 4
Abeokuta 62 E 4
Aberaeron 6 B 1
Aberchirder 2 C 3
Aberdare 6 C 2
Aberdare National Park 65 F 5
Aberdares → Nyanda Rua 65 F 5
Aberdeen 2 C 3
Aberdeen (Airport) 2 C 3
Aberdeen (S.D., U.S.A.) 76 G 2
Aberdeen (South Africa) 66 C 6
Aberdeen (WA, U.S.A.) 76 B 2
Aberdeen [Andaman Is.] 41 F 5
Aberdeen Lake 73 RS 3
Aberdyfi 6 B 1
Aberedew 6 C 1
Aberfeldy 3 C 3

Aberffraw 6 B 1
Aberfoyle 49 H 3
Abergavenny 6 C 2
Abergele 6 C 1
Abergynolwyn 6 C 1
Aberkenfig 6 C 3
Abermule 6 C 1
Abersoch 6 B 1
Abersychan 6 C 2
Abertillery 6 C 2
Aberystwyth 6 B 1
Abez' 25 M 2
Abganerevo 21 F 1
Abhā' 61 G 5
Abhar (Iran) 23 E 1
Abi Addi 65 F 2
Abidjan 62 D 4
Ab-i-Istada 35 H 4
Abilene 76 G 5
Abingdon 7 D 2
Abinskaya 21 E 2
Abisko 16 G 2
Abitibi 75 L 5
Abja-Paluoja 17 HJ 4
Abkit 37 T 3
Ablngton 3 C 4
Abnūb 60 E 3
Abo, Massif d' 63 H 1
Aboisso 62 D 4
Aboke 64 E 3
Abomey 62 E 4
Abong Abong, Gunung 42 A 3
Abong Mbang 63 G 5
Aborigen, Pik 37 R 3
Aborlan 43 E 2
Abou Deïa 63 H 3
Abou Goulem 63 J 3
Abovyan 21 F 2
Aboyne 3 C 3
Abqaiq (Saudi Arabia) 23 E 4
Abqayq → Buqayq 61 H 3
Abraham's Bay 79 H 3
Abrantes 18 B 4
Abreu e Lima 87 K 2
'Abrī 60 E 4
Abrolhos, Arquipélago dos 87 J 4
Abruka 17 H 4
Abruzzo 19 F 3
Absaroka Range 76 DE 2–3
Abū ad Duhūr (Syria) 22 B 2
Abū al Abyadh (United Arab
   Emirates) 23 F 4
Abū al Bukhush (United Arab
   Emirates) 23 F 4
Abū 'Alī (Saudi Arabia) 23 E 4
Abū 'Arish 61 G 5
Abū Bahr 61 H 4
Abū Ballas 60 D 4
Abū Daghmah (Syria) 22 C 1
Abū Darbah (Egypt) 22 A 3
Abu Dhabi (United Arab Emirates)
   23 FG 4
Abū Dulayq 60 E 5
Abū Ḥadrīyah (Saudi Arabia)
   23 E 4
Abū Ḥamad 60 E 5
Abū Ḥasan, Jabal 61 G 5
Abū Jābirah 60 D 6
Abū Jifān (Saudi Arabia) 23 E 4
Abū Jubayhah 60 E 6
Abū Kamāl (Syria) 22 C 2
Abū Madd, Ra's 60 F 4
Abū Maṭarīq 60 D 6
Abu Mendi 64 F 2
Abū Mūsa' (Iran) 23 G 4
Abū Njaym 59 J 2
Abū Qumayyis, Ra's (United Arab
   Emirates) 23 F 4
Abu Road 40 B 3
Abū Rubayq 61 F 4
Abū Rujmayn, Jabal 60 F 2
Abū Sa'fan (Saudi Arabia) 23 F 4
Abū Shajarah, Ra's 60 F 4
Abū Shanab 60 D 6
Abu Simbel → Abu Sunbul 60 E 4
Abū Sukhayr (Saudi Arabia)
   22 D 3
Abū Sunbul 60 E 4
Abū Tabari 60 D 5
Abū Ṭīj 60 E 3
Abū Tulayh 60 E 5
Abū 'Uruq 60 E 5
Abū Zabad 60 D 6

Abū Ẓaby (United Arab Emirates)
   23 FG 4
Abū Zanīmah (Egypt) 22 A 3
Abufari 85 F 5
Abuja 63 F 4
Abumombazi 64 C 4
Abunã 86 C 3
Abunã (Rondônia, Brazil) 84 E 5
Abūqrīn 59 J 2
Abuya Myeda 65 F 2
Abwong 64 E 3
Aby, Lagune 62 D 4
Abyad 60 D 6
Abyad, Jabal 60 D 5
Abyad, Ra's al (Saudi Arabia)
   22 BC 5
Abyār 'Alī (Saudi Arabia) 22 C 4
Abydos 60 E 3
Abyek 34 E 3
Ābyek (Iran) 23 F 2
Åbyn 16 H 2
Abyy 37 QR 2
Acadia, Cape 75 M 3
Acadia National Park 77 N 3
Acadie 75 OP 6
Açailândia 85 J 4
Acajutla 78 DE 5
Acalayong 63 FG 5
Acámbaro 78 B 3–4
Acandí 84 C 2
Acaponeta 78 A 3
Acapulco 78 B 4
Acará 85 J 4
Acarai, Serra 85 G 3
Acaraú 87 HJ 1
Acaraú 87 J 1
Acari (Brazil) 87 J 2
Acarí (Peru) 86 B 4
Acarigua 84 E 2
Acatlán de Osorio 78 C 4
Acayucan 78 C 4
Accomac 77 L 4
Accra 62 DE 4
Accrington 5 D 3
Acebuches 78 B 2
Acerra 19 F 3
Achaguas 84 E 2
Achalpur 40 C 3
Achao 89 B 7
Achar 88 E 5
Achavanich 2 C 2
Achegour 63 G 2
Acheloós 20 B 3
Acheng 39 J 1
Achiemore 2 B 2
Achikouya, Plateau des
   63 GH 6
Achikulak 21 F 2
Achill 14 A 4
Achiltibuie 2 B 2
Achim 15 E 4
Achinsk 36 EF 4
Achintee 2 B 3
Achit Nuur 36 F 6
Achnasaul 3 B 3
Achnasheen 2 B 2
Achuyevo 21 E 1
Acı Gölü 20 C 3
Acil Barké 62 C 3
Acipayam 20 C 3
Acireale 19 G 4
Acklins Island 79 H 3
Acle 7 E 1
Aconcagua, Cerro 88 BC 5
Acopiara 87 J 2
Acorizal 86 E 4
Acorn Hoek 67 E 4
Acquasanta Terme 19 F 3
Acqui Terme 19 E 3
Acre 84 C 2
Acre 86 C 3
Acre (Israel) 22 B 2
Acri 19 G 4
Actaeon Group 53 F 4
Actopan 78 C 3
Açu 87 J 2
Açude Araras 87 H 1
Açude Orós 87 J 2
Acuracay 84 D 5
Ad Ḍab'ah 60 D 2
Ad Dabbah 60 E 5
Ad Dafīnah 61 G 4

Ad Ḍafrah (United Arab Emirates)
   23 F 5
Ad Dahnā' (Saudi Arabia) 23 DE 4
Ad Ḍāli' 61 GH 6
Ad Damazin 60 E 6
Ad' Dāmir 60 E 5
Ad Dammām (Saudi Arabia)
   23 EF 4
Ad Dār al Hamrā' (Saudi Arabia)
   22 BC 4
Ad Darb 61 G 5
Ad Dawādimī (Saudi Arabia)
   22 D 4
Ad Dawḥah (Qatar) 23 F 4
Ad Dawr (Iraq) 22 D 2
Ad Dayr (Egypt) 22 A 4
Ad Dibdibah (Saudi Arabia)
   23 E 3–4
Ad Diffah 59 K 2
Ad Dikākah 61 J 5
Ad Dilam (Saudi Arabia) 23 E 5
Ad Dindar 60 E 6
Ad Dirīyah (Saudi Arabia) 23 E 4
Ad Dīwanīyah (Iraq) 23 D 3
Ad Du'ayn 60 D 6
Ad Duwayd 60 D 6
Ad Duwayd (Saudi Arabia)
   22 CD 3
Ad Duwaym 60 E 6
Ad Ouzzeïne 62 E 2
Ada (Ghana) 62 E 4
Ada (OK, U.S.A.) 77 G 5
Ada Burnu 21 D 3
Adaba 65 F 3
'Adad 65 H 3
Adādle 65 G 3
Adafer 58 CD 5
Adair, Bahia 78 D 5
Adak (AK, U.S.A.) 72 B 5
Adak (Sweden) 16 G 2
'Adale 65 H 4
Ådalen 16 G 3
Adam, Mount 89 DE 9
Adama Nazareth → Adama 65 F 3
Adamantina 87 F 5
Adamaoua 63 G 4
Adamello 19 F 2
Adamoua, Massif de l' 63 G 4
Adams Bridge 40 C 6
Adams Peak 40 D 6
Adamstown 53 G 4
Adana 21 E 3
Adang, Teluk 42 E 4
Adapazarı 20 D 2
Adarama 60 E 5
Adare, Cape 91
Adavale 49 G 4
Adaut 43 H 5
Adavalle 49 G 4
Adda 19 E 2
Addis Ababa 65 F 3
Addis Alam 65 F 3
Addis Derra 65 F 2
Addis Zemen 65 F 2
Adelaide (South Africa) 66 D 6
Adelaide (South Australia) 49 F 5
Adelaide Island 91
Adelaide Peninsula 73 S 2
Adelaide River 48 E 1
Adelaye 64 C 3
Adele Island 48 C 2
Adélie Coast 91
Aden 61 H 6
Aden, Gulf of 61 H 6
Aderbissinat 63 F 2
Adh Dhahībāt 59 H 2
Adh Dhayd (United Arab
   Emirates) 23 G 4
Adhan, Jabal (United Arab
   Emirates) 23 G 4
Adi 64 E 4
Adi Arkai 65 F 2
Adi Kaie 65 F 2
Adi, Pulau 43 H 4
Adi Quala 65 F 2
Adi Ugri 65 F 2
Adiaké 62 D 4
Adige 19 F 2
Adigrat 65 F 2
Adıgüzel Barajı 20 C 3
Adilabad 40 C 4
Adilcevaz 21 F 3
Adirondack Mountains 77 M 3
Adıyaman 21 E 3
Adjud 20 C 1

Adler 21 E 2
Admer, Erg d' 59 G 4
Admiralty 72 L 4
Admiralty Gulf 48 D 1
Admiralty Island National
   Monument 72 L 4
Admiralty Islands 50 E 2
Admiralty Mountains 91
Ado 62 E 4
Ado Ekiti 63 F 4
Adok 64 E 3
Adolphus Island 48 D 2
Adonara, Pulau 43 F 5
Adoni 40 C 4
Adour 18 C 3
Adra 18 C 4
Adrano 19 F 4
Adrar (Algeria) 58 E 3
Adrar (Algeria) 59 G 3–4
Adrar des Iforas 62 E 1–2
Adrar Sotuf 58 B 4
Adré 63 J 3
Adria 19 F 2
Adrian 77 K 3
Adriatic Sea 19 FG 3
Adulis 65 F 1
Adusa 64 D 4
Advie 2 C 3
Adwa 65 F 2
Ady-Kit, Gora 36 G 2
Adycha 37 P 2
Adygalakh 37 R 3
Adyge-Khabl' 21 F 2
Adyk 21 G 1
Adzhar 21 F 2
Adzhima 37 P 6
Adzopé 62 D 4
Adz'va 25 L 2
Adzva 25 M 2
Aegean Sea 20 C 3
Aesculapium 20 C 3
Afade 63 G 3
Afao, Mount 59 G 3
Affak (Iraq) 23 D 2
Affollé 58 C 5
Afghanistan 35 GH 4
Afgöye 65 H 4
'Afif (Saudi Arabia) 22 D 4–5
Afikpo 63 F 4
Aflou 59 F 2
Afmadow 65 G 4
Afogados da Ingazeira 87 J 2
Afognak 72 G 4
Afore 50 E 3
Afrêra, Lake 65 G 2
African Islands 65 J 5
Afşin 21 E 3
Afsluitdijk 14 E 4
Aftout 58 C 5
Afuá 85 H 4
Afyonkarahisar 20 D 3
Agadem 63 G 2
Agadez 63 F 2
Agadir 58 D 2
Agadyr' 25 O 6
Agailás 58 C 4
Agalta, Sierra de 78 E 4
Agana 52 A 2
Agapa 36 E 1
Agapa 36 E 1
Agapitovo 25 R 2
Agapovka 25 L 5
Agara 21 F 2
Agaro 65 F 3
Agartala 41 F 3
Agata 36 F 2
Agata, Ozero 36 F 2
Agats 43 J 5
Agattu 72 A 5
Agawa Bay 74 L 6
Agbaja 63 F 4
Agboville 62 D 4
Agdam 34 D 2
Agdary 36 L 3
Agde 18 D 3
Agdz 58 D 2
Agen 18 D 3
Agepsta 21 F 2
Agha Jari 31
Agha Jārī 34 E 4
Agha Jārī (Iran) 23 EF 3
Aghireşu 20 B 1
Aghrejit 58 C 4
Agía Pelagía 20 B 3
Aginskoye 36 FG 4

Aginskoye **36** K 5
Agmar **58** C 3
Agmumuit **58** B 4
Agnew **48** C 4
Agnibilékrou **62** D 4
Agnita **20** B 1
Agön **16** G 3
Agordat **65** F 1
Agout **18** D 3
Agoza **63** J 2
Agra **40** C 2
Ágreda **18** C 3
Ağrı **21** F 3
Agrigento **19** F 4
Agrihan **52** A 1
Agrínion **20** B 3
Agrour Sfaya **58** C 4
Agto **75** R 2
Agua Blanca **89** C 6
Água Branca (Alagoas, Brazil)
　87 J 2
Agua Branca (Piauí, Brazil) **87** H 2
Água Clara **87** F 5
Agua Prieta **76** E 5
Agua Vermelha, Reprêsa
　87 FG 4–5
Aguachica **84** D 2
Aguaclara **84** D 3
Aguadas **84** C 2
Aguadulce **84** B 2
Aguapeí, Serra do **86** E 4
Aguaray **86** D 5
Aguarico **84** C 4
Águas Formosas **87** H 4
Águeda **18** B 3
Aguelhok **62** E 2
Aguelt el Melha **58** D 4
Aguelt Némadi **58** C 5
Aguemour **59** FG 3
Aguenit **58** C 4
Agueraktem **58** D 4
Aguerguer **58** B 4
Aguezi Tigu **63** G 1
Aguilar de Campóo **18** C 3
Aguilas **18** C 4
Aguililla **78** B 4
Aguja, Cerro **89** B 7
Agulhas, Cape **66** C 6
Agulhas Negras, Pico das **87** H 5
Agung, Gunung **42** E 5
Aguscalientes **78** B 3
Agustín Codazzi **84** D 1–2
Ağva **20** C 2
Agvali **21** G 2
Aha Hills **66** C 3–4
Ahaggar **59** G 4
Ahar **34** D 3
Ahe **53** F 3
Ahiri **40** D 4
Ahlat **21** F 3
Ahmadabad **40** B 3
Ahmadnagar **40** BC 4
Ahmadpur East **35** J 5
Ahmadpur West **35** J 5
Ahmar Mountains **65** G 3
Ahmeyim **58** C 4
Ahnet **59** F 4
Ahome **76** E 6
Ahram (Iran) **23** F 3
Ahraura **40** D 3
Ahrensburg **15** F 4
Ähtäri **16** H 3
Ähtärinjärvi **16** H 3
Ahtaung **41** G 4
Ähtävänjoki **16** H 3
Ahunui **53** F 4
Åhus **17** F 4
Ahvāz **34** D 4
Ahvāz (Iran) **23** E 3
Ahvenanmaa **17** GH 3
Ahwar **61** H 6
Ai-Ais **66** B 5
Aiapuá **85** F 4
Aigoual, Mont **18** D 3
Aigua **88** F 5
Aigues-Mortes **18** D 3
Aiguilete, Cerro **89** B 9
Aiguillon **18** D 3
Aihui **37** N 5
Aiken **77** K 5
Ailao Shan **38** D 6
Aileu **43** G 5
Ailigandí **84** C 2
Ailinginae **52** C 2
Ailinglapalap **52** C 2
Aillik **75** Q 4
Ailsa Craig **3** B 4
Ailuk **52** C 2
Aim **37** O 4
Aimorés **87** H 4
Aimorés, Serra dos **87** H 4
Ain **19** E 2
Aïn Afalelah **59** G 4
'Ain al Khaleifa **60** D 3
'Ain al Wādī **60** D 3
Aïn Amenas **59** G 3

Aïn Amguel **59** FG 4
Aïn Athil **58** C 4
Aïn Azaoua **59** G 3
Aïn Beïda **59** G 1
Aïn ben Tili **58** D 3
Ain Beni Mathar **58** E 2
Aïn Ebeggi **59** G 4
Aïn Ekker **59** G 4
Aïn el Barka **58** D 3
Aïn el Hadjadj **59** G 3
Aïn Ezzane **59** H 4
Aïn Galakka **63** H 2
Aïn Guezzam **59** G 5
Aïn Ouzzal **59** F 4
Aïn Safra **58** C 5
Aïn Sefra **58** E 2
Aïn Souf **59** F 3
Aïn Taya **18** D 4
Aïn Témouchent **58** E 1
Aïn Tidjoubar **59** F 3
Aïn Tiguelguemine **59** F 3
Aïn Ziza **59** F 4
Ainaro **43** G 5
Aïnaži **17** H 4
Aínos Óros **20** B 3
Ainsdale **5** D 3
Aïoun Abd el Malek **58** D 4
Aioun el Atrouss **58** D 5
Aiquile **86** C 4
Aïr **63** F 2
Air Force Island **75** N 2
Air Musi **42** B 4
Airão **85** F 4
Aird of Sleat **3** B 3
Airdrie **3** C 4
Aire, River **5** E 3
Aireborough **5** E 3
Aire-sur-l'Adour **18** CD 3
Airolo **19** E 2
Airth **3** C 3
Aisaita **65** G 2
Aiscia **65** G 2
Aisega **50** E 3
Aishalton **85** G 3
Aishihik **72** K 3
Aisne **18** D 2
Aïssa, Djebel **58** E 2
Aitana, Pico **18** C 4
Aitape **50** D 2
Aith **2** C 2
Aitolikón **20** B 3
Aitutaki **53** E 4
Aiud **20** B 1
Aix-en-Provence **19** E 3
Aix-les-Bains **19** E 2
Aiyaíon Pélagos **20** C 3
Aíyina **20** B 3
Aiyion **20** B 3
Aizawl **41** F 3
Aizuwakamatsu **39** M 3
Aj Bogd Uul **36** FG 7
Aj Bogd Uul **38** BC 2
Aja, Jabal (Saudi Arabia) **22** C 4
Ajab Shīr **34** D 3
Ajaccio **19** E 3
Ajajú **84** D 3
'Ajā'iz **61** K 5
Ajanta Range **40** C 3
Ajdābiyā **59** K 2
Ajdīr, Ra's **59** H 2
Ajigasawa **39** L 2
Ajir, Mont **63** F 2
Ajka **20** A 1
'Ajlūn (Jordan) **22** B 2
'Ajmah, Jabal al (Egypt) **22** A 3
'Ajmān (United Arab Emirates)
　23 G 4
Ajmer **40** B 2
Ajo **76** D 5
Ajo, Cabo de **18** C 3
Ajoewa **85** G 3
Aju, Kepulauan **43** H 3
Ak Dağ **20** C 3
Ak Dağ **20** C 3
Ak Dağ (Turkey) **21** E 3
Ak Dağ (Turkey) **21** F 2
Ak Dovurak **36** F 5
Akabli **59** F 3
Akademii, Zaliv **37** P 5
Akal **60** F 5
Akalkot **40** C 4
Akanthou **21** D 3
Akanthou (Cyprus) **22** A 2
Akarnaniká Ori **20** B 3
Akaroa **51** Q 9
'Akasha **60** E 4
Akashi **39** K 4
Akbaba Tepe **21** E 3
Akbaytal, Pereval **35** J 3
Akbulak **24** L 5
Akçaabat **21** E 2
Akçadağ **21** E 3
Akçakale **21** E 3
Akçakale (Turkey) **22** C 1
Akçakara Dağı **21** F 3
Akçakışla **21** E 3

Akçakoca **20** D 2
Akcha **35** H 3
Akchar, Dunes de l' **58** C 4
Akchatau **25** O 6
Akdağmadeni **21** E 3
Akelamo **43** G 3
Aketi **64** C 4
Akelo **64** E 3
Akespe **34** G 1
Akhalkalaki **21** F 2
Akhaltsikhe **21** F 2
Akharnaí **20** B 3
Akhdar, Jabal al **61** K 4
Akhdar, Wādī al (Saudi Arabia)
　22 B 4
Akhiny **36** J 5
Akhisar **20** C 3
Akhmīm **60** E 3
Akhsu **34** D 2
Akhtarīn (Syria) **22** B 1
Akhtubinsk **24** J 6
Akhtyrka **24** F 5
Akimiski **75** L 5
Akimovka **21** E 1
Akita **39** M 3
Akjoujt **58** C 5
Akka **58** D 3
Akkabak **35** G 1
Akkajaure **16** G 2
'Akko (Israel) **22** B 2
Akköy **20** C 3
Akkul' **35** J 2
Aklavik **72** K 2
Aklé Aouana **58** D 5
Akmenrags **17** H 4
Akmeqit **35** K 3
Akobo **64** E 3
Akobo **64** E 3
Akok **63** F 5
Akola **40** C 3
Akongkür **35** K 2
Akonolinga **63** G 5
Akosombo Dam **62** D 4
Akot (India) **40** C 3
Akot (Sudan) **64** E 3
Akpatok **75** O 3
Akqi **35** K 2
Ákra Akritas **20** B 3
Ákra Ambelos **20** B 3
Ákra Áraxos **20** B 3
Akra Arnauti **21** D 3
Akra Arnauti (Cyprus) **22** A 2
Akra Gata **21** D 4
Akra Gata (Cyprus) **22** A 2
Akra Greco **21** D 4
Akra Greco (Cyprus) **22** B 2
Ákra Kafirévs **20** BC 3
Ákra Kambanós **20** BC 3
Ákra Kánestron **20** B 3
Ákra Kastéllos **20** C 3
Ákra Lithinon **20** B 4
Ákra Maléas **20** B 3
Akra Okhthonia **20** B 3
Akra Pinnes **20** B 2
Ákra Pláka **20** C 2
Ákra Sidheros **20** C 3
Ákra Soúnion **20** B 3
Ákra Spátha **20** B 3
Ákra Taínaron **20** B 3
Akranes **16** A 3
Akrapkir **21** E 3
Akreïdil **58** B 5
Akritas, Ákra **20** B 3
Akron **77** K 3
Aksai Chin **35** K 3
Aksaray **21** D 3
Aksay **21** F 1
Aksay **24** K 5
Aksay Kazakzu Zizhixian **38** B 3
Aksayqin Hu **35** L 3
Akşehir **20** D 3
Akşehir Gölü **20** D 3
Akseki **21** D 3
Aksenovo-Zilovskoye **36** L 5
Aksha **36** K 5
Akshiy **35** G 1
Akstafa **21** G 2
Aksu (Turkey) **20** D 3
Aksu (China) **35** L 2
Aksu (U.S.S.R.) **25** O 5
Aksu (U.S.S.R.) **25** P 6
Aksu He **35** L 2
Aksuat **25** Q 6
Aksum **65** F 2
Aksumbe **35** H 2
Aktash **35** H 3
Aktasty **25** M 5
Aktau (Iraq) **23** E 3
Aktau, Gora **35** G 2
Akto **35** K 3
Aktobe **34** E 2
Aktogay **25** OP 6
Aktogay **25** P 6
Aktumsyk **34** F 1

Aktyubinsk **25** L 5
Akula **64** C 4
Akun **72** D 5
Akure **63** F 4
Akureyri **16** B 2
Akutan **72** D 5
Akwanga **63** F 4
Akyab **41** F 3
Akyazı **20** D 2
Akzhal **25** Q 6
Akzhar **35** J 2
Akzhaykyn, Ozero **35** H 1–2
Al Jazā'ir **59** F 1
Al Qāhirah **60** E 2
Al 'Urūq al Mu' taridah **61** J 4
Al 'Abbāsīyah **60** E 6
Al Abyad, Ra's **59** G 1
Al Abyār **59** K 2
Al 'Adam **59** K 2
Al 'Agabah as Şaghīrah (Egypt)
　22 A 4
Al Ahmadī (Kuwait) **23** E 3
Al Akhḍar, Al Jabal **59** K 2
Al 'Amādīyah (Iraq) **22** D 1
Al 'Amārah (Iraq) **23** E 3
Al 'Aqabah (Jordan) **22** B 3
Al 'Aqaylah **59** J 2
Al 'Aqīq **61** G 4
Al 'Arabīyah (Saudi Arabia)
　23 EF 4
Al Arabīyah as Su'ûdīyah → Saudi
　Arabia **61** GH 4
Al 'Araj **60** D 3
Al 'Arīsh (Egypt) **22** AB 3
Al 'Armah (Saudi Arabia) **23** DE 4
Al Arţāwīyah (Saudi Arabia)
　23 D 4
Al 'Aşāb (United Arab Emirates)
　23 G 5
Al Ashkharah **61** K 4
Al 'Āshūrīyah (Iraq) **22** D 3
Al 'Assāfīyah (Saudi Arabia)
　22 C 3
Al' Athāmīn (Iraq) **22** D 3
Al 'Aţrun **60** D 5
Al 'Awāliq **61** H 6
Al 'Awāriq **61** H 4
Al 'Awaynāt **59** H 3
Al Awshazīyah (Saudi Arabia)
　22 CD 4
Al 'Ayn (United Arab Emirates)
　23 G 4
Al Ayn (Sudan) **60** D 5
Al Aziziyah **59** H 2
Al Bāb (Syria) **22** B 1
Al Badārī **60** E 3
Al Badi' (Saudi Arabia) **61** H 4
Al Bādī (Iraq) **22** C 2
Al Bahr al Mayyit (Jordan) **22** B 3
Al Bahrah (Kuwait) **23** E 3
Al Bahrayn **60** D 3
Al Balyanā **60** E 3
Al Barkāt **59** H 4
Al Barrah (Saudi Arabia) **23** D 4
Al Başrah (Iraq) **23** E 3
Al Baţhā' (Iraq) **23** D 3
Al Baţīn (Saudi Arabia) **23** F 5
Al Bāţin (Iraq) **22** D 2
Al Batinah (Oman) **61** K 4
Al Bāţinah (Saudi Arabia) **23** E 4
Al Batrūn (Lebanon) **22** B 2
Al Bawīţī **60** D 3
Al Bayādh **61** H 4
Al Bayḍā' (Libya) **59** K 2
Al Bayḍā' (S. Yemen) **61** H 6
Al Bid' (Saudi Arabia) **22** B 3
Al Bi'r (Saudi Arabia) **22** B 3
Al Birk **61** G 5
Al Birkah **61** G 4
Al Brayqah **59** JK 2
Al Buhayrah al Murrah al Kubrā
　(Egypt) **22** A 3
Al Burayj (Syria) **22** B 2
Al Buraymi (Oman) **23** G 4
Al Burdī **59** L 2
Al Burmah **59** G 2
Al Buţayn (Saudi Arabia) **23** D 4
Al Dab'iyyah (United Arab
　Emirates) **23** FG 4
Al Fallūjah (Iraq) **22** D 2
Al Farīdah (United Arab Emirates)
　23 G 4
Al Fāshir **60** D 6
Al Fashn **60** E 3
Al Fatḥah (Iraq) **22** D 2
Al Faw (Iraq) **23** E 3
Al Fawwārah (Saudi Arabia)
　22 D 4
Al Fayyūm **60** E 3
Al Fāzih **61** G 6
Al Fifi **60** C 6
Al Fuḥayhīl (Kuwait) **23** E 3
Al Fuhūd (Iraq) **23** E 3
Al Fujayrah (United Arab
　Emirates) **23** G 4

Al Fūlah **60** D 6
Al Fuqahā **59** J 3
Al Furāt (Syria) **22** C 2
Al Fuwayrit (Qatar) **23** F 4
Al Gā¢a **60** E 4
Al Galhak **60** E 6
Al Gharbi **59** H 2
Al Ghāt (Saudi Arabia) **23** D 4
Al Ghaydah **61** J 5
Al Ghayl **61** H 4
Al Ghazālah (Saudi Arabia) **22** C 4
Al Ghrayfah **59** H 3
Al Ghurdaqah (Egypt) **22** AB 4
Al Ghuwairīyah (Qatar) **23** F 4
Al Ḥabakah (Saudi Arabia) **22** D 3
Al Haḍabat al Ma'āzah **60** E 3
Al Ḥaddār **61** H 4
Al Ḥadhālīl (Saudi Arabia)
　22–23 D 3
Al Ḥadīdah **61** J 4
Al Ḥadīthah (Iraq) **22** CD 2
Al Hadr (Iraq) **22** D 2
Al Hā'ir (Saudi Arabia) **23** E 4
Al Hajar al Gharbī **61** K 4
Al Hajar ash Sharqī **61** K 4
Al Ḥalfāyah (Iraq) **23** E 3
Al Ḥamād **22** C 2–3
Al Ḥamādah al Ḥamrā' **59** H 3
Al Ḥammām (Iraq) **22** D 3
Al Ḥamrā' (Saudi Arabia) **22** C 5
Al Ḥamrā', al Ḥamādah **59** H 3
Al Ḥanākīyah (Saudi Arabia)
　22 C 4
Al Ḥanīsh al Kabīr **61** G 6
Al Ḥanīyah (Iraq) **23** DE 3
Al Ḥarīq (Saudi Arabia) **23** E 5
Al Ḥarrah (Jordan) **22** BC 3
Al Ḥarrah (Saudi Arabia) **22** C 3
Al Ḥarrah (Syria) **22** B 2
Al Ḥarūj al Aswad **59** J 3
Al Ḥasa (Jordan) **22** B 3
Al Ḥasā' (Saudi Arabia) **23** EF 4
Al Ḥasakah (Syria) **22** C 1
Al Ḥasan (Iraq) **22** D 2
Al Ḥasānī (Saudi Arabia) **22** B 4
Al Ḥawātah **60** EF 6
Al Ḥawīyah **61** G 4
Al Ḥawjā' (Saudi Arabia) **22** C 3
Al Ḥawrah **61** H 6
Al Ḥawtah **61** H 4
Al Ḥawwārī **59** K 4
Al Ḥayy (Iraq) **23** DE 2
Al Ḥayz **60** D 3
Al Hibāk **61** J 4–5
Al Hijaz (Saudi Arabia) **22** BC 4
Al Hillah (Iraq) **23** D 2
Al Hillah (Saudi Arabia) **23** E 5
Al Hillah (Sudan) **60** D 6
Al Hinnāh (Saudi Arabia) **23** E 4
Al Hirmil (Lebanon) **22** B 2
Al Hoceima **58** E 1
Al Hout (Saudi Arabia) **23** E 3
Al Ḥudaydah **61** G 6
Al Hufrah (Libya) **59** J 3
Al Hufrah (Saudi Arabia)
　22 BC 3–4
Al Hufūf (Saudi Arabia) **23** E 4
Al Hūj (Saudi Arabia) **22** C 3
Al Hunayy (Saudi Arabia) **23** E 4
Al Ḥusayhisah **60** E 6
Al Ḥuwaymī **61** H 6
Al Ḥuwayyit (Saudi Arabia) **22** C 4
Al Huwwah **61** H 4
Al Iglim al Janūbīyah **64** DE 3
Al Ikhwān **61** G 4
Al Ikhwān (Egypt) **22** B 4
Al 'Iraq **22** D 2
Al 'Iraq al 'Arabi (Iraq) **23** DE 2–3
Al 'Irq **59** K 3
Al 'Irqah **61** H 6
Al 'Isāwīyah (Saudi Arabia) **22** B 3
Al Iskandarīyah (Egypt) **60** DE 2
Al Iskandarīyah (Iraq) **22** D 2
Al Ismā'īlīyah (Egypt) **22** A 3
Al Jabal al Akhḍar **59** K 2
Al Jabalayn **60** E 6
Al Jadīdah (Saudi Arabia) **23** E 4
Al Jafr (Jordan) **22** B 3
Al Jāfūrah (Saudi Arabia) **23** F 4–5
Al Jaghbūb **59** K 3
Al Jahrah (Kuwait) **23** E 3
Al Jalāmīd (Saudi Arabia) **22** C 3
Al Jamalīyah (Qatar) **23** F 4
Al Jamm **59** H 1
Al Jardāwīyah (Saudi Arabia)
　22 D 4
Al Jarid, Shaţţ **59** G 2
Al Jawārah **61** K 5
Al Jawb (Saudi Arabia) **23** F 5
Al Jawf (Saudi Arabia) **22** C 3
Al Jawf → Al Kufrah **59** K 4
Al Jaylī **60** E 5
Al Jazīrah **60** E 6
Al Jazīrah (Iraq) **22** CD 2
Al Jībān (Saudi Arabia) **23** F 5
Al Jifārah (Saudi Arabia) **23** D 5

Al Jiwā' (United Arab Emirates) 23 FG 5
Al Jīzah 60 E 2
Al Jubayl (Saudi Arabia) 23 E 4
Al Jubaylah (Saudi Arabia) 23 E 4
Al Jufrah Oasis → Wahat al Jufrah 59 J 3
Al Jufrah, Wāhat 59 J 3
Al Julayqah (Saudi Arabia) 23 E 4
Al Jumaymah (Iraq) 22 D 3
Al Junaynah 60 C 6
Al Junaynah 61 G 4
Al Jurayd 23 EF 4
Al Kabā'ish (Iraq) 23 E 3
Al Kāf 59 G 1
Al Kahfah (Saudi Arabia) 22 D 4
Al Kāmilīn 60 E 5
Al Karak (Jordan) 22 B 3
Al Karnak (Egypt) 22 A 4
Al Kawah 60 E 6
Al Kāzimīyah (Iraq) 22 D 2
Al Khābūrah 61 K 4
Al Khalīl 22 B 3
Al Khālis (Iraq) 23 D 2
Al Khalūf 61 K 4
Al Khandaq 60 E 5
Al Khārijah 60 E 3
Al Kharj (Saudi Arabia) 23 E 5
Al Khartum 60 E 5
Al Khartūm Bahrī 60 E 5
Al Khasab (Oman) 23 G 4
Al Khatam (United Arab Emirates) 23 G 5
Al Khatt (United Arab Emirates) 23 G 4
Al Khawr (Qatar) 23 F 4
Al Khazna (United Arab Emirates) 23 G 4
Al Khidr 61 H 2
Al Khidr (Iraq) 23 D 3
Al Khīsah (Saudi Arabia) 23 F 4
Al Khubar (Saudi Arabia) 23 F 4
Al Khufayfīyah (Saudi Arabia) 23 D 4
Al Khums 59 H 2
Al Khunfah (Saudi Arabia) 22 C 3
Al Khunn 61 H 4
Al Khuraybah 61 H 5
Al Khurmah 61 G 4
Al Khuwayr (Qatar) 23 F 4
Al Kidn 61 J 4
Al Kifl (Iraq) 22 D 2
Al Kilh Sharq (Egypt) 22 A 4
Al Kir'ānah (Qatar) 23 F 4
Al Kirbekan 60 E 5
Al Kubar (Syria) 22 C 2
Al Kūfah (Iraq) 22 D 2
Al Kufrah 59 K 4
Al Kufrah, Wāhāt 59 K 4
Al Kūm (Syria) 22 C 2
Al Kumayt (Iraq) 23 E 2–3
Al Kuntillah (Egypt) 22 B 3
Al Kūt (Iraq) 23 D 2
Al Kuwayt (Kuwait) 23 E 3
Al Labbah (Saudi Arabia) 22 CD 3
Al Lādhiqīyah (Syria) 22 B 2
Al Lagowa 60 D 6
Al Layyah 60 F 5
Al Līfīyah (Iraq) 22 D 3
Al Lisāfah (Saudi Arabia) 23 E 4
Al Līth 61 G 4
Al Luhayyah 61 G 5
Al Lussuf (Iraq) 22 D 3
Al Madīna (Iraq) 23 E 3
Al Madīnah (Saudi Arabia) 22 C 4
'Al Madōw 65 H 2
Al Mafraq (Jordan) 22 B 2
Al Maghrah 60 D 2
Al Mahallah al Kubrā 60 E 2
Al Mahārīg 60 E 3
Al Mahāwiyah 61 G 4
Al Mahdīyah 59 H 1
Al Mahmūdīyah (Iraq) 22 D 2
Al Mahrah 61 J 5
Al Majann (Saudi Arabia) 23 F 5
Al Majarr el Kabīr (Iraq) 23 E 3
Al Majma'ah (Saudi Arabia) 23 D 4
Al Makhaylī 59 K 2
Al Maks al Qibli 60 E 4
Al Mallāhah al Bahrīyah 59 H 2
Al Mallāhah al Gharbīyah 59 H 2
Al Manadir (Oman) 23 G 5
Al Manadir (United Arab Emirates) 23 G 5
Al Manāmah 23 F 4
Al Manāqil 60 E 6
Al Manshāh 60 E 3
Al Mansūrah 60 E 2
Al Ma'qil (Iraq) 23 E 3
Al Māqnah (Saudi Arabia) 22 B 3
Al Maqrūn 59 J 2
Al Maqtā' (United Arab Emirates) 23 G 4
Al Marj 59 K 2
Al Ma'rūf 59 J 3

Al Mas'ānīyah (Saudi Arabia) 22 D 3
'Al Maskād 65 H 2
Al Matnah 60 EF 6
Al Mawsil (Iraq) 22 D 1
Al Mayādīn (Syria) 22 C 2
Al Mayyāh (Saudi Arabia) 22 D 4
Al Mazra'ah (Jordan) 22 B 3
Al Mellem 64 D 3
Al Midhnab (Saudi Arabia) 22 D 4
Al Milh, Ra's 59 L 2
Al Mintirīb 61 K 4
Al Minyā 60 E 3
Al Mīqdādīyah (Iraq) 23 D 2
Al Mubarraz (Saudi Arabia) 23 E 4
Al Mubarraz (United Arab Emirates) 23 F 4
Al Mudarraj (Saudi Arabia) 22 C 4
Al Mudawwarah (Saudi Arabia) 22 B 3
Al Mughayrā' (Saudi Arabia) 22 B 3
Al Mughayrā' (United Arab Emirates) 23 F 5
Al Muglad 60 D 6
Al Muharraq 23 F 4
Al Mukallā 61 H 6
Al Mukhā 61 G 6
Al Muknīn 59 H 1
Al Munastir 59 H 1
Al Murabbā' (Saudi Arabia) 22 D 4
Al Musannāh (Saudi Arabia) 23 E 3
Al Musawwart as Safra' 60 E 5
Al Musayjid (Saudi Arabia) 22 C 4
Al Musayyib (Iraq) 22 D 2
Al Muwayh 61 G 4
Al Muwaylih (Saudi Arabia) 22 B 4
Al Nasser (Egypt) 22 A 4
Al Qa'āmīyāt 61 H 5
Al Qadārif 60 F 6
Al Qaddāhīyah 59 J 2
Al Qadīmah 61 F 4
Al Qadmūs (Syria) 22 B 2
Al Qaffay (United Arab Emirates) 23 F 4
Al Qahmah 61 G 5
Al Qā'iyah (Saudi Arabia) 23 D 4
Al Qalībah (Saudi Arabia) 22 B 3
Al Qāmishlī (Syria) 22 C 1
Al Qantarah (Egypt) 22 A 3
Al Qarābullī 59 H 2
Al Qārah (Saudi Arabia) 22 C 3
Al Qardah 59 H 3
Al Qaryāt Darj Zāwiya 59 H 2
Al Qaryatayn (Syria) 22 B 2
Al Qasr 60 D 3
Al Qasrayn 59 G 1
Al Qatīf (Saudi Arabia) 23 E 4
Al Qatn 61 H 5
Al Qatrānī (Jordan) 22 B 3
Al Qatrūn 59 H 3–4
Al Qay'īyah (Saudi Arabia) 22 D 4
Al Qayrawān 59 GH 1
Al Qaysūmah (Saudi Arabia) 22 D 3
Al Qaysūmah (Saudi Arabia) 23 E 3
Al Qunaytirah (Syria) 22 B 2
Al Qunfudhah 61 G 5
Al Qurayni 61 J 4
Al Qurayyah (Saudi Arabia) 22 B 3
Al Qurayyah 61 K 4
Al Qurnah (Iraq) 23 E 3
Al Qusaymah (Egypt) 22 AB 3
Al Qusayr (Syria) 22 B 2
Al Qusayr (Egypt) 22 B 4
Al Qūsīyah 60 E 3
Al Qūsūrīyah (Saudi Arabia) 22 D 5
Al Qutayfah (Syria) 22 B 2
Al Qutaynah 60 E 6
Al Quwārah (Saudi Arabia) 22 D 4
Al Quwayīyah (Saudi Arabia) 23 D 4
Al Quwayr (Iraq) 22 D 1–2
Al Qwārshah 59 J 2
Al Rabyānah, Wāhāt 59 K 4
Al Rayyān (Qatar) 23 F 4
Al Shagra (Qatar) 23 F 4
Al Tāzirbū, Wāhāt 59 K 3
Al 'Ubaylah 61 J 4
Al Ubayyid 60 E 6
Al 'Udaysāt (Egypt) 22 A 4
Al Ugsur (Egypt) 22 A 4
Al 'Ulā (Saudi Arabia) 22 C 4
Al 'Uqayr (Saudi Arabia) 23 E 4
Al Urayq (Saudi Arabia) 22 C 3
Al Urdun 23 B 3
Al 'Uthmānīyah (Saudi Arabia) 23 E 4
Al 'Uwaynidhīyah (Saudi Arabia) 22 B 4
'Al 'Uwayqīlah (Saudi Arabia) 22 CD 3

Al 'Uyūn (Saudi Arabia) 22 C 4
Al 'Uzayr (Iraq) 23 E 3
Al Wāhah 59 K 3
Al Wajh (Saudi Arabia) 22 B 4
Al Wakrah (Qatar) 23 F 4
Al Wannān (Saudi Arabia) 23 E 4
Al Warī'ah (Saudi Arabia) 23 E 4
Al Wāsitah 60 E 3
Al Watyah 59 H 2
Al Wazz 60 D 5
Al Widyān (Iraq) 22 C 3
Al Wīgh 59 J 4
Al Wīgh, Ramlat 59 J 4
Al Zukum (United Arab Emirates) 23 F 4
Ala, Monti di 19 E 3
Alabama 77 J 5
Alabama 77 J 5
Alaca 21 DE 2
Alaçam 21 E 2
Alaçam Dağları 20 C 3
Alachakh 37 P 4
Alachevo 37 T 3
Alacrán 78 E 3
Aladağ (Turkey) 21 DE 3
Aladağ (Turkey) 21 F 3
Aladža manastir 20 C 2
Alagir 21 F 2
Alagoas 87 J 2
Alagoinhas 87 J 3
Alagón (Spain) 18 B 3–4
Alagón (Spain) 18 C 3
Alahanpanjang 42 B 4
Alahärmä 16 H 3
Alaid 37 T 5
Alaita 65 G 2
Alajärvi 16 H 3
Alajuela 78 F 5
Alakanuk 72 E 3
Alakol', Ozero 25 Q 6
Alakurtti 16 K 2
'Alam al Rūm, Ra's 60 D 2
Alamagan 52 A 1
Alamitos, Sierra de los 78 B 2
Alamogordo 76 E 5
Alamos 76 E 6
Alamos, Sierra 78 B 2
Alamosa 76 E 4
Åland 17 GH 3
Ålands hav 17 G 4
Alaniemi 16 J 2
Alantika Mountains 63 G 4
Alanya 21 D 3
Alaotra, Lac 67 H 3
Alapaha River 77 K 5
Alapayevsk 25 M 4
Alaplı 20 D 2
Alarçon, Embalse de 18 C 4
Alas, Selat 42 E 5
Alaşehir 20 C 3
Alaska 72 FH 2
Alaska, Gulf of 72 HJ 4
Alaska Peninsula 72 E 4
Alaska Range 72 GH 3
Alassio 19 E 3
Alatau Shankou 35 L 1
Alatna 72 G 2
Alatri 19 F 3
Alatyr' 24 J 5
Alava, Cape 76 A 2
Alaverdi 21 F 2
Alavijeh (Iran) 23 F 2
Alavus 16 H 3
Al'Awsajīyah (Saudi Arabia) 22 D 4
Alayh (Lebanon) 22 B 2
Alaykël' 35 J 2
Alayskiy Khrebet 35 J 3
Alayunt 20 D 3
Alazani 21 G 2
Alazeya 37 S 1
Alazeyskoye Ploskogor'ye 37 R 2
Alb, Crișul 20 B 1
Alba 19 E 3
Alba Iulia 20 B 1
Albacete 18 C 4
Albanel, Lac 75 N 5
Albania 20 AB 2
Albano Laziale 19 F 3
Albany (Australia) 48 B 5
Albany (GA, U.S.A.) 77 K 5
Albany (N.Y., U.S.A.) 77 M 3
Albany (Ontario, Can.) 74 L 5
Albany (OR, U.S.A.) 76 B 3
Albany Downs 49 H 4
Albardón 88 C 5
Albatross Bay 49 G 1
Albatross Plateau 99 D 3
Albatross Point 51 Q 8
Albemarle Sound 77 L 4
Alberga River 48 E 4
Albert Edward Bay 73 R 2
Albert, Lake (Uganda/Zaire) 64 E 4
Albert Lake (OR, U.S.A.) 76 BC 3
Albert Lea 77 H 3

Albert Nile 64 E 4
Albert River (Queensland, Austr.) 49 F 2
Alberta 73 OP 5
Alberti 88 DE 6
Albertkanaal 14 DE 4
Albertville 19 E 2
Albi 18 D 3
Albina 85 H 2
Alborán 18 C 4
Ålborg 17 F 4
Albox 18 C 4
Albro 49 H 3
Ålbū 'Alī (Iraq) 22 D 2
Albuquerque 76 E 4
Albuquerque, Cayos de 79 F 5
Albury 49 H 6
Alcácer do Sal 18 B 4
Alcalá 18 B 4
Alcalá 18 C 3
Alcalá de Chivert 18 D 3
Alcalá la Real 18 C 4
Alcamo 19 F 4
Alcañices 18 B 3
Alcañiz 18 C 3
Alcántara 85 K 4
Alcántara, Embalse de 18 B 4
Alcantarilla 18 C 4
Alcaraz 18 C 4
Alcaraz, Sierra de 18 C 4
Alcaudete 18 C 4
Alcázar de San Juan 18 C 4
Alciéni 63 G 6
Alcira 18 C 4
Alcobaça 87 J 4
Alcobendas 18 C 3
Alcolea del Pinar 18 C 3
Alcoutim 18 B 4
Alcoy 18 C 4
Alcudia 18 D 4
Aldabra Islands 65 H 6
Aldama 76 E 6
Aldan 37 N 4
Aldan 37 O 3
Aldano-Uchurskiy Khrebet 37 N 4
Aldanskoye Nagor'ye 37 MN 4
Aldarhaan 36 G 6
Aldbourne 7 D 2
Aldbrough 5 E 3
Aldeburgh 7 E 1
Alderley Edge 5 D 3
Alderney 7 C 3
Alderney 14 C 5
Aldershot 7 D 2
Aldingham 5 D 2
Aldoma 37 P 4
Aldridge 7 D 1
Aleg 58 C 5
Alegrete 88 E 4
Aleknagik 72 F 4
Aleksandriya (Ukraine, U.S.S.R.) 21 D 1
Aleksandrov 24 G 4
Aleksandrov Gay 24 J 5
Aleksandrovsk 25 M 4
Aleksandrovskiy 36 L 5
Aleksandrovskoye 21 F 2
Aleksandrovskoye 25 P 3
Aleksandrovskoye 25 QR 6
Aleksandrovsk-Sakhalinskiy 37 Q 5
Alekseyevka (Kazakhstan, U.S.S.R.) 25 O 5
Alekseyevka (Kazakhstan, U.S.S.R.) 25 QR 6
Alekseyevka (U.S.S.R.) 24 GH 5
Alekseyevka (U.S.S.R.) 37 M 3
Alekseyevo 37 R 1
Alekseyevsk 36 J 4
Aleksikovo 24 H 5
Aleksinac 20 B 2
Além Paraíba 87 H 5
Alemania (Argentina) 88 C 4
Alemania (Chile) 88 B 4
Alençon 18 D 2
Alenquer 85 H 4
Alépé 62 D 4
Aleppo (Syria) 22 B 1
Aléria 19 E 3
Alerta 86 B 3
Alès 18 D 3
Aleshki 36 H 4
Alessandria 19 E 3
Ålestrup 17 E 4
Ålesund 16 E 3
Aleutian Basin 99 C 2
Aleutian Islands 72 AC 4
Aleutian Range 72 F 4
Aleutian Trench 99 D 2
Alexander Archipelago 72 K 4
Alexander Bay 66 B 5
Alexander Island 91
Alexandra 50 P 10
Alexandra Channel 41 F 5
Alexandra Falls 73 O 3
Alexandria (Australia) 49 F 2

Alexandria (Egypt) 60 E 2
Alexandria (LA, U.S.A.) 77 H 5
Alexandria (MD, U.S.A.) 77 L 4
Alexandria (Romania) 20 BC 2
Alexandria (South Africa) 66 D 6
Alexandria (U.K.) 3 B 4
Alexandrina, Lake 49 F 6
Alexandroúpolis 20 C 2
Aley 25 Q 5
Aleysk 25 Q 5
Alfabia, Sierra de 18 D 4
Alfambra 18 C 3
Alfaro (Ecuador) 84 C 4
Alfaro (Spain) 18 C 3
Alferovka 25 P 5
Alfios 20 B 3
Alföld 20 AB 1
Alford (Grampian) 2 C 3
Alford (Lincolnshire) 7 E 1
Alfreton 7 D 1
Alga 34 F 1
Algama 37 N 4
Alganskaya 37 W 3
Algarrobo 89 B 2
Algarrobo del Águila 89 C 6
Algarve 18 B 4
Algasovo 24 H 5
Algeciras 18 B 4
Alger → Al Jazā'ir 59 F 1
Algeria 58–59 EF 3
Alghero 19 E 3
Algibe 18 B 4
Algiers 59 F 1
Algoa Bay 66 D 6
Algona 77 H 3
Alhama de Murcia 18 C 4
Alī al Gharbī (Iraq) 23 E 2
'Alī ash Sharqi (Iraq) 23 E 2
Ali Bayramly 34 DE 3
Ali Sabjeh 65 G 2
'Alī Shāh 'Avaz (Iran) 23 F 2
'Alīābād (Iran) 23 E 2
'Alīābād (Iran) 23 F 1
'Alīābād (Iran) 23 G 1
Alīābād (Iran) 23 G 3
Alīābād (Iran) 34 EF 3
'Alīābād, Kūh-e (Iran) 23 F 2
Aliákmon 20 B 2
Alibag 40 B 4
Alibey, Ozero 20 D 1
Alibo 65 F 3
Alicante 18 C 4
Alice 76 G 6
Alice, Punta dell' 19 G 4
Alice River 49 H 3
Alice Springs 48 E 3
Alichur 35 J 3
Alicudi 19 F 4
Aligarh 40 C 2
Aligüdarz (Iran) 23 E 2
Alijūq, Kūh-e (Iran) 23 F 3
Alikayası 21 E 3
Alim 50 E 2
Alima 63 H 6
Alindao 64 C 3
Alingsås 17 F 4
Alinskoye 25 R 3
Alipur 35 J 5
Alipur Duar 40 E 2
Aliskerovo 37 V 2
Alitak, Cape 72 FG 4
Aliwal North 66 D 6
Aljustrel 18 B 4
Alkmaar 14 D 4
Allada 62 E 4
Allahabad 40 D 2
Allahüekber Dağı 21 F 2
Allakaket 72 G 2
Allakh-Yun' 37 P 3
Allanmyo 41 G 4
Allanridge 66 D 5
'Allāqī, Wādī al 60 E 4
Alldays 66 D 4
Allegheny Mountains 77 KL 4
Allegheny Plateau 77 K 4
Allegheny River 77 L 3
Allen, Lough 4 AB 2
Allende 78 B 2
Allentown 77 L 3
Allenwood 4 B 3
Alleppey 40 C 6
Aller 15 E 4
Allevard 19 E 2
Alliance 76 F 3
Allier 18 D 2
Alligator River, East 48 E 1
Alligator River, South 48 E 1
Alloa 3 C 3
Allonby 5 D 2
Allonnes 18 D 2
Allora 49 J 4
Alma 75 N 6
Almada 18 B 4
Almadén 18 C 4

Almalyk **35** H 2
Almansa **18** C 4
Almazán **18** C 3
Almaznyy **36** K 3
Almeirim **85** H 4
Almelo **14** E 4
Almenara **87** H 4
Almenara, Sierra de la **18** C 4
Almendra, Embalse de **18** B 3
Almendralejo **18** B 4
Almería **18** C 4
Almería, Golfo de **18** C 4
Al'met'yevsk **24** K 5
Älmhult **17** F 4
Almina, Punta **58** D 1
Almirante **84** B 2
Almirante Brown **91**
Almirante Montt, Golfo **89** B 9
Almirós **20** B 3
Almodôvar **18** B 4
Almogasta **88** C 4
Almonte **18** B 4
Almora **40** CD 2
Almoustarat **62** D 2
Almuñécar **18** C 4
Almus **21** E 2
Alness **2** B 3
Alney, Gora **37** TU 4
Alnmouth **5** E 2
Alnön **16** G 3
Alnwick **5** E 2
Alo **63** J 3
Alofi (Cook Is.) **52** D 4
Alofi (Wallis and Futuna) **52** D 3
Alomata **65** F 2
Along **41** F 2
Alongshan **37** M 5
Alónnisos **20** B 3
Alor, Pulau **43** F 5
Alor, Selat **43** F 5
Alor Setar **42** B 2
Álora **18** C 4
Alotau **49** J 1
Alotau **51** F 4
Alpachiri **89** D 6
Alpena **77** K 2
Alpercatas, Serra das **85** JK 5
Alpes Mancelles **18** C 2
Alpha **49** H 3
Alpha River **49** H 3
Alphonse **65** J 6
Alpi Carniche **19** F 2
Alpi Dolomitiche **19** F 2
Alpi Marittime **19** E 3
Alpi Orobie **19** EF 2
Alpine (TX, U.S.A.) **76** F 5
Alpine (WY, U.S.A.) **76** D 3
Alqueva, Barragem de **18** B 4
Als **17** EF 5
Alsask **73** Q 5
Alsasua **18** C 3
Alsfeld **15** E 4
Alsh, Lake **2** B 3
Al'skiy Khrebet **37** P 5
Alsten **16** F 2
Alston **5** D 2
Alta **16** H 2
Alta Gracia **88** D 5
Altaelva **16** H 2
Altafjorden **16** H 1
Altagracia de Orituco **84** E 2
Altai **36** EF 6
Altamachi **86** C 4
Altamaha River **77** K 5
Altamira **85** H 4
Altamont **76** B 3
Altamura **19** G 3
Altan **36** J 6
Altanbulag **36** J 5
Altaqracia **84** D 1
Altar **76** D 5
Altas, Rías **18** B 3
Altat **36** F 4
Altata **76** E 7
Altatump **25** M 3
Altay (China) **35** M 1
Altay (Mongolia) **36** G 6
Altay (U.S.S.R.) **25** N 3
Altay (U.S.S.R.) **25** R 5
Altay Shan **35** M 1
Altayskiy **25** QR 5
Altdorf **19** E 2
Altenburg **15** F 4
Altevatnet **16** G 2
Altıntaş **20** D 3
Altiplanicie Mexicana **78** B 2
Altiplano **86** C 4
Altkirch **19** E 2
Altmark **15** F 4
Altmühl **15** F 5
Altnaharra **2** B 2
Alto Araguaia **87** F 4
Alto Chicapa **66** B 2
Alto Garças **87** F 4
Alto Molócuè **67** F 3
Alto Paraguai **86** E 3

Alto Parnaíba **87** G 2
Alto Purus **86** B 2–3
Alto Río Senguerr **89** B 8
Alto Sucuriú **87** F 4
Alto Turi **87** G 1
Alto Zaza **66** B 1
Alto-Alentejo **18** B 4
Alton (IL, U.S.A.) **77** H 4
Alton (U.K.) **7** D 2
Alton Downs **49** F 4
Altoona **77** L 3
Altrincham **5** D 3
Altun Ha **78** E 4
Âltūn Kūprī (Iraq) **22** D 2
Altun Shan **38** AB 3
Alturas **78** B 3
Altus **76** G 5
Altynasar **35** G 1
Alu **51** G 3
Alucra **21** E 2
Aluk **64** D 3
'Alūla **65** J 2
Alüm (Iran) **23** E 2
Aluminé **89** B 6
Alupka **21** D 2
Alur **40** C 4
'Âlūs (Iraq) **22** D 2
Alushta **21** D 2
Al'Uyūn (Saudi Arabia) **22** D 4
Alva (OK, U.S.A.) **76** G 4
Alva (U.K.) **3** C 3
Alvano, Kūh-e (Iran) **23** E 2
Alvarães **85** F 4
Alvdal **16** F 3
Älvdalen **16** F 3
Älvdalen **17** F 3
Alvear **88** E 4
Alvelos, Serra de **18** B 4
Alvesta **17** F 4
Alvid **2** C 3
Älvik **17** E 3
Älvkarleby **17** G 3
Alvorado **87** G 3
Alvord Valley **76** C 3
Älvsbyn **16** H 2
Alwar **40** C 2
Alxa Youqi **38** D 3
Alxa Zuoqi **38** DE 3
Alyangula **49** F 1
Alyaskitovyy **37** Q 3
Alygdzher **36** G 5
Alys-Khaya **37** P 2
Alysy-Garakh **37** Q 2
Alytus **17** H 5
Alzamay **36** G 4
Am Dam **63** J 3
Am Djéména **63** H 3
Am Guereda **63** J 3
Am Raya **63** H 3
Am Timan **63** J 3
Am Zoer **63** J 3
Amada **60** E 4
Amada Gaza **64** B 4
Amadeus, Lake **48** E 3
Amadi **64** E 3
Amadjuak Lake **75** N 2–3
Amahai **43** G 4
Amain, Monts d' **18** D 2
Amakinskiy **36** K 1
Âmâl **59** K 3
Åmål **17** F 4
Amalfi (Colombia) **84** D 2
Amalfi (Italy) **19** F 3
Amalias **20** B 3
Amambaí **87** EF 5
Amami-ō-shima **39** J 5
Amanã, Lago **85** F 4
Amangel'dy **25** N 5
Amanino **37** T 4
Amanotkel' **35** G 1
Amanu **53** F 4
Amanzimtoti **67** E 6
Amapá **85** H 3
Amapá **85** H 3
Amorgós **20** C 3
Amar **63** FG 4
'Amara **60** E 4
Amarante **87** H 2
Amârat Abū Sinn **60** EF 5
Amarillo **76** F 4
Amaro Leite **87** G 3
Amarti **65** QR 2
Amasra **21** D 2
Amasya **21** E 2
Amataurá **84** E 4
Amazar **36** M 5
Amazon **85** H 4
Amazonas **84–85** EF 4
Amazonas **85** H 4
Amba Farit **65** F 2
Ambala **40** C 1
Ambalavao **67** H 4
Ambam **63** G 5
Ambanja **67** H 2
Ambar **36** EF 2
Ambarchik **36** G 4
Ambarchik **37** U 2

Ambardakh **37** P 1
Ambarnyy **16** K 2
Ambato **84** C 4
Ambato Boény **67** H 3
Ambatofinandrahana **67** H 4
Ambatolampy **67** H 3
Ambatondrazaka **67** H 3
Ambatosoratra **67** H 3
Ambatry **67** G 4
Ambelos, Ákra **20** B 3
Amberg **15** F 5
Ambérieu-en-Bugey **19** E 2
Ambgaon **40** D 3
Ambidédi **62** B 3
Ambikapur **40** D 3
Ambilobe **67** H 2
Amble-by-the-Sea **5** E 2
Ambleside **5** D 2
Ambo **86** A 3
Amboasary **67** H 4
Ambodifototra **67** H 4
Ambohibe **67** G 4
Ambohimahasoa **67** H 4
Ambohitralanana **67** J 3
Ambon **43** G 4
Ambon, Pulau **43** G 4
Ambositra **67** H 4
Ambovombe **67** H 5
Ambre, Cap d' **67** H 2
Ambre, Montagne d' **67** H 2
Ambrim **51** J 5
Ambriz **66** A 1
Ambur **40** C 5
Amchitka **72** A 5
Amchitka Pass **72** AB 5
'Amd **61** H 5
Amderma **25** M 2
Amdo **38** B 4
Ameca **78** B 3
Amendolara **19** G 3–4
'Âmeri (Iran) **23** F 3
American Falls Reservoir **76** D 3
American Highland **91**
American Samoa **52** D 3
Americus **77** K 5
Amersham **7** D 2
Amery Ice Shelf **91**
Ames **77** H 3
Amesbury **7** D 2
Amet **40** B 2
Ametlla de Mar **18** D 3
Amfilokhia **20** B 3
Amfissa **20** B 3
Amga **37** O 3
Amgu **39** L 1
Amguema **72** B 2
Amguid **59** G 3
Amgun' **37** P 5
Amhara **65** F 2
Amherst **75** P 6
Amherst Island **77** L 3
Amiata **19** F 3
Amiens **18** D 2
Amik Gölü **21** E 3
Amili **41** G 2
'Amīnābād (Iran) **23** F 3
Amindivi Islands **40** B 5
Aminuis **66** B 4
Amirante Islands **65** J 6
Amisk Lake **73** R 5
Amka **37** Q 4
Amlia **72** C 5
Amlwch **6** B 1
'Amm Adăm **60** F 5
'Ammân (Jordan) **22** B 3
Ammanford **6** B 2
Ammarfjället **16** G 2
Ammarnäs **16** G 2
Ammokhostos → Famagusta
    21 D 3
Amo **36** H 3
Âmol (Iran) **23** F 1
Amolar **86** E 4
Amorgós **20** C 3
Amos **75** M 6
Âmot **17** E 4
Amour, Djebel **59** F 2
Amourj **58** D 5
Amoy **39** G 6
Ampanihy **67** G 4
Amparafaravola **67** H 3
Ampitsikanana **67** H 2
Amposta **18** D 3
Ampthill **7** D 1
'Amrân **61** G 5
Amravati **40** C 3
Amri **35** H 5
'Amrit (Syria) **22** B 2
Amritsar **40** C 1
Amroha **40** C 2
Amsâ'ad **59** K 2
Amsterdam (Netherlands) **14** DE 4
Amsterdam (N.Y., U.S.A.) **77** M 3
Amstetten **19** F 2
Amtkeli **21** F 2
Âmūda (Syria) **22** C 1

Amu-Dar'ya **35** G 2
Amudat **64** E 4
Amukta Pass **72** C 5
Amulrea **3** C 3
Amundsen Gulf **73** N 1
Amundsen Sea **91**
Amundsen-Scott **91**
Amungen **16** G 3
Amuntai **42** E 4
Amur **37** P 5
Amursk **37** P 5
Amvrakikos Kólpos **20** B 3
Amysakh **36** L 2
An Nabatīyah at Tahta (Lebanon)
    22 B 2
An Nabk (Syria) **22** B 2
An Nabk Abū Qasr (Saudi Arabia)
    22 C 3
An Nafidah **19** F 4
An Nafūd (Saudi Arabia) **22** CD 3
An Nāfūrah **59** K 3
An Nāhiyah (Iraq) **22** C 2
An Najaf (Iraq) **22** D 2–3
An' Nakhl (Egypt) **22** AB 3
An Nāmūs, Jabal **59** J 3–4
An Nashshāsh (United Arab
    Emirates) **23** FG 5
An Nashwawh (Iraq) **23** E 3
An Nāsirīyah (Iraq) **23** E 3
An Nhon **41** J 5
An Nu'ayrīyah (Saudi Arabia)
    23 E 4
An Nuhūd **60** D 6
An Nu'mān (Saudi Arabia) **22** B 4
An Nu'mānīyah (Iraq) **23** D 2
An Nuqayr (Saudi Arabia) **23** E 4
An Nūwfalīyah **59** J 2
An Tuc **41** J 5
An Uaimh Navan **4** B 3
An Xian **38** D 4
Ana Maria, Golfo de **79** G 3
Anabar **36** K 1
Anabarskiy Zaliv **36** KL 1
Anabarskoye Ploskogor'ye
    36 J 1–2
Anaco **85** F 2
Anaconda **76** D 2
Anadoli **20–21** CD 3
Anadyr' **37** X 3
Anadyr' **37** X 3
Anadyrskaja Nizmennost' **37** X 2
Anadyrskiy Liman **37** X 3
Anadyrskiy Zaliv **37** Y 3
Anadyrskiy Zaliv **72** B 3
Anadyrskoye Ploskogor'ye
    37 VW 2
Anáfi **20** C 3
Anáfjället **16** F 3
Anaghit **65** F 1
Anagni **19** F 3
'Ânah (Iraq) **22** C 2
Anáhuac **78** C 2
Anaï **59** H 4
Anaimalai Hills **40** C 5
Anajás **85** J 4
Anajatuba **87** H 1
Anakapalle **40** D 4
Anaklia **21** F 2
Anaktuvuk Pass **72** G 2
Analalava **67** H 2
Anamá **85** F 4
Anambas, Kepulauan **42** C 3
Anamur **21** D 3
Anamur Burnu **21** D 3
Anamur Burum (Turkey) **22** A 2
Anamuryum **21** D 3
Anangravnen, Sopka **37** U 4
Anantapur **40** C 5
Anantnag **35** K 4
Anan'yev **20** C 1
Anapa **21** E 2
Anapka **37** U 3
Anápolis **87** G 4
Anapu **85** H 4
Anãr (Iran) **23** G 3
Anārak (Iran) **23** F 2
Anarisfjällen **16** F 3
Anatahan **52** A 1
Anatolia **20–21** D 3
Añatuya **88** D 4
Anauá **85** F 3
Anavarza **21** E 3
Anavelona **67** G 4
Anavilhanas, Arquipélago das
    85 F 4
'Anazah, Jabal (Iraq) **22** C 2
Anbyŏn **39** J 3
Ancares, Sierra de **18** B 3
Ancasti, Sierra de **88** C 4
Ancenis **18** C 2
Ancha **37** P 3
Anchor Bay **76** B 4
Anchorage **72** H 3
Anci **39** G 3
Ancohuma **86** C 4
Ancon (Ecuador) **84** B 4

Ancón (Peru) **86** A 3
Ancona **19** F 3
Ancuabe **67** F 2
Ancud **89** B 7
Ancud, Golfo de **89** B 7
Anda **39** J 1
Andacollo (Argentina) **89** B 6
Andacollo (Chile) **88** B 5
Andahuaylas **86** B 3
Andalgala **88** C 4
Åndalsnes **16** E 3
Andalucía **18** BC 4
Andaman Islands **41** F 5
Andaman Sea **41** G 5–6
Andamooka **49** F 5
Andapa **67** H 2
Andara **66** C 3
Andarab **35** H 3
Andaraí **87** H 3
Andeg **24** K 2
Andenes **16** G 2
Andéranboukane **62** E 2
Anderson (IN, U.S.A.) **77** J 3–4
Anderson (N.W.T., Can.) **72** M 2
Anderson (S.C., U.S.A.) **77** K 5
Anderstorp **17** F 4
Andes (Colombia) **84** C 2
Andes Mountains **81** C 2–6
Andevoranto **67** H 3
Andfjorden **16** G 2
Andhra Pradesh **40** C 4
Andikira **20** B 3
Andikíthira **20** B 3
Andilamena **67** H 3
Andilanatoby **67** H 3
Andīmeshk **34** D 4
Andīmeshk (Iran) **23** E 2
Andípaxoi **20** AB 3
Andiria Burun **21** D 3
Andiria burun (Cyprus) **22** B 2
Andrrın **21** E 3
Andirlangar **35** L 3
Andiyskiy Khrebet **21** G 2
Andizhan **35** J 2
Andkhui **35** H 3
Andoas **84** C 4
Andomskiy Pogost **24** G 3
Andong **39** J 3
Andorra **18** D 3
Andorra la Vella **18** D 3
Andover **7** D 2
Andøya **16** G 2
Andradina **87** F 5
Andraitx **18** D 4
Andranopasy **67** G 4
André Félix National Park **64** C 3
Andreanof Islands **72** BC 5
Andreas **4** C 2
Andrepatsy **67** H 3
Andrews **76** F 5
Andreyevka **21** E 1
Andreyevka **24** K 5
Andreyevka **25** Q 6
Andreyevo-Ivanovka **20** D 1
Andreyevsk **36** KL 4
Andreyevskiy **36** KL 4
Andria **19** G 3
Andriamena **67** H 3
Andriba **67** H 3
Andringitra **67** H 4
Androka **67** G 5
Androna, Plateau de l' **67** H 3
Andropov **24** G 4
Ándros **20** B 3
Ándros **20** C 3
Andros Island **79** G 3
Androsovka **24** J 5
Androth **40** B 5
Andrushevka **17** J 5
Andryushka **37** S 2
Andselv **16** G 2
Andu Tan **42** D 2
Andudu **64** C 4
Andújar **18** C 4
Andulo **66** B 2
Andyngda **36** L 2
Aneby **17** FG 4
Anécho **62** E 4
Anéfis **62** E 2
Anegada, Bahía **89** D 7
Anegada Passage **79** K 4
Aneityum **51** JK 6
Añelo **89** C 6
Aneroft **5** D 2
Aneto, Pico de **18** D 3
Aney **63** G 2
Ang Thong **41** H 5
Angamos, Punta **86** B 5
Ang'angxi **39** H 1
Angar **43** H 4
Angara **36** F 4
Angarsk **36** H 5
Angas Downs **48** E 4
Angatau **53** F 4
Angaul **36** H 5
Angaur **43** H 2

Ânge 16 G 3
Ángel de la Guarda, Isla 76 D 6
Angel Falls 85 F 2
Angeles 43 J 1
Ângelholm 17 F 4
Angemuk, Gunung 43 J 4
Ångermanälven 16 G 3
Angers 18 C 2
Angerville (France) 18 D 2
Angical 87 H 3
Angijak Island 75 P 2
Angikuni Lake 73 S 3
Angkor 41 H 5
Angle 6 B 2
Anglem, Mount 50 P 10
Anglesey 6 B 1
Angmagssalik 90
Angmering 7 D 2
Ango 64 D 4
Angoche 67 G 3
Angol 89 B 6
Angola 160 BC 2
Angola Basin 98 B 4
Angónia, Planalto de 67 E 2
Angoram 50 D 2
Angostura 76 E 6
Angostura, Salto 84 D 3
Angoulême 18 D 2
Angouma 63 G 5
Angra do Heroismo 58 A 1
Angra dos Reis 87 H 5
Angren 35 J 2
Angu 64 C 4
Anguil 89 D 6
Anguilla 79 K 4
Anguille, Cape 75 PQ 6
Angul 40 E 3
Angumu 64 D 5
Anguo 38 G 3
Angutikha 25 R 2
Anh Son 41 J 4
Anholt 17 F 4
Anhua 38 F 5
Anhui 39 G 4
Aniak 72 F 3
Aniakchak National Monument
    and Preserve 72 F 4
Anié 62 E 4
Animas Peak 76 E 5
Anina 20 B 1
Aniva 37 Q 6
Aniva, Mys 37 Q 6
Aniva, Zaliv 37 Q 6
Anivorano-Nord 67 H 2
Aniwa 51 J 5
Anjala 17 J 3
Anjou 18 C 2
Anjouan 67 G 2
Anjozorobe 67 H 3
Anju 39 J 3
Anjuman 35 J 3
Anka 63 F 3
Ankacho 36 J 3
Ankang 38 E 4
Ankara 21 D 2–3
Ankaramena 67 H 4
Ankavandra 67 H 3
Ankazoabo 67 G 4
Ankazobe 67 H 3
Ankerika 67 H 3
'Ankhor (Somalia) 65 H 2
Anklam 15 F 4
Anklesvar 40 B 3
Ankober 65 F 3
Ankofa 67 H 3
Ankoro 64 D 6
Ankpa 63 F 4
Anlong 38 E 5
Anlu 38 F 4
Ånn 16 F 3
Ann Arbor 77 K 3
Ann, Cape 91
Anna (IL, U.S.A.) 77 J 4
Anna (U.S.S.R.) 24 H 5
Anna Plains 48 C 2
Annaba 59 G 1
Annai 85 G 3
Annalong 4 C 2
Annan 5 D 2
Annandale 49 H 3
Annapolis 77 L 4
Annapurna 40 D 2
Annbank 3 B 4
Annean, Lake 48 B 4
Annecy 19 E 2
Annemasse 19 E 2
Annenskiy-Most 24 G 3
Anning 38 D 6
Anniston 77 J 5
Annobón 63 F 6
Annonay 19 D 2
Anoka 77 H 2
Anori 85 F 4
Anoshkinsk 37 N 1
Anou 62 E 2

Anoumaba 62 D 4
Anou-n Bidek 59 F 5
Anqing 39 G 4
Ansâb (Saudi Arabia) 23 D 3
Ansariye, Jabal al (Syria) 22 B 2
Ansas 43 J 4
Ansbach 15 F 5
Anserma 84 C 2
Anshan 39 H 2
Anshun 38 E 5
Ansina 88 E 5
Ansley 76 G 3
Anson Bay 48 D 1
Ansongo 62 E 2
Anston 7 D 1
Anstruther 3 C 3
Ansudu 43 J 4
Anta 86 B 3
Anta, Cachoeira de 85 F 5
Antakya 21 E 3
Antakya (Turkey) 22 B 1
Antalaha 67 J 2
Antalya 20 D 3
Antalya Körfezi 20 D 3
Antananarivo 67 H 3
Antanimora 67 H 4
Antarctic Peninsula 91
Antas 88 F 4
Antela, Laguna de 18 B 3
Antequera 18 C 4
Antequera 86 E 5
Anthony 76 E 5
Anthony Lagoon 48 F 2
Antibes 19 E 3
Anticosti, Île d' 75 P 6
Antifer, Cap d' 18 CD 2
Antigonish 75 P 6
Antigua 79 K 4
Antigua and Barbuda 79 KL 4
Antigua Guatemala 78 D 5
Antillas Mayores 79 HJ 4
Antillas Menores 79 K 5
Antioche, Pertuis d' 18 C 2
Antiope 52 D 4
Antioquia 84 C 2
Antipayuta 25 P 2
Antipinskiy 37 N 1
Antipodes Islands 91
Antlāt 59 K 2
Antnäs 16 H 2
Antofagasta 86 B 5
Antofagasta de la Sierra 88 C 4
Antofalla, Salar de 88 C 4
Antofalla, Volcán 88 C 4
Antongil, Baie d' 67 HJ 3
Antonina 88 G 4
Antônio Bezerra 87 J 1
Antonio de Biedma 89 C 8
Antonovo 34 E 1
Antonto 88 D 4
Antrim 4 B 2
Antrim Mountains 4 B 2
Antrodoco 19 F 3
Antsakabary 67 H 2
Antsalova 67 G 3
Antseranana 67 H 2
Antsirabe 67 H 3
Antsohihy 67 H 2
Antu 39 J 2
Antufash 61 G 5
Antwerpen 14 D 4
Antykan 37 O 5
Añueque, Sierra 89 C 7
Anupgarh 40 B 2
Anuradhapura 40 D 6
Anuta 51 J 4
Anvik 72 E 3
Anxi (Fujian, China) 39 G 5
Anxi (Gansu, China) 38 C 2
Anxiang 38 F 5
Anxious Bay 48 E 5
Anyama 62 D 4
Anyang 38 F 3
Anyuan 38 G 5
A'nyemaqen Shan 38 CD 3–4
An'yudin 25 L 3
Anyue 38 E 4
Anyuysk 37 U 2
Anyuyskiy Khrebet, Severnyy
    37 UW 2
Anyuyskiy Khrebet, Yuzhnyy
    37 UV 2
Anzhero-Sudzhensk 25 R 4
Ao Ban Don 41 G 6
Aoga-shima 39 L 4
Aomori 39 M 2
Aosta 19 E 2
Aoudaghost 58 C 5
Aoudéras 63 F 2
Aouinat Legraa 58 D 3
Aouker (Mali) 58 E 4
Aouker (Mauritania) 58 CD 5
Aoulef el Arab 58–59 F 3
Aoumou 51 J 6
Apacha 37 T 5
Apahida 20 B 1

Apalachee Bay 77 K 6
Apan 78 C 4
Apaporis 84 D 4
Aparecida do Tabuado 87 F 4
Aparri 43 J 1
Apataki 53 F 4
Apatin 20 A 1
Apatity 16 K 2
Apatzingán 78 B 4
Ape 17 J 4
Apeldoorn 14 E 4
Apere 86 C 3
Aphrodisias 20 C 3
Api (Nepal) 40 D 2
Api (Zaire) 64 D 4
Api, Gunung 43 E 5
Api, Tanjung 42 C 3
Apia 52 D 3
Apiacás, Serra dos 86 E 2–3
Apiai 87 G 5
Apiaú, Serra do 85 F 3
Apinajé 87 G 3
Apio 51 H 3
Apizaco 78 C 4
Apo, Mount 43 G 2
Apolinario Saravia 86 D 5
Apollo Bay 49 G 6
Apollonia 59 K 2
Apolo 86 C 3
Aporé 87 F 4
Aporé 87 F 4
Aporema 85 H 3
Apóstoles 88 E 4
Apostolovo 21 D 1
Apoteri 85 G 3
Appalachian Mountains
    77 KM 3–4
Appennino Calabro 19 G 4
Appennino Ligure 19 E 3
Appennino Lucano 19 G 3–4
Appennino Tosco-Emiliano 19 F 3
Appenzell 19 E 2
Appin 3 B 3
Appleby 5 D 2
Applecross 2 B 3
Appleton 77 J 3
Appollonia → Süsah 59 K 2
Approuague 85 H 3
Aprilia 19 F 3
Apsheronsk 21 E 2
Apt 19 E 3
Apucarana 87 F 5
Apuka 37 W 3
Apuka Chukotskaya 37 W 3
Apure 84 D 2
Apurimac 86 B 3
Āqā Bābā (Iran) 23 E 1
Aqā 'Atabah 59 H 3
Aqdā (Iran) 23 F 2
'Aqīq 60 F 5
Āqotāq (Iran) 23 E 1
Aqrah (Iraq) 22 D 1
Aqrin, Jabal (Saudi Arabia) 22 C 3
Aquibi, Cachoeira 87 E 3
Aquidauana 86 E 5
'Ar 'ar, Wādi (Saudi Arabia)
    22 C 3
Ar Horqin Qi 39 H 2
Ar Rachidiya 58 E 2
Ar Radīsīyah Bahrī (Egypt) 22 A 4
Ar Rahad 60 F 6
Ar Rahad 60 E 6
Ar Rahhālīyah (Iraq) 22 D 2
Ar Ramādī (Iraq) 22 D 2
Ar Ramlah (Jordan) 22 B 3
Ar Rank 60 E 6
Ar Raqqah (Syria) 22 C 2
Ar Rāqūbah 59 J 3
Ar Rass (Saudi Arabia) 22 D 4
Ar Rawdatayn (Kuwait) 23 E 3
Ar Rastān (Syria) 22 B 2
Ar Rawdah 61 G 4
Ar Rawdah 61 H 6
Ar Rawdah (Saudi Arabia) 22 C 4
Ar Rawdatayn (Kuwait) 23 E 3
Ar Rāwuk 61 H 5
Ar Rayhānī (Oman) 23 G 5
Ar Rayyān 61 H 5
Ar Rifā' (Qatar) 23 F 4
Ar Rifā'ī (Iraq) 23 E 3
Ar Rihāb (Iraq) 23 D 3
Ar Rimāh (Saudi Arabia) 23 E 4
Ar Rimāl 61 J 4
Ar Riyād (Saudi Arabia) 23 E 4
Ar Rub al Khali 61 HJ 4–5
Ar Rubad 61 F 4
Ar Rumaythah (Iraq) 23 D 3
Ar Rumaythah (Qatar) 23 F 4
Ar Ruqi (Saudi Arabia) 23 E 3
Ar Rusāfah (Syria) 22 C 2
Ar Rusayris 60 E 6
Ar Rutbah (Iraq) 22 C 2
Ar Ruwaydah (Saudi Arabia)
    22 D 4
Ar Ruways (Qatar) 23 F 4
Ar Ruways (United Arab
    Emirates) 23 F 4

Ara 18 C 3
'Arabah, Wādi al (Jordan) 22 B 3
Arabatskaya Strelka 21 E 1
Arabestān (Iran) 23 E 3
Arabian Basin 98 B 3
Arabian Desert → As Şaḥrā' ash
    Sharqīyah 60 E 3
Arabian Sea 93
Araç 21 D 2
Araçá 85 F 3
Aracaju 87 J 3
Aracati 87 J 1
Araçatuba 87 F 5
Aracena, Sierra de 18 B 4
Árachthos 20 B 3
Araçuai 87 H 4
Arad 20 B 1
Arada 63 J 2
'Arādah (United Arab Emirates)
    23 F 5
Aradanskiy Khrebet 36 F 5
Arafali 65 F 1
Arafura, Laut 43 HJ 5
Arafura Sea 43 HJ 5
Arafura Shelf 99 C 4
Aragarças 87 F 4
Aragats 21 F 2
Aragon 18 C 3
Aragón 18 C 3
Aragua de Barcelona 85 F 2
Aragua de Maturín 85 F 2
Araguacema 85 HJ 5
Araguaçu 87 G 3
Araguaia 85 J 5
Araguaia, Parque Nacional do
    87 FG 3
Araguaiana 87 F 4
Araguaína 85 J 5
Araguari (Amapá, Brazil) 85 H 3
Araguari (Minas Gerais, Brazil)
    87 G 4
Araguatins 85 J 5
Arak (Algeria) 59 F 3
Arāk (Iran) 23 E 2
Araka 63 H 2
Arakaka 85 G 2
Arakan Yoma 41 F 3–4
Araks 34 D 3
Aral 35 L 2
Aral'sk 35 G 1
Aral'skoye More 34–35 FG 2
Aralsul'fat 35 G 1
Aramac 49 H 3
Arambaza 84 D 4
Ārān (Iran) 23 F 2
Aran Islands 14 AB 4
Aranda de Duero 18 C 3
Arandai 43 H 4
Arandelovac 20 B 2
Aranjuez 18 C 3
Aranos 66 B 4
Aranuka 52 C 3
Aranyaprathet 41 H 5
Araouane 62 D 2
Arapa, Lago 86 B 4
Arapari 85 J 5
Arapey 88 E 5
Arapiraca 87 J 2
Arapongas 87 F 5
Araquara 87 G 5
'Ar'ar (Saudi Arabia) 22 C 3
Araracuara, Cerros de 84 D 3–4
Araranguá 88 G 4
Araras 85 H 5
Araras, Serra das 87 F 4
Ararat (Armeniya, U.S.S.R.)
    21 FG 3
Ararat (Victoria, Austr.) 49 G 6
Ararat, Mount (Turkey) 21 F 3
Ararí 87 H 1
Araro 65 F 4
Aras 21 F 2
Aras 34 D 3
Araticu 85 J 4
Aratika 53 F 4
Arauá 87 J 3
Arauca 84 D 2
Arauco 89 B 6
Arauquita 84 D 2
Araura 84 D 2
Aravalli Range 40 B 2
Arawale Game Reserve 65 G 5
Araxá 87 G 4
Áraxos, Ákra 20 B 3
Araya 85 F 1
Arba Minch 65 F 3
'Arbat (Iraq) 23 D 2
Arbatax 19 E 4
Arboga 17 G 4
Arbon 19 E 2
Arbrā 16 G 3
Arbre du Ténéré 63 G 2
Arbroath 3 C 3
Arcachon 18 C 3
Arcata 76 B 3

Arcelia 78 B 4
Archer River 49 G 1
Archer River National Park 49 G 1
Archer's Post 65 F 4
Archidona 18 C 4
Archiestown 2 C 3
Archipelago Kerimbas 67 G 2
Archipelago of the Recherche
    48 C 5
Archipiélago de Camagüey 79 G 3
Archipiélago de Colón 84 B 6
Archipiélago de la Reina Adelaida
    89 A 9
Archipiélago de los Canarreos
    79 F 3
Archipiélago de los Chonos
    89 AB 7–8
Archipiélago de los Jardinesde la
    Reina 79 FG 3
Archipiélago Guayaneco 89 A 8
Arckaringa River 48 E 4
Arco (Italy) 19 F 2
Arco (U.S.A.) 76 D 3
Arcos 18 B 4
Arcos de Jalón 18 C 3
Arcos de Valdevez 18 B 3
Arcoverde 87 J 2
Arctic Ocean 90
Arctic Red River 72 L 2
Arctic Red River 72 L 2
Arctic Village 72 H 2
Arctowski 91
Ard aş Şawwān 60 F 2
Ard aş Şawwān (Jordan) 22 B 3
Arda 20 C 2
Ardabīl 34 D 3
Ardahan 21 F 2
Ardakān (Iran) 23 FG 2
Ardakān (Iran) 23 F 3
Ardal (Iran) 23 F 2
Ardalstangen 16 E 3
Ardatov 24 H 4
Ardee 4 B 3
Ardennes 14 E 4
Ardennes, Canal des 19 D 2
Ardentinny 3 B 3
Ardersier 2 C 3
Ardeşen 21 F 2
Ardestan (Iran) 23 F 2
Ardfern 3 B 3
Ardglass 4 C 2
Ardila 18 B 4
Ardley 7 D 2
Ardlui 3 B 3
Ardlussa 3 B 3
Ardmore 77 G 5
Ardnamurchan 3 AB 3
Ardrishaig 3 B 4
Ardrossan 3 B 4
Ards Peninsula 4 C 2
Ardvasar 3 B 3
Åre 16 F 3
Arebi 64 D 4
Areciba 89 C 8
Areia Branca 87 J 1
Arena 43 F 2
Arena, Point 76 B 4
Arenales, Cerro 89 B 8
Arenápolis 86 E 3
Arenas, Punta de 89 C 9
Arendal 17 E 4
Aréopolis 20 B 3
Arequipa 86 B 4
Arere 85 H 4
Arés 87 J 2
Åreskutan 16 F 3
Arévalo 18 C 3
Arezzaf 62 D 2
Arezzo 19 F 3
Arga 37 R 2
Argadargada 49 F 3
Arga-Emneke, Gora 37 Q 2
Argan 38 A 2
Arganda 18 C 3
Arga-Sala 36 J 2
Argens 19 E 3
Argent, Côte d' 18 C 3
Argenta 19 F 3
Argentan 18 D 2
Argentina 89 CD 6
Argentine Basin 98 A 5
Argentino, Lago 89 B 9
Argenton-sur-Creuse 18 D 2
Arges 20 C 2
Arghandab 35 H 4
Argio 65 F 3
Argo 60 E 5
Argolikós Kólpos 20 B 3
Argonne 19 DE 2
Árgos 20 B 3
Agostólion 20 B 3
Arguin, Cap d' 58 B 4
Argun' 36 L 5
Argungu 63 EF 3
Argyle, Lake 48 D 2
Argyll 3 B 3

Arholma 17 G 4
Århus 17 F 4
Ariari 84 D 3
Arias 88 D 5
Ariaú 85 G 4
Aribinda 62 D 3
Arica (Chile) 86 B 4
Arica (Colombia) 84 D 4
Arid, Cape 48 C 5
Aridal 58 C 3
Ariège 18 D 3
Ariel 89 D 6
Ariguaní 84 D 1
Arīḥā (Syria) 22 B 2
Arima 85 F 5
Arima (Trinidad and Tobago)
  85 F 1
Arinos (Mato Grosso, Brazil)
  86 E 3
Arinos (Mato Grosso, Brazil)
  86 E 3
Arinos (Minas Gerais, Brazil)
  87 G 4
Aripuanã 85 F 5
Aripuanã 85 F 5
Ariquemes 85 F 5
Ariripina 87 H 2
Arismendi 84 E 2
Arissa 65 G 2
Aritzo 19 E 4
Arivonimamo 67 H 3
Ariza 18 C 3
Arizaro, Salar de 86 C 5
Arizona (Argentina) 89 C 6
Arizona (U.S.A.) 76 D 5
Ärjäng 17 F 4
Arjasa 42 DE 5
Arjeplog 16 G 2
Arjona 84 C 1
Arka 37 Q 3
Arkadak 24 H 5
Arkadelphia 77 H 5
Arkaig, Loch 3 B 3
Arkalyk 25 N 5
Arkansas 77 H 4
Arkansas 77 H 5
Arkansas City 77 G 4
Arkanū, Jabal 59 K 4
Arkatag Shan 38 AB 3
Arkhangel 24 H 3
Arkhangel'sk 24 H 3
Arkhangel'skaya 21 F 1
Arkhangel'skoye 21 F 2
Arkhangel'skoye 24 G 5
Arkhara 37 O 6
Arkhyz 21 F 2
Arklow 4 B 3
Arkonam 40 C 5
Arlberg 19 F 2
Arles 19 D 3
Arlington (OR, U.S.A.) 76 C 2
Arlington (TX, U.S.A.) 77 G 5
Arlington (VA, U.S.A.) 77 L 4
Arlit 63 F 2
Arlon 14 E 5
Arly 62 E 3
Armadale 3 C 4
Armagh 4 B 2
Armagnac, Collines de l' 18 D 3
Arman 37 S 4
Armant 60 E 3
Armavir 21 F 1
Armenia 84 C 3
Armeniya 21 F 2
Armentieres 18 D 1
Armeria 78 B 4
Armero 84 D 2
Armidale 49 J 5
Armori 40 D 3
Armoy 4 B 2
Armstrong 74 K 5
Armur 40 C 4
Armyansk 21 D 1
Arnauti, Akra (Cyprus) 22 A 2
Arnawai 35 J 3
Arnhem 14 E 4
Arnhem Bay 49 F 1
Arnhem, Cape 49 F 1
Arnhem Land 48 EF 1
Arnhem Land Reserve 48 EF 1
Arni 40 C 5
Arno (Italy) 19 F 3
Arno (Marshall Is.) 52 C 2
Arno Bay 49 F 5
Arnold 7 D 1
Arnöy 16 H 1
Arnside 5 D 2
Ærö 17 F 5
Aroab 66 B 5
Aroche, Pico de 18 B 4
Aroma 60 F 5
Arona 50 E 3
Arorae 52 C 3
Arosa 19 E 2
Årösund 17 E 4
Arpaçay 21 F 2

Arpajon 18 D 2
Arpavla 25 M 3
Arquipélago das Anavilhanas
  85 F 4
Arquipélago dos Abrolhos 87 J 4
Arquipélago dos Bijagós 62 A 3
Arrah 40 D 2
Arraias 87 G 3
Arran 3 B 4
Arras 18 D 1
Arrecifal 84 E 3
Arrecife 58 C 3
Arrecifes 88 D 5
Arrecifes Triángulos 78 D 3
Arriaga 78 D 4
Arroio Grande 88 F 5
Arrowsmith, Mount 51 Q 9
Arroyito 88 D 5
Arroyo de las Flores 89 DE 6
Arroyo Verde 89 C 7
Arroyos y Esteros 86 E 5
Års 17 E 4
Arsenján (Iran) 23 F 3
Arsen'yev 39 K 2
Årskogen 16 G 3
Arsuk 75 S 3
Árta 20 B 3
Artá, Cuevas de 18 D 4
Artashat 21 F 3
Arteaga 78 B 4
Artem 39 K 2
Artemisa 78 F 3
Artémou 58 C 5
Artemovsk 21 E 1
Artemovsk 36 F 5
Artemovskiy 21 F 1
Artesia 76 F 5
Artherstone 7 D 1
Arthur's Town 79 G 3
Artigas 88 E 5
Artik 21 F 2
Artillery Lake 73 Q 3
Artoli 60 E 5
Artsyz 20 C 1
Artux 35 K 3
Artvin 21 F 2
Artybash 25 R 5
Artyk 37 R 3
Aru 64 E 4
Aru Islands 50 C 3
Aru, Kepulauan 43 HJ 5
Aru, Tanjung 42 E 4
Arua 64 E 4
Aruaja 84 E 5
Aruanã 87 F 3
Aruba, Isla 84 E 1
Aruma 85 F 4
Arun Qi 37 M 6
Arunachal Pradesh 41 F 2
Arundel 7 D 2
Aruppukkottai 40 C 6
Arus, Tanjung 43 F 3
Arusha 65 F 5
Arusha Chini 65 F 5
Aruwimi 64 D 4
Arvada 76 E 4
Arvagh 4 B 3
Arvayheer 38 D 1
Arvidsjaur 16 G 2
Årvika 17 F 4
Årviksand 16 GH 1
Arxan 36 L 6
Ary 36 M 1
Arys' 35 H 2
Arys, Ozero 35 H 1
Aryta 37 N 3
Arzamas 24 H 4
Arzanah (United Arab Emirates)
  23 F 4
Aržano 19 G 3
Arzgir 21 F 1
Arzhan 36 G 5
As Ḩasāwinah, Jabal 59 H 3
As Ṣa'an (Syria) 22 B 2
As Sab'ān (Syria) 22 C 4
As Ṣadr (United Arab Emirates)
  23 G 4
As Ṣafirah (Syria) 22 B 1
As Ṣāfiyah (Jordan) 22 B 3
As Ṣaḩm 61 K 4
As Ṣaḩrā' al Gharbīyah 60 D 3
As Ṣaḩrā' al Janūbīyah 60 D 4
As Ṣaḩrā' an Nūbiyah 60 E 4
As Ṣaḩrā' ash Sharqīyah (Egypt)
  22 AB 4–5
As Ṣaḩrā' at Tīh (Egypt) 22 AB 3
As Salamīyah (Saudi Arabia)
  23 E 4
As Salamīyah (Syria) 22 B 2
As Salīf 61 G 5
As Ṣāliḩīyah (Syria) 22 C 2
As Sālimīyah (Kuwait) 23 E 3
As Sallūm 60 D 2
As Salmān (Iraq) 23 D 3
As Salt (Jordan) 22 B 2
As Samāwah (Iraq) 23 D 3

As Ṣanām 61 J 4
As Sarīr 59 K 3
As Sarīr 59 K 3
As Sawdā, Jabal 59 HJ 3
As Sawrah (Saudi Arabia) 22 C 4
As Sayl al Kabīr 61 G 4
as Sibā'ī, Jabal (Egypt) 22 AB 4
As Sidrah 59 J 2
As Sidrah 59 J 2
As Silā (United Arab Emirates)
  23 F 4
As Subū' 60 E 4
As Sufāl 61 H 6
As Ṣufayyah 60 E 5
As Ṣufug (United Arab Emirates)
  23 F 5
As Ṣukhayrah 59 H 2
As Suknah (Jordan) 22 C 2
As Sulaymī (Saudi Arabia) 22 C 4
As Sulayyil 61 H 4
As Ṣulb (Saudi Arabia) 23 E 4
As Ṣummān (Saudi Arabia)
  23 DE 4
As Suwaydā' (Syria) 22 B 2
As Suwayh 61 K 4
As Ṣuwayrah (Iraq) 23 D 2
As Suways 22 A 3
Asab 66 B 5
Asaba 63 F 4
Asadabad (Afghanistan) 35 J 4
Asadābād (Iran) 23 E 2
Asadābād (Iran) 34 F 3
Asahikawa 39 M 2
'Asalūyeh (Iran) 23 F 4
Asamakka 63 F 2
Asansol 40 E 3
Åsarna 16 F 3
Asbest 25 M 4
Ascensión (Bolivia) 86 D 4
Ascension Island 54 A 5
Ascension Island 54 A 5
Aschaffenburg 15 E 5
Ascoli Piceno 19 F 3
Ascot 7 D 2
Ascotán 86 C 5
Aseda 17 G 4
Asedjrad 59 F 4
Asekseme 59 F 3
Åsele 16 G 3
Aselle 65 F 3
Åsen 16 F 3
Åsendabo 65 F 3
Asfar, Tall as (Jordan) 22 B 2
Ash Shabakah (Iraq) 22 D 3
Ash Shabb 60 D 4
Ash Shallāl al Khamis 60 E 5
Ash Shallāl ar Rābi' 60 DE 5
Ash Shallāl as Sablūkah 60 E 5
Ash Shallāl ath Thālith 60 E 5
Ash Sha'm (United Arab Emirates)
  23 G 4
Ash Shāmīyah (Iraq) 23 D 3
Ash Shāmīyah (Iraq) 23 E 3
Ash Shaqīq (Saudi Arabia) 22 C 3
Ash Shaqrā' (Saudi Arabia) 23 D 4
Ash Sha'rā' (Saudi Arabia) 22 D 4
Ash Shāriqah (United Arab
  Emirates) 23 G 4
Ash Sharmah (Saudi Arabia)
  22 B 3
Ash Sharqāt (Iraq) 22 D 2
Ash Sharqī 59 H 2
Ash Sharqīyah 61 K 4
Ash Shāṭi', Wādī 59 H 3
Ash Shaṭrah (Iraq) 23 E 3
Ash Shawbak (Jordan) 22 B 3
Ash Shiḩr 61 H 6
Ash Shinafīyah (Iraq) 23 D 3
Ash Shu'aybah (Saudi Arabia)
  22 CD 3–4
Ash Shu'bah (Saudi Arabia) 23 D 3
Ash Shumlūl (Saudi Arabia) 23 E 4
Ash Shuqayq 61 G 5
Ash Shurayf → Khaybar 61 F 3
Ash Shuraykh 60 E 5
Ash Shuwayhāt (United Arab
  Emirates) 23 F 5
Ash Shuwaykh (Kuwait) 23 E 3
Ash Shwayrif 59 H 3
Asha 25 L 4
Ashanti 62 D 4
Ashbourne 4 B 3
Ashbourne 5 E 3
Ashburton 6 C 3
Ashburton 51 Q 9
Ashburton River 48 B 3
Ashby de la Zouch 7 D 1
Ashchikol', Ozero 35 H 1
Ashdod (Israel) 22 A 3
Asheville 77 K 4
Ashford 7 E 2
Ashington 5 E 2
Ashkhabad 34 F 3
Ashkidah 59 H 3

Ashkirk 3 C 4
Ashkun 35 J 3
Ashland (KS, U.S.A.) 76 G 4
Ashland (KY, U.S.A.) 77 K 4
Ashland (OR, U.S.A.) 76 B 3
Ashland (WI, U.S.A.) 77 H 2
Ashmore Reef 48 C 1
Ashqelon (Israel) 22 B 3
Ashtabula 77 K 3
Ashtarak 21 F 2
Ashtīyān (Iran) 23 EF 2
Ashton 76 D 3
Ashton-in-Makerfield 5 D 3
Ashton-under-Lyne 5 DE 3
Ashuanipi 75 O 5
Ashuanipi Lake 75 O 5
Ashur → Assur 61 G 1
Asia, Kepulauan 43 H 3
Asilah 58 D 1
Asimiro 43 G 3
Asinara 19 E 3
Asinara, Golfo dell' 19 E 3
Asino 25 R 4
Asir, Ra's 65 J 2
Aska 40 D 4
Aşkale 21 F 3
Askaniya Nova 21 D 1
Askim 17 F 4
Askiz 36 F 5
Askja 16 B 3
Askoll 16 E 3
Asker 17 F 4
Askern 7 D 1
Askersund 17 G 4
Askvoll 16 E 3
Asmara 65 F 1
Åsnen 17 FG 4
Asni 58 D 2
Asop 40 B 2
Asosa 64 E 2
Asoteriba, Jabal 60 F 4
Asouf Mellene 59 F 3
Åspås (Iran) 23 F 3
Aspatria 3 C 4
Aspatrla 5 D 2
Aspen 76 E 4
Aspendos 20 D 3
Aspermont 76 F 5
Aspiring, Mount 50 P 9
Aspurito 84 E 2
Asqueimat 58 B 4
Assa 58 D 3
Assab 65 G 2
Assâba 58 C 5
Assale, Lake 65 G 2
Assam 41 F 2
Assaouas 63 F 2
Assaye 40 C 3
Assekaifaf 59 G 3
Assekrème 59 G 4
Assen 14 E 4
Assens 17 EF 4
Assini 62 D 5
Assiniboia 73 Q 6
Assiniboine 73 S 6
Assiniboine, Mount 73 O 5
Assiou 59 G 4
Assis 87 F 5
Assisi 19 F 3
Assodé 63 F 2
Assumption 65 H 6
Assur (Iraq) 22 D 2
Astakh 37 P 2
Åstäneh (Iran) 23 E 2
Astara 34 D 3
Astārā (Iran) 34 D 3
Asti 19 E 3
Astillero 89 C 7
Astipálaia 20 C 3
Astola 35 G 6
Astor 35 J 3
Astorga 18 B 3
Astoria 76 B 2
Astove 65 H 6
Astrakhan 34 D 1
Asturias 18 B 3
Astwood 7 D 1
Asuncion (Mariana Is.) 52 A 1
Asunción (Paraguay) 88 E 4
Aswa 64 E 4
Aswān (Egypt) 22 A 4
Aswan High Dam (Egypt) 22 A 5
Asyūt 60 E 3
At Ṭaff (United Arab Emirates)
  23 G 4
At Ṭafīlah (Jordan) 22 B 3
At Ṭā'if 61 G 4
At Tamīmī 59 K 2
At Tarhūnī, Jabal 59 K 4
At Ṭarmīyah (Iraq) 22 D 2
At Ṭawīl (Saudi Arabia) 22 C 3
At Ṭaysīyah (Saudi Arabia)
  22 D 3–4
At Ṭayyārah 60 E 6
At Ṭīb, Ra's 59 H 1
At Tin, Ra's 59 K 2

At Ṭulayḥī (Saudi Arabia) 22 D 4
At Ṭullāb 59 K 4
At Ṭūr (Egypt) 22 A 3
At Ṭurayf (Saudi Arabia) 22 C 3
At Turbah 61 G 6
At Ṭuwayshah 60 D 6
At Ṭuwayyah (Saudi Arabia)
  22 C 4
Ata 52 D 4
Atacama, Desierto do 86 C 5
Atacama, Salar de 86 C 5
Atafu 52 D 4
Ataki 20 C 1
Atakora, Chaîne de l' 62 E 3
Atakpamé 62 E 4
Atalándi 20 B 3
Atalaya 86 B 3
Atalaya, Cerro (Chile) 89 B 9
Atalaya, Cerro (Peru) 86 B 3
Atalayasa 18 D 4
Atamanon Óri 20 B 3
Atambua 43 F 5
Atangmik 75 R 3
Atar 58 C 4
Atas Bogd Uul 38 C 2
Atascadero 76 B 4
Atasu 25 O 6
Atauba 85 F 4
Atauro, Pulau 43 G 5
Ataviros 20 C 3
Atbalmin 50 D 2
'Atbarah 60 E 5
Atbarah 60 F 5
Atbasar 25 N 5
At-Bash 35 K 2
Atchafalaya Bay 77 H 6
Atchison 77 G 4
Atebubu 62 D 4
Ateca 18 C 3
Atemble 50 D 2–3
Åteshān (Iran) 23 F 2
Ath Thamad (Egypt) 22 B 3
Ath Thumāmī (Saudi Arabia)
  23 D 4
Athabasca (Alb., Can.) 73 P 4
Athabasca (Alb., Can.) 73 P 5
Athabasca, Lake 73 Q 4
Athboy 4 B 3
Athens (GA, U.S.A.) 77 K 5
Athens (TN, U.S.A.) 77 K 4
Athens → Athínai 20 B 3
Athéras 20 C 3
Atherstone 7 D 1
Atherton (Queensland, Austr.)
  49 GH 2
Atherton (U.K.) 5 D 3
Athi 65 F 5
Athi River 65 F 5
Athínai 20 B 3
Athlone 4 B 3
Athni 40 C 4
Áthos 20 B 2
Athy 4 B 3
Ati 63 H 3
Atiak 64 E 4
Atico 86 B 4
Atikokan 74 J 6
Atikonak Lake 75 P 5
Atiu 53 E 4
Atka 72 C 5
Atka (AK, U.S.A.) 72 C 5
Atka (U.S.S.R.) 37 S 3
Atkarsk 24 H 5
Atkasuk 72 F 1
Atkinson (N.C., U.S.A.) 77 L 5
Atkinson (NE, U.S.A.) 76 G 3
Atlanta 77 JK 5
Atlantic (IA, U.S.A.) 77 H 3
Atlantic City 77 M 4
Atlantic Ocean 92
Atlantic-Indian Rise 98 B 5
Atlas el Kebir 58 DE 2
Atlas el Moutaouassit 58 DE 2
Atlas es Sahir 58 D 2–3
Atlas Mountains 58 DF 2
Atlasova, Ostrov 37 ST 5
Atlin 72 L 4
Atlin Lake 72 L 4
Atmore 77 J 5
Atna Peak 73 M 5
Atocha 86 C 5
Atoka 77 G 5
Atouat 41 J 4
Atoyac de Alvarez 78 B 4
Åtran 17 F 4
Atrato 84 C 2
Atrek 34 E 3
Atsy 43 J 5
Attawapiskat 74 KL 5
Attawapiskat 74 L 5
Attawapiskat 74 K 5
Attersee 19 F 2
Attikamagen Lake 75 O 5
Attleborough 7 E 1
Attopeu 41 J 5
Attu 72 A 5

Attu 72 A 5
Attur 40 C 5
Atuel 89 C 6
Atura 64 E 4
Åtvidaberg 17 G 4
Atwick 5 E 2
Atyr-Meyite 37 O 2
Aua 50 D 2
Auadi 58 C 4
Auas Mountains 66 B 4
Auati Paraná 84 E 4
Auatu 65 G 3
Aubagne 19 E 3
Aube 19 D 2
Aubry, Lake 73 M 2
Auburn (CA, U.S.A.) 76 B 4
Auburn (ME, U.S.A.) 77 M 3
Auburn (NE, U.S.A.) 77 G 3
Auburn River 49 J 4
Aubusson 18 D 2
Auca Mahuida, Sierra 89 C 6
Auch 18 D 3
Auchenbreck 3 B 4
Auchencairn 3 C 4
Auchi 63 F 4
Auchinleck 3 B 4
Auchterarder 3 C 2
Auckland 51 Q 8
Auckland Islands 91
Aude 18 D 3
Audo Range 65 G 3
Aue 15 F 4
Augathella 49 H 4
Aughnacloy 4 B 2
Aughrabies Falls 66 C 5
Augsburg 15 F 5
Augusta (AR, U.S.A.) 77 H 4
Augusta (Australia) 48 A 5
Augusta (GA, U.S.A.) 77 K 5
Augusta (Italy) 19 G 4
Augusta (ME, U.S.A.) 77 N 3
Augustów 15 H 4
Augustus, Mount 48 B 3
Auki 51 H 3
Auld, Lake 48 C 3
Auna 63 E 3
Auning 17 F 4
Aur 52 C 2
Auraiya 40 C 2
Aurangabad 40 D 3
Aurangaband 40 C 4
Auray 18 C 2
Aure 16 E 3
Aurès, Massif de l' 59 G 1
Aurich 15 E 4
Aurilândia 87 F 4
Aurillac 18 D 3
Aurlandsfjorden 16 E 3
Aurlandsvangen 16 E 3
Aurora (CO, U.S.A.) 76 F 4
Aurora (Philippines) 43 F 2
Aurunci, Monti 19 F 3
Aus 66 B 5
Ausangate, Nevado 86 B 3
Ausert 58 C 4
Aust-Agder 17 E 4
Austin (Australia) 48 B 4
Austin (MN, U.S.A.) 77 H 3
Austin (NV, U.S.A.) 76 C 4
Austin (TX, U.S.A.) 76 G 5
Austin, Lake 48 B 4
Austral Downs 49 F 3
Australia 48–49 DF 3
Australian Alps 49 H 6
Australian Capital Territory 49 H 6
Australian-Antarctic Basin 98 B 5
Australian-Antarctic Discordance
99 C 5
Australian-Antarctic Rise 99 C 5
Austria 19 F 2
Austurhorn 16 C 3
Austvågøy 16 F 2
Autazes 85 G 4
Autlán 78 B 4
Autun 18 D 2
Auxerre 18 D 2
Auxonne 19 E 2
Auyuittuq National Park 75 OP 2
Avakubi 64 D 4
Avallon 18 D 2
Avalon Peninsula 75 R 6
Avan 34 G 1
Avanavero 85 G 3
Avaré 87 G 5
Avarua 53 E 4
Avaz 34 G 4
Ávdhira 20 B 2
Avebury 7 D 2
Avedat (Israel) 22 B 3
Aveh (Iran) 23 F 2
Aveiro 85 H 4
Aveiro (Portugal) 18 B 3
Åvej 34 D 3

Åvej (Iran) 23 E 2
Åvej, Gardaneh-ye 34 D 3
Åvej, Gardaneh-ye (Iran) 23 E 2
Avekova 37 U 3
Avellaneda 88 E 5
Avellino 19 FG 3
Averöya 16 E 3
Aversa 19 F 3
Aves, Isla de 79 K 4
Aves, Islas las 84 E 1
Avesta 17 G 3
Aveyron 18 D 3
Avezzano 19 F 3
Aviá Terai 88 D 4
Aviemore 2 C 3
Avigait 75 R 3
Avignon 19 D 3
Ávila 18 C 3
Avilés 18 B 3
Avington 49 GH 3
Avola 19 G 4
Avon Downs 49 F 2
Avon Park 77 K 6
Avon, River (Avon) 6 C 2
Avon, River (Grampian) 2 C 3
Avon, River (Warwickshire) 7 D 1
Avon River (Australia) 48 B 5
Avonmouth 6 C 2
Avranches 18 C 2
Avrora 21 D 1
Awai 63 F 4
'Awālī (Qatar) 23 F 4
Awanui 51 Q 8
Awara Plain 65 G 4
Awareh 65 G 3
Awasa 65 F 3
Awash 65 G 2
Awash 65 G 3
Awash Fish River (Namibia)
66 B 5
Awasib Mountains 66 B 5
Awaso 62 D 4
Awat 35 L 2
'Awaynat Wanīn 59 H 3
Awbārī 59 H 3
Awbārī, Idhān 59 H 3
Awdēgle 65 G 4
Awe, Loch 3 B 3
Awjilah 59 K 3
Awka 63 F 4
Axel Heiberg Island 90
Axi-les-Thermes 18 D 3
Axim 62 D 5
Axinim 85 G 4
Axioma 85 F 5
Axiós 20 B 2
Axminster 6 C 2
Ayabaca 84 BC 4
Ayachi, Jbel 58 E 2
Ayacucho (Argentina) 89 E 6
Ayacucho (Peru) 86 B 3
'Ayādh 61 H 6
Ayaguz 25 P 6
Ayaguz 25 Q 6
Ayakkum Hu 38 A 3
Ayakli 36 G 2
Ayamé 62 D 4
Ayamé Dam 62 D 4
Ayamonte 18 B 4
Ayan 36 F 2
Ayan 36 J 3
Ayan 36 J 4
Ayan 37 P 4
Ayanaka 37 V 3
Ayancık 21 D 2
Ayangba 63 F 4
Ayanka 37 U 3
Ayaş 21 D 2
Ayava 36 H 4
Ayaturku, Ozero 36 EF 1
Ayaviri 86 B 3
Ayaya 37 O 3
Aydın 20 C 3
Aydıncık 21 D 3
Aydingkol Hu 38 AB 2
Aydyrlinskiy 25 L 5
Ayelu 65 G 2
Ayerbe 18 C 3
Ayers Rock → Uluru National
Park 48 E 4
Áyion Óros 20 B 2
Áyios Evstrátios 20 C 3
Áyios Kirikos 20 C 3
Áyios Nikólaos 20 C 3
Aykhal 36 K 2
Aylesbury 7 D 2
Aylmer Lake 73 Q 3
Aylsham 7 E 1
'Ayn al 'Ajalīyah 61 H 4
'Ayn al Baydā' (Syria) 22 BC 2
'Ayn al Ghazāl 59 K 4
'Ayn 'Aysa (Syria) 22 C 1
'Ayn Dāllah 60 D 3
Ayn Dār (Saudi Arabia) 23 E 4
Ayn Dīwār (Turkey) 22 CD 1
'Ayn, Ra's al (Syria) 22 C 1

'Ayn Sifnī (Iraq) 22 D 1
'Ayn Sukhnah (Egypt) 22 A 3
'Ayn Zuwayyah 59 K 4
Ayna 18 C 4
'Aynabo 65 H 3
Ayni 35 H 3
'Aynīn 61 G 4
Ayod 64 E 3
Ayon 37 V 2
Ayorou 62 E 3
Ayr (Australia) 49 H 2
Ayr (U.K.) 3 B 4
Ayrag Nuur 36 F 6
Ayrancı 21 D 3
Ayrshire Downs 49 G 3
Aysary 25 O 5
Ayshirak 25 O 6
Aytos 20 C 2
Aytré 18 C 2
Ayuán-Tepuí 85 F 2
Ayutla 78 C 4
Ayutthaya 41 H 5
Ayvacık 20 C 3
Ayvacık 21 E 2
Ayvalık 20 C 3
Az Daro 65 F 2
Az Tibaghbagh 60 D 3
Az Zāb al Kabīr (Iraq) 22 D 1
Az Zāb as Şaghīr (Iraq) 22 D 2
Az Zabdānī (Syria) 22 B 2
Az Zafīr 61 G 5
Az Zahrah 59 J 3
Az Zahrān (Saudi Arabia) 23 EF 4
Az Zallāq 23 F 4
Az Zaqāzīq 60 E 2
Az Zarqā' (United Arab Emirates)
23 F 4
Az Zarqā' (Jordan) 22 B 2
Az Zāwiyah 59 H 2
Az Zaydab 60 E 5
Az Zaydīyah 61 G 5
Az Zaytūn 60 D 3
Az Zilfī (Saudi Arabia) 23 D 4
Az Zubayr (Iraq) 23 E 3
Az Zugar 61 G 6
Āzādshahr (Iran) 23 G 1
Azaila 18 C 3
Azambuja 18 B 4
Azamgarh 40 D 2
Azanka 25 M 4
Azaouad 62 D 2
Azaouak, Vallée de l' 62 E 2
Āzarān 34 D 3
Azare 63 G 3
A'zāz 22 B 1
Azbine 63 F 2
Azdavay 21 D 2
Azéffal, Dunes de l' 58 BC 4
Azelik 63 F 2
Azemmour 58 D 2
Azennezal 58 F 4
Azerbaydzhan 34 D 2
Azilal 58 D 2
Aznā (Iran) 23 E 2
Azogues 84 C 4
Azopol'ye 24 J 2
Azores 58 A 1
Azoum 63 J 3
Azov 21 E 1
Azovskiy Kanal 21 EF 1
Azovskoye More 21 E 1
Azovy 25 N 3
Azozo 65 F 2
Azraq ash Shīshān (Jordan) 22 B 3
Azrou 58 D 2
Azrow 35 H 4
Aztec ruins 76 E 4
Azua 79 H 4
Azuaga 18 B 4
Azuero, Península de 84 B 2
Azul 89 E 6
Azul, Cordillera 84 C 5
Azur, Côte d' 19 E 3
Azzaba 59 G 1
Azzel Matti, Sebkha 58 F 3
Azzuwaytīnah 59 JK 2

B

B Bua Chum 41 H 4
Ba Dong 41 J 6
Ba' qūbah (Iraq) 23 D 2
Ba Xian 38 E 5
Ba Xian 39 G 3
Baa 43 F 6
Baä 48 C 1
Ba'abdā (Lebanon) 22 B 2
Ba'ādwēyn 65 H 3
Baan Baa 49 H 5
Bāb (United Arab Emirates) 23 F 5
Bāb al Māndab 61 G 6
Baba Burnu 20 D 2
Baba Burun 20 C 3
Bābā Heydar (Iran) 23 F 2

'Ayn Sifnī (Iraq) 22 D 1
Babaculândia 85 J 5
Babadag 20 C 2
Babaeski 20 C 2
Babahoyo 84 C 4
Babai Gaxun 38 D 2
Babanūsah 60 D 6
Babar, Kepulauan 43 G 5
Babi, Pulau 42 A 3
Babine 73 M 4
Babine Lake 73 M 5
Babino Polje 19 G 3
Babo 43 H 4
Babol (Iran) 23 F 1
Bābol Sar (Iran) 23 F 1
Baborigame 76 E 6
Baboua 64 AB 3
Babushkin 36 J 5
Babuyan 43 E 1–2
Babuyan 43 J 1
Babuyan Channel 43 J 1
Babylon (Iraq) 22 D 2
Bac Can 41 J 3
Bac Ninh 41 J 3
Bac Quang 41 H 3
Bacabal (Maranhão, Brazil)
87 GH 1
Bacabal (Pará, Brazil) 85 G 5
Bacajá 85 H 4
Bacan, Pulau 43 G 4
Bacău 20 C 1
Bachaquero 84 D 2
Bachu 35 K 3
Back 2 A 2
Back 73 S 2
Bačka Palanka 20 A 1
Bačka Topola 20 AB 1
Bačkovski Manastir 20 BC 2
Bacolod 43 F 1
Bacton 7 E 1
Bacup 5 D 3
Bād (Iran) 23 F 2
Bad Aussee 19 F 2
Bad Godesberg 15 E 4
Bad Hersfeld 15 E 4
Bad Homburg 15 E 4
Bad Ischl 19 F 2
Bad Kissingen 15 F 4
Bad Kreuznach 15 E 5
Bad Reichenhall 15 F 5
Bad Schwartau 15 F 4
Bad Tölz 15 F 5
Badagara 40 BC 5
Badagri 62 E 4
Badain Jaran Shamo 38 D 2
Badajós 85 J 4
Badajoz, Lago 85 F 4
Badajoz 18 B 4
Badakhshan 35 J 3
Badalona 18 D 3
Badami 40 C 4
Badanah (Saudi Arabia) 22 C 3
Badarma 36 H 4
Badcall 2 B 2
Badda 65 F 3
Baden (Austria) 19 G 2
Baden (Ethiopia) 65 F 1
Baden (Switzerland) 19 E 2
Baden-Baden 15 E 5
Baden-Württemberg 15 E 5
Badenoch 3 B 3
Badgastein 19 F 2
Badin 35 H 6
Bādiyat ash Shām 22 BC 2
Badjawa 43 F 5
Badlands 76 F 2
Badluarach 2 B 3
Bado 43 J 5
Badoumbé 62 B 3
Badr Hunayn (Saudi Arabia)
22 C 5
Badulla 40 D 6
Badyarikha 37 R 2
Badzhal 37 O 5
Badzhal'skiy Khrebet 37 O 5
Baena 18 C 4
Baeza (Ecuador) 84 C 4
Baeza (Spain) 18 C 4
Baf → Paphos 21 D 4
Bafa Gölü 20 C 3
Bafang 63 FG 4
Bafatá 62 B 3
Baffin Bay 90
Baffin Island 75 NO 2
Bafia 63 G 5
Bafing 62 B 3
Bafing Makana 62 BC 3
Bafoulabé 62 B 3
Bafoussam 63 G 4
Bāfq (Iran) 23 G 3
Bāfq, Kūh-e (Iran) 23 G 3

Bafra 21 E 2
Bafra Burnu 21 E 2
Bāft (Iran) 23 G 3
Bafwaboli 64 D 4
Bafwasende 64 D 4
Baga 63 G 3
Baga Sola 63 G 3
Bagadzha 36 L 3
Bagalkot 40 C 4
Bagam 63 F 2
Bagamoyo 65 F 6
Baganalakh 36 L 3
Bagansiapapi 42 B 3
Bagata 64 B 5
Bagdarin 36 K 5
Bagé 88 F 5
Bagerovo 21 E 1
Baghdād (Iraq) 22 D 2
Bagh-e Malek (Iran) 23 E 3
Bagheria 19 F 4
Bāghin (Iran) 23 G 3
Baghlan 35 H 3
Bagley 77 G 2
Bağlum 21 D 2
Bagn 17 E 3
Bagnères-de-Bigorre 18 D 3
Bagoé 62 C 3
Bagrationovsk 23 F 3
Bagrax → Bohu 35 M 2
Bagre 85 H 4
Bagshot 7 D 2
Bagua 84 C 5
Baguia 43 G 5
Baguio 43 J 1
Baguirmi 63 H 3
Bagusi 43 J 4
Bagzane, Monts 63 F 2
Bahadale 65 F 5
Bahama Islands 79 H 3
Bāhār (Iran) 23 E 2
Bahar Dar 65 F 2
Bahariya Oasis → Wāhat al
Bahariyah 60 D 3
Bahau 42 B 3
Bahaur 42 D 4
Bahawalnagar 35 J 5
Bahawalpur 35 J 5
Bahçe 21 E 2
Bahçe (Turkey) 22 B 1
Bahi 64 F 6
Bahía (Argentina) 89 C 8
Bahía (Brazil) 87 H 3
Bahía → Salvador (Brazil) 87 J 3
Bahía Adair 76 D 5
Bahía Anegada 89 D 7
Bahía Ballenas 76 D 6
Bahía Blanca 89 D 6
Bahía Blanca 89 D 6
Bahía Coatzacoalcos 78 D 4
Bahía Concepcíon 76 D 6
Bahía Darwin 89 AB 8
Bahía de Amatique 78 D 4
Bahía de Campeche 78 D 4
Bahía de Caráquez 84 B 4
Bahía de Chetumal 78 E 4
Bahía de Coronado 78 F 6
Bahía de La Paz 76 D 7
Bahía de Petacalco 78 B 4
Bahía de San Jorge 76 D 5
Bahía de San Quintín 76 C 5
Bahía de Santa Elena 76 E 6
Bahía de Santa María 76 E 6
Bahía de Sechura 84 B 5
Bahía de Tepoca 76 D 5
Bahía de Topolobampo 76 E 6
Bahía Dulce 78 C 4
Bahía Grande 89 C 9
Bahía, Islas de la 78 E 4
Bahía Kino 76 D 6
Bahía Laura 89 C 8
Bahía Magdalena 76 D 7
Bahía Negra 86 E 5
Bahía Otway 89 B 9
Bahía Pargua 89 B 7
Bahía Rosario 76 C 6
Bahía Samborombón 89 E 6
Bahía San Luis Gonzaga 76 D 6
Bahía Santa Ines 76 D 6
Bahía Sebastián Vizcaíno 76 D 6
Bahías, Cabo dos 89 CD 8
Bahindi 85 J 4
Bahr al Abyad 60 E 6
Bahr al 'Arab 60 D 6
Bahr al Azraq 60 E 6
Bahr al Ghazāl 64 DE 3
Bahr al Jabal 64 E 3
Bahr al Milh (Iraq) 22 D 2
Bahr Aouk 64 B 3
Bahr ar Rimāl al 'Azīm 60 D 3
Bahr ath Tharthār (Iraq) 22 D 2
Bahr el Ghazal 63 H 2–3
Bahrah 61 H 4
Bahraich 40 D 2
Bahrain 23 F 4
Bahrat Hims (Syria) 22 B 2

Bahrayn, Khalĭjal (Saudi Arabia) 23 F 4
Bāhu Kālāt 35 G 5
Bai Thuong 41 J 4
Baía de Maputo 67 E 5
Baía de Paranaguá 88 G 4
Baía de Setúbal 18 B 4
Baía de Sofala 67 EF 4
Baía de Todos os Santos 87 J 3
Baía do Bengo 66 A 1
Baía dos Tigres 66 A 3
Baía Farta 66 A 2
Baia Mare 20 B 1
Baião 85 J 4
Baíbokoum 63 H 4
Baicang 41 F 1
Baicheng 35 L 2
Baicheng 39 H 1
Baie aux Feuilles 75 O 4
Baie Comeau 75 O 6
Baie d'Antongil 67 HJ 3
Baie d'Audierne 18 C 2
Baie de Corisco 63 F 5
Baie de la Seine 18 C 2
Baie de Lannion 18 C 2
Baie de Rupert 75 LM 5
Baie Diana 75 O 3
Baie du Poste 75 N 5
Baie Mosquito 75 M 3
Baie Payne 75 O 4
Baie Trinité 75 O 6
Baie Verte 75 Q 6
Baie-des-Moutons 75 Q 5
Baihe 38 F 4
Baikal, Lake 36 J 5
Baikha 25 R 3
Bailang 36 M 6
Baildon 5 E 3
Baile Átha Cliath 14 B 4
Baile Atha Cliath 4 B 3
Bailén 18 C 4
Băileşti 20 B 2
Bailieborough 4 B 3
Bailique, Ilha 85 J 3
Ba-Illi 63 H 3
Bailundo 66 B 2
Baima 38 D 4
Baimuru 50 D 3
Bainang 40 E 2
Bainbridge 5 D 2
Bainbridge 77 K 5
Bain-de-Bretagne 18 C 2
Baing 43 F 6
Baingoin 40 E 1
Baiquan 37 N 6
Bā'ir (Jordan) 22 B 3
Baird Inlet 72 E 3
Baird Mountains 72 E 2
Baird Peninsula 75 M 2
Bairiki 52 C 2
Bairin Youqi 39 G 2
Bairin Zuoqi 39 GH 2
Bairkum 35 H 2
Bairndale 49 H 6
Bais 43 F 2
Baisha 38 E 7
Baixo-Alentejo 18 B 4
Baixo-Longa 66 B 3
Baiyanghe 35 M 2
Baiyer River 50 D 3
Baiyü 38 C 4
Baiyuda 60 E 5
Baiyuda Desert → Şaḥrā' Bayyūḍah 60 E 5
Baja 20 A 1
Baja California Norte 76 C 5
Baja California Sur 76 D 6
Baja de Marajó 85 J 4
Bājah 59 G 1
Bajas, Rías 18 B 3
Bājgīrān 34 F 3
Bajitpur 41 F 3
Bajun Islands 65 G 5
Baka 64 E 4
Bakadzhitsite 20 C 2
Bakal 25 L 5
Bakala 64 C 3
Bakanas 35 K 2
Bakar 19 F 2
Bakayan, Gunung 42 E 3
Bakchar 25 Q 4
Bake 42 B 4
Bakel 62 B 3
Baker (CA, U.S.A.) 76 C 4
Baker (MT, U.S.A.) 76 F 2
Baker (OR, U.S.A.) 76 C 3
Baker (Pacific Ocean, U.S.A.) 52 D 2
Baker, Canal 89 B 8
Baker Lake 73 S 3
Baker Lake (Australia) 48 D 4
Baker Lake (N.W.T., Can.) 73 S 3
Bakersfield 76 C 4
Bakewell 7 D 1
Bakharden 34 F 3
Bakhardok 34 F 3

Bākharz 34 G 4
Bakhchisaray 21 D 2
Bakhma (Iraq) 22 D 1
Bakhmach 24 F 5
Bakhta 35 R 3
Bakhta 25 R 3
Bakhtegān, Daryācheh-ye (Iran) 23 FG 3
Baki 63 J 2
Bakinskikh Komissarov, Imeni 26 34 DE 3
Bakir 20 C 3
Bakırdağı 21 E 3
Bakkaflói 16 C 2
Bako (Ethiopia) 65 F 3
Bako (Ivory Coast) 62 C 4
Bakony 20 A 1
Bakouma 64 C 3
Bakoye 62 C 3
Baksanges 21 F 2
Baku 34 DE 2
Bakungan 42 A 3
Bakuriani 21 F 2
Bakwa M'Bule 64 C 5
Bal Hāf 61 H 6
Bal Qaf 59 J 3
Bala 6 C 1
Bala (Guinea) 62 C 3
Bala (Senegal) 62 B 3
Balā (Turkey) 21 D 3
Bala (U.K.) 6 C 1
Bala (U.S.S.R.) 37 O 2
Bālā Bolūk 35 G 4
Bala Murghab 35 G 3
Balabac 42 E 2
Balabac 42 E 2
Balabac Strait 42 E 2
Balabak Dağları 21 E 2
Ba'labakk (Lebanon) 22 B 2
Ba'labakk, Ra's (Syria) 22 B 2
Balabalangan, Kepulauan 42 E 4
Bal'ad 65 H 4
Balad (Iraq) 22 D 2
Balad Rūz (Iraq) 23 D 2
Bālādeh (Iran) 23 F 3
Baladek 37 O 5
Baladīyat 'Adan 61 H 6
Balagannakh 37 O 2
Balagannoye 37 R 4
Balaghat 40 D 3
Balaghat Range 40 C 4
Balaguer 18 D 3
Balakhna 24 H 4
Balakhnya 36 H 1
Balakhta 36 F 4
Balaklava 21 D 2
Balakleya 24 G 6
Balakovo 24 J 5
Balama 67 F 2
Balambangam 42 E 2
Balas 42 E 4
Balashov 24 H 5
Balasore 40 E 3
Balassagyarmat 20 A 1
Balāt 60 D 3
Balaton 20 A 1
Balaurin 43 F 5
Balazhal 25 Q 6
Balazote 18 C 4
Balbi, Mount 51 F 3
Balblair 2 B 3
Balboa 84 C 2
Balbriggan 4 B 3
Balcarce 89 E 6
Balclutha 50 P 10
Balcombe 7 D 2
Bald Head 48 B 6
Balde 88 C 5
Baldock 7 D 2
Baldy Peak 76 E 5
Bale 65 G 3
Baleares, Islas 18 D 3–4
Balearic Islands 18 D 3
Baleia, Ponta da 87 J 4
Baleine, Grande Rivière de la 75 M 4–5
Baleine, Rivière à la 75 O 4
Baler 43 J 1
Balerno 3 C 4
Baley 36 L 5
Balezino 24 K 4
Balgazin 36 G 5
Balguntay 35 M 2
Balho 65 G 2
Bali 42 DE 5
Bali, Laut 42 E 5
Balia 62 B 4
Balık Gölü 21 F 3
Balıkesir 20 C 3
Balikpapan 42 E 4
Balikpapan, Gunung 42 E 4
Balikpapan, Teluk 42 E 4
Balimbing 43 EF 2
Balimo 50 D 3
Balintang Channel 43 J 1

Balis (Syria) 22 BC 2
Baliza 87 F 4
Balkan Mountains 20 C 2
Balkashino 25 N 5
Balkh 35 H 3
Balkhab 35 H 3
Balkhash 25 O 6
Balkhash, Ozero 25 OP 6
Ballachulish 3 B 3
Balladonia 48 C 5
Ballangen 16 G 2
Ballantrae 4 C 2
Ballard, Lake 48 C 4
Ballater 3 C 3
Ballaugh 4 C 2
Ballé 62 C 2
Ballenas, Bahía 76 D 6
Ballenita, Punta 88 B 4
Balleny Islands 91
Ballia 40 D 2
Ballina (Australia) 49 J 4
Ballina (Rep. of Ireland) 14 B 4
Ballinamore 4 B 2
Ballingarry 4 AB 3
Ballinger 76 G 5
Ballinrobe 14 B 4
Ballintra 4 A 2
Ballitore 4 B 3
Balloch 2 B 3
Ballon 4 B 3
Balls Pyramid 49 K 5
Ballybofey 4 B 2
Ballycarry 4 C 2
Ballycastle 4 B 2
Ballyclare 4 B 2
Ballygalley 4 C 2
Ballygawley 4 B 2
Ballyhaunis 14 B 4
Ballyhornan 4 C 2
Ballykelly 4 B 2
Ballymahon 4 B 3
Ballymena 4 B 2
Ballymoney 4 B 2
Ballynahinch 4 C 2
Ballynahowan 4 B 3
Ballynure 4 C 2
Ballyragget 4 B 3
Ballyroan 4 B 3
Ballyshannon 4 A 2
Balmedie 2 C 3
Balmoral Castle 3 C 3
Balnacoil 2 C 2
Balneario Claromecó 89 DE 6
Balombo 66 AB 2
Balonne River 49 H 4
Balotra 40 B 2
Balovale 66 C 2
Balrampur 40 D 2
Balranald 49 G 5
Balrath 4 B 3
Balş 20 B 2
Balsas 85 J 5
Balsas (Maranhão, Brazil) 87 G 2
Balsas (Maranhão, Brazil) 87 G 2
Balsas (Mexico) 78 C 4
Balsas, Rio 78 B 4
Balta 20 C 1
Balta Brăilei 20 C 1–2
Balta Ialomiţei 20 C 2
Balta sound 2 D 1
Baltasar Brum 88 E 5
Baltaţi 20 C 1
Baltic Sea 17 GH 4
Baltım 60 E 2
Baltimore (MD, U.S.A.) 77 L 4
Baltimore (South Africa) 66 D 4
Baltinglass 4 B 3
Baltiskaya Grjada 17 HJ 4–5
Baltistan 35 K 3
Baltiysk 17 GH 5
Baltray 4 B 3
Baluchistan 34–35 FG 3
Balurghat 40 E 2
Balvard (Iran) 23 G 3
Balvi 17 J 4
Balya 20 C 3
Balygychan 37 S 3
Balyksa 25 R 5
Bam 34 F 5
Bam Posht 35 G 5
Bama 63 G 3
Bamako 62 C 3
Bāmbā (Libya) 59 K 2
Bamba (Mali) 62 D 2
Bamba (Zaire) 62 D 3
Bambafouga 62 B 3
Bambama 63 G 6
Bambangando 66 C 3
Bambari 64 C 3
Bambaroo 49 H 2
Bamberg 15 F 5
Bambesa 64 D 4

Bambesi 64 E 3
Bambey 62 A 3
Bambio 64 B 4
Bamboi 62 D 4
Bambouti 64 D 3
Bambouto, Monts 63 G 4
Bamburgh 5 E 2
Bamenda 63 G 4
Bamford 7 D 1
Bamingui 64 B 3
Bamingui 64 C 3
Bamingui-Bangoran, Parc National du 64 BC 3
Bamiyan 35 H 4
Bampūr 35 G 5
Ban Ban 41 H 4
Ban Don 41 J 5
Ban Kniet 41 J 5
Ban Me Thuot 41 J 5
Ban Na San 41 G 6
Ban Nabo 41 J 4
Ban Ngon 41 H 4
Ban Sao 41 H 4
Ban Sop Huai Hai 41 G 4
Ban Taup 41 J 4
Banaadir 65 GH 4
Banaba 51 J 2
Bañados de Izozog 86 D 4
Banagher 4 B 3
Banagi 64 EF 5
Banalia 64 D 4
Banamba 62 C 3
Banana 49 J 3
Banana Islands 62 B 4
Bananal, Ilha do 87 F 3
Bananga 41 F 6
Banas 40 C 2
Banās, Ra's (Egypt) 22 B 5
Banat 20 B 1
Banaz 20 C 3
Banbar 38 B 4
Banbridge 4 B 2
Banbury 7 D 1
Banc du Geyser 67 H 2
Banchory 3 C 3
Banco Chinchorro 78 E 4
Banco de Serrana 79 G 5
Banco Quitasueño 79 F 5
Banco Serranilla 79 G 4
Bancoran 43 E 2
Bancroft 75 M 6
Band Boni 34 F 5
Band Qīr (Iran) 23 E 3
Banda 40 C 3
Banda 40 D 2
Banda Aceh 42 A 2
Banda Elat 43 H 5
Banda, Kepulauan 43 G 4
Banda, Laut 43 GH 5
Banda Sea 43 GH 5
Bandahara, Gunung 42 A 3
Bandama 62 D 4
Bandama Blanc 62 C 4
Bandan Kūh 35 G 4
Bandar Abbas (Iran) 23 G 4
Bandar Ma'shur (Iran) 23 E 3
Bandar Seri Begawan 42 D 3
Bandar Shāh (Iran) 23 E 1
Bandarban 41 F 3
Bandar-e Chārak (Iran) 23 G 4
Bandar-e Chāru 34 E 5
Bandar-e Chāru (Iran) 23 FG 4
Bandar-e Deylam (Iran) 23 E 3
Bandar-e Gaz (Iran) 23 F 1
Bandar-e Khomeynī (Iran) 23 E 3
Bandar-e Lengeh 34 E 5
Bandar-e Lengeh (Iran) 23 G 4
Bandar-e Māh Shahr (Iran) 23 E 3
Bandar-e Māqām (Iran) 23 F 4
Bandar-e Moghūyeh (Iran) 34 E 5
Bandar-e Moghūyeh (Iran) 23 FG 4
Bandar-e Rig (Iran) 23 F 3
Bandar-e Shah → Bandar-e Torkeman 34 G 3
Bandar-e Shahpur → Bandar-e Khomeyni 34 D 4
Bandar-e Torkeman (Iran) 23 G 1
Bandar-e-Anzalī 34 DE 3
Bandarlampung 42 C 5
Bandarpunch 40 C 1
Bandau 42 E 2
Bandeira 87 H 5
Bandeirante 87 F 3
Bandera 88 D 4
Bandiagara 62 D 3
Band-i-Amir 35 H 3
Band-i-Baba 35 G 4
Band-i-Baian 35 H 4
Bandırma 20 C 2
Band-i-Turkestan 35 GH 3
Bandundu 64 B 5
Bandundu 64 B 5
Bandung 42 C 5

Baneh 34 D 3
Baneh (Iran) 23 D 2
Banemo 43 G 3
Banes 79 G 3
Banff 73 O 5
Banff (U.K.) 2 C 3
Banff National Park 73 O 5
Banfora 62 CD 3
Bang Hieng 41 J 4
Bang Mun Nak 41 H 4
Bang Saphan Yai 41 GH 5
Banga 64 C 6
Bangadi 64 D 4
Bangalore 40 C 5
Banganté 63 G 4
Bangar 42 E 3
Bangassou 64 C 4
Bangeta, Mount 50 E 3
Banggai 43 F 4
Banggai, Kepulauan 43 F 4
Banggi 42 E 2
Banggong Co 40 CD 1
Bangka, Pulau 42 C 4
Bangka, Selat 42 C 4
Bangkalan 42 D 5
Bangkaru, Pulau 42 A 3
Bangko 42 B 4
Bangkok 41 H 5
Bangkok, Bight of 41 H 5
Bangladesh 41 F 3
Bangor (ME, U.S.A.) 77 N 3
Bangor (U.K.) 4 C 2
Bangsund 16 F 3
Bangui 64 B 4
Bangui (Philippines) 43 J 1
Banguru 64 D 4
Bangweulu Swamps 66 D 2
Banhã 60 E 2
Banhine National Park 67 E 4
Bani 62 C 3
Banī 79 H 4
Bani Bangou 62 E 2–3
Banī Forūr (Iran) 23 G 4
Bani, Jbel 58 D 3
Banī Ma' ārid 61 H 5
Banī Mazār 60 E 3
Banī Suwayf 60 E 3
Banī Tonb (Iran) 23 G 4
Banī Walīd 59 H 2
Baniara 51 E 3
Banihal Pass 35 K 4
Bāniyās (Lebanon) 22 B 2
Bāniyās (Syria) 22 B 2
Bāniyās [Golan Heights] 22 B 2
Banja Koviljača 19 G 3
Banja Luka 19 G 3
Banjarmasin 42 DE 4
Banjul 62 A 3
Banka 40 E 3
Bankas 62 D 3
Bankeryd 17 F 4
Banket 67 E 3
Banks Island (Br. Col., Can.) 72 L 5
Banks Island (Canada) 73 N 1
Banks Island (Queensland, Austr.) 49 G 1
Banks Islands (Vanuatu) 51 J 4
Banks Lake 76 C 2
Banks Peninsula 51 Q 9
Banks Strait 50 L 9
Bankura 40 E 3
Banmauk 41 G 3
Bann, River 4 B 2
Bannockburn 3 C 3
Bannu 35 J 4
Bāno 16 G 2
Bansi 40 D 2
Banská Bystrica 15 G 5
Banstead 7 D 2
Banswara 40 B 3
Bantaeng 43 E 5
Bantry 14 B 4
Bantry Bay 14 AB 4
Banu 35 H 3
Banyo 63 G 4
Banyuls-sur-Mer 18 D 3
Banyuwangi 42 D 5
Banzare Coast 91
Banzart 59 GH 1
Bao Bilia 63 J 2
Bao Ha 41 H 3
Bao Loc 41 J 5
Baode 38 F 3
Baodi 39 G 3
Baoding 38 G 3
Baofeng 38 F 4
Baoji 38 E 4
Baokang 38 F 4
Baoqing 39 K 1
Baoro 64 B 3
Baoshan 38 C 5
Baotou 38 E 2
Baoulé 58 D 6
Baoulé 62 C 3
Baoxing 38 D 4

Baoying 39 G 4
Bap 40 B 2
Bapatla 40 D 4
Baqam (Iran) 23 F 2
Baqen 38 B 4
Bāqerābād (Iran) 23 F 2
Baquedano 86 C 5
Bar 20 A 2
Bar Harbor 77 N 3
Bara 63 G 3
Bara Banki 40 D 2
Barabai 42 E 4
Barabinsk 25 P 4
Barabinskaya Step' 25 P 5
Baracaldo 18 C 3
Baragoi 65 F 4
Bārah 60 E 6
Barahona 79 H 4
Barail Range 41 F 2
Baraka 65 F 1
Barakāt 60 E 6
Barakkul' 25 N 5
Baram 42 D 3
Baramanni 85 G 2
Baramula 35 J 4
Baran (India) 40 C 2
Baran (U.S.S.R.) 17 K 5
Barangbarang 43 F 5
Barani 62 D 3
Baranikha, Malaya 37 V 2
Baranoa 84 C 1
Baranof 72 K 4
Baranovichi 17 J 5
Baranovka 24 J 5
Barão de Capanema 86 E 3
Barão de Melgaço 86 E 4
Barão de Melgaco 86 D 3
Barapasi 43 J 4
Baratang 41 F 5
Barati 43 F 5
Baraunda 40 D 2
Barãwe 65 G 4
Barbacena 87 H 5
Barbacoas 84 C 3
Barbados 79 K 5
Barbar 60 E 5
Bárbara 84 D 4
Barbas, Cabo 58 B 4
Barbastro 18 D 3
Barbate de Franco 18 B 4
Barberton 77 K 3
Barberton (South Africa) 67 E 5
Barbezieux 18 C 2
Barbosa 84 D 2
Barbuda 79 K 4
Barcaldine 49 H 3
Barce → Al Marj 59 K 2
Barcellona 19 FG 4
Barcelona 85 F 2
Barcelona (Spain) 18 D 3
Barcelonette 19 E 3
Barcelos 85 F 4
Barcoo or Cooper Creek 49 F 4
Barcoo River 49 G 3
Barcoo River 49 H 3
Barda del Medio 89 C 6
Bardaï 63 H 1
Bardejov 15 H 5
Bārdēre 65 G 4
Bardeskan 34 F 3
Bardonecchia 19 E 2
Bardsey Island 6 B 1
Barēda 65 J 2
Bareilly 40 CD 2
Barents Sea 24 GH 2
Barentsovo More 24 GJ 1
Barentu 65 F 1
Barfleur, Pointe de 18 C 2
Bårgå 16 G 2
Barga 40 D 1
Bārgāl 65 J 2
Barganshahr (Iran) 23 E 3
Bargarh 40 D 3
Bargoed 6 C 2
Barguzin 36 J 5
Barguzinskiy Khrebet 36 JK 4–5
Barhaj 40 D 2
Barham 7 E 2
Barhau 42 B 5
Bari 19 G 3
Bari, Mola di 19 G 3
Bari Sadri 40 B 3
Bari, Terra di 19 G 3
Baria 84 E 3
Barīdi, Ra's (Saudi Arabia) 22 B 4
Barikiwa 65 F 6
Barīm 61 G 6
Barinas 84 DE 2
Baring, Cape 73 O 2
Baringo, Lake 65 F 4
Baripada 40 E 3
Bariri 87 G 5
Bariri, Represa 87 G 5
Bāris 60 E 4
Barisal 41 F 3
Barisan, Pegunungan 42 B 4

Barito, Sungai 42 D 4
Barkä' 61 K 4
Barkam 38 D 4
Barkan, Ra's-e (Iran) 23 E 3
Barkley, Lake 77 J 4
Barkly East 66 D 6
Barkly Tableland 49 F 2
Barkly West 66 C 5
Barkol Kazak Zizhixian 38 B 2
Barladağı 20 D 3
Bar-le-Duc 19 DE 3
Barlee, Lake 48 B 4
Barlee Range 48 B 3
Barletta 19 G 3
Barma 43 H 4
Barmby Moor 5 E 3
Barmer 40 B 2
Barmera 49 G 5
Barmouth 6 B 1
Barnard Castle 5 E 2
Barnaul 25 Q 5
Barnes Ice Cap 75 N 1–2
Barnsley 5 E 3
Barnstaple 6 BC 2
Barnstaple or Bideford Bay 6 B 2
Baro (Ethiopia) 64 E 3
Baro (Nigeria) 63 F 4
Baroda → Vadodara 40 B 3
Barong 38 C 4
Barotseland 66 C 3
Barouéli 62 C 3
Barq al Bishārīyīn 60 E 5
Barquisimeto 84 DE 1
Barra (Airport) 3 A 3
Barra (Bahía, Brazil) 87 H 3
Barra (U.K.) 3 A 3
Barra da Estiva 87 H 3
Barra do Corda 87 G 2
Barra do Dande 66 A 1
Barra do Garças 87 F 4
Barra do Ribeiro 88 F 5
Barra do São Manuel 85 G 5
Barra dos Coqueiros 87 J 3
Barra Head 3 A 3
Barra Patuca 78 F 4
Barraba 49 J 5
Barracão do Barreto 85 G 5
Barragem da Rocha de Galé 18 B 4
Barragem de Alqueva 18 B 4
Barragem de Sobradinho 87 H 3
Barranca (Peru) 84 C 4
Barranca (Peru) 84 C 6
Barrancabermeja 84 D 2
Barrancas 85 F 2
Barranqueras 88 E 4
Barranquilla 84 C 1
Barraute 75 M 6
Barreiras 87 H 3
Barreirinha 85 G 4
Barreirinhas 87 H 1
Barreiro 18 B 4
Barreiros 87 JK 2
Barren 41 F 5
Barren Island, Cape 51 L 9
Barren Islands 72 G 4
Barrenitos 78 B 2
Barretos 87 G 5
Barrhead 73 P 5
Barrhead (U.K.) 3 B 4
Barrhill 3 B 4
Barri 6 C 2
Barrie 75 LM 7
Barrington 75 MN 7
Barrocão 87 H 4
Barrow (AK, U.S.A.) 72 F 1
Barrow (Argentina) 89 DE 6
Barrow (Rep. of Ireland) 14 B 4
Barrow Creek 48 E 3
Barrow Island 48 A 3
Barrow, Point 72 FG 1
Barrow Range 48 D 4
Barrow, River 4 B 3
Barrow-in-Furness 5 D 2
Barry 6 C 3
Barsa-Kel'mes, Ostrov 34 F 1
Barsi 40 C 4
Barstow 76 C 5
Bar-sur-Aube 19 D 2
Bartallah (Iraq) 22 D 1
Bartazuga, Jabal 60 E 4
Bartibougou 62 E 3
Bartica 85 G 2
Bartın 21 D 2
Bartlesville 77 G 4
Barton-upon-Humber 5 E 3
Barton-upon-Humber 7 D 1
Bartow 77 K 6
Barú, Volcán 84 B 2
Bāruni 40 E 2
Baruun Urt 38 F 1
Barvas 2 A 2
Barwa 40 D 3
Barwani 40 B 3
Barwon River 49 H 4
Barycz 15 G 4
Barylas 37 O 2
Barzas 25 R 4

Barzūk (Iran) 23 F 2
Bāsa'idū (Iran) 23 G 4
Basankusu 64 BC 4
Basauri 18 C 3
Basekpio 64 CD 4
Basel 19 E 2
Bashi Haixia 39 H 6
Bashkend 21 G 2
Basian 43 F 4
Basilan 43 F 2
Basilan City 43 F 2
Basildon 7 E 2
Basílio 88 F 5
Basingstoke 7 D 2
Başkale 21 F 3
Baskatong, Réservoir 75 MN 6
Baskil 21 E 3
Baskol' 25 P 5
Basmat 40 C 4
Baso, Pulau 42 B 4
Basoko 64 C 4
Basongo 64 C 5
Basra (Iraq) 23 E 3
Bass Strait 50 KL 8
Bassano del Grappa 19 F 2
Bassari 62 E 4
Bassas da India 67 F 4
Basse Santa Su 62 B 3
Bassein 41 F 4
Bassein → Vasai 40 B 4
Basse-Terre (Saint
   Christopher-Nevis) 79 K 4
Basseterre (Saint
   Christopher-Nevis) 79 K 4
Bassikounou 58 D 5
Bassila 62 E 4
Bassin de Rennes 18 C 2
Bassin de Thau 18 D 3
Basso, Plateau de 63 J 2
Bastak (Iran) 23 G 4
Bastam (Iran) 23 G 1
Bastevarri 16 H 2
Basti 40 D 2
Bastia 19 E 3
Basto, Terra de 18 B 3
Bastrop 77 H 5
Bastuträsk 16 G 3
Basuto 66 D 3
Baswa 40 C 2
Bata 63 F 5
Batabano, Golfo del 78–79 F 3
Batagay 37 OP 2
Batagay-Alyta 37 O 2
Batai, Gunung 42 BC 5
Bataklık Gölü 21 D 3
Batala 40 BC 1
Batalha 18 B 4
Batam, Pulau 42 B 3
Batama (U.S.S.R.) 36 H 5
Batama (Zaire) 64 D 4
Batamay 37 N 3
Batamshinskiy 25 L 5
Batan Islands 39 H 6
Batang 38 C 4
Batang (Indonesia) 42 C 5
Batang Hari 42 B 4
Batanga 63 F 6
Batangafo 64 B 3
Batangas 43 F 1
Batanta, Pulau 43 H 4
Batara 64 B 3
Batavia 88 C 3
Bataysk 21 EF 1
Batchawana Mountain 74 L 6
Batchelor 48 E 1
Batemans Bay 49 J 6
Bateria, Cachoeira da 85 G 3
Bath (ME, U.S.A.) 77 N 3
Bath (U.K.) 6 C 2
Batha 63 H 3
Batha 63 H 3
Bathgate 3 C 4
Bathurst (Canada) 75 O 6
Bathurst (N.S.W., Austr.) 49 H 5
Bathurst, Cape 72 LM 1
Bathurst → Banjul 62 A 3
Bathurst Inlet 73 Q 2
Bathurst Inlet 73 Q 2
Bathurst Island (N.T., Austr.)
   48 D 1
Bathurst Island (The Arctic) 90
Batié 62 D 4
Batie 65 G 2
Bātin, Wādi al (Iraq) 23 E 3
Batkanu 62 B 4
Bātlāq-e Gavkhūnī (Iran) 23 F 2
Batley 5 E 3
Batman 21 F 3
Batman 21 F 3
Batn al Hajar 60 E 4
Batna 59 G 1
Batoka 66 D 3
Batomga 37 P 4
Baton Rouge 77 H 5

Baton-le-Clay 7 D 2
Batopilas 76 E 6
Batouri 63 G 5
Batrā, Jabal (Saudi Arabia) 22 B 4
Båtsfjord 16 J 1
Battambang 41 H 5
Batti Malv 41 F 6
Batticaloa 40 D 6
Battinga 64 C 3
Battle 73 P 5
Battle (U.K.) 7 E 2
Battle Creek 77 J 3
Battle Harbour 75 Q 5
Battle Mountain 76 C 3
Batu 65 F 3
Batu Pahat 42 B 3
Batu Puteh, Gunung 42 B 3
Batui 43 F 4
Batulantee, Gunung 42 E 5
Batumi 21 F 2
Batuputih 43 E 3
Baturaja 42 B 4
Baturino 25 R 4
Baturinskaya 21 E 1
Baturité 87 J 1
Bau 42 D 3
Baubau 43 F 5
Baucau 43 G 5
Bauchi 63 F 3
Bauchi Plateau 63 FG 3–4
Baud 18 C 2
Baudó 84 C 2
Baudó, Serranía de 84 C 2
Bauhinia Downs 49 H 3
Baula 43 F 4
Bauld, Cape 75 Q 5
Baumann, Pic 62 E 4
Baunei 19 E 3
Baunt 36 K 4
Bauple 49 J 4
Baures 86 D 3
Bauru 87 G 5
Baús 87 F 4
Bauska 17 H 4
Bautzen 15 F 4
Bavaria 15 F 5
Bavispe 76 E 5
Bāw 60 E 6
Bawdsey 7 E 1
Bawean, Pulau 42 D 5
Bawku 62 D 3
Bawmi 41 F 4
Bawn 65 G 2
Bawtry 5 E 3
Baxoi 38 C 4
Bay Bulls 75 R 6
Bay City (MI, U.S.A.) 77 K 3
Bay City (TX, U.S.A.) 77 G 6
Bay de Verde 75 R 6
Bay Lorne 49 G 6
Bay of Bengal 40–41 EF 4
Bay of Biscay 18 C 2–3
Bay of Fundy 75 O 6–7
Bay of Gods Mercy 73 U 3
Bay of Islands 75 Q 6
Bay of Plenty 51 R 8
Bay Springs 77 HJ 5
Bayamo 79 G 3
Bayan 36 J 6
Bayan Har Shan 38 CD 4
Bayan Har Shankou 38 C 4
Bayan Mod 38 D 2
Bayan Obo 38 E 2
Bayana 40 C 2
Bayan-Adraga 36 K 6
Bayan-Agt 36 H 6
Bayan-Aul 25 P 5
Bayanbaraat 38 E 1
Bayanbulag 36 G 6
Bayanbulak 35 L 2
Bayanchandman 36 J 6
Bayandalay 38 D 2
Bayanday 36 J 5
Bayanga 64 B 4
Bayangol 36 H 5
Bayanhongor 36 H 6
Bayanmönh 38 E 1
Bayan-Öndör 38 C 2
Bayan-Öndör 38 D 1
Bayantsagaan 38 E 1
Bayantsogt 36 J 6
Bayan-Uul 36 G 6
Bayan-Uul 36 K 6
Bayat 21 D 2
Bayāz 34 F 4
Bayāz (Iran) 23 G 3
Bayāzeh (Iran) 23 G 2
Bayburt 21 F 2
Baychunas 34 E 1
Baydaratskaya Guba 25 N 2
Baydrag Gol 36 G 5
Bayerischer Wald 15 F 5
Bayern 15 F 5
Bayeux 18 C 2

Bayhān al Qişāb 61 H 6
Bayındır 20 C 3
Bayjī (Iraq) 22 D 2
Baykal 36 H 5
Baykal, Ozero 36 J 5
Baykalovo 25 N 4
Baykal'skiy Khrebet 36 J 4–5
Baykal'skoye 36 JK 4
Baykal'skoye Nagor'ye, Severo
   36 K 4
Baykan 21 F 3
Bay-Khak 36 F 5
Baykit 36 G 3
Baykitskiy 36 G 3
Baykonur 35 H 1
Baymak 25 L 5
Baynūnah (United Arab Emirates)
   23 F 5
Bayo Nuevo 79 G 4
Bayombong 43 J 1
Bayonne 18 C 3
Bayovar 84 B 5
Bayram-Ali 35 G 3
Bayramiç 20 C 3
Bayreuth 15 F 5
Bayrūt (Lebanon) 22 B 2
Baysa 36 K 5
Bay-Syut 36 G 5
Bayt al Faqīh 61 G 6
Bayt Lahm (Israel) 22 B 3
Baytik Shan 35 N 1
Baytown 77 H 5–6
Bayunglincir 42 B 4
Bayy al Kabīr, Wādi 59 H 2
Bayyūdah, Şahrā' 60 E 5
Baza 18 C 4
Bazar Dyuzi, Gora 34 D 2
Bazarnyy Syzgan 24 J 5
Bazaruto National Park 67 F 4
Bazhong 38 E 4
Baztán 18 C 3
Beach 76 F 2
Beachy Head 7 E 2
Beacon 48 B 5
Beaconsfield 7 D 2
Beagle Bay 48 C 2
Beagle, Canal 89 C 9
Beagle Gulf 48 DE 1
Beal 5 E 2
Beal Range 49 G 4
Bealanana 67 H 2
Beaminster 6 C 2
Beampingaratra 67 H 4
Bear Cape 75 P 6
Bear Island 90
Bear Lake 76 D 3
Bear Lodge Mountains 76 EF 3
Bearpaw Mountains 76 E 2
Bearskin Lake 74 J 5
Beas 40 C 1
Beas de Segura 18 C 4
Beata, Cabo 79 H 4
Beatrice 77 G 3
Beatrice, Cape 49 F 1
Beatton 73 N 4
Beatton River 73 N 4
Beatty 76 C 4
Beattyville 75 M 6
Beau-Bassin 67 K 6
Beaucaire 19 D 3
Beaucanton 75 M 6
Beaufort 42 E 2
Beaufort 77 K 5
Beaufort Sea 72 JL 1
Beaufort West 66 C 6
Beaujolais, Monts du 19 D 2
Beaulieu 7 D 2
Beauly 2 B 3
Beauly Firth 2 B 3
Beaumaris 6 B 1
Beaumont (France) 18 C 2
Beaumont (TX, U.S.A.) 77 H 5
Beaune 19 DE 2
Beaupré 75 N 6
Beausejour 73 S 5
Beauvais 18 D 2
Beaver (AK, U.S.A.) 72 H 2
Beaver (Sask., Can.) 73 Q 5
Beaver (UT, U.S.A.) 76 D 4
Beaver Dam 77 J 3
Beaver Island 77 J 2
Beaverton 76 B 2
Beawar 40 B 2
Beazley 88 C 5
Bebedouro 87 G 5
Beberibe 87 J 1
Bebington 5 D 3
Becan 78 E 4
Beccles 7 E 1
Bečej 20 B 1
Becerreá 18 B 3
Béchar 58 E 2
Becharof Lake 72 F 4
Becharof National Monument
   72 F 4
Bechevin Bay 72 E 4

Beck Row 7 E 1
Beckfoot 5 D 2
Beckley 77 K 4
Beckum 15 E 4
Bedale 5 E 2
Bedeli 65 F 3
Bedford (IN, U.S.A.) 77 J 4
Bedford (PA, U.S.A.) 77 L 3
Bedford (U.K.) 7 D 1
Bedfordshire 7 D 1
Bedirli 21 E 3
Bedlington 5 E 2
Bednodem'yanovsk 24 H 5
Bedoba 36 G 4
Bedourie 49 F 3
Bedworth 7 D 1
Beech Grove 77 J 4
Beecroft Head 49 J 5–6
Beenleigh 49 J 4
Be'er Sheva 22 B 3
Beeston 7 D 1
Beetaloo 48 E 2
Beeville 76 G 6
Befale 64 C 4
Befandriana 67 G 4
Befandriana 67 H 3
Bega 49 H 6
Begambanj 41 F 3
Begejski Kanal 20 B 1
Bègle 18 C 3
Begna 17 E 3
Begoml' (U.S.S.R.) 17 J 5
Behâbâd (Iran) 23 G 3
Behbehân (Iran) 23 EF 3
Behleg 38 B 3
Behring Point 79 G 3
Behshahr (Iran) 23 F 1
Bei Hulsan Hu 38 C 3
Bei Shan 38 C 2
Bei'an 37 N 6
Beibu Wan 41 J 3
Beichuan 38 D 4
Beida 59 K 2
Beihai 38 E 6
Beijing 39 G 2
Beiliu 38 F 6
Beilu Heyan 38 B 4
Beilul 65 G 2
Beïnamar 63 H 4
Beinn Dearg 2 B 3
Beinn Dhorain 2 C 2
Beipiao 39 H 2
Beira 67 EF 3
Beirut (Lebanon) 22 B 2
Beishan 38 C 2
Beitbridge 66 D 4
Beith 3 B 4
Beitstad 16 F 3
Beitun 35 M 1
Beizhen 39 G 3
Beizhen 39 H 2
Beja 18 B 4
Beja 85 J 4
Bejaïa 59 F 1
Béjar 18 B 3
Beji 35 H 5
Bekabad 35 H 2
Bekasi 42 C 5
Bekdash 34 E 2
Békéscsaba 20 B 1
Bekily 67 H 4
Bekodoka 67 H 3
Bekopaka 67 G 3
Bekwai 62 D 4
Bel Guerdane 58 C 3
Bel Haïrane 59 G 2
Bela 35 H 5
Bela 40 D 2
Béla Bérim 63 G 2
Bela Crkva 20 B 2
Bela Dila 40 D 4
Bela Polanka 20 B 2
Bela Vista (Angola) 66 A 1
Bela Vista (Brazil) 86 E 5
Bela Vista (Mozambique) 67 E 5
Bélabo 63 G 5
Belaga 42 D 3
Bel'Agach 25 Q 5
Belaia Sancai 64 F 2
Belaka 64 C 5
Belang 43 FG 3
Belawan 42 A 3
Belaya 24 K 4
Belaya 37 W 2
Belaya (U.S.S.R.) 21 F 2
Belaya Glina 21 F 1
Belaya Kalitva 21 F 1
Belaya Tserkov 24 F 6
Belcher Islands 75 L 4
Belcik 21 E 3
Belcoo 4 B 2
Bełczyna 15 G 4
Belebey 24 K 5
Beled Wêyne 65 H 4

Belém (Amazonas, Brazil) 84 E 4
Belem (Mexico) 76 D 6
Belem (Mozambique) 67 F 2
Belém (Pará, Brazil) 85 J 4
Belém de São Francisco 87 J 2
Belén (Argentina) 88 C 4
Belén (Colombia) 84 C 3
Belen (N.M., U.S.A.) 76 E 5
Belén (Paraguay) 86 E 5
Beleuli 34 F 2
Belfast 4 C 2
Belfast (Airport) 4 B 2
Belfast (Aldergrove) 4 B 2
Belfast Lough 4 C 2
Belfield 76 F 2
Belford 5 E 2
Belfort 19 E 2
Belgaum 40 B 4
Belgium 14 DE 4
Belgorod 24 G 5
Belgorod-Dnestrovskiy 20 CD 1
Belgrade 20 B 2
Beli 63 G 4
Beli Drim 20 B 2
Beli Manastir 19 G 2
Belice 19 F 4
Belikh (Syria) 22 C 1
Belimbing 42 B 5
Belin 18 C 3
Belinga 63 G 5
Belingwe → Mberengwa 66 D 4
Belinskiy 24 H 5
Belinyu 42 C 4
Belitung, Pulau 42 C 4
Belize 78 E 4
Belize City 78 E 4
Belize River 78 E 4
Bélizon 85 H 3
Beljanica 20 B 2
Bel'kachi 37 O 4
Bell 75 M 6
Bell Bay 74 L 1
Bell Peninsula 73 V 3
Bell Ville 88 D 5
Bella Bella 73 M 5
Bella Coola 73 M 5
Bella Vista (Argentina) 88 E 4
Bellac 18 D 2
Bellaco 88 E 5
Bellanagh 4 B 3
Bellary 40 C 4
Bellavista (Peru) 84 C 4
Bellavista (Peru) 84 C 5
Bellbrook 49 J 5
Belle Fourche River 76 F 3
Belle Glade 77 K 6
Belle Ile 18 C 2
Belle Isle 75 QR 5
Belle Isle, Strait of 75 Q 5
Belle Yella 62 B 4
Belleek 4 A 2
Bellegarde 19 E 2
Bellehiglash 2 C 3
Belleville (France) 19 DE 2
Belleville (IL, U.S.A.) 77 J 4
Belleville (KS, U.S.A.) 76 G 4
Belleville (Ontario, Can.) 75 M 7
Bellevue (NE, U.S.A.) 77 G 3
Bellevue (WA, U.S.A.) 76 B 2
Belley 19 E 2
Bellin 75 N 3
Bellingen 49 J 5
Bellingham 5 D 2
Bellingham 76 B 2
Bellingshausen 91
Bellingshausen Sea 91
Bellinzona 19 E 2
Bello 84 C 2
Bellona 51 G 4
Bellot Strait 73 T 1
Belluno 19 F 2
Bellyk 36 F 5
Belmonte 87 J 4
Belmonte (Portugal) 18 B 3
Belmonte (Spain) 18 C 4
Belmopan 78 E 4
Belmount 2 D 1
Belo Horizonte (Minas Gerais, Brazil) 87 H 4
Belo Horizonte (Pará, Brazil) 85 H 5
Belo Jardim 87 J 2
Belo Monta 85 H 4
Bologolovoye 37 T 4
Belogorsk 21 D 2
Belogorsk (U.S.S.R.) 37 N 5
Belogor'ye 25 N 3
Belogradčik 20 B 2
Beloit 77 J 3
Belokholunitskiy 24 K 4
Belomorsk 16 K 3
Belopol'ye 24 F 5
Belorechensk 21 F 2
Beloretsk 25 L 5
Belorussiya 17 J 5
Belorusskaya Gryada 17 J 5

Belo-sur-Mer 67 G 4
Belo-sur-Tsiribihina 67 G 3
Belot, Lac 73 M 2
Belousovka 20 D 1
Belovo 25 R 5
Beloyarovo 37 N 5
Beloye More 24 G 2
Beloye Ozero 21 G 1
Beloye Ozero 24 G 3
Belozerka 21 D 1
Belozersk 24 G 4
Belper 5 E 3
Belsay 5 E 2
Beltana 49 F 5
Belterra 85 G 4
Bel'tsy 20 C 1
Belturbet 4 B 2
Belukha, Gora 25 R 5–6
Belush'ya Guba 24 K 1
Belyando River 49 H 3
Belyayevka 20 D 1
Belyy 24 F 4
Belyy Yar 25 R 4
Bełżyce 15 H 4
Bemaraha, Plateau du 67 GH 3
Bembe 66 A 1
Bembridge 7 D 2
Bemidji 77 G 2
Bempton 5 E 2
Ben (Iran) 23 F 2
Ben Ahmadu 58 C 3
Ben Hee 2 B 2
Ben Hope 2 B 2
Ben Klibreck 2 B 2
Ben Lawers 3 B 3
Ben Lomond 3 B 3
Ben Macdhui 3 C 3
Ben Mehidi 59 E 3
Ben More 3 AB 3
Ben More Assynt 2 B 2
Ben Nevis 3 B 3
Ben Wyvis 2 B 3
Bena Dibile 64 C 5
Benáb (Iran) 23 E 1
Benalla 49 H 6
Benares 40 D 2
Benavente 18 B 3
Benbecula 2 A 3
Benbecula (Airport) 2 A 3
Bencubbin 48 B 5
Bend 76 B 3
Bendaja 62 B 4
Bende 63 F 4
Bendela 64 B 5
Bendemeer 49 J 5
Bender Bâyla 65 J 3
Bender Cassim → Bōsāso 65 H 2
Bender Mur'anyo 65 HJ 2
Bender Siyada 65 H 2
Bendery 20 C 1
Bendigo 49 G 6
Benešov 15 F 5
Benevento 19 FG 3
Bengal 40 E 3
Bengal, Bay of 40–41 EF 4
Bengal, West 40 E 3
Bengara 42 E 3
Bengbis 63 G 5
Bengbu 39 G 4
Benghazi 59 JK 2
Benghisa Point 19 F 4
Bengkalis 42 B 3
Bengkalis, Pulau 42 B 3
Bengkulu 42 B 4
Bengo, Baía do 66 A 1
Bengtsfors 17 F 4
Benguela 66 A 2
Benguela Current 93
Benguerir 58 D 2
Beni (Bolivia) 86 C 3
Beni (Zaire) 64 D 4
Beni Abbès 58 E 2
Beni Mellal 58 D 2
Beni Ounif 58 E 2
Beni Saf 58 E 1
Beni Suef → Banī Suwayf 60 E 3
Benicarló 18 D 3
Benicasim 18 D 3
Benidorm 18 CD 4
Benin 62 E 3–4
Benin, Bight of 62 E 4
Benin City 63 F 4
Benito Juárez 78 D 4
Benjamin Constant 84 D 4
Benjamin Corrilla 89 CD 6
Benkelman 76 F 3
Benkovac 19 G 3
Benllech 6 B 1
Bennichab 58 B 5
Benoud 58 F 2
Bénoué 63 G 4
Bénoué National Park 63 G 4
Benoy 63 H 4
Bensané 62 B 3
Bensheim 15 E 5
Benson 76 D 5

Bent 34 F 5
Bentaeng 43 F 5
Bentiaba 66 A 2
Bentinck 41 G 5
Bentinck Island (Queensland, Austr.) 49 F 2
Bentiu 64 E 3
Bentley 5 E 3
Bento Gonçalves 88 F 4
Benton 77 H 5
Bentong 42 B 3
Benue 63 F 4
Benxi 39 H 2
Beo 43 G 3
Beograd 20 B 2
Beoumi 62 C 4
Beppu 39 K 4
Bera 40 E 3
Beraketa 67 H 4
Berati 20 A 2
Berau, Teluk 43 H 4
Berbera 65 H 2
Berbérati 64 B 4
Berca 20 C 1
Berchogur 34 F 1
Berchtesgaden 15 F 5
Berck 18 D 1
Berdale 65 G 4
Berdâle 65 H 3
Berdichev 17 J 6
Berdoba 63 J 2
Berdsk 25 Q 5
Berdyansk 21 E 1
Berdyuzh'ye 25 N 4
Bere Regis 7 C 2
Beregovo 20 B 1
Bereina 50 E 3
Bereko 65 F 5
Berekum 62 D 4
Berenice → Mīnā' Baranīs 60 EF 4
Berens 73 S 5
Berens River 73 S 5
Berettyóújfalu 20 B 1
Bereza 17 J 5
Bereznegovatoye 21 D 1
Berezniki 24 L 4
Berezovka (Russia, U.S.S.R.) 25 Q 4
Berezovka (Russia, U.S.S.R.) 36 L 4
Berezovka (Russia, U.S.S.R.) 37 T 2
Berezovka (Ukraine, U.S.S.R.) 20 D 1
Berezovo 25 N 3
Berezovo 37 W 3
Berezovskaya 24 H 5
Berezovskiy 25 L 5
Berezovskiy 25 R 4
Berg 16 F 3
Berga 18 D 3
Bergama 20 C 3
Bergamo 19 EF 2
Bergby 17 G 3
Bergen (F.R.G.) 15 F 4
Bergen (Norway) 17 DE 3
Bergerac 18 D 3
Bergkvara 17 G 4
Bergland 66 B 4
Bergö 16 H 3
Bergslagen 17 F 3
Bergviken 16 G 3
Berhala, Selat 42 B 4
Berhampore 40 E 3
Berhampur 40 D 4
Berīkān (Iran) 23 F 3
Berikul'skiy 25 R 4
Bering Glacier 72 J 3
Bering Land Bridge National Preserve 72 C 3
Bering Sea 72 CD 3–4
Bering Strait 72 CD 2–3
Beringarra 48 B 4
Beringovskiy 37 X 3
Berislav 21 D 1
Berkakit 37 M 4
Berkane 58 E 2
Berkeley 76 B 4
Berkner Island 91
Berkovisa 20 B 2
Berkshire 7 D 2
Berlevåg 16 J 1
Berlin 15 F 4
Berlin (N.H., U.S.A.) 77 M 3
Bermeja, Punta 89 D 7
Bermeja, Sierra 18 B 4
Bermejo 88 C 5
Bermejo 88 C 5
Bermejo (Argentina) 88 D 4
Bermen, Lac 75 O 5
Bermeo 18 C 3
Bermuda Islands 79 K 1
Bern 19 E 2
Bernalillo 76 E 4
Bernardo de Irigoyen 88 F 4

Bernasconi 89 D 6
Bernay 18 D 2
Bernburg 15 F 4
Berne 19 E 2
Berner Alpen 19 E 2
Berneray 2 A 3
Bernier Island 48 A 3
Bernina 19 E 2
Bernkastel-Kues 15 E 5
Bernstorffs Isfjord 75 T 3
Béroroha 67 H 4
Beroubouaye 62 E 3
Beroun 15 F 5
Berovo 20 B 2
Berre, Étang de 19 E 3
Berrechid 58 D 2
Berri (Saudi Arabia) 23 E 4
Berriane 59 F 2
Berriedale 2 C 2
Berry 18 D 2
Berry Islands 79 G 2
Berseba 66 B 5
Bershad 20 C 1
Bertolínia 87 H 2
Bertoua 63 G 5
Beru 52 C 3
Beruri 85 F 4
Beruwala 40 CD 6
Berwick-upon-Tweed 5 E 2
Besalampy 67 G 3
Besançon 19 E 2
Besar, Gunung 42 E 4
Besar, Pulau 43 F 5
Beskidy Zachodny 15 GH 5
Beslan 21 F 2
Besna Kobila 20 B 2
Besni 21 E 3
Bessarabiya 20 C 1
Bessbrook 4 B 2
Bessemer 77 J 5
Bessines-sur-Gartempe 18 D 2
Besskorbnaya 21 F 2
Bestamak 25 P 6
Bestepeler Geçidi 21 E 3
Bestobe 25 O 5
Bestuzhevo 24 H 3
Bestyakh 37 MN 2
Bestyakh 37 O 3
Beswick 48 E 1
Bēsyuke 37 N 2
Bet She'an (Israel) 22 B 2
Betafo 67 H 3
Betamba 64 C 5
Betanzos 18 B 3
Bétaré Oya 63 G 4
Bethal 66 D 5
Bethan (OK, U.S.A.) 76 G 4
Bethanie 66 B 5
Bethany 77 H 3
Bethel 72 E 3
Bethersden 7 E 2
Bethesda 6 B 1
Bethlehem (South Africa) 66 D 5
Bethlehem → Bayt Lahm 60 EF 2
Bethor 65 F 2
Bethulie 66 D 6
Béthune 18 D 1
Betioky 67 G 4
Betling Sib 41 F 3
Betong (Indonesia) 42 D 3
Betong (Thailand) 41 H 6
Betoota 49 G 4
Betou 63 H 5
Betpak-Dala 25 O 6
Betpak-Dala 35 HJ 1
Betroka 67 H 4
Betsiboka 67 H 3
Bettiah 40 D 2
Bettles 72 G 2
Bettola 19 E 3
Bettyhill 2 B 2
Betul 40 C 3
Betwa 40 C 2
Betws-y-Coed 6 C 1
Beulah 6 C 1
Beveridge 52 D 4
Beverley (U.K.) 5 E 3
Beverley (Western Australia) 48 B 5
Bexhill 7 E 2
Bey Dağları 20 CD 3
Beyânlu (Iran) 23 E 1
Beykoz 20 C 2
Beyla 62 C 4
Beyneu 34 F 1
Beyoneisu-retsugan 39 L 4
Beypazarı 21 D 2
Beypore 40 C 5
Beyra 65 H 3
Beyram (Iran) 23 F 4
Beyşehir 21 D 3
Beyşehir Gölü 20 D 3
Beysug 21 F 1
Bezaha 67 G 4
Bezdez 15 G 4

Bezhanitskaya Vozvyshennost' 17 J 4
Bezhanitsy 17 K 4
Bezhetsk 24 G 4
Béziers 18 D 3
Bezmein 34 F 3
Beznosova 36 H 5
Bhadarwah 35 K 4
Bhadgaon 40 E 2
Bhadohi 40 D 2
Bhadrachalam 40 D 4
Bhadrajan 40 B 2
Bhadrakh 40 E 3
Bhadravati 40 C 5
Bhagalpur 40 E 3
Bhakkar 35 J 4
Bhalki 40 C 4
Bhamo 41 G 3
Bhandara 40 C 3
Bhanrer Range 40 C 3
Bharatpur 40 C 2
Bharatpur 40 D 3
Bharuch 40 B 3
Bhatinda 40 BC 1
Bhatpara 40 E 3
Bhavnagar 40 B 3
Bhawanipatna 40 D 4
Bhilwara 40 BC 2
Bhima 40 C 4
Bhind 40 C 2
Bhiwani 40 C 2
Bhongir 40 C 4
Bhopal 40 C 3
Bhopalpatnam 40 D 4
Bhor 40 B 4
Bhuban 40 E 3
Bhuban Hills 41 F 3
Bhubaneswar 40 E 3
Bhuj 40 A 3
Bhumiphol Dam 41 G 4
Bhusawal 40 C 3
Bhutan 41 F 2
Biak (Indonesia) 43 F 4
Biak (Papua New Guinea) 43 J 4
Biak, Pulau 43 J 4
Biała Podlaska 15 H 4
Białogard 15 G 4
Białowieża 15 H 4
Białystok 15 H 4
Bianco 19 G 4
Biankouma 62 C 4
Biaora 40 C 3
Biaro, Pulau 43 G 3
Biarritz 18 C 3
Biasca 19 E 2
Bibā 60 E 3
Bibai 39 M 2
Bibala 66 A 2
Bibémi 63 G 4
Biberach 15 EF 5
Bibi Hakimeh (Iran) 23 F 3
Bibiani 62 D 4
Bicester 7 D 2
Bichura 36 J 5
Bickerton Island 49 F 1
Bickleigh 6 C 3
Bicuari National Park 66 AB 3
Bida 63 F 4
Bida Zayed (United Arab Emirates) 23 FG 5
Bidar 40 C 4
Biddeford 77 MN 3
Biddulph 7 C 1
Bideford 6 B 2
Bidon 5 (Algeria) 59 F 4
Bidzhan 37 O 6
Bié 66 B 2
Biebrza 15 H 4
Biel 19 E 2
Bielefeld 15 E 4
Biella 19 E 2
Bielsk Podlaski 15 H 4
Bielsko-Biała 15 G 5
Bien Hoa 41 J 5
Bienville, Lac 75 N 4
Biferno 19 F 3
Bifoum 63 G 6
Big Bald Mountain 75 O 6
Big Bell 48 B 4
Big Belt Mountains 76 D 2
Big Bend National Park 76 F 6
Big Cypress National Preserve 77 K 6
Big Delta 72 H 3
Big Falls 77 H 2
Big Island 75 N 3
Big Quill Lake 73 R 5
Big Rapids 77 J 3
Big River 73 Q 5
Big Sand Lake 73 S 4
Big Sheep Mountains 76 E 2
Big Sioux 77 G 3
Big Smoky Valley 76 C 4
Big Snowy Mountains 76 E 2
Big Spring 76 F 5
Big Trout Lake 73 J 5

Big Trout Lake 74 K 5
Big Trout Lake (Ontario, Can.) 74 K 5
Biga 20 C 2
Bigbury Bay 6 C 2
Biger 36 G 6
Biggar 3 C 4
Biggar 73 Q 5
Biggleswade 7 D 1
Bighorn 76 E 2
Bighorn Basin 76 E 3
Bighorn Lake 76 E 3
Bighorn Mountains 76 E 3
Bight of Bangkok 41 H 5
Bight of Benin 62 E 4
Bigi 64 C 4
Bignona 62 A 3
Bigobo 64 D 6
Bihać 19 G 3
Bihar 40 E 2
Bihar 40 E 3
Biharamulo 64 E 5
Bijapur 40 C 4
Bijār 34 D 3
Bijār (Iran) 23 E 2
Bijawar 40 C 3
Bijeljina 19 G 3
Bijelo Polje 20 AB 2
Bijiang 38 C 5
Bijie 38 E 5
Bijnor 40 C 2
Bijoutier 65 J 6
Bikaner 40 B 2
Bikar 52 C 2
Bikin 37 O 6
Bikin 37 P 6
Bikini 52 C 2
Bikoro 64 B 5
Bilād Banī Bū 'Alī 61 K 4
Bilād Ghāmid 61 G 5
Bilād Zahrān 61 G 4
Bilala 63 G 6
Bilanga 62 E 3
Bilaspur 40 D 3
Bilauktaung Range 41 G 5
Bilbao 18 C 3
Bilbury 7 D 2
Bil'chir 36 K 5
Bileća 19 G 3
Bilecik 20 C 2
Bilesha Plain 65 G 4
Bili 64 C 4
Bili 64 D 4
Bilibino 37 V 2
Biling La 40 D 1
Bilir 37 O 2
Billabalong 48 B 4
Billericay 7 E 2
Billesdon 7 D 1
Billiluna 48 D 2
Billingham 5 E 2
Billinghay 5 E 3
Billings 76 E 2
Billingsfors 17 F 4
Billingshurst 7 D 2
Billingsley 6 C 1
Bilma 63 G 2
Bilma, Grand Erg de 63 G 2
Bilo Gora 19 G 2
Biloela 49 J 3
Biloku 85 G 3
Biloxi 77 J 5
Biltine 63 J 3
Bilugyun 41 G 4
Bilyarsk 24 JK 5
Bima 43 E 5
Bimbéréke 62 E 3
Bimberi, Mount 49 H 6
Bimbila 62 D 4
Bimbo 64 B 4
Bimini Islands 79 G 2
Bimlipatam 40 D 4
Bin Ghanīmah, Jabal 59 J 3–4
Bin Ghashir 59 H 2
Bin Qirdān 59 H 2
Bin Xian 38 E 3
Bin Xian 39 G 3
Bin Xian 39 J 1
Bin Yauri 63 EF 3
Bīnab (Iran) 23 E 1
Binaiya, Gunung 43 G 4
Binatang 42 D 3
Binbrook 7 D 1
Binchuan 38 D 5
Binder 36 K 6
Bindura 67 E 3
Binga (Zaire) 64 C 4
Binga (Zaire) 66 D 3
Binga, Monte 67 E 3
Bingara 49 J 4
Bingen 15 E 5
Bingham 77 N 2
Binghamton 77 L 3
Bingley 5 E 3
Bingöl 21 F 3
Binh Son 41 J 4

Binhai 39 GH 4
Bini Erdi 63 H 1
Binjai 42 A 3
Binjai 42 C 3
Binnaway 49 H 5
Binongko, Pulau 43 F 5
Bint Bayyah 59 H 3
Bintan, Pulau 42 B 3
Bintuan 42 B 4
Bintulu 42 D 3
Bintuni, Teluk 43 H 4
Binyang 38 E 6
Bío Bío 89 B 6
Biograd na Moru 19 G 3
Bioko 63 F 5
Bir 40 C 4
Bi'r Abraq (Egypt) 22 B 5
Bi'r Abū al Ḥusayn 60 E 4
Bi'r Abū Algharab 59 H 2
Bi'r Abū Gharādiq 60 D 2
Bi'r Abū Hashim (Egypt) 22 AB 5
Bi'r Abū Mingat 60 D 3
Bi'r Adh Dhikār 59 K 3
Bi'r al 'Abd (Egypt) 22 A 3
Bi'r al Ḥakīm 59 K 2
Bi'r al Ḥamrā' 59 H 2
Bi'r al Hisw (Saudi Arabia) 22 C 4
Bi'r al Jadīd (Saudi Arabia) 22 C 4
Bi'r al Khamsah 60 D 2
Bi'r al Mrabba'ab (Syria) 22 C 2
Bi'r al Mushayqīq 59 H 2
Bi'r al Mushayqīq (Tunisia) 59 GH 2
Bi'r al Qurayyah (Egypt) 22 A 4
Bi'r 'Allāq 59 H 2
Bi'r ar Rāh (Iraq) 22 C 2
Bi'r ar Rūmān 59 G 2
Bi'r Arjā' (Saudi Arabia) 22 C 4
Bi'r Bayah (Egypt) 22 B 4
Bi'r Baydā (Saudi Arabia) 22 B 4
Bi'r Baylī 60 D 2
Bi'r Bin Ghunaymah 59 K 2
Bi'r Bū Ḥawsh 59 K 3
Bi'r Bū Zurayyq 59 K 3
Bir Chali 58 D 4
Bi'r Dibis 60 D 4
Bi'r Djedid 59 G 2
Bi'r Dūfān 59 H 2
Bir ed Deheb 58 E 3
Bir el Ater 59 G 2
Bir el Hadjaj 58 E 3
Bir el Khzaim 58 D 4
Bir el Ksaib 62 C 1
Bir Enzaran 58 C 4
Bi'r Fajr (Saudi Arabia) 22 B 3
Bi'r Fardān 61 H 4
Bi'r Fu'ād 60 D 2
Bir Gandus 58 B 4
Bir Gara 63 H 3
Bi'r Ghawdah 61 G 4
Bi'r Ḥabs adh Dhur'ānī 59 K 2
Bi'r Ḥasanah (Egypt) 22 AB 3
Bi'r Ḥaymir (Saudi Arabia) 22 C 4
Bi'r Ibn Sarrār 61 G 5
Bir Igueni 58 C 4
Bi'r Kusaybah 60 E 4
Bir Lehlú 58 D 3
Bir Lehmar 58 C 3
Bi'r Misāhah 60 D 4
Bir Moghreim 58 C 3
Bi'r Murr 60 E 4
Bi'r Nāhid 60 D 2
Bi'r Nasīf 61 F 4
Bi'r Nasīf (Saudi Arabia) 22 C 4
Bir Ould Brini 58 E 3
Bir Ounane 62 D 1
Bir Rhoraffa 59 G 2
Bi'r Safājah (Egypt) 22 AB 4
Bi'r Saḥrā' 60 D 4
Bi'r Salālah 60 F 5
Bi'r Sayyālah (Egypt) 22 A 4
Bi'r Shalatayn 60 F 4
Bi'r Sīdī Madhkūr 59 H 2
Bi'r Ṭarfāwī (Egypt) 60 D 4
Bi'r Ṭarfāwī (Sudan) 60 E 4
Bi'r Tlākshīn 59 H 2
Bi'r 'Umm Fawākhīr (Egypt) 22 A 4
Bi'r 'Umm Sa'īd (Egypt) 22 A 3
Bi'r Ungāt 60 E 4
Bi'r Wurshah 59 K 2
Bir Zreigat 58 D 4
Bira 37 O 6
Bira 37 P 6
Birab 43 J 5
Birāk at Tahtāni, Tall (Syria) 22 C 1
Birakan 37 O 6
Birao 64 C 2
Biratnagar 40 E 2
Birch Creek 72 H 2
Birch Lake 74 J 5
Birch Mountains 73 P 4
Bird 73 T 4
Birdsville 49 F 4
Birdum River 48 E 2

Birecik 21 E 3
Birecik (Turkey) 22 C 1
Birekte 36 L 2
Bireuen 42 A 2
Birgham 3 C 4
Birikao → Būr Gābo 65 G 5
Birilyussy 36 F 4
Birini 64 C 3
Bīrjand 34 F 4
Birkat Nasser (Egypt) 22 A 5
Birkat Qārūn 60 E 3
Birkenhead 5 D 3
Birket Fatmé 63 H 3
Birksgate Range 48 DE 4
Bīrlad 20 C 1
Bīrlad 20 C 1
Birmingham (Airport) 7 D 1
Birmingham (AL, U.S.A.) 77 J 5
Birmingham (U.K.) 7 D 1
Birni 62 E 3–4
Birni Ngaoure 62 E 3
Birni Nkonni 63 EF 3
Birnie 52 D 3
Birnin Gwari 63 F 3
Birnin Kebbi 63 E 3
Birnin Kudu 63 F 3
Birobidzhan 37 O 6
Birr 4 B 3
Birrindudu 48 D 2
Birsilpur 40 B 2
Birsk 24 L 4
Biru 38 B 4
Biruni 34 G 2
Biryusa 36 G 4
Biryusinsk 36 G 4
Biržai 17 HJ 4
Birzebbuga 19 F 4
Bisaccia 19 G 3
Bisalpur 40 D 2
Bisbee 76 DE 5
Bischofshofen 19 F 2
Biscay, Bay of 18 C 2–3
Bisceglie 19 G 3
Biscarrosse, Étang de 18 C 3
Biscoe Islands 91
Bisekera 37 X 3
Bishan 38 E 5
Bishārīyīn, Barq al 60 E 5
Bishnath 41 F 2
Bishop 76 C 4
Bishop Auckland 5 E 2
Bishop Rock 14 B 5
Bishop's Falls 75 Q 6
Bishops Stortford 7 E 2
Bishr 59 J 2
Bishrī, Jabal al (Syria) 22 C 2
Bishui 37 M 5
Biskia 65 F 1
Biskra 59 G 2
Bislig 43 G 2
Bismarck 76 F 2
Bismarck Archipelago 50–51 EF 2
Bismarck Range 50 DE 2–3
Bismarck Sea 50–51 EF 2
Bismil 21 F 3
Bison 76 F 2
Bīsotūn (Iran) 23 E 2
Bispfors 16 G 3
Bissau 62 A 3
Bissett 73 S 5
Bissikrima 62 B 3
Bistcho Lake 73 NO 4
Bistrica 20 B 2
Bistriţa 20 B 1
Bistriţa 20 C 1
Bitam 63 G 5
Bitburg 14 E 5
Bitchana 65 F 2
Bitkiné 63 H 3
Bitlis 21 F 3
Bitlis Dağları 21 F 3
Bitola 20 B 2
Bitonto 19 G 3
Bitterfeld 15 F 4
Bitterfontein 66 B 6
Bitterroot Range 76 D 2–3
Bittou 62 DE 3
Biu 63 G 3
Bivolari 20 C 1
Bivolu, Virful 20 C 1
Biwa-ko 39 L 3
Biya 25 R 5
Biyang 38 F 4
Biyārjomand 34 F 3
Biyārjomand (Iran) 23 G 1
Biylikol, Ozero 35 J 2
Biyo Kaboba 65 G 2
Biysk 25 R 5
Bizerta 59 GH 1
Bjala Slatina 20 B 2
Bjargtangar 16 A 2
Bjästa 16 G 3
Bjelašnica 20 A 2
Bjelovar 19 G 2
Bjerkvik 16 G 2

Björkö 16 H 3
Björna 16 G 3
Björnafjorden 17 E 3
Björneborg 16 H 3
Björnevatn 16 J 2
Björnöya 90
Bjurholm 16 G 3
Bjuröklubb 16 H 3
Bjuv 17 F 4
Bla 62 C 3
Black Bull 4 B 3
Black Escarpment 66 B 5
Black Hills 76 F 3
Black Isle 2 B 3
Black Lake 73 R 4
Black Mountain 77 K 4
Black Mountains 6 C 1–2
Black Range 76 E 5
Black River Falls 77 HJ 3
Black Rock Desert 76 C 3
Black Sea 21 DE 2
Black Volta 62 D 4
Blackall 49 H 3
Blackbull (Queensland, Austr.) 49 G 2
Blackburn 5 D 3
Blackburn, Mount 72 J 3
Blackfoot 76 D 3
Blacklion 4 B 2
Blacklunans 3 D 3
Blackpool 5 D 3
Blackrock 4 B 3
Blackrock 4 B 3
Blackthorn 7 D 2
Blackwater 6 A 1
Blackwater (Queensland, Austr.) 49 H 3
Blackwater (Rep. of Ireland) 14 B 4
Blackwater, River 7 E 2
Blackwaterfoot 3 B 4
Blackwell 76 G 4
Blackwood River 48 B 5
Blaenau Ffestiniog 6 C 1
Blaenavon 6 C 2
Blåfjellhatten 16 F 3
Blagodarnoye 21 F 1
Blagodatnoye 20 D 1
Blagodatnyy 39 L 1
Blagoevgrad 20 B 2
Blagoveshchenka 25 PQ 5
Blagoveshchensk 24 KL 4
Blagoveshchensk 37 N 5
Blain 18 C 2
Blaine 77 H 2
Blair 77 G 3
Blair Atholl 3 C 3
Blairgowrie 3 C 3
Blaj 20 B 1
Blakeney 7 E 2
Blanc, Cap (Mauritania) 58 B 4
Blanca, Cordillera 84 C 5
Blanca, Laguna 89 B 9
Blanchard 5 D 2
Blanco, Cape 76 AB 3
Blanco, Lago 89 C 9
Blanda 16 B 2
Blandford Forum 7 C 2
Blanes 18 D 3
Blangy-sur-Bresle 18 D 2
Blansko 15 G 5
Blantyre 67 E 3
Blåsjön, Stora 16 F 3
Blåskavlen 16 E 3
Blato 19 G 3
Blåvands Huk 17 E 4
Blaydon 5 E 2
Blaye 18 C 2
Bleadon 6 C 3
Bled 19 F 2
Blei, Monti 19 F 4
Blekinge 17 FG 4
Blenheim 51 Q 9
Blessington 4 B 3
Bletchley 7 D 2
Bleus, Monts 64 E 4
Blida 59 F 1
Blind River 74 L 6
Blitar 42 D 5
Blitta 62 E 4
Bloemfontein 66 D 5
Bloemhof 66 D 5
Bloemhof Dam 66 D 5
Blois 18 D 2
Blönduós 16 AB 2
Bloomington (IL, U.S.A.) 77 J 3
Bloomington (IN, U.S.A.) 77 J 4
Bloomington (MN, U.S.A.) 77 H 3
Blora 42 D 5
Blosseville Coast 90
Blouberg 66 D 4
Bloxham 7 D 1

Blubberhouses 5 E 3
Blue Mountain Lake 77 LM 3
Blue Mountain Peak 79 G 4
Blue Mountains 49 J 5
Blue Mountanis National Park 49 J 5
Blue Mud Bay 49 F 1
Blue Nile 60 E 6
Blue Ridge 77 KL 4
Blue Stack Mountains 4 A 2
Bluefield 77 K 4
Bluefields 78 F 5
Bluenose Lake 73 O 2
Bluff 50 P 10
Bluff Knoll 48 B 5
Bluff Point 48 A 4
Blumenau 88 G 4
Blyth 5 E 2
Blythe 76 D 5
Blytheville 77 J 4
Bo 62 B 4
Bo Duc 41 J 5
Bo Hai 39 GH 3
Bo River 64 D 3
Bo Trach 41 J 4
Bo Xian 38 G 4
Boa Esperança, Reprêsa 87 H 2
Boa Vista (Cape Verde) 62 B 6
Boa Vista (Pará, Brazil) 85 G 4
Boa Vista (Roraima, Brazil) 85 F 3
Boac 43 F 1
Boaco 78 E 5
Boane 67 E 5
Boano, Pulau 43 G 4
Boarhills 3 C 3
Boat of Garten 2 C 3
Boatasyn 37 Q 5
Boath 2 B 3
Boatman 49 H 4
Bobai 38 EF 6
Bobangi 64 B 5
Bobât (Iran) 23 G 3
Bobbili 40 D 4
Bobo Dioulasso 62 D 3
Bobonazo 84 C 4
Bobonong 66 D 4
Bobrinets 21 D 1
Bobrov 24 H 5
Bobruysk 17 J 5
Boby, Pic 67 H 4
Boca, Cachoeira da 85 GH 5
Boca de la Serpiente 85 F 2
Boca del Guafo 89 AB 7
Boca del Rio 76 E 6
Bôca do Acre 84 E 5
Bôca do Curuquetê 84 E 5
Bôca do Jari 85 H 4
Bôca do Moaço 84 E 5
Boca Grande 85 FG 2
Boca Mavaca 84 E 3
Boca Raton 77 L 6
Bocage Vendéen 18 C 2
Bocaiúva 87 H 4
Bocaranga 64 B 3
Bocas del Toro 84 B 2
Bochnia 15 H 5
Bochum 15 E 4
Bocoio 66 A 2
Boconó 84 DE 2
Boçsa 20 B 1
Boda 64 B 4
Bodaybo 36 K 4
Boddam 2 D 2
Boddington 48 B 5
Bodélé 63 H 2
Boden 16 H 2
Bodensee 19 E 2
Bodmin 6 B 2
Bodmin Moor 6 B 2
Bodö 16 F 2
Bodoquena, Serra da 86 E 5
Bodrum 20 C 3
Boduna 64 B 3
Boën 18 D 2
Boende 64 C 5
Boffa 62 B 3
Bog of Allen 4 B 3
Bogachevka 37 U 5
Bogale 41 G 4
Bogalusa 77 J 5
Bogan River 49 H 5
Bogandé 62 DE 3
Bogangolo 64 B 3
Bogbonga 64 B 4
Bogcang Zangbo 40 E 1
Bogda Feng 35 M 2
Bogda Shan 35 MN 2
Bogdan 20 B 2
Bogen 16 G 2
Bogense 17 F 4
Bogetkol'skiy 25 M 5
Boggabilla 49 HJ 4
Boggeragh Mountains 14 B 4
Boghari → Ksar el Buokhari 59 F 1
Boghra Dam 35 GH 4

Bogia 50 D 2
Bognor Regis 7 D 2
Bogo 43 F 1
Bogodukhov 24 G 5
Bogol Manya 65 G 4
Bogor 42 C 5
Bogoroditsk 24 G 5
Bogorodskoye 24 K 4
Bogorodskoye 37 Q 5
Bogotá 84 D 3
Bogotol 25 R 4
Bogöy 16 G 2
Bogra 40 E 3
Boguchany 36 G 4
Bogué 58 C 5
Boguslav 24 F 6
Boğzlıyan 21 E 3
Bohai Haixia 39 H 3
Bohemia 15 F 5
Bohemia Downs 48 D 2
Bohicon 62 E 4
Böhmerwald 15 F 5
Bohodoyou 62 C 4
Bohol 43 F 2
Bohol Sea 43 F 2
Bohu 35 M 2
Bohuslän 17 F 4
Boiaçu 85 F 4
Boim 85 G 4
Boipeba, Ilha 87 J 3
Bois 87 F 4
Bois, Lac des 73 N 2
Boise 76 C 3
Boise City 76 F 4
Boise River 76 C 3
Boissevain 73 S 6
Boizenburg 15 F 4
Bojador, Cabo 58 C 3
Bojnürd 34 F 3
Bojonegoro 42 D 5
Bojuro 88 F 5
Bok 50 E 3
Boka Kotorska 20 A 2
Bokani 63 F 4
Bokatola 64 B 5
Boké 62 B 3
Bokhapcha 37 S 3
Boki 63 G 4
Boknafjorden 17 E 4
Boko 63 G 6
Bokora Game Reserve 64 E 4
Bokoro 63 H 3
Bokote 64 C 5
Bokpyin 41 G 5
Boksitogorsk 24 F 4
Bokspits 66 C 5
Bokungu 64 C 5
Bokwankusu 64 C 5
Bol (Chad) 63 G 3
Bol (Yugoslavia) 19 G 3
Bolafa 64 C 4
Bolaiti 64 C 5
Bolama 62 A 3
Bolan Pass 35 H 5
Bolangir 40 D 3
Boldon 5 E 2
Bole (China) 35 L 2
Bole (Ethiopia) 65 F 3
Bole (Ghana) 62 D 4
Bolesławiec 15 G 4
Bolgatanga 62 D 3
Bolgrad 20 C 1
Boli 39 K 1
Bolia 64 B 5
Boliden 16 H 3
Bolinao 43 H 1
Bolintin Vale 20 C 2
Boliohutu, Gunung 43 F 3
Bolívar (Argentina) 89 D 6
Bolívar (Colombia) 84 C 3
Bolívar, Cerro 85 F 2
Bolívar, Pico 84 D 2
Bolivia 86 CD 4
Bolkar Dağları 21 D 3
Bolkhov 24 G 5
Bolléne 19 D 3
Bollnäs 16 G 3
Bollon 49 H 4
Bollstabruk 16 G 3
Bolmen 17 F 4
Bolnisi 21 F 2
Bolobo 64 B 5
Bologna 19 F 3
Bolognesi 86 B 3
Bologoye 24 F 4
Bologur 37 O 3
Bolomba 64 B 4
Bolombo 64 C 5
Bolon' 37 P 5
Bolon', Ozero 37 P 6
Bolotnoye 25 Q 4
Bolsena, Lago di 19 F 3
Bol'shaya Belozerka 21 D 1
Bol'shaya Chernigovka 24 JK 5
Bol'shaya Glushitsa 24 K 5
Bol'shaya Lepetikha 21 D 1

Bol'shaya Murta 36 F 4
Bol'shaya Novoselka 21 E 1
Bol'shaya Orlovka 21 F 1
Bol'shaya Pyssa 24 J 3
Bol'shaya Vladimirovka 25 P 5
Bol'shaya Yerema 36 J 3
Bol'shenarymskoye 25 Q 6
Bol'sheokinskoye 36 H 4
Bol'sheretsk 37 T 5
Bol'shezemel'skaya Tundra 24–25 KM 2
Bol'shiye Khatymy 37 M 4
Bol'shiye Klyuchsishchi 24 J 5
Bol'shiye Lar'yak 25 Q 3
Bol'shiye Shogany 25 M 3
Bol'shiye Uki 25 O 4
Bol'shoy 37 T 1
Bol'shoy Anyuy 37 U 2
Bol'shoy Balkhan, Khrebet 34 EF 3
Bol'shoy Begichev, Ostrov 36 KL 1
Bol'shoy Berezovy, Ostrov 17 J 3
Bol'shoy Kavkaz 21 FG 2
Bol'shoy Lyakhovskiy, Ostrov 37 Q 1
Bol'shoy Nimnyr 37 MN 4
Bol'shoy Oloy 37 TU 2
Bol'shoy Onguren 36 J 5
Bol'shoy Patom 36 KL 3–4
Bol'shoy Pit 36 F 4
Bol'shoy Porog 36 F 2
Bol'shoy Salym 25 O 3
Bol'shoy Shantar, Ostrov 37 P 4–5
Bol'shoy Uluy 36 F 4
Bol'shoy Yenisey 36 G 5
Bol'shoy Yeravnoye, Ozero 36 K 5
Bol'shoye Vlasyevo 37 Q 5
Bol'shoye Morskoye, Ozero 37 T 1
Bolsón de Mapimi 78 B 2
Bolsover 7 D 1
Bolton 5 D 3
Bolu 20 D 2
Bolungarvík 16 A 2
Boluntay 38 B 3
Bolvadin 20 D 3
Bolvanskiy Nos, Mys 25 LM 1
Bolzano 19 F 2
Bom 50 E 3
Bom Comercio 84 E 5
Bom Jardim 84 E 5
Bom Jesus 87 H 2
Bom Jesus da Gurguéia, Serra 87 H 2
Bom Jesus da Lapa 87 H 3
Bom Retiro 88 G 4
Boma 63 G 7
Bomassa 63 H 5
Bombala 49 H 6
Bombarral 18 B 4
Bombay 40 B 4
Bomberai 43 H 4
Bombéré 64 B 4
Bombo 64 E 4
Bomboma 64 B 4
Bomdila 41 F 2
Bomi 38 C 5
Bomi Hills 62 B 4
Bomili 64 D 4
Bömlo 17 DE 4
Bomokandi 64 D 4
Bomongo 64 B 4
Bomu 64 C 4
Bona, Mount 72 J 3
Bonaire, Isla 84 E 1
Bonampak 78 D 4
Bonanza 78 F 5
Bonaparte Archipelago 48 C 1
Bonar Bridge 2 B 3
Bonavista 75 R 6
Bonavista Bay 75 R 6
Bondo 64 C 4
Bondo 64 C 3
Bondowoso 42 D 5
Bône → Annaba 59 G 1
Bone, Teluk 43 F 4
Bonelohe 43 F 5
Boneng 41 H 4
Bo'ness 3 C 3
Bonete, Cerro 88 C 4
Bong Mountains 62 C 4
Bonga 65 F 3
Bongabong 43 F 1
Bongandanga 64 C 4
Bongka 43 F 4
Bongo 63 G 6
Bongor 63 H 3
Bongos, Massif des 64 C 3
Bongou 64 C 3
Bongouanou 62 D 4
Boni Game Reserve 65 G 5
Bonifacio 19 E 3
Bonifacio, Strait of 19 E 3
Bonifati, Capo 19 G 4

Bonin Islands 27 R 7
Bonito 86 E 5
Bonkoukou 62 E 3
Bonn 15 E 4
Bonners Ferry 76 C 2
Bonnet Plume 72 L 2–3
Bonneville Saltflats 76 D 3
Bonnie Rock 48 B 5
Bonny 63 F 5
Bonobono 42 E 2
Bontang 42 E 3
Bonthe 62 B 4
Bontoc 43 J 1
Bonwapitse 66 D 4
Bonyhád 20 A 1
Boogardie 48 B 4
Boola 62 C 4
Boolaloo 48 B 3
Booligal 49 GH 5
Boologooro 48 A 3
Boon 74 L 6
Böön Tsagaan Nuur 38 C 1
Boonah 49 J 4
Boone 77 H 3
Boongoondoo 49 H 3
Boonville 77 H 4
Booroorban 49 G 5
Boothby, Cape 91
Boothia, Gulf of 73 T 1
Boothia Peninsula 73 T 1
Bootle 5 D 2
Bootle 5 D 3
Booué 63 G 5–6
Bophuthatswana 66 C 5
Bopolu 62 B 4
Boqueirão 88 F 5
Boquete 84 B 2
Boquillaqas del Carmen 78 B 2
Bor (Sudan) 64 E 3
Bor (Turkey) 21 D 3
Bor (U.S.S.R.) 24 H 4
Bor (Yugoslavia) 20 B 2
Bora-Bora 53 E 4
Borah Peak 76 D 3
Borama 65 G 3
Borås 17 F 4
Borasambar 40 D 3
Borâzjân (Iran) 23 F 3
Borçka 21 F 2
Bordeaux 18 CD 3
Borders 3 C 4
Bordertown 49 G 6
Bordj Bou Arreridj 59 F 1
Bordj Fly Sainte Marie 58 E 3
Bordj Messouda 59 G 2
Bordj Moktar 59 F 4
Bordj Omar Driss 59 G 3
Bordj Sif Fatima 59 G 2
Borgå 17 J 3
Borgarnes 16 A 3
Börgefjellet 16 F 2
Borgholm 17 G 4
Borgo 64 B 4
Borinage 14 E 4
Borisav 15 H 5
Borisoglebsk 24 H 5
Borisov 17 J 5
Borisovka 35 H 2
Borispol 24 F 5
Borja 19 G 3
Borja 84 C 4
Borjas Blancas 18 D 3
Borkou 63 H 2
Borlänge 17 FG 3
Borlu 20 C 3
Borneo 42 DE 3
Bornholm 17 F 5
Bornu 63 G 3
Bornwee Head 14 B 4
Boro 64 D 3
Borodino 36 G 4
Borodyanka 24 E 5
Borohoro Shan 35 L 2
Boroko 43 F 3
Borolgustakh 36 M 2
Boromo 62 D 3
Borong, Khrebet 37 P 2
Borongan 43 G 1
Bororen 49 J 3
Borotou 62 C 4
Boroughbridge 5 E 2
Borovichi 17 J 4
Borovichi 24 FG 4
Borovlyanka 25 Q 5
Borovo 19 G 2
Borovoye 25 O 5
Borovskiy 25 N 4
Borovskoye 25 M 5
Borrän 65 H 2
Borrby 17 F 4
Borris 4 B 3
Borrisoleigh 4 B 3
Borroloola 49 F 2
Borşa 20 B 1
Börselv 16 J 1

Borshchev (Ukraine, U.S.S.R.) 24 E 6
Borshchovochnyy Khrebet 36 KL 5
Borshckev (Ukraine, U.S.S.R.) 20 C 1
Borsippa (Iraq) 22 D 2
Borth 6 B 1
Boru 37 Q 1
Borüjen (Iran) 23 F 3
Borüjerd (Iran) 23 E 2
Borzhomi 21 F 2
Bőrzsöny 20 A 1
Borzya 36 L 5
Bosa 19 E 3
Bosaga 25 O 6
Bosanska Gradiška 19 G 2
Bosanska Krupa 19 G 3
Bosanski Novi 19 G 2
Bosanski Petrovac 19 G 3
Bosanski Samac 19 G 2
Bösäso 65 H 2
Bosbury 6 C 1
Boscastle 6 B 2
Bose 38 E 6
Boseki 64 B 5
Boshan 39 G 3
Boshnyakovo 37 Q 6
Boshrûyeh 34 F 4
Bosilegrad 20 B 2
Boskamp 85 G 2
Bosna 19 G 3
Bosna 20 C 2
Bosnik 43 J 4
Bosobolo 64 B 4
Bosporus 20 C 2
Bosque Bonito 76 E 5
Bossangoa 64 B 3
Bossé Bangou 62 E 3
Bossembele 64 B 3
Bossemptélé Il 64 B 3
Bossier City 77 H 5
Bosso 63 G 3
Bossut, Cape 48 C 2
Bostan 35 H 4
Bostandyk 24 J 6
Bosten Hu 38 A 2
Boston (MA, U.S.A.) 77 M 3
Boston (U.K.) 7 DE 1
Boston Mountains 77 H 4
Botan 21 F 3
Botev 20 C 2
Botevgrad 20 B 2
Bothaville 66 D 5
Bothel 5 D 2
Botletle 66 C 4
Botlikh 21 G 2
Botomoyu 36 L 3
Botrange 14 E 4
Botoşani 20 C 1
Botswana 66 CD 4
Botte Donato 19 G 4
Bottesford 7 D 1
Bottrop 14 E 4
Botucatu 87 G 5
Botuobuya, Ulakhan 36 K 3
Botwood 75 QR 6
Bou Arfa 58 E 2
Bou Djéhiba 62 D 2
Bou Garfa 58 D 3
Bou Ismaïl 18 D 4
Bou Izakarn 58 D 3
Bou Kadir 18 D 4
Bou Naga 58 C 5
Bou Rjeima 58 BC 5
Bou Saâda 59 F 1
Bouaflé 62 C 4
Bouaké 62 D 4
Bouala 64 B 3
Bouali (Burkina) 64 B 4
Bouali (Gabon) 63 G 6
Bouânane 58 E 2
Bouar 64 B 3
Boubandjida 63 GH 4
Boubandjida National Park 63 GH 4
Boubin 15 F 5
Boubout 58 E 3
Bouca 64 B 3
Boucle de Baoulé, Parc National de la 62 C 3
Boudenib 58 E 2
Boufarik 18 D 4
Bougainville (Papua New Guinea) 51 G 3
Bougainville Reef 49 H 2
Bougainville Strait (Solomon Is.) 51 G 3
Bougainville Strait (Vanuatu) 51 J 5
Bougaroun, Cap 59 G 1
Bougie → Bejaïa 59 F 1
Bougouni 62 C 3
Bougtob 58 EF 2
Bouïra 59 F 1
Boulanouar 58 B 4

Boulder (Australia) **48** C 5
Boulder (U.S.A.) **76** F 3
Boulia **49** F 3
Boulogne-sur-Mer **18** D 1
Boulouli **62** C 2
Bouloupari **51** J 6
Boulsa **62** D 3
Boultoum **63** G 3
Bouly **58** C 5
Boumdeïd **58** C 5
Boun Neua **41** H 3
Bouna **62** D 4
Boundiali **62** C 4
Boundji **63** GH 6
Boundou **62** B 3
Boundoukou **62** D 4
Bounoum **62** A 2
Bountiful **76** D 3
Bounty Islands **91**
Bourail **51** J 6
Bourem **62** D 2
Bouressa **62** E 1
Bourg **19** E 2
Bourganeuf **18** D 2
Bourges **18** D 2
Bourget, Lac du **19** E 2
Bourgogne **19** DE 2
Bourgogne, Canal de **18** D 2
Bourgoin-Jallieu **19** E 2
Bourke **49** H 5
Bourne **7** D 1
Bournemouth **7** D 2
Bournemouth (Airport) **7** D 2
Bouroum **62** D 3
Bourton-on-the-Water **7** D 2
Bourtoutou **63** J 3
Boussens **18** D 3
Bousso **63** H 3
Bouvet Island **91**
Bouza **63** F 3
Bovril **88** E 5
Bow **73** P 5
Bowen (Argentina) **88** C 5
Bowen (Australia) **49** H 2
Bowes **5** C 2
Bowkan (Iran) **23** E 1
Bowland Forest **5** D 2–3
Bowling Green **77** J 4
Bowling Green, Cape **49** H 2
Bowman **76** F 2
Bowman Bay **75** MN 2
Bowmore **3** A 4
Bowral **49** J 5
Boxholm **17** G 4
Boxing **39** G 3
Boyabat **21** D 2
Boyabo **64** B 4
Boyang **39** G 5
Boyang Hu **38** G 5
Boyarka **36** G 1
Boyarsk **36** J 4
Boyle **14** B 4
Boyne, River **4** B 3
Boyuibe **86** D 5
Boz Daği **20** C 3
Bozdağ **21** D 3
Bozdoğan **20** C 3
Bozeman **76** D 2
Bozene **64** B 4
Bozkır **21** D 3
Bozok Platosu **21** DE 3
Bozouls **18** D 3
Bozoum **64** B 3
Bozova **21** E 3
Bozshakul' **25** OP 5
Bozüyük **20** D 3
Bra **19** E 3
Brač **19** G 3
Bracadale **2** A 3
Bracciano, Lago di **19** F 3
Bräcke **16** G 3
Brački Kanal **19** G 3
Brackley **7** D 1
Bracknell **7** D 2
Bracora **3** B 3
Brad **20** B 1
Bradano **19** G 3
Bradda Head **4** C 2
Bradenton **77** K 6
Bradford (PA, U.S.A.) **77** L 3
Bradford (U.K.) **5** E 3
Bradford-on-Avon **7** C 2
Bradley Reefs **51** H 3
Bradshaw **48** E 2
Brady **76** G 5
Brady Mountains **76** G 5
Brae **2** D 1
Braemar **3** C 3
Bragado **88** D 6
Bragança **18** B 3
Bragança **85** J 4
Bragina **37** X 3
Brahman Baria **41** F 3
Brahmaputra **41** F 2

Brăila **20** C 1
Brailsford **7** D 1
Brainerd **77** H 2
Braintree **7** E 2
Braithwaite Point **48** E 1
Bräk **59** H 3
Brakna **58** C 5
Brålanda **17** F 4
Bramdean **7** D 2
Brämön **16** G 3
Brampton **75** L 7
Brampton (U.K.) **5** D 2
Brancaster **7** E 1
Brandberg **66** A 4
Brandberg West Mine **66** A 4
Brande **17** E 4
Brandenburg **15** F 4
Brandon **5** E 2
Brandon **7** E 1
Brandon **73** S 6
Brandsby **5** E 2
Brandvlei **66** C 6
Braniewo **15** GH 4
Branston **7** D 1
Brantford **75** L 7
Brás **85** G 4
Bras d'Or Lake **75** PQ 6
Brasil, Planalto do **87** H 4
Brasiléia **86** C 3
Brasília **87** G 4
Brasília Legal **85** G 4
Brasília, Parque Nacional do **87** G 4
Braslav **17** J 4
Braşov **20** C 1
Brass **63** F 5
Brassey, Mount **48** E 3
Bratca **20** B 1
Bratislava **15** G 5
Bratsk **36** H 4
Bratskoye Vodokhranilishche **36** H 4
Bratslav **20** C 1
Brattleboro **77** M 3
Brattvåg **16** E 3
Braţul Borcea **20** C 2
Braţul Chilia **20** C 1
Braţul Cremenea **20** C 2
Braţul Sfintu Gheorghe **20** C 1–2
Braunau am Inn **19** F 2
Braunschweig **15** F 4
Braunton **6** B 2
Brava **62** AB 7
Bråviken **17** G 4
Bravo, Cerro **84** C 5
Brawley **76** C 5
Bray **75** M 2
Bray (South Africa) **66** C 5
Bray (U.K.) **4** B 3
Brazil **86–87** EG 3
Brazil Basin **98** A 4
Brazil Current **92**
Brazo Casiquiare **84** E 3
Brazos River **77** G 5
Brazzaville **63** GH 6
Brčko **19** G 3
Brda **15** G 4
Brdy **15** F 5
Brea, Cerros de la **84** B 4
Breadalbane **3** B 3
Breaden, Lake **48** D 4
Bready **4** B 2
Breaza **20** C 1
Brebes **42** C 5
Brechin **3** C 3
Breckenridge **76** G 5
Brecknock, Península **89** B 9
Breclav **15** G 5
Brecon **6** C 2
Breda **14** D 4
Bredasdorp **66** C 6
Bredbyn **16** G 3
Brede **7** E 2
Bredy **25** M 5
Bregenz **19** E 2
Breiðafjörður **16** A 2
Breiðdalur **16** C 3
Breivikbotn **16** H 1
Brejo (Maranhão, Brazil) **87** H 1
Brejo (Piauí, Brazil) **87** H 2
Brekken **16** F 3
Brekstad **16** EF 3
Bremangerlandet **16** D 3
Bremen **15** E 4
Bremer Bay **48** B 5
Bremer Bay **48** B 5
Bremerhaven **15** E 4
Bremerton **76** B 2
Brenner **19** F 2
Brenta, Gruppo di **19** F 2
Brentwood **7** E 2
Brescia **19** F 2
Bressanone **19** F 2
Bressay **2** D 1
Brest (France) **18** C 2

Brest (U.S.S.R.) **17** H 5
Brestova **19** F 2
Bretagne **18** C 2
Breteuil **18** D 2
Breton, Pertuis **18** C 2
Brett, Cape **51** Q 8
Breueh, Pulau **42** A 2
Breves **85** H 4
Brevik **17** E 4
Brevoort Island **75** P 3
Brewarrina **49** H 4–5
Brewerville **62** B 4
Brewster, Kap **90**
Brewton **77** J 5
Brezhnev **24** K 4
Brežice **19** G 2
Brézina **59** F 2
Bria **64** C 3
Briançon **19** E 3
Briare, Canal de **18** D 2
Brichany **20** C 1
Bride **4** C 2
Bridestowe **6** B 2
Bridge of Earn **3** C 3
Bridge of Gaur **3** B 3
Bridge of Orhy **3** B 3
Bridgend **2** C 3
Bridgend **3** A 4
Bridgend (Mid-Glamorgan) **6** C 2
Bridgend (Rep. of Ireland) **4** B 2
Bridgeport (CA, U.S.A.) **76** C 4
Bridgeport (CT, U.S.A.) **77** M 3
Bridger Peak **76** E 3
Bridgetown (Australia) **48** B 5
Bridgetown (Barbados) **79** KL 5
Bridgewater **75** P 7
Bridgnorth **6** C 1
Bridgwater **6** C 2
Bridgwater Bay **6** C 2
Bridlington **5** E 2
Bridlington Bay **5** E 2
Bridport **6** C 2
Brig **19** E 2
Brigg **5** E 3
Brigham City **76** D 3
Brighouse **5** E 3
Bright **49** H 6
Brightlingsea **7** E 2
Brighton **7** D 2
Brignoles **19** E 2
Brigstock **7** D 1
Brijuni **19** F 3
Brikama **62** A 3
Brindisi **19** G 3
Brinkene **58** E 3
Brinklow **7** D 1
Brisbane **49** J 4
Bristol **6** C 2
Bristol (Airport) **6** C 2
Bristol (TN, U.S.A.) **77** K 4
Bristol Bay **72** EF 4
Bristol Channel **6** C 2
Britânia **87** F 4
British Columbia **73** MN 4–5
British Isles **92**
British Mountains **72** JK 2
Brits **66** D 5
Britstown **66** C 6
Brive **18** D 2
Briviesca **18** C 3
Brixham **6** C 2
Brixton **6** C 2
Brno **15** G 5
Broad Bay **2** A 2
Broad Sound **49** H 3
Broadback **75** M 5
Broadclyst **6** C 3
Broadford **3** A 4
Broadstairs **7** E 2
Broadus **76** EF 2
Broadview **73** R 5
Broadway **6** C 3
Broadway **7** D 1
Broadwey **6** C 2
Broadwindsor **6** C 3
Brochet **73** R 4
Brochet, Lake **73** R 4
Brocken **15** F 4
Brockenhurst **7** D 2
Brockman, Mount **48** B 3
Brock's Creek **48** E 1
Brockville **75** M 7
Brod **20** B 2
Broderick Falls **64** EF 4
Brodick **3** B 4
Brodnica **15** G 4
Brody **17** J 5
Broken Hill **49** G 5
Brokhovo **37** ST 4
Brokopondo **85** G 3
Bromölla **17** F 4
Bromyard **6** C 1
Brönderslev **17** F 4
Bronnikovo **25** N 4
Brönnøysund **16** F 2
Bronte **19** F 4

Brooke's Point **42** E 2
Brookfield **77** H 4
Brookhaven **77** H 5
Brookings (CA, U.S.A.) **76** B 3
Brookings (S.D., U.S.A.) **77** G 3
Brookland **7** E 2
Brooks **73** P 5
Brooks Range **72** FH 2
Brookston **77** H 2
Brookton **48** B 5
Brookville **49** H 3
Broom, Loch **2** B 3
Broome **48** C 2
Broome, Mount **48** D 2
Brora **2** C 2
Brora, River **2** B 2
Brough **5** D 2
Brough Head **2** C 2
Broughshane **4** B 2
Broughton **5** D 3
Broughton **7** D 1
Broughton in Furness **5** D 2
Broughton Island **75** P 2
Broughtown **2** C 2
Broutona, Ostrov **37** S 6
Brovst **17** E 4
Brown Lake **73** T 2
Brown River (Queensland, Austr.) **49** G 2
Browne Range Nature Reserve **48** CD 3–4
Brownfield **76** F 5
Brownhills **7** D 1
Browning **76** D 2
Brownsville **77** G 6
Brownwood **76** G 5
Browse Island **48** C 1
Broxburn **3** C 4
Bruce Crossing **77** J 2
Bruce, Mount **48** B 3
Bruce Peninsula **75** L 7
Bruchsal **15** E 5
Bruck **19** G 2
Brückenau **15** EF 4
Brugge **14** D 4
Brumado **87** H 3
Bruncio **19** F 2
Bruneau **76** C 3
Brunei **42** D 2
Brunflo **16** FG 3
Brunsbüttel **15** E 4
Brunswick **77** K 5
Brunswick Bay **48** C 2
Brunswick, Peninsula de **89** B 9
Bruny **50** L 9
Brus, Laguna de **78** F 4
Brusilovka **24** KL 5
Brusovo **25** R 3
Brusque **88** G 4
Brussels **14** DE 4
Brusset, Erg **63** FG 2
Bruxelles **14** DE 4
Bruzual **84** E 2
Bryan **77** G 5
Bryan Coast **91**
Bryanka **36** F 3
Bryansk **24** F 5
Bryanskoye **21** G 2
Brydekirk **3** C 4
Bryne **17** E 4
Bryn'kovskaya **21** E 1
Bryukhovetskaya **21** E 1
Bryungyadinskiye Gory **37** PQ 3
Brza Palanka **20** B 2
Brzeg **15** G 4
Bu Craa **58** C 3
Bũ Hạsă' (United Arab Emirates) **23** F 5
Bu Khanum **41** H 5
Bu Tu Suay **41** J 5
Bua Yai **41** H 4
Buandougou **62** C 4
Buapinang **43** F 4
Buba **62** A 3
Bubanza **64** D 5
Bubaque **62** A 3
Būbīyān (Kuwait) **23** E 3
Bucak **20** D 3
Bucaramanga **84** D 2
Buccaneer Archipelago **48** C 2
Buchan **2** D 3
Buchan Ness **2** D 3
Buchanan **62** B 4
Buchanan, Lake (Queensland, Austr.) **49** H 3
Buchanan, Lake (TX, U.S.A.) **76** G 5
Buchanan, Lake (Western Australia) **48** C 4
Buchardo **88** D 5
Bucharest **20** C 2
Bucharest = Bucureşti **20** C 2
Buchlyvrie **3** B 3
Buchs **19** E 2
Buck, Lake **48** E 2

Buckeye **76** D 5
Buckfastleigh **6** C 2
Buckhaven **3** C 3
Buckie **2** C 3
Buckingham **7** D 2
Buckingham Bay **49** F 1
Buckinghamshire **7** D 2
Buckland **7** E 1
Buckland **72** E 2
Buckland Tableland **49** H 3
Buckley **6** C 1
Buckley **6** C 1
Bucknall **7** D 1
Buco Zau **63** G 6
Bucureşti **20** C 2
Bucyrus **77** K 3
Bud Bud **65** H 4
Budacu, Virful **20** C 1
Budapest **20** A 1
Budaun **40** C 2
Bude **6** B 2
Bude Bay **6** B 2
Budennovka **24** K 5
Budennovsk **21** F 2
Búðardalur **16** A 2
Budjala **64** B 4
Budleigh Salterton **6** C 2
Buea **63** F 5
Buen Pasto **89** C 8
Buena Vista **84** E 2
Buenaventura (Colombia) **84** C 3
Buenaventura (Mexico) **76** E 6
Buenavista **76** E 7
Buendia, Embalse de **18** C 3
Buengas **66** B 1
Buenópolis **87** H 4
Buenos Aires **88** E 5
Buenos Aires, Lago **89** B 8
Buffalo (N.W.T., Can.) **73** P 3
Buffalo (N.Y., U.S.A.) **77** L 3
Buffalo (OK, U.S.A.) **76** G 4
Buffalo (S.D., U.S.A.) **76** F 2
Buffalo (WY, U.S.A.) **76** E 3
Buffalo Lake **73** OP 3
Buffalo Narrows **73** Q 4
Buftea **20** C 2
Bug **15** H 4
Buga **84** C 3
Bugala Island **64** E 5
Bugene **64** E 5
Bugel, Tanjung **42** D 5
Bugarach, Pech de **18** D 3
Bugarikhta **36** KL 5
Bugat **36** H 6
Bugel, Tanjung **42** D 5
Bugene **64** E 5
Bugojno **19** G 3
Bugorkan **36** J 3
Bugöynes **16** J 2
Bugrino **24** J 2
Bugsuk **42** E 2
Bugt **37** M 6
Bugul'deyka **36** J 5
Bugul'ma **24** K 5
Buguruslan **24** K 5
Buh He **38** C 3
Buhayrat al Asad (Syria) **22** C 1–2
Buhayrat Shārī (Iraq) **22** D 2
Buhera **67** E 3
Bühödle **65** H 3
Bui Dam **62** D 4
Builth Wells **6** C 1
Buinsk **24** J 5
Buir Nur **36** L 6
Buitepos **66** B 4
Buítrago del Lozoya **18** C 3
Bujaraloz **18** CD 3
Bujaru **85** J 4
Buje **19** F 2
Bujumbura **64** D 5
Buka **51** F 3
Bukachacha **36** L 5
Bukadaban Feng **38** B 3
Bukakata **64** E 5
Bukama **64** D 6
Bukanskoye **25** Q 5
Bukantau, Gory **35** G 3
Bukavu **64** D 5
Bukene **64** E 5
Bukhara **35** G 3
Bukit Gandadiwata **43** EF 4
Bukit Harun **42** E 3
Bukit Kambuno **43** EF 4
Bukit Masurai **42** B 4
Bukit Mawa **42** D 3
Bukit Raya **42** D 4
Bukit Sulat **43** G 3
Bukittinggi **42** B 4
Bukoba **64** E 5
Bukukun **36** K 6
Bukuru **63** F 4
Bukwimba **64** E 5
Būl, Kūh-e (Iran) **23** F 3
Bula **43** H 4
Bulambuk **36** G 5
Bulan **43** F 1
Bulancak **21** E 2

Bulandshahr 40 C 2
Bulanik 21 F 3
Būlāq 60 E 3
Bulawayo 66 D 4
Bulayevo 25 O 5
Buldan 20 C 3
Buldana 40 C 3
Buldir 72 A 5
Bulgan 36 F 6
Bulgan 36 H 6
Bulgan 36 K 6
Bulgaria 20 C 2
Buli 43 G 3
Buli, Teluk 43 G 3
Bulki 65 F 3
Bull Shoals Lake 77 H 4
Bulla Regia 19 E 4
Bullahār 65 G 2
Bullfinch 48 B 5
Bullion Mountains 76 C 5
Bullita 48 E 2
Bulloo River 49 G 4
Bulnes 89 B 6
Bulo Berde 65 H 4
Bulolo 50 E 3
Bulucan 21 E 3
Bulukumba 43 F 5
Bulun 37 N 1
Bulun 37 Q 4
Bulun 37 T 2
Bulungu 64 B 5
Bumba 64 B 6
Bumba 64 C 4
Bumbulan 43 F 3
Bumbuli 64 C 5
Bumbuna 62 B 4
Bun Yun 41 H 4
Buna 65 F 4
Bunbeg 4 A 2
Bunbury 48 B 5
Bunclody 4 B 3
Buncrana 4 B 2
Bunda 64 E 5
Bunda Bunda 49 G 3
Bundaberg 49 J 3
Bundesrepublik Deutschland
  15 EF 5
Bundi 40 C 2
Bundooma 48 E 3
Bunessan 3 A 3
Bung Sai 41 J 4
Bungay 7 E 1
Bungku 43 F 4
Bungo-suidō 39 K 4
Buni 63 G 3
Bunia 64 E 4
Bunji 35 JK 3
Bunkeya 66 D 2
Bunkie 77 H 5
Buntingford 7 E 2
Buntok 42 DE 4
Bünyan 21 E 3
Buol 43 F 3
Buolkalakh 36 L 1
Buorkhaya, Guba 37 O 1
Buorkhaya, Mys 37 O 1
Buotama 37 N 3
Bupul 50 D 3
Buqayq (Saudi Arabia) 23 E 4
Buqda Kōsār 65 G 4
Buqūm, Ḥarrat al 61 G 4
Bur 36 J 4
Būr Dab 65 H 3
Būr Gābo 65 G 5
Būr Hakkaba 65 G 4
Būr Saʿīd (Egypt) 22 A 3
Būr Sūdān 60 F 5
Bura 65 F 5
Buram 60 D 6
Buran 25 R 6
Burang 40 D 1
Buraʾo 65 H 3
Buraq (Syria) 22 B 2
Buraydạ (Saudi Arabia) 22 D 4
Burbage 7 D 2
Burdekin River 49 H 2
Burdēre 65 H 4
Burdur 20 D 3
Burdur Gölü 20 CD 3
Burdwan 40 E 3
Bure, River 7 E 1
Bureå 16 H 3
Burei 64 F 3
Bureinskiy, Khrebet 37 O 5
Büren 36 H 6
Bureya 37 N 6
Bureya 37 O 5
Burfjord 16 H 2
Burford 7 D 2
Burg 15 F 4
Burg Sãfītã (Syria) 22 B 2
Burgakhcha 37 Q 3
Burgan 31
Burgas 20 C 2
Burgaski zaliv 20 C 2
Burgdorf 19 E 2

Burgeo 75 Q 6
Burgersdorp 66 D 6
Burgess Hill 7 D 2
Burgfjället 16 G 3
Burgh le Marsh 5 F 3
Burghausen 19 F 2
Burghead 2 C 3
Burgos (Mexico) 78 C 3
Burgos (Spain) 18 C 3
Burgsvik 17 G 4
Burhan Budai Shan 38 C 3
Burhaniye 20 C 3
Burhanpur 40 C 3
Burias 43 F 1
Buribay 25 L 5
Burica, Punta 78 F 6
Burin Peninsula 75 Q 6
Buriram 41 H 5
Buriti 86 E 4
Buritizal, Cachoeira do 85 H 3
Burj at Tuyūr 60 D 4
Burjasot 18 C 4
Burji 65 F 3
Burke River 49 F 3
Burketown (Queensland, Austr.)
  49 F 2
Burkhala 37 RS 3
Burkhaybyt 37 P 2
Burkina 62 D 3
Burla 25 P 5
Burley 76 D 3
Burlington (CO, U.S.A.) 76 F 4
Burlington (IA, U.S.A.) 77 H 3
Burlington (N.Y., U.S.A.) 77 M 3
Burlyu-Tobe 25 P 6
Burma 41 FG 3
Burmantovo 25 M 3
Burnett River 49 J 3–4
Burney 76 B 3
Burnham 6 C 2
Burnham-on-Crouch 7 E 2
Burnie 50 L 9
Burnley 5 D 3
Burnmouth 3 C 4
Burns 76 C 3
Burns Lake 73 M 5
Burnside 73 PQ 2
Burntisland 3 C 3
Burntwood 73 S 4
Burqān (Kuwait) 23 E 3
Burqin 35 M 1
Burra (Nigeria) 63 F 3
Burra (South Australia) 49 F 5
Burray 2 C 2
Burriana 18 C 4
Burruyacú 88 D 4
Burry Port 6 B 2
Bursa 20 C 2
Burtnieku ezers 17 J 4
Burton 5 D 2
Burton, Lac 75 M 5
Burton Latimer 7 D 1
Burton upon Trent 7 D 1
Burträsk 16 H 3
Buru, Pulau 43 G 4
Burūm 61 H 6
Burunday 35 K 2
Burundi 64 DE 5
Bururi 64 D 5
Burutu 63 F 4
Burwash 7 E 2
Burwell 7 E 1
Bury 5 D 3
Bury St. Edmunds 7 E 1
Burye 65 F 2
Busalla 19 E 3
Busanga (Zaire) 64 C 5
Busanga (Zaire) 66 D 2
Busanga Swamp (Zambia) 66 D 2
Buşayrah (Syria) 22 C 2
Büshehr 34 E 5
Büshehr (Iran) 23 F 3
Būshgãn (Iran) 23 F 3
Bushimaie 64 C 6
Bushman Land 66 B 5
Bushmills 4 B 2
Busia 64 E 4
Businga 64 C 4
Busira 64 B 5
Buskerud 17 E 3
Busko-Zdrój 15 H 4
Buskul' 25 M 5
Busse 37 N 5
Busselton 48 A 5
Bussol', Proliv 37 S 6
Bustakh, Ozero 37 Q 1
Busu Djanoa 64 C 4
Busu Gongo 64 C 4
Busu Melo 64 C 4
Busuanga 43 EF 1
Bususulu 64 C 4
Buta 64 C 4
Buta Ranquil 89 C 6
Butajira 65 F 3
Butang Group 41 G 6
Butare 64 DE 5

Butaritari 52 C 2
Bute 3 B 4
Butemba 64 E 4
Butembo 64 D 4
Butere 64 E 4
Butha Qi 37 M 6
Buthidaung 41 F 3
Butía 88 F 5
Butiaba 64 E 4
Butiama 64 E 5
Butkan 24 J 3
Butler 4 B 2
Butlers Bridge 4 B 2
Butt of Lewis 2 A 2
Butte 76 D 2
Butte de Vaudémont 19 E 2
Buttermere 5 E 2
Butterworth (Malaysia) 42 B 2
Butterworth (South Africa) 66 D 6
Button Bay 73 T 4
Button Islands 75 P 3
Butuan 43 G 2
Butung, Pulau 43 F 4
Buturlinovka 24 H 5
Butuy 36 K 5
Buwayrāt al Ḥasūn 59 J 2
Buxton 5 E 3
Buxton 77 L 4
Buy 24 H 4
Buyant-Ovoo 38 E 2
Buynaksk 34 D 2
Buyo 62 C 4
Buyr Nuur 36 L 6
Büyük Ağrı Dağı 21 F 3
Büyük Menderes 20 C 3
Buyunda 37 S 3
Buzachi, Poluostrov 34 E 1–2
Buzău 20 C 1
Buzău 20 C 1
Buzet 19 F 2
Būzhãn (Iran) 23 E 2
Buzi 67 F 3
Buzi 67 E 4
Buzluk Dağı 21 E 2
Buzuluk 24 K 5
Bwendi 64 D 4
Byblos (Lebanon) 22 B 2
Byczyna 15 G 4
Bydgoszcz 15 G 4
Byfleet 7 D 2
Bygdeå 16 H 3
Bygdeträsket 16 H 3
Bygdin 64 C 8
Byglandsfjord 17 E 4
Byglandsfjorden 17 E 4
Bykhov 24 F 5
Bykle 17 E 4
Bykov 37 Q 6
Bykovo 24 J 3
Bykovskiy 37 NO 1
Bykyldak 25 OP 6
Bylchau 6 C 1
Bylkyldak 25 OP 6
Bylot Island 90
Bynoe River (Queensland, Austr.)
  49 G 2
Byraya-Tas, Vozvyshennost'
  36 M 1
Byrd Station 91
Byrka 36 L 5
Byro 48 B 4
Byrock 49 H 5
Byron Bay 49 J 4
Byron, Cape 49 J 4
Byron, Isla 89 A 8
Byrranga, Gory 36 GH 1
Byserovo 24 K 4
Byske 16 H 3
Byskeälven 16 H 2
Bystraya 37 T 5
Bystrinskiy Golets, Gora 36 J 6
Bytantay 37 O 2
Bytča 15 G 5
Bytom 15 G 4
Bytów 15 G 4
Byuchennyakh 37 QR 3
Byxelkrok 17 G 4
Byzantium 49 H 4
Bzīmah 59 K 4
Bzybskiy Khrebet 21 F 2

C

Ca Na 41 J 5
Caacupé 88 E 4
Caaguazu 88 E 4
Caála 66 B 2
Caatinga (Minas Gerais, Brazil)
  87 G 4
Cáatingas 87 GH 2
Caazapa 88 E 4
Caballeria, Cabo de 18 D 3
Caballo Res. 76 E 5
Caballococha 84 D 4
Cabanatuan 43 J 1
Čabar 19 F 2
Cabeceiras 87 G 4

Cabedelo 87 K 2
Cabeza del Buey 18 BC 4
Cabezas 86 D 4
Cabildo (Argentina) 89 D 6
Cabildo (Chile) 88 B 5
Cabimas 84 D 1
Cabinda 63 G 7
Cabinda 63 G 7
Cabinet Mountains 76 C 2
Cabo Barbas 58 B 4
Cabo Blanco 89 C 8
Cabo Bojador 58 C 3
Cabo Camarón 78 EF 4
Cabo Cassiporé 85 H 3
Cabo Catoche 78 E 3
Cabo Choros 88 B 4
Cabo Corrientes (Argentina)
  89 E 6
Cabo Corrientes (Colombia) 84 C 2
Cabo Cruz 79 G 4
Cabo das Correntes 67 F 4
Cabo de Ajo 18 C 3
Cabo de Caballeria 18 D 3
Cabo de Cala Figuera 18 D 4
Cabo de Creus 18 D 3
Cabo de Finisterre 18 B 3
Cabo de Formentor 18 D 3–4
Cabo de Gata 18 C 4
Cabo de Hornos 89 C 10
Cabo de la Nao 18 D 4
Cabo de Palos 18 C 4
Cabo de Peñas 18 B 3
Cabo de Salinas 18 D 4
Cabo de San Francisco 84 B 3
Cabo de Santa Maria
  (Mozambique) 67 E 5
Cabo de Santa Maria (Portugal)
  18 B 4
Cabo de Santa Marta 66 A 2
Cabo de Santa Marta Grande
  88 G 4
Cabo de São Brás 66 A 1–2
Cabo de São Roque 87 J 2
Cabo de São Tomé 87 H 5
Cabo de São Vicente 18 B 4
Cabo de Sines 18 B 4
Cabo de Tortosa 18 D 3
Cabo Delgado 67 G 2
Cabo Deseado 89 AB 9
Cabo dos Bahías 89 CD 8
Cabo Engaño 79 J 4
Cabo Espichel 18 B 4
Cabo Francés 78 F 3
Cabo Freu 18 D 4
Cabo Frio 87 H 5
Cabo Frio 87 H 5
Cabo Gloucester 89 B 9
Cabo Gracias a Dios 78 F 4–5
Cabo Gurupi 85 J 3
Cabo Ledo 66 A 1
Cabo Maguarinho 85 J 4
Cabo Manglares 84 C 3
Cabo Marzo 84 C 2
Cabo Mondego 18 B 3
Cabo Norte 85 J 3
Cabo Orange 85 H 3
Cabo Ortegal 18 B 3
Cabo Pantoja 84 CD 4
Cabo Pasado 84 B 4
Cabo Polonio 88 F 5
Cabo Quedal 89 B 7
Cabo Quilán 89 AB 7
Cabo Raper 89 A 8
Cabo Raso 89 C 7
Cabo Rojo (Mexico) 78 C 3
Cabo Rojo (Puerto Rico) 79 J 4
Cabo San Antonio (Argentina)
  89 E 6
Cabo San Antonio (Cuba) 78 EF 3
Cabo San Diego 89 C 9
Cabo San Juan 63 F 5
Cabo San Lorenzo 84 B 4
Cabo San Lucas 76 E 7
Cabo San Rafael 79 J 4
Cabo Santa Elena 78 E 5
Cabo Touriñán 18 B 3
Cabo Trafalgar 18 B 4
Cabo Verde 62 AB 6
Cabo Vírgenes 89 C 9
Cabonga, Réservoir 75 M 6
Caboolture 49 J 4
Cabora Bassa 67 E 3
Cabora Bassa, Lago 67 E 3
Caborca 76 D 5
Cabot Strait 75 Q 6
Cabourg 18 CD 2
Cabras, Stagno di 19 E 4
Cabrera 18 D 4
Cabrera, Sierra de la 18 B 3
Cabriel 18 C 3–4
Cabrobó 87 J 2
Cabruta 84 E 2
Cabuyaro 84 D 3
Caçador 88 F 4

Čačak 20 B 2
Caçapava do Sul 88 F 5
Cacequi 88 EF 4
Cáceres (Brazil) 86 E 4
Cáceres (Colombia) 84 CD 2
Cáceres (Spain) 18 B 4
Cacharí 89 E 6
Cachi, Nevado de 86 C 5
Cachimbo 85 H 5
Cachimbo, Serra do 85 G 5
Cachinal 86 C 5
Cachingues 66 B 2
Cachoeira 87 J 3
Cachoeira Alta 87 F 4
Cachoeira Aquibi 87 E 3
Cachoeira Cantagalo 85 H 5
Cachoeira Capinzal 85 G 3
Cachoeira da Bateria 85 G 3
Cachoeira da Boca 85 GH 5
Cachoeira da Conceição 85 F 5
Cachoeira das Capoeiras 85 G 5
Cachoeira das Ilhas 85 G 4
Cachoeira das Sete Quedas 85 G 5
Cachoeira de Anta 85 F 5
Cachoeira de Paulo Afonso 87 J 2
Cachoeira do Buritizal 85 H 3
Cachoeira do Chacorão 85 G 5
Cachoeira do Infermo 85 G 4
Cachoeira do Pimenta 85 F 3
Cachoeira do Rafael 86 D 3
Cachoeira do Rebojo 85 G 5
Cachoeira do Sul 88 F 5
Cachoeira do Tereraimbu 85 H 5
Cachoeira dois de Novembro
  85 F 5
Cachoeira dos Índios 85 F 3
Cachoeira dos Patos 85 FG 5
Cachoeira Figueira 85 G 5
Cachoeira Grande 85 G 3
Cachoeira Maranhão 85 G 4
Cachoeira Pereira 85 G 4
Cachoeiro de Itapemirim 87 HJ 5
Cachos, Punta 88 B 4
Cacine 62 A 3
Cacolo 66 B 2
Caconda 66 B 2
Cacuaco 66 A 1
Cacula 66 A 2
Caculé 87 H 3
Caçumba, Ilha 87 J 4
Cacuso 66 B 1
Cadamstown 4 B 3
Cadaqués 18 D 3
Cadarga 49 J 4
Cadena del Pantiacolla 86 B 3
Cader Idris 6 C 1
Cadí, Sierra del 18 D 3
Cadillac 77 J 3
Cadiz (Philippines) 43 F 1
Cádiz (Spain) 18 B 4
Cádiz, Golfo de 18 B 4
Caen 18 C 2
Caerleon 6 C 2
Caernarfon 6 B 1
Caernarfon Bay 6 B 1
Caerphilly 6 C 2
Caesarea (Israel) 22 B 2
Caete 87 H 4
Caetite 87 H 3
Cagayan 43 J 1
Cagayan de Oro 43 F 2
Cagayan Islands 43 F 2
Cagayan Sulu 43 E 2
Cagliari 19 E 4
Cagnes 19 E 3
Cagua 84 E 1
Caguas 79 J 4
Caguén 84 D 3
Caha Mountains 14 B 4
Cahama 66 A 3
Cahersiveen 14 AB 4
Cahore Point 6 A 1
Cahore Point 14 B 4
Cahors 18 D 3
Cai Nuoc 41 HJ 6
Caia 67 F 3
Caiabis, Serra dos 86 E 3
Caianda 66 C 2
Caiapó, Serra do 87 F 4
Caiapônia 87 F 4
Caibarién 79 G 3
Caicara 84 E 2
Caico 87 J 2
Caicos Islands 79 H 3
Caicos Passage 79 H 3
Cailloma 86 B 4
Caiman Point 43 H 1
Cainde 66 A 3
Cairndow 3 B 3
Cairngorm Mountains 2 C 3
Cairnryan 3 B 4
Cairns 49 H 2
Cairo 60 E 2
Caister-on-Sea 7 E 1
Caistor 5 E 3
Caiundo 66 B 3

Cajamarca 84 C 5
Cajazeiras 87 J 2
Cajuapara 85 J 4
Caka 38 C 3
Çakırgöl Dağ 21 EF 2
Çakmak 21 D 3
Čakovec 19 G 2
Cakrani 20 A 2
Çal 20 C 3
Cala Figuera, Cabo de 18 D 4
Cala Ratjada 18 D 4
Calabar 63 F 4
Calabozo 84 E 2
Calabria 19 G 4
Calabro, Apennino 19 G 4
Calafat 20 B 2
Calafate 89 B 9
Calagua Islands 43 F 1
Calahorra 18 C 3
Calai 66 B 3
Calais 18 D 4
Calakmul 78 D 4
Calama 85 F 5
Calama (Chile) 86 C 5
Calamar 84 D 3
Calamarca 86 C 4
Calamian Group 43 E 1
Calamocha 18 C 3
Calanaque 85 F 4
Calanda 18 C 3
Calandula 66 B 1
Calang 42 A 3
Calapan 43 F 1
Călăraşi 20 C 2
Calatayud 18 C 3
Calatrava, Campo de 18 C 4
Calayan 43 J 1
Calbayog 43 FG 1
Calbuco 89 B 7
Calchaquí 88 D 4
Calçoene 85 H 3
Calcutta 40 E 3
Caldas 84 C 2
Caldas da Rainha 18 B 4
Caldbeck 5 D 2
Caldeirão, Serra de 18 B 4
Calder Bridge 5 C 2
Caldera 88 B 4
Calderina 18 C 4
Caldicot 6 C 2
Çaldıran 21 F 3
Çaldwell 76 C 3
Caldy Island 6 B 2
Caledon 4 B 2
Caledonia 77 H 3
Caledonian Canal 3 B 3
Caleta Buena 86 A 3
Caleta Clarencia 89 C 9
Caleta Olivia 89 C 8
Calf of Man 4 C 2
Calgary 3 A 3
Calgary 73 P 5
Cali 84 C 3
Caliente 76 D 4
California 76 BC 3–5
California Current 92
California, Golfo de 76 DE 5–7
Calilegua 86 CD 5
Calimere, Point 40 C 5
Calingasta 88 BC 5
Callabonna, Lake 49 F 4
Callac 18 C 2
Callafo 65 G 3
Callan 14 B 4
Callander 3 B 3
Callao 86 A 3
Callernish 2 A 2
Callytharra Springs 48 B 4
Calne 7 C 2
Calpe 18 D 4
Caltagirone 19 F 4
Caltanissetta 19 F 4
Calulo 66 B 2
Caluquembe 66 A 2
Calvi 19 E 3
Calvinia 66 BC 6
Cam Ranh 41 J 5
Cama 78 F 5
Camabatela 66 B 1
Camacá 87 J 4
Camacupa 66 B 2
Camaguán 84 E 2
Camagüey 79 G 3
Camagüey, Archipiélago de 79 G 3
Camaná 86 B 4
Camapuã 87 F 4
Camaquã 88 F 5
Camaquã 88 F 5
Camará 85 F 4
Camararé 86 E 3
Camarat, Cap 19 E 3
Camargo 86 C 5
Camariñas 18 B 3
Camarón, Cabo 78 EF 4

Camarones (Argentina) 89 C 7
Camarones (Chile) 86 B 4
Camas 18 B 4
Camatindi 86 D 5
Camaxilo 66 B 1
Cambados 18 B 3
Cambay → Khambhat 40 B 3
Camberley 7 D 2
Cambodia 41 HJ 5
Camboon 49 J 4
Camborne 6 B 2
Cambrai 18 D 1
Cambrian Mountains 6 C 1
Cambridge (Airport) 7 E 1
Cambridge (ID, U.S.A.) 76 C 3
Cambridge (Jamaica) 79 G 4
Cambridge (MA, U.S.A.) 77 M 3
Cambridge (MD, U.S.A.) 77 L 4
Cambridge (U.K.) 7 E 1
Cambridge Bay 73 QR 2
Cambridge Downs 49 G 3
Cambridge Gulf 48 D 1
Cambridgeshire 7 D 1
Cambuci 87 H 5
Cambulo 66 C 1
Cambundi-Catembo 66 B 2
Camden 77 H 5
Camden Bay 72 HJ 1
Cameia 66 C 2
Cameia National Park 66 C 2
Camelford 6 B 2
Camerino 19 F 3
Cameron 77 H 2
Cameron Hills 73 O 4
Cameroon 63 FG 4
Cameroon, Mont 63 F 5
Cametá 85 J 4
Camiguin 43 F 2
Camiguin 43 J 1
Camiña 86 C 4
Camiranga 85 J 4
Camiri 86 D 5
Camisea 86 B 3
Čamlıbel Gečidi 21 E 2
Cammarata 19 F 4
Camocim 87 H 1
Camoió 87 J 2
Camolin 6 A 1
Camoola 49 G 3
Camooweal (Queensland, Austr.)
   49 F 2
Camopi 85 H 3
Camorta 41 F 6
Camotes Sea 43 F 1
Camp Century 90
Camp Verde 76 D 5
Campana 88 E 5
Campana, Isla 89 A 8
Campanario 89 BC 6
Campas 87 GH 3–4
Campbell, Cape 51 Q 9
Campbell Island 91
Campbell Plateau 99 C 5
Campbell River 73 M 6
Campbellpore 35 J 4
Campbellton 75 O 6
Campbelltown (N.S.W., Austr.)
   49 J 5
Campbeltown (U.K.) 4 C 2
Campeche 78 D 4
Campeche 78 D 4
Campeche, Bahia de 78 D 4
Camperdown 49 G 6
Campidano 19 E 4
Campiglia Marittima 19 F 3
Campina Grande 87 J 2
Campina Verde 87 G 4
Campinas 87 G 5
Campo 63 F 5
Campo Belo 87 G 5
Campo Corral 84 D 2
Campo de Calatrava 18 C 4
Campo de Criptana 18 C 4
Campo de Diauaruru 87 F 3
Campo de Montiel 18 C 4
Campo Formoso 87 H 3
Campo Gallo 88 D 4
Campo Grande 87 F 5
Campo Maior 87 H 1
Campo Mourão 87 F 5
Campo Quijano 86 C 5
Campo Troso 84 E 3
Campobasso 19 FG 3
Campomarino 19 G 3
Campos 87 GH 3–4
Campos 87 H 5
Campos Novos 88 F 4
Campos Sales 87 HJ 2
Campsie Fells 4 C 1
Camrose 73 P 5
Camsell 73 O 3
Camsell Portage 73 PQ 4
Camucuio 66 A 2
Çan (Turkey) 20 C 3
Çan (Turkey) 21 F 3
Can Tho 41 J 6

Canacassala 66 A 1
Canada 72–75
Canada Basin 99 D 1
Cañada de Gómez 88 D 5
Cañada Oruro 86 D 5
Cañada Verde → Villa Huidobro
   88 D 5
Canadian 76 F 4
Canadian River 76 F 4
Canadian River North 76 G 4
Canaima 85 F 2
Canaima, Parque Nacional 85 F 2
Çanakkale 20 C 2
Çanakkale Boğazı 20 C 2–3
Canal Baker 89 B 8
Canal Beagle 89 C 9
Canal de Ballenas 76 D 6
Canal de Bourgogne 18–19 D 2
Canal de Briare 18 D 2
Canal de la Marne à la Saône
   19 E 2
Canal de la Mona 79 J 4
Canal de Sainte-Lucie 79 K 5
Canal de Yucatán 78 E 3
Canal des Ardennes 18–19 D 2
Canal des Ardennes 19 D 2
Canal do Norte 85 H 3
Canal do Sul 85 HJ 4
Canal du Midi 18 D 3
Canal Moraleda 89 B 7
Canale Cavour 19 E 2
Canale di Sicilia 19 F 4
Canale di Malta 19 F 4
Canalejas 89 C 6
Canama 84 D 5
Canamari 86 C 3
Cananea 76 DE 5
Cananéia 87 G 5
Cananguchal 84 C 3
Canapiari, Cerro 84 E 3
Cañaveral 18 B 4
Canaveral, Cape 77 KL 6
Canavieiras 87 J 4
Canberra 49 H 6
Canby 77 G 3
Canchas 88 B 4
Canchyuaya, Cerros de 84 D 5
Cancún 78 E 3
Candamom Hills 40 C 6
Çandarlı 20 C 3
Candeias 87 J 3
Candelaria 78 D 4
Çandili Tepe 21 E 3
Cando 76 G 2
Candoí 88 F 4
Canéla (Goiás, Brazil) 87 G 3
Canela (Río Grande do Sul, Brazil)
   88 F 4
Canelones 88 E 5
Cañete (Chile) 89 B 6
Cañete (Peru) 86 A 3
Cangamba 66 C 2
Cangandala 66 B 1
Canguçu 88 F 5
Cangumbe 66 B 2
Cangwu 38 F 6
Cangyuan 38 C 6
Cangzhou 39 G 3
Caniapiscau 75 N 5
Caniapiscau, Lac 75 O 5
Canicatti 19 F 4
Canık Dağları 21 E 2
Canindé (Amazonas, Brazil)
   84 D 5
Canindé (Ceará, Brazil) 87 J 1
Canipiscau 75 O 4
Çankırı 21 D 2
Cann River 49 H 6
Canna 3 A 3
Cannanore 40 BC 5
Cannes 19 E 3
Cannich 2 B 3
Canning Basin 48 C 2
Cannington 6 C 3
Cannock 7 C 1
Canoas 88 F 4
Canobie 49 G 2
Canon City 76 E 4
Canonbie 3 C 4
Canora 73 R 5
Canosa 19 G 3
Canso 75 P 6
Canso, Strait of 75 P 6
Canta 86 A 3
Cantabrian Mountains 18 BC 3
Cantagalo, Cachoeira 85 H 5
Cantaura 85 F 2
Canterbury 7 E 2

Canterbury Bight 51 Q 9
Canterbury Plains 51 Q 9
Cantilan 43 G 2
Canto do Buriti 87 H 2
Canton (China) 38 F 6
Canton (MS, U.S.A.) 77 HJ 5
Canton (OH, U.S.A.) 77 K 3
Cantù 19 E 2
Cantwell 72 H 3
Cañuelas 88 E 6
Canumã 85 G 4
Canumã (Amazonas, Brazil)
   85 FG 5
Canumã (Amazonas, Brazil)
   85 G 4
Canutama 85 F 5
Canvey 7 E 2
Canyon 76 F 4
Cao Bang 41 J 3
Cao Xian 38 G 4
Caombo 66 B 1
Caonguyen Dac Lac 41 J 5
Càorle 19 F 2
Cap Blanc (Mauritania) 58 B 4
Cap Blanc → Ra's al Abyad 59 G 1
Cap Bon → Ra's at Ţīb 59 H 1
Cap Bougar'oûn 59 G 1
Cap Camarat 19 E 3
Cap Corse 19 E 3
Cap Croisette 19 DE 3
Cap d'Ambre 67 H 2
Cap d'Antifer 18 CD 2
Cap d'Arguin 58 B 4
Cap de Fer 59 G 1
Cap de Gaspé 75 P 6
Cap de la Hague 18 C 2
Cap Drâa 58 C 3
Cap Est 67 J 3
Cap Ferret 18 C 3
Cap Fréhel 18 C 2
Cap Gris-Nez 18 D 1
Cap Hopes Advance 75 O 3
Cap Juby 58 C 3
Cap Lopez 63 F 6
Cap Masoala 67 J 3
Cap Prince de Galles 75 N 3
Cap Rhir 58 CD 2
Cap Roxo 62 A 3
Cap Saint-André 67 G 3
Cap Spartel 58 D 1
Cap Timiris 58 B 5
Cap Tres Forcas 58 E 1
Cap Verga 62 B 3
Cap Vert 62 A 3
Cap Vohimena 67 GH 5
Cap Wolstenholme 75 M 3
Capaccio 19 G 3
Capaia 66 C 1
Capanaparo 84 E 2
Capanema 85 J 4
Capão Bonito 87 G 5
Capatárida 84 D 1
Cap-de-la-Madeleine 75 N 6
Cap-de-Nouvelle France 75 N 3
Cape Abyssal Plain 98 B 5
Cape Acadia 75 M 3
Cape Adare 91
Cape Agulhas 66 C 6
Cape Alava 76 A 2
Cape Alitak 72 FG 4
Cape Anguille 75 PQ 6
Cape Ann 91
Cape Arid 48 C 5
Cape Arid National Park 48 C 5
Cape Arnhem 49 F 1
Cape Baring 73 O 2
Cape Barren Island 50 L 9
Cape Basin 98 B 5
Cape Bathurst 72 LM 1
Cape Bauld 75 QR 5
Cape Bear 75 P 6
Cape Beatrice 49 F 1
Cape Blanco 76 AB 3
Cape Boothby 91
Cape Bossut 48 C 2
Cape Bowling Green 49 H 2
Cape Breton Highlands National
   Park 75 P 6
Cape Breton Island 75 Q 6
Cape Brett 51 Q 8
Cape Byron 49 J 4
Cape Ca Mau 41 H 6
Cape Campbell 51 Q 9
Cape Canaveral 77 KL 6
Cape Capricorn 49 J 3
Cape Catastrophe 49 F 6
Cape Chapman 73 U 2
Cape Charles (Newfoundl., Can.)
   75 QR 5
Cape Charles (VA, U.S.A.) 77 L 4
Cape Chelyuskin 90
Cape Chidley 75 P 3
Cape Churchill 73 T 4
Cape Clear 14 B 4
Cape Coast 62 D 4

Cape Cod 77 N 3
Cape Cod Bay 77 MN 3
Cape Columbine 66 B 6
Cape Colville 73 T 2
Cape Comorin 40 C 6
Cape Constantine 72 EF 4
Cape Coral 77 K 6
Cape Cornwall 6 B 2
Cape Cretin 50 E 3
Cape Croker 48 E 1
Cape Cross 66 A 4
Cape Cuvier 48 A 3
Cape Dalhousie 72 L 1
Cape Darnley 91
Cape de la Hague 7 D 3
Cape Dennison 91
Cape Dominion 75 M 2
Cape Dorchester 75 M 2
Cape Dorset 75 MN 3
Cape du Couedic 49 F 6
Cape Dyer 75 P 2
Cape Egmont 51 Q 8
Cape Engaño 43 J 1
Cape Farewell 51 Q 9
Cape Farquhar 48 A 3
Cape Fear 77 L 5
Cape Felix 73 S 2
Cape Finniss 48 E 5
Cape Flattery (Queensland,
   Austr.) 49 H 1
Cape Flattery (WA, U.S.A.)
   76 AB 2
Cape Foulwind 51 Q 9
Cape Freels 75 R 6
Cape Fria 66 A 3
Cape Girardeau 77 J 4
Cape Grenville (Queensland,
   Austr.) 49 G 1
Cape Grim 50 K 9
Cape Guardafui 65 J 2
Cape Halkett 72 G 1
Cape Harrison 75 Q 5
Cape Hatteras 77 LM 4
Cape Henrietta Maria 75 L 4
Cape Herluf Trolle 75 T 3
Cape Hooper 75 O 2
Cape Hope 73 O 2
Cape Horn 89 C 10
Cape Howe 49 J 6
Cape Inscription 48 A 4
Cape Jaffa 49 F 6
Cape Jones 73 T 3
Cape Kattaktoc 75 O 4
Cape Keer-Weer (Queensland,
   Austr.) 49 G 1
Cape Kellett 73 M 1
Cape Kendall 73 U 3
Cape Kidnappers 51 R 8
Cape Knox 72 L 5
Cape Krusenstern National
   Monument 72 DE 2
Cape Lambert 51 F 2
Cape Lambton 73 MN 1
Cape Latouche Treville 48 C 2
Cape Leeuwin 48 A 5
Cape Lévêque 48 C 2
Cape Lisburne 72 D 2
Cape Lisburne 72 DE 2
Cape Londonderry 48 D 1
Cape Lookout 77 L 5
Cape Low 73 UV 3
Cape Maria van Diemen 51 Q 7
Cape Matapan 20 B 3
Cape May 77 M 4
Cape Melville (Queensland,
   Austr.) 49 G 1
Cape Mendocino 76 AB 3
Cape Mercy 75 P 3
Cape Meredith 89 D 9
Cape Michelsen 73 R 1
Cape Mohican 72 D 3
Cape Monze → Ras Muari 35 H 6
Cape Morris Jesup 90
Cape Naturaliste 48 A 5
Cape Negrais 41 F 4
Cape Nelson 49 G 6
Cape Nelson (Papua New Guinea)
   51 E 3
Cape Newenham 72 E 4
Cape North (Nova Scotia, Can.)
   75 P 6
Cape Norvegia 91
Cape of Good Hope 66 B 6
Cape Otway 49 G 6
Cape Palliser 51 R 9
Cape Palmas 62 C 5
Cape Parry 73 N 1
Cape Pembroke 89 E 9
Cape Pembroke (Ontario, Can.)
   75 L 3
Cape Poinsett 91
Cape Portland 50 L 9
Cape Prince Alfred 73 M 1
Cape Prince of Wales 72 D 2
Cape Providence 50 P 10
Cape Province 66 CD 6

Cape Queen 75 M 3
Cape Race 75 R 6
Cape Raper 75 O 2
Cape Ray 75 Q 6
Cape River 49 H 3
Cape Rodney (AK, U.S.A.) 72 D 3
Cape Rodney (Papua New Guinea) 50 E 4
Cape Romanzof 72 D 3
Cape Runaway 51 R 8
Cape Sable 75 O 7
Cape Sable (FL, U.S.A.) 77 K 6
Cape Saint Francis 66 CD 6
Cape Saint George 75 PQ 6
Cape Saint George (Papua New Guinea) 51 F 2
Cape Saint James 72 L 5
Cape Saint Lucia 67 E 5
Cape San Agustin 43 G 2
Cape San Blas 77 J 6
Cape Scott 48 D 1
Cape Scott 72 M 5
Cape Smith 75 M 3
Cape Southampton 73 UV 3
Cape Spencer 49 F 6
Cape Swinburne 73 RS 1
Cape Tatnam 73 TU 4
Cape Three Points 62 D 5
Cape Town 66 B 6
Cape Van Diemen 48 D 1
Cape Verde 62 AB 6
Cape Verde (Senegal) 58 B 6
Cape Walsingham 75 P 2
Cape Wessel 49 F 1
Cape Wickham 50 K 8
Cape Wilson 73 VW 2
Cape Wrath 2 B 2
Cape Wrottesley 73 N 1
Cape Yakataga 72 J 4
Cape York 49 G 1
Cape York Peninsula (Queensland, Austr.) 49 G 1
Cape Zhelaniya 90
Capel 7 D 2
Capelinha 87 H 4
Capello 50 D 2
Cap-Haïtien 79 H 4
Capibara 84 E 3
Capilla 88 E 5
Capim 85 J 4
Capim 85 J 4
Capinota 86 C 4
Capinzal, Cachoeira 85 G 5
Capitán Arturo Prat 91
Capitan Bado 86 E 5
Capitán Meza 88 E 4
Capivara, Reprêsa da 87 F 5
Capo Bonifati 19 G 4
Capo Carbonara 19 E 4
Capo Circeo 19 F 3
Capo delle Colonne 19 G 4
Capo di Pula 19 E 4
Capo Gallo 19 F 4
Capo Linaro 19 F 3
Capo Mannu 19 E 3
Capo Marargiu 19 E 3
Capo Murro di Porco 19 G 4
Capo Palinuro 19 FG 3
Capo Passero 19 G 4
Capo Punta Granitola 19 F 4
Capo San Marco 19 E 4
Capo Santa Maria di Leuca 19 G 4
Capo Scaramia 19 F 4
Capo Sferracavallo 19 E 4
Capo Spartivento 19 E 4
Capo Testa 19 E 3
Capo Vaticano 19 G 4
Capoeiras, Cachoeira das 85 G 5
Capoompeta 49 J 4
Cappercleuch 3 C 4
Capraia 19 E 3
Capreol 75 L 6
Capri 19 F 3
Capricorn, Cape 49 J 3
Capricorn Channel 49 J 3
Capricorn Group 49 J 3
Caprivi Game Park 66 C 3
Caprivi Strip 66 C 3
Captains Flat 49 H 6
Captieux 18 C 3
Capunda 66 B 2
Caquetá 84 D 4
Car Nicobar 41 F 6
Carabaya, Cordillera de 86 B 3
Caracal 20 B 2
Caracaraí 85 F 3
Caracas 84 E 1
Caracol 87 H 2
Caraga 43 G 2
Carahue 89 B 6
Carajari 85 H 4
Carajás, Serra dos 85 H 4–5
Caramulo, Serra do 18 B 3
Caranapatuba 85 F 5
Carandotta 49 F 3
Carangola 87 H 5

Caransbeş 20 B 1
Carantuohill 14 AB 4
Carapajó 85 J 4
Caraquet 75 P 6
Caratasca, Laguna de 78 F 4
Caratinga 87 H 4
Carauari 84 E 4
Caravaca 18 C 4
Caravelas 87 J 4
Caraveli 86 B 4
Caraz 84 C 5
Carazinho 88 F 4
Carballo 18 B 3
Carbonara, Capo 19 E 4
Carboneras 18 C 4
Carbonia 19 E 4
Carbost 2 A 3
Carbury 4 B 3
Carcajou 73 O 4
Carcans-Plage 18 C 2
Carcar Mountains → Karkār 65 H 3
Carcaraña 88 D 5
Carcassonne 18 D 3
Carcross 72 K 3
Cárdenas (Cuba) 79 F 3
Cárdenas (Mexico) 78 C 3
Cardiel, Lago 89 B 8
Cardiff 6 C 2
Cardiff (Airport) 6 C 2
Cardigan 6 B 1
Cardigan Bay 6 B 1
Cardona 18 D 3
Cardozo 88 E 5
Cardston 73 P 6
Carei 20 B 1
Careiro 85 G 4
Carentan 18 C 2
Carey 76 D 3
Carey, Lake 48 C 4
Cargèse 19 E 3
Carhaix-Plouguer 18 C 2
Carhué 89 D 6
Cariati 19 G 4
Caribbean Sea 79 GJ 4
Caribou 77 N 2
Caribou Lake, North 74 J 5
Caribou Mountains (Alb., Can.) 73 O 4
Caribou Mountains (Br. Col., Can.) 73 N 5
Carimbula 66 BC 1
Cariñena 18 C 3
Carinhanha 87 H 3
Carinish 2 A 3
Cariparé 87 G 3
Caripito 85 F 1
Caritianas 85 F 5
Carius 87 J 2
Carleton Place 75 M 6
Carletonville 66 D 5
Carlingford 4 B 2
Carlingford Lough 4 B 2
Carlisle 5 D 2
Carloforte 19 E 4
Carlos Casares 89 D 6
Carlos Chagas 87 H 4
Carlow 4 B 3
Carloway 2 A 2
Carlsbad (CA, U.S.A.) 76 C 5
Carlsbad (N.M., U.S.A.) 76 F 5
Carlsberg Ridge 98 B 3
Carlton 7 D 1
Carlton Hill 48 D 2
Carlyle 73 R 6
Carmacks 72 K 3
Carmagnola 19 E 2
Carmarthen 6 B 2
Carmarthen Bay 6 B 2
Carmaux 18 D 3
Carmel 76 B 4
Çarmeli 20 C 3
Carmelo 88 E 5
Carmen 88 E 4
Carmen Alto 86 BC 5
Carmen de Patagones 89 D 7
Carmen, Isla 76 D 6
Carmensa 89 C 6
Carmi 77 J 4
Carmila 49 H 3
Carmona 18 B 4
Carmyllie 3 D 3
Carnac 18 C 2
Carnamah 48 B 4
Carnamore 4 B 2
Carnaross 4 B 3
Carnarvon 48 A 3
Carnarvon 66 C 6
Carnarvon Range 48 C 4
Carnbee 3 C 3
Carncastle 4 C 2
Carndonagh 4 B 2
Carnegie 48 C 4
Carnegie, Lake 48 C 4
Carnew 4 B 3
Carnforth 5 D 2

Carniche, Alpi 19 F 2
Carnlough 4 C 2
Carno 6 C 1
Carnot 64 B 3
Carnoustie 3 C 3
Carnsore Point 6 A 1
Carnwath 3 C 4
Carolina 85 J 5
Carolina (Ecuador) 84 C 3
Carolina Beach 77 L 5
Caroline (Kiribati) 53 EF 3
Caroline Basin 99 C 3
Caroline Islands 52 AB 2
Carondelet 52 D 3
Caroní 85 F 2
Carora 84 DE 1
Carpathians 20 BC 1
Carpaţii Meridionali 20 B 1–2
Carpentaria, Gulf of 49 F 1
Carpentras 19 E 3
Carpi 19 F 3
Carpina 87 J 2
Carrara 19 E 3
Carrazedo 85 H 4
Carrbridge 2 C 3
Carrera 86 E 5
Carreta, Punta 86 A 3
Carrick 4 C 2
Carrickart 4 B 2
Carrickboy 4 B 3
Carrickfergus 4 C 2
Carrickmacross 4 B 3
Carrick-on-Shannon 4 AB 3
Carrillo 78 B 2
Carrión de los Condes 18 C 3
Carrizal (Colombia) 84 D 1
Carrizal (Mexico) 76 E 5
Carrizal Bajo 88 B 4
Carrizo Springs 76 G 6
Carrizos 76 E 5
Carrizozo 76 E 5
Carroll 77 H 3
Carrollton 77 J 5
Carron, Loch 2 B 3
Carronbridge 3 C 4
Carrowkeel 4 B 2
Carryduff 4 C 2
Carsaig 3 B 3
Çarşamba 21 D 3
Çarşamba 21 E 2
Carson 76 B 2
Carson City 76 C 4
Carsphairn 3 B 4
Cartagena (Colombia) 84 C 1
Cartagena (Spain) 18 C 4
Cartago 84 C 3
Cartago (Costa Rica) 78 F 6
Carter, Mount (Queensland, Austr.) 49 G 1
Carthage (MO, U.S.A.) 77 H 4
Carthage (Tunisia) 19 F 4
Carthage (Tunisia) 59 H 1
Carthago (IL, U.S.A.) 77 H 3
Cartier Island 48 C 1
Cartmel 5 D 2
Cartwright 75 Q 5
Caruaru 87 J 2
Carúpano 85 F 1
Carutapera 85 J 4
Carvoeiro 85 F 4
Casa Branca 87 G 5
Casa Grande 76 D 5
Casa Nova 87 H 2
Casablanca 58 D 2
Casablanca (Chile) 88 B 5
Casal Velino 19 G 3
Casalbordino 19 F 3
Casale Monferrato 19 E 2
Casalmaggiore 19 F 3
Casalvasco 86 E 4
Casamance 62 A 3
Casanare 84 D 2
Casaux, Étang de 18 C 3
Casbas 89 D 6
Cascade 76 C 3
Cascade Range 76 B 2–3
Cascadia Basin 99 D 2
Cascavel 87 F 5
Cascina 19 F 3
Caserta 19 F 3
Casey 91
Casiguran 43 F 1
Casiguran 43 J 1
Casilda 88 D 5
Casino 49 J 4
Cáslav 15 G 5
Casma 84 C 5
Casper 76 E 3
Caspian Depression 34 DE 1
Caspian Sea 34 DE 2–3
Caspian Sea (Iran) 23 F 1
Cassai 66 C 2
Cassai Sul 66 C 2
Cassamba 66 C 2
Cassiar 72 L 4
Cassiar Mountains 72 M 4

Cassilândia 87 F 4
Cassinga 66 B 3
Cassino 88 F 5
Cassino (Italy) 19 F 3
Cassiporé, Cabo 85 H 3
Cassongue 66 A 2
Castañar, Sierra del 18 C 4
Castanhal 85 J 4
Castanho 85 F 5
Castaño 88 C 5
Castel di Sangro 19 F 3
Castelarrasin 18 D 3
Castellabate 19 F 3
Castellammare, Golfo di 19 F 4
Castellane 19 E 3
Castellaneta 19 G 3
Castelli 89 E 6
Castelló 18 D 4
Castellón 18 D 4
Castelnau-de-Médoc 18 C 2
Castelnaudary 18 D 3
Castelo Branco 18 B 4
Castelo de Vide 18 B 4
Castelvetrano 19 F 4
Castets 18 C 3
Castiglione 19 F 3
Castilla (Chile) 88 B 4
Castilla (Peru) 84 B 5
Castilla la Nueva 18 C 3–4
Castilla la Vieja 18 C 3
Castillejo 18 B 3
Castillo, Cerro 89 B 8
Castillo Incasico de Ingapirca 84 C 4
Castillo, Pampa del 89 C 8
Castillonnes 18 D 3
Castillos 88 F 5
Castle Cary 6 C 2
Castle Douglas 4 D 2
Castlebar 14 B 4
Castlebay 3 A 3
Castlebellingham 4 B 3
Castleblayney 4 B 2
Castlebridge 6 A 1
Castlecomer 4 B 3
Castledawson 4 B 2
Castlederg 4 B 2
Castledermot 4 B 3
Castleellis 6 A 1
Castlefinn 4 B 2
Castleford 5 E 3
Castlegar 73 O 6
Castlemaine 49 G 6
Castlemartin 6 B 2
Castlereagh Bay 48 F 1
Castlereagh River 49 H 5
Castlerigg 5 D 2
Castleside 5 E 2
Castletown 2 C 2
Castletown 4 B 3
Castletown 4 B 3
Castletown 4 C 2
Castlewellan 4 BC 2
Castor 73 P 5
Castres 18 D 3
Castries (Saint Lucia) 79 K 5
Castro (Chile) 89 B 7
Castro (Paraná, Brazil) 87 G 5
Castro Daire 18 B 3
Castro del Río 18 C 4
Castro Verde 18 B 4
Castro-Urdiales 18 C 3
Castrovillari 19 G 4
Castuera 18 B 4
Casuarina, Mount 48 D 1
Casula 67 E 3
Çat 21 F 3
Cat Island 79 GH 3
Cat Lake 74 J 5
Catabola 66 B 2
Catacaos 84 B 5
Cataguases 87 H 5
Çatak 21 F 3
Catalão 87 G 4
Catalina, Punta 89 C 9
Catalonia 18 D 3
Çatalzeytin 21 D 2
Catamarca 88 C 4
Catamayo 84 BC 4
Catanduanes 43 F 1
Catanduva 87 G 5
Catania 19 G 4
Catanzaro 19 G 4
Cataratas del Iguazú 88 F 4
Catastrophe, Cape 49 F 6
Catauera 85 G 4
Catbalogan 43 FG 1
Catende 87 J 2
Caterham 7 D 2
Catete 66 A 1
Catherine, Mount 76 D 4
Catinzaco 88 C 4
Catió 62 A 3
Catisimiña 85 F 3
Catlodge 3 B 3

Cato Island and Bank 49 K 3
Catoche, Cabo 78 E 3
Catora 86 D 4
Catriló 89 D 6
Catrimani 85 F 3
Catrimani 85 F 3
Catterick 5 E 2
Catterline 3 D 3
Catuane 67 E 5
Catuile 66 C 3
Catuna 88 C 5
Catur 67 F 2
Cauaburi 84 E 3
Cauca 84 C 2
Caucasia 84 CD 2
Caucasus Mountains 21 F 2
Caudry 18 D 1
Caulonia 19 G 4
Caungula 66 B 1
Cauquenes 89 B 6
Caura 85 F 2
Causapscal 75 O 6
Caussade 18 D 3
Causse de Gramat 18 D 3
Causse de Limogne 18 D 3
Causse du Larzac 18 D 3
Cautário 86 D 3
Cauvery 40 C 5
Cavaillon 19 D 3
Cavalcante 87 G 3
Cavally 62 C 4
Cavan 4 B 3
Cavan 4 B 3
Cavarzere 19 F 2
Çavdarhisar 20 C 3
Cavell 74 K 5
Caviana, 85 HJ 3
Cavignac 18 C 2
Cavili 43 F 2
Cavour, Canale 19 E 2
Cavtat 19 G 3
Çavuşcu Gölü 21 D 3
Çavuşçu Gölü 21 D 3
Cawell 74 K 5
Çay 20 D 3
Cay Sal 79 F 3
Cayambe 84 C 3
Cayambe 84 C 3
Çaycuma 21 D 2
Çayeli 21 F 2
Cayenne 85 H 3
Çayıralan 21 E 3
Çayırhan 20 D 2
Cayman Brac 79 G 4
Cayman Islands 79 FG 4
Cayo Arenas 78 D 3
Cayo Nuevo 78 D 3
Cayos Arcas 78 D 3
Cayos de Albuquerque 79 F 5
Cayos de Roncador 79 G 5
Cayos Miskitos 78 F 5
Caythorpe 7 D 1
Cazombo 66 C 2
Cazongo 63 G 7
Ceanannus Mor 4 B 3
Ceará 87 J 1
Ceara Abyssal Plain 98 A 3
Ceará Mirim 87 J 2
Ceballos 78 B 2
Cebollar 88 C 4
Cebollatí 88 F 5
Cebu 43 F 1
Cebu 43 F 2
Čechy 15 F 4
Cecina 19 F 3
Cedar City 76 D 4
Cedar Creek Reservoir 77 G 5
Cedar Falls 77 H 3
Cedar Key 77 K 6
Cedar Lake 73 RS 5
Cedar Rapids 77 H 3
Cedar River 77 H 3
Cedros, Isla 76 C 6
Ceduna 48 E 5
Cefalù 19 F 4
Cefn-Mawr 6 C 1
Cegléd 20 A 1
Cejal 84 E 3
Čekerek 21 E 2–3
Çekerek 21 E 2
Çelaya 78 B 3
Celebes 43 EF 4
Celebes Sea 43 F 3
Çelebi 21 D 3
Celestún 78 D 3
Çelikhan 21 E 3
Celje 19 G 2
Celle 15 F 4
Celorico da Beira 18 B 3
Celtic Sea 14 B 4
Celtic Shelf 98 A 2
Çeltikçi Geçidi 20 D 3
Çemişgezek 21 E 3

Cemmaes 6 C 1
Cenajo, Embalse de 18 C 4
Cencia 65 F 3
Cendrawasih 43 H 4
Cendrawasih, Teluk 43 HJ 4
Centenario 89 C 6
Center 77 H 5
Centerville 77 H 3
Cento 19 F 3
Central 3 B 3
Central African Republic 64 BC 3
Central America 92
Central Arctic District 73 QR 1
Central Brahui Range 35 H 5
Central, Cordillera (Colombia) 84 C 2–3
Central, Cordillera (Peru) 84 C 5
Central Kalahari Game Reserve 66 C 4
Central Makran Range 35 GH 5
Central Pacific Basin 99 D 3
Central Range (Papua New Guinea) 50 D 2–3
Central Siberian Plateau 36 GK 3
Centralia 76 B 2
Centreville 77 H 5
Čepin 19 G 2
Cepu 42 D 5
Ceram 43 G 4
Cercal 18 B 4
Cereal 73 P 5
Ceremai, Gunung 42 C 5
Ceres (Brazil) 87 G 4
Ceres (South Africa) 66 B 6
Cereté 84 C 2
Cerf 65 J 6
Cerignola 19 G 3
Çerkeş 21 D 2
Čermenika 20 B 2
Cernavoda 20 C 2
Cerne Abbas 6 C 3
Černi vrukh 20 B 2
Cerra Viejo 76 D 5
Cerralvo, Isla 76 E 7
Cerritos 78 BC 3
Cerro Aconcagua 88 BC 5
Cerro Agua Caliente 78 A 2
Cerro Aguja 89 B 7
Cerro Aiguilete 89 B 9
Cerro Ángel 78 B 3
Cerro Arenales 89 B 8
Cerro Atalaya (Chile) 89 B 9
Cerro Atalaya (Peru) 86 B 3
Cerro Azul 78 C 4
Cerro Blanco 76 E 6
Cerro Bolívar 85 F 2
Cerro Bonete 88 C 4
Cerro Bravo 84 C 5
Cerro Canapiari 84 E 3
Cerro Candelaria 78 B 3
Cerro Castillo 89 B 8
Cerro Champaquí 88 D 5
Cerro Chato 89 B 7
Cerro Chirripó 78 F 6
Cerro Chochis 86 E 4
Cerro Cibuta 76 D 5
Cerro Coan 84 C 5
Cerro Coatepetl 78 C 4
Cerro Cojudo Blanco 89 C 8
Cerro Colorado 76 C 5
Cerro Colorado 89 C 7
Cerro Cónico 89 B 7
Cerro de la Asunción 78 C 3
Cerro de la Encantada 76 CD 5
Cerro de las Mesas 78 CD 4
Cerro de Pasco 86 A 3
Cerro de Punta 79 J 4
Cerro de San Felipe 18 C 3
Cerro de Tocorpuri 86 C 5
Cerro Dedo 89 B 7
Cerro del Tigre 78 BC 3
Cerro del Toro 88 C 4
Cerro Desmoronado 78 AB 3
Cerro el Cóndor 88 C 4
Cerro el Nevado 84 D 3
Cerro el Potro 88 C 4
Cerro Galán 88 C 4
Cerro Grande 78 B 3
Cerro Guaiquinima 85 F 2
Cerro Hudson 89 B 8
Cerro La Ardilla 78 B 3
Cerro Largo 88 EF 4
Cerro Las Casitas 76 E 7
Cerro Las Minas 78 E 5
Cerro Lechiguiri 78 C 4
Cerro Lejia 86 C 5
Cerro León 86 D 5
Cerro Marahuaca 84 E 3
Cerro Mariquita 78 C 3
Cerro Mato 84 E 2
Cerro Mercedario 88 BC 5
Cerro Mesa 89 B 8
Cerro Mohinora 76 E 6
Cerro Morado 86 CD 5
Cerro Morado 86 CD 5
Cerro Moreno 86 B 5

Cerro Munchique 84 C 3
Cerro Murallón 89 B 8
Cerro Negro 89 C 7
Cerro Nevado 89 C 6
Cerro Nuevo Mundo 86 C 5
Cerro O'Higgins 89 B 8
Cerro Ojos del Salado 88 C 4
Cerro Paine Medio 89 B 9
Cerro Payún 89 C 6
Cerro Peña Nevada 78 C 3
Cerro Piedra 89 B 6
Cerro Potosí 78 B 2–3
Cerro San Lorenzo 89 B 8
Cerro San Valentín 89 B 8
Cerro Santiago 79 F 6
Cerro Santiago 88 B 2
Cerro Tetari 84 D 2
Cerro Toroni 86 C 4
Cerro Tres Cruces 78 D 4
Cerro Tres Picos 89 D 6
Cerro Tunari 86 C 4
Cerro Veijo 84 C 4
Cerro Ventana 76 E 7
Cerro Yavi 84 E 2
Cerro Yucuyácua 78 C 4
Cerro Yumari 84 E 3
Cerros de Araracuara 84 D 3–4
Cerros de Canchuaya 84 D 5
Cerros de la Brea 84 B 4
Cervera 18 D 3
Cervia 19 F 3
Cesano 19 F 3
Cesena 19 F 3
Cēsis 17 J 4
Česká Lípa 15 F 4
Česká Třebova 15 G 5
České Budějovice 15 F 5
Českézemě 15 FG 5
Český les 15 F 5
Çeşme 20 C 3
Cess 62 C 4
Cessford 71
Cessnock 49 J 5
Cetina 19 G 3
Cetinje 20 A 2
Çetinkaya 21 E 3
Cetraro 19 G 4
Cetteville 77 G 4
Ceuta 58 D 1
Ceva-i-Ra 52 C 4
Cévennes 18 D 3
Ceyhan 21 E 3
Ceyhan 21 E 3
Ceyhan (Turkey) 22 B 1
Ceylânpınar (Turkey) 22 C 1
Ceylon 40 D 6
Cézallier 18 D 2
Chabas 88 D 5
Chăboksar (Iran) 23 F 1
Chaca 86 B 4
Chacabuco 88 D 5
Chacance 86 BC 5
Chachani, Nevado 86 B 4
Chachapoyas 84 C 5
Chachoengsao 41 H 5
Chachro 35 J 5
Chaco Austral 88 D 4
Chaco Boreal 86 D 5
Chaco Central 86 DE 6
Chaco, Parque Nacional de 88 E 4
Chacorão, Cachoeira do 85 G 5
Chad 63 H 3
Chad 63 HJ 3
Chad, Lake 63 G 3
Chadan 36 F 5
Chădegăn (Iran) 23 F 2
Chadileuvú 89 C 6
Chadiza 67 E 2
Chadobets 36 G 4
Chadobets 36 GH 4
Chadron 76 F 3
Chagai 35 G 5
Chagai Hills 35 G 5
Chagda 37 O 4
Chagdo Kangri 40 D 1
Chagford 6 C 3
Chaghcharăn 35 H 4
Chagny 19 D 2
Chagodoshcha 24 G 4
Chagos Archipelago 28 F 7
Chaguaramas 84 E 2
Chagyl 34 F 2
Chah Bahār 35 G 5
Chahah Burjak 35 G 4
Chai Badan 41 H 5
Chai Buri 41 H 4
Chaibassa 40 E 3
Chaillu, Massif du 63 G 6
Chainat 41 GH 4
Chaîne de l'Atakora 62 E 3
Ch'aio-ko-li Feng 35 K 3
Chaiyaphum 41 H 4
Chajari 88 E 5
Chak Chak 64 D 3
Chakari 66 D 3
Chake Chake 65 FG 6

Chakhansur 35 G 4
Chakva 21 F 2
Chakwal 35 J 4
Chala 86 B 4
Chalabesa 67 E 2
Chalalais 2 A 2
Chalbi Desert 65 F 4
Chălesban (Iran) 23 E 2
Chaleur Bay 75 OP 6
Chalhuanca 86 B 3
Chalía 89 B 8
Chaling 38 F 5
Chalisgaon 40 C 3
Challapata 86 C 4
Challenger Deep 99 C 3
Challis 76 D 3
Chalna 40 E 3
Châlons-sur-Marne 19 D 2
Chalon-sur-Saône 19 DE 2
Chaltyr' 21 E 1
Chălūs (Iran) 23 F 1
Cham 15 F 5
Chama 67 E 2
Chamais 66 B 5
Chaman 35 H 4
Chamaya 84 C 5
Chamba (India) 40 C 1
Chamba (Tanzania) 67 F 2
Chambal 40 C 2
Chamberlain River 48 D 2
Chambéry 19 E 2
Chambeshi 67 E 2
Chambishi 66 D 2
Chamchamăl (Iraq) 23 D 2
Chamela 78 B 4
Chamiapatna 40 C 5
Chamical 88 C 5
Chamo, Lake 65 F 3
Chamoli 40 C 1
Chamonix 19 E 2
Chamouchouane 75 N 6
Champa 40 D 3
Champagne 19 DE 2
Champagne 19 DE 2
Champanha 85 G 5
Champaquí, Cerro 88 D 5
Champdoré, Lac 75 O 4
Champlain, Lake 77 M 3
Champotón 78 D 4
Chamrajnagar 40 C 5
Chamutete 66 B 3
Chan Chan 84 C 5
Chañaral 88 B 4
Chanc Changmar 40 C 1
Chanchur 36 J 5
Chanco 89 B 6
Chandalar 72 H 2
Chandalar 72 H 2
Chandarnagar 40 E 3
Chandausi 40 C 2
Chandeleur Islands 77 J 6
Chanderi 40 C 3
Chandler 75 P 6
Chandmani 38 C 1
Chandpur 41 F 3
Chandrakona 40 E 3
Chandrapur 40 C 4
Chanf 35 G 5
Chang Jiang 39 G 4
Changane 67 E 4
Changara 67 E 3
Changbai Shan 39 J 2
Changcheng [Chinese Wall] 38 E 3
Changchun 39 J 2
Changdao 39 H 3
Changde 38 F 5
Changfeng 39 G 4
Changhua 39 GH 6
Changji 35 M 2
Changjiang 38 E 7
Changjin 39 J 2
Changli 39 G 3
Changling 39 H 2
Changlung 35 K 4
Changning 38 CD 6
Changsha 38 F 5
Changshan 39 G 5
Changshu 39 H 4
Changshun 38 E 5
Changting 38 G 5
Changtu 39 H 2
Changwu 38 E 3
Changzhi 38 F 3
Changzhou 39 G 4
Channel Islands (U.K.) 7 C 3
Channel Islands (U.K.) 14 C 5
Channel Islands (U.S.A.) 76 C 5
Channel Port aux Basques 75 Q 6
Channing 76 F 4
Chantada 18 B 3
Chanthaburi 41 H 5
Chantilly 18 D 2
Chantrey Inlet 73 S 2
Chany 25 P 4
Chany, Ozero 25 P 5

Chao Hu 39 G 4
Chao, Isla 84 C 5
Chao Xian 39 G 4
Chao'an 38 G 6
Chaor He 39 H 1
Chaoyang 38 G 6
Chaoyang 39 GH 2
Chaoyangcun 37 MN 5
Chaozhong 37 M 5
Chapa 37 N 4
Chapa Tong 41 F 3
Chapada das Mangabeiras 87 G 2–3
Chapada Diamantina 87 H 3
Chapada dos Veadeiros, Parque Nacional do 87 G 3
Chapadão dos Gerais 87 G 4
Chapadinha 87 H 1
Chapala 78 B 3
Chapala, Lago de 78 B 3
Chapanda 37 O 4
Chaparral 84 C 3
Chapayevo 24 K 5
Chapayevsk 24 J 5
Chapayev-Zheday 36 L 3
Chapchachi 24 J 6
Chapelton 3 B 4
Chapiquy 88 E 5
Chapleau 74 L 6
Chaplinka 21 D 1
Chaplygin 24 GH 5
Chapman, Cape 73 U 2
Chapoma 24 GH 2
Chapra 40 DE 2
Chaqui 86 C 4
Char 58 C 4
Chara 36 L 4
Chara 36 L 4
Chara 36 L 4
Charagua 86 D 4
Charaña 86 C 4
Charcas 78 B 3
Charcot Island 91
Chard 73 P 4
Chard (U.K.) 6 C 2
Chărdagh (Iran) 23 E 1
Chardara 35 H 2
Chardăvol (Iran) 23 E 2
Chardzhou 35 G 3
Charente 18 C 2
Chari 40 C 1
Charikar 35 H 3
Charing 7 E 2
Charity 85 G 2
Charkabozh 24 K 2
Charkayuvom 24 KL 2
Charleroi 14 DE 4
Charles 75 N 3
Charles, Cape (Newfoundl., Can.) 75 QR 5
Charles City 77 H 3
Charles Louis, Pegunungan 43 J 4
Charles Peak 48 C 5
Charlesbourg 75 N 6
Charleston (S.C., U.S.A.) 77 L 5
Charleston (W.V., U.S.A.) 77 K 4
Charleville 49 H 4
Charleville-Mézières 19 DE 2
Charlotte 77 KL 4
Charlotte Amalie 79 K 4
Charlotte Harbor 77 K 6
Charlottenberg 17 F 4
Charlottesville 77 L 4
Charlottetown 75 P 6
Charlton 7 C 2
Charlton 49 G 6
Charlton 75 LM 5
Charlwelton 7 D 1
Charmes 19 E 2
Charouïne 58 E 3
Charsadda 35 J 4
Charshanga 35 H 3
Charsk 25 Q 6
Charters Towers 49 H 3
Chartres 18 D 2
Chartreuse, Grande 19 E 2
Chăru, Bandar-e (Iran) 23 FG 4
Charyn 35 K 2
Charysh 25 Q 5
Charyshskoye 25 Q 5
Chascomus 88 E 6
Chasel'ka 25 Q 2
Chashniki 17 J 5
Chasico 89 C 7
Chasma Barrage 35 J 4
Chasnachorr, Gora 16 K 2
Chasŏng 39 J 2
Chasovnya Uchurskaya 37 O 4
Chăt 34 F 3
Chatal Balkan 20 C 2
Chatanga 36 K 5
Châteaubriant 18 C 2
Château-Chinon 18 D 2
Château-du-Loir 18 D 2

Châteaudun 18 D 2
Châteaulin 18 C 2
Châteauneuf-sur-Loire 18 D 2
Châteauroux 18 D 2
Chateau-Salins 19 E 2
Château-Thierry 18 D 2
Chateaux-Arnoux 19 E 3
Châtellerault 18 D 2
Chatham (New Brunswick, Can.) 75 O 6
Chatham (New Zealand) 51 S 9
Chatham (Ontario, Can.) 77 K 3
Chatham (U.K.) 7 E 2
Chatham Islands 51 S 9
Chatham Strait 72 L 4
Châtillon-sur-Seine 19 D 2
Chatkal 35 J 2
Chato, Cerro 89 B 7
Chatra 40 D 3
Chatrapur 40 E 4
Chattahoochee 77 JK 5
Chattahoochee River 77 JK 5
Chattanooga 77 J 5
Chatteris 7 E 1
Chatyrkel', Ozero 35 JK 2
Chau Phu 41 J 5
Chauchaiñeu, Sierra 89 C 7
Chauk 41 F 3
Chaullay 86 B 3
Chaumont 19 DE 2
Chaunskaya Guba 37 VW 2
Chauny 18 D 2
Chaura 41 F 6
Chaves 85 HJ 4
Chaves (Portugal) 18 B 3
Chávica 84 D 3
Chavuma 66 C 2
Chayatyn, Khrebet 37 P 5
Chaydakh 37 O 2
Chayek 35 J 2
Chayia (Iraq) 22 C 2
Chaykovskiy 24 KL 4
Chayvo, Zaliv 37 Q 5
Chazhegovo 24 K 3
Chazón 88 D 5
Cheb 15 F 4
Chebarkul' 25 M 4–5
Cheboksary 24 J 4
Chech, Erg 58 E 3–4
Chechaouen 58 D 1
Checheng 39 H 6
Chech'on 39 J 3
Chechuysk 36 J 4
Cheddar 6 C 3
Cheduba 41 F 4
Cheffadene 63 G 2
Cheg 58 C 3
Chegdomyn 37 O 5
Chegga (Algeria) 59 G 2
Chegga (Mauritania) 58 D 3
Cheghelvandi (Iran) 23 E 2
Chegutu 66 DE 3
Chegytun 72 C 2
Chehariz (Iraq) 23 E 2
Chehel Păyeh 34 F 4
Cheikria 58 D 3
Cheil, Ra's el 65 HJ 3
Cheju 39 J 4
Cheju-do 39 J 4
Cheju-haehyŏp 39 J 4
Chekhov 37 Q 6
Chekunda 37 O 5
Chekurovka 37 N 1
Chekuyevo 24 G 3
Chela, Serra da 66 A 3
Chelan, Lake 76 C 2
Cheleken 34 E 3
Chelforó 89 C 6
Chélia, Djebel 59 G 1
Chelkar 34 F 1
Chelleh Khăneh, Kūh-e (Iran) 23 E 1
Chełm 15 H 4
Chełmno 15 G 4
Chelmsford 7 E 2
Chelmuzhi 24 G 3
Chełmża 15 G 4
Chelosh 25 R 5
Cheltenham 7 CD 2
Chelyabinsk 25 M 4
Chelyuskin, Cape 90
Chemal 25 R 5
Chemba 67 E 3
Chembe 66 D 2
Chemdal'sk 36 H 4
Chemer 24 F 5
Chemillé 18 C 2
Chemult 76 B 3
Chen Barag Qi 36 L 6
Chenab 41 F 4
Chenachane 58 E 3
Chenărbăshi (Iran) 23 E 2
Chencoyi 78 D 4
Cheng Xian 38 E 4
Cheng'an 38 F 3

Chengcheng 38 E 3
Chengde 39 G 2
Chengdu 38 D 4
Chenggong 38 D 5
Chengjiang 38 D 6
Chengkou 38 E 4
Chengmai 38 F 7
Chengzitan 39 H 3
Chenxi 38 F 5
Chenzhou 38 F 5
Cheom Ksan 41 H 5
Chepen 84 C 5
Chepes 88 C 5
Chepstow 6 C 2
Cher 18 D 2
Cherangani Mountains 64 F 4
Cherbaniani Reef 40 B 5
Cherbourg 18 C 2
Cherchell 59 F 1
Cherdyn' 24 L 3
Cheremkhovo 36 H 5
Cherendey 36 L 3
Cherepanovo 25 Q 5
Chereponi 62 DE 3
Cherepovets 24 G 4
Chergui, Chott Ech 58 EF 2
Cherhill 7 D 2
Chéri 63 G 3
Cherkashina 36 J 4
Cherkassy 24 F 6
Cherkessk 21 F 2
Cherlak 25 O 5
Cherlakskiy 25 O 5
Chernaya 24 L 2
Chernaya 36 EF 1
Chernigov 24 F 5
Chernigovka 21 E 1
Chernigovka 39 K 2
Chernikovsk 24 L 5
Chernobyl 24 F 5
Chernogorsk 36 F 5
Chernolesskaya 37 P 3
Chernomorskoye 21 D 1
Chernoostrovskoye 25 R 3
Chernovskiye Kopi 36 K 5
Chernovtsy 20 C 1
Chernushka 24 L 4
Chernut'yevo 24 J 3
Cherny 34 D 1
Chernyakhovsk 17 H 5
Chernyanka 24 G 5
Chernyshevsk 36 L 5
Chernyshevskiy 36 K 3
Chernyy Ostrov 36 F 3
Chernyy Rynok 21 G 2
Chernyye Brat'ya, Ostrova 37 S 6
Chernyye Zemli 21 G 1
Cherokee 77 GH 3
Cherokees, Lake O' The 77 H 4
Cherskiy Range 37 Q 2
Cherskogo, Khrebet 36 KL 5
Chertkovo 24 H 6
Chertsey 7 D 2
Cherven 17 J 5
Chervlennaya 21 G 2
Chervonograd 17 HJ 5
Chervonoye, Ozero 17 J 5
Chervonoznamenka 20 D 1
Chervyanka 36 G 4
Cherwell, River 7 D 2
Chesapeake Bay 77 L 4
Chesapeake Bay Bridge-Tunnel
    77 LM 4
Chesham 7 D 2
Cheshire 5 D 3
Chëshskaya Guba 24 J 2
Cheshunt 7 D 2
Chester 5 D 3
Chesterfield 7 D 1
Chesterfield, Iles 52 B 4
Chesterfield Inlet 73 T 3
Chesterfield Inlet 73 TU 3
Chesterfield Islands 52 B 4
Chesterfield, Récifs et Iles 49 K 2
Chester-le-Street 5 E 2
Chesters 3 C 4
Chesuncook Lake 77 N 2
Chetlat 40 B 5
Chetumal 78 E 4
Chetumal, Bahia de 78 E 4
Chetvertyy Kuril'skiy Proliv
    37 ST 5–6
Cheugda 37 O 5
Cheulik 37 P 2
Cheviot (New Zealand) 51 Q 9
Cheviot Hills 5 D 2
Chewton Mendip 6 C 3
Cheyenne 76 F 3
Cheyenne River 76 F 3
Cheyenne Wells 76 F 4
Cheyne Bay 48 B 5
Chhatarpur 40 C 3
Chhindwara 40 C 3
Chiamboni, Ra's 65 G 5
Chiang Dao 41 G 4

Chiang Kham 41 H 4
Chiang Khan 41 H 4
Chiang Mai 41 G 4
Chiang Rai 41 G 4
Chiang Saen 41 H 3
Chiange 66 A 3
Chiapas 78 D 4
Chiatura 21 F 2
Chiavari 19 E 3
Chiayi 39 H 6
Chiba 39 M 3
Chibabava 67 E 4
Chibagalakh 37 PQ 2
Chibemba 66 A 3
Chibia 66 A 3
Chibit 25 R 5
Chibougamau 75 N 6
Chibougamau, Lac 75 N 6
Chibuto 67 E 4
Chibwe 66 D 2
Chicago 77 J 3
Chicamba 63 G 6–7
Chicapa 66 C 1
Chic-Chocs, Mounts 75 O 6
Chicha 63 H 2
Chichagof 72 K 4
Chichaoua 58 D 2
Chichas, Cordillera de 86 C 4–5
Chicheng 39 G 2
Chichén-Itzá 78 E 3
Chichester 7 D 2
Chichester Range National Park
    48 B 3
Chickasha 76 G 5
Chicken 72 J 3
Chiclana de la Frontera 18 B 4
Chiclayo 84 C 5
Chico (CA, U.S.A.) 76 B 4
Chico (Chile) 89 C 7
Chico (Chile) 89 C 8
Chicoana 88 C 4
Chicomba 66 A 2
Chicomo 67 E 4
Chiconono 67 F 2
Chicoutimi 75 N 6
Chicualacuala 67 E 4
Chicuma 66 A 2
Chidambaram 40 CD 5
Chidenguele 67 E 4
Chideock 6 C 3
Chidley, Cape 75 P 3
Chiemsee 15 F 5
Chiengi 66 D 1
Chieti 19 F 3
Chieveley 7 D 2
Chifeng 39 G 2
Chifre, Serra do 87 H 4
Chifunde 67 E 2
Chigamane 67 E 4
Chiganak 25 O 6
Chignik 72 F 4
Chigorodó 84 C 2
Chigubo 67 E 4
Chihli, Gulf of 39 GH 3
Chihuahua 76 E 6
Chiili 35 H 2
Chik Ballapur 40 C 5
Chikan 36 J 5
Chikayevo 37 W 3
Chikhacheva 37 R 1
Chikmagalur 40 C 5
Chikoy 36 J 5
Chikwawa 67 E 3
Chilabombwe 66 D 2
Chilas 35 J 3
Chilaw 40 C 6
Chilca, Cordillera de 86 B 4
Chilca, Punta de 86 A 3
Childers 49 J 4
Childress 76 F 5
Chile 88–89 B 4–6
Chile Basin 99 E 3
Chile Chico 89 B 8
Chilecito 88 C 4
Chilete 84 C 5
Chilgir 21 G 1
Chilham 7 E 2
Chilik 35 K 2
Chilimanzi 67 E 3
Chilipa de Alvarez 78 C 4
Chilka Lake 40 E 4
Chillagoe 49 G 2
Chillán 89 B 6
Chillar 89 E 6
Chillicothe (MO, U.S.A.) 77 H 4
Chillicothe (OH, U.S.A.) 77 K 4
Chiloé, Isla de 89 B 7
Chiloquin 76 B 3
Chilpancingo 78 BC 4
Chiltern Hills 7 D 2
Chiluage 66 C 1
Chilumba 67 E 2
Chilwa, Lake 67 F 3
Chimala 64 E 6
Chimalavera 66 A 2

Chimalginskiy Khrebet 37 Q 2
Chimaltenango 78 D 5
Chimán 84 C 2
Chimanimani 67 E 3
Chimbay 34 F 2
Chimborazo 84 C 4
Chimbote 84 C 5
Chimbwingombi 67 E 2
Chimeyevo 25 N 4
Chimishliya 20 C 1
Chimkent 35 H 2
Chimoio 67 E 3
Chimoio, Planalto de 67 E 3
Chimtarga 35 H 3
Chin 41 F 3
China 38 DF 4
Chinandega 78 E 5
Chincha Alta 86 A 3
Chinchilla 49 J 4
Chinchilla de Monte-Aragon
    18 C 4
Chinchorro, Banco 78 E 4
Chindagatuy 25 R 6
Chinde 67 F 3
Chin-do 39 J 4
Chindu 38 C 4
Chindwin 41 F 3
Chinese Wall 38 E 3
Chingirlau 24 K 5
Chingola 66 D 2
Chinguetti 58 C 4
Chinguil 63 H 3
Chinhae 39 J 3
Chinhoyi 66 DE 3
Chínipas 76 E 6
Chinju 39 J 3
Chinko 64 C 3
Chinnur 40 C 4
Chinon 18 D 2
Chinsali 67 E 2
Chintalnar 40 D 4
Chioco 67 E 3
Chioggia 19 F 2
Chipata 67 E 2
Chipepo 66 D 3
Chiperone 67 F 3
Chipili 66 D 2
Chipindo 66 B 2
Chipinge 67 E 4
Chipogolo 65 F 6
Chipoia 66 B 2
Chippenham 7 C 2
Chippewa Falls 77 H 3
Chippewa, Lake 77 H 2
Chipping Camden 7 D 1
Chipping Norton 7 D 2
Chipping Ongar 7 E 2
Chipping Sodbury 6 C 2
Chipurupalle 40 D 4
Chiquián 86 A 2–3
Chiquitos, Llanos de 86 D 4
Chirala 40 D 4
Chirchik 35 HJ 2
Chiredzi 67 E 4
Chirfa 63 G 1
Chiriguaná 84 D 2
Chiriguanos 86 D 5
Chirikof 72 F 4
Chirinda 36 H 2
Chirinkotan, Ostrov 37 S 6
Chiriquí 84 B 2
Chiriquí, Golfo de 84 B 2
Chirk 6 C 1
Chiromo 67 F 3
Chirpan 20 C 2
Chirundu 66 D 3
Chisamba 66 D 2
Chishmy 24 L 5
Chishui 38 E 5
Chishui He 38 E 5
Chisimaio → Kismäyu 65 G 5
Chiskovo 36 G 3
Chistoozernoye 25 P 5
Chistopol 24 K 4
Chita 36 K 5
Chitado 66 A 3
Chitambo 67 E 2
Chitato 66 C 1
Chitembo 67 B 2
Chitina 72 J 3
Chitina 72 J 3
Chitipa 67 E 1
Chitokoloki 66 C 2
Chitradurga 40 C 5
Chitral 35 J 3
Chitré 84 B 2
Chittagong 41 F 3
Chittaurgarh 40 C 3
Chittoor 40 C 5
Chiume 66 C 1
Chiume 66 C 1
Chiure 67 G 2
Chiure Novo 67 F 2
Chiuta, Lago 67 F 2
Chivasso 19 E 2
Chivay 86 B 4

Chivilcoy 88 D 5
Chizha 24 H 2
Chkalovo 25 O 5
Cho Ra 41 J 3
Choba 65 F 4
Chobe National Park 66 C 3
Chobham 7 D 2
Chochis, Cerro 86 E 4
Chocontá 84 D 2
Chocope 84 C 5
Chodzież 15 G 4
Choele Choel 89 CD 6
Choggia 19 F 2
Choique 89 D 6
Choiseul 51 G 3
Choix 76 E 6
Chojna 15 F 4
Chojnice 15 G 4
Choke Mountains 65 F 2
Choknar 35 JK 2
Chokurdakh 37 R 1
Chókwè 67 E 4
Chola Shan 38 C 4
Cholet 18 C 2
Cholila 89 B 7
Chollerton 5 D 2
Choluteca 78 E 5
Choma 66 D 3
Chomo Yummo 40 E 2
Chomutov 15 F 4
Chon Buri 41 H 5
Chon Thanh 41 J 5
Chona 36 J 3
Ch'ŏnan 39 J 3
Chondon 37 P 1
Chone 84 B 4
Chong Kal 41 H 5
Ch'ŏngjin 39 JK 2
Ch'ŏngju 39 J 3
Chŏngju 39 J 3
Chongkü 38 C 4
Chongming Dao 39 H 4
Chongoroi 66 A 2
Chongqing 38 E 5
Chongup 39 J 3
Chongxin 38 E 3
Chongzuo 38 E 6
Chŏnju 39 J 3
Chonos, Archipiélago de los
    89 AB 7–8
Chop 20 B 1
Chorito, Sierra del 18 C 4
Chorley 5 D 3
Chorolque 86 C 5
Choros, Cabo 88 B 4
Chorregon 49 G 3
Chorrillos 86 A 3
Chorrochó 87 J 2
Ch'ŏrwŏn 39 J 3
Chŏshi 39 M 3
Chosica 86 A 3
Chos Malal 89 BC 6
Choszczno 15 G 4
Chota 84 C 5
Chota Udaipur 40 B 3
Chotanagpur 40 DE 3
Chott Ech Chergui 58 EF 2
Chott el Hodna 59 F 1
Chott el Rharsa 59 G 2
Chott Melrhir 59 G 2
Chott Merouane 59 G 2
Choum 58 C 4
Choybalsan 36 K 6
Christchurch 51 Q 9
Christchurch (U.K.) 7 D 2
Christiana 66 D 5
Christian Sound 72 KL 4
Christie Bay 73 PQ 3
Christmas Island 42 C 6
Chtakal'skiy Khrebet 35 J 2
Chu 35 J 2
Chu 35 J 2
Chu Xian 39 G 4
Chu Yang Sin 41 J 5
Chubut 89 C 7
Chuchukan 36 L 3
Chucuito 86 BC 4
Chucul 88 D 5
Chudinovo 25 M 5
Chudleigh Park 49 G 2
Chudovo 17 K 4
Chudskoye Ozero 17 J 4
Chugach Mountains 72 H 3
Chuginadak 72 C 5
Chuhuichupa 76 E 6
Chu-Iliyskiye Gory 35 JK 2
Chukai 42 B 3
Chukar 36 L 3
Chukchagirskoye, Ozero 37 P 5
Chukchi Sea 72 CD 2
Chuken 37 P 6
Chukhloma 24 H 4
Chukoch'ye 37 T 2
Chukotsk Peninsula 90
Chukotsk Range 90

Chukotskiy, Mys 72 C 3
Chukotskiy Poluostrov 72 BC 2
Chukuchany 37 R 2
Chula Vista 76 C 5
Chulak-Kurgan 35 HJ 2
Chulakovka 21 D 1
Chulasa 24 J 3
Chulitna 72 H 3
Chulkovo 25 R 3
Chul'man 37 M 4
Chulmleigh 6 C 3
Chulucanas 84 BC 5
Chulym 25 Q 4
Chulym 25 QR 4
Chulym 36 F 4
Chum 25 M 2
Chum Phae 41 H 4
Chumakovo 25 P 4
Chumbicha 88 C 4
Chumek 25 R 6
Chumerna 20 C 2
Chumikan 37 OP 5
Chumphon 41 G 5
Chumysh 25 Q 5
Chuña 88 C 4
Chuna 36 G 4
Ch'unch'ŏn 39 J 3
Chundzha 35 K 2
Chunga 66 D 2
Ch'ungju 39 J 3
Chungking → Chongqing 38 E 5
Ch'ungmu 39 J 4
Chunhua 39 K 2
Chunskiy 36 G 4
Chunya (Tanzania) 64 E 6
Chunya (U.S.S.R.) 36 G 3
Chuor Phnum Kravanh 41 H 5
Chupa 16 K 2
Chüplü (Iran) 23 E 1
Chuquibamba 84 D 2
Chuquibamba 86 B 4
Chuquicamata 86 C 5
Chuquillanquí 84 C 5
Chur 19 E 2
Churapcha 37 O 3
Church Stoke 6 C 1
Church Stretton 6 C 1
Churchill 73 ST 4
Churchill 75 P 5
Churchill (Man., Can.) 73 T 4
Churchill (Sask., Can.) 73 R 4
Churchill, Cape 73 T 4
Churchill Falls 75 P 5
Churchill Lake 73 Q 4
Churchill Mountains 91
Churchill Peak 73 N 4
Churchtown 6 A 1
Chureg-Tag, Gora 36 F 5
Churia Range 40 E 2
Churkino 24 H 3
Churu 40 C 2
Churuguara 84 DE 1
Churún Merú 85 F 2
Chushal 35 K 4
Chushkakyl' 34 F 1
Chusovaya 25 L 4
Chusovoy 25 L 4
Chusovskoy 24 L 3
Chute-des-Passes 75 N 6
Chutes de Katende 64 C 4
Chutes de la Lufira 64 D 6
Chutes de Livingstone 63 G 7
Chutes Ngaliema 64 D 4
Chutes Tembo 64 B 6
Chuval 25 L 3
Chuvanskiye Gory 37 V 3
Chuvanskoye Petushkova 37 W 2
Chuxiong 38 D 5
Chuy Cevolleti 88 F 5
Chuya 36 K 4
Chuya 36 K 4
Chuyengo 36 H 3
Chybydat 36 M 3
Chyul'be 37 O 4
Chyulu Range 65 F 5
Ciamis 42 C 5
Cianjur 42 C 5
Cianorte 87 F 5
Cibuta, Cerro 76 D 5
Cicero Dantas 87 J 3
Ćićevac 20 B 2
Cide 21 D 2
Ciechanów 15 H 4
Ciego de Ávila 79 G 3
Ciénaga 84 D 1
Cienfuegos 79 F 3
Cieza 18 C 4
Çifteler 20 D 3
Cifuentes 18 C 3
Cihanbeyli 21 D 3
Cihanbeyli Platosu 21 D 3
Cihara 42 C 5
Cihuatlán 78 B 4
Cijara, Embalse de 18 BC 4
Cijulang 42 C 5

Cilacap 42 C 5
Çıldır 21 F 2
Çıldır Gölü 21 F 2
Cilo Dağı 21 F 3
Cimahi 42 C 5
Cimarron 76 G 4
Çimen Dağı 21 E 3
Cimone 19 F 3
Cîmpia Bărăganului 20 C 1–2
Cîmpia Burnazului 20 C 2
Cîmpia Turzii 20 B 1
Cîmpina 20 C 1
Cîmpulung Moldovenesc 20 C 1
Cina, Tanjung 42 BC 5
Çinar 21 F 3
Cinca 18 D 3
Cincinnati 77 K 4
Cinco Saltos 89 C 6
Çine 20 C 3
Cintalapa de Figueroa 78 D 4
Cinto, Monte 19 E 3
Cintra, Golfo de 58 B 4
Cipolletti 89 C 6
Circeo, Capo 19 F 3
Circle (AK, U.S.A.) 72 J 2
Circle (MT, U.S.A.) 76 E 2
Cirebon 42 C 5
Cirencester 7 D 2
Ciriè 19 E 2
Ciro Marina 19 G 4
Cirque Mountain 75 P 4
Cisco 76 G 5
Ciskei 66 D 6
Cisnădie 20 B 1
Cisne, Islas del 78 F 4
Cisnéros (Colombia) 84 D 2
Citac, Nevado 86 AB 3
Citlaltépetl, Volcán 78 C 4
Citrusdal 66 B 6
Citta del Vaticano 19 F 3
Città di Castello 19 F 3
Ciucasu, Virful 20 C 1
Ciudad Acuña 78 B 2
Ciudad Altamirano 78 B 4
Ciudad Bolívar 85 F 2
Ciudad Bolivia 84 DE 2
Ciudad Camargo 76 E 6
Ciudad Cuauhtémoc 78 D 4
Ciudad de Dolores Hidalgo 78 BC 3
Ciudad de Nutrias 84 DE 2
Ciudad de Rio Grande 78 B 3
Ciudad del Carmen 78 D 4
Ciudad del Maíz 78 C 3
Ciudad Guayana 85 F 2
Ciudad Guzmán 78 B 4
Ciudad Hidalgo (Mexico) 78 BC 4
Ciudad Hidalgo (Mexico) 78 D 5
Ciudad Juárez 78 E 5
Ciudad Lerdo 78 B 2
Ciudad Madero 78 C 3
Ciudad Mante 78 C 3
Ciudad Mendoza 78 C 4
Ciudad Obregón 76 E 6
Ciudad Ojeda 84 D 1
Ciudad Piar 85 F 2
Ciudad Real 18 C 4
Ciudad Río Bravo 78 C 2
Ciudad Valles 78 C 3
Ciudad Victoria 78 C 3
Ciudadela 18 D 3
Ciudad-Rodrigo 18 B 3
Civa Burnu 21 E 2
Civita Castellana 19 F 3
Civitanova Marche 19 F 3
Civitavecchia 19 F 3
Çivril 20 C 3
Cizre 21 F 3
Cizre (Turkey) 22 D 1
Clachan 3 B 4
Clacton-on-Sea 7 E 2
Cladich 3 B 3
Claggan 3 B 3
Claire Coast 91
Claire Engle Lake 76 B 3
Claire, Lake 73 P 4
Clamecy 18 D 2
Clanwilliam 66 B 6
Claonaig 3 B 4
Clara 4 B 3
Claraz 89 E 6
Clare 49 F 5
Clarence, Isla 89 B 9
Clarence Strait 72 L 4
Clarence Strait (N.T., Austr.) 48 E 1
Clarence Town 79 H 3
Clarendon 76 F 5
Clarenville 75 R 6
Claresholm 73 P 5
Clarinda 77 H 3
Clarion Fracture Zone 99 D 3
Clark Fork 76 C 2
Clark Hill Lake 77 K 5
Clark, Lake 72 F 3
Clark, Mount 73 N 3

Clark River 49 H 2
Clarke 50 L 9
Clarke Range 49 H 3
Clarksburg 77 KL 4
Clarksdale 77 H 5
Clarkston 76 C 2
Clarksville 77 J 4
Claro 87 F 4
Claughton 5 D 2
Claveria 43 J 1
Clay Belt 74–75 LM 5
Clay Cross 5 E 3
Clay Head 4 C 2
Claydon 7 E 1
Clear Lake 76 B 3
Clear Lake 76 B 4
Clearfield 76 D 3
Clearwater 77 K 6
Clearwater Mountains 76 C 2
Cleethorpes 5 EF 3
Clere, Mount 48 B 4
Clermont 49 H 3
Clermont-Ferrand 18 D 2
Clevedon 6 C 2
Cleveland (MS, U.S.A.) 77 H 5
Cleveland (OH, U.S.A.) 77 K 3
Cleveland Hills 5 E 2
Cleveland, Mount 76 D 2
Clew Bay 14 AB 4
Cliffe 7 E 2
Clifton 5 D 2
Clifton 77 J 4
Clifton Hills 49 F 4
Clinton 73 N 5
Clinton (IA, U.S.A.) 77 H 3
Clinton (OK, U.S.A.) 76 G 4
Clinton-Colden Lake 73 Q 3
Clipperton 53 H 2
Clipperton Fracture Zone 99 D 3
Clitheroe 5 D 3
Cloates, Point 48 A 3
Clodomira 88 D 4
Clogh Mills 4 B 2
Cloghan 4 B 3
Clogher 4 B 3
Clonbulloge 4 B 3
Cloncurry 49 FG 3
Cloncurry River 49 G 2–3
Clones 4 B 3
Clonmany 4 B 2
Clonmel 14 B 4
Clonmore 4 B 3
Clontibret 4 B 3
Cloppenburg 15 E 4
Cloquet 77 H 2
Clorinda 88 E 4
Closeburn 3 C 4
Cloud Peak 76 E 3
Clough 4 C 2
Cloughton 5 E 2
Clousta 2 D 1
Clovelly 6 B 2
Clovis 76 F 5
Clwyd 5 D 3
Clyde (N.W.T., Can.) 75 O 1
Clydebank 3 B 4
Clynnog-fawr 5 B 1
Cnossus 20 C 3
Côa 18 B 3
Coagh 4 B 2
Coahuila 78 B 2
Coal River 73 M 4
Coalcoman, Sierra de 78 B 4
Coalinga 76 B 4
Coalisland 4 B 2
Coalville 7 D 1
Coan, Cerro 84 C 5
Coaraci 87 J 3
Coari 85 F 4
Coari 85 F 4
Coast Mountains 72–73 LM 4–5
Coast of Labrador 75 PQ 4–5
Coast Range (Queensland, Austr.) 49 J 4
Coast Ranges (U.S.A.) 76 B 3–4
Coatbridge 3 B 4
Coatepec 78 C 4
Coats Island 73 V 3
Coats Land 91
Coatzacoalcos 78 D 4
Coatzacoalcos, Bahia 78 D 4
Coba 78 E 3
Cobán 78 D 4
Cobar 49 H 5
Cobh 14 B 4
Cobija 86 C 3
Cobourg Peninsula 48 E 1
Cobquecura 89 B 6
Cobue 67 EF 2
Coburg 15 F 4
Cocachacra 86 B 4
Cocamá 86 B 3
Cochabamba 86 C 4

Cochin 40 C 6
Cochinoca 86 C 5
Cochrane (Chile) 89 B 8
Cochrane (Man., Can.) 73 R 4
Cochrane (Ontario, Can.) 75 L 6
Cockburn 49 G 5
Cockburnspath 3 C 4
Cockenzie and Port Seton 3 C 4
Cockerham 5 D 3
Cockermouth 5 D 2
Cocklebiddy 48 D 5
Coco Channel 41 F 5
Coco I. 84 A 2
Coco, Isla del 84 A 2
Coco Island (Costa Rica) 80 B 2
Coco Islands 41 F 5
Coco o Segovia, Rio 78 EF 5
Cocoa 77 K 6
Cocobeach 63 FG 5
Côcos 87 H 3
Cocula 78 B 3
Cocuy, Sierra Nevada de 84 D 2
Codajás 85 F 4
Codford 7 D 2
Codigoro 19 F 3
Codlea 20 C 1
Codó 87 H 1
Cody 76 E 3
Coelemu 89 B 6
Coen (Queensland, Austr.) 49 G 1
Coeroenie 85 G 3
Coesfeld 15 E 4
Coetivy 65 K 6
Coeur d'Alene 76 C 2
Coffin Bay 49 F 5
Coff's Harbour 49 J 5
Cofrentes 18 C 4
Coggeshall 7 E 2
Cognac 18 C 2
Cogne 19 E 2
Cohaique 89 B 8
Cohaique Alto 89 B 8
Coimbatore 40 C 5
Coimbra 18 B 3
Coin 18 C 4
Coipasa, Salar de 86 C 4
Cojimies 84 B 3
Cojudo Blanco, Cerro 89 C 8
Cojutepeque 78 E 5
Col de Larche 19 E 3
Col de Perthus 18 D 3
Col de Tende 19 E 3
Colac 49 G 6
Colalao del Valle 88 C 4
Colan-Conhué 89 C 7
Colatina 87 H 4
Colby 4 C 2
Colchester 7 E 2
Cold Bay 72 E 4
Cold Lake 73 P 5
Cold Norton 7 E 2
Coldstream 3 C 4
Coleman 76 G 5
Coleman River 49 G 2
Coleraine 4 B 2
Coles Bay 50 L 9
Colesberg 66 D 6
Coleshill 7 D 1
Colfax 76 C 2
Colhué Huapí, Lago 89 C 8
Colima 78 B 4
Colinas (Goiás, Brazil) 87 G 3
Colinas (Maranhão, Brazil) 87 H 2
Coll 3 A 3
Collahuasi 86 C 5
College 72 H 3
College Station 77 G 5
Colli Euganei 19 F 2
Collie 48 B 5
Collier Bay 48 C 2
Collier Ranges National Park 48 B 3
Collines de la Puisaye 18 D 2
Collines de l'Armagnac 18 D 3
Collines de l'Artois 18 D 1
Collines du Perche 18 D 2
Collines du Sancerrois 18 D 2
Collingham 7 D 1
Collingwood (New Zealand) 51 Q 9
Collingwood (Ontario, Can.) 75 M 7
Collinson Peninsula 73 R 1–2
Collinsville 49 H 3
Collipulli 89 B 6
Collo 19 E 4
Collon 4 B 3
Colmar 19 E 2
Colmena 88 D 4
Colmenar Viejo 18 C 3
Colmonell 3 B 4
Colne 5 D 3
Cologne → Köln 15 E 4

Cololo, Nevado 86 C 4
Colombia 84 DE 3
Colombia (São Paulo, Brazil) 87 G 5
Colombo 40 C 6
Colon (Argentina) 88 D 5
Colón (Argentina) 88 E 5
Colón (Cuba) 79 F 3
Colón (Panamá) 84 C 2
Colón, Archipiélago de 84 B 6
Colona 48 E 5
Colonet 76 C 5
Colonia Catriel 89 C 6
Colonia Dalmacia 88 E 4
Colonia del Sacramento 88 E 5
Colonia Josefa 89 C 6
Colonia Las Heras 89 C 8
Colonia Morelos 76 E 5
Colonne, Capo delle 19 G 4
Colonsay 3 A 3
Colorado (Argentina) 89 D 6
Colorado (AZ, U.S.A.) 76 D 5
Colorado (TX, U.S.A.) 77 G 5–6
Colorado (U.S.A.) 76 EF 4
Colorado, Cerro (Argentina) 89 C 7
Colorado, Cerro (Mexico) 76 C 5
Colorado, Pico 88 C 4
Colorado Plateau 76 DE 4
Colorado Springs 76 F 4
Colotlán 78 B 3
Colquechaca 86 C 4
Colsterworth 7 D 1
Columbia (MO, U.S.A.) 77 H 4
Columbia (S.C., U.S.A.) 77 K 5
Columbia (TN, U.S.A.) 77 J 4
Columbia (WA, U.S.A.) 76 BC 2
Columbia Falls 76 D 2
Columbia, Mount 73 O 5
Columbia Mountains 73 NO 5
Columbia Plateau 76 C 3
Columbine, Cape 66 B 6
Columbria 49 H 3
Columbus (GA, U.S.A.) 77 J 5
Columbus (IN, U.S.A.) 77 J 4
Columbus (MS, U.S.A.) 77 J 5
Columbus (NE, U.S.A.) 76 G 3
Columbus (OH, U.S.A.) 77 K 4
Columbus (TX, U.S.A.) 77 G 6
Colville 72 G 2
Colville, Cape 73 T 2
Colville Channel 51 R 8
Colville Lake 73 MN 2
Colville Lake 73 MN 2
Colwyn Bay 6 C 1
Colyton 6 C 3
Comacchio 19 F 3
Comai 41 F 2
Comalcalco 78 D 4
Comandante Luis Piedrabuena 89 BC 8–9
Comandante Salas 88 C 5
Comănești 20 C 1
Comayagua 78 E 5
Combarbala 88 B 5
Comber 4 C 2
Combermere Bay 41 F 4
Comeragh Mountains 14 B 4
Comet 49 H 3
Comet River 49 H 3
Comilla 41 F 3
Comitán de Dominguez 78 D 4
Commander Islands 90
Commentry 18 D 2
Commercy 19 E 2
Committee Bay 73 U 2
Como 19 E 2
Como, Lago di 19 E 2
Comodoro Rivadavia 89 C 8
Comondú 76 D 6
Comorin, Cape 40 C 6
Comoros 67 G 2
Compiègne 18 D 2
Compton 7 D 2
Comrie 3 C 3
Con Son 41 J 6
Con Vidal 89 E 6
Cona 41 F 2
Cona Niyeo 89 C 7
Conakry 62 B 4
Concarneau 18 C 2
Conceição, Cachoeira da 85 F 5
Conceição da Barra 87 J 4
Conceição do Araguaia 85 J 3
Concepción (Argentina) 88 C 4
Concepción (Bolivia) 86 C 3
Concepción (Bolivia) 86 D 3
Concepción (Chile) 89 B 6
Concepción (Paraguay) 86 E 5
Concepción, Bahía 78 C 3
Concepción del Oro 78 B 3
Concepción del Uruguay 88 E 5
Conception Bay 75 R 6
Conception Bay (Namibia) 66 A 4
Conception, Point 76 B 5

Conchi 86 C 5
Conchos, Rio 76 EF 6
Concord 77 M 3
Concórdia (Amazonas, Brazil) 84 E 4
Concordia (Argentina) 88 E 5
Concordia (KS, U.S.A.) 76 G 4
Concordia (Mexico) 78 A 3
Concordia (Peru) 84 C 4
Conda 66 A 2
Condamine 49 J 4
Conde 87 J 3
Condobolin 49 H 5
Condom 18 D 3
Condon 76 C 2
Condor, Cordillera del 84 C 4
Condoto 84 CD 4
Conecuh River 77 J 5
Conegliano 19 F 2
Conejera 18 D 4
Conejo 76 D 7
Conero 19 F 3
Conghua 38 F 6
Congleton 7 C 1
Congo 63 H 6
Congo 63 H 6
Congresbury 6 C 3
Cónico, Cerro 89 B 7
Coningsby 5 E 3
Conn Lake 75 N 1
Conn, Lough 14 B 4
Connah's Quay 6 C 1
Connaught 14 B 4
Connecticut 77 M 3
Connellsville 77 L 3
Connemara, Mountains of 14 AB 4
Connor, Mount 48 D 1
Conrad 76 D 2
Conrad Rise 98 B 5
Conroe 77 G 5
Conselheiro Lafaiete 87 H 5
Consett 5 E 2
Constância dos Baetas 85 F 5
Constanța 20 C 2
Constantina 18 B 4
Constantine 59 G 1
Constantine, Cape 72 EF 4
Constantine, Cape 72 F 4
Constitución 89 B 6
Contai 40 E 3
Contamana 84 CD 5
Contão 85 F 3
Cóntas 87 H 3
Contreras, Embalse de 18 C 4
Contreras, Puerto de 18 C 4
Contwoyto Lake 73 PQ 2
Convención 84 D 2
Convoy 4 B 2
Conway (AR, U.S.A.) 77 H 4
Conway (S.C., U.S.A.) 77 L 5
Conway Reef 52 C 4
Conwy 6 C 1
Conza, Sella di 19 G 3
Coober Pedy 48 E 4
Cooch Behar 40 E 2
Cook 48 E 5
Cook Inlet 72 G 3
Cook Islands 52 E 3
Cook, Mount 51 Q 9
Cook Mountains 91
Cook Strait 51 QR 9
Cookes Peak 76 E 5
Cookstown 4 B 2
Cooktown 49 H 2
Coolgardie 48 C 5
Coolibah 48 D 1
Coolidge 76 D 5
Cooma 49 H 6
Coombe Bisset 7 D 2
Coombe Martin 6 BC 2
Coon Rapids 77 H 2
Coonabarabran 49 H 5
Coonamble 49 H 5
Coondapoor 40 B 5
Coongoola 49 H 4
Coonoor 40 C 5
Cooper Creek 49 G 4
Coorow 48 B 4
Cooroy 49 J 4
Coos Bay 76 B 3
Coosa River 77 J 5
Cootamundra 49 H 5
Cootehill 4 B 2
Copahue 89 B 6
Copan 78 E 5
Copana 84 E 4
Copenhagen 17 F 4
Copiapó 88 BC 4
Čöpköy 20 C 2
Copper 72 J 3
Copper Center 72 H 3
Copper Cliff 75 L 6
Copper Harbor 77 J 2
Copper Queen 66 D 3
Copperbelt 66 D 2
Coppermine 73 OP 2

Coppermine 73 OP 2
Copplestone 6 C 3
Coqên 40 E 1
Coquet, River 5 E 2
Coquimbo 88 B 4
Corabia 20 B 2
Coral Harbour 73 UV 3
Coral Sea 52 B 3–4
Coral Sea Islands Territory 49 HJ 1–2
Corantijn 85 G 3
Corato 19 G 3
Corbridge 5 DE 2
Corby 7 D 1
Corcaigh 14 B 4
Corcovado, Golfo 89 B 7
Corcovado, Volcán 89 B 7
Cordele 77 K 5
Cordilheiras, Serra das 85 J 5
Cordillera Azul 84 C 5
Cordillera Blanca 84 C 5
Cordillera Cantábrica 18 BC 3
Cordillera Central (Colombia) 84 C 2–3
Cordillera Central (Dominican Rep.) 79 H 4
Cordillera Central (Peru) 84 C 5
Cordillera Central (Philippines) 43 J 1
Cordillera, Costa de la 84 E 2
Cordillera de Carabaya 86 B 3
Cordillera de Chichas 86 C 4–5
Cordillera de Chilca 86 B 4
Cordillera de Huanzo 86 B 3
Cordillera de la Costa 84 E 2
Cordillera de Lípez 86 C 5
Cordillera de Mérida 84 D 2
Cordillera del Condor 84 C 4
Cordillera Domeyko 86 C 5
Cordillera Isabella 78 EF 5
Cordillera Negra 84 C 5
Cordillera Occidental 86 BC 3–4
Cordillera Occidental (Colombia) 84 C 2–3
Cordillera Oriental 86 BC 3–5
Cordillera Oriental (Colombia) 84 CD 2–3
Cordillera Real (Bolivia) 86 C 4
Cordillera Real (Ecuador) 84 C 4
Cordillera Vilcabamba 86 B 3
Córdoba (Argentina) 88 D 5
Córdoba (Mexico) 78 C 4
Córdoba (Spain) 18 BC 4
Córdoba, Sierra de 88 D 5
Cordova (AK, U.S.A.) 72 H 3
Córdova (Peru) 86 A 3
Corfe Castle 7 C 2
Corfu 20 A 3
Corguinno 87 E 4
Coria 18 B 4
Corigliano Calabro 19 G 4
Corinda (Queensland, Austr.) 49 F 2
Coringa Islands 49 J 2
Corinth (Greece) 20 B 3
Corinth (MS, U.S.A.) 77 J 5
Corinto 87 H 4
Corisco, Baie de 63 F 5
Corisco Island 63 F 5
Cork (Queensland, Austr.) 49 G 3
Cork (Rep. of Ireland) 14 B 4
Corleone 19 F 4
Çorlu 20 C 2
Cornafulla 4 AB 3
Cornelio 76 D 6
Cornélio Procópio 87 F 5
Cornelius Grinnel Bay 75 P 3
Corner Brook 75 Q 6
Cornhill 2 C 3
Corno Grande 19 F 3
Cornwall (Ontario, Can.) 75 MN 6
Cornwall (U.K.) 6 B 2
Coro 84 E 1
Coroatá 87 H 1
Corocoro 86 C 4
Coroico 86 C 4
Coromandel Coast 40 D 5
Coromandel Peninsula 51 R 8
Coronado, Bahía de 78 F 6
Coronation 73 P 5
Coronation Gulf 73 P 2
Corondo 88 D 5
Coronel 89 B 6
Coronel Dorrego 89 D 6
Coronel Fabriciano 87 H 4
Coronel Falcón 89 D 6
Coronel Oviedo 88 E 4
Coronel Pringles 89 D 6
Coronel Suárez 89 D 6
Corongo 84 C 5
Coropuna, Nevado 86 B 4
Corozal 78 E 4
Corozal 84 CD 2
Corpus 88 E 4
Corpus Christi 77 G 6
Corque 86 C 4

Corquin 78 E 5
Corral 89 B 6
Corrales 88 E 5
Corran 3 B 3
Corrente (Bahía, Brazil) 87 H 3
Corrente (Piauí, Brazil) 87 G 3
Correntes 87 F 4
Correntes, Cabo das 67 F 4
Correntina 87 GH 3
Corrib, Lough 14 B 4
Corrientes 84 C 4
Corrientes (Argentina) 88 E 4
Corrientes (Argentina) 88 E 4
Corrientes (Peru) 84 C 4
Corrientes, Cabo (Argentina) 89 E 6
Corrientes, Cabo (Colombia) 84 C 2
Corrigin 48 B 5
Corryong 49 H 6
Corse 19 E 3
Corse, Cap 19 E 3
Corsica 19 E 3
Corsicana 77 G 5
Corte 19 E 3
Corte Alto 89 B 7
Cortegana 18 B 4
Cortez (Spain) 18 C 3
Cortez (U.S.A.) 76 E 4
Cortona 19 F 3
Corubal 62 B 3
Coruche 18 B 4
Çoruh 21 F 2
Çoruh Dağları 21 F 2
Çorum 21 D 2
Corumba (Goiás, Brazil) 87 G 4
Corumbá (Mato Grosso do Sul, Brazil) 86 E 4
Corumbá de Goiás 87 G 4
Corunna 18 B 3
Coruripe 87 J 3
Corvallis 76 B 3
Corvo 58 A 1
Corwen 6 C 1
Corwen 6 C 1
Cosamaloapan 78 C 4
Coshocton 77 K 3
Cosmoledo Group 65 H 6
Cosne-sur-Loire 18 D 2
Costa Blanca 18 C 4
Costa Blanca 18 C 4
Costa Brava 18 D 3
Costa de la Luz 18 B 4
Costa de Mosquitos 78 F 5
Costa del Azahar 18 D 3–4
Costa del Sol 18 C 4
Costa Dorada 18 D 3
Costa Rica 78 EF 6
Costa Verde 18 B 3
Cotabato 43 F 2
Cotagaita 86 C 5
Cotahuasi 86 B 4
Côte d'Argent 18 C 3
Côte d'Azur 19 E 3
Côte de l'Ile de France 18 D 2
Côte d'Ivoire → Ivory Coast 62 CD 4
Côte d'Or 19 D 2
Coteau du Missouri 76 FG 2
Cotentin 18 C 2
Cotherstone 49 H 3
Cotonou 62 E 4
Cotopaxi 84 C 4
Cotswold Hills 7 C 2
Cottbus 15 F 4
Cottica 85 H 3
Cottingham 5 E 3
Cotulla 76 G 6
Coubre, Pointe de la 18 C 2
Couhé 18 CD 2
Čoukkarašša 16 H 2
Coulommiers 18 D 2
Council 72 E 3
Council Bluffs 77 GH 3
Coupar Angus 3 C 3
Courantyne 85 G 3
Courland 17 H 4
Courmayeur 19 E 2
Courtenai 73 M 6
Courtown 6 A 1
Coutances 18 C 2
Coutras 18 CD 2
Couvin 14 D 4
Cove 2 B 3
Coventry 7 D 1
Coverack 6 B 2
Covilhã 18 B 3
Covington (GA, U.S.A.) 77 K 5
Covington (KY, U.S.A.) 77 K 4
Covington (TN, U.S.A.) 77 J 4
Covington (VA, U.S.A.) 77 L 4
Cowal 3 B 3
Cowal, Lake 49 H 5
Cowan, Lake 48 C 5
Cowargarze 38 C 4

Cowbridge 6 C 2
Cowdenbeath 3 C 3
Cowell 49 F 5
Cowes 7 D 2
Cowfold 7 D 2
Cowra 49 H 5
Cox's Bazar 41 F 3
Coy Aike 89 C 9
Coyame 76 E 6
Coyle → Coig 89 B 9
Coylton 3 B 4
Coyotitan 76 E 7
Cracow 15 H 4
Cracow 49 J 4
Cradock 66 D 6
Crai 6 C 3
Craig (AK, U.S.A.) 72 L 4
Craig (CO, U.S.A.) 76 E 3
Craigavon 4 B 2
Craigavon 4 B 2
Craighouse 3 B 4
Craigie 3 B 4
Craignure 3 B 3
Craigs Range 49 J 4
Crail 3 C 3
Craiova 20 B 2
Cramlington 5 E 2
Crampel 58 E 2
Crampel → Kaga Bandoro 64 B 3
Cranbrook 73 O 6
Cranbrook (Western Australia) 48 B 5
Cranford 4 B 2
Cranleigh 7 D 2
Craolândia 85 J 5
Crary Mountains 91
Crasna 20 B 1
Crater Lake 76 B 3
Cratère du Nouveau-Québec 75 N 3
Cratéus 87 H 2
Crathie 3 D 3
Crato (Amazonas, Brazil) 85 F 5
Crato (Ceará, Brazil) 87 J 2
Cravo Norte 84 E 2
Crawford 76 F 3
Crawfordjohn 3 C 4
Crawfordsville 77 J 3
Crawley 7 D 2
Crazy Peak 76 D 2
Creaggan 3 B 3
Creagorry 2 A 3
Crediton 6 C 2
Cree 73 Q 4
Cree Lake 73 Q 4
Creel 76 E 6
Creetown 3 B 4
Creggan 4 B 2
Creggans 3 B 3
Creil 18 D 2
Cremona 19 F 2
Crepori 85 G 5
Cres 19 F 3
Crescent City 76 B 3
Cressage 6 C 1
Crest 19 DE 3
Creston 77 H 3
Crestview 77 J 5
Crêt de la Neige 19 E 2
Crete 20 BC 3
Cretin, Cape 50 E 3
Creus, Cabo de 18 D 3
Creuse 18 D 2
Crevillente 18 C 4
Crewe 5 D 3
Crewkerne 6 C 2
Crianlarich 3 B 3
Crinan Canal 3 B 3
Cristal, Monts de 63 G 5
Cristalândia 87 G 3
Cristino Castro 87 H 2
Cristmas Island 53 E 2
Cristóbal, Colón Pico 84 D 1
Crişul Alb 20 B 1
Crişul Repede 20 B 1
Crkvena Planina 20 B 2
Crna Gora 20 A 2
Crna Gora 20 B 2
Crna Reka 20 B 2
Crni Drim 20 B 2
Črni Vrh (Yugoslavia) 19 G 2
Crni Vrh (Yugoslavia) 19 G 3
Croatia 19 G 2
Crockett 77 G 5
Croft-on-Tees 5 E 2
Croissette, Cap 19 DE 3

Croker, Cape 48 E 1
Croker Island 48 E 1
Cromarty 2 BC 3
Cromarty Firth 2 B 3
Cromer 7 E 1
Crook 5 E 2
Crooked Creek 72 F 3
Crooked Island 79 H 3
Crooked Island Passage 79 GH 3
Crookham 5 D 2
Crookham Hill 7 E 2
Crookston 77 G 2
Crosby 4 C 2
Crosby (N.D., U.S.A.) 76 F 2
Crosby (U.K.) 5 D 3
Cross (Nigeria) 63 F 4
Cross, Cape 66 A 4
Cross City 77 K 6
Cross Fell 5 D 2
Cross Lake 73 S 5
Cross Sound 72 K 4
Crossett 77 H 5
Crossgar 4 C 2
Crossgates 3 C 3
Crosshill 3 B 4
Crossmaglen 4 B 2
Crotone 19 G 4
Crow Agency 76 E 2
Crow Lake 74 J 6
Crowell 76 G 5
Crowland 7 D 1
Crowley 77 H 5
Crowley Ridge 77 H 4
Crowling 5 D 3
Crown Prince Frederik Island 73 U 2
Crows Nest 49 J 4
Crowsnest Pass 73 OP 6
Croxton 7 D 1
Croyde 6 B 2
Croydon 7 D 2
Croydon 49 G 2
Crozon 18 C 2
Cruden Bay 2 D 3
Crudgington 6 C 1
Crumlin 4 B 2
Cruz Alta 88 F 4
Cruz Alta (Argentina) 88 D 5
Cruz, Cabo 79 G 4
Cruz del Eje 88 D 5
Cruz Grande (Chile) 88 B 4
Cruz Grande (Mexico) 78 C 4
Cruzeiro 87 G 5
Cruzeiro do Oeste 87 F 5
Cruzeiro do Sul 84 D 5
Crymych 6 B 2
Crynant 6 C 3
Crystal Brook 49 F 5
Ctesiphon (Iraq) 23 D 2
Cu Lao Cham 41 J 4
Cu Lao Hon 41 J 5
Cu Lao Re 41 J 4
Cua Rao 41 H 4
Cuale 66 B 1
Cuamba 67 F 2
Cuando Cubango 66 BC 3
Cuangar 66 B 3
Cuango 66 B 1
Cuango 66 B 1
Cuanza 66 B 1
Cuanza Norte 66 AB 1
Cuanza Sul 66 AB 2
Cuareim 88 E 4
Cuarteron Reef 42 D 2
Cuarto 88 D 5
Cuauhtémoc 76 E 6
Cuba 79 F 3
Cubal 66 A 2
Cubango 66 B 3
Cubati 66 B 3
Cubuk 21 D 2
Cuchi 66 B 2
Cuchi 66 B 2
Cuchilla de Santa Ana 88 EF 5
Cuchilla Grande 88 EF 5
Cuchillo-Có 89 D 6
Cuchumatanes, Sierra de los 78 D 4
Cuckfield 7 D 2
Cucuí 84 E 3
Cucumbi 66 B 2
Cucurpe 76 D 5
Cúcuta 84 D 2
Cuddalore 40 CD 5
Cuddapah 40 C 5
Cudi Dağı 21 F 3
Cue 48 B 4
Cuéllar 18 C 3
Cuemba 66 B 2
Cuenca (Ecuador) 84 C 4
Cuenca (Spain) 18 C 3
Cuencamé de Ceniceros 78 B 3
Cuerda del Pozo, Embalse de la 18 C 3
Cuernavaca 78 BC 4
Cuero 77 G 6

Cuevas de Artá 18 D 4
Cuevo 86 D 5
Cufra Oasis → Wāhāt al Kufrah 59 K 4
Cuiabá 86 E 4
Cuiabá 86 E 4
Cuiari 84 E 3
Cuilapa 78 D 5
Cuillin Hills 2 A 3
Cuillin Sound 3 A 3
Cuilo 66 B 1
Cuilo 66 B 1
Cuima 86 B 2
Cuito Cuanavale 66 B 3
Cuiuni 85 F 4
Cujmir 20 B 2
Cukurca 21 F 3
Cukurca (Turkey) 22 D 1
Culan 18 D 2
Culbokie 2 B 3
Culcairn 49 H 6
Culdaff 4 B 2
Culgoa River 49 H 4
Culiacán 76 E 7
Culion 43 F 1
Cullen 2 C 3
Cullera 18 C 4
Cullman 77 J 5
Cullompton 6 C 2
Cullybackey 4 B 2
Culrain 2 B 3
Culswick 2 D 1
Cultowa 49 G 5
Cults 2 C 3
Culuene 87 F 3
Culver, Point 48 C 5
Cumaná 85 F 1
Cumaria 84 D 5
Cumbal 84 C 2
Cumberland 77 L 4
Cumberland Islands 49 H 3
Cumberland, Lake (KY, U.S.A.) 77 J 4
Cumberland Lake (Sask., Can.) 73 R 5
Cumberland Peninsula 75 OP 2
Cumberland Plateau 77 JK 4
Cumberland River 77 J 4
Cumberland Sound 75 O 2
Cumbernauld 3 B 4
Cumbrian Mountains 5 D 2
Cûmina 85 G 4
Cuminapanema 85 GH 4
Cuminestown 2 C 3
Cummins 49 F 5
Cumnock 3 B 4
Çumra 21 D 3
Cunani 85 H 3
Cunco 89 B 6
Cunene 66 A 3
Cunene 66 B 3
Cuneo 19 E 3
Cungena 48 E 5
Cunnamulla 49 H 4
Cunningham 3 B 4
Cupar 3 C 3
Cupica 84 C 2
Cuprija 20 B 2
Curaçao, Isla 84 E 1
Curacautin 89 B 6
Curanilahue 89 B 6
Curaray 84 CD 4
Curare 84 E 3
Curcubata, Virful 20 B 1
Curdimurka 49 F 4
Curepipe 67 K 6
Curepto 89 B 6
Curiapo 85 F 2
Curicó 89 B 5–6
Curicuriari 84 E 4
Curimatá 87 H 2–3
Curious, Mount 48 A 4
Curiplaya 84 C 3
Curitiba 88 FG 4
Curnamona 49 F 5
Curoca 66 A 3
Currais Novos 87 J 2
Curralinho 85 J 4
Currie 49 G 6
Currie 50 K 8
Curtea de Argeş 20 BC 1
Curtici 20 B 1
Curtina 88 E 5
Curtis 52 D 5
Curtis Channel 49 J 3
Curtis Island 49 J 3
Curuá 85 H 5
Curuá (Pará, Brazil) 85 H 4
Curuá, Ilha 85 J 3
Curuá Una 85 H 4
Curuaí 85 G 4
Curuçá 85 J 3
Curuçambaba 85 J 4
Curuguaty 86 E 5
Curumu 85 H 4
Curupá 85 J 5

Curupira, Sierra de 84–85 EF 3
Cururupu 85 K 4
Curuzú Cuatiá 88 E 4
Curvelo 87 H 4
Cushendun 4 B 2
Cushina 4 B 3
Cushing 77 G 4
Cushing, Mount 73 M 4
Cusset 18 D 2
Cutervo 84 C 5
Cutral-Có 89 C 6
Cuttack 40 E 3
Cuvelai 66 B 3
Cuvette 63 H 6
Cuvier, Cape 48 A 3
Cuxhaven 15 E 4
Cuya 86 B 4
Cuyo Islands 43 F 1
Cuyuni 85 G 2
Cuzco 86 B 3
Cuzna 18 C 4
Cwmbran 6 C 2
Cwmffrwd 6 B 2
Cyangugu 64 D 5
Cyclades 20 C 3
Cynwyl Elfed 6 B 2
Cypress Hills 73 PQ 6
Cyprus 21 D 3
Cyprus 22 AB 2
Cyrenaica 59 K 2
Cyrene 59 K 2
Cyrene → Shahhāt 59 K 2
Cyrus (Iran) 23 E 3
Cyrus Field Bay 75 P 3
Czechoslovakia 15 G 5
Czeremcha 15 H 4
Czersk 15 G 4
Częstochowa 15 G 4

D

Da Hinggan Ling 39 GH 1–2
Da Lat 41 J 5
Da Nang 41 J 4
Da Qaidam 38 C 3
Da Yunhe 39 G 4
Da'an 39 H 1
Daba Shan 38 E 4
Dabaga 65 F 6
Dabajuro 84 D 1
Dabakala 62 D 4
Dabat 65 F 2
Dabbāgh, Jabal (Saudi Arabia) 22 B 4
Dabeiba 84 C 2
Dabhoi 40 B 3
Dabie Shan 38 G 4
Dabnou 63 F 3
Dabo 42 B 4
Dabola 62 B 3
Daborōw 65 H 3
Dabou 62 D 4
Daboya 62 E 3
Dabrash 20 B 2
Dabu 38 G 6
Dābuleni 20 B 2
Dacca 40 E 3
Dachau 15 F 5
Dadali 51 G 3
Dadu 35 H 5
Dadu He 38 D 5
Dadynskoye, Ozero 21 FG 1
Daet 43 F 1
Dafang 38 E 5
Dafeng 39 H 4
Daflas 41 F 2
Daga Medo 65 G 3
Daga Post 64 E 3
Dagabur 65 G 3
Dagadzhik 34 E 3
Dagana (Chad) 63 H 3
Dagana (Senegal) 62 A 2
Dagary 36 K 4
Dagash 60 E 5
Dağbası 21 E 3
Dagi 37 Q 5
Daguan 38 D 5
Dagupan 43 J 1
Dagur 38 C 3
Dagworth 49 G 2
Dagzê 41 F 2
Dagzê Co 40 E 1
Dagzhuka 40 E 2
Dahabān 61 F 4
Dahanu 40 B 4
Dahei He 38 F 2
Daheiding Shan 37 NO 6
Dahl al Furayy (Saudi Arabia) 23 E 4
Dahlak Archipelago 65 G 1
Dahlak Kebir 65 G 1
Dahongliutan 35 K 3
Dahra (Algeria) 18 D 4
Dahra (Senegal) 62 A 2

Dahūk (Iraq) 22 D 1
Dahy, Nafūd ad 61 GH 4
Dai 51 H 3
Dai Xian 38 F 3
Daïa 59 F 2
Daicheng 39 G 3
Daik-u 41 G 4
Daimier 18 C 4
Daingean 4 B 3
Dainkog 38 C 4
Daintree River National Park 49 G 2
Daireaux 89 D 6
Dairen 39 H 3
Dairsle 3 C 3
Daitō-shotō 39 K 5
Daiyun Shan 39 G 5–6
Dajarra 49 F 3
Dak Kon 41 J 5
Dakala 62 E 3
Dakar 62 A 3
Dakha 40 E 3
Dakhla 58 B 4
Dakhla Oasis → Wāhāt ad Dākhilah 60 D 3
Dakhlet Nouadhibou 58 B 4
Dako 62 D 2
Dakoro 63 F 3
Dakovo 19 G 2
Daktuy 37 N 5
Dákura 78 F 5
Dala 66 C 2
Dalaba 62 B 3
Dalad Qi 38 E 2
Dalai Nur 39 G 2
Dalälven 17 G 3
Dalaman 20 C 3
Dalāmī 60 E 6
Dalandzadgad 38 DE 2
Dalanjargalan 38 E 1
Dalarna 17 F 3
Dalbandin 35 G 5
Dalbeattie 3 C 4
Dalby 49 J 4
Dalbyrdakh 37 P 2
Dale 17 E 3
Dale Hollow Lake 77 JK 4
Dalen 17 E 4
Daletme 41 F 3
Dalgonally 49 G 3
Dalhalvaig 2 C 2
Dalhart 76 F 4
Dalhousie 75 O 6
Dalhousie, Cape 72 L 1
Dali 38 D 5
Dali 38 EF 4
Dalian → Lüda 39 H 3
Dalias 18 C 4
Daliburgh 2 A 3
Dalj 19 G 2
Daljaʼ 60 E 3
Dalkeith 3 C 4
Dall 72 L 5
Dall Lake 72 E 3
Dallas 2 C 3
Dallas 77 G 5
Dalli 40 D 3
Dallol Bosso 62 E 3
Dalmā' (United Arab Emirates) 23 F 4
Dalmaj, Hawr (Iraq) 23 D 2
Dalmally 3 B 3
Dalmellington 3 B 4
Dalnaspidal 3 B 3
Dalnavie 2 B 3
Dal'negorsk 39 L 2
Dal'nerechensk 39 K 1
Dal'nyaya 37 Q 6
Daloa 62 C 4
Dalou Shan 38 E 5
Dalqān (Saudi Arabia) 23 D 4
Dalqū 60 E 4
Dalrymple, Mount 49 H 3
Dals Långed 17 F 4
Dalsfjorden 16 D 3
Dalsland 17 F 4
Dalstroy 37 P 3
Dalton 3 C 4
Dalton 77 K 5
Daltonganj 40 D 3
Dalton-in-Furness 5 D 2
Daluo 38 D 6
Dalupiri 43 J 1
Dalvik 16 B 2
Dalwallinu 48 B 5
Dalwinnie 3 B 3
Daly Bay 73 U 3
Daly River 48 E 1
Daly Waters 48 E 2
Daman 40 B 3
Dāmaneh (Iran) 23 F 2
Damanhūr 60 DE 2
Damar, Pulau 43 G 4
Damar, Pulau 43 G 5
Damara 64 B 3

Damaraland 66 B 4
Damascus (Syria) 22 B 2
Dāmāsh (Iran) 23 E 1
Damaturu 63 G 3
Damāvand (Iran) 23 F 2
Damāvand, Qolleh-ye 34 E 3
Damba 66 B 1
Dambarta 63 F 3
Dame Marie, Cap 79 H 4
Damietta → Dumyāt 60 E 2
Damīr Qābū (Syria) 22 CD 1
Damlataş 21 D 3
Damoh 40 C 3
Damot 65 H 3
Dampier 48 B 3
Dampier Archipelago 48 B 3
Dampier Land 48 C 2
Dampier, Selat 43 H 4
Dampier Strait 50 E 3
Damqawt 61 J 5
Damxung 41 F 1
Dan Gulbi 63 F 3
Dan Sai 41 H 4
Dan Xian 38 E 7
Dana 37 U 3
Danakil Depression → Kobar Sink 65 G 2
Danakil Plain 65 G 2
Danan 65 G 3
Danané 62 C 4
Danau Toba 42 A 3
Danau Towuti 43 F 4
Danba 38 D 4
Dandarah (Egypt) 22 A 4
Dande 66 A 1
Dandeldhura 40 D 2
Dandeli 40 B 4
Dandong 39 H 2
Danells Fjord 75 T 3
Danfa 62 C 3
Danfeng 38 F 4
Danforth 77 N 2
Dang Krien 41 J 5
Dangara 35 H 3
Dangchang 38 D 4
Dange 66 B 1
Danghe Nanshan 38 C 3
Dangila 62 F 2
Dangriga 78 E 4
Dangshan 39 G 4
Dangyang 38 F 4
Daniel 76 D 3
Daniell 48 C 5
Daniel's Harbour 75 Q 5
Danielskuil 66 C 5
Danilov 24 H 4
Danilovka 24 H 5
Daning 38 F 3
Danjiangkou Shuiku 38 F 4
Danjo-guntō 39 J 4
Dank (Oman) 23 G 5
Dankhar 40 C 1
Danlí 78 E 5
Danmark 17 E 4
Danmarks Havn 90
Dannevirke 51 R 9
Danompari 42 E 3
Dante 65 J 2
Dantewara 40 D 4
Danu 51 F 2
Danube 20 C 1
Danure 3 B 4
Danville (IL, U.S.A.) 77 J 3
Danville (KY, U.S.A.) 77 K 4
Danville (VA, U.S.A.) 77 L 4
Danzhai 38 E 5
Dao 43 F 1
Dao Tho Chy 41 G 5
Dao Timni 63 G 1
Dao Xian 38 F 5
Daocheng 38 D 5
Daora 58 C 3
Daoukro 62 D 4
Daoura 58 E 2
Dapango 62 E 3
Dapchi 63 G 3
Daphabum 41 G 2
Dapoli 40 B 4
Daqing 39 J 1
Dar al Homr 60 D 6
Dar el Beida 58 CD 2
Dar el Kouti 64 C 3
Dar es Salaam 65 F 6
Dar Hamar 60 D 6
Dar Nūbah 60 DE 6
Dar Rounga 64 C 2–3
Dar Sila 63 J 3
Darʼā (Syria) 22 B 2
Dārāb 34 E 5
Dārāb (Iran) 23 G 3
Darabani 20 C 1
Daraçya Yarımadası 20 C 3
Darāfisah 60 E 6

Daraj 59 H 2
Dāran (Iran) 23 F 2
Darapap 50 D 2
Darasun 36 K 5
Darāw (Egypt) 22 A 4
Darazo 63 G 3
Darband 34 F 4
Darbhanga 40 E 2
Dārboruk 65 G 3
Darda 19 G 2
Dardanelle Lake 77 H 4
Dardanelles 20 C 3
Dardanelles 20 C 3
Darende 21 E 3
Darfo Boario Terme 19 EF 2
Dārfūr 60 C 6
Darganata 35 G 2
Dargaville 51 Q 8
Dargo 49 H 6
Dargol 62 E 3
Darhan 36 J 6
Darhan Muminggan Lianheqi 38 F 2
Darién 84 C 2
Darién, Golfo del 84 C 2
Darién, Serranía del 84 C 2
Dar'inskiy 25 O 6
Darius (Iran) 23 EF 3
Darjeeling 40 E 2
Darkan 48 B 5
Darkhovīn (Iran) 23 E 3
Darlag 38 C 4
Darlfield 7 D 1
Darling Downs 49 H 4
Darling Range 48 B 5
Darling River 49 G 5
Darlington 5 E 2
Darlot, Lake 48 C 4
Darłowo 15 G 4
Darmstadt 15 E 5
Darnah 59 K 2
Darnley Bay 73 N 2
Darnley, Cape 91
Daroca 18 C 3
Darreh Gaz 34 F 3
Darsi 40 C 4
Dartford 7 E 2
Dartmoor 6 BC 2
Dartmouth 75 P 7
Dartmouth (U.K.) 6 C 2
Daru 50 D 3
Daruba 43 G 3
Darūneh (Iran) 23 G 2
Daruvar 19 G 2
Darvaza 34 F 2
Darvel 3 B 4
Darvel, Teluk 43 E 3
Darvi 36 F 6
Darwen 5 D 3
Darweshan 35 G 4
Darwin (Argentina) 89 C 6
Darwin (Australia) 48 E 1
Darwin, Bahía 89 AB 8
Darwin, Isla 84 B 6
Darwin, Port 48 E 1
Dāryāch-ye 35 G 4
Daryācheh-ye Bakhtegān 34 E 5
Daryācheh-ye Bakhtegān (Iran) 23 FG 3
Daryācheh-ye Hāmūn-e Hīrmand 35 G 4
Daryācheh-ye Mahārlū (Iran) 23 F 3
Daryācheh-ye Namak (Iran) 23 F 2
Daryācheh-ye Orūmīyeh (Iran) 23 D 1
Daryācheh-ye Tashk 34 E 5
Daryācheh-ye Tashk (Iran) 23 FG 3
Daryā-ye Māzandarān 34 E 3
Darya-ye Panj 35 J 3
Dās (United Arab Emirates) 23 F 4
Dashbalbar 36 K 6
Dasht (Iran) 34 F 3
Dasht (Pakistan) 35 G 5
Dasht Āb (Iran) 23 G 3
Dashtak (Iran) 23 F 3
Dasht-e Kavīr (Iran) 23 FG 2
Dasht-e Lūt (Iran) 23 G 2
Dasht-e Naomid 34–35 G 4
Dasht-i Arbu Lut 35 G 5
Dasht-i Tahlab 35 G 5
Dashtiari 35 G 5
Dasht-i-Margo 35 G 4
Dasht-i-Nawar 35 H 4
Daspalla 40 D 3
Dastgardān (Iran) 23 G 2
Dasuya 40 C 1
Datça 20 C 3
Date 39 M 2
Datha 40 B 3
Datia 40 C 2
Datian 39 G 5
Datong 31
Datong 38 D 3

Datong 38 F 2
Datong 39 H 1
Datong Shan 38 CD 3
Datta 37 Q 6
Datu Piang 43 F 2
Datu, Teluk 42 D 3
Datumakuta 42 E 3
Dăuarzan 34 F 3
Daugava 17 H 4
Daugav'pils 17 J 4
Daulat Yar 35 H 3
Daulatabad 35 GH 3
Daule 84 B 4
Daule 84 C 4
Daung Kyun 41 G 5
Dauphin 73 R 5
Dauphin Lake 73 R 5
Dauphin Lake 73 S 5
Dauphiné 19 E 3
Daura 63 F 3
Daurskoye 36 F 4
Davangere 40 C 5
Davao 43 G 2
Davao Gulf 43 G 2
Dāvar Panāh 35 G 5
Dāvarān, Kūh-e (Iran) 23 G 3
Dāvarzan (Iran) 23 G 1
Davenport 77 HJ 3
Davenport Downs 49 G 3
Daventry 7 D 1
David 84 B 2
Davidson Mountains 72 J 2
Davies, Mount 48 D 4
Davis (Antarctica) 91
Davis (CA, U.S.A.) 76 B 4
Davis Inlet 73 P 4
Davis River 48 C 3
Davis Sea 91
Davis Strait 75 Q 2
Davlekanovo 24 K 5
Davos 19 E 2
Davydov Brod 21 D 1
Dawa 65 G 4
Dawāsir, Wādī ad 61 G 4
Dawes Range 49 J 3
Dawhat as Salwā (Qatar) 23 F 4
Dawlish 6 C 2
Dawna Range 41 G 4
Dawqah (Oman) 61 J 5
Dawqah (Saudi Arabia) 61 G 5
Dawson 72 K 3
Dawson Creek 73 N 4
Dawson Inlet 73 T 3
Dawson, Isla 89 B 9
Dawson Range 72 K 3
Dawson River 49 HJ 3
Dawu 38 D 4
Dawu 38 F 4
Dax 18 C 3
Daxian 38 E 4
Daxin 38 E 6
Daxing 39 G 3
Daxue Shan 38 D 4–5
Daya Abeidi 62 C 1
Daya Hamami 58 C 4
Dayangshu 37 M 6
Dayao 38 D 5
Dayet en Naharat 62 D 2
Daym Zubayr 64 D 3
Dayong 38 F 5
Dayr az Zawr (Syria) 22 C 2
Dayr Ḥāfir (Syria) 22 B 1
Dayr, Jabal ad 60 E 6
Dayrūt 60 E 3
Dayton 77 K 4
Daytona Beach 77 K 6
Dayu 38 F 5
Dayyīnah (United Arab Emirates) 23 F 4
Dazhu 38 E 4
Dazjā 34 F 3
Dazjā (Iran) 23 G 2
Dazkırı 20 C 3
Dazu 38 E 5
De Aar 66 C 6
De Behagle → Lai 63 H 4
De Brie 67 H 3
de Gras, Lac 73 P 3
De Grey River 48 C 3
De Jong, Tanjung 43 J 5
De Kalb 77 J 3
De Kalk 66 B 4
De Land 77 K 6
De Long Mountains 72 E 2
De Peré 77 J 3
De Queen 77 H 5
De Ridder 77 H 5
Dead Sea (Jordan) 22 B 3
Deadhorse 72 GH 1
Deal 7 E 2
Deal Island (Victoria, Austr.) 49 H 6
De'an 38 G 5
Dean 73 M 5
Deán Funes 88 D 5
Dease 72 M 4

Dease Arm 73 N 2
Dease Lake 72 L 4
Dease Strait 73 Q 2
Death Valley 76 C 4
Death Valley National Monument 76 C 4
Debak 42 D 3
Debaltsevo 21 E 1
Debao 38 E 6
Debar 20 B 2
Debark 65 F 2
Debdou 58 E 2
Debenham 7 E 1
Dębica 15 H 4
Dęblin 15 H 4
Dębno 15 F 4
Débo, Lac 62 D 2
Deborah, Lake 48 B 5
Deboyne Island 51 F 4
Debra Birhan 65 F 3
Debra Libanos 65 F 3
Debra Markos 65 F 2
Debra Sina 65 F 3
Debra Tabor 65 F 2
Debra Zeit 65 F 3
Debrecen 20 B 1
Decamere 65 F 1
Decatur (AL, U.S.A.) 77 J 5
Decatur (IL, U.S.A.) 77 J 4
Decazeville 18 D 3
Deccan 40 CD 3–5
Decelles, Réservoir 75 M 6
Decepción 91
Dechang 38 D 5
Děčín 15 F 4
Deda 20 B 1
Dedegöl Dağı 20 D 3
Dedo, Cerro 89 B 7
Dédougou 62 D 3
Dedovichi 17 J 4
Dedu 37 N 6
Dedza 67 E 2
Dee, River (Clwyd) 6 C 1
Dee, River (Grampian) 2 C 3
Deep Well 48 E 3
Deer Lake 75 Q 6
Deer Lake (Ontario, Can.) 74 J 5
Deer Lodge 76 D 2
Deering 72 E 2
Deering, Mount 48 D 3
Deesa 40 B 2
Defah 59 K 3
Defferrari 89 E 6
Defirou 63 H 1
Dêgê 38 C 4
Degema 63 F 5
Dêgên 41 F 1
Degerfors 17 F 4
Deggendorf 15 F 5
Deh Bārez 34 F 5
Deh Bīd (Iran) 23 F 3
Deh Dasht (Iran) 23 EF 3
Deh Mollā (Iran) 23 EF 3
Deh Shū 35 G 4
Dehaj 34 E 4
Dehaj (Iran) 23 G 3
Dehak 35 G 5
Dehaq (Iran) 23 F 2
Dehdez (Iran) 23 F 3
Deh-e Namak (Iran) 23 F 2
Deh-e Shīr (Iran) 23 F 3
Dehgolān (Iran) 23 E 2
Dehlorān (Iran) 23 E 2
Dehra Dun 40 C 1
Dehua 39 G 5
Dehui 39 J 2
Deingueri, Mont 64 D 3
Dej 20 B 1
Dejiang 38 E 5
Dekar 66 C 4
Dekese 64 C 5
Dekina 63 F 4
Dékoa 64 B 3
Del Campillo 88 D 5
Del City 76 G 4
Del Norte 76 E 4
Del Rio 76 F 6
Delabole 6 B 2
Delarof Islands 72 B 5
Delaware 77 L 4
Delaware Bay 77 L 4
Delaware River 77 L 3
Delcommune, Lac 66 D 2
Delegate 49 H 6
Delémont 19 E 2
Delft (Netherlands) 14 D 4
Delft (Sri Lanka) 40 C 6
Delgado, Cabo 67 G 2
Delger 36 G 6
Delgereh 38 F 1
Delgerhaan 36 HJ 6
Delgerhaan 38 DE 1
Delgerhangay 38 D 1
Delgerhet 38 F 1
Delgertsogt 38 E 1
Delhi 40 C 2

Deliblatska Peščara 20 B 1–2
Deličal Dağı 20 C 2–3
Delice 21 D 3
Delicias 76 E 6
Delicirmak 21 D 2–3
Delījān (Iran) 23 F 2
Delingha 38 C 3
Dellen 16 G 3
Dellys 59 F 1
Delmenhorst 15 E 4
Delnice 19 F 2
Delorme, Lac 75 O 5
Delos → Dhílos 20 C 3
Delphi 20 B 3
Delphi → Dhelfoi 20 B 3
Delsbo 16 G 3
Delta (CO, U.S.A.) 76 E 4
Delta (UT, U.S.A.) 76 D 4
Delta del Ebro 18 D 3
Delta Downs 49 G 2
Delta Dunării 20 CD 1
Delta Dunării 20 D 1
Delta Junction 72 H 3
Delvin 4 B 3
Delvina 20 AB 3
Delyankyr 37 R 3
Delyatin 20 B 1
Demanda, Sierra de la 18 C 3
Demavend, Mount 34 E 3
Demavend, Mount (Iran) 23 F 2
Demba 64 C 6
Dembi 65 F 3
Dembia 64 C 3
Dembidollo 64 E 3
Deming 76 E 5
Demini 85 F 3
Demir Kapija 20 B 2
Demirci 20 C 3
Demırköprü Barajı 20 C 3
Demmin 15 F 4
Demnate 58 D 2
Democracia 85 F 5
Demopolis 77 J 5
Dempo, Gunung 42 B 4
Dêmqog 40 C 1
Demre 20 C 3
Dem'yanka 25 O 4
Dem'yanovka 25 N 5
Dem'yanskoye 25 N 4
Den Helder 14 D 4
Denain 18 D 1
Denali 72 H 3
Denali National Park and Preservative 72 G 3
Denali National Park and Preserve 72 H 3
Denau 35 H 3
Denbigh 6 C 1
Dendang 42 C 4
Dendi 65 F 3
Denezhkin Kamen', Gora 25 L 3
Denezhkino 25 R 2
Deng Deng 63 G 4
Deng Xian 38 F 4
Dêngqên 38 C 4
Denham 48 A 4
Denham Sound 48 A 4
Denia 18 D 4
Deniliquin 49 G 6
Denio 76 C 3
Denison (IA, U.S.A.) 77 G 3
Denison (TX, U.S.A.) 77 G 5
Denison, Mount 72 G 4
Denizli 20 C 3
Denkou 38 E 2
Denmark 17 E 4
Denmark (Australia) 48 B 5
Denmark Strait 90
Dennison, Cape 91
Denpasar 42 E 5
Denton 7 D 1
Denton 77 G 5
D'Entrecasteaux Islands 51 F 3
D'Entrecasteaux, Point 48 AB 5
Denver 76 F 4
Deo 63 G 4
Deogarh 40 D 3
Deoghar 40 E 3
Deolali 40 B 4
Deori 40 C 3
Depoe Bay 76 B 3
Depósita 85 F 3
Deprésion del Balsas 78 BC 4
Dépression du Mourdi 63 J 2
Deputatskiy 37 P 2
Deqên 38 C 5
Deqing 38 F 6
Der, Lac du 19 D 2
Dera Bugti 35 H 5
Dera Ghazi Khan 35 HJ 4
Dera Ismail Khan 35 J 4
Deraheib 60 F 4
Derajat 35 J 4
Derbeke 37 P 2
Derbent 34 D 2
Derbent 35 H 3

Derbino 36 F 4
Derbisaka 64 C 3
Derby (Australia) 48 C 2
Derby (U.K.) 7 D 1
Derbyshire 7 D 1
Derdap 20 B 2
Dereköy 20 C 2
Dergachi 24 J 5
Derik 21 F 3
Derm 66 B 4
Dermott 77 H 5
Derna → Darnah 59 K 2
Dêrong 38 C 5
Derrybeg 4 A 2
Derryveagh Mountains 4 A 2
Dersingham 7 E 1
Derudeb 60 F 5
Derventa 19 G 3
Dervock 4 B 2
Derwent, River (U.K.) 5 E 2
Derwent River (Tasmania, Austr.) 50 L 9
Deryabino 25 Q 1
Derzhavinsk 25 N 5
Des Moines 77 H 3
Des Moines River 77 H 3
Desaguadero (Argentina) 88 C 5
Desaguadero (Bolivia) 86 C 4
Désappointement, Îles du 53 F 3
Desborough 7 D 1
Descalvado 86 E 4
Deschambault Lake 73 R 5
Deseado 89 C 8
Deseado, Cabo 89 AB 9
Desengaño, Punta 89 C 8
Desert Center 76 C 5
Desierto de Sechura 84 B 5
Desierto de Vizcaíno 76 D 6
Desierto do Atacama 86 C 5
Desna 24 F 5
Desolación, Isla 89 AB 9
Desrouches, Île 65 J 6
Dessau 15 F 4
Dessye 65 F 2
Destruction Bay 72 K 3
Deta 20 B 1
Detmold 15 E 4
Detroit 77 K 3
Détroit de Jacques-Cartier 75 P 6
Détroit d'Honguedo 75 P 6
Detroit Lakes 77 G 2
Dett 66 D 3
Dettifoss 16 B 2
Deutsche Bucht 15 E 4
Deutsche Demokratische Republik 15 F 4
Deva 20 B 1
Devakottai 40 C 6
Devarkonda 40 C 4
Devecı Dağı 21 E 2–3
Develi 21 E 3
Deveron, River 2 C 3
Devikot 40 B 2
Devils Elbow 3 C 3
Devil's Island 85 H 2
Devils Lake 76 G 2
Devils Paw 72 L 4
Devizes 7 D 2
Devli 40 C 2
Devnya 20 C 2
Devolli 20 B 2
Devon 6 C 2
Devon Island 90
Devonport 52 A 5
Devonport (New Zealand) 51 Q 8
Devonport (Tasmania, Austr.) 50 L 9
Devrek 21 D 2
Devres 21 D 2
Dewangiri 41 F 2
Dewsbury 5 E 3
Dexing 39 G 5
Dexter 77 K 5
Dey Dey, Lake 48 E 4
Deyang 38 D 4
Deyhuk 34 F 4
Deynau 35 G 2
Deyyer (Iran) 23 F 4
Dez (Iran) 23 E 2
Dez Gerd (Iran) 23 F 3
Dezfūl (Iran) 23 E 2
Dezhneva, Mys 72 D 2
Dezhou 39 G 3
Dháfni 20 B 3
Dhahab (Egypt) 22 B 3
Dhahran (Saudi Arabia) 23 EF 4
Dhahran → Az Ẓahrān 61 HJ 3
Dhamār 61 G 6
Dhamra 40 E 3
Dhamtari 40 D 3
Dhanbad 40 E 3
Dhang Range 40 D 2
Dhangain 40 D 2
Dhankuta 40 E 2
Dhar 40 C 3
Dhar Adrar 58 C 4

Dhar Oualata 58 D 5
Dhar Tagant 58 C 5
Dhar Tichit 58 D 5
Dharinavaram 40 C 5
Dharmapuri 40 C 5
Dharmjaygarh 40 D 3
Dharwar 40 C 4
Dhaulagiri 40 D 2
Dhenkanal 40 E 3
Dhelfoí 20 B 3
Dhiavlos Thásou 20 BC 2
Dhíavlos Zakínthou 20 B 3
Dhílos 20 C 3
Dhírfis Óros 20 B 3
Dhisoron Óros 20 B 2
Dhofar → Ẓufār 61 J 5
Dholpur 40 C 2
Dhomokós 20 B 3
Dhone 40 C 4
Dhoraji 40 B 3
Dhubāb 61 G 6
Dhule 40 B 3
Dhulian 40 E 3
Dhwanr 61 G 6
Diabakagna 62 B 3
Diable, Île du 85 H 2
Diablo Range 76 B 4
Diaca 67 F 2
Diafarabe 62 C 3
Dialafara 62 B 3
Dialakoto 62 B 3
Diamante (Argentina) 88 D 5
Diamante (Italy) 19 G 4
Diamante, Punta del 78 C 4
Diamantina (Minas Gerais, Brazil) 87 H 4
Diamantina (Queensland, Austr.) 49 G 3
Diamantina Lakes 49 G 3
Diamantina Fracture Zone 98 C 5
Diamantino 86 E 3
Diamond Harbour 40 E 3
Diamond Jenness Peninsula 73 OP 1
Diamond Peak 76 C 4
Diamou 62 B 3
Diamounguel 62 B 2
Dian Chi 38 D 6
Diana, Baie 75 O 3
Dianbai 38 F 6
Dianjiang 38 E 4
Dianópolis 87 G 3
Diapaga 62 E 3
Dibā (United Arab Emirates) 23 G 4
Dībagah (Iraq) 22 D 2
Dibang 41 G 2
Dibaya 64 C 6
Dibaya-Lubue 64 B 5
Dibella 63 G 2
Dibete 66 D 4
Dibo 65 G 3
Dibrugarh 41 FG 2
Dibsī ʿAfnān (Syria) 22 BC 2
Dickinson 76 F 2
Dicle 21 F 3
Didcot 7 D 2
Didiéni 62 C 3
Didwana 40 B 2
Didyma 20 C 3
Die 19 E 3
Diébougou 62 D 3
Diego Ramírez, Islas 89 BC 10
Diéké 62 C 4
Diéma 62 C 3
Dien Bien Phu 41 H 3
Diepholz 15 E 4
Dieppe 18 D 2
Di'er Songhua Jiang 39 J 2
Dif 65 G 4
Diffa 63 G 3
Digba 64 D 4
Digby 75 O 7
Dighir 40 C 4
Digne 19 E 3
Digoin 18 D 2
Digos 43 G 2
Digranes 16 C 2
Digul, Sungai 43 J 5
Dihang 41 G 2
Dijlāh (Iraq) 23 D 2
Dijon 19 E 2
Dik 63 H 4
Dikanäs 16 G 2
Dikeneye 66 D 4
Dikhil 65 G 2
Dikili 20 C 3
Dikmen 21 E 2
Dıkmen Dağı 21 D 2
Dikodougou 62 C 4
Dikson 90
Dikwa 63 G 3
Dilaram 35 G 4

Dili 43 G 5
Dilizhan 21 FG 2
Dilj 19 G 2
Dilla 65 F 3
Dillia 63 G 2
Dillia Téfidinga 63 G 2
Dilling 60 D 6
Dillingham 72 F 4
Dillon 76 D 2
Dilly 62 C 2
Dilolo 66 C 2
Dimashq (Syria) 22 B 2
Dimbelenge 64 C 6
Dimbokro 62 D 4
Dimboola 49 G 6
Dimitrovgrad 20 B 2
Dimitrovgrad 20 C 2
Dimitrovgrad 24 JK 5
Dimitrya Lapteva, Proliv 37 Q 1
Dimona (Israel) 22 B 3
Dimovo 20 B 2
Dīn (Iran) 23 G 4
Dinagat 43 G 1
Dinangourou 62 D 3
Dinant 14 DE 2
Dınar 20 D 3
Dīnār, Kūh-e (Iran) 23 F 3
Dinara Planina 19 G 3
Dinard 18 C 2
Dinas Powis 6 C 3
Dinder National Park 60 F 6
Dindigul 40 C 5
Dindiza 67 E 4
Dindori 40 D 3
Ding Xian 38 FG 3
Dinga 64 B 6
Dingbian 38 E 3
Dinggyê 40 E 2
Dinghai 39 H 4
Dingle 14 A 4
Dingle Bay 14 A 4
Dingtao 38 G 3–4
Dinguiraye 62 B 3
Dingwall 2 B 3
Dingxi 38 D 3
Dingxian 38 F 3
Dingxing 38 G 3
Dinh Lap 41 J 3
Diniapur 41 F 2
Dinokwe 66 D 4
Dinskaya 21 E 1
Dīṇsōr 65 G 4
Diois, Massif du 19 E 3
Dioka 62 B 3
Diomida, Ostrova 72 D 2
Diona 63 J 2
Dionísio Cerqueira 88 F 4
Diouloulou 62 A 3
Dioundiou 62 E 3
Dioura 62 C 3
Diourbel 62 A 3
Dipkarpas 21 D 3
Dipkarpas (Cyprus) 22 B 2
Dipolog 43 F 2
Dir 35 J 3
Diré 62 D 2
Diredawa 65 G 3
Dirico 66 C 3
Dirk Hartog Island 48 A 4
Dirkou 63 G 2
Dirranbandi 49 H 4
Dirs 61 G 5
Disappointment, Lake 48 C 3
Dishnā (Egypt) 22 A 4
Disko 90
Disko Bugt 90
Disna 17 J 4
Dispur 41 F 2
Diss 7 E 1
District of Columbia (D.C., U.S.A.) 77 L 4
District of Fort Smith 73 P 3
District of Inuvik 72 LM 2
District of Keewatin 73 TU 2–3
Distrito Federal 87 G 4
Ditdak 41 F 6
Diu 40 B 3
Dīvāndarreh (Iran) 23 E 1
Divénié 63 G 6
Divinópolis 87 GH 5
Divisor, Serra do 84 D 5
Divisoria 17 J 4
Divnogorsk 36 F 4
Divnoye 21 F 1
Divo 62 C 4
Divriği 21 E 3
Dīvrūd (Iran) 23 F 1
Dixon Entrance 72 L 5
Diyālā (Iraq) 23 D 2
Diyarbakır 21 F 3
Diyarbakır Havzası 21 F 3
Diza 21 G 3
Dja 63 G 5
Djado 63 G 1
Djado, Plateau du 63 G 1

Djafou 59 F 3
Djaja Peak 43 J 4
Djaja Peak 50 C 2
Djako 64 C 3
Djamaa 59 G 2
Djambala 63 G 6
Djanet 59 G 4
Djaret 59 F 3
Djaul 51 F 2
Djebel Aïssa 58 E 2
Djebel Amour 59 F 2
Djebel Chélia 59 G 1
Djebel Edough 19 E 4
Djebel Onk 59 G 2
Djebel Ounane 59 G 3
Djebel Telerhteba 59 G 4
Djebobo 62 E 4
Djédaa 63 H 3
Djedi 59 F 2
Djelfa 59 F 2
Djéma 64 D 3
Djemila 59 G 1
Djenienbou Rezg 58 E 2
Djénné 62 D 3
Djerba → Jarbah 59 H 2
Djerem 63 G 4
Djéroual 63 H 3
Djibo 62 D 3
Djibouti 65 G 2
Djibouti 65 G 2
Djiguéni 58 D 5
Djikdjik 63 J 2
Djilbabo Plain 65 F 4
Djokupunda 64 C 6
Djolu 64 C 4
Djombo 64 C 4
Djougou 62 E 4
Djoum 63 G 5
Djourab, Erg du 63 H 2
Djugu 64 E 4
Djúpivogur 16 C 3
Dmanisi 21 F 2
Dnepr 24 F 6
Dneprodzerzhinsk 21 D 1
Dnepropetrovsk 21 E 1
Dneprovskiy Liman 20 D 1
Dneprovsko-Bugskiy Kanal
  17 HJ 5
Dnestr 20 C 1
Dnestrovskiy Liman 20 D 1
Dno 17 K 4
Dô, Lac 62 D 2
Doa 67 E 3
Doany 67 H 2
Doba (Chad) 63 H 4
Doba (China) 40 E 1
Dobbiaco 19 F 2
Dobel 65 F 4
Dobele 17 H 4
Döbeln 15 F 4
Doblas 89 D 6
Dobo 43 H 5
Doboj 19 G 3
Dobreta Turnu Severin 20 B 2
Dobrogea 20 C 2
Dobrowolski 91
Dobroye 37 R 7
Dobrudzhanska Plato 20 C 2
Dobruja 20 C 2
Dobryanka 24 L 4
Doce 87 H 4
Docking 7 E 1
Docksta 16 G 3
Doctor Arroyo 78 B 3
Dod Ballapur 40 C 5
Doda Betta 40 C 5
Dodecanese 20 C 3
Dodge City 76 F 4
Dodman Point 6 B 2
Dodoma 65 F 6
Dofa 43 G 4
Dog Creek 73 N 5
Dogai Coring 40 E 1
Doğankent 21 E 3
Dogger Bank 14 D 4
Doghārūn 35 G 4
Dõgo 39 K 3
Dogonbādān (Iran) 23 F 3
Dogondoutchi 63 E 3
Doğu Karadeniz Dağlari 21 EF 2
Doğubayazıt 21 F 3
Doguéraoua 63 F 3
Dogwaya 60 EF 5
Do'gyaling 40 E 1
Doha (Qatar) 23 F 4
Dohad 40 B 3
Dohazan 41 F 3
Dõhõ Nugālēd 65 H 3
Doi Inthanon 41 G 4
Doilungdêqen 41 F 2
Dois de Novembro, Cachoeira
  85 F 5
Dois Irmãos 85 J 5
Dois Irmãos, Serra 87 H 2
Doka (Indonesia) 43 H 5
Doka (Sudan) 60 F 6

Dokka 17 F 3
Doko 64 D 4
Dokshitsy 17 J 5
Dokuchayevsk 21 E 1
Dolak Island 50 C 3
Dolanog 6 C 1
Dolbeau 75 N 6
Dôle 19 E 2
Doleib Hill 64 E 3
Dolgellau 6 C 1
Dolgiy, Ostrov 25 LM 2
Dolgiy-Most 36 G 4
Dolinsk 37 Q 6
Dolinskaya 21 D 1
Dolni Dŭbnik 20 B 2
Dolo 65 G 4
Dolon, Pereval 35 K 2
Dolores (Argentina) 89 E 6
Dolores (Uruguay) 88 E 5
Dolphin and Union Strait 73 OP 2
Dolphinton 3 C 4
Dolwyddelan 6 C 1
Dolzhanskaya 21 E 1
Dom Aquino 87 F 4
Dom Cavati 87 H 4
Dom, Kūh-e (Iran) 23 F 2
Dom Pedrito 88 F 5
Doma Peaks 50 D 3
Domadare 65 G 4
Domaniç 20 C 3
Domažlice 15 F 5
Domba 38 C 4
Dombarovskiy 25 L 5
Dombås 16 E 3
Dombóvár 20 A 1
Domeyko 86 C 5
Domeyko, Cordillera 86 C 5
Dominica 79 K 4
Dominica Passage 79 K 4
Dominican Republic 79 J 3–4
Dominion, Cape 75 M 2
Domino 75 Q 5
Domiongo 64 C 5
Domo → Damot 65 H 3
Domo (Mali) 62 D 2
Domodossola 19 E 2
Dompierre 18 D 2
Dompu 43 E 5
Domuyo, Volcán 89 BC 6
Don (Mexico) 76 E 6
Don (U.S.S.R.) 24 H 6
Don Benito 18 B 4
Don Khi 41 H 4
Don, River (Grampian) 2 C 3
Don, River (S. Yorkshire) 5 E 3
Donadeu 88 D 4
Donaghadee 4 C 2
Donald 49 G 6
Donau 15 E 5
Donauwörth 15 F 5
Doncaster 5 E 3
Dondo (Angola) 66 A 1
Dondo (Indonesia) 43 F 4
Dondo (Mozambique) 67 E 3
Dondra Head 40 D 6
Donegal 4 AB 2
Donegal Bay 14 B 4
Donegal Mountains 14 B 4
Donets Basin 12
Donets Basin 21 E 1
Donets, Severskiy 21 F 1
Donetsk 21 E 1
Donetskiy Kryazh 21 E 1
Donetskiy Kryazh 21 EF 1
Donfeng 39 J 2
Dong Ha 41 J 4
Dong Hai 39 HJ 5
Dong He 38 D 2
Dong Hoi 41 J 4
Dong Jiang 38 FG 6
Dong Khe 41 J 3
Dong Nai 41 J 5
Dong Taijnar Hu 38 B 3
Dong Ujimqin Qi 39 G 1
Donga 63 G 4
Dongara 48 AB 4
Dongargarh 40 D 3
Dongchuan 38 D 5
Donges 18 C 2
Dongfang 38 E 7
Donggala 43 E 4
Donggi Cona 38 C 3
Donggou 39 H 3
Donghai 39 G 4
Donghai Dao 38 F 6
Dongkalang 43 F 3
Donglan 38 E 6
Donglük 38 A 3
Dongning 39 K 2
Dongo (Angola) 66 B 2
Dongo (Zaire) 64 B 4
Dongo (Zaire) 64 B 6
Dongou 63 H 5
Dongoura 62 C 3
Dongping 39 G 3
Dongshan 39 G 6

Dongshan Dao 39 G 6
Dongsheng 38 EF 3
Dongtai 39 H 4
Dongtou 39 H 5
Dongwe 66 C 2
Dongxiang 38 G 5
Dongying 39 G 3
Dongzhen 38 D 3
Dongzhi 39 G 4
Dönna 16 F 2
Donja Brela 19 G 3
Donji Miholjac 19 G 2
Donji Vakuf 19 G 3
Donjek 72 K 3
Donnybrook 48 B 5
Donskoye 21 F 1
Donuzlav, Ozero 21 D 1
Doocharry 4 A 2
Doonerak, Mount 72 H 2
Door Peninsula 77 J 3
Dora Baltea 19 E 2
Dora, Lake 48 C 3
Doramarkog 38 C 4
Dorbod 39 H 1
Dorchester 6 C 2
Dorchester, Cape 75 M 2
Dordogne 18 D 3
Dordrecht 14 D 4
Dore Lake 73 Q 5
Dore, Monts 18 D 2
Dores do Indaiá 87 G 4
Dori 62 D 3
Doring 66 B 6
Dorking 7 D 2
Dormidontovka 37 P 6
Dornbin 19 E 2
Dornoch 2 B 3
Dornoch Firth 2 B 3
Dornod 36 K 6
Dornogovï 38 EF 2
Doro (Indonesia) 43 G 3
Doro (Mali) 62 D 2
Dorogobuzh 24 F 5
Dorogorskoye 24 H 2
Dorohoi 20 C 1
Drokiya 20 C 1
Dorotea 16 G 3
Dorovitsa 24 J 4
Dorra (Saudi Arabia) 23 E 3
Dorre Island 48 A 4
Dorrigo 49 J 5
Dorset 6–7 C 2
Dortmund 15 E 4
Dörtyol 21 E 3
Dörtyol (Turkey) 22 B 1
Doruma 64 D 4
Doruokha 36 K 1
Dos de Mayo 84 D 5
Dosatuy 36 L 5
Doshi 35 H 3
Dosso 62 E 3
Dossor 34 E 1
Dothan 77 J 5
Douai 18 D 1
Douala 63 FG 5
Douandago 64 B 3
Douaumont 18 D 1
Doubs 19 E 2
Doubtful Sound 50 P 10
Douentza 62 D 3
Dougga 59 G 1
Douglas (AK, U.S.A.) 72 L 4
Douglas (AZ, U.S.A.) 76 E 5
Douglas (South Africa) 66 C 5
Douglas (U.K.) 4 C 2
Douglas (WY, U.S.A.) 76 EF 3
Doumbouene 63 J 3
Doumé 63 G 5
Douna 62 D 3
Doune 3 B 3
Dounreay 2 C 2
Dourada, Serra 87 G 3
Dourado, Monte 85 H 4
Dourados 87 F 5
Dourbali 63 H 3
Douro 18 B 3
Dove, River 7 D 1
Dover (DE, U.S.A.) 77 L 4
Dover (U.K.) 7 E 2
Dover, Strait of 14 D 4
Dovre 16 E 3
Dovrefjell 16 E 3
Dow Dehak (Iran) 23 F 2
Dow Rūd (Iran) 23 E 2
Dow Sar 34 D 3
Dow Sar (Iran) 23 E 2
Dowa 67 E 2
Dowlatābād 34 F 5
Dowlatābād (Iran) 23 G 3
Downham Market 7 E 1
Downhill 4 B 2
Downpatrick 4 C 2
Downtown 7 D 2
Dowra 4 B 2
Dozois, Réservoir 75 M 6

Drâa, Cap 58 C 3
Drâa, Hamada du 58 D 3
Drâa, Wadi 58 D 3
Drabat 'Ali, Ra's 61 J 5
Drac 19 E 3
Dragan 16 FG 3
Drăgăşani 20 B 2
Dragonera 18 D 4
Dragör 17 F 4
Draguignan 19 E 3
Drain 76 B 3
Drake 49 J 4
Drake Passage 91
Drake Strait 89 CD 10
Drakensberg 66 DE 4
Drakensberg 66 D 5
Drakensberg (Lesotho) 66 D 5–6
Dráma 20 B 2
Drammen 17 F 4
Drangajökull 16 A 2
Drangedal 17 E 4
Drangsnes 16 A 2
Dranka 37 U 4
Draperstown 4 B 2
Dras 35 K 4
Drau 19 F 2
Drava 19 G 2
Dráva 20 A 1
Dravograd 19 G 2
Drawa 15 G 4
Drawsko, Jezioro 15 G 4
Drayton 49 J 4
Drayton Valley 73 O 5
Drean 19 E 4
Dresden 15 F 4
Dreux 18 D 2
Drevsjö 16 F 3
Drina 19 G 3
Drini 20 B 2
Driva 16 E 3
Drniš 19 G 3
Dröbak 17 F 4
Drogheda 4 B 3
Drogobych 15 H 5
Droichead Nua 4 B 3
Droitwich 7 C 1
Dromore 4 B 2
Dronfield 5 E 3
Dronning 35 J 3
Drosh 35 J 3
Drumbeg 2 B 2
Drumclog 3 B 4
Drumfree 4 B 2
Drumheller 73 P 5
Drumlithe 3 D 3
Drummnod 76 D 2
Drummond Range 49 H 3
Drummondville 75 N 6
Drummore 4 C 2
Drumnadrochit 2 B 3
Drumod 4 B 3
Drumshanbo 4 A 2
Druskininkai 17 H 5
Druzhba 20 C 2
Druzhbovka 21 D 1
Druzhina 37 R 2
Druzhkovka 21 E 1
Druzhnaya 91
Druzhnaya II 91
Drvar 19 G 3
Drvenik 19 G 3
Drweca 15 G 4
Dry River 48 E 2
Dry Tortugas 77 K 7
Dryanovo 20 C 2
Dryden 74 J 6
Drymen 3 B 3
Drysdale River 48 D 1–2
Drysdale River National Park
  48 D 2
Dschang 63 F 4
Du Bois 77 L 3
du Couedic, Cape 49 F 6
Duaringa 49 H 3
Dubai → Dubayy 61 JK 3
Dubawnt 73 R 3
Dubawnt Lake 73 R 3
Dubayy (United Arab Emirates)
  23 G 4
Dubbo 49 H 5
Dubenskiy 24 L 5
Dubica 19 G 2
Dublin (Airport) 4 B 3
Dublin (GA, U.S.A.) 77 K 5
Dublin (Rep. of Ireland) 4 B 3
Dubna 24 G 4
Dubna 24 G 5
Dubno 17 J 5
Dubossary 20 C 1
Dubovka 24 J 6
Dubovskoye 21 F 1
Dubreka 63 B 4
Dubrovitsa 17 J 5
Dubrovnik 19 G 3
Dubrovnoye 25 NO 4

Dubuque 77 H 3
Duc de Gloucester, Îles du 53 F 4
Duchesne 76 D 3
Duchess 49 F 3
Ducie 53 G 4
Dudhi 40 D 3
Dudinka 25 R 2
Dudley 7 C 1
Dŭdo 65 J 3
Dudub 65 H 3
Dudypta 36 F 1
Duékoué 62 C 4
Dueré 87 G 3
Duero 18 C 3
Duff Islands 51 J 3
Dufftown 2 C 3
Duga-Zapadnaya, Mys 37 R 4
Dugi Otok 19 F 3
Dugo Selo 19 G 2
Duhūn Tarsū 59 J 4
Duifken Point 49 G 1
Duirinish 2 A 3
Duisburg 14 E 4
Duitama 84 D 2
Dujuma 65 G 4
Duk Fadiat 64 E 3
Duk Faiwil 64 E 3
Dukagjini 20 A 2
Dukān (Iraq) 23 D 2
Dukana 65 F 4
Duke of York Bay 73 UV 2
Dukhān (Qatar) 23 F 4
Duki 65 F 3
Duki (U.S.S.R.) 37 P 5
Dukou 38 D 5
Duku 63 G 3
Dukwe 66 D 4
Dulan 38 C 3
Dulce 88 D 4
Dulce, Bahia 78 C 4
Dulce, Golfo 78 F 6
Dul'durga 36 K 5
Duleek 4 B 3
Dulga-Kyuyel' 36 K 3
Dulgalakh 37 O 2
Dulla 65 F 3
Duluth 77 H 2
Dŭmā 60 F 2
Dumaguete 43 F 2
Dumai 42 B 3
Dumanlı Dağı 21 F 3
Dumaran 43 EF 1
Dumaring 42 E 3
Dumayr (Syria) 22 B 2
Dumbarton 3 B 4
Dumboa 63 G 3
Dumfries 3 C 4
Dumfries and Galloway 3 BC 4
Dumont d'Urville 91
Dumpu 50 E 3
Dumraon 40 D 2
Dumyāt 60 F 2
Dun Laoghaire 4 B 3
Duna 20 A 1
Dunaföldvár 20 A 1
Dunajec 15 GH 5
Dunan 2 B 3
Dunántúl 20 A 1
Dunărea 20 C 1
Dunaujváros 20 A 1
Dunav 20 B 2
Dunay 36 M 1
Dunay 39 K 2
Dunayevtsy 24 E 6
Dunbar (Australia) 49 G 2
Dunbar (U.K.) 3 C 3
Dunbeath 2 C 2
Dunblane 3 C 3
Dunboyne 4 B 3
Duncan 76 G 5
Duncan Passage 41 F 5
Duncansby Head 2 C 2
Dunchurch 7 D 1
Duncow 3 C 4
Dundalk 4 B 2
Dundalk Bay 4 B 3
Dundas, Lake 48 C 5
Dundas Strait 48 E 1
Dundee (Airport) 3 C 3
Dundee (South Africa) 66 E 5
Dundee (U.K.) 3 C 3
Dundgovï 38 E 1
Dundonald 4 C 2
Dundonnell 2 B 3
Dundrennan 3 C 4
Dundwa Range 40 D 2
Dunecht 2 C 3
Dunedin 51 Q 10
Dunes de l'Akchar 58 C 4
Dunes de l'Azéffal 58 BC 4
Dunfanaghy 4 B 2
Dunfermline 3 C 3
Dungannon 4 B 2
Dungarpur 40 B 3
Dungas 63 F 3
Dungeness 7 E 2

133

Dungiven 4 B 2
Dungog 49 J 5
Dungu 64 D 4
Dungul 60 E 4
Dunholme 7 D 1
Dunhua 39 J 2
Dunhuang 38 B 2
Dunkeld 3 C 3
Dunkerque 14 D 4
Dunkirk 77 L 3
Dunkur 64 F 2
Dunkwa 62 D 4
Dunlavin 4 B 3
Dunleer 4 B 3
Dunlewy 4 A 2
Dunmanway 14 B 4
Dunmarra 48 E 2
Dunmurry 4 B 2
Dunnet 2 C 2
Dunnet Head 2 C 2
Dunoon 3 B 4
Dunqulah al 'Ordi 60 E 5
Dunqulah al Qadīmah 60 DE 5
Dunqunāb 60 F 4
Dunrankin 74 L 6
Duns 3 C 4
Dunsby 7 D 1
Dunsmuir 76 B 3
Dunstable 7 D 2
Dunvegan Head 2 A 3
Duolun 39 G 2
Duong Dong 41 H 5
Duque de York 89 A 9
Dura Europos (Syria) 22 C 2
Durack Range 48 D 2
Durağan 21 DE 2
Durance 19 E 3
Durand 51 J 6
Durango (CO, U.S.A.) 76 E 4
Durango (Mexico) 78 AB 3
Durango (Spain) 18 C 3
Durant 77 G 5
Duratón 18 C 3
Durazno 88 E 5
Durban 67 E 5
Durdevac 19 G 2
Düren 14 E 4
Durg 40 D 3
Durgapur (Bangla Desh) 41 F 2
Durgapur (India) 40 E 3
Durham (N.C., U.S.A.) 77 L 4
Durham (U.K.) 5 E 2
Durham Downs 49 G 4
Durmä (Saudi Arabia) 23 E 4
Durmitor 20 A 2
Durness 2 B 2
Duro Europos → As Şālihīyah 61 G 2
Duroy 36 L 5
Durresi 20 A 2
Durrow 4 B 3
Dursunbey 20 C 3
Duruksi 65 H 3
Durusu Gölü 20 C 2
Durūz, Jabal ad (Syria) 22 B 2
D'Urville Island 51 Q 9
D'Urville Sea 91
Dusa Mareb 65 H 3
Dushak 34 G 3
Dushan 38 E 5
Dushanbe 35 H 3
Dushekan 36 J 3
Dusheti 21 F 2
Düsseldorf 14 E 4
Dutch Harbor 72 D 5
Dutlwe 66 C 4
Duved 16 F 3
Duvno 19 G 3
Duvogero 16 K 3
Duwayhin (United Arab Emirates) 23 F 4
Duwisib 66 B 5
Duwwäh 61 K 4
Duye 64 D 4
Duyun 38 E 5
Düz 59 G 2
Düzce 20 D 2
Dvina, Severnaya 24 H 3
Dvinskaya Guba 24 G 2–3
Dvurechnaya 24 G 6
Dwarka 40 A 3
Dworshak Reservoir 76 C 2
Dyadmo 36 J 4
Dyatkovo 24 F 5
Dyatlovo 17 J 5
Dyce 2 C 3
Dyersburg 77 J 4
Dyfed 6 B 2
Dygdy-Sise, Khrebet 37 O 4
Dyje 15 G 5
Dyke 2 C 3
Dykehead 3 C 4
Dykh Tau 21 F 2
Dylewska Góra 15 GH 4
Dymechurch 7 E 2
Dyrhólaey 16 B 3

Dysnų Ežeras 17 J 4
Dytike Rodhopi 20 B 2
Dyurmen'tobe 35 G 1
Dyurtyuli 24 K 4
Dzag 36 G 6
Dzamïn Uüd 38 F 2
Dzaoudzi 67 H 2
Dzavhan Gol 36 F 6
Dzenzik, Mys 21 E 1
Dzerzhinsk (Belorussiya, U.S.S.R.) 17 J 5
Dzerzhinsk (Russia, U.S.S.R.) 24 H 4
Dzerzhinskaya, Gora 17 J 5
Dzerzhinskoye 25 Q 6
Dzerzhinskoye 36 G 4
Dzhagdy, Khrebet 37 O 5
Dzhaki-Unakhta Yakbyyana,Khrebet 37 OP 5–6
Dzhaksy 25 N 5
Dzhalagash 35 G 1
Dzhalal-Abad 35 J 2
Dzhalampyr 35 H 3
Dzhalilabad 34 D 3
Dzhalinda 37 M 5
Dzhaltyr 25 N 5
Dzhambul 25 M 5
Dzhambul 25 O 6
Dzhambul 35 J 2
Dzhamm 37 O 1
Dzhanga 34 E 2
Dzhankoy 21 D 1
Dzhanybek 24 J 6
Dzhardzhan 37 MN 2
Dzharkurgan 35 H 3
Dzhava 21 F 2
Dzhebariki 37 P 3
Dzhebel 34 E 3
Dzhelinde 36 K 1
Dzhetygara 25 M 5
Dzhezkazgan 35 H 1
Dzhigirbent 35 G 2
Dzhigudzhak 37 T 3
Dzhirgatal' 35 J 3
Dzhizak 35 H 2
Dzhubga 21 E 2
Dzhugdzhur, Khrebet 37 OP 4
Dzhugdzhur Range 37 Q 4
Dzhungarskiy Alatau, Khrebet 25 PQ 6–7
Dzhunkun 36 K 3
Dzhurin 20 C 1
Dzhurun 34 F 1
Dzhusaly 35 G 1
Dzibalchén 78 E 4
Dzierżoniów 15 G 4
Dzioua 59 G 2
Dziuche 78 E 4
Dzungaria 35 M 1
Dzüünbayan 38 E 2
Dzuunbulag 38 FG 1

E

Eagle (AK, U.S.A.) 65 J 6
Eagle (Seychelles) 72 J 3
Eagle Lake (CA, U.S.A.) 76 B 3
Eagle Lake (Ontario, Can.) 74 J 6
Eagle Pass 76 FG 6
Eagle Peak 76 C 3
Eagle River 72 H 3
Eagle Summit 72 H 2
Ear Falls 74 J 5
Earlish 2 A 3
Earls Barton 7 D 1
Earlsferry 3 C 3
Earn, Loch 3 B 3
Easington 5 F 3
Easingwold 5 E 2
Easley 77 K 5
East Alligator River 48 E 1
East Antarctica 91
East Bay 73 V 3
East Berlin 15 F 4
East Brent 6 C 3
East Cape 51 R 8
East China Sea 39 HJ 5
East Croachy 2 B 3
East Dean 7 E 2
East Dereham 7 E 1
East Falkland 89 E 9
East Grinstead 7 E 2
East Kilbride 3 B 4
East London (South Africa) 66 D 6
East Midlands (Airport) 7 D 1
East Pacific Basin 99 D 4
East Pacific Ridge 99 D 5
East Point 77 JK 5
East Retford 5 E 3
East Siberian Sea 37 S 1
East Siberian Sea 90
East Sussex 7 E 2
East Turkistan 28 FG 2–3
East Wittering 7 D 2

Eastbourne 7 E 2
Eastend 73 Q 6
Easter Island 53 H 4
Easter Ross 2 B 3
Eastern Ghats 35 CD 3–5
Eastern Ghats 40 D 4
Eastern Nara River 35 H 5
Eastleigh 7 D 2
Eastmain 75 M 5
Eastman 77 K 5
Eastoft 7 D 1
Easton 77 L 3
Eastport 77 N 3
Eastry 7 E 2
Eastwood 7 D 1
Eatonville 76 B 2
Eau Claire 77 H 3
Eau-Claire, Lac à l' 75 N 4
Eauripik 52 A 2
Ebano 78 C 3
Ebbw Vale 6 C 2
Ebe 37 Q 3
Ebe-Basa 37 NO 3
Ebebiyin 63 G 5
Ebeltoft 17 F 4
Eber Gölü 20 D 3
Eberswalde 15 F 4
Ebinur Hu 35 L 1
Ebla (Syria) 22 B 2
Ebo 66 A 2
Ebola 64 C 4
Eboli 19 G 3
Ebolowa 63 G 5
Ebombo 64 D 6
Ebon 52 C 2
Ebony 66 AB 4
Ebro 18 C 3
Ebro 18 C 3
Ebro, Delta del 18 D 3
Ebro, Embalse del 18 C 3
Ebyakh 37 S 2
Ecbatana (Iran) 23 E 2
Eccles 3 C 4
Eccles 5 D 3
Ech Cheliff 59 F 1
Echdeiria 58 C 3
Echeng 38 FG 4
Echmiadzin 21 F 2
Echo Bay 73 O 2
Echuca 49 G 6
Écija 18 B 4
Eckernförde 15 EF 4
Eckerö 17 G 3
Ecuador 84 B 4
E'cueils, Pointe aux 75 M 4
Ed 17 F 4
Ed Damer → Ad' Dämir 60 E 5
Eday 2 C 2
Edchera 58 C 3
Edd 65 G 2
Eddaré 58 D 4
Eddéki 63 H 2
Edderton 2 B 3
Eddleston 3 C 4
Ede 63 E 4
Edéa 63 FG 5
Edefors 16 H 2
Edel Land 48 A 4
Eden (N.S.W., Austr.) 49 H 6
Eden, River 5 D 2
Edenburg 66 D 5
Edenderry 4 B 3
Edenton 77 L 4
Eder 15 E 4
Edgar Range 48 C 2
Edgell 75 P 3
Edgemont 76 F 3
Edgeöya 90
Edgeworthstown 4 B 3
Edhessa 20 B 2
Edina 77 H 3
Edinburgh 3 C 4
Edinburgh (Airport) 3 C 4
Edinga 63 H 2
Edirne 20 C 2
Edjeleh 59 GH 3
Edmonds 76 B 2
Edmonton 73 P 5
Edmundston 75 O 6
Edough, Djebel 19 E 4
Edounga 63 G 6
Edremit 20 C 3
Edremit Körfezi 20 C 3
Edson 73 O 5
Eduni, Mount 72 LM 3
Edward, Lake 64 D 5
Edward River 49 G 1
Edwards Creek 49 F 4
Edwards Plateau 76 FG 5–6
Edzhen 37 P 3
Edzo 73 O 3
Eek 72 E 3
Eenhana 66 B 3
Efate 51 J 5

Eferding 19 F 2
Efes 20 C 3
Effingham 77 J 4
Eflâni 21 D 2
Eforie 20 C 2
Eg Glab Tiguesmat 58 D 3–4
Egan Range 76 CD 4
Egaña 89 E 6
Egbe 63 F 4
Egegik 72 F 4
Eger 20 B 1
Egerton, Mount 48 B 3
Eggan 63 F 4
Eggum 16 F 2
Egilsstaðir 16 C 2
Egil_ngham 5 E 2
Eğridir 20 D 3
Eğridir Gölü 20 D 3
Eguata 83 H 4
Egvekinot 72 B 2
Egypt 60 DE 4
Eha Amufu 63 F 4
Ehcel 62 E 2
Ei Loutone, Mont 63 G 1
Eiao 53 F 3
Eibar 18 C 3
Eidet 16 F 3
Eidfjord 17 E 3
Eidslandet 16 E 3
Eidsvåg 16 E 3
Eidsvoll 17 F 3
Eifel 14 E 4
Eigg 3 A 3
Eight Degree Channel 40 B 6
Eights Coast 91
Eighty Mile Beach 48 C 2
Eigrim, Jabal 60 F 5
Eildon 49 H 6
Einasleigh 49 G 2
Einasleigh River 49 G 2
Eindhoven 14 DE 4
Eindpaal 66 B 5
Eire 14 B 4
Eiríksjökull 16 A 3
Eirunepé 84 DE 5
Eisenach 15 EF 4
Eisenerz 19 F 2
Eisenhüttenstadt 15 F 4
Eisenstadt 19 G 2
Ejeda 67 G 4
Ejin Horo Qi 38 E 3
Ejin Qi 38 D 2
Ejura 62 D 4
Ekarma, Ostrov 37 S 6
Ekecik Dağı 21 D 3
Ekenäs [Tammisaari] 17 H 4
Eket 63 F 5
Ekibastuz 25 P 5
Ekimchan 37 O 5
Ekoli 64 C 5
Ekonda 36 H 2
Eksjö 17 G 4
Ekwan 64 L 5
El Aaiún 58 C 3
El Aatf 58 B 4
El Abiodh Sidi Cheikh 58 F 2
El Adeb Larache 59 G 3
El Affroum 18 D 4
El Agreb 59 G 2
El Alamein → Al 'Alamayn 60 D 2
El Alamo 76 C 5
El Alia 59 G 2
El Arahal 18 B 4
El Arâich → Larache 58 D 1
El Aricha 58 E 2
El Arrouch 19 E 4
El Attar 59 F 2
El Banco 84 D 2
El Barco 18 B 3
El Barco de Ávila 18 BC 3
El Baul 84 E 2
El Bayadh 59 F 2
El Bema 59 F 4
El Bir → Teouit 59 G 3
'El Būr 65 H 4
El Burgo de Osma 18 C 3
El Buro 78 B 2
El Caín 89 C 7
El Cajon 76 FG 5–6
El Callao 85 F 2
El Canelo 78 BC 3
El Carmen (Bolivia) 86 D 3
El Carmen (Colombia) 84 C 2
El Carre 65 G 3

El Casco 78 B 2
El Centro 76 C 5
El Cerito 84 C 3
El Cerro 86 D 4
El Chorro 86 D 5
El Cocuy 84 D 2
El Cóndor, Cerro 88 C 4
El Cuy 89 C 6
El Dab 65 H 3
El Daoud 58 D 4
El Der 65 G 3
'El Dẹre 65 H 4
El Descanso 76 C 5
El Difícil 84 D 2
El Diviso 84 C 3
El Djouf 58 D 4
El Dorado 85 F 2
El Dorado (AR, U.S.A.) 77 H 5
El Dorado (KS, U.S.A.) 77 G 4
El Dorado (Mexico) 76 E 7
El Eglab 58 DE 3
El Encanto 84 D 4
El Eulma 59 G 1
El Farsia 58 D 3
El Fasher 60 D 5
El Ferrol del Caudillo 18 B 3
El Fud 65 G 3
El Fuerte 78 B 3
'El Gâl 65 J 2
El Gassi 59 G 2
El Goléa 59 F 2
El Goran 65 G 3
El Guamo 84 C 3
El Guettara 62 D 1
El Hachchana 59 F 3
El Hajeb 58 D 2
'El Hạmurre 65 H 3
El Hank 58 D 4
El Homr 59 F 3
El Jadida 58 D 2
El Jicaral 78 E 5
El Kala 59 G 1
El Kantara 59 G 1
El Kelaa 58 D 2
El Kharga → Al Khārijah 60 E 3
El Khnâchích 58 E 4
El Kseïbat 58 E 3
El Lagodei → Qardo 65 H 3
'El Maestrazgo 18 CD 3
El Mahia 62 D 1
El Maitén 89 B 7
El Mamoun 62 D 2
El Mansour 58 E 3
El Mayoco 89 B 7
El Medo 65 G 3
El Meghaïer 59 G 2
El Mereié 58 D 5
El Messir 63 H 2
El Milhéas 58 D 3
El Milia 19 E 4
El Mirador 78 E 4
El Moïnane 58 C 5
El Mreiti 58 D 4
El Mreyer 58 D 4
El Mzereb 58 D 4
El Mzerif 62 D 1
El Niabo 65 H 2
El Nido 43 E 1
El Nihuil 89 C 5
El Novillo 76 DE 6
El Obeid 60 E 6
El Odre 89 C 6
El Oso 84 E 3
El Oued 59 G 2
El Ousseukh 59 F 2
El Palmito 78 A 2
El Palquí 88 B 5
El Paso 76 E 5
El Pico 86 D 4
El Pilar 85 F 1
El Pintado 86 D 5
El Portugues 84 C 5
El Porvenir (Panamá) 84 C 2
El Porvenir (Venezuela) 84 E 2
El Potosí (Mexico) 78 B 3
El Potro, Cerro 88 C 4
El Progreso 78 E 4
El Puerto 76 D 6
El Puerto de Santa María 18 B 4
El Real 84 C 2
El Reno 76 G 4
El Safiya 60 E 5
El Salto 78 A 3
El Salvador 78 DE 5
El Sauca 78 D 7
El Seibo 79 J 4
El Sharana 48 E 1
El Soberbio 88 F 4
El Sueco 76 E 6
El Tigre (Colombia) 84 E 3
El Tigre (Venezuela) 85 F 2
El Tocuyo 84 E 2
El Tofo 88 B 4
El Tránsito 88 B 4

El Trapiche 84 C 3
El Triumfo 76 D 7
El Tuito 78 A 3
El Tunal 88 D 4
El Tuparro, Parque Nacional 84 E 2
El Turbio 89 B 9
El Valle 84 C 2
El Vigía 84 D 2
El Wak 65 G 4
Elassón 20 B 3
Elat (Israel) 22 B 3
Eláti 20 B 3
Elato 52 A 2
Elâziğ 21 E 3
Elba 19 F 3
El'ban 37 P 5
Elbasani 20 A 2
Elbe 15 F 4
Elbert, Mount 76 E 4
Elbeyli 22 B 1
Elbistan 21 E 3
Elblåg 15 G 4
Elbow 73 Q 5
Elbrus 21 F 2
Elburz Mountains 34 EF 3
Elburz Mountains (Iran) 23 FG 1
Elche 18 C 4
Elcho Island 48 F 1
Elda 18 C 4
El'dikan 37 P 3
Eldorado (Argentina) 88 EF 4
Eldoret 64 F 4
Elëja 17 H 4
Elektrostal' 24 G 4
Elele 63 F 4
Elemi Triangle 64 EF 4
Elephant Butte Reservoir 76 E 5
Elephant Island 91
Elesbão Veloso 87 H 2
Eleuthera Island 79 G 2
Elevtheroúpolis 20 B 2
Elgåhogna 16 F 3
El'gakan 37 M 4
Elghena 65 F 1
El'gi 37 Q 3
Elgin (OR, U.S.A.) 76 C 2
Elgin (U.K.) 2 C 3
El'ginskoye Ploskogor'ye 37 PQ 2
Elgol 2 A 3
Elgon, Mount 64 E 4
El'gyay 36 L 3
El'gygytgyn, Ozero 37 W 2
Elham 7 E 2
Eliase 43 H 5
Elikón Óros 20 B 3
Elila 64 D 5
Elila 64 D 5
Elim 72 E 3
Elingampangu 64 C 5
Elisabethtown 77 J 4
Elisenvaara 16 J 3
Eliseu Martins 87 H 2
Eliseyna 20 B 2
Elista 21 F 1
Elizabeth 49 F 5
Elizabeth City 77 L 4
Elizabeth Falls 73 Q 4
Elizabeth, Mount 48 D 2
Ełk 15 H 4
Elk City 76 G 4
Elkhart 77 J 3
Elkhorn River 76 G 3
Elkhovo 20 C 2
Elkins 77 L 4
Elko 76 C 3
Elku Kalns 17 J 4
Ell, Lake 48 D 4
Ellef Ringnes Island 90
Ellenabad 40 B 2
Ellendale 76 G 2
Ellensburg 76 B 2
Ellesmere 6 C 1
Ellesmere Island 90
Ellesmere Port 5 D 3
Ellesmere Port 5 D 3
Ellice Islands 52 C 3
Ellila 63 J 2
Ellington 5 E 2
Elliot (Australia) 48 E 2
Elliot (South Africa) 66 D 6
Elliot, Mount 49 H 2
Ellisburg 77 L 3
Elliston 49 E 5
Ellon 2 C 3
Ellsworth Land 91
Ellsworth Mountains 91
Elmadağ 21 D 3
Elmalı 20 C 3
Elmalı Dağı 21 DE 3
Elmhurst 77 J 3
Elmira 77 L 3
Elmshorn 15 EF 4
Elne 18 D 3
Elorza 84 E 2
Eloy 76 D 5

Elphin 2 B 2
Elphinstone 49 H 3
Elsdon 5 D 2
Elsen Nur 38 B 3
Elsey 48 E 1
Elsrickle 3 C 4
Eltanin Fracture Zone System 99 D 5
Eltisley 7 D 1
Elton 7 D 1
Elton 24 J 6
Elva 17 J 4
Elvanfoot 3 C 4
Elvas 18 B 4
Elverum 17 F 3
Elvira 84 D 5
Elvire River 48 D 2
Ely (MN, U.S.A.) 77 H 2
Ely (NV, U.S.A.) 76 D 4
Ely (U.K.) 7 E 1
Ema Jõgi 17 J 4
Emali 65 F 5
Emämrüd 34 EF 3
Emämrüd (Iran) 23 G 1
Emämzadeh 'Abbās (Iran) 23 E 2
Emämzädeh Nasrod Dīn (Iran) 23 E 2
Emån 17 G 4
Emas, Parque Nacional do 87 F 4
Emba 34 F 1
Emba 34 F 1
Embalse de Alarcón 18 C 4
Embalse de Alcántara 18 B 4
Embalse de Almendra 18 B 3
Embalse de Buendía 18 C 3
Embalse de Cenajo 18 C 4
Embalse de Cijara 18 BC 4
Embalse de Contreras 18 C 4
Embalse de Entrepeñas 18 C 3
Embalse de Gabriel y Galan 18 B 3
Embalse de la Cuerda del Pozo 18 C 3
Embalse de la Sotonera 18 C 3
Embalse de Mequinenza 18 CD 3
Embalse de Ricobayo 18 B 3
Embalse de Valdecañas 18 BC 4
Embalse de Yesa 18 C 3
Embalse del Ebro 18 C 3
Embalse del Guárico 84 E 2
Embalse del Río Negro 88 EF 5
Embalse Ezequiel Ramos Mexia 89 C 6
Embalse Florentino Ameghino 89 C 7
Embarcación 86 D 5
Embarras Portage 73 P 4
Embira 84 D 5
Embleton 5 E 2
Embu 65 F 5
Emden 15 E 4
Emei Shan 38 D 5
Emel'dzak 37 N 4
Emerald 49 H 3
Emerson 73 S 6
Emet 20 C 3
Emgayet 59 H 3
Emi Fezzane 63 G 2
Emi Koussi 63 H 2
Emi Lulu 63 G 1
Emiliano Zapata 78 D 4
Emin 35 L 1
Emira 51 F 2
Emirdağ 20 D 3
Emmaboda 17 G 4
Emmaste 17 H 4
Emmen 14 E 4
Emmet 49 G 3
Emmett 76 C 3
Emmonak 72 E 3
Emo 4 B 3
Emory Peak 76 F 6
Empalme 76 D 6
Empangeni 67 E 5
Empedrado (Argentina) 88 E 4
Empedrado (Chile) 89 B 6
Emperor Seamount Chain 99 C 2
Empoli 19 F 3
Emporia (KS, U.S.A.) 77 G 4
Emporia (VA, U.S.A.) 77 L 4
Ems 15 E 4
Emumägi 17 J 4
Emyvale 4 B 2
Enånger 16 G 3
Enard Bay 2 B 2
Enarotali 43 J 4
Encarnación 88 E 4
Enchi 62 D 4
Encinal 76 G 6
Encón 88 C 5
Encontrados 84 D 2
Encounter Bay 49 F 6
Encruzilhada do Sul 88 F 5
Enda Salassie 65 F 2
Ende 43 F 5

Endeavour 49 H 2
Endeavour Strait 49 G 1
Enderbury 52 D 3
Enderby Abyssal Plain 98 B 5
Enderby Land 91
Endicott Mountains 72 G 2
Endon 7 C 1
Endwell 77 L 3
Endybal 37 O 2
Energia 89 E 6
Enez 20 C 2
Enfer, Portes d' 64 D 6
Enfield 4 B 3
Enfield 7 D 2
Engaño, Cabo 79 J 4
Engaño, Cape 43 J 1
Engel's 24 J 5
Engerdyakh 36 L 3
Engershatu 65 F 1
Enggano, Pulau 42 B 5
Engiabaia 65 F 2
English Bazar 40 E 3
English Channel 7 D 2
Engozero 16 K 2
Engozero, Ozero 16 K 2
Engure 17 H 4
Enibé 63 J 2
Enid 76 G 4
Eniwetok 52 B 2
Enji 58 D 5
Enkan 37 Q 4
Enkan, Mys 37 Q 4
Enkeldoorn 67 E 3
Enköping 17 G 4
Enmore 85 G 2
Enna 19 F 4
Ennadai 73 R 3
Ennadai Lake 73 R 3
Ennedi 63 J 2
Ennis 14 B 4
Enniscorthy 6 A 1
Enniscorthy 14 B 4
Enniskerry 4 B 3
Enniskillen 2 B 2
Ennistymon 14 B 4
Ennore 40 D 5
Enns 19 F 2
Enns 19 F 2
Enns 19 F 2
Eno 16 K 3
Enontekiö 16 H 2
Enrekang 43 EF 4
Enschede 14 E 4
Ensenada 76 C 5
Enshi 38 E 4
Entebbe 64 E 4
Enterkinfoot 3 C 4
Enterprise (N.W.T., Can.) 73 O 3
Enterprise (OR, U.S.A.) 76 C 2
Entre Rios (Amazonas, Brazil) 85 G 4
Entre Ríos (Bolivia) 86 D 5
Entre Ríos (Pará, Brazil) 85 H 5
Entrepeñas, Embalse de 18 C 3
Entroncamento 18 B 4
Entrevaux 19 E 3
Enugu 63 F 4
Enugu Ezike 63 F 4
Enurmino 72 C 2
Envigado 84 CD 2
Envira 84 D 5
Enyamba 64 D 5
Enyamkulam 40 C 6
Enyellé 63 H 5
Eolie o Lipari, Isole 19 F 4
Epanomi 20 B 2
Epéna 63 H 5
Épernay 18 D 2
Ephesus 20 C 3
Epi 51 J 5
Epidhavros 20 B 3
Épinal 19 E 2
Epira 85 G 2
Episkopi 21 D 4
Episkopi (Cyprus) 22 A 2
Epping 7 E 2
Epsom 7 D 2
Epukiro 66 B 4
Epukiro 66 C 4
Epuyén 89 B 7
Epworth 7 D 1
Eqlīd (Iran) 23 F 3
Équateur 64 BC 4
Equatoria 64 DE 3–4
Equatorial Guinea 63 F 5
Er Hai 38 D 5
Er Rif 58 E 2
Er Roseires → Ar Rusayris 60 E 6
Er rout Sanihida 63 G 1
Eraclea 19 G 3
Erap 50 E 3
Erba, Jabal 60 F 4
Erbaa 21 F 3
Erbeskopf 15 E 5
Erbil (Iraq) 22 D 1
Erçek 21 F 3

Erçek Gölü 21 F 3
Erciş 21 F 3
Erciyas Daği 21 E 3
Érd 20 A 1
Erdaogou 38 B 4
Erdek 20 C 2
Erdemli 21 D 3
Erdemli (Turkey) 22 B 1
Erdene 38 F 3
Erdenedalay 38 DE 1
Erdene 38 F 3
Eereentsav 36 L 6
Ereğli (Turkey) 20 D 2
Ereğli (Turkey) 21 D 3
Erenhaberga Shan 35 LM 2
Erenhot 38 F 2
Erentepe 21 F 3
Erepecu, Lago de 85 G 4
Eresma 18 C 3
Erfoud 58 E 2
Erfurt 15 F 4
Erg Afarag 59 F 4
Erg Atouila 62 D 1
Erg Brusset 63 FG 2
Erg Chech 58 E 3–4
Erg d'Admer 59 G 4
Erg de Ténéré 63 G 2
Erg du Djourab 63 H 2
Erg el Ahmar 58 E 4
Erg er Raoui 58 E 3
Erg Iabès 58 E 3
Erg Iguidi 58 DE 3
Erg in Sakkane 62 D 1
Erg N-Ataram 59 F 4
Ergani 21 E 3
Ergedzhey 36 L 3
Ergene 20 C 2
Ergli 17 J 4
Ergun He 36 M 5
Ergun Youqi 36 M 5
Ergun Zuoqi 37 M 5
Eriba 60 F 5
Eriboll 2 B 2
Eriboll, Loch 2 B 2
Eric 75 O 5
Erice 19 F 4
Ericeira 18 B 4
Erichsen Lake 75 L 1
Ericht, Loch 3 B 3
Eridu (Iraq) 23 D 3
Erie 77 K 3
Erie Canal 77 L 3
Erie, Lake 77 K 3
'Erigabo 65 H 2
Erikub 52 C 2
Erimbet 35 G 2
Erimo-misaki 39 M 2
Erinpura 40 B 2
Eriskay 3 A 3
Eritrea 65 FG 2
Erkowit 60 F 5
Erlangen 15 F 5
Erldunda 48 E 4
Ermelo 66 DE 5
Ermenek 21 D 3
Ermera 43 FG 5
Ermesinde 18 B 3
Ermil 60 D 6
Ermióni 20 B 3
Ermoupolis 20 B 3
Erne, River 4 A 2
Ernest Legouvé 53 E 5
Erode 40 C 5
Erongo 66 B 4
Erongo Mountains 66 B 4
Erota 65 F 1
Erozionnyy 37 R 2
Errego 67 F 3
Errogie 2 B 3
Erromanga 51 J 5
Ertai 35 N 1
Ertil 24 H 5
Ertix He 35 M 1
Eruh 21 F 3
Erundu 66 B 4
Eryuan 38 C 5
Erzgebirge 15 F 4
Erzin 36 G 5
Erzincan 21 E 3
Erzurum 21 F 3
Erzurum-Kars Yaylâsı 21 F 2
Esa-ala 51 F 3
Esbjerg 19 E 4
Esbo 17 H 3
Escada 87 J 2
Escalante 76 D 4
Escalón 78 B 2
Escalona 18 C 3
Escanaba 77 J 2
Escatrón 18 C 3
Esch [sur-Alzette] 19 E 2
Eschan 37 R 3
Eschwege 15 F 4
Escondido 76 C 5

Escorial, Serra do 87 H 3
Escrick 5 E 3
Escudo, Puerto de 18 C 3
Escuintla 78 D 5
Eséka 63 G 5
Eşenler Daği 21 D 3
Esfahan (Iran) 23 F 2
Esfandärän (Iran) 23 F 3
Esfandiar (Iran) 23 EF 3
Eshowe 67 E 5
Eshtehärd (Iran) 23 F 2
Esk River 50 L 9
Eskdale 3 C 4
Eskifjörður 16 C 2
Eskilstuna 17 G 4
Eskimo Lakes 72 L 2
Eskimo Point 73 T 3
Eskipazar 21 D 2
Eskişehir 20 D 3
Esla 18 B 3
Eslämäbad (Iran) 23 E 2
Eslöv 17 F 4
Eşme 20 C 3
Esmeralda 84 E 3
Esmeralda, Isla 89 A 8
Esmeraldas 84 BC 3
Esmeraldas 84 C 3
España 18 C 4
Española, 84 B 6
Espanola 76 E 4
Esperance 48 C 5
Esperance Bay 48 C 5
Esperanza (Antarctica) 91
Esperanza (Argentina) 88 D 5
Esperanza (Mexico) 76 E 6
Esperanza (Peru) 84 D 5
Espichel, Cabo 18 B 4
Espigão Mestre 87 G 3
Espinal 84 D 3
Espinal 86 E 4
Espinar 86 B 3
Espinazo del Diablo, Sierra 78 A 3
Espinhaço, Serra do 87 H 4
Espinho 18 B 3
Espírito Santo (Brazil) 87 HJ 4
Espíritu Santo (Vanuatu) 51 J 5
Esplanada 87 J 3
Espoo 17 H 3
Espungabera 67 E 4
Esquel 89 B 7
Esquina 88 E 5
Esquinapa de Hidalgo 78 A 3
Essaouira 58 CD 2
Essen 15 E 4
Essendon, Mount 48 C 3
Essequibo 85 G 3
Essex 7 E 2
Essex Mountain 76 E 3
Esslingen 15 E 5
Esso 37 T 4
Essouk 62 E 2
Est, Cap 67 J 3
Estados, Isla de los 89 D 9
Estahbänät (Iran) 23 G 3
Estância 87 J 3
Estancias, Sierra de la 18 C 4
Estarreja 18 B 3
Estats, Pic d' 18 D 3
Estcourt 66 D 5
Este 19 F 2
Estelí 78 E 5
Estella 18 C 3
Estepona 18 BC 4
Estero de Agiabampo 76 E 6
Esteros 86 D 5
Esteros del Iberá 88 E 4
Estevan 73 R 6
Estherville 77 GH 3
Estoniya 17 H 4
Estrecho de Gibraltar 18 B 4
Estrecho de le Maire 89 CD 9–10
Estrecho de Magallanes 89 B 9
Estrecho Nelson 89 AB 9
Estreito, Reprêsa do 87 G 4–5
Estrela, Serra da (Mato Grosso, Brazil) 87 G 4
Estrêla, Serra de (Portugal) 18 B 3
Estrella 18 C 4
Estremadura 18 B 4
Estremoz 18 B 4
Estrondo, Serra do 85 J 5
Esztergom 20 A 1
Etadunna 49 F 4
Etah 40 C 2
Étain 19 E 2
Étampes 18 D 2
Étang de Berre 19 DE 3
Étang de Biscarrosse 18 C 3
Étang de Cazaux 18 C 3
Étang de Leucate 18 D 3
Étang de Sigean 18 D 3
Étang d'Hourtin 18 C 2
Etawah 40 C 2
Etengua 66 A 3
Ethel Creek 48 C 3
Ethiopia 65 FG 3

Ethiopian Plateau 65 FG 3
Etna 19 G 4
Etolin 72 L 4
Etolin Strait 72 DE 3–4
Etosha National Park 66 B 3
Etosha Pan 66 B 3
Etoumbi 63 GH 6
Ettington 7 D 1
Etykan 37 R 2
Etzná Tixmucuy 78 D 4
Euca 85 H 3
Eucla 48 D 5
Eudora 77 H 5
Eufaula 77 J 5
Eufaula Lake 77 G 4
Eugene 76 B 3
Eugenia, Punta 76 C 6
Eugmo 16 H 3
Eungella National Park 49 H 3
Euphrates (Iraq) 22 C 2
Eura 16 H 3
Eure 18 D 2
Eureka (CA, U.S.A.) 76 B 3
Eureka (NV, U.S.A.) 76 C 4
Europa (Réunion) 67 G 4
Europa, de Picos 18 C 3
Europa, Picos de 18 C 3
Europa, Punta de 18 B 4
Euskirchen 14 E 4
Euston 49 G 5
Eutin 15 F 4
Eva 85 G 4
Evans, Lac 75 M 5
Evans Strait 73 V 3
Evanston (IL, U.S.A.) 77 J 3
Evanston (WY, U.S.A.) 76 D 3
Evansville 77 J 4
Evaz (Iran) 23 F 4
Evenequén 85 F 3
Evensk 37 T 3
Everard, Lake 49 F 5
Everard Range 48 E 4
Evercreech 6 C 3
Everest, Mount 40 E 2
Everett 76 B 2
Everett Mountains 75 O 3
Everglades City 77 K 6
Everglades National Park
77 K 6
Evergreen 77 J 5
Evesham 7 D 1
Evijärvi 16 H 3
Evinayong 63 FG 5
Evje 17 E 4
Évora 18 B 4
Évreux 18 D 2
Evros 20 C 2
Evstratios, Ayios 20 C 3
Évvoia 20 B 3
Evzono 20 B 2
Ewaso Ngiri 65 F 4
Ewasse 51 F 3
Ewe, Loch 2 B 3
Ewenkizu Zizhqi 36 L 6
Ewes 3 C 4
Ewirgol 35 M 2
Ewo 63 GH 6
Exaltacion 86 C 3
Excelsior Springs 77 H 4
Exe, River 6 C 2
Executive Committee Range 91
Exeter 6 C 2
Exeter Sound 75 P 2
Exford 6 C 3
Exmoor 6 C 2
Exmouth (Australia)
48 A 3
Exmouth (U.K.) 6 C 2
Exmouth Gulf 48 A 3
Expedition Range 49 H 3
Exton 6 C 3
Extremadura 18 B 4
Extremo 86 BC 3
Exuma Cays 79 G 3
Exuma Sound 79 G 3
Eyakit-Tërdë 36 K 2
Eyasi, Lake 64 E 5
Eye 7 D 1
Eye 7 E 1
Eye Peninsula 2 A 2
Eyemouth 3 C 4
Eygurande 18 D 2
Eyik 36 L 2
Eyjafjallajökull 16 A 3
Eyjafjörður 16 B 2
Eyl 65 H 3
Eynsham 7 D 2
Eyrarbakki 16 A 3
Eyre 48 D 5
Eyre, Lake 49 F 4
Eyre Peninsula 49 F 5
Eyre River 49 F 3
Eysturoy 14 A 1
Eyvänakï (Iran) 23 F 2
Ezequiel Ramos Mexia, Embalse
89 C 6

Ezine 20 C 3
Ezinepazarı 21 E 2
Ezop, Gora 37 S 3

F

F. D. Roosevelt Lake 76 C 2
Fabala 62 C 4
Fabens 76 E 5
Faber Lake 73 O 3
Fåborg 17 F 4
Fabriano 19 F 3
Facatativa 84 D 3
Fachi 63 G 2
Facundo 89 B 8
Fada 63 J 2
Fada Niamtougou 62 E 3
Fādilī (Saudi Arabia) 23 E 4
Faenza 19 F 3
Faeroe Islands 14 A 1
Fafa (Burkina) 64 B 3
Fafa (Mali) 62 E 2
Fafan 65 G 3
Făgăraş 20 BC 1
Fagernes 16 E 3
Fagersta 17 G 3
Fagita 43 H 4
Fagnano, Lago 89 C 9
Faguibine, Lac 62 D 2
Fahūd 61 K 4
Faial 58 A 1
Fair Bluff 77 L 5
Fair Isle 2 D 2
Fair Ness 75 N 3
Fairbanks 72 H 3
Fairborn 77 K 4
Fairbourne 6 C 1
Fairfield 76 B 3
Fairmont (MN, U.S.A.) 77 H 3
Fairmont (W.V., U.S.A.) 77 L 4
Fairview 49 G 2
Fairweather, Mount 72 K 4
Faisalabad 35 J 4
Faith 76 F 2
Faizabad (Afghanistan) 35 J 3
Faizabad (India) 40 D 2
Fajr, Wādī (Saudi Arabia) 22 BC 3
Fakahina 53 F 4
Fakaofo 52 D 3
Fakarava 53 F 4
Fakenham 7 E 1
Fakfak 43 H 4
Fakhr (Iran) 23 F 3
Fakse Bugt 17 F 4
Fakse Ladeplats 17 F 4
Faku 39 H 2
Falaba 62 B 4
Falagh 64 E 3
Falaise 18 CD 2
Falaise de Tiguidit 63 F 2
Falakrón Óros 20 B 2
Falam 41 F 3
Falcarragh 4 A 2
Fălciu 20 C 1
Falconara Marittima 19 F 3
Falcone, Punta 19 E 3
Faléa 62 B 3
Falémé 62 B 3
Faleshty 20 C 1
Falfield 6 C 3
Falfurrias 76 G 6
Falkenberg 17 F 4
Falkirk 3 C 3
Falkland Islands 89 DE 9
Falkland Sound 89 DE 9
Falköping 17 F 4
Fall River 77 M 3
Fallon 76 C 4
Falls City 77 G 3
Falmouth 6 B 2
Falmouth Bay 6 B 2
False Bay 66 B 6
False Pass 72 E 5
Falso Cabo de Hornos 89 C 10
Falster 17 F 5
Falstone 5 D 2
Falterona 19 F 3
Fălticeni 20 C 1
Falun 17 G 3
Famagusta 21 D 3
Famagusta (Cyprus) 22 AB 2
Famatina 88 C 4
Famatina, Sierra de 88 C 4–5
Fan si Pan 41 H 3
Fana 62 C 3
Fanchang 39 G 4
Fandriana 67 H 4
Fang Xian 38 F 4
Fangak 64 E 3
Fangataufa 53 F 4
Fangcheng 38 F 4
Fangcheng 38 E 6
Fangliao 39 H 6
Fangshan 39 G 3

Fangzheng 39 J 1
Fanö 17 E 4
Fano 19 F 3
Fanö Bugt 17 E 4
Faraba 62 B 3
Faradje 64 D 4
Farafangana 67 H 4
Farāfirah, Wāhāt al 60 D 3
Farafra Oasis → Wāhāt al
Farāfirah 60 D 3
Farah 35 G 4
Farah Rud 35 G 4
Farahābad (Iran) 23 F 1
Farallon de Medinilla 52 A 1
Farallon de Pajaros 52 A 1
Faranah 62 B 3
Farasān, Jazā'ir 61 G 5
Faraulep 52 A 2
Farāyid, Jabal al (Egypt) 22 B 5
Farcău, Virful 20 B 1
Fardes 18 C 4
Fardrum 4 B 3
Fareham 7 D 2
Farewell 72 G 3
Farewell, Cape 51 Q 9
Fargo (GA, U.S.A.) 77 K 5
Fargo (N.D., U.S.A.) 76 G 2
Faribault, Lac 75 N 4
Faridabad 40 C 2
Faridpur 40 E 3
Fārigh, Wādī 59 K 2
Färila 16 G 3
Farim 62 A 3
Faringdon 7 D 2
Fāris (Egypt) 22 A 4
Farkhato 35 HJ 3
Farkovo 25 R 2
Farkwa 65 F 6
Farmahīn (Iran) 23 E 2
Farmington (MN, U.S.A.) 77 M 3
Farmington (N.M., U.S.A.) 76 E 4
Farnborough 7 D 2
Farnham 7 D 2
Farnworth 5 D 3
Fårö 17 G 4
Faro 85 G 4
Faro (Cameroon) 63 G 4
Faro (N.W.T., Can.) 72 L 3
Faro (Portugal) 18 B 4
Faro National Park 63 G 4
Faro, Sierra del 18 B 3
Fårösund 17 G 4
Farquhar, Cape 48 A 3
Farquhar Group 65 J 7
Farrars Creek 49 G 3
Farrāshband (Iran) 23 F 3
Fārs (Iran) 23 F 3
Farsi 35 G 4
Fārsī (Iran) 23 F 4
Farsö 17 E 4
Farsund 17 E 4
Fartak, Ra's 61 J 5
Fasā (Iran) 23 F 3
Fasad 61 J 5
Fasano 19 G 3
Fastov 24 E 5
Fataka 51 J 4
Fatehabad 40 C 2
Fatehgarh 40 CD 2
Fatehpur 40 D 2
Fath (United Arab Emirates)
23 G 4
Fatick 62 A 3
Fatsa 21 E 2
Fatu Hiva 53 F 3
Fatu Hutu 53 F 3
Fatunda 64 B 5
Faūrei 20 C 1
Fauro 51 G 3
Fauske 16 G 2
Faux Cap 67 H 5
Favara 19 F 4
Favignana 19 F 4
Fawley 7 D 2
Faxaflói 16 A 3
Faya-Largeau 63 H 2
Fayd (Saudi Arabia) 22 D 4
Fayetteville (AR, U.S.A.) 77 H 4
Fayetteville (N.C., U.S.A.) 77 L 5
Faylakah (Kuwait) 23 E 3
Faysh Khābūr (Iraq) 22 D 1
Fayu 52 B 2
Fazei 63 G 2
Fazilka 40 B 1
Fazrān (Saudi Arabia) 23 E 4
Fdérik 58 C 4
Fear, Cape 77 L 5
Feathertop, Mount 49 H 6
Fécamp 18 D 2
Federación 88 E 5

Federal Republic of Germany
15 E 4
Federated States of Micronesia
52 AB 2
Fedorovka 25 M 5
Fehmarn 15 F 4
Feicheng 39 G 3
Feijó 84 D 5
Feira 67 E 3
Feira de Santana 87 J 3
Feixiang 38 FG 3
Feke 21 E 3
Feklistova, Ostrov 37 P 4–5
Felanitx 18 D 4
Feldbach 19 G 2
Feldberg 15 E 5
Feldkirch 19 E 2
Felipe Carrillo Puerto 78 E 4
Felix, Cape 73 S 2
Felixlândia 87 H 4
Felixstowe 7 E 2
Feltre 19 F 2
Feltwell 7 E 1
Femer Bælt 17 F 5
Femund 16 F 3
Fen He 38 F 3
Fenaroa 65 F 2
Fener Burnu 21 E 2
Feng Xian 38 E 4
Feng Xian 39 G 4
Fengcheng 39 H 2
Fengdu 38 E 5
Fenghuang 38 E 5
Fengjie 38 E 4
Fengning 39 G 2
Fengqing 38 CD 6
Fengqiu 38 F 3
Fengrun 39 G 3
Fengshuba Shuiku 38 G 6
Fengshui Shan 37 M 5
Fengtai 39 G 4
Fengxiang 38 E 4
Fengxin 38 G 5
Fengzhen 38 F 2
Feni Islands 51 F 2
Fenoarivo Atsinanana 67 HJ 3
Fensfjorden 16 DE 3
Fentani, Monti dei 19 FG 3
Fenxi 38 F 3
Fenyang 38 F 3
Fenyi 38 F 5
Feodosiya 21 E 1
Feolin Ferry 3 A 4
Fer, Cap de 59 G 1
Ferbane 4 B 3
Ferdows 34 F 4
Fereidoon (Iran) 23 EF 3
Feren 16 F 3
Ferfer 65 H 3
Fergana 35 J 2
Fergana Basin 35 J 2
Ferganskiy Khrebet 35 J 2
Fergus Falls 77 G 2
Fergus St. 2 D 3
Ferguson Lake 73 Q 2
Fergusson 51 F 3
Fergusson River 48 E 1
Ferjukot 16 A 3
Ferkéssédougou 62 C 4
Ferlo 62 B 3
Fermo 19 F 3
Fermoselle 18 B 3
Fernandina, 84 B 6
Fernando de la Mora 88 E 4
Fernando de Noronha Island
81 G 3
Fernando Póo → Bioko 63 F 5
Fernandópolis 87 FG 5
Ferrara 19 F 3
Ferreira Gomes 85 H 3
Ferrenafe 84 C 5
Ferret, Cap 18 C 3
Ferriday 77 H 5
Ferryden 3 D 3
Fertilia 19 E 3
Feshi 64 B 6
Festus 77 H 4
Feteşti 20 C 2
Fethiye 20 C 3
Fethiye Körfezi 20 C 3
Fetisovo 34 E 2
Fetlar 2 D 1
Fès 58 E 2
Feshi 64 B 6
Fezzan 59 HJ 3
Ffestiniog 6 C 1
Fiambalá 88 C 4
Fianarantsoa 67 H 4
Fianga 63 H 4
Fich 65 G 3
Fiche 65 F 3
Fichtelgebirge 15 F 4
Ficksburg 66 D 5
Fidenza 19 F 3
Fieri 20 A 2

Fierras 16 G 2
Fiery Cross Reef 42 D 2
Fife 3 C 3
Fife Ness 3 C 3
Fifth Cataract → Ash Shallāl al
Khamis 60 E 5
Figeac 18 D 3
Figtree 66 D 4
Figueira, Cachoeira 85 G 5
Figueira da Foz 18 B 3
Figueras 18 D 3
Figuig 58 E 2
Fiji 52 C 4
Fiji Islands 52 C 4
Filadélfia 85 J 5
Filadélfia (Paraguay) 86 D 5
Filchner Ice Shelf 91
Filey 5 E 2
Filiaşi 20 B 2
Filiatra 20 B 3
Filicudi 19 F 4
Filingué 62 E 3
Filipstad 17 F 4
Filtu 65 G 3
Fimbul Ice Shelf 91
Fimi 64 B 5
Fin (Iran) 23 F 2
Fincham 7 E 1
Finchley 7 D 2
Findhorn 2 C 3
Findhorn, River 2 C 3
Findlay 77 K 3
Findon 7 D 2
Fingoè 67 E 3
Finike 20 D 3
Finisterre, Cabo de 18 B 3
Finke 48 E 4
Finke Flood Flats River 49 F 4
Finke Gorge National Park 48 E 3
Finke, Mount 48 E 5
Finke River 48 E 4
Finland 16 J 3
Finland, Gulf of 17 HJ 4
Finlay 73 MN 4
Finlay Forks 73 N 4
Finley 49 H 6
Finnie Bay 75 M 2
Finniss, Cape 48 E 5
Finnmark 16 H 2
Finnmarksvidda 16 H 2
Finnskogen 17 F 3
Finnsnes 16 G 2
Finnveden 17 F 4
Fins 61 K 4
Finspång 17 G 4
Finsterwalde 15 F 4
Fintona 4 B 2
Finvoy 4 B 2
Fionnphort 3 A 3
Fiordland National Park 50 P 9–10
Firat 21 E 3
Firenze 19 F 3
Firghia 62 B 3
Firkachi 63 G 2
Firmat 88 D 5
Firminy 18 D 2
Firovo 24 F 4
Firozabad 40 C 2
Firozpur 40 BC 1
First Cataract → Sadd al Aswān
60 E 4
Firth of Clyde 3 B 4
Firth of Forth 3 C 3
Firth of Inverness 2 B 3
Firth of Lorn 3 B 3
Firth of Tay 3 C 3
Fīrūz Kūh (Iran) 23 F 2
Fīrūzābād (Iran) 23 E 2
Fīrūzābād (Iran) 23 F 3
Fīrūzābād (Iran) 23 F 3
Fischersbrunn 66 A 4
Fish River 49 F 2
Fish River (South Africa) 66 C 6
Fisher Strait 73 V 3
Fishguard 6 B 2
Fishkåfjället 16 F 3
Fiskárdhon 20 B 3
Fiskenæsset 75 R 3
Fitful Head 2 D 2
Fitri, Lac 63 H 3
Fitz Roy 89 C 8
Fitz Roy, Monte 89 B 8
Fitzcarrald 86 B 3
Fitzgerald 73 P 4
Fitzgerald River National Park
48 B 5
Fitzroy Crossing 48 D 2
Fitzroy River (Queensland, Austr.)
49 J 3
Fitzroy River (Western Australia)
48 C 2
Fiumicino 19 F 3
Fivemiletown 4 B 2
Fivizzano 19 EF 3
Fizi 64 D 5

Fizuli **34** D 3
Fjällbacka **17** F 4
Fjällfjällen **16** F 2
Fkih Ben Salah **58** D 2
Flacq **67** K 6
Fladdabister **2** D 1
Flagler Beach **77** K 6
Flagstaff **76** D 4
Flamborough Head **5** E 2
Flamenco (Argentina) **89** D 7
Flamenco (Chile) **88** B 4
Flamenco, Isla **89** D 7
Flaming Gorge Reservoir **76** E 3
Flanders **14** D 4
Flannan Isles **2** A 2
Flasher **76** F 2
Flåsjön **16** G 3
Flat **72** F 3
Flat Island **42** E 1
Flatey **16** A 2
Flateyri **16** A 2
Flathead Lake **76** D 2
Flattery, Cape (Queensland, Austr.) **49** H 1
Flattery, Cape (WA, U.S.A.) **76** AB 2
Fleet **7** D 2
Fleetwood (Queensland, Austr.) **49** H 3
Fleetwood (U.K.) **5** D 3
Flekkefjord **17** E 4
Flen **17** G 4
Flensburg **15** E 4
Flers **18** C 2
Flesberg **17** E 4
Fleurance **18** D 3
Flevoland **14** E 4
Flin Flon **73** R 5
Flinders **50** L 8
Flinders Bay **48** B 5
Flinders Chase National Park **49** F 6
Flinders Island **49** H 6
Flinders Passage **49** H 2
Flinders Range **49** F 5
Flinders Ranges National Park **49** FG 5
Flinders Reefs **49** H 2
Flinders River **49** G 2
Flint (Kiribati) **53** E 3
Flint (MI, U.S.A.) **77** K 3
Flint (U.K.) **5** D 3
Flint Hills **77** G 4
Flint River **77** K 5
Flinton **49** H 4
Flintry **3** C 3
Flisa **17** F 3
Flisegga **17** E 4
Florac **18** D 3
Floraville (Queensland, Austr.) **49** F 2
Florence (AL, U.S.A.) **77** J 5
Florence (Italy) **19** F 3
Florence (OR, U.S.A.) **76** B 3
Florence (S.C., U.S.A.) **77** KL 5
Florencia **84** C 3
Florentino Ameghino **89** C 7
Florentino Ameghino, Embalse **89** C 7
Flores (Azores) **58** A 1
Flores (Guatemala) **78** E 4
Flores (Indonesia) **43** F 5
Flores, Laut **43** EF 5
Flores Sea **43** EF 5
Floreshty **20** C 1
Floriano **87** H 2
Floriano Pleixoto **84** E 5
Florianópolis **88** G 4
Florida (Cuba) **79** G 3
Florida (Uruguay) **88** E 5
Florida (U.S.A.) **77** K 6
Florida Islands **51** GH 3
Florida Keys **77** K 7
Floridablanca **84** D 2
Flórina **20** B 2
Florø **16** E 3
Flotta **2** C 2
Fluk **43** G 4
Flumendosa **19** E 4
Fly River **50** D 3
Flying Fish Cove **42** C 6
Foča **19** G 3
Fochi **63** H 2
Fochimi **63** H 2
Foci del Po **19** F 2–3
Focşani **20** C 1
Foggaret ez Zoua **59** F 3
Foggia **19** G 3
Foggo **63** G 3
Fogo **75** R 6
Fogo (Cape Verde) **62** B 7
Fohnsdorf **19** F 2
Foix **18** D 3
Fokku **63** E 3
Folakara **67** H 3
Folda **16** F 2

Folégandros **20** B 3
Foley (Botswana) **66** D 4
Foley (N.W.T., Can.) **75** M 2
Foleyet **74** L 6
Folgefonni **17** E 3–4
Foligno **19** F 3
Folkestone **7** E 2
Folkingham **7** D 1
Folkston **77** K 5
Folldal **16** EF 3
Föllinge **16** F 3
Fomboni **67** G 2
Fomich **36** J 1
Fomin **21** F 1
Fond du Lac **73** QR 4
Fond du Lac (WI, U.S.A.) **77** J 3
Fond du-Lac (Sask., Can.) **73** Q 4
Fongen **16** F 3
Fonseca, Golfo de **78** E 5
Fontainebleau **18** D 2
Fontas **73** N 4
Fonte Boa **84** D 4
Fonte do Pau-d'Agua **86** E 3
Fontenay-le-Comte **18** C 2
Fontstown **4** B 3
Fontur **16** C 2
Fonualei **52** D 4
Foraker, Mount **72** G 3
Forbes **49** H 5
Forcados **63** F 4
Ford City **76** C 4
Förde **16** E 3
Fördefjorden **16** DE 3
Fordham **7** E 1
Fordingbridge **7** D 2
Fordyce **2** C 3
Forecariah **62** B 4
Forest **77** J 5
Forest Fawr **6** C 2
Forest of Dean **6** C 2
Forestville **75** O 6
Forêt d'Ecouves **18** C 2
Forez, Plaine du **18** D 2
Forfar **3** C 3
Forgandenny **3** C 3
Forín Linares **86** D 5
Forkas **62** E 3
Forli **19** F 3
Formby **5** D 3
Formentera **18** D 4
Formentor, Cabo de **18** D 3–4
Formia **19** F 3
Formigas **58** A 1
Formosa (Argentina) **88** E 4
Formosa (Goiás, Brazil) **87** G 4
Formosa (Taiwan) **39** H 6
Formosa do Rio Prêto **87** G 3
Formosa, Serra **87** E 3
Formosa Strait **39** GH 5–6
Formosa Strait → Taiwan Haixia **39** GH 5–6
Formoso **87** G 3
Formoso **87** G 3
Fornæs **17** F 4
Föroyar **14** A 1
Forres **2** C 3
Forrest **48** D 5
Forrest City **77** H 5
Forsayth **49** G 2
Forshaga **17** F 4
Forsinard **2** C 2
Forsmark **17** G 3
Forsnäs **16** G 2
Forssa **17** H 3
Forst **15** F 4
Fort Albany **75** L 5
Fort Archambault → Sarh **63** H 4
Fort Assiniboine **73** OP 5
Fort Augustus **2** B 3
Fort Beaufort **66** D 6
Fort Benton **76** D 2
Fort Black **73** Q 4
Fort Bragg **76** B 4
Fort Bridger **76** D 3
Fort Brussaux → Markounda **64** B 3
Fort Charlet → Djanet **59** G 4
Fort Chipewyan **73** P 4
Fort Collins **76** F 3
Fort Collinson **73** O 1
Fort de Polignac → Illizi **59** G 3
Fort Dodge **77** H 3
Fort Edward **77** M 3
Fort Flatters → Bordj Omar Driss **59** G 3
Fort Foureau → Kousseri **63** G 3
Fort Frances **74** J 6
Fort Franklin **73** N 2
Fort Gardel → Zaouatallaz **59** G 4
Fort Good Hope **72** M 2
Fort Gouraud → Fdérik **58** C 4
Fort Hope **74** K 5
Fort Kent **75** O 6
Fort Knox **77** J 4
Fort Lamy → N'Djamena **63** H 3

Fort Laperrine → Tamanrasset **59** G 4
Fort Lauderdale **77** L 6
Fort Liard **73** N 3
Fort Mackay **73** P 4
Fort Macleod **73** P 6
Fort Madison **77** H 3
Fort McMahon → El Homr **59** F 3
Fort McMurray **73** P 4
Fort McPherson **72** L 2
Fort Miribel **59** F 3
Fort Morgan **76** F 3
Fort Motylinski → Tarahouahout **59** G 4
Fort Myers **77** K 6
Fort Nelson **73** N 3
Fort Nelson **73** N 4
Fort Norman **73** M 3
Fort Peck **76** E 2
Fort Peck Dam **76** E 2
Fort Peck Lake **76** E 2
Fort Pierce **77** KL 6
Fort Portal **64** DE 4
Fort Providence **73** O 3
Fort Qu'Appelle **73** R 5
Fort Randell Dam **76** G 3
Fort Resolution **73** OP 3
Fort Rupert **75** M 5
Fort Saint James **73** N 5
Fort Saint John **73** N 4
Fort Saskatchewan **73** P 5
Fort Scott **77** H 4
Fort Severn **74** K 4
Fort Shevchenko **34** E 2
Fort Simpson **73** N 3
Fort Smith (Alb., Can.) **73** P 4
Fort Smith (OK, U.S.A.) **77** H 4
Fort Stockton **76** F 5
Fort Sumner **76** F 5
Fort Trinquet → Bir Moghrein **58** C 3
Fort Vermilion **73** O 4
Fort Victoria → Masvingo **67** E 4
Fort Walton Beach **77** J 5
Fort Wayne **77** J 3
Fort Wellington **85** G 2
Fort William **3** B 3
Fort Worth **76** G 5
Fort Yukon **72** J 2
Fortaleza (Ceará, Brazil) **87** J 1
Fortaleza (Pará, Brazil) **85** G 5
Fortaleza de Ituxi **84** E 5
Fortaleza de Santa Teresa **88** F 5
Fort-Carnot **67** H 4
Fort-Chimo **75** O 4
Fort-de-France **79** K 5
Fortescue River **48** B 3
Fort-George **75** M 5
Forth, River **3** B 3
Fortín Carlos Antonio López **86** E 5
Fortin Coronel Eugenio Garay **86** D 5
Fortín Falcon **86** E 5
Fortín Galpón **86** E 4
Fortín General Aquino **86** E 5
Fortín General Pando **86** E 4
Fortín Ingavi **86** D 4
Fortín Lavalle **88** D 4
Fortín Madrejón **86** E 5
Fortín Madrejoncito **86** E 5
Fortín Ravelo **86** E 4
Fortín Rojas Silva **86** E 5
Fortín Suárez Arana **86** DE 4
Fortín Uno **89** C 6
Fortrose **2** B 3
Fortune Bay **75** Q 6
Fortuneswell **6** C 2
Forūr (Iran) **23** G 4
Fosdyke **7** D 1
Foshan **38** F 6
Fosna **16** F 3
Foso **62** D 4
Fossano **19** E 3
Fossil Bluff **91**
Foster **49** H 6
Foster, Mount **72** K 4
Fougamou **63** G 6
Fougères **18** C 2
Foul Bay → Khalīj Foul **60** F 4
Foula **2** D 1
Foula Morie **62** B 3
Fouladou **62** AB 3
Foulalaba **62** C 3
Foulden **3** C 4
Foulness Island **7** E 2
Foulwind, Cape **51** Q 9
Foum el Hassan **58** D 2
Foum Zguid **58** D 2
Foumban **63** G 4
Foundiougne **62** A 3
Four Mountains, Islands of **72** CD 5
Fourmies **18** D 1
Fourth Cataract → Ash Shallāl ar Rābi' **60** E 5

Fouta Djallon **62** B 3
Fouta Ferlo **62** B 2
Foveaux Strait **50** P 10
Fowey **6** B 2
Fowlers Bay **48** E 5
Fowlers Bay **48** E 5
Fowman **34** D 3
Fox Islands **72** D 5
Fox River **77** J 3
Foxe Basin **73** VW 2
Foxe Channel **75** M 3
Foxe Peninsula **75** M 3
Foyers **2** B 3
Foyle, Lough **4** B 2
Foyle, River **4** B 2
Foz do Breu **84** D 5
Foz do Copeá **85** F 4
Foz do Gregório **84** D 5
Foz do Iguaçu **88** F 4
Foz do Jordão **84** D 5
Foz do Jutaí **84** E 4
Foz Tarauacá **84** E 5
Fraga **18** D 3
Frampton **6** C 3
Franca **87** G 5
Francés, Cabo **78** F 3
Francavilla **63** G 6
Francis Case, Lake **76** FG 3
Francisco de Orellana (Ecuador) **84** C 4
Francisco de Orellana (Peru) **84** D 4
Francisco Escárcega **78** D 4
Francistown **66** D 4
Francofonte **19** FG 4
Francs Peak **76** E 3
Frankenberg **15** E 4
Frankfort (KY, U.S.A.) **77** J 4
Frankfort (MI, U.S.A.) **77** J 3
Frankfurt am Main **15** E 4
Frankfurt an der Oder **15** F 4
Franklin Bay **73** M 1–2
Franklin Lake **73** S 2
Franklin Mountains **73** MN 2–3
Franklin Strait **73** S 1
Fransfontein **66** A 4
Fransfontein Mountains **66** B 4
Franz **74** L 6
Franz Josef Land **90**
Fraser **73** N 5
Fraser, Mount **48** B 4
Fraser or Great Sandy Island **49** J 4
Fraser Plateau **73** N 5
Fraser Range **48** C 5
Fraserburg (South Africa) **66** C 6
Fraserburgh (U.K.) **2** D 3
Fraserdale **75** L 6
Frauenfeld **19** E 2
Fray Bentos **88** E 5
Freckleton **5** D 3
Fredericia **17** EF 4
Frederick Hills **48** F 1
Frederick Reef **49** J 3
Fredericksburg **77** L 4
Fredericton **75** O 6
Frederik IX-Land **75** R 2
Frederik VI-Coast **90**
Frederiksdal **75** S 3
Frederikshavn **17** F 4
Frederikssund **17** F 4
Fredrikstad **79** J 4
Fredônia **84** C 2
Fredrika **16** G 3
Fredrikshamn **17** J 3
Fredrikstad **17** F 4
Fredvang **16** F 2
Freeling Heights **49** F 5
Freels, Cape **75** R 6
Freeport (IL, U.S.A.) **77** J 3
Freeport (TX, U.S.A.) **77** GH 6
Freeport City **79** G 2
Freetown **62** B 4
Fréhel, Cap **18** C 2
Freiberg **15** F 4
Freiburg **15** E 5
Freilassing **15** F 5
Freirina **88** B 4
Freising **15** F 5
Freistadt **19** F 2
Freital **15** F 4
Fréjus **19** E 3
Fremantle **48** B 5
French Guiana **85** H 3
French Polynesia **53** F 4
Frenchman **73** Q 6
Frenda **59** F 1
Fresco (Ivory Coast) **62** C 5
Fresco **85** H 5
Freshford **4** B 3
Freshwater **7** D 2
Fresia **89** B 7

Fresnillo **78** B 3
Fresno **76** B 4
Freu, Cabo **18** D 4
Freycinet Peninsula **50** L 9
Fria **62** B 3
Fria, Cape **66** A 3
Frías **88** C 4
Fribourg **19** E 2
Fridaythorpe **5** E 2
Friedberg **19** G 2
Friesach **19** F 2
Friesland **14–15** E 4
Frinton **7** E 2
Frio, Cabo **87** H 5
Friockheim **3** D 3
Frisian Islands **14** E 4
Fritsa, Proliv **37** R 6
Frobisher Bay **75** O 3
Frobisher Bay **75** O 3
Frobisher Lake **73** Q 4
Frolovo **24** H 6
Frome **7** C 2
Frome, Lake **49** F 5
Front Range **76** E 3–4
Fronteiras **87** H 2
Frontera **78** D 4
Fronteras **76** E 5
Frosinone **19** F 3
Frösö **16** F 3
Frotín Cañada Oruro **86** D 5
Froxfield **7** D 2
Fröya **16** E 3
Fröysjöen **16** D 3
Frozen Strait **73** V 2
Frunze **35** J 4
Frunzovka **20** C 1
Fruška Gora **20** A 1
Frutal **87** G 4
Frýdek Mistek **15** G 5
Fryken, Övre **17** F 3
Ftéri **20** B 3
Fu Xian **38** E 3
Fu Xian **39** H 3
Fu'an **39** G 5
Fubo **63** G 7
Fuchou **39** G 5
Fuchuan **38** F 6
Fuding **39** H 5
Fuengirola **18** C 4
Fuente de Cantos **18** B 4
Fuentes **18** B 4
Fuentesaúco **18** B 3
Fuerte Olimpo **86** E 5
Fuerteventura **58** C 3
Fuga **43** J 1
Fuglafjorður **14** A 1
Fugong **38** C 5
Fugou **38** F 4
Fugu **38** F 3
Fuhai **35** M 1
Fuhaymi (Iraq) **22** CD 2
Fuji **39** L 3
Fujian **39** G 5
Fujin **37** O 6
Fuji-san **39** L 3–4
Fujiyama **39** LM 4
Fūka **60** D 2
Fukang **35** M 2
Fukue **39** J 4
Fukue-jima **39** J 4
Fukui **39** L 3
Fukuoka **39** JK 4
Fukushima **39** LM 2
Fukushima **39** M 3
Fukuyama **39** K 4
Fūlād Mahalleh (Iran) **23** FG 1
Fulda **15** E 4
Fuling **38** E 5
Fulton **89** E 6
Fulufjället **16** F 3
Funabashi **39** M 3
Funafuti **52** C 3
Funafuti **52** CD 3
Funäsdalen **16** F 3
Funchal **58** B 2
Fundación **84** D 1
Fundão **18** B 3
Fundão **87** H 4
Fundy, Bay of **75** O 6–7
Funhaiouro **67** E 4
Funing **38** E 6
Funing **39** G 4
Funing **39** GH 4
Funiu Shan **38** F 4
Funnel River **49** H 3
Funsi **62** D 3
Fuping **38** E 4
Fuping **38** F 3
Fuqing **39** G 5
Furana **59** F 4
Furancungo **67** E 2
Furano **39** M 2
Furawiyah **60** C 5
Fürg (Iran) **23** G 3
Furmanov **24** H 4
Furmanovka **35** J 2

Furmanovo 24 JK 6
Furnas Dam 87 G 5
Furnas, Reprêsa de 87 G 5
Furneaux Group 50 L 9
Furneaux Group 52 A 5
Furqlus (Syria) 22 B 2
Fürstenfeld 19 G 2
Fürstenfeldbrück 15 F 5
Fürstenwalde 15 F 4
Fürth 15 F 5
Furth im Wald 15 F 5
Furudal 16 G 3
Furukawa 39 M 3
Fury and Hecla Strait 74 L 1–2
Fusagasugá 84 D 3
Fushë-Lura 20 B 2
Fushun 39 H 2
Fusong 39 J 2
Fusui 38 E 6
Futa, Passo della 19 F 3
Futa Ruím 89 BC 7
Futuna (Vanuatu) 51 K 5
Futuna (Wallis and Futuna) 52 D 3
Fuwaris (Saudi Arabia) 23 E 3
Fuxian Hu 38 D 6
Fuxin 39 H 2
Fuyang 38 G 4
Fuyu 37 M 6
Fuyu 39 H 1
Fuyuan (China) 38 D 5
Fuyuan (U.S.S.R.) 37 O 6
Fuyun 35 M 1
Fuzhou 38 G 5
Fyn 17 F 4
Fyne, Loch 3 B 3
Fyresvatn 17 E 4
Fyrsjön 16 G 3
Fyvie 2 C 3

G

Gabba' 65 J 3
Gabbs 76 C 4
Gabela 66 A 2
Gabès 59 H 2
Gabon 63 F 5
Gabon 63 G 6
Gaborone 66 D 4
Gaboto 88 D 5
Gabras 60 D 6
Gabredarre 65 G 3
Gabrey, Vozvyshennost' 36 F 1
Gabriel Strait 75 O 3
Gabriel y Galan, Embalse de
  18 B 3
Gabrovo 20 C 2
Gacé 18 D 2
Gach Sārān (Iran) 23 F 3
Gacko 19 G 3
Gada 63 F 3
Gadamai 60 F 5
Gadame 64 E 3
Gäddede 16 F 3
Gadê 38 C 4
Gadhap 35 H 5
Gadsden 77 J 5
Gadūk, Gardaneh-ye (Iran) 23 F 2
Gadwal 40 C 4
Gaeta 19 F 3
Gaeta, Golfo di 19 F 3
Gaferut 52 A 2
Gaffney 77 K 4
Gafsa 57
Gafsa → Qafsah 59 G 2
Gag, Pulau 43 G 4
Gagan 51 F 3
Gagarin 24 F 4
Gagere 63 F 3
Gagnoa 62 C 4
Gagnon 75 O 5
Gagra 21 F 2
Gagshor 24 JK 3
Gahkom 23 G 3
Gai Xian 39 H 2
Gaibanda 40 E 2
Gaillac 18 D 3
Gaillimh 14 B 4
Gaimán 89 C 7
Gainesville (FL, U.S.A.) 77 K 6
Gainesville (GA, U.S.A.) 77 K 5
Gainesville (TX, U.S.A.) 77 G 5
Gainsborough 7 D 1
Gairdner, Lake 49 F 5
Gairloch 2 B 3
Gaizina Kalns 17 J 4
Gakankoy 37 T 4
Gakarosa 66 C 5
Gakona 72 H 3
Gal Tardo 65 H 4
Gala (Greece) 20 C 2
Gala (Tibet, China) 40 E 2
Galadi (Ethiopia) 65 H 3
Galadi (Nigeria) 63 F 3
Galán, Cerro 88 C 4

Galana 65 F 5
Galanino 36 F 4
Galápagos Islands 84 B 6
Galashiels 3 C 4
Galathea Deep 52 D 5
Galaţi 20 C 1
Galatina 19 G 3
Galbraith 49 G 2
Galdhöpiggen 16 E 3
Galeana 76 E 5
Galeana (Mexico) 78 C 3
Galeh Dār (Iran) 23 F 4
Galela 43 G 3
Galena 72 F 3
Galera, Punta 89 B 7
Galesburg 77 H 3
Gali 21 F 2
Galich 24 H 4
Galicia (Poland) 15 H 5
Galicia (Spain) 18 B 3
Galilee, Lake 49 H 3
Galiléia 87 H 4
Galimyy 37 T 3
Gälka'yo 65 H 3
Gallan Head 2 A 2
Gallarate 19 E 2
Galle 40 D 6
Gallego 18 C 3
Gallegos 89 B 9
Gallinas, Punta 84 D 1
Gallipoli 19 G 3
Gällivare 16 H 2
Gallo 18 C 3
Gallo, Capo 19 F 4
Gallo Mountains 76 E 5
Galloway 3 B 4
Gallup 76 E 4
Galole 65 F 5
Galty Mountains 14 B 4
Galveston 77 H 6
Galveston Bay 77 H 6
Gálvez 88 D 5
Galway 14 B 4
Galway Bay 14 B 4
Gam 66 C 4
Gama 89 D 7
Gama, Isla 89 D 7
Gamarri, Lake 65 G 2
Gamba (Gabon) 63 F 6
Gamba (Tibet, China) 40 E 2
Gambaga 62 D 3
Gambeila 64 E 3
Gambell 72 C 3
Gambia 62 A 3
Gambie 62 B 3
Gambier Islands 53 FG 6
Gamboma 63 H 6
Gamboola 49 G 2
Gamboula 64 B 4
Gamkunoro, Gunung 43 G 3
Gamleby 17 G 4
Gamlingay 7 D 1
Gammelstad 16 H 2
Gamo Gofa 65 F 3
Gamud 65 F 4
Gamvik 16 J 1
Gan Jiang 38 G 5
Ganale 65 G 3
Ganaly 37 T 5
Ganda 66 A 2
Gandadiwata, Bukit 43 EF 4
Gandajika 64 C 6
Gandak 40 D 2
Gandaua 35 H 5
Gander 75 R 6
Gandesa 18 D 3
Gandhi Sagar Dam 40 C 3
Gandhinagar 40 B 3
Gandi 63 F 3
Gandía 18 C 4
Gand-i-Zirreh 35 G 5
Gandu 87 J 3
Ganeb 58 C 5
Ganetti 60 E 5
Ganga 40 E 2
Ganga, Mont de 63 G 4
Ganga, Mouths of the 40–41 EF 3
Gangakher 40 C 4
Gangan 89 C 7
Ganganagar 40 B 2
Gangapur 40 C 2
Gangara 63 F 3
Gangaw 41 F 3
Gangawati 40 C 4
Gangca 38 D 3
Gangdisê Shan 40 DE 1
Ganges 40 E 3
Ganges Cone 98 B 3
Ganghar 40 C 3
Gangmar Co 40 D 1
Gangotri 40 C 1
Gangtok 40 E 2
Gangu 38 E 4
Gani 43 G 4
Ganina Gar' 36 F 4

Gannan 37 M 6
Gannat 18 D 2
Gannett Peak 76 DE 3
Ganquan 38 E 3
Gansu 38 DE 3
Gant 12
Ganta 62 C 4
Gantang 38 D 3
Ganyesa 66 C 5
Ganzhou 38 F 5
Ganzurino 36 J 5
Gao 62 D 2
Gao Xian 38 D 5
Gao'an 38 G 5
Gaohe 38 F 6
Gaolan 38 D 3
Gaoligong Shan 38 C 5
Gaolou Ling 38 E 5–6
Gaomi 39 GH 3
Gaona 88 D 3
Gaoping 38 F 3
Gaotai 38 C 3
Gaotang 39 G 3
Gaoua 62 D 3
Gaoual 62 B 3
Gaoyi 38 F 3
Gaoyou 39 G 4
Gaoyou Hu 39 G 4
Gaozhou 38 F 6
Gap 19 E 3
Gapan 43 J 1
Gar 40 C 1
Gara'ad 65 H 3
Garachiné 84 C 2
Garai 35 J 3
Garaina 50 E 3
Garamba National Park 64 D 4
Garangan (Iran) 23 F 3
Garanhuns 87 J 2
Garantah 42 E 5
Garar, Plaine de 63 J 3
Garara 50 E 3
Garba Härrey 65 G 4
Garberville 76 B 3
Garbokaray 36 G 5
Garboldisham 7 E 1
Garbosh, Kūh-e (Iran) 23 EF 2
Garco 40 E 1
Garda, Lago di 19 F 2
Gardaneh-ye Avej 34 D 3
Gardaneh-ye Avej (Iran) 23 E 2
Gardaneh-ye Gadūk (Iran) 23 F 2
Gardaneh-ye Kandovān (Iran)
  23 F 1
Gardaneh-ye Khāneh Sorkh (Iran)
  23 G 3
Gardaneh-ye Kowlī Kosh (Iran)
  23 F 3
Garden City 76 F 4
Gardermoen 17 F 3
Gardez 35 H 4
Gardiner 76 D 2
Gardo → Qardo 65 H 3
Gardula 65 F 3
Garelochhead 3 B 3
Gareloi 65 J 1
Garet el Djenoun 59 G 3
Gargano, Promontorio del 19 G 3
Gargnäs 16 G 2
Gargouna 62 DE 2
Gari 25 M 4
Garies 66 B 6
Garissa 65 FG 5
Garkida 63 G 3
Garlieston 3 B 4
Garmal 65 J 3
Garmdasht (Iran) 23 E 3
Garmisch-Partenkirchen 15 F 5
Garmsar 34 E 3
Garmsar (Iran) 23 F 2
Garnett 77 G 4
Garonne 18 D 3
Garoua (Cameroon) 63 G 4
Garoua (Niger) 63 G 3
Garoua Boulai 63 G 4
Garöwe 65 H 3
Garphyttan 17 G 4
Garri, Kūh-e (Iran) 23 E 2
Garrison 4 A 2
Garrison Dam 76 F 2
Garry Bay 73 U 2
Garry Lake 73 R 2
Garsen 65 F 5
Garsila 60 C 6
Garstang 5 D 3
Garth 6 C 1
Garut 42 C 5
Garvagh 4 B 2
Garvagh 4 B 3
Garvald 3 C 4
Garve 2 B 3
Garwa 40 D 3
Garwolin 15 H 4
Gary 77 J 3
Garyn' 36 J 4
Garza 88 D 4

Garze 38 C 4
Garzón 84 C 3
Gas Hu 38 B 3
Gasan-Kuli 34 E 3
Gascogne 18 CD 3
Gascoyne Junction 48 B 4
Gascoyne River 48 A 3
Gashagar 63 G 3
Gashaka 63 G 4
Gasht 35 G 5
Gashua 63 G 3
Gashun 21 F 1
Gaspar, Selat 42 C 4
Gaspé 75 P 6
Gaspé, Cap de 75 P 6
Gaspé, Péninsule de 75 O 6
Gassi Touil 59 G 2
Gassol 63 G 4
Gastello, Iméni 37 R 3
Gastonia 77 K 4
Gastre 89 C 7
Gästrikland 17 G 3
Gata, Akra (Cyprus) 22 A 2
Gata, Cabo de 18 C 4
Gata, Sierra de 18 B 3
Gatamaran 50 L 9
Gatchina 17 K 4
Gatehouse of Fleet 3 B 4
Gates of the Arctic National Park
  and Preserve 72 G 2
Gateshead (N.W.T., Can.) 73 S 1
Gateshead (U.K.) 5 E 2
Gatineau Park 75 M 6
Gatooma → Kadoma 66 D 3
Gattinara 19 E 2
Gatton 49 J 4
Gatvand (Iran) 23 E 2
Gatwick (Airport) 7 D 2
Gauani 65 G 2
Gauhati 41 F 2
Gauja 17 H 4
Gaula 16 E 3
Gauldalen 16 F 3
Gaurdak 35 H 3
Gaurihar 40 CD 2
Gausta 17 E 4
Gauttier, Pegunungan 43 J 4
Gäv Kosh (Iran) 23 E 2
Gavanka 37 T 4
Gaväter 35 G 5
Gāvbandi (Iran) 23 F 4
Gavbūs, Kūh-e (Iran) 23 FG 4
Gávdhos 20 B 4
Gave de Pau 18 C 3
Gävle 17 G 3
Gävlebukten 17 G 3
Gawler 49 F 5
Gawler Ranges 49 F 5
Gaxun Nur 38 D 2
Gaya (India) 40 E 3
Gaya (Niger) 63 F 3
Gaya (Nigeria) 63 F 3
Gaydon 7 D 1
Gaylord 77 K 2
Gayndah 49 J 4
Gayny 24 K 3
Gaysin 20 C 1
Gayvoron 20 D 1
Gaz (Iran) 23 F 2
Gaza → Ghazzah 60 E 2
Gaza Strip 22 AB 3
Gazammi 63 G 3
Gazaoua 63 F 3
Gazelle Peninsula 51 F 2
Gaziantep 21 E 3
Gaziantep (Turkey) 22 B 1
Gaziantep Yaylasi 21 E 3
Gazimur 36 L 5
Gazimurskiy Zavod 36 L 5
Gazipaşa 21 D 3
Gazli 35 G 2
Gbarnga 62 C 4
Gboko 63 F 4
Gcoverega 66 C 3
Gdańsk 15 G 4
Gdansk, Gulf of 15 G 4
Gdov 17 J 4
Gdynia 15 G 4
Gearhart Mountain 76 B 3
Gebe, Pulau 43 G 4
Gebze 20 C 2
Gechia 64 F 3
Gedi 65 F 5
Gediz 20 C 3
Gediz 20 C 3
Gedser 17 F 5
Geelong 49 G 6
Geelvink Channel 48 A 4
Gefara Plain → Jifārah Plain
  59 H 2
Gegamskiy Khrebet 21 G 2–3
Gê'gyai 40 D 1
Geidam 63 G 3
Geigar 60 E 6
Geikie 73 R 4

Geilo 17 E 3
Geiranger 16 E 3
Geita 64 E 5
Gejiu 31
Gejiu 38 D 6
Gel 64 D 3
Gelai 65 F 5
Gelendzhik 21 E 2
Gelibolu 20 C 2
Gelibolu Yarimadasi 20 C 2
Gellinsör 65 H 3
Gelsenkirchen 15 E 4
Gemena 64 B 4
Gemerek 21 E 3
Gemlik 20 C 2
Gemlik Körfezi 20 C 2
Gemona 19 F 2
Gemsbok National Park 66 C 4–5
Gemuru 42 E 4
Genç 21 F 3
Gencek 20 D 3
Geneina → Al Junaynah 60 C 6
General Acha 89 D 6
General Alvear (Argentina)
  89 C 5–6
General Alvear (Argentina)
  89 DE 6
General Belgrano 89 E 6
General Belgrano II 91
General Belgrano III 91
General Bernardo O'Higgins 91
General Bravo 78 C 2
General Carrera, Lago 89 B 8
General Chaves 89 D 6
General Conesa 89 CD 7
General Daniel Cerri 89 D 6
General Guido 89 E 6
General La Madrid 89 D 6
General Lavalle 89 E 6
General Madariaga 89 E 6
General Martín Miguel de Güemes
  86 D 5
General Paz 88 E 4
General Pico 89 D 6
General Pinedo 88 D 4
General Pinto 88 D 5
General Roca 89 C 6
General San Martin 91
General Santos 43 G 2
General Treviñe 78 C 2
General Trias 76 E 5
General Vargas 88 F 4
General Villegas 88 D 6
Geneva (N.Y., U.S.A.) 77 L 3
Genève 19 E 2
Gengma 38 C 6
Genichesk 21 DE 1
Genil 18 C 4
Genoa 19 E 3
Genova 19 E 3
Genova, Golfo di 19 E 3
Genovesa Isla 84 B 6
Gent 14 D 4
Genteng 42 C 5
Genyem 50 CD 2
Geographe Bay 48 B 5
Geographe Channel 48 A 3
Geok-Tepe 34 F 3
Georg von Neumayer 91
George (Quebec, Can.) 75 O 4
George (South Africa) 66 C 6
George, Lake (FL, U.S.A.) 77 K 6
George, Lake (N.Y., U.S.A.)
  77 M 3
George, Lake (Uganda) 64 E 5
George, Lake (Western Australia)
  48 C 3
George Town (Malaysia) 42 AB 2
George Town (Tasmania, Austr.)
  50 L 9
George V Coast 91
George VI Sound 91
George West 76 G 6
Georgetown (Cayman Is.) 79 F 4
Georgetown (Gambia) 62 B 3
Georgetown (Guyana) 85 G 2
Georgetown (Queensland, Austr.)
  49 G 2
Georgetown (S.C., U.S.A.) 77 L 5
Georgetown (The Bahamas) 79 G 3
Georgetown (TX, U.S.A.) 76 G 5
Georgia (U.S.A.) 77 K 5
Georgia (U.S.S.R.) 21 F 2
Georgian Bay 75 L 6
Georgina River 49 F 3
Georgiu-Dezh 24 G 5
Georgiyevka 25 Q 6
Georgiyevka 35 K 2
Georgiyevsk 21 F 2
Gera 15 F 4
Gerais, Chapadão dos 87 G 4
Geral de Goiás, Serra 87 G 3
Geral do Paraná, Serra 87 G 3
Geral ou Grande, Serra 87 G 3
Geral, Serra 88 F 4

Geraldine (New Zealand) 51 Q 9
Geraldine (Western Australia)
 48 A 4
Geraldton (Ontario, Can.) 74 K 6
Geraldton (Western Australia)
 48 A 4
Gerãs, Serra do 18 B 3
Gerasimovka 25 O 4
Gerba 37 S 3
Gerbichi, Gora 36 J 2
Gercüş 21 F 3
Gerðar 16 A 3
Gerede 21 D 2
Geriban → 'El Ḥamurre 65 H 3
Gering 76 F 3
Gerlachovský Štit 15 H 5
Gerlogubi 65 GH 3
Gerlovo 20 C 2
German Democratic Republic
 15 F 4
Germânia 86 BC 3
Germania 88 D 5
Germi 34 D 3
Germi 34 E 4
Germi (Iran) 23 G 2
Gerona 18 D 3
Gerze 21 DE 2
Gêrzê 40 D 1
Gesoa 50 D 3
Gestro, Webbe 65 G 3
Gesunda 17 F 3
Gesunden 16 G 3
Getafe 18 C 3
Gettysburg 76 G 2
Getúlio Vargas 88 F 4
Getz Ice Shelf 91
Geumpang, Krueng 42 A 3
Gevaş 21 F 3
Gevgelija 20 B 2
Geyik Dağı 21 D 3
Geyser, Banc du 67 H 2
Geysir 16 A 3
Geyve 20 D 2
Ghadāmis 59 G 2
Ghadduwah 59 H 3
Ghadīr ar Razzah 59 J 3
Ghaghara 40 D 2
Ghana 62 D 4
Ghanadah, Ra's (United Arab
 Emirates) 23 G 4
Ghanzi 66 C 4
Gharaqābād (Iran) 23 EF 2
Ghardaïa 59 F 2
Ghārib, Jabal (Egypt) 22 A 3
Gharib, Ra's (Egypt) 22 A 3
Gharyān 59 H 2
Ghāt 59 H 4
Ghats, Eastern 40 CD 3–5
Ghats, Western 40 BC 4–5
Ghawar 34 D 6
Ghawar (Saudi Arabia) 23 E 4
Ghayl Bā Wāzīr 61 H 6
Ghayl Bin Ymayn 61 H 5
Ghazaouet 58 E 1
Ghaziabad 40 C 2
Ghazipur 40 D 2
Ghazni 35 H 4
Ghazzah 22 B 3
Ghedo 65 F 3
Ghelemso 65 G 3
Ghemi, Jabal 64 E 3
Gheorghe Gheorghiu-Dej 20 C 1
Gheorghieni 20 C 1
Gherla 20 B 1
Ghimbi 64 F 3
Ghizao 35 H 4
Ghizar 35 J 3
Ghubaysh 60 D 6
Ghubbat al Qamar 61 J 5
Ghubbat Ṣawqirah 61 K 5
Ghudāf, Wādī al (Iraq) 22 D 2
Ghurāb, Jabal al (Syria) 22 C 2
Ghurayrah 61 G 5
Ghurd Abū Muḥarrik 60 D 3
Ghurian 35 G 4
Giamame → Jamāme 65 G 4
Giannutri 19 F 3
Gibara 79 G 3
Gibb River 48 D 2
Gibeon 66 B 5
Gibostad 16 G 2
Gibraltar 18 B 4
Gibraltar, Estrecho de 18 B 4
Gibraltar, Strait of 18 B 4
Gibson 48 C 5
Gibson Desert 48 C 3
Gichgeniyn Nuruu 36 FG 6
Giddings 77 G 5
Gideå 16 G 3
Gideån 16 G 3
Gidgi, Lake 48 D 4
Gidole → Gardula 65 F 3
Gien 18 D 2
Giessen 15 E 4
Gift Lake 73 O 4
Gifthorn 15 F 4

Gifu 39 L 3
Gigant 21 F 1
Giganta, Sierra de la 76 D 6
Gigha 3 B 4
Giglio 19 F 3
Gijón 18 B 3
Gila 76 D 5
Gila Bend 76 D 5
Gīlān-e Gharb (Iran) 23 DE 2
Gilbert Islands 52 C 2–3
Gilbert River 49 G 2
Gilbert River 49 G 2
Gilberton 49 G 2
Gilbués 87 G 2
Gilé 67 F 3
Giles 48 D 4
Gilford 4 B 2
Gilgandra 49 H 5
Gilgau 20 B 1
Gilgil 65 F 5
Gilgit 35 J 3
Gilgunnia 49 H 5
Gill 5 E 2
Gillam 73 T 4
Gillen, Lake 48 C 4
Gillette 76 E 3
Gillian, Lake 75 M 2
Gillingham 7 E 2
Gilo 64 E 3
Gilroy 76 B 4
Gilvān (Iran) 23 E 1
Gilwern 6 C 3
Gilyuy 37 N 4
Gimli 73 S 5
Gimolskoye, Ozero 16 K 3
Gingin 48 B 5
Gingoog 43 G 2
Ginir 65 G 3
Ginzo de Limia 18 B 3
Gioher → Jōwhar 65 H 4
Gioia 19 G 3
Gioia Tauro 19 G 4
Gir Forest 40 B 3
Giralia 48 A 3
Girardot 84 D 3
Girdle Ness 2 CD 3
Giresun 21 E 2
Giri 64 B 4
Giridih 40 E 3
Girishk 35 G 4
Girna 40 C 3
Girne 21 D 3
Girne (Cyprus) 22 A 2
Girón 84 C 2
Gironde 18 C 2
Girvan 3 B 4
Girvas 16 K 3
Gisborne 51 R 8
Gisburn 5 D 3
Gisenye 64 D 5
Gislaved 17 F 4
Gistral 18 B 3
Gitarama 64 DE 5
Gitega 64 E 5
Gitu (Iran) 23 E 2
Giuba → Juba 65 G 4
Giulianova 19 F 3
Giurgiu 20 C 2
Givors 19 D 2
Giza 60 DE 3
Gizhduvan 35 G 2
Gizhiga 37 U 3
Gizhiginskaya Guba 37 T 3
Gizo 51 G 3
Giżycko 15 H 4
Gjiri i Drinit 20 A 2
Gjiri i Karavastase 20 A 2
Gjiri i Vlorã 20 A 2
Gjirokastra 20 B 2
Gjøgur 16 B 2
Gjøvik 17 F 3
Glace Bay 75 Q 6
Glaciares, Parque Nacional los
 89 B 8
Glacier Bay 72 K 4
Glacier Bay National Park and
 Preserve 72 K 4
Glacier Lake 73 T 5
Glacier National Park (MT,
 U.S.A.) 76 D 2
Glacier Peak 76 B 2
Gladstone 49 J 3
Gladstone 77 J 2
Gláma 16 A 2
Glåma 17 F 3
Glamis 3 D 3
Glanaman 6 C 3
Glarryford 4 B 2
Glarus 19 E 2
Glasgow (Airport) 3 B 4
Glasgow (KY, U.S.A.) 77 J 4
Glasgow (MT, U.S.A.) 76 E 2
Glasgow (U.K.) 3 B 4
Glasier 89 C 7
Glastonbury 6 C 2
Glazov 24 K 4

Glebe 4 B 2
Gleib Chileh 58 C 4
Gleisdorf 19 G 2
Glen Canyon National Recreation
 Area 76 D 4
Glen Garry 3 B 3
Glen Innes 49 J 4
Glen Lyon 3 B 3
Glen More 2–3 B 3
Glenavy 4 B 2
Glenbarr 3 B 4
Glencaple 3 C 4
Glencarse 3 C 3
Glendale 76 D 5
Glendive 76 F 2
Glenfarg 3 C 3
Glenfarne 4 A 2
Glenfinnan 3 B 3
Glenham 4 C 2
Glenhope 51 Q 9
Glenluce 3 B 4
Glennallen 72 H 3
Glenormiston 49 F 3
Glenrock 76 E 3
Glenrothes 3 C 3
Glens Falls 77 M 3
Glentham 7 D 1
Glenwood Springs 76 E 4
Glina 19 G 2
Glittertind 16 E 3
Gliwice 15 G 4
Globe 76 D 5
Głogów 15 G 4
Glomfjord 16 F 2
Glommersträsk 16 GH 2
Gloppet 16 H 3
Glorieuses, Iles 67 H 2
Glossop 5 E 3
Glottof, Mount 72 G 4
Gloucester (Australia) 49 J 5
Gloucester (MA, U.S.A.) 77 M 3
Gloucester (U.K.) 7 C 2
Gloucester, Cabo 89 B 9
Gloucestershire 7 C 2
Glubokiy 21 F 1
Glubokoye 17 J 4
Glubokoye 25 Q 5
Glücksburg 15 E 4
Glukhov 24 F 5
Glusha 17 J 5
Glusk 17 J 5
Glybokaya 20 C 1
Glynn 4 C 2
Gmelinka 24 J 5
Gmünd 19 F 2
Gmünd 19 G 2
Gmunden 19 F 2
Gnarp 16 G 3
Gniben 17 F 4
Gniezno 15 G 4
Gniloaksayskaya 21 F 1
Gnjilane 20 B 2
Gnowangerup 48 B 5
Goa 40 B 4
Goageb 66 B 5
Goalpara 41 F 2
Goaso 62 D 4
Goba 65 G 3
Gobabeb 66 B 4
Gobabis 66 B 4
Gobernador Crespo 88 D 5
Gobernador Gregores 89 BC 8
Gobi 38 EF 2
Gochas 66 B 4
Godalming 7 D 2
Godār-e Sorkh (Iran) 23 G 2
Godar-i-Shah 35 G 5
Godavari 40 D 4
Godavari, Mouths of the 40 D 4
Godavari, Mouths of the 40 D 4
Godby 17 H 3
Goðafoss 16 B 2
Godhra 40 B 3
Godinlave 65 H 3
Godmanchester 7 D 1
Godoy Cruz 88 C 5
Gods Lake 73 T 5
Gods Lake 73 T 5
Gods Mercy, Bay of 73 U 3
Gods River 73 T 4
Godthåb 75 R 3
Godthåbfjord 75 R 3
Godwar 40 B 2
Goe 50 D 3
Goéland, Lac au 75 M 5–6
Goélands, Lac aux 75 P 4
Goes 14 D 4
Gofitskoye 21 F 1
Gogebic Range 77 J 2
Goginan 6 C 1
Gogland, Ostrov 17 J 3
Gogolevskiy 25 O 5
Gogrial 64 D 3
Gogu, Virful 20 B 1
Gogui 62 C 2
Goiandira 87 G 4

Goianesia 87 G 4
Goiânia 87 G 4
Goianorte 85 J 5
Goiás 87 G 3
Goiás (Goiás, Brazil) 87 G 4
Göinge 17 F 4
Góis 18 B 3
Gojam 65 F 2
Gojra 35 J 4
Gökçe Ada 20 C 2–3
Gökırmak 21 D 2
Göksu 21 D 3
Göksu (Turkey) 21 E 3
Göksu (Turkey) 21 F 3
Göksum 21 E 3
Göktepe 20 C 3
Gokwe 66 D 3
Gol 17 E 3
Gol Tappeh (Iran) 23 D 1
Golaghat 41 F 2
Golan Heights 22 B 2
Golaya Pristan 21 D 1
Golconda 76 C 3
Gölcük 20 C 2
Gold Coast 62 DE 5
Gold Coast (Australia) 49 J 4
Gold Rock 74 J 6
Goldap 15 H 4
Golden 73 O 5
Golden Gate 76 B 4
Golden Hinde 73 M 6
Golden Vale 14 B 4
Goldfield 76 C 4
Goldsboro 77 L 4
Goldsworthy 48 B 3
Göle 21 F 2
Goleniów 15 FG 4
Golets Skalistyy, Gora 37 O 4
Golets-Inyaptuk, Gora 36 K 4
Golets-Longdor, Gora 36 L 4
Golets-Purpula, Gora 36 K 4
Golets-Skalistyy, Gora 36 LM 4
Golfe de la Gonâve 79 H 4
Golfe de Saint-Florent 19 E 3
Golfe de Saint-Malo 18 C 2
Golfe de Tadjourah 65 G 2
Golfe du Lion 18–19 D 3
Golfito 78 F 6
Golfo Almirante Montt 89 B 9
Golfo Aranci 19 E 3
Golfo Corcovado 89 B 7
Golfo de Almeria 18 C 4
Golfo de Ana María 79 G 3
Golfo de Ancud 89 B 7
Golfo de Cádiz 18 B 4
Golfo de California 76 DE 5–7
Golfo de Chiriquí 84 B 2
Golfo de Cintra 58 B 4
Golfo de Fonseca 78 E 5
Golfo de Guacanayabo 79 G 3
Golfo de Guayaquil 84 B 4
Golfo de Honduras 78 E 4
Golfo de los Mosquitos 84 B 2
Golfo de Nicoya 78 F 6
Golfo de Panamá 84 C 2
Golfo de Paria 85 F 1
Golfo de Penas 89 B 8
Golfo de Rosas 18 D 3
Golfo de San Jorge 18 D 3
Golfo de Tehuantepec 78 D 4
Golfo de Valencia 18 C 3
Golfo de Venezuela 84 D 1
Golfo del Batabano 78–79 F 3
Golfo del Darién 84 C 2
Golfo del Papagayo 78 E 5
Golfo dell'Asinara 19 E 3
Golfo di Castellammare 19 F 4
Golfo di Gaeta 19 F 3
Golfo di Genova 19 E 3
Golfo di Manfredonia 19 G 3
Golfo di Palmas 19 E 4
Golfo di Policastro 19 G 4
Golfo di Salerno 19 F 3
Golfo di Squillace 19 G 4
Golfo di Taranto 19 G 3–4
Golfo Dulce 78 F 6
Golfo Ladrillero 89 A 8
Golfo Nuevo 89 D 7
Golfo San Jorge 89 C 8
Golfo San Matías 89 D 7
Golfo Trinidad 89 A 8
Gölgeli Dağları 20 C 3
Gölhisar 20 C 3
Golija 20 B 2
Goljak 20 B 2
Goljama Syutkya 20 B 2
Gölköy 21 E 2
Golmud 38 B 3
Golmud He 38 BC 3
Golo 19 E 3
Gololcha 65 G 3
Gölören 21 D 3
Golovanevsk 20 D 1
Golovin 72 E 3
Golovnino 39 N 2

Golovskoye 36 J 4
Golpayegan (Iran) 23 F 2
Gölpazari 20 D 2
Golspie 2 C 3
Golubac 20 B 2
Golubovka 25 O 5
Golyam Perelik 20 B 2
Golyam Persenk 20 B 2
Golyama 20 B 2
Golyayevka 24 H 5
Golygino 37 T 5
Golyshmanovo 25 N 4
Goma 64 D 5
Gomati 40 D 2
Gombe 63 G 3
Gombi 63 G 3
Gomel 24 F 5
Gomera 58 B 3
Goméz Palacio 78 B 2
Gomo 40 E 1
Gomo Co 40 E 1
Gomo Gomo 43 HJ 5
Gonäbäd 34 F 4
Gonaïves 79 H 4
Gonam 37 O 4
Gonam 37 O 4
Gonâve, Golfe de la 79 H 4
Gonâve, Ile de la 79 H 4
Gonbad-e Qābus 34 EF 3
Gonda 40 D 2
Gondal 40 B 3
Gondar 65 F 2
Gondia 40 D 3
Gondomar 18 B 3
Gönen 20 C 2
Gonfirth 2 D 1
Gongan 38 F 4
Gongbo' gyamda 38 B 5
Gongga Shan 38 D 5
Gonggar 41 F 2
Gonghe 38 D 3
Gonglee 62 C 4
Gongliu 35 L 2
Gongola 63 G 3
Gongpoquan 38 C 2
Gongshan 38 C 5
Goñi 88 E 5
Gonjo 38 C 4
Gonzales 78 C 3
Good Hope, Cape of 66 B 6
Goodhouse 66 B 5
Gooding 76 CD 3
Goodland 76 F 4
Goodnews Bay 72 E 4
Goodooga 49 H 4
Goole 5 E 3
Goolgowi 49 H 5
Goomalling 48 B 5
Goondiwindi 49 HJ 4
Goongarrie 48 C 5
Goonyella 49 H 3
Goose Bay 75 P 5
Goose Lake 76 B 3
Göppingen 15 E 5
Gora Adyarta 36 G 2
Gora Aktau 35 G 2
Gora Alney 37 TU 4
Gora Arga-Emneke 37 Q 2
Gora Bazar Dyuzi 34 D 2
Gora Belukha 25 R 5–6
Gora Bystrinskiy Golets 36 J 6
Gora Chureg-Tag 36 F 5
Gora Denezhkin Kamen' 25 L 3
Gora Dzerzhinskaya 17 J 5
Gora Ezop 37 S 3
Gora Fisht 21 E 2
Gora Gerbichi 36 J 2
Gora Golets Skalistyy 37 O 4
Gora Golets-Inyaptuk 36 K 4
Gora Golets-Longdor 36 L 4
Gora Golets-Purpula 36 K 4
Gora Golets-Skalistyy 36 LM 4
Gora Isherim 25 L 3
Gora Ivao 37 RS 6
Gora Kamen 36 FG 2
Gora Kamen 36 FG 2
Gora Kekurnaya 37 V 3
Gora Kelil'vun 37 V 2
Gora Khil'mi 37 S 1
Gora Khoydype 25 N 2
Gora Konus 37 O 4
Gora Konzhakovskiy Kamen'
 25 LM 4
Gora Kovriga 24 J 2
Gora Kroviga 36 F 3
Gora Kurkure-Bazhi 25 R 5
Gora Kuytun 25 R 6
Gora Ledyanaya 37 W 3
Gora Lopatina 37 Q 5
Gora Medvezh'ya 37 P 6
Gora More-Iz 25 M 2
Gora Moskva 36 F 5
Gora Munku-Sardyk 36 GH 5
Gora Nachikinskaya 37 U 4
Gora Narodnaya 25 LM 2
Gora Nelkuchan 37 P 3

Gora Ostryak 37 W 3
Gora Pal-Pal 37 VW 3
Gora Pay-Yer 25 M 2
Gora Pobeda 37 R 2
Gora Pshish 21 F 2
Gora Pyat'kovende 37 T 2
Gora Shunak 25 O 6
Gora Shunak 35 J 1
Gora Skaliskaya 36 D 1
Gora Skalistaya 36 D 1
Gora Sokhondo 36 K 6
Gora Sokhor 36 J 5
Gora Syuge-Khaya 37 P 2
Gora Taklaun 37 Q 3
Gora Tardoki Yani 37 P 6
Gora Tel'pos-Iz 25 L 3
Gora Terpukhoy 37 VW 2
Gora Topko 37 P 4
Gora Volna 37 T 3
Gora Yamantau 25 L 5
Gora Yebe-Khay 36 KL 1
Gora Yenashimski Pol'kan
    36 F 3–4
Góra Zamkowa 15 H 4
Gora Zubets 37 X 3
Goragorskiy 21 G 2
Gorakhpur 40 D 2
Goransko 20 A 2
Gorda 76 B 4
Gördes 20 C 3
Gordil 64 C 3
Gordion 21 D 3
Gordium 21 D 3
Gordon (NE, U.S.A.) 76 F 3
Gordon (WI, U.S.A.) 77 H 2
Gordon Downs 48 D 2
Gordon Lake 73 P 3
Gordon River 50 L 9
Gordonvale 49 H 2
Goré (Chad) 63 H 4
Gore (Ethiopia) 64 F 3
Gore (New Zealand) 50 P 10
Gorebridge 3 C 4
Görele 21 E 2
Gorelova 37 T 2
Göreme 21 D 3
Gorey 4 B 3
Gorg 34 F 5
Gorgān (Iran) 23 G 1
Gorgin (Iran) 23 E 1
Gorgona (Italy) 19 E 3
Gorgona, Isla 84 C 3
Gorgora 65 F 2
Gorgoram 63 G 3
Gori 21 F 2
Goring 7 D 2
Gorizia 19 F 2
Gorjanci 19 G 2
Gorkha 40 D 2
Gorki 25 N 2
Gor'kiy 24 H 4
Gor'kovskoye Vodokhranilishche
    24 H 4
Görlitz 15 F 4
Gorlovka 21 E 1
Gormanstown 50 L 9
Gorna Oryakhovitsa 20 C 2
Gornji Vakuf 19 G 3
Gorno Slinkina 25 N 4
Gorno-Altaysk 25 QR 5
Gorno-Chuyskiy 36 K 4
Gorno-Filinskoye 25 N 3
Gornostakhskiy Khrebet 37 P 3–4
Gornozavodsk 37 Q 6
Gornyak 25 Q 5
Gornyy 37 P 5
Gornyy Kazymsk 25 N 2
Gorodenka 20 C 1
Gorodets 24 H 4
Gorodnitsa 17 J 5
Gorodnya 24 F 4
Gorodok 17 J 4
Gorodovikovsk 21 F 1
Goroka 58 E 3
Goromay 37 Q 5
Gorom-Gorom 62 D 3
Gorongosa 67 E 3
Gorongosa National Park 67 E 3
Gorongosa, Serra da 67 E 3
Gorontalo 43 F 3
Goroshikha 25 R 2
Górowo Haweckie 15 H 4
Gorrahei 65 G 3
Gorseinon 6 B 2
Gorstan 2 B 3
Gortantaoid 3 A 4
Goru, Virful 20 C 1
Gory Bukantau 35 G 2
Gory Byrranga 36 GH 1
Gory Kul'dzhuktau 35 G 2
Gory Oloyskiye 37 U 2
Gory Putorana 36 FH 2
Gory Świetokrzyskie 15 H 4
Gory Ulutau 35 H 1
Gory Ushkan'iy 37 X 2
Gory Ushurakchan 37 U 2

Gory Yermentau 25 O 5
Goryachegorsk 25 R 4
Goryachenskiy 24 K 5
Goryachiy Klyuch 21 E 2
Goryachiy Klyuch 37 S 3
Goryn' 17 J 5
Gorzów Wielkopolski 15 G 4
Goschen Strait 51 F 4
Gosford 49 J 5
Gosforth 5 C 2
Goshogawara 39 LM 2
Goslar 15 F 4
Gospic 19 G 3
Gosport 7 D 2
Gossi 62 D 2
Gossinga 64 D 3
Goste Delčhev 20 B 2
Gostivar 20 B 2
Gostynin 15 G 4
Göta älv 17 F 4
Göta kanal 17 F 4
Götaland 17 FG 4
Gotaru 40 B 2
Göteborg 17 F 4
Gotel Mountains 63 G 4
Götene 17 F 4
Gotha 15 F 4
Gothenburg (NE, U.S.A.) 76 FG 3
Gothenburg (Sweden) 17 F 4
Gotheye 62 E 3
Gotland 17 G 4
Gotō-rettō 39 J 4
Gotowasi 43 G 3
Gotska Sandön 17 GH 4
Gōtsu 39 K 3
Göttingen 15 EF 4
Gottwaldov 15 G 5
Goubéré 64 D 3
Goubon 63 H 1
Goudge 88 C 5
Goudiri 62 B 3
Goudoumaria 63 G 3
Goulburn 49 H 5
Goulburn Islands 48 E 1
Gould, Mount 48 B 4
Goulimime 58 C 3
Goumbou 62 C 3
Goundam 62 D 2
Goundi 63 H 4
Gouradi 63 H 2
Gourara 58 F 3
Gourcy 62 D 3
Gourdon 18 D 3
Gouré 63 G 3
Gourin 18 C 2
Gourma 62 E 3
Gourma-Rarous 62 D 2
Gouro 63 H 2
Gourock 3 B 4
Gourounsi 62 D 3
Gouzon 18 D 2
Gove (Angola) 66 B 2
Gove (Australia) 47
Gove Peninsula 49 F 1
Govena, Poluostrov 37 V 4
Goverla 20 B 1
Governador Valadares 87 H 4
Governor's Harbour 79 G 2
Goviałtay 38 C 1
Govorovo 37 N 1
Gower (U.K.) 6 B 2
Goya 88 E 4
Göynük 20 D 2
Goz Beïda 63 J 3
Gozha Co 40 D 1
Gozo 19 F 4
Graaff Reinet 66 C 6
Grabo 62 C 5
Gračac 19 G 3
Grace, Lake 48 B 5
Gracehill 4 B 2
Gracias a Dios, Cabo 78 F 5
Graciosa 58 A 1
Gradaús 85 H 5
Gradaús, Serra dos 85 H 5
Grado (Italy) 19 F 2
Grado (Spain) 18 B 3
Grafing 15 F 5
Grafton 49 J 4
Grafton (N.D., U.S.A.) 76 G 2
Grafton, Islas 89 B 9
Graham (Br. Col., Can.) 72 L 5
Graham (Ontario, Can.) 74 J 6
Graham Land 91
Grahamstown 66 D 6
Grain Coast 62 BC 4–5
Grajaú 85 J 5
Grajaú 87 G 2
Grajewo 15 H 4
Gramat 18 D 3
Gramat, Causse de 18 D 3
Grampian 2 C 3
Grampian Mountains 3 B 3
Gran Antiplanicie Central 89 C 8
Gran Canaria 58 B 3

Gran Chaco 86 D 5
Gran Laguna Salada 89 C 7
Gran Morelos 76 E 5
Gran Paradiso 19 E 2
Gran Pilastro 19 F 2
Gran Río 85 G 3
Gran Sasso d'Italia 19 F 3
Granada (Nicaragua) 78 E 5
Granada (Spain) 18 C 4
Grænalón 16 B 3
Granard 4 B 3
Granby 75 N 6
Grand Bahama Island 79 G 2
Grand Ballon 19 E 2
Grand Bank 75 Q 6
Grand Bassam 62 D 4–5
Grand Béréby 62 C 5
Grand Canal 14 B 4
Grand Canal (China) 39 G 3
Grand Canal (Rep. of Ireland)
    4 B 3
Grand Canyon 76 D 4
Grand Canyon 76 D 4
Grand Canyon National Park
    76 D 4
Grand Cayman 79 F 4
Grand Cess 62 C 5
Grand Coulee 76 C 2
Grand Coulee Dam 76 C 2
Grand Erg de Bilma 63 GH 2
Grand Erg Occidental 58–59 E 2–3
Grand Erg Oriental 59 G 2–3
Grand Falls 75 Q 6
Grand Forks 76 G 2
Grand Island 76 G 3
Grand Junction 76 E 4
Grand Lahou 62 CD 5
Grand Lake 75 O 6
Grand Lake 75 O 6
Grand Lieu, Lac de 18 C 2
Grand Manan 75 O 7
Grand Marais (MN, U.S.A.)
    77 HJ 2
Grand Passage 51 H 5
Grand Popo 62 E 4
Grand Portage 77 J 2
Grand Rapids (Man., Can.) 73 S 5
Grand Rapids (MI, U.S.A.) 77 J 3
Grand Rapids (MN, U.S.A.)
    77 H 2
Grand River 77 J 3
Grand Santi 85 H 3
Grand Teton 76 D 3
Grand Traverse Bay 77 JK 2–3
Grand Turk 79 H 3
Grand Valley 76 E 4
Grand Wintersberg 19 E 2
Grande Cache 73 O 5
Grande Chartreuse 19 E 2
Grande Comore 67 G 2
Grande, Ilha 87 H 5
Grande Prairie 73 O 4
Grande Ridge 98 A 5
Grande Rivière de la Baleine
    75 M 4–5
Grande Ronde River 76 C 2
Grande, Sierra (Mexico) 78 B 2
Grandin, Lake 73 O 3
Grandioznyy, Pik 36 G 5
Grândola 18 B 4
Grândola, Serra de 18 B 4
Graneros 88 B 5
Grange 5 E 2
Grangemouth 3 C 3
Grange-over-Sands 5 D 2
Grängesberg 17 F 3
Grangeville 76 C 2
Granite City 77 J 4
Granite Peak 76 C 3
Granite Peak (MT, U.S.A.) 76 E 2
Granitola, Capo Punta. 19 F 4
Granja 87 H 1
Gränna 17 F 4
Granön 16 G 3
Grant 76 F 3
Grantham 7 D 1
Grantownon Spey 2 C 3
Grants 76 E 4
Grants Pass 76 B 3
Granville 18 C 2
Granville Lake 73 R 4
Graskop 67 E 5
Grasmere 5 D 2
Grasse 19 E 3
Gråsten 17 E 5
Graulhet 18 D 3
Gravatá 87 J 2
Grave, Pointe de 18 C 2
Gravelbourg 73 Q 6
Gravesend 7 E 2
Gravina 19 G 3
Gray 19 E 2
Grayling 77 K 3
Grayrigg 5 C 2
Grays 7 E 2

Grays Harbor 76 B 2
Graz 19 G 2
Grdelica 20 B 2
Great Abaco Island 79 G 2
Great Artesian Basin 49 G 3–4
Great Australian Bight 48 DE 5
Great Ayton 5 E 2
Great Baddow 7 E 2
Great Barrier Island 51 R 8
Great Barrier Reef 49 H 1–2
Great Basin 76 C 3–4
Great Bear 73 N 2
Great Bear Lake 73 NO 2
Great Bend 76 G 4
Great Berg 66 B 6
Great Bernera 2 A 2
Great Bitter Lake (Egypt) 22 A 3
Great Dalby 7 D 1
Great Discovery Reef 42 D 1
Great Dividing Range 49 HJ 3–4
Great Dividing Range 49 HJ 4–6
Great Driffield 5 E 2
Great Dunmow 7 E 2
Great Exhibition Bay 51 Q 7
Great Exuma Island 79 G 3
Great Falls 76 D 2
Great Fisher Bank 14 D 3
Great Harwood 5 D 3
Great Inagua Island 79 H 3
Great Indian Basin 98 B 4
Great Indian Desert 40 B 2
Great Karas Mountains 66 B 5
Great Karroo 66 C 6
Great Khingan Mountains
    39 GH 1–2
Great Lake 50 L 9
Great Malvern 7 C 1
Great Mountains 66 A 3
Great North East Channel 50 D 3
Great Pee Dee River 77 L 5
Great Plain of the Koukdjuak
    75 N 2
Great Plains 73 OQ 4–5
Great Plains 76 F 2–4
Great Ponton 7 D 1
Great Ruaha 65 F 6
Great Salt Lake 76 D 3
Great Salt Lake Desert 76 D 3
Great Sampford 7 E 2
Great Sand Sea → Baḥr ar Rimāl al
    Azīm 60 D 3
Great Sandy Desert 48 C 3
Great Sandy Island → Fraser
    Island 49 J 3–4
Great Scarcies 62 B 4
Great Sitkin 72 B 5
Great Slave Lake 73 P 3
Great Torrington 6 B 2
Great Victoria Desert 48 D 4
Great Victoria Desert Nature
    Reserve 48 DE 4–5
Great Wall of China 38 E 3
Great Yarmouth 7 E 1
Greater Antilles 79 GJ 3–4
Greater London 7 D 2
Greater Manchester 5 D 3
Greater Sunda Islands 29 JK 7
Greatham 5 E 2
Grebbestad 17 F 4
Grebenka 24 F 5
Gréboun, Mont 63 F 1
Greco, Akra (Cyprus) 22 AB 2
Greece 20 B 3
Greeley (CO, U.S.A.) 76 F 3
Greeley (NE, U.S.A.) 76 G 4
Green (OR, U.S.A.) 76 B 3
Green Bay 77 J 3
Green Bay (WI, U.S.A.) 77 J 2–3
Green Island (New Zealand)
    51 Q 10
Green Islands (Papua New Guinea)
    51 F 2
Green River (KY, U.S.A.) 77 J 4
Green River (Papua New Guinea)
    50 D 2
Green River (UT, U.S.A.) 76 D 4
Green River (UT, U.S.A.) 76 DE 4
Green River (WY, U.S.A.)
    76 DE 3
Greencastle 4 B 2
Greenhead 5 D 2
Greenisland 4 C 3
Greenland 90
Greenland Sea 90
Greenlaw 3 C 4
Greenloaning 3 C 3
Greenock 3 B 4
Greenough River 48 B 4
Greensboro (GA, U.S.A.) 77 K 5
Greensboro (N.C., U.S.A.) 77 L 4
Greenvale (Queensland, Austr.)
    49 GH 2
Greenville 77 N 2
Greenville (AL, U.S.A.) 77 J 5
Greenville (Liberia) 62 C 4–5

Greenville (MS, U.S.A.) 77 H 5
Greenville (N.C., U.S.A.) 77 L 4
Greenville (S.C., U.S.A.) 77 K 5
Greenville (TX, U.S.A.) 77 G 5
Greenwood 77 K 5
Greetham 7 D 1
Gregorio 84 D 5
Gregory Downs (Queensland,
    Austr.) 49 F 2
Gregory, Lake (South Australia)
    49 F 4
Gregory, Lake (Western Australia)
    48 B 4
Gregory, Lake (Western Australia)
    48 D 3
Gregory Range 49 G 2
Gregory River (Queensland,
    Austr.) 49 F 2
Greifswald 15 F 4
Grein 19 F 2
Greitz 15 F 4
Gremikha 24 G 2
Grená 17 F 4
Grenada 79 K 5
Grenada (MS, U.S.A.) 77 J 5
Grenadine Islands 79 K 5
Grenchen 19 E 2
Grenen 17 F 4
Grenoble 19 E 2
Grense-Jakobselv 16 K 2
Grenville, Cape 49 G 1
Gresford 6 C 1
Gresik 42 D 5
Gretna 4 D 2
Grevená 20 B 2
Greven 14 E 4
Grévenbroich 14 E 4
Grévenmacher 19 E 2
Grey Islands 75 QR 5
Grey Range 49 G 4
Greymouth 51 Q 9
Greystoke 5 D 2
Greystones 4 B 3
Greytown 67 E 5
Grico 84 E 2
Griffin 77 K 5
Griffith 49 H 5
Grigoriopol' 20 C 1
Grim, Cape 50 K 9
Grimari 64 C 3
Grime's Graves 7 E 1
Grimsá 16 A 3
Grimsby 5 E 3
Grímsey 16 B 2
Grimshaw 73 O 4
Grímsstaðir 16 B 2
Grimstad 17 E 4
Grímsvötn 16 B 3
Grindavik 16 A 3
Grindon 5 D 2
Grindsted 17 E 4
Grinnell 77 H 3
Grintavec 19 F 2
Griqatown 66 C 5
Gris-Nez, Cap 18 D 1
Grisslehamn 17 G 3
Grizim 58 E 3
Grmeč 19 G 3
Groblersdal 66 D 5
Grodekovo 39 K 2
Grodno 17 H 5
Groix, Ile de 18 C 2
Grójec 15 H 4
Gronau 14 E 4
Gröndalen 16 F 3
Grong 16 F 3
Groningen (Netherlands) 14 E 4
Groningen (Surinam) 85 G 2
Grønnedal 75 S 3
Groot River 66 C 6
Groot Vloer 66 C 5
Groot Winter Berg 66 D 6
Groote Eylandt 49 F 1
Grootfontein 66 B 3
Gros Morne 75 Q 6
Grosebay 2 A 3
Grosser Arber 15 F 5
Grosseto 19 F 3
Grossglockner 19 F 2
Groswater Bay 75 Q 5
Grötvær 16 G 2
Grotli 16 E 3
Grottaglie 19 G 3
Grotte de Lascaux 18 D 2
Groumania 62 D 4
Group, Actaeon 53 F 4
Grovfjord 16 G 2
Groznyy 21 G 2
Grubišno Polje 19 G 2
Grudziądz 15 G 4
Gruesa, Punta 86 B 5
Gruinart 3 A 4
Grums 17 F 3
Grünau 66 B 5
Grundy 77 K 4
Gruñidera 78 B 3
Gruppo di Brenta 19 F 2
Gruziya 21 F 2

Gryada Khara-Tas 36 J 1
Gryazi 24 H 5
Gryazovets 24 G 4
Grycksbo 17 G 3
Grythyttan 17 F 4
Grytviken 91
Gua Musang 42 B 3
Guacamayas 84 D 3
Guacanayabo, Golfo de 79 G 3
Guacara 84 E 1
Guadalajara (Mexico) 78 B 3
Guadalajara (Spain) 18 C 3
Guadalcanal 51 G 3
Guadalén 18 C 4
Guadalmena 18 C 4
Guadalquivir 18 C 4
Guadalupe (Mexico) 78 B 3
Guadalupe (Mexico) 78 C 2
Guadalupe Bravos 76 E 5
Guadalupe, Isla de 76 C 6
Guadalupe Mountains 76 EF 5
Guadalupe River 77 G 6
Guadalupe, Sierra de 18 B 4
Guadarrama, Sierra de 18 C 3
Guadelope (Spain) 18 C 3
Guadeloupe (Lesser Antilles)
   79 K 4
Guadeloupe Passage 79 K 4
Guadiana 18 B 4
Guadiana 18 C 4
Guadiana 18 C 4
Guadix 18 C 4
Guafo, Boca del 89 AB 7
Guafo, Isla 89 AB 7
Guaíba 88 F 5
Guaina 85 F 2
Guainia 84 E 3
Guaiquinima, Cerro 85 F 2
Guaíra 87 F 5
Guaiúba 87 J 1
Guajará Mirim 86 CD 3
Guajaturaba 85 F 5
Guajira, Península de 84 D 1
Gualaquiza 84 C 4
Gualeguay 88 DE 5
Gualeguaychú 88 E 5
Gualicho, Salina del 89 D 7
Guallatiri 86 C 4
Guam 52 A 2
Guamá 85 J 4
Guamblin, Isla 89 A 7
Guaminí 89 D 6
Guamo 79 G 3
Guampi, Sierra de 84 E 2
Guamúchil 76 E 6
Gu'an 39 G 3
Guan Xian 38 D 4
Guanajuato 78 B 3
Guanambi 87 H 3
Guanape, Isla 84 C 5
Guanare 84 E 2
Guanare 84 E 2
Guanarito 84 E 2
Guandacol 88 C 4
Guane 78 F 3
Guang'an 38 E 4
Guangchang 38 G 5
Guangde 39 G 4
Guangdong 38 F 6
Guanghan 38 D 4
Guanghe 38 D 3
Guanghua 38 F 4
Guangji 38 G 5
Guangling 38 F 3
Guangnan 38 DE 6
Guangning 38 F 6
Guangshan 38 F 4
Guangxi Zhuangzu Zizhiqu 38 E 6
Guangyuan 38 E 4
Guangze 39 G 5
Guangzhou 38 F 6
Guanhães 87 H 4
Guanling 38 E 5
Guantánamo 79 H
Guantao 38 G 3
Guanyun 39 G 4
Guapí 84 C 3
Guapó 87 G 4
Guaporé (Río Grande do Sul,
   Brazil) 88 F 4
Guaporé (Rondônia, Brazil) 86 D 3
Guaqui 86 C 4
Guarabira 87 J 2
Guaranda 84 C 4
Guarapari 87 H 5
Guarapuava 88 F 4
Guaratuba 88 G 4
Guarda 18 B 3
Guardafui, Cape 65 J 2
Guardal 18 C 4
Guardia Mitre 89 D 7
Guardo 18 C 3
Guarenas 84 E 1
Guárico 84 E 2
Guárico, Embalse del 84 E 2
Guasave 76 E 6

Guascama, Punta 84 C 3
Guasdualito 84 D 2
Guasipati 85 F 2
Guasopa 51 F 3
Guatemala 78 D 4
Guatemala 78 DE 5
Guaviare 84 E 3
Guaxupé 87 G 5
Guayabal 84 E 2
Guayabero 84 D 3
Guayaneco, Archipiélago 89 A 8
Guayaquil 84 C 4
Guayaquil, Golfo de 84 B 4
Guayaramerin 86 C 3
Guaymallén 88 C 5
Guaymas 76 D 6
Guba (U.S.S.R.) 24 F 3
Guba (Zaire) 66 D 2
Guba Buorkhaya 37 O 1
Guba Gusinaya 37 RS 1
Gubakha 25 L 4
Guban 65 GH 2
Gubba 64 F 2
Gubbio 19 F 3
Gubin 15 F 4
Gubio 63 G 3
Gubkin 24 G 5
Guchin-Us 38 D 1
Gudar, Sierra de 18 C 3
Gudauta 21 F 2
Gudbrandsdalen 16 EF 3
Guddu Barrage 35 HJ 5
Gudenå 17 E 4
Gudermes 21 G 2
Gudivada 40 D 4
Gudiyattam 40 C 5
Güdül 21 D 2
Gudur 40 C 5
Gudvangen 16 E 3
Guebwiller 19 E 2
Guékédou 62 B 4
Guelb er Richât 58 C 4
Guélengdeng 63 H 3
Guelma 59 G 1
Guelph 75 L 7
Guelta Zemmur 58 C 3
Guem 62 D 2
Guémar 59 G 2
Guéné 62 E 3
Guénéné-Penfao 18 C 2
Güera 58 B 4
Guéra 60 B 6
Guéra 63 H 3
Guéra, Massif de 63 H 3
Guérande 18 C 2
Guerara 59 F 2
Guercif 58 E 2
Guéréda 63 J 3
Guéret 18 D 2
Guernsey 7 C 3
Guernsey 14 C 5
Guernsey (Airport) 7 C 3
Guérou 58 C 5
Guerrero 78 B 4
Guerzim 58 E 3
Guga 37 P 5
Gügerd, Kūh-e (Iran) 23 F 2
Gughe 65 F 3
Guguan 52 A 1
Gui Jiang 38 F 6
Gui Xian 38 E 6
Guiana Highlands 85 FH 3
Guibes 66 B 5
Guichi 39 G 4
Guide 38 D 3
Guider 63 G 4
Guidimouni 63 F 3
Guiding 38 E 5
Guidjiba 63 G 4
Guidong 38 F 5
Guiers, Lac de 62 A 2
Guiglo 62 C 4
Guijá 67 E 4
Guijuelo 18 B 3
Guildford 7 D 2
Guilin 38 F 5
Guillaume Delisle, Lac 75 M 4
Guilvinec 18 C 2
Guimarães 18 B 3
Guimaras 43 F 1
Guinan 38 D 3
Guinea 62 B 3
Guinea Basin 98 A 3
Guinea Equatorial 63 F 5
Guinea, Gulf of 63 EF 5
Guinea-Bissau 62 AB 3
Güines 79 F 3
Guingamp 18 C 2
Guinguinéo 62 A 3
Guir 62 D 2
Guiratinga 87 F 4
Guiria 85 F 1
Guisanbourg 85 H 3
Guisborough 5 E 2
Guita Koulouba 64 C 3

Guitiriz 18 B 3
Guitri 62 C 4
Guiuan 43 G 1
Guixi 39 G 5
Guiyang 38 E 5
Guizhou 38 E 5
Gujar Khan 35 J 4
Gujarat 40 B 3
Gujranwala 35 J 4
Gujrat 35 J 4
Gukovo 21 F 1
Gulang 38 D 3
Gulbarga 40 C 4
Gulbene 17 J 4
Gul'cha 35 J 2
Gülek Boğazı 21 D 3
Gulf of Aden 61 H 6
Gulf of Alaska 72 HJ 4
Gulf of Aqaba → Khalīj al 'Aqabah
   60 E 3
Gulf of Boothia 73 T 1
Gulf of Bothnia 16 GH 3
Gulf of Carpentaria 49 F 1
Gulf of Chihli 39 GH 3
Gulf of Danzig 15 G 4
Gulf of Finland 17 H 4
Gulf of Guinea 63 EF 5
Gulf of Khambhat 40 B 3–4
Gulf of Kutch 40 A 3
Gulf of Maine 77 N 3
Gulf of Mannar 40 C 6
Gulf of Martaban 41 G 4
Gulf of Mexico 78 DE 2
Gulf of Ob 25 O 2
Gulf of Oman 34 F 5–6
Gulf of Oman 61 K 4
Gulf of Papua 50 DE 3
Gulf of Riga 17 H 4
Gulf of Saint Lawrence 75 P 6
Gulf of Sirt 59 J 2
Gulf of Suez 22 A 3
Gulf of Suez → Khalīj as Suways
   60 E 3
Gulf of Thailand 41 H 5
Gulf of Tonkin 41 J 4
Gulf of Venice 19 F 2
Gulf Saint Vincent 49 F 6
Gulf Stream 92
Gulfport 77 J 5
Gulgong 49 H 5
Gulian 37 M 5
Gulin 38 E 5
Gulistan 35 H 2
Guliya Shan 37 M 6
Gulkana 72 H 3
Gulkhari (Iran) 23 F 3
Gull Lake 73 Q 5
Gullane 3 C 3
Gullfoss 16 B 3
Gullkrona fjärd 17 H 4
Gullspång 17 F 4
Güllük 20 C 3
Gülnar 21 D 3
Gülşehir 21 D 3
Gul'shad 25 O 6
Guluguba 49 HJ 4
Gulu 64 E 4
Gülübovo 20 C 2
Guluguba 49 HJ 4
Gulwe 65 F 3
Gulya 36 M 5
Gulyaypole 21 E 1
Gumbiri, Jabal 64 E 4
Gumbiro 67 F 2
Gumel 63 F 3
Gummi 63 F 3
Gumuru 64 E 3
Gümüşane Dağları 21 E 2
Gümüşhane 21 E 2
Guna (Ethiopia) 65 F 2
Guna (India) 40 C 3
Gunda 36 K 3
Gundagai 49 H 6
Gundji 64 C 4
Gundoğmuş 21 D 3
Güneydoğu Toroslar 21 EF 3
Gungu 64 B 3
Guni 63 F 4
Gunib 34 D 2
Gunnar 73 Q 4
Günnariyn 38 D 1
Gunnarn 16 G 3
Gunnedah 49 HJ 5
Gunnison 76 E 4
Guntakal 40 C 4
Guntersville Lake 77 J 5
Guntur 40 D 4
Gunung Abong Abong 42 A 3
Gunung Agung 42 E 5
Gunung Angemuk 43 J 4
Gunung Api 43 E 5
Gunung Bakayan 42 E 3
Gunung Balikpapan 42 E 4
Gunung Bandahara 42 A 3
Gunung Batai 42 BC 5
Gunung Batu Puteh 42 B 3
Gunung Batulantee 42 E 5

Gunung Besar 42 E 4
Gunung Binaiya 43 G 4
Gunung Boliohutu 43 F 3
Gunung Ceremai 42 C 5
Gunung Dempo 42 B 4
Gunung Gamkunoro 43 G 3
Gunung Gueredong 42 A 3
Gunung Kaubalatmada 43 G 4
Gunung Kerinci 42 B 4
Gunung Kinabalu 42 E 2
Gunung Klabat 43 G 3
Gunung Kongkemul 42 E 3
Gunung Kwoka 43 H 4
Gunung Lawit 42 D 3
Gunung Leuser 42 A 3
Gunung Lewotobi 43 F 5
Gunung Liangpran 42 D 3
Gunung Lokilalaki 43 F 4
Gunung Lompobatang 43 F 5
Gunung Maling 43 F 3
Gunung Marapi 42 B 4
Gunung Mekongga 43 F 4
Gunung Menyapa 42 E 3
Gunung Mulu 43 DE 3
Gunung Mutis 43 F 5
Gunung Niut 42 CD 3
Gunung Ogoamas 43 F 3
Gunung Pangrango 42 C 5
Gunung Peuetsagu 42 A 3
Gunung Rinjani 42 E 5
Gunung Saran 42 D 4
Gunung Sarempaka 42 E 4
Gunung Sinabung 42 A 3
Gunung Sitoli 42 A 3
Gunung Slamet 42 C 5
Gunung Sombang 42 E 3
Gunung Sorikmerapi 42 A 3
Gunung Tahan 42 B 3
Gunung Talakmau 42 B 3
Gunung Tambora 43 E 5
Gunung Tentolomatinan 43 F 3
Gunung Wanggameti 43 EF 6
Gunung Waukara 43 E 4
Gunungsugih 42 C 4
Guoiret es Soud 59 F 3
Guoyang 38 G 4
Gurah 36 H 5
Gurara 63 F 4
Gurban Obo 38 F 2
Gurbantünggüt Shamo 35 M 1–2
Gurdaspur 40 C 1
Gurdim 34 FG 5
Gurgan (Iran) 23 G 1
Gurgaon 40 C 2
Gurgei, Jabal 60 C 6
Gurgueia 87 H 2
Gurha 40 B 2
Guri Dam 85 F 2
Gurimatu 50 D 3
Gürlevik Dağı 21 E 3
Guro 67 E 3
Gürpınar 21 F 3
Gurskoye 37 P 5
Guru Sikhar 40 B 3
Gürüš 67 F 3
Gürün 21 E 3
Gurupá 85 H 4
Gurupi (Brazil) 85 J 4
Gurupí (Goiás, Brazil) 87 G 3
Gurupi, Cabo 85 J 3
Gurupi, Serra do 85 J 4–5
Guruve 67 E 3
Guruzala 40 C 4
Gurvan Sayhan Uul 38 D 2
Gurvanbulag 36 H 6
Gur'yev 34 E 1
Gur'yevsk 25 R 5
Gusau 63 F 3
Güselyurt (Cyprus) 22 A 2
Gusev 17 H 5
Gushi 38 G 4
Gushiago 62 D 4
Gusikha 36 J 1
Gusinaya, Guba 37 RS 1
Gusinaya Zemlya, Poluostrov
   24 K 1
Gusinoozersk 36 J 5
Gusinoye Ozero 36 J 5
Gus'Khrustal'nyy 24 GH 4
Gusmp, Ostrov 37 U 1–2
Guspini 19 E 4
Güssing 19 G 2
Gustavus 72 K 4
Güstrow 15 F 4
Guthrie (OK, U.S.A.) 76 G 4
Guthrie (TX, U.S.A.) 76 F 5
Gutian 39 G 5
Gutii, Virful 20 B 1
Guyana 85 G 3
Guyenne 18 CD 3
Guyra 49 J 5
Guyuan 38 E 3

Guyuan 39 G 2
Guzar 35 H 3
Güzelhisar 20 C 3
Güzelyurt 21 D 3
Güzhān (Iran) 23 E 2
Guzhang 38 EF 5
Guzhen 39 G 4
Gvardeysk 17 H 5
Gvardeyskoye 21 D 1
Gvarv 17 E 4
Gwa 41 F 4
Gwadabawa 63 F 3
Gwadar 35 G 5
Gwai 66 D 3
Gwalior 40 C 2
Gwanda 66 D 4
Gwane 64 D 4
Gwatar Bay 35 G 5–6
Gwda 15 G 4
Gwebin 41 F 3
Gwent 6 C 2
Gweru 66 D 3
Gweta 66 D 4
Gwyddelwern 6 C 1
Gwynedd 6 BC 1
Gya La 40 E 2
Gyaca 38 B 5
Gyangzê 40 E 2
Gyaring 38 C 3
Gyaring Co 40 E 1
Gyaring Hu 38 C 4
Gyda 25 P 1
Gydanskaya Guba 25 P 1
Gydanskiy Poluostrov 25 P 1–2
Gyirong 40 E 2
Gyitang 38 C 4
Gympie 49 J 4
Gyöngyös 20 A 1
Győr 20 A 1
Győr 20 A 1
Gypsum Point 73 O 3
Gypsumville 73 S 5
Gyula 20 B 1
Gyurgyan 34 E 2

H

Ha Dong 41 J 3
Ha Giang 41 J 3
Ha Noi 41 J 3
Ha Tien 41 H 5
Ha Tinh 41 J 4
Haanhöniy Uul 36 F 6
Haanja Kõrgustik 17 J 4
Ha'apai Group 52 D 4
Haapajärvi 16 HJ 3
Haapavesi 16 J 3
Haapsalu 17 H 4
Haarlem 14 D 4
Haast 50 P 9
Habahe 35 M 1
Habarūt 61 J 5
Habas 58 C 3
Habashīyah, Jabal 61 J 5
Habaswein 65 FG 4
Habay (Alb., Can.) 73 O 4
Habay (Somalia) 65 G 4
Habbān 61 H 6
Hābbānīyah (Iraq) 22 D 2
Hābbānīyah, Hawral (Iraq) 22 D 2
Habiganj 41 F 3
Habīt Awlād Muhammad 59 H 2
Habshān (United Arab Emirates)
   23 F 5
Hachijō-jima 39 LM 4
Hachinohe 39 M 2
Hacıbektaş 21 D 3
Hadabat al Jilf al Kabīr 60 D 4
Hadada, Jabal 60 D 4
Hadārībah, Ra's al 60 F 4
Hadan, Harrat 61 G 4
Hadd, Ra's al 61 KL 4
Haddā' 61 F 4
Hadded 65 H 2
Haddington 3 C 4
Haddiscop 7 E 1
Hadejia 63 F 3
Hadejia 63 G 3
Hadeland 17 F 3
Hadera (Israel) 22 B 2
Haderslev 17 E 4
Hādh Banī Zaynān 61 H 4
Hadiboh 61 J 2
Hadid, Jabal 59 K 4
Hadilik 35 M 3
Hadim 21 D 3
Hadjer el Hamis 63 GH 3
Hadjer Kamaran 63 J 3
Hadjer Mardi 63 J 3
Hadjer Mornou 63 J 2
Hadjer Telfane 63 H 3
Hadjout 18 D 3
Hadleigh 7 E 1
Hadley Bay 73 Q 1
Hadramawt 61 H 5

141

Hadrian's Wall 5 D 2
Hadsund 17 F 4
Haeju 39 J 3
Ḥafar al 'Atk (Saudi Arabia)
  23 E 4
Ḥafar al Bāṭin (Saudi Arabia)
  23 E 3
Hafik 21 E 3
Ḥafīrat al 'Aydā (Saudi Arabia)
  22 C 4
Ḥafīt (Oman) 23 G 4–5
Ḥafīt, Jabal (United Arab
  Emirates) 23 G 4
Hafnarfjörður 16 A 3
Haft Gel (Iran) 23 E 3
Ḥāfūn 65 J 2
Ḥāfūn, Ra's 65 J 2
Hag 'Abdullah 60 E 6
Hagadera 65 G 4
Hagari 40 C 5
Hagemeister 72 E 4
Hagen 15 E 4
Hagerstown 77 L 4
Hagfors 17 F 3
Häggenås 16 G 3
Hags Head 14 AB 4
Hague, Cap de la 18 C 2
Haguenau 19 E 2
Hagunia 58 C 3
Hai Duong 41 J 3
Hai He 39 G 3
Hai Phong 41 J 3
Hai'an 39 H 4
Haicheng 39 H 2
Haifa (Israel) 22 B 2
Haifeng 38 G 6
Haikang 38 EF 6
Haikou 38 F 6–7
Ḥā'il (Saudi Arabia) 22 C 4
Hailakandi 41 F 3
Hailar 36 L 6
Hailar He 36 M 6
Hailin 39 J 2
Hailing Dao 38 F 6
Hailong 39 HJ 2
Hailsham 7 E 2
Hailun 37 N 6
Hailuoto 16 H 2
Haimen 39 H 4
Hainan Dao 38 F 7
Haines 72 K 4
Haines Junction 72 K 3
Haiqing 37 O 6
Haïti 79 H 4
Haivare 50 D 3
Haiyan 38 D 3
Haiyang 39 H 3
Haiyuan 38 E 3
Haizhou Wan 39 G 4
Hajar, Tall al (Syria) 22 B 2
Hajārah, Sahrā' al 22–23 D 3
Hajdúböszörmény 20 B 1
Hajduság 20 B 1
Hajhir, Jabal 65 J 2
Hajipur 40 E 2
Hājjīābād 34 F 5
Hājjīābād (Iran) 23 G 3
Hājjīābād (Iran) 23 G 3
Hājjīābād-e Māsīleh (Iran) 23 F 2
Hajmah 61 K 4–5
Haka 41 F 3
Hakkâri 21 F 3
Hakkâri Dağları 21 F 3
Hakkas 16 H 2
Hakodate 39 M 2
Haku-san 39 L 3
Ḥalab (Syria) 22 B 1
Halab (Iran) 23 E 1
Ḥalabjah (Iraq) 23 DE 2
Ḥalā'ib 60 F 4
Halali 66 B 3
Halbā (Lebanon) 22 B 2
Halberstadt 15 F 4
Halcon, Mount 43 F 1
Halden 17 F 4
Haldia 40 E 3
Haldia 40 E 3
Haldwani 40 C 2
Hale, Mount 48 B 4
Hales 7 E 1
Halesowen 7 C 1
Halesworth 7 E 1
Halfeti 21 E 3
Ḥalī 61 G 5
Halia 40 D 3
Halicarnassus 20 C 3
Halifax 75 P 7
Halifax (Queensland, Austr.)
  49 H 2
Halifax (U.K.) 5 E 3
Halifax Bay 49 H 2
Halifax, Mount 49 H 2
Ḥalīl 34 F 5
Ḥalīn 65 H 3
Halkett, Cape 72 G 1
Halkirk 2 C 2

Hall 72 C 3
Hall Beach 73 V 2
Hall Islands 52 B 2
Hall Lake 73 V 2
Hall Peninsula 75 O 3
Halland 17 F 4
Ḥallat' Ammār (Saudi Arabia)
  22 B 3
Halle 15 F 4
Halleberg 17 F 4
Hällefors 17 F 4
Hallettsville 77 G 6
Halley Bay 91
Hallingdalselva 17 E 3
Hallingskarvet 17 E 3
Hällnäs 16 G 3
Halls Creek 48 D 2
Hallsberg 17 G 4
Hallstahammar 17 G 4
Hallstatt 19 F 2
Hallstavik 17 G 3
Halmahera 43 G 3
Halmahera, Laut 43 G 4
Halmstad 17 F 4
Hals 17 F 4
Hälsingeskogen 16 G 3
Hälsingland 16 G 3
Halsön 16 H 3
Halti 16 H 2
Haltwhistle 5 D 2
Halwell 6 C 3
Ham 63 H 3
Hamab 66 B 5
Hamada de Tindouf 58 D 3
Hamada de Tinrhert 59 G 3
Hamada du Drâa 58 D 3
Hamada du Guir 58 E 2
Hamada el Haricha 58 E 4
Hamada Mangueni 63 G 1
Hamada Safia 58 E 4
Hamada Tounassine 58 DE 3
Hamadān (Iran) 23 E 2
Ḥamādat Tingharat 59 H 3
Ḥamāh (Syria) 22 B 2
Hamamatsu 39 L 4
Hamar 17 F 3
Hamarro Hadad 65 G 3
Hămaşu Mare, Vîrful 20 C 1
Hamātah, Jabal (Egypt) 22 B 4
Hambantota 40 D 6
Hamburg 15 F 4
Hamd, Wādī al (Saudi Arabia)
  22 B 4
Ḥamdah 61 G 5
Ḥamdānah 61 G 5
Häme 16 HJ 3
Hämeenlinna 16 HJ 3
Hämeenselkä 16 H 3
Hamelin Pool 48 A 4
Hamelin Pool 48 A 4
Hameln 15 E 4
Hamersley Range 48 B 3
Hamersley Range National Park
  48 B 3
Hamgyŏng-sanmaek 39 J 2
Hamhŭng 39 J 3
Hami 38 B 2
Ḥamīd (Iran) 23 E 3
Ḥamīdīyeh (Iran) 23 E 3
Hamilton (Bermuda Is.) 79 K 1
Hamilton (MT, U.S.A.) 76 D 2
Hamilton (New Zealand) 51 R 8
Hamilton (Ontario, Can.) 75 M 7
Hamilton (Queensland, Austr.)
  49 G 3
Hamilton (U.K.) 3 BC 4
Hamilton (Victoria, Austr.) 49 G 6
Hamilton River 49 G 3
Ḥamīm, Wādī 59 K 2
Hamina [Fredrikshamn] 17 J 3
Hamirpur 40 D 2
Hamm 15 E 4
Ḥammādat Mānghīnī 59 H 4
Ḥammam al 'Alīl (Iraq) 22 D 1
Ḥammām al Anf 59 H 1
Ḥammāmāt 59 H 1
Hammami 58 C 4
Hammar, Hawr al (Iraq) 23 E 3
Hammarstrand 16 G 3
Hammerdal 16 FG 3
Hammerfest 16 H 1
Hammond (IN, U.S.A.) 77 J 3
Hammond (LA, U.S.A.) 77 H 5
Hammur Koke 65 G 3
Hamodji 63 G 2
Hamoyet, Jabal 60 F 5
Hampden 51 Q 10
Hampshire 7 D 2
Hamra 16 G 3
Hamrân (Iran) 23 D 1
Ḥamrat ash Shaykh 60 D 6
Hamrīn, Jabal (Iraq) 22–23 D 2
Hamuku 43 HJ 4
Hamum i Mashkel 35 G 5

Hāmun-e Hīrmand 35 G 4
Hāmūn-e Jaz Mūriān 34 F 5
Han 62 D 3
Han Jiang 38 G 6
Han Shui 38 F 4
Hanahan 77 L 5
Ḥanak (Saudi Arabia) 22 B 4
Hanamaki 39 M 3
Hanang 64 EF 5
Hanbogd 38 E 2
Hanceville 73 N 5
Hancheng 38 F 3
Hanchuan 38 F 4
Handan 38 F 3
Handen 17 G 4
Handeni 65 F 6
Hanegev (Israel) 22 B 3
Hangay 36 G 6
Hangayn Nuruu 36 GH 6
Hanggin Houqi 38 E 2
Hanggin Qi 38 E 3
Hangö [Hanko] 17 H 4
Hangu (China) 39 G 3
Hangu (Pakistan) 35 J 4
Hangya 38 C 3
Hangzhou 39 H 4
Hangzhou Wan 39 H 4
Hanh 36 H 5
Ḥanjūrah, Ra's (United Arab
  Emirates) 23 G 4
Hankasalmi 16 J 3
Hanko 17 H 4
Hankoniemi 17 H 4
Hanksville 76 D 4
Hanle 35 K 4
Hanna 73 P 5
Hannah Bay 75 LM 5
Hannibal 77 H 4
Hannover (F.R.G.) 15 E 4
Hanöbukten 17 FG 4
Hanover (F.R.G.) 15 E 4
Hanover (South Africa) 66 C 6
Hanover, Islas 89 AB 9
Hanstholm 17 E 4
Hantengri Feng 35 L 2
Hantzsch 75 N 2
Hanumangarh 40 B 2
Han-Uul 36 L 6
Hanuy Gol 36 H 6
Hanyuan 38 D 5
Hanzhong 38 E 4
Hao 53 F 4
Haouach 63 J 2
Haoud el Hamra 59 G 2
Haparanda 16 H 2
Hapo 43 G 3
Hapur 40 C 2
Ḥaql (Saudi Arabia) 22 B 3
Ḥaql (Saudi Arabia) 22 B 3
Har Hu 38 C 3
Har Nuur 36 F 6
Har Sai Shan 38 C 3
Har Us Nuur 36 F 6
Hara 36 J 6
Hara Fanna 65 G 3
Haraa Gol 36 J 6
Ḥarad 61 G 5
Ḥaradh (Saudi Arabia) 23 E 4
Haraiki 53 F 4
Harand (Iran) 23 F 2
Harar 65 G 3
Harardēre 65 H 4
Harare 67 E 3
Hararge 65 GH 3
Harāsīs, Jiddat al 61 K 4–5
Harāwah 59 J 2
Har-Ayrag 38 E 2
Haraz Djoumba 63 H 3
Harāzah, Jabal 60 E 6
Harazé 63 J 4
Harbel 62 B 4
Harbin 39 J 1
Harbor Beach 77 K 3
Harbour Breton 75 Q 6
Harbour Grace 75 R 6
Harda 40 C 3
Hardangerfjorden 17 E 3–4
Hardangerjøkulen 17 E 3
Hardangervidda 17 E 3
Hardap Dam 66 B 4
Hardin 76 E 2
Hardoi 40 D 2
Hardwar 40 C 2
Harēri Mālin Warfā 65 H 4
Harga 64 C 3
Hargeysa 65 G 3
Hari, Batang 42 B 4
Hari Kurk 17 H 4
Hari Rud 35 G 4
Ḥarib 61 H 6
Harihari 51 Q 9
Harike Barrage 40 C 1
Ḥarīm 22 B 1
Haringhat 41 F 3
Haripur 35 J 4
Harjavalta 16 H 3

Härjedalen 16 F 3
Harlech 6 B 1
Harleston 7 E 1
Harlingen (Netherlands) 14 E 4
Harlingen (TX, U.S.A.) 77 G 6
Harlow 7 E 2
Harmak 35 G 4
Harmalīyah (Saudi Arabia) 23 E 4
Harmancık 20 C 3
Harmånger 16 G 3
Harnai 35 H 4
Harney Basin 76 BC 3
Harney Lake 76 C 3
Harney Peak 76 F 3
Härnön 16 G 3
Härnösand 16 G 3
Haroldswick 2 D 1
Haröyfjorden 16 E 3
Harpenden 7 D 2
Harper 62 C 5
Harper, Mount 72 J 3
Harqin Qi 39 G 2
Ḥarrat al Buqūm 61 G 4
Ḥarrat al Kishb 61 G 4
Ḥarrat al 'Uwayrid (Saudi Arabia)
  22 B 4
Ḥarrat ar Rahāh (Saudi Arabia)
  22 B 4
Ḥarrat Ḥadan 61 G 4
Ḥarrat Ithnayn (Saudi Arabia)
  22 C 4
Ḥarrat Khaybar (Saudi Arabia)
  22 C 4
Ḥarrat Kuramā (Saudi Arabia)
  22 C 4
Ḥarrat Lunayyir (Saudi Arabia)
  22 B 4
Ḥarrat Nawāṣīf 61 G 4
Ḥarrat Rahat 61 G 4
Harricana 75 M 5
Harrington Harbour 75 Q 5
Harris 2 A 3
Harrisburg 77 L 3
Harrismith 66 D 5
Harrison 77 H 4
Harrison Bay 72 G 1
Harrison, Cape 75 Q 5
Harrisonburg 77 L 4
Harrisville 77 K 3
Harrogate 5 E 3
Harry S. Truman Reservoir 77 H 4
Harshö 65 H 2
Harsim (Iran) 23 E 2
Harsin (Iran) 23 E 2
Harşit 21 E 2
Harsprånget 16 GH 2
Harstad 16 G 2
Harsvik 16 E 3
Hart 5 E 2
Hartbees 66 C 5
Hartfield 7 E 2
Hartford 77 M 3
Hartland 6 B 2
Hartland Point 6 B 2
Hartlepool 5 E 2
Hartley → Chegutu 66 DE 3
Hartola 16 J 3
Harts Range 48 E 3
Hartsville 77 K 5
Hartz Mountains National Park
  50 L 9
Harvey (N.D., U.S.A.) 76 G 2
Harvey (Western Australia) 48 B 5
Harwich 7 E 2
Haryana 40 C 2
Harz 15 F 4
Hasalbag 35 K 3
Hasan Langī 34 F 5
Ḥasanābad (Iran) 23 FG 3
Ḥasanābād (Iran) 23 EF 1
Hasançelebi 21 E 3
Hasār 34 F 5
Hasekiyata 20 C 2
Haséré Vokré 63 G 4
Haslemere 7 D 2
Hassan 40 C 5
Hasse 15 E 4
Hassela 16 G 3
Hassi Barouda 59 F 3
Hassi Bel Guebbour 59 G 3
Hassi Bou Akba 58 D 3
Hassi Bou Krechba 59 G 3
Hassi Bou Zid 59 F 3
Hassi Chaamba 58 E 3
Hassi Djafou 59 F 2
Hassi el Hadadra 59 F 2
Hassi el Krenig 59 F 3
Hassi Erg Sedra 59 F 2
Hassi Fokra 58 E 2
Hassi Habadra 59 F 3
Hassi Imoulaye 59 G 3
Hassi Inifel 59 F 3
Hassi Insokki 59 F 3
Hassi Krezrez 59 F 3

Hassi Marroket 59 F 2
Hassi Messaoud 59 G 2
Hassi Ouchen 58 F 2
Hassi R'Mel 59 F 2
Hassi Serouenout 59 G 4
Hassi Tartrat 59 G 3
Hassi Timellouline 59 G 3
Hassi Tin Fouchaye 59 G 3
Hassi Zemmoul 58 D 3
Hassi Zirara 59 F 2
Hässleholm 17 F 4
Hastings 7 D 1
Hastings (MN, U.S.A.) 77 H 3
Hastings (NE, U.S.A.) 76 G 3
Hastings (New Zealand) 51 R 8
Hastings (U.K.) 7 E 2
Hasvik 16 H 1
Ḥasy Hague 59 H 3
Hat Hin 41 H 3
Hat Yai 41 H 6
Hatanbulag 38 E 2
Hatch Beauchamp 6 C 3
Haṭeg 20 B 1
Hatfield 7 D 2
Hatgal 36 G 5
Hatherleigh 6 B 2
Hathras 40 C 2
Ḥāṭibah, Ra's 60 F 4
Hatisar 41 F 2
Hatta 40 C 3
Hattah 49 G 5
Hatteras, Cape 77 L 4
Hatteras, Cape 77 LM 4
Hatteras Island 77 LM 4
Hattfjelldal 16 F 2
Hatton 2 D 3
Hatton Bank 98 A 2
Hatutu 53 F 3
Hauberg Mountains 91
Haud 65 GH 3
Hauge 17 E 4
Haugesund 17 DE 4
Haugsdorf 19 G 2
Haukeligrend 17 E 4
Haukipudas 16 HJ 2
Haukivesi 16 J 3
Haukivuori 16 J 3
Hauraki Gulf 51 R 8
Hausa 58 C 3
Hausruck 19 F 2
Hauterive 75 O 6
Haute-Saône, Plateau de 19 E 2
Hauts Plateaux 58 EF 2
Haut-Zaïre 64 CD 4
Havana 77 K 7
Havana 79 F 3
Havant 7 D 2
Havel 15 F 4
Havelock 41 F 5
Haverfordwest 6 B 2
Haverhill (MA, U.S.A.) 77 M 3
Haverhill (U.K.) 7 E 1
Havern 16 G 3
Havířov 15 G 5
Havlíčkův Brod 15 G 5
Havøysund 16 H 1
Havran 20 C 3
Havre 76 E 2
Havre-Saint-Pierre 75 P 5
Havsa 20 C 2
Havza 21 E 2
Hawaii 53 E 1
Hawaii 53 E 1
Hawaiian Islands 53 E 1
Hawaiian Ridge 99 D 3
Ḥawalli (Kuwait) 23 E 3
Ḥawār (Qatar) 23 F 4
Hawera 51 Q 8
Hawes 5 D 2
Hawi 53 E 1
Hawick 3 C 4
Hawke Bay 51 R 8
Hawke Harbour 75 Q 5
Hawker 49 F 5
Hawkhurst 7 E 2
Hawkers Gate 49 G 4
Hawkinge 7 E 2
Hawkshead 5 D 2
Hawkwood 49 J 4
Hawmat as Sūq 59 H 2
Hawng Luk 41 G 3
Hawr al Ḥābbānīyah (Iraq) 22 C 2
Hawr al Hammar (Iraq) 23 E 3
Hawr as S'adīyah (Iraq) 23 E 2
Hawr as Suwayqīyah (Iraq) 23 E 2
Hawr Dalmaj (Iraq) 23 D 2
Ḥawrā' 61 H 5
Ḥawrān, Wādī (Iraq) 22 C 2
Hawthorne 76 C 4
Haxey 7 D 1
Hay 73 O 4
Hay (N.S.W., Austr.) 49 G 5
Hay River (N.T., Austr.) 49 F 3
Hay River (N.W.T., Can.) 73 O 3

Haybān 60 E 6
Haybān, Jabal 60 E 6
Haydon Bridge 5 D 2
Hayes 73 T 4
Hayes, Mount 72 H 3
Hayjān 61 G 5
Hayl (Oman) 23 G 4
Hayl, Wādi al (Syria) 22 C 2
Hayle 6 B 2
Haymana 21 D 3
Haymana Platosu 21 D 3
Hay-on-Wye 6 C 1
Hayraboly 20 C 2
Hayrān 61 G 5
Hays 76 G 4
Hayward 76 B 4
Haywards Heath 7 D 2
Haywood, Mount 73 N 3
Hayyā 60 F 5
Hazar Gölü 21 E 3
Hazarajat 35 H 4
Hazard 77 K 4
Hazaribagh 40 E 3
Hazaribagh Range 40 D 3
Hazebrouck 18 D 1
Hazel Grove 5 D 3
Hazelton 73 M 4
Hazeva (Israel) 22 B 3
Hazhdanahr 35 H 3
Hazlehurst 77 K 5
Hazleton 77 L 3
Hazlett, Lake 48 D 3
Hazrah, Ra's al (United Arab
   Emirates) 23 F 4
Hazro 21 F 3
He Xian 38 F 6
Head of Bight 48 E 5
Heales-ville 49 H 6
Heanor 7 D 1
Hearne 77 G 5
Hearst 74 L 6
Heathfield 7 E 2
Heathrow (Airport) 7 D 2
Hebburn 5 E 2
Hebei 39 G 3
Hebel 49 H 4
Hebi 38 F 3
Hebian 38 F 3
Hebron (Newfoundl., Can.) 75 P 4
Heby 17 G 4
Hecate Strait 72 L 5
Hechi 38 E 6
Hechuan 38 E 4
Heckington 7 D 1
Hede 16 F 3
Hedemora 17 G 3
Hedmark 16 F 3
Hedon 5 E 3
Heerenveen 14 E 4
Hefa (Israel) 22 B 2
Hefei 39 G 4
Hegang 37 NO 6
Hegura-jima 39 L 3
Heide (F.R.G.) 15 E 4
Heide (Namibia) 66 B 4
Heidelberg 15 E 5
Heidenheim 15 F 5
Heilbron 66 D 5
Heilbronn 15 E 5
Heiligenblut 19 F 2
Heiligenstadt 15 F 4
Heilong Jiang 37 O 6
Heilongjiang 39 JK 1
Heimaey 16 A 3
Heimahe 38 C 3
Heimdal 16 EF 3
Heinola 16 J 3
Heinrkut 41 FG 2
Heishan 39 H 2
Heishui 38 D 4
Hejaz (Saudi Arabia) 22 B 4
Hejian 39 G 3
Hejiang 38 E 5
Hejing 35 M 2
Heka 38 C 3
Hekimhan 21 E 3
Hekla 16 B 3
Helagsfjället 16 F 3
Helan 38 E 3
Helan Shan 38 E 3
Helen Reef 43 H 3
Helena (AR, U.S.A.) 77 H 5
Helena (MT, U.S.A.) 76 D 2
Helensburgh 3 B 3
Helensville 51 Q 8
Helgeland 16 F 2
Helgoland 15 E 4
Helgoländer Bucht 15 E 4
Helikarnassos 20 C 3
Hella 16 A 3
Hellas 20 B 3
Hellifield 5 D 2
Hellin 18 C 4
Hells Canyon 76 C 2
Hell-Ville 67 H 2
Helmand 35 G 4

Helmeringhausen 66 B 5
Helmsdale 2 C 2
Helmsley 5 E 2
Helmstedt 15 F 4
Helong 39 J 2
Helsby 5 D 3
Helsingborg 17 F 4
Helsingfors 17 J 3
Helsingör 17 F 4
Helsinki 17 J 3
Helston 6 B 2
Helvellyn 5 D 2
Helwan → Hulwān 60 E 3
Hemel Hempstead 7 D 2
Hemnesberget 16 F 2
Hemsby 7 E 1
Hemse 17 G 4
Hemsö 16 G 3
Henan 38 D 4
Henan 38 F 4
Henares 18 C 3
Henbury 48 E 3
Hendek 20 D 2
Henderson 76 C 4
Henderson (N.C., U.S.A.) 77 L 4
Henderson (Pacific Ocean, U.K.)
   53 G 4
Henderson (TX, U.S.A.) 77 H 5
Hendersonville (N.C., U.S.A.)
   77 K 4
Hendersonville (TN, U.S.A.)
   77 J 4
Hendījan (Iran) 23 E 3
Hendorābi (Iran) 23 F 4
Hendrik Verwoerd Dam 66 D 6
Hendriktop 85 G 3
Henfield 7 D 2
Heng Shan 38 F 3
Heng Shan 38 F 5
Heng Xian 38 E 6
Hengām (Iran) 23 G 4
Henganon 50 E 3
Hengduan Shan 38 C 5
Hengshan 38 D 4
Hengshan 38 F 5
Hengshui 38 G 3
Hengue 66 B 2
Hengyang 38 F 5
Henik Lakes 73 S 3
Henley-in-Arden 7 D 1
Henley-on-Thames 7 D 2
Hennan 16 G 3
Henrietta Maria, Cape 75 L 4
Henry Kater Peninsula 75 O 2
Henryetta 77 G 4
Henties Bay 66 A 4
Hentiy 36 J 6
Hentiyn Nuruu 36 J 6
Henzada 41 G 4
Hepu 38 E 6
Hequ 38 F 3
Heraklia 60 F 1
Herakol Dağı 21 F 3
Herald Cays 49 H 2
Herat 35 G 4
Herault 18 D 3
Herbert 73 Q 5
Herbert River 49 F 3
Herberton 47
Hercegnovi 20 A 2
Hercegovina 19 G 3
Herðubreið 16 B 2
Heredia 78 F 5
Hereford (TX, U.S.A.) 76 F 5
Hereford (U.K.) 6 C 1
Hereford and Worcester 6–7 C 1
Hereheretue 53 F 4
Herford 15 E 4
Herlen Gol 36 K 6
Herlen He 36 L 6
Herluf Trolle, Cape 75 T 3
Herm 7 C 3
Herma Ness 2 D 1
Hermanas 78 B 2
Hermanos, Islas los 85 F 1
Hermanus 66 B 6
Hermidale 49 H 5
Hermiston 76 C 2
Hermit Islands 50 E 2
Hermon, Mount (Lebanon) 22 B 2
Hermosillo 76 D 6
Hernandarias 88 EF 4
Hernani 18 C 3
Herne Bay 7 E 2
Herning 17 E 4
Heroica Alvarado 78 C 4
Heroica Tlapacoyan 78 C 4
Herrera 88 D 4
Herrera de Pisuerga 18 C 3
Herrljunga 17 F 4
Herschel 72 K 2
Hertford 7 DE 2
Hertfordshire 7 D 2
Hervey Bay 49 J 3–4
Herzliyya (Israel) 22 B 2
Hesāmābād (Iran) 23 E 2

Hesār (Iran) 23 F 3
Heshun 38 F 3
Hess 72 L 3
Hessen 15 E 4
Heswall 5 D 3
Hexham 5 D 2
Hexigten Qi 39 G 2
Heydarābād (Iran) 23 D 1
Heydarābād (Iran) 23 G 3
Heysham 5 D 2
Heyuan 38 F 6
Heywood (U.K.) 5 D 3
Heywood (Victoria, Austr.) 49 G 6
Heze 38 G 3
Hezheng 38 D 3
Hialeah 77 K 6
Hibbing 77 H 2
Hibernia Reef 48 C 1
Hickley 7 D 1
Hidaka-sammyaku 39 M 2
Hidalgo 78 C 3
Hidalgo del Parral 76 E 6
Hidrolândia 87 G 4
Hierro 58 B 3
Higginsville 48 C 5
High Level 73 O 4
High Point 77 L 4
High Prairie 73 O 4
High River 73 P 5
High Wycombe 7 D 2
Higham Ferrers 7 D 1
Highampton 6 B 2
Highland 2 B 3
Highrock Lake (Man., Can.)
   73 RS 4
Highrock Lake (Sask., Can.)
   73 Q 4
Highworth 7 D 2
Higuerote 84 E 1
Higüey 79 J 4
Hiitola 16 J 3
Hiiumaa 17 H 4
Hijar 18 C 3
Hikurangi 51 R 8
Hila 43 G 5
Hildesheim 15 EF 4
Hill Bank 78 E 4
Hill Grove 49 H 2
Hill Island Lake 73 Q 3
Hill of Fearn 2 C 3
Hill of Tara 4 B 3
Hillborough 7 E 1
Hillcrest Center 76 C 4
Hilleröd 17 F 4
Hillingdon 7 D 2
Hillsboro (IL, U.S.A.) 77 HJ 5
Hillsboro (TX, U.S.A.) 77 G 5
Hillsborough 4 B 2
Hillside 3 D 3
Hillston 49 H 5
Hillswick 2 D 1
Hilltown 4 B 2
Hilo 53 E 1
Hilvan 21 E 3
Hilversum 14 DE 4
Himā' 61 G 5
Himā Darīyah, Jabal (Saudi
   Arabia) 22 C 4
Himachal Pradesh 40 C 1
Himalayas 40–41 CF 1–2
Himanka 16 H 3
Himara 20 A 2
Himatnagar 40 B 3
Himi 39 L 3
Himmerland 17 E 4
Himmetdede 21 E 3
Himo 65 F 5
Hims (Syria) 22 B 2
Hin Heup 41 H 4
Hinchin Brook 72 H 3
Hinchinbrook Island 49 H 2
Hindarun 40 C 2
Hindhead 7 D 2
Hindmarsh, Lake 49 G 6
Hindon 7 C 2
Hindu Kush 35 HJ 3
Hindubagh 35 H 4
Hindupur 40 C 5
Hindustan 28 FG 4
Hinganghat 40 C 3
Hingol 35 H 5
Hingoli 40 C 4
Hinnöya 16 G 2
Hinobaan 43 F 2
Hinton 73 O 5
Hirado 39 J 4
Hirakud Reservoir 40 D 3
Hirara 39 J 6
Hirfanlı Barajı 21 D 3
Hirhafok 59 G 4
Hiriyur 40 C 5
Hirosaki 39 LM 2
Hiroshima 39 K 4
Hirson 18 D 2
Hirtshals 17 E 4

Hirvensalmi 16 J 3
Hirwaun 6 C 2
Hirwaun 6 C 3
Hīs 65 H 2
Hismā (Saudi Arabia) 22 B 3
Hisn al 'Abr 61 H 5
Hispaniola 79 H 4
Hissar 40 C 2
Histon 7 E 1
Hitachi 39 M 3
Hitchin 7 D 2
Hite 76 D 4
Hitra 16 E 3
Hiva Oa 53 F 3
Hjälmaren 17 G 4
Hjelmsöya 16 H 1
Hjerkinn 16 E 3
Hjo 17 F 4
Hjörring 17 E 4
Hlatikulu 67 E 5
Ho 62 E 4
Ho Chi Minh 41 J 5
Hoa Binh 41 HJ 3
Hoachanas 66 B 4
Hoai Nhon 41 J 5
Hoanib 66 A 3
Hoare Bay 75 P 2
Hoaseb Store 66 B 4
Hobart (OK, U.S.A.) 76 G 4
Hobart (Tasmania, Austr.) 50
   L 9
Hobbs 76 F 5
Hobo 84 C 3
Hobo Shamo 38 E 2
Hoboksar 35 M 1
Hobro 17 EF 4
Hoburgen 17 G 4
Hobyā 65 H 3
Hochfeld 66 B 4
Hochschwab 19 G 2
Hodal 40 C 2
Hodda 65 J 2
Hoddesdon 7 E 2
Hodeida 61 G 6
Hodgson Downs 48 E 2
Hodh 58 D 5
Hódmezővásárhely 20 B 1
Hodna, Chott el 59 F 1
Hodna, Monts du 59 F 1
Hodnall 6 C 1
Hodnet 6 C 1
Hodonin 15 G 5
Hof 15 F 4
Höfðakaupstaður 16 AB 2
Höfn 16 B 3
Hofors 17 G 3
Hofsá 16 B 2
Hofsjökull 16 B 3
Höfu 39 K 4
Höganäs 17 F 4
Hogback Mountain 76 D 3
Hoggar 59 F 4
Hoggar → Ahaggar 59 G 4
Högstegia 16 EF 3
Hoh Sai Hu 38 B 3
Hoh Xil Hu 38 B 3
Hōhang-nyöng 39 J 2
Hohe Acht 19 E 1
Hohe Tauern 19 F 2
Hohes Venn 14 E 4
Hohhot 38 F 2
Hohoe 62 E 4
Hoi An 41 J 4
Hoi Xuan 41 J 3
Hoima 64 E 4
Hokitika 51 Q 9
Hokkaidō 39 M 2
Hokksund 17 E 4
Hokmābād 34 F 3
Hol 17 E 3
Hol Hol 65 G 2
Holanda 86 C 3
Holbæk 17 F 4
Holbox, Isla 78 E 3
Holbrook 7 E 2
Holbrook 76 D 5
Holdenville 77 G 4
Holdrege 76 G 3
Hole Narcipur 40 C 5
Holford 6 C 3
Holguín 79 G 3
Holitna 72 F 3
Höljes 17 F 3
Hollabrunn 19 G 2
Holland 77 J 3
Hollandsbird 66 A 4
Hollick-Kenyon Plateau 91
Holly Springs 77 HJ 5
Hollywood 4 B 3
Hollywood (CA, U.S.A.) 76 C 5
Hollywood (FL, U.S.A.) 77 L 6
Holman Island 73 O 1
Hólmavik 16 A 2

Holme-on-Spalding-Moor 5 E 3
Holmes Reefs 49 H 2
Holmestrand 17 EF 4
Holmfirth 5 E 3
Holmhead 3 B 4
Holmön 16 H 3
Holmsjön 16 FG 3
Holmsund 16 H 3
Holmudden 17 G 4
Holoog 66 B 5
Holstebro 17 E 4
Holsteinburg 75 R 2
Holsworthy 6 B 2
Holt 5 D 3
Holy Cross 72 E 3
Holy Island 6 B 1
Holy Island Lindisfarne 5 E 2
Holyhead 6 B 1
Holyoke (CO, U.S.A.) 76 F 3
Holyoke (MA, U.S.A.) 77 M 3
Holywell 6 C 1
Holywood (U.K.) 4 C 2
Homā (Iran) 23 E 2
Homa Bay 64 E 5
Homalin 41 G 3
Homāyūnshahr (Iran) 23 F 2
Hombori 62 D 2
Hombori, Monts du 62 D 2
Hombori Tondo 62 D 3
Hombre Muerto, Salar de 88 C 4
Home Bay 75 O 2
Home Hill 49 H 2
Homer 72 G 4
Homestead (FL, U.S.A.) 77 K 6
Homestead (Queensland, Austr.)
   49 H 3
Homewood 77 J 5
Hommelstö 16 F 2
Homnabad 40 C 4
Homoine 67 E 4
Homoljske Planina 20 B 2
Homosassa 77 K 6
Homs 60 F 2
Homs → Al Khums 59 H 2
Hon Chong 41 H 5
Hon Gai 41 J 3
Hon Khoci 41 J 6
Hon Panjang 41 H 6
Honavar 40 B 5
Honda 84 D 2
Hondeklip Baai 66 B 6
Honduras 78 E 5
Hönefoss 17 F 3
Honey Lake 76 B 3
Hong Kong 38 FG 6
Honghe 38 D 6
Hongliuhe 38 B 2
Hongliuyuan 38 BC 2
Hongor 38 F 1
Hongqizhen 38 E 7
Hongsa 41 H 4
Hongshui He 38 E 6
Honguedo, Détroit d' 75 P 6
Hongyuan 38 D 4
Hongze 39 G 4
Hongze Hu 39 G 4
Honiara 51 G 3
Honington 7 D 1
Honiton 6 C 2
Honkajoki 16 H 3
Honnali 40 C 5
Honningsvåg 16 J 1
Honolulu 53 E 1
Honrubia 18 C 4
Honshū 39 KL 3
Hood, Mount 76 B 2
Hood Point 48 B 5
Hood River 76 B 2
Hoogeveen 14 E 4
Hooghly 40 E 3
Hook 7 D 2
Hook Island 49 H 3
Hooker Creek 48 E 2
Hoonah 72 K 4
Hooper Bay 72 D 3
Hooper, Cape 75 O 2
Hoorn 14 E 4
Hoover Dam 76 D 4
Hopa 21 F 2
Hope (AR, U.S.A.) 77 H 5
Hope (AZ, U.S.A.) 76 D 5
Hope, Cape 73 O 2
Hope, Point 72 D 2
Hopedale 75 P 4
Hopes Advance, Cap 75 O 3
Hopetoun (Victoria, Austr.) 49 G 6
Hopetoun (Western Australia)
   48 C 5
Hopetown 66 C 5
Hopewell Islands 75 M 4
Hopin 41 G 3
Hopkins, Lake 48 D 3
Hopkinsville 77 J 4
Hopton 7 E 1
Hoquiam 76 B 2
Hora Kalifo 65 G 3

Horasan 21 F 2
Hordaland 17 E 3
Hordio → Hurdiyo 65 J 2
Horgen 19 E 2
Horgos 20 A 1
Hörh Uul 38 E 2
Horinger 38 F 2
Horizon Deep 52 D 4
Horley 7 D 2
Horlick Mountains 91
Hormoz (Iran) 23 G 4
Hormoz, Kūh-e (Iran) 23 G 4
Hormoz [ö] (Iran) 23 G 4
Hormuz, Strait of 23 G 4
Horn (Austria) 19 G 2
Horn (Iceland) 16 A 2
Horn, Cape 89 C 10
Horn Islands 52 D 3
Horn Plateau 73 O 3
Hornad 15 H 5
Hornavan 16 G 2
Hornby Bay 73 O 2
Horncastle 5 E 3
Hörnefors 16 G 3
Hornell 77 L 3
Hornepayne 74 K 6
Hornos, Cabo de 89 C 10
Hornos, Falso Cabo de 89 C 10
Hornsea 5 E 3
Hornslandet 16 G 3
Horqin Youyi Qianqi 39 H 1
Horqin Youyi Zhongqi 39 H 1
Horqin Zuoyi Houqi 39 H 2
Horqin Zuoyi Zhongqi 39 H 2
Horqueta 86 E 5
Horred 17 F 4
Horsely 7 D 2
Horsens 17 EF 4
Horsey 7 E 1
Horsham 7 D 2
Horsham 49 G 6
Hortobágy 20 B 1
Horton 73 N 2
Hosalay 21 D 2
Hose Mountains 42 D 3
Hosenofu 59 K 4
Hoseynābād (Iran) 23 F 2
Hoseynīyeh (Iran) 23 E 3
Hoshab 35 G 5
Hoshangabad 40 C 3
Hoskins 51 F 3
Hospet 40 C 4
Hospitalet de Llobregat 18 D 3
Hosseina 65 F 3
Hoste, Isla 89 C 10
Hot 41 G 4
Hot Springs 76 F 3
Hot Springs 77 H 5
Hotagen 16 F 3
Hotan 35 K 3
Hotan He 35 L 2–3
Hotazel 66 C 5
Hoting 16 G 3
Hottah Lake 73 O 2
Houei Sai 41 H 3
Houghton 77 J 2
Houghton Lake 77 K 3
Houlton 77 N 2
Houma (China) 38 F 3
Houma (LA, U.S.A.) 77 H 6
Houndé 62 D 3
Hourn, Loch 3 B 3
Hourtin, Étang d' 18 C 2
House, Mount 48 D 2
Houston 77 G 5
Houtman Abrolhos 48 A 4
Houxia 35 M 2
Hovd 36 F 6
Hovd 38 D 2
Hovd Gol 36 F 6
Hove 7 D 2
Hoveyzeh (Iran) 23 E 3
Hövsgöl 38 E 2
Hövsgöl Nuur 36 H 5
Howar 60 D 5
Howard 49 J 4
Howden 5 E 3
Howe, Cape 49 J 6
Howland (ME, U.S.A.) 77 N 2
Howland (Pacific Ocean, U.S.A.)
  52 D 2
Howrah 40 E 3
Howth Head 4 BC 3
Hox Xil Shan 38 AB 3
Hoxne 7 E 1
Hoxud 38 A 2
Hoy 2 C 2
Höyanger 16 E 3
Hoylake 5 D 3
Hoyos 18 B 3
Höytiäinen 16 J 3
Hozat 21 E 3
Hpunhpu 41 G 2
Hradec Králové 15 G 4
Hraun 16 BC 3
Hron 15 G 5

Hrubieszow 15 H 4
Hrvatska 19 G 2
Hsi-hseng 41 G 3
Hsinchu 39 H 6
Hsinying 39 H 6
Hsipaw 41 G 3
Hu Men 38 F 6
Hu Xian 38 E 4
Hua Hin 41 GH 5
Hua Sai 41 H 6
Hua Xian (Guangdong, China)
  38 F 6
Hua Xian (Shanxi, China) 38 E 4
Hua Xian (Shanxi, China) 38 F 3
Hua'an 39 G 5
Huachinango 78 C 3
Huacho 84 C 6
Huachuan 37 O 6
Huacrachuco 84 C 5
Huade 38 F 2
Huadian 39 J 2
Huahine 53 EF 4
Huahuapán 78 A 3
Huai'an 38 F 2
Huaibei 39 G 4
Huaibin 38 G 4
Huaide 39 H 2
Huaihua 38 E 5
Huaiji 38 F 6
Huailai 38 G 2
Huainan 39 G 4
Huairen 38 F 3
Huaiyin 39 G 4
Huajuapan de León 78 C 4
Hualien 39 H 6
Huallaga 84 C 5
Huallanca 84 C 5
Hualong 38 D 3
Huambo 66 B 2
Huambo 66 B 2
Huan Xian 38 E 3
Huanan 39 K 1
Huancabamba 84 C 5
Huancané 86 C 4
Huancavelica 86 A 3
Huancayo 86 A 3
Huanchaca, Serranía de 86 D 3
Huanchasa 86 C 5
Huang Hai 39 H 3
Huang He 39 G 3
Huang Shan 39 G 4
Huang Shui 38 D 3
Huang Xian 39 H 3
Huangchuan 38 G 4
Huanghe Kou 39 G 3
Huanghetan 38 C 3
Huanghua 39 G 3
Huangling 38 E 3
Huangliu 38 E 7
Huanglong 38 EF 3
Huangshi 38 G 4
Huangyan 39 H 5
Huangyangzhen 38 D 3
Huangyuan 38 D 3
Huangzhong 38 D 3
Huanren 39 HJ 2
Huanta 86 B 3
Huánuco 84 C 5
Huanzo, Cordillera de 86 B 3
Huaping 38 D 5
Huara 86 C 4
Huaral 86 A 3
Huaraz 84 C 5
Huariaca 86 A 3
Huarmey 84 C 6
Huasago 84 C 4
Huascarán, Nevado 84 C 5
Huasco 88 B 4
Huashixia 38 C 3
Huatabampo 76 E 6
Huating 38 E 3
Huautla 78 C 3
Huayllay 86 A 3
Huayuri, Pampa de 86 A 3
Huazhou 38 F 6
Hubbart Point 73 T 4
Hubei 38 F 4
Hubli 40 C 4
Hucal 89 D 6
Huckitta 48 F 3
Hucknall Torkard 7 D 1
Hudat 65 F 3
Huddersfield 5 E 3
Huddun 65 H 3
Huddur Hadama 65 G 4
Huder 37 M 6
Hudiksvall 16 G 3
Hudson 77 M 3
Hudson Bay 74 KL 3–4
Hudson Bay (Sask., Can.) 73 R 5
Hudson, Cerro 89 B 8
Hudson Strait 75 N 3
Hudson's Hope 73 N 4
Hue 41 J 4
Huehuetenango 78 D 4
Huelma 18 C 4

Huelva 18 B 4
Huercal-Ovéra 18 C 4
Huesca 18 C 3
Huéscar 18 C 4
Ḥufrat an Naḥās 64 C 3
Hugh Town 6 A 3
Hughenden 49 G 3
Hughes (AK, U.S.A.) 72 G 2
Hughes (South Australia) 48 D 5
Hugo 77 G 5
Hui Xian 38 E 4
Hui'an 39 G 5
Huiarau Range 51 R 8
Huib High Plateau 66 B 5
Huichang 38 G 5
Huicholes, Sierra de los 78 B 3
Hŭich'on 39 J 2
Huidong 38 F 6
Huihe 36 L 6
Huŝla 66 AB 2
Huila 84 C 3
Huilai 38 G 6
Huili 38 D 5
Huimin 39 G 3
Huinan 39 J 2
Huishui 38 E 5
Huiten Nur 38 B 3
Huittinen 16 H 3
Huixtla 78 D 4
Huize 38 D 5
Hŭksan-chedo 39 HJ 4
Hukuntsi 66 C 4
Hulan 39 J 1
Ḥulayfā (Saudi Arabia) 22 C 4
Huld 38 E 1
Hulin 39 K 1
Hull 75 M 6
Hultsfred 17 G 4
Hulun Buir Meng 36 LM 6
Hulun Nur 36 L 6
Ḥulwān 60 E 3
Huma 37 N 5
Huma He 37 M 5
Humahuaca 86 C 5
Humaitá (Amazonas, Brazil)
  85 F 5
Humaitá (Paraguay) 88 E 4
Humansdorp 66 C 6
Humara, Jabal al 60 E 5
Humay 86 A 3
Humber Bridge 5 E 3
Humber, River 5 E 3
Humberside 5 E 3
Humberston 7 E 1
Humboldt (Sask., Can.) 73 R 5
Humboldt (TN, U.S.A.) 77 J 4
Humboldt River 76 C 3
Humeburn 49 H 4
Humenné 15 H 5
Humpata 66 A 2
Hūn 59 J 3
Hun He 39 H 2
Hun Xieng Hung 41 H 3
Húnaflói 16 A 2
Hunan 38 F 5
Hunchun 39 K 2
100 Mile House 73 N 5
Hunedoara 20 B 1
Hungary 20 A 1
Hungerford (Queensland, Austr.)
  49 G 4
Hungerford (U.K.) 7 D 2
Hŭngnam 39 J 3
Huni Valley 62 D 4
Hunjiang 39 J 2
Hunnebostrand 17 F 4
Hunsrück 15 E 5
Hunstad 16 G 2
Hunsur 40 C 5
Hunte 15 E 4
Hunter 50 K 9
Hunter, Ile 51 K 6
Hunter's Bay 41 F 3–4
Huntingdon 7 D 1
Huntington 77 K 4
Huntly 2 C 3
Huntspill 6 C 3
Huntsville (AL, U.S.A.) 77 J 5
Huntsville (Ontario, Can.) 75 M 6
Huntsville (TX, U.S.A.) 77 G 5
Hunyuan 38 F 3
Hunza 35 J 3
Huo Xian 38 F 3
Huocheng 35 L 2
Huolongmen 37 N 6
Huon 51 H 5
Huon Gulf 50 E 3
Huon Peninsula 50 E 3
Huong Khe 41 J 4
Huong Thuy 41 J 4
Huoshan 38 G 4
Hur 34 F 4
Huraymilāh (Saudi Arabia) 23 E 4
Hurdiyo 65 J 2
Hure 41 J 2
Hure Qi 39 H 2
Huri Hills 65 F 4

Huron 76 G 3
Huron, Lake 77 K 3
Huron Mountains 77 J 2
Hurricane 76 D 4
Hurst 77 G 5
Hurstpierpoint 7 D 2
Húsavík 16 B 2
Hushinish 2 A 3
Huşi 20 C 1
Huskvarna 17 F 4
Huslia 72 F 2
Husum (F.R.G.) 15 E 4
Husum (Sweden) 16 G 3
Hutag 36 H 6
Hutchinson (KS, U.S.A.) 76 G 4
Hutchinson (MN, U.S.A.)
  77 GH 3
Ḥuth 61 G 5
Huthi 41 G 4
Hutou 39 K 1
Hutton Cranswick 5 E 3
Hutton, Mount 49 H 4
Hutubi 35 M 2
Huzhou 39 H 4
Hvammstangi 16 AB 2
Hvar 19 G 3
Hvarski Kanal 19 G 3
Hveragerði 16 A 3
Hveravellir 16 B 3
Hvide Sande 17 E 4
Hvita 16 B 3
Hvitá 16 B 3
Hvítárvatn 16 AB 3
Hwang Ho 39 G 3
Hwange 66 D 3
Hwange National Park 66 D 3
Hyannis 77 MN 3
Hyargas Nuur 36 F 6
Hyden 48 B 5
Hyderabad (India) 40 C 4
Hyderabad (Pakistan) 35 H 5
Hyères 19 E 3
Hyères, Iles d' 19 E 3
Hyesan 39 J 2
Hyltebruk 17 F 4
Hyrra Banda 64 C 3
Hyrynsalmi 16 J 3
Hysham 76 E 2
Hythe 7 D 2
Hythe 7 E 2
Hyūga 39 K 4
Hyvinge 17 H 3
Hyvinkää 17 H 3

I

Iacó 86 C 3
Iaçu 87 H 3
Iakora 67 H 4
Ialomiţa 20 C 2
Iaripo 85 H 3
Iaşi 20 C 1
Iauaretê 84 E 3
Iba 43 HJ 1
Ibadan 62–63 E 4
Ibagué 84 C 3
Ibaiti 87 F 5
Ibar 20 B 2
Ibarra 84 C 3
Ibb 61 G 6
Ibba 64 D 4
Ibembo 64 C 4
Ibenga 63 H 5
Iberá, Esteros del 88 E 4
Iberia 86 C 3
Iberville, Lac d' 75 N 4
Ibestad 16 G 2
Ibi 63 F 4
Ibiapaba, Serra da 87 H 1–2
Ibiara 87 J 2
Ibicaraí 87 J 4
Ibicuí 88 E 4
Ibicuy 88 E 5
Ibipetuba 87 H 3
Ibitiara 87 H 3
Íbiza 18 D 4
Ibiza 18 D 4
Ibn Qawrah 61 J 5
Ibo 67 G 2
Ibonma 43 H 4
Ibotirama 87 H 3
Iboundji, Mont 63 G 6
Ibrā' 61 K 4
Ibrah, Wādī 60 C 6
Ibrāhīm, Jabal 61 G 4
'Ibrī 61 K 4
Ibrīm 60 E 4
Ibsley 7 D 2
Ibstock 7 D 1
Içá (Amazonas, Brazil) 84 E 4
Ica (Peru) 86 A 3
Içana 84 E 3
Icana (Amazonas, Brazil) 84 E 3
Icapuí 87 J 1
Icatu 87 H 1

İçel 21 D 3
Iceland 16 A 3
Icepê 87 F 5
Icha 37 T 4
Ichaf 58 D 3
Ichalkaranji 40 B 4
Ichchapuram 40 D 4
Ichera 36 J 4
Ichibusa-yama 39 K 4
Ichig → Chegga 58 D 3
Ichigemskiy Khrebet 37 UV 3
Ichinskaya Sopka 37 T 4
Ichnya 24 F 5
Ico 87 J 2
Icoca 66 B 1
Icoraci 85 J 4
Icy Cape 72 E 1
Idabel 77 H 5
Idah 63 F 4
Idaho 76 CD 3
Idaho Falls 76 D 3
Idän 65 H 3
Íday 63 G 3
'Idd al Ghanam 60 C 6
Idd el Sharqi (Qatar) 23 F 4
Idel 16 K 3
Idelès 59 G 4
Idélimen 62 E 2
Idfū (Egypt) 22 A 4
Idhān Awbārī 59 H 3
Idhān Murzuq 59 H 4
Ídhi Óros 20 BC 3
Ídhra 20 B 3
Idikel 63 F 2
Idil 21 F 3
Idiofa 64 B 5
Idku 63 F 2
Idlib (Syria) 22 B 2
Idre 16 F 3
Idrī 59 H 3
Idrija 19 F 2
Idutywa 66 D 6
Idyum 37 O 4
Iema 63 E 3
Ierápetra 20 C 3
Ierisós 20 B 2
Ierisou, Kólpos 20 B 2
Iesi 19 F 3
Iet 65 G 4
Iezerul, Virful 20 B 1
Ifag 65 F 3
Ifakara 65 F 6
Ifalik 52 A 2
Ifanadiana 67 H 4
Ife 63 E 4
Iférouane 63 F 2
Ifetesene 59 F 3
Ifinga 64 F 6
Ifjord 16 J 1
Ifon 63 F 4
Iganga 64 E 4
Igara Paraná 84 D 4
Igarapava 87 G 4
Igarapé-Açu 85 J 4
Igarka 25 R 2
Igatimí 86 E 5
Igatpuri 40 B 4
Igbetti 63 E 4
Igdet, Jbel 58 D 2
Iğdır (Turkey) 21 F 3
Igdir (Iran) 34 D 3
Ige 38 B 3
Iggesund 16 G 3
Ighil Mgoun, Jbel 58 D 2
Iglesia 88 C 5
Iglesias 19 E 4
Igli 58 E 2
Ignace 74 J 6
Ignashino 37 M 5
İğneada 20 C 2
Igoumenitsá 20 B 3
Igra 24 K 4
Igrim 25 M 3
Iguaçu 88 F 4
Iguaçu, Parque Nacional do 88 F 4
Iguala 78 C 4
Igualada 18 D 3
Igualdade 84 E 4
Iguassú Falls 88 F 4
Iguatu 87 J 2
Iguazú, Cataratas del 88 F 4
Iguéla 63 F 6
Iguetti, Sebkha 58 D 3
Iguidi, Erg 58 DE 3
Iguigik 72 F 4
Igusi 66 D 3
Ih Bogd Uul 38 CD 2
Ihirene 59 F 4
Ihosy 67 H 4
İhsaniye 20 D 3
Ihtamir 36 H 6
Ii 16 J 2
Iijoki 16 J 2
Iisalmi 16 J 3
Iivaara 16 J 2
Ijebu Ode 63 E 4

Ijsselmeer 14 E 4
Ijuí 88 F 4
Ikaalinen 16 H 3
Ikalamavony 67 H 4
Ikali 64 C 5
Ikanda 64 C 5
Ikaría 20 C 3
Ikatskiy Khrebet 36 K 5
Ikeda 39 M 2
Ikeja 62 E 4
Ikela 64 C 5
Ikerre 63 F 4
Ikey 36 H 5
Iki Burul 21 F 1
Ikom 63 F 4
Ikomba 67 E 1
Ikongo 65 F 6
Ikot Ekpene 63 F 4
Ikryanoye 21 G 1
Ikungi 64 E 6
Ikungu 64 E 6
Ila 63 EF 4
Ilabaya 86 B 4
Ilad 65 H 2
Ilaferh 59 F 4
Ilaferh 59 F 4
Ilagan 43 J 1
Ilam (Iran) 23 E 2
Ilan 39 H 6
Ilanskiy 36 G 4
Ilaro 62 E 4
Ilatan 63 E 2
Iława 15 G 4
Ilbenge 37 M 3
Ilchester 6 C 3
Île à Vache 79 H 4
Île d'Anticosti 75 P 6
Ile de France 18 D 2
Ile de France, Côte de l' 18 D 2
Ile de Groix 18 C 2
Ile de la Gonâve 79 H 4
Île de la Madeleine 75 P 6
Île de la Tortue 79 H 3
Île de Ré 18 C 2
Île de Sable 52 B 4
Ile des Noefs 65 J 6
Ile des Pins 51 J 6
Île Desrouches 65 J 6
Île d'Oléron 18 C 2
Ile d'Ouessant 18 B 2
Île du Diable 85 H 2
Ile d'Yeu 18 C 2
Ile Hunter 51 K 6
Ile Matthew 51 K 6
Ile Tidra 58 B 5
Ile Walpole 51 J 6
Ile-à-la-Crosse 73 Q 4
Ilebo 64 C 5
Ilek 24 L 5
Ilemera 64 E 5
Iles Belep 51 H 5
Iles Chesterfield 52 B 4
Îles de Los 62 B 4
Iles d'Hyères 19 E 3
Îles du Désappointement 53 F 3
Îles du Duc de Gloucester 53 F 4
Îles du Roi Georges 53 F 3
Iles Glorieuses (Réunion) 67 H 2
Iles Loyauté 51 J 6
Îles Palliser 53 F 4
Ilesha 62 E 4
Ilford 73 S 4
Ilfracombe 6 B 2
Ilgaz 21 D 2
Ilgaz Dağları 21 D 2
Ilgın 21 D 3
Ilha Bailique 85 J 3
Ilha Caçumba 87 J 4
Ilha Caviana 85 HJ 3
Ilha Curuá (Amapá, Brazil) 85 J 3
Ilha da Inhaca 67 E 5
Ilha de Maracá 85 HJ 3
Ilha de Marajó 85 HJ 3
Ilha de Orango 62 A 3
Ilha de Santa Catarina 88 G 4
Ilha de São Sebastião 87 GH 5
Ilha de Tinharé 87 J 3
Ilha do Bananal 87 F 3
Ilha Grande 87 H 5
Ilha Grande (Brazil) 84 E 4
Ilha Grande do Gurupá 85 H 4
Ilha Janaucu 85 HJ 3
Ilha Mexiana 85 J 3
Ilha Queimada 87 G 5
Ilha Santa Carolina 67 F 4
Ilha Tupinambaranas 85 G 4
Ilha Vamizi 67 G 2
Ilhas, Cachoeira das 85 G 4
Ilhas de São João 85 K 4
Ilhas Selvagens (Portugal) 58 B 2
Ilhea Point 66 A 4
Ilhéus 87 J 3
Ili 25 P 7
Ili 35 L 2
Ili He 35 L 2
Ilia 20 B 1

Iliamna 72 G 4
Iliamna Lake 72 F 4
İliç 21 E 3
Il'ich 35 H 2
Ilidza 19 G 3
Iligan 43 F 2
Iligan Bay 43 F 2
Ilim 36 H 4
Ilimniir 37 S 2
Ilimsk 36 H 4
Ilimskiy, Ust'-, Vodokhranilishche
    36 H 4
Ilinskiy 37 Q 6
Ilinsky 16 K 3
Ilir 36 H 4
Ilirgytkin, Ozero 37 T 1
Ilirney 37 V 2
Ilirska Bistrica 19 F 2
Il'ka 36 J 5
Ilkeston 7 D 1
Ilkley 5 E 3
Illana Bay 43 F 2
Illapel 88 B 5
Illéla 63 F 3
Illescas 18 C 3
Illimani, Nevado 86 C 4
Illinois 77 J 3–4
Illinois River 77 H 4
Illizi 62 E 3
Illo 62 E 3
Ilmajoki 16 H 3
Il'men, Ozero 17 K 4
Ilminster 6 C 2
Ilmuvye 37 W 3
Ilo 86 B 4
Iloilo 43 F 1
Ilok 19 G 2
Ilomantsi 16 K 3
Ilorin 63 E 4
Ilots de Bass 53 F 4
Ilovlinskaya 24 H 6
Il'pi 37 W 3
Il'pyrskiy 37 U 4
Ilskiy 21 E 2
Ilubabor 64 EF 3
Ilunde 64 E 6
Ilwaki 43 G 5
Ilych 24 L 3
Ilyichovsk 20 D 1
Ima 36 L 4
Imabari 39 K 4
Imām al Ḥamzah (Iraq) 23 D 3
Iman 39 L 1
Imandra, Ozero 16 K 2
Imari 39 JK 4
Imasa 60 F 5
Imataca, Serranía de 85 F 2
Imatra 16 J 3
Imbituba 88 G 4
Imenas 62 E 2
Imeni 26 Bakinskikh Komissarov
    34 DE 3
Imeni Bakinskikh Komissarov
    34 DE 3
Iméni Gastello 37 R 3
Iméni Lazo 37 S 3
Iméni Mariny 37 R 3
Iméni Poliny Osipenko 37 P 5
Imese 64 B 4
Imgytskoye Boloto 25 O 4
Imi 65 G 3
Imileton 5 D 2
Imi n'Tanoute 58 D 2
Imilac 86 C 5
Imilili 58 B 4
Imishli 34 D 3
Immingham 5 E 3
Imola 19 F 2
Imonda 50 D 2
Imotski 19 G 3
Imperatriz (Amazonas, Brazil)
    84 E 5
Imperatriz (Maranhão, Brazil)
    85 J 5
Imperia 19 E 3
Impfondo 63 H 5
Imphal 41 F 3
Imphy 18 D 2
Imralı 20 C 2
İmranlı 21 E 3
İmroz 20 C 2
İmroz 20 C 2
Imst 19 F 2
Imtän (Syria) 22 B 2
Imtonzha 37 N 2
In Abalene 62 E 2
In Akhmed 62 D 2
In Alay 62 D 2
In Allarène Gérigéri 63 F 2
In Azaoua 63 F 1
In Belbel 59 F 3
In Beriem 62 DE 2
In Dagouber 62 D 1
In Edek 63 E 2
In Gall 63 F 2
In Ouagar 63 F 2
In Ouelene 63 F 2

In Rhar 59 F 3
In Salah 59 F 3
In Tadreft 63 F 2
In Talak 62 E 2
In Tebezas 62 E 2
In Zekouane 62 E 2
Inagua Island, Great 79 H 3
Inagua Island, Little 79 H 3
Inajá 87 J 2
Inanwatan 43 H 4
Inanya 37 S 3
Iñapari 86 C 3
Inari 16 J 2
Inarigda 36 J 3
Inarijärvi 16 J 2
Inca 18 D 4
Inca de Oro 88 C 4
İnce Burnu 21 D 2
İncekum Burnu 21 D 3
Inch 4 B 3
Inchadamph 2 B 2
Inchiri 58 C 5
Inch'ŏn 39 J 3
Inchôpe 67 E 3
Indalsälven 16 G 3
Indargarh 40 C 2
Independence (KS, U.S.A.) 77 G 4
Independence (MO, U.S.A.)
    77 H 4
Independencia, Isla 86 A 3
Independenta 20 C 1
Inderagiri, Sungai 42 B 4
Inderapura 42 B 4
Inderborskiy 34 E 1
India 40 CD 3
Indian Harbour 75 Q 5
Indian Ocean 93
Indian Springs 76 C 4
Indiana 77 J 3
Indianapolis 77 J 4
Indiaroba 87 J 3
Indias Occidentales 79 H 3
Indiga 24 J 2
Indigirka 37 R 2
Indigirskaya Nizmennost' 37 QR 2
Indija 20 B 1
Índios, Cachoeira dos 85 F 3
Indispensable Reefs 52 B 3
Indispensable Strait 51 H 3
Indonesia 42–43 DG 4
Indore 40 C 3
Indramayu 42 C 5
Indravati 40 D 4
Indre 18 D 2
Indus 35 H 6
Indus Cone 98 B 3
İnebolu 21 D 2
İnecik 20 C 2
İnecik 20 C 2
İnegöl 20 C 2
Inezgane 58 D 2
Infermo, Cachoeira do 85 G 4
Inga 64 A 6
Ingatestone 7 E 2
Ingawa 63 F 3
Ingelstad 17 F 4
Ingende 63 H 6
Ingeniero Jacobacci 89 C 7
Ingeniero Luiggi 89 D 6
Ingham 49 H 2
Ingleton 5 D 2
Inglewood 49 J 4
Ingoda 36 K 5
Ingoldmells 7 E 1
Ingólfshöfði 16 B 3
Ingolstadt 15 F 5
Ingomer 48 E 4
Ing-Puta-Yaun-Pugol 25 O 3
Ingrid Christensen Coast 91
Inguisivi 86 C 4
Ingul 21 D 1
Ingulets 21 D 1
Ingulets 21 D 1
Inguri 21 F 2
Inhaca, Ilha de 67 E 5
Inhambane 67 F 4
Inhaminga 67 F 3
Inharrime 67 F 4
Inhassôro 67 F 4
Inhaúmas 87 GH 3
Inhumas 87 G 5
Inírida 84 E 3
Inishowen 4 B 2
Inishowen Head 4 B 2
Inishtrahull 4 B 2
Injune 49 H 4
Inkerman 49 G 2
Inkisi-Kisantu 64 B 6
Inklin 72 L 4
Inle, Lake 41 G 3
Inn 15 F 5
Innamincka 49 G 4
Innellan 3 B 4
Inner Hebrides 3 A 3
Inner Mongolia 38 E 2–3
Inner Sound 2 B 3

Innerleithen 3 C 4
Innisfail (Queensland, Austr.)
    49 H 2
Innokent'evka 37 O 6
Innokent'yevka 37 P 6
Innsbruck 19 F 2
Innset 16 G 2
Inobonto 43 F 3
Inongo 64 B 5
Inoni 63 H 6
Inorunie 49 G 2
Inowrocław 15 G 4
Inriko 20 C 2–3
Interlaken 19 E 2
Interview 41 F 5
Intletovy 25 P 3
Intuto 84 D 4
Inuvik 72 L 2
Inuvik, District of 72 LM 2
Inveralligin 2 B 3
Inveraray 3 B 3
Inverarity 3 D 3
Inverbervie 3 C 3
Invercargill (New Zealand) 50 P 10
Inverell 49 J 4
Invergarry 3 B 3
Invergordon 2 B 3
Inverie 3 B 3
Inverkeilor 3 D 3
Inverkeithing 3 C 3
Inverkip 3 B 3
Inverkirkaig 2 B 2
Invermoriston 2 B 3
Inverness 2 B 3
Inverness (Airport) 2 B 3
Inverurie 2 C 3
Inverway 48 D 2
Investigator Shoal 42 D 2
Investigator Strait 49 F 6
Inya 25 Q 4
Inya 25 R 5
Inya 37 R 3
Inyanga 67 E 3
Inyangani 67 E 3
Inyati 66 D 3
Inyonga 64 E 6
Inza 24 J 5
Ioánnina 20 B 3
Iolotan 35 G 3
Ioma 50 E 3
Iona (Angola) 66 A 3
Iona (U.K.) 3 A 3
Iona National Park 66 A 3
Iona Peres 85 HJ 4
Iongo 66 B 1
Ionian Islands 20 A 3
Ionian Sea 20 AB 3
Iónioi Nísoi 20 A 3
Iónion Pélagos 20 AB 3
Iony, Ostrov 37 Q 4
Íos 20 C 3
Íos 20 C 3
Iō-shima 39 K 4
Iosser 24 K 3
Iowa 77 H 3
Iowa City 77 H 3
Ipala 64 E 5
Ipameri 87 G 4
Ipatinga 87 H 4
Ipatovo 21 F 1
Ipiales 84 C 3
Ipiaú 87 J 3
Ipiranga 84 E 4
Ípiros 20 B 3
Ipixuna (Amazonas, Brazil) 84 D 5
Ipixuna (Amazonas, Brazil) 85 F 5
Ipoh 42 B 3
Iporá 87 F 4
Ippy 64 C 3
İpsala 20 C 2
Ipstones 7 D 1
Ipswich (Australia) 49 J 4
Ipswich (U.K.) 7 E 1
Ipu 87 H 1
Ipun, Isla 89 B 7
Iquape 87 G 5
Iquique 86 B 5
Iquitos 84 D 4
Iracoubo 85 H 2
Irafshan 35 G 5
Iraí 88 F 4
Iráklion 20 C 3
Iran 34 EF 4
Iran, Pegunungan 42 D 3
Iranshahr 35 G 5
Irapa 85 F 1
Irapuato 78 B 3
Iraq 22 CD 2
Irati 88 F 4
Îrawan, Wâdī 59 H 3
Irbeni Väin 17 H 4

Irbid (Jordan) 22 B 2
Irbit 25 M 4
Irebu 64 B 5
Irecê 87 H 3
Iret' 37 S 3
Irgiz 24 J 5
Irgiz 35 G 1
Irharen 59 F 4
Irharhar 59 G 3
Irharharene 59 G 3
Irharrhar 59 G 4
Irhazer Ouan Agadez 63 F 2
Irherm 58 D 2
Irian Jaya 43 HJ 4
Iriba 63 J 2
Iriklinskiy 25 L 5
Iringa 65 F 6
Iriomote-jima 39 H 6
Iriona 78 EF 4
Iriri 85 H 4
Irish Sea 4 C 3
Iritsoka 67 H 4
Irkeneyeva 36 G 4
Irkut 36 H 5
Irkutsk 36 H 5
Irlam 5 D 3
İrmasan Geçidi 20 D 3
Irminger Basin 98 A 2
Irnijärvi 16 J 2
Iroise 18 BC 2
Iron gate → Portile de Fier 20 B 2
Iron Knob 49 F 5
Iron Mountain 77 J 2
Iron Mountains 4 B 2
Iron Range 49 G 1
Irosin 43 F 1
'Irq al Idrīsī 59 K 4–5
'Irq al Mazḥūr (Saudi Arabia)
    22 D 4
Irq Jahām (Saudi Arabia) 23 E 4
Irrawaddy 41 G 4
Irrawaddy, Mouths of the 41 FG 4
Irrigi 62 CD 2
Irthlingborough 7 D 1
Irtuia 85 J 4
Irtysh 25 N 4
Irtysh 25 O 5
Irtyshskoye 25 O 5
Irumu 64 D 4
Irún 18 C 3
Irves Šaurums 17 H 4
Irvine 3 B 4
Irvinestown 4 B 2
Irving 77 G 5
Is, Jabal 60 EF 4
Isa 63 F 3
Isá Khel 35 J 4
Īsā, Ra's 61 G 5
Isabel 76 F 2
Isabela (Ecuador) 84 B 6
Ísafjörður 16 A 2
Isahaya 39 K 4
Isaka 64 E 5
Isakogorka 24 GH 3
Isalo, Massif de l' 67 H 4
Isandja 64 C 5
Isanga 64 C 5
Isangi 64 C 4
Isanlu Makatu 63 F 4
Isaouane N-Irharharene 59 G 3
Isar 15 F 5
Isayevskiy 36 G 1
Ischia 19 F 3
Iscia Baidoa → Isha Baydąbo
    65 G 4
Ise 39 L 4
Isefjord 17 F 4
Iséo, Lago d' 19 F 2
Isere 19 DE 2
Isernia 19 F 3
Iset' 25 M 4
Ise-wan 39 L 4
Iseyin 62 E 4
Isfahan → Esfahan (Iran) 23 F 2
Isfendiyar Dağlari 21 D 2
Isha Baydąbo 65 G 4
Isherim, Gora 25 L 3
Isherton 85 G 3
Ishigaki 39 H 6
Ishikari-wan 39 M 2
Ishikawa 39 J 5
Ishikhly 34 D 3
Ishim 25 N 4
Ishim 25 O 4
Ishimbay 24 L 5
Ishimskaya Step' 25 O 5
Ishinomaki 39 M 3
Ishkamish 35 H 3
Ishkashim 35 J 3
Ishull i Sazanit 20 A 2
Isigny-sur-Mer 18 C 2
Išiklar Dağı 20 C 2
Isikli Gölü 20 CD 3
Isil'kul 25 O 5
Isinga 36 K 5

Isiolo 65 F 4
Isipingo Beach 67 E 5–6
Isiro 64 D 4
Isisford 49 G 3
Isit' 37 N 3
Iskamen', Khrebet 72 B 2
Iskander 35 H 2
İskenderun 21 E 3
İskenderun (Turkey) 22 B 1
İskenderun Körfezi 21 E 3
İskenderun Körfezi (Turkey) 22 B 1
İskilip 21 D 2
Iskitim 25 Q 5
Iskup 25 R 3
Iskŭr 20 B 2
Iskushuban 65 J 2
Iskut River 72 L 4
Isla Ángel de la Guarda 76 D 6
Isla Aruba 84 E 1
Isla Bonaire 84 E 1
Isla Byron 89 A 8
Isla Campana 89 A 8
Isla Carmen 76 D 6
Isla Cedros 76 C 6
Isla Cerralvo 76 E 7
Isla Chao 84 C 5
Isla Clarence 89 B 9
Isla Curaçao 84 E 1
Isla Darwin 84 B 6
Isla Dawson 89 B 9
Isla de Altamura 76 E 7
Isla de Aves 79 K 4
Isla de Chiloé 89 B 7
Isla de Coiba 84 B 2
Isla de Cozumel 78 E 3
Isla de Guadelupe 76 C 6
Isla de la Juventud 78 F 3
Isla de los Estados 89 D 9
Isla de Margarita 85 F 1
Isla de Ometepe 78 EF 5
Isla de Providencia 79 F 5
Isla de San Ignacio 76 E 6
Isla de Santa Margarita 76 D 7
Isla de Vieques 79 JK 4
Isla del Coco 84 A 2
Isla del Maíz 78 F 5
Isla del Rey 84 C 2
Isla Desolación 89 AB 9
Isla Esmeralda 89 A 8
Isla Española 84 B 6
Isla Fernandina 84 B 6
Isla Genovesa 84 B 6
Isla Gorgona (Colombia) 84 C 3
Isla Grande de Tierra del Fuego 89 C 9
Isla Guafo 89 AB 7
Isla Guamblin 89 A 7
Isla Guañape 84 C 5
Isla Holbox 78 E 3
Isla Hoste 89 C 10
Isla Independencia 86 A 3
Isla Ipun 89 B 7
Isla Isabela (Ecuador) 84 B 6
Isla Jicarón 84 B 2
Isla Jorge Montt 89 AB 9
Isla La Blanquilla 85 F 1
Isla La Orchila 84 E 1
Isla La Tortuga 84 E 1
Isla Lennox 89 C 10
Isla Lobos de Tierra 84 B 5
Isla Los Roques 84 E 1
Isla Madre de Dios 89 AB 9
Isla Magdalena (Chile) 89 B 7
Isla Magdalena (Mexico) 76 D 7
Isla Malpelo 84 B 3
Isla Marchena 84 B 6
Isla Melchor 89 B 8
Isla Mocha 89 B 6
Isla Mona 79 J 4
Isla Montague 76 D 5
Isla Mornington 89 A 8
Isla Noir 89 B 9
Isla Nueva 89 C 10
Isla Picton 89 C 10
Isla Pinta 84 B 6
Isla Puna 84 B 4
Isla Riesco 89 B 9
Isla San Cristóbal 84 B 6
Isla San José 76 DE 6
Isla San Marcos 76 D 6
Isla San Salvador 84 B 6
Isla Sangayán 86 A 3
Isla Santa Cruz 84 B 6
Isla Santa Inés 89 B 9
Isla Santa María 84 B 6
Isla Stewart (Chile) 89 B 9
Isla Tiburon 76 D 6
Isla Tobago 85 F 1
Isla Trinidad (Argentina) 89 D 6
Isla Trinidad (Trinidad and Tobago) 85 F 1
Isla Wellington 89 AB 8
Isla Wolf 84 B 6
Isla-Cristina 18 B 4
Islamabad 35 J 4

Ísland 16 AB 3
Island Lake 73 T 5
Island Lake 73 T 5
Island Magee 4 C 2
Islands, Bay of 75 Q 6
Islands of Four Mountains 72 CD 5
Islas Baleares 18 D 3–4
Islas Canarias 58 B 3
Islas de la Bahía 78 E 4
Islas de los Riachos 89 D 6
Islas de Sotavento 79 JK 5
Islas de Sotavento 84 E 1
Islas del Cisne (Honduras) 78 F 4
Islas Diego Ramírez 89 BC 10
Islas Grafton 89 B 9
Islas Hanover 89 AB 9
Islas las Aves 84 E 1
Islas Lobos de Afuera 84 B 5
Islas los Hermanos 85 F 1
Islas los Monjes 84 D 1
Islas los Testigos 85 F 1
Islas Malvinas 89 DE 9
Islas Malvinas → Falkland Islands 89 DE 9
Islas Rennell 89 B 9
Islas Wollaston 89 C 10
Islay 3 A 4
Islay (Airport) 3 A 4
Isle 18 D 2
Isle of Man 4 C 2
Isle of Man (Airport) 4 C 2
Isle of Portland 6 C 2
Isle of Sheppey 7 E 2
Isle of Wight 7 D 2
Isle Royale 77 J 2
Isles of Scilly 6 A 3
Îsles Tristao 62 A 3
Islip 7 D 2
Islivig 2 A 2
Isluga 86 C 4
Ismailia → Al Ismā'īlīyah 60 E 2
Isnā 60 E 3
Isoka 64 E 6
Isole Egadi 19 F 4
Isole Eolie o Lipari 19 F 4
Isole Pelagie 59 H 1
Isole Ponziane 19 F 3
Isole Tremiti 19 G 3
Isosyöte 16 J 2
İsparta 20 D 3
İspir 21 F 2
Israel 22 B 3
Issano 85 G 2
Issia 62 C 4
Issoire 18 D 2
Issoudun 18 D 2
Issyk-Kul, Ozero 35 K 2
İstabūlat (Iraq) 22 D 2
İstanbul 20 C 2
İstanbul 20 C 2
İstanbul Boğazi 20 C 2
Isteren 16 F 3
Isthmus of Kra 41 G 5
Istiaía 20 B 3
Istmina 84 C 2
Istmo de Panamá 84 C 2
Istmo de Tehuantepec 78 D 4
Isto, Mount 72 J 2
Istra 19 F 2
Istria 20 C 2
Itabaiana (Paraíba, Brazil) 87 J 2
Itabaiana (Sergipe, Brazil) 87 J 3
Itabapoana 87 H 5
Itaberaba 87 H 3
Itabira 87 H 4
Itaboca 85 F 4
Itabuna 87 J 3
Itacaiúna 87 F 2
Itacajá 85 J 5
Itacarambi 87 H 3–4
Itacaré 87 J 3
Itacoatiara 85 G 4
Itaete 87 H 3
Itaguajé 87 F 5
Itaguí 84 C 2
Itaituba 85 G 4
Itajaí 88 G 4
Itaka 36 L 5
Italia 19 FG 3
Italy 19 F 3
Itamataré 85 J 4
Itambé 87 H 4
Itambé, Pico de 87 H 4
Itampolo 67 G 4
Itapaci 87 G 3
Itaparica 87 J 3
Itaparica, Ilha 87 J 3
Itapemirim 87 H 5
Itaperucu Mirim 87 H 1
Itaperuna 87 H 5
Itapetim 87 J 2
Itapetinga 87 HJ 4
Itapetininga 87 G 5
Itapicura 87 H 2
Itapinima 85 F 5
Itapipoca 87 J 1

Itapiranga (Amazonas, Brazil) 85 G 4
Itapiranga (Santa Catarina, Brazil) 88 F 4
Itapiúna 87 J 1
Itaporã 85 J 5
Itaporanga 87 J 2
Itaquari 87 H 5
Itaqui 88 E 4
Itaquyry 87 EF 5
Itararé 87 G 5
Itarsi 40 C 3
Itaruma 87 F 4
Itatupã 85 H 4
Itaum 87 EF 5
Itaúna 87 H 5
Itaúnas 87 J 4
Itbāy 60 F 4–5
Itchen Lake 73 P 2
Iténez 86 D 3
Iteshi-Teshi, Lake 66 D 3
Ithaca 77 L 3
Itháki 20 B 3
Ithnayn, Harrat 61 FG 3
Ithra (Saudi Arabia) 22 BC 3
Itigi 64 E 6
Itiquira 86 E 4
Itirucu 87 H 3
Itiúba, Serra de 87 HJ 3
Itivdleg 75 R 2
Itoko 64 C 5
Itongafeno 67 H 3
Itu 63 F 4
Itu Aba 42 D 1
Ituberá (Bahía, Brazil) 87 J 3
Ituí 84 D 5
Ituiutaba 87 G 4
Itula 64 D 5
Itumbiara 87 G 4
Itungi 64 E 6
Itupiranga 85 J 5
Iturama 87 F 4
Iturbe 86 C 5
Ituri 64 D 4
Iturup, Ostrov 37 R 6–7
Ituxi 84 E 5
Itzehoe 15 E 4
Iul'tin 72 B 2
Ivaí 87 F 5
Ivaíporã 87 F 5
Ivakoany, Massif de l' 67 H 4
Ivalo 16 J 2
Ivalojoki 16 J 2
Ivangorod 17 J 4
Ivangrad 20 A 2
Ivanhoe 49 G 5
Ivaničgrad 19 G 2
Ivanjska 19 G 3
Ivankov 24 E 5
Ivano-Frankovsk 24 D 6
Ivanovka 17 J 4
Ivanovka 24 K 5
Ivanovka 25 Q 6
Ivanovka 37 N 5
Ivanovo 24 H 4
Ivao, Gora 37 RS 6
Ivashka 37 U 4
Ivdel' 25 M 3
Ivigtut 75 S 3
Ivindo 63 G 5
Ivinheima 87 F 5
Ivohibe 67 H 4
Ivory Coast 62 CD 4
Ivory Coast 62 CD 5
Ivrea 19 E 2
Ivujivik 75 M 3
Iwaki 39 M 3
Iwakuni 39 K 4
Iwanai 39 M 2
Iwo 63 E 4
Iwo Jima 27 R 7
Iwŏn 39 J 2
Ixiamas 86 C 3
Ixtan 85 G 4
Ixworth 7 E 1
Iya 36 G 5
'Iyāl Bakhīt 60 D 6
Izamal Balankanche 78 E 3
Izberbash 34 D 2
Īzeh (Iran) 23 F 3
Izhevsk 24 K 4
Izhma 24 K 3
Izhorskaya Vozvyshennost' 17 J 4
Izkī 61 K 4
Izmail 20 C 1
İzmir 20 C 3
İzmir Körfezi 20 C 3
İzmit 20 C 2
İzmit Körfezi 20 C 2
İznik Gölü 20 C 2
Izobil'noye 21 F 1
Izozog, Bañados de 86 D 4
Iztočni Rodopi 20 C 2
Izuhara 39 J 4

Izu-shotō 39 M 4
Izyndy 34 F 1
Izyum 24 G 6

J

Jaala 16 J 3
Jaama 17 J 4
Jääsjärvi 16 J 3
Jabal Abadab 60 F 5
Jabal 'Abd al ' Azīz 61 F 1
Jabal 'Abd al 'Aziz 21 EF 3
Jabal 'Abd al 'Aziz (Syria) 22 C 2
Jabal 'Abd al 'Aziz (Syria) 22 C 2
Jabal Abū Hasan 61 G 5
Jabal Abū Rujmayn (Syria) 22 BC 2
Jabal Abyad 60 D 5
Jabal ad Dayr 60 E 6
Jabal ad Durūz (Syria) 22 B 2
Jabal Adhan (United Arab Emirates) 23 G 4
Jabal Ajā' (Saudi Arabia) 22 C 4
Jabal al 'Ajmah (Egypt) 22 A 3
Jabal al Akhdar 61 K 4
Jabal al Ansariye (Syria) 22 B 2
Jabal al Awliyā' 60 E 5
Jabal al Farāyid (Egypt) 22 B 5
Jabal al Ghurāb (Syria) 22 C 2
Jabal al Humara 60 E 5
Jabal al Kū' (Saudi Arabia) 23 E 4
Jabal al Lawz (Saudi Arabia) 22 B 3
Jabal al Ung 19 E 4
Jabal al 'Urf (Egypt) 22 A 4
Jabal al 'Uwaynāt 60 D 4
Jabal an Nabī Shu' ayb 61 G 5
Jabal an Nāmūs 59 J 3–4
Jabal an Nir (Saudi Arabia) 22 D 4–5
Jabal 'Anazah (Iraq) 22 C 2
Jabal Aqrin (Saudi Arabia) 22 C 3
Jabal Arkanū 59 K 4
Jabal as Hasāwinah 59 H 3
Jabal as Sawdā 59 HJ 3
Jabal as Sibā'ī (Egypt) 22 AB 4
Jabal ash Shām 61 K 4
Jabal ash Shām (Oman) 61 JK 5
Jabal ash Shām (Oman) 61 K 4
Jabal ash Shargī (Syria) 22 B 2
Jabal ash Shaykh (Lebanon) 22 B 2
Jabal ash Shifā' (Saudi Arabia) 22 B 3
Jabal Asoteriba 60 F 4
Jabal at Tanf (Syria) 22 C 2
Jabal at Tarhūni 59 K 4
Jabal at Tubayq (Saudi Arabia) 22 B 3
Jabal az Zannah (United Arab Emirates) 23 F 4
Jabal Bartazuga 60 E 4
Jabal Batrā (Saudi Arabia) 22 B 4
Jabal Bin Ghanīmah 59 J 3–4
Jabal Dabbāgh (Saudi Arabia) 22 B 4
Jabal Eigat 60 EF 4
Jabal Eigrim 60 F 5
Jabal Erba 60 F 4
Jabal Ghemi 64 E 3
Jabal Gumbiri 64 E 4
Jabal Gurgei 60 C 6
Jabal Habashīyah 61 J 5
Jabal Hadada 60 D 4
Jabal Hadid 59 K 4
Jabal Hafit (United Arab Emirates) 23 G 4
Jabal Hajhir 65 J 2
Jabal Hamātah (Egypt) 22 B 4
Jabal Hamoyet 60 F 5
Jabal Hamrīn (Iraq) 22–23 D 2
Jabal Harāzah 60 E 6
Jabal Haybān 60 E 6
Jabal Himā Dariyah (Saudi Arabia) 22 C 4
Jabal Ibrāhīm 61 G 4
Jabal Is 60 EF 4
Jabal Kātrīna (Egypt) 22 AB 3
Jabal Katul 60 D 6
Jabal Kinyeti 64 E 4
Jabal Kissū 60 D 4
Jabal Kurur 60 E 4
Jabal Lado 64 E 3
Jabal Lotuke 64 E 4
Jabal Lubnān (Lebanon) 22 B 2
Jabal Mahrāt 61 J 5
Jabal Manda 64 C 3
Jabal Marrah 60 C 6
Jabal Nafūsah 59 H 2
Jabal Natityāy 60 E 4
Jabal Nuqay 59 J 4
Jabal Nuqrus (Egypt) 22 B 4
Jabal Oda 60 F 4
Jabal Qarā' 61 J 5

Jabal Radwā (Saudi Arabia) 22 BC 4
Jabal Rāf (Saudi Arabia) 22 C 3
Jabal Rahib 60 D 5
Jabal Ramm (Jordan) 22 B 3
Jabal Sabidana 60 F 5
Jabal Sabīr 61 G 6
Jabal Sāq (Saudi Arabia) 22 D 4
Jabal Shā'ib al Banāt (Egypt) 22 A 4
Jabal Shammar (Saudi Arabia) 22 CD 4
Jabal Sharshar 60 E 4
Jabal Sinjār (Iraq) 22 C 1
Jabal Tageru 60 D 5
Jabal Teljo 60 D 6
Jabal Thāmir 61 H 6
Jabal Thanīyah 61 H 5
Jabal Tlētē Ouate Gharbī (Syria) 22 C 2
Jabal Tuwayq (Saudi Arabia) 23 D 4
Jabal Waddān 59 J 3
Jabal Yu 'Alliq (Egypt) 22 A 3
Jabalón 18 C 4
Jabalpur 40 CD 3
Jabālyah 22 B 3
Jabjabah, Wādī 60 E 4
Jablah (Syria) 22 B 2
Jablanica 19 G 3
Jablaničko Jezero 19 G 3
Jablonec 15 G 4
Jaboatão 87 J 2
Jaboticabal 87 G 5
Jabrīn (Iran) 23 F 4
Jabung, Tanjung 42 B 4
Jaburu 85 F 5
Jaca 18 C 3
Jacaré 85 H 4
Jacareacanga 85 G 5
Jacaretinga 85 G 5
Jacarézinho 87 G 5
Jáchal 88 C 4
Jaciara 87 F 4
Jaciparaná 85 F 5
Jack Mountain 76 B 2
Jackpot 76 D 3
Jacksboro 76 G 5
Jackson (MI, U.S.A.) 77 K 3
Jackson (MS, U.S.A.) 77 H 5
Jackson (TN, U.S.A.) 77 J 4
Jackson Head 50 P 9
Jackson Lake 76 D 3
Jackson, Mount (Antarctica) 91
Jackson, Mount (Western Australia) 48 B 5
Jacksonville (FL, U.S.A.) 77 K 5
Jacksonville (IL, U.S.A.) 77 J 4
Jacksonville (N.C., U.S.A.) 77 L 5
Jacksonville (TX, U.S.A.) 77 GH 5
Jacksonville Beach 77 K 5
Jacob Lake 76 D 4
Jacobabad 35 H 5
Jacobina 87 H 3
Jacona 78 B 4
Jacques Cartier, Détroit de 75 P 6
Jacuí 88 F 4
Jacuipe 87 HJ 3
Jacundá (Pará, Brazil) 85 H 4
Jacundá (Pará, Brazil) 85 J 4
J.A.D. Jensens Nunatakker 75 S 3
Jada 63 G 4
Jadal 63 E 2
Jadīd Ra's al Fīl 60 D 6
Jādū 59 H 2
Jaén 18 C 4
Jaffa → Tel Aviv-Yafo 60 E 2
Jaffa, Cape 49 F 6
Jaffna 40 D 6
Jafjaf as Saghīr 59 K 4
Jagdalpur 40 D 4
Jagdaqi 37 M 5
Jagersfontein 66 CD 5
Jaggang 40 C 4
Jagtial 40 C 4
Jaguaquara 87 J 3
Jaguarão 88 F 5
Jaguarari 87 HJ 3
Jaguari 88 F 4
Jaguariaíva 87 FG 5
Jaguaribe 87 J 2
Jaguaribe 87 J 2
Jagüé 88 C 4
Jahām, 'Irq 61 H 3
Jahrom (Iran) 23 F 3
Jaice 19 G 3
Jailo, Selat 43 G 3–4
Jailolo 43 G 3
Jailolo, Selat 43 G 4
Jaina 78 D 3
Jainca 38 D 3
Jaipur 40 C 2
Jaisalmer 40 B 2
Jājarm (Iran) 23 G 1
Jakarta 42 C 5

Jakhan 40 A 3
Jakobshavn 90
Jakobstad 16 H 3
Jakpa 63 EF 4
Jakupica 20 B 2
Jalaid Qi 39 H 1
Jalalabad 35 J 4
Jalalpur Pirwala 35 J 5
Jalapa 78 E 5
Jalapa Enríquez 78 C 4
Jalasjärvi 16 H 3
Jalaun 40 C 2
Jaldessa 65 G 3
Jales 87 F 5
Jalgaon 40 C 3
Jalib Shahab (Iraq) 23 DE 3
Jalībah (Iraq) 23 E 3
Jalingo 63 G 4
Jalisco 78 B 3
Jālitah 59 G 1
Jalkot 35 J 3
Jalna 40 C 4
Jalo Oasis → Wāhāt Jālū 59 K 3
Jalón 18 C 3
Jalor 40 B 2
Jalostotitlán 78 B 3
Jalpa 78 B 3
Jalpaiguri 40 E 2
Jālū 59 K 3
Jālū, Wāhāt 59 K 3
Jaluit 52 C 2
Jalūlā' (Iraq) 23 D 2
Jam (Iran) 23 F 4
Jam (Iran) 23 G 2
Jama 84 B 4
Jamaica 79 G 4
Jamaica Channel 79 GH 4
Jamalpur 41 F 3
Jamāme 65 G 4
Jamanixim 85 G 5
Jamari 85 F 5
Jamari 85 F 5
Jamba 66 B 2
Jambi 42 B 4
Jamboaye 42 A 3
Jambuair, Tanjung 42 A 2
Jambusar 40 B 3
James 76 G 3
James Bay 75 L 5
James River (VA, U.S.A.) 77 L 4
James Ross Strait 73 S 1–2
Jamestown (N.D., U.S.A.) 76 G 2
Jamestown (N.Y., U.S.A.) 77 L 3
Jamestown (South Australia)
   49 F 5
Jamiltepec 78 C 4
Jamkhandi 40 C 4
Jamkhed 40 C 4
Jammer Bugt 17 E 4
Jammu 35 K 4
Jammu and Kashmir 35 K 4
Jamnagar 40 B 3
Jampur 35 J 5
Jämsä 16 HJ 3
Jamsah (Egypt) 22 A 4
Jämsänkoski 16 HJ 3
Jamshedpur 40 E 3
Jämtland 16 F 3
Jamuna 40 E 2–3
Jamundí 84 C 3
Jan Mayen Island 90
Jan Mayen Ridge 98 A 1
Janā' 23 EF 4
Janakpur 40 E 2
Janaúba 87 H 4
Janaucu, 85 HJ 3
Jandaia 87 FG 4
Jandaq 34 E 4
Jandaq (Iran) 23 G 2
Jándula 18 C 4
Janesville 77 J 3
Janīn [Westbank] 22 B 2
Janjira 40 B 4
Jannatabad 35 G 3
Janos 76 E 5
Jansenville 66 C 6
Januária 87 H 4
Jaora 40 C 3
Japan 39 L 3
Japan, Sea of 39 KL 3
Japan Trench 99 C 2
Japiim 84 D 5
Japurá 84 E 4
Japurá 84 E 4
Japvo Mountain 41 F 2
Jaqué 84 C 2
Jarābulus (Syria) 22 C 1
Jaraguá 87 G 4
Jaramillo 89 C 8
Jarandilla 18 B 3
Jaranwala 35 J 4
Jarash (Jordan) 22 B 2
Jarbah 59 H 2
Jardim 86 E 5
Jardine River National Park 49 G 1

Jardines de la Reina, Archipiélago
   de los 79 FG 3
Jæren 17 E 4
Jærens rev 17 DE 4
Jargalant 38 FG 1
Jargalant → Hovd 36 F 6
Jari 85 H 3
Jarjīs 59 H 2
Jarlshof 2 D 2
Jarny 19 E 2
Jarocin 15 G 4
Jarosław 15 H 4
Järpen 16 F 3
Jarrahdale 47
Jarrow 5 E 2
Jartai 38 E 3
Jaru 86 D 3
Jarud Qi 39 H 2
Järvenpää 17 J 3
Jarvis 53 E 3
Järvsö 16 G 3
Jashpurnagar 40 D 3
Jasikan 62 E 4
Jasīra 65 H 4
Jāsk 34 F 5
Jasło 15 H 5
Jason Islands 89 D 9
Jasper 73 O 5
Jasper (AL, U.S.A.) 77 J 5
Jasper (TX, U.S.A.) 77 H 5
Jasper National Park 73 O 5
Jassan (Iraq) 23 D 2
Jastrzebie Zdrój 15 G 5
Jászberény 20 A 1
Jászság 20 AB 1
Jataí 87 F 4
Jatapu 85 G 4
Jath 40 C 4
Jatisiri, Pulau 42 E 4
Jativa 18 C 4
Jatobá 85 H 4
Jatobal 85 HJ 4
Jatuarana 85 F 5
Jaú (Amazonas, Brazil) 85 F 4
Jaú (São Paulo, Brazil) 87 G 5
Jaua, Meseta del Cerro 85 F 2–3
Jauaperi 85 F 3
Jauja 86 A 3
Jaumave 78 C 3
Jaunjelgava 17 J 4
Jaunpur 40 D 2
Jaupaci 87 F 4
Java 42 C 5
Java Sea 42 C 5
Java Trench 99 C 4
Javānrūd (Iran) 23 E 2
Javari 84 D 4
Jávea 18 D 4
Javhlant → Uliastay 36 G 6
Javor 20 A 2
Javorie 15 G 5
Javorie 20 A 1
Javorová skála 15 F 5
Jävre 16 H 2
Jawa 42 CD 5
Jawi 42 C 4
Jaya, Puncak 43 J 4
Jayanca 84 C 5
Jayapura 50 D 2
Jayawijaya, Pegunungan 43 J 4
Jāyezān (Iran) 23 E 3
Jazā' ir Farasān 61 G 5
Jazā' ir Khurīyā Murīya 61 K 5
Jazīrat Wādī Jimāl (Egypt) 22 B 4
Jazvān (Iran) 23 E 1
Jbel Ayachi 58 E 2
Jbel Bani 58 D 3
Jbel Igdet 58 D 2
Jbel Ighil Mgoun 58 D 2
Jbel Lekst 58 D 3
Jbel Mousaaou Salah 58 E 2
Jbel Ouarkziz 58 D 3
Jbel Sarhro 58 D 2
Jbel Tidirhine 58 E 2
Jbel Toubkal 58 D 2
Jebba 63 E 4
Jebel 59 K 3
Jeberos 84 C 5
Jeci 67 EF 2
Jedburgh 5 D 2
Jedda → Jiddah 61 F 4
Jedrzejów 15 H 4
Jefferson City 77 H 4
Jefferson, Mount (NV, U.S.A.)
   76 C 4
Jefferson, Mount (OR, U.S.A.)
   76 B 3
Jefferson River 76 D 2
Jega 63 E 3
Jēkabpils 17 J 4
Jelenia Góra 15 G 4
Jelgava 17 H 4
Jelica 20 B 2
Jelling 17 E 4
Jelow Gir (Iran) 23 E 2
Jemaja, Pulau 42 C 3

Jember 42 D 5
Jembongan 42 E 2
Jen 63 G 4
Jena 15 F 4
Jeneponto 43 E 5
Jenny 85 G 2
Jenny Lind Island 73 R 2
Jens Munk Island 75 L 2
Jequié 87 H 3
Jequitinhonha 87 H 4
Jequitinhonha 87 H 4
Jerada 58 E 2
Jérémie 79 H 4
Jeremoabo 87 J 3
Jerez de Garcia Salinas 78 B 3
Jerez de la Frontera 18 B 4
Jerez de los Caballeros 18 B 4
Jerik 43 H 4
Jerisjärvi 16 H 2
Jerome 76 D 3
Jerruck 35 H 5
Jersey 7 C 3
Jersey 14 C 5
Jersey (Airport) 7 C 3
Jerumenha 87 H 2
Jerusalem 22 B 3
Jervis Bay 49 J 6
Jesenice 19 F 2
Jesenice 19 G 3
Jessheim 17 F 3
Jessore 40 E 3
Ještěd 15 F 4
Jesup 77 K 5
Jesus Carranza 78 C 4
Jesús María 88 D 5
Jevnaker 17 F 3
Jeyhūn (Iran) 23 G 4
Jeypore 40 D 4
Jezercës 20 A 2
Jezioro Drawsko 15 G 4
Jezioro Gardno 15 G 4
Jezioro Gopło 15 G 4
Jezioro Jeziorak 15 G 4
Jezioro Koronowski 15 G 4
Jezioro Łebsko 15 G 4
Jezioro Mamry 15 H 4
Jezioro Miedwie 15 F 4
Jezioro Sniardwy 15 H 4
Jhabua 40 B 3
Jhalawar 40 C 3
Jhang Sadar 35 J 4
Jhansi 40 C 2
Jhelum 35 J 4
Jhelum 35 J 4
Jhunjhunu 40 C 2
Jia Xian 38 F 3
Jiahe 38 F 5
Jialing Jiang 38 E 4
Jiamusi 39 K 1
Ji'an 38 F 5
Ji'an (N. Korea) 39 J 2
Jianchang 39 GH 2
Jianchuan 38 CD 5
Jiande 39 G 5
Jiang'an 38 DE 5
Jiangao Shan 38 C 5
Jiangbiancun 38 G 5
Jiangcheng 38 D 6
Jiangchuan 38 D 6
Jiange 38 E 4
Jianghua 38 F 5
Jiangjin 38 E 5
Jiangle 39 G 5
Jiangling 38 F 4
Jiangmen 38 F 6
Jiangsu 39 GH 4
Jiangxi 38 G 5
Jiangyin 39 H 4
Jiangyong 38 F 5
Jiangyou 38 D 4
Jianli 38 F 5
Jianning 38 G 5
Jian'ou 39 G 5
Jianping 39 G 2
Jianshi 38 E 4
Jianshui 38 D 6
Jianyang 38 D 4
Jianyang 39 G 5
Jiaocheng 38 F 3
Jiaohe 39 J 2
Jiaonan 39 H 3
Jiaozuo 38 F 3
Jiashan 39 G 4
Jiashi 35 K 3
Jiaxing 39 H 4
Jiayin 37 O 6
Jiayu 38 F 5
Jiayuguan 38 C 3
Jibāl ash Sharāh (Jordan) 22 B 3
Jibiya 63 F 3
Jicarón, Isla 84 B 2
Jiddah 61 F 4
Jiddat al Harāsīs 61 K 4–5
Jidong 39 K 1
Jiekkevarre 16 GH 2
Jiešjavrre 16 HJ 2

Jiexi 38 G 6
Jiexiu 38 F 3
Jieyang 38 G 6
Jieznas 17 H 5
Jifārah Plain 59 H 2
Jiftūn (Egypt) 22 AB 4
Jigzhi 38 D 4
Jihlava 15 G 5
Jija Sarai 35 G 4
Jijel 59 G 1
Jijiga 65 G 3
Jijona 18 C 4
Jiloca 18 C 3
Jilin 39 HJ 2
Jilin 39 J 2
Jilin Hada Ling 39 J 2
Jiloca 18 C 3
Jimāl, Wādī (Egypt) 22 B 4
Jimbolia 20 B 1
Jimena de la Frontera 18 B 4
Jiménez 78 B 2
Jimma 65 F 3
Jimo 39 H 3
Jimsar 35 M 2
Jin Xian 38 G 3
Jin Xian 39 H 2
Jin Xian 39 H 3
Jinan 39 G 3
Jincheng 38 F 3
Jinchuan 38 D 4
Jind 40 C 2
Jing Xian 38 E 5
Jing Xian 39 G 4
Jingbian 38 E 3
Jingde 39 G 4
Jingdezhen 39 G 5
Jinggu 38 D 6
Jinghai 39 G 3
Jinghong 38 D 6
Jingle 38 F 3
Jingmen 38 F 4
Jingning 38 E 3
Jingpo Hu 39 J 2
Jingtai 38 D 3
Jingyu 39 J 2
Jingyuan 38 D 3
Jinhua 39 GH 5
Jining 38 F 2
Jining 39 G 3
Jinja 64 E 4
Jinkouhe 38 D 5
Jinotega 78 E 5
Jinotepe 78 E 5
Jinping 38 D 6
Jinping 38 E 5
Jinsha 38 E 5
Jinsha Jiang 38 D 5
Jinshan 39 H 4
Jinshi 38 F 5
Jinst 38 D 1
Jinta 38 C 3
Jinxi 39 H 2
Jinxiang 39 G 3–4
Jinyang 38 D 5
Jinzhai 38 G 4
Jinzhou 39 H 2
Jiparaná 85 F 5
Jipijapa 84 B 4
Jirjā 60 E 3
Jirwān (Saudi Arabia) 23 F 5
Jishan 38 F 3
Jishou 38 E 5
Jishui 38 G 5
Jisr ash Shughūr (Syria) 22 B 2
Jiu 20 B 2
Jiujiang 38 G 5
Jiulong 38 D 5
Jiuquan 38 C 3
Jiutai 39 J 2
Jiwani, Ras 35 G 6
Jiwen 37 M 5
Jixi 39 K 1
Jize 38 FG 3
Joaçaba 88 F 4
Joal-Fadiout 62 A 3
Joanes 85 J 4
Joanésia 87 H 4
João Pessoa 87 K 2
João Pinheiro 87 G 4
Joaquín V. González 88 D 4
Jódar 18 C 4
Jodhpur 40 B 2
Joensuu 16 JK 3
Jōetsu 39 L 3
Jōgeva 17 J 4
Joghatāy (Iran) 23 G 1
Joghatāy, Kūh-e (Iran) 23 G 1
Johannesburg 66 D 5
John Day 76 C 3
John Day River 76 C 3
John, Mount 48 D 2
John o' Groats 2 C 2
Johnshaven 3 D 3
Johnson 76 F 4

Johnson City (TN, U.S.A.) 77 K 4
Johnson City (TX, U.S.A.) 76 G 5
Johnsonburg 77 L 3
Johnsons Crossing 72 L 3
Johnston (Pacific Ocean, U.S.A.)
   52 D 1
Johnston (U.K.) 6 B 2
Johnstone 3 B 4
Johnstonebridge 3 C 4
Johnstown 4 B 3
Johnstown 77 L 3
Johor Baharu 42 B 3
Joigny 18 D 2
Joinville 88 G 4
Joinville 19 DE 2
Joinville Island 91
Jokk 16 H 2
Jokkmokk 16 GH 2
Jökulsá 16 B 2–3
Jökulsá á Dal 16 BC 2
Jökulsá á Fjöllum 16 B 2
Jolfa 34 D 3
Joliette 75 N 6
Jolo 43 F 2
Jolo Island 43 F 2
Jombang 42 D 5
Jomda 38 C 4
Jonava 17 H 4
Jonê 38 D 4
Jones, Cape 73 T 3
Jonesboro 77 H 4
Jonglei 64 E 3
Jonglei Canal 64 E 3
Jonk 40 D 3
Jönköping 17 F 4
Jonquière 75 N 6
Jontoy 65 G 5
Jonuta 78 D 4
Joplin 77 H 4
Jordan 22 B 2–3
Jordan 22 B 3
Jordan (MT, U.S.A.) 76 E 2
Jordan Valley 76 C 3
Jordânia 87 HJ 4
Jorge Montt, Isla 89 AB 9
Jorhat 41 F 2
Jörn 16 H 2
Joroinen 16 J 3
Jørpeland 17 E 4
Jos 63 F 4
Jos Plateau 63 F 4
Jos Sodarso, Pulau 43 J 5
José de San Martín 89 B 7
Joseph Bonaparte Gulf 48 D 1
Joseph Lake 75 O 5
Josephstaal 50 E 2
Joshua Tree National Monument
   76 C 5
Josselin 18 C 2
Jostedalen 16 E 3
Jostedalsbreen 16 E 3
Jotunheimen 16 E 3
Joutsa 16 J 3
Joutseno 16 J 3
Jow Kār (Iran) 23 E 2
Jōwhar 65 H 4
Jreïda 58 B 5
Ju Xian 39 G 3
Juaba 85 J 4
Juan Aldama 78 B 3
Juan de Nova 67 G 3
Juan Fernández Islands 81 B 6
Juan José 88 D 4
Juan L. Lacaze 88 E 5
Juancheng 38 G 3
Juanjuí 84 C 5
Juankoski 16 J 3
Juárez 89 E 6
Juarez, Ciudad 76 E 5
Juarez, Sierra de 76 C 5
Juarzon 62 C 4
Juàzeiro 87 H 2
Juàzeiro do Norte 87 J 2
Juba (Somalia) 65 G 4
Jūbā (Sudan) 64 E 4
Jubaland 65 G 4
Jubayl (Egypt) 22 A 3
Jubayl (Lebanon) 22 B 2
Jubayt 60 F 5
Jubayt 60 F 5
Jubbah (Saudi Arabia) 22 C 3
Jubilee Lake 48 D 4
Jubileo 88 E 5
Juby, Cap 58 C 3
Júcar 18 C 4
Juçara 87 F 4
Juchitan de Zaragoza 78 D 4
Jucurucú 87 J 4
Judayyīdat al Hamīr (Saudi Arabia)
   22 C 3
Judayyidat 'Ar'ar (Saudi Arabia)
   22 C 3
Juelsminde 17 F 4
Jugoslavija → Yugoslavia 19 G 3
Juhaym (Iraq) 23 D 3
Juigalpa 78 E 5

Juiz de Fora 87 H 5
Juktån 16 G 2
Julaca 86 C 5
Juli 86 C 4
Julia Creek 49 G 3
Juliaca 86 B 4
Julianatop 85 G 3
Julianehåb 75 S 3
Julimes 76 E 6
Jullundur 40 C 1
Jumanggoin 38 C 4
Jumayrah (United Arab Emirates) 23 G 4
Jumbo 65 G 5
Jumilla 18 C 4
Jumla 40 D 2
Jun Bulen 39 G 1
Jun Xian 38 F 4
Junagadh 40 B 3
Junagarh 40 D 4
Junan 39 G 3
Junction 76 G 5
Junction City 77 G 4
Jundah 49 G 3
Jundiaí 87 G 5
Jundûbah 59 G 1
Juneau 72 L 4
Junee 49 H 5
Jungar Qi 38 F 3
Junggar Pendi 35 M 1
Junín (Argentina) 88 D 5
Junín (Chile) 86 B 4
Junín (Peru) 86 A 3
Junín de los Andes 89 B 6–7
Junín, Lago de 86 A 3
Jûniyah (Lebanon) 22 B 2
Junlian 38 D 5
Junosuando 16 H 2
Junqueiro 87 J 2
Junsele 16 G 3
Juoksengi 16 H 2
Jupiá, Reprêsa de 87 F 5
Juquiá 87 G 5
Jura (Switzerland) 19 E 2
Jura (U.K.) 3 B 3
Juradó 84 C 2
Juratishki 17 J 5
Juraybî'at (Iraq) 23 D 3
Juraybî'at (Saudi Arabia) 23 E 4
Jurbarkas 17 H 4
Jurby Head 4 C 2
Jurhen Ul Shan 38 B 4
Jurien Bay 48 A 5
Jurm 35 J 3
Jûrmala 17 H 4
Juruá 84 E 4
Juruá (Amazonas, Brazil) 84 E 4
Juruena 86 E 3
Juruena 86 E 3
Jurumirim, Reprêsa de 87 G 5
Juruti 85 G 4
Justo Daract 88 C 5
Jutaí (Amazonas, Brazil) 84 E 4
Jutaí (Amazonas, Brazil) 84 E 5
Jutiapa 78 E 5
Juticalpa 78 E 5
Jutland 17 E 4
Juuka 16 J 3
Juva 16 J 3
Juventud, Isla de la 78 F 3
Jûybår (Iran) 23 F 1
Jûyom (Iran) 23 FG 3
Južhni Rodopi 20 C 2
Juzna Morava 20 B 3
Juzur Qarqannah 59 H 2
Jylland 17 E 4
Jyväskylä 16 J 3

K

Kaabong 64 E 4
Kaakhka 34 F 3
Kaamanen 16 J 2
Kaarta 62 C 3
Kaba 43 J 5
Kabaena, Pulau 43 F 5
Kabakly 35 G 3
Kabala 62 B 4
Kabale 64 D 5
Kabalebo Reservoir 85 G 3
Kabali 43 F 4
Kabalo 64 D 6
Kabambare 64 D 5
Kabanjahe 42 A 3
Kabanovka 24 K 5
Kaban'ya 37 P 6
Kabardinka 21 E 2
Kabare 64 D 5
Kabarega Falls 64 E 4
Kabasalan 43 F 2
Kåbåw 59 H 2
Kabba 63 F 4
Kåbdalis 16 G 2
Kaberamaido 64 E 4
Kabinakagami Lake 74 L 6

Kabinda 64 C 6
Kabîr Kûh (Iran) 23 E 2
Kabkåbîyah 60 C 6
Kabna 60 E 5
Kabo 64 B 3
Kabompo 66 C 2
Kabompo 66 C 2
Kabondo Dianda 64 D 6
Kabongo 64 D 6
Kabûd Råhang (Iran) 23 E 2
Kabûdîyåh, Ra's 59 H 1
Kabul 35 H 4
Kabuli 50 E 2
Kabunda 66 D 2
Kabushiya 60 E 5
Kabwe 66 D 2
Kabwe Katanda 64 C 6
Kabylie 59 G 1
Kacha 21 D 2
Kacha Kuh 35 G 5
Kachalinskaya 24 H 6
Kaché 63 H 3
Kachia 63 F 4
Kachikattsy 37 NO 3
Kachikau 66 C 4
Kachin 41 G 2
Kachiry 25 P 5
Kachkanar 25 L 4
Kachreti 21 G 2
Kachug 36 J 5
Kaçkar Dagı 21 F 2
Kada 63 H 2
Kadali 36 K 4
Kadan Kyun 41 G 5
Kade 62 D 4
Kadeï 64 B 4
Kadiana 62 C 3
Kadina 49 F 5
Kadinhanı 21 D 3
Kadiolo 62 C 3
Kadiri 40 C 5
Kadirli 21 E 3
Kadiyevka 21 E 1
Kadmat 40 B 5
Kadoka 76 F 3
Kadoma 66 D 3
Kadonkani 41 G 4
Kåduglî 60 D 6
Kaduna 63 F 3
Kadur 40 C 5
Kadusam 41 G 2
Kadyr-Egi-Tayga, Khrebet 36 G 5
Kadzherom 24 L 3
Kaédi 58 C 5
Kaélé 63 G 3
Kaesõng 39 J 3
Kåf (Saudi Arabia) 22 B 3
Kafakumba 64 C 6
Kafan 34 D 3
Kafanchan 63 F 4
Kaffrine 62 A 3
Kafia Kingi 64 C 3
Kafirévs, Åkra 20 B 3
Kafirévs, Åkra 20 BC 3
Kafta 65 F 2
Kafu 64 E 4
Kafue 66 D 2
Kafue 66 D 3
Kafue Dam 66 D 3
Kafue National Park 66 D 3
Kafue National Park 66 D 3
Kafulwe 66 D 1
Kafura 64 E 5
Kaga 39 L 3
Kaga Bandoro 64 B 3
Kagalaska 72 B 5
Kagal'nitskaya 21 EF 1
Kagaluk 75 P 4
Kagan 35 G 3
Kagera 64 E 5
Kağızman 21 F 2
Kagmar 60 E 6
Kagoshima 39 JK 4
Kagua 50 D 3
Kagul 20 C 1
Kahak (Iran) 23 E 1
Kahal Tabelbala 58 E 3
Kahama 64 E 5
Kahan 35 H 5
Kahe 65 F 5
Kahemba 64 B 6
Kahia 64 D 6
Kahoolawe 53 E 1
Kahramanmaraş 21 E 3
Kahrûyeh (Iran) 23 F 3
Kai Besar, Pulau 43 H 5
Kai Kecil, Pulau 43 H 5
Kai, Kepulauan 43 H 5
Kai Xian 38 E 4
Kaiama 63 E 4
Kaibobo 43 G 4
Kaidu He 35 M 2
Kaieteur Falls 85 G 2
Kaifeng 38 FG 4
Kaikohe 51 Q 8
Kaikoura 51 Q 9

Kailahun 62 B 4
Kaili 38 E 5
Kailu 39 H 2
Kaimana 43 H 4
Kaimur Range 40 D 3
Kainantu 50 E 3
Kainji Dam 63 EF 4
Kainji Reservoir 63 E 3
Kaintragarh 40 D 3
Kaipara Harbour 51 Q 8
Kaiping 38 F 6
Kairouan → Al Qayrawån 59 GH 1
Kairuku 50 E 3
Kaiserslautern 15 E 5
Kaitaia 51 Q 8
Kaithal 40 C 2
Kaiti 65 F 5
Kaitumälven 16 G 2
Kaiwatu 43 G 5
Kaiyang 38 E 5
Kaiyuan 38 D 6
Kaiyuan 39 H 2
Kaiyuh Mountains 72 F 3
Kajaani 16 J 3
Kajabbi 49 G 3
Kajaki Dam 35 H 4
Kajiado 65 F 5
Kajo Kaji 64 E 4
Kajura 63 F 3
Kaka (Ethiopia) 65 F 3
Kåkå (Sudan) 60 E 6
Kakada 63 H 2
Kakamas 66 C 5
Kakamega 64 EF 4
Kakana 41 F 6
Kakata 62 BC 4
Kakdwip 40 E 3
Kakenge 64 C 5
Kakhonak 72 G 4
Kakhovka 21 D 1
Kakhovskoye Vodokhranilishche 21 D 1
Kakhtana 37 T 4
Kåkî (Iran) 23 E 1
Kakinada 40 D 4
Kakisa 73 O 3
Kakisa Lake 73 O 3
Kakonko 64 E 5
Kakpin 62 D 4
Kaktovik 72 J 1
Kakuma 64 F 4
Kakumbi 67 E 2
Kakya 65 F 5
Kala 64 E 6
Kalabagh 35 J 4
Kalabahi 43 F 5
Kalabáka 20 B 3
Kalabakan 42 E 3
Kalabana 62 C 3
Kalabo 66 C 3
Kalach 24 H 5
Kalachinsk 25 O 4
Kalach-na-Donu 24 H 6
Kaladan 41 F 3
Kaladan 41 F 3
Kalahari 66 C 4
Kalahari Gemsbok National Park 66 C 5
Kalahasti 40 CD 5
Kalai-Khumb 35 J 3
Kalai-Mor 35 G 3
Kalajoki 16 H 3
Kalakan 36 L 4
Kalámai 20 B 3
Kalamazoo 77 J 3
Kalambo Falls 64 E 6
Kalamitskiy Zaliv 21 D 2
Kalampising 42 E 3
Kalanchak 21 D 1
Kalanshiyû 59 K 3
Kalao, Pulau 43 F 5
Kalaong 43 F 2
Kalaotoa, Pulau 43 F 5
Kalar 36 L 4
Kalar 36 L 4
Kalarash 20 C 1
Kalasin (Indonesia) 42 D 3
Kalasin (Thailand) 41 H 4
Kalat 40 A 2
Kalåteh (Iran) 23 G 1
Kalaus 21 F 2
Kalavárdha 20 C 3
Kalávrita 20 B 3
Kalaw 41 G 3
Kalbarri 48 A 4
Kalbarri National Park 48 A 4
Kalbinskiy Khrebet 25 Q 6
Kaldbakur 16 A 2
Kaldfarnes 16 G 2
Kale 20 C 3
Kale (Turkey) 20 D 3
Kale (Turkey) 21 E 2
Kale (Turkey) 21 E 3
Kål-e Shûr 34 F 3

Kalecik 21 D 2
Kalegauk 41 G 4
Kalehe 64 D 5
Kalemie 64 D 6
Kalemyo 41 F 3
Kalene Hill 66 C 2
Kalevala 16 K 2
Kalewa 41 F 3
Kalgа 36 L 5
Kalgoorlie 48 C 5
Kali 40 D 2
Kalianda 42 C 5
Kaliganj 41 F 3
Kalima 64 D 5
Kalimantan 42 DE 3
Kálimnos 20 C 3
Kálimnos 20 C 3
Kalingapatam 40 D 4
Kalinin 24 G 4
Kalinin 34 F 2
Kaliningrad 17 H 5
Kalinino 21 F 2
Kalinkovichi 17 J 5
Kalinovik 19 G 3
Kaliro 64 E 4
Kalis 65 H 3
Kalispell 76 D 2
Kalix 16 H 2
Kalixälven 16 H 2
Kalkah 49 G 1
Kalkan 20 C 3
Kalkfeld 66 B 4
Kalkfontein 66 C 4
Kalkrand 66 B 4
Kall 16 F 3
Kallaktjåkkå 16 G 2
Kallavesi 16 J 3
Kallinge 17 G 4
Kallonis, Kólpos 20 C 3
Kallsjön 16 F 3
Kalmar 17 G 4
Kalmarsund 17 G 4
Kalmykovo 34 E 1
Kalni 41 F 3
Kalnik 19 G 2
Kaloko 64 D 6
Kalol 40 B 3
Kalole 64 D 5
Kalolio 43 F 4
Kalomo 66 D 3
Kalpa 40 C 1
Kalpákion 20 B 3
Kalpeni 40 B 5
Kalpi 40 C 2
Kalpin 35 K 2
Kalskag 72 F 3
Kalsubai 40 B 4
Kaltag 72 F 3
Kaltungo 63 G 4
Kalukalukuang, Pulau 42 E 5
Kalulushi 66 D 2
Kalumburu 48 D 1
Kalundborg 17 F 4
Kalush 24 D 6
Kalutara 40 C 6
Kalvarija 17 H 5
Kalya 25 L 3
Kalya 64 D 6
Kalyazin 24 G 4
Kam Summa 65 G 4
Kama (U.S.S.R.) 24 K 4
Kama (Zaire) 64 D 5
Kamaï 59 J 4
Kamaishi 39 M 3
Kamal 42 D 5
Kamalampa 64 E 6
Kamalia 51 J 4
Kaman 21 D 3
Kamanjab 66 B 3
Kamanyola 64 D 5
Kamarån 61 G 5
Kamaran, Hadjer 63 J 3
Kamard 35 H 3
Kamareddi 40 C 4
Kamaria Falls 85 G 2
Kamashi 35 H 3
Kambalda 48 C 5
Kambal'naya Sopka 37 T 5
Kambanós, Åkra 20 BC 3
Kambia 62 B 4
Kambove 66 D 2
Kambuno, Bukit 43 EF 4
Kambût 59 K 2
Kamchatka 37 TU 4
Kamchatka, Poluostrov 37 S 4–5
Kamchatskiy Poluostrov 37 U 4
Kamchatskiy Zaliv 37 U 4
Kamčija 20 C 2
Kamčiyska Plato 20 C 2
Kamen, Gora 36 FG 2

Kamende 64 C 6
Kamenets-Podolskiy 20 C 1
Kamenjak, Rt 19 F 3
Kamenka 24 G 5
Kamenka 24 H 2
Kamenka 24 H 5
Kamenka 36 G 4
Kamen-na-Obi 25 Q 5
Kamennogorsk 16 J 3
Kamennomostskiy 21 F 2
Kamennoye, Ozero 16 K 3
Kamennyy, Khrebet 37 UV 3
Kamenolomni 21 EF 1
Kamensk 36 J 5
Kamenskoye 37 V 3
Kamensk-Shakhtinskiy 21 F 1
Kamensk-Ural'skiy 25 M 4
Kames 3 B 4
Kameshki 37 U 3
Kamet 40 D 1
Kamieskroon 66 B 6
Kamileroi (Queensland, Austr.) 49 H 2
Kamina 64 D 6
Kaminak Lake 73 S 3
Kaminuriak Lake 73 S 3
Kamituga 64 D 5
Kamkaly 35 J 2
Kamla 40 E 2
Kamloops 73 N 5
Kamnik 19 F 2
Kamnrokan 36 K 4
Kamo 21 FG 2
Kamoa Mountains 85 G 3
Kampala 64 E 4
Kampanda 66 C 2
Kampar 42 B 3
Kampar, Sungai 42 B 3
Kampen 14 E 4
Kampene 64 D 5
Kamphaeng Phet 41 G 4
Kampot 41 H 5
Kamptee 40 C 3
Kampti 62 D 4
Kampuchea 41 HJ 5
Kampungtengah 42 D 4
Kamsack 73 R 5
Kamsar 62 B 3
Kamskoye Vodokhranilishche 24 L 4
Kamundan 41 H 4
Kåmyårån (Iran) 23 E 2
Kamyshevatskaya 21 E 1
Kamyshin 24 HJ 5
Kamyshlov 25 M 4
Kamyshnyy 25 M 5
Kamyshovaya Bukhta 21 D 2
Kamyzyak 34 D 1
Kan (Burma) 41 F 3
Kan (Iran) 23 F 2
Kan (Sudan) 64 E 3
Kan (U.S.S.R.) 36 G 4
Kanaapscow 75 M 5
Kanab 76 D 4
Kanaga 72 B 5
Kanairiktok 75 P 5
Kanå'is, Ra's al 60 D 2
Kananga 64 C 6
Kanangra Boyd National Park 49 H 5
Kanayka 25 Q 6
Kanazawa 39 L 3
Kanbalu 41 G 3
Kanchanaburi 41 G 5
Kanchipuram 40 CD 5
Kandagach 34 F 1
Kandahar 35 H 4
Kandalaksha 16 K 2
Kandalakshskaya Guba 16 K 2
Kandale 64 B 6
Kandangan 42 DE 4
Kandavu 52 C 4
Kande 62 E 4
Kandi 62 E 3
Kandi, Tanjung 43 F 3
Kandıra 20 D 2
Kandla 40 B 3
Kandovån, Gardaneh-ye (Iran) 23 F 1
Kandreho 67 H 3
Kandrian 51 EF 3
Kandukur 40 CD 4
Kandy 40 D 6
Kandychan 37 RS 3
Kane Fracture Zone 98 A 2–3
Kanem 63 GH 3
Kane Xian 38 E 4
Kanga 65 F 6
Kangaba 62 C 3
Kangal 21 E 3
Kangalassy 37 N 3
Kangâmiut 75 R 2
Kangån 34 F 5

Kangan (Iran) 23 F 4
Kangan (Iran) 23 F 4
Kangar 42 B 2
Kangare 62 C 3
Kangaroo Island 49 F 6
Kangasala 16 H 3
Kangasniemi 16 J 3
Kangävar (Iran) 23 E 2
Kangaz 20 C 1
Kangbao 38 F 2
Kangchenjunga 40 E 2
Kangding 38 D 5
Kangean, Kepulauan 42 E 5
Kangeeak Point 75 P 2
Kangen 64 E 3
Kangerlussuaq 75 RS 2
Kangetet 65 F 4
Kanggup'o 39 J 2
Kanggye 39 J 2
Kangle 38 D 3
Kangmar 40 E 1
Kangmar 40 E 2
Kangnŭng 39 J 3
Kango 63 G 5
Kangping 39 H 2
Kangrinboqe Feng 40 D 1
Kangto 41 F 2
Kangynin 72 B 2
Kanhan 40 C 3
Kani 62 C 4
Kaniama 64 C 6
Kaniet Islands 50 E 2
Kanigiri 40 C 4
Kanin Nos 24 H 2
Kanin Nos, Mys 24 H 2
Kanin, Poluostrov 24 HJ 2
Kaningo 65 F 5
Kaninskiy Bereg 24 H 2
Kanioumé 62 D 2
Kanjiža 20 B 1
Kankaanpää 16 H 3
Kankakee 77 J 3
Kankan 62 C 3
Kanker 40 D 3
Kankesanturai 40 D 6
Kankossa 58 C 5
Kankunskiy 37 N 4
Kanmaw Kyun 41 G 5
Kannapolis 77 KL 4
Kannauj 40 CD 2
Kannonkoski 16 J 3
Kannus 16 H 3
Kano 63 F 3
Kanona 67 E 2
Kanovlei 66 B 3
Kanowit 42 D 3
Kanoya 39 K 4
Kanozero, Ozero 16 K 2
Kanpur 40 CD 2
Kansanshi 66 D 2
Kansas 76 G 4
Kansas City 77 H 4
Kansk 36 G 4
Kansŏng 39 J 3
Kantang 41 G 6
Kantaralak 41 H 5
Kantchari 62 E 3
Kantche 63 F 3
Kantemirovka 24 G 6
Kantishna 72 G 3
Kanturk 14 B 4
Kanuku Mountains 85 G 3
Kanye 66 CD 4
Kanyu 66 C 4
Kanzenze 66 D 2
Kaohsiung 39 GH 6
Kaolack 62 A 3
Kaoma 66 C 2
Kaouadja 64 C 3
Kaouar 63 G 2
Kap Arkona 15 F 4
Kap Brewster 90
Kap Cort Adelaer 75 T 3
Kap Farvel 75 T 4
Kapanga 64 C 6
Kapar (Iran) 23 E 1
Kaparhã (Iran) 23 E 3
Kapatu 67 E 1
Kapchagay 35 K 2
Kapchagayskoye
  Vodokhranilishche 35 K 2
Kapfenberg 19 G 2
Kapıdağı Yarımadası 20 C 2
Kapili 41 F 2
Kapingamarangi 52 B 2
Kapiri Moposhi 66 D 2
Kapisigdlit 75 RS 3
Kapiskau 74 L 5
Kapit 42 D 3
Kapitanskaya Zaseka 37 PQ 3
Kapitonovka 24 F 6
Kapka, Massif du 63 J 2
Kapoe 41 G 6
Kapoeta 64 E 4
Kapombo 66 C 2
Kapona 64 D 6

Kaposvár 20 A 1
Kapp 17 F 3
Kapsukas 17 H 5
Kapterko 63 J 2
Kapuas, Sungai 42 C 4
Kapuas, Sungai 42 D 4
Kapuskasing 74 L 6
Kapustoye 16 K 2
Kaputir 64 F 4
Kara 25 MN 2
Kara 25 MN 2
Kara Dağ 21 D 3
Kara Dağı 21 EF 3
Kara Sea 25 M 1
Kara Tepe 21 D 3
Kara-Balty 35 J 2
Karabas 25 O 6
Karabas 25 P 6
Karabekaul 35 G 3
Karabiga 20 C 2
Karabil', Vozvyshennost' 35 G 3
Kara-Bogaz-Gol,Zaliv 34 E 2
Karabük 21 D 2
Karabulak 25 Q 6
Karabutak 34 G 1
Karaca Dağ 21 E 3
Karacaköy 20 C 2
Karacapey 20 C 2
Karacasu 20 C 3
Karachayevsk 21 F 2
Karachev 24 FG 5
Karachi 35 H 6
Karad 40 B 4
Karadoruk 21 E 3
Karadzha 21 D 1
Karaftit 36 K 5
Karaga 37 U 4
Karagan 36 M 5
Karaganda 25 O 6
Karagayly 25 P 6
Karaginskiy, Ostrov 37 U 4
Karaginskiy Zaliv 37 U 4
Karagüney Dağları 21 DE 2
Karaikkudi 40 C 5
Karaisalı 21 E 3
Karaitivu 40 C 6
Karaj 34 E 3
Karaj (Iran) 23 F 2
Kara-Kala 34 F 3
Karakax He 35 K 3
Karakeçi 21 E 3
Karakelong, Pulau 43 G 3
Karakoçan 21 F 3
Karakoin, Ozero 35 H 1
Karakolka 35 K 2
Karakoram 35 JK 3–4
Karakore 65 G 2
Karakorum 36 H 6
Karakorum Shankou 35 K 3
Karaköse 21 F 3
Karakuduk 25 P 5
Karakul' 35 G 3
Karakul' 35 J 3
Karakum, Peski 34 E 1
Karakumskiy Kanal 35 G 3
Karakumy, Peski 34–35 FG 3–4
Karakuwisa 66 B 3
Karalundi 48 B 4
Karam 36 J 4
Karamagay 35 M 1
Karaman 21 D 3
Karamay 35 L 1
Karamea 51 Q 9
Karamea Bight 51 Q 9
Karamet Niyaz 35 G 3
Karamıkbataklığı 20 D 3
Karamiran He 35 M 3
Karamiran Shankou 35 M 3
Karamysheva 36 GH 4
Karān (Saudi Arabia) 23 EF 4
Karand (Iran) 23 E 2
Karapınar 21 D 3
Karasburg 66 B 5
Karashoky 25 P 5
Karasjåkka 16 H 2
Karasjok 16 HJ 3
Karasu (Turkey) 20 D 2
Karasu (Turkey) 21 F 3
Karasu-Aras Dağları 21 F 3
Karasuk 25 P 5
Karatal 25 P 6
Karatan 25 R 6
Karataş 25 K 5
Karataş (Turkey) 22 B 1
Karataş Burnu 21 DE 3
Karatau 35 J 2
Karatau, Khrebet 35 H 2
Karatepe 21 E 3
Karathuri 41 G 5
Karatj 16 G 2
Karatobe 34 E 1
Karatogay 34 F 1
Karaton 34 E 1
Karaul 25 Q 1
Karauli 40 C 2

Karaulkel'dy 34 F 1
Karavat 51 F 2
Karawa 64 C 4
Karawang 42 C 5
Karayulgun 35 L 2
Karazhal 25 O 6
Karazhingil 25 O 6
Karbalā' (Iraq) 22 D 2
Kårböle 16 FG 3
Karcag 20 B 1
Karchyk, Poluostrov 37 V 2
Kardhámila 20 C 3
Kardhítsa 20 B 3
Kärdla 17 H 4
Kareliya 16 K 3
Karema 64 E 6
Karen 41 F 5
Karen 41 G 4
Karenga 36 L 5
Karepino 24 L 3
Karesuando 16 H 2
Karet 58 D 4
Kargalinskaya 21 G 2
Karganay 37 X 2
Kargasok 25 Q 4
Kargat 25 Q 4
Kargı 21 D 2
Kargil 35 K 4
Kargopol' 24 G 3
Karhijärvi 16 H 3
Kari 63 G 3
Kariai 20 B 2
Kariba 66 D 3
Kariba Dam 66 D 3
Kariba, Lake 66 D 3
Karibib 66 B 4
Karigasniemi 16 J 2
Karikal 40 C 5
Karimata, Pulau 42 C 4
Karimata, Selat 42 C 4
Karimganj 41 F 3
Karimnagar 40 C 4
Karimunjawa, Pulau 42 D 5
Karin 65 H 2
Karin 65 H 2
Karis 17 H 3
Karisimbi 64 D 5
Káristos 20 B 3
Karjaa 17 H 3
Karjala 16 K 3
Karkabat 65 F 1
Karkar 50 E 2
Karkār 65 H 3
Karkaralinsk 25 OP 6
Karkas, Kūh-e (Iran) 23 F 2
Karkheh (Iran) 23 E 2
Karkinitskiy Zaliv 21 D 1
Karkūmā, Ra's (Saudi Arabia)
  22 B 4
Karla Marksa, Pik 35 J 3
Karleby 16 H 3
Karlik Shan 38 B 2
Karlino 15 G 4
Karliova 21 F 3
Karl-Marx-Stadt 15 F 4
Karlobag 19 G 3
Karlovac 19 G 2
Karlovy Vary 15 F 4
Karlsborg 17 F 2
Karlshamn 17 FG 4
Karlskoga 17 FG 4
Karlskrona 17 G 4
Karlsöarna 17 G 4
Karlsruhe 15 E 5
Karlstad (MN, U.S.A.) 77 G 2
Karlstad (Sweden) 17 F 4
Karluk 72 F 4
Karma 62 E 3
Karmah 60 E 5
Karmala 40 C 4
Karmøy 17 DE 4
Karnafuli Reservoir 41 F 3
Karnal 40 C 2
Karnali 40 D 2
Karnataka 40 C 4
Karnobat 20 C 2
Karokpi 41 G 4
Karong 41 F 2
Karonga 67 E 1
Karonie 48 C 5
Karora 65 G 5
Karossa, Tanjung 43 E 5
Karoy 25 O 6
Kárpathos 20 C 3
Kárpathos 20 C 3
Karpenision 20 B 3
Kars 21 F 2
Kars Platosu 21 F 2
Karsakpay 35 H 1
Kärsämäki 16 J 3
Kärsava 17 J 4
Karshi 35 H 3
Karskiye Vorota, Proliv 24–25 L
Karskoye More 25 M 1
Karstula 16 HJ 3
Kartal 20 C 2

Kartaly 25 LM 5
Karthago 59 H 1
Kartun 39 K 1
Karufa 43 H 4
Karuma National Park 64 E 4
Karumba 49 G 2
Kārun (Iran) 23 E 3
Kārūn (Iran) 23 F 3
Karungi 16 H 2
Karungu 64 E 5
Karunjie 48 D 2
Karunki 16 H 2
Karur 40 C 5
Karvia 16 H 3
Karvina 15 G 5
Karwar 40 B 5
Karwi 40 D 2
Karym 25 N 3
Karymskoye 36 K 5
Karynzharyk, Peski 34 E 2
Karzala 24 K 5
Kaş (Turkey) 20 C 3
Kas (Sudan) 60 C 6
Kas (U.S.S.R.) 25 R 4
Kas Kong 41 H 5
Kas Rong 41 H 5
Kasai 64 B 5
Kasai Occidental 64 C 6
Kasai Oriental 64 C 5–6
Kasaji 66 C 2
Kasama 67 E 2
Kasane 66 CD 3
Kasanga 64 E 6
Kasangulu 64 B 5
Kasaragod 40 B 5
Kasba Lake 73 R 3
Kasba Tadla 58 D 2
Kas'bi 35 GH 3
Kasempa 66 D 2
Kasenga 66 D 2
Kasenye 64 E 4
Kasese (Uganda) 64 E 4
Kasese (Zaire) 64 D 5
Kasganj 40 C 2
Kashaf 34 G 3
Kāshān (Iran) 23 F 2
Kashi 35 K 3
Kashimbo 66 D 2
Kashipur 40 C 2
Kashiwazaki 39 L 3
Kashken Teniz 25 O 6
Kāshmar 34 F 3
Kashmor 35 H 5
Kashyukulu 64 D 6
Kasimov 24 H 5
Kasindi 64 D 4
Kasiruta, Pulau 43 G 4
Kasisty 36 K 1
Kaskaskia River 77 J 4
Kaskelen 35 K 2
Kaskinen 16 H 3
Kaskö 16 H 3
Kasli 25 M 4
Kasongo 64 D 5
Kasongo-Lunda 64 B 6
Kásos 20 C 3
Kaspi 21 F 2
Kaspiysk 34 D 2
Kaspiyskiy 21 G 1
Kaspiyskoye More 34 E 1
Kasr, Ra's 60 F 5
Kassalā 60 F 5
Kassándra 20 B 2
Kassándras, Kólpos 20 B 2–3
Kassel 15 E 4
Kasserine → Al Qasrayn 59 G 1
Kastamonu 21 D 2
Kastaneaí 20 C 2
Kastéllion 20 B 3
Kastellós, Ákra 20 C 3
Kastoria 20 B 2
Kástron 20 BC 3
Kasuku 64 D 5
Kasulu 64 E 5
Kasumbalesa 66 D 2
Kasumkent 34 D 2
Kasungan 42 D 4
Kasungu 67 E 2
Kasungu National Park 67 E 2
Kasur 35 J 4
Kata 36 H 4
Kataba 66 C 3
Kataeregi 63 F 4
Katagum 63 G 3
Katako-Kombe 64 CD 5
Katanga 57
Katangli 37 Q 5
Katanning 48 B 5
Katavi Plain Game Reserve 64 E 6
Katav-Ivanovsk 25 L 5
Katawaz 35 H 4
Katchall 41 F 6
Katchiungo 66 B 2
Katea 64 D 6

Katende Falls 64 C 6
Katenga 64 D 6
Katerini 20 B 2
Katesh 64 F 5
Katete 67 E 2
Katha 41 G 3
Katherine 48 E 1
Katherine Gorge National Park
  48 E 1
Katherine River 48 E 1
Kathiawar 40 B 3
Kathīri 61 H 5
Kathleen Falls 48 E 1
Kathua 35 K 4
Kati 62 C 3
Katihar 40 E 2
Katima Mulilo 66 C 3
Katima Rapids 66 C 3
Katiola 62 CD 4
Katla 16 B 3
Katlanovo 20 B 2
Katmai, Mount 72 FG 4
Katmai National Park and
  Preserve 72 G 4
Katmandu 40 E 2
Katompi 64 D 6
Katondwe 67 E 3
Katonga 64 E 4
Katon-Karagay 25 R 6
Katoomba 49 J 5
Katowice 15 G 4
Kātrīna, Jabal (Egypt) 22 AB 3
Katrine, Loch 3 B 3
Katrineholm 17 G 4
Katshi 64 D 6
Katsina 63 F 3
Katsina 63 F 4
Kattaktoc, Cape 75 O 4
Kattakurgan 35 H 3
Kattavia 20 C 3
Kattegat 17 F 4
Katul, Jabal 66 D 6
Katulu 65 G 4
Katumba 64 D 6
Katun' 25 R 5
Katunskiy Khrebet 25 R 5–6
Katunskiy Khrebet 25 R 6
Katyl'ga 25 P 4
Katyryk 36 G 1
Kau, Teluk 43 G 3
Kauai 53 E 1
Kaubalatmada, Gunung 43 G 4
Kaufbeuren 15 F 5
Kauhajoki 16 H 3
Kauhava 16 H 3
Kaukkwe Hills 41 G 3
Kaukonen 16 J 2
Kaukura 53 F 4
Kaula 53 E 1
Kaulishishi 66 D 3
Kaunas 17 H 5
Kaunispää 16 J 2
Kauno Marios 17 H 5
Kaura Namoda 63 F 3
Kaustinen 16 H 3
Kautokeino 16 H 2
Kavacha 37 V 3
Kavadarci 20 B 2
Kavaja 20 A 2
Kavak (Turkey) 20 C 2
Kavak (Turkey) 21 E 2
Kavak (Turkey) 21 E 3
Kavak Daği 20 C 3
Kavalerovo 39 KL 2
Kavali 40 D 5
Kaval'kan 37 P 4
Kaválla 20 B 2
Kavār (Iran) 23 F 3
Kavīr (Iran) 23 F 2
Kavīr, Dasht-e (Iran) 23 FG 2
Kavir-e Abarqu (Iran) 23 F 3
Kavir-e Marvast (Iran) 23 G 3
Kavīr-e Namak 34 F 4
Kavīr-e Namak (Iran) 23 G 1
Kavir-e Sirjān (Iran) 23 G 3
Kavkaz 21 F 2
Kawa 60 E 5
Kawalusu, Pulau 43 F 3
Kawambwa 66 D 1
Kawardha 40 D 3
Kawerau 51 R 8
Kawich Peak 76 C 4
Kawio, Kepulauan 43 F 3
Kawkareik 41 G 4
Kawm Umbū (Egypt) 22 A 4
Kawthaung 41 G 5
Kax He 35 L 2
Kaxgar He 35 K 3
Kaya 62 D 3
Kayah 41 G 4
Kayak (AK, U.S.A.) 72 J 4
Kayak (U.S.S.R.) 36 H 1
Kayambi 67 E 1
Kayan 42 E 3

Kayan, Sungai 42 E 3
Kayankulam 40 C 6
Kayenta 76 D 4
Kayes 62 B 3
Kayf, Tall (Iraq) 22 D 1
Kaygy 25 M 5
Kaynar 25 P 6
Kayoa, Pulau 43 G 3
Kayseri 21 E 3
Kayuagung 42 BC 4
Kayyerkan 25 R 2
Kaz Dağı 20 C 3
Kazachinskoye 36 F 4
Kazachinskoye 36 J 4
Kazach'ye 37 P 1
Kazakh 21 G 2
Kazakhskiy Melkosopochnik
25 NP 6
Kazakhstan 35 FH 1
Kazalinsk 35 G 1
Kazan' 24 J 4
Kazan (N.W.T., Can.) 73 S 3
Kazan Islands (Japan) 27 QR 7
Kazandzik 34 F 3
Kazanka 21 D 1
Kazanlı 21 D 3
Kazanlük 20 C 2
Kazanskoye 25 NO 4
Kazantip, Mys 21 E 1
Kazantsevo 25 Q 1–2
Kazarman 35 J 2
Kazatin 24 E 6
Kazbek 21 F 2
Kāzerūn (Iran) 23 F 3
Kazgorodok 25 N 5
Kazhim 24 K 3
Kazi Magomed 34 D 2
Kāzımkarabekir 21 D 3
Kazincbarcika 20 B 1
Kaztalovka 24 J 6
Kazungula 66 D 3
Kazym 25 N 3
Kazymskaya 25 N 3
Kazymskiy Mys 25 N 3
Kazzān ar Rusayris 60 E 6
Ke Bao 41 J 3
Ké Macina 62 C 3
Kéa 20 B 3
Kéa 20 B 3
Keady 4 B 2
Keal 7 E 1
Keams Canyon 76 D 4
Kearney 76 G 3
Kearns 76 D 3
Keban Gölü 21 E 3
Kebbi 63 E 3
Kébémer 62 A 2
Kebnekaise 16 G 2
Kebumen 42 C 5
Kecskemét 20 AB 1
Keda 21 F 2
Kédainiai 17 H 4
Kediat Idjil 58 C 4
Kediri 42 D 5
Kedjaman 42 D 3
Kedong 37 N 6
Kédougou 62 B 3
Kedva 24 K 3
Kedzierzyn Koźle 15 G 4
Keele 73 M 3
Keele Peak 72 LM 3
Keeling 37 N 6
Keer-Weer, Cape 49 G 1
Keestekraal 66 D 5
Keetmanshoop 66 B 5
Keewatin 74 HJ 6
Keewatin, District of 73 TU 2–3
Kefa 65 F 3
Kefallinía 20 B 3
Kéfalos 20 C 3
Kefamanau 43 F 5
Keffi 63 F 4
Kefken 20 D 2
Keflavík 16 A 3
Kegalla 40 CD 6
Kégashka 75 P 5
Kegen' 35 K 2
Kegulta 21 F 1
Kehl 15 E 5
Kehsi Mansam 41 G 3
Keighley 5 DE 3
Keila 17 H 4
Keimoes 66 C 5
Keiss 2 C 2
Keitele 16 J 3
Keith (South Australia) 49 G 6
Keith (U.K.) 2 C 3
Keith Arm 73 N 2
Keke Usun, Ozero 21 G 1
Keketa 50 D 3
Kekurnaya, Gora 37 V 3
Kel' 37 N 2
Kelam 65 F 4
Kelan 38 F 3
Kelang 42 B 3

Kelang, Pulau 43 G 4
Kelantan 42 B 2
Kělcyra 20 B 2
Kele 37 O 3
Kélekam 63 G 3
Keles 20 C 3
Keli Hāji Ibrāhīm (Iraq) 23 D 1
Kelil'vun, Gora 37 V 2
Kelkit 21 E 2
Kelkit 21 E 2
Kellé 63 G 6
Kellerberrin 48 B 5
Kellett, Cape 73 M 1
Kellog (U.S.S.R.) 25 R 3
Kellogg (ID, U.S.A.) 76 C 2
Kelloselkä 16 J 2
Kells 4 B 2
Kells 4 B 3
Kélo 63 H 4
Kelolokan 42 E 3
Kelowna 73 O 6
Kelsey 73 S 4
Kelsey Bay 73 M 5
Kelso (U.K.) 5 D 2
Kelso (WA, U.S.A.) 76 B 2
Kel'terskiy Khrebet 37 N 3
Keluang 42 B 3
Kelyehed 65 H 3
Kem' 16 K 3
Kem' 16 K 3
Kemah 21 E 3
Kemalpaşa (Turkey) 20 C 3
Kemalpaşa (Turkey) 21 F 2
Kembé 64 C 4
Kemble 7 D 2
Kemboma 63 G 5
Kemer 20 C 3
Kemer 20 D 3
Kemer Barajı 20 C 3
Kemerovo 25 R 4
Kemi 16 H 2
Kemijärvi 16 J 2
Kemijärvi 16 J 2
Kemijoki 16 J 2
Kemkra 37 P 4
Kemp, Lake 76 G 5
Kempele 16 HJ 3
Kempendyayi 36 L 3
Kemps Bay 79 G 3
Kempsey 49 J 5
Kempt, Lac 75 N 6
Kempten 15 F 5
Ken 40 D 3
Ken Thao 41 H 4
Kenadsa 58 E 2
Kenai 72 G 3
Kenai Fjords National Park 72 H 4
Kenai Mountains 72 G 4
Kenai Peninsula 72 GH 4
Kenaliasam 42 B 4
Kencha 37 P 3
Kendal 5 D 2
Kendall, Cape 73 U 3
Kendallville 77 JK 3
Kendari 43 F 4
Kendawangan 42 CD 4
Kendigué 63 H 3
Kendyrlik 25 R 6
Kenema 62 B 4
Kenga 25 Q 4
Kenge 64 B 5
Kengere 66 D 2
Kengtung 41 G 3
Kenhardt 66 C 5
Kéniéba 62 B 3
Kenilworth 7 D 1
Kenitra 58 D 2
Keniut 37 X 3
Kenkeme 37 N 3
Kenmare (N.D., U.S.A.) 76 F 2
Kenmare (Rep. of Ireland) 14 B 4
Kenmore 3 D 3
Kenn Reef 49 K 3
Kerrville 76 G 5
Kennedy Range National Park
48 B 3
Kennet, River 7 D 2
Kennett 77 H 4
Kennewick 76 C 2
Kenninghall 7 E 1
Kennya 37 P 3
Keno Hill 72 K 3
Kenogami 74 K 5
Kenora 74 J 6
Kensaleyre 2 A 3
Kent (Sierra Leone) 62 B 4
Kent (U.K.) 7 E 2
Kent Peninsula 73 Q 2
Kentau 35 H 2
Kentucky 77 J 4
Kentucky Lake 77 J 4
Kentucky River 77 K 4
Kenya 65 F 4
Kenya, Mount 65 F 5
Keokuk 77 H 3
Keonihargarh 40 E 3

Kep i Gjuhës 20 A 2
Kep i Rodonit 20 A 2
Kepahiang 42 B 4
Kepe 16 K 2
Kepi 43 J 5
Kepno 15 G 4
Keppyul'skaya 37 P 4
Keptin 37 M 3
Kepulauan Aju 43 H 3
Kepulauan Anambas 42 C 3
Kepulauan Aru 43 HJ 5
Kepulauan Asia 43 H 3
Kepulauan Babar 43 G 5
Kepulauan Balabalangan 42 E 4
Kepulauan Banda 43 G 4
Kepulauan Banggai 43 F 4
Kepulauan Kai 43 H 5
Kepulauan Kangean 42 E 5
Kepulauan Kawio 43 FG 3
Kepulauan Leti 43 G 5
Kepulauan Lingga 42 B 3–4
Kepulauan Lingga 42 BC 4
Kepulauan Mapia 43 HJ 3
Kepulauan Mentawai 42 A 4
Kepulauan Nanusa 43 G 3
Kepulauan Natuna 42 C 3
Kepulauan Obi 43 G 4
Kepulauan Palau 43 H 2
Kepulauan Riau 42 BC 3
Kepulauan Sangihe 43 G 3
Kepulauan Seram Laut 43 H 4
Kepulauan Sula 43 FG 4
Kepulauan Talaud 43 G 3
Kepulauan Tambelan 42 C 3
Kepulauan Tanimbar 43 H 5
Kepulauan Tenggara 43 G 5
Kepulauan Togian 43 F 4
Kepulauan Tukangbesi 43 F 5
Kepulauan Watubela 43 H 4
Kerala 40 C 5
Kerama-rettō 39 J 5
Kerandin 42 BC 4
Kerang 49 G 6
Kerava 17 J 3
Kerch' 21 E 1
Kerchel' 25 M 4
Kerchenskiy Proliv 21 E 1–2
Kerchevskiy 24 L 4
Kerekhtyakh 37 N 3
Kerema 50 E 3
Kerempe Burnu 21 D 2
Keren 65 F 1
Keret', Ozero 16 K 3
Kerets, Mys 24 G 2
Kerewan 62 A 3
Kerguelen-Gaussberg Ridge 98 B 5
Keri Kera 60 E 6
Kericho 64 F 5
Kerimäki 16 J 3
Kerimbas, Archipelago 67 G 2
Kerinci, Gunung 42 B 4
Kerion 20 B 3
Keriske 37 O 2
Keriya He 35 L 3
Keriya Shankou 35 L 3
Kerkennah Islands → Juzur
Qarqannah 59 H 2
Kerki 24 K 3
Kerki 35 GH 3
Kérkira 20 A 3
Kérkira 20 A 3
Kerkour Nourene, Massif du
63 J 2
Kermadec Islands 52 D 4–5
Kermadec Trench 99 D 5
Kermān 34 F 4
Kermānshāh (Iran) 23 E 2
Kermānshāhān (Iran) 23 G 3
Kerme Körfezi 20 C 3
Kermit 76 F 5
Kérouané 62 C 4
Kerrobert 73 PQ 5
Kerrville 76 G 5
Kershader 2 A 2
Kertamulia 42 C 4
Kerteh 42 B 3
Kerulen 36 K 6
Kerzaz 58 E 3
Kesagami Lake 75 L 5
Kesälahti 16 J 3
Keşan 20 C 2
Kesen'numa 39 M 3
Kesh 4 B 2
Keshan 37 N 6
Keshvar (Iran) 23 E 2
Keskin 21 D 3
Kessingland 7 E 1
Kestenga 16 K 2
Keswick 5 D 2
Keszthely 20 A 1
Ket' 25 Q 4
Ket' 36 F 4
Keta 62 E 4
Keta, Ozero 36 F 2
Ketanda 37 Q 3
Ketapang 42 CD 4

Ketchikan 72 L 4
Ketchum Mountain 76 F 5
Kete 62 E 4
Ket-Kap, Khrebet 37 O 4
Ketmen', Khrebet 35 KL 2
Ketou 62 E 4
Ketoy, Ostrov 37 S 6
Ketrzyn 15 H 4
Kettering 7 D 1
Kettle River Range 76 C 2
Keul' 36 H 4
Keuruu 16 H 3
Keuruunselkä 16 HJ 3
Kew 79 H 3
Kewagama 75 M 6
Kewanee 77 H 3
Keweenaw Peninsula 77 J 2
Key Largo 77 KL 6
Key West 77 K 7
Keyano 75 N 5
Keynsham 6 C 2
Keystone Lake 77 G 4
Kezhma 36 H 4
Kezi 66 D 4
Kghoti 66 C 4
Khabalakh 36 K 3
Khabarikha 24 K 2
Khabarovsk 37 P 6
Khabary 25 P 5
Khabr, Kūh-e (Iran) 23 G 3
Khābūr (Syria) 22 C 1
Khachmas 34 D 2
Khadki 40 B 4
Khafji (Saudi Arabia) 23 E 3
Khafjī, Ra's al (Saudi Arabia)
23 E 3
Khafs Banbān (Saudi Arabia)
23 E 4
Khaipur 35 J 5
Khairagarh 40 D 3
Khairpur 35 J 5
Khairpur 40 A 2
Khaishi 21 F 2
Khāīz, Kūh-e (Iran) 23 F 3
Khajuri Kach 35 H 4
Khakh (Iran) 23 F 2
Khakhar 37 P 4
Khakhea 66 C 4
Khakhsyn 37 M 2
Khakriz 37 M 2
Khalach 35 G 3
Khalatse 35 K 4
Khalesavoy 25 P 3
Khalīj al 'Aqabah 22 B 3
Khalīj al Bahrayn (Saudi Arabia)
23 F 4
Khalīj as Suways 22 A 3
Khalīj Foul (Egypt) 22 B 5
Khalīj Maşīrah 61 K 5
Khalīj Sirt 59 J 2
Khalkhāl 34 D 3
Khálki 20 C 3
Khalkidhiki 20 B 2
Khalkís 20 B 3
Khal'mer-Yu 25 M 2
Khalturin 24 J 4
Khalygras 37 N 2
Kham Keut 41 H 4
Khamaky 36 K 3
Khamar Daban, Khrebet 36 HJ 5
Khambhat 40 B 3
Khambhat, Gulf of 40 B 3–4
Khambi Yakha 25 O 2
Khamgaon 40 C 3
Khamir 61 G 5
Khamis Mushayt 61 G 5
Khammam 40 D 4
Khampa 36 L 3
Khampa 37 M 3
Khamra 36 K 3
Khamsara 36 G 5
Khamseh (Iran) 23 E 1
Khān al Baghdādī (Iraq) 22 CD 2
Khān Ruhābah (Iraq) 22 D 3
Khān Shaykhūn (Syria) 22 B 2
Khanabad 35 H 3
Khanapur 40 B 4
Khānaqīn (Iraq) 23 D 2
Khandagayty 36 F 5
Khandwa 40 C 3
Khandyga 37 P 3
Khangarh 35 J 5
Khanglasy 25 M 3
Khangokurt 25 M 3
Khanh Hung 41 J 6
Khani 36 M 4
Khánia 20 B 3
Khaniadhana 40 C 2
Khanion, Kólpos 20 B 3
Khanka, Ozero 39 K 1–2
Khannya 36 L 2
Khanovey-Sede 25 P 2
Khanpur 35 J 5
Khanskoye Ozero 21 E 1
Khantau 35 J 2

Khantayka 25 R 2
Khantayskoye, Ozero 36 F 2
Khantayskoye Vodokhranilishche
25 RS 2
Khanty-Mansiysk 25 N 3
Khanu 41 G 4
Khanyangda 37 Q 4
Khanyardakh 37 N 3
Khānzīr, Ra's 65 H 2
Khao Lang 41 G 6
Khao Luang 41 G 6
Khao Sai Dao Tai 41 H 5
Khapa 40 C 3
Khapalu 35 K 3
Khapcheranga 36 K 6
Khappyrastakh 37 M 4
Khar al Amaya (Iraq) 23 E 3
Khār Kūh (Iran) 23 F 3
Khara 36 G 5
Khara Astakh 36 K 3
Khara-Aldan 37 O 3
Kharabali 21 G 1
Kharagpur 40 E 3
Kharagun 36 K 5
Kharakas 20 BC 4
Kharampur 25 P 3
Khārān (Iran) 34 F 5
Kharan (Pakistan) 35 G 5
Kharan (Pakistan) 35 H 5
Kharānaq 34 EF 4
Kharānaq (Iran) 23 G 2
Kharānaq, Kūh-e (Iran) 23 G 2
Kharanor 36 L 5
Khara-Tala 37 ST 2
Khara-Tas, Gryada 36 J 1
Kharaulakhskiy Khrebet 37 N 1
Kharauz 36 J 5
Kharga Oasis → Wāhāt al
Khārijah 60 E 3–4
Kharik 36 H 5
Kharimkotan, Ostrov 37 ST 6
Kharīt, Wādi al (Egypt) 22 B 4–5
Khārk (Iran) 23 F 3
Khārk (Iran) 23 F 3
Kharkov 24 G 6
Kharlovka 24 G 2
Kharlu 16 K 3
Kharmanli 20 C 2
Kharoti 35 H 4
Kharovsk 24 H 4
Kharstan 37 Q 1
Kharsysk 21 E 1
Khartaksho 35 K 4
Khartoum 60 E 5
Khartoum North → Al Khartūm
Bahrī 60 E 5
Kharutayuvam 25 LM 2
Kharwar 35 H 4
Khasan 39 K 2
Khasavyurt 21 G 2
Khash (Afghanistan) 35 G 4
Khāsh (Iran) 35 G 5
Khash Desert 35 G 4
Khash Rud 35 G 4
Khashgort 25 N 2
Khashm al Qirbah 60 F 6
Khashm Mishraq (Saudi Arabia)
23 DE 4
Khashuri 21 F 2
Khasi Jaintia 41 F 2
Khaskovo 20 C 2
Khatanga 40 B 3
Khatanga 36 H 1
Khatangskiy Zaliv 36 JK 1
Khataren 37 T 3
Khatyngnakh 37 O 3
Khatyrka 37 X 3
Khatystakh 36 M 4
Khāvar (Iran) 23 E 3
Khawr Abū Habl 60 E 6
Khawr al Fakkān (United Arab
Emirates) 23 G 4
Khawr āl Juhaysh 61 J 4
Khawr al Mufattah (Saudi Arabia)
23 E 3
Khaya 37 P 3
Khaybar (Saudi Arabia) 22 C 4
Khaybar, Harrat 61 FG 3
Khaydarken 35 J 3
Khaylino 37 V 3
Khaylyulya 37 U 4
Khazzān Jabal al Awliyā' 60 E 5–6
Khe Bo 41 HJ 4
Khe Sanh 41 J 4
Kheda 40 B 3
Khelyulya 16 K 3
Khemchik 36 F 5
Khemis Miliana 59 F 1
Khemisset 58 D 2
Khemmarat 41 H 4
Khenchela 59 G 1
Khenifra 58 D 2

Kheri 40 D 2
Kherpuchi 37 P 5
Khersan (Iran) 23 F 3
Kherson 21 D 1
Khesh 35 H 4
Kheta 25 Q 2
Kheta 36 G 1
Kheta 36 H 1
Khetta, Levaya 25 O 3
Kheyräbäd 34 F 5
Kheyräbäd (Iran) 23 E 3
Kheyräbäd (Iran) 23 G 3
Khibiny 16 K 2
Khilchipur 40 C 3
Khil'mi, Gora 37 S 1
Khilok 36 J 5
Khilok 36 K 5
Khimki 24 G 4
Khíos 20 C 3
Khíos 20 C 3
Khirbat Isrīyah (Syria) 22 BC 2
Khlong Makham 41 H 5
Khmelev 24 F 5
Khmel'nik 24 E 6
Khmel'nitskiy 24 E 6
Khobol'chan 37 Q 2
Khodzha Mubarek 35 H 3
Khodzheyli 34 F 2
Khoe 37 Q 5
Khogali 64 D 3
Khok Kloi 41 G 6
Khokhropar 35 J 5
Khokiley 25 Q 2
Kholm (Afghanistan) 35 H 3
Kholm (U.S.S.R.) 17 K 4
Kholmogory 24 H 3
Kholmsk 37 Q 6
Kholodnoye 25 M 3
Kholzun, Khrebet 25 Q 5
Khomän 34 DE 3
Khomas Highland 66 B 4
Khomeyn (Iran) 23 F 2
Khomeyni, Bandar-e (Iran) 23 E 3
Khomokashevo 36 HJ 3
Khon Kaen 41 H 4
Khong 41 J 5
Khong Sedone 41 J 4
Khongkhoyuku 37 O 3
Khongo 37 S 3
Khonj (Iran) 23 F 4
Khonsär (Iran) 23 F 2
Khonu 37 O 2
Khonu 37 Q 2
Khoper 24 H 5
Khoppuruo 36 L 4
Khor 37 P 6
Khor 37 P 6
Khor Anghar 65 G 2
Khora 20 B 3
Khoräsän 34 F 4
Khorat Plateau 41 H 4
Khorb el Ethel 58 D 3
Khordogoy 36 L 3
Khorgo 36 K 1
Khorinsk 36 J 5
Khorintsy 36 M 3
Khorixas 66 A 4
Khorog 35 J 3
Khoronkhu 37 O 3
Khoronnokh 36 LM 2
Khorram (Iran) 23 E 1
Khorramäbäd (Iran) 23 E 2
Khorramshahr (Iran) 23 E 3
Khorsäbäd (Iraq) 22 D 1
Khosheutovo 21 G 1
Khoshyeylaq (Iran) 23 G 1
Khosrowäbäd (Iran) 23 E 3
Khosta 21 EF 2
Khotin 20 C 1
Khouribga 58 D 2
Khovu-Aksy 36 F 5
Khowrjän (Iran) 23 F 3
Khowst 35 H 4
Khoydype, Gora 25 N 2
Khrami 21 F 2
Khrebet Bol'shoy Balkhan
   34 EF 3
Khrebet Borong 37 P 2
Khrebet Bureinskiy 37 O 5
Khrebet Chayatyn 37 P 5
Khrebet Cherskogo 36 KL 5
Khrebet Cherskogo 37 P 1–2
Khrebet Chingiz-Tau 25 P 6
Khrebet Dygdy-Sise 37 O 4
Khrebet Dzhagdy 37 O 5
Khrebet Dzhaki-Unakhta
   Yakbyyana 37 OP 5–6
Khrebet Dzhugdzhur 37 OP 4
Khrebet Dzhungarskiy Alatau
   25 PQ 6–7
Khrebet Iskaten' 72 B 2
Khrebet Kadyr-Egi-Tayga 36 G 5
Khrebet Kamennyy 37 UV 3
Khrebet Karatau 35 H 2
Khrebet, Katunski 25 R 5–6

Khrebet Ket-Kap 37 O 4
Khrebet Ketmen' 35 KL 2
Khrebet Khamar Daban 36 HJ 5
Khrebet Kholzun 25 Q 5
Khrebet Khugdyungda 36 G 2
Khrebet Kivun 37 P 5
Khrebet Kodar 36 L 4
Khrebet Kolymskiy 37 SU 3
Khrebet Kopet-Dag 34 F 3
Khrebet Koryakskiy 37 VW 3
Khrebet Kungey Alatau 35 K 2
Khrebet Mayskiy 37 O 4–5
Khrebet Narymskiy 25 QR 6
Khrebet Nuratau 35 H 2
Khrebet Orulgan 37 N 2
Khrebet Pay-Khoy 25 M 2
Khrebet Pekul'ney 37 WX 2
Khrebet Pribrezhnyy 37 P 4
Khrebet Rarytkin 37 WX 2
Khrebet Rarytkin 37 WX 3
Khrebet Saur 25 QR 6
Khrebet Semme-Dahan 37 P 3
Khrebet Sette-Daban 37 P 3
Khrebet Suntar Khayata 37 PQ 3
Khrebet Taaga 37 N 4
Khrebet Talasskiy Alatau 35 J 2
Khrebet Tarbagatay 25 Q 6
Khrebet Taskyl 36 G 5
Khrebet Tas-Kystabys 37 QR 3
Khrebet Terskey Alatau 35 K 2
Khrebet Tukuringra 37 N 5
Khrebet Turana 37 O 5
Khrebet Udokan 36 L 4
Khrebet Ulakhan-Chistay
   37 QR 2–3
Khrebet Ulan-Burgasy 36 J 5
Khrebet Umnyn Syverma 36 GH 2
Khrebet Verkhoyanskiy 37 N 2–3
Khrebet Yam-Alin' 37 OP 5
Khrebet Yankan 36 L 4
Khrebet Yuzhno Chuyskiy 25 R 6
Khroma 37 Q 1
Khromskaya Guba 37 R 1
Khrom-Tau 25 L 5
Khrustal'nyy 39 KL 2
Khudoseya 25 Q 2–3
Khudumelapye 66 C 4
Khudzhakh 37 R 3
Khuff 59 J 3
Khuff (Saudi Arabia) 22 B 4
Khugdyungda, Khrebet 36 G 2
Khugiani 35 H 4
Khuis 35 C 5
Khulga 25 M 3
Khulkhuta 21 G 1
Khulna 40 E 3
Khulo 21 F 2
Khummi, Ozero 37 P 5
Khürab (Iran) 23 F 3
Khurai 40 C 3
Khüran (Iran) 23 G 4
Khurays (Saudi Arabia) 23 E 4
Khurayt 60 D 6
Khurchan 37 S 4
Khurda 40 E 3
Khurīyä Murīyä, Jazä'ir 61 K 5
Khurja 40 C 2
Khurmalik 35 G 4
Khurr, Wädī al (Saudi Arabia)
   22 C 3
Khurramshahr (Iran) 23 E 3
Khursanīyah (Saudi Arabia) 23 E 4
Khushab 35 J 4
Khust 20 B 1
Khutse 66 C 4
Khuwayy 60 D 6
Khuzdar 35 H 5
Khūzestän (Iran) 23 E 3
Khuzhir 36 J 5
Khväf 34 FG 4
Khväf 34 G 4
Khvalynsk 24 J 5
Khvojeh, Küh-e (Iran) 23 E 2
Khvor (Iran) 23 G 2
Khvormüj (Iran) 23 F 3
Khvormüj, Küh-e (Iran) 23 F 3
Khvoy 34 D 3
Khwaja Amran 35 H 4
Khyber Pass 35 J 4
Kia 51 G 3
Kiama 64 B 6
Kiamba 43 F 2
Kiambi 64 D 6
Kiana 72 E 2
Kiantajärvi 16 J 2
Kiapulka 64 D 6
Kiäseh (Iran) 23 F 1
Kibaha 65 F 6
Kibamba 64 D 5
Kibangou 63 G 6
Kibau 64 F 6
Kibaya 65 F 6
Kiberege 65 F 6
Kiberg 16 K 1
Kiboko 65 F 5
Kibombo 64 D 5

Kibondo 64 E 5
Kibre Mengist 65 F 3
Kibris → Cyprus 21 D 3
Kibungu 64 E 5
Kibuye 64 D 5
Kibwezi 65 F 5
Kibworth Harcourt 7 D 1
Kicevo 20 B 2
Kichi Kichi 63 H 2
Kichiga 37 U 4
Kicking Horse Pass 73 O 5
Kidal 62 E 2
Kidatu 65 F 6
Kidderminster 7 C 1
Kidepo National Park 64 E 4
Kidira 62 B 3
Kidnappers, Cape 51 R 8
Kidsgrove 7 C 1
Kidwelly 6 B 2
Kiel 15 F 4
Kielce 15 H 4
Kielder 5 D 2
Kieler Bucht 15 F 4
Kienge 66 D 2
Kieta 51 G 3
Kiffa 58 C 5
Kifissós 20 B 3
Kifrī (Iraq) 22 D 2
Kifri (Iraq) 23 D 2
Kigali 64 E 5
Kiği 21 F 3
Kigille 64 E 3
Kigilyakh 37 Q 1
Kignan 62 C 3
Kigoma 64 D 5
Kihelkonna 17 H 4
Kihnu 17 H 4
Kii-hantö 39 L 4
Kiik 25 O 6
Kii-suidö 39 KL 4
Kikai-jima 39 JK 5
Kikiakki 25 Q 3
Kikinda 20 B 1
Kikládhes 20 C 3
Kikori 50 D 3
Kikwit 64 B 6
Kil 17 F 4
Kilafors 16 G 3
Kilakkarai 40 C 6
Kilambé 78 E 5
Kīlan (Iran) 23 F 2
Kilberry 3 B 4
Kilberry 4 B 3
Kilbirnie 3 B 4
Kilbrannan Sound 3 B 4
Kilbride 2 A 3
Kilbride 3 B 3
Kilbride 4 B 3
Kilbuck Mountains 72 F 3
Kilchoan 3 A 3
Kilchu 39 J 2
Kilcogy 4 B 3
Kilcormac 4 B 3
Kilcoy 49 J 4
Kilcreggan 3 B 4
Kilcullen 4 B 3
Kildare 4 B 3
Kil'din, Ostrov 16 K 2
Kildrummy 2 C 3
Kilembe 64 C 6
Kili 52 C 2
Kilibo 62 E 4
Kilifi 65 F 5
Kilimanjaro 65 F 5
Kilimanjaro National Park 65 F 5
Kilinailau Islands 51 G 2
Kilindini 65 F 5
Kilindoni 65 F 6
Kilis (Turkey) 22 B 1
Kilitbahir 20 C 2
Kiliya 20 C 1
Kilkampton 6 B 2
Kilkee 14 B 4
Kilkeel 4 B 3
Kilkenny 4 B 3
Kilkis 20 B 2
Killarney 14 B 4
Killashandra 4 B 2
Killeen 76 G 5
Killelu 65 G 2
Killin 3 B 3
Killinek 75 O 3
Kíllini Óros 20 B 3
Killmacrenan 4 B 2
Killough 4 C 2
Kilmaluag 2 A 3
Kil'mez' 24 K 4
Kil'mez 24 K 4
Kilmore 49 H 6
Kilombero 65 F 6
Kilosa 65 F 6

Kilpisjärvi 16 H 2
Kilp-Javr 16 K 2
Kilrea 4 B 2
Kiltan 40 B 5
Kiltoom 4 B 3
Kilur Karim (Iran) 23 F 3
Kilwa 64 D 6
Kilwa Kisiwani 65 F 6
Kilwa Kivinje 65 F 6
Kilwa Masoko 65 F 6
Kilwaughter 4 B 2
Kilwinning 3 B 4
Kilyos 20 C 2
Kimaan 43 J 5
Kimba 49 F 5
Kimball 76 G 3
Kimball, Mount 72 J 3
Kimbe Bay 51 F 3
Kimberley (South Africa) 66 CD 5
Kimberley (Western Australia)
   48 C 2
Kimberley Downs 48 C 2
Kimberley Plateau 48 D 2
Kimbolton 7 D 1
Kimch'aek 39 J 2
Kimch'on 39 J 3
Kimhandu 65 F 6
Kimi (Cameroon) 63 G 4
Kimi (Greece) 20 B 3
Kimito 17 H 3
Kimongo 63 G 6
Kimovsk 24 G 5
Kimparana 62 BC 3
Kimpese 64 A 6
Kimry 24 G 4
Kimvula 64 B 6
Kinabalu, Gunung 42 E 2
Kinabatangan 42 E 2
Kinawley 4 B 2
Kinbrace 2 C 2
Kincardine 2 B 3
Kinchang 41 G 2
Kinchega National Park 49 G 5
Kinda (Sweden) 17 G 4
Kinda (Zaire) 64 C 6
Kindamba 63 G 6
Kindambi 64 C 6
Kindat 41 F 3
Kinder 77 H 5
Kindersley 73 Q 5
Kindia 62 B 4
Kindu 64 D 5
Kineshma 24 H 4
King 50 K 8
King Christian IX Land 90
King Christian X Land 90
King City 76 B 4
King Edward VII Falls 85 G 3
King Frederik VIII Land 90
King George Islands 75 M 4
King George Sound 48 B 6
King Island 49 G 6
King Leopold Ranges 48 CD 2
King Sound 48 C 2
King William Island 73 S 2
King Williams Town 66 D 6
Kingaroy 49 J 4
Kingarth 3 B 4
Kinghorn 3 C 3
Kingisepp (U.S.S.R.) 17 J 4
Kingisepp (Estoniya, U.S.S.R.)
   17 H 4
Kingman (AZ, U.S.A.) 76 D 4
Kingman (Pacific Ocean, U.S.A.)
   52 E 2
Kingombe 64 D 5
Kingombe 64 D 5
Kingoonya 49 F 5
King's Lynn 7 E 1
Kings Peak (CA, U.S.A.) 76 B 3
Kings Peak (UT, U.S.A.) 76 DE 3
King's Somborne 7 D 2
Kingsbridge 6 C 2
Kingsclere 7 D 2
Kingscote 49 F 6
Kingscourt 4 B 3
Kingskerswell 6 C 3
Kingsmill Group 52 C 3
Kingsport 77 K 4
Kingsteignton 6 C 2
Kingston 75 M 7
Kingston (Jamaica) 79 G 4
Kingston (Norfolk Is., Austr.)
   52 E 2
Kingston (N.Y., U.S.A.) 77 M 3
Kingston (South Australia) 49 F 6
Kingston Peak 76 C 4
Kingston upon Hull 5 E 3
Kingston Upon Thames 7 D 2
Kingstown 79 K 5
Kington 6 C 1
Kingussie 3 BC 3

Kiniama 66 D 2
Kinkala 63 G 6
Kinlochewe 2 B 3
Kinlochleven 3 B 3
Kinmaw 41 F 4
Kinna 17 F 4
Kinnaird's Head 2 D 3
Kinnegad 4 B 3
Kinnekulle 17 F 4
Kinoosao 73 R 4
Kinross 3 C 3
Kinsale 14 B 4
Kinsarvik 17 E 3
Kinshasa 64 B 5
Kinston 77 L 4
Kintampo 62 D 4
Kintap 42 E 4
Kintinku 64 EF 6
Kintyre 3 B 4
Kinyangiri 64 E 5
Kinyeti, Jabal 64 E 4
Kinzia 64 B 5
Kipaka 64 D 5
Kiparissiakós Kolpós 20 B 3
Kipawa, Lac 75 M 6
Kipembawe 64 E 6
Kipili 64 E 6
Kipini 65 G 5
Kipnuk 72 E 4
Kippen 3 B 3
Kipushi 66 D 2
Kirakira 51 H 4
Kirané 62 B 2
Kiraz 20 C 3
Kirbey 36 H 2
Kirbey 36 K 2
Kircubbin 4 C 2
Kirdimi 63 H 2
Kirenga 36 J 4
Kirensk 36 J 4
Kirghiz Steppe 34–35 FG 1
Kirgiz Step' 34–35 FH 1
Kirgiziya 35 JK 2
Kirgizskiy Khrebet 35 J 2
Kiri 64 B 5
Kiribati 52 DE 3
Kırıkhan 21 E 3
Kırıkhan (Turkey) 22 B 1
Kırıkkale 21 D 3
Kirikos, Ayios 20 C 3
Kirillovka 21 E 1
Kirimati 53 E 2
Kirishi 17 K 4
Kiritimati 53 E 2
Kiritimati 53 E 2
Kirk Michael 4 C 2
Kırkağaç 20 C 3
Kirkbampton 5 D 2
Kirkbean 3 C 4
Kirkby 5 D 3
Kirkby in Ashfield 7 D 1
Kirkby Lonsdale 5 D 2
Kirkby Stephen 5 C 2
Kirkby Thore 5 D 2
Kirkbymoorside 5 E 2
Kirkcaldy 3 C 3
Kirkcolm 3 B 4
Kirkconnel 3 B 4
Kirkcudbright 3 BC 4
Kirkee → Khadki 40 B 4
Kirkenes 16 K 2
Kirkham 5 D 3
Kirkhill 2 B 3
Kirkintilloch 3 B 4
Kirkjubæjarklaustur 16 B 3
Kirkland 3 C 2
Kirkland Lake 75 L 6
Kirkmichael 3 J 3
Kirkpatrick, Mount 91
Kirksville 77 H 3
Kirktown of Auchterless 2 C 3
Kirktown of Culsalmond 2 C 3
Kirkūk (Iraq) 22 D 2
Kirkwall 2 C 2
Kirkwall (Airport) 2 C 2
Kirkwhelpington 5 E 2
Kirkwood (MO, U.S.A.) 77 H 4
Kirkwood (South Africa) 66 D 6
Kırlangıç Burnu 20 D 3
Kirov 24 F 5
Kirov 24 J 4
Kirovabad 34 D 2
Kirovakan 21 F 2
Kirovo Chepetsk 24 K 4
Kirovograd 21 D 1
Kirovsk 16 K 2
Kirovsk 17 K 4
Kirovsk 34 G 3
Kirovskiy 35 K 2
Kirovskiy 37 T 5
Kirovskiy 39 K 1
Kirriemuir 3 C 3
Kirs 24 K 4
Kırşehir 21 D 3

Kirtachi 62 E 3
Kirthar Range 35 H 5
Kirtlebridge 3 C 4
Kirton 7 D 1
Kiruna 16 H 2
Kirundu 64 D 5
Kir'yanovskaya Kontora 36 H 4
Kisa 17 G 4
Kisabi 64 D 6
Kisaki 65 F 6
Kisalföld 20 A 1
Kisambo 64 B 6
Kisangani 64 D 4
Kisangire 65 F 6
Kisar, Pulau 43 G 5
Kiselevsk 25 R 5
Kishangarh 40 B 2
Kishangarh 40 BC 2
Kishb, Ḥarrat al 61 G 4
Kishi 62 E 4
Kishinev 20 C 1
Kishorganj 41 F 3
Kishtwar 35 K 4
Kisii 64 E 5
Kisiju 65 F 6
Kısılırmak 21 D 2
Kısır Dağı 21 F 2
Kiska 72 A 5
Kiska Volcano 72 A 5
Kiskőei Viztároló 20 B 1
Kiskőrös 20 A 1
Kiskunfélegyháza 20 A 1
Kiskunhalas 20 AB 1
Kislovodsk 21 F 2
Kismāyu 65 G 5
Kisoro 64 DE 5
Kissidougou 62 B 4
Kissū, Jabal 60 D 4
Kisumu 64 E 5
Kisvárda 20 B 1
Kita 62 C 3
Kitab 35 H 3
Kita-daitō-jima 39 K 5
Kitai, Ozero 20 C 1
Kitakyushū 39 JK 4
Kitale 64 F 4
Kitami 39 M 2
Kitami-sanchi 39 M 2
Kitanda 64 D 6
Kitangari 67 F 2
Kitangiri, Lake 64 E 5
Kitchener 75 L 7
Kitee 16 K 3
Kiteiyab 60 E 4
Kitete 64 E 6
Kitgum 64 E 4
Kíthira 20 B 3
Kíthira 20 B 3
Kithnos 20 B 3
Kitimat 72 M 5
Kitimat Ranges 72–73 M 5
Kitinen 16 J 2
Kitoboynyy 37 S 6
Kitoy 36 H 5
Kit's Coty House 7 E 2
Kitsman 20 C 1
Kittanning 77 KL 3
Kittilä 16 H 2
Kitui 65 F 5
Kitunda 64 E 6
Kitwe 66 D 2
Kitzbühel 19 F 2
Kitzbüheler Alpen 19 F 2
Kiunga (Kenya) 65 G 5
Kiunga (Papua New Guinea) 50 D 3
Kiuruvesi 16 J 3
Kivak 72 C 3
Kivalina 72 E 2
Kivijärvi 16 HJ 3
Kivik 17 F 4
Kiviõli 17 J 4
Kivu 64 D 5
Kivu, Lake 64 D 5
Kivun, Khrebet 37 P 5
Kiwaba N'zogi 66 B 1
Kiya 25 R 4
Kīyāmakī Dāgh 34 D 3
Kiyeng-Kyuyel' 37 S 2
Kiyeng-Kyuyel', Ozero 36 JK 1
Kiyev 24 F 5
Kiyevka 25 O 5
Kiyevka 39 K 2
Kiyevskoye Vodokhranilishche 24 F 5
Kıyıköy 20 C 2
Kiyma 25 N 5
Kizel 25 L 4
Kizema 24 H 3
Kizha 36 J 5
Kizhinga 36 J 5
Kızıl Dağ 21 D 3
Kızıl Tepe 20 D 2
Kızılcahamam 21 D 2
Kızılırmak 21 E 2
Kizilirmak 21 E 3

Kizil'skoye 25 L 5
Kızıltepe 21 F 3
Kızıltepe (Turkey) 22 C 1
Kizimen, Sopka 37 U 4
Kizimi 63 H 2
Kizlyar 21 G 2
Kizlyarskiy Zaliv 21 G 2
Kizyl-Arvat 34 F 3
Kizyl-Atrek 34 E 3
Kizyl-Su 34 E 3
Kjöllefjord 16 J 1
Kjölur 16 B 3
Kjöpsvik 16 G 2
Klabat, Gunung 43 G 3
Kladanj 19 G 3
Kladno 15 F 4
Klagan 42 E 2
Klagenfurt 19 F 2
Klaipėda 17 H 4
Klamath Falls 76 B 3
Klamath Mountains 76 B 3
Klamath River 76 B 3
Klamono 43 H 4
Klarälven 17 F 3
Klatovy 15 F 5
Klawer 66 B 6
Klea → Abū Tulayh 60 E 5
Klein Aub 66 B 4
Kleinsee 66 B 5
Klerksdorp 66 D 5
Klevan' 17 J 5
Klichka 36 L 5
Klin 24 G 4
Klina 20 B 2
Klintehamn 17 G 4
Klintsovka 24 J 5
Klintsy 24 F 5
Klipgat 66 C 4
Klippan 17 F 4
Klit 17 E 4
Kłodzko 15 G 4
Kłomnice 15 G 4
Klondike Plateau 72 K 3
Klosi 20 B 2
Klotz, Lac 75 N 3
Klotz, Mount 72 K 2
Kluane Lake 72 K 3
Kluane National Park 72 K 3
Kluczbork 15 G 4
Klukhorskiy Pereval 21 F 2
Klyavlino 24 K 5
Klyazma 24 H 4
Klyuchevaya 24 H 2
Klyuchevskaya Sopka 37 U 4
Klyuchi 36 K 5
Klyuchr 37 U 4
Knack 2 A 2
Knaresborough 5 E 2
Knarsdale 5 D 2
Kneža 20 B 2
Knighton 6 C 1
Knin 19 G 3
Knittelfeld 19 FG 2
Knjaževac 20 B 2
Knock 2 C 3
Knösen 17 EF 4
Knosós 20 C 3
Knottingley 5 E 3
Knowle 7 D 1
Knox, Cape 72 L 5
Knox Coast 91
Knoxville (IA, U.S.A.) 77 H 3
Knoxville (TN, U.S.A.) 77 K 4
Knoydart 3 B 3
Knud Rasmussen Land 90
Knutsford 5 D 3
Knutsford 6 C 1
Knyazhevo 24 H 4
Knysna 66 C 6
Ko Chan 41 G 6
Ko Chang 41 H 5
Ko Kut 41 H 5
Ko Lanta 41 G 6
Ko Phangan 41 H 6
Ko Phuket 41 G 6
Ko Samui 41 G 6
Ko Samui 41 H 6
Ko Tao 41 GH 5
Ko Tarutao 43 F 4
Ko Way 41 H 6
Koal 63 H 3
Koartac 75 N 3
Koba 42 C 4
Koba 43 J 5
Kobar Sink 65 G 2
Kobbo 65 F 2
Kobdo → Hovd 36 F 6
Kōbe 39 KL 4
Köbenhavn 17 F 4
Kobenni 58 D 5
Koblenz 15 E 4
Koboldo 37 O 5
Kobrin 17 H 5
Kobroor, Pulau 43 H 5
Kobuk 72 EF 2
Kobuk 72 F 2

Kobuk Valley National Park 72 F 2
Kobuleti 21 F 2
Kobyai 37 N 3
Koca Çal 21 D 3
Koca Çay 20 C 3
Kocaeli 20 CD 2
Kočani 20 B 2
Kocasu 20 C 3
Koch 75 M 2
Kochechum 36 G 2
Kochegarovo 36 L 4
Kochenga 36 H 4
Kochevo 24 K 4
Kōchi 39 K 4
Kochikha 36 G 1
Koçhisar Ovası 21 D 3
Kochkorka 35 K 2
Koçhmar 20 C 2
Kochmes 25 M 2
Kochubey 21 G 2
Kock 15 H 4
Kodar, Khrebet 36 L 4
Kodar, Khrebet 36 L 4
Kodi 43 E 5
Kodiak 72 G 4
Kodiak Island 72 G 4
Kodima 24 H 3
Kodino 24 GH 3
Kodok 64 E 3
Kodori, Mys 21 F 2
Kodyma 20 D 1
Kodžha Balkan 20 C 2
Koel 40 D 3
Köes 66 B 5
Kofçaz 20 C 2
Koffiefontein 66 C 5
Kofiau, Pulau 43 GH 4
Köflach 19 G 2
Koforidua 62 D 4
Koggala 40 D 6
Kogil'nik 20 C 1
Kogon 62 B 3
Koh i Qaisar 35 G 4
Kohat 35 J 4
Koh-Hisar 35 H 3–4
Koh-i-Baba 35 H 4
Kohima 41 F 2
Koh-i-Mazar 35 H 4
Koh-i-Pantar 35 H 5
Koh-i-Sangan 35 GH 4
Kohistan 35 J 3
Kohlu 35 H 5
Kohtla-Järve 17 J 4
Kohunlich 78 E 4
Koitere 16 K 3
Kojonup 48 B 5
Kojūr (Iran) 23 F 1
Kokalaat 35 G 1
Kokand 35 J 2
Kokaral, Ostrov 34 FG 1
Kokas 43 H 4
Kokcha 35 H 3
Kokchetav 25 N 5
Kokemäenjoki 16 H 3
Kokemäki 16 H 3
Kokkola 16 H 3
Koko 64 F 2
Koko Nor 38 D 3
Kokoda 50 E 3
Kokomo 77 J 3
Kokonau 43 J 4
Kokong 66 C 4
Kokora, Ozero 36 H 1
Kokpekty 25 Q 6
Koksaray 35 H 2
Kokshaga 24 J 4
Koksoak 75 O 4
Kokstad 66 D 6
Koktuma 25 Q 6
Kokuora 37 Q 1
Kok-Yangak 35 J 2
Kola 16 K 2
Kola 16 K 2
Kola Peninsula 24 G 2
Kolahun 62 BC 4
Kolai 35 J 3
Kolaka 43 F 4
Kolar 40 C 5
Kolar Gold Fields 40 C 5
Kolari 16 H 2
Kolbachi 37 M 5
Kolbio 65 G 5
Kolda 62 B 3
Kolding 17 E 4
Kole 64 C 5
Kole 64 D 4
Koléa 18 D 4
Kolepom Island 43 J 5
Kolesnoye 20 D 1
Kolesovo 37 S 1
Kolff, Tanjung 43 J 5
Kolguyev, Ostrov 24 J 2
Kolhapur 40 B 4
Koli 16 J 3

Koliganek 72 F 4
Kolka 17 H 4
Kolkasrags 17 H 4
Kollegal 40 C 5
Kollumúli 16 C 2
Kolmanskop 66 AB 5
Kolmården 17 G 4
Kolmogorovo 36 F 4
Köln 15 E 4
Kolo 15 G 4
Kołobrzeg 15 G 4
Kologi 60 E 6
Kolokani 62 C 3
Koloko 62 C 3
Kololo 65 G 3
Kolombangara 51 G 3
Kolomna 24 G 4
Kolomyya 20 C 1
Kolondieba 62 C 3
Kolonia 52 E 1
Kolonodale 43 F 4
Kolosovka 25 O 4
Kolozero, Ozero 16 K 2
Kolpakovo 37 T 5
Kolpashevo 25 Q 4
Kolpino 17 K 4
Kol'skiy, Poluostrov 24 G 2
Koluton 25 N 5
Kolva 24 L 2
Kolvitskoye, Ozero 16 K 2
Kolwa 35 G 5
Kolwezi 66 D 2
Kolyma 37 T 2
Kolyma Range 37 U 3
Kolymskaya 37 T 2
Kolymskaya 37 V 2
Kolymskaya Nizmennost' 37 ST 2
Kolymskiy, Khrebet 37 SU 3
Kolymskoye Nagor'ye 37 S 3
Kolyshley 24 H 5
Kolyuchinskaya Guba 72 C 2
Kolyvan' 25 Q 5
Koma 65 F 3
Komadugu Gana 63 G 3
Komadugu Yobe 63 G 3
Komandorski Islands 27 TU 4
Komandorskije Ostrova 27 TU 4
Komarichi 24 F 5
Komárno 15 G 5
Komarom 20 A 1
Komati Poort 67 E 5
Komatsu 39 L 3
Komba 64 C 4
Kombat 66 B 3
Kombissiguiri 62 D 3
Kombolcha 65 FG 2
Komdi 41 G 1
Kome 64 E 5
Kome Island 64 E 5
Komelek 37 O 3
Komfane 43 HJ 5
Komló 20 A 1
Kommunarka 25 R 2
Kommunarsk 21 E 1
Kommunist 37 X 3
Kommunizma, Pik 35 J 3
Komodo, Pulau 43 E 5
Komoé 62 D 3
Komoé, Parc National de la 62 D 4
Komono 63 G 6
Komoran, Pulau 43 J 5
Komotiní 20 C 2
Kompas Berg 66 C 6
Kompong Cham 41 J 5
Kompong Chhnang 41 H 5
Kompong Som 41 H 5
Kompong Speu 41 H 5
Kompong Sralao 41 J 5
Kompong Thom 41 J 5
Kompot 43 F 3
Komrat 20 C 1
Komsa 25 R 3
Komsomolets 25 M 5
Komsomol'sk 35 G 3
Komsomol'skiy 25 M 2
Komsomol'skiy 34 E 1
Komsomolskiy 21 G 1
Komsomol'sk-na-Amure 37 P 5
Komusan 39 JK 2
Kon Plong 41 J 5
Kona 65 F 3
Konakovo 24 G 4
Konarak 40 E 4
Konda 25 M 3
Konda 43 H 4
Kondagaon 40 D 4
Kondakova 37 T 2
Kondakovo 37 S 2
Kondinin 48 B 5
Kondoa 65 F 5
Kondon 37 P 5
Kondopoga 24 F 3

Kondor 34 F 3
Kondut 48 B 5
Konetsbor 24 L 3
Konevits, Ostrov 16 K 3
Konevo 24 F 3
Kong 62 D 4
Kong Frederik VI-Kyst 75 T 3
Konginskiye Gory 37 T 3
Kongkemul, Gunung 42 E 3
Kongola 66 C 3
Kongolo 64 D 6
Kongor 64 E 3
Kongsberg 17 EF 4
Kongsvinger 17 F 3
Kongur Shan 35 K 3
Kongwa 65 F 6
Koni, Poluostrov 37 S 4
Koni, Poluostrov 37 S 4
Koniaker 62 B 3
Konin 15 G 4
Konitsa 20 B 2
Konjed Jān (Iran) 23 F 2
Könkämä älv 16 H 2
Konkan 40 B 4
Konko 66 D 2
Konkouré 62 B 3
Konkudera 36 K 4
Konosha 24 H 3
Konoshchel'ye 25 R 2
Konotop 24 F 5
Konqi He 38 A 2
Konosha 24 H 3
Końskié 15 H 4
Konstantinovka 21 E 1
Konstantinovskiy 21 F 1
Konstanz 15 E 5
Kontagora 63 F 3
Kontcha 63 G 4
Kontiomäki 16 J 3
Kontum 41 J 5
Konus, Gora 37 O 4
Konya 21 D 3
Konya Ovası 21 D 3
Konza 65 F 5
Konzaboy 37 T 2
Konzhakovskiy Kamen', Gora 25 LM 4
Kookynie 48 C 4
Kooline 48 B 3
Koolivoo, Lake 49 F 3
Koonalda 48 D 5
Koör 43 H 4
Koorda 48 B 5
Kootenay 73 O 5–6
Kootenay National Park 73 O 5
Kooussa 62 C 4
Kop Geçidi 21 F 2
Kopanovka 21 G 1
Kópasker 16 B 3
Kópavogur 16 A 3
Koper 19 F 2
Kopervik 17 DE 4
Kopet-Dag, Khrebet 34 F 3
Kopeysk 25 M 5
Köping 17 G 4
Koplik 20 A 2
Köpmanholmen 16 G 3
Koppang 16 F 3
Kopparberg 17 FG 4
Koprivnica 19 G 2
Kopychintsy 24 E 6
Kop'yevo 25 R 5
Kopylovka 25 Q 4
Kor (Iran) 23 F 3
Koralpe 19 FG 2
Koramlik 35 M 3
Korangi 35 H 6
Koraput 40 D 4
Korarou, Lac 62 D 2
Korba 40 D 3
Korbach 15 E 4
Korbol 63 H 3
Korça 20 B 2
Korchino 25 Q 5
Korčula 19 G 3
Korčulanski Kanal 19 G 3
Kord Kūy 34 E 3
Kord Kūy (Iran) 23 G 1
Kord Sheykh (Iran) 23 F 3
Kordān (Iran) 23 F 2
Kordestān 34 D 3
Kordestān (Iran) 23 E 2
Kordofan → Kurdufān 60 DE 6
Kords 34 FG 5
Korea Strait 39 J 4
Korelaksha 16 K 2
Korennoye 36 J 1
Korenovsk 21 F 1
Korenshty 20 C 1
Korets 17 J 5
Korf 37 V 3
Korfa, Zaliv 37 V 3–4
Korfovskiy 37 P 6
Korgen 16 F 2
Korhogo 62 C 4
Korienza 62 D 2
Korim 43 J 4

Korinthiakós Kólpos 20 B 3
Kórinthos 20 B 3
Koriolei 65 G 4
Kōriyama 39 M 3
Korkino 25 M 5
Korkino 36 J 5
Korkodon 37 ST 3
Korkodon 37 T 3
Korkut 21 F 3
Korkuteli 20 D 3
Korla 35 M 2
Korliki 25 Q 3
Kormakiti Bur (Cyprus) 22 A 2
Kormakiti Burnu 21 D 3
Kornat 19 FG 3
Korneuburg 19 G 2
Kórnik 15 G 4
Kornilovo 25 Q 5
Koro (Fiji) 52 C 4
Koro (Ivory Coast) 62 C 4
Koro (Mali) 62 D 3
Koro Kidinga 63 H 2
Koro Toro 63 H 2
Korobovskiy 25 P 6
Köroğlu Dağları 21 D 2
Köroğlu Tepe 21 D 2
Korogwe 65 F 6
Koroit 49 G 6
Koror 43 H 2
Kőrös 20 B 1
Korosten 17 J 5
Korostyshev 17 J 5
Korostyshev 24 E 5
Korovin Volcano 72 C 5
Korpilahti 16 J 3
Korpilombolo 16 H 2
Korsakov 37 Q 6
Korsfjorden 17 DE 3
Korshunovo 36 K 4
Korskrogen 16 G 3
Korsnäs 16 H 3
Korsör 17 F 4
Kort Creek 40 A 3
Koryak Range 37 W 3
Koryakskaya Sopka 37 T 5
Koryakskiy Khrebet 37 VW 3
Koryazhma 24 J 3
Kos 20 C 3
Kos 20 C 3
Kosa (Mauritania) 58 D 5
Kosa (U.S.S.R.) 36 J 5
Kosa Fedotova 21 E 1
Koschagyl 34 E 1
Kościan 15 G 4
Kosciusko 77 J 5
Kosciusko, Mount 49 H 6
Kose 17 J 4
Köse Dağı 21 E 2
Kosha 60 E 4
Kosh-Agach 25 R 6
Kosi 40 C 2
Košice 15 H 5
Koskuduk 35 K 2
Kosmaj 20 B 2
Kosŏng 39 J 3
Kosovo Polje 20 B 2
Kosovska Mitrovica 20 B 2
Kossou, Lac de 62 CD 4
Kossovo 17 J 5
Kostajnica 19 G 2
Kostamus 16 K 3
Koster 66 D 5
Kostino 25 R 2
Kostomuksa 16 K 3
Kostopol' 17 J 5
Kostroma 24 H 4
Kostroma 24 H 4
Kostrzyn 15 F 4
Kos'yu 25 L 2
Koszalin 15 G 4
Kot Kapura 40 B 1
Kota 40 C 2
Kota Baharu (Malaysia) 42 B 2
Kota Belud 42 E 2
Kota Kinabalu 42 E 2
Kota Tinggi 42 B 3
Kotaagung 42 B 5
Kotabaharu (Indonesia) 42 D 4
Kotabaru 42 E 4
Kotamobagu 43 F 3
Kotapad 40 D 4
Kotchandpur 40 E 3
Kotcho, Lake 71
Koteasro 35 H 4
Kotel'nich 24 J 4
Kotel'nikovo 21 F 1
Kotel'nyy, Ostrov 37 P 1
Kotido 65 E 4
Kotikovo 37 Q 6
Kotka 17 J 3
Kotkino 25 P 4
Kotlas 24 J 3
Kotli 35 J 4
Kotlik 72 E 3

Kotlina Sandomierska 15 H 4
Koto 37 P 6
Koton Karifi 63 F 4
Kotor 20 A 2
Kotor Varoš 19 G 3
Kotovsk 20 C 1
Kotovsk 20 C 1
Kotovsk 24 H 5
Kotri Allahrakhio 35 H 6
Kotr-Tas 34 F 1
Kötschach 19 F 2
Kottagudem 40 D 4
Kottayam 40 C 6
Kotto 64 C 3
Kotton 65 J 3
Kotturu 40 C 5
Kotu Group 52 D 4
Kotuy 36 H 1
Kotuykan 36 HJ 1
Kotzebue 72 E 2
Kotzebue Sound 72 E 2
Kouango 64 C 3
Kouba Modounga 63 H 2
Koudougou 62 D 3
Kouéré 62 D 3
Koufey 63 G 3
Kougaberge 66 C 6
Kouilou 63 G 6
Kouki 64 B 3
Koukourou 64 C 3
Koulamoutou 63 G 6
Koulen 41 H 5
Koulikoro 62 C 3
Koumac 51 H 6
Koumala 49 H 3
Koumameyong 63 G 5
Koumbia 62 B 3
Koumbi-Saleh 58 D 5
Koumongou 62 E 3
Koumpentoum 62 B 3
Koumra 63 H 4
Koundara 62 B 3
Koundian 62 B 3
Koundougou 62 D 3
Koungheul 62 AB 3
Koungou, Monts 63 G 6
Kounradskiy 25 O 6
Koupéla 62 DE 3
Kourou 85 H 2
Kouroussa 62 B 3
Kousséri 62 B 3
Koutiala 62 C 3
Koutous 63 FG 3
Kouvola 16 J 3
Kova 36 H 4
Kova 36 H 4
Kovač 20 A 2
Kovdor 16 K 2
Kovdozero, Ozero 16 K 2
Kovel' 17 HJ 5
Kovinskaya Gora 36 H 4
Kovriga, Gora 24 J 2
Kovrizhka 37 U 3
Kovrov 24 H 4
Kovylkino 24 H 5
Kowares 66 A 3
Kowloon 38 FG 6
Kowt-e Ashrow 35 HJ 4
Koyandy 25 P 6
Köyceğis 20 C 3
Koyda 24 H 2
Koyukuk 72 F 2
Koyukuk 72 FG 2
Koyulhisar 21 E 2
Kozaklı 21 E 3
Kozan 21 E 3
Kozáni 20 B 2
Kozel'sk 24 G 5
Kozhevnikovo 25 Q 4
Kozhevnikovo 36 K 1
Kozhim 25 L 2
Kozhozero, Ozero 24 G 3
Kozhva 24 L 2
Kozlu 20 D 2
Kozul'ka 36 F 4
Kozyrevsk 37 T 4
Kpandu 62 DE 4
Kpessi 62 E 4
Kra 62 E 4
Kra Buri 41 G 5
Kra, Isthmus of 41 G 5
Krafla 16 B 2
Kragerö 17 E 4
Kragujevac 20 B 2
Krak des Chevaliers (Syria) 22 B 2
Krakor 41 H 5
Kraków 15 GH 4
Kralendijk 84 E 1
Kraljevica 19 F 2
Kraljevo 20 B 2
Kramatorsk 21 E 1
Kramfors 16 G 3
Kranj 19 F 2

Krapina 19 G 2
Krasilov 24 E 6
Krasino 24 K 1
Kraskino 39 K 2
Krāslava 17 J 4
Krasnaya Polyana 21 F 2
Krasnaya Yaranga 37 X 3
Krasnaya Yaranga 72 C 2
Krasneno 37 W 3
Kraśnik 15 H 4
Krasnoarmeysk 21 E 1
Krasnoarmeysk 24 HJ 5
Krasnoarmeysk 25 N 5
Krasnoarmeyskiy 21 F 1
Krasnodar 21 E 2
Krasnogorsk 37 Q 6
Krasnograd 24 G 6
Krasnogvardeyskoye 21 D 1
Krasnogvardeyskoye 21 F 1
Krasnoje Selo 17 J 4
Krasnokamsk 24 KL 4
Krasnokutskoye 25 OP 5
Krasnoperekopsk 21 D 1
Krasnosel'kup 25 Q 2
Krasnoslobodsk 24 HJ 6
Krasnoturansk 36 F 5
Krasnotur'insk 25 M 4
Krasnoufimsk 25 L 4
Krasnoural'sk 25 M 4
Krasnousol'skiy 24 L 5
Krasnovishersk 24 L 3
Krasnovodsk 34 E 2
Krasnovodskoye Poluostrov 34 E 2
Krasnoyarovo 37 N 5
Krasnoyarsk 36 F 4
Krasnoyarskiy 25 L 5
Krasnoyarskoye
  Vodokhranilishche 36 F 5
Krasnoye 21 F 1
Krasnoye, Ozero 37 W 3
Krasnoye Znamya 35 G 3
Krasnozatonskiy 24 K 3
Krasnozerskoye 25 PQ 5
Krasnoznamenskoye 25 N 5
Krasnystaw 15 H 4
Krasnyy Chikoy 36 J 5
Krasnyy Kut 24 J 5
Krasnyy Luch 21 E 1
Krasnyy Sulin 21 EF 1
Krasnyy Yar 24 HJ 5
Krasnyy Yar 25 N 5
Krasnyy Yar 25 Q 4
Krasnyy Yar 34 D 1
Krasnyy-Yar 25 O 4
Kratie 41 J 5
Kratovo 20 B 2
Kray Lesov 37 U 2
Krayište 20 B 2
Krefeld 14 E 4
Kremastá, Limni 20 B 3
Kremenchug 24 F 6
Kremenchugskoye
  Vodokhranilishche 24 F 6
Kremenets 17 J 5
Kremmling 76 E 3
Krems 19 G 2
Kreshchenka 25 Q 4
Kresta, Zaliv 72 B 2
Kresti 24 F 4
Krest-Khal'dzhayy 37 O 3
Krestovaya 36 K 4
Krestovka 24 K 2
Krestovskiy, Ostrov 37 U 1
Krestovyy Pereval 21 F 2
Kresty 36 E 1
Kretinga 17 H 4
Kreuztal 15 E 4
Kribi 63 F 5
Krichev 24 F 5
Kričhim 20 B 2
Kril'on, Mys 37 Q 6
Krimml 19 F 2
Krishna 40 C 4
Krishna, Mouths of the 40 D 4
Krishnagiri 40 C 5
Krishnanagar 40 E 3
Kristiansand 17 E 4
Kristianstad 17 F 4
Kristiansund 16 E 3
Kristiinankaupunki 16 H 3
Kristineberg 16 G 2
Kristinehamn 17 F 4
Kristinestad 16 H 3
Kristinovka 20 C 1
Kríti 20 BC 3
Kritikón Pélagos 20 BC 3
Kriva Palanka 20 B 2
Krivoy Rog 21 D 1
Krk 19 F 2
Krnov 15 G 4
Kroken 16 F 2
Krokodil River 66 D 4
Krokom 16 F 3
Kroměříž 15 G 5
Kronotskaya Sopka 37 T 5

Kronotski 37 U 5
Kronotskiy, Mys 37 U 4–5
Kronotskiy Poluostrov 37 U 5
Kronotskiy Zaliv 37 U 5
Kronotskoye Ozero 37 TU 5
Kronshtadt 17 J 4
Kroonstad 66 D 5
Kropotkin 21 F 1
Kropotkin 36 L 4
Krosno 15 H 5
Krotoszyn 15 G 4
Krotovka 24 K 5
Kroviga, Gora 36 F 3
Krško 19 G 2
Krstača 20 B 2
Krueng Geumpang 42 A 3
Kruger National Park 67 E 4
Krugersdorp 66 D 5
Krugloye 21 E 1
Krui 42 B 5
Krung Thep 41 H 5
Kruså 17 E 5
Kruševac 20 B 2
Krusne Hory 15 F 4
Krutinka 25 O 4
Kruzenshterna, Proliv 37 S 6
Kruzof 72 K 4
Kryazh Chernycheva 25 LM 2
Kryazh Kula 37 O 2
Kryazh Polousnyy 37 PQ 2
Kryazh Ulakhan-Sis 37 S 1–2
Krym (Ukraine, U.S.S.R.) 21 D 1
Krym (Ukraine, U.S.S.R.) 21 E 1
Krymsk 21 E 1–2
Krymskiye Gory 21 D 2
Krzyż 15 G 4
Ksabi 58 E 3
Ksar Chellala 59 F 1
Ksar el Barka 58 C 5
Ksar el Boukhari 59 F 1
Ksar el Kebir 58 D 2
Ksar Torchane 58 C 4
Ksen'yevka 36 L 5
Ksour, Monts des (Algeria) 58 EF 2
Ksour, Monts des (Tunisia) 59 GH 2
Kü', Jabal al (Saudi Arabia) 23 E ‹
Kuala Belait 42 D 3
Kuala Dungun 42 B 3
Kuala Kangsar 42 B 3
Kuala Kapuas 42 D 4
Kuala Kerai 42 B 2
Kuala Lipis 42 B 3
Kuala Lumpur 42 B 3
Kuala Pilah 42 B 3
Kuala Rompin 42 B 3
Kuala Selangor 42 B 3
Kuala Terengganu 42 B 2
Kualakeriau 42 D 3
Kualakurun 42 D 4
Kualamanjual 42 D 4
Kualapembuang 42 D 4
Kualasimpang 42 A 3
Kualatungkal 42 B 4
Kuamut 42 E 2
Kuancheng 39 G 2
Kuandian 39 H 2
Kuantan 42 B 3
Kuba 21 F 2
Kuba (Azerbaydzhan, U.S.S.R.) 34 D 2
Kuban' 21 E 1
Kubaysah (Iraq) 22 D 2
Kubbe 16 G 3
Kubbum 60 C 6
Kubenskoye, Ozero 24 G 4
Kubkain 50 D 2
Kubumesaäi 42 E 3
Kuching 42 D 3
Kudara 35 J 3
Kūdasht (Iran) 23 E 2
Kudat 42 E 2
Kudaw 41 G 3
Kudremukh 40 BC 5
Kudryashevo 25 Q 4
Kudu-Kyuyel't 36 LM 4
Kudus 42 D 5
Kudymkar 24 K 4
Kufra Oases 59 K 4
Kufstein 19 F 2
Kugmallit Bay 72 L 2
Kugul'ta 21 F 1
Kuhaylī 60 E 5
Kūhbonān (Iran) 23 G 3
Küh-e Ālādāgh 34 F 3
Küh-e 'Alīābād (Iran) 23 F 2
Küh-e Alījūq (Iran) 23 F 3
Küh-e Alvano (Iran) 23 E 2
Küh-e Bāfq (Iran) 23 G 3
Küh-e Bazmān 34 F 5
Küh-e Biābān 34 F 5
Küh-e Bozqūsh 34 D 3
Küh-e Būl (Iran) 23 F 3
Küh-e Chehel Dokhtarān 35 G 4

Küh-e Chelleh Khāneh (Iran) 23 E 1
Küh-e Darband 34 F 4
Küh-e Dāvārān (Iran) 23 G 3
Küh-e Dīnār (Iran) 23 F 3
Küh-e Dom (Iran) 23 F 2
Küh-e Garbosh (Iran) 23 EF 2
Küh-e Garri (Iran) 23 E 2
Küh-e Gāvbūs 34 E 5
Küh-e Gāvbūs (Iran) 23 FG 4
Küh-e Gügerd 34 E 3–4
Küh-e Gügerd (Iran) 23 F 2
Küh-e Hormoz (Iran) 23 G 4
Küh-e Jebal Bārez 34 F 5
Küh-e Joghatāy (Iran) 23 G 1
Küh-e Kalat 34 F 4
Küh-e Karkas (Iran) 23 F 2
Küh-e Khabr (Iran) 23 G 3
Küh-e Khāīz (Iran) 23 F 3
Küh-e Kharānaq (Iran) 23 G 2
Küh-e Khormūj 34 E 5
Küh-e Khvojeh 34 F 3
Küh-e Khvojeh (Iran) 23 E 2
Küh-e Khvormūj (Iran) 23 F 3
Küh-e Kūhrān 34 F 4
Küh-e Kūkalār (Iran) 23 F 3
Küh-e Lāleh Zār 34 F 5
Küh-e Malek Sīāh 35 G 5
Küh-e Masāhīm (Iran) 23 G 3
Küh-e Nāy Band 34 F 4
Küh-e Safīd (Iran) 23 E 2
Küh-e Shah Jahān 34 F 3
Küh-e Sorkh 34 EF 4
Küh-e Sorkh 34 F 3
Küh-e Sorkh (Iran) 23 G 2
Küh-e Tābask (Iran) 23 F 3
Küh-e Taftān 35 G 5
Kūhestak 34 F 5
Kūhhā ye Zagros (Iran) 23 EF 2–3
Kūhhā Zagros 34 DE 4
Kūhhā-ye Bashākerd 34 F 5
Kūhhā-ye Genū (Iran) 23 G 4
Kūhhā-ye Qorūd 34 E 4
Kūhhā-ye Qorūd (Iran) 23 FG 2–3
Kūhhā-ye-Sabalān 34 D 3
Kuhmo 16 J 3
Kuhmoinen 16 J 2
Kūhpāyeh 34 F 4
Kūhpāyeh (Iran) 23 F 2
Kui Nua 41 GH 5
Kuikkavaara 16 J 3
Kuiseb 66 B 4
Kuito 66 B 2
Kuiu 72 L 4
Kuivaniemi 16 J 2
Kujani Game Reserve 62 D 4
Kujawy 15 G 4
Kuji 39 M 2
Kükalär, Küh-e (Iran) 23 F 3
Kukan 37 O 6
Kukawa 63 G 3
Kukësi 20 B 2
Kukhtuy 37 Q 4
Kukushka 37 N 5
Kula 20 C 3
Kula Kangri 41 F 2
Kulagino 34 E 1
Kulakovo 36 F 4
Kulakshi 34 F 1
Kulaneh 35 G 5
Kulanoy 34 F 1
Kulbus 60 C 6
Kul'chi 37 P 5
Kuldīga 17 H 4
Kuldja 35 L 2
Kul'dzhuktau, Gory 35 G 2
Kule 60 C 4
Kulen Vakuf 19 G 3
Kulenjin (Iran) 23 E 2
Kulgera 48 E 2
Kulinda 36 H 3
Kulinda 36 J 3
Kullen 17 F 4
Kulmasa 62 D 4
Kulmbach 15 F 4
Kulp 21 F 3
Kul'sary 34 E 1
Kul'skiy 36 J 5
Kultay 34 E 1
Kultsjön 16 G 3
Kultuk 36 H 5
Kulu (Turkey) 21 D 3
Kulu (U.S.S.R.) 37 R 3
Kuludzhun 25 Q 6
Kululli 65 G 2
Kululu 64 E 6
Kulunda 25 P 5
Kulundinskaya Step' 25 P 5
Kulundinskoye, Ozero 25 PQ 5
Kulyab 35 HJ 3
Kum Kuduk 38 B 2
Kuma (Russia, U.S.S.R.) 16 K 2
Kuma (Russia, U.S.S.R.) 21 G 2
Kumagaya 39 L 3
Kumai 42 D 4
Kumai, Teluk 42 D 4

Kumak 25 M 5
Kumakh-Surt 37 N 1
Kumakhta 36 K 5
Kumamoto 39 K 4
Kumanovo 20 B 2
Kumara 37 N 5
Kumasi 62 D 4
Kumawa, Pegunungan 43 H 4
Kumba 63 F 5
Kumbakonam 40 C 5
Kumbe 50 CD 3
Kumbo 63 G 4
Kum-Dag 34 E 3
Kumdah 61 H 4
Kume-jima 39 J 5
Kumertau 24 KL 5
Kuminskiy 25 N 4
Kumla 17 FG 4
Kumluca 20 D 3
Kumo 63 G 3
Kumon Range 41 G 2
Kumonda 36 G 4
Kumora 36 K 4
Kumta 40 B 5
Kumu 64 D 4
Kümüx 38 A 2
Kunar 35 J 4
Künas 35 L 2
Kunashak 25 M 4
Kunda 17 J 4
Kunda Hills 40 C 5
Kunda-dia-Baze 66 B 1
Kundelungu, Monts 64 D 6–7
Kundelungu National Park 66 D 2
Kundur, Pulau 42 B 3
Kunduz 35 H 3
Kunene 66 A 3
Kunes 16 J 1
Künes He 35 L 2
Kungälv 17 F 4
Kungasalakh, Ozero 36 JK 1
Kungey Alatau, Khrebet 35 K 2
Kungrad 34 F 2
Kungsbacka 17 F 4
Kungu 64 B 4
Kungur 24 L 4
Kungur Tuk 36 G 5
Kungurri 49 H 3
Kungyangon 41 G 4
Kunhing 41 G 3
Kunjirap Daban 35 K 3
Kunlong 41 G 3
Kunlun Shan 35 KM 3
Kunlun Shankou 38 B 3
Kunming 38 D 5
Kunsan 39 J 3
Kuntshankoi 64 C 5
Kuntuk 37 R 4
Kununurra 48 D 2
Kunwak 73 S 3
Kunya 63 F 3
Kunyao 64 F 4
Kunya-Urgench 34 F 2
Kuocang Shan 39 H 5
Kuonamka 36 J 2
Kuonara 36 M 2
Kuop 52 B 2
Kuopio 16 J 3
Kuorboaivi 16 J 2
Kuoyka 36 M 1
Kupa 19 G 2
Kupang 43 F 6
Kupang, Teluk 43 F 5–6
Kupiano 50 E 4
Kupino 25 P 5
Kupiškis 17 J 4
Kupreanof 72 L 4
Kupyansk 24 G 6
Kuqa 35 L 2
Kura 21 F 2
Kura 21 G 2
Kura (Nigeria) 63 F 3
Kura (U.S.S.R.) 34 D 2
Kuragino 36 F 5
Kuramā, Ḥarrat 61 G 4
Kurashasayskiy 24 L 5
Kurashiki 39 K 4
Kuraymah 60 E 5
Kurayn 23 EF 4
Kurbatovo 36 F 4
Kurbulik 36 J 5
Kurchum 25 Q 6
Kurdistan 34 CD 3
Kurdufān 60 DE 6
Kŭrdžhali 20 C 2
Küre 21 D 2
Kure 39 K 4
Kureyka 25 RS 2
Kurgaldzhino 25 O 5
Kurgalski, Mys 17 J 4
Kurgan 25 N 4
Kurganinsk 21 F 2
Kurgan-Tyube 35 H 3
Kurgasyn 35 H 1
Kuria 52 C 2
Kuria Muria Islands 61 K 5

Kurikka 16 H 3
Kuril Islands 37 S 6
Kuril Trench 99 C 2
Kurilovka 24 J 5
Kuril'sk 37 R 6
Kuril'skiye Ostrova 37 RS 6
Kurkure-Bazhi, Gora 25 R 5
Kurleya 36 L 5
Kurmuk 60 E 6
Kurnool 40 C 4
Kuro Siwo 93
Kuroiso 39 M 3
Kuro-shima 39 J 4
Kurovskiy 37 N 5
Kurram 35 J 4
Kursavka 21 F 2
Kuršenai 17 H 4
Kursk 24 G 5
Kurskaja Kosa Neringa 17 H 4
Kurskaya 21 F 2
Kurski Zaliv 17 H 4
Kursu 16 J 2
Kuršumlija 20 B 2
Kuršunlu 21 D 2
Kuršunlu Dağı 21 E 3
Kurtalan 21 F 3
Kurtamysh 25 M 5
Kürtī 60 E 5
Kuru 64 D 3
Kuru Dağı 20 C 2
Kurucaşile 21 D 2
Kuruçay 21 E 3
Kuruktag 38 A 2
Kurum 50 E 2
Kuruman 66 C 5
Kuruman 66 C 5
Kurume 39 K 4
Kurumkan 36 K 5
Kurunegala 40 CD 6
Kurung 36 L 3
Kurupka 72 C 3
Kurur, Jabal 60 E 4
Kur'ya 24 L 3
Kur'ya 25 Q 5
Kur'ya 36 E 1
Kurzeme 17 H 4
Kuş Gölü 20 C 2
Kuşada Körfezi 20 C 3
Kusadası 20 C 3
Kusaie 52 B 2
Kushchevskaya 21 E 1
Kusheriki 63 F 3
Küshik, Tall (Syria) 22 C 1
Kushimoto 39 L 4
Kushiro 39 M 2
Kushka 35 G 3
Kushkushara 24 H 3
Kushmurun 25 MN 5
Kushmurun, Ozero 25 M 5
Kushva 25 L 4
Kuskokwim 72 E 3
Kuskokwim Bay 72 E 4
Kuskokwim Mountains 72 F 3
Kusma 40 D 2
Kussharo-ko 39 M 2
Kustanay 25 M 5
Küstī 60 E 6
Kut (Iran) 23 E 3
Kūt Abdollah (Iran) 23 E 3
Kuta 63 F 4
Kütahya 20 C 3
Kutai, Sungai 42 E 4
Kutaisi 21 F 2
Kutan 21 G 2
Kutana 37 O 4
Kutch 40 AB 3
Kutch, Gulf of 40 A 3
Kutch, Rann of 40 AB 3
Kutima 36 J 4
Kutina 19 G 2
Kutno 15 G 4
Kutop'yegan 25 NO 2
Kutru 40 D 4
Kuttusvaara 16 J 2
Kutu 64 B 5
Kutulik 36 H 5
Kutum 60 C 6
Kuuli-Mayak 34 E 2
Kuusamo 16 J 2
Kuusankoski 16 J 3
Kuusivaara 16 H 2
Kuutse Mägi 17 J 4
Kuvango 66 B 2
Kuwait 23 E 3
Kuwait (Kuwait) 23 E 3
Kuya 24 H 2
Kuybyshev 24 K 5
Kuybyshev 25 P 4
Kuybyshevo 37 R 6
Kuybyshevskiy 25 N 5
Kuybyshevskoye
    Vodokhranilishche 24 JK 5
Kuygan 25 O 6
Küysanjaq (Iraq) 23 D 1
Kuytun 35 M 2
Kuytun (U.S.S.R.) 36 H 5

Kuytun, Gora 25 R 6
Kuytun He 35 L 2
Kuyucuk Dağı 20 D 3
Kuyumba 36 G 3
Kuz'movka 25 S 3
Kuznetsk 24 J 5
Kuznetsk Basin 31
Kuznetskiy Alatau 25 R 4–5
Kuzomen 24 G 2
Kvabé 63 H 4
Kvalöy 16 G 2
Kvalöya 16 H 1
Kvalsund 16 H 1
Kvænangen 16 H 1
Kvareli 21 G 2
Kvarner 19 F 2–3
Kvarnerič 19 F 3
Kvarnbergsvattnet 16 F 3
Kverkfjöll 16 B 3
Kvichak 72 F 4
Kvichak Bay 72 F 4
Kvikkjokk 16 G 2
Kvinesdal 17 E 4
Kvissleby 16 G 3
Kviteseid 17 E 4
Kwa 64 B 5
Kwa Mtoro 64 EF 6
Kwahu Plateau 62 D 4
Kwaja Ali 35 G 4
Kwajalein 52 C 2
Kwakoegron 85 G 2
Kwale (Kenya) 65 F 5
Kwale (Nigeria) 63 F 4
Kwamisa 62 D 4
Kwamouth 64 B 5
Kwangju 39 J 3
Kwango 64 B 5
Kwangsi Chuang 38 E 6
Kwanmo-bong 39 JK 2
Kwatisore 43 HJ 4
Kwekwe 66 D 3
Kwenge 64 B 6
Kwethluk 72 E 3
Kwidzyn 15 G 4
Kwigillingok 72 E 4
Kwikila 50 E 3
Kwilu 64 B 5
Kwilu 64 B 6
Kwitaro 85 G 3
Kwoka, Gunung 43 H 4
Kyabram 49 GH 6
Kyaikkami 41 G 4
Kyaikto 41 G 4
Kyaka 64 E 5
Kyakhta 36 J 5
Kyancutta 49 F 5
Kyango 64 D 3
Kyaukkyi 41 G 4
Kyaukme 41 G 3
Kyaukpyu 41 F 4
Kyaukse 41 G 3
Kyauktaw 41 F 3
Kybartai 17 H 5
Kycham-Kyuyel' 37 R 2
Kychema 24 H 2
Kyeintali 41 F 4
Kyela 64 E 6
Kyelanq 40 C 1
Kyenjojo 64 E 4
Kyffhäuser 15 F 4
Kyjov 15 G 5
Kyle of Lochalsh 2 B 3
Kylerhea 2 B 3
Kylestrome 2 B 2
Kyll 19 E 1
Kymijoki 17 J 3
Kynnefjäll 17 F 4
Kynuna 49 G 3
Kyoga, Lake 64 E 4
Kyong 41 G 3
Kyŏnggi-man 39 HJ 3
Kyŏngju 39 J 3
Kyōto 39 L 3
Kyrbykan 37 N 3
Kyren 36 H 5
Kyrkheden 17 F 3
Kyrksœteröra 16 E 3
Kyrönjoki 16 H 3
Kyrösjärvi 16 H 3
Kyrta 24 L 3
Kyrynniky 36 L 3
Kyshtovka 25 P 4
Kyshtym 25 M 4
Kystatam 36 M 2
Kytalyktakh 37 OP 2
Kyuekh-Bulung 36 KL 2
Kyungyaung 41 G 4
Kyushe 34 F 1
Kyūshū 39 K 4
Kyustendil 20 C 2
Kyusyur 37 N 1
Kyzas 25 R 5
Kyzyk 34 E 2

Kyzyl 25 R 5
Kyzyl 36 F 5
Kyzylart, Pereval 35 J 3
Kyzyldyykan 35 H 1
Kyzyl-Kiya 35 J 2
Kyzylkiya 25 P 6
Kyzyl-Kommuna 35 H 1
Kyzylkum, Peski 35 G 2
Kyzylkum, Peski 35 GH 2
Kyzylrabot 35 J 3
Kyzyl-Suluo 37 P 3
Kyzyl-Syr 37 NO 3
Kyzyltau 25 O 6
Kyzyluy 35 H 1
Kyzyl-Yllyk 36 K 3
Kyzylzhar 35 G 1
Kzyl-Dzhar 35 H 1
Kzyl-Orda 35 H 2
Kzyltu 25 O 5

L

La Asunción 85 F 1
La Babia 78 B 2
La Banda 88 D 4
La Barca 78 B 2
La Barge 76 DE 3
La Blanquilla, Isla 85 F 1
La Bureba 18 C 3
La Cadena 78 B 2
La Campina 18 BC 4
La Canourgue 18 D 3
La Carlota 43 F 1
La Carlota 88 D 5
La Carolina 18 C 4
La Cebollera 18 C 3
La Ceiba (Honduras) 78 E 4
La Ceiba (Venezuela) 84 D 2
La Charité-sur-Loire 18 D 2
La Châtre 18 D 2
La Chaux-de-Fonds 19 E 2
La Chorrera 84 BC 2
La Chorrera 84 D 4
La Ciotat 19 E 3
La Cocha 88 C 4
La Colorada 76 D 6
La Concepción 84 D 1
La Coronilla 88 F 5
La Coruña 18 B 3
La Crosse 77 H 3
La Cruz (Argentina) 88 E 4
La Cruz (Costa Rica) 78 E 5
La Cruz (Mexico) 76 E 7
La Cruz (Uruguay) 88 E 5
La Cuesta 78 B 2
La Cueva 89 B 6
La Digue 65 K 5
La Dorada 84 D 2
La Escala 18 D 3
La Esmeralda 86 D 5
La Esperanza (Argentina) 89 C 6
La Esperanza (Bolivia) 86 D 3
La Estrada 18 B 3
La Estrella 86 D 5
La Flèche 18 CD 2
La Flor 78 F 5
La Forestière 85 H 2
La Fría 84 D 2
La Fuente de San Esteban 18 B 3
La Glória 84 D 2
La Gran Sabana 85 F 2–3
La Grand-Combe 18 D 3
La Grande 76 C 2
La Grande Rivière 75 MN 5
La Grange 77 J 5
La Granja 18 C 3
La Gruta 88 F 4
La Guaira 84 E 1
La Guardia (Argentina) 88 C 4
La Guardia (Bolivia) 86 D 4
La Guardia (Spain) 18 B 3
La Habana 79 F 3
La Huacan 78 B 4
La Japonesa 89 C 6
La Junta (Bolivia) 86 D 4
La Junta (CO, U.S.A.) 76 F 4
La Junta (Mexico) 76 E 6
La Libertad 78 E 5
La Ligua 88 B 5
La Linea 18 B 4
La Loche 73 Q 4
La Maddalena 19 E 3
La Maiella 19 F 3
La Malbaie 75 N 6
La Mancha 18 C 4
La Marina 18 C 4
La Mariscala 88 F 5
La Marmora 19 E 4
La Marque 77 G 6
La Mauricie National Park 75 N 6
La Merced 88 C 4
La Montaña 86 B 2–3
La Mosquitia 78 F 4–5
La Negra 86 B 5

La Orchila, Isla 84 E 1
La Oroya 86 A 3
La Palma (Panamá) 84 C 2
La Palma [Canary Islands] 58 B 3
La Palma del Condado 18 B 4
La Paloma 88 F 5
La Paragua 85 F 2
La Paz (Argentina) 88 C 5
La Paz (Argentina) 88 E 5
La Paz (Bolivia) 86 C 4
La Paz (Mexico) 76 D 7
La Paz, Bahia de 76 D 7
La Pedrera 84 DE 4
La Pelada 88 D 5
La Perouse Strait 37 Q 6
La Pesca 78 E 3
La Piedad 78 B 3
La Pine 76 B 3
La Plata 88 E 5–6
La Puebla de Cazalla 18 B 4
La Puerta 88 D 5
La Puntilla 84 B 4
La Quemada 78 B 3
La Quiaca 86 C 5
La Raya Abra 86 B 3
La Réole 18 CD 3
La Ribera 18 C 3
La Rioja (Argentina) 88 C 4
La Rioja (Spain) 18 C 3
La Robla 18 B 3
La Roche 51 J 6
La Rochelle 18 C 2
La Roche-sur-Yon 18 C 2
La Roda 18 C 4
La Romana 79 J 4
La Ronge 73 Q 4
La Sabana (Argentina) 88 D 4
La Sabana (Colombia) 84 E 3
La Salina 76 D 5
La Salle 77 J 3
La Sarre 75 M 6
La Serena (Chile) 88 B 4
La Serena (Spain) 18 B 4
La Seyne-sur-Mer 19 E 3
La Solana 18 C 4
La Souterraine 18 D 2
La Spezia 19 EF 3
La Tagua 84 CD 3
La Teste 18 C 3
La Tortuga, Isla 84 E 1
La Tuque 75 N 6
La Unión 84 C 3
La Unión (Chile) 89 B 7
La Union (El Salvador) 78 E 5
La Union (Mexico) 78 B 4
La Unión (Spain) 18 C 4
La Urbana 84 E 2
La Vega 89 EF 3
La Venta 78 D 4
La Ventana 78 B 3
La Ventura 78 B 3
La Viña 84 C 5
La Zarca 78 B 2
Laa an der Thaya 19 G 2
Laba 21 F 2
Labang 42 D 3
Labaz, Ozero 36 G 1
Labazhskoye 24 K 2
Labbezenga 62 E 2
Labe (Czechoslovakia) 15 F 4
Labé (Guinea) 62 B 3
Labelle 75 N 6
Labengke, Pulau 43 F 4
Labenne 18 C 3
Labouheyre 18 C 3
Laboulaye 88 D 5
Labrador 75 NO 4
Labrador Basin 98 A 2
Labrador City 75 O 5
Labrador, Coast of 75 PQ 4–5
Labrador Current 92
Labrador Sea 75 QR 4
Lábrea 85 F 3
Labrieville 75 O 6
Labuan (Indonesia) 42 C 5
Labuan (Malaysia) 42 DE 2
Labuha 43 G 4
Labuhanbajo 43 EF 5
Labuhanbilik 42 B 3
Labutta 41 F 4
Labuya 37 S 2
Labytnangi 25 N 2
Lac 20 A 2
Lac à l'Eau-Claire 75 MN 4
Lac à l'Eau-Claire 75 N 4
Lac Alaotra 67 H 3
Lac Albanel 75 N 5
Lac Allard 75 P 5
Lac au Goéland 75 M 5–6
Lac aux Goélands 75 P 4
Lac Belot 73 M 2
Lac Bermen 75 O 5

Lac Bienville 75 N 4
Lac Brochet 73 R 4
Lac Burton 75 M 5
Lac Caniapiscau 75 O 5
Lac Champdoré 75 O 4
Lac Chibougamau 75 N 6
Lac Couture 75 N 3
Lac de Grand Lieu 18 C 2
Lac de Gras 73 P 3
Lac de Guiers 62 A 2
Lac de Kossou 62 CD 4
Lac de Neuchâtel 19 E 2
Lac Débo 62 D 2
Lac Delcommune 66 D 2
Lac Delorme 75 O 5
Lac des Bois 73 N 2
Lac d'Iberville 75 N 4
Lac Dô 62 D 2
Lac du Bourget 19 E 2
Lac du Der 19 D 2
Lac Evans 75 M 5
Lac Faguibine 62 D 2
Lac Faribault 75 N 4
Lac Fitri 63 H 3
Lac Guillaume Delisle 75 M 4
Lac Kempt 75 N 6
Lac Kipawa 75 M 6
Lac Klotz 75 N 3
Lac Korarou 62 D 2
Lac La Biche 73 P 5
Lac la Martre 73 O 3
Lac la Martre 73 O 3
Lac la Ronge 73 R 4
Lac Le Moyne 75 O 4
Lac Léman 19 E 2
Lac Mai-Ndombe 64 B 5
Lac Manouane 75 N 5
Lac Maunoir 73 MN 2
Lac Mégantic 75 N 6
Lac Minto 75 N 4
Lac Mistassini 75 N 5
Lac Moero 64 D 6
Lac Musquaro 75 P 5
Lac Nantais 75 N 3
Lac Naococane 75 NO 5
Lac Niangay 62 D 2
Lac Nichicum 75 N 5
Lac Opiscotéo 75 O 5
Lac Payne 75 N 4
Lac Peribonca 75 N 5
Lac Plétipi 75 N 5
Lac Sakami 75 M 5
Lac Seul 74 J 5
Lac Tassialouc 75 N 4
Lac Tshangalele 66 D 2
Lac Tumba 64 B 5
Lac Upemba 64 D 6
Lac Wakuach 75 O 4
Lacanau 18 C 2
Lacantún, Rio 78 D 4
Lacaune, Monts de 18 D 3
Laccadive Islands 40 B 5
Lacepede Bay 49 F 6
Lacepede Islands 48 C 2
Lacerdónia 67 F 3
Lacha, Ozero 24 G 3
Lachay, Punta 84 C 6
Lachlan River 49 GH 5
Lâçin 21 D 2
Lackawanna 77 L 3
Lacombe 73 P 5
Lacq 12
Lacs des Loups Marins 75 N 4
Lacul Razelm 20 C 2
Lacul Sinoe 20 C 2
Ladakh Range 35 K 4
Ladário 86 E 4
Laddicea 20 C 3
Ladik 21 E 2
Ladismith 66 C 6
Lãdiz 35 G 5
Lado, Jabal 64 E 3
Ladoga, Lake 16 K 3
Ladong 38 E 6
Ladozhskoye Ozero 16 K 3
Ladrillero, Golfo 89 A 8
Ladu 41 F 2
Ladybrand 66 D 5
Ladyga 25 R 2
Ladysmith 66 D 5
Ladyzhenka 25 N 5
Ladzhanur 21 F 2
Lae (Marshall Is.) 52 C 2
Lae (Papua New Guinea) 50 E 3
Laea 43 F 4
Laem Ngop 41 H 5
Lafayette (IN, U.S.A.) 77 J 3
Lafayette (LA, U.S.A.) 77 H 5
Laffan, Ra's (Qatar) 23 F 4
Lafia 63 F 4
Lafiagi 63 EF 4
Lâft (Iran) 23 G 4
Laful 41 F 6
Laga Hida 65 G 3
Lagan 17 F 4
Lagarto 87 J 3

Lagash (Iraq) 23 E 3
Lågen 16 E 3
Laggan 3 B 3
Laggan, Loch 3 B 3
Laghouat 59 F 2
Laghy 4 A 2
Lago Agrio 84 C 4
Lago Amanã 85 F 4
Lago Arapa 86 B 4
Lago Argentino 89 B 9
Lago Badajós 85 F 4
Lago Blanco 89 C 9
Lago Buenos Aires 89 B 8
Lago Cabora Bassa 67 E 3
Lago Cardiel 89 B 8
Lago Chiuta 67 F 2
Lago Colhué Huapí 89 C 8
Lago da Pedra 85 J 4
Lago de Chapala 78 B 3
Lago de Erepecu 85 G 4
Lago de Junín 86 A 3
Lago de Manacapuru 85 F 4
Lago de Managua 78 E 5
Lago de Maracaibo 84 D 1–2
Lago de Nicaragua 78 E 5
Lago de Poopó 86 C 4
Lago de San Luis 86 D 3
Lago de Yojoa 78 E 5
Lago del Coghinas 19 E 3
Lago del Toro 89 B 9
Lago di Bolsena 19 F 3
Lago di Bracciano 19 F 3
Lago di Como 19 E 2
Lago di Garda 19 F 2
Lago di Lesina 19 G 3
Lago di Varano 19 G 3
Lago d'Iséo 19 E 2
Lago d'Orta 19 E 2
Lago Fagnano 89 C 9
Lago General Carrera 89 B 8
Lago Llanguihue 89 B 7
Lago Maggiore 19 E 2
Lago Mandioré 86 E 4
Lago Musters 89 C 8
Lago Nahuel Huapi 89 B 7
Lago Novo 85 H 3
Lago O'Higgins 89 B 8
Lago Omodeo 19 E 3
Lago Piorini 85 F 4
Lago Posadas 89 B 8
Lago Pueyrredón 89 B 8
Lago Rogagua 86 C 3
Lago San Martín 89 B 8
Lago Titicaca 86 C 4
Lago Trasimeno 19 F 3
Lago Uiñaimarca 86 C 4
Lago Viedma 89 B 8
Lagoa dos Patos 88 F 5
Lagoa Feia 87 H 5
Lagoa Mangueira 88 F 5
Lagoa Mirim 88 F 5
Lagonoy Gulf 43 F 1
Lagos (Greece) 20 C 2
Lagos (Nigeria) 62 E 4
Lagos (Portugal) 18 B 4
Lagos de Moreno 78 B 3
Lagosa 64 E 6
Lagrange 48 C 2
Laguiole 18 D 3
Laguna 88 G 4
Laguna Blanca 89 B 9
Laguna Concepción 86 D 4
Laguna de Antela 18 B 3
Laguna de Brus 78 F 4
Laguna de Caratasca 78 F 4
Laguna de Chiriquí 84 B 2
Laguna de Perlas 78 F 5
Laguna de Santa Maria 76 E 5
Laguna de Tamiahua 78 C 3
Laguna de Términos 78 D 4
Laguna Madre (Mexico) 78 C 2–3
Laguna Madre (TX, U.S.A.) 77 G 6
Laguna Mar Chiquita 88 D 5
Laguna Merín 88 F 5
Laguna Morales 78 C 3
Laguna Uberaba 86 E 4
Laguna Veneta 19 F 2
Lagunas (Chile) 86 BC 5
Lagunas (Peru) 84 C 5
Lagune Aby 62 D 4
Lagune Ndogo 63 F 6
Lagune Nkomi 63 F 6
Lagunillas 84 D 1
Lagunillas 86 D 4
Lagunitos 84 B 4
Laha 37 M 6
Lahad Datu 43 E 2
Lahat 42 B 4
Lahe 41 G 2
Lahewa 42 A 3
Lahij 61 G 6
Lãhijãn (Iran) 23 F 1
Laholm 17 F 4
Laholmsbukten 17 F 4
Lahore 35 J 4

Lahr 15 E 5
Lahti 16 J 3
Lai 63 H 4
Lai Chau 41 H 3
Laiagam 50 D 3
Laide 2 B 3
Laihia 16 H 3
Lai-hka 41 G 3
Laingsburg 66 C 6
Lainioälven 16 H 2
Lairg 2 B 2
Lairi 63 H 3
Lais 42 B 4
Laisamis 65 F 4
Laisvall 16 G 2
Laitila 17 H 3
Laiwu 39 G 3
Laiwui 43 G 4
Laixi 39 H 3
Laiyang 39 H 3
Laiyuan 38 F 3
Laizhou Wan 39 G 3
Lajes (Río Grande do Norte, Brazil) 87 J 2
Lajes (Santa Catarina, Brazil) 88 F 4
Lak Boggal 65 F 4
Lak Bor 65 G 4
Lak Dera 65 FG 4
Lake Abaya 65 F 3
Lake Abbe 65 G 2
Lake Abitibi 75 M 6
Lake Afrêra 65 G 2
Lake Albert (OR, U.S.A.) 76 BC 3
Lake Albert (Uganda/Zaire) 64 E 4
Lake Alexandrina 49 F 6
Lake Alsh 2 B 3
Lake Amadeus 48 E 3
Lake Annean 48 B 4
Lake Argyle 48 D 2
Lake Assale 65 G 2
Lake Athabasca 73 Q 4
Lake Aubry 73 M 2
Lake Auld 48 C 3
Lake Austin 48 B 4
Lake Baikal 36 J 5
Lake Ballard 48 C 4
Lake Bangweulu 66 D 2
Lake Baringo 65 F 4
Lake Barkley 77 J 4
Lake Barlee 48 B 4
Lake Berryessa 76 B 4
Lake Big Sand, 73 S 4
Lake Birch, 74 J 5
Lake Blanche (South Australia) 49 F 4
Lake Blanche (Western Australia) 48 C 3
Lake Breaden 48 D 4
Lake Brown, 73 T 2
Lake Buchanan (Queensland, Austr.) 49 H 3
Lake Buchanan (TX, U.S.A.) 76 G 5
Lake Buchanan (Western Australia) 48 C 4
Lake Buck 48 E 3
Lake Callabonna 49 F 4
Lake Carey 48 C 4
Lake Cargelligo 49 H 5
Lake Carnegie 48 C 4
Lake Chad 63 G 3
Lake Chamo 65 F 3
Lake Champlain 77 M 3
Lake Charles 77 H 5
Lake Chelan 76 B 2
Lake Chilwa 67 F 3
Lake Chippewa 77 H 2
Lake City (FL, U.S.A.) 77 K 5
Lake City (N.C., U.S.A.) 77 L 5
Lake Claire 73 P 4
Lake Clark 72 G 3
Lake Clark National Park and Preserve 72 G 3
Lake Cowal 49 H 5
Lake Cowan 48 C 5
Lake Cumberland 77 JK 4
Lake Darlot 48 C 4
Lake Deborah 48 B 5
Lake Dey Dey 48 E 4
Lake Disappointment 48 C 3
Lake District 5 D 2
Lake Dora 48 C 3
Lake Dundas 48 C 5
Lake Eaton 48 E 3
Lake Edward 64 D 5
Lake Ell 48 D 4
Lake Erie 77 K 3
Lake Everard 49 F 5
Lake Eyasi 64 E 5
Lake Eyre 49 F 4
Lake Eyre Basin 49 F 4
Lake Francis Case 76 FG 3
Lake Frome 49 F 5
Lake Gairdner 49 F 5

Lake Galilee 49 H 3
Lake Gamarri 65 G 2
Lake George (FL, U.S.A.) 77 K 6
Lake George (N.Y., U.S.A.) 77 M 3
Lake George (Uganda) 64 E 5
Lake George (Western Australia) 48 C 3
Lake Gidgi 48 D 4
Lake Gillen 48 C 4
Lake Gillian 75 M 2
Lake Gordon, 73 P 3
Lake Grace 48 B 5
Lake Grandin 73 O 3
Lake Gregory (South Australia) 49 F 4
Lake Gregory (Western Australia) 48 A 4
Lake Gregory (Western Australia) 48 D 3
Lake Harbour 75 O 3
Lake Havasu City 76 D 5
Lake Hazlett 48 D 3
Lake Hopkins 48 D 3
Lake Huron 77 K 3
Lake Inle 41 G 3
Lake Iteshi-Teshi 66 D 3
Lake Jackson 77 G 6
Lake Kariba 66 D 3
Lake Kemp 76 G 5
Lake King 48 B 5
Lake Kitangiri 64 E 5
Lake Kivu 64 D 5
Lake Koocanusa 76 D 2
Lake Koolivoo 49 F 3
Lake Kopiago 50 D 3
Lake Kotcho 71
Lake Kutubu 50 D 3
Lake Kyoga 64 E 4
Lake Laberge 72 K 3
Lake Ladoga 16 K 3
Lake Ladoga 16 K 3
Lake Lapage 48 C 5
Lake Lefroy 48 C 5
Lake Lucas 48 D 3
Lake Macdonald 48 D 3
Lake Machattie 49 FG 3
Lake Mackay 48 D 3
Lake Magenta 48 B 5
Lake Maitland 48 C 4
Lake Malawi 67 E 2
Lake Manitoba 73 S 5
Lake Manyara 65 F 5
Lake Marion 77 K 5
Lake Mason 48 B 4
Lake Maurice 48 E 4
Lake Mburu 64 E 5
Lake Mc Leod 48 A 3
Lake Mead 76 D 4
Lake Mead National Recreation Area 76 CD 4
Lake Melville 75 Q 5
Lake Michigan 77 J 3
Lake Minchumina 72 G 3
Lake Minigwal 48 C 4
Lake Missisa, 74 K 5
Lake Monger 48 B 4
Lake Moore 48 B 4
Lake Moultrie 77 K 5
Lake Murray (Papua New Guinea) 50 D 3
Lake Murray (Papua New Guinea) 50 D 3
Lake Murray (S.C., U.S.A.) 77 K 5
Lake Mweru 64 D 6
Lake Nabberu 48 C 4
Lake Nash 49 F 3
Lake Nasser (Egypt) 22 A 5
Lake Natron 65 F 5
Lake Neale 48 E 3
Lake Ngami 66 C 4
Lake Nipigon 74 K 6
Lake Nipissing 75 LM 6
Lake Nyanga 48 D 4
Lake Nyasa 67 E 2
Lake O' The Cherokees 77 H 4
Lake Oahe 76 FG 2
Lake of the Ozarks 77 H 4
Lake of the Woods 74 H 6
Lake Okeechobee 77 K 6
Lake Onega 24 G 3
Lake Ontario 77 L 3
Lake Owyhee 76 C 3
Lake Oxford 73 S 4–5
Lake Peipus 17 J 4
Lake Pend Oreille 76 C 2
Lake Philippi 49 F 3
Lake Placid 77 M 3
Lake Pontchartrain 77 HJ 5
Lake Powell 76 D 4
Lake Raeside 48 C 4
Lake Rason 48 C 4
Lake Rebecca 48 C 5
Lake River 75 L 5
Lake Rosa 79 H 3

Lake Rudolf 65 F 4
Lake Rukwa 64 E 6
Lake Rutanzige 64 D 5
Lake Rutanzige → Lake Edward 64 D 5
Lake Saint Joseph 74 J 5
Lake Saint Lucia 67 E 5
Lake Saint-Jean 75 N 6
Lake Sakakawea 76 F 2
Lake Scugog 75 M 7
Lake Seabrook 48 B 5
Lake Shala 65 F 3
Lake Shepperd 48 C 4
Lake Shibogama, 74 K 5
Lake Simcoe 75 M 7
Lake Stefanie 65 F 4
Lake Superior 77 J 2
Lake Tahiryuak, 73 P 1
Lake Tahoe 76 C 4
Lake Tana 65 F 2
Lake Tanganyika 64 DE 6
Lake Taupo 51 R 8
Lake Te Anau 50 P 10
Lake Throssel 48 C 4
Lake Timagami 75 L 6
Lake Timiskaming 75 M 6
Lake Tobin 48 D 3
Lake Torrens 49 F 5
Lake Turkana 65 F 4
Lake Victoria 64 E 5
Lake Volta 62 DE 4
Lake Wakatinu 50 P 10
Lake Wanaka 50 P 9
Lake Waukarlycarly 48 C 3
Lake Way 48 C 4
Lake White 48 D 3
Lake Wills 48 D 3
Lake Windermere 5 D 2
Lake Winnebago 77 J 3
Lake Winnibigoshish 77 H 2
Lake Winnipeg 73 S 5
Lake Winnipegosis 73 RS 5
Lake Winnipesaukee 77 M 3
Lake Woods 48 E 2
Lake Worth 77 L 6
Lake Xau 66 C 4
Lake Yamma Yamma 49 G 4
Lake Yeo 48 C 4
Lake Zwai 65 F 3
Lakefield 49 G 1
Lakeland 77 K 6
Lakenheath 7 E 1
Lakes Entrance 49 H 6
Lakes, Eskimo 72 L 2
Lakes National Park 51 Q 9
Lakeview 76 BC 3
Lakewood (CO, U.S.A.) 76 E 4
Lakewood (OH, U.S.A.) 77 K 3
Lakhdenpokh 16 K 3
Lakhimpur 40 D 2
Lakhnadon 40 C 3
Lakhpat 40 A 3
Lakki 35 J 4
Lakon 51 J 4
Lakonikos Kólpos 20 B 3
Lakota 62 C 4
Laksefjorden 16 J 1
Lakselv 16 J 1
Lakshadweep 40 B 5
Lakuramau 51 F 2
Lala Musa 35 J 4
Lalago 64 E 5
Lalara 63 G 5
Lãleli Geçidi 21 E 3
Lalereh, Tanjung 43 E 4
Lãlí (Iran) 23 E 2
Lalibela 65 F 2
Lalin 18 B 3
Lalitpur 40 C 3
Lam Chi 41 H 4
Lam Pao Reservoir 41 H 4
Lama Kara 62 E 4
Lama, Ozero 36 F 2
Lama Shillindi 65 G 4
Lamar 76 F 4
Lamarque 89 C 6
Lamas 84 C 5
Lamballe 18 C 2
Lambaréné 63 FG 6
Lambay Island 4 BC 3
Lambayeque 84 B 5
Lamberhurst 7 E 2
Lambert, Cape 51 F 2
Lambert Glacier 91
Lamberts Bay 66 B 6
Lambley 5 D 2
Lambon 51 F 2
Lambourne 7 D 2
Lambton, Cape 73 MN 1
Lamé 63 G 4
Lamego 18 B 3
Lamesa 76 F 5
Lamezia Terme 19 G 4
Lamia 12
Lamía 20 B 3
Lamington 3 C 4

Lamington National Park 49 J 4
Lammermoor 49 G 3
Lammermuir Hills 3 C 4
Lamon Bay 43 F 1
Lamont 77 K 5
Lamotrek 52 A 2
Lamotte-Beuvron 18 D 2
Lampang 41 G 4
Lampasas 76 G 5
Lampazos de Naranjo 78 BC 2
Lampeter 6 B 1
Lamphun 41 G 4
Lamu 65 G 5
Lamud 84 C 5
Lan Hsu 39 H 6
Lanai 53 E 1
Lanark 3 C 4
Lanbi Kyun 41 G 5
Lancang 38 C 6
Lancang Jiang 38 D 6
Lancashire 5 D 3
Lancaster (CA, U.S.A.) 76 C 5
Lancaster (U.K.) 5 D 2
Lancelin 48 B 5
Lanchkhuti 21 F 2
Lanciano 19 F 3
Lanco 89 B 6
Łańcut 15 H 4
Landau 15 F 5
Landeck 19 F 2
Landegode 16 F 2
Lander 76 E 3
Landerneau 18 C 2
Landete 18 C 4
Landfall 41 F 5
Land's End 6 B 2
Landshut 15 F 5
Landskrona 17 F 4
Landsort 17 G 4
Landsortsdjupet 17 G 4
Lanesborough 4 B 3
Lang Shan 38 E 2
Lang Son 41 J 3
Lang Suan 41 G 6
La'nga Co 40 D 1
Langa Langa 64 B 5
Långan 16 F 3
Langanes 16 BC 2
Langarfoss 16 C 2
Langdon 76 G 2
Lange Berg 66 B 6
Langeberg 66 BC 6
Langeland 17 F 5
Längelmävesi 16 H 3
Langenhagen 15 E 4
Langesund 17 E 4
Langholm 5 D 2
Langjökull 16 B 3
Langkawi 42 A 2
Langkon 42 E 2
Langlade 75 M 6
Langlo River 49 H 4
Langogne 18 D 3
Langon 18 C 3
Langöya 16 F 2
Langqên Zangbo 40 CD 1
Langreo 18 B 3
Langres 19 E 2
Langres, Plateau de 19 E 2
Langry 37 Q 5
Langsa 42 A 3
Långsele 16 G 3
Långseleån 16 G 3
Languedoc 18 D 3
Langzhong 38 E 4
Lanin, Parque Nacional 89 B 6
Lanin, Volcán 89 B 6
Lanji 40 D 3
Lannemezan 18 D 3
Lannion 18 C 2
Lannion, Baie de 18 C 2
Lanping 38 C 5
Lansdowne House 74 K 5
Lanshan 38 F 5
Lansing (MI, U.S.A.) 77 JK 3
Lansing (N.W.T., Can.) 72 L 3
Lansjärv 16 H 2
Lanxi 39 G 5
Lanzarote 58 C 3
Lanzhou 38 D 3
Lao Cai 41 H 3
Lao Ling 39 J 2
Laoag 43 J 1
Laoang 43 G 1
Laodikeia 20 C 3
Laoha He 39 G 2
Laohekou 38 F 4
Laois 4 B 3
Laon 18 D 2
Laos 41 HJ 4
Laouni 59 G 4
Laoye Ling 39 J 2
Lapa 88 G 4
Lapage, Lake 48 C 5
Lapai 63 F 4
Lapalisse 18 D 2

Lapford 6 C 3
Lapinig 43 G 1
Lapinlahti 16 J 3
Lápithos 21 D 3
Lápithos (Cyprus) 22 A 2
Lapland 16 H 2
Lappajärvi 16 H 3
Lappeenranta 16 J 3
Lappi 16 J 2
Lapri 37 MN 4
Laprida (Argentina) 88 D 4
Laprida (Argentina) 89 D 6
Lapseki 20 C 2
Laptev Sea 37 NO 1
Laptevo 24 G 5
Laptevykh, More 36 MN 1
Lapua 16 H 3
Laqīyat al Arba'in 60 D 4
Laqīyat 'Umran 60 D 5
L'Aquila 19 F 3
Lār 34 E 5
Lār (Iran) 23 G 4
Lar Koh 35 G 4
Larache 58 D 1
Laragh 4 B 3
Laragne 19 E 3
Lārak (Iran) 23 G 4
Laramate 86 B 3
Laramie 76 E 3
Laramie Mountains 76 E 3
Laramie River 76 E 3
Laranjal 85 G 4
Larantuka 43 F 5
Larat 43 H 5
Lärbro 17 G 4
Larche, Col de 19 E 3
Lærdalsøyri 16 E 3
Larde 67 F 3
Laredo (Spain) 18 C 3
Laredo (TX, U.S.A.) 76 G 6
Lārestān (Iran) 23 FG 4
Lārestān (Iran) 23 G 2
Largoward 3 C 3
Largs 3 B 4
Lárisa 20 B 3
Larkana 35 H 5
Larlomkriny 25 O 4
Larnaca 21 D 4
Larnaca (Cyprus) 22 A 2
Lárnax → Larnaca 21 D 4
Larne 4 C 2
Larned 76 G 4
Larrey Point 48 B 2
Larrimah 48 E 2
Larsa (Iraq) 23 D 3
Larsen Ice Shelf 91
Larvik 17 F 4
Lar'yak 25 Q 3
Larzac, Causse du 18 D 3
Lās 'Ānōd 65 H 3
Las Bonitas 84 E 2
Las Cejas 88 D 4
Las Coloradas 89 B 6
Las Cruces 76 E 5
Lās Dāred 65 H 2
Lās Dawa 65 H 2
Las Flores 89 E 6
Las Lajas 89 BC 6
Las Lanjitas 86 D 5
Las Lomitas 86 D 5
Las Marismas 18 B 4
Las Martinetas 89 C 8
Las Mestenas 78 B 2
Las Palmas 58 B 3
Las Palomas 76 E 5
Las Piedras 88 E 5
Las Pipinas 88 E 6
Las Plumas 89 C 7
Lās Qoray 65 H 2
Las Tablas 84 B 2
Las Tinajas 88 D 4
Las Tórtolas 88 C 4
Las Vegas (N.M., U.S.A.) 76 E 4
Las Vegas (NV, U.S.A.) 76 C 4
Lascaux, Grotte de 18 D 2
Lāsh-e Joveyn 35 G 4
Lashio 41 G 3
Lashkar 40 C 2
Lashkar Gāh 35 G 4
Lasia, Pulau 42 A 3
Lāsjerd (Iran) 23 F 2
Læsø 17 F 4
Lasolo 43 F 4
Lassen Peak 76 B 3
Last Mountain Lake 73 R 5
Lastoursville 63 G 6
Lastovo 19 G 3
Latacunga 84 C 4
Latady Island 91
Latakia (Syria) 22 B 2
Lätäseno 16 H 2
Latgale 17 J 4
Latgales Augstiene 17 J 4
Latheron 2 C 2
Lātīā'ān (Iran) 23 G 4
Latina 19 F 3

Latouche Treville, Cape 48 C 2
Latouma 63 G 1
Latronico 19 G 3
Latur 40 C 4
Latviya 17 J 4
Lau 63 G 4
Lau Group 52 D 4
Lauder 3 C 4
Lauenburg 15 F 4
Laughlin Peak 76 F 4
Lauhavuori 16 H 3
Laukaa 16 J 3
Launceston 52 A 5
Launceston (Tasmania, Austr.) 50 L 9
Launceston (U.K.) 6 B 2
Launggyaung 41 G 2
Laura 49 G 2
Laurel (MS, U.S.A.) 77 J 5
Laurel (MT, U.S.A.) 76 E 2
Laurencekirk 3 C 3
Laurentian Scarp 75 M 6
Lauria 19 G 3–4
Laurie River 73 R 4
Lauro Retiro 88 G 4
Lausanne 19 E 2
Lausitz 15 F 4
Laut Arafura 43 HJ 5
Laut Bali 42 C 1
Laut Banda 43 GH 5
Laut Flores 43 E 5
Laut Halmahera 43 G 4
Laut Jawa 42 CD 4
Laut Maluku 43 G 4
Laut, Pulau 42 E 4
Laut Seram 43 GH 4
Laut, Selat 42 E 4
Laut Sulawesi 43 F 3
Laut Timor 43 G 6
Lautaro 89 B 6
Laval (France) 18 C 2
Laval (Quebec, Can.) 75 N 6
Lavalle 88 C 5
Lāvān (Iran) 23 F 4
Lavapié, Punta 89 B 6
Lävar Meydän 34 E 4
Lavenham 7 E 1
Laverton 48 C 4
Lavezares 43 F 1
Lavia 16 H 3
Lavka Integralsoyuza 37 V 2
Lavras 87 G 5
Lavrentiya 72 C 2
Lávrion 20 B 3
Lavumisa 67 E 5
Law 64 E 3
Lāw 64 E 3
Lawas 42 E 3
Lawdar 61 H 6
Lawele 43 F 5
Lawers 3 B 3
Lawit, Gunung 42 D 3
Lawksawk 41 G 3
Lawn Hill (Queensland, Austr.) 49 F 2
Lawn Hill Creek (Queensland, Austr.) 49 F 2
Lawqah (Saudi Arabia) 22 D 3
Lawra 62 D 3
Lawrence 77 G 4
Lawrenceburg 77 J 4
Lawton 76 G 5
Lawz, Jabal al (Saudi Arabia) 22 B 3
Laxå 17 F 4
Laxey 4 C 2
Laxey Bay 4 C 2
Laxo 2 D 1
Layar, Tanjung 42 E 4
Laydennyy, Mys 24 J 2
Laylá 61 H 4
Layton 76 D 3
Laytown 4 B 3
Lazarev 37 Q 5
Lazarevac 20 B 2
Lazarevskoye 21 E 2
Lāzeh (Iran) 23 F 4
Lazo Dolinovka 37 T 4
Lazo, Iméni 37 S 3
Le Blanc 18 D 2
Le Creusot 19 D 2
Le Havre 18 CD 2
Le Locle 19 E 2
Le Maire, Estrecho de 89 CD 9–10
Le Mans 18 D 2
Le Mars 77 G 3
Le Mont-Saint-Michel 18 C 2
Le Moyne, Lac 75 O 4
Le Palais 18 C 2
Le Puy 18 D 2
Le Tanargue 18 D 3
Le Thillot 19 E 2
Le Tréport 18 D 1
Le Verdon-sur-Mer 18 C 2
Leaden Roding 7 E 2

Leadenham 7 D 1
Leadhills 3 C 4
Leadville 76 E 4
Leake, Mount 48 D 2
Le'an 38 G 5
Leatherhead 7 D 2
Leavenworth 77 GH 4
Łeba 15 G 4
Lebak 43 F 2
Lebanon (Lebanon) 22 B 2
Lebanon (MO, U.S.A.) 77 H 4
Lebanon (PA, U.S.A.) 77 L 3
Lebedin 24 F 5
Lebedyan' 24 G 5
Lebo 64 C 4
Lebombo Mountains 67 E 4–5
Lębork 15 G 4
Lebrija 18 B 4
Lebu 89 B 6
Lebyazh'ye 25 P 5
Lecce 19 G 3
Lecco 19 E 2
Lech 15 F 5
Lechang 38 F 5
Lechkhumskiy Khrebet 21 F 2
Leckemy 4 B 2
Léconi 63 G 6
Ledaig 3 B 3
Ledbury 6 C 1
Ledesma 18 B 3
Ledo, Cabo 66 A 1
Leduc 73 P 5
Ledyanaya, Gora 37 W 3
Lee 5 D 2
Leebotwood 6 C 1
Leeds 5 E 3
Leeds Bradford (Airport) 5 E 3
Leedstown 6 B 2
Leek 5 DE 3
Leer 15 E 4
Leeuwarden 14 E 4
Leeuwin, Cape 48 A 5
Leeward Islands (French Polynesia) 53 E 4
Leeward Islands (West Indies) 79 K 4
Léfini 63 H 6
Léfini Reserve 63 H 6
Lefke → Levka 21 D 3
Lefkoniko 21 D 3
Lefkoniko (Cyprus) 22 A 2
Lefkosa → Nicosia 21 D 3
Lefroy, Lake 48 C 5
Leganés 18 C 3
Legaspi 43 F 1
Legbourne 7 E 1
Legerwood 3 C 4
Legges Tor 50 L 9
Legnago 19 F 2
Legnano 19 E 2
Legnica 15 G 4
Legune 48 D 2
Leh 35 K 4
Léhamba 63 G 6
Lehi 76 D 3
Lehututu 66 C 4
Leibnitz 19 G 2
Leicester 7 D 1
Leicestershire 7 D 1
Leichardt River (Queensland, Austr.) 49 F 2
Leiden 14 D 4
Leigh 5 D 3
Leigh Creek 49 F 5
Leighlinbridge 4 B 3
Leighton Buzzard 7 D 2
Leikanger 16 E 3
Leine 15 E 4
Leipzig 15 F 4
Leiria 18 B 4
Leirvik 17 E 4
Leisler, Mount 48 D 3
Leiston 7 E 1
Leith 3 C 4
Leitrim 4 AB 2
Leixlip 4 B 3
Leiyang 38 F 5
Leizhou Bandao 38 E 6
Leizhou Wan 38 F 6
Leje 14 D 4
Leka 16 F 2
Lékana 63 G 6
Lekemti → Nekemt 65 F 3
Lekey 63 G 6
Lekhainá 20 B 3
Lekitobi 43 F 4
Lekki Lagoon 63 E 4
Leknes 16 F 2
Lekrisovo 25 P 3
Leksand 17 F 3
Leksozero, Ozero 16 K 3
Lekst, Jbel 58 D 3
Leksvik 16 F 3
Lelång 17 F 4

Lelant 6 B 2
Lelekovka 21 D 1
Leles 15 H 4
Lelewau 43 F 4
Leling 39 G 3
Lelinta 43 GH 4
Léman, Lac 19 E 2
Lembolovskaya Vozvyshennost' 17 JK 3
Lemesós → Limassol 21 D 4
Lemgo 15 E 4
Lemieux Islands 75 P 3
Lemluia 58 C 3
Lemmon 76 F 2
Lemmon, Mount 76 D 5
Lemoro 43 F 4
Lemos 85 H 4
Lempa, Rio 78 E 5
Lempäälä 16 H 3
Lemreway 2 A 2
Lemtybozh 24 L 3
Lemvig 17 E 4
Len Malaäs 43 H 4
Lena 37 N 1
Lendalfoot 3 B 4
Lendava 19 G 2
Lendery 16 K 3
Lenger 35 H 2
Lengshuijiang 38 F 5
Lengua de Vaca, Punta 88 B 5
Lenham 7 E 2
Lenina, Pik 35 J 3
Leninabad 35 HJ 2
Leninakan 21 F 2
Leningrad 17 K 4
Leningradskaya 21 E 1
Leningradskaya 91
Leninka 37 X 3
Lenino 21 E 1
Leninogorsk 24 K 5
Leninogorsk 25 Q 5
Leninsk 21 F 1
Leninskiy 37 N 4
Leninskoye 37 O 6
Len'ki 25 Q 5
Lenkoran' 34 D 3
Lennard River 48 C 2
Lennox, Isla 89 C 10
Leno-Angarskoye Plato 36 HJ 4
Lensk 36 K 3
Lentekhi 21 F 2
Lentiira 16 J 3
Lentini 19 F 4
Lentua 16 JK 3
Léo 62 D 3
Leoben 19 F 2
Leominster 6 C 1
León 18 B 3
León (Mexico) 78 B 3
León (Nicaragua) 78 E 5
León (Spain) 18 B 3
León, Cerro 86 D 5
Leon, Montes de 18 B 3
León Nuevo (Mexico) 78 C 2
Leonardville 66 B 4
Leonora 48 C 4
Leopold and Astrid Coast 91
Leopoldina 87 H 5
Leopoldo de Bulhões 87 G 4
Leovo 20 C 1
Lepar, Pulau 42 C 4
Lepe 18 B 4
Lepel' 17 J 5
Lephepe 66 D 4
Leping 39 G 5
Lepini, Monti 19 F 3
Lepiske 37 N 2
Lepsy 25 P 6
Leptis Magna 59 H 2
Lercara Friddi 19 F 4
Léré (Chad) 63 G 4
Lere (Nigeria) 63 F 3
Lérida (Colombia) 84 D 3
Lérida (Spain) 18 D 3
Lerma 18 C 3
Lermontovskiy 21 F 2
Lermoos 19 F 2
Léros 20 C 3
Lerum 17 F 4
Lerwick 2 D 1
Les Cayes 79 H 4
Les Coëvrons 18 C 2
Les Escoumins 75 O 6
Les Landes 18 C 3
Les Sables-d'Olonne 18 C 2
Lesina, Lago di 19 G 3
Lesjöfors 17 F 4
Leskino 36 C 1
Leskovac 20 B 2
Lesmahagow 3 C 4
Lesnaya 37 TU 4
Lesnoy 25 N 4
Lesogorsk 37 Q 6
Lesosibirsk 36 F 4

Lesotho 66 D 5
Lesozavodsk 39 K 1
Lesozavodskiy 16 K 2
Lesparre-Médoc 18 C 2
L'Esperance Rock 52 D 5
Lessebo 17 G 4
Lesser Antilles 79 K 4–5
Lesser Khingan Mountains 37 N 6
Lesser Slave Lake 73 OP 4
Lesser Sunda Islands 43 FG 5
Lestijärvi 16 H 3
Lestijoki 16 H 3
Lesueur, Mount 48 B 5
Lésvos 20 C 3
Leszno 15 G 4
Letchworth 7 D 2
Letha Range 41 F 3
Lethbridge 73 P 6
Lethem 85 E 3
Leti, Kepulauan 43 G 5
Leticia 84 D 4
Leting 39 G 3
Letlhakane 66 D 4
Letlhakeng 66 C 4
Letnerechenskiy 16 K 3
Letnyaya Zolotitsa 24 G 3
Letong 42 C 3
Letovice 15 G 4
Letsok-aw Kyun 41 G 5
Letterbreen 4 B 2
Letterkenny 4 B 2
Léua 66 C 2
Leuca 19 G 4
Leucate, Étang de 18 D 3
Leunovo 24 H 3
Leurbost 2 A 2
Leuser, Gunung 42 A 3
Levadhia 20 B 3
Levanger 16 F 3
Levante, Riviera di 19 E 3
Levanzo 19 F 4
Levas 34 D 2
Levaya Khetta 25 O 2–3
Leven 3 C 3
Leven 5 E 3
Leven, Loch 3 C 3
Leven 5 E 3
Lévêque, Cape 48 C 2
Leverkusen 15 E 4
Lévézou 18 D 3
Levice 15 G 5
Levin 51 R 9
Levis 75 N 6
Levka 21 D 3
Levka (Cyprus) 22 A 2
Levká Óri 20 B 3
Levkás 20 B 3
Levkosia → Nicosia 21 D 3
Levokumskoye 21 F 2
Levski 20 C 2
Lewe 41 G 4
Lewes 7 E 2
Lewis 2 A 2
Lewiston (ID, U.S.A.) 76 C 2
Lewiston (ME, U.S.A.) 77 N 3
Lewistown (MI, U.S.A.) 77 K 3
Lewistown (MT, U.S.A.) 76 E 2
Lewistown (PA, U.S.A.) 77 L 3
Lewotobi, Gunung 43 F 5
Lexington (KY, U.S.A.) 77 K 4
Lexington (N.C., U.S.A.) 77 KL
Leyburn 5 E 2
Leye 38 E 6
Leyland 5 D 3
Leysdown on Sea 7 E 2
Leyte 43 F 1
Lezha 20 A 2
Lezhi 38 DE 4
Lézignan-Corbieres 18 D 3
L'gov 24 G 5
Lhanbryde 2 C 3
Lhari 38 B 4
Lhasa 41 F 2
Lhasa He 41 F 1
Lhazê 40 E 2
Lhazhong 40 E 1
Lhok Seumawe 42 A 2
Lhoksukon 42 A 2–3
Lhorong 38 C 4
Lhozhag 41 F 2
Lhünze 38 B 5
Lhünzhub 41 F 1
Li Xian 38 D 4
Li Xian 38 E 4
Li Xian 38 F 5
Lia 64 B 3
Lian Xian 38 F 6
Liancheng 38 G 5
Lianga 43 G 2
Lianghe 38 C 6
Liangpran, Gunung 42 D 3
Lianhua Shan 38 G 6
Lianjiang 38 EF 6
Lianjiang 39 G 5
Lianping 38 F 6
Lianyin 37 M 5

Lianyungang 39 GH 4
Liao He 39 H 2
Liaodong Bandao 39 H 3
Liaodong Wan 39 H 2
Liaoning 39 H 2
Liaoyang 39 H 2
Liaoyuan 39 HJ 2
Liard 73 N 3
Liard River 73 M 4
Libby 76 C 2
Libenge 64 B 4
Liberal 76 F 4
Liberec 15 G 4
Liberia 62 BC 4
Liberia (Costa Rica) 78 E 5
Libertade 87 F 3
Libertador General San Martín
  86 D 5
Libo 38 E 5
Libobo, Tanjung 43 G 4
Liboi 65 G 4
Libourne 18 CD 3
Librazhdi 20 B 2
Libreville 63 F 5
Libro Point 43 E 1
Libya 59 HK 3
Libyan Desert 60 CD 3–4
Licata 19 F 4
Lice 21 F 3
Lichfield 7 D 1
Lichinga 67 F 2
Lichinga, Planalto de 67 F 2
Lichtenburg 66 D 5
Lichuan 38 E 4
Licosa, Punta 19 F 3
Lida (Japan) 39 L 3
Lida (U.S.S.R.) 17 J 5
Liden 16 G 3
Lidgate 7 E 1
Lidhorikion 20 B 3
Lido di Ostia 19 F 3
Lidzbark Wármiński 15 H 4
Liebig, Mount 48 E 3
Liechtenstein 19 EF 2
Liége 14 E 4
Lieksa 16 K 3
Lielupe Musa 17 H 4
Lienart 64 D 4
Lienz 19 F 2
Liepāja 17 H 4
Lierne 16 F 3
Liestal 19 E 2
Lievestuoreenjärvi 16 J 3
Lievre 75 M 6
Liffey, River 4 B 3
Lifford 4 B 2
Lifou 51 J 6
Lifton 6 B 2
Līgatne 17 H 4
Ligeni Shkodrës 20 A 2
Ligonha 67 F 3
Ligure, Appennino 19 E 3
Ligurian Sea 19 E 3
Ligwera 67 F 2
Lihir Group 51 F 2
Lihou Reef and Cays 49 J 2
Lijiang 38 D 5
Likasi 66 D 2
Likati 64 C 4
Likenäs 17 F 3
Likiep 52 C 2
Likoro 63 F 3
Likoto 64 C 5
Likouala 63 H 5
Likouala 63 H 5
Likouala aux Herbes 63 GH 5
Likwangoli 64 E 3
Liling 38 F 5
Lilla Edet 17 F 4
Lille 18 D 1
Lille Bælt 17 EF 4
Lillebonne 18 D 2
Lillehammer 16 F 3
Lillesand 17 E 4
Lilleström 17 F 4
Lillhärdal 16 F 3
Lilloet 73 N 5
Lilongwe 67 E 2
Liloy 43 F 2
Lim 20 A 2
Lima (MT, U.S.A.) 76 D 3
Lima (OH, U.S.A.) 77 K 3
Lima (Peru) 86 A 3
Lima (Portugal) 18 B 3
Limache 88 B 3
Līmah (Oman) 23 G 4
Limal 86 D 5
Limassol 21 D 4
Limassol (Cyprus) 22 A 2
Limavady 4 B 2
Limay 89 C 6
Limay Mahuida 89 C 6
Limbaži 17 H 4

Limbe 67 F 3
Limboto 43 F 3
Limburg 15 E 4
Limedsforsen 17 F 3
Limeira 87 G 5
Limerick 14 B 4
Limfjorden 17 E 4
Liminka 16 HJ 3
Limmen Bight 48 F 1
Límni 20 B 3
Limni Kremastá 20 B 3
Límni Mikre Prëspa 20 B 2
Limni Trikhonis 20 B 3
Limni Vegorritis 20 B 2
Limni Zistonis 20 C 2
Limningen 16 F 3
Limnos 20 C 3
Limoeiro 87 J 2
Limoges 18 D 2
Limogne, Causse de 18 D 3
Limon (CO, U.S.A.) 76 F 4
Limón (Costa Rica) 78 F 5
Limone Piemonte 19 E 3
Limoquije 86 CD 4
Limousin 18 D 2
Limoux 18 D 3
Limpopo 66 D 4
Limpopo 67 E 4
Limuru 65 F 5
Lin Xian 38 F 3
Linaälven 16 H 2
Līnah (Saudi Arabia) 22 D 3
Linakhamari 16 K 2
Lin'an 39 G 4
Linapacan Strait 43 E 1
Linares (Chile) 89 B 6
Linares (Mexico) 78 C 3
Linares (Spain) 18 C 4
Linaro, Capo 19 F 3
Lincang 38 D 6
Lincoln 7 D 1
Lincoln (Argentina) 88 D 5
Lincoln (IL, U.S.A.) 77 J 3
Lincoln (NE, U.S.A.) 77 G 3
Lincoln City 76 B 2
Lincoln Sea 90
Lincoln Wolds 5 E 3
Lincolnshire 7 D 1
Lindau 15 E 5
Linde 36 M 2
Linden 85 G 2
Lindenows Fjord 75 T 3
Linderödsåsen 17 F 4
Lindesberg 17 FG 4
Lindesnes 17 E 4
Lindhos 20 C 3
Lindi (Tanzania) 65 F 6–7
Lindi (Zaire) 64 D 4
Line Islands 53 E 2–3
Linfen 38 F 3
Lingao 38 E 7
Lingayan Gulf 43 H 1
Lingayen 43 H 1
Lingen 15 E 4
Lingfield 7 E 2
Lingga, Kepulauan 42 B 3–4
Lingga, Kepulauan 42 BC 4
Lingga, Pulau 42 B 4
Lingling 38 F 5
Lingomo 64 C 4
Lingqiu 38 F 3
Lingshan 38 E 6
Lingshi 38 F 3
Lingshui 38 F 7
Lingsugur 40 C 4
Linguère 62 AB 2
Lingwu 38 E 3
Lingyuan 39 G 2
Linh Cam 41 J 4
Linhai 39 H 5
Linhares 87 J 4
Linhe 38 E 2
Linhpa 41 G 2
Linköping 17 G 4
Linkou 39 K 1
Linlithgow 3 C 4
Linnhe, Loch 3 B 3
Linosa 19 F 4
Linquan 38 G 4
Lins 87 G 5
Linshu 39 G 4
Lintan 38 D 4
Lintao 38 D 3
Linton 7 E 1
Linton 76 G 2
Lintong 38 E 4
Linxi 39 G 2
Linxia 38 D 3
Linyanti 66 C 3
Linyi (Shandong, China) 39 G 3
Linyi (Shanxi, China) 38 F 3
Linz 19 F 2
Linze 38 CD 3
Lion, Golfe du 18–19 D 3
Liondo 64 C 5
Lioppa 43 G 5

Liouesso 63 H 5
Lipa 43 F 1
Lipari 19 FG 4
Lipatkain 42 B 3
Lipéité 63 H 5
Lipetsk 24 GH 5
Lípez, Cordillera de 86 C 5
Liphook 7 D 2
Lipin Bor 24 G 3
Liping 38 E 5
Lipkany 20 C 1
Lipno 15 G 4
Lipova 20 B 1
Lipovtsy 39 K 2
Lipu 38 F 6
Lira 64 E 4
Liranga 63 H 6
Lircay 86 B 3
Lisa 20 A 2
Lisabata 43 G 4
Lisala 64 C 4
Lisbellaw 4 B 2
Lisboa 18 B 4
Lisbon (N.D., U.S.A.) 76 G 2
Lisbon (Portugal) 18 B 4
Lisburn 4 B 2
Lisburne, Cape 72 D 2
Lishi 38 F 3
Lishu 39 H 2
Lishui 39 G 5
Lisichansk 24 G 6
Lisieux 18 D 2
Liskeard 6 B 2
L'Isle-Jourdain 18 D 3
L'Isle-sur-la-Sorgue 19 E 3
Lismanovy 25 P 3
Lismore (N.S.W., Austr.) 49 J 4
Lismore (U.K.) 3 B 3
Lisnacree 4 B 3
Lisnaskea 4 B 2
Liss 7 D 2
Listafjorden 17 E 4
Lištica 19 G 3
Litang 38 CD 4
Litang 38 E 6
Litang Qu 38 D 5
Lithgow 49 HJ 5
Lithinon, Ákra 20 B 4
Lithuania 17 H 4
Litke 24 L 1
Litke 37 Q 5
Litoměřice 15 F 4
Litovko 37 P 6
Little Abaco Island 79 G 2
Little Aden 61 G 6
Little Andaman 41 F 5
Little Cayman 79 F 4
Little Colorado 76 E 4
Little Desert National Park 49 G 6
Little Falls 77 H 2
Little Grand Rapids 73 ST 5
Little Inagua Island 79 H 3
Little Karroo 66 C 6
Little Minch 2 A 3
Little Missouri River 76 F 2
Little Nicobar 41 F 6
Little Ouse, River 7 E 1
Little Pamir 35 J 3
Little Rock 77 H 5
Little Sitkin 72 A 5
Little Smoky River 73 O 5
Little Tanaga 72 BC 5
Littlefield 76 F 5
Littlehampton 7 D 2
Littlemill 2 C 3
Littleport 7 E 1
Littleton 76 E 4
Litva 17 H 4
Liuhe 39 J 2
Liujia Xia 38 D 3
Liuku 38 C 5
Liupanshui 38 D 5
Liushuquan 38 B 2
Liuwa Plain 66 C 2
Liuyuan 38 C 2
Liuzhou 38 E 6
Līvāni 17 J 4
Livengood 72 H 2
Liveringa 48 C 2
Livermore, Mount 76 F 5
Liverpool (Airport) 5 D 3
Liverpool (Nova Scotia, Can.)
  75 P 7
Liverpool (U.K.) 5 D 3
Liverpool Bay 72 LM 1–2
Liverpool Range 49 J 5
Livingston (MT, U.S.A.) 76 D 2
Livingston (Newfoundl., Can.)
  75 O 5
Livingston (U.K.) 3 C 4
Livingstone 66 D 3
Livingstone Falls 63 G 7
Livingstone Memorial 67 E 2
Livingstone Mountains 64 E 6
Livingstonia 67 E 2

Livny 24 G 5
Livoniya 17 J 4
Livorno 19 EF 3
Livradois, Monts du 18 D 2
Liwale 65 F 6
Liwonde 67 F 2–3
Liyang 39 G 4
Lizard 6 B 3
Lizard Point 6 B 3
Lizarda 85 J 5
Ljig 20 B 2
Ljubeli 19 F 2
Ljubinje 19 G 3
Ljubljana 19 F 2
Ljubovija 20 A 2
Ljugarn 17 G 4
Ljungan 16 F 3
Ljungaverk 16 G 3
Ljungby 17 F 4
Ljungdalen 16 F 3
Ljungskile 17 F 4
Ljusdal 16 G 3
Ljusnan 16 G 3
Ljusne 16 G 3
Ljusterö 17 G 4
Llaima, Volcán 89 B 6
Llanaber 5 B 1
Llanaelhaearn 5 B 1
Llanbedr 5 B 1
Llanberis 5 B 1
Llanbrynmair 6 C 1
Llandefaelog 5 B 1
Llandeilo 6 B 2
Llandinam 6 C 1
Llandovery 6 C 2
Llandrindod Wells 6 C 1
Llandudno 4 D 3
Llandyfaelog 6 B 2
Llanelli 6 B 2
Llanes 18 C 3
Llanfaelog 5 B 1
Llanfaethlu 5 B 1
Llanfair Clydogau 6 C 1
Llanfairfechan 4 D 3
Llanfyllin 6 C 1
Llangadfan 6 C 1
Llangadog 6 C 1
Llangefni 6 B 1
Llanglydwen 6 B 2
Llangoed 5 B 1
Llangollen 6 C 1
Llangorse 6 C 3
Llangranog 6 B 1
Llangullo 6 C 1
Llangurig 6 C 1
Llanidloes 6 C 1
Llanilar 6 B 1
Llanllyfni 5 B 1
Llano Estacado 76 F 5
Llano River 76 G 5
Llanon 6 B 1
Llanos 84 DE 2–3
Llanos de Chiquitos 86 D 4
Llanos de Moxos 86 CD 4
Llanos de Tabasco y Campeche
  78 D 4
Llanos de Tamaulipas 78 C 2
Llanos de Urgel 18 D 3
Llanquihue, Lago 89 B 7
Llanrhaeadr-ym-Mochnant 6 C 1
Llanrhystud 6 B 1
Llanrwst 6 C 1
Llanstephan 6 B 2
Llanta 88 C 4
Llantrisant 6 C 2
Llantrisant 6 C 3
Llantwit Major 6 C 3
Llanwddyn 6 C 1
Llanwenog 6 B 1
Llanwnen 6 C 1
Llanwrda 6 C 3
Llanwrtyd-Wells 6 C 1
Lledrod 6 C 1
Lleyn 6 B 1
Llica 86 C 4
Llico 89 B 5
L'Ile Rousse 19 E 3
Lluchmayor 18 D 4
Llullaillaco, Volcán 86 C 5
Lo Nakpo 41 F 2
Loa 86 C 5
Loaita Island 42 D 1
Loanda 63 F 6
Loandjili 63 G 6
Loange 64 C 6
Loanhead 3 C 4
Loano 19 E 3
Lobatse 66 D 5
Lobaye 64 B 4
Loberia 89 E 6
Lobito 66 A 2
Lobitos 84 B 4
Lobos 88 E 5
Lobos de Afuera, Islas 84 B 5
Lobos de Tierra, Isla 84 B 5

Lobva 25 M 4
Locarno 19 E 2
Loch Arkaig 3 B 3
Loch Awe 3 B 3
Loch Broom 2 B 3
Loch Carron 2 B 3
Loch Doon 3 B 4
Loch Earn 3 B 3
Loch Eriboll 2 B 2
Loch Ericht 3 B 3
Loch Etive 3 B 3
Loch Ewe 2 B 3
Loch Fyne 3 B 3
Loch Hourn 3 B 3
Loch Katrine 3 B 3
Loch Laggan 3 B 3
Loch Leven 3 C 3
Loch Linnhe 3 B 3
Loch Lochy 3 B 3
Loch Lomond 3 B 3
Loch Long 3 B 3
Loch Maree 3 B 3
Loch Morar 3 B 3
Loch Ness 2 B 3
Loch Nevis 3 B 3
Loch Rannoch 3 B 3
Loch Shiel 3 B 3
Loch Shin 2 B 2
Loch Snizort 2 A 3
Loch Sunart 3 B 3
Loch Tay 3 B 3
Loch Torridon 2 B 3
Lochaber 3 B 3
Lochailort 3 B 3
Lochaline 3 B 3
Lochboisdale 2 A 3
Lochdon 3 B 3
Lochearnhead 3 B 3
Locheport 2 A 3
Locherben 3 C 4
Lochgair 3 B 3
Lochgilphead 3 B 3
Lochinver 2 B 2
Lochmaddy 2 A 3
Lochnagar 3 C 3
Lochranza 3 B 4
Lochy, Loch 3 B 3
Lock 49 F 5
Lockerbie 3 C 4
Lockhart River Mission 49 G 1
Lockton 5 E 2
Locminé 18 C 2
Locri 19 G 4
Lod (Israel) 22 B 3
Loddon River 49 G 6
Lodève 18 D 3
Lodeynoye Pole 24 F 3
Lodi 19 E 2
Lödingen 16 G 2
Lodja 64 C 5
Lödöse 17 F 4
Lodwar 64 F 4
Łodz 15 G 4
Loelli 64 E 3
Loeriesfontein 66 B 6
Lofa 62 B 4
Lofoten 16 F 2
Lofsdalen 16 F 3
Loftus 5 E 2
Lofty Ranges, Mount 49 F 5
Loga 62 E 3
Logan 76 D 3
Logan, Mount 72 J 3
Logan Mountains 72 M 3
Logansport 77 J 3
Logg 3 B 4
Logone 63 H 3–4
Logone Birni 63 G 3
Logoualé 62 C 4
Logroño 18 C 3
Logrosán 18 B 4
Lögstör 17 E 4
Lögumkloster 17 E 4
Lögurinn 16 C 2
Lohardaga 40 D 3
Lohit 41 G 2
Lohja 17 H 3
Lohjanjärvi 17 H 3
Lohjanselkä 17 H 3
Loholoho 43 F 4
Loikaw 41 G 4
Loimaa 17 H 3
Loimijoki 17 H 3
Loir 18 C 2
Loir, Vaux du 18 D 2
Loire 18 C 2
Loire, Val de 18 D 2
Loja 18 C 4
Loja 84 C 4
Loji 43 G 4
Lojo 17 H 3
Loka (Sudan) 64 E 4
Loka (Zaire) 64 B 4
Lokan tekojärvi 16 J 2
Lokandu 64 D 5
Lokaw 64 C 5

Löken 17 F 4
Lokgwabe 66 C 4
Lokhpodgort 25 N 2
Lokichar 65 F 4
Lokichokio 64 E 4
Lokilalaki, Gunung 43 F 4
Lokka 16 J 2
Lökken (Denmark) 17 E 4
Lökken (Norway) 16 E 3
Loknya 17 K 4
Loko (Burkina) 64 B 4
Loko (Nigeria) 63 F 4
Lokoja 63 F 4
Lokomo 63 H 5
Lokoro 64 C 5
Lokosovo 25 O 3
Loks Land 75 P 3
Loksa 17 J 4
Lokshak 37 O 5
Lokwa-Kangole 65 F 4
Lol 64 D 3
Lola 62 C 4
Loliondo 65 F 5
Lolland 17 F 5
Lolo 64 C 4
Loloda 43 G 3
Lolodorf 63 G 5
Lolowau 42 A 3
Lom (Bulgaria) 20 B 2
Lom (Cameroon) 63 G 4
Lom Sak 41 H 4
Loma Bonita 78 C 4
Loma Mountains 62 B 4
Loma Negra, Planicie de la 89 C 6
Lomami 64 C 4
Lomas 86 B 4
Lomas Coloradas 89 C 7
Lomas de Zamora 88 E 6
Lombarda, Serra 85 H 3
Lombarton 4 C 2
Lomblen, Pulau 43 F 5
Lombok 42 E 5
Lombok, Selat 42 E 5
Lomé 62 E 4
Lomela 64 C 5
Lomela 64 C 5
Loméméti 51 J 5
Lomié 63 G 5
Lomond, Loch 3 B 3
Lomonosov 17 J 4
Lomonosovka 25 N 5
Lomovoye 24 GH 3
Lomphat 41 J 5
Lompobatang, Gunung 43 F 5
Lompoc 76 B 5
Łomźa 15 H 4
Loncoche 89 B 6
Loncopue 89 B 6
Londiani 64 F 5
London 75 L 7
London (U.K.) 7 DE 2
Londonderry 4 B 2
Londonderry 89 B 10
Londonderry, Cape 48 D 1
Londonderry, Isla (Chile) 89 B 9
Londrina 87 F 5
Lone Pine 76 C 4
Long Akah 42 DE 3
Long Bay 77 L 5
Long Beach (CA, U.S.A.) 76 C 5
Long Beach (N.Y., U.S.A.) 77 M 3
Long Beach (WA, U.S.A.) 76 B 2
Long Eaton 7 D 1
Long Island (Papua New Guinea) 50 E 3
Long Island (Quebec, Can.) 75 M 5
Long Island (The Bahamas) 79 G 3
Long Lake 74 K 6
Long, Loch 3 B 3
Long Marston 5 E 3
Long Melford 7 E 1
Long Range Mountains 75 Q 6
Long Stratton 7 E 1
Long Valley 76 D 5
Long Xian 38 E 4
Long Xuyen 41 J 5
Longa (Angola) 66 A 2
Longa (Angola) 66 B 2
Longa (Brazil) 87 H 1
Longbleh 42 E 3
Longchuan 38 C 6
Longde 38 E 3
Longford (Tasmania, Austr.) 50 L 9
Longford (U.K.) 4 B 3
Longformacus 3 C 4
Longframlington 5 E 2
Longhai 39 G 6
Longhoughton 5 E 2
Longhua 39 G 2
Longhui 38 F 5
Longitudinal, Valle 89 B 6
Longjiang 37 M 6
Longkou 39 GH 3

Longlac 74 K 6
Longleju 42 E 3
Longlin 38 E 6
Longling 38 C 6
Longmanhill 2 C 3
Longmen 38 F 6
Longmont 76 F 3
Longmorn 2 C 3
Longnan 38 FG 6
Longnor 7 D 1
Longquan 39 G 5
Longreach 49 G 3
Longridge 5 D 3
Longs Peak 76 E 3
Longsegah 42 E 3
Longshan 38 E 5
Longsheng 38 F 5
Longshou Shan 38 D 3
Longside 2 D 3
Longtoft 5 E 2
Longtown 3 C 4
Longview (TX, U.S.A.) 77 GH 5
Longview (WA, U.S.A.) 76 B 2
Longwy 19 E 2
Longxi 38 D 3
Longyan 38 G 5
Longyao 38 G 3
Longzhou 38 E 6
Lonkin 41 G 2
Lons-le-Saunier 19 E 2
Lonton 41 G 2
Lontra 85 H 4
Loo 21 E 2
Looc 43 F 1
Lookout, Cape 77 L 5
Lookout Ridge 72 F 2
Loolmalasin 65 F 5
Loongana 48 D 5
Loop Head 14 AB 4
Lop 35 L 3
Lop Buri 41 H 5
Lop Nur 38 B 2
Lopari 64 C 4
Lopatin 34 D 2
Lopatina, Gora 37 Q 5
Lopatka 37 T 6
Lopatka, Mys 37 T 5
Lopatki 25 N 5
Lopcha 37 M 4
Lopez, Cap 63 F 6
Lopphavet 16 H 1
Loppi 17 H 3
Lopud 19 G 3
Lopydino 24 K 3
Lora 35 H 4
Lora del Río 18 B 4
Loralai 35 H 4
Lorca 18 C 4
Lord Howe Island 49 K 5
Lord Mayor Bay 73 TU 2
Lordegán (Iran) 23 F 3
Lordsburg 76 E 5
Lorengau 50 E 2
Lorestán (Iran) 23 E 2
Loreto 76 D 6
Loreto 84 D 4
Loreto (Maranhão, Brazil) 85 JK 5
Loreto (Mexico) 78 B 3
Lorica 84 C 2
Lorient 18 C 2
Lorn 3 B 3
Lörrach 15 E 5
Lorraine 19 E 2
Lorton 5 E 2
Lorugumu 64 F 4
Los 16 G 3
Los Alamos 76 E 4
Los Alerges, Parque Nacional 89 B 6
Los Andes 88 B 5
Los Ángeles (Chile) 89 B 6
Los Angeles 76 BC 5
Los Antiguos 89 B 8
Los Blancos 88 D 4
Los Frentones 88 D 4
Los Gatos 76 B 4
Los, Îles de 62 B 4
Los Juríes 88 D 4
Los Lagos 89 B 6
Los Lavaderos 78 C 3
Los Menucos 89 C 7
Los Mochis 76 E 6
Los Monegros 18 C 3
Los Palacios 78 F 3
Los Paraguas, Parque Nacional 89 B 6
Los Pozos 88 BC 4
Los Reyes de Salgado 78 B 4
Los Roques, Islas 84 E 1
Los Teques 84 E 1
Los Vilos 88 B 5
Losap 52 B 2
Lošinj 19 F 3

Losinoborskaya 25 R 4
Lospalos 43 G 5
Lossiemouth 2 C 3
Lost Trail Pass 76 D 2
Lostwithiel 6 B 2
Losuia 51 F 3
Losuwo 43 G 3
Lot 18 D 3
Lota 89 B 6
Loto 64 C 5
Lotta 16 J 2
Lotuke, Jabal 64 E 4
Lou 50 E 2
Loubomo 63 G 6
Loubuzhuang 38 A 3
Loudéac 18 C 2
Loudun 18 D 2
Loué 18 C 2
Louga 62 A 2
Lough Allen 4 A 2
Lough Conn 14 B 4
Lough Foyle 4 B 2
Lough Neagh 4 B 2
Lough Ree 4 B 3
Lough Sheelin 4 B 3
Lough Swilly 4 B 2
Loughborough 7 D 1
Loughton 7 E 2
Louhans 19 E 2
Louis Trichardt 66 DE 4
Louisa 77 K 4
Louisa Reef 42 D 2
Louisiade Archipelago 49 J 1
Louisiade Archipelago 51 F 4
Louisiana 77 H 5
Louisville 77 J 4
Loukhi 16 K 2
Loukolela 63 H 6
Loulan Yiji 38 A 2
Loum 63 FG 5
Loup 76 G 3
Loups Marins, Lacs des 75 N 4
Lourdes 18 C 3
Loustín 15 F 4
Louth (Australia) 49 H 5
Louth (Lincolnshire U.K.) 5 EF 3
Louth (Rep. of Ireland) 4 B 3
Loutrá Killinis 20 B 3
Louviers 18 D 2
Louwater 66 B 4
Lövånger 16 H 3
Lovat 17 K 4
Lovech 20 B 2
Loveland 76 E 3
Lovell 76 E 3
Lovelock 76 C 3
Loviisa 17 J 3
Lovington 76 F 5
Lovisa 17 J 3
Lovozero 16 L 2
Lovozero, Ozero 16 L 2
Lóvua 66 C 1
Lóvua 66 C 2
Low, Cape 73 UV 3
Lowa 64 D 5
Lowa 64 D 5
Lowell 77 M 3
Lower California 76 D 6
Lower Hutt 51 R 9
Lower Lough Erne 4 B 2
Lower Post 72 M 4
Lower Red Lake 77 H 2
Lower Tunguska River 36 F 3
Lowestoft 7 E 1
Lowicz 15 G 4
Lowshán (Iran) 23 E 1
Loxton (South Africa) 66 C 6
Loxton (South Australia) 49 G 5
Loyalty Islands 51 J 6
Loyauté, Iles 51 J 6
Loyoro 64 E 4
Lozére, Mont 18 D 3
Loznica 20 A 2
Lozovaya 25 P 5
Loz'va 25 M 4

Luangwa Valley Game Reserve 67 E 2
Luanping 39 G 2
Luanshya 66 D 2
Luanza 64 D 6
Luapala 66 D 2
Luarca 18 B 3
Luashi 66 C 2
Luau 66 C 2
Luba 63 F 5
Lubalo 66 B 1
Luban 15 G 4
Lubānas Ezers 17 J 4
Lubang Islands 43 EF 1
Lubango 66 A 2
Lubao 64 D 6
Lubartów 15 H 4
Lübbenau 15 F 4
Lubbock 76 F 5
Lübeck 15 F 4
Lubefu 64 C 5
Lubefu 64 C 5
Lubero 64 D 5
Lubika 64 D 6
Lubilash 64 C 6
Lubin 15 G 4
Lublin 15 H 4
Lubnān, Jabal (Lebanon) 22 B 2
Lubny 24 F 5
Luboń 15 G 4
Lubondaie 64 D 6
Lubuagan 43 J 1
Lubudi 64 D 6
Lubue 64 B 5
Lubuklinggau 42 B 4
Lubumbashi 66 D 2
Lubutu 64 D 5
Lubwe 66 D 2
Lucala 66 B 1
Lucala 66 B 1
Lucania, Mount 72 J 3
Lucano, Appenino 19 G 3
Lucapa 66 C 1
Lucas 86 B 3
Lucas, Lake 48 D 3
Lucca 19 F 3
Luce Bay 4 C 2
Lucea 79 G 4
Lucena (Philippines) 43 F 1
Lucena (Spain) 18 C 4
Lučenec 15 G 5
Lucera 19 G 3
Lucero 76 E 5
Luchulingo 67 F 2
Lüchun 38 D 6
Lucira 66 A 2
Luckenwalde 15 F 4
Lucker 5 E 2
Lucknow 40 D 2
Lucksta 16 G 3
Lucon 18 C 2
Lucusse 66 C 2
Lucy Creek 49 F 3
Lüda 39 H 3
Ludborough 5 EF 3
Ludbreg 19 G 2
Lüderitz 66 AB 5
Lüderitz Bay 66 AB 5
Ludgavan 6 B 2
Ludgershall 7 D 2
Ludgorsko Plato 20 C 2
Ludhiana 40 C 1
Ludian 38 D 5
Ludington 77 J 3
Ludlow 6 C 1
Ludogorie 20 C 2
Luduş 20 B 1
Ludvika 17 G 3
Ludwigsburg 15 E 5
Ludwigshafen 15 E 5
Ludwigslust 15 F 4
Ludza 17 J 4
Luebo 64 C 6
Lueki 64 D 5
Luena (Angola) 66 B 2
Luena (Angola) 66 C 2
Luena (Zaire) 64 D 6
Luena (Zambia) 67 E 2
Luena Flats 66 C 2
Luengue 66 C 3
Luepa 85 F 2
Lüeyang 38 E 4
Lufeng 38 D 5
Lufeng 38 G 6
Lufico 66 A 1
Lufira 64 D 6
Lufira, Chutes de la 64 D 6
Lufira Falls 64 D 6
Luga 17 J 4
Luga 17 J 4
Lugano 19 E 2
Lugansk → Voroshilovgrad 21 E 1
Luganville 51 J 5
Lugards Falls 65 F 5
Lugela 67 F 3

Lugenda 67 F 2
Lugnaquillia 4 B 3
Lugnvik 16 G 3
Lugo 18 B 3
Lugoj 20 B 1
Lugovoy 35 J 2
Lugovskiy 36 K 4
Lugton 3 B 4
Luhin Sum 39 G 1
Luhuo 38 D 4
Lui 66 B 1
Luia 66 C 1
Luiana 66 C 3
Luiana 66 C 3
Luilaka 64 C 5
Luimneach 14 B 4
Luing 3 B 3
Luino 19 E 2
Luiro 16 J 2
Luís Correia 87 H 1
Luis d'Abreu → Calchaguí 88 D 4
Luishia 66 D 2
Luiza 64 C 6
Luizi 64 D 6
Lujiang 39 G 4
Lukanga Swamp 66 D 2
Lukashkin Yar 25 P 3
Lukenie 64 B 5
Lukeville 76 D 5
Lukolela (Congo) 64 B 5
Lukolela (Zaire) 64 C 6
Lukonzolwa 64 D 6
Lukovit 20 B 2
Łukow 15 H 4
Lukoyanov 24 H 4
Lukuga 64 D 6
Lukuka 63 G 7
Lukumburu 64 F 6
Lukuni 64 B 6
Lukusashi 67 E 2
Luleå 16 H 2
Luleälven 16 H 2
Lüleburgaz 20 C 2
Luliang 38 D 5
Lüliang Shan 38 F 3
Lulimba 64 D 5
Lulonga 64 B 4
Lulonga 64 B 4
Lulu (Saudi Arabia) 23 E 3
Lulua 64 C 6
Lulworth Cove 7 C 2
Luma Cassai 66 B 2
Lumajangdong Co 40 D 1
Lumbala Kaquengue 66 C 2
Lumbala N'guimbo 66 C 2
Lumberton 77 L 5
Lumbo 67 G 3
Lumbovka 24 H 2
Lumbrales 18 B 3
Lumding 41 F 2
Lumsden 50 P 10
Lumuna 64 D 5
Lumut, Tanjung 42 C 4
Lunayyir, Ḥarrat 60 F 3
Luncarty 3 C 3
Lund 17 F 4
Lunda Norte 66 C 1
Lunda Sul 66 C 2
Lundazi 67 E 2
Lundevatn 17 E 4
Lundi → Runde 67 E 4
Lundie 3 C 3
Lundu 42 C 3
Lundy Island 6 B 2
Lune, River 5 D 2
Lüneburg 15 EF 4
Lüneburger Heide 15 EF 4
Lunel 18 D 3
Lunéville 19 E 2
Lunga 66 D 2
Lunggar 40 D 1
Lungleh 41 F 3
Lungue-Bungo 66 B 2
Luni 40 B 2
Luninets 17 J 5
Lunkho 35 J 3
Lunovayam 37 U 3
Lunsar 62 B 4
Lunsemfwa 66 D 2
Luntai 35 L 2
Luo He 38 E 3
Luobei 37 O 6
Luocheng 38 E 6
Luochuan 38 E 3
Luodian 38 E 5
Luoding 38 F 6
Luofu 64 D 5
Luohe 38 F 4
Luonan 38 F 4
Luong Nam Tha 41 H 3
Luonteri 16 J 3
Luoshan 38 FG 4
Luoyang 38 F 4
Luoyuan 39 GH 5
Luozi 63 G 6

Lupan Shan 38 E 3
Lupane 66 D 3
Lupeni 20 B 1
Luperón 79 H 4
Lupire 66 B 2
Luputa 64 C 6
Lūq 65 G 4
Luqu 38 D 4
Luquan 38 D 5
Luquembo 66 B 2
Lure, Montagne de 19 E 3
Lurgan 4 B 2
Luribay 86 C 4
Lurín 86 A 3
Lurio 67 F 2
Lurio 67 G 2
Lusaka 66 D 3
Lusambo 64 C 5
Lusanga 64 B 5
Lusangi 64 D 5
Lush, Mount 48 D 2
Lushan 38 D 4
Lushi 38 F 4
Lushnja 20 A 2
Lushoto 65 F 5
Lushui 38 C 5
Lüshun 39 H 3
Lusitano 66 B 1
Lusk 76 F 3
Lusk (Rep. of Ireland) 4 B 3
Luss 3 B 3
Lussanvira 87 F 5
Lustrafjorden 16 E 3
Lūt, Dasht-e (Iran) 23 G 2
Lutembo 66 C 2
Luton 7 D 2
Luton (Airport) 7 D 2
Lutong 42 D 3
Lutshima 64 B 6
Lutsk 17 J 5
Lutterworth 7 D 1
Lutuai 66 C 2
Luusua 16 J 2
Luvua 64 D 6
Luvuei 66 C 2
Luwegu 65 F 6
Luwingu 66 D 2
Luwuk 43 F 4
Luxembourg 14 E 5
Luxembourg 14 E 5
Luxi 38 C 6
Luxi 38 D 6
Luxor (Egypt) 22 A 4
Luza 24 J 3
Luza 24 J 3
Luzern 19 E 2
Luzhai 38 E 6
Luzhou 38 E 5
Luziânia 87 G 4
Luzilândia 87 H 1
Luzino 25 QR 2
Luzon 43 J 1
Luzon Strait 43 J 1
Lvov 24 D 6
L'vovka 25 P 4
Lyady 17 J 4
Lyakhovskiy, Bol'shoy, Ostrov
    37 Q 1
Lyakhovskiy, Malyy, Ostrov
    37 Q 1
Lyakhovskiye Ostrova 37 P 1
Lyamin 25 O 3
Lybster 2 C 2
Lycksele 16 G 3
Lydd 7 E 2
Lydd (Airport) 7 E 2
Lydenburg 66 DE 5
Lydham 6 C 1
Lydney 6 C 2
Lygyy, Mys 36 LM 1
Lyme Bay 6 C 2
Lyme Regis 6 C 2
Lymington 7 D 2
Lympne (Airport) 7 E 2
Lynchburg 77 L 4
Lynd 49 G 2
Lynd River 49 G 2
Lyndhurst (Queensland, Austr.)
    49 G 2
Lyndhurst (U.K.) 7 D 2
Lyndon River 48 A 3
Lyneham 7 D 2
Lyness 2 C 2
Lyngdal 17 E 4
Lyngen 16 H 2
Lyngseidet 16 H 2
Lynmouth 6 C 2
Lynn Canal 72 K 4
Lynn Lake 73 R 4
Lynton 6 C 2
Lynx Lake 73 Q 3
Lyon 19 DE 2
Lyon Inlet 73 V 2
Lyonnais, Monts du 19 D 2
Lyons River 48 B 3

Lysefjorden 17 E 4
Lysekil 17 F 4
Lyskovo 24 H 4
Łyso Gory 15 H 4
Lys've 25 L 4
Lysye Gory 24 H 5
Lytham St. Anne's 5 D 3
Lytton 73 N 5
Lyuban' 17 K 4
Lyubar 17 J 6
Lyubertsy 24 G 4
Lyubeshov 17 J 5
Lyuboml 17 H 5
Lyucha 36 G 3
Lyudinovo 24 FG 5
Lyuri 37 W 3

M

Ma'āmīr (Iraq) 23 E 3
Ma'ān (Jordan) 22 B 3
Maanselkä 16 J 3
Ma'anshan 39 G 4
Maarianhamina 17 H 3
Ma'arrat an Nu'mān (Syria) 22 B 2
Maas 14 E 4
Maasin 43 F 1
Maastricht 14 E 4
Maaza Plateau → Al Hadabat
    alMa'āzah 60 E 3
Mabaia 66 A 1
Mabalane 67 E 4
Ma'bar 61 G 6
Mabaruma 85 G 2
Mablethorpe 7 E 1
Mabote 67 E 4
Mabrous 63 G 1
Mabrūk 59 J 3
Mabuasehube 66 C 5
Mabuki 64 E 5
Ma'būs Yūsuf 59 K 3
Mac Kenzie Bay 91
Mac Kinlay River 49 G 3
Mac Pherson Range 49 J 4
Mac Robertson Land 91
Maca, Monte 89 B 8
Macadam Plains 48 B 4
Macaé 87 H 5
Macaíba 87 J 2
Macalister River 49 H 6
Macaloge 67 F 2
MacAlpine Lake 73 R 2
Macao 38 F 6
Macapá 85 H 3
Macará (Peru) 84 B 4
Macarena, Parque Nacional de la
    84 D 3
Macas 84 C 4
Macau 87 J 2
Macaúba 87 F 3
Macauley 52 D 4–5
Macaya, Pic de 79 H 4
Macclesfield 5 D 3
Macdonald, Lake 48 D 3
Macdonnell Ranges 48 E 3
Macduff 2 C 3
Macedo de Cavaleiros 18 B 3
Maceió 87 J 2
Macenta 62 C 4
Macerata 19 F 3
Mach 35 H 5
Macha 36 L 4
Machacamarca 86 C 4
Machachi 84 C 4
Machaíla 67 E 4
Machakos 65 F 5
Machala 84 C 4
Machar Marshes 64 E 3
Machattie, Lake 49 FG 3
Machaze 67 E 4
Machece 67 F 3
Macheke 67 E 3
Macheng 38 FG 4
Machera 21 D 4
Machevna 37 W 3
Machilipatnam 40 D 4
Machiques 84 D 1
Machrihanish 3 B 4
Machupicchu 86 B 3
Machynlleth 6 C 1
Macia 67 E 5
Măcin 20 C 1
Macina 62 D 3
Maçka 21 E 2
Mackay 49 H 3
Mackay, Lake 48 D 3
Mackenzie 72 LM 2
Mackenzie 73 N 3
Mackenzie Bay 72 K 2
Mackenzie King Island 90
Mackenzie Mountains
    72–73 LM 2–3
Mackenzie River 49 H 3
Mackinaw City 77 K 2
Mackinnon Road 65 F 5

Maclean 49 J 4
Macmillan 72 L 3
Macmillan Pass 72 L 3
Macocola 66 B 1
Macomer 19 E 3
Macomia 67 FG 2
Mâcon (France) 19 D 2
Macon (GA, U.S.A.) 77 K 5
Macon (MS, U.S.A.) 77 J 5
Macondo 66 C 2
Macosqvin 4 B 2
Macquarie Harbour 50 L 9
Macquarie Island 91
Macquarie River 49 H 5
Macujer 84 D 3
Macumba 49 F 4
Macusani 86 B 3
Macuze 67 F 3
Mačva Podluzje 20 A 2
Ma'dabā (Jordan) 22 B 3
Madadi 63 J 2
Madagali 63 G 3
Madagascar 67 G 3
Madā'in Sālih (Saudi Arabia)
    22 C 4
Madama 63 G 1
Madan 12
Madang 50 E 3
Madanīyīn 59 H 2
Madaoua 63 F 3
Madarounfa 63 F 3
Madau 51 F 3
Madawaska Highlands 75 M 6
Madaya 41 G 3
Madd, Ra's Abū (Saudi Arabia)
    22 B 4
Maddaloni 19 F 3
Madeir 64 D 3
Madeira (Brazil) 85 F 4–5
Madeira (Portugal) 58 B 2
Madeleine, Île de la 75 P 6
Maden 21 E 3
Maden 21 F 2
Madeniyet 25 P 6
Madeniyet 34 F 2
Madera 76 B 4
Madero, Puerto del 18 C 3
Madesimo 19 E 2
Madetkoski 16 J 2
Madhipura 40 E 2
Madhubani 40 E 2
Madhupur Jungle 41 F 3
Madhya Pradesh 40 CD 3
Madidi 86 C 3
Madimba 64 B 5
Madina 62 B 3
Madīnat ash Sha'b 61 G 6
Madingo-Kayes 63 G 6
Madingou 63 G 6
Madirovalo 67 H 3
Madison (IN, U.S.A.) 77 J 4
Madison (MN, U.S.A.) 77 G 2
Madison (WI, U.S.A.) 77 J 3
Madison River 76 D 2
Madisonville (KY, U.S.A.) 77 J 4
Madisonville (TX, U.S.A.) 77 G 5
Madiun 42 D 5
Madjingo 63 G 5
Mado Gashi 65 F 4
Madoi 38 C 4
Madonie 19 F 4
Madrakah 61 FG 4
Madrakah, Ra's al 61 K 5
Madras (India) 40 D 5
Madras (OR, U.S.A.) 76 B 3
Madre de Dios 86 C 3
Madre de Dios 86 C 3
Madre de Dios, Isla 89 AB 9
Madre del Sur, Sierra 78 B 4
Madre Oriental, Sierra 78 BC 2–3
Madre, Sierra 78 D 4
Madrid 18 C 3
Madridejos 18 C 4
Madrona, Sierra 18 C 4
Madura, Pulau 42 D 5
Madura, Selat 42 D 5
Madurai 40 C 6
Madurantakam 40 C 5
Madyan (Saudi Arabia) 22 B 4
Madzha 24 K 3
Mae Hong Son 41 G 4
Mae Nam Mun 41 H 4
Mae Nam Nan 41 H 4
Mae Nam Yom 41 G 4
Mae Rim 41 G 4
Mae Sariang 41 G 4
Mae Sot 41 G 4
Maebashi 39 L 3
Maes Howe 2 C 2
Maesteg 6 C 2
Maevatanana 67 H 3
Maéwo 51 J 5
Mafeking 66 D 5
Mafeteng 66 D 5
Mafia Island 65 FG 6

Mafikeng ÄMmbathoÅ 66 D 5
Mafra 88 FG 4
Magadan 37 S 4
Magadi 65 F 5
Magallanes, Estrecho de 89 B 9
Magalo 65 G 3
Maganey 4 B 3
Magangué 84 D 2
Maganja 67 F 3
Magaria 63 F 3
Magarida 51 E 4
Magburaka 62 B 4
Magdagachi 37 N 5
Magdala 65 F 2
Magdalena (Bolivia) 86 D 3
Magdalena (Colombia) 84 D 1–2
Magdalena (Mexico) 76 D 5
Magdalena, Bahia 76 D 7
Magdalena, Isla (Chile) 89 B 7
Magdalena, Isla (Mexico) 76 D 7
Magdalena, Punta 84 C 3
Magdeburg 15 F 4
Magelang 42 C 5
Magellan, Strait of 89 BC 9
Magenta 19 E 2
Magenta, Lake 48 B 5
Mageröya 16 J 1
Maggiorasca 19 E 3
Maggiore, Lago 19 E 2
Maghāgha 60 E 3
Maghama 58 C 5
Maghera 4 B 2
Magherafelt 4 B 2
Maghnia 58 E 2
Maglaj 19 G 3
Maglie 19 G 3
Magnitogorsk 25 L 5
Magnolia 77 H 5
Magnor 17 F 4
Mago 37 Q 5
Mágoè 67 E 3
Magor 6 C 3
Magosa → Famagusta 21 D 3
Magpie 75 P 6
Magta Lahjar 58 C 5
Maguarinho, Cabo 85 J 4
Magude 67 E 4
Maguiresbridge 4 B 2
Magumeri 63 G 3
Măgura Priei 20 B 1
Magwe 41 G 3
Magyarország 20 A 1
Magyichaung 41 F 3
Māh Shahr, Bandar (Iran) 23 E 3
Maha Sarakham 41 H 4
Mahābād (Iran) 23 D 1
Mahabalipuram 40 D 5
Mahabe 67 H 3
Mahabharat Range 40 E 2
Mahabo 67 G 3
Mahadday Wēyne 65 H 4
Mahadeo Hills 40 C 3
Mahadeo Range 40 B 4
Mahagi 64 E 4
Mahajamba 67 H 3
Mahajan 40 B 2
Mahajanga 67 H 3
Mahakam, Sungai 42 E 3
Mahalapye 66 D 4
Mahalevona 67 J 3
Mahallāt (Iran) 23 F 2
Māhān 34 F 4
Mahanadi 40 DE 3
Mahanoro 67 H 3
Maharashtra 40 BC 4
Mahārlū, Daryācheh-ye (Iran)
    23 F 3
Mahās 65 H 4
Mahasamund 40 D 3
Mahatalaky 67 H 4
Mahatsanary 67 G 5
Mahavavy 67 H 3
Mahbés 58 D 3
Mahbubnagar 40 C 4
Mahd adh Dhahab (Saudi Arabia)
    22 C 5
Mahdah (Oman) 23 G 4
Mahdia (Algeria) 59 F 1
Mahdia (Guyana) 85 G 2
Mahè 40 C 5
Mahébourg 67 K 6
Mahendragirii 40 D 4
Mahenge 65 F 6
Mahesana 40 B 3
Maheshwar 40 C 3
Mahi 40 B 3
Mahi 40 B 3
Mahia Peninsula 51 R 8
Mahin 63 E 4
Mahkene 16 F 3
Mahlabalini 67 E 5
Mahmūdābād (Iran) 23 F 1
Mahmudiye 20 D 3
Mahmud-Raqi 35 HJ 3
Māhneshān (Iran) 23 E 1
Mahnomen 77 G 2

Mahón 18 D 4
Mahrāt, Jabal 61 J 5
Mahuva 40 B 3
Mahwa 40 C 2
Mahyār (Iran) 23 F 2
Mai Munene 64 C 6
Maiana 52 C 2
Maïao 53 F 4
Maicao 84 D 1
Maicurú 85 H 4
Maidenhead 7 D 2
Maidens 3 B 4
Maidstone 7 E 2
Maiduguri 63 G 3
Maigudo 65 F 3
Maihar 40 D 3
Maijdi 41 F 3
Maikala Range 40 D 3
Maiko 64 D 5
Maiko National Park 64 D 5
Maimana 35 G 3
Main 15 E 5
Main Barrier Range 49 G 5
Main Channel 77 K 2
Maínalon Óros 20 B 3
Mai-Ndombe, Lac 64 B 5
Maine 77 N 2
Maine, Gulf of 77 N 3
Maïné Soroa 63 G 3
Mainland (Orkney Is., U.K.) 2 C 2
Mainland (Shetland Is., U.K.) 2 D 1
Mainling 38 B 5
Mainoru 48 E 1
Mainpuri 40 C 2
Maintirano 67 G 3
Mainz 15 E 5
Maio 62 B 6
Maipo, Volcán 88 C 5
Maipú (Argentina) 89 E 6
Maipú (Chile) 88 B 5
Maipuco 84 D 4
Maiquetía 84 E 1
Maisi, Punta 79 H 3
Maiskhal 41 F 3
Maitengwe 66 D 4
Maitland (N.S.W., Austr.) 49 J 5
Maitland (South Australia) 49 F 5
Maitland, Lake 48 C 4
Maiyu, Mount 48 D 2
Maíz, Isla del 78 F 5
Maizhokunggar 38 B 5
Maizuru 39 L 3
Majagual 84 D 2
Majardah 19 EF 4
Majdanpek 20 B 2
Majene 43 E 4
Majērtēn 65 HJ 3
Majevica 19 G 3
Maji 64 F 3
Majune 67 F 2
Majuriã 84 E 5
Majuro 52 C 2
Maka 62 B 3
Makā Rūd (Iran) 23 F 1
Makabana 63 G 6
Makalamabedi 66 C 4
Makale (Ethiopia) 65 F 2
Makale (Indonesia) 43 E 4
Makalu, Mount 40 E 2
Makambako 64 EF 6
Makanchi 25 Q 6
Makanrushi, Ostrov 37 S 6
Makanza 64 B 4
Makari 63 G 3
Makari Mountains 64 D 6
Makarikari 66 D 4
Makarikha 25 L 2
Makarov 37 Q 6
Makarova 36 DE 1
Makarovo 24 H 5
Makarovo 36 J 4
Makaryev 24 H 4
Makassar 43 E 5
Makassar, Selat 42 E 4
Makassar Strait 42 E 4
Makat 34 E 1
Makatea 53 F 4
Makaw 41 G 2
Makay, Massif du 67 H 4
Makedhonía 20 F 2
Makedonija 20 B 2
Makemo 53 F 4
Makeni 62 B 4
Makeyevka 21 E 1
Makgadikgadi Pan 66 D 4
Makgadikgadi Pans Game Reserve 66 CD 4
Makhachkala 34 D 2
Makharadze 21 F 2
Makhfar al Buşayyah (Iraq) 23 D 3
Makhfar al Ḥammām (Syria) 22 C 2
Makhmūr (Iraq) 22 D 2
Maki 43 H 4
Makian, Pulau 43 G 3

Makinsk 25 O 5
Makkah 61 FG 4
Makkovik 75 Q 4
Maknassy 59 G 2
Makó 20 B 1
Makokou 63 G 5
Makoli 66 D 3
Makongolosi 64 E 6
Makopse 21 E 2
Makorako 51 R 8
Makoua 63 H 6
Makovskoye 25 R 2
Makrai 40 C 2
Makran 34–35 FG 5
Makri 40 D 4
Maksimkiy Yar 25 R 4
Maksimovka 39 L 1
Makteir 58 C 4
Mākū 34 C 3
Makū (Iran) 23 F 3
Makumbi 64 C 6
Makunduchi 65 F 6
Makung 39 G 6
Makunza 64 C 6
Makurazaki 39 JK 4
Makurdi 63 F 4
Makushin Volcano 72 D 5
Makushino 25 N 4
Makuyuni 65 F 5
Makwa 51 J 2
Mal 58 C 5
Malå 16 G 2
Mala 86 A 3
Malá Fatra 15 G 5
Mala Kapela 19 G 2–3
Malabang 43 F 2
Malabar Coast 40 BC 5–6
Malabo 63 F 5
Malacacheta 85 FG 3
Malacca, Strait of 42 B 3
Malacky 15 G 5
Malad City 76 D 3
Málaga 18 C 4
Malagarasi 64 E 5–6
Malagasy Republic 67 G 3
Malagón 18 C 4
Malahide 4 B 3
Malaimbandy 67 H 4
Malaita 51 H 3
Malakāl 64 E 3
Malakanagiri 40 D 4
Malakand 35 J 4
Malam 50 D 3
Malang 42 D 5
Malangen 16 G 2
Malanje 66 B 1
Malanville 62 E 3
Malao 51 J 5
Mälaren 17 G 4
Malargue 89 C 6
Malaripo 85 H 3
Malaspina (Argentina) 89 C 7
Malaspina Glacier 72 J 4
Malatayur, Tanjung 42 D 4
Malatya 21 E 3
Malatya Dağları 21 E 3
Malawi 67 E 2
Malāwī (Iran) 23 E 2
Malawi, Lake 67 E 2
Malawi National Park 67 E 2
Malawiya 60 F 5
Malax 16 H 3
Malaya 42 B 3
Malaya Baranikha 37 V 2
Malaya Sos'va 25 M 3
Malaya Vishera 24 F 4
Malaya Viska 20 D 1
Malawa 40 C 3
Malaybalay 43 G 2
Malāyer (Iran) 23 E 2
Malaysia 42 CD 2
Malazgirt 21 F 3
Malbon 49 G 3
Malbork 15 G 4
Malbrán 88 D 4
Malcolm 48 C 4
Malda 40 E 2
Malden 53 E 3
Maldives 40 B 6
Maldon 7 E 2
Malé 19 F 2
Male 28 F 6
Malé Karpaty 15 G 5
Maléas, Ákra 20 B 3
Maléha 62 C 3
Malei 67 F 3
Malek 64 E 3
Malek Kandī (Iran) 23 DE 1
Malekābād (Iran) 23 EF 2
Malekula 51 J 5
Malema 67 F 2
Maleta 36 J 5
Maleyevo 36 G 4
Maleza 84 E 3

Malgobek 21 F 2
Malgomaj 16 G 3
Malha 60 D 5
Malheur Lake 76 C 3
Mali 62 CD 2–3
Mali (Guinea) 62 B 3
Mali Hka 41 G 2
Mali i Gribës 20 A 2
Mali i Ostrovicës 20 B 2
Mali i Tomorit 20 B 2
Mali Kanal 20 A 1
Mali Kyun 41 G 4
Mali Lošinj 19 F 3
Maliana 43 G 5
Malianjing 38 C 2
Malik 43 F 4
Malik Naro 35 G 5
Malik, Wādī al 60 D 5
Malili 43 F 4
Malimba, Monts 64 D 6
Malin 17 J 5
Malin Head 4 B 2
Malindi 65 G 5
Maling, Gunung 43 F 3
Malinovka 25 R 4
Malinovoye Ozero 25 PQ 5
Malinyi 65 F 6
Malipo 38 D 6
Malita 43 G 2
Malka 21 F 2
Malkachan 37 S 4
Malkaïli (Iran) 23 E 2
Malkara 20 C 2
Malkhanskiy Khrebet 36 JK 5
Mallacoota 49 H 6
Mallaig 3 B 3
Mallani 40 B 2
Mallawī 60 E 3
Mallery Lake 73 S 3
Mallorca 18 D 4
Malm 16 F 3
Malmberget 16 H 2
Malmesbury (South Africa) 66 B 6
Malmesbury (U.K.) 7 C 2
Malmö 17 F 4
Maloca 85 G 3
Maloca 85 H 5
Maloca de Indios 86 E 3
Maloca do Gonçalo 85 G 5
Maloelap 52 C 2
Malole 67 E 2
Malolos 43 F 1
Malonga 66 C 2
Malorita 17 H 5
Maloshuyka 24 G 3
Malosofiyevka 21 D 1
Måløy 16 D 3
Malozemel'skaya Tundra 24 JK 2
Malpas 5 D 3
Malpelo, Isla 84 B 3
Malpura 40 C 2
Malta 19 F 4
Malta (MT, U.S.A.) 76 E 2
Maltahöhe 66 B 4
Maltby 5 E 3
Malton 5 E 2
Maluku 43 G 4
Maluku, Laut 43 G 3
Malumfashi 63 F 3
Malunda 43 E 4
Malung 17 F 3
Malūt 60 E 6
Malvan 40 B 4
Malvinas, Islas → Falkland Islands 89 DE 9
Malwa 40 C 3
Maly Kavkaz 21 FG 2
Malya 64 E 5
Malykay 36 L 3
Malyovitsa 20 B 2
Malyshevka 25 QR 2
Malyy Anyuy 37 U 2
Malyy Lyakhovskiy, Ostrov 37 Q 1
Malyy Yenisey 36 FG 5
Malyye Derbety 21 FG 1
Malyye Derbety 34 CD 1
Mama 36 K 4
Mamagota 51 G 3
Mamaia 20 C 2
Mamakan 36 K 4
Mamara 86 B 3
Mambajao 43 F 2
Mambasa 64 D 4
Mamberamo, Sungai 43 J 4
Mambéré 64 B 4
Mambili 63 H 5
Mambilima Falls 66 D 2
Mamburao 43 F 1
Mamfe 63 F 4
Mamiña 86 C 4
Mamlyutka 25 N 5
Mammamattawe 74 L 5
Mamonovo 17 H 5

Mamonta, Poluostrov 36 C 1
Mamoré 86 C 3
Mamou 62 B 3
Mamoun 64 C 2
Mampikony 67 H 3
Mampodre 18 BC 3
Mampong 62 D 4
Mamry, Jezioro 15 H 4
Mamué 66 A 2
Mamuju 43 E 4
Mamuno 66 C 4
Man 62 C 4
Man Na 41 G 3
Mana (French Guiana) 85 H 3
Mana (U.S.S.R.) 36 F 4
Manacacías 84 D 3
Manacapuru 85 F 4
Manacapuru, Lago de 85 F 4
Manacor 18 D 4
Manado 43 F 3
Managua 78 E 5
Managua, Lago de 78 E 5
Manakara 67 H 4
Manakau 51 Q 9
Manam 50 E 2
Manama 23 F 4
Manambao 67 G 3
Mananara 67 H 3
Mananara ÅRiverÅ 67 H 4
Manandréa 67 G 4
Manangoora 49 F 2
Mananjary 67 H 4
Manankoro 62 C 3
Manantenina 67 H 4
Manantiales 88 D 4
Manapouri 50 P 10
Manāqīsh (Kuwait) 23 E 3
Manas (Bhutan) 41 F 2
Manas (China) 35 M 2
Manas He 35 M 2
Manas Hu 35 M 1
Manaslu 40 D 2
Manatuto 43 G 5
Manaus 85 FG 4
Manavgat 20 D 3
Manbij (Syria) 22 BC 1
Mancha Blanca 89 C 7
Mancheng 38 FG 3
Manchester 5 D 3
Manchester (Airport) 5 D 3
Manchuria 39 HJ 2
Manciano 19 F 3
Mancınık 21 E 3
Mancınık Dağı 20 C 3
Mancınık Dağı 20 C 3
Máncora 84 B 4
Mand (Iran) 23 F 3
Manda 67 E 2
Manda Hills 40 B 3
Manda Island 65 G 5
Manda, Jabal 64 C 3
Mandabe 67 G 4
Mandal (Mongolia) 36 H 6
Mandal (Norway) 17 E 4
Mandalay 41 G 3
Mandalgovĭ 38 E 1
Mandalī (Iraq) 23 D 2
Mandal-Ovoo 38 D 2
Mandalya Körfezi 20 C 3
Mandan 76 F 2
Mandaon 43 F 1
Mandaoua 63 G 3
Mandar, Teluk 43 E 4
Mandara Mountains 63 G 3
Mandas 19 E 4
Mandasor 40 B 3
Mandawa 65 F 6
Mandera 65 G 4
Mandeville 79 G 4
Mandi 40 C 1
Mandiana 62 C 3
Mandimba 67 F 2
Mandinga 84 C 2
Mandingues, Monts 62 B 3
Mandioli, Pulau 43 G 4
Mandioré, Lago 86 E 4
Mandjafa 63 H 3
Mandji 63 G 6
Mandla 40 D 3
Mandö 17 E 4
Mandor 42 C 3
Mandora 48 C 2
Mandoúdhion 20 B 3
Mandritsara 67 H 3
Mandurah 48 B 5
Manduria 19 G 3
Mandvi 40 A 3
Mandya 40 C 5
Manendragarh 40 D 3
Maneromango 65 F 6
Manevichi 17 J 5
Manfalut 60 E 3
Manfredonia 19 G 3
Manfredonia, Golfo di 19 G 3

Manga (Minas Gerais, Brazil) 87 H 3
Manga (Niger/Chad) 63 GH 3
Mangabeiras, Chapada das 87 G 2–3
Mangai 64 B 5
Mangaia 53 E 4
Mangalia 20 C 2
Mangalmé 63 H 3
Mangalore 40 B 5
Mangareva 53 G 4
Manggawitu 43 H 4
Mangit 34 G 2
Mangkalihat, Tanjung 43 E 3
Manglar Alto 84 B 4
Manglares, Cabo 84 C 3
Mangnai 38 D 3
Mangoche 67 EF 2
Mangoky 67 G 4
Mangole, Pulau 43 G 4
Mangueigne 63 J 3
Mangueira, Lagoa 88 F 5
Mangui 37 M 5
Manguinho, Ponta do 87 J 3
Manguredjipa 64 D 4
Mangut 36 K 6
Mangyshlak, Poluostrov 34 E 2
Manhan 36 F 6
Manhattan 77 G 4
Manhica 67 E 5
Manhuacu 87 H 5
Maní (Colombia) 84 D 3
Mani (Zaire) 64 D 6
Manianko 62 C 3
Manica 67 E 3
Manicaland 67 E 3
Manicoré 85 F 5
Manicouagan 75 O 5
Manicouagan, Réservoir 75 O 5
Maniema 57
Manifa (Saudi Arabia) 23 E 4
Maniganggo 38 C 4
Manihi 53 F 3
Manihiki 52 E 3
Manila 43 F 1
Manimbaya, Tanjung 43 E 4
Maningrida 48 E 1
Maninian (Guinea) 62 C 4
Manipa, Pulau 43 G 4
Manipa, Selat 43 G 4
Manipur 41 F 3
Manipur 41 F 3
Manisa 20 C 3
Manises 18 C 4
Manistique 77 J 2
Manitoba 73 S 5
Manitoba, Lake 73 S 5
Manitou Springs 76 F 4
Manitoulin Island 74 L 6
Manitowoc 77 J 3
Maniwaki 75 M 6
Manizales 84 C 2
Manja 67 G 4
Manjacaze 67 E 4
Manjakandriana 67 H 3
Manjil (Iran) 23 E 1
Manjimup 48 B 5
Manjra 40 C 4
Mankato 77 H 3
Mankhere 40 D 3
Mankim 63 G 5
Mankono 62 C 4
Manlay 38 E 2
Manley Hot Springs 72 G 2
Manlleu 18 D 3
Manmad 40 BC 3
Manna 42 B 4
Mannahill 49 F 5
Mannar 40 C 6
Mannheim 15 E 5
Manning 73 O 4
Mannu, Capo 19 E 3
Manoa 84 E 5
Manokwari 43 H 4
Manombo 67 G 4
Manompana 67 HJ 3
Manonga 64 E 5
Manono 64 D 6
Manorcunningham 4 B 2
Manoron 41 G 5
Manosque 19 E 3
Manouane 75 N 6
Manouane, Lac 75 N 5
Manp'ojin 39 J 2
Manra 52 D 3
Manresa 18 D 3
Mansa 66 D 2
Mansa Konko 62 A 3
Mansehra 35 J 4
Mansel Island 75 L 3
Mansfield (OH, U.S.A.) 77 K 3
Mansfield (U.K.) 5 E 3
Mansfield Woodhouse 7 D 1
Mansi 41 G 3
Mansle 18 D 2
Mansôa 62 A 3

Mansūri (Iran) 23 E 3
Mansūri (Iran) 23 E 3
Manta 84 B 4
Mantalingajan, Mount 42 E 2
Mantaro 86 B 3
Mantecal 84 E 2
Manteo 77 L 4
Mantes-la-Jolie 18 D 2
Mantiqueira, Serra da 87 GH 5
Mantova 19 F 2
Mäntsälä 17 J 3
Mänttä 16 H 3
Mäntyharju 16 J 3
Manú 86 B 3
Manu Ranipur 40 C 2
Manua Islands 52 D 3
Manuae 53 E 4
Manuae (Society Is.) 53 E 4
Manuangi 53 F 4
Manuel Benavides 78 B 2
Manuel Urbano 84 E 5
Manuelzinho 85 H 5
Manui, Pulau 43 F 4
Mānūk, Tall (Iraq) 22 C 2
Manukau 51 Q 8
Manus 50 E 2
Manwat 40 C 4
Man'ya 25 M 3
Manyame 67 E 3
Manyara, Lake 65 F 5
Manych 21 F 1
Manych Gudilo, Ozero 21 F 1
Manychskaya Vpadina 21 F 1
Manyoni 64 E 6
Manzanares 18 C 4
Manzanillo (Cuba) 79 G 3
Manzanillo (Mexico) 78 B 4
Manzarīyeh (Iran) 23 F 2
Manzhouli 36 L 6
Manzil Bū Ruqaybah 59 GH 1
Manzini 67 E 5
Manzurka 36 J 5
Mao 79 H 4
Mao, Pulau 43 G 5
Maoke Mountains 50 D 2
Maoke, Pegunungan 43 J 4
Maoming 38 F 6
Maowen 38 D 4
Mapaga 43 EF 4
Mapai 67 E 4
Mapam Yumco 40 D 1
Mapanza 66 D 3
Maper 64 DE 3
Mapi 43 J 5
Mapia, Kepulauan 43 HJ 3
Mapinhane 67 F 4
Mapire 85 F 2
Mapireme 85 H 3
Mapiripana 84 D 3
Maple Creek 73 Q 6
Mapmakers Seamounts 99 C 3
Maprik 50 D 2
Mapuera 85 G 4
Maputo 67 E 5
Maputo 67 E 5
Maputo, Baía de 67 E 5
Māqām, Bandar-e (Iran) 23 F 4
Maqar an Na'am (Iraq) 22 C 3
Maqên 38 D 4
Maqên Gangri 38 C 4
Maqu 38 D 4
Maquan He 40 D 2
Maquela do Zombo 66 B 1
Maquinchao 89 C 7
Mar Chiquita, Laguna 88 D 5
Mar del Plata 89 E 6
Mar Menor 18 C 4
Mar, Serra do 88 G 4
Mara 64 E 5
Mara 64 E 5
Mara Bridge 64 F 5
Maraã 84 E 4
Marabá 85 J 5
Marabahan 42 DE 4
Maracá, Ilha de 85 HJ 3
Maracaçume 85 J 4
Maracaibo 84 D 1
Maracaibo, Lago de 84 D 1–2
Maracaju 87 F 5
Maracaju, Serra de 86–87 EF 5
Maracanã 85 J 4
Maracanaquará, Planalto 85 H 3–4
Maracás 87 H 3
Maracay 84 E 1
Marādah 37 J 3
Maradi 63 F 3
Marāgheh 34 D 3
Maragogipe 87 J 3
Marāh (Saudi Arabia) 23 D 4
Marahuaca, Cerro 84 E 3
Marais Breton 18 C 2
Marajó, Baja de 85 J 4
Marajó, Ilha de 85 HJ 4
Marakei 52 C 2
Maralal 65 F 4
Maralaleng 66 C 5

Marali 64 B 3
Maralik 21 F 2
Maralinga 48 E 5
Maramasike 51 H 3
Maramba 66 D 3
Maran 42 B 3
Maranã (Iraq) 23 D 2
Marānd 34 D 3
Marandellas → Marondera 67 E 3
Marang 42 B 2
Maranguape 87 J 1
Maranhão (Brazil) 87 GH 2
Maranhão (Goiás, Brazil) 87 G 3
Maranhão, Cachoeira 85 G 4
Maranoa River 49 H 4
Marañón 84 C 4
Marão 67 E 4
Marão, Serra do 18 B 3
Maraoue 62 C 4
Marapi, Gunung 42 B 4
Marargiu, Capo 19 E 3
Marari 84 E 5
Mărăşeşti 20 C 1
Maratea 19 G 4
Marathon 20 B 3
Marathon (Ontario, Can.) 74 K 6
Marathon (TX, U.S.A.) 76 F 5
Maraú 87 J 3
Marauá 84 E 4
Marávia, Planalto de 67 E 2
Maravovo 51 G 3
Marāwah 59 K 2
Marawi (Philippines) 43 F 2
Marawī (Sudan) 60 E 5
Marāwih (United Arab Emirates) 23 F 4
Maraxó Paiá 85 G 3
Maraza 34 D 2
Marbella 18 C 4
Marble Bar 48 B 3
Marble Canyon 76 D 4
Marble Hall 66 D 4
Marburg 15 E 4
Marcala 78 E 5
Marcelino Ramos 88 F 4
March (Austria) 19 G 2
March (U.K.) 7 E 1
Marche 19 F 3
Marche, Plateaux de la 18 D 2
Marchena, 84 B 6
Marchena 18 B 4
Marcigny 18 D 2
Marcos Juárez 88 D 5
Marcus Baker, Mount 72 H 3
Mardan 35 J 4
Mardi, Hadjer 63 J 3
Mardin 21 F 3
Mardin Eşigi 21 F 3
Maré 51 J 6
Marechal Deodoro 87 J 2
Maree, Loch 2 B 3
Mareeba (Queensland, Austr.) 49 GH 2
Mareg 65 H 4
Maréna 62 C 3
Marendego 65 F 6
Marennes 18 C 2
Marettimo 19 F 4
Marfa 76 F 5
Marganets 21 D 1
Margaret River (Western Australia) 48 A 5
Margaret River (Western Australia) 48 D 2
Margarida 86 E 5
Margarita, Isla de 85 F 1
Margaritovo 39 K 2
Margate (South Africa) 66 DE 6
Margate (U.K.) 7 E 2
Margherita → Jamāme 65 G 4
Margherita di Savona 19 G 3
Margie 73 P 4
Margilan 35 J 2
Margyang 40 E 2
Marhoum 58 E 2
Mari (Burma) 41 G 2
Mari (Papua New Guinea) 50 D 3
Mari (Syria) 22 C 2
Maria (Tuamotu Is.) 53 F 4
Maria (Tubuai Is.) 53 E 4
Maria Grande 88 E 5
Maria Island 49 F 1
María Teresa (Argentina) 88 D 5
Maria Theresa (Pacific Ocean) 53 E 5
Maria van Diemen, Cape 51 Q 7
Mariakani 65 F 5
Mariana Islands 52 A 1
Mariana Trench 99 C 3
Marianao 79 F 3
Marias River 76 D 2
Mariato, Punta 84 B 2
Mariazell 19 G 2
Maribor 19 G 2
Marico 66 D 4
Maricourt 75 N 3

Marīdī 64 D 4
Marie Byrd Land 91
Marie-Galante 79 K 4
Mariehamn 17 H 3
Mariental 66 B 4
Mariestad 17 F 4
Marietta 77 K 5
Mariga 63 F 3
Marignane 19 E 3
Mariinsk 25 R 4
Mariinskoye 37 Q 5
Marília 87 G 5
Marillana 48 B 3
Marimba 66 B 1
Marina Gorka 17 J 5
Marinduque 43 F 1
Marinette 77 J 2
Maringa (Paraná, Brazil) 87 F 5
Maringa (Zaire) 64 C 4
Marīnjab (Iran) 23 F 2
Marinuma 84 E 3
Mariny, Iméni 37 R 3
Marion (IA, U.S.A.) 77 H 3
Marion (IL, U.S.A.) 77 J 4
Marion (IN, U.S.A.) 77 J 3
Marion (OH, U.S.A.) 77 K 3
Marion Downs 49 F 3
Marion, Lake 77 K 5
Marion Reef 49 J 2
Maripa 84 E 2
Mariscal Estigarribia 86 D 5
Maritsa 20 C 2
Marittime, Alpi 19 E 3
Mariu 50 D 3
Marīvañ (Iran) 23 E 2
Marīyyah (United Arab Emirates) 23 F 5
Märjamaa 17 H 4
Marjan (Saudi Arabia) 23 E 3
Marka 65 GH 4
Markam 38 C 5
Markapur 40 C 4
Markaryd 17 F 4
Market Deeping 7 D 1
Market Drayton 5 D 3
Market Harborough 7 D 1
Market Lavington 7 D 2
Market Rasen 5 E 3
Market Weighton 5 E 3
Markethill 4 B 2
Markha 36 K 2
Markha 36 L 3
Markha 37 M 3
Markham Bay 75 N 3
Markit 35 K 3
Marko 16 G 2
Markounda 64 B 3
Markovo 25 R 3
Markovo 37 W 3
Marlborough (Guyana) 85 G 2
Marlborough (Queensland, Austr.) 49 HJ 3
Marlborough (U.K.) 7 D 2
Marlin 77 G 5
Marlow 7 D 2
Marmagao 40 B 4
Marmande 18 D 3
Marmara 20 C 2
Marmara Denizi 20 C 2
Marmara Gölü 20 C 3
Marmaris 20 C 3
Marmelos 85 F 5
Marmolada 19 F 2
Marne 18 D 2
Marne à la Sane, Canal de la 19 E 2
Mårnes 16 F 2
Marnpat 40 D 3
Maro 63 H 2
Maro 63 H 4
Maroa 84 E 3
Maroantsetra 67 H 3
Marolambo 67 H 4
Maromandia 67 H 2
Maromokotro 67 H 2
Marondera 67 E 3
Maroni 85 H 3
Maros 43 F 4
Maroua 63 G 3
Marovoay 67 H 3
Marowijne 85 H 3
Marqab, Qal 'at al (Syria) 22 B 2
Marqâdah (Syria) 22 C 2
Marquesas Islands 53 F 3
Marquette 77 J 2
Marra Mountains 60 C 6
Marracuene 67 E 5
Marradi 19 F 3
Marrah, Jabal 60 C 6
Marrakech 58 D 2
Marrawah 50 K 9
Marree 49 F 4
Marrero 77 H 6
Marresale 25 N 2

Marromeu 67 F 3
Marrupa 67 F 2
Marsa al' Alam (Egypt) 22 B 4
Marsa al Uwayjah 59 J 2
Marsa Fatma 65 G 2
Marsa Sha'b 60 F 4
Marsa Taklai 65 F 1
Marsa 'Umm Ghayj (Egypt) 22 B 4
Marsabit 65 F 4
Marsabit National Reserve 65 F 4
Marsala 19 F 4
Marsden 5 E 3
Marsden 49 H 5
Marseille 19 E 3
Marsfjället 16 G 2
Marsh Harbour 79 G 2
Marsh Island 77 H 6
Marshall (AK, U.S.A.) 72 E 3
Marshall (Liberia) 62 B 4
Marshall (MN, U.S.A.) 77 G 3
Marshall (TX, U.S.A.) 77 H 5
Marshall Islands 52 BC 2
Marshall River 49 F 3
Marshalltown 77 H 3
Marshalstown 6 A 1
Marshfield 77 J 3
Märsta 17 G 4
Marstrand 17 F 4
Marta 19 F 3
Martaban 41 G 4
Martaban, Gulf of 41 G 4
Martap 63 G 3
Martapura 42 B 4
Martapura 42 DE 4
Martés, Sierra de 18 C 4
Martigny 19 E 2
Martigues 19 DE 3
Martin (Czechoslovakia) 15 G 5
Martin (U.S.A.) 76 F 3
Martín de Loyola 89 C 6
Martina Franca 19 G 3
Martínez de la Torre 78 C 3
Martinique 79 K 5
Martinique Passage 79 K 5
Martinsburg 77 L 4
Martinsville 77 KL 4
Marton 7 D 1
Marton 51 R 9
Martos 18 C 4
Martre, Lac la 73 O 3
Martti 16 J 2
Martūbah 59 K 2
Martuk 24 L 5
Martuni 21 G 2
Martyn 35 L 2
Marudi 42 D 3
Mārūn (Iran) 23 E 3
Marunga 51 F 3
Marungu, Monts 64 D 6
Marusthali 40 B 2
Marutea 53 F 4
Marv Dasht (Iran) 23 F 3
Marvast (Iran) 23 G 3
Marvast, Kavīr-e (Iran) 23 G 3
Marvejols 18 D 3
Marwar Junction 40 B 2
Mary 35 G 3
Mary Tavy 6 B 2
Maryborough (Queensland, Austr.) 49 J 4
Maryborough (Victoria, Austr.) 49 G 6
Marydale 66 C 5
Mar'yevka 25 N 5
Maryland 77 L 4
Maryport 5 D 2
Marystown 75 R 6
Marysville (CA, U.S.A.) 76 B 4
Marysville (KS, U.S.A.) 77 G 4
Maryville 77 H 3
Marywell 3 D 3
Marzafal 62 D 2
Marzo, Cabo 84 C 2
Masaguru 67 F 2
Masāhīm, Kūh-e (Iran) 23 G 3
Masai Steppe 65 F 5
Masaka 64 E 5
Masākin 59 H 1
Masalasef 63 H 3
Masalembo, Pulau 42 D 5
Masally 34 D 3
Masamba 43 F 4
Masan 39 J 3
Masasi 67 F 2
Masaya 78 E 5
Masbate 43 F 1
Masbate Island 43 F 1
Mascara 58 EF 1
Mascarene Islands 67 K 6
Mascota 78 B 3
Masela, Pulau 43 GH 5
Maseru 66 D 5
Masfinto 65 F 2
Mashaba 67 E 4
Mashabīi (Saudi Arabia) 22 B 4

Mashaki 35 H 4
Mashala 64 C 6
Masham 5 E 2
Mashan 38 E 6
Mashewa 65 F 5
Mashhad 34 F 3
Mashīz 34 F 5
Mashīz (Iran) 23 G 3
Mashkel 35 G 5
Māshkid 35 G 5
Mashonaland 67 E 3
Mashoro 66 D 4
Mashra'ar Raqq 64 D 3
Masīlah, Wādī al 61 J 5
Masi-Manimba 64 B 5
Masimbu 43 E 4
Masindi 64 E 4
Masīrah 61 K 4
Masīrah, Khalīj 61 K 5
Masisea 84 D 5
Masisi 64 D 5
Masjed Soleymān (Iran) 23 E 3
Maskanah (Syria) 22 B 2
Maslovare 19 G 3
Maslovo 25 M 3
Maslyanskoye 25 O 4
Maso 62 D 4
Masoala, Cap 67 J 3
Masohi 43 G 4
Mason City 77 H 3
Mason, Lake 48 B 4
Masqat 61 K 4
Massa 19 F 3
Massa Marittima 19 F 3
Massachusetts 77 M 3
Massafra 19 G 3
Massaguet 63 H 3
Massakori 63 H 3
Massangena 67 E 4
Massango 66 B 1
Massapé 87 H 1
Massau 51 E 2
Massava 25 M 3
Massawa 65 F 1
Massawarat es Sufra → Al Musawwarāt as Safra' 60 E 5
Massena 77 M 3
Massénya 63 H 3
Masset 72 L 5
Massif Central 18 D 2–3
Massif d'Abo 63 H 1
Massif de Guéra 63 H 3
Massif de l'Adamoua 63 G 4
Massif de l'Aurès 59 G 1
Massif de l'Isalo 67 H 4
Massif de l'Ivakoany 67 H 4
Massif de l'Ouarsenis 59 F 1
Massif de Takolokouzet 63 F 2
Massif de Tarazit 63 F 1
Massif de Termit 63 G 2
Massif des Bongos 64 C 3
Massif du Chaïllu 63 G 6
Massif du Diois 19 E 3
Massif du Kapka 63 J 2
Massif du Kerkour Nourene 63 J 2
Massif du Makay 67 H 4
Massif du Pelvoux 19 E 3
Massif du Tamgué 62 B 3
Massif du Tondou 64 C 3
Massif du Tsaratanana 67 H 2
Massif du Yadé 64 B 3
Massigui 62 C 3
Massinga 67 F 4
Massingir 67 E 4
Masslo 65 F 3
Mastābah 61 F 4
Masteksay 34 E 1
Masterton 51 R 9
Mastuj 35 J 3
Mastung 35 H 5
Mastūrah 60 F 4
Masuda 39 K 4
Masuika 64 C 6
Māsūleh (Iran) 23 E 1
Masulipatnam → Machilipatnam 40 D 4
Masurai, Bukit 42 B 4
Masvingo 67 E 4
Masyāf (Syria) 22 B 2
Mata Amarilla 89 B 8
Mata Gassile 65 G 4
Matabeleland 66 D 3–4
Matachewan 75 L 6
Matachic 76 E 6
Matadi 64 A 6
Matador 76 F 5
Matagalpa 78 E 5
Matagalpa, Rio Grande de 78 F 5
Matagami 75 M 6
Matagorda Island 77 G 6
Mataiva 53 F 3
Matakana 49 H 5
Matala 66 B 2
Matale 40 D 6
Matam 62 B 3
Matameye 63 F 3

Matamoros 78 B 2
Matamoros 78 C 2
Ma'ṭan as Sārah 59 K 4
Ma'ṭan Bishārah 59 K 4
Ma'tan Bū at Tifl 59 K 3
Matancita 76 D 6
Matandu 65 F 6
Matane 75 O 6
Matankari 63 E 3
Matanzas 79 F 3
Matanzilla, Pampa de la 89 C 6
Matão, Serra do 85 H 5
Maṭār (Saudi Arabia) 23 E 4
Matara (Ethiopia) 65 F 2
Matara (Peru) 84 C 5
Matara (Sri Lanka) 40 D 6
Mataram 42 E 5
Matarani 86 B 4
Mataranka 48 E 1
Matarca 84 D 4
Matārimah, Ra's (Egypt) 22 A 3
Matarka 58 E 2
Mataró 18 D 3
Matatiele 66 D 6
Matatila Dam 40 C 2
Mata-Utu 52 D 3
Matay 25 P 6
Mategua 86 D 3
Matehuala 78 B 3
Matera 19 G 3
Mátészalka 20 B 1
Matetsi 66 D 3
Matfors 16 G 3
Matheson 75 L 6
Mathry 6 B 2
Mathura 40 C 2
Mati 43 G 2
Matiakouali 62 E 3
Matimbuka 67 F 2
Matinha 85 J 4
Matir 59 G 1
Matla 40 E 3
Matlock 5 E 3
Mato, Cerro 84 E 2
Mato Grosso 86–87 EF 3
Mato Grosso (Mato Grosso, Brazil) 86 E 3
Mato Grosso do Sul 86–87 EF 4
Matopo Hills 66 D 4
Matozinhos 18 B 3
Mátra 20 AB 1
Maṭrah 61 K 4
Matru 62 B 4
Matrūh 60 D 2
Matsesta 21 EF 2
Matsu (Japan) 39 M 2
Matsu (Taiwan) 39 H 5
Matsudo 39 M 3
Matsue 39 K 3
Matsumoto 39 L 3
Matsusaka 39 L 4
Matsuyama 39 K 4
Mattancheri 40 C 6
Matterhorn (Switzerland) 19 E 2
Matterhorn (U.S.A.) 76 C 3
Matthew, Ile 51 K 6
Matthew Town 79 H 3
Matthews Range 65 F 4
Matthew's Ridge 85 G 2
Maṭṭī, Sabkhat 61 J 4
Mattoon 77 J 4
Matu 42 D 3
Matua, Ostrov 37 S 6
Matucana 86 A 3
Maturín 85 F 2
Matveyev-Kurgan 21 E 1
Matyl'ka 25 R 3
Matyshevo 24 H 5
Matyushkinskaya 25 P 4
Mau 40 D 3
Mau Range 65 F 5
Maúa 67 F 2
Maubeuge 18 D 1
Maubin 41 G 4
Maude 49 G 5
Maués 85 G 4
Maués Açu 85 G 4
Maug 52 A 1
Mauganj 40 D 3
Maughold Head 4 C 2
Maui 53 E 1
Mauke 53 E 4
Mauléon 18 C 2
Maulvi Bazar 41 F 3
Maumere 43 F 5
Maun 66 C 4
Mauna Kea 53 E 1
Mauna Loa 53 E 1
Maungmagan Island 41 G 5
Maunoir, Lac 73 MN 2
Maupihaa 53 E 4
Maupin 76 B 2
Maupiti 53 E 4
Mauralasan 42 E 3
Maurice, Lake 48 E 4
Mauritania 58 CD 5

Mauritius 67 K 6
Mauron 18 C 2
Mavasjaure 16 G 2
Mavinga 66 BC 3
Mavue 67 E 4
Mavume 67 E 4
Mavuradonha Mountains 67 E 3
Mawa, Bukit 42 D 3
Mawa'afaq 61 JK 5
Mawei 39 G 5
Mawkmai 41 G 3
Mawlaik 41 F 3
Mawqaq (Saudi Arabia) 22 C 4
Mawson 91
Mawson Coast 91
Maxcanu 78 DE 3
Maxixe 67 F 4
May Pen 79 G 4
May River 50 D 2
Maya 37 O 4
Maya Mountains 78 E 4
Maya, Pulau 42 C 4
Mayaguana Island 79 H 3
Mayaguana Passage 79 H 3
Mayagüez 79 J 4
Mayahi 63 F 3
Mayama 63 GH 6
Mayámey (Iran) 23 G 1
Mayang 38 E 5
Mayapán 78 E 3
Maybole 4 C 2
Mayd 65 H 2
Maydān (Iraq) 23 D 2
Maydī 61 G 5
Mayenne 18 C 2
Mayenne 18 C 2
Maykain 25 P 5
Maykop 21 F 2
Maylykum 35 H 1
Maymak 35 J 2
Maymakan 37 P 4
Maymecha 36 H 1
Maymyo 41 G 3
Mayn 37 W 3
Mayna 36 F 5
Maynas 84 C 4
Mayno-Amamkut 37 X 3
Maynooth 4 B 3
Maynopil'gyno 37 X 3
Mayo 72 K 3
Mayo Daga 63 G 4
Mayo Mayo 86 C 3
Mayo, Mountains of 14 B 4
Mayoko 63 G 6
Mayon 43 F 1
Mayor Buratovich 89 D 6
Mayor-Krest 37 Q 2
Mayotte 67 H 2
Mayraira Point 43 HJ 1
Maysk 25 P 4
Mayskiy 21 F 2
Mayskiy 37 N 5
Mayskiy, Khrebet 37 O 4–5
Mayskoye 25 P 5
Maysville 77 L 5
Mayum La 40 D 1
Mayumba 63 G 6
Mayvale 49 H 4
Mayya 37 O 3
Maza 89 D 6
Mazabuka 66 D 3
Mazagão 85 H 4
Mazalet 63 F 2
Mazalij (Saudi Arabia) 23 E 4
Mazamet 18 D 3
Mazar 35 K 3
Mazara dell Vallo 19 F 4
Mazar-i-Sharif 35 H 3
Mazarredo 89 C 8
Mazaruni 85 FG 2
Mazatenango 78 D 5
Mazatlán 78 A 3
Mažeikiai 17 H 4
Mazirbe 17 H 4
Mazoe 67 E 3
Mazomeno 64 D 5
Mazong Shan 38 C 2
Mazowe 67 E 3
Mazowsze 15 H 4
Mazrub 60 D 6
Mazunga 66 D 4
Mazury 15 H 4
Mbabane 67 E 5
Mbahiakro 62 D 4
Mbaiki 64 B 4
Mbakaou Reservoir 63 G 4
Mbaké 62 A 3
Mbala (Burkina) 64 C 3
Mbala (Zambia) 67 E 1
Mbale 64 E 4
Mbalmayo 63 G 5
Mbamba Bay 67 E 2
Mbandaka 64 B 4
Mbang, Monts 63 G 4

Mbanga 63 F 5
M'banza Congo 66 A 1
Mbanza-Ngungu 64 B 6
Mbarara 64 E 5
Mbari 64 C 3
Mbé 63 G 4
Mbengwi 63 F 4
Mberengwa 66 D 4
Mbeya 64 E 6
Mbigou 63 G 6
Mbinda 63 G 6
Mbinga 67 F 2
Mbini 63 F 5
Mbini 63 G 5
Mbini 63 G 5
Mbizi 67 E 4
M'Boi 64 C 3
Mbokou 64 D 3
M'Boli 64 C 4
Mboma 63 G 5
Mbomou 64 C 4
Mbouda 63 FG 4
Mbour 62 A 3
Mbout 58 C 5
Mbozi 64 E 6
Mbrés 64 BC 3
M'bridge 66 A 1
Mbuji-Mayi 64 C 6
Mbulu 64 F 5
Mburu, Lake 64 E 5
Mburucuyá 88 E 4
Mbuyuni 65 F 6
Mc Arthur River 48–49 F 2
Mc Grath 72 F 3
Mc Leod, Lake 48 A 3
Mc Leod Lake 73 N 5
Mc Murdo 91
Mc Murdo Sound 91
McAlester 77 G 5
McAllen 76 G 6
McArthur River 48 F 2
McBeth Fjord 75 O 2
McCamey 76 F 5
McCammon 76 D 3
McCarthy 72 J 3
McComb 77 H 5
McCook 76 F 3
McDame 72 M 4
McDermitt 76 C 3
McGill 76 D 4
McGregor 77 H 2
Mcherrah 58 E 3
Mchinja 65 F 6
Mchinji 67 E 2
McKean 52 D 3
McKeand 75 O 3
McKeesport 77 L 3
McKenzie Island 74 J 5
McKinley, Mount 72 G 3
McKinley Park 72 H 3
McKinney 77 G 5
McLeod Bay 73 P 3
M'Clintock 73 T 4
M'Clintock Channel 73 R 1
McLoughlin, Mount 76 B 3
M'Clure Strait 73 O 1
McPherson 76 G 4
McVicar Arm 73 O 2
Mdandu 64 EF 6
Mdennah 58 D 4
Mead, Lake 76 D 4
Meade 72 F 1–2
Meade Peak 76 D 3
Meadow 48 A 4
Meadow Lake 73 Q 5
Mealhada 18 B 3
Mealy Mountains 75 Q 5
Meander River 73 O 4
Meare 6 C 3
Meath 4 B 3
Meaux 18 D 2
Meavaig 2 A 3
Mecanhelas 67 F 3
Mecca 61 FG 4
Mechelen 14 D 4
Mecheria 58 E 2
Mechigmenskiy Zaliv 72 C 2
Mecklenburg 15 F 4
Mecklenburger Bucht 15 F 4
Meconta 67 F 3
Mecrihan 21 E 3
Mecsek 20 A 1
Mecuburi 67 F 2
Mecúfi 67 G 2
Mecula 67 F 2
Mecumbura 67 E 3
Medaguine 59 F 2
Medak 40 C 4
Médala 58 D 5
Medan 42 A 3
Medano 88 C 5
Médanos 88 E 5
Medanos 89 D 6
Medbourne 7 D 1
Médéa 59 F 1

Medellín 84 CD 2
Medelpad 16 G 3
Mederdra 58 B 5
Medétsız 21 D 3
Medford 76 B 3
Medgidia 20 C 2
Medi 64 E 3
Mediaş 20 B 1
Medical Lake 76 C 2
Medicine Bow 76 E 3
Medicine Hat 73 P 5
Medicine Lodge 76 G 4
Medigan 25 R 5
Medina (Saudi Arabia) 22 C 4
Medina del Campo 18 C 3
Medinipur 40 E 3
Mediterranean Sea 11 HL 8–9
Mediterranean Sea 22 A 2
Medje 64 D 4
Medjerda, Monts de la 59 G 1
Mednogorsk 25 L 5
Mêdog 38 C 5
Médouneu 63 G 5
Medveditsa 24 H 5
Medvezh'i, Ostrova 37 U 1
Medvezhiy Var 36 F 1
Medvezh'ya, Gora 37 P 6
Medvezh'yegorsk 24 FG 3
Medway, River 7 E 2
Meeberrie 48 B 4
Meekatharra 48 B 4
Meeker 76 E 3
Meenaclady 4 A 2
Meerut 40 C 2
Mega (Ethiopia) 65 F 4
Mega (Indonesia) 43 H 4
Mega, Pulau 42 B 4
Megalopolis 20 B 3
Meganom, Mys 21 E 2
Meganom, Mys 21 E 2
Mégara 20 B 3
Megasani Hill 40 E 3
Megève 19 E 2
Meghalaya 41 F 2
Megid 59 K 3
Megion 25 P 3
Megra 24 G 3
Megra 24 H 2
Meguidene 59 F 3
Meguinenza, Embalse de 18 CD 3
Mehadia 20 B 2
Mehar 35 H 5
Mehdīshahr (Iran) 23 F 2
Mehrābād (Iran) 23 E 1
Mehrān (Iran) 23 E 2
Mehrān (Iran) 23 G 4
Mehrīz (Iran) 23 G 3
Mehtar Lam 35 J 4
Mei Xian 38 G 5
Meia Meia 65 F 6
Meiganga 63 G 4
Meigle 3 D 3
Meiktila 41 G 3
Meishan 38 D 5
Meissen 15 F 4
Meissner 15 E 4
Meitan 38 E 5
Mejillones 86 B 5
Mékambo 63 G 5
Mekerrhane, Sebkha 59 F 3
Mekhé 62 A 2
Meknès 58 D 2
Meko 62 E 4
Mekong 41 J 5
Mekong, Mouths of the 41 J 6
Mekongga, Gunung 43 F 4
Mekoryuk 72 D 3
Mekrou 62 E 3
Mêladên 65 H 2
Melaka 42 B 3
Melanesia 51 FJ 2–3
Melawi, Sungai 42 D 4
Melbourn 7 E 1
Melbourne (Australia) 49 G 6
Melbourne (FL, U.S.A.) 77 KL 6
Melchor, Isla 89 B 8
Melchor Múzquiz 78 B 2
Melchor Ocampo 78 B 4
Melendiz Dağı 21 D 3
Melenki 24 H 4
Meletsk 36 F 4
Meleuz 24 L 5
Mélèzes, Rivière aux 75 N 4
Melfi (Chad) 63 H 3
Melfi (Italy) 19 G 3
Melfort 73 Q 5
Melilla 58 E 1
Melimoyo, Monte 89 B 7
Melinca 89 B 7
Melipilla 88 B 5
Melitopol' 21 E 1
Melk 19 G 2
Melksham 7 C 2
Mellan-Fryken 17 F 4
Mellen 77 H 2
Mellerud 17 F 4

Mellish Reef 49 K 2
Mellit 60 D 6
Mellouline 59 F 4
Melmerby 5 D 2
Mel'nichnaya 25 R 2
Melo 88 F 5
Melolo 43 F 5
Melrhir, Chott 59 G 2
Melrose (U.K.) 5 D 2
Melrose (U.S.A.) 76 D 2
Melsetter → Chimanimani 67 E 3
Melsungen 15 E 4
Meltaus 16 HJ 2
Meltham 5 E 3
Melton Constable 7 E 1
Melton Mowbray 7 D 1
Meluco 67 F 2
Melun 18 D 2
Melvich 2 C 2
Melville 73 R 5
Melville Bay 90
Melville, Cape 49 G 1
Melville Fracture Zone 98 B 5
Melville Hills 73 N 2
Melville Island 48 E 1
Melville Island 90
Melville, Lake 75 Q 5
Melville Peninsula 73 V 2
Melville Sound 73 Q 2
Melyuveyem 37 W 3
Meman 41 J 5
Mêmar Co 40 D 1
Memba 67 G 2
Memboro 43 E 5
Memmingen 15 EF 5
Mempawah 42 C 3
Memphis (Egypt) 60 E 3
Memphis (TN, U.S.A.) 77 J 4
Memsie 2 C 3
Mena (AR, U.S.A.) 77 H 5
Mena (U.S.S.R.) 24 F 5
Menai Bridge 6 B 1
Menai Strait 6 B 1
Ménaka 62 E 2
Menawashei 60 D 6
Mencué 89 C 7
Mendawai, Sungai 42 D 4
Mende 18 D 3
Mendi (Ethiopia) 64 F 3
Mendi (Papua New Guinea) 50 D 3
Mendip Hills 6 C 2
Mendocino, Cape 76 B 3
Mendoza (Argentina) 88 C 5
Mendoza (Peru) 84 C 5
Mene Grande 84 D 2
Menemen 20 C 3
Menez Hom 18 C 2
Mengcheng 39 G 4
Méngen 21 D 2
Mengene Dağı 21 F 3
Menghai 38 D 6
Mengla 38 D 6
Menglian 38 C 6
Mengzi 38 D 6
Meniet 59 F 3
Menihek Lakes 75 O 5
Menindee 49 G 5
Meningie 49 F 6
Menkere 36 M 3
Menkere 37 MN 2
Menominee 77 J 2
Menongue 66 B 2
Menorca 18 D 3
Menouarar 58 E 2
Men'shikova, Mys 25 LM 1
Men'shikova, Ostrov 37 PQ 5
Mentasta Lake 72 J 3
Mentawai, Kepulauan 42 A 4
Mentawai, Selat 42 A 4
Mentese 20 C 3
Mentok 42 C 4
Menyamya 50 E 3
Menyapa, Gunung 42 E 3
Menyuan 38 D 3
Menza 36 J 6
Menzel Bourgiba → Manzil Bū Ruquaybah 59 GH 1
Menzelinsk 24 K 4
Menzies 48 C 4
Menzies, Mount 91
Meon stoke 7 D 2
Meopham 7 E 2
Meoqui 76 E 6
Mepistskaro 21 F 2
Meponda 67 E 2
Meppel 14 E 4
Meppen 15 E 4
Mepuze 67 E 4
Merak 42 C 5
Merāker 16 F 3
Merangngau 42 D 4
Merano 19 F 2
Merauke 50 D 3
Mercadal 18 D 4
Mercara 40 C 5
Merced 76 B 4

Mercedario, Cerro 88 BC 5
Mercedes (Argentina) 88 C 5
Mercedes (Argentina) 88 E 4
Mercedes (Uruguay) 88 E 5
Merceditas 88 BC 4
Merĉes 84 E 5
Merchants Bay 75 P 2
Mercy Bay 73 O 1
Mercy, Cape 75 P 3
Meredith, Cape 89 D 9
Meredoua 59 F 3
Merefa 24 G 6
Merenga 37 T 3
Mereworth 7 E 2
Merga → Nukhaylak 60 D 5
Mergenevo 34 E 1
Mergui 41 G 5
Mergui Archipelago 41 G 5
Meriç 20 C 2
Mérida (Mexico) 78 E 3
Mérida (Spain) 18 B 4
Mérida (Venezuela) 84 D 2
Mérida, Cordillera de 84 D 2
Meriden 7 D 1
Meridian 77 J 5
Meridja 58 E 2
Mérignac 18 C 3
Merikarvia 16 H 3
Merín, Laguna 88 F 5
Meringur 49 G 5
Merinos 88 E 5
Merir 43 H 3
Merivale River 49 H 4
Merkushino 25 N 4
Merkushura Strelka 37 R 1
Meroe 60 E 5
Merouane, Chott 59 G 2
Merredin 48 B 5
Merrick 3 B 4
Merril 77 J 2
Merriman 76 F 3
Merritt 73 N 5
Merritt Island 77 KL 6
Merseburg 15 F 4
Mersey, River 5 D 3
Merseyside 5 D 3
Mersin 21 D 3
Mersin (Turkey) 22 B 1
Mersing 42 B 3
Mērsrags 17 H 4
Merta 40 B 2
Merthyr Tydfil 6 C 2
Merti 65 F 4
Mértola 18 B 4
Mertole Maryam 65 F 2
Merton 6 B 2
Meru (Kenya) 65 F 4
Meru (Tanzania) 65 F 5
Meru Game Reserve 65 F 4
Merutai 42 E 3
Merzifon 21 E 2
Mesa, Cerro 89 B 8
Mesa de San Carlos 76 CD 6
Mesa de Yambí 84 D 3
Mesabi Range 77 H 2
Mesapo 42 E 2
Mescalero 76 E 5
Meschede 15 E 4
Mescit Daği 21 F 2
Meseied 58 C 3
Meseta Central 78 B 3
Meseta de Chiapas 78 D 4
Meseta de Somuncurá 89 C 7
Meseta del Cerro Jaua 85 F 2–3
Mesetas de las Vizcachas 89 B 9
Meskou 63 H 2
Mesmiyah (Syria) 22 B 2
Mesolóngion 20 B 3
Mesopotamia (Iraq) 22–23 CD 2–3
Mesquite 77 G 5
Messaad 59 F 2
Messalo 67 F 2
Messengue 67 E 4
Messerian 34 E 3
Messina (Italy) 19 FG 4
Messina (South Africa) 66 D 4
Messina, Stretto di 19 G 4
Messiniakós Kólpos 20 B 3
Messo 25 P 2
Messoyakha 25 PQ 2
Mesta 20 B 2
Mesters Vig 90
Meta 84 DE 2
Meta Incognita Peninsula 75 O 3
Metairie 77 H 5–6
Metal, Mont du 59 G 4
Metán 88 D 4
Metangula 67 EF 2
Metapan 78 E 5
Metaponto 19 G 3
Meteghan 75 O 7
Metemma 64 F 2
Meteor Depth 98 A 5
Meteran 51 F 2
Méthana 20 B 3
Methven 3 C 3

Metković 19 G 3
Metlakatla 72 L 4
Metlika 19 G 2
Metlili Chaamba 59 F 2
Metro 42 C 5
Métsevon, Zigos 20 B 3
Metu 64 F 3
Metz 19 E 2
Meulaboh 42 A 3
Meureudu 42 A 2
Meuse 19 E 2
Mevagissey 6 B 2
Mexborough 5 E 3
Mexiana, 85 J 3
Mexicali 76 CD 5
Mexican Hat 76 E 4
Mexico 78 C 3
Mexico (MO, U.S.A.) 77 H 4
México City 78 BC 4
Mexico, Gulf of 78 DE 2
Meyanobab 43 H 5
Meybod (Iran) 23 F 2
Meydān-e Gel 34 EF 5
Meydān-e Gel (Iran) 23 G 3
Meyeihido 58 B 4
Meyísti 20 C 3
Meymeh (Iran) 23 E 2
Meymeh (Iran) 23 F 2
Meyo Centre 63 G 5
Mezada (Israel) 22 B 3
Mezcalapa, Rio 78 D 4
Mezdra 20 B 2
Mezen' 24 HJ 2
Mezen' 24 HJ 2
Mezenskaya Guba 24 H 2
Mezenskiy 36 G 1
Mezhdurechensk 25 R 5
Mezhdurechenskiy 25 N 4
Mezhdusharskiy, Ostrov 24 K 1
Mezhevaya 21 E 1
Mežica 19 F 2
Mezötúr 20 B 1
Mezraa 21 E 2
Mfanganu 64 E 5
Mgachi 37 Q 5
Mgera 65 F 6
Mgori 64 EF 5
Mhow 40 C 3
Miajadas 18 B 4
Miaméré 64 C 3
Miami (AZ, U.S.A.) 76 D 5
Miami (FL, U.S.A.) 77 K 6
Miami (OK, U.S.A.) 77 H 4
Miami Beach 77 L 6
Miān Āb (Iran) 23 E 2–3
Mian Kalai 35 J 4
Miancaowan 38 C 3
Mianchi 38 F 4
Miāndarreh (Iran) 23 F 2
Miāndowāb (Iran) 23 D 1
Miandrivazo 67 H 3
Mianduhe 37 M 6
Miāneh (Iran) 23 E 1
Miāneh (Iran) 23 E 1
Miani Hor 35 H 5
Mianning 38 D 5
Mianwali 35 J 4
Mianyang 38 D 4
Mianzhu 38 D 4
Miaodao Qundao 39 H 3
Miao'ergou 35 L 1
Miarinarivo 67 H 3
Miaru 50 E 3
Miass 25 LM 5
Miass 25 M 4
Miastko 15 G 4
Micaune 67 F 3
Micay 84 C 3
Michalovce 15 H 5
Michelsen, Cape 73 R 1
Michelson, Mount 72 H 2
Micheweni 65 FG 5
Michigan 77 JK 2–3
Michigan City 77 J 3
Michigan, Lake 77 J 3
Michipicoten Bay 74 K 6
Michipicoten Island 74 K 6
Michoacán 78 B 4
Mičhurin 20 C 2
Michurinsk 24 G 5
Micronesia 52 BC 2–3
Mid Glamorgan 6 C 2
Mid Yell 2 D 1
Midai, Pulau 42 C 3
Mid-Atlantic Ridge 98 A 2–5
Middelburg 14 D 4
Middelburg (South Africa) 66 C 5
Middelburg (South Africa) 66 D 6
Middelfart 17 EF 4
Middelwit 66 D 4
Middle Alkali Lake 76 C 3
Middle America Trench 99 D 3
Middle Andaman 41 F 5
Middlesboro 77 K 4
Middlesbrough 5 E 2
Middlesmoor 5 E 2

Middleton 5 D 2
Middleton 5 D 3
Middleton 7 E 1
Middleton-in-Teesdale 5 D 2
Middleton-on-the-Wolds 5 E 3
Middletown 4 B 2
Middletown 77 JK 4
Middlewich 5 D 3
Midelt 58 E 2
Miðsandur 16 A 3
Midhurst 7 D 2
Midi, Canal du 18 D 3
Mid-Indian Ridge 98 B 4
Midland (MI, U.S.A.) 77 K 3
Midland (Ontario, Can.) 75 M 7
Midland (TX, U.S.A.) 76 F 5
Midongy Atsimo 67 H 4
Midsummer Norton 6 C 2
Midway I. 102 B 3
Midwest 76 E 3
Midyat 21 F 3
Midžor 20 B 2
Miedwie, Jezioro 15 F 4
Międzyrzec Podlaski 15 H 4
Międzyrzecz 15 G 4
Miekojärvi 16 HJ 2
Mielan 18 D 3
Mielec 15 H 4
Mielno 15 G 4
Miercurea Ciuc 20 C 1
Mieres 18 B 3
Mierzeja Helska 15 G 4
Mierzeja Wiślana 15 G 4
Miesso 65 G 3
Migiurtinia 65 HJ 2
Miguel Alves 87 H 1
Mihăilesti 20 C 2
Mihalıçcık 20 D 3
Mihuru 67 F 2
Mijares 18 C 3
Mijdahah 61 H 6
Mikha Tskhakaya 21 F 2
Mikhalkino 37 U 2
Mikhaylov 24 G 5
Mikhaylovgrad 20 B 2
Mikhaylovka 21 G 1
Mikhaylovka 24 H 5
Mikhaylovka 34 D 1
Mikhaylovskiy 25 PQ 5
Mikínai 20 B 3
Mikindani 67 FG 2
Mikino 37 U 3
Mikkeli 16 J 3
Míkonos 20 C 3
Mikré Prěspa, Límni 20 B 2
Mikumi 65 F 6
Mikumi National Park 65 F 6
Mikun' 24 JK 3
Mikuni-sanmyaku 39 L 3
Mila 19 E 4
Miladunmadulu Atoll 40 B 6
Milagro 84 C 4
Milan 19 EF 2
Milando Reserve 66 B 1
Milange 67 F 3
Milano 19 E 2
Milás 20 C 3
Milazzo 19 FG 4
Milcan Tepe 21 E 3
Mildenhall 7 E 1
Mildura 49 G 5
Mile 38 D 6
Miléai 20 B 3
Miles 49 HJ 4
Miles City 76 E 2
Milet 20 C 3
Milford 76 D 4
Milford Haven 6 B 2
Milford Sound 50 P 9
Milgun 48 B 4
Milh, Bahr al (Iraq) 22 D 2
Mili 52 C 2
Milk 76 E 2
Milkovo 37 T 5
Mill 75 M 3
Millau 18 D 3
Mille Lacs Lake 77 H 2
Milledgeville 77 K 5
Millerovo 24 H 6
Millevaches, Plateau de 18 D 2
Millford 8 C 2
Millicent 49 FG 6
Millington 77 J 4
Millisle 4 C 2
Millom 5 D 2
Millport 3 B 4
Mills Lake 73 O 3
Millstatt 19 F 2
Millstream 48 B 3
Milltown 2 C 3
Milltown 4 B 2
Milltownpass 4 B 3
Millwood Lake 77 H 5
Milly Milly (Western Australia)
  48 B 4

Milngavie 3 B 4
Milo 62 C 3
Mílos 20 B 3
Milparinka 49 G 4
Milton (N.C., U.S.A.) 77 L 4
Milton (N.S.W., Austr.) 49 J 6
Milton Abbot 6 B 2
Milton Keynes 7 D 1
Miltou 63 H 3
Miluo 38 F 5
Milwaukee 77 J 3
Milwaukie 76 B 2
Milyatino 24 F 5
Mimizan 18 C 3
Mimongo 63 G 6
Min Jiang 38 D 5
Min Jiang 39 G 5
Min Shan 38 D 4
Min Xian 38 D 4
Mina 36 F 5
Mīnā' 'Abd Allāh (Kuwait) 23 E 3
Mīnā' al 'Ahmadī (Kuwait) 23 E 3
Mīnā' Baranīs (Egypt) 22 B 5
Mina Jabal 'Alī (United Arab
  Emirates) 23 G 4
Mina, Mont 62 C 3
Mīnā' Sa'ūd (Saudi Arabia) 23 E 3
Mīnāb 34 F 5
Minahassa Peninsula 43 F 3
Minamata 39 JK 4
Minami-daitō-jima 39 K 5
Minas (Indonesia) 42 B 3
Minas (Uruguay) 88 EF 5
Minas Gerais 87 GH 4
Minas Novas 87 H 4
Minas, Sierra de las 78 E 4
Minatitlán 78 D 4
Minbu 41 F 3
Minbya 41 F 3
Mincha 88 B 5
Mincio 19 F 2
Mindanao 43 FG 2
Mindelo 62 B 6
Minden (F.R.G.) 15 E 4
Minden (LA, U.S.A.) 77 H 5
Minderoo 48 B 3
Mindif 63 G 3
Mindoro 43 F 1
Mindoro Strait 43 F 1
Mindorou 63 G 5
Mindyak 25 L 5
Mine Head 14 B 4
Minehead 6 C 2
Mineiros 87 F 4
Mineral Wells 76 G 5
Mineral'nyye Vody 21 F 2
Minerva Reefs 52 D 4
Minfeng 35 L 3
Minga 66 D 2
Mingan 75 P 5
Mingary 49 G 5
Mingechaur 34 D 2
Mingechaurskoye
  Vodokhranilishche 34 D 2
Mingenew 48 B 4
Mingin Range 41 G 3
Mingo Lake 75 N 3
Mingon 41 G 3
Mingshui 38 C 2
Mingshui 39 J 1
Mingteke 35 K 3
Mingualy 3 A 3
Mingxi 39 G 5
Minhe 38 D 3
Minho 18 B 3
Minicoy 40 B 6
Minigwal, Lake 48 C 4
Minilya 48 A 3
Minilya River 48 A 3
Ministro João Alberto 87 F 3
Minle 38 D 3
Minna 63 F 4
Minneapolis (KS, U.S.A.) 76 G 4
Minneapolis (MN, U.S.A.) 77 H 3
Minnedosa 73 S 5
Minnesota 77 GH 2
Minnesota River 77 G 2–3
Minnigaf 3 B 4
Miño 18 B 3
Minot 76 F 2
Minqin 38 D 3
Minqing 39 G 5
Minsin 41 G 2
Minsk 17 J 5
Minster 7 E 2
Minster 7 E 2
Minto 72 K 3
Minto (Fed. States of Micronesia)
  52 B 2
Minto Inlet 73 O 1
Minto, Lac 75 N 4
Minūdasht 34 F 3
Minusinsk 36 F 5
Minvoul 63 G 5
Minwakh 61 H 5

Miquan 35 M 2
Miquelon 75 M 6
Miquelon 75 Q 6
Mir 63 G 3
Mira 19 F 2
Mirabad 35 G 4
Mirador 87 H 2
Miraflores 84 D 3
Miraj 40 B 4
Miramar 89 E 6
Mirambeau 18 C 2
Miramichi Bay 75 P 6
Miramont-de-Guyenne 18 D 3
Miran 38 A 3
Miraña 84 D 4
Miranda 86 E 5
Miranda 86 E 5
Miranda de Ebro 18 C 3
Mirandela 18 B 3
Mirandola 19 F 3
Mirapinima 85 F 4
Miravalles, Volcán 78 F 5
Miravete, Puerto de 18 B 4
Mirbāt 61 J 5
Mirdita 20 AB 2
Mirgorod 24 F 6
Miri 42 D 3
Miriam Vale 49 J 3
Mirim, Lagoa 88 F 5
Mirina 20 C 3
Mirnoye 25 R 3
Mirnyy 36 K 3
Mirnyy 91
Mirpur 35 J 4
Mirpur Khas 35 H 5
Mirria 63 F 3
Mirsali 35 M 2
Mirtna 49 H 3
Mirtóon Pélagos 20 B 3
Mirzapur 40 D 2
Misgar 35 J 3
Mish'āb, Ra's al (Saudi Arabia)
  23 E 3
Mishan 39 K 1
Mishkino 24 L 4
Misima Island 49 J 1
Misima Island 51 F 4
Misión Cavinas 86 C 3
Miskah (Saudi Arabia) 22 D 4
Miskitos, Cayos 78 F 5
Miskolc 20 B 1
Mismār 60 F 5
Misool, Pulau 43 H 4
Miṣr 60 DE 4
Misrāta 59 HJ 2
Misrātah, Ra's 59 J 2
Missinaibi 74 L 5
Missisa Lake 74 K 5
Mississippi 77 H 5
Mississippi 77 HJ 5
Mississippi Delta 77 J 6
Missoula 76 D 2
Missour 58 E 2
Missouri 77 H 4
Missouri 77 H 4
Mistassini, Lac 75 N 5
Misti, Volcán 86 B 4
Mistrás 20 B 3
Misty Fjords National Monument
  72 L 4
Mitchell 76 G 3
Mitchell (Queensland, Austr.)
  49 H 4
Mitchell, Mount 77 K 4
Mitchell River 49 G 2
Mitchell River (Queensland,
  Austr.) 49 G 2
Mitchell River (Victoria, Austr.)
  49 H 6
Miteja 65 F 6
Mithimna 20 C 3
Mitiaro 53 E 4
Mitilíni 20 C 3
Mitina 24 J 2
Mitla 78 C 4
Mito 39 M 3
Mitomoni 67 EF 2
Mitra 63 F 3
Mitsinjo 67 H 3
Mittellandkanal 15 E 4
Mittersill 19 F 2
Mitú 84 D 3
Mitumba 84 E 6
Mitumba, Monts 64 D 5–6
Mitwaba 64 D 6
Mityayevo 25 M 3
Mitzic 63 G 5
Mius 21 E 1
Mivec 58 C 3
Miyāh, Wādi al (Syria) 22 C 2
Miyake-jima 39 LM 4
Miyako 39 M 3
Miyako-jima 39 J 6
Miyakonojō 39 K 4
Miyako-rettō 39 H 6

Miyaly **34** E 1
Miyazaki **39** K 4
Miyi **38** D 5
Miyun **39** G 2
Mizan Teferi **64** F 3
Mizdah **59** H 2
Mizen Head **14** AB 4
Mizhi **38** F 3
Mizil **20** C 2
Mizoram **41** F 3
Mizque **86** D 4
Mizusawa **39** M 3
Mjölby **17** G 4
Mjöndalen **17** E 4
Mjösa **17** F 3
Mkangira **65** F 6
Mkasu **65** F 6
Mkata **65** F 6
Mkoani **65** F 6
Mkokotoni **65** F 6
Mkomazi **65** F 5
Mkomazi Game Reserve **65** F 5
Mkuku **66** D 2
Mkulwe **64** E 6
Mkushi **66** D 2
Mladá Boleslav **15** F 4
Mladenovac **20** B 2
Mlala Hills **64** E 6
Mława **15** H 4
Mleihas **58** D 4
Mleti **21** F 2
Mljet **19** G 3
Mljetski kanal **19** G 3
Mlnta **63** G 5
Mmadinare **66** D 4
Mmbatho **66** D 5
Mo i Rana **16** F 2
Moa **62** B 4
Moab **76** E 4
Moabi **63** G 6
Moʿalla (Iran) **23** F 2
Moamba **67** E 5
Moanda (Gabon) **63** G 6
Moanda (Zaire) **63** G 7
Moate **4** B 3
Moatize **67** E 3
Moba **64** D 6
Mobārakeh (Iran) **23** F 2
Mobaye **64** C 4
Mobayi-Mbongo **64** C 4
Mobeka **64** B 4
Moberly **77** H 4
Mobile **77** J 5
Mobile Bay **77** J 5
Mobridge **76** F 2
Mocajuba **85** J 4
Moçambique **67** G 3
Mocambique Basin **98** B 5
Mocha → Al Mukhā **61** G 6
Mocha, Isla **89** B 6
Mochudi **66** D 4
Mocímboa da Praia **67** G 2
Mockfjärd **17** FG 3
Môco, Morro de **66** AB 2
Mocoa **84** C 3
Mococa **87** G 5
Moctezuma **76** E 6
Moctezuma **78** B 3
Mocuba **67** F 3
Modane **19** E 2
Model Town **35** J 4
Modena (Italy) **19** F 3
Modena (U.S.A.) **76** D 4
Modesto **76** B 4
Modica **19** F 4
Modjamboli **64** C 4
Modowi **43** H 4
Modra **63** H 1
Modriča **19** G 3
Modur Daği **21** F 3
Moe **49** H 6
Moelfre **5** B 1
Moelv **16** F 3
Moengo **85** H 2
Moero, Lac **64** D 6
Moffat **3** C 4
Moga **64** D 5
Mogadiscio → Muqdisho **65** H 4
Mogadishu **65** H 4
Mogadouro, Serra do **18** B 3
Mogāl (Iran) **23** F 1
Mogaung **41** G 2
Mogdy **37** O 5
Mogi das Cruzes **87** G 5
Mogilev **17** JK 5
Mogilev Podol'skiy **20** C 1
Mogil-Mogil **49** H 4
Mogi-Mirim **87** G 5
Mogincual **67** G 3
Mogocha **36** LM 5
Mogochin **25** Q 4
Mogogh **64** E 3
Mogok **41** G 3
Mogotoyevo, Ozero **37** R 1
Mogoyn **36** G 6

Mogoytui **36** KL 5
Mogu **65** G 4
Moguqi **37** M 6
Mogzon **36** K 5
Mohács **20** A 1
Mohall **76** F 2
Mohammadābād (Iran) **23** G 3
Mohammedia **58** D 2
Mohe **37** M 5
Moheda **17** F 4
Moheli **67** G 2
Mohenjo Daro **35** H 5
Mohican, Cape **72** D 3
Mohill **4** B 3
Mohon Peak **76** D 5
Mohona **40** C 2
Mohoro **65** F 6
Moidart **3** B 3
Mointy **25** O 6
Moise **75** O 5
Moisie **75** O 5
Moissac **18** D 3
Moïssala **63** H 4
Moitaco **85** F 2
Mojácar **18** C 4
Mojave **76** C 4
Mojave Desert **76** C 4
Mojiang **38** D 6
Mojjo **65** F 3
Moju **85** J 4
Mokambo **66** D 2
Mokhotlong **66** D 5
Mokhovaya **37** T 5
Mokil **52** B 2
Moklakan **36** L 4
Mokokchung **41** F 2
Mokolo **63** G 3
Mokpʼo **39** J 4
Mokra Gora **20** B 2
Mokwa **63** E 4
Mol **14** E 4
Mola di Bari **19** G 3
Molagno **78** C 3
Molat **19** F 3
Molchanovo **25** Q 4
Mold **6** C 1
Moldava **20** C 1
Moldaviya **20** C 1
Molde **16** E 3
Moldefjorden **16** E 3
Moldes **88** D 5
Moldova Nouă **20** B 2
Moldoveanu, Virful **20** B 1
Mole Game Reserve **62** D 4
Molegbe **64** C 4
Moleke **64** B 5
Molepolole **66** D 4
Molfetta **19** G 3
Molina (Argentina) **88** C 5
Molina (Chile) **89** B 6
Molina de Aragón **18** C 3
Molina de Segura **18** C 4
Moline **77** H 3
Moling **41** F 2
Moliro **64** E 6
Molkābād (Iran) **23** F 2
Molkom **17** F 4
Mollendo **86** B 4
Molochansk **21** E 1
Molochnyy Liman **21** E 1
Molodechno **17** J 5
Molodezhnaya **91**
Molodo **36** M 2
Molodogvardeyskaya **25** O 5
Molokai **53** E 1
Molokai Fracture Zone **99** D 2
Molong **49** H 5
Molopo **66** C 5
Molotovo **21** F 2
Moloundou **63** H 5
Molteno **66** D 6
Moluccas **43** G 4
Molus Ridge **98** A 1
Moma (Mozambique) **67** F 3
Moma (U.S.S.R.) **37** QR 2
Mombaça **87** J 2
Mombasa **65** FG 5
Mombetsu **39** M 2
Mombi New **41** F 3
Mombo **65** F 5
Mombotuta Falls **66** D 2
Momboyo **64** B 5
Momi **64** D 5
Mompono **64** C 4
Mompós **84** D 2
Momskiy Khrebet **37** QR 1–2
Momskiy Khrebet **37** QR 2
Mön **17** F 5
Mon **41** G 4–5
Mon Yul **41** F 2
Mona, Canal de la **79** J 4
Mona, Isla **79** J 4
Mona Quimbundo **66** B 1
Monach Isles **2** A 3
Monaco **19** E 3

Monaghan **4** B 2
Monahans **76** F 5
Monapo **67** G 2
Monarch Mountain **73** M 5
Monashee Mountains **73** O 5
Monasterevin **4** B 3
Monastery of Saint Catherine
  (Egypt) **22** AB 3
Monatélé **63** G 5
Monbetsu **39** M 2
Moncalieri **19** E 2–3
Moncayo, Sierra del **18** C 3
Monchegorsk **16** K 2
Mönchen-Gladbach **14** E 4
Monclova **78** B 2
Moncton **75** O 6
Mondego **18** B 3
Mondego, Cabo **18** B 3
Mondjuko **64** C 5
Mondo **63** H 3
Mondoñedo **18** B 3
Mondovi **19** E 3
Mondragone **19** F 3
Mondy **36** H 5
Money **41** K 4
Moneygall **4** B 3
Moneymore **4** B 2
Moneyslane **4** B 2
Monfalcone **19** F 2
Monforte **18** B 4
Mong Cai **41** J 3
Mong Hang **41** G 3
Mong Hpayak **41** G 3
Mong La **41** G 3
Mong Lin **41** H 3
Mong Loi **41** H 3
Mong Yai **41** G 3
Monga **64** C 4
Mongala **64** C 4
Mongalla **64** E 3
Mongbwalu **64** D 4
Monger, Lake (Western Australia)
  48 B 4
Monghyr **40** E 2
Mongo (Chad) **63** H 3
Mongo (Sierra Leone) **62** B 4
Mongol Ard Uls **36** GH 6
Mongolia **36** GH 6
Mongolo **36** J 2
Mongono **63** G 5
Mongonu **63** G 3
Mongororo **63** J 3
Mongu **66** C 3
Móngua **66** B 3
Monguel **58** C 5
Mönhhaan **38** F 1
Monichkirchen **19** G 2
Monigotes **88** D 5
Monjes, Islas los **84** D 1
Monkey Bay **67** EF 2
Monkey River **78** E 4
Monkira **49** G 3
Monkoto **64** C 5
Monmouth **6** C 2
Mono (Solomon Is.) **51** G 3
Mono (Togo) **62** E 4
Mono Lake **76** C 3
Monolithos **20** C 3
Monong **66** C 4
Monopoli **19** G 3
Monor **20** A 1
Monou **63** J 2
Monreal del Campo **18** C 3
Monreale **19** F 4
Monroe (LA, U.S.A.) **77** H 5
Monroe (MI, U.S.A.) **77** K 3
Monroe (N.C., U.S.A.) **77** K 5
Monrovia **62** B 4
Mons **14** D 4
Monsanto **18** B 3
Monse **43** F 4
Monsefú **84** C 5
Mönsterås **17** G 4
Mont Afao **59** G 3
Mont Aigoual **18** D 3
Mont Ajir **63** F 2
Mont aux Sources **66** D 5
Mont Blanc **19** E 2
Mont Cameroon **62** F 5
Mont de Ganga **63** G 4
Mont Deingueri **64** D 3
Mont du Metal **59** G 4
Mont Ei Loutone **63** G 1
Mont Gréboun **63** F 1
Mont Iboundji **63** G 6
Mont Jacques-Cartier **75** OP 6
Mont Joli **75** O 6
Mont Kavendou **62** B 3
Mont Lozére **18** D 3
Mont Mézenc **18** D 3
Mont Mina **62** C 3
Mont Mpelé **63** G 6
Mont Ngoua **64** C 4
Mont Niéndkoué **62** C 4
Mont Panié **51** H 6
Mont Pelat **19** E 3

Mont Pinçon **18** C 2
Mont Tahat **59** G 4
Mont Tembo **63** G 5
Mont Tonkou **62** C 4
Mont Ventoux **19** E 3
Mont Zedness **58** C 4
Montagne d'Ambre **67** H 2
Montagne de Lure **19** E 3
Montagne Pelée **79** K 5
Montague **72** H 4
Montague, Isla **76** D 5
Montalbán **18** C 3
Montalegre **18** B 3
Montana **76** DE 2
Montargis **18** D 2
Montauban **18** C 2
Montauban **18** D 3
Montbard **19** D 2
Montbeliard **19** E 2
Montbrison **18** D 2
Montceau-les-Mines **18** D 2
Mont-de-Marsan **18** C 3
Monte Pascoal, Parque Nacional
  de **87** J 4
Monte Alban **78** C 4
Monte Alegre **85** H 4
Monte Azul **87** H 4
Monte Bello Islands **48** AB 3
Monte Binga **67** E 3
Monte Carlo **19** E 3
Monte Carmelo **87** G 4
Monte Caseros **88** E 5
Monte Cinto **19** E 3
Monte Claros **87** H 4
Monte Comán **88** C 5
Monte Cristo **86** D 3
Monte d'Oro **19** E 3
Monte Dourado **85** H 4
Monte Fitz Roy **89** B 8
Monte Lindo **86** E 5
Monte Maca **89** B 8
Monte Melimoyo **89** B 7
Monte Negro Falls **66** A 3
Monte Quemado **88** D 4
Monte Rosa **19** E 2
Monte Santo **85** J 5
Monte Sarmiento **89** B 9
Monte Tronador **89** B 7
Monte Zeballos **89** B 8
Montech **18** D 3
Montecristi **79** H 4
Montecristo **19** F 3
Montego Bay **79** G 4
Montejinnie **48** E 2
Montelimar **19** D 3
Montemoreos **78** C 2
Montemor-o-Novo **18** B 4
Montenegro **88** F 4
Montepuez **87** F 2
Montepulciano **19** F 3
Monterado **42** C 3
Monterey **76** B 4
Monterey Bay **76** B 4
Montería **84** C 2
Montero **86** D 4
Monterotondo **19** F 3
Monterrey **78** BC 2
Montes Altos **85** J 5
Montes de Leon **18** B 3
Montes de Toledo **18** C 4
Montes Universales **18** C 3
Montes Vascos **18** C 3
Montesilvano **19** F 3
Montevideo **88** EF 5–6
Montgomery **6** C 1
Montgomery **77** J 5
Monthey **19** E 2
Monti Aurunci **19** F 3
Monti dei Frentani **19** FG 3
Monti di Ala **19** E 3
Monti Iblei **19** F 4
Monti Lepini **19** F 3
Monti Peloritani **19** FG 4
Monti Sabini **19** F 3
Monti Volsini **19** F 3
Monticello **76** E 4
Montiel, Campo de **18** C 4
Montigny-le-Roi **19** E 2
Montigny-les-Metz **19** E 2
Montijo, Golfo de **79** F 6
Montilla **18** C 4
Mont-Louis **18** D 2
Montluçon **18** D 2
Montmagny **75** NO 6
Montoro **18** C 4
Montpelier (ID, U.S.A.) **76** D 3
Montpelier (VT, U.S.A.) **77** M 3
Montpéllier **18** D 3
Montréal **75** N 6
Montreal Lake **73** QR 5
Montréjeau **18** D 3
Montreux **19** E 2
Montrose (U.K.) **3** C 3
Montrose (U.S.A.) **76** E 4
Monts Bagzane **63** F 2

Monts Bambouto **63** G 4
Monts Bleus **64** E 4
Monts Chic-Chocs **75** O 6
Monts d'Amain **18** D 2
Monts d'Arrée **18** C 2
Monts d'Aubrac **18** D 3
Monts de Cristal **63** G 5
Monts de la Medjerda **59** G 1
Monts de Lacaune **18** D 3
Monts de Toura **62** C 4
Monts des Ksour (Algeria) **58** EF 2
Monts des Ksour (Tunisia)
  59 GH 2
Monts des Oulad Naïl **59** F 2
Monts Dore **18** D 2
Monts du Beaujolais **19** D 2
Monts du Hodna **59** FG 1
Monts du Hombori **62** D 2
Monts du Livradois **18** D 2
Monts du Lyonnais **19** D 2
Monts Koungou **63** G 6
Monts Kundelungu **64** D 6–7
Monts Malimba **64** D 6
Monts Mandingues **62** B 3
Monts Marungu **64** D 6
Monts Mbang **63** G 4
Monts Mitumba **64** D 5–6
Monts Moukandé **63** G 6
Monts Mugila **64** D 6
Monts Nimba **62** C 4
Monts Notre-Dame **75** O 6
Monts Otish **75** N 5
Monts Tamgak **63** F 2
Monts Tarouadji **63** F 2
Monts Timétrine **62** D 2
Montsalvy **18** D 3
Montsant, Sierra de **18** D 3
Montseck, Sierra del **18** D 3
Montseny, Sierra de **18** D 3
Montserrat **79** K 4
Monveda **64** C 4
Monviso **19** E 3
Monywa **41** G 3
Monza **19** E 2
Monze **66** D 3
Monzón **18** D 3
Moonie **49** J 4
Moonie River **49** H 4
Moonta **49** F 5
Moor of Rannoch **3** B 3
Moora **48** B 5
Mooraberree **49** G 4
Moore, Lake **48** B 4
Moorea **53** EF 4
Moorfoot Hills **3** C 4
Moorhead **77** G 2
Moorlands **49** F 6
Moorreesburg **66** B 6
Moose **75** L 5
Moose Jaw **73** Q 5
Moose Pass **72** H 3
Moosehead Lake **77** N 2
Moosomin **73** R 5
Moosonee **75** L 5
Mopeia **67** F 3
Mopipi **66** CD 4
Mopti **62** D 3
Moqokorei **65** H 4
Moquegua **86** B 4
Mora (Cameroon) **63** G 3
Mora (Spain) **18** C 4
Mora (Sweden) **17** F 3
Mora de Ebro **18** D 3
Moraca **20** A 2
Moradabad **40** C 2
Morado, Cerro **86** CD 5
Morafenobe **67** G 3
Morąg **15** G 4
Moraleda, Canal **89** B 7
Moraleya **18** B 3
Moramanga **67** H 3
Moran **76** D 3
Morant Cays **79** G 4
Morane **53** F 4
Morar, Loch **3** B 3
Morata, Puerto de **18** C 3
Moratuwa **40** C 6
Morava (Czechoslovakia) **15** G 5
Morava (Western Australia) **48** B 4
Morava (Yugoslavia) **20** B 2
Moraviţa **20** B 1
Morawa **48** B 4
Morawhanna **85** G 2
Moray Firth **2** C 3
Morbi **40** B 3
Mordaga **36** M 5
Morden **73** S 6
Mordovo **24** H 5
Möre **17** G 4
More Laptevykh **36** MN 1
Morden **73** S 6
Möre og Romsdal **16** E 3
Morebath **67** G 3
Morecambe **5** D 2
Morecambe Bay **5** D 2
Moree **49** H 4
Morehead **50** D 3
Morehead City **77** L 5

Moreira 85 F 4
More-Iz, Gora 25 M 2
Morelia 78 B 4
Morelos 78 C 4
Morena 40 C 2
Morena, Sierra 18 BC 4
Morenci 76 E 5
Moreni 20 C 1–2
Moreno (Argentina) 89 B 6
Moreno (Peru) 84 C 5
Moreno National Park 89 B 8
Moreno, Parque Nacional 89 B 8
Moresby 72 L 5
Moreton 49 G 1
Moreton Island 49 J 4
Moretonhampstead 6 C 3
Moreton-in-Marsch 7 D 2
Morgan 49 F 5
Morgan City 77 H 6
Morganton 77 K 4
Morges 19 E 2
Morges 21 E 2
Mori (China) 38 B 2
Mori (Japan) 39 M 2
Moriarty 76 E 4
Morichal 84 D 3
Moriki 63 F 3
Morin Dawa 37 M 6
Morioka 39 M 3
Morjärv 16 H 2
Morkoka 36 K 2
Morlaix 18 C 2
Morley 5 E 3
Mormanno 19 G 4
Morne Diablotin 79 K 4
Mornington Abyssal Plain 99 D 5
Mornington, Isla 89 A 8
Mornington Island (Queensland, Austr.) 49 F 2
Morno 62 D 4
Mornou, Hadjer 63 J 2
Moro Gulf 43 F 2
Morobe 50 E 3
Morocco 58 D 2
Moroga 24 G 4
Morogoro 65 F 6
Moroleón 78 B 3
Morombe 67 G 4
Mörön 36 H 6
Morón (Cuba) 79 G 3
Morón (Spain) 18 B 4
Morón (Venezuela) 84 E 1
Morona 84 C 4
Morondava 67 G 4
Morondo 62 C 4
Moroni 67 G 2
Moroshechnoye 37 T 4
Morotai, Pulau 43 G 3
Morotai, Selat 43 G 3
Moroto 64 E 4
Moroto, Mount 64 EF 4
Morozovsk 21 F 1
Morpará 87 H 3
Morpeth 5 E 2
Morphou → Güzelyurt 21 D 3
Morrinhos 87 G 4
Morrinhos 87 H 1
Morris 73 S 6
Morro de Chapéu 87 H 3
Morro de Môco 66 AB 2
Morro do Sinal 87 E 3
Morro, Punta 88 B 4
Mörrum 17 F 4
Morrumbala 67 F 3
Morrumbene 67 F 4
Mors 17 E 4
Morshansk 24 H 5
Mörsil 16 F 3
Morskaya 37 X 3
Mortagne-sur-Sèvre 18 C 2
Mortain 18 C 2
Morteros 88 D 5
Mortesoro 60 E 6
Mortlake 49 G 6
Mortlock Islands 52 B 2
Moruya 49 J 6
Morven 49 H 4
Morvern 3 B 3
Morville 6 C 1
Morwell 49 H 6
Moryakovskiy Zaton 25 Q 4
Morzelândia 87 F 3
Mosby 17 E 4
Moscow 24 G 4
Moscow (ID, U.S.A.) 76 C 2
Mosel 15 E 4
Moselle 14 E 5
Moselle 19 E 2
Moses Lake 76 C 2
Moses Point 72 E 3
Moseyevo 24 J 2
Mosgiel 50 Q 10
Moshchnyy, Ostrov 17 J 4
Moshi 65 F 5
Mosina 15 G 4
Mosjöen 16 F 2

Moskal'vo 37 Q 5
Moskenesöya 16 F 2
Moskosel 16 G 2
Moskva 24 G 4
Moskva, Gora 36 F 5
Mosomane 66 D 4
Mosonmagyaróvár 20 A 1
Mosquera 84 C 3
Mosquito, Baie 75 M 3
Mosquitos, Costa de 78 F 5
Mosquitos, Golfo de los 84 B 2
Moss 17 F 4
Mossaka 63 H 6
Mosselbaai 66 C 6
Mossendjo 63 G 6
Mossoró 87 J 2
Moss-side 4 B 2
Mossuril 67 G 2
Most 15 F 4
Mostaganem 58 EF 1
Mostar 19 G 3
Mostardas 88 F 5
Mostrim 4 B 3
Mosty 17 H 5
Mostyn 43 E 3
Mosul 61 G 1
Mösvatn 17 E 4
Mota 65 F 2
Motajica 19 G 2–3
Motala 17 G 4
Motherwell 3 C 4
Motihari 40 DE 2
Motilla del Palancar 18 C 4
Motovskiy Zaliv 16 K 2
Motril 18 C 4
Motru 20 B 2
Motu One 53 E 4
Motueka 51 Q 9
Motul 78 E 3
Motutunga 53 F 4
Motykleyka 37 R 4
Mouchard 19 E 2
Moudjéria 58 C 5
Mouila (Algeria) 58 E 3
Mouila (Gabon) 63 G 6
Mouka 64 C 3
Moukandé, Monts 63 G 6
Moul 63 G 2
Moulhoulé 65 G 2
Moulins 18 D 2
Moulmein 41 G 4
Moulouya 58 E 2
Moultrie 77 K 5
Moultrie, Lake 77 K 5
Moundou 63 H 4
Mount Adam 89 DE 9
Mount Airy 77 K 4
Mount Amundsen 91
Mount Anglem 50 P 10
Mount Apo 43 G 2
Mount Ararat 21 F 3
Mount Arrowsmith 51 Q 9
Mount Aspiring 50 P 9
Mount Assiniboine 73 O 5
Mount Augustus 48 B 3
Mount Balbi 51 F 3
Mount Bangeta 50 E 3
Mount Barker 48 B 5
Mount Bimberi 49 H 6
Mount Blackburn 72 J 3
Mount Bona 72 J 3
Mount Brassey 48 E 3
Mount Brockman 48 B 3
Mount Broome 48 D 2
Mount Bruce 48 B 3
Mount Brukkaros 66 B 5
Mount Carter 49 G 1
Mount Casuarina 48 D 1
Mount Catherine 76 D 4
Mount Charles 4 A 2
Mount Christie 48 E 5
Mount Clark 73 N 3
Mount Clere 48 B 4
Mount Cleveland 76 D 2
Mount Columbia 73 O 5
Mount Connor 48 D 1
Mount Cook 51 Q 9
Mount Coolon 49 H 3
Mount Curious 48 A 4
Mount Cushing 73 M 4
Mount Dalrymple 49 H 3
Mount Darwin 67 E 3
Mount Davies 48 D 4
Mount Deering 48 D 3
Mount Demavend 23 F 2
Mount Demavend (Iran) 23 F 2
Mount Denison 72 G 4
Mount Doonerak 72 H 2
Mount Douglas 49 H 3
Mount Eba 49 F 5
Mount Eduni 72 LM 3
Mount Egerton 48 B 3
Mount Egmont 51 Q 8
Mount Elbert 76 E 4
Mount Elgon 64 E 4
Mount Elizabeth 48 D 2

Mount Elliot (Queensland, Austr.) 49 H 2
Mount Erebus 91
Mount Essendon 48 C 3
Mount Everest 40 E 2
Mount Fairweather 72 K 4
Mount Feathertop 49 H 6
Mount Finke 48 E 5
Mount Foraker 72 G 3
Mount Forel 90
Mount Forest 75 L 7
Mount Foster 72 K 4
Mount Fraser (Western Australia) 48 B 4
Mount Frere 66 D 6
Mount Gambier 49 FG 6
Mount Giluwe 50 D 3
Mount Gimie 79 K 5
Mount Glottof 72 G 4
Mount Godwin Austin 35 K 3
Mount Gould 48 B 4
Mount Hagen 50 D 3
Mount Halcon 43 F 1
Mount Hale (Western Australia) 48 B 4
Mount Halifax (Queensland, Austr.) 49 H 2
Mount Harper 72 J 3
Mount Hawkes 91
Mount Hayes 72 H 3
Mount Haywood 73 N 3
Mount Hermon (Lebanon) 22 B 2
Mount Hillaby 85 G 1
Mount Hood 76 B 2
Mount Hope 49 F 5
Mount House 48 D 2
Mount Hutton 49 H 4
Mount Isa 49 F 3
Mount Isto 72 J 2
Mount Jackson 48 B 5
Mount Jackson 91
Mount Jefferson (NV, U.S.A.) 76 C 4
Mount Jefferson (OR, U.S.A.) 76 B 3
Mount John 48 D 2
Mount Katmai 72 FG 4
Mount Kenya 65 F 5
Mount Kenya National Park 65 F 5
Mount Kimball 72 J 3
Mount Kirkpatrick 91
Mount Klotz 72 K 2
Mount Kosciusko 49 H 6
Mount Leake 48 D 3
Mount Leisler 48 D 3
Mount Lemmon 76 D 5
Mount Lesueur 48 B 5
Mount Liebig 48 E 3
Mount Livermore 76 F 5
Mount Lofty Ranges 49 F 5
Mount Logan 72 J 3
Mount Lucania 72 J 3
Mount Lush 48 D 2
Mount Magnet 48 B 4
Mount Maiyu 48 D 2
Mount Makalu 40 E 2
Mount Mantalingajan 42 E 2
Mount Marcus Baker 72 H 3
Mount McKinley 72 G 3
Mount McLoughlin 76 B 3
Mount Menzies 91
Mount Michelson 72 H 2
Mount Mitchell 77 K 4
Mount Molloy (Queensland, Austr.) 49 GH 2
Mount Morgan 49 J 3
Mount Moroto 64 EF 4
Mount Mowbullan 49 J 4
Mount Murchison (Western Australia) 48 B 4
Mount Nurri 49 H 5
Mount Nyiru 65 F 4
Mount Oglethorpe 77 K 5
Mount Olga 43 E 4
Mount Olympos → Kato Olimbos 20 B 3
Mount Olympus 76 B 2
Mount Omatako 66 B 4
Mount Ord 48 D 2
Mount Ossa 50 L 9
Mount Ossa 52 A 5
Mount Owen 51 Q 9
Mount Palomar 76 C 5
Mount Pattullo 72 LM 4
Mount Pinos 76 C 4–5
Mount Pleasant (MI, U.S.A.) 77 J 3
Mount Pleasant (UT, U.S.A.) 76 D 4
Mount Pulog 43 J 1
Mount Queen Bess 73 N 5
Mount Ragang 43 F 2
Mount Rainier 76 B 2
Mount Ratz 72 L 4
Mount Redcliffe 48 C 4
Mount Ritter 76 C 4

Mount Robe 49 G 5
Mount Roberts 49 J 4
Mount Robson 73 NO 5
Mount Roosevelt 73 M 4
Mount Saint Elias 72 J 3
Mount Saint Helens 76 B 2
Mount Samuel 48 E 2
Mount Sandiman 48 B 3
Mount Sanford 72 J 3
Mount Shasta 76 B 3
Mount Shenton 48 C 4
Mount Singleton 48 B 4
Mount Sir Alexander 73 N 5
Mount Sir James MacBrian 72 M 3
Mount Sir Thomas 48 D 4
Mount Smythe 73 MN 4
Mount Springer 75 N 6
Mount Squires 48 D 4
Mount Sulen 50 D 2
Mount Sunflower 76 F 4
Mount Tama 66 A 2
Mount Taylor 76 E 4
Mount Thuillier 41 F 6
Mount Tipton 76 D 4
Mount Tom White 72 J 3
Mount Torbert 72 G 3
Mount Travers 51 Q 9
Mount Trumbull 76 D 4
Mount Usborne 89 E 9
Mount Veniaminof 72 EF 4
Mount Vernon (Australia) 48 B 3
Mount Vernon (IL, U.S.A.) 77 J 4
Mount Vernon (KY, U.S.A.) 77 K 4
Mount Vernon (OH, U.S.A.) 77 K 3
Mount Vernon (WA, U.S.A.) 76 B 2
Mount Victoria (Burma) 41 F 3
Mount Victoria (Papua New Guinea) 50 E 3
Mount Vsevidof 72 D 5
Mount Waddington 73 M 5
Mount Washington 77 M 3
Mount Whitney 76 C 4
Mount Wilhelm 50 D 3
Mount Willoughby 48 E 4
Mount Wilson 76 C 5
Mount Woodroffe 48 E 4
Mount Wrightson 76 D 5
Mountain Ash 6 C 2
Mountain Grove 77 H 4
Mountain Home 76 C 3
Mountain Village 72 E 3
Mountains of Connemara 14 AB 4
Mountains of Mayo 14 B 4
Mountfield 4 B 2
Mountjoy 4 B 2
Mountmellick 4 B 3
Mountrath 4 B 3
Mount's Bay 6 B 2
Moura 85 F 4
Mourão 18 B 4
Mourdi, Dépression du 63 J 2
Mourdiah 62 C 3
Mourenx 18 C 3
Mournei 60 C 6
Mourne Mountains 4 BC 2
Mourra 63 J 3
Mousaaou Salah, Jbel 58 E 2
Mouscron 14 D 4
Mousehole 6 B 2
Moussoro 63 H 3
Mouths of the Amazon 85 J 3
Mouths of the Danube 20 CD 1
Mouths of the Ganges 40–41 EF 3
Mouths of the Godavari 40 D 4
Mouths of the Indus 40 A 3
Mouths of the Irrawaddy 41 FG 4
Mouths of the Krishna 40 D 4
Mouths of the Mekong 41 J 6
Mouths of the Orinoco 85 FG 2
Moûtiers 19 E 2
Moutong 43 F 3
Mouydir 59 F 4
Mouyondzi 63 G 6
Movas 76 E 6
Moville 4 B 2
Mowbullan, Mount 49 J 4
Möwe Bay 66 A 3
Moxico 66 BC 2
Moxico 66 C 2
Moxos, Llanos de 86 CD 4
Moyahua 78 B 3
Moyale 65 F 4
Moyamba 62 B 4
Moyen Atlas 58 DE 2
Moyeni 66 D 6
Moyero 36 H 2
Moygashel 4 B 2
Moyo, Pulau 42 E 5
Moyobamba 84 C 5
Moyowosi 64 E 5
Moyto 63 H 3
Moyu 35 K 3
Moyvally 4 B 3

Moyvore 4 B 3
Mozambique 67 EF 3
Mozambique Channel 67 FG 3–4
Mozdok 21 FG 2
Mozharka 36 F 5
Mozhga 24 K 4
Mozyr' 17 J 5
Mpala 64 D 6
Mpanda 64 E 6
Mpé 63 G 6
Mpelé, Mont 63 G 6
Mpika 67 E 2
Mporokosa 66 DE 1
Mpouya 63 H 6
Mpui 64 E 6
Mpulungu 66 E 1
Mpwapwa 65 F 6
Mrągowa 15 H 4
Mrakovo 24 L 5
Mrewa 67 E 3
Msäk Mallat 59 H 3–5
Msäk Mastäfat 59 H 3
Msata 65 F 6
M'Sila 59 F 1
Msoro 67 E 2
Mstislavl' 24 F 5
Mtabatuba 67 E 5
Mtakuja 64 E 6
Mtama 67 F 2
Mtandi 65 F 6
Mtegere 65 F 6
Mtera 65 F 6
Mtito Andei 65 F 5
Mtoko 67 E 3
Mtsensk 24 G 5
Mtskheta 21 F 2
Mtwara 67 G 2
Mu Us Shamo 38 E 3
Mualang 42 D 3
Muanã 85 J 4
Muang 41 H 5
Muang Loei 41 H 4
Muang Long 41 G 4
Muang Moc 41 H 4
Muang Nan 41 H 4
Muang Ngao 41 G 4
Muang Oi 41 H 4
Muang Phayao 41 G 4
Muang Phrae 41 H 4
Muanza 67 EF 3
Muar 42 E 3
Muara 42 E 2–3
Muara Teweh 42 D 4
Muaraaman 42 B 4
Muarabenangin 42 E 4
Muarabungo 42 B 4
Muaraenim 42 B 4
Muaramawai 42 E 3
Muarapangean 42 E 3
Muarapayang 42 E 4
Muarasiberut 42 A 4
Muaratebo 42 B 4
Muarawahau 42 E 3
Muari, Ras 35 H 6
Muaro 42 B 4
Muasdale 3 B 4
Mubarak (Iran) 23 G 4
Mubende 64 E 4
Mubi 63 G 3
Mucajaí 85 F 3
Much Wenlock 6 C 1
Muchalls 3 D 3
Muchinga Escarpment 67 E 2
Muck 3 A 3
Muckle Roe 2 D 1
Mucojo 67 G 2
Muconda 66 C 2
Mucubela 67 F 3
Mucur 21 D 3
Mucura 85 F 4
Mucuri 87 H 4
Mucurici 87 H 4
Mucusso 66 C 3
Muda 67 E 3
Mudan Jiang 39 J 1–2
Mudanjiang 39 JK 2
Mudanya 20 C 2
Muddy Gap 76 E 3
Mudgee 49 H 5
Mudhol 40 C 4
Mudon 41 G 4
Mudug 65 H 3
Mudurnu 20 D 2
Muecate 67 F 2
Mueda 67 F 2
Muff 4 B 2
Mufu Shan 38 F 5
Mufulira 66 D 2
Muganskaya Step' 34 D 3
Mugattạ 60 F 6
Mugila, Monts 64 D 6
Muğla 20 C 3
Mugodzhary 34 F 1
Muhagiriya 60 D 6
Muḥaiwir (Iraq) 22 C 2
Muḥammad Qawl 60 F 4

Muhammad, Ra's (Egypt) 22 B 4
Muhammadgarh 40 C 3
Mühlhausen 15 F 4
Mühlig-Hofmann Mountains 91
Muhos 16 J 3
Muhu 17 H 4
Muhulu 64 D 5
Muhuwesi 67 F 2
Mui Bai Bung 41 H 6
Mui Ca Mau 41 H 6
Muié 66 C 2
Muine Bheag 4 B 3
Muir of Ord 2 B 3
Muirkirk 3 B 4
Muiron Islands 48 A 3
Muite 67 F 2
Mujimbeji 66 C 2
Mukachevo 20 B 1
Mukah 42 D 3
Mukdahan 41 H 4
Mukden 39 J 2
Mukhino 37 N 5
Mukho 39 J 3
Mukhomornoye 37 W 2
Mukhor-Shibir' 36 J 5
Mukinbudin 48 B 5
Mukoba 64 C 6
Mukomuko 42 B 4
Muktinath 40 D 2
Mukur 34 E 1
Mukur (Afghanistan) 35 H 4
Mukwe 66 C 3
Mula 18 C 4
Mulainagiri 40 C 5
Mulaly 25 P 6
Mulan 39 J 1
Mulanje 67 F 3
Mulata 65 G 3
Mulchatna 72 F 3
Mulchén 89 B 6
Mulde 15 F 4
Mulegé 76 D 6
Mulegé, Sierra de 76 D 6
Mulenda 64 D 5
Mulevala 67 F 3
Mulga Park 48 E 4
Mulgrave Island 50 D 4
Mulhacén 18 C 4
Mulhouse 19 E 2
Muli 38 D 5
Muling 39 K 2
Muling He 39 K 1
Mull 3 B 3
Mull of Galloway 4 C 2
Mull of Kintyre 3 B 4
Mull of Oa 4 B 2
Mullaittivu 40 D 6
Mullaley 49 HJ 5
Muller, Pegunungan 42 D 3
Mullet Peninsula 14 A 4
Mullewa (Western Australia)
    48 B 4
Müllheim 15 E 5
Mulligan River 49 F 4
Mullingar 4 B 3
Mullion 6 B 2
Mulobezi 66 D 3
Mulonga 64 D 6
Multan 35 J 4
Multanovy 25 O 3
Multia 16 H 3
Mulu, Gunung 42 DE 3
Mulym'ya 25 M 3
Mumbué 66 B 2
Mumbwa 66 D 2
Mumena 66 D 2
Mumra 34 D 1
Muna 36 M 2
Muna, Pulau 43 F 5
Munabao 40 B 2
Munamägi 17 J 4
Munayly 34 EF 1
München 15 F 5
Munchique, Cerro 84 C 3
Muncho Lake 73 M 4
Muncie 77 JK 3
Mundar 37 R 2
Munday 76 G 5
Münden 15 E 4
Mundesley 7 E 1
Mundford 7 E 1
Mundo Nôvo 87 H 3
Mundra 40 A 3
Mundrabilla 48 D 5
Munducurus 85 G 4
Mundybash 25 R 5
Mungar 49 J 4
Mungbere 64 D 4
Mungo 66 B 2
Munhango 66 B 2
Munich 15 F 5
Munîfah (Saudi Arabia) 23 E 4
Munkedal 17 F 4
Munkfors 17 F 4
Munkhafad al Qattârah 60 D 3

Munku-Sardyk, Gora 36 GH 5
Munlochy 2 B 3
Munster 14 B 4
Münster 15 E 4
Muntenia 20 C 2
Munţii Almajului 20 B 1–2
Munţii Apuseni 20 B 1
Munţii Bihorului 20 B 1
Munţii Calimanului 20 BC 1
Munţii Harghita 20 C 1
Munţii Metaliferi 20 B 1
Munţii Poiana Ruscă 20 B 1
Munţii Rodnei 20 B 1
Munţii Sebeşului 20 B 1
Munţii Zărandului 20 B 1
Munugudzhak 37 U 3
Munzur Silsilesi 21 E 3
Muodoslompolo 16 H 2
Muojärvi 16 J 2
Muong Hiem 41 H 3
Muong Khoua 41 H 3
Muong Khuong 41 H 3
Muong Lam 41 HJ 4
Muong Nong 41 J 4
Muong Sai 41 H 3
Muong Sen 41 H 4
Muong Sing 41 H 3
Muong Son 41 H 3
Muong Te 41 H 3
Muonio 16 H 2
Muonioälven 16 H 2
Muonionjoki 16 H 2
Mupa National Park 66 B 3
Muqaddam 60 E 5
Muqayshit 61 J 4
Muqdisho 65 H 4
Muqshin 61 J 5
Mur 19 G 2
Mura 19 G 2
Muradiye 21 F 3
Murakami 39 L 3
Murallón, Cerro 89 B 8
Murana 43 H 4
Murang'a 65 F 5
Murashi 24 J 4
Murat (France) 18 D 2
Murat (Turkey) 21 F 3
Murat Daği 20 C 3
Muratlı 20 C 2
Muratlı 20 C 2
Murau 19 F 2
Muravera 19 E 4
Mürcheh Khvort (Iran) 23 F 2
Murchison Falls 64 E 4
Murchison, Mount 48 B 4
Murchison River 48 AB 4
Murcia 18 C 4
Murdo 76 F 3
Mureş 20 B 1
Muret 18 D 3
Murfreesboro 77 J 4
Murgab 35 G 3
Murgaš 20 B 2
Murgash 20 B 2
Murghab 35 G 3
Murgon 49 J 4
Murgoo 48 B 4
Murguba 63 G 3
Murguz 21 G 2
Muriaé 87 H 5
Murici 87 J 2
Muriége 66 C 1
Murilo 52 B 2
Murin'ya 36 J 5
Muritz 17 F 4
Mürjän (Iran) 23 F 3
Murjek 16 H 2
Murkong Selek 41 FG 2
Murmansk 16 K 2
Murmashi 16 K 2
Murmino 24 H 5
Murnau 15 F 5
Murom 24 H 4
Muromtsevo 25 P 4
Muroran 39 M 2
Muros 18 B 3
Muros y Noya, Rio de 18 B 3
Muroto 39 K 4
Murphysboro 77 J 4
Murrah 60 E 4
Murray (KY, U.S.A.) 77 J 4
Murray (UT, U.S.A.) 76 D 3
Murray Bridge 49 F 6
Murray Downs 48 E 3
Murray Fracture Zone 99 D 2
Murray Islands 50 D 3
Murray, Lake 77 K 5
Murray, Lake (Papua New Guinea)
    50 D 3
Murray River 49 G 5
Murraysburg 66 C 6
Murro di Porco, Capo 19 G 4
Murrumbidgee River 49 H 5
Mursala, Pulau 42 A 3
Murshidabad 40 E 3

Murska Sobota 19 G 2
Murta 36 F 4
Murten 19 E 2
Murukta 36 H 2
Mururoa 53 F 4
Murwara 40 D 3
Murwillumbah 49 J 4
Murzuq 59 H 3
Muş 21 F 3
Muša 17 H 4
Musa Qala 35 G 4
Mûsâ, Wâdi (Jordan) 22 B 3
Musadi 64 C 5
Musala 20 B 2
Musallah (Iraq) 22 D 2
Musallam (Iraq) 23 E 3
Musan 39 J 2
Musandam Peninsula (Oman)
    23 G 4
Musao 64 D 6
Musayîd (Qatar) 23 F 4
Musaymir 61 G 6
Muscat 61 K 4
Musgrave 49 G 1
Musgrave Ranges 48 E 4
Mushâsh (Saudi Arabia) 23 E 4
Mushâsh al 'Ashâwî (Saudi Arabia)
    23 E 4
Mushayrib, Ra's (United Arab
    Emirates) 23 F 4
Mushie 64 B 5
Musi, Air 42 B 4
Mûsiân (Iran) 23 E 2
Muskegon 77 J 3
Muskegon River 77 J 3
Muskogee 77 GH 4
Musoma 64 E 5
Musquaro, Lac 75 P 5
Mussa Ali 65 G 2
Mussafah (United Arab Emirates)
    23 G 4
Musselburgh 3 C 4
Musselburgh 3 C 4
Musselshell River 76 E 2
Mussende 66 B 2
Mussidan 18 D 2
Mustafa 37 P 3
Mustafakemalpaşa 20 C 3
Mustahil 65 G 3
Mustang 40 D 2
Musters, Lago 89 C 8
Mustla 17 J 4
Mustvee 17 J 4
Muswellbrook 49 J 5
Mût (Egypt) 60 D 3
Mut (Turkey) 21 D 3
Mutá, Ponta de 87 J 3
Mûtaf, Ra's al (Iran) 23 F 4
Mutanda 66 D 2
Mutarara 67 F 3
Mutare 67 E 3
Mutayyin 61 G 5
Mutha 65 F 5
Mutis, Gunung 43 F 5
Mutnovskaya Sopka 37 T 5
Mutoray 36 H 3
Mutriba (Kuwait) 23 E 3
Mutsamudu 67 G 2
Mutshatsha 66 C 2
Mutsu-wan 39 M 2
Muttaburra 49 G 3
Mutusjärvi 16 J 2
Muurasjärvi 16 J 3
Muurola 16 HJ 2
Muwale 64 E 6
Muxaluando 66 A 1
Muxima 66 A 1
Muya 36 K 4
Muya 36 L 4
Muyezerskiy 16 K 3
Muyinga 64 E 5
Muynak 34 F 2
Muynkum, Peski 35 J 2
Muyumba 64 D 6
Muzaffarabad 35 J 4
Muzaffargarh 35 J 4–5
Muzaffarnagar 40 C 2
Muzaffarpur 40 DE 2
Muzhi 41 G 4
Muzillac 18 C 2
Muztag 35 L 3
Muztag 35 M 3
Muztagata 35 K 3
Mvolo 64 D 3
Mvomero 65 F 6
Mvoung 63 G 5
Mwadingusha 66 D 2
Mwangalala 67 E 2
Mwanya 67 E 2
Mwanza (Tanzania) 64 E 5
Mwanza (Zaire) 64 D 6
Mwatate 65 F 5
Mweelrea 14 B 4
Mweka 64 C 5
Mwene Biji 64 C 6
Mwene Ditu 64 C 6

Mwenesi 67 E 4
Mwenezi 67 E 4
Mwenga 64 D 5
Mweru, Lake 66 D 1
Mwimba 64 C 6
Mwinilunga 66 C 2
My Tho 41 J 5
My Trach 41 J 5
Mya 59 F 2
Myakit 37 S 3
Myaksa 24 G 4
Myanaung 41 G 4
Myaundzha 37 R 3
Myaungmya 41 F 4
Mycenae 20 B 3
Mydroilyn 6 B 1
Myingyan 41 G 3
Myinmoletkat 41 G 5
Myinmu 41 G 3
Myitkyina 41 G 2
Myitta 41 G 5
Myittha 41 G 3
Mymensingh 41 F 3
Myn-Aral 25 O 6
Mynbulak 35 G 2
Myndagayy 37 O 3
Mýrar 16 A 3
Mýrdalsjökull 16 B 3
Myre 16 F 2
Myrtle Beach 77 L 5
Mys Aniva 37 Q 6
Mys Bolvanskiy Nos 25 M 1
Mys Buorkhaya 37 O 1
Mys Chukotskiy 72 C 3
Mys Dezhneva 72 D 2
Mys Duga-Zapadnaya 37 R 4
Mys Dzenzik 21 E 1
Mys Enkan 37 Q 4
Mys Kanin Nos 24 H 2
Mys Kazantip 21 E 1
Mys Kerets 24 G 2
Mys Kodori 21 F 2
Mys Kril'on 37 Q 6
Mys Kronotskiy 37 U 4–5
Mys Kurgalski 17 J 4
Mys Laydennyy 24 J 2
Mys Lopatka 37 T 5
Mys Lygyy 36 LM 1
Mys Meganom 21 E 2
Mys Men'shikova 25 LM 1
Mys Olyutorskiy 37 VW 4
Mys Ostrovnoy 37 T 3
Mys Peschanyy 34 E 2
Mys Pitsunda 21 EF 2
Mys Ratmanova 24–25 L 1
Mys Sarych 21 D 2
Mys Sengiri 34 E 2
Mys Shipunskiy 37 TU 5
Mys Svatoy Nos 37 P 1
Mys Svyatoy Nos 24 GH 2
Mys Svyatoy Nos 24 H 2
Mys Taran 17 GH 4–5
Mys Tarkhankut 21 D 1
Mys Taygonos 37 U 3
Mys Terpeniya 37 QR 6
Mys Tolstoy 37 T 4
Mys Uengan 25 N 1
Mys Yelizavety 37 Q 5
Mys Yuzhnyy 37 T 4
Mysen 17 F 4
Mysore 40 C 5
Mysovaya 37 T 2
Myszków 15 G 4
Mývatn 16 B 2
Myylybulak 25 P 6
Mze 15 F 5
Mzenga 65 F 6
Mziha 65 F 6
Mzimba 67 E 2
Mzuzu 67 E 2

N

Na Baek 41 H 4
Naab 15 F 5
Naama 58 EF 2
Naandi 64 D 3
Naantali 17 H 3
Naas 4 B 3
Naast 2 B 3
Näätämöjoki 16 J 2
Näätämöjoki 16 J 2
Naba 41 G 3
Nabadid 65 G 3
Nabbe ru, Lake 48 C 4
Naberera 65 F 5
Nabha 40 C 1
Nabî Shu'ayb, Jabal an 61 G 5
Nabire 65 G 3
Nabk al Gharbî (Saudi Arabia)
    22 B 3
Nabou 62 D 3
Nabq (Egypt) 22 B 3
Nâbul 59 H 1

Nâbulus [West Bank] 22 B 2
Nacala 67 G 2
Nacala 67 G 2
Nacarôa 67 F 2
Nachana 40 B 2
Nachikinskaya, Gora 37 U 4
Nachingwea 67 F 2
Nachod 15 G 4
Nachuge 41 F 5
Nachvak Fiord 75 P 4
Nacozari 76 E 5
Nacunday 88 EF 4
Nådendal 17 H 3
Nadiad 40 B 3
Nădlac 20 B 1
Nador 58 E 1
Nadvoitsy 16 K 3
Nadvornaya 20 B 1
Nadym 25 O 2
Nadym 25 O 3
Nafada 63 G 3
Naft Khâneh (Iraq) 23 D 2
Naft-e Safîd (Iran) 23 E 3
Naft-e Shah (Iran) 23 D 2
Naftshahr (Iran) 23 D 2
Nafuce 63 F 3
Nafûd ad Dahy 61 GH 4
Nafûd al 'Urayq (Saudi Arabia)
    22 D 4
Nafûd as Sirr (Saudi Arabia)
    22–23 D 4
Nafûd as Surrah 61 G 4
Nafûd qunayfîdhah (Saudi Arabia)
    23 D 4
Nafûsah, Jabal 59 H 2
Nafy (Saudi Arabia) 22 D 4
Nag 35 G 5
Naga 43 F 1
Naga Hills 41 FG 2
Nagai 72 E 5
Nagaland 41 F 2
Nagano 39 L 3
Nagaoka 39 L 3
Nagappattinam 40 CD 5
Nagarzê 41 F 2
Nagasaki 39 J 4
Nagato 39 K 4
Nagaur 40 B 2
Nagavati 40 D 4
Nagda 40 C 3
Nagercoil 40 C 6
Nagichot 64 E 4
Nago 39 J 5
Nagornyy 37 N 4
Nagor'ye Sangilen 36 G 5
Nagoya 39 L 3
Nagpur 40 C 3
Nagqu 38 B 4
Nagyatád 20 A 1
Nagykanizsa 20 A 1
Nagykőrös 20 AB 1
Naha 39 J 5
Nahan 40 C 1
Nahang 35 G 5
Nahanni Butte 73 N 3
Nahanni National Park 73 M 3
Naharîyya (Israel) 22 B 2
Nahâvand (Iran) 23 E 2
Na'hîmâbâd (Iran) 23 G 3
Nahr ad Dindar 60 EF 6
Nahr al Lîtânî (Lebanon) 22 B 2
Nahr an Nîl (Egypt) 22 A 4
Nahr 'Um (Iraq) 23 E 3
Nahuel Huapi, Lago 89 B 7
Nahuel Huapi, Parque Nacional
    89 B 7
Nahuel Niyeu 89 C 7
Nai 51 E 2
Nai Ga 41 G 2
Naikliu 43 F 5
Nailsea 6 C 3
Nailsworth 7 C 2
Na'îmâbâd (Iran) 23 G 1
Naiman Qi 39 H 2
Nä'in (Iran) 23 F 2
Nä'in (Iran) 34 E 4
Nain 75 P 4
Naini Tal 40 C 2
Nairn 2 C 3
Nairobi 65 F 5
Naissaar 17 H 4
Naita 64 F 3
Naivasha 65 F 5
Naj' Hammâdi 60 E 3
Najafâbâd (Iran) 23 F 2
Najd (Saudi Arabia) 22 CD 4
Najera 18 C 3
Najibabad 40 C 2
Najin 39 K 2
Najmah (Saudi Arabia) 23 F 4
Najrân 61 G 5
Nakamti → Nekemt 65 F 3
Nakanno 36 J 3
Naka-no-shima 39 K 3
Nakasongola 64 E 4
Nakatsu 39 K 4

Nakfa 65 F 1
Nakhichevan' 21 FG 3
Nakhichevan' 34 CD 3
Nakhodka 25 O 2
Nakhodka 25 P 2
Nakhodka 39 K 2
Nakhon Nayok 41 H 5
Nakhon Pathom 41 G 5
Nakhon Phanom 41 H 4
Nakhon Ratchasima 41 H 5
Nakhon Sawan 41 GH 4
Nakhon Si Thammarat 41 G 6
Nakina 74 K 5
Nakło 15 G 4
Naknek 72 F 4
Nako 62 D 3
Nakonde 67 E 1
Nakop 66 B 5
Nakskov 17 F 5
Näkten 16 F 3
Näkten 16 F 3
Nakuru 65 F 5
Nalayh 36 J 6
Nalázi 67 E 4
Nal'chik 21 F 2
Näldsjön 16 F 3
Näldsjön 16 F 3
Nalgimskaya 37 VW 3
Nalgonda 40 C 4
Nallamala Range 40 C 4
Nallıhan 20 D 2
Nālūt 59 H 2
Nam Ca Dinh 41 H 4
Nam Can 41 J 6
Nam Co 41 F 1
Nam Dinh 41 J 3
Nam Ou 41 H 3
Nam Phang 41 H 4
Nam Phong 41 H 4
Nam Teng 41 G 3
Namaacha 67 E 5
Namacunde 66 B 3
Namacurra 67 F 3
Namak, Daracheh-ye (Iran) 23 F 2
Namak, Kavir-e (Iran) 23 G 1
Namaki (Iran) 23 G 3
Namakzar-e Shadad 34 F 4
Namaland 66 B 3
Namanga 65 F 5
Namangan 35 J 2
Namanyere 64 E 6
Namapa 67 G 2
Namaponda 67 G 3
Namaqualand 66 B 5
Namarrói 67 F 3
Namasagali 64 E 4
Namatanai 51 F 2
Nambour 49 J 4
Namche Bazar 40 E 2
Namdalen 16 F 3
Nametil 67 F 3
Namib Desert 66 AB 3–5
Namib Desert Park 66 AB 4
Namibe 66 A 3
Namibe Reserve 66 A 3
Namibia 66 B 4
Namiquipa 76 E 6
Namjagbarwa Feng 38 C 5
Namkham 41 G 3
Namlan Pan 41 G 3
Namlea 43 G 4
Namling 40 E 2
Namoi River 49 H 5
Namoluk 52 B 2
Namonuito 52 A 2
Namorik 52 C 2
Namoya 64 D 5
Nampa 76 C 3
Nampala 62 C 2
Namp'o 39 HJ 3
Nampula 67 F 3
Namrole 43 G 4
Namru 40 D 1
Namsang 41 G 3
Namsê La 40 D 2
Namsen 16 F 2–3
Namsos 16 F 3
Namsvattnet 16 F 2
Namton 41 G 3
Namtsy 37 N 3
Namtu 41 G 3
Namu 52 C 2
Namuli 67 F 3
Namuno 67 F 2
Namur 14 DE 4
Namutoni 66 B 3
Namwala 66 D 3
Namwŏn 39 J 3
Namy 37 O 2
Namya Ra 41 G 2
Namyit Island 42 D 1
Nan Hulsan Hu 38 C 3
Nan Ling 38 EF 5
Nana Kru 62 C 5
Nanaimo 73 N 6
Nanam 39 JK 2

Nanambinia 48 C 5
Nanao 39 L 3
Nancha 37 N 6
Nanchang 38 G 5
Nancheng 38 G 5
Nanchong 38 E 4
Nanchuan 38 E 5
Nancowry 41 F 6
Nancy 19 E 2
Nanda Devi 40 D 1
Nandan 38 E 6
Nander 40 C 4
Nandod 40 B 3
Nandu Jiang 38 E 7
Nandurbar 40 B 3
Nandyal 40 C 4
Nanfeng 38 G 5
Nang Xian 38 B 5
Nanga Emboko 63 G 5
Nanga Parbat 35 J 3
Nangakelawit 42 D 3
Nangapinoh 42 D 4
Nangatayap 42 D 4
Nangin 41 G 5
Nangnim-sanmaek 39 J 2
Nangong 38 G 3
Nangqên 38 C 4
Nanguneri 40 C 6
Nanhua 38 D 5
Nanhui 39 H 4
Nanjian 38 D 5
Nanjiang 38 E 4
Nanjing 39 G 4
Nankang 38 F 5
Nanking → Nanjing 39 G 4
Nankova 66 B 3
Nanle 38 G 3
Nannine 48 B 4
Nanning 38 E 6
Nannup 48 B 5
Nanortalik 75 S 3
Nanpan Jiang 38 D 6
Nanpara 40 D 2
Nanpi 39 G 3
Nanping 38 D 4
Nanping 39 G 5
Nansei-shotō 39 J 5
Nansha Qundao 42 D 2
Nanshan Islands 42 D 2
Nansikan, Ostrov 37 PQ 4
Nansio 64 E 5
Nantais, Lac 75 N 3
Nantes 18 C 2
Nanton 73 P 5
Nantong 39 H 4
Nantou 39 H 6
Nantucket Island 77 N 3
Nantucket Sound 77 MN 3
Nantulo 67 F 2
Nantwich 5 D 3
Nantwich 6 C 1
Nantyffyllon 6 C 3
Nantyglow 6 C 2
Nanumanga 52 C 3
Nanumea 52 C 3
Nanuque 87 HJ 4
Nanusa, Kepulauan 43 G 3
Nanwei Dao 42 D 2
Nanxiong 38 F 5
Nanyang 38 F 4
Nanyuki 65 F 4
Nanzhang 38 F 4
Nanzhao 38 F 4
Nanzhil 66 D 3
Nao, Cabo de la 18 D 4
Naococane, Lac 75 N 5
Naoli He 37 O 6
Náousa 20 B 2
Napaku 42 E 3
Napalkovo 25 OP 1
Napana 37 T 4
Napas 25 Q 4
Napassoq 75 R 2
Napata 60 E 5
Nape 41 J 4
Napido 43 J 4
Napier 51 R 8
Napier Mountains 91
Naples (FL, U.S.A.) 77 K 6
Naples (Italy) 19 F 3
Napo 38 E 6
Napo (Peru) 84 D 4
Napoli 19 F 3
Napperby 48 E 3
Napuka 53 F 3
Naqa 60 E 5
Naqadeh (Iran) 23 D 1
Naqb, Ra's an (Jordan) 22 B 3
Naqsh-e Rostam (Iran) 23 F 3
Nara (Japan) 39 L 4
Nara (Mali) 62 C 2
Nara (Pakistan) 35 H 6
Naracoorte 49 G 6
Naran 36 G 6
Naran 38 F 1
Naranjos 78 C 3

Narasapur 40 D 4
Narasun 36 K 5
Narathiwat 41 H 6
Narayanganj 41 F 3
Narberth 6 B 2
Nærbö 17 E 4
Nærbö 17 E 4
Narbonne 18 D 3
Narborough 7 E 1
Nares Strait 90
Naretha 48 C 5
Narew 15 H 4
Narmada 40 B 3
Narman 21 F 2
Narnaul 40 C 2
Naroch 17 J 5
Narodnaya, Gora 25 LM 2
Naro-Fominsk 24 G 4
Narok 65 F 5
Narooma 49 J 6
Narowal 35 J 4
Närpes 16 H 3
Närpiö 16 H 3
Narrabri 49 HJ 5
Narrandera 49 H 5
Narrogin 48 B 5
Narromine 49 H 5
Narsimhapur 40 C 3
Narsinghgarh 40 C 3
Narsinghpur 40 E 3
Narssalik 75 S 3
Narssaq 75 R 3
Narssaq 75 S 3
Narssarssuaq 75 ST 3
Nāruja 20 C 1
Narungombe 65 F 6
Narva 17 J 4
Narvik 16 G 2
Narvski Zaliv 17 J 4
Narwietooma 48 E 3
Nar'yan Mar 24 K 2
Narym 25 Q 4
Narymskiy, Khrebet 25 QR 6
Naryn 35 JK 2
Naryn 35 K 2
Naryn 36 G 5
Narynkol' 35 KL 2
Nås 17 F 3
Nås 17 F 3
Näsåker 16 G 3
Näsåker 16 G 3
Nasarawa 63 F 4
Nāsăud 20 B 1
Nashtarūd (Iran) 23 F 1
Nashville 77 J 4
Našice 19 G 2
Näsijärvi 16 H 3
Näsijärvi 16 H 3
Nasik 40 B 3
Nāsir 64 E 3
Nasirabad (India) 40 B 2
Nasirabad (Pakistan) 35 H 5
Naskaupi 75 P 5
Nasmah 59 H 2
Nasmgani 40 D 3
Nasrābād (Iran) 23 F 2
Nass 72 M 4
Nassau (Cook Is.) 52 D 3
Nassau (The Bahamas) 79 G 2
Nasser, Birkat (Egypt) 22 A 5
Nasser, Lake (Egypt) 22 A 5
Nassian 62 D 4
Nässjö 17 FG 4
Nastapoka Islands 75 M 4
Næstved 17 F 4
Nasva 17 K 4
Nata 66 D 4
Nata 66 D 4
Natal 87 JK 2
Natal (Amazonas, Brazil) 85 F 5
Natal (Indonesia) 42 A 3
Natal (South Africa) 66–67 E 5
Natara 37 MN 3
Natashquan 75 P 5
Natashquan 75 QR 5
Natchez 77 H 5
Natchitoches 77 H 5
Nathdwara 40 B 3
Natīh 61 K 4
Natitingou 62 E 3
Natityāy, Jabal 60 E 4
Natividade 87 G 3
Natkyizin 41 G 5
Natron, Lake 65 F 5
Natrūn, Wādī an 60 DE 2
Nattaung 41 G 4
Nattavaara 16 H 2
Natuna Besar 42 C 3
Natuna, Kepulauan 42 C 3
Natuna Utara 42 C 3
Naturaliste, Cape 48 A 5
Naturaliste Channel 48 A 4
Naturno 19 F 2
Nauchas 66 B 4
Nauja Bay 75 M 2

Naujoji-Akmene 17 H 4
Naukluft 66 B 4
Naul 4 B 3
Naumburg 15 F 4
Naungpale 41 G 4
Naupe 84 C 5
Nā'ūr (Jordan) 22 B 3
Naurskaya 21 G 2
Nauru 51 J 2
Naurzum 25 M 5
Naushahro Firoz 35 H 5
Naushki 36 J 5
Nauta 84 D 4
Nautanwa 40 D 2
Nava 78 B 2
Navahermosa 18 C 4
Navajo Reservoir 76 E 4
Naval 43 F 1
Navalmoral de la Mata 18 B 4
Navarra 18 C 3
Navassa 79 G 4
Navia (Argentina) 88 C 5
Navia (Spain) 18 B 3
Navidad 88 B 5
Naviraí 87 F 5
Navlya 24 F 5
Năvodari 20 C 2
Navoi 35 H 2
Navojoa 76 E 6
Navolato 76 E 7
Navolok 24 G 3
Navplion 20 B 3
Navrongo 62 D 3
Navsari 40 B 3
Navtlug 21 G 2
Nawabganj 40 D 2
Nawabshah 35 H 5
Nāwah 35 H 4
Nawalgarh 40 C 2
Nawāsīf, Harrat 61 G 4
Naws, Ra's 61 K 5
Náxos 20 C 3
Nāy Band (Iran) 23 F 4
Nāy Band, Ra's-e (Iran) 23 F 4
Nayakhan 37 T 3
Nayarit 78 B 3
Nayarit, Sierra 78 B 3
Nayland 7 E 2
Nayoro 39 M 2
Naystenyarvi 16 K 3
Nazaré 18 B 4
Nazaré (Bahía, Brazil) 87 J 3
Nazaré (Goiás, Brazil) 85 J 5
Nazareth (Peru) 84 C 5
Nazarovka 24 H 5
Nazarovo 36 F 4
Nazas 78 B 2
Nazca 86 B 3
Nazca Ridge 99 E 4
Naze 39 J 5
Nazerat (Israel) 22 B 2
Nazilli 20 C 3
Nazimovo 36 F 4
Nazina 25 P 3
Nazira 41 F 2
Nazmiye 21 EF 3
Nazran' 21 F 2
Nazwa 61 K 4
Nchelenge 66 D 1
Ncheu 67 E 2
Ndala 64 E 5
N'dalatando 66 A 1
Ndali 62 E 4
Ndélé 64 C 3
Ndélélé 63 G 5
Ndendé 63 G 6
Ndeni 51 J 4
Ndindi 63 G 6
N'Djamena 63 H 3
Ndjolé 63 G 6
Ndogo, Lagune 63 G 6
Ndola 66 D 2
Ndoro 63 G 6
Ndrhamcha, Sebkha de 58 BC 5
Ndu 64 C 4
Nea (Norway) 16 F 3
Nea (Solomon Is.) 51 J 4
Nea Filippías 20 B 3
Néa Zíkhni 20 B 2
Neagh, Lough 4 B 2
Neagh, Lough 14 B 4
Neale, Lake 48 E 3
Neápolis 20 B 2
Neápolis 20 B 3
Near Islands 72 A 5
Neath 6 C 2
Nebbou 62 D 3
Nebine River 49 H 4
Nebit-Dag 34 E 3
Neblina, Pico da 84 E 3
Nebo 49 H 3
Nebolchi 24 F 4
Nebraska 76 FG 3
Nebraska City 77 G 3

Nechako 73 N 5
Nechako Plateau 73 N 5
Nechako Reservoir 73 M 5
Nechi 84 D 2
Neckar 15 E 5
Necochea 89 E 6
Nédéley 63 H 2
Nedong 41 F 2
Needles 76 CD 5
Nefedovo 25 O 4
Neftah 59 G 2
Neftegorsk 21 EF 2
Neftegorsk 24 K 5
Neftekamsk 24 K 4
Neftekumsk 21 F 2
Neftelensk 35 J 4
Nefteyugansk 25 O 3
Nefyn 5 B 1
Negage 66 B 1
Negala 62 C 3
Negelli 65 F 3
Negomano 67 F 2
Negombo 40 C 6
Negotin 20 B 2
Negotka 25 Q 4
Negra, Cordillera 84 C 5
Negra, Punta 84 B 5
Negra, Serra 85 J 5
Negrais, Cape 41 F 4
Négrine 59 G 2
Negritos 84 B 4
Negro, Cerro 89 C 7
Negro, Río (Brazil) 85 F 4
Negro, Rio (Uruguay) 88 EF 5
Negros 43 F 2
Negru Vodă 20 C 2
Nehãvand 34 D 3
Nehãvand (Iran) 23 E 2
Nehbandan 34 FG 4
Nehe 37 MN 6
Nehoiu 20 C 1
Nehone 66 B 3
Nei Monggol Zizhiqu 38 DG 2
Neige, Crêt de la 19 E 2
Neijiang 38 E 5
Neilton 76 B 2
Neiqiu 38 F 3
Neiva 84 CD 3
Nejanilini Lake 73 S 4
Nejd (Saudi Arabia) 22 CD 5
Nejo 64 F 3
Neka (Iran) 23 F 1
Nekemt 65 F 3
Nekrasovka 39 L 2
Neksikan 37 R 3
Neksö 17 G 4
Nelemnoye 37 S 2
Nel'gese 37 O 2
Nelichu 64 E 3
Nelidovo 24 F 4
Nel'kan 37 P 4
Nel'keskan 36 M 2
Nelkuchan, Gora 37 P 3
Nellore 40 CD 5
Nel'ma 37 P 6
Nelson (Br. Col., Can.) 73 O 6
Nelson (Man., Can.) 73 S 5
Nelson (New Zealand) 51 Q 9
Nelson (U.K.) 5 D 3
Nelson, Cape 49 G 6
Nelson, Estrecho 89 AB 9
Nelson Head 73 N 1
Nelson Island 72 D 3
Nelspruit 67 E 5
Nelyaty 36 L 4
Néma 58 D 5
Neman 17 HJ 5
Nembrala 43 F 6
Nemira, Vîrful 20 C 1
Némiscau 75 M 5
Nemours → Ghazaouet 58 E 1
Nemrutdağı 21 E 3
Nemunas 17 H 4
Nemuro 39 N 2
Nemuy 37 P 4
Nen Jiang 39 H 1
Nenana 72 H 3
Nenana 72 H 3
Nendo 51 J 4
Nene, River 7 E 1
Nengonengo 53 F 4
Nenjiang 37 N 6
Nenthead 5 D 2
Néon Karlovásion 20 C 3
Nepa 36 J 4
Nepa 36 J 4
Nepal 40 D 2
Nepalganj 40 D 2
Nepeña 84 C 5
Nephi 76 D 4
Nepoko 64 D 4
Nera 37 Q 3
Nérac 18 D 3
Nercha 36 L 5
Nerchinsk 36 L 5
Nerchinskiy Khrebet 36 L 5

Nerekhta 24 H 4
Neretva 19 G 3
Neringa-Nida 17 H 4
Neriquinha 66 C 3
Neris 17 HJ 5
Neroy 36 G 5
Nerpich'ye, Ozero 37 T 2
Nerpio 18 C 4
Nerva 18 B 4
Nes' 24 H 2
Nesbyen 17 E 3
Nesebŭr 20 C 2
Nesjöen 16 F 3
Neskaupstaður 16 C 2
Nesna 16 F 2
Ness, Loch 2 B 3
Nesscliffe 6 C 1
Nesterov 17 H 5
Nesterovo 36 J 5
Neston 6 C 1
Néstos 20 B 2
Nesvizh 17 J 5
Netanya (Israel) 22 B 2
Netherlands 14 DE 4
Netherlands Antilles 79 K 4
Netherlands Antilles 84 E 1
Netrakona 41 F 3
Nettilling Lake 75 N 2
Nettlebed 7 D 2
Nettuno 19 F 3
Neubrandenburg 15 F 4
Neuchâtel 19 E 2
Neuchâtel, Lac de 19 E 2
Neufchâteau 19 E 2
Neufchâtel-en-Bray 18 D 2
Neum 19 G 3
Neumarkter Sattel 19 F 2
Neumünster 15 F 4
Neunkirchen (Austria) 19 G 2
Neuquen 89 C 6
Neuquén 89 C 6
Neuruppin 15 F 4
Neusiedler See 19 G 2
Neustrelitz 15 F 4
Nevada (MO, U.S.A.) 77 H 4
Nevada (U.S.A.) 76 C 4
Nevada, Cerro el 84 D 3
Nevada, Sierra (Spain) 18 C 4
Nevada, Sierra (U.S.A.) 76 BC 4
Nevado Ausangate 86 B 3
Nevado, Cerro 89 C 6
Nevado Chachani 86 B 4
Nevado Citac 86 AB 3
Nevado Cololo 86 C 4
Nevado Coropuna 86 B 4
Nevado de Cachi 86 C 5
Nevado de Colima 78 B 4
Nevado Huascarán 84 C 5
Nevado Illimani 86 C 4
Nevado Sajama 86 C 4
Nevado Salcantay 86 B 3
Nevado Salluyo 86 C 3
Nevado, Sierra del 89 C 6
Nevado Yerupajá 86 A 3
Neve, Serra da 66 A 2
Nevel' 17 K 4
Nevel'sk 37 Q 6
Nevel'skogo, Proliv 37 Q 5
Never 37 M 5
Nevers 18 D 2
Nevesinje 19 G 3
Nevinnomyssk 21 F 2
Nevis 79 K 4
Nevis, Loch 3 B 3
Nevon 36 H 4
Nevşehir 21 D 3
Nev'yansk 25 M 4
New Albany 77 J 4
New Amsterdam 85 G 2
New Bedford 77 M 3
New Bern 77 L 4
New Braunfels 76 G 6
New Britain 51 F 3
New Brunswick (Canada) 75 O 6
New Brunswick (N.J., U.S.A.) 77 LM 3
New Buffalo 77 J 3
New Busuanga 43 E 1
New Caledonia 51 H 6
New Castle 77 K 3
New Cumnock 4 C 2
New Delhi → Delhi 40 C 2
New England 77 MN 3
New England Range 49 J 5
New Forest 7 D 2
New Galloway 3 B 4
New Georgia 51 G 3
New Georgia Sound 51 G 3
New Glasgow 75 P 6
New Guinea 45 CD 3
New Guinea 52 A 3
New Hampshire 77 M 3
New Hampton 77 H 3
New Hanover 51 F 2
New Haven 77 M 3
New Hebrides 51 J 5

New Hunstanton 7 E 1
New Iberia 77 H 6
New Ireland 51 F 2
New Jersey 77 LM 4
New Liskeard 75 LM 6
New Liskeard 77 K 2
New London 77 M 3
New Luce 3 B 4
New Meadows 76 C 2
New Mexico 76 E 5
New Milton 7 D 2
New Norcia 48 B 5
New Norfolk 50 L 9
New Orleans 77 J 5–6
New Plymouth 51 Q 8
New Providence Island 79 G 3
New Quay 6 B 1
New Richmond 75 O 6
New River (Guyana) 85 G 3
New River (W.V., U.S.A.) 77 K 4
New Rockford 76 G 2
New Romney 7 E 2
New Scone 3 C 3
New Siberian Islands 90
New Smyrna Beach 77 KL 6
New South Wales 49 GH 5
New Stuvahok 72 F 4
New Ulm 77 H 3
New Westminster 73 N 6
New York 77 L 3
New York (N.Y., U.S.A.) 77 M 3
New Zealand 51 R 9
New Zealand 51 R 9
Newala 67 F 2
Newark 77 K 3
Newark (N.J., U.S.A.) 77 M 3
Newark (OH, U.S.A.) 77 K 3
Newark-on-Trent (U.K.) 7 D 1
Newberry 77 J 2
Newbiggin by the Sea 5 E 2
Newbliss 4 B 2
Newbridge-on-Wye 6 C 1
Newburgh 2 D 3
Newburgh (N.Y., U.S.A.) 77 M 3
Newburgh (U.K.) 3 C 3
Newbury 7 D 2
Newby Bridge 5 D 2
Newcastle 4 C 2
Newcastle 75 O 6
Newcastle (Airport) 5 E 2
Newcastle (N.S.W., Austr.) 49 J 5
Newcastle (South Africa) 66 D 5
Newcastle (WY, U.S.A.) 76 F 3
Newcastle Waters 48 E 2
Newcastle Emlyn 6 B 1
Newcastle River 48 E 2
Newcastleton 3 C 4
Newcastle-under-Lyme 5 D 3
Newcastle-upon-Tyne 5 E 2
Newenham, Cape 72 E 4
Newfoundland 75 Q 5
Newfoundland 75 QR 6
Newgrange 4 B 3
Newhaven 7 DE 2
Newick 7 E 2
Newmachar 2 C 3
Newman 48 B 3
Newmarket 7 E 1
Newmill 3 C 4
Newmilns 3 B 4
Newnham Frampton 6 C 3
Newport (AR, U.S.A.) 77 H 4
Newport (Gwent, U.K.) 6 C 2
Newport (Isle of Wight) 7 D 2
Newport (OR, U.S.A.) 76 B 3
Newport (Salop, U.K.) 6 C 1
Newport (VT, U.S.A.) 77 M 3
Newport (WA, U.S.A.) 76 C 2
Newport Beach 76 C 5
Newport Pagnell 7 D 1
Newport-on-Tay 3 C 3
Newquay 6 B 2
Newry (N.T., Austr.) 48 D 2
Newry (U.K.) 4 B 2
Newton 3 C 4
Newton 5 D 3
Newton 77 H 3
Newton Abbot 6 C 2
Newton Aycliffe 5 E 2
Newton Flotman 7 E 1
Newton on Trent 7 D 1
Newton Poppleton 6 C 3
Newton Stewart 4 C 2
Newton-le-Willows 5 D 3
Newtonmore 3 B 3
Newtown 6 C 1
Newtown Forbes 4 B 3
Newtown Mt. Kennedy 4 B 3
Newtownabbey 4 B 2
Newtownards 4 C 2
Newtownhamilton 4 B 2
Newtownstewart 4 B 2
Neya 24 H 4
Neyestãnak (Iran) 23 F 2
Neyland 6 B 2
Neyriz 34 E 5

Neyriz (Iran) 23 G 3
Neyshãbūr 34 F 3
Nezhin 24 F 5
Ngabé 63 H 6
Ngala 63 G 3
Ngambé 63 G 5
Ngami, Lake 66 C 4
Ngamiland 66 C 3
Ngamring 40 E 2
Ngangala 64 E 4
Ngangerabeli Plain 65 G 5
Ngangla Ringco 40 D 1
Nganglong Kangri 40 D 1
N'gangula 66 A 2
Ngangzê Co 40 E 1
Ngaoundal 63 G 4
Ngaoundéré → Guidjiba 63 G 4
Ngara 64 E 5
Ngathainggyaung 41 F 4
Ngatik 52 B 2
Ngatokae 51 G 3
Ngidinga 64 B 6
Ngo 63 H 6
Ngoc Linh 41 J 4
Ngoïla 63 G 5
Ngoko 63 H 5
Ngom Qu 38 C 4
Ngomeni, Ras 65 G 5
Ngong 65 F 5
Ngoring 38 C 4
Ngoring Hu 38 C 4
Ngorongoro Crater 64 F 5
Ngoua, Mont 64 C 3
Ngoui 62 B 2
Ngounié 63 G 6
Ngouri 63 H 3
Ngourou 64 C 3
Ngourti 63 G 2
Ngoussi 59 G 2
Ngoywa 64 E 6
Nguara 63 H 3
Ngudu 64 E 5
Nguigmi 63 G 3
Ngum 41 H 4
Nguni 65 F 5
Nguru 63 G 3
Nguyen Binh 41 J 3
Ngwale 67 F 2
Ngwane 67 E 5
Nha Trang 41 J 5
Nhachengue 67 F 4
Nhambiquara 86 E 3
Nhamundá 85 G 3
Nhamundá 85 G 4
Nharea 66 B 2
Nhill 49 G 6
Nhommarath 41 J 4
Nhulunbuy 49 F 1
Niafounke 62 D 2
Niagara Falls 77 L 3
Niagara River 77 L 3
Niagassola 62 C 3
Niah 42 D 3
Niakaramandougou 62 C 4
Niamey 62 E 3
Niaming 62 C 3
Niandan Koro 62 C 3
Niangara 64 D 4
Niangay, Lac 62 D 2
Niangoloko 62 D 3
Nia-Nia 64 D 4
Nianzishan 37 M 6
Niari 63 G 6
Nias, Pulau 42 A 3
Niassa 67 F 2
Niau 53 F 4
Nibāk (Saudi Arabia) 23 F 4
Nicaragua 78 EF 5
Nicaragua, Lago de 78 E 5
Nice 19 E 3
Nichalakh 37 QR 1
Nichicun, Lac 75 N 5
Nicholas Channel 79 G 3
Nicholls Town 79 G 2
Nicholson River 49 F 2
Nickerie 85 G 2
Nickol Bay 48 B 3
Nicobar Islands 41 F 6
Nicocli 84 C 2
Nicosia 21 D 3
Nicosia (Cyprus) 22 A 2
Nicotera 19 G 4
Nicoya 78 E 5
Nicoya, Golfo de 78 F 6
Nicoya, Península de 78 E 6
Nicuadala 67 F 3
Nida 15 H 4
Nidd, River 5 E 3
Nidelva 17 E 4
Nido, Sierra del 76 E 6
Nidym 36 G 3
Nidzica 15 H 4
Niebüll 15 E 4
Niecka Sieradzka 15 G 4
Nieddu 19 E 3

Niedere Tauern 19 F 2
Niedersachsen 15 E 4
Niefang 63 G 5
Niellé 62 C 3
Niellim 63 H 4
Niemba 64 D 6
Niemba 64 D 6
Niemisel 16 H 2
Nienburg 15 E 4
Niéndkoué, Mont 62 C 4
Niéré 63 J 3
Niete Mountains 62 C 4
Nieuw Amsterdam 85 H 2
Nieuw Nickerie 85 G 2
Nieuwoudtville 66 B 6
Nieves 86 C 3
Niğde 21 D 3
Nigenãn 34 F 4
Niger (River) 63 F 4
Niger Delta 63 F 5
Nigeria 63 FG 4
Nigg 2 C 3
Nighasan 40 D 2
Nihau 53 E 1
Nihiru 53 F 4
Nihoa 52 E 1
Niigata 39 L 3
Niihama 39 K 4
Niitsu 39 L 3
Nĩjar 18 C 4
Nijmegen 14 E 4
Nikel' 16 K 2
Nikkaluokta 16 G 2
Nikki 62 E 4
Nikolayev 20 D 1
Nikolayevka 21 D 1
Nikolayevka 25 N 5
Nikolayevo 17 J 4
Nikolayevskiy 24 J 5
Nikolayevskiy 37 N 5
Nikolayevsk-na-Amure 37 Q 5
Nikol'sk 24 J 4
Nikol'sk 24 J 5
Nikol'sk 36 F 4
Nikolski 72 D 5
Nikol'skiy 35 H 1
Nikol'skoye 21 G 1
Nikopol (Bulgaria) 20 B 2
Nikopol (U.S.S.R.) 21 D 1
Nĩkpey (Iran) 23 E 1
Niksar 21 E 2
Nikshahr 35 G 5
Nikšic 20 A 2
Nikumaroro 52 D 3
Nila, Pulau 43 G 5
Nilakka 16 J 3
Nile (Egypt) 22 A 4
Niles 77 J 3
Nili 59 F 2
Nilka 35 L 2
Nilo Peçanha 85 H 5
Nilsiä 16 J 3
Nimach 40 B 3
Nimba, Monts 62 C 4
Nimbe 63 F 5
Nimes 18 D 3
Nimmitabel 49 H 6
Nimrũd (Iraq) 22 D 1
Nimule 64 E 4
Nin 19 G 3
Nincheng 39 G 2
Ninda 66 C 2
Nine Degree Channel 40 B 6
Ninety East Ridge 98 B 5
Ninety Mile Beach 49 H 6
Nineveh (Iraq) 22 D 1
Ninfas, Punta 89 D 7
Ninfield 7 E 2
Ning Xian 38 E 3
Ningaloo 48 A 3
Ningbo 39 H 5
Ningde 39 G 5
Ningdu 38 G 5
Ninghai 39 H 5
Ningi 63 F 3
Ningjing Shan 38 C 4
Ninglang 38 D 5
Ningming 38 E 6
Ningnan 38 D 5
Ningshan 38 E 4
Ningwu 38 F 3
Ningxia Huizu Zizhiqu 38 E 3
Ningxiang 38 F 5
Ninh Binh 41 J 3
Ninhue 89 B 6
Ninigo Group 52 A 3
Ninigo Islands 50 D 2
Ninyako-Vogumma 25 P 1
Niobrara River 76 FG 3
Nioki 64 B 5
Niokolo Koba, Parc National du 62 B 3
Niono 62 C 3
Nioro 62 A 3

Nioro du Sahel 62 C 2
Niort 18 C 2
Niou 62 D 3
Niout 58 D 5
Nipa 85 F 2
Nipani 40 B 4
Nipawin 73 R 5
Nipigon 74 K 6
Nipigon, Lake 74 K 6
Nipissing, Lake 75 LM 6
Nippur (Iraq) 23 D 2
Nir, Jabal an (Saudi Arabia) 22 D 4–5
Nirmal 40 C 4
Nirmal Range 40 C 4
Niš 20 B 2
Nisãb (S. Yemen) 61 H 6
Nisãb → Ansãb 61 G 3
Nišava 20 B 2
Niscemi 19 F 4
Nishino'omote 39 K 4
Nísiros 20 C 3
Nisko 15 H 4
Nísoi Strofádhes 20 B 3
Nisser 17 E 4
Nissum Bredning 17 E 4
Nissum Fjord 17 E 4
Nitchequon 75 N 5
Niterói 87 H 5
Nithsdale 3 C 4
Nitiya 37 P 4
Nitra 15 G 5
Nitsa 25 M 4
Niuafo'ou 52 D 4
Niuato Putapu 52 D 4
Niue 52 D 4
Niugini 50 E 3
Niulakita 52 C 3
Niut, Gunung 42 D 3
Niutao 52 C 3
Niutoushan 39 G 4
Nivala 16 H 3
Nivernais 18 D 2
Nivskiy 16 K 2
Niwbwich 5 B 1
Nĩyabãd (Iran) 23 E 2
Nĩza (Iran) 23 G 3
Nizamabad 40 C 4
Nizhmozero 24 G 3
Nizhnaya Pesha 24 J 2
Nizhneangarsk 36 J 4
Nizhnegorskiy 21 D 1
Nizhne-Kamchatsk 37 U 4
Nizhne-Ozernaya 37 U 4
Nizhneshadrino 36 F 4
Nizhnetambovskoye 37 P 5
Nizhneudinsk 36 G 5
Nizhnevartovskoye 25 P 3
Nizhneyansk 37 P 1
Nizhneye Bugayevo 24 K 2
Nizhneye Karelina 36 J 4
Nizhniy Baskunchak 24 J 6
Nizhniy Chir 24 H 6
Nizhniy Kholtoson 36 H 5
Nizhniy Kuranakh 37 MN 4
Nizhniy Lomov 24 H 5
Nizhniy Pyandzh 35 H 3
Nizhniy Tagil 25 M 4
Nizhniy Tsasuchey 36 L 5
Nizhniy Yenangsk 24 J 4
Nizhniye Kresty 37 U 2
Nizhnyaya Mgla 24 HJ 2
Nizhnyaya Omka 25 O 4
Nizhnyaya Poyma 36 G 4
Nizhnyaya Tavda 25 N 4
Nizhnyaya Tunguska 36 F 3
Nizhnyaya Voch' 24 K 3
Nizhnyaya Zolotitsa 24 H 2
Nizina Podlaska 15 H 4
Nizip 7 E 3
Nizip (Turkey) 22 B 1
Nízke Tatry 15 G 5
Nizmennost' 35 G 2
Njinjo 65 F 6
Njombe 64 EF 6
Njonbe 64 E 6
Njudung 17 F 4
Njunes 16 G 2
Njurunda 16 G 3
Njutånger 16 G 3
Nkai 66 D 3
Nkambe 63 G 4
Nkawkaw 62 D 4
Nkayi 63 G 6
Nkhata Bay 67 E 2
Nkhotka-Kota 67 E 2
Nkolabona 63 G 5
Nkomi, Lagune 63 F 6
Nkongsamba 63 G 5
Nkurenkuru 66 B 3
Nkusi 64 E 4
Nkwalini 67 E 5
Nmai Hka 41 G 2
No. 10 Station 60 E 5
No. 5 Station 60 E 4
Noakhali 41 F 3

Noanamá 84 C 3
Noatak 72 E 2
Noatak 72 EF 2
Noatak National Preserve 72 F 2
Nobel 75 L 6
Nobeoka 39 K 4
Nobéré 62 D 3
Nobres 86 E 3
Noccundra 49 G 4
Noefs, Ile des 65 J 6
Nogal Valley → Dōhō Nugāléd
  65 H 3
Nogales 76 D 5
Nogales 76 D 5
Nogayskiye Step' 21 G 2
Nogent-le-Rotrou 18 D 2
Noginsk 24 G 4
Noginskiy 36 F 3
Nogliki 37 Q 5
Nogoya 88 D 5
Nogueira, Serra da 18 B 3
Nohar 40 B 2
Noir, Isla 89 B 9
Noirmoutier 18 C 2
Nojane 66 C 4
Nok Kundi 35 G 5
Nokaneng 66 C 3
Nokia 16 H 3
Nokou 63 G 3
Nokra 65 F 1
Nokrek Peak 41 F 1
Nokrek Peak 41 F 1
Nola 64 B 4
Nolinsk 24 J 4
Nomad 50 D 3
Nombre de Dios 78 B 3
Nome 72 D 3
Nomgon 38 D 2
Nomhon 38 C 3
Nömrög 36 G 6
Nomtsas 66 B 4
Nomuka Group 52 D 4
Nomwin 52 B 2
Nonacho Lake 73 Q 3
Nonburg 24 K 2
Nondugl 50 D 3
Nong Khai 41 H 4
Nongoma 67 E 5
Nonoava 76 E 6
Nonouti 52 C 3
Noonkanbah 48 C 2
Noordoewer 66 B 5
Noordzeekanaal 14 D 4
Noorvik 72 E 2
Nora 17 F 4
Norberg 17 G 3
Nordaustlandet 90
Norden 15 E 4
Nordenham 15 E 4
Norderstedt 15 E 4
Nordfjord 16 E 3
Nordfjordeid 16 E 3
Nordfold 16 FG 2
Nordfriesische Inseln 15 E 4
Nordhausen 15 F 4
Norðöyar 14 A 1
Nordkapp 16 J 1
Nordkinn 16 J 1
Nordkinnhalvöya 16 J 1
Nordkjosbotn 16 GH 2
Nord-Kvalöy 16 G 1
Nordland 16 F 2
Nordmaling 16 GH 3
Nordostrundingen 90
Nord-Ostsee-Kanal 15 E 4
Nordöyane 16 E 3
Nordre Strömfjord 75 R 2
Nordreisa 16 H 2
Nord-Tröndelag 16 F 3
Nordvik 36 K 1
Nore, River 4 B 3
Norefjell 17 E 3
Norfolk (NE, U.S.A.) 76 G 3
Norfolk (U.K.) 7 E 1
Norfolk (VA, U.S.A.) 77 L 4
Norfolk Islands 52 C 4
Norfolk Lake 77 H 4
Norge 16 F 2
Nori 25 O 2
Noril'sk 25 R 2
Norkai, Pulau 43 HJ 5
Normal 77 J 3
Norman 76 G 4
Norman River 49 G 2
Normanby Island 49 J 1
Normanby Island 51 F 4
Normandie 18 CD 2
Normanton 49 G 2
Norquin 89 B 6
Norquinco 89 B 7
Norra Kvarken 16 H 3
Norra Storfjället 16 G 2
Norrahammar 17 F 4
Norråker 16 G 3
Norrbotten 16 GH 2
Norresundby 17 F 4

Norris Lake 77 K 4
Norrköping 17 G 4
Norrland 16 FG 3
Norrtälje 17 G 4
Norseman 48 C 5
Norsjö (Norway) 17 E 4
Norsjö (Sweden) 16 G 3
Norsk 37 O 5
Norsoup 51 J 5
Norte, Cabo 85 J 3
Norte, Canal do 85 H 3
Norte, Punta 89 E 6
Nortelândia 86 E 3
North Adams 77 M 3
North Andaman 41 F 5
North Arm 73 P 3
North Atlantic Drift 92
North Aulatsivik Island 75 P 4
North Battleford 73 Q 5
North Bay 75 M 6
North Belcher Islands 75 L 4
North Bend 76 B 3
North Berwick 3 C 3
North Canadian River 76 G 4
North, Cape (Nova Scotia, Can.)
  75 P 6
North Cape (New Zealand) 51 Q 7
North Cape (Norway) 16 J 1
North Caribou Lake 74 J 5
North Carolina 77 L 4
North Cascades National Park
  76 B 2
North Channel 74 L 6
North Channel (U.K.) 4 C 2
North Dakota 76 FG 2
North Danger Reef 42 D 1
North Downs 7 E 2
North Foreland 7 E 2
North Fork Pass 72 K 3
North Geomagnetic Pole 90
North Highlands 76 B 4
North Horr 65 F 4
North Island 51 Q 8
North Korea 39 K 2
North Lakhimpur 41 F 2
North Las Vegas 76 C 4
North Little Rock 77 H 5
North Loup River 76 F 3
North Magnetic Pole 90
North Minch 2 B 2
North Pacific Basin 99 D 2
North Platte 76 F 3
North Platte 76 F 3
North Platte River 76 E 3
North Point 50 L 8
North Pole 90
North River 73 T 4
North Roe 2 D 1
North Rona 2 B 2
North Ronaldsay 2 C 2
North Saskatchewan 73 PQ 5
North Sea 14 D 3
North Sentinel 41 F 5
North Slope 72 FH 2
North Stradbroke Island 49 J 4
North Taranaki Bight 51 Q 8
North Thompson 73 O 5
North Tolsta 2 A 2
North Tyne, River 5 D 2
North Uist 2 A 3
North Walsham 7 E 1
North West Cape 48 A 3
North West Highlands 2–3 B 3
North West River 75 P 5
Northallerton 5 E 2
Northam (Australia) 48 B 5
Northam (South Africa) 66 D 4
Northam (U.K.) 6 B 2
Northampton (U.K.) 7 D 1
Northampton (Western Australia)
  48 A 4
Northamptonshire 7 D 1
Northcliff 48 B 5
Northeast Cape 72 D 3
Northeast Providence Channel
  79 G 2
Northeim 15 F 4
Northern Cook Islands 52 E 3
Northern Dvina River 24 H 3
Northern Indian Lake 73 S 4
Northern Ireland 4 B 2
Northern Mariana Islands 52 B 1
Northern Perimeter Highway
  84 D 4–5
Northern Perimeter Highway
  85 G 3
Northern Territory 48 E 2–3
Northfield 77 H 3
Northiam 7 E 2
Northleach 7 D 2
Northton 2 A 3
Northumberland 5 DE 2
Northumberland Islands 49 J 3
Northumberland Strait 75 P 6
Northway Junction 72 J 3
Northwest Pacific Basin 99 C 2

Northwest Territories (Canada)
  73 NT 2
Northwich 5 D 3
Norton (KS, U.S.A.) 76 F 4
Norton (VA, U.S.A.) 77 K 4
Norton (Zimbabwe) 67 E 3
Norton Bay 72 E 3
Norton Sound 72 E 3
Norvegia, Cape 91
Norwalk 77 K 3
Norway 16 F 2
Norway (WI, U.S.A.) 77 J 2
Norway Bay 73 R 1
Norway House 73 S 5
Norwegian Basin 98 A 1
Norwegian Sea 11 FH 2
Norwich 7 E 1
Norwich (Airport) 7 E 1
Noshiro 39 L 2
Noshul' 24 J 3
Nosok 25 Q 1
Nosovaya 24 K 2
Nosovka 24 F 5
Nosovshchina 24 G 3
Nosratābād 34 F 5
Nossa Senhora da Glória 84 D 5
Nossob 66 B 4
Nossob 66 C 5
Nosy Barren 67 G 3
Nosy Boraha 67 H 3
Nosy Mitsio 67 H 2
Nosy-Bé 67 H 2
Nosy-Varika 67 H 4
Nota 16 J 2
Noteć 15 G 4
Noto 19 FG 4
Notodden 17 E 4
Noto-hantō 39 L 3
Notorskoye 37 O 3
Notre Dame Bay 75 QR 6
Notre Dame, Monts 75 O 6
Nottawasaga Bay 75 L 7
Nottaway 75 M 5
Nottingham (Ontario, Can.)
  75 M 3
Nottingham (U.K.) 7 D 1
Nottinghamshire 7 D 1
Nouadhibou 58 B 4
Nouadhibou, Dakhlet 58 B 4
Nouakchott 58 B 5
Nouamrhar 58 B 5
Nouméa 51 J 6
Noumin He 37 M 6
Nouna 62 D 3
Noupoort 66 D 6
Nouveau Comptoir 75 M 5
Nouvelle France, Cap de 75 N 3
Nouvelle-Calédonie 51 H 6
Nova 87 H 2
Nova Andradino 87 F 5
Nova Caipemba 66 A 1
Nova Cruz 87 J 2
Nova Friburgo 87 H 5
Nova Gorica 19 F 2
Nova Gradiška 19 G 2
Nova Iguaçu 87 H 5
Nova Lamego 62 B 3
Nova Lima 87 H 5
Nova Mambone 67 F 4
Nova Olinda do Norte 85 G 4
Nova Scotia 75 OP 6–7
Nova Sento Sé 87 H 2
Nova, Serra 85 F 4
Nova Sofala 67 EF 4
Nova Varoš 20 A 2
Nova Venécia 87 H 4
Nova Vida 86 D 3
Nova Zagora 20 C 2
Novabad 35 HJ 3
Novara 19 E 2
Novaya Igirma 36 H 4
Novaya Kakhovka 21 D 1
Novaya Kazanka 24 J 6
Novaya Lyalya 25 M 4
Novaya Odessa 20 D 1
Novaya Ushitsa 20 C 1
Novaya Ussuri 37 P 6
Novaya Zemlya 24 L 1
Novaya Zemlya 90
Nové Zámky 15 G 5
Novelda 18 C 4
Novembro, Cachoeira dois de
  85 F 5
Novgorod 17 K 4
Novgorod Severskiy 24 F 5
Novgorodka 17 J 4
Novgorodka 21 D 1
Novi Ligure 19 E 3
Novi Pazar (Bulgaria) 20 C 2
Novi Pazar (Yugoslavia) 20 B 2
Novi Sad 20 AB 1
Novi Vinodolski 19 FG 2
Novigrad 19 F 2
Novikovo 37 Q 6
Novillero 78 A 3

Novo Acôrdo 85 H 4
Novo Aripuanã 85 FG 5
Novo Arkhangelsk 20 D 1
Novo Hamburgo 88 F 4
Novo Horizonte 87 G 5
Novo, Lago 85 H 3
Novo Pskov 24 G 6
Novo Sagres 43 G 5
Novo Sergeyevka 24 K 5
Novo Troitskoye 21 D 1
Novo Ukrainka 20 D 1
Novo Uzensk 24 J 5
Novoaleksandrovsk 21 F 1
Novoalekseyevka 21 D 1
Novoaltaysk 25 Q 5
Novoanninskiy 24 H 5
Novoazovskoye 21 E 1
Novobiryusinskiy 36 G 4
Novobogatinskoye 34 E 1
Novobogdanovka 21 DE 1
Novocherkassk 21 EF 1
Novodolinka 25 O 5
Novogeorgiyevka 37 N 5
Novograd-Volynskiy 17 J 5
Novogrudok 17 J 5
Novokazalinsk 35 G 1
Novokhoperskiy 24 H 5
Novokocherdyk 25 M 5
Novokubansk 21 F 1
Novokuybyshevsk 24 J 5
Novokuznetsk 25 R 5
Novolazarevskaya 91
Novoletov'ye 36 H 1
Novoluzino 25 R 2
Novolynsk 15 H 4
Novomariinka 36 G 4
Novomikhaylovskoye 21 E 2
Novomirgorod 20 D 1
Novomoskovsk 21 E 1
Novomoskovsk 24 G 5
Novonikol'skoye 25 P 4
Novonikolskoye 25 NO 4
Novoorsk 25 L 5
Novopavlovskoye 36 K 5
Novopokrovskaya 21 F 1
Novopolotsk 17 J 4
Novorossiysk 21 E 2
Novorybnoye 36 HJ 1
Novo-selitsa 20 C 1
Novoselovo 36 F 4
Novoshakhtinsk 21 E 1
Novosibirsk 25 Q 4
Novosibirskiye Ostrova → New
  Siberian Islands 27 QR 2
Novosibirskoye
  Vodokhranilishche 25 Q 5
Novosokol'niki 17 JK 4
Novotroitsk 25 L 5
Novotroitskoye 35 J 2
Novotsimlyanskiy 21 F 1
Novoveselyy 21 F 1
Novovorontsovka 21 D 1
Novovolynsk 15 H 4
Novovoskresenovka 37 N 5
Novoyugino 25 PQ 4
Novozhilovskaya 24 K 3
Novozybkov 24 F 5
Novvy Bug 21 D 1
Nový Jičín 15 G 5
Novy Uzen' 34 E 2
Novyy 25 R 4
Novyy 36 J 1
Novyy Afon 21 F 2
Novyy Bor 24 K 2
Novyy Karymkary 25 N 3
Novyy Oskol 24 G 5
Novyy Port 25 O 2
Novyy Tanguy 36 H 4
Novyy Vasyugan 25 P 4
Now Bandegān (Iran) 23 FG 3
Now Gombād (Iran) 23 F 2
Now Shahr (Iran) 23 F 1
Nowa Ruda 15 G 4
Nowa Sól 15 G 4
Nowbarān 34 D 3
Nowbarān (Iran) 23 E 2
Nowdesheh 34 D 3
Nowdesheh (Iran) 23 E 2
Nowfel Iow Shātow (Iran) 23 F 2
Nowgong 41 F 2
Nowitna 72 FG 3
Nowo Korczyn 15 H 4
Nowogard 15 G 4
Nowra 49 J 5
Nowrangapur 40 D 4
Nowshera 35 J 4
Nowy Dwór 15 H 4
Nowy Sącz 15 H 5
Nowy Targ 15 H 5
Noya 18 B 3
Noyek (Iran) 23 G 1
Noyon 38 D 2

Nozay 18 C 2
Nsa 59 F 2
Nsanje 67 F 3
Nsawam 62 D 4
Nsok 63 G 5
Nsombo 66 D 2
Nsukka 63 F 4
Nsuta 62 D 4
Ntadembele 64 B 5
Ntakat 58 C 5
Ntem 63 G 5
Ntui 63 G 5
Nu Jiang 38 C 5–6
Nu Shan 38 C 5
Nuaib 58 D 3
Nuanetsi → Mwenezi 67 E 4
Nuba Mountains → Dar Nūbah
  60 DE 4
Nubia 60 E 5
Nubian Desert → As Ṣaḥrā' an
  Nūbiyah 60 E 4
Nūbiyah 60 DE 5
Nūbiyah, As Ṣaḥrā' an 60 E 4
Nueces River 76 G 6
Nueifed 58 C 4
Nueltin Lake 73 S 3
Nueva Alejandría 84 D 5
Nueva Antioqia 84 E 2
Nueva Esperanza 86 D 4
Nueva Galia 88 C 5–6
Nueva Gerona 78 F 3
Nueva Imperial 89 B 6
Nueva, Isla 89 C 10
Nueva Lubecka 89 BC 7
Nueva Rosita 78 B 2
Nueva San Salvador 78 DE 5
Nueve de Julio 88 D 6
Nuevitas 79 G 3
Nuevo Berlin 88 E 5
Nuevo Casas Grandes 76 E 5
Nuevo, Golfo 89 D 7
Nuevo Laredo 78 BC 2
Nuevo León 78 BC 2
Nuevo Mundo, Cerro 86 C 5
Nuevo Rocafuerte 84 C 4
Nugāl 65 H 3
Nuguria Islands 51 FG 2
Nui 52 C 3
Nuiqsut 72 G 1
Nujiang 38 C 4–5
Nukey Bluff 49 F 5
Nukhayb (Iraq) 22 D 2
Nukhaylak 60 D 5
Nuku Hiva 53 F 3
Nuku'alofa 52 D 4
Nukufetau 52 C 3
Nukuhu 51 E 3
Nukulaelae 52 C 3
Nukumanu Islands 51 G 2
Nukunau 52 C 3
Nukunonu 52 D 3
Nukuoro 52 B 2
Nukus 34 F 2
Nulato 72 F 3
Nullagine 48 C 3
Nullarbor 48 E 5
Nullarbor Plain 48 DE 5
Nulloocha 49 G 3
Num, Pulau 43 J 4
Numan 63 G 4
Numancia 43 G 2
Numazu 39 L 4
Numbulwar Mission 48 F 1
Numedal 17 E 3
Numfor, Pulau 43 H 4
Numkaub 66 B 3
Numto 25 O 3
Numurkah 49 H 6
Nundle 49 J 5
Nundu 64 D 5
Nuneaton 7 D 1
Nungnain Sum 39 G 1
Nungo 67 F 3
Nunivak Island 72 D 3
Nunkun 35 K 4
Nuntherungie 49 G 5
Nunyamo 72 C 2
Nuorajärvi 16 K 3
Nuorgam 16 J 1
Nuoro 19 E 3
Nūq (Iran) 23 G 3
Nuqay, Jabal 59 J 4
Nuqrah (Saudi Arabia) 22 C 4
Nuqrus, Jabal (Egypt) 22 B 4
Nuquí 84 C 2
Nūr (Iran) 23 G 3
Nur Dağları 21 E 3
Nura 25 O 5
Nura 25 O 6
Nūrābād (Iran) 23 F 3
Nurata 35 H 2
Nuratau, Khrebet 35 H 2
Nurek 35 H 3
Nuremberg 15 F 5

Nurhak Daği 21 E 3
Nūrī 60 E 5
Nuristan 35 J 3
Nurlat 24 K 5
Nurmes 16 J 3
Nürnberg 15 F 5
Nurney 4 B 3
Nurpur 40 C 1
Nurri, Mount 49 H 5
Nusaybin 21 F 3
Nusaybin (Turkey) 22 C 1
Nushagak 72 F 4
Nushki 35 H 5
Nutak 75 P 4
Nuuk 75 R 3
Nuupas 16 J 2
Nuwara Eliya 40 D 6
Nuwaybi'al Muzayyinah (Egypt)
 22 B 3
Nuweveldreeks 66 C 6
Nxai Pan National Park 66 C 3
Nyaake 62 C 5
Nyabéssan 63 G 5
Nyabing 48 B 5
Nyahanga 64 E 5
Nyahua 64 E 6
Nyahururu 65 F 5
Nyainqentanglha Shan 38 B 4
Nyainrong 38 B 4
Nyakakangaga 64 E 5
Nyakanazi 64 E 5
Nyåker 16 G 3
Nyaksimvol' 25 M 3
Nyala 60 D 6
Nyalam 40 E 2
Nyalikungu 64 E 5
Nyamandhlovu 66 D 3
Nyamboma Rapids 66 C 2
Nyamboyto 25 Q 2
Nyamirembe 64 E 5
Nyamlell 60 E 5
Nyamtumbo 67 F 2
Nyanda Rua 65 F 5
Nyandoma 24 H 3
Nyanga 63 FG 6
Nyanga 63 G 6
Nyanga, Lake 48 D 4
Nyangana 66 C 3
Nyanza 64 D 5
Nyasa, Lake 67 E 2
Nyaungu 41 F 3
Nyayba 37 O 1
Nyazepetrovsk 25 L 4
Nyborg 17 F 4
Nybro 17 G 4
Nybster 2 C 2
Nyda 25 O 2
Nyêmo 41 F 2
Nyeri 65 F 5
Nyerol 64 E 3
Nyika Plateau 67 E 2
Nyima 40 E 1
Nyimba 67 E 2
Nyingchi 38 B 5
Nyiregyháza 20 B 1
Nyiri Desert 65 F 5
Nyiru, Mount 65 F 4
Nykarleby 16 H 3
Nyköbing (Denmark) 17 E 4
Nyköbing (Denmark) 17 F 4
Nyköbing (Denmark) 17 F 5
Nyköping (Sweden) 17 G 4
Nylstroom 66 D 4
Nymagee 49 H 5
Nynäshamn 17 G 4
Nyngan 49 H 5
Nyon 19 E 2
Nyong 63 G 5
Nyrob 24 L 3
Nysa 15 G 4
Nyslott 16 J 3
Nyssa 76 C 3
Nystad 17 H 3
Nytva 24 L 4
Nyuk, Ozero 16 K 3
Nyuksenitsa 24 H 3
Nyukzha 37 M 4
Nyunzu 64 D 6
Nyurba 36 L 3
Nyurol'skiy 25 P 4
Nyuya 36 K 3
Nyuya 36 L 3
Nyvrovo 37 Q 5
Nyyiskiy Zaliv 37 Q 5
Nzambi 63 G 6
Nzara 64 D 4
Nzébéla 62 C 4
Nzega 64 E 5
Nzérékoré 62 C 4
N'zeto 66 A 1

O

Oahe Dam 76 F 3
Oahe, Lake 76 F 2
Oahu 53 E 1
Oak Hills 49 H 2
Oak Ridge 77 K 4
Oakbank 49 G 5
Oakey 49 J 4
Oakford 6 C 3
Oakham 7 D 1
Oakland (CA, U.S.A.) 76 B 4
Oakland (MD, U.S.A.) 77 L 4
Oakley 76 F 4
Oakover River 48 C 3
Oakridge 76 B 3
Oakville 75 M 7
Oamaru 51 Q 10
Oasis 76 D 3
Oates Coast 91
Oatlands 50 L 9
Oaxaca 78 C 4
Oaxaca de Juárez 78 C 4
Ob 25 N 2
Oba 74 L 6
Obala 63 G 5
Oban (New Zealand) 50 P 10
Oban (U.K.) 3 B 3
Oban Hills 63 F 4
Obanazawa 39 LM 3
Obando 84 E 3
Obbia 65 H 3
Obeh 35 G 4
Obeliai 17 J 4
Oberonovac 20 AB 2
Oberpfälzer Wald 15 F 5
Obervellach 19 F 2
Obi, Kepulauan 43 G 4
Obi, Pulau 43 G 4
Obi, Selat 43 G 4
Óbidos 85 G 4
Obihiro 39 M 2
Obil'noye 21 F 1
Oblivskaya 24 H 6
Obluch'ye 37 O 6
Oblukovino 37 T 4
Obninsk 24 G 4
Obo 38 D 3
Obo 64 D 3
Obock 65 G 2
Obodovka 20 C 1
Obokote 64 D 5
Oborniki 15 G 4
Obouya 63 H 6
Oboyan' 24 G 5
Obozerskiy 24 H 3
Obruk Platosu 21 D 3
Obshchiy Syrt 24 KL 5
Obskaya Guba 25 O 1–2
Obuasi 62 D 4
Obubra 63 F 4
Obudu 63 F 4
Obzor 20 C 2
Ocala 77 K 6
Ocampo 76 E 6
Ocaña (Colombia) 84 D 2
Ocaña (Spain) 18 C 4
Occidental, Cordillera 86 BC 3–4
Occidental, Cordillera (Colombia)
 84 C 2–3
Ocean City 77 L 4
Ocean Falls 73 M 5
Ocean Island 51 J 2
Ochakov 20 D 1
Ochamchire 21 F 2
Ocher 24 K 4
Ochil Hills 3 C 3
Ockelbo 17 G 3
Ocmulgee River 77 K 5
Ocoña 86 B 4
Oconee 77 K 5
Oconee 77 K 5
Ocotlán 78 B 3
Ocotlán de Morelos 78 C 4
Ocreza 18 B 4
Ocumare del Tuy 84 E 1
Oda 62 D 4
Oda, Jabal 60 F 4
Ódáðahraun 16 B 2–3
Odalen 17 F 3
Ödate 39 M 2
Odawara 39 L 3–4
Odda 17 E 3
Odder 17 F 4
Odemira 18 B 4
Ödemiş 20 C 3
Odendaalsrus 66 D 5
Odense 17 F 4
Oder 15 F 4
Ödeshög 17 FG 4
Odessa (TX, U.S.A.) 76 F 5
Odessa (U.S.S.R.) 20 D 1
Odiel 18 B 4
Odienné 62 C 4
Ödmården 17 G 3
Odorheiu Secuiesc 20 C 1

Odra 15 FG 4
Odra 15 G 4
Ödwêyne 65 H 3
Odžak 19 G 2
Odzala National Park 63 GH 5
Oeiras 87 H 2
Oelwein 77 H 3
Oeno 53 G 4
Oenpelli 48 E 1
Of 21 F 2
Ofanto 19 G 3
Offaly 4 B 3
Offenbach 15 E 4
Offenburg 15 E 5
Offord D'Arcy 7 D 1
Oficina 85 F 2
Ofotfjorden 16 G 2
Og Aguelt Abd el Jebar 58 D 4
Oga 39 L 3
Ogaden 65 GH 3
Oga-hanto 39 L 3
Ōgaki 39 L 3
Ogallala 76 F 3
Ogbomosho 63 E 4
Ogden 76 D 3
Ogdensburg 77 LM 3
Oghroud 59 G 2
Ogilvie Mountains 72 JK 2
Oginskiy Kanal 17 J 5
Oglanly 34 E 3
Oglat Beraber 58 E 2
Oglat el Fersig 58 D 4
Oglio 19 F 2
Ogmore 49 H 3
Ognev Yar 25 P 4
Ognon 19 E 2
Ogoamas, Gunung 43 F 3
Ogoja 63 F 4
Ogoki 74 K 5
Ogoki Reservoir 74 K 5
Ogon 62 E 4
Ogooué 63 G 6
Ogoron 37 N 5
Ogr → Sharafah 60 D 6
Ogre 17 H 4
Ogulin 19 G 2
Oguma 63 F 4
Ogun 62 E 4
Ogurchinskiy, Ostrov 34 E 3
Ogwashi Uku 63 F 4
Ohakune 51 R 8
Ohanet 59 G 3
O'Higgins, Cerro 89 B 8
O'Higgins, Lago 89 B 8
Ohio 77 K 3
Ohio 77 K 4
Ohopoho 66 A 3
Ohře 15 F 4
Ohrid 20 B 2
Ohridskojezero 20 B 2
Oiapoque 85 H 3
Oiapoque 85 H 3
Oijärvi 16 J 2
Oilgate 6 A 1
Oise 18 D 2
Ōita 39 K 4
Öjebyn 16 H 2
Ojinaga 78 B 2
Ojo de Agua 88 D 4
Ojos del Salado, Cerro 88 C 4
Oka 24 H 4
Oka 36 H 5
Okaba 43 J 5
Okahandja 66 B 4
Okahao 66 A 3
Okak Islands 75 P 4
Okakarara 66 B 4
Okanagan Lake 73 NO 6
Okapa 50 E 3
Okaputa 66 B 4
Okara 35 J 4
Okaukuejo 66 B 3
Okavango 66 C 3
Okavango Swamp 66 C 3
Okavarumendu 66 B 4
Okaya 39 L 3
Okayama 39 K 3–4
Okazaki 39 L 4
Okazize 66 B 4
Okeechobee, Lake 77 K 6
Okehamptom 6 B 2
Okene 63 F 4
Okha (India) 40 A 3
Okha (U.S.S.R.) 37 Q 5
Ókhi Oros 20 B 3
Okhota 37 Q 3
Okhotsk 37 Q 4
Okhotsk, Sea of 37 R 4
Okhotskiy Perevoz 37 P 3
Okhotskoye More 37 QS 4
Okhthonia, Ákra 20 B 3
Okinawa-jima 39 J 5
Okinoerabu-jima 39 J 5
Oki-shotō 39 K 3

Okitipupa 63 EF 4
Oklahoma 76–77 G 4
Oklahoma City 77 G 4
Oknitsa 20 C 1
Okollo 64 E 4
Okombahe 66 B 4
Okondja 63 G 6
Okonogan 73 O 6
Okorukambe 66 B 4
Okoyo 63 H 6
Okstindan 16 F 2
Oktemberyan 21 F 2
Oktwin 41 G 4
Oktyabr'skiy 21 F 1
Oktyabr'skiy 36 F 5
Oktyabr'skiy 36 G 4
Oktyabr'skiy 37 N 4
Oktyabr'skiy 37 Q 5
Oktyabr'skiy 37 T 5
Oktyabrskiy 24 K 5
Oktyabrskiy 37 N 5
Oktyabr'skoye 24 GH 5
Oktyabr'skoye 25 N 3
Okurchan 37 S 4
Okushiri-tō 39 L 2
Okuta 62 E 4
Ola 37 S 4
Ólafsfjörður 16 B 2
Ólafsvík 16 A 3
Olancha 76 C 4
Olanchito 78 E 4
Öland 17 G 4
Olanga 16 K 2
Olanga 16 K 2
Olary 49 G 5
Olathe 77 H 4
Olavarría 89 DE 6
Oława 15 G 4
Olbia 19 E 3
Old Bahama Channel 79 G 3
Old Cherrabun 48 D 2
Old Crow 72 K 2
Old Crow 72 K 2
Old Gidgee 48 B 4
Old Harbor 72 G 4
Old Mkushi 66 D 2
Old Wives Lake 73 Q 5
Oldcastle 4 B 3
Oldenburg (F.R.G.) 15 E 4
Oldham 5 D 3
Oldhamstocks 3 C 4
Oldmeldrum 2 C 3
Olds 73 P 5
Oldshoremore 2 B 2
Olekma 36 M 4
Olekminsk 36 LM 3
Olekminskiy Stanovik 36 LM 5
Olekmo-Charskoye Nagor'ye
 36 LM 4
Olema 24 J 3
Olenegorsk 16 K 2
Olenëk 36 K 2
Olenëk 36 M 1
Olenëkskiy Zaliv 36 M 1
Olenevod 37 T 4
Olenevod 37 WX 3
Olenitsa 16 KL 2
Olen'ya Rechka 36 F 5
Oléron, Ile d' 18 C 2
Oleśnica 15 G 4
Olevsk 17 J 5
Ol'ga 39 KL 2
Olga, Mount 48 E 4
Ol'ginka 21 E 1
Ölgiy 36 F 6
Ol'gopol' 21 D 1
Ol'gopol 20 C 1
Olhão 18 B 4
Oliana 18 D 3
Olib 19 F 3
Olifants 67 E 4
Olifantshoek 66 C 5
Olimarao 52 A 2
Olímbía 20 B 3
Ólimbos 20 B 2–3
Ólimbos 20 C 3
Olímpia 87 G 5
Olinda 87 K 2
Olindina 87 J 3
Olite 18 C 3
Oliva (Argentina) 88 D 5
Oliva (Spain) 18 C 4
Oliveira 87 H 5
Olivença 67 EF 2
Olkusz 15 G 4
Ollagüe 86 C 5
Ollagüe, Volcán 86 C 5
Olmos 84 C 5
Olney 7 D 1
Olochi 36 L 5
Olofström 17 F 4
Olomouc 15 G 5
Olonets 16 K 3

Olongapo 43 HJ 2
Oloron-Sainte-Marie 18 C 3
Olot 18 D 3
Olovo 19 G 3
Olovyannaya 36 L 5
Oloyskiye Gory 37 U 2
Olshammar 17 F 4
Olsztyn 15 H 4
Olsztynek 15 H 4
Olt 20 B 2
Olten 19 E 2
Oltenia 20 B 2
Olteniţa 20 C 2
Oltu 21 F 2
Olvera 18 B 4
Olympia (U.S.A.) 76 B 2
Olympia → Olimbia 20 B 3
Olympic National Park 76 B 2
Olympus 20 B 3
Olympus, Mount 76 B 2
Olyutorka 37 V 3
Olyutorskiy 37 VW 3
Olyutorskiy Gory 37 W 3
Olyutorskiy, Mys 37 V 4
Olyutorskiy Poluostrov 37 W 3
Olyutorskiy Zaliv 37 V 3
Om' 25 Q 4
Omagh 4 B 3
Omaguas 84 D 4
Omaha 77 G 3
Oman 61 JK 4–5
Oman, Gulf of 34 F 5–6
Oman, Gulf of 61 K 4
Omarama 50 P 9
Omaruru 66 A 4
Omaruru 66 B 4
Omatako 66 B 4
Omatako, Mount 66 B 4
Omate 86 B 4
Omatjete 66 B 4
Ombai, Selat 43 G 5
Ombi, Selat 43 G 5
Ombombo 66 A 3
Omboué 63 F 6
Ombrone 19 F 3
Ombu 40 E 1
Omchali 34 E 2
Omdurman 60 E 5
Omeleut 37 W 3
Omeo 49 H 6
Ometepe, Isla de 78 E 5
Ometepec 78 C 4
Omili 20 C 3
Omineca Mountains 73 M 4
Omiš 19 G 3
Omitara 66 B 4
Ōmiya 39 L 3
Ommanney Bay 73 R 1
Ömnödelger 36 K 6
Ömnögoví 38 D 2
Omo 65 F 3
Omodeo, Lago 19 E 3
Omolon 37 T 2
Omolon 37 U 2
Omoloy 36 L 3
Omoloy 37 O 1
Omsk 25 O 4–5
Omsukchan 37 T 3
Omsukchanskiy Gory 37 T 3
Omu, Virful 20 C 1
Omulew 15 H 4
Ōmura 39 J 4
Ōmuta 39 K 4
Omutinskiy 25 N 4
Omutninsk 24 K 4
Ona Dikonde 64 C 5
Onamia 77 H 2
Onang 43 F 4
Onawa 77 G 3
Onayena 66 B 3
Onbingwin 41 G 5
Oncócua 66 A 3
Ondangwa 66 B 3
Ondaruza Falls 66 A 3
Ondava 15 H 5
Ondekaremba 66 B 4
Ondjiva 66 B 3
Ondo 63 E 4
Ondor Sum 38 F 2
Öndörhaan 36 K 6
Ondorkara 35 M 1
Öndörshireet 36 H 6
Ondozero, Ozero 16 K 3
Onega 24 G 3
Onega 24 G 3
O'Neill 76 G 3
Onekotan, Ostrov 37 ST 6
Oneonta 77 M 3
Onesi 66 A 3
Onezhskaya Guba 24 G 3
Onezhskoye, Ozero 24 G 3
Ongiyn Gol 38 D 1
Ongjin 39 J 3
Ongniud Qi 39 G 2
Ongole 40 D 4
Onguday 25 R 5
Oni 21 F 2

Onilahy 67 G 4
Onitsha 63 F 4
Onk,Djebel 59 G 2
Onkuchakh 36 KL 2
Ono-i-Lau Islands 52 CD 4
Onomichi 39 K 4
Onon 36 L 5
Onon Gol 36 K 6
Onotoa 52 C 3
Onovgay 37 T 4
Onsala 17 F 4
Onseepkans 66 B 5
Onslow 48 B 3
Onslow Bay 77 L 5
Ontario (Canada) 74 JL 5
Ontario (OR, U.S.A.) 76 C 3
Ontario, Lake 77 L 3
Onteniente 18 C 4
Ontojärvi 16 J 3
Ontong Java 51 G 3
Oodnadatta 49 F 4
Ookiep 66 B 5
Ooldea 48 E 5
Oologah Lake 77 G 4
Oorindi 49 G 3
Oostende 14 D 4
Ootacamund 40 C 5
Opala (U.S.S.R.) 37 T 5
Opala (Zaire) 64 C 5
Opanake 40 D 6
Opari 64 E 4
Opasatika 74 L 6
Opatija 19 F 2
Opava 15 G 5
Opelousas 77 H 5
Ophir 72 F 3
Opienge 64 D 4
Opis (Iraq) 22 D 2
Opiscotéo, Lac 75 O 5
Opobo 63 F 5
Opochka 17 J 4
Opoczno 15 GH 4
Opole 15 G 4
Oporto 18 B 3
Oposhnya 24 F 6
Opotiki 51 R 8
Opp 77 J 5
Oppdal 16 EF 3
Oppland 16 E 3
Opportunity 76 C 2
Oputo 76 E 5
Or, Côte d' 19 D 2
Oradea 20 B 1
Öræfajökull 16 B 3
Òrah 59 J 3
Orahovica 19 G 2
Orai 40 C 2
Oran 58 E 1
Orange (Australia) 49 H 5
Orange (France) 19 D 3
Orange (Namibia) 66 B 5
Orange (TX, U.S.A.) 77 H 5
Orange, Cabo 85 H 3
Orange Free State 66 D 5
Orange Park 77 K 5
Orange Walk 78 E 4
Orango, Ilha de 62 A 3
Oranienburg 15 F 4
Oranje 66 B 5
Oranje Gebergte 85 GH 3
Oranjemund 66 B 5
Oranjestad 84 E 1
Oranzherei 21 G 1
Orapa 66 D 4
Orbetello 19 F 3
Orbigo 18 B 3
Orbost 49 H 6
Orcadas 91
Ord, Mount 48 D 2
Ord River 48 D 2
Ord River Dam 48 D 2
Ordenes 18 B 3
Ordoquif 89 D 6
Ordos Plateau 38 E 3
Ordu 21 E 2
Ordynskoye 25 Q 5
Ordzhonikidze 21 E 2
Ordzhonikidze 21 FG 2
Ordzhonikidzeabad 35 HJ 3
Orealla 85 G 2
Orebić 19 G 3
Örebro 17 G 4
Oregon 76 BC 3
Oregon Inlet 77 LM 4
Öregrund 17 G 3
Orekhov 21 E 1
Orekhovo 20 B 2
Orekhovo Zuyevo 24 G 4
Orel' 21 D 1
Orel 24 G 5
Orel', Ozero 37 P 5
Orellana (Peru) 84 C 4
Orellana (Peru) 84 C 5
Orem 76 D 3
Oren 20 C 3
Orenburg 24 K 5

Orense 18 B 3
Orestiás 20 C 2
Öresund 17 F 4
Orford 7 E 1
Organ Peak 76 E 5
Organ Pipe Cactus National
  Monument 76 D 5
Organã 18 D 3
Orgeyev 20 C 1
Órgiva 18 C 4
Orhaneli 20 C 3
Orhangazi 20 C 2
Orhon Gol 36 H 6
Ori 87 J 2
Orick 76 B 3
Oriental, Cordillera 86 BC 3–5
Oriental, Cordillera (Colombia)
  84 CD 2–3
Oriente 89 D 6
Orihuela 18 C 4
Orillia 75 M 7
Orimattila 17 J 3
Orinduik 85 F 3
Orinoco (Colombia) 84 E 2
Orissa 40 DE 3
Orissaare 17 H 4
Oristano 19 E 4
Orivesi 16 H 3
Orivesi 16 J 3
Oriximiná 85 G 4
Orizaba 78 C 4
Orjen 20 A 2
Orkadalen 16 EF 3
Orkanger 16 E 3
Örkelljunga 17 F 4
Orkla 16 E 3
Orkney (South Africa) 66 D 5
Orkney Islands 2 C 2
Orlando 77 K 6
Orléans 18 D 2
Orlik 36 G 5
Orlovskaya 37 V 3
Orlu 63 F 4
Ormara 35 G 5
Ormoc 43 F 1
Órmos Almiroú 20 B 3
Ormskirk 5 D 3
Orne 18 C 2
Örnö 17 G 4
Örnsköldsvik 16 G 3
Oro, Monte d' 19 E 3
Orobie, Alpi 19 EF 2
Orocué 84 D 3
Orodara 62 CD 3
Orofino 76 C 2
Örög Nuur 36 F 5
Orog Nuur 38 D 1
Orogrande 76 E 5
Oroluk 52 B 2
Oromocto 75 O 6
Oron (Nigeria) 63 F 5
Oron (U.S.S.R.) 36 L 4
Orona 52 D 3
Oropesa 18 B 4
Oropesa 18 CD 3
Oroqen Zizhiqi 37 M 5
Oroquieta 43 F 2
Óros Ossa 20 B 3
Orosei 19 E 3
Oroszlány 20 A 1
Orotukan 37 S 3
Oroville (CA, U.S.A.) 76 B 4
Oroville (WA, U.S.A.) 76 C 2
Oroyëk 37 S 3
Orphir 2 C 2
Orpington 7 E 2
Orqohan 37 M 6
Orr 77 H 2
Orrefors 17 G 4
Orroroo 49 F 5
Orsa 16 F 3
Orsa Finnmark 16 F 3
Orsasjön 16 F 3
Orsha 17 K 5
Orsk 25 L 5
Orşova 20 B 2
Örsta 16 E 3
Orta 21 D 2
Ortã, Lago d' 19 E 2
Ortaca 20 C 3
Ortegal, Cabo 18 B 3
Orthez 18 C 3
Ortigueira 18 B 3
Ortiz 76 D 6
Ortles 19 F 2
Orto-Ayan 37 NO 1
Orton 5 C 2
Ortona 19 F 3
Ortonville 77 G 2
Oruhito 66 A 3
Orulgan, Khrebet 37 N 2
Orūmīyeh 34 D 3
Orūmīyeh, Daryācheh-ye (Iran)
  23 D 1
Orungo 64 E 4
Oruro 86 C 4

Orust 17 F 4
Orvault 18 C 2
Orvieto 19 F 3
Osa 24 L 4
Osa 36 H 5
Osa, Península de 78 F 6
Ōsaka 39 L 4
Osakarovka 25 O 5
Ōsaka-wan 39 L 4
Osam 20 B 2
Osborne 76 G 4
Osby 17 F 4
Osceola 77 H 3
Osen 16 F 3
Osensjöen 16 F 3
Osh 35 J 2
Osha 25 O 4
Oshakati 66 B 3
Oshawa 75 M 7
Oshikango 66 B 3
Ō-shima 39 L 2
Oshivelo 66 B 3
Oshkosh 77 J 3
Oshmarino 36 D 1
Oshmyany 17 J 5
Oshnavīyeh (Iran) 23 D 1
Oshogbo 63 EF 4
Oshtoran Kūh (Iran) 23 E 2
Oshtorīnān (Iran) 23 E 2
Oshwe 64 B 5
Osijek 19 G 2
Osimo 19 F 3
Osinniki 25 R 5
Osinovka 25 Q 6
Osinovo 25 R 3
Osipovichi 17 J 5
Osire 66 B 4
Oskaloosa 77 H 3
Oskamull 3 A 3
Oskarshamn 17 G 4
Oskarström 17 F 4
Oskino 36 J 3
Öskjuuvatn 16 B 2
Oskoba 36 H 3
Oslo 17 F 4
Oslob 43 F 2
Oslofjorden 17 F 4
Osmanabad 40 C 4
Osmancık 21 DE 2
Osmaneli 20 D 2
Osmaniye 21 E 3
Osmaniye (Turkey) 22 B 1
Os'mino 17 J 4
Osmotherley 5 E 2
Osmyanskaya Vozvyshennost'
  17 J 5
Osnabrück 15 E 4
Osor 19 F 3
Osorno 89 B 7
Osoyoos 73 NO 6
Osøyra 17 E 3
Ospito 84 E 2
Osprey Reef (Queensland, Austr.)
  49 H 1
Ossa, Mount 50 L 9
Ossa, Mount 52 A 5
Ossa, Óros 20 B 3
Osse 84 E 3
Ossora 37 U 4
Ostashkov 24 F 4
Östavall 16 G 3
Österdalälven 16 F 3
Österdalen 16 F 3
Östergötland 17 F 4
Östersund 16 FG 3
Ostfriesische Inseln 14–15 E 4
Östhammar 17 G 3
Östhavet 16 JK 1
Östmark 17 F 3
Ostrava 15 G 5
Ostroda 15 GH 4
Ostrogozhsk 24 GH 5
Ostrołeka 15 H 4
Ostroshitski Gorodok 17 J 5
Ostrov (Czechoslovakia) 15 F 4
Ostrov (Romania) 20 C 2
Ostrov (Russia, U.S.S.R.) 17 J 4
Ostrov Atlasova 37 ST 5
Ostrov Barsa-Kel'mes 34 F 1
Ostrov Beringa 27 T 4
Ostrov Bol'shoy Begichev
  36 KL 1
Ostrov Bol'shoy Berezovy 17 J 3
Ostrov Bol'shoy Lyakhovskiy
  37 Q 1
Ostrov Bol'shoy Shantar 37 P 4–5
Ostrov Broutona 37 S 6
Ostrov Chirinkotan 37 S 6
Ostrov Dolgiy 25 LM 2
Ostrov Ekarma 37 S 6
Ostrov Feklistova 37 P 4–5
Ostrov Gogland 17 J 3
Ostrov Gusmp 37 U 1–2
Ostrov Iony 37 Q 4
Ostrov Iturup 37 R 6–7

Ostrov Karaginskiy 37 U 4
Ostrov Ketoy 37 S 6
Ostrov Kharimkotan 37 ST 6
Ostrov Kil'din 16 KL 2
Ostrov Kokaral 34 FG 1
Ostrov Kolguyev 24 J 2
Ostrov Konevits 16 K 3
Ostrov Kotel'nyy 37 P 1
Ostrov Krestovskiy 37 U 1
Ostrov Makanrushi 37 S 6
Ostrov Malyy Lyakhovskiy 37 Q 1
Ostrov Matua 37 S 6
Ostrov Mednyy 27 TU 4
Ostrov Men'shikova 37 PQ 5
Ostrov Mezhdusharskiy 24 K 1
Ostrov Moshchnyy 17 J 4
Ostrov Nansikan 37 Q 4
Ostrov Ogurchinskiy 34 E 3
Ostrov Onekotan 37 ST 6
Ostrov Paramushir 37 T 5
Ostrov Peschanyy 36 L 1
Ostrov Rasshua 37 S 6
Ostrov Raykoke 37 S 6
Ostrov Semenovskiy 37 O 1
Ostrov Shiashkotan 37 S 6
Ostrov Shumshu 37 T 5
Ostrov Simushir 37 S 6
Ostrov Stolbovoy 37 P 1
Ostrov Urup 37 S 6
Ostrov Valaam 16 K 3
Ostrov Vaygach 25 L 1
Ostrov Vozrozhdeniya 34 F 1
Ostrov Zav'yalova 37 RS 4
Ostrova Chernyye Brat'ya 37 S 6
Ostrova Diomida 72 D 2
Ostrova Medvezh'i 37 R 1
Ostrova Solovetskiye 24 G 2
Ostrova Srednego 37 S 6
Ostrova Tyulen'i 34 E 1–2
Ostrovnoy 37 U 4
Ostrovnoy, Mys 37 T 3
Ostrovnoy 37 TU 5
Ostrovnoye 37 U 2
Ostrovul Letea 20 C 1
Ostrovul Sfintu Gheorghe 20 C 1–2
Ostrow Mazowiecka 15 H 4
Ostrow Wielkopolski 15 G 4
Ostrowiec Świetokrzyski 15 H 4
Ostryak, Gora 37 W 3
Ostrzeszow 15 G 4
Ostuni 19 G 3
Ōsumi-shotō 39 JK 4
Osuna 18 BC 4
Os'van' 24 L 2
Osvejskoje, Ozero 17 J 4
Oswego 77 L 3
Oswestry 6 C 1

Otar 35 K 2
Otaru 39 M 2
Otautau 50 P 10
Otava 15 F 5
Otavalo 84 C 3
Otavi 66 B 3
Otchinjau 66 A 3
Otepää Kõrgustik 17 J 4
Otgon 36 G 6
Othonoí 20 A 3
Oti 62 E 4
Oti-daitō-jima 39 K 6
Otish, Monts 75 N 5
Otjiha'vara 66 B 4
Otjikondo 66 B 3
Otjimbingwe 66 B 4
Otjinene 66 B 4
Otjinoko 66 B 4
Otjipatera Mountains 66 B 4
Otjitambi 66 AB 3
Otjituuo 66 B 4
Otjiwarongo 66 B 4
Otjovazandu 66 AB 3
Otjozondjou 66 B 4
Otjozondu 66 B 4
Otkrytyy 37 M 4
Otley 5 E 2
Otočac 19 G 3
Otog Qi 38 E 3
Otoño 89 D 6
Otoskwin 74 JK 5
Otra 17 E 4
Otradnaya 21 F 2
Otradnoye 37 T 5
Otranto 20 A 2
Otshandi 66 A 3
Otshikuku 66 B 3
Ot-Siyen 36 M 1
Otsu 39 L 4
Otta 16 E 3
Ottadalen 16 E 3
Ottawa 75 M 6
Ottawa 75 MN 6
Ottawa (KS, U.S.A.) 77 G 4
Ottawa Islands 75 L 4
Ottenby 17 G 4
Otter Creek 77 K 6
Otterburn 5 D 2
Ottery St. Mary 6 C 2

Ottumwa 77 H 3
Oturkpo 63 F 4
Otuwe 66 B 4
Otway, Bahía 89 B 9
Otway, Cape 49 G 6
Otwock 15 H 4
Ötz 19 F 2
Ou Neua 41 H 3
Ouachita Mountains 77 GH 5
Ouad Naga 58 B 5
Ouadane 58 C 4
Ouaddaï 63 J 3
Ouagadougou 62 D 3
Ouahigouya 62 D 3
Ouahran → Oran 58 E 1
Ouaka 64 C 3
Oualam 62 E 3
Oualata 58 D 5
Oualidia 58 D 2
Ouallene Bordj 59 F 4
Ouan Taredert 59 G 3
Ouanary 85 H 3
Ouanda-Djallé 64 C 3
Ouando 64 D 3
Ouango 64 C 4
Ouangolodougou 62 CD 4
Ouani 63 H 2
Ouaqui 85 H 3
Ouarane 58 CD 4
Ouargaye 62 DE 3
Ouargla 59 G 2
Ouarkziz, Jbel 58 D 3
Ouarra 64 D 3
Ouarsenis, Massif de l' 59 F 1
Ouarzazate 58 D 2
Ouassou 62 B 3
Ouatcha 63 F 3
Oubangui 63 H 5
Oudeïka 62 D 2
Oudje 59 G 2
Oudong 41 H 5
Oudtshoorn 66 C 6
Oued Rhiou 59 F 1
Oued Zem 58 D 2
Oueïta 63 J 2
Ouéllé 62 D 4
Ouémé 62 E 4
Ouessant, Ile de 18 B 2
Ouesso 63 H 5
Ouezzane 58 D 2
Ougarou 62 E 3
Ouham 63 H 4
Ouidah 62 E 4
Ouirigué 78 E 4
Ouistreham 18 C 2
Oujaf 58 D 5
Oujda 58 E 2
Oujeft 58 C 4
Oulad Naïl, Monts des 59 F 2
Oulainen 16 HJ 3
Oulankajoki 16 J 2
Ould Yenjé 58 C 5
Ouled Djellal 59 G 2
Oulossébougou 62 C 3
Oulu 16 J 2
Oulujärvi 16 J 3
Oulujoki 16 J 3
Oum Chalouba 63 J 2
Oum el Asell 58 E 4
Oum el Bouaghi 59 G 1
Oum er Rbia 58 D 2
Oum Hadjer 63 H 3
Oumé 62 C 4
Oumm ed Droûs Guebli, Sebkhet
  58 C 4
Oumm ed Droûs Telli, Sebkha
  58 C 4
Ounane, Djebel 59 G 3
Ounasjoki 16 H 2
Oundle 7 D 1
Ounianga Kebir 63 J 2
Ounianga Serir 63 J 2
Ounissoui Baba 63 G 2
Ouricuri 87 HJ 2
Ourinhos 87 G 5
Ouro Prêto 87 H 5
Ourthe 14 E 4
Ōu-sanmyaku 39 M 2–3
Ouse, River (N. Yorkshire) 5 E 3
Ouse, River (Norfolk) 7 E 1
Oust 18 C 2
Outagouna 62 E 2
Outaouais 75 M 6
Outapi 66 A 3
Outardes, Rivière aux 75 O 5–6
Outat Oulad el Haj 58 E 2
Outer Hebrides 2 A 3
Outjo 66 B 4
Outlook 73 Q 5
Outokumpu 16 J 3
Outwell 7 E 1
Ouvéa 51 J 6
Ouyen 49 G 5–6
Ovacık 21 D 3

Ovacık 21 E 3
Ovada 19 E 3
Ovalle 88 B 5
Ovamboland 66 B 3
Oveng 63 G 5
Överbygd 16 G 2
Overhalla 16 F 3
Överkalix 16 H 2
Overland Park 77 H 4
Övertorneå 16 H 2
Överuman 16 FG 2
Oviedo (Haiti) 79 H 4
Oviedo (Spain) 18 B 3
Oviksfjällen 16 F 3
Övre Ardal 16 E 3
Övre Fryken 17 F 3
Övre Soppero 16 H 2
Ovruch 17 J 5
Ovsyanka 37 N 5
Ovul 51 F 3
Owando 63 H 6
Owatonna 77 H 3
Owen, Mount 51 Q 9
Owen Sound 75 L 7
Owen Stanley Range 50 E 3
Owendo 63 FG 5
Owensboro 77 J 4
Owerri 63 F 4
Owo 63 F 4
Owosso 77 K 3
Owyhee 76 C 3
Owyhee, Lake 76 C 3
Owyhee River 76 C 3
Ox Mountains 14 B 4
Oxberg 16 F 3
Oxelösund 17 G 4
Oxford (MS, U.S.A.) 77 J 5
Oxford (U.K.) 7 D 2
Oxford Lake 73 S 4–5
Oxfordshire 7 D 2
Oxton 3 C 4
Oya Siwo 93
Oyapock 85 H 3
Oyash 25 Q 4
Oyem 63 G 5
Öyeren 17 F 4
Oykel Bridge 2 B 3
Oykel, River 2 B 3
Oymyakon 37 Q 3
Oyo (Nigeria) 62 E 4
Oyo (Sudan) 60 F 4
Oyón 86 A 3
Oyonnax 19 E 2
Oyotung 37 R 1
Oyshilik 25 Q 6
Oyster Cliffs 66 A 5
Öystese 17 E 3
Oysurdakh 37 S 2
Oytal 35 J 2
Oyun-Khomoto 37 P 2
Ozamiz 43 F 2
Ozark 77 J 5
Ozark Plateau 77 H 4
Ozarks, Lake of the 77 H 4
Ózd 20 B 1
Ozernaya 37 U 4
Ozernovskiy 37 T 5
Ozero Agata 36 F 2
Ozero Akzhaykyn 35 H 1–2
Ozero Alakol' 25 Q 6
Ozero Alibey 20 D 1
Ozero Arys 35 H 1
Ozero Aschikol' 35 H 1
Ozero Ayaturku 36 EF 1
Ozero Balkhash 25 OP 6
Ozero Baykal 36 J 5
Ozero Biylikol' 35 J 2
Ozero Bolon' 37 P 6
Ozero Bol'shoy Yeravnoye 36 K 5
Ozero Bolsjoj Morskoye 37 T 1
Ozero Bustakh 37 Q 1
Ozero Chany 25 P 5
Ozero Chatyrkel' 35 JK 2
Ozero Chervonoye 17 J 5
Ozero Chukchagirskoye 37 P 5
Ozero Dadynskoye 21 FG 1
Ozero Donuzlav 21 D 1
Ozero El'gygytgyn 37 W 2
Ozero Engozero 16 K 2
Ozero Gimolskoye 16 K 3
Ozero Ilirgytkin 37 T 1
Ozero Il'men 17 K 4
Ozero Imandra 16 K 2
Ozero Issyk-Kul 35 K 2
Ozero Kamennoye 16 K 3
Ozero Kanozero 16 K 2
Ozero Karakoin 35 H 1
Ozero Keke Usun 21 G 1
Ozero Keret' 16 K 2
Ozero Keta 36 F 2
Ozero Khanka 39 K 1–2
Ozero Khantayskoye 36 F 2
Ozero Khummi 37 P 5
Ozero Kitai 20 C 1
Ozero Kiyeng-Kyuyel' 36 JK 1

Ozero Kokora 36 H 1
Ozero Kolozero 16 K 2
Ozero Kolvitskoye 16 K 2
Ozero Kovdozero 16 K 2
Ozero Kozhozero 24 G 3
Ozero Krasnoye 37 W 3
Ozero Kubenskoye 24 G 4
Ozero Kulundinskoye 25 PQ 5
Ozero Kungasalakh 36 JK 1
Ozero Kushmurun 25 M 5
Ozero Labaz 36 G 1
Ozero Lacha 24 G 3
Ozero Lama 36 F 2
Ozero Leksozero 16 K 3
Ozero Lovozero 16 L 2
Ozero Manych Gudilo 21 F 1
Ozero Markakol' 25 R 6
Ozero Mogotoyevo 37 R 1
Ozero Nerpich'ye 37 T 2
Ozero Nyuk 16 K 3
Ozero Ondozero 16 K 3
Ozero Onezhskoye 24 G 3
Ozero Orel' 37 P 5
Ozero Osvejskoje 17 J 4
Ozero Ozhogino 37 R 2
Ozero Paravani 21 F 2
Ozero Portnyagino 36 HJ 1
Ozero Purinskoye 36 E 1
Ozero Pyaozero 16 K 2
Ozero Pyasino 25 R 2
Ozero Rovkulskoye 16 K 3
Ozero Sadochye 34 F 2
Ozero Sartlan 25 PQ 4–5
Ozero Sarykamysh 34 F 2
Ozero Sarykopa 25 M 5
Ozero Sasyk 20 C 1
Ozero Sasykkol' 25 Q 6
Ozero Segozero 16 K 3
Ozero Seletyteniz 25 O 5
Ozero Sevan 21 G 2
Ozero Sonkel' 35 K 2
Ozero Sovetskoje 25 Q 2
Ozero Sredneye Kuyto 16 K 2–3
Ozero Sukhodolskoye 16 K 3
Ozero Svetloye 21 G 1
Ozero Syamozero 16 K 3
Ozero Taymyr 36 H 1
Ozero Teletskoye 25 R 5
Ozero Tengiz 25 N 5
Ozero Tikhtoozero 16 K 2
Ozero Tikshozero 16 K 2
Ozero Topozero 16 K 2
Ozero Topozero 16 K 2
Ozero Tulos 16 K 3
Ozero Ubinskoye 25 Q 4
Ozero Udyl' 37 P 5
Ozero Umbozero [Umbozero] 16 KL 2
Ozero Verkhneye Kuyto 16 K 3
Ozero Vodlozero 24 G 3
Ozero Vozhe 24 G 3
Ozero Vuoksa 16 JK 3
Ozero Vyalozero 16 L 2
Ozero Vygozero 24 G 3
Ozero Yalpukh 20 C 1
Ozero Yambuto 25 PQ 1
Ozero Yanis'yarvi 16 K 3
Ozero Yessey 36 H 2
Ozero Zaysan 25 Q 6
Ozero Zhamanakkal' 35 G 1
Ozero Zvoron 37 P 5
Ozhogina 37 R 2
Ozhogino 37 R 2
Ozhogino, Ozero 37 R 2
Ozinki 24 J 5
Ozona 76 F 5
Ozorków 15 G 4

P

Paamiut 75 R 3
Pa-an 41 G 4
Paarl 66 B 6
Paavola 16 J 3
Pab Range 35 H 5
Pabianice 15 G 4
Pabna 40 E 3
Pabradé 17 J 4
Pacaás Novos, Serra dos 86 D 3
Pacaraima, Sierra 85 F 3
Pacasmayo 84 BC 5
Pachacamac 86 A 3
Pachakshiri 41 F 2
Pachbhadra 40 B 2
Pachino 19 G 4
Pachitea 84 C 5
Pachiza 84 C 5
Pacho 84 D 2
Pachuca 78 C 3–4
Pacific Ocean 92
Pacific Ranges 73 M 5
Pacora 84 C 2
Padam 35 K 4
Padang 42 B 4
Padang 42 C 3

Padang 42 C 4
Padang, Pulau 42 B 3
Padangpanjang 42 AB 4
Padangsidempuan 42 A 3
Padany 16 K 3
Padauari 85 F 3
Paddle Prairie 73 O 4
Paderborn 15 E 4
Padilla 86 D 4
Padova 19 F 2
Padrão, Ponta do 66 A 1
Padrauna 40 D 2
Padre Island 77 G 6
Padstow 6 B 2
Paducah 77 J 4
Padula 19 G 3
Paengnyŏng-do 39 H 3
Paestum 19 FG 3
Pafuri 67 E 4
Pag 19 F 3
Paga Centa 85 H 4
Pagadian 43 F 2
Pagalu 63 F 6
Pagan 52 A 1
Pagasitikós Kólpos 20 B 3
Pagatan 42 E 4
Page 76 D 4
Pago Mission 48 D 1
Pago-Pago 52 D 3
Pagosa Springs 76 E 4
Pagri 40 E 2
Pagwi 50 D 2
Pahang, Sungai 42 B 3
Paharpur 35 J 4
Pahkaing Bum 41 G 2
Pahlavi Dezh (Iran) 23 E 2
Pai 63 G 4
Paide 17 J 4
Paignton 6 C 2
Paiguás 86 E 4
Paijánne 16 J 3
Páikon Oros 20 B 2
Paikot 40 D 3
Pailin 41 H 5
Paimio 17 H 3
Paimpol 18 C 2
Painan 42 B 4
Paine Medio, Cerro 89 B 9
Painesville (OH, U.S.A.) 77 K 3
Painesville (Western Australia) 48 B 4
Painted Desert 76 D 4
Paisley 3 B 4
Paita 84 B 5
Paithan 40 C 4
Pajala 16 H 2
Pajares, Puerto de 18 B 3
Pajatén 84 C 5
Pak Beng 41 H 4
Pak Hin Boun 41 H 4
Pak Lay 41 H 4
Pak Neun 41 H 4
Pak Phanang 41 H 6
Pak Sane 41 H 4
Pakala 40 C 5
Pakaraima Mountains 85 FG 2–3
Pakhacha 37 V 3
Paki 63 F 3
Pakima 64 C 5
Pakin 52 B 2
Pakistan 35 HJ 5
Pakokku 41 F 3
Pakpattan 35 J 4
Pakrac 19 G 2
Paks 20 A 1
Pakse 41 J 4
Pakwach 64 E 4
Pal Lahara 40 E 3
Pal Malmal 51 F 3
Pala (Burkina) 64 C 3
Pala (Chad) 63 H 4
Palacios 77 G 6
Palafrugell 18 D 3
Palagruža 19 G 3
Palaiokhóra 20 B 3
Palakollu 40 D 4
Palamau 40 D 3
Palamós 18 D 3
Palana 37 T 4
Palanan Point 43 J 1
Palanga 17 H 4
Palangkaraya 42 D 4
Palanpur 40 B 3
Palapye 66 D 4
Palatka 37 S 3
Palau 19 E 3
Palau 43 J 2
Palau 43 J 2
Palau Islands 43 H 2
Palauk 41 G 5
Palaw 41 G 5
Palawan 43 E 2
Palawan Passage 42–43 E 1–2
Palayankottai 40 C 6
Palazzo, Punta 19 E 3
Palca 86 C 4

Paldiski 17 H 4
Pale 41 F 3
Palel 41 F 3
Paleleh 43 F 3
Palembang 42 BC 4
Palencia 18 C 3
Palenque 78 D 4
Palermo 19 F 4
Palestine 22 B 2–3
Palestine (TX, U.S.A.) 77 G 5
Paletwa 41 F 3
Palghat 40 C 5
Palgrave Point 66 A 4
Pali 40 B 2
Palimé 62 E 4
Palinuro, Capo 19 FG 3
Palitana 40 B 3
Paljakka 16 J 3
Paljenik 19 G 3
Palk Strait 40 C 5–6
Palkonda Range 40 C 5
Palla Bianca 19 F 2
Pallasovka 24 J 5
Pallastunturi 16 H 2
Palliser, Cape 51 R 9
Palliser, Îles 53 F 4
Palm Bay 77 KL 6
Palm Springs 76 C 5
Palma (Mozambique) 67 G 2
Palma (Spain) 18 D 4
Palma del Río 18 B 4
Palma Soriano 79 G 3
Palmar Sur 78 F 6
Palmares 88 F 4
Palmares do Sul 88 FG 5
Palmarito 88 DE 2
Palmarola 19 F 3
Palmas Bellas 84 B 4
Palmas, Cape 62 C 5
Palmas, Golfo di 19 E 4
Palmeira 88 F 4
Palmeira dos Indios 87 J 2
Palmeirais (Piauí, Brazil) 87 H 2
Palmeiras (Goiás, Brazil) 87 G 3
Palmer (AK, U.S.A.) 72 H 3
Palmer (Antarctica) 91
Palmer Archipelago 91
Palmer Land 91
Palmerston 51 Q 10
Palmerston 52 E 4
Palmerston North 51 R 9
Palmi 19 G 4
Palmira 84 C 3
Palmyra (Pacific Ocean, U.S.A.) 52 E 2
Palmyra (Syria) 22 C 2
Palmyras Point 40 E 3
Palni 40 C 5
Palo Alto 76 B 4
Palo Santo 88 E 4
Paloemeu 85 G 3
Paloh (Indonesia) 42 C 3
Paloh (Malaysia) 42 D 3
Paloich 60 E 2
Palomar, Mount 76 C 5
Palopo 43 F 4
Palos, Cabo de 18 C 4
Pal-Pal, Gora 37 VW 3
Palpala 86 C 5
Palpetu, Tanjuna 43 G 4
Paltamo 16 J 3
Palu (Indonesia) 43 E 4
Palu (Turkey) 21 EF 3
Palwal 40 C 2
Pama 62 E 3
Pamanukan 42 C 5
Pamban Channel 40 C 6
Pamekasan 42 D 5
Pameungpeuk 42 C 5
Pamiers 18 D 3
Pamir 35 J 3
Pamlico Sound 77 L 4
Pampa 76 F 4
Pampa de Huayuri 86 A 3
Pampa de la Matanzilla 89 C 6
Pampa de las Salinas 88 C 5
Pampa del Castillo 89 C 8
Pampa del Tamarugal 86 C 5
Pampa Grande 86 D 4
Pampas (Argentina) 88–89 D 5–6
Pampas (Peru) 86 B 3
Pamplona (Colombia) 84 D 2
Pamplona (Spain) 18 C 3
Pamukan, Teluk 42 E 4
Pamukova 20 CD 2
Pamyati 36 F 4
Pan de Azúcar 88 B 4
Pan, Tierra del 18 B 3
Pan Xian 38 DE 5
Pana 63 G 6
Panagjurište 20 B 2
Panahan 42 D 4
Panaitan, Pulau 42 BC 5
Panaitolikón Óros 20 B 3
Panaji 40 B 4

Panakhaikón Óros 20 B 3
Panama 84 C 2
Panamá 84 C 2
Panama Canal 84 B 2
Panama City (FL, U.S.A.) 77 J 5
Panamá, Golfo de 84 C 2
Panamá, Istmo de 84 C 2
Panarea 19 F 4
Pančevo 20 B 2
Pančičev vrh 20 B 2
Panda (Mozambique) 67 E 4
Panda (Zaire) 64 B 4
Pandamatenga 66 D 3
Pandan 43 F 1
Pandan 43 F 1
Pandaria 40 D 3
Pandharpur 40 BC 4
Pandivere Kõrgustik 17 J 4
Pando 88 B 3
Pandokratór 20 A 3
Pandrup 17 E 4
Pandy 6 C 3
Panevežys 17 H 4
Panfilov 35 KL 2
Panga 64 D 4
Pangala 63 G 6
Pangani 65 F 5
Pangani 65 F 6
Panggoe 51 G 3
Panghkam 41 G 3
Panglang 41 G 2
Pangi 64 D 5
Pangi Range 35 JK 4
Pangkajene 43 E 4
Pangkalanbrandan 42 A 3
Pangkalanbuun 42 D 4
Pangkalpinang 42 C 4
Panglang 41 G 2
Pangnirtung 75 OP 2
Pango Aluquém 66 A 1
Pangrango, Gunung 42 C 5
Panguraran 42 A 3
Pangutaran Group 43 F 2
Panhandle 76 F 4
Pania Mutombo 64 C 6
Panié, Mont 51 H 6
Panipat 40 C 2
Panjang 42 C 5
Panjao 35 H 4
Panjbarar (Iran) 23 E 2
Panjgur 35 G 3
Panjim 40 B 4
Panjnad 35 J 5
Panjshir 35 H 3
Panjwin (Iraq) 23 D 2
Pankshin 63 F 4
P'anmunjŏm 39 J 3
Panna 40 D 3
Panopah 42 D 4
Panorama 87 F 5
Panovo 25 O 4
Panshan 39 H 2
Panshi 39 J 2
Pantanal de São Lourénço 86 E 4
Pantanal do Río Negro 86 E 4
Pantar, Pulau 43 F 5
Pantelleria 19 F 5
Pantemakassar 43 F 5
Pantiacolla, Cadena del 86 B 3
Panuco 78 C 3
Panuco, Rio 78 C 3
Panyam 63 F 4
Panzi 64 B 3
Paola 19 G 4
Paoua 64 B 3
Pap 64 E 3
Pápa 20 A 1
Papa Stour 2 D 1
Papa Westray 2 C 2
Papagayo, Golfo del 78 E 5
Papantla de Olarte 78 C 3
Papar 42 E 2
Papeete 53 F 4
Papenburg 15 E 4
Papey 16 C 3
Paphos 21 D 4
Paphos (Cyprus) 22 A 2
Papikion Óros 20 C 2
Paposo 88 B 4
Papua, Gulf of 50 DE 3
Papua New Guinea 50 E 2–3
Papun 41 G 4
Pará (Brazil) 85 GH 5
Pará → Belém 85 J 4
Parabel 25 Q 4
Parabel 25 Q 4
Paraburdoo 48 B 3
Paracatu 87 G 4
Paracel Islands 29 K 5
Paracel Islands 41 K 4
Paracuru 87 J 1
Paragould 77 H 4
Paragua 85 F 2
Paraguaçu 87 J 3
Paraguai 86 E 5
Paraguaí (Bolivia) 86 D 3

Paraguaná, Península de 84 E 1
Paraguarí 88 E 4
Paraguay 86 DE 5
Paraguay 88 E 4
Paraíba 87 J 2
Paraíba do Sul 87 H 5
Parainen 17 H 3
Paraiso, Serra do 87 F 3–4
Parakhino Poddubye 24 F 4
Parakou 62 E 4
Paramaribo 85 GH 2
Paramillo 84 C 2
Paramirim 87 H 3
Paramonga 84 C 6
Paramushir, Ostrov 37 T 5
Paraná 87 G 3
Paraná 88 E 5
Paraná (Argentina) 88 D 5
Paraná (Brazil) 87 F 5
Paraná (Goiás, Brazil) 87 G 3
Paranaguá 88 G 4
Paranaguá, Baia de 88 G 4
Paranaíba 87 F 4
Paranam 85 G 2
Paranapanema 87 F 5
Paranapiacaba, Serra do 87 G 5
Paranavai 87 F 5
Parandak (Iran) 23 F 2
Paranéstion 20 B 2
Parangaba 87 J 1
Paranhos 87 E 5
Paraoa 53 F 4
Parapetí 86 D 4
Parapol'skiy Dolina 37 V 3
Parara 43 F 4
Parati 87 H 5
Paratinga 87 H 3
Paratunka 37 T 5
Paravani, Ozero 21 F 2
Paray-le-Monial 18 D 2
Parbati 40 C 2
Parbhani 40 C 4
Parbig 25 Q 4
Parbold 5 D 3
Parc National de la Boucle De
  Baoule 62 C 3
Parc National de la Komoé 62 D 4
Parc National de la Pendjari 62 E 3
Parc National de Sinianka-Minia
  63 H 3
Parc National de Taï 62 C 4
Parc National de Wonga Wongué
  63 FG 6
Parc National de Zakouma 63 H 3
Parc National du
  Bamingui-Bangoran 64 BC 3
Parc National du Niokolo Koba
  62 B 3
Parcs Nationaux du ''W'' 62 E 3
Pardo 87 H 4
Pardubice 15 G 4
Pare Mountains 65 F 5
Parecis 86 E 3
Parecis, Serra dos 86 D 3
Pareditas 88 C 5
Pāreh (Iran) 23 E 1
Paren 37 U 3
Paren 37 U 3
Parent 75 N 6
Parepare 43 E 4
Parera 88 E 5
Párga 20 B 3
Pargas 17 H 3
Parguaza 84 E 2
Pari 21 F 2
Paria, Golfo de 85 F 1
Paria, Península de 85 F 1
Pariaguán 85 F 2
Pariaman 42 B 4
Paricatuba 85 F 4
Parichi 17 J 5
Paricutín, Volcán 78 B 4
Parigi 43 F 4
Parika 85 G 2
Parikkala 16 J 3
Parima, Sierra 85 F 3
Parinari 84 D 4
Pariñas, Punta 84 B 4
Parintins 85 G 4
Paris (France) 18 D 2
Paris (IL, U.S.A.) 77 J 4
Paris (TN, U.S.A.) 77 J 4
Paris (TX, U.S.A.) 77 G 5
Parismina 78 F 5
Parit Buntar 42 B 2
Pariti 43 F 6
Park Rapids 77 H 2
Parkano 16 H 3
Parker 76 D 5
Parkersburg 77 K 4
Parkes 49 H 5
Parkgate 3 C 4
Parkhar 35 H 3
Parkland 76 B 2
Parlakimidi 40 D 4
Parlakote 40 D 4

Parma (Italy) 19 F 3
Parma (OH, U.S.A.) 77 K 3
Parnaguá 87 H 3
Parnaíba 87 H 1
Parnaíba 87 H 1
Parnamirim 87 J 2
Parnarama 87 H 2
Parnassós Óros 20 B 3
Parnon Óros 20 B 3
Pärnu 17 H 4
Pärnu Jõgi 17 HJ 4
Parola 16 H 3
Paromay 37 Q 5
Paroo River 49 GH 4
Paropamisus 35 G 4
Páros 20 BC 3
Parpaillon 19 E 3
Parque Arqueológico 84 C 3
Parque Nacional Canaima 85 F 2
Parque Nacional da Quiçama
  66 A 1
Parque Nacional de Chaco 88 E 4
Parque Nacional de la Macarena
  84 D 3
Parque Nacional de Monte Pascoal
  87 J 4
Parque Nacional do Araguaia
  87 FG 3
Parque Nacional do Brasília 87 G 4
Parque Nacional do Chapada dos
  Veadeiros 87 G 3
Parque Nacional do Emas 87 F 4
Parque Nacional do Iguaçu 88 F 4
Parque Nacional el Tuparro 84 E 2
Parque Nacional Lanin 89 B 6
Parque Nacional Los Alerges
  89 B 6
Parque Nacional los Glaciares
  89 B 8
Parque Nacional Los Paraguas
  89 B 6
Parque Nacional Moreno 89 B 8
Parque Nacional Nahuel Huapi
  89 B 7
Parque Nacional Simón Bolivar
  84 D 2
Parral 89 B 6
Parras de la Fuente 78 B 2
Parras, Sierra de 78 B 2
Parrita 78 F 6
Parry Bay 73 V 2
Parry, Cape 73 N 1
Parry Islands 90
Parry Peninsula 73 MN 2
Parseta 15 G 4
Parshino 36 K 4
Partabpur 40 D 3
Pårtetjåkkå 16 G 2
Parthenay 18 CD 2
Partille 17 F 4
Partinico 19 F 4
Partizansk 39 K 2
Partizanske 15 G 5
Partizanskoye 36 F 4
Partney 7 E 1
Paru 85 H 4
Paru de Oeste 85 G 3
Paruro 86 B 3
Parvatipuram 40 D 4
Paryang 40 D 2
Parys 66 D 5
Pas de Calais 14 D 4
Pasadena 76 C 5
Pasado, Cabo 84 B 4
Pasaje 84 C 4
Pasangkayu 43 E 4
Pāsārgād (Iran) 23 F 3
Pasarwajo 43 F 5
Pasawng 41 G 4
Pascagoula 77 J 5
Paşcani 20 C 1
Pasekudah 40 D 6
Pashkovo 37 O 6
Pashskiy-Perevoz 24 F 3
Pashtun Zarghūn 35 G 4
Pasinler 21 F 3
Pasir Mas 42 B 2
Pasirpengarayan 42 AB 3
Pasni 35 G 5
Paso de Indios 89 C 7
Paso de los Libres 88 E 4
Paso de los Toros 88 E 5
Paso de los Vientos 79 H 3–4
Paso de Pino Hachado 89 B 6
Paso de San Francisco 88 C 4
Paso del Limay 89 BC 7
Paso Río Mayo 89 B 8
Paso Socompa 86 C 5
Pass of Brander 3 B 3
Pass of Drumochter 3 BC 3
Pass of Glen Coe 3 B 3
Pass of Killiecrankie 3 C 3
Passagem 87 H 3
Passau 15 F 5
Passero, Capo 19 G 4
Passo della Futa 19 F 3

Passo della Spluga 19 E 2
Passo della Stelvio 19 F 2
Passo dello Scalone 19 G 4
Passo di Resia 19 F 2
Passo Fundo 88 F 4
Passos 87 G 5
Pastaza 84 C 4
Pasteur 88 D 6
Pasto 84 C 3
Pasto Grande 85 F 5
Pastos Bons 87 H 2
Paštrik 20 B 2
Pasul Mestecănis 20 C 1
Pasul Predeal 20 C 1
Pasul Turnu Roşu 20 B 1
Pasuruan 42 D 5
Pasvalys 17 H 4
Pasvikelva 16 J 2
Patacamaya 86 C 4
Patagonia 89 BC 7–9
Patan (India) 40 B 3
Patan (Nepal) 40 E 2
Patani 43 G 3
Patāven (Iran) 23 F 3
Pate 65 G 5
Pate Island 65 G 5
Pategi 63 F 4
Pateley Bridge 5 E 2
Patensie 66 C 6
Paterno 19 F 4
Paterson 77 LM 3
Pathankot 40 C 1
Pathfinder Reservoir 76 E 3
Pathiu 41 G 5
Patía 84 C 3
Patiala 40 C 1
Pativilca 84 C 6
Patkaglik 35 M 3
Pátmos 20 C 3
Patna 3 B 4
Patna 40 E 2
Patnagarh 40 D 3
Patnos 21 F 3
Patomskoye Nagor'ye 36 KL 4
Patonga 64 E 4
Patos 87 J 2
Patos, Cachoeira dos 85 FG 5
Patos de Minas 87 G 4
Patos, Lagoa dos 88 F 5
Patquía 88 C 5
Pátrai 20 B 3
Patraikós Kólpos 20 B 3
Patras 20 B 3
Patricio Lynch 89 A 8
Patrington 5 E 3
Patrocínio 87 G 4
Pattani 41 H 6
Pattaya 41 H 5
Patten Escarpment 99 D 2
Pattle 41 K 4
Pattullo, Mount 72 LM 4
Patú 87 J 2
Patuakhali 41 F 3
Patuca, Rio 78 F 4
Patvinsuo 16 K 3
Pau 18 C 3
Pau d'Arco 85 J 5
Pauillac 18 C 2
Pauini 84 E 5
Pauini 84 E 5
Pauksa Taung 41 F 4
Paulatuk 73 N 2
Paulina Peak 76 B 3
Paulistana 87 H 2
Paulo Afonso 87 J 2
Paulo Afonso, Cachoeira de 87 J 2
Pauls Valley 77 G 5
Paungde 41 G 4
Pauri 40 C 1
Pausa 86 B 4
Pauto 84 D 2
Păveh (Iran) 23 E 2
Pavia 19 E 2
Păvilosta 17 H 4
Pavlikeni 20 C 2
Pavlodar 25 P 5
Pavlof Islands 72 E 5
Pavlof Volcano 72 E 4
Pavlograd 21 E 1
Pavlovka 25 O 5
Pavlovo 24 H 4
Pavlovsk 25 Q 5
Pavlovskaya 21 E 1
Pavlysh 24 F 6
Pavón 84 D 3
Pavullo nel Frignano 19 F 3
Pawahku 41 G 2
Pawan, Sungai 42 D 4
Pawut 41 G 5
Paxoí 20 AB 3
Paxson 72 H 3
Payakumbuh 42 B 4
Pay-Khoy, Khrebet 25 M 2
Payne, Baie 75 O 4
Payne, Lac 75 N 4
Paynes Find 48 B 4

Paysandú 88 E 5
Payson 76 D 4
Payturma 36 F 1
Payún, Cerro 89 C 6
Pay-Yer, Gora 25 M 2
Paz de Aripora 84 D 2
Păzanān (Iran) 23 EF 3
Pazar 21 F 2
Pazarcık 21 E 3
Pazardžik 20 B 2
Pazaryeri 20 C 3
Pazña 86 C 4
Peace Point 73 P 4
Peace River 73 O 4
Peace River 73 O 4
Peace River 73 P 4
Peacehaven 7 E 2
Peach Springs 76 D 4
Peacock Hills 73 PQ 2
Peaima Falls 85 F 2
Peak District 5 E 3
Peaked Mountain 77 N 2
Pearl 77 J 5
Pearsall 76 G 6
Pearsoll Peak 76 AB 3
Peary Land 90
Pebane 67 F 3
Pebas 84 D 4
Pebble Island 89 E 9
Peć 20 B 2
Peca 19 F 2
Pech de Bugarach 18 D 3
Pechenga 16 K 2
Pecherakh 25 M 3
Pechora 24 K 2
Pechora 24 L 2
Pechorskaya Guba 24 KL 2
Pechorskoye More 24 KL 2
Pechory 17 J 4
Pecos 76 F 5
Pecos 76 F 5
Pecos Plains 76 F 5
Pécs 20 A 1
Pededze 17 J 4
Pedernales (Ecuador) 84 B 3
Pedernales (Venezuela) 85 F 2
Pedirka 48 F 4
Pedo La 40 D 2
Pedra Lume 62 B 6
Pedras Negras 86 D 3
Pedreiras 87 GH 1
Pedriceña 78 B 2
Pedro Afonso 85 J 5
Pedro Cays 79 G 4
Pedro de Valdivia 86 BC 5
Pedro Gomes 87 F 4
Pedro Juan Caballero 86 E 5
Pedro Luro 89 D 6
Pedro R. Fernández 88 E 4
Pedroso, Sierra del 18 B 4
Peebles 3 C 4
Peel (N.W.T., Can.) 72 L 2
Peel (U.K.) 4 C 2
Peera Peera Poolanna Lake 49 F 4
Pegasus Bay 51 Q 9
Pegu 41 G 4
Pegu Yoma 41 G 3–4
Pegunungan Barisan 42 B 4
Pegunungan Charles Louis 43 J 4
Pegunungan Gauttier 43 J 4
Pegunungan Iran 42 D 3
Pegunungan Jayawijaya 43 J 4
Pegunungan Kumawa 43 H 4
Pegunungan Maoke 43 J 4
Pegunungan Muller 42 D 3
Pegunungan Schwaner 42 D 4
Pegunungan Sudirman 43 J 4
Pegunungan Tamrau 43 H 4
Pegunungan van Rees 43 J 4
Pegunungan Weyland 43 J 4
Pegysh 24 K 3
Pehuajó 89 D 6
Pei Xian 39 G 4
Peine 15 F 4
Peipus, Lake 17 J 4
Peixe (Goiás, Brazil) 87 G 3
Peixe (São Paulo, Brazil) 87 F 5
Pejantan, Pulau 42 C 3
Pekalongan 42 C 5
Pekanbaru 42 B 3
Pekin 40 C 1
Peking 39 G 2
Pekkala 16 J 2
Pekon 41 G 4
Pekorica 20 A 2
Pekul'ney, Khrebet 37 WX 2
Pekul'veyem 37 X 3
Pelabuanratu 42 C 5
Pelabuanratu, Teluk 42 C 5
Pelagie, Isole 59 H 1
Pelagonija 20 B 2
Pélagos 20 B 3
Pelaihari 42 D 4
Pelat, Mont 19 E 3
Peleaga, Virful 20 B 1
Peleduy 36 K 4

Peleliu 43 H 2
Peleng, Pulau 43 F 4
Peleng, Selat 43 F 4
Peleniya 20 C 1
Pelican 72 K 4
Pelican Narrows 73 R 4
Pelinaion Óros 20 C 3
Peliny Osipenko, Iméni 37 P 5
Pelješac 19 G 3
Pelkosenniemi 16 J 2
Pellegrini 89 D 6
Pello 16 H 2
Pelly 72 L 3
Pelly Bay 73 T 2
Pelly Bay 73 U 2
Pelly Crossing 72 K 3
Pelly Mountains 72 L 3
Peloponnese 20 B 3
Pelopónnisos 20 B 3
Peloritani, Monti 19 FG 4
Pelotas (Río Grande do Sul, Brazil)
  88 F 5
Pelotas (Santa Catarina, Brazil)
  88 F 4
Pelvoux, Massif du 19 E 3
Pelym 25 M 3
Pemalang 42 C 5
Pemangkat 42 C 3
Pemarung, Pulau 42 E 4
Pematangsiantar 42 A 3
Pemba (Mozambique) 67 G 2
Pemba (Zambia) 66 D 3
Pemba Island (Tanzania) 65 FG 6
Pemberton 48 B 5
Pembina 76 G 2
Pembroke (Ontario, Can.) 75 M 6
Pembroke (U.K.) 6 B 2
Pembroke, Cape 89 E 9
Pembroke, Cape (N.W.T., Can.)
  75 L 3
Pembuang 42 D 4
Peña, Sierra de la 18 C 3
Peñafiel 18 C 3
Penally 6 B 2
Peñaranda de Bracamonte 18 BC 3
Penarie 49 G 5
Peñarroya Pueblonuevo 18 B 4
Penarth 6 C 2
Peñas, Sierra de 18 B 4
Peñas, Golfo de 89 B 8
Pencader 6 B 2
Pend Oreille 76 C 2
Pend Oreille, Lake 76 C 2
Pendembu 62 B 4
Pender 48 C 2
Pendjari, Parc National de la
  62 E 3
Pendleton 76 C 2
Pendzhikent 35 H 3
Pene Mende 64 D 5
Penedo 87 J 3
Peng'an 38 E 4
Penge 64 D 5
Penghu Liedaoo 39 G 6
Penglai 39 H 3
Pengshui 38 E 5
Pengze 38 G 5
Penicuik 3 C 4
Penida, Pulau 42 E 5
Península Brecknock 89 B 9
Península de Azuero 84 B 2
Península de Brunswick 89 B 9
Península de Guajira 84 D 1
Península de Nicoya 78 E 6
Península de Osa 78 F 6
Península de Paraguaná 84 DE 1
Península de Paria 85 F 1
Península de Taitao 89 AB 8
Península de Yucatán → Yucatán
  Península 78 E 3–4
Península Tres Montes 89 A 8
Península Valdés 89 D 7
Péninsule de Gaspé 75 O 6
Peninsula Salentina 19 G 3
Penisola Salentina 19 G 3
Penitente, Serra do 85 J 5
Pénjamo 78 B 3
Penmaenmawr 6 C 1
Penn Hills 77 L 3
Pennan 2 C 3
Penner 40 C 5
Pennine Chain 5 DE 2–3
Pennsylvania 77 L 3
Penny Ice Cap 75 O 2
Penobscot Bay 77 N 3
Penola 49 G 6
Peñón Blanco 78 B 3
Penong 48 E 5
Penonomé 84 B 2
Penrhyn 53 E 3
Penrith 5 D 2
Penryn 6 B 3
Pensacola 77 J 5
Pensacola Mountains 91
Pensiangan 42 E 3
Pensilva 6 B 2

Pentecost 51 J 5
Penticton 73 O 6
Pentland 49 H 3
Pentland Firth 2 C 2
Pentland Hills 3 C 4
Pentrefoelas 6 C 1
Penukonda 40 C 5
Penwegon 41 G 4
Penza 24 H 5
Penzance 6 B 2
Penzhino 37 V 3
Penzhinskaya Guba 37 U 3
Penzhinskiy Khrebet 37 VW 3
Peoria 77 J 3
Pepa 64 DE 6
Pepel 62 B 4
Pequizeiro 85 J 5
Perabumulih 42 B 4
Perales, Puerto de 18 B 3
Percé 75 P 6
Perche, Collines du 18 D 2
Percival Lakes 48 C 3
Pereira 84 C 3
Pereira Barreto 87 F 5
Pereira, Cachoeira 85 G 4
Pereirinha 85 G 5
Perekop 21 D 1
Pereshchepino 24 FG 6
Pereval Akbaytal 35 J 3
Pereval Dolon 35 K 2
Pereval Kyzylart 35 J 3
Pereval Torugart 35 K 2
Pereval Yablonitse 20 BC 1
Perevolotskiy 24 K 5
Pérez 88 C 4
Pergamino 88 D 5
Pergamon 20 C 3
Perge 20 D 3
Perho 16 H 3
Péribonca 75 N 6
Peribonca, Lac 75 N 5
Pericos 76 E 6
Périgueux 18 D 2
Perijá, Sierra de 84 D 1–2
Perim Island → Barīm 61 G 6
Perito Moreno 89 B 8
Peritoró 87 H 1
Perković 19 G 3
Perlas, Laguna de 78 F 5
Perm 24 L 4
Përmeti 20 B 2
Pernambuco 87 J 2
Pernambuco → Recife 87 K 2
Pernik 20 B 2
Péronne 18 D 2
Perote 78 C 4
Perpignan 18 D 3
Perranporth 6 B 2
Perros-Guirec 18 C 2
Perry 77 K 5
Perry Island 73 R 2
Perryton 76 F 4
Perryville 72 F 4
Persembe 21 E 2
Persepolis (Iran) 23 F 3
Perseverancia 86 D 3
Persia 23 F 2
Persian Gulf 23 F 3–4
Pertek 21 E 3
Perth (Australia) 48 B 5
Perth (U.K.) 3 C 3
Perth-Andover 75 O 6
Perthus, Col de 18 D 3
Pertuis 19 E 3
Pertuis Breton 18 C 2
Pertuis d'Antioche 18 C 2
Peru 84 C 5
Peru Basin 99 E 4
Peru Current 92
Peru-Chile Trench 98 A 4–5
Perugia 19 F 3
Peruíbe 87 G 5
Perušić 19 G 3
Pervari 21 F 3
Pervomaysk (Russia, U.S.S.R.)
  20 D 1
Pervomaysk (Russia, U.S.S.R.)
  24 H 5
Pervomayskiy (Kazakhstan,
  U.S.S.R.) 25 Q 5
Pervomayskiy (Russia, U.S.S.R.)
  24 H 3
Pervoural'sk 25 L 4
Pervyy Kamen' 37 U 2
Pesaro 19 F 3
Pescadores 39 G 6
Pescara 19 F 3
Pescara 19 F 3
Peschanyy, Mys 34 E 2
Peschanyy, Ostrov 36 L 1
Peschici 19 G 3
Pescoraro 19 G 4
Peshawar 35 J 4
Peshchanopskoye 21 F 1
Peshkopi 20 B 2
Peski 35 G 3

Peski Karakum 34 E 1
Peski Karakumy 34–35 FG 3
Peski Karynzharyk 34 E 2
Peski Kyzylkum 35 GH 2
Peski Muyunkum 35 J 2
Peski Priaral'skiye Karakumy
  35 G 1
Peski Sary Ishikotrau 25 P 6
Peso da Régua 18 B 3
Pesochny 17 K 3
Pesqueira 87 J 2
Pessac 18 C 3
Pestovo 24 G 4
Pestravka 24 J 5
Pestraya Dresva 37 T 3
Petacalco, Bahia de 78 B 4
Petäjävesi 16 J 3
Petare 84 E 1
Petatlán 78 B 4
Petén 78 D 4
Petenwell Lake 77 J 3
Peter I Island 91
Peter Lake 73 T 3
Peter Pond Lake 73 Q 4
Peterborough (Ontario, Can.)
  75 M 7
Peterborough (South Australia)
  49 F 5
Peterborough (U.K.) 7 D 1
Peterhead 2 D 3
Peterlee 5 E 2
Petermann Ranges 48 D 4
Peteroa 89 BC 6
Petersburg (AK, U.S.A.) 72 L 4
Petersburg (VA, U.S.A.) 77 L 4
Petersfield 7 D 2
Peterstow 6 C 3
Petilia Policastro 19 G 4
Petites Pyrénées 18 D 3
Petit-Mécatina, Rivière du 75 PQ 5
Petitot 73 N 4
Petitsikapau Lake 75 O 5
Petkula 16 J 2
Petlad 40 B 3
Peto 78 E 3
Petorca 88 B 5
Petra (Jordan) 22 B 3
Petra Azul 87 H 4
Petra Velikogo, Zaliv 39 K 2
Petrel 91
Petrela 20 A 2
Petrified Forest National Park
  89 C 8
Petrikov 17 J 5
Petrikovka 21 DE 1
Petrila 20 B 1
Petrinja 19 G 2
Petrodvorets 17 J 4
Petrolândia 87 J 2
Petrolina 87 H 2
Petronell 19 G 2
Petropavlovka 36 J 5
Petropavlovka 37 N 5
Petropavlovsk 25 NO 5
Petropavlovsk-Kamchatskiy
  37 T 5
Petropavlovskoye 25 QR 5
Petropavlovskoye 36 J 4
Petropavelovka 25 Q 6
Petrópolis 87 H 5
Petroşeni 20 B 1
Petroso 19 F 3
Petrova Gora 19 G 2
Petrovac 20 A 2
Petrovsk 24 J 5
Petrovskaya 21 E 1
Petrovskiy Yam 24 G 3
Petrovsk-Zabaykal'skiy 36 J 5
Petrozavodsk 24 FG 3
Petsamo 16 K 2
Petukhovo 25 N 4
Petworth 7 D 2
Peuetsagu, Gunung 42 A 3
Peureulak 42 A 3
Pevek 90
Pevensey 7 E 2
Peza 24 J 2
Pezas 25 R 5
Pézenas 18 D 3
Pfaffenhofen 15 F 5
Pforzheim 15 E 5
Phalaborwa 67 E 4
Phalodi 40 B 2
Phaltan 40 B 4
Phan Rang 41 J 5
Phan Thiet 41 J 5
Phangnga 41 G 6
Phanom Dang Raek 41 H 5
Phatthalung 41 H 6
Phenix City 77 J 5
Phet Buri 41 G 5
Phetchabun 41 H 4
Phiafay 41 J 5
Phichit 41 H 4

Philadelphia 77 M 4
Philae 60 E 4
Philip Smith Mountains 72 H 2
Philippeville → Skikda 59 G 1
Philippi 20 B 2
Philippi, Lake 49 F 3
Philippine Basin 99 C 3
Philippines 43 FG 1
Philipstown 66 C 6
Phillack 6 B 2
Phillipsburg 76 G 4
Phitsanulok 41 H 4
Phnom Aural 41 H 5
Phnom Penh 41 H 5
Phoenix (AZ, U.S.A.) 76 D 5
Phoenix Islands 52 D 3
Phong Nha 41 J 4
Phong Saly 41 H 3
Phrao 41 G 4
Phu Dien Chau 41 J 4
Phu Ly 41 J 3
Phu My 41 J 5
Phu Set 41 J 4
Phu Tho 41 J 3
Phu Vinh 41 J 6
Phuket 41 G 6
Phulbani 40 D 3
Phum Khvao 41 HJ 5
Phum Siem 41 H 5
Phumi Kroy 41 J 5
Phung Hiep 41 J 6
Phuoc Le 41 J 5
Piacá 85 J 5
Piacenza 19 EF 2–3
Piana Mwanga 64 D 6
Pianguan 38 F 3
Pianosa 19 F 3
Pianosa 19 G 3
Piara Açu 85 H 5
Piatra Neamţ 20 C 1
Piauí 87 H 2
Piave 19 F 2
Pibor Post 64 E 3
Pic Baumann 62 E 4
Pic Boby 67 H 4
Pic de la Selle 79 H 4
Pic de Macaya 79 H 4
Pic d'Estats 18 D 3
Pic Tousside 63 H 1
Pica 86 C 5
Picacho del Centinela 78 B 2
Picardie 18 D 2
Pichanal 86 D 5
Pichilemu 89 B 5
Pichilingue 76 DE 7
Pichimá 84 C 3
Pickering 5 E 2
Pickle Lake 74 J 5
Pickwick Lake 77 J 4
Pico 58 A 1
Pico Aitana 18 C 4
Pico Bolívar 84 D 2
Pico Bonito 78 E 4
Pico Colorado 88 C 4
Pico Cristóbal Colón 84 D 1
Pico da Neblina 84 E 3
Pico das Agulhas Negras 87 H 5
Pico de Aneto 18 D 3
Pico de Aroche 18 B 4
Pico de Itambé 87 H 4
Pico de Santa Isabel 63 F 5
Pico de Teide 58 B 3
Pico de Tio 62 C 4
Pico de Tomé 63 F 5
Pico Rondón 85 F 3
Pico San Juan 79 F 3
Pico Tamacuarí 84 E 3
Pico Truncado 89 C 8
Picos 87 H 2
Picos de Europa 18 C 3
Picota 84 C 5
Picton, Isla 89 C 10
Pictou 75 P 6
Picún Leufú 89 C 6
Pidurutalagala 40 D 6
Piedecuesta 84 D 2
Piedmont (MO, U.S.A.) 77 H 4
Piedra, Cerro 89 B 6
Piedra Sola 88 E 5
Piedrabuena 18 C 4
Piedrahita 18 C 3
Piedras Negras 78 B 2
Pieksämäki 16 J 3
Pielavesi 16 J 3
Pielinen 16 J 3
Pierowall 2 C 2
Pierre 76 FG 3
Pierrelatte 19 D 3
Piesapa 43 J 4
Pieskehaure 16 G 2
Piešt'any 15 G 5
Piet Retief 67 E 5
Pietarsaari 16 H 3
Pietermaritzburg 66 DE 5
Pietersburg 66 D 4
Pietrosu, Virful 20 BC 1

Pietroşul, Virful 20 BC 1
Pigawasi 64 E 5
Pigeon Hole 48 E 2
Pigué 89 D 6
Pihlajavesi 16 J 3
Pihtipudas 16 J 3
Pik Aborigen 37 R 3
Pik Grandioznyy 36 G 5
Pik Karla Marksa 35 J 3
Pik Kommunizma 35 J 3
Pik Lenina 35 J 3
Pik Pobedy 35 KL 2
Pik Revolyutsii 35 J 3
Pikangikum 74 J 5
Pikelot 52 A 2
Pikes Peak 76 E 4
Piketberg 66 B 6
Pikhtovka 25 Q 4
Pikounda 63 H 5
Pila (Argentina) 89 E 6
Piła (Poland) 15 G 4
Pila, Sierra de la 18 C 4
Pilão Arcado 87 H 3
Pilar 88 E 4
Pilar (Alagoas, Brazil) 87 J 2
Pilar (Argentina) 88 D 5
Pilas Group 43 F 2
Pilatus 19 E 2
Pilcaniyeu 89 BC 7
Pilcomayo 86 DE 5
Pilica 15 H 4
Pilion Óros 20 B 3
Pilis 20 A 1
Piloncilo Mountains 76 E 5
Pilos 20 B 3
Pilot Peak 76 D 3
Pilot Rock 76 C 2
Pil'tun 37 Q 5
Pil'tun, Zaliv 37 Q 5
Pim 25 O 3
Pimenta Bueno 86 D 3
Pimenta, Cachoeira do 85 F 3
Pimental 85 G 4
Pimentel (Peru) 84 B 5
Pinang, Pulau 42 B 2
Pínar del Rio 79 F 3
Pinarbaşi 21 E 3
Pinarello 19 E 3
Pınarhisar 20 C 2
Piñas 88 C 5
Pincher Creek 73 P 6
Pinchincha 84 C 3
Pinçon, Mont 18 C 2
Pindaíba 87 F 3
Pindaré 87 G 1
Pindaré Mirim 87 G 1
Pindhos Óros 20 B 2–3
Pindi Gheb 35 J 4
Pindobal 85 J 4
Pindorama 87 G 3
Pine Bluff 77 H 5
Pine Bluffs 76 F 3
Pine Creek 48 E 1
Pine Falls 73 S 5
Pine Island Bay 91
Pine Pass 73 N 4
Pine Point 73 P 3
Pine Ridge 76 F 3
Pinega 24 H 3
Pinega 24 J 3
Pinerolo 19 E 3
Pinetown 67 E 5
Ping'anyi 38 D 3
Pingbian 38 D 5
Pingchang 38 E 4
Pingdingshan 38 F 4
Pingdu 39 H 3
Pingelap 52 B 2
Pingelly 48 B 5
Pingguo 38 E 6
Pinghu 39 H 4
Pingjiang 38 F 5
Pingliang 38 E 3
Pinglu 38 F 4
Pingluo 38 E 3
Pingnan 38 F 6
Pingquan 39 G 2
Pingshan 38 F 3
Pingtan 39 GH 5
Pingtang 38 E 6
Pingtung 39 H 6
Pingwu 38 D 4
Pingxiang 38 E 6
Pingxiang 38 F 5
Pingyang 39 H 5
Pingyao 38 F 3
Pingyuan 39 G 3
Pinheiro 85 J 4
Pinheiro Machado 88 F 5
Pini, Pulau 42 A 3
Piníos 20 B 3
Pinjang 43 F 3
Pink Mountain 73 N 4

Pinlebu 41 G 3
Pinnaroo 49 G 6
Pinnes, Akra 20 B 2
Pino Hachado, Paso de 89 B 6
Pinos, Mount 76 C 4–5
Pinos-Puente 18 C 4
Pinrang 43 E 4
Pinsk 17 J 5
Pinta, 84 B 6
Pintados 86 BC 5
Pinto 88 D 4
Pinyug 24 J 3
Pio 51 H 4
Pio IX 87 H 2
Piombino 19 F 3
Pioner 25 R 4
Pionki 15 H 4
Piorini, Lago 85 F 4
Piotrków Trybunalski 15 G 4
Pipar 40 B 2
Pipestone 77 G 3
Pipmouacan, Réservoir 75 N 6
Piquiá 84 E 4
Piquiri 87 F 5
Pir Panjal Range 35 J 4
Pīr Tāj (Iran) 23 E 2
Pira 62 E 4
Piracicaba 87 G 5
Piracuruca 87 H 1
Piraeus → Piraiévs 20 B 3
Piraiévs 20 B 3
Pirámide 89 B 8
Pirámide El Triunfo 88 D 4
Piran 19 F 2
Piranhas 87 F 4
Piranhas 87 J 2
Pirapemas 87 H 1
Pirapora 87 H 4
Pires do Río 87 G 4
Pirgos 20 B 3
Piriá 85 H 4
Pirimapuan 43 J 5
Pirin 20 B 2
Piripiri 87 H 1
Pirmasens 15 E 5
Pirna 15 F 4
Pirot 20 B 2
Pirovano 89 D 6
Piru 43 G 4
Piryatin 24 F 5
Pisa 19 F 3
Pisac 86 B 3
Pisagua 86 B 4
Pisco 86 A 3
Písek 15 F 5
Pishan 35 K 3
Pishin 35 H 4
Pīshvā (Iran) 23 F 2
Piso Firme 86 D 3
Pissila 62 D 3
Pisté 78 E 3
Pisticci 19 G 3
Pistoia 19 F 3
Pisuerga 18 C 3
Pita 62 B 3
Pitaga 75 O 5
Pitalito 84 C 3
Piteå 16 H 2
Piteälven 16 H 2
Piterka 24 J 5
Piteşti 20 B 2
Pithapuram 40 D 4
Pithara 48 B 5
Pithiviers 18 D 2
Pitibhit 40 C 2
Pitkul' 16 K 2
Pitkyaranta 16 K 3
Pitlochry 3 C 3
Pitlyar 25 N 2
Pitomača 19 G 2
Pitrufquén 89 B 6
Pitsunda, Mys 21 F 2
Pitt 51 S 9
Pitt Island (Br. Col., Can.) 72 L 5
Pittenween 3 C 3
Pittsburg (KS, U.S.A.) 77 H 4
Pittsburgh (PA, U.S.A.) 77 L 3
Pittsfield (IL, U.S.A.) 77 H 4
Pittsfield (MA, U.S.A.) 77 M 3
Pituri River 49 F 3
Piuí 87 G 5
Pium 87 G 3
Piura 84 B 5
Pivan' 37 P 5
Pizacoma 86 C 4
Pizzo Calabro 19 G 4
Placentia 75 R 6
Placentia Bay 75 R 6
Placer 43 F 1
Placetas 79 G 3
Plaine de Garar 63 J 3
Plaine des Flandres 18 D 1
Plaine du Forez 18 D 2
Plaines et Seuil du Poitou 18 D 2

Plainview 76 F 5
Plake 20 B 2
Plakhino 25 R 2
Plampang 42 E 5
Planalto 87 H 3
Planalto Central 87 G 4
Planalto da Borborema 87 J 2
Planalto de Angónia 67 E 2
Planalto de Chimoio 67 E 3
Planalto de Lichinga 67 F 2
Planalto de Marávia 67 E 2
Planalto do Brasil 87 H 4
Planalto do Mato Grosso
  86–87 EF 3–4
Planalto Maracanaquará 85 H 3–4
Planet Deep 51 F 3
Planeta Rica 84 C 2
Planicie de la Loma Negra 89 C 6
Plasencia 18 B 3
Plast 25 M 5
Plastun 39 L 2
Plastunka 21 E 2
Platanal 85 F 3
Plate, River 89 EF 6
Plateau de Basso 63 J 2
Plateau de Haute-Saône 19 E 2
Plateau de l'Androna 67 H 3
Plateau de Langres 19 E 2
Plateau de Millevaches 18 D 2
Plateau des Achikouya 63 GH 6
Plateau du Bemaraha 67 GH 3
Plateau du Djado 63 G 1
Plateau du Tademaït 59 F 3
Plateau du Tchigai 63 G 1
Plateau Laurentien 75 NQ 5
Plateau of Tibet 48 DE 1
Plateaux 63 H 6
Plateaux de la Marche 18 D 2
Plati 20 B 2
Plato 84 D 2
Plato Syverma 36 G 3
Plato Ustyurt 34 F 2
Plato Yagtali 36 G 2
Platte 65 K 6
Platte 76 F 3
Platterville 77 H 3
Plattsburg 77 M 3
Plattsmouth 77 G 3
Plau 15 F 4
Plauen 15 F 4
Plaviņas 17 J 4
Plavsk 24 G 5
Playa Azul 78 B 4
Playas 84 B 4
Playgreen Lake 73 S 5
Playitas 84 D 2
Plaza Huincul 89 C 6
Pleasanton 76 G 6
Pleiku 41 J 5
Plentywood 76 EF 2
Plesetsk 24 H 3
Pleshchenitsy 17 J 5
Pleşu, Vîrful 20 B 1
Pleszew 15 G 4
Plétipi, Lac 75 N 5
Pleven 20 B 2
Plibo 62 C 5
Plitvice 19 G 3
Pljevlja 20 A 2
Ploča, Rt 19 G 3
Ploče 19 G 3
Płock 15 GH 4
Ploiești 20 C 2
Plomárion 20 C 3
Plomb du Cantal 18 D 2
Plouguerneau 18 BC 2
Plovdiv 20 BC 2
Pluckley 7 E 2
Plumpton 5 D 2
Plumridge Lake 48 D 4
Plumtree 66 D 4
Plunge 17 H 4
Plymouth (Montserrat) 79 K 4
Plymouth (U.K.) 6 B 2
Plymouth Sound 6 B 2
Plyussa 17 J 4
Plyussa 17 J 4
Plzeň 15 F 5
Plzeňská Pahorkatina 15 F 5
Pô (Burkina) 62 D 3
Po (Italy) 19 F 3
Pobè (Benin) 62 E 4
Pobé (Burkina) 62 D 3
Pobeda, Gora 37 R 2
Pobedino 37 Q 6
Pobedy, Pik 35 KL 2
Pobrežhiye 20 C 2
Pocatello 76 D 3
Pochala 64 E 3
Pochinok 24 F 5
Pochtovaya 37 R 3
Pocklington Reef 51 G 4
Poços 87 H 3
Pocoma 86 B 4
Poconé 86 E 4
Pocono Mountains 77 M 3

Poços de Caldas 87 G 5
Podgornoye 25 Q 4
Podgornyy 37 R 6
Podkagernoye 37 U 3
Podkamennaya Tungusku 36 FG 3
Podlesnoye 24 J 5
Podlužje 20 B 2
Podol'sk 24 G 4
Podor 62 B 2
Podosinovets 24 J 3
Podporozh'ye 24 FG 3
Podravska Slatina 19 G 2
Podresovo 25 N 4
Podtësovo 36 F 4
Pod'yelanka 36 H 4
Podyuga 24 H 3
Pofadder 66 B 5
Poggibonsi 19 F 3
Pogibi 37 Q 5
Pogórze Karpackie 15 H 5
Pogoso 64 B 6
Pogradeci 20 B 2
Pogranichnoye 37 Q 5
P'ohang 39 J 3
Pohjanmaa 16 J 3
Poi 41 F 2
Poiana Mare 20 B 2
Poie 64 C 5
Poinsett, Cape 91
Point Arena 76 B 4
Point Baker 72 L 4
Point Barrow 72 FG 1
Point Calimere 40 C 5
Point Cloates 48 A 3
Point Conception 76 B 5
Point Culver 48 CD 5
Point D'Entrecasteaux 48 AB 5
Point Hope 72 D 2
Point Hope 72 D 2
Point Kadami 64 E 4
Point Lake 73 P 2
Point Lay 72 E 2
Point of Ayre 4 C 2
Point of Stoer 2 B 2
Point Pleasant 77 M 4
Point Stuart 48 E 1
Pointe aux E'cueils 75 M 4
Pointe de Barfleur 18 C 2
Pointe de Grave 18 C 2
Pointe de la Coubre 18 C 2
Pointe de l'Est 75 P 6
Pointe de Penmarch 18 BC 2
Pointe de Saint-Gildas 18 C 2
Pointe de Saint-Mathieu 18 BC 2
Pointe des Monts 75 O 6
Pointe du Croisic 18 C 2
Pointe du Raz 18 BC 2
Pointe Louis-XIV 75 L 5
Pointe Noire 63 G 6
Pointe-à-Pitre 79 K 4
Poissonnier Point 48 B 2
Poitiers 18 D 2
Poitou 18 CD 2
Poitou, Plaines et seeuil du 18 D 2
Poivre Islands 65 J 6
Pojeierze Pomorskie 15 G 4
Pojezierze Mazurskie 15 H 4
Pokaran 40 B 2
Pokhara 40 D 2
Pokhodsk 37 TU 2
Pokhvistnevo 24 K 5
Poko 64 D 4
Pokontopugol 25 Q 3
Pokrovsk 37 N 3
Pokrovskoye 21 E 1
Pola de Siero 18 B 3
Poland 15 G 4
Polatlı 21 D 3
Polcura 89 B 6
Pol-e Safid (Iran) 23 F 1
Polegate 7 E 2
Polei Monu 41 J 5
Polesie Lubelskie 15 H 4
Polessk 17 H 5
Polesskoye 17 J 5
Polesworth 7 D 1
Polesye 17 J 5
Polevskoy 25 M 4
Polewali 43 E 4
Polgovskoye 25 N 4
Pōlgyo 39 J 4
Poli 63 G 4
Policastro, Golfo di 19 G 4
Policoro 19 G 3
Poligus 36 F 3
Polillo Islands 43 J 2
Polillo Strait 43 J 1
Pólis 21 D 3
Pólis (Cyprus) 22 A 2
Polist' 17 K 4
Polistena 19 G 4
Poliyiros 20 B 2
Pollachi 40 C 5
Pollensa 18 D 4

Polnovat 25 N 3
Pologi 21 E 1
Polonio, Cabo 88 F 5
Polonnaruwa 40 D 6
Polonnoye 17 J 5
Polotsk 17 J 4
Polousnyy, Kryazh 37 PQ 2
Polovniki 24 K 3
Polperro 6 B 2
Polska 15 G 4
Polson 76 D 2
Poltava 24 F 6
Poltavka 25 O 5
Põltsamaa 17 J 4
Polunochnoye 25 MN 3
Poluostrov Buzachi 34 E 1–2
Poluostrov Govena 37 V 4
Poluostrov Gusinaya Zemlya
  24 JK 1
Poluostrov Kamchatka 37 S 4–5
Poluostrov Kanin 24 HJ 2
Poluostrov Karchyk 37 V 2
Poluostrov Kol'skiy 24 G 2
Poluostrov Koni 37 S 4
Poluostrov Mamonta 36 C 1
Poluostrov Mangyshlak 34 E 2
Poluostrov Pyagina 37 S 4
Poluostrov Rybachiy 16 K 2
Poluostrov Shirokostan 37 PQ 1
Poluostrov Shmidta 37 Q 5
Poluostrov Taygonos 37 U 3
Poluostrov Taymyr 36 FH 1
Poluostrov Yamal 25 NO 1
Polür (Iran) 23 F 2
Polür (Iran) 23 F 2
Poluy 25 N 2
Polvijärvi 16 J 3
Polwarth 3 C 4
Pol'yanovo 25 N 3
Polyarnik 72 B 2
Polyarnyy (Kamchatka, U.S.S.R.)
  37 R 1
Polyarnyy (Kola Pen., U.S.S.R.)
  16 K 2
Polyarnyy Ural 25 MN 2
Polynesia 53 EG 2–4
Poman 88 C 4
Pombal (Bahía, Brazil) 87 J 3
Pombal (Paraíba, Brazil) 87 J 2
Pombal (Portugal) 18 B 4
Pomerania 15 FG 4
Pomeroy 4 L 3
Pomio 52 B 3
Pommersche Bucht 15 F 4
Pomona 76 C 5
Pomorie 20 C 2
Pomoshnaya 20 D 1
Pomozdino 24 K 3
Pompei 19 F 3
Pompeyevka 37 O 6
Ponape 52 B 2
Ponca City 77 G 4
Ponce 79 J 4
Pondicherry 40 CD 5
Ponente, Rivera di 19 E 3
Ponérihouen 51 J 6
Ponferrada 18 B 3
Pongkolaero 43 F 5
Pongo 64 D 3
Pongo Manserichi 84 C 4
Pongola 67 E 5
Ponnani 40 C 5
Ponnyadaung Range 41 F 3
Ponomarevka 24 KL 5
Ponoy 24 G 2
Ponoy 24 H 2
Pons (France) 18 C 2
Pons (Spain) 18 D 3
Pont de Suert 18 D 3
Ponta da Baleia 87 J 4
Ponta das Salinas 66 A 2
Ponta de Mutá 87 J 3
Ponta Delgada 58 A 1
Ponta do Manguinho 87 J 3
Ponta do Padrão 66 A 1
Ponta Grossa 88 F 4
Ponta Porã 86–87 EF 5
Pontant 89 D 6
Pontarddulais 6 C 2
Pontarlier 19 E 2
Pontassieve 19 F 3
Pont-Audemer 18 D 2
Pontchartrain, Lake 77 H 5
Pontchartrain, Lake 77 HJ 5
Pontchâteau 18 C 2
Ponte de Pedra 86 E 3
Ponte do Lima 18 B 3
Ponte Nova 87 H 5
Pontefract 5 E 3
Ponteland 5 E 2
Ponterwyd 6 C 1
Pontes-e-Lacerda 86 E 4
Pontevedra 18 B 3
Pontiac (IL, U.S.A.) 77 J 3
Pontianak 42 C 4
Pontine Mountains 21 F 2

Pont-l'Abbé 18 C 2
Pontremoli 19 E 3
Pontrilas 6 C 3
Pontsticill 6 C 3
Pontypool 6 C 2
Pontypridd 6 C 2
Ponza 19 F 3
Ponzari 24 H 5
Ponziane, Isole 19 F 3
Poochera 48 E 5
Pool 63 H 6
Pool Maleb 64 B 5
Pool ó Muckhart 3 C 3
Poole 7 C 2
Poona 40 B 4
Poopó 86 C 4
Poopó, Lago de 86 C 4
Poorman 72 F 3
Popa Taung 41 G 3
Popacateptl, Volcan 78 C 4
Popar Hill 74 J 5
Popayán 84 C 3
Poperechnoye 36 K 5
Popigay 36 J 1
Popigay 36 K 1
Poplar Bluff 77 H 4
Popokabaka 64 B 6
Popondetta 50 E 3
Popovo 20 C 2
Poprad 15 H 5
Poptún 78 E 4
Poquis 86 C 5
Porahat 40 E 3
Porangatu 87 G 3
Porbandar 40 A 3
Porco 86 C 4
Porcuna 18 C 4
Porcupine 72 J 2
Porcupine Plain 72 K 2
Pordenone 19 F 2
Poretta 19 E 3
Pórfido, Punta 89 D 7
Pori 16 H 3
Porirua 51 R 9
Porjus 16 H 2
Porkhov 17 J 4
Porkkala 17 H 4
Porlamar 85 F 1
Porlock 6 C 3
Pornic 18 C 2
Porog 24 G 3
Porog 24 L 3
Porog Bol'shoy 36 H 1
Poronaysk 37 Q 6
Porosozero 16 K 3
Porpoise Bay 91
Porrentruy 19 E 2
Porsangen 16 J 1
Porsanger Plain 16 J 1
Porsangerhalvöya 16 HJ 1
Porsgrunn 17 EF 4
Porsuk 20 D 3
Porsuk Barajı 20 D 3
Port Alberni 73 N 6
Port Alfred 66 D 6
Port Alice 73 M 5
Port Angeles 76 B 2
Port Antonio 79 G 4
Port Arthur (Tasmania, Austr.)
  50 L 9
Port Arthur (TX, U.S.A.) 77 H 6
Port Arthur → Lüshun 39 H 3
Port Askaig 3 A 4
Port au Prince 79 H 4
Port Augusta 49 F 5
Port Blair 41 F 5
Port Blandford 75 R 6
Port Burwell 75 P 3
Port Chalmers 51 Q 10
Port Charlotte 77 K 6
Port Darwin (Falkland Is., U.K.)
  89 E 9
Port Darwin (N.T., Austr.) 48 E 1
Port Davey 50 L 9
Port Douglas 49 H 2
Port Edward 66 DE 6
Port Elgin 75 L 7
Port Elizabeth 66 D 6
Port Ellen 3 A 4
Port Erin 4 C 2
Port Étienne → Nouadhibou
  58 B 4
Port Fairy 49 G 6
Port Gentil 63 F 6
Port Glasgow 3 B 4
Port Graham 72 G 4
Port Harcourt 63 F 5
Port Hardy 73 M 5
Port Hawkesbury 75 P 6
Port Hedland 48 B 3
Port Heiden 72 F 4
Port Hope Simpson 75 QR 5
Port Huron 77 K 3
Port Isaac 6 B 2
Port Jackson 51 R 8
Port Katon 21 E 1
Port Keats 48 D 1

Port Láirge 14 B 4
Port Laoise 4 B 3
Port Lavaca 77 G 6
Port Lincoln 49 F 5
Port Logan 3 B 4
Port Loko 62 B 4
Port Macquarie 49 J 5
Port Menier 75 P 6
Port Moller 72 E 4
Port Moresby 50 E 3
Port Nelson 73 T 4
Port Nelson 74 J 4
Port Nelson 74 J 4
Port Nolloth 66 B 5
Port of Ness 2 A 2
Port of Spain 85 F 1
Port Ontario 77 L 3
Port Pegasus 50 P 10
Port Phillip Bay 49 GH 6
Port Pirie 49 F 5
Port Radium 71
Port Radium 73 O 2
Port Said (Egypt) 22 A 3
Port Saint Joe 77 J 6
Port Saint Johns 66 DE 6
Port Saunders 75 Q 5
Port Shepstone 66 DE 6
Port Simpson 72 LM 5
Port Sudan → Bür Südan 60 F 5
Port Sulphur 77 J 6
Port Talbot 6 C 2
Port Victoria 64 E 4–5
Port Wakefield 49 F 5
Port William 3 B 4
Portachuelo 86 D 4
Portadown 4 B 2
Portaferry 4 C 2
Portage la-Prairie 73 S 5
Portalegre 18 B 4
Portales 76 F 5
Portarlington 4 B 3
Portavogie 4 C 2
Port-Bergé-Vao Vao 67 H 3
Port-Bou 18 D 3
Port-Cartier 75 O 5
Porteira 85 G 4
Portel 18 B 4
Portel 85 H 4
Porterville 76 C 4
Portes d'Enfer 64 D 6
Port-Eynon 6 B 2
Porth 6 C 3
Porthcawl 6 C 2
Porthleven 6 B 2
Portile de Fier 20 B 2
Portimão 18 B 4
Portishead 6 C 2
Portița 20 C 2
Portland (ME, U.S.A.) 77 N 3
Portland (N.S.W., Austr.) 49 H 5
Portland (OR, U.S.A.) 76 B 2
Portland (Victoria, Austr.) 49 G 6
Portland Bill 6 C 2
Portland, Cape 50 L 9
Port-la-Nouvelle 18 D 3
Port-Louis (Guadeloupe) 79 K 4
Port-Louis (Mauritius) 67 K 6
Portmarnock 4 B 3
Portnaguran 2 A 2
Portnahaven 3 A 4
Portnockie 2 C 3
Port-Nouveau-Québec 75 O 4
Portnyagino, Ozero 36 HJ 1
Pôrto (Brazil) 87 H 1
Porto (Corse, France) 19 E 3
Porto (Portugal) 18 B 3
Pôrto Acre 84 E 5
Pôrto Alegre 63 F 5–6
Pôrto Alegre 85 H 4
Pôrto Alegre (Amazonas, Brazil)
  84 E 5
Pôrto Alegre (Mato Grosso do Sul,
  Brazil) 87 F 1
Pôrto Alegre (Río Grande do Sul,
  Brazil) 88 FG 5
Porto Amboim 66 A 2
Pôrto Artur 87 F 3
Porto Azzurro 19 F 3
Pôrto Barra 87 F 5
Pôrto Camargo 87 F 5
Porto Cervo 19 E 3
Pôrto Conceição 86 E 4
Pôrto da Barca 85 H 4–5
Pôrto de Moz 85 H 4
Pôrto de Pedras 87 J 2
Pôrto dos Gauchos 86 E 3
Pôrto dos Meinacos 87 F 3
Porto Empedocle 19 F 4
Pôrto Esperança 86 E 4
Pôrto Esperidião 86 E 4
Pôrto Grande 85 H 3
Pôrto Jofre 86 E 4
Pôrto Lucena 88 EF 4
Pôrto Mendes 87 F 5
Pôrto Murtinho 86 E 5
Pôrto Nacional 87 G 3

Porto Novo (Benin) 62 E 4
Porto Novo (India) 40 CD 5
Pôrto Santana 85 H 3
Pôrto Santo 58 B 2
Porto Santo Stefano 19 F 3
Pôrto São José 87 F 5
Pôrto Seguro 87 J 4
Porto Tolle 19 F 3
Porto Torres 19 E 3
Pôrto União 88 F 4
Pôrto Valter 84 D 5
Pôrto Velho 85 F 5
Portobello (Spain) 18 B 3
Portobelo (Panamá) 84 C 2
Portoferraio 19 F 3
Portogruaro 19 F 2
Pörtom 16 H 3
Porto-Vecchio 19 E 3
Portoviejo 84 BC 4
Portpatrick 4 C 2
Portraine 4 B 3
Portreath 6 B 2
Portree 2 A 3
Portrush 4 B 2
Portsalon 4 B 2
Portsmouth (N.H., U.S.A.) 77 M 3
Portsmouth (OH, U.S.A.) 77 K 4
Portsmouth (U.K.) 7 D 2
Portsmouth (VA, U.S.A.) 77 L 4
Portsoy 2 C 3
Portstewart 4 B 2
Porttipahdan tekojärvi 16 J 2
Portugal 18 B 3
Portugalete 18 C 3
Porvenir 89 BC 9
Porvoo 17 J 3
Pos Poluy 25 N 2
Posadas 88 E 4
Poschiavo 19 F 2
Posht-e Badam (Iran) 23 G 2
Posio 16 J 2
Positos 86 D 5
Poso 43 F 4
Posof 21 F 2
Pospelikha 25 Q 5
Posse 87 G 3
Possel 64 B 3
Possesion 66 AB 5
Post Bobonazo 84 C 4
Postavy 17 J 4
Poste Maurice Cortier 59 F 4
Poste Weygand 58 EF 4
Poste-de-la-Baleine 75 M 4
Postmasburg 66 C 5
Pôsto Alto Manissauá 87 F 3
Posto Cunambo 84 C 4
Postojna 19 F 2
Postville 75 Q 5
Potapovo 25 R 2
Potchefstroom 66 D 5
Potenza 19 G 3
Potes 18 C 3
Potgietersrus 66 D 4
Potholes Reservoir 76 C 2
Poti (Brazil) 87 H 2
Poti (Gruziya, U.S.S.R.) 21 F 2
Potiskum 63 G 3
Potnarhvin 51 J 5
Potomac River 77 L 4
Potosi (Bolivia) 86 C 4
Potrerillos 88 C 4
Potsdam 15 F 4
Potters Bar 7 D 2
Pottstown 77 L 3
Pou Bia 41 H 4
Pou Loi 41 H 3
Pou Miang 41 H 4
Pou San 41 H 4
Poulaphouca Reservoir 4 B 3
Pouso Alegre (Mato Grosso, Brazil) 86 E 3
Pouso Alegre (Minas Gerais, Brazil) 87 G 5
Povenets 24 F 3
Povlen 20 A 2
Póvoa de Varzim 18 B 3
Povungnituk 75 M 3
Powassan 75 M 6
Powder River 76 E 2
Powell Creek 48 E 2
Powell, Lake 76 D 4
Powell River 73 N 6
Powys 6 C 1
Poxoreu 87 F 4
Poya 51 J 6
Poyarkovo 37 N 6
Poyntz Pass 4 B 2
Poza Rica de Hidalgo 78 C 3
Pozantı 21 DE 3
Požarevac 20 B 2
Pozdeyevka 37 N 5
Pozega 20 AB 2
Pozharskoye 39 K 1
Poznań 15 G 4
Pozo Almonte 86 C 5
Pozo del Molle 88 D 5

Pozo del Tigre 86 D 5
Pozzuoli 19 F 3
Prabuty 15 G 4
Prachuap Khiri Khan 41 GH 5
Praděd 15 G 4
Pradera 84 C 3
Prades 18 D 3
Prado 87 J 4
Prague 15 FG 4
Praha → Prague 15 FG 4
Praia 62 B 7
Praia Albandão 88 F 5
Praia Azul 66 A 3
Prainha 85 F 5
Prainha 85 H 4
Prairie du Chien 77 H 3
Prakhon Chai 41 H 5
Prapat 42 A 3
Pratapgarh 40 B 3
Prato 19 F 3
Pratt 76 G 4
Praya 42 E 5
Prechistoye 24 F 4
Predgornoye 21 G 2
Predivinsk 36 F 4
Pregolya 17 H 5
Prek Kak 41 J 5
Premuda 19 F 3
Prenjsi 20 B 2
Prentice 77 H 2
Prenzlau 15 F 4
Preobrazhenka 36 J 3
Preparis 41 F 5
Preparis Nourth Channel 41 F 4
Preparis South Channel 41 F 5
Přerov 15 G 5
Presa de la Boquilla 76 EF 6
Presa Falcon 78 C 2
Presa Miguel Alemán 78 C 4
Presa Netzahualcyótl 78 D 4
Prescott 76 D 5
Presidencia Roque Sáenz-Peña 88 D 4
Presidente Dutra 87 H 2
Presidente Epitácio 87 F 5
Presidente Murtinho 87 F 4
Presidente Prudente 87 F 5
Preslav 20 C 2
Presnogor'kovka 25 N 5
Presnovka 25 N 5
Prešov 15 H 5
Prespansko Jezero 20 B 2
Presque Isle 77 N 2
Prestatyn 6 C 1
Prestatyn 6 C 1
Prestea 62 D 4
Presteigne 6 C 1
Preston 76 D 3
Preston (U.K.) 5 D 3
Preston Candover 7 D 2
Prestonburg 77 K 4
Prestonpans 3 C 4
Prestwick 3 B 4
Prestwick (Airport) 3 B 4
Prêto 87 G 4
Prêto do Igapó Açu 85 F 4
Pretoria 66 D 5
Prévesa 20 B 3
Prey Veng 41 J 5
Priangarskoye Plato 36 G 4
Priaral'skiye Karakumy, Peski 35 G 1
Priazovskaya Vozvyshennost' 21 E 1
Pribilof Islands 72 D 4
Priboj 20 A 2
Pribrezhnyy, Khrebet 37 P 4
Price 76 D 4
Prichard 77 J 5
Prichernomorskaya Nizmennost' 21 D 1
Priekule 17 H 4
Priene 20 C 3
Prieska 66 C 5
Prieta, Sierra 76 D 5
Prievidza 15 G 5
Prijedor 19 G 3
Priluki 24 F 5
Priluki 24 H 3
Primavera 91
Primeira Cruz 87 H 1
Primorsk 17 J 3
Primorsk 21 E 1
Primorskiy 21 E 1
Primorskiy Khrebet 36 HJ 5
Primorsko-Akhtarsk 21 E 1
Primorskoye 21 E 1

Primošten 19 G 3
Primrose Lake 73 Q 4–5
Prince Albert 73 Q 5
Prince Albert (South Africa) 66 C 6
Prince Albert Mountains 91
Prince Albert National Park 73 Q 5
Prince Albert Peninsula 73 O 1
Prince Albert Road 66 C 6
Prince Albert Sound 73 OP 1
Prince Alfred, Cape 73 M 1
Prince Charles Island 75 M 2
Prince Charles Mountains 91
Prince Edward Island (Canada) 75 P 6
Prince Edward Islands (Antarctica) 91
Prince George 73 N 5
Prince of Wales, Cape 72 D 2
Prince of Wales Island 73 S 1
Prince of Wales Island (AK, U.S.A.) 72 L 4
Prince of Wales Island (Queensland, Austr.) 49 G 1
Prince of Wales Strait 73 O 1
Prince Patrick Island 90
Prince Rupert 72 L 5
Prince William Sound 72 H 3
Princes Risborough 7 D 2
Princess Astrid Coast 91
Princess Charlotte Bay 49 G 1
Princess Martha Coast 91
Princess Ragnhild Coast 91
Princess Royal Island 72 M 5
Princeton 73 N 6
Princeton (IN, U.S.A.) 77 J 4
Princeton (MO, U.S.A.) 77 H 3
Princetown 6 C 3
Príncipe 63 F 5
Príncipe da Beira 86 D 3
Prineville 76 B 3
Prins Christians Sund 75 T 3
Prinzapolka 78 F 5
Priozersk 16 K 3
Pripet Marshes 17 J 5
Pripolyarnyy Ural 25 LM 3
Pripyat' 17 J 5
Prirechnyy 16 K 2
Priština 20 B 2
Pritzwalk 15 F 4
Privas 19 D 3
Privolzhskaya Vozvyshennost' 24 J 5
Privolzhskiy 34 D 1
Priyutnoye 21 F 1
Priyutovo 24 K 5
Prizren 20 B 2
Proddatur 40 C 5
Progreso 78 E 3
Prohod Vrăška čuka 20 B 2
Prokhladnyy 21 F 2
Prokhorkino 25 P 4
Prokop'yevo 36 H 4
Prokop'yevsk 25 R 5
Prokuplje 20 B 2
Proletariy 17 K 4
Proletarskaya 21 F 1
Proletarskiy 24 G 5
Proliv Bussol' 37 S 6
Proliv Dmitriya Lapteva 37 Q 1
Proliv Fritsa 37 R 6
Proliv Karskiye Vorota 24–25 L 1
Proliv Karskiye Vorota 24 L 1
Proliv Kruzenshterna 37 S 6
Proliv Nevel'skogo 37 Q 5
Proliv Sannikova 37 PQ 1
Proliv Yugorskiy Shar 25 LM 2
Prome 41 G 4
Promissão, Reprêsa 87 G 5
Promontoire Portland 75 LM 4
Promontorio del Gargano 19 G 3
Promyshlennaya 25 R 5
Propria 87 J 3
Propriano 19 E 3
Proserpine 49 H 3
Prosna 15 G 4
Prosperidad 43 G 2
Prospikhino 36 G 4
Prosser 76 B 2
Prostějov 15 G 5
Protochnoye 25 N 3
Provadija 20 C 2
Provence 19 E 3
Providence (R.I., U.S.A.) 77 M 3
Providence (Seychelles) 65 J 6
Providence, Cape 50 P 10
Providencia, Isla de 79 F 5
Providência, Serra da 86 D 3
Provideniya 72 C 3
Provincetown 77 N 3
Provincias Vascongadas 18 C 3
Provins 18 D 2
Provo 76 D 3
Prozor 19 G 3
Prudhoe 5 E 2
Prudhoe Bay 72 H 1

Pruszków 15 H 4
Prut 20 C 1
Pruzhany 17 H 5
Pryazha 24 F 3
Prydz Bay 91
Przemyśl 15 H 5
Przeworsk 15 H 4
Przheval'sk 35 K 2
Psará 20 C 3
Pshada 21 E 2
Pshino Ob 25 Q 4
Pshish 21 E 2
Pshish, Gora 21 F 2
Pskov 17 J 4
Pskovskoye Ozero 17 J 4
Ptich 17 J 5
Ptolemaïs (Greece) 20 B 2
Ptolemais → Ţulmaythah (Libya) 59 K 2
Ptuj 19 G 2
Puán 89 D 6
Pubei 38 E 6
Pucallpa 84 CD 5
Pucará 86 D 4
Pucheng 39 G 5
Pucheveem 37 W 2
Pucioasa 20 C 1
Puckeridge 7 D 2
Pudasjärvi 16 J 2
Pudino 25 P 4
Pudozh 24 G 3
Pudsey 5 E 3
Pudukkottai 40 C 5
Puebla 78 C 4
Puebla 78 C 4
Puebla de Alcocer 18 BC 4
Pueblo 76 F 4
Pueblo Hundido 88 C 4
Puelches 89 C 6
Puelén 89 C 6
Puente Alto 88 BC 5
Puente-Genil 18 C 4
Pu'er 38 D 6
Puerto Acosta 86 C 4
Puerto Adela 87 EF 5
Puerto Aisén 89 B 8
Puerto Alegre 86 D 3
Puerto Angel 78 C 4
Puerto Arista 78 D 4
Puerto Armuelles 84 B 2
Puerto Asís 84 C 3
Puerto Ayacucho 84 E 2
Puerto Baqueriza Moreno 84 B 6
Puerto Barrios 78 E 4
Puerto Bermúdez 86 B 3
Puerto Berrio 84 D 2
Puerto Boyacá 84 D 2
Puerto Caballas 86 A 3
Puerto Cabello 84 E 1
Puerto Cabezas 78 F 5
Puerto Carreño 84 E 2
Puerto Casade 86 E 5
Puerto Chicama 84 BC 5
Puerto Cisnes 89 B 7
Puerto Coig 89 C 9
Puerto Colombia 84 C 1
Puerto Cortés 78 E 4
Puerto Cumarebo 84 E 1
Puerto de Contreras 18 C 4
Puerto de Mazarrón 18 C 4
Puerto de Miravete 18 B 4
Puerto de Morata 18 C 3
Puerto de Pajares 18 B 3
Puerto de Perales 18 B 3
Puerto de Torre Miró 18 C 3
Puerto de Villatoro 18 B 3
Puerto del Escudo 18 C 3
Puerto del Madeiro 18 C 3
Puerto del Rosario 58 C 3
Puerto Deseado 89 C 8
Puerto Escondido 78 C 4
Puerto Esperanza 88 F 4
Puerto Estrella 84 D 1
Puerto Etén 84 BC 5
Puerto Grether 86 D 4
Puerto Guaraní 86 E 5
Puerto Harberton 89 C 9
Puerto Heath 86 C 3
Puerto Huitoto 84 D 3
Puerto Iguazu 88 EF 4
Puerto Juárez 78 E 3
Puerto la Concordia 84 D 3
Puerto la Cruz 85 F 1
Puerto la Paz 86 D 5
Puerto Leguizamo 84 D 4
Puerto Leigue 86 D 3
Puerto Lempira 78 F 4
Puerto Libertad 76 D 6
Puerto Limón 84 D 3
Puerto Lobos 89 C 7
Puerto López 84 D 1
Puerto Madero 78 D 5
Puerto Madryn 89 C 7
Puerto Magdalena 76 D 7
Puerto Maldonado 86 C 3
Puerto Montt 89 B 7

Puerto Nariño 84 E 3
Puerto Natales 89 B 9
Puerto Nuevo 84 E 2
Puerto Ordaz 85 F 2
Puerto Padilla 86 B 3
Puerto Páez 84 E 2
Puerto Patillos 86 B 5
Puerto Patiño 86 C 4
Puerto Pinasco 86 E 5
Puerto Pirámides 89 D 7
Puerto Plata 79 HJ 4
Puerto Portillo 84 D 5
Puerto Princesa 43 E 2
Puerto Reyes 86 E 5
Puerto Rico (Argentina) 88 F 4
Puerto Rico (Bolivia) 86 C 3
Puerto Rico (Colombia) 84 CD 3
Puerto Rico (U.S.A.) 79 J 4
Puerto Rico Trench 98 A 3
Puerto Rondón 84 D 2
Puerto Sastre 86 E 5
Puerto Siles 86 C 3
Puerto Somport 18 C 3
Puerto Suárez 86 E 4
Puerto Tejada 84 C 3
Puerto Umbría 84 C 3
Puerto Vallarta 78 AB 3
Puerto Varas 89 B 7
Puerto Verlarde 86 D 4
Puerto Victoria 84 D 5
Puerto Villamizar 84 D 2
Puerto Villazón 86 D 3
Puerto Visser 89 C 8
Puerto Wilches 84 D 2
Puerto Williams 89 C 10
Puerto Ybapobó 86 E 5
Puertollano 18 C 4
Pueyrredón, Lago 89 B 8
Pugachev 24 J 5
Pugal 40 B 2
Puget Sound 76 B 2
Puig Mayor 18 D 4
Puigmal 18 D 3
Puisaye, Collines de la 18 D 2
Pujehun 62 B 4
Puka 20 AB 2
Pukapuka (Cook Is.) 52 DE 3
Pukapuka (French Polynesia) 53 F 3
Pukaruha 53 F 4
Pukaskwa National Park 74 K 6
Pukatawagan 73 R 4
Pukch'ŏng 39 J 2
Puketeraki Range 51 Q 9
Puksoozero 24 H 3
Pula 19 F 3
Pula, Capo di 19 E 4
Pulap 52 A 2
Pulau Adi 43 H 4
Pulau Adonara 43 F 5
Pulau Alor 43 F 5
Pulau Alor 43 F 5
Pulau Ambon 43 G 4
Pulau Atauro 43 G 5
Pulau Babi 42 A 3
Pulau Bacan 43 G 4
Pulau Bangka 42 C 4
Pulau Bangkaru 42 A 3
Pulau Baso 42 B 4
Pulau Batam 42 B 3
Pulau Batanta 43 H 4
Pulau Bawean 42 D 5
Pulau Belitung 42 C 4
Pulau Bengkalis 42 B 3
Pulau Besar 43 F 5
Pulau Biak 43 J 4
Pulau Biaro 43 G 3
Pulau Binongko 43 F 5
Pulau Bintan 42 B 3
Pulau Boano 43 G 4
Pulau Breueh 42 A 2
Pulau Buru 43 G 4
Pulau Butung 43 F 4
Pulau Damar (L. Sunda Is.) 43 G 5
Pulau Damar [Moluccas] 43 G 4
Pulau Enggano 42 B 5
Pulau Gag 43 G 4
Pulau Gebe 43 G 4
Pulau Jatisiri 43 G 4
Pulau Jemaja 42 C 3
Pulau Jos Sodarso 43 J 5
Pulau Kabaena 43 F 5
Pulau Kai Besar 43 H 5
Pulau Kai Kecil 43 H 5
Pulau Kalaotoa 43 F 5
Pulau Kalukalukuang 42 E 5
Pulau Karakelong 43 G 3
Pulau Karimata 42 C 4
Pulau Karimunjawa 42 D 5
Pulau Kasiruta 43 G 4
Pulau Kawalusu 43 F 3
Pulau Kayoa 43 G 3
Pulau Kelang 43 G 4
Pulau Kisar 43 G 5
Pulau Kobroor 43 H 5

Pulau Kofiau 43 GH 4
Pulau Komodo 43 E 5
Pulau Komoran 43 J 5
Pulau Komoran 50 C 3
Pulau Kundur 42 B 3
Pulau Labengke 43 F 4
Pulau Lasia 42 A 3
Pulau Laut 42 E 4
Pulau Lepar 42 C 4
Pulau Lingga 42 B 4
Pulau Lomblen 43 F 5
Pulau Madura 42 D 5
Pulau Makian 43 G 3
Pulau Mandioli 43 G 4
Pulau Mangole 43 G 4
Pulau Manipa 43 G 4
Pulau Manui 43 F 4
Pulau Mao 43 G 5
Pulau Masalembo 42 D 5
Pulau Masela 43 GH 5
Pulau Maya 42 C 4
Pulau Mega 42 B 4
Pulau Midai 42 C 3
Pulau Misool 43 H 4
Pulau Morotai 43 G 3
Pulau Moyo 42 E 5
Pulau Muna 43 F 5
Pulau Mursala 42 A 3
Pulau Nias 42 A 3
Pulau Nila 43 G 5
Pulau Num 43 J 4
Pulau Numfor 43 H 4
Pulau Obi 43 G 4
Pulau Padang 42 B 3
Pulau Panaitan 42 B 5
Pulau Pantar 43 F 5
Pulau Pejantan 42 C 3
Pulau Peleng 43 F 4
Pulau Pemarung 42 E 4
Pulau Penida 42 E 5
Pulau Pinang 42 B 2
Pulau Pini 42 A 3
Pulau Rakata 42 C 5
Pulau Rangsang 42 B 3
Pulau Rinja 43 E 5
Pulau Romang 43 G 5
Pulau Roti 43 F 6
Pulau Rupat 42 B 3
Pulau Salawati 43 H 4
Pulau Samosir 42 A 3
Pulau Sanana 43 G 4
Pulau Sanding 42 B 4
Pulau Sangeang 43 E 5
Pulau Sangihe 43 G 3
Pulau Sawu 43 F 6
Pulau Sayang 43 G 3
Pulau Sebanka 42 BC 3
Pulau Sebatik 42–43 E 3
Pulau Sebuku 42 E 4
Pulau Selaru 43 H 5
Pulau Selatan 42 B 4
Pulau Selayar 43 F 5
Pulau Semau 43 F 6
Pulau Sepanjang 42 E 5
Pulau Serasan 42 C 3
Pulau Sermata 43 G 5
Pulau Siberut 42 A 4
Pulau Sibutu 43 E 3
Pulau Simeulue 42 A 3
Pulau Simuk 42 A 3
Pulau Singkep 42 B 4
Pulau Spayua 42 A 4
Pulau Subi 42 C 3
Pulau, Sungai 43 J 5
Pulau Supiori 43 J 4
Pulau Tahulandang 43 FG 3
Pulau Taliabu 43 FG 4
Pulau Tanahbala 42 A 4
Pulau Tanahjampea 43 F 5
Pulau Tanahmasa 42 A 4
Pulau Tebingtinggi 42 B 3
Pulau Terentang 42 E 4
Pulau Trangan 43 H 5
Pulau Tuangku 42 A 3
Pulau Tubelai 43 G 4
Pulau Utara 43 J 5
Pulau Waigeo 43 H 4
Pulau Wangiwangi 43 F 5
Pulau Weh 42 A 2
Pulau Wetar 43 G 5
Pulau Wokam 43 H 5
Pulau Workai 43 HJ 5
Pulau Wowoni 43 F 4
Pulau Yamdena 43 H 5
Pulau Yapen 43 J 4
Puławy 15 H 4
Pulicat 40 D 5
Pulkkila 16 J 3
Pullman 76 C 2
Pulo Anna 43 H 3
Pulog, Mount 43 J 1
Pulonga 24 H 2
Pulozero 16 K 2
Pulton-Le-Fylde 5 D 3
Pułtusk 15 H 4
Pulusuk 52 A 2

Puluwat 52 A 2
Puma Yumco 41 F 2
Pumpsaint 6 C 1
Puna de Atacama 86 C 5–6
Puná, Isla 84 B 4
Punakha 40 E 2
Puncak Jaya 43 J 4
Puncak Trikora 43 J 4
Punda Milia 67 E 4
Punduga 24 H 3
Pune 40 B 4
Punia 64 D 5
Puning 38 G 6
Punjab 40 BC 1
Punkaharju 16 J 3
Puno 86 B 4
Punta Alegre 79 G 3
Punta Almina 58 D 1
Punta Alta 89 D 6
Punta Angamos 86 B 5
Punta Arenas 89 B 9
Punta Ballenita 88 B 4
Punta Bermeja 89 D 7
Punta Burica 78 F 6
Punta Cachos 88 B 4
Punta Carreta 86 A 3
Punta Catalina 89 C 9
Punta, Cerro de 79 J 4
Punta Colorada 88 B 4
Punta de Arenas 89 C 9
Punta de Chilca 86 A 3
Punta de Europa 18 BC 4
Punta de Mata 85 F 2
Punta del Diamante 78 BC 4
Punta Delgada 89 D 7
Punta Delgado 89 C 9
Punta dell' Alice 19 G 4
Punta Desengaño 89 C 8
Punta Eugenia 76 C 6
Punta Falcone 19 E 3
Punta Fijo 84 D 1
Punta Galera 89 B 7
Punta Gallinas 84 D 1
Punta Gorda (Belize) 78 E 4
Punta Gorda 17 H 3
Punta Gorda (Nicaragua) 78 F 5
Punta Gorda, Bàhía de 78 F 5
Punta Gruesa 86 B 5
Punta Guascama 84 C 3
Punta Lachay 84 C 6
Punta Lavapié 89 B 6
Punta Lengua de Vaca 88 B 5
Punta Licosa 19 F 3
Punta Magdalena 84 C 3
Punta Maisí 79 H 3
Punta Mala 84 C 2
Punta Mariato 84 B 2
Punta Medanosa 89 CD 8
Punta Morro 88 B 4
Punta Negra 84 B 5
Punta, Ninfas 89 D 7
Punta Norte 89 E 6
Punta Palazzo 19 E 3
Punta Pariñas 84 B 4
Punta Pórfido 89 D 7
Punta Poro 88 E 4
Punta Prieta 76 D 6
Punta Rasa 89 D 7
Punta Rieles 86 E 5
Punta Roja 89 CD 7
Punta Rotja 18 D 4
Punta Sarga 58 B 4
Punta Stilo 19 G 4
Punta Sur 89 E 6
Punta Topocalma 88 B 5
Punta Verde 78 F 6
Puntarenas 78 EF 6
Puolanka 16 J 3
Puper 43 H 4
Puqi 38 F 5
Puquio 86 B 3
Puquios 88 C 4
Pur 25 P 2
Pura 36 E 1
Pura 36 E 1
Puracé 84 C 3
Purcell Mountains 73 O 5
Purdy Islands 50 E 2
Puri 40 E 4
Puri 66 B 1
Purificación 84 D 3
Purikari Neem 17 J 4
Purinskoye, Ozero 36 E 1
Purna 40 C 3
Purnea 40 E 2
Pursat 41 H 5
Purton 7 D 2
Purtuniq 75 N 3
Purukcahu 42 D 4
Purulia 40 E 3
Purus 85 F 4
Puruvesi 16 J 3
Purwakarta 42 C 5
Pusan 39 J 3
Pushchino 37 T 5
Pushkin 17 K 4
Pushkino 24 J 5

Pusht-i-Rud 35 G 4
Pusteci 20 B 2
Pustoretsk 37 U 3
Pustoshka 17 J 4
Puszcza Notecka 15 G 4
Putao 41 G 2
Putian 39 G 5
Putina 86 C 3
Puting, Tanjung 42 D 4
Putla de Guerrero 78 C 4
Putnok 20 B 1
Putorana, Gory 36 FH 2
Puttalam 40 C 6
Puttenham 7 D 2
Puttgarden 15 F 4
Putumayo 84 D 4
Putussibau 42 D 3
Puulavesi 16 J 3
Puy Crapaud 18 C 2
Puy de Dôme 18 D 2
Puy de Sancy 18 D 2
Puyang 38 G 3
Puyo 84 C 4
Puzla 24 K 3
Pwani 65 F 6
Pweto 64 D 6
Pwllheli 6 B 1
Pyagina, Poluostrov 37 S 4
Pyakupur 25 P 2–3
Pyal'ma 24 G 3
Pyandzh 35 H 3
Pyaozero, Ozero 16 K 2
Pyapon 41 G 4
Pyasina 36 E 1
Pyasino, Ozero 25 R 2
Pyatigorsk 21 F 2
Pyatigory 24 KL 3
Pyatikhatki 21 D 1
Pyatistennoy 37 TU 2
Pyat'kovende, Gora 37 T 2
Pyawbwe 41 G 3
Pygmalion Point 41 F 6
Pyhäjärvi 16 J 3
Pyhäjärvi 17 H 3
Pyhäjoki 16 HJ 3
Pyhäntä 16 J 3
Pyhäselkä 16 JK 3
Pyhätunturi 16 J 2
Pyinmana 41 G 4
Pyl'karamo 25 Q 3
Pym 25 O 3
Pymta 37 T 5
P'yŏnggang 39 J 3
P'yŏngyang 39 HJ 3
Pyramid Lake 76 C 3–4
Pyramids 60 E 3
Pyrénées 18 CD 3
Pyshchug 24 J 4
Pytalovo 17 J 4
Pyu 41 G 4

Q

Qābis 59 H 2
Qābis, Khalīj 59 H 2
Qabr Hūd 61 H 5
Qaderābād (Iran) 23 F 3
Qādir Karam (Iraq) 23 D 2
Qāḍub 65 J 2
Qā'emshahr (Iran) 23 F 1
Qafṣah 59 G 2
Qagan (Nei Monggul Zizhiqu, China) 36 L 6
Qagan Nur (Nei Monggul Zizhiqu, China) 38 F 2
Qagan Nur (Qinghai, China) 38 C 3
Qagan Tohoi 38 B 3
Qagcaka 40 D 1
Qahar Youyi Houqi 38 F 2
Qahar Youyi Qianqi 38 F 2
Qahremānshahr (Iran) 23 E 2
Qaidam He 38 C 3
Qaidam Pendi 38 BC 3
Qal 'at al Husn (Syria) 22 B 2
Qal'at al Marqab (Syria) 22 B 2
Qal' at Dīzah (Iraq) 23 D 1
Qal' at Sukkar (Iraq) 23 E 3
Qala'an Nahl 60 E 6
Qala-Nau 35 G 4
Qālat 35 H 4
Qal'at Abū Ghār (Iraq) 23 DE 3
Qal'at al Akhdar (Saudi Arabia) 22 B 4
Qal'at al Mu'azam (Saudi Arabia) 22 BC 4
Qal'at Bīshah 61 G 4
Qal'at Sālih (Iraq) 23 E 3
Qal'eh (Iran) 23 G 1
Qal'eh Asgar (Iran) 23 G 3
Qal'eh-ye Now (Iran) 23 E 2
Qalīb ash Shuyūkh (Kuwait) 23 E 3
Qallābāt 60 F 6
Qamalung 38 C 4
Qamar, Ghubbat al 61 J 5

Qamata 66 D 6
Qamdo 38 C 4
Qamīnis 59 JK 2
Qanāt as Suways (Egypt) 22 A 3
Qandala 65 H 2
Qapqal 35 L 2
Qaqortog 75 S 3
Qar Wagēr 65 H 2
Qārah 60 D 3
Qarah Dāgh (Iraq) 22 D 1
Qarah Dāgh 34 D 3
Qārā', Jabal 61 J 5
Qara Tarai 35 H 4
Qarānqū 34 D 3
Qarqi 35 M 2
Qārūn, Birkat 60 E 3
Qaryat al Gharab (Iraq) 23 D 3
Qaryat al 'Ulyā (Saudi Arabia) 23 E 4
Qasa Murg 35 G 4
Qaṣr Ahmād 59 J 2
Qasr al Azraq (Jordan) 22 B 3
Qaṣr al Hayr (Syria) 22 BC 2
Qasr al Khūbbaz (Iraq) 22 D 2
Qaṣr as Ṣabīyah (Kuwait) 23 E 3
Qaṣr bū Hādī 59 J 2
Qasr Burqu' (Jordan) 22 BC 2
Qaṣr Farāfirah 60 D 3
Qasr Hamām 61 H 4
Qasr-e Qand 35 G 5
Qasr-e Shīrīn (Iran) 23 DE 2
Qatar 23 F 4
Qatif (Saudi Arabia) 23 E 4
Qatlīsh 34 F 3
Qatrūyeh (Iran) 23 G 3
Qattara Depression 60 D 3
Qawām al Hamzah (Iraq) 23 D 3
Qawz Abū ṭlū' 60 E 5
Qawz Rajab 60 F 5
Qāyen 34 F 4
Qaysān 60 E 6
Qayyārah (Iraq) 22 D 2
Qazvīn (Iran) 23 F 1
Qeshm 34 F 5
Qeshm 34 F 5
Qeshm [ö] (Iran) 23 G 4
Qeshm [ort] (Iran) 23 G 4
Qeydār (Iran) 23 E 1
Qeydū (Iran) 23 F 2
Qeys (Iran) 23 F 4
Qezel Owzan (Iran) 23 E 1
Qezi'ot (Israel) 22 B 3
Qian Gorlos 39 H 2
Qian Shan 39 H 2–3
Qian'an 39 H 1
Qianjiang 38 E 5
Qianning 38 D 4
Qianwei 38 D 5
Qianxi 38 E 5
Qianyang 38 F 5
Qiaojia 38 D 5
Qiaowan 38 C 2
Qichun 38 G 4
Qidong 39 H 4
Qiemo 35 M 3
Qift (Egypt) 22 A 4
Qijiang 38 E 5
Qijiaojing 38 B 2
Qila Ladgasht 35 G 5
Qila Saifullah 35 H 4
Qilian 38 D 3
Qilian Shan 38 CD 3
Qimantag 38 B 3
Qimen 39 G 5
Qin Xian 38 F 3
Qinā (Egypt) 22 A 4
Qina, Wādī (Egypt) 22 A 4
Qin'an 38 E 4
Qing He 38 E 3
Qing Jiang 38 F 4
Qing Zang Gaoyuan 40 DE 1
Qingchuan 38 E 4
Qingdao 39 H 3
Qinggang 39 J 1
Qinghai 38 C 3
Qinghai Hu 38 D 3
Qinghe 35 N 1
Qingjiang (Jiangsu, China) 39 G 4
Qingjiang (Jiangxi, China) 38 G 5
Qinglong 38 DE 5
Qinglong (Hebei, China) 39 G 2
Qingshen 38 D 5

Qingshuihe 38 F 3
Qingxu 38 F 3
Qingyang 38 E 3
Qingyuan 39 H 2
Qinhuangdao 39 GH 3
Qinling Shan 38 EF 4
Qinliu 38 G 5
Qinzhou 38 E 6
Qionghai 38 F 7
Qionglai 38 D 4
Qionglai Shan 38 D 4
Qiongshan 38 F 7
Qiongzhou Haixia 38 EF 6
Qiqiar 36 M 5
Qir (Iran) 23 F 3
Qira 35 L 3
Qirdi (Saudi Arabia) 23 E 4
Qirjat Shemona (Israel) 22 B 2
Qirjat Yam (Israel) 22 B 2
Qiryat Gat (Israel) 22 B 3
Qirzah 59 H 2
Qishn 61 J 5
Qishrān 61 FG 4
Qitai 35 M 2
Qitaihe 39 K 1
Qitbīt, Wādī 61 J 5
Qiyang 38 F 5
Qog Qi 38 E 2
Qog Ul 39 G 2
Qogir Feng 35 K 3
Qolleh-ye Damāvand 34 E 3
Qolleh-ye Damāvand (Iran) 23 F 2
Qoltag 38 A 2
Qom (Iran) 23 F 2
Qom (Iran) 23 F 2
Qomdo 38 D 4
Qomolangma Feng 40 E 2
Qomrūd (Iran) 23 F 2
Qomsheh 34 E 4
Qomsheh (Iran) 23 F 2–3
Qonggyai 41 F 2
Qôrnoq 75 R 3
Qorveh 34 D 3
Qorveh (Iran) 23 E 2
Qosbeh-ye Nassār (Iran) 23 E 3
Qotbābād (Iran) 23 F 3
Qotbābād 34 F 5
Qotbābād (Iran) 23 G 4
Qotur 34 D 3
Qu Xian 39 G 5
Quairading 48 B 5
Quan Dao Nam Du 41 H 6
Quan Long 41 J 6
Quan Phu Quoc 41 H 5
Quang Ngai 41 J 4
Quang Tri 41 J 4
Quang Yen 41 J 3
Quanshuigou 35 K 3
Quanzhou (Fujian, China) 39 G 6
Quanzhou (Guangxi Zhuangzu Zizhiqu, China) 38 F 5
Qu'Appelle 73 R 5
Quaraí 88 E 5
Quartu Sant' Elena 19 E 4
Quartz Mountain 76 B 3
Quartzsite 76 D 5
Quatro Ciénegas 78 B 2
Quayti 61 H 5
Qūchān 34 F 3
Queanbeyan 49 H 6
Québec 75 N 5
Québec 75 N 5
Quebracho 88 E 5
Quebracho Coto 88 D 4
Quedal, Cabo 89 B 7
Queen Bess, Mount 73 N 5
Queen, Cape 75 M 3
Queen Charlotte Islands 72 KL 5
Queen Charlotte Sound 72 LM 5
Queen Charlotte Strait 72–73 M 5
Queen Elizabeth Islands 90
Queen Fabiola Mountains 91
Queen Mary Coast 91
Queen Maud Gulf 73 R 2
Queen Maud Land 91
Queen Maud Mountains 91
Queens Channel 48 D 1
Queensferry 3 C 4
Queensland 49 GH 3
Queenstown (New Zealand) 50 P 9
Queenstown (South Africa) 66 D 6
Queenstown (Tasmania, Austr.) 50 L 9
Quehue 89 D 6
Queimada, Ilha 87 G 5
Queimadas 87 HJ 3
Quela 66 B 1
Quelimane 67 F 3
Quellén 89 B 7
Quelpart 39 J 4
Quemado 76 E 5
Quembo 66 B 2
Quemchi 89 B 7
Quemoy 39 G 6

Quemu Quemu 89 D 6
Quequén 89 E 6
Querétaro 78 BC 3
Quesada 78 F 5
Queshan 38 F 4
Quesnel 73 N 5
Quesnel Lake 73 N 5
Quetena 86 C 5
Quetta 35 H 4
Quevedo 84 C 4
Quezaltenango 78 D 5
Quezon City 43 J 2
Qui Nhon 41 J 5
Quibaxe 66 A 1
Quibdó 84 C 2
Quiberon 18 C 2
Quibili 59 G 2
Quicabo 66 A 1
Quiçama National Park 66 A 1
Quiches 84 C 5
Quiculungo 66 B 1
Quienha 66 B 2
Quiha 65 F 2
Quihita 66 A 3
Quiindy 88 E 4
Quila 76 E 7
Quilán, Cabo 89 B 7
Quilberry 49 H 4
Quilca 86 B 4
Quilco 89 D 6
Quilenda 66 A 2
Quilengues 66 A 2
Quilino 88 D 5
Quillabamba 86 B 3
Quillacollo 86 C 4
Quillagua 86 BC 5
Quillaicillo 88 B 5
Quillota 88 B 5
Quilon 40 C 6
Quilpie 49 G 4
Quimbele 66 B 1
Quimilí 88 D 4
Quimper 18 C 2
Quince Mil 86 B 3
Quincy 77 H 4
Quines 88 C 5
Quingey 19 E 2
Quinhagak 72 E 4
Quiñones 76 D 7
Quintana Roo 78 E 3–4
Quintanar de la Orden 18 C 4
Quinto 88 D 5
Quionga 67 G 2
Quipapá 87 J 2
Quipungo 66 A 2
Quirima 66 B 2
Quirinópolis 87 F 4
Quissanga 67 G 2
Quissico 67 EF 4
Quitasueño, Banco 79 F 5
Quiterajo 67 G 2
Quito 84 C 4
Quivilla 84 C 5
Quixadá 87 J 1
Quixeramobim 87 J 2
Qujing 38 D 5
Qulansiyah 65 J 2
Qulaybiah 59 H 1
Qulbān Layyah (Iraq) 23 E 3
Qumarlêb 38 C 4
Qumarrabdūn 38 B 4
Qumbu 66 D 6
Qunayfidhah, Nafūd 61 GH 4
Qu'nyido 38 C 4
Quoich 73 T 3
Quorn 49 F 5
Qūr al Hulwāt (Saudi Arabia)
    22 C 3
Qurdūd 60 D 6
Qurnat as Sawdā' (Lebanon)
    22 B 2
Qūs (Egypt) 22 A 4
Qusaybah (Iraq) 22 C 2
Qusayr ad Daffah 59 K 2
Qusum 38 B 5
Qüxü 41 F 2
Quyang 38 F 3
Quynh Luu 41 J 4
Qyteti Stalin 20 B 2

R

Raab 19 G 2
Raahe 16 H 3
Rääkkylä 16 J 3
Raasay 2 A 3
Rab 19 F 3
Rába 20 A 1
Raba 43 E 5
Rabak 60 E 6
Rabal 43 HJ 5
Rabalou 18 D 4
Rabat (Malta) 19 F 4
Rabat (Morocco) 58 D 2

Rabaul 51 F 2
Rabiah (Iraq) 22 D 1
Rābigh 61 F 4
Rabka 15 H 5
Rabocheostrovsk 16 K 2
Rabyānah 59 K 4
Rabyānah, Ramlat 59 JK 4
Racconigi 19 E 3
Race, Cape 75 R 6
Rach Gia 41 HJ 5–6
Rachid 58 C 5
Racine 77 J 3
Radā' 61 GH 6
Rădăuţi 20 C 1
Radebeul 15 F 4
Radeče 19 G 2
Radekhov 17 HJ 5
Radhanpur 40 B 3
Radisson 75 M 5
Radom 15 H 4
Radom (Sudan) 64 C 3
Radomir 20 B 2
Radomsko 15 G 4
Radöy 16 D 3
Radstock 6 C 2
Radun 17 J 5
Radviliškis 17 H 4
Radville 73 R 6
Radwā, Jabal (Saudi Arabia)
    22 BC 4
Radzyń Podlaski 15 H 4
Rae 73 O 3
Rae Bareli 40 D 2
Raeside, Lake 48 C 4
Raevavae 53 F 4
Rāf, Jabal (Saudi Arabia) 22 C 3
Rafael, Cachoeira do 86 D 3
Rafaela 88 D 5
Rafah 22 B 3
Rafaï 64 C 3
Raffili Rapids 64 D 3
Rafhā (Saudi Arabia) 22 D 3
Rafsanjān (Iran) 23 G 3
Raga 64 D 3
Ragam 63 F 3
Ragang, Mount 43 F 2
Ragay Gulf 43 F 1
Ragged Island Range 79 G 3
Raglan 6 C 3
Ragusa 19 F 4
Raha 43 F 4
Rahad al Bardī 60 C 6
Rahāh, Harrat ar 60 F 3
Raharney 4 B 3
Rahat, Harrat 61 G 4
Raheita 65 G 2
Rahib, Jabal 60 D 5
Rahimyar Khan 35 J 5
Raia 18 B 4
Raiatea 53 E 4
Raichur 40 C 4
Raiganj 40 E 2
Raigarh 40 D 3
Raimangal 40 E 3
Rainbow Peak 76 C 3
Rainier, Mount 76 B 2
Rainy Lake 74 J 6
Raipur 40 D 3
Raisen 40 C 3
Raisio 17 H 3
Raiwind 35 J 4
Raj Nandgaon 40 D 3
Rajabasa 42 B 5
Rajada 87 H 2
Rajahmundry 40 D 4
Rajakoski 16 J 2
Rajang 42 D 3
Rajanpur 35 J 5
Rajapalaiyam 40 C 6
Rajapur 40 B 4
Rajasthan 40 BC 2
Rajasthan Canal 40 B 2
Rajgarh 40 C 2
Rajgarh 40 C 3
Rajinac 19 FG 3
Rajkot 40 B 3
Rajmahal Hills 40 E 3
Rajshahi 40 E 3
Rajura 40 C 4
Raka 40 E 2
Raka Zangbo 40 E 2
Rakahanga 52 E 3
Rakata, Pulau 42 C 5
Rakhmanoviskoye 25 R 6
Rakhov 20 B 1
Rakhsh (United Arab Emirates)
    23 F 4
Rakitnoye 17 J 5
Rakkestad 17 F 4
Rakoko 66 C 3
Rakops 66 C 4
Rakshan 35 G 5
Rakulka 24 HJ 3
Råkvåg 16 E 3
Rakvere 17 J 4

Ra's-al Kūh 61 K 3
Raleigh 77 L 4
Raleigh Bay 77 L 5
Ralik Chain 52 C 2
Rām Allāh [Westbank] 22 B 3
Rama 78 F 5
Ramādah 59 H 2
Ramalho, Serra do 87 H 3
Ramallo 88 D 5
Ramanathapuram 40 C 6
Ramapo Deep 27 R 6
Ramasaig 2 A 3
Ramatlabama 66 CD 5
Ramblon 88 C 5
Rambouillet 18 D 2
Rambutyo 50 E 2
Ramea 75 Q 6
Rameswaram 40 C 6
Ramgarh (Bangla Desh) 41 F 3
Ramgarh (India) 40 E 3
Ramgul 35 J 3
Rāmhormoz (Iran) 23 E 3
Ramkola 40 D 3
Ramlān (Saudi Arabia) 23 E 4
Ramlat al Wīgh 59 J 4
Ramlat as Sab'atayn 61 H 5
Ramlat Dahm 61 H 5
Ramlat Hagolan 22 B 2
Ramlat Rabyānah 59 JK 4
Ramlat Yām 61 H 5
Ramlu 65 G 2
Ramm, Jabal (Jordan) 22 B 3
Ramnagar 40 D 3
Ramo 65 G 3
Ramokgwebana 66 D 4
Ramotswa 66 D 4
Rampart 72 G 2
Rampur 40 C 2
Rampur 40 D 3
Ramree 41 F 4
Rams (United Arab Emirates)
    23 G 4
Rāmsar (Iran) 23 F 1
Ramsele 16 G 3
Ramsey 74 L 6
Ramsey (Cambridgeshire) 7 D 1
Ramsey (Isle of Man) 4 C 2
Ramsey Bay 4 C 2
Ramsey Island 6 B 2
Ramseycleuch 3 C 4
Ramsgate 7 E 2
Rāmshīr (Iran) 23 E 3
Ramsjö 16 G 3
Ramsund 16 G 2
Ramu 65 G 4
Ramu River 50 D 2
Ramvik 16 G 3
Rañadoiro, Sierra de 18 B 3
Rancagua 88 B 5
Rance 18 C 2
Rancha de Caça dos Tapiúnas
    86 E 3
Rancharia 87 F 5
Ranchi 40 E 3
Rancul 88 D 6
Rand Rifles 66 A 4
Randalstown 4 B 2
Randers 17 F 4
Randijaure 16 G 2
Randsfjorden 17 F 3
Råneå 16 H 2
Råneälven 16 H 2
Ranelva 16 F 2
Ranérou 62 B 2
Rangamati 41 F 3
Rangantamiang 42 D 4
Ranger 76 G 5
Rangia 41 F 2
Rangiroa 53 F 3
Rangkasbitung 42 C 5
Rangoon 41 G 4
Rangpur 40 E 2
Rangsang, Pulau 42 B 3
Rania 40 B 2
Ranibennur 40 C 5
Ranikhet 40 C 2
Rāniyah (Iraq) 23 D 1
Ranken River 49 F 3
Ranken Store 49 F 2
Rankin Inlet 73 T 3
Rann of Kutch 40 AB 3
Rannes 49 HJ 3
Ranohira 67 H 4
Ranon 51 J 5
Ranong 41 G 6
Ranongga 51 G 3
Ransaren 16 G 2
Ransiki 43 H 4
Ranskill 7 D 1
Rantabe 67 H 3
Rantasalmi 16 J 3
Rantau 42 E 4
Rantauprapat 42 AB 3
Ranua 16 J 2
Raohe 37 O 6

Raoui, Erg er 58 E 3
Raoul 52 D 4
Rapa 53 F 4
Rapa Nui 53 H 4
Rapadalen 16 G 2
Rapallo 19 E 3
Raper, Cabo 89 A 8
Raper, Cape 75 O 2
Rapid City 76 F 3
Rappang 43 EF 4
Rapulo 86 C 3
Raraka 53 F 4
Raroïa 53 F 4
Rarotonga 53 E 4
Rarytkin, Khrebet 37 WX 3
Ra's Abū Madd (Saudi Arabia)
    22 B 4
Ra's Abū Qumayyis (United Arab
    Emirates) 23 F 4
Ra's Abū Sawmah (Egypt) 22 B 4
Ra's Abū Shajarah 60 F 4
Ra's ad Daqm 61 K 5
Ra's Ajdīr 59 H 2
Rås al Abyad (Saudi Arabia)
    22 BC 5
Ra's al Abyad (Tunisia) 59 G 1
Ra's al 'Ayn (Syria) 22 C 1
Ra's al Hadāribah 60 F 4
Ra's al Hadd 61 KL 4
Ra's al Hazrah (United Arab
    Emirates) 23 F 4
Ra's al Kanā'is 60 D 2
Ra's al Khafjī (Saudi Arabia)
    23 E 3
Ra's al Khaymah (United Arab
    Emirates) 23 G 4
Ra's al Madrakah 61 K 5
Ra's al Milh 59 L 2
Ra's al Mish'āb (Saudi Arabia)
    23 E 3
Ra's al Mūtaf (Iran) 23 F 4
Ra's 'Alam al Rūm 60 D 2
Ra's an Naqb (Jordan) 22 B 3
Ra's as Saffānīyah (Saudi Arabia)
    23 E 3
Ra's as Sidr (Egypt) 22 A 3
Ra's ash Shaykh (Saudi Arabia)
    22 B 3
Ra's Asir 65 J 2
Ra's at Tanāqīb (Saudi Arabia)
    23 E 4
Ra's at Tannūrah (Saudi Arabia)
    23 F 4
Ra's at Ṭīb 59 H 1
Ra's at Tin 59 K 2
Ra's az Zawr (Saudi Arabia)
    23 E 4
Ra's Ba'labakk (Syria) 22 B 2
Ra's Banās (Egypt) 22 B 5
Ra's Barīdī (Saudi Arabia) 22 B 4
Ra's Chiamboni 65 G 5
Ras Dashan 65 F 2
Ra's Durbat ' Alī 61 J 5
Ra's el Cheil 65 HJ 3
Ras el Ma 62 D 2
Ra's Fartak 61 J 5
Ra's Ghanadah (United Arab
    Emirates) 23 G 4
Ra's Ghārib (Egypt) 22 A 3
Ra's Hāfūn 65 J 2
Ra's Hanjūrah (United Arab
    Emirates) 23 G 4
Ra's Hātībah 60 F 4
Ras Jiwani 35 G 6
Ra's Kabūdīyah 59 H 1
Ra's Karkūmā (Saudi Arabia)
    22 B 4
Ra's Kasr 60 F 5
Ra's Khānzir 65 H 2
Ra's Laffān (Qatar) 23 F 4
Ra's Lānūf 59 J 2
Ra's Matārimah (Egypt) 22 A 3
Ra's Misrātah 59 J 2
Ras Muari 35 H 6
Ra's Muhammad (Egypt) 22 B 4
Ra's Mushayrib (United Arab
    Emirates) 23 F 4
Ra's Naws 61 K 5
Ra's Ngomeni 65 G 5
Ra's Qattārah 60 D 7
Ra's Rakan (Qatar) 23 F 4
Ras Rawura 67 G 2
Ra's Sharbithāt 61 K 5
Ra's Sura 65 H 2
Ra's Zayt (Egypt) 22 A 4
Rasa, Punta 89 D 7
Ra's-e Barkan (Iran) 23 E 3
Ra's-e Nāy Band (Iran) 23 F 4
Rashād 60 E 6
Rashīd 60 E 2
Rasht (Iran) 23 E 1
Raskoh 35 G 5
Rasmussen Basin 73 ST 2
Rason, Lake 48 C 4
Rasshevatskaya 21 F 1

Rasshua, Ostrov 37 S 6
Rasskazovo 24 H 5
Rassokha 37 S 2
Rastigaissa 16 J 1
Råstojaure 16 H 2
Rasūl 34 F 5
Rasul (Iran) 23 G 4
Rat 72 A 5
Rat Buri 41 G 5
Rat Islands 72 A 5
Ratak Chain 52 C 2
Ratangarh 40 B 2
Rath 40 C 2
Ráth Luirc 14 B 4
Rathangan 4 B 3
Rathdrum 4 B 3
Rathenow 15 F 4
Rathfriland 4 B 2
Rathlin Island 4 B 2
Rathmelton 4 B 1
Rathnew 4 B 3
Rathowen 4 B 3
Ratlam 40 C 3
Ratmanova, Mys 24–25 L 1
Ratmanova, Ostrov 72 D 2
Ratnagiri 40 B 4
Ratnapura 40 D 6
Ratno 17 H 5
Raton 76 F 4
Ratqah, Wadi ar (Iraq) 22 C 2
Ratta 25 Q 3
Rattray 3 D 3
Rattray Head 2 D 3
Rättvik 17 G 3
Ratz, Mount 72 L 4
Raub 42 B 3
Rauch 89 E 6
Rauchua 37 V 2
Raufarhöfn 16 B 2
Raufoss 17 F 3
Raúl Leoni, Represa 85 F 2
Rauma 16 H 3
Rauma (Norway) 16 E 3
Raumo 16 H 3
Raupelyan 72 C 2
Raurkela 40 D 3
Ravahere 53 F 4
Ravānsar (Iran) 23 E 2
Rāvar (Iran) 23 G 3
Rava-Russkaya 17 H 5
Ravelsbach 19 G 2
Ravenna 19 F 3
Ravensburg 15 EF 5
Ravenshoe (Queensland, Austr.)
    49 GH 2
Ravensthorpe 48 C 5
Ravensworth 5 E 2
Ravi 35 J 4
Ravnina 35 G 3
Rāwah (Iraq) 22 CD 2
Rawaki 52 D 3
Rawalpindi 35 J 4
Rawandūz (Iraq) 23 D 1
Rawas 43 H 4
Rawdah (Iraq) 22 C 2
Rawicz 15 G 4
Rawlinna 48 D 5
Rawlins 76 E 3
Rawson 89 D 7
Rawtenstall 5 D 3
Rawura, Ras 67 G 2
Ray, Cape 75 Q 6
Raya, Bukit 42 D 4
Rayachoti 40 C 5
Rayadrug 40 C 5
Rayagada 40 D 4
Rayak (Lebanon) 22 B 2
Rāyāt (Iraq) 23 D 1
Raychikhinsk 37 N 6
Raykoke, Ostrov 37 S 6
Rayleigh 7 E 2
Raymond 76 B 2
Raymondville 77 G 6
Rayón 78 C 3
Rayong 41 H 5
Razan 34 D 3
Rāzān (Iran) 23 E 2
Razan (Iran) 23 E 2
Razdan 21 F 2
Razdel'naya 20 D 1
Razdolinsk 36 F 3
Razdol'noye 21 D 1
Razdolnoye 37 S 3
Razeh (Iran) 23 E 2
Razgrad 20 C 2
Razlog 20 B 2
Razmak 35 J 4
Ré, Ile de 18 C 2
Read 73 P 2
Reading 7 D 2
Reaghstown 4 B 3
Real, Cordillera 84 C 4
Real del Padre 88 C 5
Realico 88 D 6
Rèálmont 18 D 3
Reao 53 G 4

Reata 78 B 2
Reay 2 C 2
Rebbenesöy 16 G 1
Rebecca, Lake 48 C 5
Rebi 43 H 5
Rebiana Sand Sea → Ramlat
   Rabyānah 59 JK 4
Rebojo, Cachoeira do 85 G 5
Reboly 16 K 3
Rebun-tō 39 M 1
Recalde 89 D 6
Recaș 20 B 1
Rechitsa 24 F 5
Rechna Doab 35 J 4
Recife 87 K 2
Récifs de L'Astrolabe 51 J 5
Recifs d'Entrecasteaux 51 H 5
Récifs et Iles Chesterfield 49 K 2
Reconquista 88 DE 4
Recreio 85 G 5
Recreo 88 D 4
Recuay 84 C 5
Red Bank 77 J 4
Red Basin 38 E 4
Red Bay (Newfoundl., Can.)
   75 Q 5
Red Bay (U.K.) 4 C 2
Red Bluff 76 B 3
Red Cloud 76 G 3
Red Deer 73 P 5
Red Deer River (Alb., Can.) 73 P 5
Red Deer River (Sask., Can.)
   73 R 5
Red Devil 72 F 3
Red Hill (New Zealand) 51 Q 9
Red Hill (South Australia) 49 F 5
Red Hills 76 G 4
Red Lake 73 J 5
Red Lake 74 J 5
Red Lodge 76 E 2
Red Oak 77 GH 3
Red River (LA, U.S.A.) 77 H 5
Red River (MN, U.S.A.) 77 G 2
Red Rock River 76 D 3
Red Rosses 6 B 2
Red Sea 60 F 3–4
Red Water 73 P 5
Red Wing 77 H 3
Redcar 5 E 2
Redcliffe 49 J 4
Redcliffe, Mount 48 C 4
Redding 76 B 3
Redditch 7 D 1
Redenção da Gurguéia 87 H 2
Redfield 76 G 3
Redhill 7 D 2
Redland 2 C 2
Redlands 76 C 5
Redon 18 C 2
Redoubt Volcano 72 G 3
Redruth 6 B 2
Ree, Lough 4 B 3
Reedham 7 E 1
Reef Islands 51 J 4
Reepham 7 E 1
Refahiye 21 E 3
Refresco 88 C 4
Regar 35 H 3
Regencia 87 J 4
Regensburg 15 F 5
Reggane 58 EF 3
Reggio di Calabria 19 G 4
Reggio nell'Emilia 19 F 3
Reghin 20 B 1
Regina 73 R 5
Regina 85 H 3
Registan 35 GH 4
Regocijo 78 AB 3
Rehoboth 66 B 4
Reigate 7 D 2
Reigate 7 D 2
Reighton 5 E 2
Reims 18 D 2
Reina Adelaida, Archipiélago de la
   89 A 9
Reindeer 73 R 4
Reindeer Lake 73 R 4
Reine 16 F 2
Reinoksfjellet 16 G 2
Reinosa 18 C 3
Reisaelva 16 H 2
Reitoru 53 F 4
Reitz 66 D 5
Rekinniki 37 U 3
Reliance 73 Q 3
Relizane 58 F 1
Remansão 85 HJ 4
Remanso 87 H 2
Rembang 42 D 3
Remeshk 34 F 5
Rémire 85 H 3
Remiremont 19 E 2
Remontnoye 21 F 1
Ren Xian 38 FG 3
Rena 16 F 3
Renascença 84 E 4

Rendova 51 G 3
Rendsburg 15 EF 4
Renfrew 75 M 6
Renfrew Heights 3 B 4
Rengat 42 B 4
Rengma Hills 41 F 2
Rengo 88 B 5
Reni 20 C 1
Renmark 49 G 5
Rennell 51 H 4
Rennell, Islas 89 B 9
Rennes 18 C 2
Rennie Lake 73 Q 3
Reno (Italy) 19 F 3
Reno (U.S.A.) 76 B 4
Renqiu 39 G 3
Renshou 38 D 5
Renton 76 B 2
Reo 43 F 5
Repartição 85 G 4
Repartimento 85 G 4
Replot 16 H 3
Repolovo 25 N 3
Reprêsa Agua Vermelha
   87 FG 4–5
Reprêsa Bariri 87 G 5
Reprêsa Boa Esperança 87 H 2
Reprêsa da Capivara 87 F 5
Reprêsa de Furnas 87 G 5
Reprêsa de Jupi 87 F 5
Reprêsa de Jurumirim 87 G 5
Reprêsa de Xavantes 87 F 5
Reprêsa do Estreito 87 G 4–5
Reprêsa Promissão 87 G 5
Represa Raúl Leoni 85 F 2
Reprêsa Três Marias 87 G 4
Republic 76 C 2
Republic of Ireland 14 B 4
Republican River 76 G 3
Repulse Bay 73 U 2
Repulse Bay 73 U 2
Repvåg 16 J 1
Requena 18 C 4
Requena 84 D 4
Reşadiye 21 E 2
Reşadiyel Yarımadası 20 C 3
Réservoir Baskatong 75 MN 6
Réservoir Cabonga 75 M 6
Réservoir Decelles 75 M 6
Réservoir Dozois 75 M 6
Réservoir Gouin 75 MN 6
Réservoir Manicouagan 75 O 5
Réservoir Pipmouacan 75 N 6
Reservoir Rocklands 49 G 6
Reshteh-ye Esfarāyeh 34 F 3
Reshteh-ye Kūhhā-ye Alborz
   (Iran) 23 F 1
Resia, Passo di 19 F 2
Resistencia 88 DE 4
Reşiţa 20 B 1
Resolution 50 P 10
Resolution Island 75 P 3
Resolven 6 C 3
Resplendor 87 H 4
Reston 3 C 4
Retalhuleu 78 D 5
Rethel 19 D 2
Rethimnon 20 B 3
Retkucha 37 W 2
Retz 19 G 2
Réunion 67 K 6
Reus 18 D 3
Reut 20 C 1
Reutlingen 15 E 5
Reutte 19 F 2
Revantazón 84 B 5
Revda 16 K 2
Revda 25 L 4
Revelstoke 73 O 5
Revesby 7 D 1
Revilla Gigedo 72 L 4
Revilla Gigedo Islands 69 G 8
Revin 19 D 2
Revolyutsii, Pik 35 J 3
Revsundssjön 16 FG 3
Revue 67 E 3
Rewa 40 D 3
Rewari 40 C 2
Rexburg 76 D 3
Rey 34 E 3
Rey (Iran) 23 F 2
Rey Bouba 63 G 4
Rey, Isla del 84 C 2
Reyes 86 C 3
Reyhanlı 21 E 3
Reyhanli (Turkey) 22 B 1
Reykjahlíð 16 B 2
Reykjanes 16 A 3
Reykjavik 16 B 3
Reynaldo Cullen 88 D 5
Reynosa 78 C 2
Rezé 18 C 2
Rēzekne 17 J 4
Rezovo 20 C 2
Rezvān (Iran) 23 G 4
Rhages (Iran) 23 F 2

Rhallamane 58 CD 4
Rhallamane, Sebkha de 58 D 4
Rhandirmwyn 6 C 1
Rharis 59 F 3
Rharsa, Chott el 59 G 2
Rhayader 6 C 1
Rhein 14 E 4
Rhemilès 58 E 3
Rhewl 6 C 1
Rhiconich 2 B 2
Rhinelander 77 J 2
Rhinmal 40 B 2
Rhino Camp 64 E 4
Rhir, Cap 58 CD 2
Rhiw 5 B 1
Rhode Island 77 M 3
Rhodes 20 C 3
Rhodes Grave 66 D 4
Rhodesia → Zimbabwe
   66–67 DE 3
Rhodope Mts 20 BC 2
Rhondda 6 C 2
Rhône 19 D 3
Rhos 6 B 2
Rhossili 6 B 2
Rhourde el Baguel 59 G 2
Rhuddlan 5 D 3
Rhuis 18 C 2
Rhyl 6 C 1
Rhymney 6 C 2
Rhynie 2 C 3
Rī Shahr (Iran) 23 F 3
Ría de Muros y Noya 18 B 3
Ría de Santa Marta 18 B 3
Ría de Vigo 18 B 3
Ri-Aba 63 F 5
Riachão 85 J 5
Riachão do Jacuípe 87 J 3
Riacho de Santana 87 H 3
Riachos, Islas de los 89 D 6
Rianápolis 87 G 4
Riangnom 64 E 3
Rías Altas 18 B 3
Rías Bajas 18 B 3
Riasi 35 J 4
Riau, Kepulauan 42 B 3
Riaza 18 C 3
Ribadeo 18 B 3
Ribamar 87 H 1
Ribas do Río Pardo 87 F 5
Ribáuè 67 F 2
Ribe 17 E 4
Ribeira 87 G 5
Ribeira Brava 62 B 6
Ribeira Grande 62 A 6
Ribeirão Prêto 87 G 5
Ribeiro Gonçalves 87 G 2
Ribera 19 F 4
Riberalta 86 C 3
Ribnica 19 F 2
Riccall 5 E 3
Riccione 19 F 3
Rich 58 E 2
Richard Collinson Inlet 73 P 1
Richard Toll 62 A 2
Richard's Bay 67 E 5
Richardson Mountains 72 K 2
Richfield 76 D 4
Richland 76 C 2
Richmond (CA, U.S.A.) 76 B 4
Richmond (Queensland, Austr.)
   49 G 3
Richmond (South Africa) 66 C 6
Richmond (U.K.) 5 E 2
Richmond (VA, U.S.A.) 77 L 4
Richmond Hill 75 M 7
Ricklean 16 H 3
Rickmansworth 7 D 2
Ricobayo, Embalse de 18 B 3
Ridgewell 7 E 1
Riding Mountain National Park
   73 R 5
Ridsdale 5 D 2
Ried 19 F 2
Riesa 15 F 4
Riesco, Isla 89 B 9
Rietavas 17 H 4
Rietfontein (Namibia) 66 C 4
Rietfontein (South Africa) 66 C 5
Rieti 19 F 3
Rifstangi 16 B 2
Rig Rig 63 G 3
Riga 17 H 4
Riga, Gulf of 17 H 4
Rigachikun 63 F 3
Riggins 76 C 2
Rigolet 75 Q 5
Rihand Dam 40 D 3
Riihimäki 17 HJ 3
Riiser-Larsen Ice Shelf 91
Riiser-Larsen Peninsula 91
Rijau 63 F 3
Rijeka 19 F 2
Riley 76 C 3
Rimatara 53 E 4

Rimavská Sobota 15 H 5
Rimbo 17 G 4
Rimini 19 F 3
Rimnicu Sǎrat 20 C 1
Rîmnicu Vîlcea 20 B 1–2
Rimouski 75 O 6
Rinbung 40 E 2
Rinchinlhümbe 36 G 5
Rinconada 86 C 5
Ringe 17 F 4
Ringerike 17 EF 3
Ringford 3 B 4
Ringgold Isles 52 D 4
Ringhkung 41 G 2
Ringim 63 F 3
Ringköbing 17 E 4
Ringköbing Fjord 17 E 4
Ringládes 20 AB 3
Ringsend 4 B 2
Ringvassöy 16 G 2
Ringwood 7 D 2
Rinihue 89 B 6
Rinja, Pulau 43 E 5
Rinjani, Gunung 42 E 5
Río Balsas 78 B 4
Río Branco 84 E 5
Río Branco 85 F 3
Río Branco (Uruguay) 88 F 5
Río Branco do Sul 88 G 4
Río Bravo del Norte 76 EF 5–6
Río Bravo del Norte 78 C 2
Río Brilhanter 87 EF 5
Río Bueno 89 B 7
Río Casca 87 H 5
Río Chico (Argentina) 89 C 8
Río Chico (Venezuela) 84 E 1
Río Claro 87 G 5
Río Coco o Segovia 78 F 5
Río Colorado (Argentina) 89 D 6
Río Conchos 76 EF 6
Río Cuarto 88 CD 5
Rio das Mortes 87 F 3
Río de Janeiro 87 H 5
Rio de Janeiro 87 H 5
Río de la Plata 88 E 5–6
Río de las Piedras 86 B 3
Rio de Oro 58 BC 4
Río del Rey 63 F 5
Río do Sul 88 G 4
Río Gallegos 89 C 9
Rio Grande 76 G 6
Río Grande (Argentina) 89 C 9
Río Grande (Bahía, Brazil) 87 H 3
Río Grande (Brazil) 87 G 4
Río Grande (Río Grande do Sul,
   Brazil) 88 F 5
Rio Grande de Matagalpa 78 F 5
Rio Grande de Santiago 78 B 3
Rio Grande de Tarija 86 D 5
Río Grande do Norte 87 J 2
Río Grande do Sul 88 EF 4
Rio Grande Fracture Zone 98 A 5
Río Grande o'Guapay 86 D 4
Río Hondo 88 D 4
Rio Lacantún 78 D 4
Río Lagartos 78 E 3
Rio Largo 87 J 2
Rio Lempa 78 E 5
Río Mezcalapa 78 D 4
Río Muerto 88 D 4
Río Mulatos 86 C 4
Río Negrinho 88 FG 4
Río Negro (Argentina) 89 D 6–7
Río Negro (Brazil) 85 F 4
Río Negro (Uruguay) 88 EF 5
Rio Negro, Pantanal do 86 E 4
Río Pardo 87 G 4
Rio Patuca 78 F 4
Río Real 87 J 3
Rio San Juan 78 F 5
Rio Siquia 78 F 5
Río Sonora 76 D 6
Río Tercero 88 D 5
Río Tinto 87 J 2
Río Turbio Mines 89 B 9
Rio Usumacinta 78 D 4
Río Verde (Goiás, Brazil) 87 F 4
Río Verde (Mato Grosso do Sul,
   Brazil) 87 F 5
Río Verde de Mato Grosso 87 F 4
Rio Viejo 78 E 5
Rio Yaqui 76 E 6
Ríobamba 84 C 4
Ríohacha 84 D 1
Rioja 84 C 5
Riom 18 D 2
Rion 20 B 3
Rioni 21 F 2
Ríosucio 84 C 2
Ríoverde (Ecuador) 84 C 3
Rioverde (Mexico) 78 BC 3
Ríozinho 84 E 4
Ripley 7 D 1
Ripley (N.Y., U.S.A.) 77 L 3
Ripley (U.K.) 5 E 2
Ripley (W.V., U.S.A.) 77 K 4

Ripoll 18 D 3
Ripon 5 E 2
Riposto 19 G 4
Risan 20 A 2
Risasi 64 D 5
Risca 6 C 2
Rishiri-tō 39 M 1
Rīshmūk (Iran) 23 F 3
Risör 17 E 4
Risöyhamn 16 FG 2
Risti 17 H 4
Ristiina 16 J 3
Ristijärvi 16 J 3
Ristna Neem 17 H 4
Ritchie's Archipelago 41 F 5
Rito 66 B 3
Ritsa 21 F 2
Ritter, Mount 76 C 4
Ritzville 76 C 2
Rivadavia (Argentina) 86 D 5
Rivadavia (Chile) 88 B 4
Rivas 78 E 5
River Aire 5 E 3
River Avon (Avon) 6 C 2
River Avon (Grampian) 2 C 3
River Avon (Warwickshire) 7 D 1
River Bann 4 B 2
River Barrow 4 B 3
River Blackwater 7 E 2
River Boyne 4 B 3
River Brora 2 B 2
River Bure 7 E 1
River, Cape 49 H 3
River Cess 62 BC 4
River Cherwell 7 D 2
River Coquet 5 E 2
River Dee (Clwyd) 6 C 1
River Dee (Grampian) 2 C 3
River Derwent 5 E 2
River Deveron 2 C 3
River Don (Grampian) 2 C 3
River Don (S. Yorkshire) 5 E 3
River Dove 5 E 3
River Eden 5 D 2
River Erne 4 A 2
River Exe 6 C 2
River Farrar 2 B 3
River Findhorn 2 C 3
River Forth 3 B 3
River Foyle 4 B 2
River Humber 5 E 3
River Kennet 7 D 2
River Liffey 4 B 3
River Little Ouse 7 E 1
River Lune 5 D 2
River Medway 7 E 2
River Mersey 5 D 3
River Nene 7 E 1
River Nidd 5 E 3
River Nore 4 B 3
River North Tyne 5 D 2
River Ouse (N. Yorkshire) 5 E 3
River Ouse (Norfolk) 7 E 1
River Oykel 2 B 2
River Plate 89 EF 6
River Ribble 5 D 3
River Severn (Gloucestershire)
   6 C 2
River Severn (Powys) 6 C 1
River Shannon 4 B 3
River Slaney 4 B 3
River South Tyne 5 D 2
River Stour 7 E 2
River Suir 4 B 3
River Swale 5 E 2
River Tamar 6 B 2
River Tay 3 C 3
River Tees 5 E 2
River Teifi 6 B 1
River Teme 6 C 1
River Teviot 3 C 4
River Thames 7 E 2
River Torridge 6 B 2
River Towy 6 B 2
River Trent 7 D 1
River Tweed 3 C 4
River Tyne 5 E 2
River Ure 5 E 2
River Waveney 7 E 1
River Wear 5 D 2
River Welland 7 D 1
River Wey 7 D 2
River Wharfe 5 E 3
River Witham 7 D 1
River Wye 6 C 1–2
River Yare 7 E 1
Rivera (Argentina) 89 D 6
Rivera (Uruguay) 88 E 5
Riverina 49 GH 5
Rivers Inlet 73 M 5
Riversdale 66 C 6
Riverside 76 C 5
Riverstown 4 B 3
Riverton (Man., Can.) 73 S 5

Riverton (New Zealand) 50 P 10
Riverton (WY, U.S.A.) 76 E 3
Rivesaltes 18 D 3
Riviera di Levante 19 E 3
Riviera di Ponente 19 E 3
Rivière à la Baleine 75 O 4
Rivière aux Feuilles 75 N 4
Rivière aux Mélèzes 75 N 4
Rivière aux Outardes 75 O 5
Rivière du Petit-Mécatina 75 PQ 5
Rivière-du-Loup 75 O 6
Rivoli 19 E 2
Rivungo 66 C 3
Riwoqê 38 C 4
Riyadh (Saudi Arabia) 23 E 4
Riyān 61 H 6
Riza (Iran) 23 G 2
Rize 21 F 2
Rize Dağları 21 F 2
Rizhao 39 G 3
Rizhskiy Zaliv 17 H 4
Rizokarpásso → Dipkarpas 21 D 3
Rjukan 17 E 4
Rjuven 17 E 4
Rkiz 58 B 5
Ro 41 J 4
Road Town 79 K 4
Roag 2 A 3
Roan Plateau 76 E 4
Roanne 18 D 2
Roanoke 77 L 4
Roanoke Rapids 77 L 4
Roanoke River 77 L 4
Roatán 78 E 4
Robat Karīm (Iran) 23 F 2
Robāt-e Khān (Iran) 23 G 2
Robāt-e Kord (Iran) 23 G 2
Robāt-e Tork (Iran) 23 F 2
Robāt-e-Khān 34 F 4
Robbah 59 G 2
Robben Island 66 B 6
Robe 49 F 6
Robe, Mount 49 G 5
Robert Butte 91
Robert Lee 76 F 5
Roberts, Mount 49 J 4
Robertsfield 62 BC 4
Robertsfors 16 H 3
Robertsport 62 B 4
Robi 65 F 3
Robin Hood's Bay 5 E 2
Robinson Crusoe 89 A 5
Robinson Ranges (Western
  Australia) 48 B 4
Robinson River 49 F 2
Robinstown 4 B 3
Robore 86 E 4
Robson, Mount 73 O 5
Robstown 76 G 6
Roccaraso 19 F 3
Rocha 88 F 5
Rocha de Galé, Barragem da
  18 B 4
Rochdale 5 D 3
Rochefort 18 C 2
Rocher River 73 P 3
Rocher Thomasset 53 F 3
Rochester 5 D 2
Rochester (MN, U.S.A.) 77 H 3
Rochester (N.H., U.S.A.) 77 M 3
Rochester (N.Y., U.S.A.) 77 L 3
Rochester (U.K.) 7 E 2
Rochlitzer Berg 15 F 4
Rocigalgo 18 BC 4
Rock Hill 77 K 5
Rock Island 77 H 3
Rock River 77 J 3
Rock Springs 76 E 3
Rockall Bank 98 A 2
Rockcliffe 3 C 4
Rockefeller Plateau 91
Rockford 77 J 3
Rockhampton 49 HJ 3
Rockhampton Downs 48 F 2
Rockingham (N.C., U.S.A.)
  77 L 5
Rockingham (Western Australia)
  48 B 5
Rocklands Reservoir 49 G 6
Rockport (CA, U.S.A.) 76 B 4
Rockport (TX, U.S.A.) 77 G 6
Rockstone 85 G 2
Rockville 77 L 4
Rocky Mount 77 L 4
Rocky Mountain House 73 O 5
Rocky Mountain National Park
  76 E 3
Rocky Mountains 69 FH 4–6
Rödby Havn 17 F 5
Roddickton 75 Q 5
Rodel 2 A 3
Rodeo (AZ, U.S.A.) 76 E 5
Rodeo (Mexico) 78 B 2
Rodez 18 D 3
Rodholivos 20 B 2
Rodhopi, Dytike 20 B 2

Ródhos 20 C 3
Ródhos 20 C 3
Rodina 36 G 4
Rodionovo 24 L 2
Rodney, Cape (AK, U.S.A.)
  72 D 3
Rodopi 20 BC 2
Rodrigues 84 D 5
Roebourne 48 B 3
Roebuck Bay 48 C 2
Roes Welcome Sound 73 U 2–3
Roeselare 14 D 4
Rogachev 17 J 5
Rogagua, Lago 86 C 3
Rogaland 17 E 4
Rogart 2 B 3
Rogaška Slatina 19 G 2
Rogen 16 F 3
Rogers City 77 K 2
Rogers Peak 76 D 4
Roggeveld Berge 66 BC 6
Rognan 16 FG 2
Rogovskaya 21 E 1
Rogozhina 20 A 2
Rogue River 76 B 3
Rohrbach 21 F 2
Rohri 35 H 5
Rohtak 40 C 2
Roi Et 41 H 4
Roi Georges, Îles du 53 F 3
Roja, Punta 89 CD 7
Rojas 88 D 5
Rojo, Cabo 79 J 4
Rokan, Sungai 42 B 3
Rokeby 49 G 1
Rokel 62 B 4
Rolândia 87 F 5
Röldal 17 E 4
Rolla (MO, U.S.A.) 77 H 4
Rolla (N.D., U.S.A.) 76 G 2
Rolleston 49 H 3
Rolvenden 7 E 2
Rolvsöya 16 H 1
Roma 19 F 3
Roma (Queensland, Austr.) 49 H 4
Romaine 75 P 5
Roman 20 C 1
Roman Kosh 21 D 2
Romanche Fracture Zone 98 A 3
Romang, Pulau 43 G 5
Romania 20 BC 1
Romanova 36 H 4
Romanovka 24 H 5
Romanovka 36 K 5
Romans-sur-Isère 19 E 2
Romanzof, Cape 72 D 3
Romanzof Mountains 72 J 2
Romblon 43 F 1
Rome (GA, U.S.A.) 77 J 5
Rome (Italy) 19 F 3
Rome (N.Y., U.S.A.) 77 L 3
Rome (OR, U.S.A.) 76 C 3
Romerike 17 F 3
Romilly-sur-Seine 18 D 2
Rommani 58 D 2
Romny 24 F 5
Römö 17 E 4
Romont 19 E 2
Romorantin-Lanthenay 18 D 2
Romsdal 16 E 3
Romsey 7 D 2
Rona 2 B 3
Ronaldsway 4 C 2
Ronas Hill 2 D 1
Ronay 2 A 3
Roncador 51 G 3
Roncador, Cayos de 79 G 5
Roncador, Serra do 87 F 3
Roncesvalles 18 C 3
Ronda (China) 35 K 3
Ronda (Spain) 18 BC 4
Rondane 16 EF 3
Rondas das Salinas 86 D 4
Rönde 17 F 4
Rondón, Pico 85 F 3
Rondônia 86 D 3
Rondônia 86 D 3
Rondonópolis 87 F 4
Rong Xian 38 D 5
Rong Xian 38 F 6
Rongan 49 H 5
Rongcheng 39 H 3
Ronge, Lac la 73 R 4
Rongelap 52 C 2
Rongerik 52 C 2
Rongjiang 38 E 5
Rongklang Range 41 F 3
Rongshui 38 E 5
Rönne 17 F 4
Ronne Ice Shelf 91
Ronneby 17 G 4
Ronuro 87 F 3
Rooikop 66 AB 4
Roorkee 40 C 2
Roosevelt 86 D 3

Roosevelt Island 91
Roosevelt, Mount 73 M 4
Roper River 48 E 1
Roper River 48 EF 1
Ropi 16 H 2
Roquetas de Mar 18 C 4
Roraima (Brazil) 85 F 3
Roraima (Venezuela) 85 F 2
Rori 40 C 2
Rosa 67 E 1
Rosa, Lake 79 H 3
Rosamorada 78 A 3
Rosario 78 A 3
Rosario (Argentina) 88 D 5
Rosario (Chile) 86 B 5
Rosário (Maranhão, Brazil) 87 H 1
Rosario (Paraguay) 86 E 5
Rosario, Bahía 76 C 6
Rosario de la Frontera 88 D 4
Rosario de Lerma 88 C 4
Rosario del Tala 88 E 5
Rosário do Sul 88 F 5
Rosário Oeste 86 E 3
Rosarito 76 D 6
Rosas, Golfo de 18 D 3
Roscoff 18 C 2
Roscommon 4 A 3
Roscommon 14 B 4
Roscrea 4 B 3
Roseau 79 K 4
Roseburg 76 B 3
Rosenberg 77 G 6
Rosenheim 15 F 5
Rosetown 73 Q 5
Rosetta → Rashīd 60 E 2
Rosh Pinah 66 B 5
Rosignol 85 G 2
Roşiori de Vede 20 C 2
Roskilde 17 F 4
Roslagen 17 G 4
Roslavl' 24 F 5
Roslyn 76 B 2
Ross (Canada) 72 L 3
Ross (Senegal) 62 A 2
Ross Ice Shelf 91
Ross Island 91
Ross River 72 L 3
Ross Sea 91
Rossan Point 14 B 4
Rossano 19 G 4
Rossel Island 51 F 4
Rossell y Rius 88 E 5
Rössing 66 A 4
Rosslare 6 A 1
Rosslare 14 B 4
Rosslare Harbour 6 A 1
Rosslea 4 B 2
Rosso 58 B 5
Rossön 16 G 3
Ross-on-Wye 6 C 2
Rossosh 24 G 5
Rössvatn 16 F 2
Rosta 16 G 2
Rostam (United Arab Emirates)
  23 F 4
Rostam Kalā (Iran) 23 F 1
Rostami (Iran) 23 F 3
Rostāq (Iran) 23 FG 4
Rosthern 73 Q 5
Rostock 15 F 4
Rostonsölkä 16 H 2
Rostov 24 G 4
Rostov-na-Donu 21 EF 1
Rostrevor 4 B 2
Roswell 76 F 5
Rosyth 3 C 3
Rota 18 B 4
Rota 52 A 2
Rothbury 5 E 2
Rothera 91
Rotherham 5 E 3
Rothes 2 C 3
Rothesay 3 B 4
Rothwell 5 E 3
Roti, Pulau 43 F 6
Roti, Selat 43 F 6
Rotja, Punta 18 D 4
Roto 49 H 5
Rotorua 51 R 8
Rotterdam 14 D 4
Rottweil 15 E 5
Rotuma 52 C 3
Roubaix 18 D 1
Rouen 18 D 2
Roughsike 5 D 2
Roughton 7 E 1
Rousay 2 C 2
Rouyn 75 M 6
Rovaniemi 16 J 2
Rovdino 24 H 3
Rovereto 19 F 2
Rovigo 19 F 2

Rovinj 19 F 2
Rovkulskoye, Ozero 16 K 3
Rovno 17 J 5
Rovnoye 24 J 5
Rovuma 67 F 2
Rowanburn 3 C 4
Rowley 75 M 2
Rowley Shoals 48 B 2
Rowsley 7 D 1
Roxas (Philippines) 43 E 1
Roxas (Philippines) 43 F 1
Roxburgh 50 P 10
Roxen 17 G 4
Roxo, Cap 62 A 3
Roy 76 F 4
Roy Hill 48 C 3
Royal Canal 4 B 3
Royal Leamington Spa 7 D 1
Royal Tunbridge Wells 7 E 2
Royan 18 C 2
Roybridge 3 B 3
Royston 7 D 1
Rozhdestvenskoye 24 J 4
Rozhkao 21 F 2
Rožňava 15 H 5
Rozovka 21 E 1
Roztocze 15 H 4
Rt Kamenjak 19 F 3
Rt Ploča 19 G 3
Rtanj 20 B 2
Rtishchevo 24 H 5
Ruacana Falls 66 AB 3
Ruaha National Park 64 E 6
Ruahine Range 51 R 8–9
Ruapehu 51 R 8
Ruapuke 50 P 10
Ruawai 51 Q 8
Rubeho Mountains 65 F 6
Rubi 64 D 4
Rubiku 20 A 2
Rubinéia 87 F 5
Rubio 84 D 2
Rubondo 64 E 5
Rubtsovsk 25 Q 5
Ruby 72 F 3
Ruby Mountains 76 C 3
Rūd Sar (Iran) 23 F 1
Rūdak (Iran) 23 F 3
Rudall River National Park 48 C 3
Rudao 39 H 4
Rudauli 40 D 2
Rudbar 35 G 4
Rūdbār (Iran) 23 E 1
Rudkøbing 17 F 5
Rudnaya Pristan' 39 L 2
Rudnik 20 B 2
Rudnya 24 F 4–5
Rudnyy 25 M 5
Rudolf, Lake 65 F 4
Rudong 39 H 4
Rudwick 7 D 2
Rudyard 76 D 2
Rufā'ah 60 E 6
Ruffec 18 D 2
Rufford 5 D 3
Rufiji 65 F 6
Rufino 88 D 5
Rufisque 62 A 3
Rufunsa 66 D 3
Rugby (N.D., U.S.A.) 76 G 2
Rugby (U.K.) 7 D 1
Rugeley 5 D 3
Rügen 15 F 4
Rugley 7 CD 1
Ruhea 40 E 2
Ruhengeri 64 DE 5
Ruhnu 17 H 4
Ruhr 15 E 4
Ruhuhu 67 EF 2
Rui Barbosa 87 H 3
Rui'an 39 H 5
Ruijin 38 G 5
Ruili 38 C 6
Rujm al Mudhari (Iraq) 22 C 2
Rujmayn, Jabal Abū (Syria)
  22 BC 2
Rukumkot 40 D 2
Rukwa, Lake 64 E 6
Rum 3 A 3
Rum Cay 79 H 3
Rum Jungle 48 E 1
Ruma 20 A 2
Rumādah 61 G 6
Rumāila (Iraq) 23 E 3
Rumaylah 60 E 6
Rumbalara 48 E 4
Rumbek 64 DE 3
Rumia 15 G 4
Rummah, Wādī ar (Saudi Arabia)
  22 D 4
Rumoi 39 M 2
Rumphi 67 E 2
Runan 38 F 4
Runaway, Cape 51 R 8
Runcorn 5 D 3
Runde 67 E 4

Rundu 66 B 3
Rungu 64 D 4
Rungwa 64 E 6
Rungwa 64 E 6
Rungwa West 64 E 6
Rungwe 64 E 6
Runn 17 G 3
Ruo Shui 38 C 2
Ruokolahti 16 J 3
Ruoqiang 38 A 3
Ruovesi 16 H 3
Rupanco 89 B 7
Rupara 66 B 3
Rupat, Pulau 42 B 3
Rupert (ID, U.S.A.) 76 D 3
Rupert (Quebec, Can.) 75 M 5
Rupert, Baie de 75 LM 5
Rupnagar 40 B 2
Ruponda 67 F 2
Rurrenabaque 86 C 3
Rurutu 53 E 4
Rusakovo 37 U 4
Rusanovo 24 L 1
Rusape 67 E 3
Ruse 20 C 2
Ruşeţu 20 C 2
Rush 4 B 3
Rushan 39 H 3
Rushan (U.S.S.R.) 35 J 3
Rushden 7 D 1
Rushi (Iraq) 23 E 3
Rusinga 64 E 5
Russas 87 J 1
Russell 73 R 5
Russell (New Zealand) 51 Q 8
Russell Islands 51 G 3
Russell Range 48 C 5
Russellville (AL, U.S.A.) 77 J 5
Russellville (AR, U.S.A.) 77 H 4
Russkaya 39 L 1
Russkaya 91
Rustak 35 H 3
Rustavi 21 G 2
Rustenburg 66 D 5
Ruston 77 H 5
Ruswarp 5 E 2
Rutana 64 E 5
Rutanzige, Lake 64 D 5
Ruteng 43 F 5
Rutenga 67 E 4
Rutherglen 3 B 4
Ruthin 5 D 3
Rutland 41 F 5
Rutog 40 C 1
Rutshuru 64 D 5
Ruvu 65 F 6
Ruvuma 67 F 2
Ruvuma 67 F 2
Ruwaybah 60 D 5
Ruwenzori National Park 64 DE 5
Ruwenzori Range 64 E 4
Ruzayevka 24 H 5
Ruzayevka 25 N 5
Ruzhnikova 37 T 2
Ruzitgort 25 MN 3
Ruzizi 64 D 5
Ružomberok 15 G 5
Rwanda 64 DE 5
Ryābād (Iran) 23 G 1
Ryan 76 G 5
Ryazan' 24 G 5
Ryazhsk 24 G 5
Rybachiy, Poluostrov 16 K 2
Rybach'ye 35 K 2
Rybinsk → Andropov 24 G 4
Rybinskoye Vodokhranilishche
  24 G 4
Rybnik 15 G 4
Rybnitsa 20 C 1
Rybnovsk 37 Q 5
Ryde 7 D 2
Rye 7 E 2
Ryegate 76 E 2
Ryfylke 17 E 4
Ryhope 5 E 2
Ryl'sk 24 F 5
Ryn Peski 24 J 6
Ryōtsu 39 L 3
Rytterknegten 17 G 4
Ryukyu Islands 39 J 5
Rzepin 15 FG 4
Rzeszów 15 H 4
Rzhev 24 F 4

S

Sa Dec 41 J 5
Sa Huynh 41 J 5
Sa Madre Occidental 78 AB 2–3
Sa Oui 41 H 5
Sa'ādatābād 34 F 5
Sa'ādatābād (Iran) 23 F 3
Sa'ādatābād (Iran) 23 F 3

Saale 15 F 4
Saalfeld 15 F 4
Saanen 19 E 2
Saarbrücken 15 E 5
Sääre 17 H 4
Saaremaa 17 H 4
Saarijärvi 16 J 3
Saariselkä 16 J 2
Saarlouis 14 E 5
Saavedra 89 D 6
Šabac 20 A 2
Sabadell 18 D 3
Sabah 42 E 2
Sabak 42 B 3
Sabang 43 E 3
Sabán 84 E 2
Sabana 84 D 3
Sabanalarga 84 C 1
Sabang 42 A 2
Sabang 43 E 3
Sabanözü 21 D 2
Săbăoani 20 C 1
Sabará 87 H 4
Sabari 40 D 4
Sabāya 61 G 5
Sabaya 86 C 4
Sabderat 64 F 1
Sabhā' (Saudi Arabia) 61 G 4
Sabhā (Jordan) 22 B 2
Sabhā (Libya) 59 H 3
Sabhā, Wāhāt 59 H 3
Sabidana, Jabal 61 F 5
Sabina Shoal 42 E 2
Sabinas 78 B 2
Sabinas Hidalgo 78 B 2
Sabine 77 H 5
Sabini, Monti 19 F 3
Sabīr, Jabal 61 G 6
Sābirīyah (Kuwait) 23 E 3
Sabkhat al Bardawīl (Egypt) 22 A 3
Sabkhat Albū Gharz (Iraq) 22 C 2
Sabkhat Maṭṭī (United Arab Emirates) 23 F 5
Sable, Cape 75 O 7
Sable, Cape 77 K 6
Sable, Île de 52 B 4
Sable Island 75 P 7
Sablinskoye 21 F 2
Sæböl 16 A 2
Sabonkafi 63 F 3
Sábor 18 B 3
Sabou 62 D 3
Sabozo 63 G 1
Sabrātah 59 H 2
Sabres 18 C 3
Sabrina Coast 91
Sabun 25 Q 3
Sæby 17 F 4
Sabyā' 61 G 5
Sabyndy 25 O 5
Sabzevār (Iran) 23 G 1
Saca, Vīrful 20 C 1
Sacajawea Peak 76 C 2
Sacanana 89 C 7
Sacavém 18 B 4
Sacco 19 F 3
Sacedón 18 C 3
Săcele 20 C 1
Sachkhere 21 F 2
Sachs Harbour 73 N 1
Sachsen 15 F 4
Saco 76 B 4
Sacramento 76 B 4
Sacramento Mountains 76 E 5
Sacramento Valley 76 B 3–4
Sacuriuiná 86 E 3
Sad ad Darbandī Khān (Iraq) 23 D 2
Sad ad Dūkān (Iraq) 23 D 1–2
Sad Bi'Ar (Syria) 22 B 2
Sad Kharv (Iran) 23 G 1
Sadabá 18 C 3
Sa'dah 61 G 5
Sadani 65 F 6
Sadberge 5 E 2
Sadd al Aswān (Egypt) 22 A 4
Saddajaure 16 G 2
Saddell 3 B 4
Saddle Peak 41 F 5
Sadiya 41 G 2
S'adīyah, Hawr as (Iraq) 23 E 2
Sado 18 B 4
Sadochye, Ozero 34 F 2
Sadon 21 F 2
Sado-shima 39 L 3
Sadovoye 21 F 1
Safané 62 D 3
Ṣafāqis 59 H 2
Safed Khirs 35 J 3
Safed Koh 35 GH 4
Saffānīyah, Ra's as (Saudi Arabia) 23 E 3
Säffle 17 F 4
Safford 76 E 5
Saffron Walden 7 E 1
Safi 58 D 2

Safid Dasht (Iran) 23 E 2
Safīd, Kūh-e (Iran) 23 E 2
Safīd Rūd (Iran) 23 E 1
Safonovo 24 F 4
Safonovo 24 J 2
Safonovo 37 X 3
Safrā' al Asyāh (Saudi Arabia) 22 D 4
Safrā' as Sark (Saudi Arabia) 22 D 4
Safranbolu 21 D 2
Safwān (Iraq) 23 E 3
Saga (China) 40 E 2
Saga (Japan) 39 K 4
Saga (U.S.S.R.) 25 M 5
Sagaing 41 G 3
Sagala 62 C 3
Sagan 35 K 3
Sagar 40 C 3
Sagar 40 E 3
Sagastyr 37 N 1
Sagavanirktok 72 H 2
Sage 76 D 3
Saggart 4 B 3
Saghād (Iran) 23 F 3
Saginaw 77 K 3
Saginaw Bay 77 K 3
Sagiz 34 E 1
Sagleipie 62 C 4
Saglek Bay 75 P 4
Saglouc 75 M 3
Sagres 18 B 4
Sagu (Indonesia) 43 F 5
Sagu (Romania) 20 B 1
Sagua de Tánamo 79 H 3
Sagua la Grande 79 G 3
Saguache 76 E 4
Saguenay 75 NO 6
Saguia el Hamra 58 C 3
Saguia el Hamra 58 C 3
Sagunto 18 C 4
Sagwon 72 H 2
Sahagún (Colombia) 84 C 2
Sahagún (Spain) 18 B 3
Sahara 58–59 EG 4
Saharanpur 40 C 2
Saharsa 40 E 2
Sahiwal 35 J 4
Sahl Rakbah 61 G 4
Sahlābad 34 F 4
Saḥneh (Iran) 23 E 2
Sahrā' al Hajārah (Iraq) 22–23 D 3
Saḥrā' Bayyūḍah 60 E 5
Sahuaripa 76 E 6
Sahuayo de Diaz 78 B 4
Sahul Shelf 99 C 4
Sai Yok 41 G 5
Saiapoun 41 H 4
Saibai 50 D 3
Said Bundas 64 C 3
Saïda 58 F 2
Sa'īdābād (Iran) 23 G 3
Sa'īdīyeh (Iran) 23 E 1
Saidor 50 E 3
Saidpur 40 E 2
Saigon 41 J 5
Saihan Toroi 38 D 2
Saiki 39 K 4
Saimaa 16 J 3
Saimaan kanava 16 J 3
Sain Alto 78 B 3
Sā'īn Dezh (Iran) 23 E 1
Saindak 35 G 5
Saint Alban's (Newfoundl., Can.) 75 Q 6
St. Albans (U.K.) 7 D 2
Saint Albans (VT, U.S.A.) 77 M 3
Saint Albert 73 P 5
St. Andrews 3 C 3
Saint Ann's Bay 79 G 4
Saint Anthony 75 QR 5
Saint Arnaud 49 G 6
St. Asaph 6 C 1
Saint Augustin Saguenay 75 Q 5
Saint Augustine 77 K 6
St. Austell 6 B 2
St. Austell Bay 6 B 2
St. Blazey 6 B 2
St. Brides Bay 6 B 2
St. Bride's Major 6 C 3
St. Buryan 6 B 2
Saint Catherine, Monastery of 60 E 3
St. Catherine's Point 7 D 2
Saint Christopher 79 K 4
Saint Clair River 77 K 3
St. Clears 6 B 2
Saint Cloud 77 H 2
St. Columb Major 6 B 2
St. Croix 79 JK 4
St. David's 6 B 2
St. David's Head 6 B 2
St. Dennis 6 B 2
St. Dogmaels 6 B 1
Saint Elias, Mount 72 J 3
Saint Elias Mountains 72 K 3

Saint Félicien 75 N 6
Saint Flores National Park 64 C 3
Saint Francis 76 F 4
Saint Francis Bay 66 A 5
Saint Francis, Cape 66 CD 6
Saint Francois 65 J 6
Saint Francois Mountains 77 H 4
St. Gallen 19 E 2
Saint George (AK, U.S.A.) 72 D 4
Saint George (Queensland, Austr.) 49 H 4
Saint George (UT, U.S.A.) 76 D 4
Saint George, Cape 75 PQ 6
Saint George, Cape (Papua New Guinea) 51 F 2
Saint George's 79 K 5
Saint Georges 85 H 3
Saint George's Bay 75 Q 6
St. George's Channel 6 B 1
Saint George's Channel 51 F 2–3
St. Germans 6 B 2
Saint Helena 54 B 6
Saint Helena Bay 66 B 6
St. Helens 5 D 3
Saint Helens, Mount 76 B 2
St. Helier 7 C 3
St. Helier 14 C 5
Saint Ignace 77 K 2
Saint Ignace Island 74 K 6
St. Issey 6 B 2
St. Ives (Cambridgeshire) 7 D 1
St. Ives (Cornwall) 6 B 2
St. Ives Bay 6 B 2
Saint James, Cape 72 L 5
Saint Jérôme 75 N 6
Saint John (Canada) 75 O 6
Saint John (Liberia) 62 C 4
Saint John River 75 O 6
Saint John's (Antigua) 79 K 4
Saint John's (Canada) 75 R 6
Saint Johns (AZ, U.S.A.) 76 E 5
St. John's Chapel 5 D 2
Saint Johns River (FL, U.S.A.) 77 K 5–6
Saint Johnsbury 77 M 3
St. Johnstown 4 B 2
Saint Joseph (MI, U.S.A.) 77 J 3
Saint Joseph (MO, U.S.A.) 77 H 4
Saint Joseph (Seychelles) 65 J 6
Saint Joseph, Lake 74 J 5
St. Just 6 B 2
Saint Kitts and Nevis 79 K 4
Saint Kitts [Saint Christopher] 79 K 4
Saint Laurent 85 H 2
Saint Lawrence 49 H 3
Saint Lawrence, Gulf of 75 P 6
Saint Lawrence Island 72 C 3
Saint Lawrence River 75 O 6
Saint Léonard 75 O 6
Saint Louis (MO, U.S.A.) 77 H 4
Saint Lucia 79 K 5
Saint Lucia, Cape 67 E 5
Saint Lucia, Lake 67 E 5
St. Magnus Bay 2 D 1
St. Margaret's at Cliffe 7 E 2
St. Margaret's Hope 2 C 2
St. Marks 77 K 5
Saint Mary Peak 49 F 5
St. Mary's (U.K.) 6 A 3
Saint Marys 2 C 2
Saint Marys 50 L 3
St. Marys (AK, U.S.A.) 72 E 3
Saint Mary's Bay 75 R 6
Saint Matthew 72 E 3
Saint Matthias Group 51 F 2
Saint Maurice 75 N 6
St. Mawes 6 B 2
Saint Michael 72 E 3
Saint Michaels 76 E 4
St Moritz 19 E 2
St. Neots 7 D 1
St. Niklaas 14 D 4
Saint Paul (AK, U.S.A.) 72 D 4
Saint Paul (Alb., Can.) 73 P 5
Saint Paul (Liberia) 62 B 4
Saint Paul (MN, U.S.A.) 77 H 3
St. Peter and St. Paul Rocks 81 G 2
St. Peter Port 7 C 3
St. Peter Port 14 C 5
Saint Petersburg 77 K 6
Saint Pierre 75 Q 6
Saint Pierre (Seychelles) 65 J 6
Saint Pierre et Miquelon 75 Q 6
St. Roch Basin 73 ST 2
Saint Stephen 75 O 6
Saint Thomas (Ontario, Can.) 75 L 7
Saint Vincent 79 K 5
Saint Vincent, Gulf 49 F 6
Saint Vincent Passage 79 K 5
St. Walburg 73 Q 5
St. Weonards 6 C 3
Saint-Amand-Mont-Rond 18 D 2
Saint-André, Cap 67 G 3

Saint-Avold 19 E 2
Saint-Barthélemy 79 K 4
Saint-Brieuc 18 C 2
Saint-Calais 18 D 2
Saint-Chamond 19 D 2
Saint-Claude 19 E 2
Saint-Cyr-sur-Loire 18 D 2
Saint-Denis (France) 18 D 2
Saint-Denis (Réunion) 67 K 6
Saint-Denis-d'Oléron 18 C 2
Saint-Dié 19 E 2
Saint-Dizier 19 DE 2
Saint-Elie 85 H 3
Sainte Genevieve 77 H 4
Sainte Lucie, Canal de 79 K 5
Saintes 18 C 2
Saintes-Maries-de-la-Mer 19 D 3
Sainte-Thérèse 75 MN 6
Saint-Étienne 18 D 2
Saintfield 4 C 2
Saint-Florent, Golfe de 19 E 3
Saint-Flour 18 D 2
Saint-Gaudens 18 D 3
Saint-Georges 75 NO 6
Saint-Gildas, Pointe de 18 C 2
Saint-Jean 75 N 6
Saint-Jean, Lake 75 N 6
Saint-Jean-d'Angély 18 C 2
Saint-Jean-de-Luz 18 C 3
Saint-Jean-de-Monts 18 C 2
Saint-Junien 18 D 2
Saint-Lô 18 C 2
Saint-Louis (Senegal) 62 A 2
Saint-Malo 18 C 2
Saint-Marc 79 H 4
Saint-Martin 79 K 4
Saint-Martin-Vésubie 19 E 3
Saint-Nazaire 18 C 2
Saint-Omer 18 D 1
Saint-Paul (Réunion) 67 K 6
Saint-Péray 19 D 3
Saint-Pierre (Réunion) 67 K 6
Saint-Pons 18 D 3
Saint-Quentin 18 D 2
Saint-Savin 18 D 2
Saint-Seine-l'Abbaye 19 DE 2
Saint-Thomas (Puerto Rico) 79 JK 4
Saint-Tropez 19 E 3
Saint-Yrieix-la-Perche 18 D 2
Saipal 40 D 2
Saipan 52 A 1
Sajama 19 E 4
Sajīd 61 G 5
Sajzī (Iran) 23 F 2
Saka 65 F 5
Sakabinda 66 CD 2
Sakai 39 L 4
Sakākah (Saudi Arabia) 22 C 3
Sakakawea, Lake 76 F 2
Sakala Kõrgustik 17 J 4
Sakami 75 M 5
Sakami, Lac 75 M 5
Sakami River 75 N 5
Sakania 66 D 2
Sakar 20 C 2
Sakaraha 67 G 4
Sakarat Daği 21 E 2
Sakaraya 20 D 3
Sakarya 20 D 2
Sakashima-guntō 39 HJ 6
Sakata 39 L 3
Sakçağöz 21 E 3
Sakchu 39 J 2
Saké 62 E 4
Såkevare 16 G 2
Sakhalin 37 Q 5
Sakhalinskiy Zaliv 37 Q 5
Sakhandzha 37 N 2
Sakht Sar (Iran) 23 F 1
Saki 21 D 1
Sakoli 40 D 3
Sakon Nakhon 41 H 4
Sakrivier 66 C 6
Saksaul'skiy 35 G 1
Sakti 40 D 3
Säkylä 16 H 3
Sal 21 F 1
Sal (Cape Verde) 62 B 6
Sala 17 G 4
Sala Andong Tuk 41 H 5
Sala Consilina 19 G 3
Sala y Gómes 89 H 4
Salaca 17 H 4
Salacgrīva 17 H 4
Salada 78 B 2
Salada, Gran Laguna 89 C 7
Saladillo 89 E 6
Salado 88 D 4
Salado 89 C 6
Salaga 62 D 4
Salagle 65 G 4
Salair 25 R 5

Salairskiy Kryazh 25 R 5
Salal 63 H 3
Salālah (Oman) 61 J 5
Salālah (Sudan) 60 F 4
Salamá 78 D 4
Salamanca (Mexico) 78 B 3
Salamanca (Spain) 18 B 3
Salamat 63 J 3
Salamina 84 C 2
Salamis (Cyprus) 21 D 3
Salamis (Cyprus) 22 AB 2
Salamis (Greece) 20 B 3
Salar de Antofalla 88 C 4
Salar de Arizaro 86 C 5
Salar de Atacama 86 C 5
Salar de Coipasa 86 C 4
Salar de Hombre Muerto 88 C 4
Salar de Uyuni 86 C 5
Salas 18 B 3
Salaverry 84 C 5
Salavina 88 D 4
Salbris 18 D 2
Salcantay, Nevado 86 B 3
Salchininkai 17 J 5
Salcombe 6 C 2
Saldanha 66 B 6
Saldus 17 H 4
Sale (Australia) 49 H 6
Salé (Morocco) 58 D 2
Sale (U.K.) 5 D 3
Sālehābād (Iran) 23 E 2
Salekhard 25 N 2
Salem (IL, U.S.A.) 77 J 4
Salem (India) 40 C 5
Salem (OR, U.S.A.) 76 B 3
Salemi 19 F 4
Salen 3 B 3
Sälen 16 F 3
Salentina, Penisola 19 G 3–4
Salerno 19 FG 3
Salerno, Golfo di 19 F 3
Sales 85 H 5
Saletekri 40 D 3
Salford 5 D 3
Salgótarján 20 AB 1
Salgueiro 87 J 2
Salhus 17 E 3
Sali (Algeria) 58 E 3
Sali (Argentina) 88 C 4
Sali (Yugoslavia) 19 FG 3
Salida 76 E 4
Salihli 20 C 3
Salima 67 E 2
Salīmah, Wāhāt 60 D 4
Salin 41 F 3
Salina (Italy) 19 F 4
Salina (KS, U.S.A.) 76 G 4
Salina (UT, U.S.A.) 76 D 4
Salina del Gualicho 89 D 7
Salina Grande 89 C 6
Salinas 76 B 4
Salinas (Ecuador) 84 B 4
Salinas (Minas Gerais, Brazil) 87 H 4
Salinas, Cabo de 18 D 4
Salinas de Hidalgo 78 B 3
Salinas Grandes 88 CD 4–5
Salinas Peak 76 E 5
Salinas, Ponta das 66 A 2
Salinitas 86 B 5
Salinópolis 85 J 4
Salisbury (Canada) 75 M 3
Salisbury (MD, U.S.A.) 77 L 4
Salisbury (U.K.) 7 D 2
Salisbury → Harare 67 E 3
Salisbury Plain 7 CD 2
Salkhad (Syria) 22 B 2
Salla 16 J 2
Salling 17 E 4
Salloway 2 D 1
Sallūm 60 F 5
Salluyo, Nevado 86 C 3
Sallyana 40 D 2
Salmās 34 C 3
Salmi 16 K 3
Salmon 76 D 2
Salmon Arm 73 O 5
Salmon Mountains 76 B 3
Salmon River 76 CD 2
Salmon River Mountains 76 CD 2–3
Salo (Burkina) 64 B 4
Salo (Finland) 17 H 3
Salò (Italy) 19 F 2
Salon-de-Provence 19 E 3
Salong, Tûnel-e- 35 H 3
Salonga National Park 64 C 5
Salonica 20 B 2
Salonta 20 B 1
Salop 6 C 1
Salor 18 B 4
Salou 18 D 3
Saloum 62 A 3

Salpausselkä 16 J 3
Sal-Rei 62 B 6
Salsbruket 16 F 3
Sal'sk 21 F 1
Salso 19 F 4
Salsomaggiore Terme 19 E 3
Salt 18 D 3
Salt Fork Brazos 76 FG 5
Salt Lake (Queensland, Austr.)
   49 F 3
Salt Lake City 76 D 3
Salt Lakes 48 B 4
Salt Lakes 48 C 3
Salt Range 35 J 4
Salt River 76 D 5
Salt River (South Africa) 66 C 6
Salta 86 C 5
Saltash 6 B 2
Saltburn 5 E 2
Saltcoats 3 B 4
Saltdalselva 16 G 2
Salten 16 G 2
Saltfjellet 16 G 2
Saltfjorden 16 F 2
Saltfleet 5 F 3
Saltillo 78 B 2
Salto (Uruguay) 88 E 5
Salto Angostura 84 D 3
Salto da Divisa 87 J 4
Salto das Sete Quedas 87 F 5
Salto del Guaira 87 EF 5
Salton Sea 76 C 5
Salue Timpaus, Selat 43 F 4
Salumbar 40 B 3
Salur 40 D 4
Salvador (Brazil) 87 J 3
Salvador (Libya) 63 G 1
Salvatierra (Mexico) 78 B 3
Salvatierra (Spain) 18 C 3
Salwā (Qatar) 23 F 4
Salwá Baḥrī (Egypt) 22 A 4
Salween 41 G 4
Sal'yany 34 D 3
Salzach 19 F 2
Salzburg 19 F 2
Salzgitter 15 F 4
Salzwedel 15 F 4
Sam Neua 41 H 3
Sam Rayburn Reservoir 77 H 5
Sam Son 41 J 4
Samagaltay 36 G 5
Samāh (Libya) 59 J 3
Samāh (Saudi Arabia) 23 D 3
Samaipata 86 D 4
Samak, Tanjung 42 C 4
Samales Group 43 F 2
Samalga Pass 72 D 5
Samālūt 60 E 3
Samaná 79 J 4
Samandağ 21 E 3
Samandgi (Turkey) 22 B 1
Samangan 35 H 3
Samani 39 M 2
Samar 43 G 1
Samar Sea 43 F 1
Samara, Russia, U.S.S.R.) 24 K 5
Samara (Ukraine, U.S.S.R.) 21 E 1
Samarai 51 F 4
Samaríapo 84 E 2
Samarinda 42 E 4
Samarkand 35 H 3
Sāmarrā' (Iraq) 22 D 2
Samarskoye 25 Q 6
Samastipur 40 E 2
Samate 43 H 4
Samaúma 84 E 5
Samba 64 C 4
Samba 64 D 5
Samba Caju 66 B 1
Sambaliung 42–43 E 3
Sambalpur 40 D 3
Sambar, Tanjung 42 CD 4
Sambas 42 D 3
Sambava 67 J 2
Sambhar 40 C 2
Samboja 42 E 4
Sambor (Kampuchea) 41 J 5
Samborombón, Bahía 89 E 6
Sambre 18 D 1–2
Sambu 42 B 3
Sambuan 42 E 4
Samburg 25 P 2
Samch'ŏnp'o 39 J 4
Same (Indonesia) 43 G 5
Same (Tanzania) 65 F 5
Samfya 66 D 2
Sámi 20 B 3
Sami Ghar 35 H 4
Samīrah (Saudi Arabia) 22 C 4
Samka 41 G 3
Samnū 59 HJ 3
Samo Alto 88 B 5
Samoa Islands 52 D 3
Samobor 19 G 2

Samokov 20 B 2
Sámos 20 C 3
Samosir, Pulau 42 A 3
Samothráki 20 C 2
Samothráki 20 C 2
Sampaga 43 E 4
Sampford Peverell 6 C 3
Sampit 42 D 4
Sampit, Teluk 42 D 4
Sampun 51 F 3
Sampwe 64 D 6
Samrong 41 H 5
Samsang 40 D 1
Samsø 17 F 4
Samsun 21 E 2
Samthar 40 C 2
Samuel, Mount 48 E 2
Samus' 25 QR 4
Samut Prakan 41 H 5
Samut Songkhram 41 H 5
San (Mali) 62 D 3
San (Poland) 15 H 4
San'ā' 61 G 5
San Agustin, Cape 43 G 2
San Agustin de Valle Fértil 88 C 5
S. Ambrosio Island 81 C 5
San Andrés 79 F 5
San Andrés del Rabanedo 18 B 3
San Andres Mountains 76 E 5
San Andrés Tuxtla 78 D 4
San Angelo 76 F 5
San Antonia de Cortés 78 E 4–5
San Antonio 76 G 6
San Antonio 84 E 3
San Antonio (Chile) 88 B 5
San Antonio (Portugal) 58 A 1
San Antonio (Uruguay) 88 E 5
San Antonio Abad 18 D 4
San Antonio Bay 77 G 6
San Antonio, Cabo (Argentina)
   89 E 6
San Antonio, Cabo (Cuba) 78 F 3
San Antonio de Caparo 84 D 2
San Antonio de los Cobres 86 C 5
San Antonio del Tachira 84 D 2
San Antonio Oeste 89 D 7
San Bernadetto del Tronto 19 F 3
San Bernardino 76 C 5
San Bernardino (Chile) 88 BC 5
San Bernardo (Mexico) 76 D 6
San Blas 76 E 6
San Blas 78 A 3
San Blas 78 B 2
San Blas, Cape 77 J 6
San Borja 86 C 3
San Borjas, Sierra de 76 D 6
San Buenaventura 78 B 2
San Carlos (Argentina) 88 C 4
San Carlos (Argentina) 88 C 5
San Carlos (Chile) 89 B 6
San Carlos (Mexico) 78 C 3
San Carlos (Nicaragua) 78 F 5
San Carlos (Philippines) 43 F 1
San Carlos (Uruguay) 88 EF 5
San Carlos (Venezuela) 84 E 2
San Carlos de Bariloche 89 B 7
San Carlos de Río Negro 84 E 3
San Carlos del Zulia 84 D 2
San Casme 88 E 4
San Cataldo 19 F 4
San Clemente 76 C 5
San Clemente Island 76 C 5
San Cristóbal (Argentina) 88 D 5
San Cristóbal (Dominican Rep.)
   79 HJ 4
San Cristobal (Galápagos Is.,
   Ecuador) 84 B 6
San Cristóbal (Solomon Is.) 51 H 4
San Cristóbal (Venezuela) 84 D 2
San Cristóbal de las Casas 78 D 4
San Custodio 84 E 3
San Diego 76 C 5
San Diego, Cabo 89 C 9
San Dimitri Point 19 F 4
San Dona di Piave 19 F 2
San Estanislao 86 E 5
San Esteban de Gormaz 18 C 3
San Felipe (Chile) 88 B 5
San Felipe (Colombia) 84 E 3
San Felipe (Mexico) 76 D 5
San Felipe (Mexico) 78 B 3
San Felipe (Venezuela) 84 E 1
San Felipe, Cerro de 18 C 3
San Feliu 18 D 3
San Felíu de Guixols 18 D 3
S. Félix Island 81 B 5
San Fernando (Chile) 89 B 5
San Fernando (Mexico) 78 C 3
San Fernando (Philippines) 43 J 1
San Fernando (Spain) 18 B 4
San Fernando (Trinidad and
   Tobago) 85 F 1
San Fernando de Apure 84 E 2
San Fernando de Atabapo 84 E 3
San Francisco 76 B 4

San Francisco (Argentina) 88 D 5
San Francisco, Cabo de 84 B 3
San Francisco de Arriba 78 B 2
San Francisco de Macorís 79 HJ 4
San Francisco del Chanar 88 D 4
San Francisco del Monte de Oro
   88 C 5
San Francisco del Oro 76 E 6
San Francisco del Rincón 78 B 3
San Francisco Javier 18 D 4
San Francisco, Paso de 88 C 4
San Gil 84 D 2
San Giovanni in Fiore 19 G 4
San Gregorio (Chile) 89 B 9
San Gregorio (Uruguay) 88 E 5
San Hilario 76 D 7
San Ignacio (Argentina) 89 E 6
San Ignacio (Belize) 78 E 4
San Ignacio (Bolivia) 86 C 3
San Ignacio (Mexico) 76 D 6
San Ignacio (Paraguay) 88 E 4
San Ignacio, Isla de 76 E 6
San Isidro (Argentina) 88 DE 5
San Isidro (Costa Rica) 78 F 6
San Isidro (Peru) 84 C 4
San Jacinto 84 C 2
San Javier (Argentina) 88 D 5
San Javier (Bolivia) 86 D 4
San Javier (Chile) 89 B 6
San Javier (Spain) 18 C 4
San Javier (Uruguay) 88 E 5
San Joaquín 86 D 3
San Joaquin River 76 BC 4
San Joaquin Valley 76 BC 4
San Jorge (Colombia) 84 C 2
San Jorge (Solomon Is.) 51 G 3
San Jorge, Bahia de 76 D 5
San Jorge, Golfo 89 C 8
San Jorge, Golfo de 18 D 3
San Jose (CA, U.S.A.) 76 B 4
San José (Costa Rica) 78 F 6
San José (Guatemala) 78 D 5
San Jose (Philippines) 43 F 1
San Jose (Philippines) 43 J 1
San José de Amacuro 85 F 2
San Jose de Buenavista 43 F 1
San José de Chiquitos 86 D 4
San José de Feliciano 88 E 5
San José de Gracia 76 E 6
San José de Guanipa 85 F 2
San José de Jáchal 88 C 5
San José de Mayo 88 E 5
San José de Ocuné 84 DE 3
San José del Cabo 76 E 7
San José del Guaviare 84 D 3
San José, Isla 76 DE 6
San Juan (Argentina) 88 C 5
San Juan (Argentina) 88 C 5
San Juan (Dominican Rep.) 79 H 4
San Juan (Peru) 86 A 4
San Juan (Puerto Rico) 79 J 4
San Juan (Venezuela) 84 E 2
San Juan Bautista (Paraguay) 88 E 4
San Juan Bautista (Spain) 18 D 4
San Juan Bautista Tuxtepec 78 C 4
San Juan, Cabo 63 F 5
San Juan de Guadalupe 78 B 3
San Juan de los Cayos 84 E 1
San Juan del Norte 78 F 5
San Juan del Rio 78 B 3
San Juan del Rio 78 BC 3
San Juan Mountains 76 E 5
San Juan, Pico 79 F 3
San Juan, Rio 78 F 5
San Juana (Venezuela) 84 E 2
San Julián 89 C 8
San Justo 88 D 5
San Lázaro, Sierra de 76 E 7
San Lorenzo (Argentina) 88 D 5
San Lorenzo (Ecuador) 84 C 3
San Lorenzo (Mexico) 76 E 7
San Lorenzo, Cabo 84 B 3
San Lorenzo, Cerro 89 B 8
San Lucas (Bolivia) 86 C 5
San Lucas (Mexico) 76 D 7
San Lucas, Cabo 76 E 7
San Luis (Argentina) 88 C 5
San Luis (Mexico) 76 D 6
San Luís (Venezuela) 84 E 1
San Luis de la Paz 78 BC 3
San Luis Gonzaga, Bahía 76 D 6
San Luis, Lago de 86 D 3
San Luis Obispo 76 B 4
San Luis Peak 76 E 4
San Luis Potosi 78 B 3
San Luis Rio Colorado 76 D 5
San Marco, Capo 19 E 4
San Marcos (Colombia) 84 C 2
San Marcos (Mexico) 78 B 3
San Marcos (Mexico) 78 C 4
San Marcos (TX, U.S.A.) 76 G 5–6
San Marcos, Isla 76 D 6
San Marino 19 F 3
San Marino 19 F 3
San Martín (Bolivia) 86 D 3

San Martín (Colombia) 84 D 3
San Martín (Spain) 18 C 3
San Martín de los Andes 89 B 7
San Martín, Lago 89 B 8
San Mateo 76 B 4
San Matías 86 E 4
San Matías, Golfo 89 D 7
San Miguel (Bolivia) 86 D 3
San Miguel (El Salvador) 78 E 5
San Miguel (Peru) 86 B 3
San Miguel de Allende 78 BC 3
San Miguel de Horcasitas 76 D 6
San Miguel de Huachi 86 C 4
San Miguel de Tucumán 88 C 4
San Miguel del Padrón 79 F 3
San Miguel Islands 43 E 2
San Miguel Sole de Vega 78 C 4
San Nicolás 88 D 5
San Nicolás (Mexico) 78 B 2
San Nicolás (Peru) 86 A 4
San Onofre 84 C 2
San Pablo (Argentina) 89 C 9
San Pablo (Bolivia) 86 C 5
San Pablo (Philippines) 43 F 1
San Pedro (Argentina) 88 D 5
San Pedro (Argentina) 88 DE 5
San Pedro (Dominican Rep.) 79 J 4
San Pédro (Ivory Coast) 62 C 5
San Pedro (Mexico) 78 B 2
San Pedro (Paraguay) 86 E 5
San Pedro de Arimena 84 D 3
San Pedro de Atacama 86 C 5
San Pedro de las Bôcas 85 F 2
San Pedro de Lloc 84 BC 5
San Pedro Pochutla 78 C 4
San Pedro, Sierra de 18 B 4
San Pedro Sula 78 E 4
San Pietro 19 E 4
San Quintin 76 C 5
San Quintin, Bahia de 76 C 5
San Rafael (Argentina) 88 C 5
San Rafael (Bolivia) 86 D 4
San Rafael (Chile) 89 B 6
San Rafael (Mexico) 78 B 2
San Rafael, Cabo 79 J 4
San Rafael Mountains 76 BC 4–5
San Ramón 86 AB 3
San Ramón de la Nueva Orán
   86 D 5
San Remo 19 E 3
San Roque 18 B 4
San Salvador (El Salvador) 78 E 5
San Salvador (Spain) 18 D 4
San Salvador de Jujuy 86 C 5
San Salvador, Isla 84 B 6
San Salvador [Watling Is.]
   79 GH 3
San Sebastian (Argentina) 89 C 9
San Sebastián (Spain) 18 C 3
San Severo 19 G 3
San Silvestre 84 D 2
San Telmo 76 C 5
San Valentin, Cerro 89 B 8
San Vicente (Mexico) 76 C 5
San Vicente (Philippines) 43 J 1
San Vicente de Cañete 86 A 3
San Vicente de la Barquerq 18 C 3
San Vicente del Raspeig 18 CD 4
Sana 19 G 3
Sanaba 62 D 3
Sanae 91
Sanāfir (Saudi Arabia) 22 B 3–4
Sanaga 63 G 5
Sanagir 40 C 2
Sanain 21 F 2
Sanak Islands 72 E 5
Sanana 43 G 4
Sanana, Pulau 43 G 4
Sanandaj 34 D 3
Sanandaj (Iran) 23 E 2
Sananduva 88 F 4
Sanāw 61 J 5
SanCarlos 84 BC 2
Sancarlos 84 E 2
Sancerrois, Collines du 18 D 2
Sánchez 79 J 4
Sanchor 40 B 3
Sancti Spíritus 79 G 3
Sand 17 E 4
Sand Cay 40 B 5
Sand Hills 76 F 3
Sand Point 72 EF 4
Sandai 42 D 3
Sandakan 42 E 2
Sandanski 20 B 2
Sandaré 62 B 3
Sandarne 16 E 3
Sanday 2 C 1
Sandbach 5 D 3
Sandbach 6 C 1
Sandefjord 17 EF 4
Sanderson 76 F 5
Sandgarth 2 C 2
Sandhead 3 B 4
Sandia 86 C 3
Sandıklı 20 D 3

San Martín (Colombia) 84 D 3
Sandila 40 D 2
Sandiman, Mount 48 B 3
Sanding, Pulau 42 B 4
Sandnes 17 E 4
Sandness 2 D 1
Sandnessjöen 16 F 2
Sandoa 64 C 6
Sandomierz 15 H 4
Sandon 7 C 1
Sandoway 41 F 4
Sandoy 14 A 1
Sandray 3 A 3
Sandringham 7 E 1
Sandspit 72 L 5
Sandstone (MN, U.S.A.) 77 H 2
Sandstone (Western Australia)
   48 B 4
Sandur 14 A 1
Sandusky 77 K 3
Sandvig 17 FG 4
Sandvika 17 F 4
Sandviken 17 G 3
Sandwich 7 E 2
Sandwich Bay (Namibia) 66 A 4
Sandwich Bay (Newfoundl., Can.)
   75 Q 5
Sandwich 2 A 3
Sandwick 2 D 2
Sandwip 41 F 3
Sandy 7 D 1
Sandy Cape 49 J 3
Sandy Desert, Great 48 C 3
Sandy Lake 73 J 5
Sandy Lake 74 J 5
Sandy Point 41 F 5
Sandykachi 35 G 3
Sånfjället 16 F 3
Sanford, Mount 72 J 3
Sanford River 48 B 4
Sanga 67 F 2
Sanga-Kyuyel' 37 Q 3
Sangamner 40 B 4
Sangar 37 N 3
Sangar (Iran) 23 E 1
Sangareddipet 40 C 4
Sangatolon 37 R 3
Sangay, Volcán 84 C 4
Sangayán, Isla 86 A 3
Sangbe 63 G 4
Sange 64 D 6
Sangeang, Pulau 43 E 5
Sanger 76 C 4
Sanggan He 38 F 2
Sanggau 42 D 3
Sangha 63 GH 5
Sangha 63 H 5
Sangihe, Kepulauan 43 G 3
Sangihe, Pulau 43 G 3
Sangilen, Nagor'ye 36 G 5
Sangin 35 G 4
Sangiyn Dalay Nuur 36 GH 6
Sangju 39 J 3
Sangkhla Buri 41 G 5
Sangkulirang, Teluk 43 E 3
Sangli 40 B 4
Sangmélima 63 G 5
Sangre de Cristo Mountains 76 E 4
Sangre Grande 85 F 1
Sangri 38 B 5
Sangrur 40 C 1
Sangue 86 E 3
Sangüesa 18 C 3
Sangzhi 38 F 5
Sanhala 62 C 4
Sanhe 36 M 5
Sanikiluaq 75 M 4
Sanin 35 H 4
Sanjawi 35 H 4
Sanjiang 38 F 5
Sanjö 39 L 3
Sankarani 62 C 3
Sankosh 40 E 2
Sankt Gotthard-Pass 19 E 2
Sankt Martin 19 G 2
Sankt Michel 16 J 3
Sankt Pölten 19 G 2
Sankt Veit an der Glan 19 F 2
Sankuru 64 C 5
Sanlúcar de Barrameda 18 B 4
Sanmen 39 H 5
Sanmenxia 38 F 4
Sanming 39 G 5
Sannär 60 E 6
Sannikova 90
Sannikova, Proliv 37 PQ 1
Sanniquellie 62 C 4
Sanok 15 H 5
Sanquhar 3 C 4
Sansanding 62 C 3
Sansanné Mango 62 E 3
Sant' Agata di Militello 19 F 4
Sant' Antioco 19 E 4
Santa 84 C 5
Santa Ana 76 D 5
Santa Ana (Bolivia) 86 C 3
Santa Ana (CA, U.S.A.) 76 C 5
Santa Ana (Ecuador) 84 BC 4

Santa Ana (El Salvador) 78 DE 5
Santa Ana (Solomon Is.) 51 H 4
Santa Ana, Cuchilla de 88 EF 5
Santa Barbara (CA, U.S.A.)
  76 B 5
Santa Barbara (Mexico) 76 E 6
Santa Barbara Channel 76 B 5
Santa Bárbara do Sul 88 F 4
Santa Carolina, Ilha 67 F 4
Santa Catalina (Argentina) 86 C 5
Santa Catalina (Chile) 88 C 4
Santa Catalina Island (CA, U.S.A.)
  76 C 5
Santa Catarina (Brazil) 88 F 4
Santa Catarina, Ilha de 88 G 4
Santa Clara (CA, U.S.A.) 76 B 4
Santa Clara (Colombia) 84 E 4
Santa Clara (Cuba) 79 F 3
Santa Clara (Mexico) 76 E 6
Santa Clotilde 84 D 4
Santa Comba 18 B 3
Santa Cruz (Amazonas, Brazil)
  84 D 5
Santa Cruz (Argentina) 89 B 9
Santa Cruz (Argentina) 89 C 9
Santa Cruz (Bolivia) 86 D 4
Santa Cruz (CA, U.S.A.) 76 B 4
Santa Cruz (Chile) 89 B 5
Santa Cruz (Costa Rica) 78 E 5
Santa Cruz (Espírito Santo, Brazil)
  87 HJ 5
Santa Cruz (Pará, Brazil) 85 H 4
Santa Cruz (Peru) 84 C 5
Santa Cruz (Philippines) 43 F 1
Santa Cruz (Philippines) 43 H 1
Santa Cruz de la Palma 58 B 3
Santa Cruz de la Zarza 18 C 4
Santa Cruz de Mudela 18 C 4
Santa Cruz de Tenerife 58 B 3
Santa Cruz del Sur 79 G 3
Santa Cruz do Río Pardo 87 G 5
Santa Cruz do Sul 88 F 4
Santa Cruz, Isla (Galápagos Is.,
  Ecuador) 84 B 6
Santa Cruz Island 76 C 5
Santa Cruz Islands (Solomon Is.)
  51 J 4
Santa Elena 84 B 4
Santa Elena, Bahía de 78 E 5
Santa Elena, Cabo 78 E 5
Santa Elena de Uairén 85 F 3
Santa Fé (Argentina) 88 D 5
Santa Fé (Goiás, Brazil) 87 F 4
Santa Fe (N.M., U.S.A.) 76 E 4
Santa Filomena 87 G 2
Santa Helena 85 JK 4
Santa Inês 85 J 4
Santa Ines, Bahía 76 D 6
Santa Inés, Isla 89 B 9
Santa Isabel 85 G 5
Santa Isabel 86 D 3
Santa Isabel (Argentina) 89 C 6
Santa Isabel (Solomon Is.) 51 G 3
Santa Isabel do Araguaia 85 J 5
Santa Isabel, Pico de 63 F 5
Santa Juana 84 E 2
Santa Júlia 85 G 5
Santa Lucía (Uruguay) 88 E 5
Santa Lucia Range 76 B 4
Santa Luzia 62 AB 6
Santa Margarita, Isla de 76 D 7
Santa Maria (Amazonas, Brazil)
  85 F 4
Santa María (Amazonas, Brazil)
  85 G 4
Santa María (Argentina) 88 C 4
Santa Maria (CA, U.S.A.) 76 B 4
Santa Maria (Portugal) 58 A 1
Santa María (Río Grande do Sul,
  Brazil) 88 F 4
Santa Maria, Bahia de 76 E 6
Santa Maria, Cabo de 18 B 4
Santa Maria, Cabo de 67 E 5
Santa María de Ipire 84 E 2
Santa Maria del Río 78 B 3
Santa Maria di Leuca, Capo 19 G 4
Santa Maria dos Marmelos 85 F 5
Santa Maria, Isla 84 B 6
Santa Marta 84 D 1
Santa Marta, Cabo de 66 A 2
Santa Marta Grande, Cabo de
  88 G 4
Santa Marta, Ría de 18 B 3
Santa Olalla del Cala 18 B 4
Santa Rita (Colombia) 84 D 3
Santa Rita (N.M., U.S.A.) 76 E 5
Santa Rita (Venezuela) 84 E 2
Santa Rita do Araguaia 87 F 4
Santa Rosa (Argentina) 85 E 2
Santa Rosa (Argentina) 89 CD 6
Santa Rosa (Argentina) 89 CD 6
Santa Rosa (Bolivia) 86 C 3
Santa Rosa (CA, U.S.A.) 76 B 4
Santa Rosa (Colombia) 84 E 3
Santa Rosa (N.M., U.S.A.) 76 F 5

Santa Rosa (Peru) 86 B 3
Santa Rosa (Río Grande do Sul,
  Brazil) 88 F 4
Santa Rosa de Cabal 84 C 3
Santa Rosa de Copán 78 E 4–5
Santa Rosa de la Roca 86 D 4
Santa Rosa Island 76 B 5
Santa Rosalia 76 D 6
Santa Sylvina 88 D 4
Santa Teresa (Espírito Santo,
  Brazil) 87 H 5
Santa Teresa (Goiás, Brazil)
  87 G 3
Santa Teresinha 87 F 3
Santa Vitória do Palmar 88 F 5
Santafé (Spain) 18 C 4
Santai 38 E 4
Santan 42 E 4
Santana 87 H 3
Santana do Livramento 88 EF 5
Santander (Colombia) 84 C 3
Santander (Spain) 18 C 3
Santañy 18 D 4
Santarém (Pará, Brazil) 85 H 4
Santarém (Portugal) 18 B 4
Santaren Channel 79 G 3
Santee River 77 L 5
Santeh (Iran) 23 E 1
Santiago (Chile) 88 BC 5
Santiago (Haiti) 79 H 4
Santiago (Panamá) 84 B 2
Santiago (Río Grande do Sul,
  Brazil) 88 F 4
Santiago, Cerro 79 F 6
Santiago da Cacém 18 B 4
Santiago de Compostela 18 B 3
Santiago de Cuba 79 G 4
Santiago de Papasquiaro 78 AB 2
Santiago del Estero 88 CD 4
Santiago, Rio Grande de 78 A 3
Santiago, Serranía de 86 DE 4
Santo Amaro 87 J 3
Santo André 87 G 5
Santo Ângelo 88 F 4
Santo Antão 62 A 6
Santo Antonio 88 F 4
Santo Antonio (São Tomé) 63 F 5
Santo António de Jesus 87 J 3
Santo Antônio do Içá 84 E 4
Santo Domingo (Argentina) 88 D 4
Santo Domingo (Cuba) 79 F 3
Santo Domingo (Dominican Rep.)
  79 J 4
Santo Domingo (Mexico) 76 D 6
Santo Tomás (Nicaragua) 78 F 5
Santo Tomás (Peru) 86 B 3
Santo Tomé (Argentina) 88 E 4
Santo Tomé de Guayana 85 F 2
Santoña 18 C 3
Santopitar 18 C 4
Santoríni 20 B 3
Santos 87 G 5
Santos Dumont (Amazonas,
  Brazil) 84 E 5
Santos Dumont (Minas Gerais,
  Brazil) 87 H 5
Sanza Pombo 66 B 1
São Antônio 85 H 5
São Bento do Norte 87 J 1–2
São Bento (Maranhão, Brazil)
  87 GH 1
São Bento (Roraima, Brazil)
  85 F 3
São Bernardo 87 H 1
São Borja 88 E 4
São Brás, Cabo de 66 A 1–2
São Carlos (Santa Catarina, Brazil)
  88 F 4
São Carlos (São Paulo, Brazil)
  87 G 5
São Christóvão 87 J 3
São Domingos 62 A 3
São Domingos 87 G 3
São Felix 87 F 3
São Felix do Xingu 85 H 5
São Francisco (Minas Gerais,
  Brazil) 87 H 4
São Francisco do Sul 88 G 4
São Gabriel 88 F 5
São Gabriel de Goiás 87 G 4
São Geraldo do Araguaia 85 J 5
Sao Hill 64 F 6
São Jerônimo, Serra de 87 EF 4
São João 87 G 5
São João da Barra 87 H 5
São João da Madeira 18 B 3
São João de Aliança 87 G 3
São João del Rei 87 H 5
São João do Araguaia 85 J 5
São João do Paraíso 87 H 4
São João do Piauí 87 H 2
São João dos Patos 87 H 2
São João, Ilhas de 85 K 4
São Joaquim (Amazonas, Brazil)
  84 E 4

São Joaquim (Santa Catarina,
  Brazil) 88 F 4
São Jorge 58 A 1
São José (Amazonas, Brazil)
  84 E 4
São José do Anauá 85 F 3
São José do Norte 88 F 5
São José do Peixe 87 H 2
São José do Rio Pardo 87 G 5
São José do Río Prêto 87 FG 5
São José dos Campos 87 G 5
São Leopoldo 88 F 4
São Lourênço 86 E 4
São Lourênço do Sul 88 F 5
Sao Lourénco, Pantanal de 86 E 4
São Luís (Maranhão, Brazil)
  87 H 1
São Luis de Cassianã 84 E 5
São Luis Gonzaga 88 E 4
São Mamede, Serra de 18 B 4
São Manuel 85 G 5
São Marcelino 84 E 3
São Mateus 87 J 4
São Miguel 58 A 1
São Miguel do Araguaia 87 F 3
São Nicolau 62 B 6
São Paulo 87 FG 5
São Paulo 87 G 5
São Paulo de Olivença 84 E 4
São Pedro do Sul 18 B 3
São Pedro do Sul 88 F 4
São Raimundo das Mangabeiras
  87 G 2
São Raimundo Nonato 87 H 2
São Romão (Amazonas, Brazil)
  84 E 5
São Romão (Minas Gerais, Brazil)
  87 G 4
São Roque, Cabo de 87 J 2
São Sebastião (Pará, Brazil) 85 H 5
São Sebastião (São Paulo, Brazil)
  87 GH 5
São Sebastião do Paraíso 87 G 5
São Sebastião, Ilha de 87 GH 5
São Sepé 88 F 5
São Tiago 62 B 6
São Tomé 85 P 6
São Tomé (São Tomé) 63 F 5
São Tomé and Principe 63 F 5
São Tomé, Cabo de 87 H 5
São Vicente 62 A 6
São Vicente 87 G 5
São Vicente, Cabo de 18 B 4
Saône 19 D 2
Saoura 58 E 3
Sápai 20 C 2
Sapanca Gölü 20 D 2
Sapé (Brazil) 87 J 2
Sape (Indonesia) 43 E 5
Sape, Selat 43 E 5
Sapele 63 F 4
Sapiéntza 20 B 3
Saponé 84 E 5
Saposoa 84 C 5
Sapporo 39 M 2
Sapri 19 G 3
Sapulpa 77 G 4
Sapulut 42 E 3
Sapwe 66 D 2
Sâq, Jabal (Saudi Arabia) 22 D 4
Sãqand (Iran) 23 G 2
Saqqez 34 D 3
Saqqez (Iran) 23 E 1
Sar Dasht (Iran) 23 D 1
Sar Dasht (Iran) 23 E 2
Sara Buri 41 H 5
Sarãb 34 D 3
Sarafére 62 D 2
Sarafjagār 34 DE 4
Sarafjagār (Iran) 23 F 2
Saraguro 84 C 4
Sarajevo 19 G 3
Sarakhs 35 G 3
Saraktash 24 L 5
Saralzhin 34 E 1
Saramati 41 FG 2
Saran' 25 O 6
Saranda 20 B 2
Sarandí del Yi 88 EF 5
Sarandí Grande 88 E 5
Sarangani Bay 43 G 2
Sarangani Islands 43 G 2
Sarangarh 40 D 3
Saranley 65 G 4
Saranpaul' 25 M 3
Saransk 24 J 5
Sarapul 24 K 4
Sarapul'skoye 37 P 6
Sarare 84 E 2
Sarasota 77 K 6
Sarata 20 C 1
Saratok 43 D 3
Saratov 24 HJ 5
Saravan 35 G 5
Saravane 41 J 4

Sarawak 42 D 3
Saray 20 C 2
Saraya 62 B 3
Sarãyã (Syria) 22 B 2
Sarayköy 20 C 3
Sarbāz 35 G 5
Sarca 19 F 2
Sarco 88 B 4
Sardalas → Al 'Awaynãt 59 H 3
Sardarshahr 40 B 2
Sardegna 19 E 3
Sardina 84 E 3
Sardinia 19 E 3
Sar-e Yazd (Iran) 23 G 3
Sarek National Park 16 G 2
Sarektjåkkå 16 G 2
Sarempaka, Gunung 42 E 4
Sarenga 65 F 2
Sarga, Punta 58 B 4
Sargasso Sea 79 JK 2
Sargatskoye 25 O 4
Sargento Lores 84 CD 4
Sargento Paixão, Serra do 86 DE 3
Sargodha 35 J 4
Sarh 63 H 4
Sarhro, Jbel 58 D 2
Sārī (Iran) 23 F 1
Saría 20 C 3
Sarıbuğday 21 E 2
Sarigan 52 A 1
Sarıkamış 21 F 2
Sarıkaya 21 E 3
Sarikei 42 D 3
Sarila 40 C 2
Sarıoğlan 21 E 3
Sar-i-Pul 35 H 3
Sarir 57
Sarīr al Qattūsah 59 J 3
Sarīr Kalanshiyū 59 K 3
Sarīr Tibistī 59 J 4
Sariwon 39 J 3
Sarıyar Barajı 20 D 2–3
Sarıyer 20 C 2
Sark 7 C 3
Sark 14 C 5
Sark, Safrã' as 61 G 3
Sarkand 25 P 6
Şarkıkáraağaç 20 D 3
Şarkışla 21 E 3
Şarköy 20 C 2
Sarlat-la-Canéda 18 D 3
Sarmi 43 J 4
Sarmiento 89 C 8
Sarmiento, Monte 89 BC 9
Särna 16 F 3
Sarneh (Iran) 23 E 2
Sarnia 74 L 7
Sarny 17 J 5
Saroako 43 F 4
Sarobi 35 H 4
Sarolangun 42 B 4
Saronikós Kólpos 20 B 3
Saronno 19 E 2
Saros Körfezi 20 C 2
Saroto 25 N 2
Sarpa 21 G 1
Sarpinskaya Nizmennost' 21 G 1
Sarpsborg 17 F 4
Sarralbe 19 E 2
Sarre 7 E 2
Sarrebourg 19 E 2
Sarreguemines 19 E 2
Sars 24 L 4
Sartang 37 O 2
Sartène 19 E 3
Sarthe 18 C 2
Sartlan, Ozero 25 PQ 4–5
Sarto 84 D 3
Sartyn'ya 25 M 3
Saruhanlı 20 C 3
Sārūq (Iran) 23 E 2
Sárvár 20 A 1
Sarvestān (Iran) 23 F 3
Sary Ishikotrau, Peski 25 P 6
Saryassiya 35 H 3
Sarych, Mys 21 D 2
Sarych, Mys 21 D 2
Saryg-Sep 36 G 5
Sarykamysh, Ozero 34 F 2
Sarykopa, Ozero 25 M 5
Saryoba 34 FG 1
Sary-Ozek 35 K 2
Sary-Shagan 25 O 6
Sarysu 35 H 1
Sary-Tash 35 J 3
Sasa Baneh 65 G 3
Sasamungga 51 G 3
Sasar, Tanjung 43 E 5
Sasaram 40 D 3
Sasebo 39 J 4
Saskatchewan 73 Q 5
Saskatchewan 73 R 5
Saskatoon 73 Q 5
Saskylakh 36 KL 1
Saslaya 78 F 5
Sason Dağları 21 F 3

Sasovo 24 H 5
Sassan (United Arab Emirates)
  23 F 4
Sassandra 62 C 5
Sassandra (River) 62 C 4
Sassari 19 E 3
Saßnitz 15 F 4
Sassuolo 19 F 3
Sas-Tobe 35 J 2
Sastre 88 D 5
Satadougou 62 B 3
Satara (India) 40 B 4
Satara (U.S.S.R.) 37 NO 2
Satawal 52 A 2
Satawan 52 B 2
Säter 17 G 3
Satipo 86 B 3
Satka 25 L 4
Satmala Range 40 C 4
Satna 40 D 3
Satoou 63 F 3
Satpura Range 40 C 3
Sattahip 41 H 5
Satthwa 41 G 4
Sattur 40 C 6
Satu Mare 20 B 1
Satun 41 H 6
Sauce 88 E 5
Sauceda Mountains 76 D 5
Saucillo 76 EF 6
Sauda Nathil (Saudi Arabia) 23 F 4
Sauðarkrókur 16 B 2
Saudi Arabia 61 GH 4
Sauiá 85 G 4
Sauk Centre 77 H 2
Saúl 85 H 3
Saulieu 18 D 2
Sault Sainte Marie 74 L 6
Saumarez Reef 49 J 3
Saumlaki 43 H 5
Saumur 18 C 2
Saunders Reef 49 J 3
Saundersfoot 6 B 2
Saur, Khrebet 25 QR 6
Saura 34 E 2
Saurimo 66 C 1
Sautar 86 B 2
Sauwald 19 F 2
Sava 20 AB 2
Savai'i 52 D 3
Savalou 62 E 4
Savanna la Mar 79 G 4
Savannah 77 K 5
Savannah River 77 K 5
Savannakhet 41 HJ 4
Savanne 74 K 6
Savant Lake 74 JK 5
Savantvadj 40 B 4
Savanur 40 C 5
Sävar 16 H 3
Säveh (Iran) 23 F 2
Savelugu 62 D 4
Saverdun 18 D 3
Saverne 19 E 2
Savigliano 19 E 3
Savino 24 K 2
Sãvirşin 20 B 1
Savitaipale 16 J 3
Savo 16 J 3
Savoie 19 E 2
Savona 19 E 3
Savonlinna 16 J 3
Savonselkä 16 J 3
Savoonga 72 C 3
Şavşat 21 F 2
Sävsjö 17 F 4
Savukoski 16 J 2
Savur 21 F 3
Saw 41 F 3
Sawah 42 E 3
Sawahlunto 42 B 4
Sawai Madhopur 40 C 2
Sawang 42 B 3
Sãwãnī Fassãnū 59 H 2
Sawankhalok 41 G 4
Sawbã 64 E 3
Sawbridgeworth 7 E 2
Sawdirī 60 D 6
Sawek 43 J 4
Sawel 4 B 2
Sawhãj 60 E 3
Sawmah, Ra's Abū (Egypt) 22 B 4
Sawmill Bay 73 O 2
Sawqirah 61 K 5
Sawston 7 E 1

Sawtayr **60** E 5
Sawtooth Mountains **77** H 2
Sawu Laut **43** F 5
Sawu, Pulau **43** F 6
Ṣawwān, Ard aṣ **60** F 2
Saxby **7** D 1
Saxmundham **7** E 1
Saxton **5** E 3
Say **62** E 3
Sayaboury **41** H 4
Sayak **25** P 6
Sayakskaya Pristan' **25** P 6
Sayán **86** A 3
Sayan Vostochnyy **36** G 5
Sayan, Zapadnyy **36** F 5
Sayang, Pulau **43** GH 3
Sayat **35** G 3
Saydā (Lebanon) **22** B 2
Saydy **37** O 2
Sayhūt **61** J 5
Saynshand **38** F 2
Sayram Hu **35** L 2
Saywūn **61** H 5
Sázava **15** F 5
Sazdy **34** D 1
Sazin **35** J 3
Sbaa **58** E 3
Scaër **18** C 2
Scafell Pike **5** D 2
Scaife Mountains **91**
Scalasaig **3** A 3
Scalea **19** G 4
Scalone, Passo dello **19** G 4
Scalpay **2** B 3
Scammon Bay **72** D 3
Scandinavia **93**
Scapa Flow **2** C 2
Ščara **15** H 4
Scaramia, Capo **19** F 4
Scarba **3** B 3
Scarborough (Trinidad and
   Tobago) **85** F 1
Scarborough (U.K.) **5** E 2
Scarp **2** A 2
Schaffhausen **15** E 5
Schärding **19** F 2
Schefferville **75** O 5
Scheibbs **19** FG 2
Schelde **14** D 4
Schenectady **77** M 3
Schiltigheim **19** E 2
Schio **19** F 2
Schklov **17** K 5
Schladming **19** F 2
Schleswig **15** E 4
Schleswig-Holstein **15** E 4
Schneeberg **15** F 4
Schönebeck **15** F 4
Schouten Islands **50** D 2
Schuls → Scoul **19** F 2
Schultz Lake **73** S 3
Schurz **76** C 4
Schwabach **15** F 5
Schwäbisch Hall **15** EF 5
Schwaner, Pegunungan **42** D 4
Schwarzwald **15** E 5
Schwatka Mountains **72** F 2
Schwaz **19** F 2
Schwedt **15** F 4
Schweinfurt **15** F 4
Schweizer Reneke **66** CD 5
Schwenningen **15** E 5
Schwerin **15** F 4
Schwyz **19** E 2
Sciacca **19** F 4
Scicli **19** F 4
Scioto River **77** K 4
Scoresby Sound **90**
Scoresbysund **90**
Scotia Ridge **98** A 5
Scotia Sea **91**
Scotlandville **77** H 5
Scott **73** Q 5
Scott (Antarctica) **91**
Scott, Cape **72** M 5
Scott, Cape (N.T., Austr.) **48** D 1
Scott City **76** F 4
Scott Island **91**
Scott Reef **48** C 1
Scottburgh **67** E 6
Scottsbluff **76** F 3
Scottsdale **76** D 5
Scottsdale (Tasmania, Austr.)
   50 L 9
Scottsville **77** J 4
Scourie **2** B 2
Scrabster **2** C 2
Scranton **77** L 3
Scugog, Lake **75** M 7
Scunthorpe **5** E 3
Scuol **19** F 2
Scutari, Lake → Skardarsko
   Jezero **20** A 2
Se Kong **41** J 4
Sea Islands **77** K 5
Sea of Azov **21** E 1

Sea of Crete **20** BC 3
Sea of Japan **39** KL 3
Sea of Marmara → Marmara
   Denizi **20** C 2
Sea of Okhotsk **37** R 4
Sea of the Hebrides **2–3** A 3
Seabra **87** H 3
Seabrook, Lake **48** B 5
Seaford **7** E 2
Seaforde **4** C 2
Seahorse Point **73** V 3
Seahouses **5** E 2
Seal **73** S 4
Seamer **5** E 2
Seaside **76** B 2
Seaton **6** C 2
Seaton Delaval **5** E 2
Seattle **76** B 2
Seba **43** F 6
Sebanka, Pulau **42** BC 3
Sebastián Vizcaino, Bahía **76** D 6
Sebatik, Pulau **42** E 3
Sebatik, Pulau **42** E 3
Sebba **62** E 3
Sébékoro **62** C 3
Sebeş **20** B 1
Sebewaing **77** K 3
Sebezh **17** J 4
Sebha → Sabhā **59** H 3
Sebha Oasis → Wāhāt Sabhā
   59 H 3
Şebinkarahisar **21** E 2
Sebjet Agsumal **58** C 4
Sebjet Aridal **58** C 3
Sebkha Azzel Matti **58** F 3
Sebkha de Ndrhamcha **58** B 5
Sebkha de Rhallamane **58** D 4
Sebkha de Timimoun **58–59** F 3
Sebkha de Tindouf **58** D 3
Sebkha Iguetti **58** D 3
Sebkha Mekerrhane **59** F 3
Sebkha Oumm ed Droûs Telli
   58 C 4
Sebkha Tah **58** C 3
Sebkhet Oumm ed Droûs Guebli
   58 C 4
Sebou **58** D 2
Sebring **77** K 6
Sebuku, Pulau **42** E 4
Secchia **19** F 3
Sechura **84** B 5
Sechura, Bahía de **84** B 5
Sechura, Desierto de **84** B 5
Second Baku **12**
Secunderabad **40** C 4
Seda **18** B 4
Sedah **43** F 6
Sedalia **77** H 4
Sedan **19** DE 2
Sedanka **72** D 5
Sedano **18** C 3
Sedbergh **5** D 2
Seddenga **60** DE 4
Sededema **37** S 2
Sedel'nikovo **25** P 4
Sédhiou **62** A 3
Sedom (Israel) **22** B 3
Sedona **76** D 5
Seeheim **66** B 5
Seend **7** C 2
Sées **18** D 2
Seesen **15** F 4
Şefaatli **21** D 3
Sefadu **62** B 4
Sefid Dasht (Iran) **23** F 2
Sefrou **58** E 2
Segag **65** G 3
Segamat **42** B 3
Segantur **42** E 3
Segbana **62** E 3
Segesta **19** F 4
Seget **43** H 4
Segezha **16** K 3
Seghe **51** G 3
Seghnān **35** J 3
Segine I-yy **37** P 3
Segorbe **18** C 4
Ségou **62** C 3
Segovia **18** C 3
Segozero, Ozero **16** K 3
Segré (France) **18** C 3
Segre (Spain) **18** D 3
Seguam **72** C 5
Séguédine **63** G 1
Séguéla **62** C 4
Seguin **76** G 6
Segula **72** A 5
Segura **18** C 4
Segura, Sierra de **18** C 4
Sehithwa **66** C 4
Sehore **40** C 3
Sehwan **35** H 5
Seil **3** B 3
Seiland **16** H 1
Seinäjoki **16** H 3
Seine **18** D 2

Seine, Baie de la **18** C 2
Sekayu **42** B 4
Seke **64** E 5
Sekena **20** B 3
Sekenke **64** E 5
Seki **20** C 3
Sekkemo **16** H 2
Sekoma **66** C 4
Sekondi-Takoradi **62** D 5
Sekondya **37** MN 2
Selaru, Pulau **43** H 5
Selassi **43** H 4
Selat Alas **42** E 5
Selat Alor **43** F 5
Selat Bangka **42** C 4
Selat Berhala **42** B 4
Selat Dampier **43** H 4
Selat Gaspar **42** C 4
Selat Jailolo **43** G 3–4
Selat Karimata **42** C 4
Selat Laut **42** E 4
Selat Lombok **42** E 5
Selat Madura **42** D 5
Selat Makassar **42** E 4
Selat Manipa **43** G 4
Selat Mentawai **42** A 4
Selat Morotai **43** G 3
Selat Obi **43** G 4
Selat Ombai **43** G 5
Selat Peleng **43** F 4
Selat Roti **43** F 6
Selat Salue Timpaus **43** F 4
Selat Sape **43** E 5
Selat Selayar **43** F 5
Selat Serasan **42** C 3
Selat Sumba **43** F 5
Selat Sunda → Sunda Strait
   42 BC 5
Selat Tiworo **43** F 4
Selat Wetar **43** G 5
Selat Yapen **43** J 4
Selatan, Pulau **42** B 4
Selatan, Tanjung **42** D 4
Selawik **72** F 2
Selawik Lake **72** F 2
Selayar, Pulau **43** F 5
Selayar, Selat **43** F 5
Selbu **16** F 3
Selbusjöen **16** F 3
Selby **76** G 2
Selby (U.K.) **5** E 3
Selçuk **20** C 3
Seldovia **72** G 4
Selebi-Pikwe **66** D 4
Selebir **37** O 2
Selemdzha **37** O 5
Selemdzhinsk **37** O 5
Selendi **20** C 3
Selenduma **36** J 5
Selenge **36** H 6
Selenge (Mongolia) **36** J 6
Selenge (Zaire) **64** B 5
Selennyakh **37** Q 2
Sélestat **19** E 2
Selety **25** O 5
Seletyteniz, Ozero **25** O 5
Selfjord **17** E 4
Selfoss **16** A 3
Selgon **37** P 6
Sélibaby **58** C 5
Selim **21** F 2
Selima Oasis → Wāhāt Salīmah
   60 D 4
Selinunte **19** F 4
Seliyarovo **25** O 3
Selizharovo **24** F 4
Selkirk **3** C 4
Selkirk Mountains **73** O 5
Sella di Conza **19** G 3
Sellafirth **2** D 1
Selle, Pic de la **79** H 4
Sellyakhskaya Guba **37** P 1
Selma (AL, U.S.A.) **77** J 5
Selma (CA, U.S.A.) **76** C 4
Selong **42** E 5
Selous Game Reserve **65** F 6
Selukwe → Shurugwi **66** DE 3
Selva **88** D 4
Selvagens, Ilhas **58** B 2
Selvānā **34** C 3
Selvas **84–85** EF 5
Selwyn **49** G 3
Selwyn Lake **73** R 3–4
Selwyn Mountains **72** LM 3
Sem Tripa **85** H 4
Semani **20** A 2
Semara **58** C 3
Semarang **42** D 5
Sematan **42** C 3
Semau, Pulau **43** F 6
Sembakung, Sungai **42** E 3
Sembé **63** G 5
Şemdinli **21** F 3

Semenovskiy, Ostrov **37** O 1
Semichi Islands **72** A 5
Semikarakorskiy **21** F 1
Semiluki **24** G 5
Semiozernoye **25** M 5
Semipalatinsk **25** Q 5
Semirara Islands **43** F 1
Semīrom (Iran) **23** F 3
Semisopochnoi **72** AB 5
Semitau **42** D 3
Semium **42** C 3
Semiyarka **25** P 5
Semiz-Bugu **25** OP 5
Semliki **64** DE 4
Semme Dahan, Khrebet **37** P 3
Semmering **19** G 2
Semnān **34** E 3
Semnān (Iran) **23** F 2
Semporna **43** E 3
Semuda **42** D 4
Sena (Bolivia) **86** C 3
Sena (Mozambique) **67** E 3
Sena Madureira **84** E 5
Senador Canedo **87** G 4
Senador Pompeu **87** J 2
Senaja **42** E 2
Senanga **66** C 3
Sendai **39** JK 4
Sendai **39** M 3
Sendai-wan **39** M 3
Sendelingsdrif **66** B 5
Sêndo **38** C 4
Senegal **62** AB 3
Sénégal (River) **62** B 2
Senekal **66** D 5
Seney **77** J 2
Senftenberg **15** F 4
Sêngê Zangbo **40** D 1
Sengiri, Mys **34** E 2
Sengkang **43** F 4
Senhor do Bonfim **87** H 3
Senigallia **19** F 3
Senja **16** G 2
Senjavin Group **52** B 2
Senkaku-shotō **39** H 5
Şenkaya **21** F 2
Senkyabasa **36** K 2
Sennaya **21** E 1
Senneterre **75** M 6
Senno **17** J 5
Sennybridge **6** C 2
Seno de Otway **89** B 9
Seno Skyring **89** B 9
Senorbì **19** E 4
Sens **18** D 2
Senta **20** B 1
Sentani **50** D 2
Sentinel Peak **73** N 5
Şenyurt **21** F 3
Şenyurt (Turkey) **22** C 1
Seo de Urgel **18** D 3
Seoni **40** C 3
Seoul **39** J 3
Sepanjang, Pulau **42** E 5
Separation Point **75** Q 5
Sepasu **42** E 3
Sepik River **50** D 2
Sepone **41** J 4
Sept-Îles **75** O 5
Sequillo **18** B 3
Sequoia National Park **76** C 4
Şerafettin Dağları **21** F 3
Seraing **14** E 4
Serakhs **35** G 3
Seram **43** G 4
Seram, Laut **43** GH 4
Seram Laut, Kepulauan **43** H 4
Serang **42** C 5
Serasan, Pulau **42** C 3
Serasan, Selat **42** C 3
Serbia **20** B 2
Serdo **65** G 2
Serdobsk **24** HJ 5
Serebryansk **25** Q 6
Serebryanskiy **16** L 2
Sered **15** G 5
Seredka **17** J 4
Şereflikoçhisar **21** D 3
Seremban **42** B 3
Serengeti National Park **64** EF 5
Serengeti Plain **64** EF 5
Serenje **67** E 3
Sergach **24** J 4
Sergelen **36** J 6
Sergeyevo **25** R 4
Sergino **25** N 3
Sergipe **87** J 3
Sergiyevka **21** F 2

Sermata, Pulau **43** G 5
Sernovodsk **24** K 5
Sernyy-Zavod **34** F 2
Séro **62** B 3
Seroglazovka **21** G 1
Serov **25** M 4
Serowe **66** D 4
Serpa **18** B 4
Serpentine Lakes **48** D 4
Serpiente, Boca de la **85** F 2
Serpukhov **24** G 5
Serra Acarai **85** G 3
Serra Bom Jesus da Gurguéia
   87 H 2
Serra Bonita **87** G 4
Serra da Bodoquena **86** E 5
Serra da Canastra **87** G 4
Serra da Chela **66** A 3
Serra da Estrela (Mato Grosso,
   Brazil) **87** F 4
Serra da Estrêla (Portugal) **18** B 3
Serra da Gorongosa **67** E 3
Serra da Ibiapaba **87** H 1–2
Serra da Mantiqueira **87** GH 5
Serra da Neve **66** A 2
Serra da Providência **86** D 3
Serra da Seringa **85** H 5
Serra da Tabatinga **87** H 3
Serra das Alpercatas **85** JK 5
Serra das Araras **87** F 4
Serra das Cordilheiras **85** J 5
Serra de Alvelos **18** B 4
Serra de Caldeirão **18** B 4
Serra de Grândola **18** B 4
Serra de Itiúba **87** HJ 3
Serra de Maracaju **86–87** EF 5
Serra de Nogueira **18** B 3
Serra de São Jerônimo **87** EF 4
Serra de São Mamede **18** B 4
Serra do Aguapeí **86** E 4
Serra do Apiaú **85** F 3
Serra do Cachimbo **85** G 5
Serra do Caiapó **87** F 4
Serra do Caramulo **18** B 3
Serra do Chifre **87** H 4
Serra do Divisor **84** D 5
Serra do Escorial **87** H 3
Serra do Espinhaço **87** H 4
Serra do Estrondo **85** J 5
Serra do Gerás **18** B 3
Serra do Gurupi **85** J 4–5
Serra do Jibāo **87** G 4
Serra do Mar **88** G 4
Serra do Marāo **18** B 3
Serra do Matāo **85** H 5
Serra do Mogadouro **18** B 3
Serra do Navio **85** H 3
Serra do Paraíso **87** F 3–4
Serra do Paranapiacaba **87** G 5
Serra do Penitente **85** J 5
Serra do Ramalho **87** H 3
Serra do Roncador **87** F 3
Serra do Sargento Paixão **86** DE 3
Serra do Tiracambu **87** G 1
Serra do Tombador **86** E 3
Serra do Uruçui **87** H 3
Serra Dois Irmāos **87** H 2
Serra dos Aimorés **87** HJ 4
Serra dos Apiacás **86** E 2–3
Serra dos Caiabis **86** E 3
Serra dos Carajás **85** H 4–5
Serra dos Gradaús **85** H 5
Serra dos Pacaás Novos **86** D 3
Serra dos Parecis **86** D 3
Serra dos Xavantes **87** G 3
Serra Dourada **87** G 3
Serra Formosa **87** E 3
Serra Geral **88** F 4
Serra Geral de Goiás **87** G 3
Serra Geral do Paraná **87** G 3
Serra Geral ou Grande **87** G 3
Serra Grande **87** H 2
Serra Lombarda **85** H 3
Serra Negra **85** J 5
Serra Nova **85** F 3
Serra Talhada **87** J 2
Serra Tumucumaque **85** H 3
Serra Urubuquara **85** H 4
Serres **19** E 3
Serrezuela **88** C 5
Serrinha **87** J 3
Serrota **18** BC 3
Sertã **18** B 4
Sértar **38** D 4
Sertavul Geçidi **21** D 3
Seruai **43** J 4

Serule 66 D 4
Seruyan, Sungai 42 D 4
Servia 20 B 2
Serwaru 43 G 5
Sêrxü 38 C 4
Seryshevo 37 N 5
Sesao 63 E 2
Sesayap 42 E 3
Sese Islands 64 E 5
Seseganaga Lake 74 K 5
Sesfontein 66 A 3
Seshachalam Hills 40 C 5
Sesheke 66 C 3
Seshia Mountains 65 F 3
Sesibi 60 E 4
Sesimbra 18 B 4
Seskarö 16 H 2
Sessa Aurunca 19 F 3
Sesto Fiorentino 19 F 3
Sestri Levante 19 E 3
Sestroretsk 17 J 3
Sesupé 17 H 5
Sesvete 19 G 2
Setana 39 L 2
Sète 18 D 3
Sete Lagoas 87 H 4
Sete Quedas, Cachoeira das 85 G 5
Sete Quedas, Salto das 87 F 5
Setermoen 16 G 2
Setesdal 17 E 4
Sétif 59 G 1
Seto-naikai 39 K 4
Settat 58 D 2
Setté Cama 63 F 6
Sette-Daban, Khrebet 37 P 3
Settle 5 D 2
Setúbal 18 B 4
Setúbal, Baía de 18 B 4
Seui 19 E 4
Seul, Lac 74 J 5
Seumanyam 42 A 3
Sevan 21 F 2
Sevan, Ozero 21 G 2
Sevarujo 86 C 4
Sevastopol' 21 D 2
Seven Pagodas → Mahabalipuram
   40 D 5
Sevenoaks 7 E 2
Sever 37 V 3
Severino Ribeiro 88 E 5
Severn (Ontario, Can.) 74 K 4
Severn Bridge 6 C 2
Severn Lake 74 JK 5
Severn, River (Gloucestershire)
   6 C 2
Severn, River (Powys) 6 C 1
Severnaya 25 S 2
Severnaya Bruingra 37 N 4
Severnaya Dvina 24 H 3
Severnaya Sos'va 25 M 3
Severnaya Zemlya 90
Severnayy 24 J 2
Severnoye 24 K 5
Severnoye 25 P 4
Severnykh 34 E 2
Severnyy 25 MN 2
Severnyy Anyuyskiy Khrebet
   37 UW 2
Severnyy Ural 25 L 3
Severo Baykal'skoye Nagor'ye
   36 K 4
Severo Sibirskaya Nizmennost'
   36 FK 1
Severodvinsk 24 G 3
Severo-Kuril'sk 37 ST 5
Severomorsk 16 K 2
Severoural'sk 25 L 3
Severo-Yeniseyskiy 36 F 3
Severskiy Donets 21 F 1
Severskiy Donets 24 G 6
Sevier 76 D 4
Sevier Desert 76 D 4
Sevilla 18 B 4
Sevlijevo 20 BC 2
Sevola 20 B 1
Sevrey 38 D 2
Seward (AK, U.S.A.) 72 H 3
Seward (NE, U.S.A.) 76 G 3
Seward Peninsula 72 E 2
Sewell 88 B 5
Seyah Band Koh 35 G 4
Sëyakha 25 NO 1
Sëyakha 25 O 1
Seychelles 65 J 5
Seychelles Bank 98 B 4
Seydän (Iran) 23 F 3
Seyðisfjörður 16 C 2
Seydişehir 21 D 3
Seyf Tāleh (Iran) 23 E 2
Seyfe Gölü 21 D 3
Seyhan 21 E 3
Seyhan (Turkey) 22 B 1
Seyhan Barajı 21 E 3
Seyitgazi 20 D 3
Seymchan 37 S 3
Seymour (IN, U.S.A.) 77 J 4

Seymour (South Africa) 66 D 6
Seymour (Victoria, Austr.) 49 H 6
Seyyedābād 35 H 4
Sežana 19 F 2
Sfax 59 H 2
Sferracavallo, Capo 19 E 4
Sfîntu Gheorghe 20 C 1
Sfîntu Gheorghe 20 CD 2
Sfîntu Gheorghe, Bratul 20 C 1
Sfîntu Gheorghe, Ostruvul 20 C 1
'S-Gravenhage 14 D 4
Sha Xian 39 G 5
Shaanxi 38 E 4
Shaartuz 35 H 3
Shaba 64 CD 6
Shabani → Zvishavane 66 D 4
Shābelle, Webi 65 G 4
Shabelsk 21 E 1
Shabunda 64 D 5
Shabwah 61 H 5
Shache 35 K 3
Shackleton Ice Shelf 91
Shackleton Range 91
Shaddādī (Syria) 22 C 1
Shādegān (Iran) 23 E 3
Shadrinsk 25 M 4
Shadwān (Egypt) 22 B 4
Shadzud 35 J 3
Shaftesbury 7 C 2
Shageluk 72 F 3
Shāghir (Syria) 22 C 1
Shagonar 36 F 5
Shāh 'Abbas (Iran) 23 F 2
Shah Alam 42 B 3
Shah Fuladi 35 H 4
Shāh Kūh 34 F 4
Shāh Zeyd (Iran) 23 F 1
Shahba (Syria) 22 B 2
Shahbandar 35 H 6
Shahdol 40 D 3
Shahhāt 59 K 2
Shahjahanpur 40 C 2
Shahjahanpur 40 CD 2
Shahmīrzad 34 E 3
Shahmīrzad (Iran) 23 F 2
Shahpur 35 J 4
Shahpura 40 B 2
Shahpura 40 D 3
Shahr Kord (Iran) 23 F 2
Shahrak 35 G 4
Shahr-e Bābak (Iran) 23 G 3
Shahr-e Khafr (Iran) 23 F 3
Shahtinsk 35 J 3
Shā'ib al Banāt, Jabal (Egypt)
   22 A 4
Sha'ïb Hasb (Saudi Arabia) 22 D 3
Sha'ïb Nisāh (Saudi Arabia) 23 E 4
Shaikh Bazit Dāgh 34 C 3
Shaim 25 M 3
Sha'ït, Wādī (Egypt) 22 A 4
Shajapur 40 C 3
Shakawe 66 C 3
Shakhrisyabz 35 H 3
Shakhtersk 21 E 1
Shakhtersk 37 Q 6
Shakhterskiy 37 X 3
Shakhtinsk 25 O 6
Shakhty 21 F 1
Shakhun'ya 24 J 4
Shaki 62 E 4
Shaksgam 35 K 3
Shaktoolik 72 E 3
Shāl (Iran) 23 E 2
Shala, Lake 65 F 3
Shalakusha 24 H 3
Shalamzār (Iran) 23 F 2
Shalānbōd 65 GH 4
Shaler Mountains 73 P 1
Shalgachëva 24 G 3
Shalgiya 25 O 6
Shali 21 G 2
Shalkar 24 K 5
Shaluli Shan 38 C 4–5
Shalunti 41 G 2
Shalya 25 L 4
Shalym 25 R 5
Shām, Jabal ash (Oman) 61 JK 5
Shām, Jabal ash (Oman) 61 K 4
Shamattawa 73 T 4
Shambār (Iran) 23 E 2
Shambe 64 E 3
Shambo 65 F 3
Shāmīyah 22 C 2
Shammar, Jabal (Saudi Arabia)
   22 CD 4
Shamokin 77 L 3
Shamrock 76 F 4
Shams (Iran) 23 G 3
Shamsī 60 D 5
Shamuhombo 64 B 6
Shamva 67 E 3
Shan 41 G 3
Shandan 38 D 4
Shandī 60 E 5
Shandong 39 G 3
Shandong Bandao 39 H 3

Shang Xian 38 E 4
Shangaly 24 H 3
Shangani 66 D 3
Shangcai 38 F 4
Shangcheng 38 FG 4
Shangchuan Dao 38 F 6
Shangdu 38 F 2
Shanghai 39 H 4
Shanghang 38 G 5
Shanglin 38 E 6
Shangnan 38 F 4
Shangombo 66 C 3
Shangqiu 38 G 4
Shangrao 39 G 5
Shangsi 38 E 6
Shangyi 38 F 2
Shangzhi 39 J 1
Shanh 36 H 6
Shani 63 G 3
Shankou 38 B 2
Shanklin 7 D 2
Shannon (Rep. of Ireland) 14 B 4
Shannon, Mouth of the 14 AB 4
Shannon, River 4 B 3
Shano 65 F 3
Shanshan 38 B 2
Shantarskiye Ostrova 37 P 4
Shantou 38 G 6
Shantung Peninsula → Shandong
   Bandao 39 H 3
Shanxi 38 F 3
Shanyin 38 F 3
Shaodong 38 F 5
Shaoguan 38 F 6
Shaoshan 38 F 5
Shaowu 39 G 5
Shaoxing 39 H 5
Shaoyang 38 F 5
Shap 5 E 2
Shapinsay 2 C 2
Shapkina 24 K 2
Shāpūr (Iran) 23 F 3
Shaqlāwah (Iraq) 22 D 1
Shaqqat al Kharītah 61 H 5
Shaqrā' 61 H 6
Shaqū (Iran) 23 G 4
Sharā 'Iwah (Qatar) 23 F 4
Sharaf (Iraq) 22 D 3
Sharafah 60 D 6
Sharāh, Jibāl ash 60 F 2
Sharak (Iran) 23 F 1
Sharan 24 K 5
Sharavogue 4 B 3
Sharbithāt, Ra's 61 K 5
Shargī, Jabal ash (Syria) 22 B 2
Sharīfābād (Iran) 23 F 2
Sharjah → Ash Shāriqah 61 K 3
Shark Bay 48 A 4
Sharlauk 34 F 3
Sharlyk 24 K 5
Shar'ya 24 J 4
Sharypovo 25 R 4
Shashamanna 65 F 3
Shashe 66 D 4
Shashe 66 D 4
Shashi 38 F 4
Shasta Lake 76 B 3
Shasta, Mount 76 B 3
Shatsk 24 H 5
Shatt al 'Arab (Iraq) 23 E 3
Shatt al Gharrāf (Iraq) 23 DE 3
Shatt al Jarīd 59 G 2
Shaunavon 73 Q 6
Shawan 35 M 2
Shawāq (Saudi Arabia) 22 B 4
Shawinigan 75 N 6
Shawnee 77 G 4
Shaybārā (Saudi Arabia) 22 B 4
Shaykh ' Uthmān 61 H 6
Shaykh Ahmad (Iraq) 23 E 2
Shaykh, Jabal Shaykh (Lebanon)
   22 B 2
Shaykh, Ra's ash 22 B 3
Shaykh Sa'd (Iraq) 23 DE 2
Shchara 17 J 5
Shchel'yayur 24 K 2
Shcherbakty 25 P 5
Shchigry 24 G 5
Shchiksoye Vdkhr. 21 E 1
Shchuchin 17 H 5
Shchuchinsk 25 N 5
Shchuch'ya 25 N 2
Shchuch'ye 25 M 4
Shea Ghimirra 64 F 3
Shebalin 21 F 1
Shebalino 25 QR 5
Shebekino 24 G 5
Sheboygan 77 J 3
Shebshi Mountains 63 G 4
Shebunino 37 Q 6

Shedgum (Saudi Arabia) 23 E 4
Shedin Peak 73 M 4
Shedok 21 F 2
Sheelin, Lough 4 B 3
Sheenjek 72 J 2
Sheerness 7 E 2
Sheet Harbour 75 P 7
Sheffield (AL, U.S.A.) 77 J 5
Sheffield (U.K.) 5 E 3
Shegarka 25 Q 4
Shehong 38 E 4
Sheikh Idris 60 E 6
Shekhawati 40 C 2
Shekhupura 35 J 4
Sheki 34 D 2
Shelār (Iran) 23 E 2
Shelburne 75 OP 7
Shelby 76 D 2
Sheldon Point 72 D 3
Shelekhov 36 H 5
Shelekhova 37 T 5
Shelikhova, Zaliv 37 T 3–4
Shelikof Strait 72 G 4
Shell Lakes 48 D 4
Shellbrook 73 Q 5
Shellharbour 49 J 5
Shelopugino 36 L 5
Shemakha 34 D 2
Shemonaikha 25 Q 5
Shenandoah National Park 77 L 4
Shenber 35 H 1
Shenchi 38 F 3
Shendam 63 F 4
Sheng Xian 39 H 5
Shenge 62 B 4
Shengsi Liedao 39 H 4
Shenkursk 24 H 3
Shenmu 38 F 3
Shenqiu 38 G 4
Shenton, Mount 48 C 4
Shenyang 39 H 2
Shenze 38 G 3
Sheopur 40 C 2
Shepetovka 17 J 5
Shepparton 49 H 6
Shepperd, Lake 48 C 4
Shepshed 7 D 1
Shepton Mallet 6 C 2
Sherborne 6 C 2
Sherbro Island 62 B 4
Sherbrooke 75 N 6
Sherda 63 H 1
Shere Hill 63 F 4
Sheridan 76 E 3
Sheringham 7 E 1
Sherkaly 25 N 3
Sherlovaya Gora 36 L 5
Sherman 77 G 5
Sherman Station 77 N 2
Sherpur 40 E 3
Sherridon 73 R 4
's-Hertogenbosch 14 E 4
Shetland Islands 2 D 1
Shevchenko 34 E 2
Shevli 37 O 5
Shevykan 36 J 5
Sheya 36 L 3
Sheyang 39 H 4
Sheyenne 76 G 2
Shiant Isles 2 A 3
Shiashkotan, Ostrov 37 S 6
Shīb Kūh (Iran) 23 F 3–4
Shibām 61 H 5
Shibarghan 35 H 3
Shibazhan 37 N 5
Shibeli, Webbe 65 G 3
Shibīn al Kawm 60 E 2
ShībKūh 34 E 5
Shibogama Lake 74 K 5
Shicheng Dao 39 H 3
Shidao 39 H 3
Shidian 38 C 6
Shifā', Jabal ash (Saudi Arabia)
   22 B 3
Shihezi 35 M 2
Shijiazhuang 38 F 3
Shikarpur 35 H 5
Shikoku 39 K 4
Shila 36 F 4
Shilabo 65 G 3
Shildon 5 E 2
Shilikarym 25 Q 6
Shilka 36 L 5
Shilka 36 L 5
Shilkan 37 R 4
Shilla 40 C 1
Shillelagh 4 B 3
Shillingstone 7 C 2
Shillong 41 F 2
Shilovo 24 H 5
Shimanovsk 37 N 5
Shimian 38 D 5
Shimizu 39 L 4
Shimo la Tewa 65 FG 5

Shimoga 40 C 5
Shimoni 65 F 5
Shimonoseki 39 JK 4
Shin, Loch 2 B 2
Shīnak pass 23 D 1
Shinās 61 K 4
Shindand 35 G 4
Shingbwiyang 41 G 2
Shingozha 25 Q 6
Shinghar 35 H 4
Shingshal 35 K 3
Shingū 39 L 4
Shinjö 39 M 3
Shinkafi 63 F 3
Shinness 2 B 2
Shinyanga 64 E 5
Ship Canal 5 D 3
Shipdham 7 E 1
Shiping 38 D 6
Shipley 5 E 3
Shippegan 75 P 6
Shipston-on-Stour 7 D 1
Shipton 5 E 2
Shipunovo 25 Q 5
Shipunskiy, Mys 37 TU 5
Shiquan 38 E 4
Shiquanhe 40 C 1
Shir Kuh 34 E 4
Shīr Kūh (Iran) 23 FG 3
Shira 25 R 5
Shirabad 35 H 3
Shirase Glacier 91
Shīrāz (Iran) 23 F 3
Shire 67 F 2
Shīrgāh (Iran) 23 F 1
Shirikrabat 35 G 2
Shīrīn Sū (Iran) 23 E 2
Shiriya-zaki 39 M 2
Shirley Mountains 76 E 3
Shirokaya Pad 37 Q 5
Shirokostan, Poluostrov 37 PQ 1
Shirokovo 36 G 4
Shirokoye 21 D 1
Shīrvān 34 F 3
Shīrvān (Iran) 23 E 2
Shisanzhan 37 MN 5
Shishaldin Volcano 72 E 5
Shishmaref 72 D 2
Shishou 38 F 5
Shithāthah (Iraq) 22 D 2
Shiveluch, Sopka 37 U 4
Shivpuri 40 C 2
Shiwa Ngandu 67 E 2
Shiwan Dashan 38 E 6
Shiyan 38 F 4
Shizong 38 D 6
Shizuishan 38 E 3
Shizuoka 39 L 4
Shkodra 20 A 2
Shlyuz 25 R 4
Shmidta, Poluostrov 37 Q 5
Shnezhnoye 21 E 1
Shoa 65 F 3
Sholapur 40 C 4
Shoptykul' 25 P 5
Shorapur 40 C 4
Shorawak 35 H 4
Shoreham-by-Sea 7 D 2
Shortandy 25 O 5
Shoshone 76 D 3
Shoshone Peak 76 C 4
Shoshong 66 D 4
Shoshoni 76 E 3
Shostka 24 F 5
Shou Xian 38 G 4
Shouguang 39 G 3
Show Low 76 E 5
Showa 91
Shoyna 24 H 2
Shpakovskoye 21 F 1
Shqiperia 20 AB 2
Shreveport 77 H 5
Shrewsbury 6 C 1
Shuangcheng 39 J 1
Shuangjiang 38 CD 6
Shuangliao 39 H 2
Shuangyang 39 J 2
Shuangyashan 39 K 1
Shu'ayt 61 J 5
Shubar-Kuduk 34 F 1
Shucheng 39 G 4
Shufu 35 K 3
Shuga 25 O 2
Shuga 25 P 5
Shugur 25 N 3
Shuguri Falls 65 F 6
Shuicheng 38 DE 5
Shulan 39 J 2
Shule 35 K 3
Shule He 38 C 2
Shulehe 38 C 2
Shulu 38 G 3
Shumagin Islands 72 F 4–5
Shumen 20 C 2
Shumerlya 24 J 4
Shumikha 25 M 4

Shumshu, Ostrov 37 T 5
Shumskiy 36 G 5
Shunak, Gora 25 O 6
Shunak, Gora 35 J 1
Shunchang 39 G 5
Shungnak 72 F 2
Shuo Xian 38 F 3
Shuolong 38 E 6
Shūr (Iran) 23 F 3
Shur (Iran) 23 G 3
Shūr Gaz 34 F 5
Shūr Kūl 34 F 5
Shūrāb 34 F 4
Shūrāb (Iran) 23 G 2
Shurinda 36 K 4
Shurugwi 66 DE 3
Shushenskoye 36 F 5
Shūshtar (Iran) 23 E 2
Shuwak 60 F 6
Shuya 16 K 3
Shuya 24 H 4
Shuyak 72 G 4
Shuyang 39 G 4
Shwäbische Alb 15 E 5
Shwebo 41 G 4
Shwegun 41 G 4
Shwegyin 41 G 4
Shweli 41 G 3
Shyok 35 K 4
Si Nho 41 J 4
Si Racha 41 H 5
Si Sa Ket 41 H 4
Si Xian 39 G 4
Sia 43 H 5
Siahan Range 35 GH 5
Sīāh-Chashmeh 34 C 3
Siāh-Kūh (Iran) 23 F 2
Siak Sri Indrapura 42 B 3
Sialk (Iran) 23 F 2
Sialkot 35 J 4
Siam 41 H 4
Sian → Xi'an 38 E 4
Siapa 84 E 3
Siargao 43 G 2
Siassi 50 E 3
Siau 43 G 3
Šiauliai 17 H 4
Siavonga 66 D 3
Siazan' 34 D 2
Sibā'ī, Jabal as 60 E 3
Sibay 25 L 5
Šibenik 19 G 3
Siberut, Pulau 42 A 4
Sibi 35 H 5
Sibigo 42 A 3
Sibirskiye Uvaly 25 NO 3
Sibirskoye Ploskogorye, Sredne
  36 FK 2–3
Sibiti 63 G 6
Sibiu 20 B 1
Sibolga 42 A 3
Sibsagar 41 FG 2
Sibu 42 D 3
Sibuguey Bay 43 F 2
Sibut 64 B 3
Sibutu, Pulau 43 E 3
Sibuyan 43 F 1
Sibuyan Sea 43 F 1
Sicasica 86 C 4
Sichon 41 G 6
Sichuan 38 CE 4
Sichuan Pendi 38 E 4
Sicilia 19 F 4
Sicilia, Canale de 19 F 4
Sicily 19 F 4
Sicuani 86 B 3
Sidamo 65 F 4
Sidaouet 63 F 2
Side 20 D 3
Sidéradougou 62 D 3
Siderno 19 G 4
Sidheros, Ákra 20 C 3
Sidhirokastrón 20 B 2
Sidhpur 40 B 3
Sidi Aïch 19 D 4
Sīdī Barrānī 60 D 2
Sidi Bennour 58 D 2
Sidi Ifni 58 C 3
Sidi Kacem 58 D 2
Sidi Krelil 59 G 2
Sidi-bel-Abbès 58 E 1
Sidikalang 42 A 3
Sidlaw Hills 3 C 3
Sidmouth 6 C 2
Sidney 73 N 6
Sidney (MT, U.S.A.) 76 F 2
Sidney (NE, U.S.A.) 76 F 3
Sidney (OH, U.S.A.) 77 K 3
Sidon (Lebanon) 22 B 2
Sidorovsk 25 Q 2
Sidr, Ra's as (Egypt) 22 A 3
Siedlce 15 H 2
Siegburg 15 E 4
Siegen 15 E 4
Siegen-Kyuyel 37 NO 3
Siem Reap 41 H 5

Siena 19 F 3
Sieradz 15 G 4
Sierpo 15 G 4
Sierra Alamos 78 B 2
Sierra Añueque 89 C 7
Sierra Auca Mahuida 89 C 6
Sierra Bermeja 18 B 4
Sierra Blanca 76 E 5
Sierra Chauchaiñeu 89 C 7
Sierra Cimaltepec 78 C 4
Sierra Colorada 89 C 7
Sierra de Agalta 78 E 4
Sierra de Alcaraz 18 C 4
Sierra de Alfabia 18 D 4
Sierra de Ancares 18 B 3
Sierra de Ancasti 88 C 4
Sierra de Aracena 18 B 4
Sierra de Coalcoman 78 B 4
Sierra de Córdoba 88 D 5
Sierra de Curupira 84–85 EF 3
Sierra de Famatina 88 C 4
Sierra de Gata 18 B 3
Sierra de Gredos 18 B 3
Sierra de Guadalupe 18 B 4
Sierra de Guadarrama 18 C 3
Sierra de Guampi 84 E 2
Sierra de Gúdar 18 C 3
Sierra de Juarez 76 C 5
Sierra de la Almenara 18 C 4
Sierra de la Cabrera 18 B 3
Sierra de la Demanda 18 C 3
Sierra de la Encantada 78 B 2
Sierra de la Giganta 76 D 6
Sierra de la Peña 18 C 3
Sierra de la Pila 18 C 4
Sierra de la Tasajera 76 E 6
Sierra de las Estancias 18 C 4
Sierra de las Minas 78 E 4
Sierra de las Tunas 76 E 6
Sierra de los Alamitos 78 B 2
Sierra de los Cuchumatanes 78 D 4
Sierra de los Huicholes 78 B 3
Sierra de Martés 18 C 4
Sierra de Montsant 18 D 3
Sierra de Montsech 18 D 3
Sierra de Montseny 18 D 3
Sierra de Mulegé 76 D 6
Sierra de Parras 78 B 2
Sierra de Perijá 84 D 2
Sierra de Rañadoiro 18 B 3
Sierra de San Borjas 76 D 6
Sierra de San Lázaro 76 E 7
Sierra de San Pedro 18 B 4
Sierra de San Vicente 18 C 3
Sierra de Segura 18 C 4
Sierra del Cadí 18 D 3
Sierra del Castañar 18 C 4
Sierra del Chorito 18 C 4
Sierra del Faro 18 B 3
Sierra del Moncayo 18 C 3
Sierra del Nevado 89 C 6
Sierra del Nido 76 E 6
Sierra del Pedroso 18 B 4
Sierra Espinazo del Diablo 78 A 3
Sierra Gorda 86 C 5
Sierra Grande (Argentina) 89 C 7
Sierra Grande (Mexico) 76 F 6
Sierra Grande (Mexico) 78 B 2
Sierra Leone 62 B 4
Sierra Madre (Mexico) 78 D 4
Sierra Madre (Philippines) 43 J 1
Sierra Madre del Sur 78 BC 4
Sierra Madre Oriental 78 BC 2–3
Sierra Madrona 18 C 4
Sierra Maestra 79 G 3
Sierra Mojada 78 B 2
Sierra Morena 18 BC 4
Sierra Nayarit 78 B 3
Sierra Nevada (Spain) 18 C 4
Sierra Nevada (U.S.A.) 76 BC 3–4
Sierra Nevada del Cocuy 84 D 2
Sierra Pacaraima 85 F 3
Sierra Parima 85 F 3
Sierra Prieta 76 D 5
Sierra Tarahumara 76 E 6
Sierra Velasco 88 C 4
Sierra Vizcaíno 76 D 6
Sierre 19 E 2
Sifani 65 G 2
Sifié 62 C 4
Sífnos 20 B 3
Sig 16 K 2
Sig 58 EF 1
Siğacik 20 C 3
Sigean, Étang de 18 D 3
Sigglesthorne 5 E 3
Sighetul Marmaţiei 20 B 1
Sighişoara 20 B 1
Sigiriya 40 D 6
Sigli 42 A 2
Siglufjörður 16 B 2
Signakhi 21 G 2
Signal Peak 76 D 5
Signy Island 91
Sigoisoinan 42 A 4
Sigovo 25 R 3

Sigsig 84 C 4
Sigtuna 17 G 4
Siguiri 62 C 3
Sigulda 17 HJ 4
Sihaung Myauk 41 F 3
Sihui 38 F 6
Siikajoki 16 J 3
Siilinjärvi 16 J 3
Siin 37 P 6
Siirt (Turkey) 21 F 3
Sikanni Chief 73 N 4
Sikar 40 C 2
Sikaram 35 H 4
Sikariman 42 AB 4
Sikasso 62 C 3
Sikéa 20 B 2
Sikéa 20 B 3
Sikerin 37 Q 2
Sikeston 77 J 4
Sikfors 16 H 2
Sikhote-Alin 37 P 6
Síkinos 20 BC 3
Síkinos 20 C 3
Sikkim 40 E 2
Siklós 20 A 1
Sikonge 64 E 6
Sikosi 66 C 3
Siktemey 37 S 2
Siktyakh 37 N 2
Sil 18 B 3
Silagui 42 A 4
Silba 19 F 3
Silchar 41 F 3
Sildagapet 16 D 3
Sile 20 C 2
Sileby 7 D 1
Silesia 15 G 4
Silet 59 F 4
Silgarhi-Doti 40 D 2
Silhouette 65 J 5
Sili 62 D 3
Silifke 21 D 3
Siligir 36 K 2
Siliguri 40 E 2
Siling Co 40 E 1
Silistra 20 C 2
Silivri 20 C 2
Siljan 17 F 3
Silkeborg 17 E 4
Sillajhuay → Cerro Toroni 86 C 4
Sillamäe 17 J 4
Sille 21 D 3
Sillian 19 F 2
Sillil 65 G 2
Silloth 3 C 4
Sillustani 86 B 4
Siloam Springs 77 H 4
Siloana Plains 66 C 3
Silom 51 F 2
Silonga 66 C 3
Silsden 5 DE 3
Siltou 63 H 2
Silup 35 G 5
Šilutė 17 H 4
Silvan 21 F 3
Silvassa 40 B 3
Silver Bank Passage 79 HJ 3
Silver City 76 E 5
Silverstone 7 D 1
Silverton 76 E 4
Silverton (N.S.W., Austr.) 49 G 5
Silves 85 G 4
Silyānah 59 G 1
Sil'yeyaki 37 Q 1
Simaleke Hilir 42 A 4
Simanggang 42 D 3
Simao 38 D 6
Simareh (Iran) 23 E 2
Simav 20 C 2
Simav 20 C 3
Simav 20 C 3
Simba 64 C 4
Simbo (Solomon Is.) 51 G 3
Simbo (Tanzania) 64 DE 5
Simcoe, Lake 75 M 7
Simenga 36 J 3
Simeulue, Pulau 42 A 3
Simferopol' 21 D 2
Sími 20 C 3
Simití 84 D 2
Simla 40 C 1
Şimleu Silvaniei 20 B 1
Simo 16 H 2
Simojärvi 16 J 2
Simojoki 16 J 2
Simojovel de Allende 78 D 4
Simón Bolivar, Parque Nacional
  84 D 2
Simonstown 66 B 6
Simpele 16 J 3
Simplicio Mendes 87 H 2
Simplon Pass 19 E 2
Simpson Desert 49 F 3
Simpson Desert National Park
  49 F 4
Simpson Hill 48 D 4

Simpson Peninsula 73 U 2
Simrishamn 17 F 4
Simuk, Pulau 42 A 3
Simushir, Ostrov 37 S 6
Sin Cow 42 D 2
Sīnā' (Egypt) 22 A 3
Sinabang 42 A 3
Sinabung, Gunung 42 A 3
Sinadaqo 65 H 3
Sinai (Egypt) 22 A 3
Sinaloa 76 E 6–7
Sinamaica 84 D 1
Sinalunga 19 F 3
Sinamaica 84 D 1
Sinazongwe 66 D 3
Sinbo 41 G 3
Sincé 84 C 2
Sincelejo 84 C 2
Sinch'am 39 J 2
Sinch'ang-ni 39 J 2
Sinclair Mine 66 B 5
Sinclairs' Bay 2 C 2
Sind 35 H 5
Sinda 37 P 6
Sindangbarang 42 C 5
Sindara 63 G 6
Sindeh, Teluk 43 F 5
Sindèr 62 E 3
Sindgi 40 C 4
Sindhuli Garhi 40 E 2
Sindor 24 K 3
Sinegorskiy 21 F 1
Sinelnikovo 21 E 1
Sines, Cabo de 18 B 4
Sinettä 16 J 2
Sinfra 62 C 4
Sing Buri 41 GH 5
Singako 63 H 4
Singapore 42 BC 3
Singapore, Strait of 42 B 3
Singaraja 42 E 5
Singen 15 E 5
Singida 64 E 5
Singitikós Kólpos 20 B 2–3
Singkaling Hkamti 41 G 2
Singkawang 42 C 3
Singkep, Pulau 42 B 4
Singkilbaru 42 A 3
Singleton 7 D 2
Singleton 49 J 5
Singleton, Mount (Western
  Australia) 48 B 4
Singö 17 G 3
Singu 41 G 3
Sinhailien 39 GH 4
Sinianka-Minia, Parc National du
  63 H 3
Siniscola 19 E 3
Siniy-Shikhan 25 M 5
Sinj 19 G 3
Sinjai 43 F 5
Sinjaja 17 J 4
Sinjār (Iraq) 22 C 1
Sinjār, Jabal 61 G 1
Sinkan 41 G 3
Sinkāt 60 F 5
Sinkiang Uighur 35 L 3
Sinn al Kadhdhāb 60 E 4
Sinnamary 85 H 2
Sinnar 40 B 4
Sinnicolau Mare 20 B 1
Sinnūris 60 E 3
Sinop 21 E 2
Sinp'o 39 J 2–3
Sinskoye 37 N 3
Šintana 20 B 1
Sintang 42 D 3
Sintra 18 B 4
Sinú 84 C 2
Sinūiju 39 HJ 2
Sinujif 65 H 3
Sinyaya 37 M 3
Sinyukha 20 D 1
Siocon 43 F 2
Siöfok 20 A 1
Sioma 66 C 3
Sion 19 E 2
Sion Mills 4 B 2
Sioux City 77 G 3
Sioux Falls 77 G 3
Sioux Lookout 74 J 5
Sipalay 43 F 2
Siping 39 H 2
Sipiwesk 73 S 4
Sipiwesk Lake 73 S 4
Siple Station 91
Sipolilo → Guruve 67 E 3
Sipora 42 A 4
Sipora, Pulau 42 A 4
Siquia, Rio 78 F 5
Siquijor 43 F 2
Siquisique 84 DE 1
Sīr Abū Nu'ayr (United Arab
  Emirates) 23 G 4
Sir Alexander, Mount 73 N 5

Sīr Banī Yās (United Arab
  Emirates) 23 F 4
Sir Edward Pellew Group 49 F 2
Sir James MacBrian, Mount
  72 M 3
Sir Thomas, Mount 48 D 4
Sira (India) 40 C 5
Sira (Norway) 17 E 4
Siracusa 19 G 4
Sirajganj 40 E 3
Sirdalen 17 E 4
Sirdalsvatn 17 E 4
Sīrdān (Iran) 23 E 1
Sire 65 F 3
Sireniki 72 C 3
Siret 20 C 1
Sirevåg 17 E 4
Sīrgān 35 G 5
Sirhān, Wādi as (Saudi Arabia)
  22 BC 3
Siri 65 F 3
Sīrīk 34 F 5
Sirino 19 G 3
Siris 40 D 3
Sirja 35 G 5
Sirjan, Kavir-e (Iran) 23 G 3
Sirkka 16 H 2
Sirnak 21 F 3
Sirohi 40 B 3
Sironj 40 C 3
Siros 20 B 3
Sirotskiy 21 F 1
Sirpur 40 C 4
Sirr, Nafūd as (Saudi Arabia)
  22–23 D 4
Sīrrī 34 E 5
Sīrrī (Iran) 23 G 4
Sirsa 40 C 2
Sirt 59 J 2
Sisak 19 G 2
Sīsakht (Iran) 23 F 3
Sishen 66 C 5
Sisimiut 75 R 2
Siskiyou Mountains 76 B 3
Sisophon 41 H 5
Sisseton 76 G 2
Sistema Iberico 18 C 3
Sistemas Béticos 18 C 4
Sisteron 19 E 3
Sistig-Khem 36 FG 5
Sistranda 16 E 3
Sitalike 64 E 6
Sitamarhi 40 E 2
Sitapur 40 D 2
Sitasjaure 16 G 2
Sitges 18 D 3
Sithonia 20 B 2
Sitka 72 K 4
Sitkalidak 72 G 4
Sitoli, Gunung 42 A 3
Sitrah 60 D 3
Sittang 41 G 4
Sittingbourne 7 E 2
Sittona 65 F 2
Sittwe 41 F 3
Situbondo 42 D 5
Siuna 78 F 5
Siuri 40 E 3
Sivaki 37 N 5
Sivas 21 E 3
Sivash 21 D 1
Sivaslı 20 C 3
Sivé 58 C 5
Siverek 21 E 3
Sivrice 21 E 3
Sivrihisar 20 D 3
Siwa Oasis → Wāhāt Sīwah 60 D 3
Sīwah 60 D 3
Siwalik Range 40 CD 1–2
Siwan 40 D 2
Siwana 40 B 2
Sixin 38 D 3
Sixth Cataract → Ash Shallāl as
  Sablūkah 60 E 5
Siya 24 H 3
Siziwang 38 F 2
Sjælland 17 F 4
Sjaunja 16 GH 3
Sjövegan 16 G 2
Sjūrjestan (Iran) 23 F 3
Skäckerfjällen 16 F 3
Skadarsko Jezero 20 A 2
Skadovsk 21 D 1
Skaftá 16 B 3
Skagatá 16 A 2
Skagen 17 F 4
Skagern 17 F 4
Skagerrak 17 E 4
Skagway 72 K 4
Skaidi 16 H 1
Skaill 2 C 2
Skala Podolskaya 20 C 1
Skaland 16 G 2
Skälderviken 17 F 4

Skaliskaya, Gora 36 D 1
Skanderborg 17 E 4
Skåne 17 F 4
Skanör 17 F 4
Skara 17 F 4
Skara Brae 2 C 2
Skærbæck 17 E 4
Skärblacka 17 G 4
Skardu 35 K 3
Skärhamn 17 F 4
Skarsöy 16 E 3
Skarstind 16 E 3
Skarsvåg 16 J 1
Skarżysko-Kamienna 15 H 4
Skeena 72 M 5
Skeena Mountains 72 M 4
Skeggöxl 16 A 2
Skegness 7 E 1
Skeiðárarsandur 16 B 3
Skeldon 85 G 2
Skeleton Coast Park 66 A 3
Skellefteå 16 H 3
Skellefteälven 16 G 2
Skelleftehamn 16 H 3
Skelmersdale 5 D 3
Skerries 4 B 3
Ski 17 F 4
Skíathos 20 B 3
Skibbereen 14 B 4
Skibotn 16 H 2
Skiddaw 5 D 2
Skidegate 72 L 5
Skidel' 17 H 5
Skien 17 E 4
Skierniewice 15 H 4
Skiftet 17 H 3
Skigersta 2 A 2
Skiíros 20 B 3
Skikda 59 G 1
Skipton 5 D 3
Skíros 20 B 3
Skive 17 E 4
Skjálfandafljót 16 B 2
Skjálfandi 16 B 2
Skjern 17 E 4
Skjervöy 16 H 1
Skjoldungen 75 T 3
Sklad 36 M 1
Škofja Loka 19 F 2
Skoghall 17 F 4
Skokholm 6 B 2
Skomer 6 B 2
Skópelos 20 B 3
Skopi 20 C 3
Skopje 20 B 2
Skorodum 25 O 4
Skorovatn 16 F 3
Skörping 17 EF 4
Skövde 17 F 4
Skovorodino 37 M 5
Skowhegan 77 M 3
Skradin 19 G 3
Skrekken 17 E 3
Skudeneshavn 17 DE 4
Skurup 17 F 4
Skutskär 17 G 3
Skvira 24 E 6
Skwentna 72 G 3
Skye 2 A 3
Slagnäs 16 G 2
Slamannan 3 C 4
Slamet, Gunung 42 C 5
Slane 4 B 3
Slaney, River 4 B 3
Slannik 20 C 2
Slano 19 G 3
Slantsy 17 J 4
Slashchevskaya 24 H 6
Śląsk 15 G 4
Slatina 20 B 2
Slautnoye 37 V 3
Slave Coast 62 E 4
Slave Lake 73 O 4
Slave River 73 P 3–4
Slavgorod 21 E 1
Slavgorod 25 P 5
Slavnoye 37 R 6
Slavonska Požega 19 G 2
Slavonski Brod 19 G 2
Slavuta 17 J 5
Slavyanka 39 K 2
Slavyansk 24 G 6
Slavyansk-na-Kubani 21 E 1
Sławno 15 G 4
Sleaford 7 D 1
Sleat 3 B 3
Sleat, Sound of 2–3 B 3
Sleeper Islands 75 L 4
Slettuheiði 16 B 2
Slieve Bloom Mountains 4 B 3
Slieve Donard 4 C 2
Sligo 14 B 4
Slite 17 G 4
Sliven 20 C 2
Slobodchikovo 24 J 3
Slobodka 20 C 1

Slobodskoy 24 K 4
Slobodzeya 20 C 1
Slobozia 20 C 2
Slochteren 12
Slocum Mountain 76 C 4
Slonim 17 J 5
Slough 7 D 2
Slovakia 15 H 5
Slovechno 17 J 5
Slovenija 19 FG 2
Slovenske Gorice 19 G 2
Slovensko 15 GH 5
Sluch' 17 J 5
Slŭnchev Bryag 20 C 2
Slunj 19 G 2
Stupia 15 G 4
Słupsk 15 G 4
Slutsk 17 J 5
Slyudyanka 36 H 5
Småland 17 G 4
Smålandsstenar 17 F 4
Smallwood Réservoir 75 P 5
Smedervo 20 B 2
Smedjebacken 17 G 3
Smela 24 F 6
Smidovich 37 O 6
Smidovich 90
Smirnovskiy 25 N 5
Smirnykh 37 Q 6
Smith 73 P 4
Smith Arm 73 N 2
Smith Bay 72 G 1
Smith Falls 75 M 7
Smithers 73 M 5
Smithfield 5 D 2
Smithsborough 4 B 2
Smithton 50 L 9
Smithtown-Gladstone 49 J 5
Smjörfjöll 16 C 2
Smögen 17 F 4
Smokey Dome 76 CD 3
Smoky Cape 49 J 5
Smoky Falls 74 L 5
Smoky Hill 76 F 4
Smoky Hills 76 G 4
Smoky River 73 O 5
Smöla 16 E 3
Smolensk 24 F 5
Smólikas Óros 20 B 2
Smolyan 20 B 2
Smooth Rock Falls 75 L 6
Smorgon' 17 J 5
Smygehamn 17 F 4
Smyrna → İzmir 20 C 3
Smythe, Mount 73 MN 4
Snaefell 4 C 2
Snæfell 16 B 3
Snæfellsjökull 16 A 3
Snæfellsnes 16 A 3
Snag 72 J 3
Snake 76 C 2
Snake Bay 48 E 1
Snake River Plain 76 D 3
Snare 73 O 3
Snåsa 16 F 3
Snåsvattnet 16 F 3
Snezhnogorsk 25 R 2
Snezhnoye 37 W 2
Snežnik 19 F 2
Śnieżka 15 G 4
Śnieżnik 15 G 4
Snigirevka 21 D 1
Snizort, Loch 2 A 3
Snöhetta 16 E 3
Snoul 41 J 5
Snow Lake 73 R 5
Snow Mountain 76 B 4
Snowbird Lake 73 R 3
Snowdon 6 B 1
Snowdrift 73 P 3
Snowville 76 D 3
Snowy Mountains 49 H 6
Snowy River 49 H 6
Snyatyn 20 C 1
Snyder 76 F 5
Soacha 84 D 3
Soahanina 67 G 3
Soalala 67 H 3
Soanierana-Ivongo 67 H 3
Soasiu 43 G 3
Soavinandriana 67 H 3
Soay 2 A 3
Soba 63 F 3
Sobat → Sawbā 64 E 3
Sobolevo 37 T 5
Sobolokh Mayan 37 MN 2
Sobopol 37 N 2
Sobradinho, Barragem de 87 H 3
Sobral 87 H 1
Socaire 86 C 5
Sochaczew 15 GH 4
Sochi 21 E 2
Society Islands 53 EF 4
Socorro (Colombia) 84 D 2
Socorro (N.M., U.S.A.) 76 E 5
Sócota 84 C 5

Socotra 65 J 2
Soda Plains 35 K 3
Sodankylä 16 J 2
Soddu 65 F 3
Söderhamn 16 G 3
Söderköping 17 G 4
Södermanland 17 G 4
Södertälje 17 G 4
Södra Kvarken 17 G 3
Soe 43 F 5
Soela Väin 17 H 4
Soest 15 E 4
Sofádhes 20 B 3
Sofala, Baía de 67 EF 4
Sofia (Madagascar) 67 H 3
Sofia → Sofiya 20 B 2
Sofiya 20 B 2
Sofiyevka 21 D 1
Sofiysk 37 O 5
Sofiysk 37 PQ 5
Sofporog 16 K 2
Sofu-gan 39 LM 5
Sog Xian 38 B 4
Sogamoso 84 D 2
Soğanlı 21 D 2
Sogda 37 O 5
Sogeri 50 E 3
Sogn og Fjordane 16 E 3
Sogndalsfjöra 16 E 3
Sognefjorden 16 E 3
Sognesjöen 16 D 3
Sogo Hills 65 F 4
Sogo Nur 38 D 2
Sogod 43 F 1
Sogolle 63 H 2
Sogom 25 N 3
Sögüt 20 D 2
Sögüt Gölü 20 CD 3
Sohag → Sawhāj 60 E 3
Soham 7 E 1
Sohano 51 FG 3
Sohm Abyssal Plain 98 A 2
Sohüksan-do 39 J 4
Soila 38 C 4
Soissons 18 D 2
Sojat 40 B 2
Sojosŏn-man 39 H 3
Sokal' 17 H 5
Sokch'o 39 J 3
Söke 20 C 3
Sokele 64 C 6
Sokhondo, Gora 36 K 6
Sokhor, Gora 36 J 5
Sokna 17 E 3
Sokodé 62 E 4
Sokol 20 A 2
Sokółka 15 H 4
Sokolo 62 C 3
Sokolov 15 F 4
Sokolozero 16 K 2
Sokone 62 A 3
Sokosti 16 J 2
Sokota 65 F 2
Sokoto 63 EF 3
Sŏl 65 H 3
Sola 17 E 4
Solai 65 F 4
Solbad Hall 19 F 2
Solberg 16 G 3
Soldatovo 37 V 3
Sölden 19 F 2
Soldotna 72 G 3
Soledad (Colombia) 84 D 1
Soledad (Venezuela) 85 F 2
Soledade (Amazonas, Brazil)
  84 E 5
Soledade (Río Grande do Sul,
  Brazil) 88 F 4
Solenoye (Russia, U.S.S.R.)
  21 F 1
Solenoye (Ukraine, U.S.S.R.)
  21 D 1
Solenzara 19 E 3
Solferino 19 F 2
Solhan 21 F 3
Soligorsk 17 J 5
Solikamsk 24 L 4
Sol'-Iletsk 24 L 5
Soliman 19 F 4
Solimões 84 E 4
Solingen 15 E 4
Solita 84 D 2
Solitaire 66 B 4
Sollas 2 A 3
Sollefteå 16 G 3
Sollerön 17 FG 3
Solling 15 E 4
Sologne Bourbonnais 18 D 2
Solok 42 B 4
Solomon Islands 51 GH 3
Solomon Sea 51 F 3
Solon 39 H 1
Solontsovo 36 KL 5
Solör 17 F 3
Solothurn 19 E 2
Solovetskiye, Ostrova 24 G 2

Solov'yevsk 36 L 5
Solov'yevsk 37 MN 5
Solta 19 G 3
Soltānābād (Iran) 23 E 3
Soltānābād 34 F 3
Soltau 15 E 4
Sol'tsy 17 K 4
Solva 6 B 2
Sölvesborg 17 FG 4
Solway Firth 3 C 4
Solwezi 66 D 2
Solyanka 36 M 3
Soma 20 C 3
Somabula 66 D 3
Somali Basin 98 B 3
Somalia 65 GH 3–4
Sombang, Gunung 42 E 3
Sombo 66 C 1
Sombor 20 A 1
Sombrerete 78 B 3
Sombrero Channel 41 F 6
Somcuţa Mare 20 B 1
Somero 17 H 3
Somerset (Australia) 49 G 1
Somerset (KY, U.S.A.) 77 K 4
Somerset (U.K.) 6 C 2
Somerset East 66 CD 6
Somersham 7 E 1
Somerton 6 C 2
Someş 20 B 1
Someşu Mare 20 B 1
Somme 18 D 1
Sommen 17 G 4
Somnath 40 B 3
Somnitel'nyy 37 P 5
Somontano 18 C 3
Somoto 78 E 5
Somuncurá, Meseta de 89 C 7
Son 40 D 3
Son 40 D 3
Son Ha 41 J 4
Son La 41 H 3
Soná 84 B 2
Sonakh 37 P 5
Sonaly 25 O 6
Sŏnch'ŏn 39 H 3
Sönderborg 17 EF 5
Sondershausen 15 F 4
Söndre Strömfjord 75 R 2
Söndre Strömfjord 75 RS 2
Sondrio 19 E 2
Sonepur 40 D 3
Sonequera 86 C 5
Song 63 G 4
Song Cau 41 J 5
Song Da 41 H 3
Song Hong 41 H 3
Song Ma 41 H 3
Songea 67 F 2
Songhua Hu 39 J 2
Songhua Jiang 39 J 1
Songjiang 39 H 4
Songkhla 41 H 6
Songling 37 M 6
Songnim 39 J 3
Songo 67 E 3
Songolo 64 A 6
Songpan 38 D 4
Songwe 64 E 6
Songxi 39 G 5
Sonid Youqi 38 F 2
Sonid Zuoqi 38 F 2
Sonipat 40 C 2
Sonkel', Ozero 35 K 2
Sonmiani 35 H 5
Sonmiani Bay 35 H 5
Sonneberg 15 F 4
Sono 85 J 5
Sonoita 76 D 5
Sonoma Peak 76 C 3
Sonora (Mexico) 76 D 6
Sonora (TX, U.S.A.) 76 F 5
Sonora, Rio 76 D 6
Sonoran Desert 76 D 5
Sonqor (Iran) 23 E 2
Sonsón 84 CD 2
Sonsonate 78 DE 5
Sonsorol Islands 43 H 2
Sop Bau 41 H 3
Sopka Anangravnen 37 U 4
Sopka Kizimen 37 U 4
Sopka Shiveluch 37 U 4
Sopochnaya Karga 36 DE 1
Sopochnoye 37 T 4
Sopot 15 G 4
Sopron 20 A 1
Sopur 35 J 4
Sor 18 B 4
Sor Kaydak 34 E 1–2
Sor Mertvyy Kultuk 34 E 1
Sör Rondane Mountains 91
Sora 19 F 3
Sorada 40 D 4
Söråker 16 G 3
Sorata 86 C 4

Sordoginskiy Khrebet 37 OP 3
Sorel 75 N 6
Sorell 50 L 9
Sörfold 16 G 2
Sorgues 19 D 3
Sorgun 21 E 3
Soria 18 C 3
Soriano 88 E 5
Sorikmerapi, Gunung 42 A 3
Sorkh, Küh-e (Iran) 23 G 2
Sorkheh 34 E 3
Sorkheh (Iran) 23 F 2
Sorn 3 B 4
Sorocaba 87 G 5
Sorochinsk 24 K 5
Sorok 36 H 5
Soroki 20 C 1
Sorolen 25 P 6
Sorong 43 H 4
Soroti 64 E 4
Söröya 16 H 1
Sörøyane 16 E 3
Sorraia 18 B 4
Sörreisa 16 G 2
Sorrento 19 F 3
Sorsatunturi 16 J 2
Sorsele 16 G 2
Sorso 19 E 3
Sorsogon 43 F 1
Sort 18 D 3
Sortavala 16 K 3
Sortland 16 FG 2
Sör-Tröndelag 16 F 3
Sörvagur 14 A 1
Sörværøy 16 F 2
Sösan 39 J 3
Sosna 36 J 3
Sosnogorsk 24 KL 3
Sosnovka 24 H 2
Sosnovka 24 J 4
Sosnovka 36 J 5
Sosnovo-Ozerskoye 36 K 5
Sosnovy Bor 17 J 4
Sosnovyy Bor 25 Q 3
Sosnovyy Mys 25 N 3
Sosnowiec 15 G 4
Sosumav 67 H 2
Sos'va 25 M 4
Sos'va, Malaya 25 MN 3
Sos'va, Severnaya 25 MN 3
Sos'vinskaya Kul'tbaza 25 M 3
Sosyka 21 EF 1
Sotavento, Islas de 84 E 1
Sotik 64 F 5
Sotkamo 16 J 3
Sotnikovskoye 21 F 1
Sotonera, Embalse de la 18 C 3
Sotouboua 62 E 4
Sotra 17 D 3
Sotsial 25 P 6
Souanké 63 G 5
Soubré 62 C 4
Soudan 49 F 2
Souf 59 G 2
Souflion 20 C 2
Soufrière (Guadeloupe) 79 K 4
Soufrière (St. Vincent) 79 K 5
Souillac 18 D 3
Souilly 19 E 2
Souk Ahras 59 G 1
Souk el Arbaa du Rharb 58 D 2
Soukouralla 62 C 2
Söul 39 HJ 3
Soumenselkä 16 H 3
Sound of Arisaig 3 B 3
Sound of Harris 2 A 3
Sound of Jura 3 B 3–4
Sound of Mull 3 B 3
Sound of Raasay 2 A 3
Sound of Sleat 2–3 B 3
Sound of Sleat 2–3 B 3
Sounfat 62 E 1
Soúnion, Ákra 20 B 3
Sountellane 63 G 2
Soure 85 J 4
Souris 73 R 6
Souris 75 P 6
Souris River 73 R 6
Sous 58 D 2
Sousa 87 J 2
Sousel 86 H 4
Sousse (Tunisia) 59 H 1
Soutergate 5 D 2
South Africa 66 CD 6
South Alligator River 48 E 1
South Andaman 41 F 5
South Atlantic Ocean 91
South Aulatsivik 75 P 4
South Australia 48–49 EF 4
South Australian Basin 99 C 5
South Bay 73 V 3
South Bend (IN, U.S.A.) 77 J 3
South Bend (WA, U.S.A.) 76 B 2
South Benfleet 7 E 2
South Brent 6 C 3
South Carolina 77 K 5

South China Sea 42 CD 2
South Dakota 76 FG 3
South Downs 7 D 2
South East Cape 50 L 9
South East Point 49 H 6
South Geomagnetic Pole 91
South Georgia 91
South Glamorgan 6 C 2
South Horr 65 F 4
South Indian Lake 73 S 4
South Island 50 P 9
South Korea 39 JK 3
South Lake Tahoe 76 C 4
South Magnetic Pole 91
South Molton 6 C 2
South Nahanni 73 M 3
South Ockenden 7 E 2
South Orkney Islands 91
South Pacific Ocean 91
South Petherton 6 C 2
South Platte 76 F 3
South Pole 91
South Ronaldsay 2 C 2
South Sandwich Islands 91
South Saskatchewan 73 PQ 5
South Shetland Islands 91
South Shields 5 E 2
South Sioux City 77 G 3
South Taranaki Bight 51 Q 8
South Tasman Rise 99 C 5
South Tyne, River 5 D 2
South Uist 2 A 3
South Wellesley Islands
   (Queensland, Austr.) 49 F 2
South Yemen 61 HJ 5–6
South Yolla Bolly Mountains
   76 B 4
South Yorkshire 5 E 3
South Zeal 6 C 3
Southampton 7 D 2
Southampton (Airport) 7 D 2
Southampton, Cape 73 UV 3
Southampton Island 73 UV 3
Southeast Indian Ridge 98 BC 5
Southend 3 B 4
Southend 73 R 4
Southend (Airport) 7 E 2
Southend-on-Sea 7 E 2
Southern Alps 51 Q 9
Southern Cook Islands 53 E 4
Southern Cross 48 B 5
Southern Indian Lake 73 S 4
Southern Uplands 3 BC 4
Southminster 7 E 2
Southport 5 D 3
Southwest Cape 50 P 10
Southwest Indian Ridge 98 B 5
Southwestern Pacific Basin 99 D 5
Southwold 7 E 1
Soutpansberg 66 D 4
Soutra Hill 50 P 10
Soven 88 C 5
Soverato 19 G 4
Sovetsk 17 H 4
Sovetsk 24 J 4
Sovetskaya 21 F 2
Sovetskaya Gavan' 37 PQ 6
Sovetskaya Rechka 25 Q 2
Sovetskiy 21 D 1
Sovetskoje, Ozero 25 Q 2
Sovetskoye 21 G 2
Soya Strait 27 R 5
Soyatita 76 E 6
Soyo 66 A 1
Sozh 24 F 5
Sozimskiy 24 K 4
Sozopol 20 C 2
Spain 18 BC 4
Spalding 7 D 1
Spanish Fork 76 D 3
Spanish Town 79 G 4
Sparbu 16 F 3
Sparks 76 C 4
Sparta → Spartí 20 B 3
Spartanburg 77 K 5
Spartel, Cap 58 D 1
Spartí 20 B 3
Spartivento, Capo 19 E 4
Spassk Dal'niy 39 K 2
Spátha, Ákra 20 B 3
Spean Bridge 3 B 3
Spearfish 76 F 3
Speke Gulf 64 E 5
Spenard 72 G 3
Spence Bay 73 T 2
Spencer 77 G 3
Spencer Bay 66 A 5
Spencer, Cape 49 F 6
Spencer Gulf 49 F 5
Spennymoor 5 E 2
Sperrin Mountains 4 B 2
Spetisbury 7 C 2
Spétsai 20 B 3
Spey, River 2 C 3
Speyer 15 E 5
Spicer Islands 75 M 2

Spiez 19 E 2
Spilsby 7 E 1
Spirit River 73 O 4
Spišská-Nová Ves 15 H 5
Spitsbergen 90
Spittal 19 F 2
Spittal of Glenshee 3 D 3
Spjelkavik 16 E 3
Split 19 G 3
Split Lake 73 S 4
Spluga, Passo della 19 E 2
Spofforth 5 E 3
Spogi 17 J 4
Spokane 76 C 2
Spoleto 19 F 3
Spong 41 J 5
Spooner 77 H 2
Spratly Island 42 D 2
Spree 15 F 4
Sprengisandur 16 B 3
Springbok 66 B 5
Springdale 75 Q 6
Springdale (AR, U.S.A.) 77 H 4
Springer 76 F 4
Springer, Mount 75 N 6
Springfield (CO, U.S.A.) 76 F 4
Springfield (IL, U.S.A.) 77 HJ 4
Springfield (MA, U.S.A.) 77 M 3
Springfield (MO, U.S.A.) 77 H 4
Springfield (OR, U.S.A.) 76 B 3
Springfield (S.D., U.S.A.) 76 G 3
Springfield (TN, U.S.A.) 77 J 4
Springfontein 66 D 5–6
Springhill 75 P 6
Springlands 85 G 2
Springs 66 D 5
Springs Junction 51 Q 9
Springsure 49 H 3
Springvale (Queensland, Austr.)
   49 GH 2
Spurn Head 5 F 3
Squamish 73 N 6
Square Islands 75 QR 5
Squillace, Golfo di 19 G 4
Squinzano 19 G 3
Squires, Mount 48 D 4
Srbija 20 B 2
Sredinnyy Khrebet 37 TU 4–5
Sredna Gora 20 B 2
Sredne Russkaya Vozvyshennost'
   24 G 5
Sredne Sibirskoye Ploskogor'ye
   36 FK 2–3
Sredne Yegorlyk 21 F 1
Srednebelaya 37 N 5
Srednego, Ostrova 37 S 6
Sredne-Kamchatsk 37 U 4
Srednekolymsk 37 S 2
Sredneye Kuyto, Ozero 16 K 2–3
Sredniy 37 S 4
Sredniy Kalar 36 L 4
Sredniy Ural 25 L 4
Sredniy Vasyugan 25 P 4
Srednyaya Itkana 37 U 3
Srednyaya Nyukzha 37 M 4
Srednyaya Olekma 36 M 4
Śrem 15 G 4
Sremska Mitrovica 20 A 2
Sretensk 36 L 5
Sri Lanka 40 D 6
Sri Madhopur 40 C 2
Sriharikota 40 D 5
Srikakulam 40 D 4
Srinagar 35 K 4
Środa Wielkopolska 15 G 4
Staaten River 49 G 2
Staaten River National Park 49 G 2
Stack Skerry 2 B 2
Stadhampton 7 D 2
Stadhavet 16 DE 3
Städjan 16 F 3
Stadlandet 16 DE 3
Staffa 3 A 3
Staffin 2 A 3
Stafford 7 C 1
Staffordshire 7 CD 1
Stagno di Cabras 19 E 4
Stainach 19 F 2
Staindrop 5 E 2
Staines 7 D 2
Stainforth 5 D 2
Staithes 5 E 2
Stalham 7 E 1
Ställdalen 17 F 4
Stalowa Wola 15 H 4
Stalybridge 5 DE 3
Stamford (CT, U.S.A.) 77 M 3
Stamford (TX, U.S.A.) 76 G 5
Stamford (U.K.) 7 D 1
Stamford Bridge 5 E 3
Stampriet 66 B 4
Stamsund 16 F 2
Stanchik 37 S 1
Standerton 66 D 5
Stanger 67 E 5
Stanke Dimitrov 20 B 2

Stanley (Falkland Is., U.K.) 89 E 9
Stanley (N.D., U.S.A.) 76 F 2
Stanley (U.K.) 5 E 2
Stanley Falls 64 D 4
Stanley Mission 73 R 4
Stanley Reservoir 40 C 5
Stannakh-Khocho 36 M 1
Stanovaya 37 T 2
Stanovka 25 O 4
Stanovoy Khrebet 36–37 LN 4
Stanovoy Nagor'ye 36 KL 4
Stanovoy Range 37 N 4
Stans 19 E 2
Stansted (Airport) 7 E 2
Stansted Mountfitchet 7 E 2
Stanthorpe 49 J 4
Stara Pazova 20 B 2
Stara Planina 20 BC 2
Stara Zagora 20 C 2
Starachowice 15 H 4
Staraya Russa 17 K 4
Staraya Vorpavla 25 N 3
Starbuck 53 E 3
Starcross 6 C 3
Stargard Szczecinski 15 G 4
Starichkova 37 V 2
Starigrad 19 G 3
Staritsa 37 Q 6
Starnberg 15 F 5
Starobel'sk 24 G 6
Starodub 24 F 5
Starogard Gdański 15 G 4
Starominskaya 21 E 1
Staromlinovka 21 E 1
Starovercheskaya 24 J 4
Staroye Linde 36 M 2
Start Bay 6 C 2
Start Point 6 C 2
Staryy Dom 37 Q 1
Staryy Krym 21 DE 1
Staryy Oskol 24 G 5
State College 77 L 3
Statesboro 77 K 5
Statesville 77 K 4
Statland 16 F 3
Staunton 77 L 4
Staunton on Wye 6 C 1
Stavanger 17 DE 4
Staveley 5 E 3
Stavern 17 F 4
Stavropol' 21 F 1
Stavropol' 21 F 2
Stavropolka 25 N 5
Stavropol'skaya Vozvyshennost'
   21 F 1
Stavrós 20 B 2
Stavroupolis 20 B 2
Stawell 49 G 6
Stawiski 15 H 4
Staxton 5 E 2
Steelport 66 DE 4
Steen River 73 O 4
Steenkool 43 H 4
Steensby Inlet 75 M 1
Stefănești 20 C 1
Stefanie, Lake 65 F 4
Stefansson Island 73 Q 1
Stegi 67 E 5
Steilrand Mountains 66 A 3
Steinach 19 F 2
Steinbach 73 S 6
Steinfeld 66 B 4
Steinfurt 15 E 4
Steinkjer 16 F 3
Steinkopf 66 B 5
Stekol'nyy 37 S 4
Stella 66 C 5
Stellenbosch 66 B 6
Stello 19 E 3
Stelvio, Passo della 19 F 2
Stenay 19 DE 2
Stendal 15 F 4
Stende 17 H 4
Stenen 20 C 3
Sténon Serifou 20 B 3
Stenton 3 C 4
Stenungsund 17 F 4
Step' Shaidara 35 H 2
Stepanakert 34 D 3
Stephens Passage 72 L 4
Stephenville 75 Q 6
Stephenville (TX, U.S.A.) 76 G 5
Stepnoye 21 F 2
Stepnyak 25 O 5
Sterkstroom 66 D 6
Sterling 76 F 3
Sterlitamak 24 KL 5
Šternberk 15 G 5
Stettiner Haff 15 F 4
Stettler 73 P 5
Steubenville 77 K 3
Stevenage 7 D 2
Stevens Point 77 HJ 3

Stevenson Entrance 72 G 4
Stevenston 3 B 4
Stewart 72 KL 3
Stewart (AK, U.S.A.) 72 M 4
Stewart Crossing 72 K 3
Stewart, Isla 89 B 9
Stewart Island (New Zealand)
   50 P 10
Stewart Islands 51 H 3
Stewart River 72 K 3
Stewart Sound 41 F 5
Stewarton 3 B 4
Stewartstown 4 B 2
Steynsburg 66 D 6
Steyr 19 F 2
Stickney 7 E 1
Stikine 72 L 4
Stikine Ranges 72 L 4
Stílis 20 B 3
Stillwater 77 G 4
Stilo, Punta 19 G 4
Stilton 7 D 1
Štip 20 B 2
Stirling 3 B 3
Stirling Creek 48 D 2
Stirling Range 48 B 5
Stirling Range National Park
   48 B 5
Štit 15 H 5
Stjernöya 16 H 1
Stjördal 16 F 3
Stockbridge 7 D 2
Stockerau 19 G 2
Stockholm 17 G 4
Stockport 5 D 3
Stocksbridge 5 E 3
Stockton 76 B 4
Stockton Lake 77 H 4
Stockton Plateau 76 F 5
Stockton-on-Tees 5 E 2
Stöde 16 G 3
Stoer 2 B 2
Stoffberg 66 D 5
Stoke Albany 7 D 1
Stokenchurch 7 D 2
Stoke-on-Trent 5 D 3
Stokesley 5 E 2
Stokksnes 16 C 3
Stokmarknes 16 F 2
Stol 20 B 2
Stolbovoy, Ostrov 37 P 1
Stolbtsy 17 J 5
Stolin 17 J 5
Ston 19 G 3
Stone 7 C 1
Stonehaven 3 C 3
Stonehenge 7 D 2
Stonehouse 3 B 4
Stoneykirk 3 B 4
Stony 72 F 3
Stony Rapids 73 Q 4
Stony River 72 F 3
Stony Stratford 7 D 1
Stony Tunguska River 36 GH 3
Stora Bjßrkvattnet 16 FG 2
Stora Lulevatten 16 G 2
Stora Sjöfallet 16 G 2
Storån 16 G 3
Storavan 16 G 2
Stord 17 E 4
Store Bælt 17 F 4
Storfjorden 16 E 3
Storington 7 D 2
Storis Passage 73 S 2
Storjšen 16 F 3
Storsjöen 16 F 3
Storsjö 16 F 3
Storsjön (Sweden) 16 F 3
Storstenfjellet 16 G 2
Storuman 16 G 2
Storvigelen 16 F 3
Storvindeln 16 G 2
Stöttingfjället 16 G 3
Stour, River 7 E 2
Stourbridge 7 C 1
Stourport 7 C 1
Stövring 17 E 4
Stow on-the-Wold 7 D 2
Stowmarket 7 E 1
Stoyba 37 O 5
Strabane 4 B 2
Strachan 3 D 3
Stradbally 4 B 3
Stradbroke Island, North 49 J 4
Stradone 4 B 3
Strahan 50 L 9
Strait of Belle Isle 75 Q 5

Strait of Bonifacio 19 E 3
Strait of Canso 75 P 6
Strait of Dover 14 D 4
Strait of Gibraltar 18 B 4
Strait of Hormuz 23 G 4
Strait of Juan de Fuca 73 MN 6
Strait of Magellan 89 BC 9
Strait of Makassar 42 E 4
Strait of Malacca 42 B 3
Strait of Singapore 42 B 3
Straits of Florida 77 KL 6–7
Straits of Mackinac 77 J 2
Strakonice 15 F 5
Stralsund 15 F 4
Strand 66 B 6
Strangford 4 C 2
Strangford Lough 4 C 2
Strängnäs 17 G 4
Stranraer 4 C 2
Strasbourg 19 E 2
Strasswalchen 19 F 2
Strat (New Zealand) 51 Q 8
Stratford 75 L 7
Stratford (TX, U.S.A.) 76 F 4
Stratford (Victoria, Austr.) 49 H 6
Stratford-upon-Avon 7 D 1
Strath Dearn 2 BC 3
Strath Earn 3 C 3
Strath Kanaird 2 B 3
Strath Spey 2 C 3
Strathaven 3 B 4
Strathbogie 2 C 3
Strathclyde 3 B 4
Strathmay 49 G 1
Strathmore (Australia) 49 G 2
Strathmore (U.K.) 3 C 3
Strathpeffer 2 B 3
Strathy Point 2 C 2
Stratton 6 B 2
Straubing 15 F 5
Straumnes 16 A 2
Straumsjöen 16 F 2
Strawberry Mountain 76 C 3
Streaky Bay 48 E 5
Street 6 C 2
Strehaia 20 B 2
Strelka 36 F 4
Strelka 37 S 3
Strelka-Chunya 36 H 3
Stretham 7 E 1
Strethy 2 B 2
Stretto di Messina 19 G 4
Stretton 48 B 5
Streymoy 14 A 1
Stříbro 15 F 5
Strickland River 50 D 3
Strimón 20 B 2
Strimonikós Kólpos 20 B 2
Strizhovo 25 O 4
Stroeder 89 D 7
Strofádhes, Nísoi 20 B 3
Strokestown 4 AB 3
Stromboli 19 FG 4
Stromeferry 2 B 3
Strömfjord, Nordre 75 R 2
Strömfjord, Söndre 75 R 2
Stromness 2 C 2
Ströms Vattudal 16 F 3
Strömsbruk 16 G 3
Strömsnäsbruk 17 F 4
Strömstad 17 F 4
Strömsund 16 G 3
Stronachlachar 3 B 3
Stronsay 2 C 2
Stronsay Firth 2 C 2
Strontian 3 B 3
Stroud 7 C 2
Struer 17 E 4
Struga 20 B 2
Struma 20 B 2
Strumica 20 B 2
Strydenburg 66 C 5
Strynsvatn 16 E 3
Stryy 24 D 6
Strzyzów 15 H 5
Stuart 72 F 3
Stuart Lake 73 MN 5
Stuart, Point 48 E 1
Studland 7 D 2
Stung Treng 41 J 5
Sturgeon Lake 74 J 6
Sturry 7 E 2
Sturt Creek 48 D 2
Sturt Desert 49 G 4
Sturt National Park 49 G 4
Sturt Plain 48 E 2
Stutterheim 66 D 6
Stuttgart 15 E 5
Stykkishólmur 16 A 2
Styr' 17 J 5
Su Xian 39 G 4
Suai 43 G 5
Suao 39 H 6
Subà'il (Iraq) 22 D 2
Subay', Uruq as 61 G 4
Subayhah (Saudi Arabia) 22 C 3

Subei Monggolzu Zizhixian 38 C 3
Subeita (Israel) 22 B 3
Subi, Pulau 42 C 3
Sublette 76 F 4
Subotica 20 A 1
Suceava 20 C 1
Suck 14 B 4
Sucre 86 CD 4
Sucuaro 84 E 3
Súćuraj 19 G 3
Sucuriju 85 J 3
Sudak 21 D 2
Sudan 60 DE 6
Sudbury 7 D 1
Sudbury 75 L 6
Sudbury (U.K.) 7 E 1
Sudd 64 E 3
Suddie 85 G 2
Sudety 15 G 4
Suðureyri 16 A 2
Suðuroy 14 A 1
Sudirman, Pegunungan 43 J 4
Sue 64 D 3
Suez 22 A 3
Suez Canal (Egypt) 22 A 3
Süf Ajjīn, Wādī 59 H 2
Şufaynah 61 G 4
Suffolk 7 E 1
Sufiän 34 D 3
Suğla Gölü 21 D 3
Sugoy 37 T 3
Suguta 65 F 4
Suhai Hu 38 B 3
Şuḩār 61 K 4
Sühbaatar 36 J 5
Sühbaatar 38 F 1
Suhl 15 F 4
Sui Xian 38 F 4
Suiá-Missu 87 F 3
Suibin 37 O 6
Suichang 39 G 5
Suichuan 38 F 5
Suide 38 F 3
Suifenhe 39 K 2
Suihua 39 J 1
Suijang 38 D 5
Suileng 39 J 1
Suining 38 E 4
Suining 39 G 4
Suipacha 86 C 5
Suir, River 4 B 3
Suixi 38 F 6
Suixi 39 G 4
Suizhong 39 H 2
Suizhou 38 F 4
Sujangarh 40 B 2
Sukabumi 42 C 5
Sukadana 42 CD 4
Sukagawa 39 LM 3
Sukaraja 42 D 4
Sukau 43 E 2
Sukeva 16 J 3
Sukhana 36 L 2
Sukhodolskoye, Ozero 16 K 3
Sukhona 24 H 4
Sukhothai 41 G 4
Sukhotinskiy 21 F 1
Sukhoy 21 F 1
Sukhumi 21 F 2
Sukkertoppen 75 R 2
Sukkozero 16 K 3
Sukkur 35 H 5
Sukma 40 D 4
Süknah 59 J 3
Sukses 66 B 4
Suksukan 37 S 3
Suksun 25 L 4
Sul, Canal do 85 HJ 4
Sula (Norway) 16 D 3
Sula (U.S.S.R.) 24 JK 3
Sula, Kepulauan 43 FG 4
Sula Sgeir 2 A 2
Sulaiman Range 35 H 4–5
Sulaimäniya (Iraq) 23 D 2
Sulak 34 D 2
Sulakyurt 21 D 2
Sulanheer 38 E 2
Sülär (Iran) 23 F 3
Sularya Dağları 20 C 3
Sulat, Bukit 43 G 3
Sulawesi 43 EF 4
Sulawesi, Laut 43 F 3
Sulb 60 E 4
Süldeh (Iran) 23 F 1
Sule Skerry 2 B 2
Sulechów 15 G 4
Sulen, Mount 50 D 2
Sulima 62 B 4
Sulina 20 C 1
Sulina 20 C 1
Sulitelma 16 G 2
Sulkava 16 J 3
Sullana 84 B 4
Sullom 2 D 1
Sullom Voe 2 D 1
Sulmona 19 F 3

Sulphur 77 H 5
Sulphur Springs 77 G 5
Sultän 59 JK 2
Sultan Dağları 20–21 D 3
Sultanhani 21 D 3
Sultanpur 40 C 1
Sultanpur 40 D 2
Sulu Archipelago 43 F 2–3
Sulu Sea 43 EF 2
Sulūq 59 K 2
Suly 25 N 5
Sulyukta 35 H 3
Sumalata 43 F 3
Sümar (Iran) 23 D 2
Sumarokovo 25 R 3
Sumatera 42 AB 3–4
Sumaúma 85 G 5
Šumava 15 F 5
Sumba 43 EF 5
Sumba, Selat 43 EF 5
Sumbawa 42 E 5
Sumbawa Besar 42 E 5
Sumbawanga 64 E 6
Sumbe 66 A 2
Sümber 38 E 1
Sumbu 67 E 1
Sumbu Game Reserve 67 E 1
Sumburgh (Airport) 2 D 2
Sumburgh Head 2 D 2
Sumedang 42 C 5
Sumenep 42 D 5
Sumesar Range 40 D 2
Sumgait 34 DE 2
Sumisu-jima 39 L 4
Sumkino 25 N 4
Summel (Iraq) 22 D 1
Summer Lake 76 BC 3
Summit Lake 73 N 4
Sumperk 15 G 5
Sumprabum 41 G 2
Sumter 77 KL 5
Sumuma 36 G 3
Sumy 24 G 5
Sumzom 38 C 5
Sun Kosi 40 E 2
Sun Valley 76 D 3
Suna 16 K 3
Suna 64 E 6
Sunamganj 41 F 2
Sunan 38 C 3
Sunart, Loch 3 B 3
Sunaysilah (Iraq) 22 CD 2
Sunbury 77 L 3
Suncho Corral 86 C 5
Sunch'ön (N. Korea) 39 J 3
Sunch'ön (S. Korea) 39 J 3
Sunda Islands 93
Sunda Strait 42 C 5
Sundarbans 40–41 EF 3
Sundargarh 40 D 3
Sunday Creek 48 E 2
Sunday Strait 48 C 2
Sundbron 16 G 3
Sunde 17 E 4
Sunderland 5 E 2
Sündiren Dağları 20 D 3
Sundsvall 16 G 3
Sunduyka 36 K 6
Sunflower, Mount 76 F 4
Sungai Barito 42 D 4
Sungai Digul 43 J 5
Sungai Inderagiri 42 B 4
Sungai Kampar 42 B 3
Sungai Kapuas 42 C 4
Sungai Kapuas 42 D 4
Sungai Kayan 42 E 3
Sungai Kutai 42 E 4
Sungai Mahakam 42 E 3
Sungai Mamberamo 43 J 4
Sungai Melawi 42 D 4
Sungai Mendawai 42 D 4
Sungai Pahang 42 B 3
Sungai Pawan 42 D 4
Sungai Pulau 43 J 5
Sungai Rokan 42 B 3
Sungai Sembakung 42 E 3
Sungai Seruyan 42 D 4
Sungai Tariku 43 J 4
Sungai Taritatu 43 J 4
Sungai Wama 43 J 4
Sungai Warenai 43 J 4
Sungaianyar 42 E 4
Sungaidareh 42 B 4
Sungaigerong 42 BC 4
Sungaiguntung 42 B 3
Sungailiat 42 C 4
Sungaipenuh 42 B 4
Sungei Patani 42 B 2
Sungguminasa 43 E 5
Sungurlu 21 D 2
Suning 39 G 3
Sunja 19 G 4
Sunjikäy 60 D 6
Sunnan 16 F 3
Sunndalen 16 E 3
Sunndalsfjorden 16 E 3

Sunndalsöra 16 E 3
Sunnfjord 16 DE 3
Suntar 36 L 3
Suntar Khayata, Khrebet 37 PQ 3
Sunwu 37 N 6
Sunyani 62 D 4
Suokonmäki 16 H 3
Suolahti 16 J 3
Suomenselkä 16 J 3
Suomi 16 J 3
Suomussalmi 16 J 3
Süo-nada 39 K 4
Suonenjoki 16 J 3
Suoyarvi 16 K 3
Superior (MT, U.S.A.) 76 D 2
Superior (WI, U.S.A.) 77 H 2
Superior, Lake 77 J 2
Supetar 19 G 3
Suphan Buri 41 GH 5
Süphan Dağı 21 F 3
Supiori, Pulau 43 J 4
Süq Suwayq (Saudi Arabia) 22 C 4
Suquṭrā 65 J 2
Şür (Lebanon) 22 B 2
Şür (Oman) 61 K 4
Sur, Punta 89 E 6
Sura 24 J 4
Sura, Ra's 65 H 2
Surabaya 42 D 5
Surahammar 17 G 4
Sürak 34 F 5
Surakarta 42 CD 5
Şürän (Syria) 22 B 2
Surar 65 G 3
Surat (India) 40 B 3
Surat (Queensland, Austr.) 49 H 4
Surat Thani 41 GH 6
Suratgarh 40 B 2
Surazh 17 K 4
Surendranagar 40 B 3
Surgut 25 O 3
Surgutikha 25 R 3
Suriapet 40 C 4
Surigao 43 G 2
Surigao Strait 43 G 1
Surin 41 H 5
Surinam 85 G 3
Sürïyah 22 BC 2
Surkhab 35 H 3
Sürmag (Iran) 23 F 3
Sürmän 59 H 2
Sürmene 21 F 2
Surovikino 24 H 6
Surrah, Nafüd as 61 G 4
Surrey 7 D 2
Sursee 19 E 2
Surskoye 24 J 5
Surte 17 F 4
Surtsey 16 A 3
Surud Ad 65 H 2
Surulangun 42 B 4
Survey Pass 72 FG 2
Susa 19 E 2
Susa (Iran) 23 E 2
Sušac 19 G 3
Susak 19 F 3
Susanino 37 Q 5
Susanville 76 B 3
Süsangerd (Iran) 23 E 3
Suşehri 21 E 2
Sušice 15 F 5
Susitna 72 G 3
Susquehanna River 77 L 3
Susques 86 C 5
Sussex 16 G 3
Sussundenga 67 E 3
Susuman 37 R 3
Susunu 43 H 4
Susurluk 20 C 3
Sut Ta 41 G 4
Sutam 37 N 4
Sutgun 37 S 2
Sutherland 66 C 6
Sutlej 35 J 4
Sutton 7 D 2
Sutton (AK, U.S.A.) 72 H 3
Sutton (W.V., U.S.A.) 77 K 4
Sutton Bridge 7 E 1
Sutton Coldfield 7 D 1
Sutton in Ashfield 5 E 3
Sutton Scotney 7 D 2
Sutton Valence 7 E 2
Sutton-on Sea 5 F 3
Suttor River 49 H 3
Sutun'ya 37 O 2
Sutwik 72 F 4
Suur Väin 17 H 4
Suur-Pakri 17 H 4
Suva 52 C 4
Suva Gora 20 B 2
Suva Planina 20 B 2
Suvasvesi 16 J 3

Suvorov 52 E 3
Suwa 39 L 3
Suwalki 15 H 4
Suwannaphum 41 H 4
Suwanose-jima 39 JK 5
Suwayqiyah, Hawr as (Iraq) 23 E 2
Suwon 39 J 3
Suzhou 39 GH 4
Suzu 39 L 3
Suzun 25 Q 5
Svalbard 90
Svalyava 15 H 5
Svalyava 20 B 1
Svappavaara 16 H 2
Svärholthalvöya 16 J 1
Svartisen 16 F 2
Svatay 37 S 2
Svatovo 24 G 6
Svatoy Nos, Mys 37 P 1
Svay Rieng 41 J 5
Svealand 17 FG 4
Sveg 16 F 3
Svegsjön 16 F 3
Svendborg 17 F 4
Svenljunga 17 F 4
Šventoji 17 J 4
Sverdlovsk 25 M 4
Sverige 16 G 3
Svetac 19 G 3
Svetlaya 37 P 6
Svetlograd 21 F 1
Svetloye, Ozero 21 G 1
Svetly 17 H 5
Svetlyy 25 M 5
Svetlyy 36 L 4
Svetlyy 37 N 4
Svetogorsk 16 J 3
Svetozarevo 20 B 2
Svidnik 15 FG 5
Svir' 24 F 3
Svirsk 36 H 5
Svishtov 20 C 2
Svitavy 15 G 5
Svobodnyy 37 N 5
Svobodnyy Port 20 D 1
Svolvær 16 FG 2
Svrljig 20 B 2
Svullrya 17 F 3
Svyatoy Nos, Mys 24 GH 2
Svyatoy Nos, Mys 24 H 2
Swadlincote 7 D 1
Swaffham 7 E 1
Swain Reefs 49 J 3
Swains 52 D 3
Swakop 66 B 4
Swakopmund 66 A 4
Swale, River 5 E 2
Swaledale 5 E 2
Swallow Reef 42 D 2
Swallowcliffe 7 C 2
Swan Hill 49 G 6
Swan Islands → Islas del Cisne 78 F 4
Swan Range 76 D 2
Swan River 73 R 5
Swanage 7 CD 2
Swanley 7 E 2
Swanlinbar 4 B 2
Swansea 6 BC 2
Swansea (Airport) 6 BC 2
Swansea Bay 6 C 2
Swartberge 66 C 6
Swatragh 4 B 2
Swaziland 67 E 5
Sweden 16 G 3
Sweet Home 76 B 3
Sweetwater 76 F 5
Sweetwater River 76 E 3
Swellendam 66 C 6
Świdnica 15 G 4
Świdnik 15 H 4
Świdwin 15 G 4
Świebodzin 15 G 4
Świecie 15 G 4
Swift Current 73 Q 5
Swift River 72 L 4
Swilly, Lough 4 B 2
Swimbridge 6 C 3
Swinburne, Cape 73 RS 1
Swindon 7 D 2
Świnoujście 15 F 4
Swinton 5 D 3
Switzerland 19 E 2
Swords 4 B 3
Syadaykharvuta 25 OP 2
Syagannakh 37 Q 2
Syalakh 37 MN 2
Syamozero, Ozero 16 K 3
Syangannakh 37 R 2
Syðri-Hagangur 16 B 2
Sydney (New Brunswick, Can.) 75 Q 6

Sydney (N.S.W., Austr.) 49 J 5
Sydney Mines 75 PQ 6
Sydpröven 75 S 3
Syktyvkar 24 JK 3
Sylacauga 77 J 5
Sylarna 16 F 3
Sylhet 41 F 3
Sylt 17 E 5
Sym 25 R 3
Sym 25 R 3
Synegey 37 OP 2
Syracuse (KS, U.S.A.) 76 F 4
Syracuse (N.Y., U.S.A.) 77 L 3
Syr-Dar'ya 35 H 2
Syrdar'ya 35 H 2
Syre 2 B 2
Syria 22 BC 2
Syriam 41 G 4
Syrian Desert 22 C 2
Sysmä 16 J 3
Sysola 24 K 3
Systengnakh 37 P 1
Sytomino 25 O 3
Syuge-Khaya, Gora 37 P 2
Syurkum 37 Q 5
Syuryakh-Dzhangy, Vozvyshennost' 36 M 1
Syuryun-Kyuyel' 37 O 2
Syväri 16 J 3
Syverma, Plato 36 G 3
Syzran 24 J 5
Szamotuły 15 G 4
Szczecin 15 F 4
Szczecinek 15 G 4
Szczytno 15 H 4
Szechwan 38 D 5
Szeged 20 A 1
Székesfehérvár 20 A 1
Szekszárd 20 A 1
Szentes 20 B 1
Szolnok 20 B 1
Szombathely 20 A 1
Szprotawa 15 G 4

T

Ta Hsai 41 G 3
Ta' izz 61 G 6
Ta Khli 41 H 4
Ta Ruang 41 H 5
Taaga, Khrebet 37 N 4
Ta'äm 61 G 5
Taarom 49 HJ 4
Tab arja (Lebanon) 22 B 2
Tabacal 86 D 5
Tâbah (Saudi Arabia) 22 CD 4
Tabaí 88 E 2
Tabajara 85 F 5
Tabankort 62 E 2
Ṭabaqah (Syria) 22 C 2
Tabar Islands 51 F 2
Tabarqah 59 G 1
Tabarsuq 19 E 4
Tabas 34 G 4
Tabas (Iran) 23 G 2
Tabasara, Serranía de 84 B 2
Tabasco 78 D 4
Täbask, Küh-e (Iran) 23 F 3
Tabatinga 84 E 3
Tabatinga, Serra da 87 H 3
Tabelbala 58 E 2
Tabelbala, Kahal 58 E 3
Tabelbalet 59 G 3
Tabelkoza 58 F 3
Tabeng 41 H 5
Taber 73 P 6
Tabernas 18 C 4
Tabernes de Valldigna 18 CD 4
Tabiteuea 52 C 3
Tabla 62 E 3
Tablas 43 F 1
Table Mountain 66 B 6
Table Rock Lake 77 H 4
Tábor 15 F 5
Tabor 37 R 1
Tabora 64 E 6
Tabou 62 C 5
Tabrïz 34 D 3
Tabuaeran 53 E 2
Tabük (Saudi Arabia) 22 B 3
Tabuleiro 85 G 5
Tabuleiro de Norte 87 J 2
Täby 17 G 4
Tacámbaro 78 B 4
Tacheng 35 L 1
Tachiumet 59 GH 3
Tachov 15 F 5
Tacloban 43 F 1
Tacna 86 B 4
Taco Pozo 88 D 4
Tacoma 76 B 2
Tacora 86 C 4
Tacuarembó 88 E 5
Tadcaster 5 E 3

Tademaït, Plateau du 59 F 3
Tadjekant 58 C 5
Tadjemout 59 F 3
Tadjetaret 59 G 4
Tadjourah 65 G 2
Tadjourah, Golfe de 65 G 2
Tadoule Lake 73 S 4
Tadpatri 40 C 5
Tadzhikistan 35 HJ 3
Taebaek-Sanmaek 39 J 3
Taegu 39 J 3
Taejŏn 39 J 3
Tafahi 52 D 4
Tafalla 18 C 3
Tafanlieh 39 H 6
Tafassasset 59 G 4
Tafassasset, Ténéré du 63 G 1
Tafermaar 43 H 5
Tafí Viejo 88 CD 4
Tafihān (Iran) 23 F 3
Tafihān (Iran) 23 F 3
Tafiré 62 CD 4
Tafo 62 D 4
Tafraoute 58 D 3
Tafresh (Iran) 23 E 2
Taft (Iran) 23 G 3
Taftanās (Syria) 22 B 2
Tagama 63 F 2
Tagan 50 D 3
Taganrog 21 E 1
Taganrogskiy Zaliv 21 E 1
Tagaung 41 G 3
Tagbilaran 43 F 2
Tageru, Jabal 60 D 5
Taggafadi 63 F 2
Taghit 58 E 2
Taghrīfat 59 J 3
Tagish Lake 72 L 3
Tagliamento 19 F 2
Tagounite 58 D 3
Taguá 87 H 3
Taguatinga 87 G 3
Tagudin 43 H 1
Taguenout Haggueret 62 D 1
Taguersimet 58 B 4
Taguienout 59 G 4
Tagula 51 F 4
Tagula Island 49 J 1
Tagula Island 51 F 4
Tagum 43 G 2
Tagus 18 B 4
Tahan, Gunung 42 B 3
Tahanea 53 F 4
Tahat, Mont 59 G 4
Tahe 37 M 5
Ṭāheri (Iran) 23 F 4
Tahifet 59 G 4
Tahiryuak Lake 73 P 1
Tahiti 53 F 4
Tahkuna Neem 17 H 4
Tahoe, Lake 76 C 4
Tahoua 63 EF 3
Tahrūd 34 F 5
Ṭaḥṭā 60 E 3
Tahtali Dağlari 21 E 3
Tahuamanu 86 C 3
Tahuata 53 F 3
Tahulandang, Pulau 43 FG 3
Tahuna 43 G 3
Taï 62 C 4
Tai Hu 39 H 4
Taï, Parc National de 62 C 4
Tai Shan 39 G 3
Tai'an 39 G 3
Tai'an 39 H 2
Taibai Shan 38 E 4
Taibus Qi 38 FG 2
Taichung 39 H 6
Taigu 38 F 3
Taihang Shan 38 F 3
Taihe 38 F 5
Taihu 38 G 4
Taikang 38 FG 4
Tailai 39 H 1
Taimani 35 G 4
Taimba 36 G 3
Tain 2 B 3
Tainan 39 GH 6
Taínaron, Ákra 20 B 3
Taining 39 G 5
Taipei 39 H 6
Taiping 39 G 4
Taiping (Malaysia) 42 B 3
Taiping Ling 36 M 6
Taipu 87 J 2
Taisetsu-zan 39 M 2
Taishan 38 F 6
Taishun 39 G 5
Taitao, Península de 89 AB 8
Taitung 39 H 6
Taivalkoski 16 J 2
Taiwan 39 H 6
Taiwan Haixia 39 GH 5–6
Taiwan Shan 39 H 6
Taiyetos Óros 20 B 3
Taiyuan 38 F 3

Taizhou 39 GH 4
Tājābād (Iran) 23 G 3
Tajarhī 59 H 4
Tajito 76 D 5
Tájo 18 B 4
Tajo 18 C 3
Tajrīsh 34 E 3
Tajrīsh (Iran) 23 F 2
Tajumulco, Volcán 78 D 4
Tak 41 G 4
Takāb (Iran) 23 E 1
Takabba 65 G 4
Takalar 43 E 5
Takamatsu 39 K 4
Takaoka 39 L 3
Takara-jima 39 J 5
Takasaki 39 L 3
Takatshwane 66 C 4
Takaungu 65 FG 5
Takazze 65 F 2
Takengon 42 A 3
Takeo 41 H 5
Takestan 34 DE 3
Takestan (Iran) 23 E 1
Taketa 64 B 5
Takhādīd (Iraq) 23 D 3
Takhta 21 F 1
Takhta-Bazar 35 G 3
Takhtabrod 25 N 5
Takhtakupyr 34 FG 2
Takhtamygda 37 M 5
Takhtayamsk 37 ST 3
Takht-e Soleiman (Iran) 23 F 1
Takht-i-Sulaiman 35 HJ 4
Taki 51 G 3
Takijuq Lake 73 P 2
Takikawa 39 M 2
Takket → Aïn el Hadjadj 59 G 3
Takla Lake 73 M 4
Takla Landing 73 M 4
Takla Makan 35 L 3
Taklaun, Gora 37 Q 3
Taklimakan Shamo 35 LM 3
Takolokouzet, Massif de 63 F 2
Takoradi → Sekondi-Takoradi
    62 D 5
Takpa Shiri 41 F 2
Takua Pa 41 G 6
Takum 63 F 4
Takume 53 F 4
Takutea 53 E 4
Tala 78 B 3
Talagante 88 B 5
Talagapa 89 C 7
Tālah 59 G 1
Talak 63 EF 2
Talakan 37 O 6
Talakmau, Gunung 42 B 3
Talandzha 37 O 6
Talara 84 B 4
Talar-i-Band 35 G 5
Talas 35 J 2
Talasea 51 EF 3
Talasskiy Alatau, Khrebet 35 J 2
Talata Mafara 63 F 3
Tala-Tumsa 37 O 2
Talaud, Kepulauan 43 G 3
Talavera de la Reina 18 C 4
Talawdī 60 E 6
Talaya 36 G 4
Talaya 37 S 3
Talca 89 B 6
Talcahuano 89 B 6
Talcher 40 E 3
Taldora 49 G 2
Taldy-Kurgan 25 P 6
Tal-e Khosravi (Iran) 23 F 3
Talēh 65 H 3
Taleh Zang (Iran) 23 E 2
Talence 18 C 3
Tālesh 34 D 3
Talgar 35 K 2
Talgath 6 C 1
Taliabu, Pulau 43 FG 4
Talima 85 G 3
Talimardzhan 35 H 3
Taliqan 35 H 3
Talitsa 25 M 4
Taliwang 42 E 5
Talkalakh (Syria) 22 B 2
Talkeetna 72 G 3
Talkeetna Mountains 72 H 3
Tall ʿAfar (Iraq) 22 D 1
Tall al Hajar (Syria) 22 B 2
Tall as Asfar (Jordan) 22 B 2
Tall as Ṣuwār (Syria) 22 C 2
Tall Birāk at Tahtāni (Syria) 22 C 1
Tall Fajāmi (Syria) 22 C 2
Tall Kayf (Iraq) 22 D 1
Tall Kūshik (Syria) 22 CD 1
Tall Mānūk (Jordan) 22 C 2
Tall Tamīr (Syria) 22 C 1
Tall ʿUwaynāt (Iraq) 22 D 1
Talladale 2 B 3
Tallahassee 77 K 5
Tallapoosa River 77 J 5

Tallinn 17 HJ 4
Tallulah 77 H 5
Tālmaciu 20 B 1
Tal'menka 25 Q 5
Talmine 2 B 2
Talmine 58 E 3
Talnakh 25 R 2
Tal'nik 37 T 4
Talo 65 F 2
Taloda 40 B 3
Talok 43 E 3
Talovka 21 G 2
Talovka 37 UV 3
Talsarnau 5 B 1
Talsi 17 H 4
Talsinnt 58 E 2
Taltal 88 B 4
Taltson 73 P 3
Taltson 73 Q 3
Taluma 37 M 4
Talvik 16 H 1
Tal-y-bont 6 C 1
Tal-y-cafn 6 C 1
Tam Ky 41 J 4
Tama, Mount 66 A 2
Tamabo Range 42 E 3
Tamada 59 F 4
Tamaia 63 F 2
Tamala 48 A 4
Tamale 62 D 4
Taman 21 E 1
Tamana 52 C 3
Tamanrasset (Algeria) 59 F 4
Tamanrasset (Algeria) 59 G 4
Tamar 40 E 3
Tamar, River 6 B 2
Támara (Colombia) 84 D 2
Tamara (Yugoslavia) 20 A 2
Tamarugal, Pampa del 86 C 5
Tamaské 63 F 3
Tamaulipas 78 C 3
Tamaya 88 B 5
Tamazunchale 78 C 3
Tamba 62 B 3
Tambacounda 62 B 3
Tambalan 42 E 3
Tambara 67 E 3
Tambelan, Kepulauan 42 C 3
Tambisan 43 E 2
Tambo (Peru) 86 B 3
Tambo (Queensland, Austr.)
    49 H 3
Tambo de Mora 86 A 3
Tambohorano 67 G 3
Tambor 66 A 3
Tambora, Gunung 43 E 5
Tamboril 87 H 1
Tambov 24 H 5
Tambovka 37 N 5
Tambre 18 B 3
Tambura 64 D 3
Tamburi 87 H 3
Tamch 36 F 6
Tamchaket 58 C 5
Tamdybulak 35 GH 2
Tame 84 D 2
Tamel Aike 89 B 8
Tamesguidat 59 F 3
Tamgak, Monts 63 F 2
Tamgué, Massif du 62 B 3
Tamil Nadu 40 C 5
Tamír, Tall (Syria) 22 C 1
Tamis 20 B 1
Tammerfors 16 H 3
Tammisaari 17 H 4
Tampa 77 K 6
Tampa Bay 77 K 6
Tampere 16 H 3
Tampico 78 C 3
Tamrau, Pegunungan 43 H 4
Tamri 58 CD 2
Tamsagbulag 39 G 1
Tamshiyacu 84 D 4
Tamsu 66 C 3
Tamu 41 F 3
Tamuin 78 C 3
Tamworth (N.S.W., Austr.) 49 J 5
Tamworth (U.K.) 7 D 1
Tan An 41 J 5
Tan Emellel 59 G 3
Tan Kena Bordj 59 G 3
Tan Tan 58 C 3
Tana 51 J 5
Tana (Kenya) 65 F 5
Tana (Norway) 16 J 1
Tana bru 16 J 1
Tana, Lake 65 F 2
Tanacross 72 J 3
Tanafjorden 16 J 1
Tanaga 72 B 5
Tanah Merah 42 B 2
Tanahbala, Pulau 42 A 4
Tanahgrogot 42 E 4
Tanahjampea, Pulau 43 F 5
Tanahmasa, Pulau 42 A 4

Tanahmerah 50 CD 3
Tanakpur 40 D 2
Tanam, Cape 73 T 4
Tanama 25 PQ 1
Tanami 48 D 2
Tanami Desert 48 E 2
Tanami Desert Wildlife Sanctuary
    48 E 3
Tanana 72 G 2
Tanana 72 H 3
Tanāqīab, Ra's at (Saudi Arabia)
    23 E 4
Tanaro 19 E 3
Tanch'ŏn 39 J 2
Tanda 62 D 4
Tandag 43 G 2
Tandaho 65 G 2
Tandaltī 60 E 6
Tāndārei 20 C 2
Tandil 89 E 6
Tandragee 4 B 2
Tane-ga-shima 39 K 4
Tanezrouft 58 E 4
Tanezrouft N-Ahenet 58–59 F 4
Tanf, Jabal at (Syria) 22 C 2
Tang 4 B 3
Tang 34 F 5
Tanga 39 F 5–6
Tanga Islands 51 F 2
Tangail 40 E 3
Tangalla 40 D 6
Tanganyika, Lake 64 DE 6
Tang-e Karam (Iran) 23 F 3
Tanger 58 D 1
Tangerang 42 C 5
Tanggula Shan 38 BC 4
Tanggula Shankou 38 B 4
Tanghe 38 F 4
Tangi → Tanger 58 D 1
Tangmai 38 C 4
Tangra Yumco 40 E 1
Tangshan 39 G 3
Tanguiéta 62 E 3
Tangwanghe 37 N 6
Tangyin 38 F 3
Tangyuan 39 J 1
Tani 41 H 5
Taniantaweng Shan 38 C 4–5
Tanimbar Islands 50 B 3
Tanimbar, Kepulauan 43 H 5
Tanjung 42 E 4
Tanjung Api 42 C 3
Tanjung Aru 42 E 4
Tanjung Arus 43 F 3
Tanjung Blitung 42 C 3
Tanjung Bugel 42 D 5
Tanjung Cangkuang 42 BC 5
Tanjung Cina 42 BC 5
Tanjung De Jong 43 J 5
Tanjung Jabung 42 B 4
Tanjung Jambuair 42 A 2
Tanjung Kandi 43 F 3
Tanjung Karossa 43 E 5
Tanjung Kolff 43 J 5
Tanjung Lalereh 43 E 4
Tanjung Layar 42 E 4
Tanjung Libobo 43 G 4
Tanjung Lumut 42 C 4
Tanjung Malatayur 42 D 4
Tanjung Mangkalihat 43 E 3
Tanjung Manimbaya 43 E 4
Tanjung Palpetu 43 G 4
Tanjung Puting 42 D 4
Tanjung Samak 42 C 4
Tanjung Sambar 42 CD 4
Tanjung Sasar 43 E 5
Tanjung Selatan 42 D 4
Tanjung Vals 43 J 5
Tanjung Waka 43 G 4
Tanjungbalai 42 AB 3
Tanjungbatu 42 E 3
Tanjungpandan 42 C 4
Tanjungpinang 42 B 3
Tanjungpusu 42 D 4
Tanjungredeb 42 E 3
Tanjungselor 42 E 3
Tankhoy 36 H 5
Tankovo 25 R 3
Tankse 35 K 4
Tanlovo 25 O 2
Tännäs 16 F 3
Tannu Ola 36 F 5
Tanoucherte 58 C 4
Tanout 63 F 3
Tanṭā 60 E 2
Tanto Adam 35 H 5
Tantoyuca 78 C 3
Tanuku 40 D 4
Tanyurer 37 X 2
Tanzania 64–65 EF 6
Tao'an 39 H 1
Taoghe 66 C 3
Taolanaro 67 H 5
Taongi 52 C 2

Taormina 19 FG 4
Taoudenni 62 D 1
Taounate 58 E 2
Taourirt (Algeria) 58 F 3
Taourirt (Morocco) 58 E 2
Taouz 58 E 2
Taoyuan 39 H 5
Tapachula 78 D 5
Tapah 42 B 3
Tapajós 85 G 4
Tapaktuan 42 A 3
Tapan 42 B 4
Tapauá 84 E 5
Tapauá 85 F 5
Tapes 88 F 5
Tapeta 62 C 4
Tapiche 84 D 5
Tapini 50 E 3
Tapirapua 86 E 3
Tappahannock 77 L 4
Tapti 40 B 3
Tapul Group 43 F 2
Tapurucuara 84 E 4
Taqbostān (Iran) 23 E 2
Ṭāqṭāq (Iraq) 23 D 2
Taquara 88 F 4
Taquari 86 E 4
Taquari 87 F 4
Tara 25 P 4
Tara (U.S.S.R.) 25 O 4
Tara (Yugoslavia) 20 A 2
Tara (Yugoslavia) 20 A 2
Tara (Zambia) 66 D 3
Taraba 63 G 4
Ṭarābulus (Lebanon) 22 B 2
Ṭarābulus (Libya) 59 H 2
Taracuá 84 E 3
Tarahouahout 59 G 4
Tarahumara, Sierra 76 E 6
Tarai 40 E 2
Tarakan 42 E 3
Tarakki 35 H 4
Tarakliya 20 C 1
Taran 25 O 1
Taran, Mys 17 G 5
Tarançon 18 C 3
Tarangire National Park 65 F 5
Taransay 2 A 3
Taranto 19 G 3
Taranto, Golfo di 19 G 3–4
Tarapacá 84 DE 4
Tarapoto 84 C 5
Tararua Range 51 R 9
Tarascon 19 D 3
Tarasovo 24 J 2
Tarat 59 G 3
Tarata (Bolivia) 86 C 4
Tarata (Peru) 86 C 4
Tarauacá 84 D 5
Tarauacá 84 D 5
Tarawa 52 C 2
Tarazi (Iran) 23 E 3
Tarazit 63 F 1
Tarazit, Massif de 63 F 1
Tarazona 18 C 3
Tarazona de la Mancha 18 C 4
Tarbagatay, Khrebet 25 Q 6
Tarbagatay Shan 35 L 1
Tarbat Ness 2 C 3
Tarbert (Strathclyde) 3 B 4
Tarbert (Western Isles) 2 A 3
Tarbes 18 D 3
Tarbet 3 B 3
Tarbū 59 J 3
Tarcoola (N.S.W., Austr.) 49 G 5
Tarcoola (South Australia) 48 E 5
Tarcutta 49 H 6
Tardoki Yani, Gora 37 P 6
Taree 49 J 5
Tareina 65 G 2
Tärendö 16 H 2
Tareya 36 F 1
Tarfaya 58 C 3
Tarfside 3 D 3
Tarhūnah 59 H 2
Ṭarīf (United Arab Emirates)
    23 F 4
Tarifa 18 B 4
Tarija 86 D 5
Tariku, Sungai 43 J 4
Tarim 35 L 2
Tarīm (S. Yemen) 61 H 5
Tarim Basin 28 FG 3
Tarim He 35 L 2
Tarim Liuchang 38 A 2
Tarime 64 E 5
Tarin Kowt 35 H 4
Ṭarīq Masūs 59 K 2
Taritatu, Sungai 43 J 4
Tarka 63 F 3
Tarkhankut, Mys 21 D 1
Tarko-Sale 25 P 3
Tarkwa 62 D 4
Tarlac 43 J 1
Tarma 86 A 3

Tarn 18 D 3
Tärnaby 16 G 2
Tarnobrzeg 15 H 4
Tarnów 15 H 4
Tarnowskie Góry 15 G 4
Taron 51 F 2
Tarou 63 H 1
Tarouadji, Monts 63 F 2
Taroudant 58 D 2
Tarpon Springs 77 K 6
Tarporley 5 D 3
Tarquí 84 CD 4
Tarquinia 19 F 3
Tarradalen 16 G 2
Tarrafal 62 B 6
Tarragona 18 D 3
Tarrasa 18 D 3
Tárrega 18 D 3
Tarso Taro 63 H 1
Tarso Tiéroko 63 H 1
Tarsū Mūsā 59 J 4
Tarsus 21 D 3
Tarsus (Turkey) 22 B 1
Tart 38 B 3
Tartagal 86 D 5
Tartas 18 C 3
Tartu 17 J 4
Tartuke 62 C 4
Tarṭūs (Syria) 22 B 2
Tarumovka 21 G 2
Tārūt (Saudi Arabia) 23 F 4
Tarutino 20 C 1
Tarutung 42 A 3
Tarves 2 C 3
Tarvin 5 D 3
Tarvo 86 D 4
Tasajera, Sierra de la 76 E 6
Tas-Buget 35 H 2
Tasedjibest 59 G 3
Tashanta 25 R 6
Tashauz 34 F 2
Tashigang 41 F 2
Tashk, Daryācheh-ye 23 FG 3
Tashk, Daryācheh-ye (Iran) 23 FG 3
Tashkent 35 H 2
Tashkepri 35 G 3
Tash-Kumyr 35 J 2
Tashkurghan 35 H 3
Tashtagol 25 R 5
Tashtyp 25 R 5
Tasikmalaya 42 C 5
Tåsjön 16 G 3
Taskan 37 S 3
Tasker 63 G 2
Taşköprü 21 D 2
Taskyl, Khrebet 36 G 5
Tas-Kystabys, Khrebet 37 Q 2
Tas-Kystabys, Khrebet 37 QR 3
Taşlıçay 21 F 3
Tasman Basin 99 C 5
Tasman Bay 51 Q 9
Tasman Peninsula 50 L 9
Tasman Sea 50 NO 8
Tasman Sea 52 B 5
Tasmania 50 L 9
Tasmania 52 A 5
Tasova 21 E 2
Tassara 63 F 2
Tassialouc, Lac 75 N 4
Tassiast 58 B 4
Tassili N-Ajjer 59 G 3
Tassili Oua-n Ahaggar 59 FG 4
Tas-Tumus 37 N 3
Tas-Tumus 37 O 1
Tastūr 19 E 4
Taşucu 21 D 3
Tasūj 34 D 3
Tas-Yuryakh 36 K 3
Tata 58 D 3
Tatabánya 20 A 1
Tatakoto 53 F 4
Tatarbunary 20 C 1
Tatarsk 25 P 4
Tatarskiy Proliv 37 Q 6
Tatau 42 D 3
Tataurovo 36 J 5
Tathlina Lake 73 O 3
Tathlīth 61 G 5
Tatos Dağları 21 F 2
Tatry 15 H 5
Tatsinskaya 21 F 1
Tatta 35 H 6
Tattershall 5 E 3
Tatty 35 J 2
Tatvan 21 F 3
Tauá 87 H 2
Tauapeçaçu 85 F 4
Tauariã 85 F 5
Taubaté 87 GH 5
Tauchik 34 E 2
Tauere 53 F 4
Taumarunui 51 R 8
Taumaturgo 84 D 5
Taung 66 CD 5
Taungdwingyi 41 G 3

Taunggon 41 G 3
Taung-gyi 41 G 3
Taunglau 41 G 3
Taungnyo Range 41 G 4
Taungup 41 F 4
Taunton 6 C 2
Taunus 15 E 4
Taupo 51 R 8
Taupo, Lake 51 R 8
Tauragé 17 H 4
Tauranga 51 R 8
Taurisano 19 G 4
Taurus Mountains → Toros Dağlari 21 D 3
Tauu Islands 51 G 2
Tauwsa Barrage 35 J 4
Tauysk 37 R 4
Tauz 21 G 2
Tavas 20 C 3
Tavastehus 16 H 3
Tavatuma 37 T 3
Tavda 25 M 4
Tavda 25 N 4
Taverner Bay 75 N 2
Taveta 65 F 5
Taviano 19 G 4
Tavistock 6 B 2
Tavolara 19 E 3
Tavoy 41 G 5
Tavşanlı 20 C 3
Tavvaskaite 16 H 2
Tavyskaya Guba 37 RS 4
Taw, River 6 C 2
Tāwarghā' 59 J 2
Tawas City 77 K 3
Tawau 42 E 3
Tawfīqīyah 64 E 3
Tawilah (Egypt) 22 AB 4
Tawitawi Group 43 F 2
Tawkar 60 F 5
Tawuq (Iraq) 22 D 2
Tawzar 59 G 2
Taxco de Alarcón 78 C 4
Taxkorgan 35 K 3
Tay, Loch 3 B 3
Tay Ninh 41 J 5
Tay, River 3 C 3
Tayabamba 84 C 5
Tayakhtakh 37 N 4
Tayandu 43 H 5
Taybola 16 K 2
Tayêgle 65 G 4
Tayga 25 QR 4
Taygonos, Mys 37 U 3
Taygonos, Poluostrov 37 U 3
Taylor 72 DE 2
Taylor, Mount 76 E 4
Taylorville 77 J 4
Taymā' (Saudi Arabia) 22 C 4
Taymura 36 G 3
Taymylyr 36 M 1
Taymyr 36 F 2
Taymyr, Ozero 36 H 1
Taymyr Peninsula 36 GH 1
Taymyr, Poluostrov 36 FH 1
Taymyra, Verkhnyaya 36 G 1
Taynuilt 3 B 3
Tayshet 36 G 4
Tayshir 36 G 6
Tayside 3 C 3
Taytay 43 E 1
Tayura 36 J 4
Taz 25 P 2
Taz 25 Q 2
Taza 58 E 2
Tāzah Khurmātū (Iraq) 22 D 2
Tazdağ 20 C 2
Tazenakht 58 D 2
Tazerbo Oasis → Wāhāt al Tāzirbū 59 K 3
Tazovskaya Guba 25 P 2
Tazovskiy 25 P 2
Tazumal 78 DE 5
Tazungdam 41 G 2
Tbilisi 21 F 2
Tbilisskaya 21 F 1
Tchabal Mbabo 63 G 4
Tchamba (Cameroon) 63 G 4
Tchamba (Togo) 62 E 4
Tchaourou 62 E 4
Tchibanga 63 G 6
Tchié 63 H 4
Tchien 62 C 4
Tchigai, Plateau du 63 G 1
Tcholliré 63 G 4
Tczew 15 G 4
Te Anau, Lake 50 P 10
Te Hapua 51 Q 7
Te Kuiti 51 R 8
Tea Tree 48 E 3
Teapa 78 D 4
Teba 43 J 4
Tebahalet 62 E 2
Teberda 21 F 2
Tébessa 59 G 1
Tebingtinggi 42 A 3

Tebingtinggi 42 B 4
Tebingtinggi, Pulau 42 B 3
Tebulos Mta 21 G 2
Tecalitlán 78 B 4
Tecate 76 C 5
Tecer Dağlari 21 E 3
Tecka 89 B 7
Tecomán 78 B 4
Tecuala 78 A 3
Tecuci 20 C 1
Tedzhen 34 FG 3
Tedzhenstroy 35 G 3
Tees, River 5 E 2
Teesdale 5 DE 2
Teesside 5 E 2
Teesside (Airport) 5 E 2
Tefé 84 E 4
Tefé 85 F 4
Tefenni 20 C 3
Tegal 42 C 5
Tegguidda In Tessoum 63 F 2
Tegina 63 F 3
Tegre 65 FG 2
Tegucigalpa 78 E 5
Tegul'det 25 R 4
Tegyul'te-Térde 37 O 3
Tehamiyam 60 F 5
Teheran → Tehrän 34 E 3
Tehi-n Isser 59 G 4
Téhini 62 D 4
Tehoru 43 G 4
Tehrän 34 E 3
Tehrän (Iran) 23 F 2
Tehuacán 78 C 4
Tehuantepec 78 C 4
Tehuata 53 F 4
Teide, Pico de 58 B 3
Teifi, River 6 B 1
Teiga Plateau 60 D 5
Teiga Plateau → Hadabat Tayga 60 D 5
Teignmouth 6 C 2
Teixeira Pinto 62 A 3
Tejo 18 B 4
Teju 41 G 2
Tekeli 35 K 2
Tekes 35 L 2
Tekes He 35 L 2
Tekija 20 B 2
Tekin 37 O 6
Tekirdağ 20 C 2
Tekman 21 F 3
Teknaf 41 F 3
Tekouiat 59 F 4
Tekro 63 J 2
Tel 40 D 3
Tel Aviv-Yafo (Israel) 22 B 2–3
Telavåg 17 D 3
Telavi 21 G 2
Telč 15 G 3
Telefomin 50 D 3
Telegraph Creek 72 L 4
Telemaco Borba 87 F 5
Telemark 17 E 4
Telén 89 C 6
Teleneshty 20 C 1
Telerhteba, Djebel 59 G 4
Teles Pires 85 G 5
Telescope Peak 76 C 4
Teletskoye, Ozero 25 R 5
Telfane, Hadjer 63 H 3
Telfel 62 D 2
Telford 5 D 3
Teli 36 F 5
Télimélé 62 B 3
Teljo, Jabal 60 D 6
Tell al 'Amârna 60 E 3
Tell al Ubaid (Iraq) 23 D 3
Teller 72 D 2
Tellicherry 40 C 5
Tello 88 C 5
Telmen Nuur 36 G 6
Telmest 58 D 2
Telok Anson 42 B 3
Teloloapan 78 C 4
Tel'pos-Iz, Gora 25 L 3
Telsen 89 C 7
Telšiai 17 H 4
Teluk Adang 42 E 4
Teluk Balikpapan 42 E 4
Teluk Berau 43 H 4
Teluk Bintuni 43 H 4
Teluk Bone 43 F 4
Teluk Buli 43 G 3
Teluk Cendrawasih 43 HJ 4
Teluk Darvel 43 E 3
Teluk Datu 42 D 3
Teluk Kau 43 G 3
Teluk Kuantan 42 B 4
Teluk Kumai 42 D 4
Teluk Kupang 43 F 5–6
Teluk Mandar 43 E 4
Teluk Pamukan 42 E 4
Teluk Pelabuanratu 42 C 5
Teluk Sampit 42 D 4
Teluk Sangkulirang 43 E 3

Teluk Sindeh 43 F 5
Teluk Tolo 43 F 4
Teluk Tomini 43 F 4
Teluk Weda 43 G 3
Telukbatang 42 CD 4
Telukbutun 42 C 3
Telukdalam 42 A 3
Téma 62 E 4
Témacine 59 G 2
Tematangi 53 F 4
Tembenchi 36 G 2
Tembenchi 36 G 3
Tembilahan 42 B 4
Temblador 85 F 2
Tembleque 18 C 4
Tembo 64 B 6
Tembo Falls 64 B 6
Tembo, Mont 63 G 5
Tembué 67 E 2
Teme, River 6 C 1
Temerin 20 AB 1
Temerloh 42 B 3
Temir 34 F 1
Temirgoyevskaya 21 EF 1
Temirtau 25 O 5
Temirtau 25 R 5
Temiscaming 75 M 6
Temki 63 H 3
Temoe 53 G 4
Temora 49 H 5
Tempa 90
Tempe 76 D 5
Tempio Pausania 19 E 3
Temple 77 G 5
Templemore 4 B 3
Templetouhy 4 B 3
Tempué 66 B 2
Temruk 21 E 1
Temryukskiy Zaliv 21 E 1
Temuco 89 B 6
Ten Degree Channel 41 F 6
Tena 84 C 4
Tenali 40 D 4
Tenasserim 41 G 5
Tenasserim 41 G 5
Tenbury Wells 6 C 1
Tenby 6 B 2
Tende, Col di 19 E 3
Tendel 58 C 5
Tendrara 58 E 2
Tendrovskaya Kosa 20–21 D 1
Tendürek Daği 21 F 3
Tenekert 62 E 2
Tenenkou 62 C 3
Ténéré 63 FG 2
Ténéré du Tafassasset 63 G 1
Ténéré, Erg de 63 G 2
Tenerife 58 B 3
Ténès 59 F 1
Teng Xian 38 F 6
Teng Xian 39 G 3
Tengchong 38 C 5
Tenggara, Kepulauan 43 G 5
Tenggarong 42 E 4
Tengger Shamo 38 D 3
Tengiz, Ozero 25 N 5
Tengushevo 24 H 5
Tenialig 58 C 4
Teniente Marsh 91
Teniente Matienzo 91
Tenke (U.S.S.R.) 36 L 3
Tenke (Zaire) 66 D 2
Tenkodogo 62 D 3
Tennant Creek 48 E 2
Tennessee 77 J 4
Tennessee River 77 J 4
Teno 89 B 5
Tenojoki 16 J 2
Tenom 42 E 2
Tenosique de Pino Suárez 78 D 4
Tenterden 7 E 2
Tenterfield 49 J 4
Tentolomatinan, Gunung 43 F 3
Tentugal 85 J 4
Teocaltiche 78 B 3
Teócaltiche 78 B 3
Teófilo Otoni 87 H 4
Teotihuacan 78 C 4
Teouit 59 G 3
Tepa 43 G 5
Tepa 50 A 3
Tepache 76 E 6
Tepatitlán 78 B 3
Tepe Gawra → Khorsâbâd 61 G 1
Tepelena 20 A 2
Tepic 78 B 3
Teplice 15 F 4
Teplik 20 C 1
Teplogorka 24 K 3
Tepoca, Bahia de 76 D 5
Tequila 78 B 3
Ter 18 D 3
Téra (Niger) 62 E 3
Tera (Portugal) 18 B 4
Teraina 53 E 2
Terakeka 64 E 3

Teramo 19 F 3
Tercan 21 F 3
Terceira 58 A 1
Terek 21 F 2
Terek 34 D 2
Terekhovka 24 F 5
Terempa 42 C 3
Terenni 58 D 5
Terenos 87 E 5
Terentang, Pulau 42 E 4
Tereraimbu, Cachoeira do 85 H 5
Teresina 87 H 2
Teresinha 85 H 3
Teresita 84 E 3
Teressa 41 F 6
Terhazza 58 D 4
Terhir 59 F 2
Teriberka 16 K 2
Teriberka 16 L 2
Terkezi 63 J 2
Terme 21 E 2
Termelli 21 D 3
Termez 35 H 3
Termini Imerese 19 F 4
Termit Kaoboul 63 G 2
Termit, Massif de 63 G 2
Termoli 19 F 3
Ternate 43 G 3
Terneuzen 14 D 4
Terney 39 L 1
Terni 19 F 3
Ternopol' 24 E 6
Terpeniya, Mys 37 QR 6
Terpeniya, Zaliv 37 Q 6
Terpugovo 25 N 4
Terpukhoy, Gora 37 VW 2
Terra de Basto 18 B 3
Terra di Bari 19 G 3
Terra Firma 66 C 5
Terra Prêta 85 G 4–5
Terra Santa 85 G 4
Terrace 72 M 5
Terracina 19 F 3
Terracy Bay 74 K 6
Terråk 16 F 2
Terralba 19 E 4
Terre Haute 77 J 4
Terre Plaine 18 D 2
Terrebonne Bay 77 H 6
Tersakan Gölü 21 D 3
Terskey Alatau, Khrebet 35 K 2
Terskiy Bereg 24 GH 2
Teruel 18 C 3
Tervola 16 H 2
Teshekpuk Lake 72 G 1
Teslin 72 L 3
Teslin 72 L 3
Teslin Lake 72 L 3–4
Tesocoma 76 E 6
Tessalit 62 E 1
Tessaoua 63 F 3
Tessenei 65 F 1–2
Tessenei 65 F 2
Testa, Capo 19 E 3
Testigos, Islas los 85 F 1
Tetari, Cerro 84 D 2
Tete 67 E 3
Tetepare 51 G 3
Tetere 51 H 3
Teteven 20 B 2
Tetiaroa 53 F 4
Teton Peak 76 D 2
Tétouan 58 D 1
Tetovo 20 B 2
Tetuan → Tétouan 58 D 1
Tetrino 24 G 2
Teuini 84 E 5
Teulada 19 E 4
Teun 43 G 5
Teverya (Israel) 22 B 2
Teviot, River 3 C 4
Teviotdale 3 C 4
Teviothead 3 C 4
Tevriz 25 O 4
Tewkesbury 7 C 2
Têwo 38 D 4
Texarkana 77 H 5
Texas (Queensland, Austr.) 49 J 4
Texas (U.S.A.) 76 FG 5
Texas City 77 H 6
Texel 14 D 4
Teya 36 F 3
Teykovo 24 GH 4
Teyuareh 35 G 4
Teziutlán 78 C 4
Tezpur 41 F 2
Tha Pla 41 H 4
Tha Tako 41 H 4
Tha Tum 41 H 4
Tha-anne 73 S 3
Thabana Ntlenyana 66 D 5
Thabazimbi 66 D 4
Thādíq (Saudi Arabia) 23 DE 4
Thagyettaw 41 G 5
Thai Binh 41 J 3

Thai Nguyen 41 J 3
Thailand 41 GH 4
Thailand, Gulf of 41 H 5
Thakhek 41 HJ 4
Thal 35 J 4
Thal Desert 35 J 4
Thalabarivat 41 J 5
Thale Luang 41 H 6
Thallon 49 H 4
Tham Khae 41 J 4
Thamad Bū Ḥashishah 59 J 3
Thamarīd 61 J 5
Thame 7 D 2
Thames (New Zealand) 51 R 8
Thames, River 7 E 2
Thâmir, Jabal 61 H 6
Thamūd 61 H 5
Thana 40 B 4
Thangoo 48 C 2
Thangool 49 J 3
Thanh Hoa 41 J 4
Thanīyah, Jabal 61 H 5
Thanjavur 40 C 5
Thann 19 E 2
Thano Bula Khan 35 H 5
Thap Sakae 41 GH 5
Thapston 7 D 1
Thar Desert 40 B 2
Tharad 40 B 3
Thargomindah 49 G 4
Tharrawaddy 41 G 4
Tharrawaw 41 G 4
Tharthār, Bahr ath (Iraq) 22 D 2
Tharthār, Wādī ath (Iraq) 22 D 2
Thásos 20 B 2
Thásos 20 B 2
Thásos 20 B 2
Thateng 41 J 4
Thaton 41 G 4
Thau, Bassin de 18 D 3
Thaungdut 41 FG 3
Thayetchaung 41 G 5
Thayetmyo 41 G 4
Thazi 41 F 4
The Alps 19 EF 2
The Bahamas 79 GH 2
The Brothers → Al Ikhwān 65 J 2
The Bush 4 B 3
The Cheviot 3 C 4
The Dalles 76 B 2
The Everglades 77 K 6
The Fens 7 DE 1
The Gambia 62 A 3
The Granites 48 E 3
The Granites 48 E 3
The Great Oasis → Wāḥāt al
    Khārijah 60 E 3–4
The Gulf 23 EF 3–4
The Hague 14 D 4
The Johnston Lakes 48 C 5
The Lizard 6 B 2
The Mearns 3 C 3
The Merse 3 C 4
The Monument 49 G 3
The Mumbles 6 B 2
The Needles 7 D 2
The North Sound 2 C 2
The Pas 73 R 5
The Solent 7 D 2
The Teeth 43 E 2
The Trossachs 3 B 3
The Twins 51 Q 9
The Valley 79 K 4
The Wash 7 E 1
The Weald 7 E 2
Thebes 20 B 3
Thebes (Egypt) 22 A 4
Theddlethorpe 7 E 1
Thedford 76 F 3
Theinkun 41 G 5
Thelon 73 S 3
Thénia 18 D 4
Theologos 20 B 2
Thermaïkos Kólpos 20 B 2–3
Thermopílai 20 B 3
Thermopolis 76 E 3
Theronsvalley 66 BC 4
Thesiger Bay 73 MN 1
Thessalía 20 B 3
Thessaloníki 20 B 2
Thetford 7 E 1
Thetford Mines 75 N 6
Thief River Falls 77 G 2
Thiel Mts. 91
Thiers 18 D 2
Thiès 62 A 3
Thiesi 19 E 3
Thika 65 F 5
Thiladummathi Atoll 40 B 6
Thimphu 40 E 2
Þingvallavatn 16 A 3
Þingvellir 16 A 3
Thio (Ethiopia) 65 G 2
Thio (New Caledonia) 51 J 6
Thionville 19 E 2
Thiou 62 D 3

Thíra 20 B 3
Thíra 20 C 3
Third Cataract → Ash Shallāl ath
    Thālith 60 E 5
Thirsk 5 E 2
Thisted 17 E 4
Thitu Island 42 D 1
Thivai 20 B 3
Thiviers 18 D 2
Þjórsá 16 B 3
Thlewiaza 73 S 3
Thoen 41 G 4
Thoeng 41 H 4
Thohoyandou 67 E 4
Thomas Shoal 42 E 2
Thomastown 4 B 3
Thomasville (AL, U.S.A.) 77 J 5
Thomasville (GA, U.S.A.) 77 K 5
Thompson 73 S 4
Thompson Falls 76 C 2
Thomson River 49 G 3
Thon Buri 41 GH 5
Thongwa 41 G 4
Thonon 19 E 2
Þórisvatn 16 B 3
Þorlákshöfn 16 A 3
Thornaby-on-Tees 5 E 2
Thornby 7 D 1
Thorne 5 E 3
Thorney 7 D 1
Thornton Cleveleys 5 D 3
Thornton Dale 5 E 2
Þórshöfn 16 B 2
Thowa 65 F 5
Thráki 20 C 2
Thrakikón Pélagos 20 BC 2
Three Forks 76 D 2
Three Hummock Island 50 L 9
Three Kings Islands 51 Q 7
Three Pagodas Pass 41 G 4
Three Points, Cape 62 D 5
Three Springs 48 B 4
Throssel, Lake 48 C 4
Thruxton 7 D 2
Thuillier, Mount 41 F 6
Thule 90
Thun 19 E 2
Thundelarra 48 B 4
Thunder Bay (Canada) 74 K 6
Thunder Bay (MI, U.S.A.) 77 K 3
Thung Luang 41 G 5
Thung Song 41 G 6
Thung Wa 41 G 6
Thüringen 15 F 4
Thüringer Wald 15 F 4
Thurles 4 B 3
Thursby 5 D 2
Thurso 2 C 2
Thurston Island 91
Thusis 19 E 2
Thwaite 5 C 2
Thy 17 E 4
Thylungra 49 G 4
Tíago 85 G 4
Tian Shan 35 KM 2
Tianchang 39 G 4
Tiandong 38 E 6
Tian'e 38 E 6
Tiangua 87 H 1
Tianjin 39 G 3
Tianjin Xingang 39 G 3
Tianjun 38 C 3
Tianlin 38 E 6
Tianmen 38 F 4
Tianmu Shan 39 G 4
Tianshifu 39 H 2
Tianshui 38 E 4
Tiantai 39 H 5
Tianyang 38 E 6
Tianzhu 38 D 3
Tiaret 59 F 1
Tiassalé 62 D 4
Tibaradine 59 F 3
Tibati 63 G 4
Tiber 19 F 3
Tiberias → Teverya 60 F 2
Tibesti 63 H 1
Tibet 40 E 1
Tibet, Plateau of 40 DE 1
Tibiri 63 E 3
Tibiri 63 E 3
Tibistī, Sarīr 59 J 4
Tibnah (Syria) 22 B 2
Tibni (Syria) 22 C 2
Tibro 17 F 4
Tiburon, Isla 76 D 6
Ticao 43 F 1
Tichit 58 D 5
Tichla 58 B 4
Ticino 19 E 2
Ticul 78 E 3
Tidaholm 17 F 4
Tiddim 41 F 3
Tideswell 7 D 1
Tidikelt Oases 59 F 3
Tidirhine, Jbel 58 E 2

Tidjettaouine 59 F 4
Tidjikdja 58 C 5
Tidra, Ile 58 B 5
Tiebissou 62 CD 4
Tiel 62 A 3
Tieli 39 J 1
Tieling 39 H 2
Tielongtan 35 K 3
Tiéme 62 C 4
Tienba 62 C 4
Tientsin 39 G 3
Tierra Blanca 78 C 4
Tierra Colorada 78 C 4
Tierra de Barros 18 B 4
Tierra de Campos 18 BC 3
Tierra del Fuego, Isla Grande de
    89 C 9
Tierra del Pan 18 B 3
Tierra del Vino 18 B 3
Tieté 87 F 5
Tifariti 58 C 3
Tifton 77 K 5
Tifu 43 G 4
Tiga 51 J 6
Tigalda 72 E 5
Tigil' 37 T 4
Tigil' 37 T 4
Tignère 63 G 4
Tigre 84 C 4
Tigres, Baía dos 66 A 3
Tigris (Iraq) 23 D 2
Tiguent 58 B 5
Tiguentourine 59 G 3
Tigui 63 H 2
Tiguidit, Falaise de 63 F 2
Tihāmat 61 E 2
Tījī 59 H 2
Tijuana 76 C 5
Tijucas 88 G 4
Tikal 78 E 4
Tikamgarh 40 C 3
Tikanlik 38 A 2
Tikaré 62 D 3
Tikchik Lakes 72 F 3
Tikhoretsk 21 F 4
Tikhtoozero, Ozero 16 K 2
Tikhvin 24 F 4
Tikkakoski 16 J 3
Tikopia 51 J 4
Tikrīt 61 G 2
Tiksha 16 K 3
Tikshozero, Ozero 16 K 2
Tiksi 37 N 1
Tilaiya Reservoir 40 E 3
Tilbeşar Ovası 21 E 3
Tilbooroo 49 H 4
Tilburg 14 E 4
Tilbury 7 E 2
Tilbury 14 E 4
Tilcara 86 C 5
Tilemsi el Fasi 58 E 3
Tilemsi, Vallée du 62 E 2
Tilia 58 F 3
Tilichiki 37 V 3
Tilin 41 F 3
Tillabéri 62 E 3
Tillamook 76 B 2
Tillanchong 41 F 6
Tillia 63 E 2
Tiloa 62 E 2
Tilogne 62 B 2
Tílos 20 C 3
Tilpa 49 G 5
Til'tim 25 M 2
Ti-m Missao 59 F 4
Timā 60 E 3
Timagami, Lake 75 L 6
Timanskiy Kryazh 24 JL 2–3
Timar 21 F 3
Timaru 51 Q 9
Timashevskaya 21 E 1
Timbákion 20 B 3
Timbauba 87 J 2
Timbédra 58 D 5
Timberscombe 6 C 3
Timbio 84 C 3
Timbo 62 BC 4
Timbuktu → Tombouctou 62 D 2
Timeiaouine 59 F 4
Timétrine 62 D 2
Timétrine, Monts 62 D 2
Timfi Óros 20 B 3
Timg'aouine 59 F 4
Timia 63 F 2
Timimoun 58 F 3
Timimoun, Sebkha de 58–59 F 3
Timir-Atakh-Tas 37 S 2
Timiris, Cap 58 B 5
Timiş 20 B 1
Timiskaming, Lake 75 M 6
Timişoara 20 B 1

Timon 87 H 2
Timor 43 G 5
Timor, Laut 43 G 6
Timor Sea 43 G 6
Timoshino 24 G 3
Timote 88 D 6
Timpton 37 N 4
Timrå 16 G 3
Timur 35 H 2
Ti-n Amzi 59 F 4
Tin Asaguid 62 E 2
Tin City 72 D 2
Tin Ethisane 62 D 2
Tin Fouye 59 G 3
Ti-n Rerhoh 59 F 4
Ti-n Taoundi 59 G 4
Ti-n Tarabine 59 G 4
Tin Tounannt 62 D 1
Ti-n Zaouâtene 59 F 4
Tinaca Point 43 G 2
Tinaco 84 E 2
Tindalo 64 E 3
Tindivanam 40 CD 5
Tindouf 58 D 3
Tindouf, Hamada de 58 D 3
Tindouf, Sebkha de 58 D 3
Tinef 59 F 4
Tineldjame 59 F 3
Tineo 18 B 3
Tinerhir 58 D 2
Tingharat, Hamādat 59 H 3
Tingkawk Sakan 41 G 2
Tingmiarmiut 75 T 3
Tingo María 84 C 5
Tingréla 62 C 3
Tingri 40 E 2
Tingsryd 17 FG 4
Tinguiririca 89 BC 5
Tingvoll 16 E 3
Tinh Gia 41 J 4
Tinharé, Ilha de 87 J 3
Tini Wells 60 C 6
Tinian 52 A 2
Tinkisso 62 BC 3
Tinnsjö 17 E 4
Tinogasta 88 C 4
Tinombo 43 F 3
Tínos 20 C 3
Tinrhert, Hamada de 59 G 3
Tinsukia 41 G 2
Tintagel 6 B 2
Tintagel Head 6 B 2
Tintane 58 C 5
Tintina 88 D 4
Ti-n-Toumma 63 G 2
Tio, Pico de 62 C 4
Tioman 42 B 3
Tione di Trento 19 F 2
Tiongui 62 C 3
Tiouardiouine Aguelman 59 G 4
Tiouilit Anagoum 58 B 5
Tipperary 4 B 3
Tipperary 14 B 4
Tipton, Mount 76 D 4
Tiptree 7 E 2
Tiquisate 78 D 5
Tiracambu, Serra do 87 G 1
Tirah 35 J 4
Tirān (Egypt) 22 B 4
Tirān (Iran) 23 F 2
Tirana 20 AB 2
Tirano 19 F 2
Tiras Mountains 66 B 5
Tiraspol' 20 C 1
Tirat Karmel (Israel) 22 B 2
Tire 20 C 3
Tirebolu 21 E 2
Tiree 3 A 3
Tiree (Airport) 3 A 3
Tirgelir 37 Q 3
Tîrgi Frumos 20 C 1
Tîrgovişte 20 C 2
Tirgu Bujor 20 C 1
Tîrgu Cărbuneşti 20 B 2
Tîrgu Jiu 20 B 1
Tîrgu Mureş 20 BC 1–2
Tîrgu Neamţ 20 C 1
Tîrgu Ocna 20 C 1
Tîrgu Secuiesc 20 C 1
Tirich Mir 35 J 3
Tiririne 59 G 4
Tiris 58 C 4
Tîrnăveni 20 B 1
Tîrnavos 20 B 3
Tiro 62 B 4
Tirol 19 F 2
Tirso 19 E 3
Tiruchirappalli 40 C 5
Tiruchendur 40 C 6
Tirunelveli 40 C 6
Tiruntán 84 D 5
Tirupati 40 C 5
Tiruppur 40 C 5
Tiruvannamalai 40 C 5

Tisa 20 A 1
Tisdale 73 R 5
Tisisat Falls 65 F 2
Tissemsilt 59 F 1
Tista 40 E 2
Tisul' 25 R 4
Tisza 20 B 1
Tiszafüred 20 B 1
Tiszántúl 20 B 1
Tit 59 F 3
Titaf 58 E 3
Tit-Ary 37 N 1
Titchfield 7 D 2
Titicaca, Lago 86 C 4
Titlagarh 40 D 3
Titograd 20 A 2
Titov Veles 20 B 2
Titov vrh 20 B 2
Titova Korenica 19 G 3
Titovo Užice 20 A 2
Titran 16 E 3
Titule 64 D 4
Titusville 77 K 6
Tiui 85 GH 3
Tivaouane 62 A 3
Tiveden 17 F 4
Tiverton 6 C 2
Tiwī 61 K 4
Tiworo, Selat 43 F 4
Tizatlan 78 C 4
Tizi n'Test 58 D 2
Tizi Ouzou 59 F 1
Tizimín 78 E 3
Tiznit 58 D 3
Tjåhumas 16 G 2
Tjeggelvas 16 G 2
Tjidtjak 16 G 2
Tjörn 17 F 4
Tjotta 16 F 2
Tjust 17 G 4
Tkhach 21 F 2
Tkibuli 21 F 2
Tkvarcheli 21 F 2
Tlalnepantla 78 C 4
Tlapa de Comonfort 78 C 4
Tlaxcala 78 C 4
Tlemcen 58 E 2
Tlemcès 63 E 2
Tlētē Ouate Gharbi, Jabal 22 C 2
Tlyarata 21 G 2
Tmassah 59 J 3
Tni Haïa 58 E 3
Toaca, Vîrful 20 C 1
Toamasina 67 H 3
Toay 89 D 6
Toba & Kakar Ranges 35 H 4
Toba, Danau 42 A 3
Tobago, Isla 85 F 1
Tobarra 18 C 4
Tobermore 4 B 2
Tobermorey 49 F 3
Tobermory 75 L 6
Tobermory (U.K.) 3 A 3
Tobi 43 H 3
Tobin, Lake 48 D 3
Tobo 43 H 4
Toboali 42 C 4
Tobol 25 M 5
Tobol 25 N 4
Tobol'sk 25 N 4
Tobruk → Ṭubruq 59 K 2
Tobseda 24 K 2
Tobysh 24 K 3
Tocantinia 85 J 5
Tocantinópolis 85 J 5
Tocantins 85 J 4
Tocapilla 85 B 5
Töcksfors 17 F 4
Toco 86 C 5
Toconao 86 C 5
Tocorpuri, Cerro de 86 C 5
Todenyang 65 F 4
Todi 19 F 3
Todmorden 5 D 3
Todos os Santos, Baia de 87 J 3
Todos Santos 76 D 7
Tofino 73 M 6
Tofte 17 F 4
Togatax 35 L 3
Togher (Roundwood) 4 B 3
Togiak 72 E 4
Togian, Kepulauan 43 F 4
Togni 60 F 5
Togo 62 E 4
Toguchin 25 Q 4
Togtoh 38 F 2
Togur 25 Q 4
Togyz 35 G 1
Tohen 65 J 2
Tohma 21 E 3
Toibalewe 41 F 5
Toijala 16 H 3
Toista 2 A 2
Toisvesi 16 J 3
Tok (AK, U.S.A.) 72 J 3

Tok (Czechoslovakia) 15 F 5
Tokaj 20 B 1
Tokara-kaikyō 39 JK 4–5
Tokara-rettō 39 J 5
Tokat 21 E 2
Tok-do 39 K 3
Tokelau Islands 52 D 3
Tokko 36 L 4
Tokma 36 J 4
Tokmak 21 E 1
Tokmak 35 K 2
Tokomaru Bay 51 R 8
Toksun 35 M 2
Toktamysh 35 JK 3
Toktogul 35 J 2
Toku-no-shima 39 J 5
Tokur 37 O 5
Tokushima 39 K 4
Tōkyō 39 L 3
Tolbazy 24 L 5
Tolbonuur 36 F 6
Tolbukhin 20 C 2
Toledo (Chile) 88 B 4
Toledo (OH, U.S.A.) 77 K 3
Toledo (Spain) 18 C 4
Toledo Bend Reservoir 77 H 5
Toledo, Montes de 18 C 4
Tolga (Algeria) 59 G 2
Tolga (Norway) 16 F 3
Toli 35 L 1
Toliara 67 G 4
Tolima 84 C 3
Tolitoli 43 F 3
Tol'ka 25 Q 3
Tollarp 17 F 4
Tollesbury 7 E 2
Tolmezzo 19 F 2
Tolmin 19 F 2
Tolo 64 B 5
Tolo, Teluk 43 F 4
Tolochin 17 J 5
Tolon 36 K 4
Tolon 37 R 4
Tolstoe 20 C 1
Tolstoy, Mys 37 T 4
Toltén 89 B 6
Toluca 78 C 4
Tol'yatti 24 J 5
Tolybay 25 M 5
Tom' 25 QR 4
Tom Price 48 B 3
Tom White, Mount 72 J 3
Tomakomai 39 M 2
Toman 77 H 3
Tomar 85 F 4
Tomar (Portugal) 18 B 4
Tomari 37 Q 6
Tómaros 20 B 3
Tomaszów Lubelski 15 H 4
Tomaszów Mazowiecki 15 H 4
Tomatin 2 C 3
Tomatlán 78 AB 4
Tombador, Serra do 86 E 3
Tombe 64 E 3
Tombigbee 77 J 5
Tomboco 66 A 1
Tombouctou 62 D 2
Tômbua 66 A 3
Tomdoun 3 B 3
Tomé 89 B 6
Tomé Açu 85 J 4
Tomé, Pico de 63 F 5
Tomelilla 17 F 4
Tomelloso 18 C 4
Tomhaggard 6 A 1
Tomini, Teluk 43 F 4
Tominian 62 D 3
Tomkinson Ranges 48 D 4
Tomma 16 F 2
Tommot 37 N 4
Tomo 84 E 2
Tompa 36 J 4
Tompo 37 P 3
Tompo (Indonesia) 43 F 3
Tompo (U.S.S.R.) 37 P 3
Tomsa 65 G 3
Tomsk 25 R 4
Tomtor 37 O 2
Tonantins 84 E 4
Tonasket 76 BC 2
Tonate 85 H 3
Tonb-e Bozorg (Iran) 23 G 4
Tonbridge 7 E 2
Tondano 43 FG 3
Tondela 18 B 3
Tønder 17 E 5
Tondibi 62 D 2
Tondou, Massif du 64 C 3
Tonekābon (Iran) 23 F 1
Tong Xian 39 G 3
Tonga 52 D 4
Tonga (Sudan) 64 E 3
Tonga Islands 52 D 4
Tonga Trench 99 D 4
Tongaat 67 E 5
Tongariro National Park 51 R 8

Tongatapu Group 52 D 4
Tongbai Shan 38 F 4
Tongcheng 39 G 4
Tongchuan 38 E 3
Tongdao 38 EF 5
Tongde 38 D 3
Tonghai 38 D 6
Tonghe 39 J 1
Tonghua 39 J 2
Tongjiang 37 O 6
Tongjoson-man 39 J 3
Tongliao 39 H 2
Tongling 39 G 4
Tongliong 38 E 5
Tonglu 39 GH 5
Tongoy 88 B 5
Tongren 38 D 3
Tongren 38 E 5
Tongsa 41 F 2
Tongshan 38 F 5
Tongta 41 G 3
Tongtian He 38 C 4
Tongue 2 B 2
Tongue of the Ocean 79 G 3
Tongulakh 37 M 3
Tongwei 38 DE 3
Tongxin 38 E 3
Tongyu 39 H 2
Tongzi 38 E 5
Tonhil 36 F 6
Tonichí 76 E 6
Tonj 64 D 3
Tonk 40 C 2
Tonkou, Mont 62 C 4
Tonle Sap 41 H 5
Tonneins 18 D 3
Tonnerre 18 D 2
Tonopah 76 C 4
Tonosí 84 B 2
Tönsberg 17 F 4
Tonstad 17 E 4
Tonya 21 E 2
Tonzang 41 F 3
Tooday 48 B 5
Tooele 76 D 3
Toompine 49 G 4
Toowoomba 49 J 4
Topchikha 25 Q 5
Topeka 77 G 4
Topki 25 R 4
Topko, Gora 37 P 4
Topliţa 20 C 1
Topocalma, Punta 88 B 5
Topoli 34 E 1
Topolinyy 37 P 3
Topolobampo 76 E 6
Topolobampo, Bahia de 76 E 6
Topozero, Ozero 16 K 2
Toppenish 76 B 2
Toprak-Kala 35 G 2
Topsham 6 C 3
Tora-Khem 36 G 5
Toranggekuduk 35 N 2
Toraya 86 B 3
Torbalı 20 C 3
Torbat-e Heydarīyeh 34 FG 3
Torbat-e Jām 34 G 3
Torbay 6 C 2
Torbert, Mount 72 G 3
Torbino 24 F 4
Torcross 6 C 3
Tordesillas 18 BC 3
Töre 16 H 2
Töreboda 17 F 4
Torekov 17 F 4
Torenberg 14 E 4
Torey 36 H 5
Torez 21 E 1
Torgau 15 F 4
Torgovoye 21 F 1
Tori 64 E 3
Toribulo 43 F 4
Torino 19 E 2
Tori-shima 39 LM 4
Torit 64 E 4
Torkeman, Bandar-e (Iran) 23 G 1
Torkovichi 17 K 4
Tormes 18 B 3
Torneå 16 H 2
Torneälven 16 H 2
Torneträsk 16 H 2
Torngat Mountains 75 P 4
Tornio 16 H 2
Tornionjoki 16 H 2
Tornquist 89 D 6
Toro (Nigeria) 63 F 3
Toro (Spain) 18 B 3
Toro, Cerro del 88 C 4
Toro Doum 63 H 2
Toro, Lago del 89 B 9
Torodi 62 E 3
Torokina 51 FG 3
Torom 37 P 5
Toroni, Cerro 86 C 4
Toronto 75 M 7
Toropets 24 F 4

Tororo 64 E 4
Toros Dağlari 21 D 3
Torpoint 6 B 2
Torquato Severo 88 F 5
Torquay 6 C 2
Torra Bay 66 A 4
Torra Miro, Puerto de 18 C 3
Torre Annunziata 19 F 3
Torre de Moncorvo 18 B 3
Torre del Greco 19 F 3
Torrejón de Ardoz 18 C 3
Torrelavega 18 C 3
Torremolinos 18 C 4
Torrens Creek 49 H 3
Torrens, Lake 49 F 5
Torrens River 49 H 3
Torrente 18 C 4
Torreón 78 B 2
Tôrres 88 G 4
Torres Islands 51 J 4
Torres Strait 49 G 1
Torres Vedras 18 B 4
Torridge, River 6 B 2
Torridon, Loch 2 B 3
Torrijos 18 C 4
Torrin 2 B 3
Torrington 49 J 4
Torrington 76 F 3
Torröjen 16 F 3
Torsby 17 F 3
Torshälla 17 G 4
Tórshavn 14 A 1
Torsken 16 G 2
Torsö 17 F 4
Tortkuduk 25 O 5
Tortola 79 K 4
Tortona 19 E 3
Tortosa 18 D 3
Tortosa, Cabo de 18 D 3
Tortue, Ile de la 79 H 3
Tortuguero 78 F 5
Tortum 21 F 2
Torud (Iran) 23 G 2
Torud 34 F 3
Torugart, Pereval 35 K 2
Torul 21 E 2
Toruń 15 G 4
Torup 17 F 4
Torzhok 24 F 4
Tosashimizu 39 K 4
Tosa-wan 39 K 4
Toscaig 2 B 3
Toscana 19 F 3
Toscanini 66 A 4
Tosenfjorden 16 F 2
Tosno 17 K 4
Toson Hu 38 C 3
Tosontsengel 36 G 6
Tossa 18 D 3
Tostado 88 D 4
Tõstamaa 17 H 4
Tostuya 36 K 1
Tosya 21 D 2
Totak 17 E 4
Totana 18 C 4
Toten 17 F 3
Toteng 66 C 4
Tõtias 65 G 4
Totland 7 D 2
Totma 24 H 4
Totnes 6 C 3
Totness 85 G 2
Totonicapan 78 D 4–5
Totoras 88 D 5
Totota 62 C 4
Totten Glacier 91
Tottori 7 D 2
Tottori 39 K 3
Touat Oases 58 E 3
Touba (Ivory Coast) 62 C 4
Touba (Senegal) 62 A 3
Toubkal, Jbel 58 D 2
Toufourine 58 DE 4
Tougan 62 D 3
Touggourt 59 G 2
Tougué 62 B 3
Touila 58 D 3
Toukoto 62 C 3
Toul 19 E 2
Toulépleu 62 C 4
Toulon 19 E 3
Toulouse 18 D 3
Toumodi 62 C 4
Tounassine 58 E 3
Tounassine, Hamada 58 DE 3
Toungo 63 G 4
Toungoo 41 G 4
Toura, Monts de 62 C 4
Touraine 18 D 2
Tourassine 58 C 4
Tourcoing 18 D 1
Touriñán, Cabo 18 B 3
Tourine 58 C 4
Tournai 14 D 4
Tournavista 84 CD 5
Tournon 19 D 2

Tournus 19 DE 2
Touros 87 J 2
Tours 18 D 2
Toury 18 D 2
Tousside, Pic 63 H 1
Toussoro 64 C 3
Touws River 66 C 6
Tow Law 5 E 2
Towada 39 M 2
Towakaima 85 G 2
Towanda 77 L 3
Towcester 7 D 1
Tower Hill 49 G 3
Towerhill River 49 G 3
Towie 2 C 3
Townsend 76 D 2
Townshend Island 49 J 3
Townsville 49 H 2
Towot 64 E 3
Towson 77 L 4
Towty, River 6 B 2
Toxkan He 35 K 2
Toyama 39 L 3
Toygunen 72 C 2
Toyohashi 39 L 4
Toyota 39 L 3
Trabzon 21 EF 2
Trafalgar, Cabo 18 B 4
Trăghan 59 H 3
Traiguén 89 B 6
Trail 73 O 6
Trairi 87 J 1
Tralee 14 B 4
Tralee Bay 14 AB 4
Tranås 17 F 4
Trancas 88 C 4
Trancoso 18 B 3
Tranemo 17 F 4
Tranent 3 C 4
Trang 41 G 6
Trangan, Pulau 43 H 5
Trani 19 G 3
Trans-Amazon Highway 84 D 5
Trans-Amazon Highway 85 H 4
Transantarctic Mountains 91
Transilvania 20 B 1
Transkei 66 D 6
Transtrand 16 F 3
Transtrandsfjällen 16 F 3
Transvaal 66 D 5
Transylvanian Alps 20 B 1–2
Trapani 19 F 4
Traralgon 49 H 6
Trarza 58 BC 3
Trasimeno, Lago 19 F 3
Trat 41 H 5
Traun 19 F 2
Traunsee 19 F 2
Travers, Mount 51 Q 9
Traverse City 77 J 3
Travesia 78 E 4
Travesia Puntana 88 C 5
Travnik 19 G 3
Trawsfynydd 6 C 1
Trayning 48 B 5
Trbovlje 19 FG 2
Třebíc 15 G 5
Trebinje 19 G 3
Trebisacce 19 G 4
Trebišóv 15 H 5
Treblinka 15 H 4
Třebon 15 F 5
Tredegar 6 C 2
Treen 6 B 2
Treffgarne 6 B 2
Trefnant 6 C 1
Tregaron 6 C 1
Tregony 6 B 2
Tregosselslets and Reefs 49 J 2
Tregynon 6 C 1
Treinta y Tres 88 EF 5
Trélazé 18 C 2
Trelew 89 CD 7
Trelleborg 17 F 4
Trelleck 6 C 3
Tremadog Bay 6 B 1
Tremiti, Isole 19 G 3
Tremonton 76 D 3
Tremp 18 D 3
Trenel 89 D 6
Trenque Lauquen 89 D 6
Trent, River 7 D 1
Trento 19 F 2
Trenton (MO, U.S.A.) 77 H 3
Trenton (N.J., U.S.A.) 77 M 3
Trepassey 75 R 6
Tres Arboles 88 E 5
Tres Arroyos 89 D 6
Tres Cerros 89 C 8
Três Corações 87 GH 5
Tres Esquinas 84 CD 3
Tres Forcas, Cap 58 E 1
Três Lagoas 87 F 5
Tres Lagos 89 B 8

Tres Marías Dam 87 G 4
Tres Montes, Península 89 A 8
Tres Picos 78 D 4
Tres Picos, Cerro 89 D 6
Tres Puentes 88 BC 4
Três Ríos 87 H 5
Tres Zapotes 78 CD 4
Treuchtlingen 15 F 5
Treviglio 19 E 2
Treviso 19 F 2
Treze Quedas 85 G 4
Trgovište 20 B 2
Triabunna 50 L 9
Trialetskiy Khrebet 21 F 2
Tríbeč Vtácnik 15 G 5
Trichur 40 C 5
Trident Shoal 42 D 1
Trier 14 E 5
Trieste 19 F 2
Triglav 19 F 2
Tríkala 20 B 3
Trikhonis Limni 20 B 3
Trikomo 21 D 3
Trikomo (Cyprus) 22 AB 2
Trikomon → Trikomo 21 D 3
Trikora, Puncak 43 J 4
Trillick 4 B 2
Trim 4 B 3
Trimdon 5 E 2
Trincomalee 40 D 6
Trindade Island 81 G 5
Třínec 15 G 5
Tring 7 D 2
Trinidad (Bolivia) 86 D 3
Trinidad (CA, U.S.A.) 76 B 3
Trinidad (CO, U.S.A.) 76 F 4
Trinidad (Colombia) 84 D 2
Trinidad (Cuba) 79 G 3
Trinidad (Uruguay) 88 E 5
Trinidad and Tobago 85 FG 1
Trinidad, Golfo 89 A 8
Trinidad, Isla 85 F 1
Trinidad, Isla (Argentina) 89 D 6
Trinity Bay 75 R 6
Trinity Bay (Australia) 49 H 2
Trinity Islands 72 G 4
Trinity River 77 G 5
Trinkitat 60 F 5
Tripoli (Lebanon) 22 B 2
Tripoli (Libya) 59 J 2
Tripolis 20 B 3
Tripolitania 59 HJ 2
Tripura 41 F 3
Tristan da Cunha 102 G 5
Tristao, Îsles 62 A 3
Trivandrum 40 C 6
Trnava 15 G 5
Trobriand or Kiriwina Islands 51 F 3
Trofimov 21 F 1
Trofimovsk 37 NO 1
Trofors 16 F 2
Trogir 19 G 3
Troglav 19 G 3
Trois Rivières 75 N 6
Trois-Pistoles 75 O 6
Troitsk 25 M 5
Troitsk 36 F 4
Troitskiy 24 K 5
Troitskiy 25 O 5
Troitskiy 36 K 5
Troitsko-Pechorsk 24 L 3
Troitskoye 20 D 1
Troitskoye 24 L 5
Troitskoye 25 Q 5
Troitskoye 37 P 6
Trolla 63 G 2
Trollhättan 17 F 4
Trollheimen 16 E 3
Trollhetta 16 E 3
Trolltindane 16 E 3
Trombetas 85 G 3–4
Tromelin 55 H 6
Tromöya 17 E 4
Troms 16 G 2
Tromsö 16 G 2
Trona 76 C 4
Tronador, Monte 89 B 7
Trondheim 16 F 3
Trondheimsfjorden 16 F 3
Troodos 21 D 4
Troodos (Cyprus) 22 A 2
Troon 3 B 4
Trosa 17 G 4
Trosh 24 L 2
Trostan 4 B 2
Trostyanets 20 C 1
Trotternish 2 A 3
Trout Lake (N.W.T., Can.) 73 N 3
Trout Lake (Ontario, Can.) 74 J 5
Trout Peak 76 E 3
Trout River 75 Q 6
Trowbridge 7 C 2
Troy 20 C 3
Troy (AL, U.S.A.) 77 J 5

Troy Peak 76 C 4
Troyan 20 B 2
Troyanski Manastir 20 B 2
Troyekurovo 24 G 5
Troyes 18 D 2
Trubchevsk 24 F 5
Truc Giang 41 J 5
Trucial Coast (United Arab
   Emirates) 23 FG 4
Trudovoye 39 K 2
Trujillo (Honduras) 78 E 4
Trujillo (Peru) 84 C 5
Trujillo (Spain) 18 B 4
Trujillo (Venezuela) 84 D 2
Truk Islands 52 B 2
Trumbull, Mount 76 D 4
Truro 75 P 6
Truro (U.K.) 6 B 2
Trusovo 24 K 2
Trust Territory of the Pacific
   Islands 52 AB·2
Truth or Consequences [Hot
   Springs] 76 E 5
Trutnov 15 G 4
Truva 20 C 3
Truyére 18 D 3
Trysil 16 F 3
Trysilelva 16 F 3
Trysilfjellet 16 F 3
Trzcianka 15 G 4
Tsagaan Üür 36 H 5
Tsagaannuur 36 E 6
Tsagaan-Uul 36 G 6
Tsagan-Nur 21 G 1
Tsageri 21 F 2
Tsaidam Basin 38 BC 3
Tsaidam Basin → Qaidam Pendi
   38 BC 3
Tsalka 21 F 2
Tsangpo 38 B 5
Tsapelka 17 J 4
Tsaratanana 67 H 3
Tsaratanana, Massif du 67 H 2
Tsaris Mountains 66 B 4
Tsatsana 66 C 3
Tsau 66 C 4
Tsaukaib 66 B 5
Tsavo 65 F 5
Tsavo National Park 65 F 5
Tsāwah 59 H 3
Tsawisis 66 B 5
Tselina 21 F 1
Tselinnoye 25 R 5
Tselinograd 25 O 5
Tsenhermandal 36 JK 6
Tsenogora 24 J 3
Tsentralno Tungusskoye Plato
   36 GH 3–4
Tsentralno Yakutskaya
   Nizmennost' 37 MN 3
Tsentral'nyy 25 R 4
Tses 66 B 5
Tsetseg 36 F 6
Tsetserleg 36 G 6
Tsetserleg 36 H 6
Tsévié 62 E 4
Tshabong 66 C 5
Tshabuta 64 C 6
Tshane 66 C 4
Tshangalele, Lac 66 D 2
Tshela 63 G 6
Tshele 64 D 5
Tshesebe 66 D 4
Tshibamba 64 C 6
Tshikapa 64 C 6
Tshilenge 64 C 6
Tshimbalanga 64 C 6
Tshimbulu 64 C 6
Tshkudu 66 C 4
Tshofa 64 D 6
Tshuapa 64 C 5
Tshwane 66 C 4
Tsiafajavona 67 H 3
Tsiazonano 67 H 3
Tsihombe 67 H 5
Tsimlyansk 21 F 1
Tsimlyanskoye Vodokhranilishche
   21 F 1
Tsineng 66 C 5
Tsinghai 38 C 4
Tsingtao 39 H 3
Tsintsabis 66 B 3
Tsipa 36 L 4
Tsipanda 37 P 4
Tsipikan 36 K 5
Tsiroanomandidy 67 H 3
Tsitondroina 67 H 3
Tskhaltubo 21 F 2
Tskhinvali 21 F 2
Tsna 17 J 5
Tsna 24 H 5
Tsodilo Hills 66 C 3
Tsu 39 L 4
Tsuchiura 39 M 3
Tsugaru-kaikyō 39 M 2

Tsumeb 66 B 3
Tsumis Park 66 B 4
Tsumkwe 66 C 3
Tsuruga 39 L 3
Tsuruoka 39 L 3
Tsushima 39 JK 4
Tsuyama 39 K 3
Tsyurupinsk 21 D 1
Tua (Portugal) 18 B 3
Tua (Zaire) 64 B 5
Tual 43 H 5
Tuamotu Archipelago 53 F 4
Tuan 41 H 3
Tuangku, Pulau 42 A 3
Tuapse 21 E 2
Tuaran 42 E 2
Tuba 36 F 5
Tuba 36 H 4
Tuba City 76 D 4
Ṭubal, Wādī at (Iraq) 22 C 2
Tuban 42 D 5
Tubarão 88 G 4
Tubayq, Jabal at (Saudi Arabia)
   22 B 3
Tubbataha Reefs 43 E 2
Tubelai, Pulau 43 G 4
Tübingen 15 E 5
Ṭubruq 59 K 2
Tubuaï 53 F 4
Tubuai Islands 53 EF 4
Tucacas 84 E 1
Tucano 87 J 3
Tucavaca 86 E 4
Tuchola 15 G 4
Tucson 76 D 5
Tucumcari 76 F 4
Tucuparé 85 G 5
Tucupita 85 F 2
Tucuruí 85 HJ 4
Tudela 18 C 3
Tudmur (Syria) 22 C 2
Tuensang 41 F 2
Tufi 50 E 3
Tugela 66 E 5
Tuguegarao 43 J 1
Tugur 37 P 5
Tuim 25 R 5
Tukangbesi, Kepulauan 43 F 5
Tukayyid (Iraq) 23 D 3
Ṭūkrah 59 K 2
Tuktoyaktuk 72 L 2
Tukums 17 H 4
Tukuringra, Khrebet 37 N 5
Tukuyu 64 E 6
Tukzar 35 H 3
Tulai 38 C 3
Tulancingo 78 C 4
Tulangbawang 42 BC 4
Tulare 76 C 4
Tulasi 40 D 4
Tulay-Kiryaka-Tas,
   Vozvyshennost' 36 JK 1
Tulbagh 66 B 6
Tulcán 84 C 3
Tulcea 20 C 1
Tulchin 20 C 1
Tulemalu Lake 73 RS 3
Tuli 66 D 4
Tulihe 37 M 5
Tullahoma 77 J 4
Tullamore 4 B 3
Tulle 18 D 2
Tulln 19 G 2
Tullner Becken 19 G 2
Tullow 4 B 3
Tullus 60 C 6
Tully 49 H 2
Tullynessie 2 C 3
Ṭulmaythah 59 K 2
Tuloma 16 K 2
Tulos, Ozero 16 K 3
Tulpan 24 L 3
Tulsa 77 G 4
Tul'skaya 21 F 2
Tuluá 84 C 3
Tuluksak 72 E 3
Tulum 78 E 3
Tulun 36 H 5
Tulungagung 42 D 5
Tumaco 84 C 3
Tumanovo 24 F 4
Tumanskiy 37 X 3
Tumany 37 T 3
Tumat 37 PQ 1
Tumatumari 85 G 2
Tumba 17 G 4
Tumba, Lac 64 B 5
Tumbarumba 49 H 6
Tumbes 84 B 4
Tumbling Waters 48 E 1
Tumcha 16 K 2
Tumd Youqi 38 F 2
Tumd Zuoqi 38 F 2

Tumen 39 J 2
Tumeremo 85 F 2
Tumkur 40 C 5
Tummel Bridge 3 C 3
Tumnin 37 PQ 6
Tump 35 G 5
Tumpat 42 B 2
Tūmū 59 H 4
Tumu 62 D 3
Tumucumaque, Serra 85 H 3
Tumupasa 86 C 3
Tunari, Cerro 86 C 4
Tunas 87 G 5
Tunas, Sierra de las 76 E 6
Tunceli 21 E 3
Tundla 40 C 2
Tunduma 64 E 6
Tunduru 67 F 2
Tundzha 20 C 2
Tūnel-e-Salong 35 H 3
Tunga 63 F 4
Tungabhadra 40 C 4
Tungaru 60 E 6
Tungku 43 E 2
Tungnaá 16 B 3
Tungokochen 36 KL 5
Tungsten 72 M 3
Tunguska, Nizhnyaya 36 F 3
Tunguska, Podkamennaya 36 FG 3
Tungus-Khaya 37 N 3
Tünhel 36 J 6
Tuni 40 D 4
Tūnis 59 GH 1
Tunisia 59 GH 2
Tunja 84 D 2
Tunnhovdfjorden 17 E 3
Tunnak 72 D 3
Tununak 72 D 3
Tunungayualok 75 P 4
Tunuyan 88 C 5
Tunxi 39 G 5
Tuŏroyri 14 A 1
Tuostakh 37 P 2
Tuotuo He 38 B 4
Tuotuo Heyan 38 B 4
Tupã 87 F 5
Tupaciguara 87 G 4
Tupanciretã 88 F 4
Tupelo 77 J 4
Tupik 36 L 5
Tupinambaranas, Ilha 85 G 4
Tupirama 85 J 5
Tupirantins 85 J 5
Tupiza 86 C 5
Tuquan 39 H 1
Túquerres 84 C 3
Tura (India) 41 F 2
Tura (Tanzania) 64 E 6
Tura (U.S.S.R.) 25 M 4
Tura (U.S.S.R.) 36 H 3
Turabah 61 G 4
Turabah (Saudi Arabia) 22 D 3
Turagua, Serranías 85 F 2
Turakh 36 M 1
Turallin 49 J 4
Turama 36 G 3
Turan 36 F 5
Tūrān (Iran) 23 G 2
Turana, Khrebet 37 O 5
Turanskaya Nizmennost
   34–35 FG 2
Turbaco 84 C 1
Turbat 35 G 5
Turbo 84 C 2
Turda 20 B 1
Ṭūreh (Iran) 23 E 2
Tureia 53 F 4
Turek 15 G 4
Turen 84 E 2
Turfan Depression 38 A 2
Turgay 35 G 1
Turgay 35 G 1
Turgayskaya Dolina 25 M 5–6
Turgayskaya Stolovaya Strana
   25 M 5
Türgen Uul 36 F 6
Tŭrgovishte 20 C 2
Turgutlu 20 C 3
Turhal 21 E 2
Türi 17 J 4
Turia 18 C 4
Turiaçu 85 J 4
Turin 19 E 2–3
Turinsk 25 M 4
Turiy Rog 39 K 1
Turka 36 J 5
Turkana 64 F 4
Turkana, Lake 65 F 4
Turkannakh 36 MN 1
Turkestan 35 H 2
Turkestanskiy Khrebet 35 H 3
Turkey 21 DE 3
Turkmeniya 34 F 3
Türkoğlu 21 E 3
Turks and Caicos Islands 79 HJ 3

Turks Island Passage 79 H 3
Turks Islands 79 H 3
Turku 17 H 3
Turkwel 64 F 4
Ṭurmus, Wādī at (Saudi Arabia)
   22 D 4
Turneffe Islands 78 E 4
Turner River 48 D 2
Turnu Măgurele 20 BC 2
Turnu Roşu, Pasul 20 B 1
Turobay 25 P 6
Turochak 25 R 5
Turpan 38 A 2
Turpan Pendi 38 A 2
Turpan Zhan 35 M 2
Turriff 2 C 3
Tursha 24 J 4
Turtkul' 35 G 2
Turtle Islands 62 B 4
Turugart Shankou 35 K 2
Turukhan 25 QR 2
Turukhansk 25 R 2
Turukta 36 L 3
Turvey 7 D 1
Tuscaloosa 77 J 5
Tutak 21 F 3
Tutayev 24 G 4
Tutbury 7 D 1
Tuticorin 40 C 6
Tutóia 87 H 1
Tutonchana 36 F 2
Tutonchana, Vozvyshennost'
   36 FG 2–3
Tutonchany 36 F 3
Tutrakan 20 C 2
Tuttle Creek Lake 77 G 4
Tüttlingen 15 E 5
Tutubu 64 E 6
Tutuila 52 D 3
Tutupaca, Volcán 86 BC 4
Tutuvawang 43 GH 5
Tutuwawang 50 A 3
Tuul Gol 36 H 6
Tuvalu 52 D 3
Ṭuwayq, Jabal (Saudi Arabia)
   23 D 4
Tuwayq, Jabal 61 H 4
Tuwawang 50 A 3
Tuxford 7 D 1
Tuxpán 78 A 3
Tuxpan de Rodríguez Cano 78 C 3
Tuxtla Gutiérrez 78 D 4
Tuy 18 B 3
Tuy Hoa 41 J 5
Tuyen Quang 41 J 3
Tuymazy 24 K 5
Tūyserkān (Iran) 23 E 2
Tuz Gölü 21 D 3
Tūz Khurmātū (Iraq) 23 D 2
Tuzla 19 G 3
Tuzla 21 DE 3
Tuzluca 21 F 2
Tuzly 20 CD 1
Tvedestrand 17 E 4
Twatt 2 C 3
Twee Rivieren 66 BC 5
Tweed, River 3 C 4
Tweedmouth 5 D 2
Tweedsmuir 3 C 4
Tweedsmuir Hills 5 D 2
Twin Falls (ID, U.S.A.) 76 D 3
Twin Falls (Newfoundl., Can.)
   75 P 5
Twin Islands 75 L 5
Twisp 76 C 2
Two Harbors 77 H 2
Twomileborris 4 B 3
Twyford 7 D 2
Twynholm 3 B 4
Tyan'-Shan' 35 JK 2
Tyatino 39 N 2
Tychkino 25 P 4
Tychy 15 G 4
Tydal 16 F 3
Tygda 37 N 5
Tyk 37 Q 5
Tyler 77 G 5
Tylkhoy 37 U 3
Tylösand 17 F 4
Tyl'skiy Khrebet 37 OP 5
Tym 25 Q 4
Tymovskoye 37 Q 5
Tynda 37 M 4
Tyndrum 3 B 3
Tyne and Wear 5 E 2
Tyne, River 5 E 2
Tynemouth 5 E 2
Tynset 16 F 3
Tyräjärvi 16 J 2
Tyre (Lebanon) 22 B 2
Tyrifjorden 17 F 4
Tyrma 37 O 5
Tyrma 37 O 5
Tyrrell Lake 73 QR 3
Tyrrhenian Sea 19 F 3–4
Tyry 37 P 3
Tysnesöy 17 E 3–4

Tysse 17 E 3
Tyssedal 17 E 3
Tyubelyakh 37 Q 2
Tyugene 37 N 3
Tyugene 37 N 3
Tyugyuren 37 Q 2
Tyukalinsk 25 O 4
Tyukhtet 25 R 4
Tyul'-Bannovka 35 J 2
Tyulen'i, Ostrova 34 E 1–2
Tyul'gan 24 L 5
Tyumen' 25 N 4
Tyumsyu 37 Q 3
Tyung 36 L 2
Tyungulyu 37 O 3
Tyuntyugur 25 MN 5
Tywyn 6 B 1
Tzaneen 66 DE 4

U

Ua Huka 53 F 3
Ua Pu 53 F 3
Uad el Jat 58 C 3
Uatumá 85 G 4
Uauá 87 J 2
Uaupés 84 E 3
Uaupés 84 E 4
Uaxactún 78 D 4
Ubá 87 H 5
Ubagan 25 N 5
Ubā'ila (Iraq) 22 C 2
Ubaitaba 87 J 3
Ubangi 64 B 4
'Ubayyid, Wādī al (Iraq) 22 CD 2
Ube 39 K 4
Ubeda 18 C 4
Uberaba 87 G 4
Uberaba, Laguna 86 E 4
Uberlândia 87 G 4
Ubiaja 63 F 4
Ubinskoye, Ozero 25 Q 4
Ubiyenka 37 W 2
Ubolratna Dam 41 H 4
Ubombo 67 E 5
Ubon Ratchathani 41 HJ 4
Ubort' 17 J 5
Ubundi 64 D 5
Ucayali 84 D 5
Uch 35 J 5
Uch Kuduk 35 G 2
Uchaly 25 L 5
Uchami 36 F 3
Uchami 36 G 3
Uch-Aral 25 Q 6
Uchiura-wan 39 M 2
Uchkulan 21 F 2
Uchur 37 O 4
Učka 19 F 3
Uckfield 7 E 2
Uda 37 O 5
Udachnaya 36 K 2
Udaipur 40 B 3
Udamalpet 40 C 5
Udanna 37 Q 2
Udaquilla 89 E 6
Udayagiri 40 C 5
Udbina 19 G 3
Uddevalla 17 F 4
Uddjaur 16 G 2
Udgir 40 C 4
Udhampur 35 K 4
Udialla 48 C 2
Udine 19 F 2
Udipi 40 B 5
Udokan, Khrebet 36 L 4
Udon Thani 41 H 4
Udskaya Guba 37 P 5
Udskoye 37 O 5
Udyl', Ozero 37 P 5
Udzha 36 L 1
Uebi Scebeli → Webi Shābelle
   65 G 4
Uebonti 43 F 4
Ueda 39 L 3
Uele 64 C 4
Uelen 72 CD 2
Uel'kal' 72 AB 2
Uelzen 15 F 4
Uengan, Mys 25 N 1
Uere 64 D 4
Ufa 24 L 4
Ufa 24 L 5
Ugab 66 A 4
Ugagli 37 N 5
Ugalla 64 E 6
Ugalla 64 E 6
Ugalla River Game Reserve 64 E 6
Uganda 64 E 4
Ugarit (Syria) 22 B 2
Ugashik 72 F 4
Ughelli 63 F 4
Uglegorsk 37 Q 6
Uglekamensk 39 K 2
Uglich 24 G 4

Uglovoya 37 NO 5
Ugol'naya 37 X 3
Ugoyan 37 N 4
Ugulan 37 T 3
Ugumun 36 L 2
Ugun 37 N 4
Ugut 25 O 3
Uherské Hradiště 15 G 5
Uig 2 A 3
Uíge 66 B 1
Uil 34 E 1
Uilpata 21 F 2
Uiñaimarca, Lago 86 C 4
Uinta Mountains 76 DE 3
Uis Mine 66 AB 4
Uitenhage 66 D 6
Ujae 52 C 2
Ujarrás 78 F 6
Ujelang 52 B 2
Ujiji 64 D 6
Ujjain 40 C 3
Ujung 43 F 5
Ujung Pandang 43 E 4–5
Ujunglamuru 43 F 4
Uk 36 G 4
Uka 37 U 4
Ukara 64 E 5
Ukelayat 37 W 3
Ukerewe 64 E 5
Ukhaydir (Iraq) 22 D 2
Ukholovo 24 H 5
Ukhta 24 K 3
Ukiah (CA, U.S.A.) 76 B 4
Ukiah (OR, U.S.A.) 76 C 2
Ukmergé 17 HJ 4
Ukraina 24 FG 6
Ukrainka 25 P 4
Uktym 24 J 3
Uku 66 A 2
Ukuma 66 B 2
Ukwaa 64 E 3
Ula 20 C 3
Ulaanbaatar 36 J 6
Ulaangom 36 F 6
Ulaanhus 36 E 6
Ulaga 37 O 2
Ulakhan Botuobuya 36 K 3
Ulakhan-Cistay, Khrebet 37 QR 2–3
Ulakhan-Kyugel' 36 KL 3
Ulakhan-Sis, Kryazh 37 S 1–2
Ulakhe 39 K 2
Ulamba 64 C 6
Ulan 38 C 3
Ulan Bator 36 J 6
Ulan Ul Hu 38 B 4
Ulanbel 35 J 2
Ulan-Burgasy, Khrebet 36 J 5
Ulan-Khol 21 G 1
Ulansuhai Nur 38 E 2
Ulan-Ude 36 J 5
Ularunda 49 H 4
Ulaş 21 E 3
Ulastay 35 M 2
Ulawa 51 H 3
Ul'ba 25 Q 5
Ul'beya 37 Q 3
Ulbeya 37 Q 4
Ulbster 2 C 2
Ulchin 39 J 3
Ulcinj 20 A 2
Ule Träsk 16 J 3
Uleåborg 16 HJ 3
Ulefoss 17 E 4
Ulety 36 K 5
Ulhasnagar 40 B 4
Uliastay 36 G 6
Uliga 52 C 2
Ulindi 64 D 5
Ullapool 2 B 3
Ullared 17 F 4
Ullatti 16 H 2
Ulldecona 18 D 3
Ullsfjorden 16 G 2
Ullswater 5 D 2
Ullŭng-do 39 K 3
Ulm 15 E 5
Ulmeni 20 C 1
Ulongué 67 E 2
Ulovo 37 S 1
Ulricehamn 17 F 4
Ulsan 39 J 3
Ulsta 2 D 1
Ulsteinvik 16 E 3
Ultevis 16 G 2
Ulu 43 G 3
Ulu 60 E 6
Ulubat Gölü 20 C 2
Uludağ 20 C 2–3
Ulugqat 35 J 3
Ulukışla 21 D 3
Ulunga 37 P 6
Ulungur He 35 M 1
Ulungur Hu 35 M 1
Ulunkhan 36 K 5

Uluru (Ayers Rock - Mount Olga) National Park 48 E 4
Ulus 21 D 2
Ulutau, Gory 35 H 1
Ulva 3 A 3
Ulverston 5 D 2
Ulvön 16 G 3
Ul'ya 37 Q 4
Ulya 37 Q 4
Ul'yankovo 24 J 4
Ul'yanovsk 24 J 5
Ul'yanovskoye 25 O 5
Uma 36 M 5
Uman' 20 D 1
Úmanak 90
Úmánaq 75 T 3
Umari 43 J 4
Umarkot 35 HJ 5
Umba 16 K 2
Umboi 50 E 3
Umbozero, Ozero 16 KL 2
Umbria 19 F 3
Umeå 16 H 3
Umeälven 16 G 3
Umiat 72 G 2
Umm al 'Abīd 59 J 3
Umm al Arānib 59 H 3
'Umm al Armad (Qatar) 23 F 4
Umm al Birak (Saudi Arabia) 22 C 5
Umm al Hayt, Wādī 61 J 5
Umm al Jamājim (Saudi Arabia) 23 D 4
Umm al Qaywayn (United Arab Emirates) 23 G 4
'Umm al Sheif (United Arab Emirates) 23 F 4
Umm as Samīm 61 K 4
'Umm at Tūz (Iraq) 22 D 2
Umm az Zumūl 61 K 4
Umm az Zumūl (United Arab Emirates) 23 G 5
Umm Bāb (Qatar) 23 F 4
Umm Badr 60 D 6
Umm Bel 60 D 6
Umm Buru 60 C 5
Umm Dafok 60 C 6
Umm Dhibbān 60 DE 6
Umm Durmān 60 E 5
Umm Hagar 65 F 2
Umm Haraz 60 C 6
Umm Inderaba 60 E 5
Umm Kaddādah 60 D 6
Umm Lahai 60 D 5
Umm Lajj (Saudi Arabia) 22 B 4
'Umm Qam'ul (United Arab Emirates) 23 G 4
Umm Qawzayn 60 D 6
Umm Rumaylah 60 E 5
Umm Ruwābah 60 E 6
'Umm Saīd (Qatar) 23 F 4
Umm Sa'id → Musay'id 61 J 4
Umm Sayyālah 60 E 6
Umm Urūmah (Saudi Arabia) 22 B 4
Umma (Iraq) 23 D 3
Umnak 72 D 5
Umnyn Syverma, Khrebet 36 GH 2
Umpilua 67 F 2
Umpulo 66 B 2
Umraniye 20 D 3
Ums 66 B 4
Umtali → Mutare 67 E 3
Umtata 66 D 6
Umuarama 87 F 5
Umvuma 67 E 3
Una 87 J 4
Una (Yugoslavia) 19 G 2
Unadilla 77 K 5
Unaí 87 G 4
Unai Pass 35 H 4
Unalakleet 72 H 3
Unalaska 72 D 5
Unapoo 2 B 2
Unari 16 J 2
'Unayzah (Jordan) 22 B 3
'Unayzah (Saudi Arabia) 22 D 4
Underberg 66 D 5
Undva Neem 17 H 4
Undyulyung 37 N 2
Unecha 24 F 5
Uneiuxi 84 E 4
Ung, Jabal al 19 E 4
Unga 72 E 4
Ungava Bay 75 O 4
Ungava, Peninsule d' 75 MN 4
Ungwatiri 60 F 5
Uniabmund 66 A 4
União (Acre, Brazil) 84 D 5
União (Maranhão, Brazil) 87 H 1
União do Vitória 88 F 4
União dos Palmares 87 J 2
Unije 19 F 3
Unimak 72 E 5
Unimak Pass 72 E 5

Unini 85 F 4
Unión 89 C 6
Union City 77 J 4
Union of Soviet Socialist Republics 24–37
Uniondale 66 C 6
United Arab Emirates 23 FG 5
United Kingdom 14 CD 3–4
United States 76–77
Unitsa 24 FG 3
Unity 73 Q 5
Universales, Montes 18 C 3
University City 77 H 4
Unkyur 37 O 2
'Unnab, Wādi al (Jordan) 22 B 3
Unnao 40 D 2
Unst 2 D 1
Unuli Horog 38 B 3
Ünye 21 E 2
Unzba 24 H 4
Unzha 24 H 4
Uoyan 36 K 4
Upanu 37 X 3
Upar Ghat 40 D 3
Upata 85 F 2
Upavon 7 D 2
Upemba, Lac 64 D 6
Upemba National Park 64 D 6
Upernavik 90
Upi 43 F 2
Upington 66 C 5
Upolu 52 D 3
Upper Arlington 77 K 3
Upper Broughton 7 D 1
Upper Klamath Lake 76 B 3
Upper Lough Erne 4 B 2
Upper Red Lake 77 H 2
Upper Tean 7 D 1
Upperlands 4 B 2
Uppingham 7 D 1
Uppland 17 G 3
Uppsala 17 G 4
Upshi 35 K 4
Upwey 6 C 2
'Uqlat as Ṣuqūr (Saudi Arabia) 22 C 4
Ur 61 H 2
Ur Suq ash Shuyūkh (Iraq) 23 DE 3
Ura Guba 16 K 2
Uracoa 85 F 2
Urad Qianqi 38 E 2
Urad Zhonghou Lianheqi 38 E 2
Urak 37 Q 4
Ural 34 E 1
Ural Mountains 25 LM 2–4
Uralovka 37 N 5
Ural'sk 24 K 5
Urambo 64 E 6
Urandangie 49 F 3
Urandi 87 H 3
Urangan 49 J 4
Uranium City 73 Q 4
Uraricoera 85 F 3
Uraricoera 85 F 3
Ura-Tyube 35 H 3
'Uray'irah (Saudi Arabia) 23 E 4
'Urayq, Nafūd al 61 G 3–4
Urbandale 77 H 3
Urbano Santos 87 H 1
Urbino 19 F 3
Urco 84 D 4
Urcos 86 B 3
Urdzhar 25 Q 6
Uré 84 C 2
Ure, River 5 E 2
Ureki 21 F 2
Uren 24 J 4
Urengoy 25 P 2
Urewera National Park 51 R 8
Urez 25 P 4
'Urf, Jabal al (Egypt) 22 A 4
Urfa 21 E 3
Urfa (Turkey) 22 C 1
Urfa Platosu 21 E 3
Urgamal 36 F 6
Urgel, Llano de 18 D 3
Urgench 34 FG 2
Ürgüp 21 D 3
Urgut 35 H 3
Urho 35 M 1
Ūrī 59 J 4
Uribe 84 D 3
Uribia 84 D 1
Urimán 85 F 2
Uritskoye 25 N 5
Uritskoye 37 M 3
Urjala 16 H 3
Urkan 37 N 5
Urla 20 C 3
Urlu Dağ 21 D 2
Urluk 36 J 5
Urmannyy 25 N 3
Urmi 37 O 5
Urmia, Lake → Daryācheh-ye Orūmīyeh 34 D 3

Urninskoye Boloto 25 O 4
Uromi 63 F 4
Uroševac 20 B 2
Urrao 84 C 2
Urshult 17 FG 4
Ursus 15 H 4
Uruaçu 87 G 3
Uruana 87 FG 4
Uruapan 78 B 4
Urubamba 86 B 3
Urubamba 86 B 3
Urubu 85 G 4
Urubupunga Dam 87 F 5
Urubuquara, Serra 85 H 4
Urucará 85 G 4
Urucu 85 F 4
Uruçuca 87 J 3
Uruçuí 87 H 2
Uruçui Prêto 87 GH 2
Uruçui, Serra do 87 H 2
Urucuia 87 G 4
Urucurituba 85 G 4
Uruguaiana 88 E 4
Uruguay 88 E 5
Uruguay 88 E 5
Uruk (Iraq) 23 D 3
Urul'ga 36 KL 5
Urumchi 35 M 2
Ürümqi 35 M 2
Urup 21 F 2
Urup, Ostrov 37 S 6
'Uruq ar Rumaylah 61 H 4
'Urūq as Subay' 61 G 4
Urusha 37 M 5
Urutágua 87 G 3
Uruwira 64 E 6
Uruzgan 35 H 4
Uryung-Khaya 36 KL 1
Uryupinsk 24 H 5
Urzhum 24 J 4
Urziceni 20 C 2
Usa 25 M 2
Uşak 20 C 3
Usakos 66 B 4
Usal'gin 37 P 5
Usambara Mountains 65 F 5
Usborne, Mount 89 E 9
Ušče 20 B 2
Usedom 15 F 4
'Usfān 61 F 4
'Ushayrah (Saudi Arabia) 23 DE 4
Ushirombo 64 E 5
Ushkan'iy, Gory 37 X 2
Ushki 37 U 4
Ushki, Zaliv 37 R 4
Ush-Tobe 25 P 6
Ushuaia 89 C 9
Ushumun 37 N 5
Ushurakchan, Gory 37 U 2
Usina 85 H 5
Usinge 64 E 6
Usk 6 C 2
Uska 40 D 2
Üsküdar 20 C 2
Usman 24 GH 5
Usmas ezers 17 H 4
Usoke 64 E 6
Usol'ye 24 L 4
Usol'ye-Sibirskoye 36 H 5
Uspenka 25 P 5
Uspenskiy 25 O 6
Uspenskoye 21 F 2
U.S.S.R. 21 F 1
Ussuri 37 O 4
Ussuriysk 39 K 2
Ust Usa 24 J 5
Ust'-Allakh 37 O 3
Ust'-Amginskoye 37 O 3
Ust'-Barguzin 36 JK 5
Ust'-Bokhapcha 37 S 3
Ust'-Bol'sheretsk 37 ST 5
Ust'-Charky 37 P 2
Ust'-Chayka 36 J 3
Ust'-Chernaya 24 K 3
Ust'-Chona 36 K 3
Ust'-Dzhegutinskaya 21 F 2
Uster 19 E 2
Usti 15 F 4
Ustica 19 F 4
Ust'-Ilimpeya 36 HJ 3
Ust'-Ilimsk 36 H 4
Ust'-Ilimskiy Vodokhranilishche 36 H 4
Ustinov 24 K 4
Ustinovka 21 D 1
Ust'-Ishim 25 O 4
Ustka 15 G 4
Ust-Kada 36 H 5
Ust'-Kamchatsk 37 U 4
Ust'-Kamenogorsk 25 Q 6
Ust'-Kamo 36 G 3
Ust'-Kan 36 F 4
Ust'-Karabula 36 G 4
Ust'-Karenga 36 L 5
Ust'-Karsk 36 L 5
Ust'-Katav 25 L 5

Ust'-Khayryuzovo 37 T 4
Ust'-Koksa 25 R 5
Ust'-Kolik'yegan 25 P 3
Ust'-Kulom 24 K 3
Ust'-Kut 36 J 4
Ust'-Kuyga 37 P 2
Ust-Labinsk 21 EF 1
Ust'-Luga 17 J 4
Ust'-Lyzha 24 L 2
Ust'-Maya 37 O 3
Ust'-Mayn 37 W 3
Ust'-Mil' 37 O 4
Ust'-Nem 24 K 3
Ust'-Nera 37 Q 3
Ust'-Olenёk 36 L 1
Ust'-Omchug 37 R 3
Ust'-Ordynskiy 36 HJ 5
Ust'-Ozernoye 25 R 4
Ust'-Paden'ga 24 H 3
Ust'-Penzhino 37 V 3
Ust'-Pit 36 F 4
Ust'-Port 25 Q 2
Ust'-Reka 24 J 3
Ustrem 25 N 3
Ust'-Shchugor 24 L 3
Ust'-Sopochnoye 37 T 4
Ust'-Sugoy 37 S 3
Ust'-Tatta 37 O 3
Ust'-Tigil 37 T 4
Ust'-Tsil'ma 24 K 2
Ust'-Tym 25 Q 3
Ust'-Ulagan 25 R 5
Ust'-Umal'ta 37 O 5
Ust'-Un'ya 37 N 5
Ust'-Ura 24 H 3
Ust'-Urgal 37 O 5
Ust'Urov 36 M 5
Ust'-Us 36 F 5
Ust'-Usa 24 L 2
Ust'-Uyskoye 25 M 5
Ustuyurt, Plato 34 F 2
Ust'-Vaga 24 H 3
Ust'-Voyampolka 37 T 4
Ust'-Vym' 24 K 3
Ust'-Vyyskaya 24 J 3
Ust'-Yudoma 37 P 4
Ust'-Yuribey 25 N 2
Usu 35 L 2
Usulután 78 E 5
Usumacinta 78 D 4
Utah 76 D 4
Utah Lake 76 D 3
Utajärvi 16 J 3
Utara, Pulau 42 B 4
Utata 36 H 5
Utena 17 J 4
Utěs 25 P 5
Utesiki 37 W 2
Utete 65 F 6
Uthai Thani 41 H 4
Uthal 35 H 5
Uthumphon Phisai 41 H 5
Utiariti 86 E 3
Utica 77 M 3
Utiel 18 C 4
Utique 19 F 4
Utirik 52 C 2
Utkholok 37 T 4
Utlängan 17 G 4
Utopia 48 E 3
Utorgosh 17 K 4
Utrecht 14 E 4
Utrera 18 B 4
Utsjoki 16 J 2
Utsunomiya 39 L 3
Utta 21 G 1
Uttar Pradesh 40 D 2
Uttaradit 41 H 4
Uttoxeter 7 D 1
Uttyakh 37 O 2
Utukok 72 E 2
Utulik 36 H 5
Utupua 51 J 4
Uulbayan 38 F 1
Uuldza 36 K 6
Uuldza Gol 36 K 6
Uusikaarlepyy 16 H 3
Uusikaupunki 17 H 3
Uusimaa 17 H 3
Uva 24 K 4
Uvá (Goiás, Brazil) 87 F 4
Uvalde 76 G 6
Uvarovo 24 H 5
Uvdal 17 E 3
Uvéa 52 D 3
Uvinza 64 E 6
Uvira 64 E 5
Uvs Nuur 36 F 5
Uwajima 39 K 4
Uwayl 64 D 3
'Uwaynāt, Jabal al 60 D 4
'Uwaynāt, Tall (Iraq) 22 D 1
'Uwayrid, Harrat al 60 F 3
Uxin Qi 38 E 3
Uxituba 85 G 4
Uxmal 78 E 3

Uy 25 M 5
Uyaly 35 G 2
Uyandi 37 Q 2
Uyandina 37 QR 2
Uyar 36 F 4
Uyēdey 37 P 1
Uyega 37 Q 3
Uyo 63 F 4
Üyönch 36 F 6
Uyuk 35 J 2
Uyuni 86 C 5
Uyuni, Salar de 86 C 5
Uzbekistan 35 GH 2
Uzbel Shankou 35 J 3
Uzen 34 E 2
Uzerche 18 D 2
Uzh 17 J 5
Uzhgorod 20 B 1
Uzhur 25 R 4
Üzī 59 J 4
Uzlovaya 24 G 5
Üzü 59 J 4
Uzungwa 65 F 6
Uzunköprü 20 C 2
Uzynkair 35 G 2

V

Vääksy 16 J 3
Vaal 66 C 5
Vaal Dam 66 D 5
Vaala 16 J 3
Vaalwater 66 D 4
Vaasa [Vasa] 16 H 3
Vác 20 A 1
Vacaria 88 F 4
Vache, Île à 79 H 4
Vadodara 40 B 3
Vadsö 16 J 1
Vadstena 17 FG 4
Vaduz 19 E 2
Vaga 24 H 3
Vågåmo 16 E 3
Vágar 14 A 1
Vågåvatn 16 E 3
Vaggeryd 17 F 4
Vågsöy 16 D 3
Váh 15 G 5
Vahitahi 53 F 4
Vaigai 40 C 6
Vailjapur 40 B 4
Vainikkala 16 J 3
Vairaatea 53 F 4
Vaitupu 52 C 3
Vakarevo 37 W 3
Vakh 25 P 3
Vaknavolok 16 JK 3
Vaku 63 G 7
Val de Loire 18 D 2
Valaam 16 K 3
Valaam, Ostrov 16 K 3
Valachia 20 BC 2
Valasské Meziříčí 15 G 5
Valcheta 89 C 7
Valdagno 19 F 2
Valday 24 F 4
Valdayskaya Vozvyshennost'
  24 F 4
Valdecañas, Embalse de 18 B 4
Valdemarsvik 17 G 4
Valdepeñas 18 C 4
Valderaduey 18 BC 3
Valdés, Península 89 D 7
Valdez 72 H 3
Val-d'Isère 19 E 2
Valdivia (Chile) 89 B 6
Valdivia (Colombia) 84 C 2
Val-d'Or 75 M 6
Valdosta 77 K 5
Vale 21 F 2
Vale of Evesham 7 CD 1
Valea lui Mihai 20 B 1
Valença 87 J 3
Valença do Piauí 87 H 2
Valence 19 DE 3
Valence-d'Apen 18 D 3
Valencia 84 E 1–2
Valencia (Spain) 18 CD 4
Valencia de Alcántara 18 B 4
Valencia, Golfo de 18 D 4
Valenciennes 18 D 1
Vălenii de Munte 20 C 1
Valentin 39 K 2
Valentine 76 F 3
Valera 84 D 2
Valga 17 J 4
Valjevo 20 B 2
Valkeakoski 16 H 3
Vall de Uxó 18 C 4
Valladolid (Mexico) 78 E 3
Valladolid (Spain) 18 C 3
Valle de la Pascua 84 E 2
Valle de Topia 78 A 2
Valle de Zaragoza 76 E 6

Valle Edén 88 E 5
Valle Grande 86 D 4
Valle Hermoso 78 C 2
Valle Longitudinal 89 B 6
Valle Salado 78 B 3
Valledupar 84 D 1
Valletta 19 F 4
Valley City 76 G 2
Valley Station 77 J 4
Valleyfield 75 N 6
Valleyview 73 O 4
Vallgrund 16 H 3
Vallorbe 19 E 2
Valls 18 D 3
Valmiera 17 J 4
Valparaíso (Chile) 88 B 5
Valparaíso (Mexico) 78 B 3
Valpovo 19 G 2
Vals, Tanjung 43 J 5
Valsjöbyn 16 F 3
Valtimo 16 J 3
Valuyevka 21 F 1
Valuyki 24 G 5
Vamizi, Ilha 67 G 2
Vammala 16 H 3
Van 21 F 3
Van Blommestein Reservoir
  85 G 3
Van Buren 77 H 4
Van Canh 41 J 5
Van Diemen, Cape 48 D 1
Van Diemen Gulf 48 E 1
Van Gölü 21 F 3
Van Horn 76 F 5
Van Ninh 41 J 5
van Rees, Pegunungan 43 J 4
Van Wert 77 K 3
Vanajavesi 16 H 3
Vanak (Iran) 23 F 3
Vanak [flod] (Iran) 23 F 3
Vanavana 53 F 4
Vanavara 36 H 3
Vancouver 73 N 6
Vancouver Island 73 M 6
Vanda 91
Vanderbijlpark 66 D 5
Vanderhoof 73 N 5
Vanderlin Island 49 F 2
Vanduzi 67 E 3
Vänern 17 F 4
Vänersborg 17 F 4
Väneshän (Iran) 23 F 2
Vang 16 E 3
Vang Vieng 41 H 4
Vangaindrano 67 H 4
Vangou 39 K 2
Vangunu 51 G 3
Vanikoro Islands 51 J 4
Vanillas 86 B 5
Vanimo 50 D 2
Vanino 37 P 6
Vankarem 72 B 2
Vanna 16 G 1
Vännäs 16 G 3
Vannes 18 C 2
Vanoua Lava 51 J 4
Vanrhynsdorp 66 B 6
Vansbro 17 F 3
Vansittart 73 V 2
Vanua Levu 52 C 4
Vanuatu 51 J 5
Vanwyksvlei 66 C 6
Vanzevat 25 N 3
Vanzhil'kynak 25 QR 3
Vapnyarka 20 C 1
Var 19 E 3
Varāmīn (Iran) 23 F 2
Varandey 24 L 2
Varangerfjorden 16 K 1–2
Varangerhalvöya 16 JK 1
Varano, Lago di 19 G 3
Varāvī (Iran) 23 F 3
Varaždin 19 G 2
Varberg 17 F 4
Varcheh (Iran) 23 F 2
Vardar 20 B 2
Varde 17 E 4
Vardö 16 K 1
Vardofjällen 16 FG 2
Värend 17 FG 4
Varenikovskaya 21 E 1
Varese 17 E 4
Vårgårda 17 F 4
Vargas 88 C 5
Vargashi 25 N 4
Varginha 87 GH 5
Varkaus 16 J 3
Värmland 17 F 4
Varna (Bulgaria) 20 C 2
Varna (U.S.S.R.) 25 M 5
Värnamo 17 F 4
Varnenski zaliv 20 C 2

Varnya 25 O 2
Varsinais Suomi 17 H 3
Värska 17 J 4
Varto 21 F 3
Värtsilä 16 K 3
Var'yegan 25 P 3
Varzaneh (Iran) 23 F 2
Várzea Grande 86 E 4
Varzi 19 E 3
Varzino 24 G 2
Varzuga 16 L 2
Varzy 18 D 2
Vasa 16 G 3
Vasai 40 B 4
Vascos, Montes 18 C 3
Vashnel 25 N 3
Vasil'kov 24 F 5
Vasilyevka 21 E 1
Vasiss 25 O 4
Vaslui 20 C 1
Väsman 17 F 3
Vassdalsegga 17 E 4
Vasta 34 D 1
Vastenjaure 16 G 2
Västerås 17 G 4
Västerbotten 16 GH 3
Västerdalälven 17 F 3
Västergötland 17 F 4
Västervik 17 G 4
Vasto 19 F 3
Västra Granberget 16 H 2
Vasyugan 25 P 4
Vatan 18 D 2
Vaternish 2 A 3
Vatersay 3 A 3
Vatican State 19 F 3
Vaticano, Capo 19 G 4
Vaticano, Città Del 19 F 3
Vatnajökull 16 B 3
Vatneyri 16 A 2
Vatoa 52 D 4
Vatomandry 67 H 3
Vatra Dornei 20 C 1
Vättern 17 F 4
Vatyna 37 W 3
Vaudémont, Butte de 19 E 2
Vaughn 76 E 5
Vaupés 84 D 3
Vaux du Loir 18 D 2
Vava'u Group 52 D 4
Vavoua 62 C 4
Vavuniya 40 D 6
Vawkavysk 17 J 5
Vaxholm 17 G 4
Växjö 17 FG 4
Vayalpad 40 C 5
Vayegi 37 W 3
Vaygach 25 L 1
Vaygach, Ostrov 25 L 1
Vayvida 36 F 3
Vaza Barris 87 J 2–3
Vazhgort 24 J 3
Veadeiros 87 G 3
Veal Renh 41 H 5
Vecht 14 E 4
Vedeno 21 G 2
Vedia 88 D 5
Vefsna 16 F 2
Vega 16 F 2
Vegorritis, Limni 20 B 2
Vegreville 73 P 5
Veijo, Cerro 84 C 4
Veinticinco del Mayo 89 C 6
Veiros 85 H 4
Vejen 17 E 4
Vejer 17 E 4
Vejle 17 E 4
Velasco, Sierra 88 C 4
Velbăždski prohod 20 B 2
Velenje 19 G 2
Velestínon 20 B 3
Velež 19 G 3
Vélez Rubio 18 C 4
Vélez-Málaga 18 C 4
Velhas 87 H 4
Veli Lošinj 19 F 3
Velichayevskoye 21 G 2
Velika Plana 20 B 2
Velikaya 17 J 4
Velikaya 37 X 3
Velikaya Kema 39 L 1
Veliki Kanal 20 A 1
Velikiy Ustyug 24 J 3
Velikiye Luki 17 K 4
Veliko Tŭrnovo 20 C 2
Velikonda Range 40 C 4–5
Vélingara 62 B 3
Velingrad 20 B 2
Vella Lavella 51 G 3
Velletri 19 F 3
Vellore 40 C 5
Velsk 24 H 3
Vel't 24 K 2
Vemdalen 16 F 3
Vemor'ye 37 Q 6
Vena Park 49 G 2
Venado Tuerto 88 D 5

Venafro 19 F 3
Venda 67 E 4
Venda Nova 87 H 4
Vendas Novas 18 B 4
Vendôme 18 D 2
Vendrell 18 D 3
Vendsyssel 17 EF 4
Veneta, Laguna 19 F 2
Venetie 72 H 2
Venezia 19 F 2
Venezuela 84–85 EF 2
Venezuela, Golfo de 84 D 1
Vengerovo 25 P 4
Vengurla 40 B 4
Veniaminof, Mount 72 EF 4
Venice 19 F 2
Vénissieux 19 DE 2
Venjan 17 F 3
Venkatapuram 40 CD 4
Vennesla 17 E 4
Venta 17 H 4
Venta de Baños 18 C 3
Ventersdorp 66 D 5
Ventimiglia 19 E 3
Ventor 7 D 2
Ventotene 19 F 3
Ventselevo 37 O 6
Ventspils 17 H 4
Ventuari 84 E 3
Ventura 76 C 5
Venus Bay 49 H 6
Vera (Argentina) 88 D 4
Vera (Spain) 18 C 4
Veracruz (Mexico) 78 C 4
Veraval 40 B 3
Verbania 19 E 2
Vercelli 19 E 2
Vercors 19 E 2–3
Verdalsöra 16 F 3
Verde 76 D 5
Verde, Cape (Senegal) 58 B 6
Verde, Costa 18 B 3
Verdun 19 E 2
Vereeniging 66 D 5
Vereshchagino 24 K 4
Verga, Cap 62 B 3
Vergara 88 F 5
Verhnedvinsk 17 J 4
Verhnevilyuyskt 36 M 3
Verkhn'aya Salda 25 M 4
Verkhne Dneprovsk 21 D 1
Verkhnearshinskiy 25 L 5
Verkhne-Avzyan 25 L 5
Verkhnebakanskiy 21 E 2
Verkhneimbatskoye 25 RS 3
Verkhne-Ozernaya 37 U 4
Verkhnetulomskiy 16 K 2
Verkhnetulomskoye
  Vodokhranilishche 16 K 2
Verkhneural'sk 25 L 5
Verkhneye Kuyto, Ozero 16 K 3
Verkhneye Nil'dno 25 M 3
Verkhneye Skoblino 25 R 4
Verkhniy Ufaley 25 M 4
Verkhnyaya Amga 37 N 4
Verkhnyaya Angara 36 K 4
Verkhnyaya Baikka 25 Q 2
Verkhnyaya Chunku 36 G 3
Verkhnyaya Pakhacha 37 V 3
Verkhnyaya Taymyra 36 G 1
Verkhnyaya Toyma 24 J 3
Verkhnyaya Vol'dzha 25 P 4
Verkholensk 36 J 5
Verkhoyansk 37 O 2
Verkhoyansk Range 37 O 3
Verkhoyanskiy Khrebet 37 N 2–3
Verme Falls 65 G 3
Vermilion Bay 74 J 5
Vermilion 20 B 3
Vermont 77 M 3
Vernal 76 E 3
Vernon (Canada) 73 O 5
Vernon (France) 18 D 2
Vernon (TX, U.S.A.) 76 G 5
Vernon, Mount (Western
  Australia) 48 B 3
Vero Beach 77 KL 6
Verona 19 F 2
Vérroia 20 B 2
Versailles 18 D 2
Vershina 25 M 3
Vershino-Darasunskiy 36 L 5
Vershino-Shakhtaminskiye 36 L 5
Vert, Cap 62 A 3
Vertiskos Óros 20 B 2
Verviers 14 E 4
Verwood 7 D 2
Veselovskoye Vodokhranilishche
  21 F 1
Veseloye 21 DE 1
Veseloye 21 E 1
Veselyy 21 F 1

Veshenskaya 24 H 6
Vesoul 19 E 2
Vest-Agder 17 E 4
Vestbygd 17 E 4
Vesterålen 16 FG 2
Vesterö Havn 17 F 4
Vestfirðir 16 A 2
Vestfjorden 16 FG 2
Vestmannaeyjar 16 A 3
Vestre Jakobselv 16 J 1
Vestvågöy 16 F 2
Vesuvio 19 F 3
Veszprém 20 A 1
Vet 66 D 5
Vétaounde 51 J 4
Vetlanda 17 G 4
Vetluga 24 J 4
Vetluzhskiy 24 J 4
Vetrenyy 37 R 3
Vettore 19 F 3
Vetvey 37 V 3
Veurne 14 D 4
Vevey 19 E 2
Vežhen 20 B 2
Vezh'yudor 24 K 3
Vezirköprü 21 E 2
Viacha 86 C 4
Viamonte 88 D 5
Viamonte 89 C 9
Viana 85 E 3
Viana (Angola) 66 A 1
Viana do Castelo 18 B 3
Viang Chan 41 H 4
Viar 18 B 4
Viareggio 19 EF 3
Vibo Valentia 19 G 4
Viborg 17 E 4
Vicari 19 F 4
Vicecommodoro Marambio 91
Vicenza 19 F 2
Vichada 84 E 3
Vichy 18 D 2
Vicksburg 77 H 5
Victor Harbour 49 F 6
Victoria (Argentina) 88 DE 5
Victoria (Australia) 49 G 6
Victoria (Canada) 73 N 6
Victoria (Chile) 89 B 6
Victoria (Guinea) 62 B 3
Victoria (Hong Kong) 38 F 6
Victoria (Malaysia) 42 E 2
Victoria (Malta) 19 F 4
Victoria (Seychelles) 65 K 5
Victoria (TX, U.S.A.) 77 G 6
Victoria de Durango 78 B 3
Victoria de las Tunas 79 G 3
Victoria Falls 66 D 3
Victoria Falls 66 D 3
Victoria Island 73 PQ 1
Victoria, Lake 64 E 5
Victoria Land 91
Victoria, Mount (Burma) 41 F 3
Victoria, Mount (Papua New
  Guinea) 50 E 3
Victoria Nile 64 E 4
Victoria River 48 E 2
Victoria River Downs 48 E 2
Victoria Strait 73 R 2
Victoria West 66 C 6
Victoriaville 75 N 6
Victorica 89 CD 6
Victorino de la Plaza 89 D 6
Victorville 76 C 5
Victory Downs 48 E 4
Vicuña Mackenna 88 D 5
Vidin 20 B 2
Vidisha 40 C 3
Vidra 20 C 2
Vidsel 16 H 2
Viduša 16 F 3
Vidzemes Augstiene 17 J 4
Vidzy 17 J 4
Viedma 89 B 8
Viedma 89 D 7
Viedma, Lago 89 B 8
Viejo, Rio 78 E 5
Vieng Pou Kha 41 H 3
Vienna (Austria) 19 G 2
Vienna (W.V., U.S.A.) 77 K 4
Vienne 18 D 2
Vienne 19 DE 2
Vientiane 41 H 4
Vientos, Paso de los 79 H 3–4
Vieques, Isla de 79 JK 4
Vierwaldstätter See 19 E 2
Vierzon 18 D 2
Viesca 78 B 2
Vieste 19 G 3
Viet Tri 41 J 3
Vietas 16 G 2
Vietnam 41 J 5
Vieux-Fort 75 Q 5
Vigan 43 J 1
Vigevano 19 E 2
Vigia 85 J 4
Vignola 19 F 3

Vigo 18 B 3
Vigo, Ría de 18 B 3
Vihanti 16 H 3
Vihoflat 15 H 5
Viiala 16 H 3
Viitasaari 16 J 3
Vijayadurg 40 B 4
Vijayawada 40 CD 4
Vijosa 20 A 2
Vik 16 B 3
Vikersund 17 E 4
Vikhorevka 36 H 4
Viking 73 P 5
Vikna 16 F 3
Vila 51 J 5
Vila Bittencourt 84 E 4
Vila Conceição 85 F 3
Vila do Porto 58 A 1
Vila Franca de Xira 18 B 4
Vila Gamito 67 E 2
Vila Nova de Gaia 18 B 3
Vila Pouca de Aquiar 18 B 3
Vila Real 18 B 3
Vila Velha (Amapá, Brazil) 85 H 3
Vila Velha (Espírito Santo, Brazil)
  87 HJ 5
Vila Velha (Portugal) 18 B 4
Vilaine 18 C 2
Viļāni 17 J 4
Vilankulo 67 F 4
Vilcabamba 86 B 3
Vilcabamba, Cordillera 86 B 3
Vıldız Dağları 20 C 2
Vileyka 17 J 5
Vilhelmina 16 G 3
Vilhena 86 D 3
Viliga-Kushka 37 T 3
Viliya 17 J 5
Viljandi 17 J 4
Vilkija 17 H 4
Vilkovo 20 C 1
Villa Abecia 86 C 5
Villa Ahumada 76 E 5
Villa Ángela 88 D 4
Villa Bella 86 C 3
Villa Colón 88 C 5
Villa Constitución 88 D 5
Villa Coronado 78 B 2
Villa de Cos 78 B 3
Villa de Guadalupe 78 B 3
Villa de Reyes 78 B 3
Villa del Rosario (Argentina)
  88 D 5
Villa del Rosario (Venezuela)
  84 D 1
Villa Dolores 88 C 5
Villa Federal 88 E 5
Villa Flores 78 D 4
Villa Frontera 78 B 2
Villa General Roca 88 C 5
Villa Guillermina 88 DE 4
Villa Hayes 86 E 5
Villa Hidalgo 78 B 2
Villa Huidobro 88 D 5
Villa Ingavi 86 D 5
Villa Iris 89 D 6
Villa María 88 D 5
Villa Martín (Bolivia) 86 C 5
Villa Matoque 88 D 4
Villa Mazán 88 C 4
Villa Minetti 88 D 4
Villa Montes 86 D 5
Villa Ocampo 78 AB 2
Villa Ocampo 88 DE 4
Villa Oliva 88 E 4
Villa Regina 89 C 6
Villa Rey 86 E 5
Villa S. Giovanni 19 G 4
Villa S. Giovanni 19 G 4
Villa Unión (Argentina) 88 C 4
Villa Union (Mexico) 78 A 3
Villa Valeria 88 CD 5
Villablino 18 B 3
Villacarrillo 18 C 4
Villacastin 18 C 3
Villach 19 F 2
Villacidro 19 E 4
Villafranca del Cid 18 C 3
Villafranca di Verona 19 F 2
Villagarcia de Arosa 18 B 3
Villaguay 88 E 5
Villahermosa 78 D 4
Villajoyosa 18 C 4
Villalba 18 B 3
Villaldama 78 B 2
Villalón de Campos 18 B 3
Villalonga 89 D 6
Villalpando 18 B 3
Villamartin (Spain) 18 B 4
Villanueva 78 B 3
Villanueva de Córdoba 18 BC 4
Villanueva de la Serena 18 B 4
Villanueva del Fresno 18 B 4
Villanueva y Geltrú 18 D 3
Villarreal de los Infantes 18 C 3–4

Villarrica (Chile) 89 B 6
Villarrica (Paraguay) 88 E 4
Villarrobledo 18 C 4
Villatoro, Puerto de 18 B 3
Villavicencio 84 D 3
Villaviciosa 18 B 3
Villazón 86 C 5
Villefranche 19 DE 2
Villena 18 C 4
Villeneuve-sur-Lot 18 D 3
Villmanstrand 16 J 3
Villupuram 40 C 5
Vil'mo 36 F 3
Vilnius 17 J 5
Vilppula 16 H 3
Vilsandi 17 H 4
Vilusi 20 A 2
Vilyuy 37 MN 3
Vilyuyskoye Plato 36 J 2
Vilyuyskoye Vodokhranilishche
  36 JK 3
Vilyuyskt 36 M 3
Vimmerby 17 G 4
Vina 63 G 4
Viña del Mar 88 B 5
Vinaroz 18 D 3
Vincennes 77 J 4
Vinces 84 C 4
Vinchina 88 C 4
Vindelälven 16 G 2
Vindeln 16 G 3
Vindhya Range 40 C 3
Vineland 77 M 4
Vingåker 17 G 4
Vinh 41 J 4
Vinh Giat 41 J 5
Vinh Linh 41 J 4
Vinh Loi 41 J 6
Vinh Long 41 J 5
Vinica (Yugoslavia) 19 G 2
Vinica (Yugoslavia) 20 B 2
Vinkovci 19 G 2
Vinnitsa 24 E 6
Vino, Tierra del 18 B 3
Vinson Massif 91
Vinstervatn 16 E 3
Vinstra 16 E 3
Vinstri 16 E 3
Viqueque 43 G 5
Virac 43 F 1
Viramgam 40 B 3
Virandozero 24 FG 3
Viranşehir 21 D 3
Viranşehir 21 EF 3
Viranşehir (Turkey) 22 C 1
Virarajendrapet 40 C 5
Virden 73 R 6
Vire 18 C 2
Virei 66 A 3
Virful Balota 20 B 1
Virful Bivolu 20 B 1
Virful Budacu 20 C 1
Virful Ciucasu 20 C 1
Virful Curcubăta 20 B 1
Virful Farcău 20 B 1
Virful Gogu 20 B 1
Virful Goru 20 C 1
Virful Gutii 20 B 1
Virful Hămaşu Mare 20 C 1
Virful Iezerul 20 B 1
Virful Moldoveanu 20 B 1
Virful Nemira 20 C 1
Virful Omu 20 C 1
Virful Peleaga 20 B 1
Virful Pietrosu 20 BC 1
Virful Pietroşul 20 BC 1
Virful Pleşu 20 B 1
Virful Saca 20 C 1
Virful Toaca 20 C 1
Virful Vlădeasa 20 B 1
Virful Vulcan 20 B 1
Virgem da Lapa 87 H 4
Virgenes, Cabo 89 C 9
Virgin Islands 79 K 4
Virginia (MN, U.S.A.) 77 H 2
Virginia (South Africa) 66 D 5
Virginia (U.K.) 4 B 3
Virginia (U.S.A.) 77 L 4
Virginia Beach 77 LM 4
Virginia Falls 73 N 3
Virihaure 16 G 2
Virojoki 16 J 3
Virovitica 19 G 2
Virrat 16 H 3
Virserum 17 G 4
Virsko More 19 FG 3
Virtsu 17 H 4
Virú 84 C 5
Virudunagar 40 C 6
Vis 19 G 3
Visalia 76 C 4
Visayan Sea 43 F 1
Visby 17 G 4
Viscount Melville Sound 73 P 1
Visegrad 20 A 2
Viseu 18 B 3

Viseu 85 J 4
Vişeu de Sus 20 B 1
Vishakhapatnam 40 D 4
Vishera 24 L 3
Vishnevka 25 O 5
Visingsö 17 F 4
Viskafors 17 F 4
Visoko 19 G 3
Visp 19 E 2
Vista Alegre (Amazonas, Brazil)
  84 E 3
Vista Alegre (Amazonas, Brazil)
  84 E 5
Vista Alegre (Roraima, Brazil)
  85 F 3
Vistula 15 G 4
Vitarte 86 A 3
Vitebsk 17 K 4
Viterbo 19 F 3
Viti Levu 52 C 4
Vitim 36 K 4
Vitim 36 K 4
Vitimskiy 36 K 4
Vitimskoye Ploskogor'ye 36 K 5
Vitolište 20 B 2
Vitoria 18 C 3
Vitória (Espírito Santo, Brazil)
  87 HJ 5
Vitória (Pará, Brazil) 85 H 4
Vitória da Conquista 87 H 3
Vitré 18 C 2
Vitry-le-François 19 D 2
Vittangi 16 H 2
Vittoria 19 F 4
Vittorio d'Africa → Shalănbōd
  65 GH 4
Vittorio Veneto 19 F 2
Viver 18 C 4
Vivero 18 B 3
Vivi 36 G 3
Viviers 19 D 3
Vivonne 49 F 6
Vivorata 89 E 6
Vizagapatam → Vishakhapatam
  40 D 4
Vizcachas, Meseta de las 89 B 9
Vizcaino, Sierra 76 D 6
Vize 20 C 2
Vizianagaram 40 D 4
Vizinga 24 JK 3
Vlădeasa, Virful 20 B 1
Vladimir 24 H 4
Vladimir 39 L 2
Vladimirovka 24 K 5
Vladimirovskiy 25 M 5
Vladimir-Volynskiy 17 H 5
Vladislavovka 21 E 1
Vladivostok 39 K 2
Vlakhina 20 B 2
Vlasenica 19 G 3
Vlissingen 14 D 4
Vlorë 20 A 2
Vltava 15 F 4
Vöcklabruck 19 F 2
Vodice 19 G 3
Vodla 24 G 3
Vodlozero, Ozero 24 G 3
Vodnjan 19 F 3
Vœune Sai 41 J 5
Vogan 62 E 4
Vogel Peak 63 G 4
Vogelsberg 15 E 4
Voghera 19 E 2–3
Vohimarina 67 J 2
Vohimena, Cap 67 GH 5
Vohipeno 67 H 4
Voi 65 F 5
Voinjama 62 C 4
Voiron 19 E 2
Vojens 17 E 4
Vojmån 16 G 3
Vojmsjön 16 G 2–3
Vojnić 19 G 2
Vojvodina 20 AB 1
Volcán Antofalla 88 C 4
Volcán Barú 84 B 2
Volcán Ceboruco 78 B 3
Volcán Citlaltépetl 78 C 4
Volcán Corcovado 89 B 7
Volcán Domuyo 89 BC 6
Volcan Irazu 78 F 5–6
Volcán Lanin 89 B 6
Volcán Las Tres Virgenes 76 D 6
Volcán Llaima 89 B 6
Volcán Llullaillaco 86 C 5
Volcán Maipo 88 C 5
Volcán Miravalles 78 EF 5
Volcán Misti 86 B 4
Volcán Ollagüe 86 C 5
Volcán Paricutín 78 B 4
Volcán Popocatéptl 78 C 4
Volcán San Juan 78 AB 3
Volcán Sangay 84 C 4
Volcán Tajumulco 78 D 4
Volcán Tutupaca 86 BC 4

Volcán Wolf 84 B 6
Volchikha 25 Q 5
Volchya 21 E 1
Volda 16 E 3
Voldafjorden 16 E 3
Volga 24 J 6
Volgo-Balt [I.V. Lenin] 24 G 3
Volgodonsk 21 F 1
Volgograd 24 H 6
Volgogradskoye
  Vodokhranilishche 24 J 6
Volikovisochnoye 24 K 2
Volkhov 17 K 4
Volkhov 17 K 4
Volkovysk 17 H 5
Volksrust 66 DE 5
Volna, Gora 37 T 3
Volnovakha 21 E 1
Volochanka 36 F 1
Volochayevka 37 O 6
Volodarskoye 25 N 5
Volodorsk 24 GH 4
Vologda 24 G 4
Volokon 36 J 4
Volokovaya 24 J 2
Volonga 24 J 2
Vólos 20 B 3
Volosovo 17 J 4
Volovets 20 B 1
Volozhin 17 J 5
Volsini, Monti 19 F 3
Vol'sk 24 J 5
Volta 62 E 4
Volta Blanche 62 D 3
Volta, Lake 62 DE 4
Volta Noire 62 D 3
Volta Redonda 87 H 5
Volta Rouge 62 D 3
Volterra 19 F 3
Volteva 24 H 3
Volturino 19 G 3
Volupai 51 E 3
Volynskaya Vozvyshennost'
  17 HJ 5
Volynskoye Polesye 17 J 5
Volzhsk 24 J 4
Volzhskiy 24 J 6
Von Frank Mountain 72 G 3
Vónitsa 20 B 3
Vopnafjörður 16 BC 2
Vopnafjörður 16 C 2
Vora 20 A 2
Vorau 19 G 2
Vordingborg 17 F 4
Vórioi Sporádhes 20 B 3
Vórios Evvoikós Kólpos 20 B 3
Vorjing 41 F 2
Vorkuta 25 MN 2
Vormsi 17 H 4
Vorob'yevo 25 P 4
Vorob'yevo 36 H 4
Vorogovo 25 R 3
Voronezh 24 GH 5
Voronovo 25 Q 4
Vorontsovka 24 H 5
Vorontsovka 36 K 4
Vorontsovo 36 D 1
Voroshilovgrad 21 EF 1
Võrts Järv 17 J 4
Võru 17 J 4
Vor'yapaul' 25 M 3
Vosges 19 E 2
Voskhod 21 F 1
Voss 16 E 3
Vostochnaya Litsa 24 G 2
Vostochno Sibirskoye More
  37 ST 1
Vostochno-Kounradskiy 25 P 6
Vostochno-Sakhalinskiy Khrebet
  37 Q 5–6
Vostochnyy 37 Q 5
Vostochnyy 37 Q 6
Vostochnyy Sayan 36 G 5
Vostok (Antarctica) 91
Vostok (Kiribati) 53 E 3
Vostok 21 F 1
Vostykhoy 25 N 3
Votkinsk 24 K 4
Votkinskoye Vodokhranilishche
  24 L 4
Vourinos Oros 20 B 2
Vouziers 19 D 2
Vowchurch 6 C 1
Voxnan 16 F 3
Voyampolka 37 T 4
Voyvozh 24 L 3
Vozhe, Ozero 24 G 3
Vozhega 24 H 3
Vozhgora 24 J 3
Voznesensk 20 D 1
Vozrozhdeniya, Ostrov 34 F 1
Vozvrashcheniye 37 Q 6
Vozvyshennost' Byraya-Tas
  36 M 1

Vozvyshennost' Gabrey 36 F 1
Vozvyshennost' Karabil' 35 G 3
Vozvyshennost'
  Syuryakh-Dahangy 36 M 1
Vozvyshennost'
  Tulay-Kiryaka-Tas 36 J 1
Vozvyshennost' Tutonchana
  36 FG 2–3
Vradiyevka 20 D 1
Vran 19 G 3
Vranje 20 B 2
Vratnica 20 B 2
Vratsa 20 B 2
Vrbas 19 G 3
Vrbovsko 19 G 2
Vrede 66 D 5
Vreed en Hoop 85 G 2
Vriddhachalam 40 C 5
Vrigstad 17 F 4
Vršac 20 B 1
Vryburg 66 CD 5
Vryheid 67 E 5
Vsetín 15 G 5
Vsevidof, Mount 72 D 5
Vsevolozhsk 17 K 3
Vucitrn 20 B 2
Vukovar 19 G 2
Vulcan, Virful 20 B 1
Vulcano 19 F 4
Vung Tau 41 J 5
Vuohijärvi 16 J 3
Vuokkijärvi 16 J 3
Vuoksa 16 J 3
Vuoksa, Lago 16 JK 3
Vuollerim 16 H 2
Vuotso 16 J 2
Vyalozero, Ozero 16 L 2
Vyaltsevo 24 H 4
Vyartsilya 16 K 3
Vyatka 24 K 4
Vyatskiye Polyany 24 K 4
Vyazemskiy 37 OP 6
Vyaz'ma 24 F 4
Vyazovka 24 J 5
Vyborg 16 J 3
Vychegda 24 J 3
Vydrino 36 G 4
Vygoda 20 D 1
Vygozero, Ozero 24 G 3
Vyksa 24 H 4
Vym' 24 K 3
Vyngapur 25 P 3
Vyritsa 17 K 4
Vyselki 21 E 1
Vyshniy-Volochek 24 FG 4
Vysokaya Parma 25 L 3
Vysokogornyy 37 P 5
Vysokoye 24 F 4
Vysotsk 17 J 3
Vytegra 24 G 3
V'yuny 25 Q 4
Vyvenka 37 V 3

W

''W'', Parcs Nationaux, du 62 E 3
Wa 62 D 3
Wa Keeney 76 F 4
Waal 14 DE 4
Wabag 50 D 3
Wabana 75 R 6
Wabara 65 G 3
Wabasca 73 P 4
Wabasca River 73 O 4
Wabash River 77 J 4
Wābirī 59 J 3
Wabowden 73 S 5
Wabrah (Saudi Arabia) 23 E 4
Wąbrzeźno 15 G 4
Waco (Quebec, Can.) 75 O 5
Waco (TX, U.S.A.) 77 G 5
Waconda Lake 76 G 4
Wad 35 H 5
Wad al Ḥaddād 60 E 6
Wad Bandah 60 D 6
Wad Ḥāmid 60 E 5
Wad Madanī 60 E 6
Wad Nimr 60 E 6
Wad Rawa 60 E 5
Waddān 59 J 3
Waddān, Jabal 59 J 3
Waddeneilanden 14 D 4
Waddenzee 14 E 4
Waddesdon 7 D 2
Waddingham 7 D 1
Waddington, Mount 73 M 5
Wadebridge 6 B 2
Wādī ad Dawāsir 61 G 4
Wādī al Akhḍar (Saudi Arabia)
  22 B 4
Wādī al 'Allāqī 60 E 4
Wādī al 'Arabah (Jordan) 22 B 3
Wādī al Bātin (Iraq) 23 DE 3
Wādī al Ghudāf (Iraq) 22 D 2

197

Wādī al Hamd (Saudi Arabia) 22 B 4
Wādī al Hayl (Syria) 22 C 2
Wādī al Khariṭ (Egypt) 22 B 4–5
Wādī al Khurr (Saudi Arabia) 22 C 3
Wādī al Malik 60 D 5
Wādī al Masīlah 61 J 5
Wādī al Miyāh (Syria) 22 C 2
Wādī al 'Ubayyiḍ (Iraq) 22 CD 2
Wādī al 'Unnab (Jordan) 22 B 3
Wādī an Naṭrūn 60 DE 2
Wādī 'Ar 'ar (Saudi Arabia) 22 C 3
Wadi ar Ratqah (Iraq) 22 C 2
Wādī ar Rummah (Saudi Arabia) 22 D 4
Wādī as Sirḥān (Saudi Arabia) 22 BC 3
Wādī ash Shāti' 59 H 3
Wādī at Ṭubal (Iraq) 22 C 2
Wādī at Ṭurmus (Saudi Arabia) 22 D 4
Wādī ath Thartār (Iraq) 22 D 2
Wādī Bayy al Kabīr 59 H 2
Wadi Drâa 58 D 3
Wādī Fajr (Saudi Arabia) 22 BC 3
Wādī Fārigh 59 K 2
Wādī Ḥalfa' 60 E 4
Wādī Ḥamīm 59 K 2
Wādī Ḥawrān (Iraq) 22 C 2
Wādī Ibrah 60 C 6
Wādī Irāwan 59 H 3
Wādī Jabjabah 60 E 4
Wādī Mūsā (Jordan) 22 B 3
Wādī Qina (Egypt) 22 A 4
Wādī Qiṭbīt 61 J 5
Wādī Sha'īt (Egypt) 22 A 4
Wādī Sūf Ajjin 59 H 2
Wādī Umm al Ḥayt 61 J 5
Wadley 77 K 5
Wadsworth 76 C 4
Wafrah (Saudi Arabia) 23 E 3
Wager Bay 73 U 2
Wagga Wagga 49 H 6
Waggabundi (Queensland, Austr.) 49 F 2
Wagin 48 B 5
Wagon Mound 76 F 4
Wagoner 77 G 4
Wągrowiec 15 G 4
Wah 35 J 4
Wahai 43 G 4
Wāḥāt ad Dākhilah 60 D 3
Wāḥāt al Baḥarīyah 60 D 3
Wāḥāt al Farāfirah 60 D 3
Wāḥāt al Jufrah 59 J 3
Wāḥāt al Khārijah 60 E 3–4
Wāḥāt al Kufrah 59 K 4
Wāḥāt al Rabyānah 59 K 4
Wāḥāt al Tāzirbū 59 K 3
Wāḥāt Jālū 59 K 3
Wāḥāt Sabhā 59 H 3
Wāḥāt Salīmah 60 D 4
Wāḥāt Sīwah 60 D 3
Wāḥāt Zighan 59 K 3
Wahidī 61 H 6
Wahni 65 F 2
Wahpeton 77 G 2
Wai 40 B 4
Waibeem 43 H 4
Waidhofen 19 F 2
Waidhofen 19 F 2
Waigama 43 G 4
Waigeo, Pulau 43 H 4
Waihi 51 R 8
Waikabubak 43 E 5
Waikasa-wan 39 KL 3
Waikato 51 R 8
Waikouaiti 51 Q 10
Waimate 51 Q 9
Wainfleet All Saints 7 E 1
Wainganga 40 C 3
Waingapu 43 F 5
Wainwright (AK, U.S.A.) 72 E 1
Wainwright (Alb., Can.) 73 P 5
Waipara 51 Q 9
Waipukuran 51 R 8
Wairoa 51 R 8
Waisai 43 H 4
Waitaki River 51 Q 9
Waitara 51 Q 8
Wājid 65 G 4
Wajir 65 G 4
Waka (Ethiopia) 65 F 3
Waka (Zaire) 64 C 4
Waka, Tanjung 43 G 4
Wakasa-wan 39 L 4
Wakayama 39 L 4
Wake 52 C 1
Wakefield 5 E 3
Wakenaam Island 85 G 2
Wakes Colne 7 E 2
Wakkanai 39 M 1
Wakre 43 H 4
Waku Kungo 66 B 2
Wakuach, Lac 75 O 4

Walaga 64 F 3
Wałbrzych 15 G 4
Wałcz 15 G 4
Walden 76 E 3
Waldia 65 F 2
Waldo 77 K 6
Waldport 76 B 3
Wales (AK, U.S.A.) 72 D 2
Wales Island (N.W.T., Can.) 73 U 2
Walewale 62 D 3
Walgett 49 H 4–5
Walgreen Coast 91
Walikale 64 D 5
Walinga 50 E 3
Walker Lake 76 C 4
Walkite 65 F 3
Wall 76 F 3
Wall Creek 48 E 4
Walla Walla 76 C 2
Wallaby Island 49 G 2
Wallaceburg 74 L 7
Wallal Downs 48 C 2
Wallaroo 49 F 5
Wallasey 5 D 3
Wallel 64 E 3
Wallendbeen 49 H 5
Wallingford 7 D 2
Wallis 52 D 3
Wallis and Futuna 52 CD 3
Walls 2 D 1
Wallsend 5 E 2
Wallsend 49 J 5
Walmer 7 E 2
Walnut Ridge 77 H 4
Walpole, Ile 51 J 6
Walrus Islands 72 EF 4
Walsall 7 D 1
Walsenburg 76 F 4
Walsh 49 G 2
Walsingham, Cape 75 P 2
Walt Disney World 77 K 6
Walterboro 77 K 5
Walton 6 C 1
Walton le Dale 5 D 3
Walvis Bay 66 A 4
Walvis Ridge 98 B 5
Wama, Sungai 43 J 4
Wamba (Kenya) 65 F 4
Wamba (Nigeria) 63 F 4
Wamba (Zaire) 64 B 6
Wamba (Zaire) 64 D 4
Wamena 43 J 4
Wami 65 F 6
Wamsisi 43 G 4
Wan 43 J 5
Wan Hsa-la 41 G 3
Wana 35 H 4
Wanaaring 49 G 4
Wanaka 50 P 9
Wanaka, Lake 50 P 9
Wanapiri 43 J 4
Wandel Sea 90
Wandinzhen 38 C 6
Wang Kai 64 D 3
Wanganella 49 GH 6
Wanganui 51 R 8
Wangaratta 49 H 6
Wangcang 38 E 4
Wanggameti, Gunung 43 EF 6
Wangi 65 G 5
Wangiwangi, Pulau 43 F 5
Wangka 41 G 4
Wangkui 39 J 1
Wangmo 38 E 5
Wangqing 39 J 2
Wanie Rukula 64 D 4
Wanigela 50 E 3
Wankaner 40 B 3
Wanle Wēyn 65 G 4
Wanneroo 48 B 5
Wanning 38 F 7
Wanor 63 G 4
Wansford 7 D 1
Wantage 7 D 2
Wanxian 38 E 4
Wanyuan 38 E 4
Wanzai 38 F 5
Wapamoiwa 51 F 3
Warangal 40 CD 4
Waratah 50 L 9
Waratah Bay 49 H 6
Warboys 7 D 1
Warbumi 43 H 4
Warburg 15 E 4
Warburton Bay 73 P 3
Warburton Mission 48 D 4
Warburton Range 48 D 4
Warburton River 49 F 4
Ward Hunt Strait 51 EF 3
Warder 65 H 3
Wardha 40 C 3
Ware 7 DE 2
Ware 73 M 4
Wareham 7 C 2
Waren 43 J 4

Warenai, Sungai 43 J 4
Warenda 49 G 3
Wargrave 7 D 2
Warialda 49 J 4
Warin Chamrap 41 HJ 4
Warley 7 C 1
Warlingham 7 D 2
Warm Springs 76 C 4
Warmbad (Namibia) 66 B 5
Warmbad (South Africa) 66 D 4
Warmfontein 66 B 5
Warminster 7 C 2
Warnemünde 15 F 4
Warner Mountains 76 B 3
Warner Peak 76 C 3
Warner Robins 77 K 5
Waroona 48 B 5
Warora 40 C 3
Warragul 49 H 6
Warrawagine 48 C 3
Warrego River 49 H 4
Warren (Australia) 49 H 5
Warren (MI, U.S.A.) 77 K 3
Warrenpoint 4 B 2
Warrenton 66 C 5
Warri 63 F 4
Warrington 5 D 3
Warrnambool 49 G 6
Warrow 49 F 5
Warrumbungle Range 49 H 5
Warsaw 15 H 4
Warshīkh 65 H 4
Warsop 5 E 3
Warszawa → Warsaw 15 H 4
Warta 15 G 4
Waru 43 H 4
Warwick (Queensland, Austr.) 49 J 4
Warwick (U.K.) 7 D 1
Warwick Channel 49 F 1
Warwickshire 7 D 1
Wasagu 63 F 3
Wasatch Range 76 D 3–4
Wasco 76 C 4
Wase 63 FG 4
Washburn 76 F 2
Washburn Lake 73 Q 2
Washim 40 C 3
Washington (D.C., U.S.A.) 77 L 4
Washington (IN, U.S.A.) 77 J 4
Washington (Kiribati) 53 E 2
Washington (U.K.) 5 E 2
Washington (U.S.A.) 76 BC 2
Washington Court House 77 K 4
Washita River 76 G 4
Washuk 35 C 5
Wasian 43 H 4
Wasior 43 H 4
Wāsiṭ (Iraq) 23 E 2
Waspám 78 F 5
Wasserburg 15 F 5
Wasua 50 D 3
Wasum 51 E 3
Watampone 43 F 4
Watan Soppeng 43 E 3–4
Watchet 6 C 2
Waterberg 66 B 4
Waterbury 77 M 3
Waterford 14 B 4
Waterhouse River 48 E 1
Waterloo (Belgium) 14 D 4
Waterloo (IA, U.S.A.) 77 H 3
Waterloo (Sierra Leone) 62 B 4
Waterlooville 7 D 2
Watersmeet 77 J 2
Waterton Lakes National Park 73 OP 6
Watertown (N.Y., U.S.A.) 77 L 3
Watertown (S.D., U.S.A.) 76 G 2
Watertown (WI, U.S.A.) 77 J 3
Waterville 77 N 3
Watford 7 D 2
Watford City 76 F 2
Wa'th 64 E 3
Watheroo 48 B 5
Watrous 73 Q 5
Watrous 76 F 4
Watsa 64 D 4
Watsi Kengo 64 C 5
Watson Lake 72 M 3
Watten 2 C 2
Watton 7 E 1
Watts Bar Lake 77 K 4
Watubela, Kepulauan 43 H 4
Wau → Wāw 64 D 3
Wauchope 48 E 3
Wauchope 49 J 5
Waukara, Gunung 43 E 4
Waukarlycarly, Lake 48 C 3
Waukegan 77 J 3
Waukesha 77 J 3
Wausau 77 J 3
Wave Hill 48 E 2
Waveney, River 7 E 1
Waverly 77 H 3

Wāw 64 D 3
Wāw al Kabīr 59 J 3
Wāw an Nāmūs 59 J 4
Wawa 74 L 6
Wawa (Nigeria) 63 E 4
Wawotobi 43 F 4
Waxxari 35 M 3
Way, Lake 48 C 4
Wayabula 43 G 3
Wayamli 43 G 3
Wayao 38 C 5
Waycross 77 K 5
Wayland 77 K 4
Wayne 77 K 4
Waza (Burma) 41 G 2
Waza (Cameroon) 63 G 3
Waza National Park 63 G 3
Wāzīn 59 H 2
Wazirabad 35 J 4
Wda 15 G 4
Wé 51 J 6
Weagamow Lake 74 J 5
Wear, River 5 D 2
Weaverham 5 D 3
Webbe Gestro 65 G 3
Webbe Shibeli 65 G 3
Webi Shābelle 65 G 4
Webster 76 G 2
Webster City 77 H 3
Weda 43 G 3
Weda, Teluk 43 G 3
Weddell 89 D 9
Weddell Sea 91
Wedel 15 E 4
Weeki Wachee 77 K 6
Weert 14 E 4
Weet Burra 2 D 1
Weh, Pulau 42 A 2
Wehterby 5 E 3
Wei He 38 E 4
Wei Xian 38 G 3
Weichang 39 G 2
Weiden 15 F 5
Weifang 39 G 3
Weihai 39 H 3
Weimar 15 F 4
Weinan 38 E 4
Weining 38 D 5
Weipa 49 C 3
Weirton 77 K 3
Weiser 76 C 3
Weishan 39 G 4
Weishan Hu 39 G 4
Weishi 38 F 4
Weissbrünn 66 A 3
Weitra 19 FG 2
Weixi 38 C 5
Weiyuan 38 D 3
Weiyuan 38 D 5
Weizhou Dao 38 E 6
Wejherowo 15 G 4
Welbourn Hill 48 E 4
Welcome Kop 66 B 6
Welkom 66 D 5
Welland, River 7 D 1
Wellesley Islands (Queensland, Austr.) 49 F 2
Wellesley Islands, South (Queensland, Austr.) 49 F 2
Wellingborough 7 D 1
Wellington (KS, U.S.A.) 76 G 4
Wellington (New Zealand) 51 R 9
Wellington (N.S.W., Austr.) 49 H 5
Wellington (NV, U.S.A.) 76 C 4
Wellington (U.K.) 6 C 2
Wellington, Isla (Chile) 89 AB 8
Wells (NV, U.S.A.) 76 C 3
Wells (U.K.) 6 C 2
Wells (VT, U.S.A.) 77 M 3
Wellsboro 77 L 3
Wellton 76 D 5
Welo 65 FG 2
Wels 19 F 2
Welshpool 6 C 1
Welwyn Garden City 7 D 2
Wem 6 C 1
Wema 64 C 5
Wembere 64 E 5
Wen Xian 38 DE 4
Wen Xian 38 F 4
Wenatchee 76 C 2
Wenchang 38 F 7
Wenchuan 38 D 4
Wendeng 39 H 3
Wendens Ambo 7 E 2
Wendling 7 E 1
Wendover (NV, U.S.A.) 76 D 3
Wendover (U.K.) 7 D 2
Wengshui 38 CD 5
Wengyuan 38 F 6
Wenjiang 38 D 4
Wenling 39 H 5
Wenlock River 49 G 1

Wenquan 35 L 2
Wenquan 38 CD 3
Wenshan 38 D 6
Wenshang 39 G 3
Wensley 5 E 2
Wensley 5 E 2
Wensleydale 5 DE 2
Wensu 35 L 2
Wentworth 49 G 5
Wenzhou 39 H 5
Wepener 66 D 5
Weri 43 H 4
Werda 66 C 5
Werribee 49 G 6
Werris Creek 49 J 5
Wesel 14 E 3
Weser 15 E 4
Wesiri 43 G 5
Weslaco 76 G 6
Wesleyville 75 R 6
Wessel, Cape 49 F 1
Wessel Islands 49 F 1
Wessington Springs 76 G 3
West Allis 77 J 3
West Antarctica 91
West Auckland 5 E 2
West Bank 22 B 2
West Bend 77 J 3
West Bengal 40 E 3
West Berlin 15 F 4
West Bridgford 7 D 1
West Bromwich 7 C 1
West Calder 3 C 4
West Cape 52 C 6
West Cape Howe 48 B 6
West Elk Mountains 76 E 4
West Falkland 89 D 9
West Fayu 52 A 2
West Felton 6 C 1
West Gernish 2 A 3
West Glamorgan 6 C 2
West Heslerton 5 E 2
West Ice Shelf 91
West Indies 79 H 3
West Irian 50 C 2
West Kilbride 3 B 4
West Memphis 77 H 4
West Meon 7 D 2
West Mersea 7 E 2
West Midlands 7 D 1
West Nicholson 66 D 4
West Palm Beach 77 L 6
West Plains 77 H 4
West Point 77 J 5
West Siberian Plain 25 OP 3
West Sussex 7 D 2
West Turkistan 28 EF 2
West Virginia 77 K 4
West Wind Drift 93
West Wyalong 49 H 5
West Yellowstone 76 D 3
West Yorkshire 5 E 3
Westbrook 77 M 3
Westbury 7 C 2
Wester Ross 2 B 3
Westerdale 5 E 2
Westerland 15 E 4
Western Australia 48 BD 3–4
Western Desert → As Ṣaḥrā' al Gharbīyah 60 D 3
Western Dvina 17 J 4
Western Ghats 40 BC 4–5
Western Isles 2 A 3
Western Port 49 GH 6
Western Sahara 58 C 4
Western Samoa 52 D 3
Westgate 49 H 4
Westleton 7 E 1
Westlock 73 P 5
Westmeath 4 B 3
Westmoreland (Queensland, Austr.) 49 F 2
Weston 77 K 4
Weston-super-Mare 6 C 2
Westport 51 Q 9
Westralian Current 93
Westray 2 C 2
Westray Firth 2 C 2
Westree 75 L 6
Westward Ho 6 B 2
Westwood 76 B 3
Wetar, Pulau 43 G 5
Wetar, Selat 43 G 5
Wetaskiwin 73 P 5
Wete 65 F 5
Wetzlar 15 E 4
Wetzstein 15 F 4
Wewak 50 D 2
Wexford 6 A 1
Wexford 14 B 4
Wey, River 7 D 2
Weybridge 7 D 2
Weyburn 73 R 6
Weyland, Pegunungan 43 J 4
Weymouth 6 C 2
Whakataki 51 R 9

Whakatane 51 R 8
Whale Cove 73 T 3
Whaley Bridge 7 D 1
Whalsay 2 D 1
Whangarei 51 Q 8
Wharfe, River 5 E 3
Wharfedale 5 DE 2
Wharton Basin 98 C 4
Wharton Lake 73 R 3
Whealer Peak 76 E 4
Wheatland 76 F 3
Wheeler (OR, U.S.A.) 76 B 2
Wheeler (Quebec, Can.) 75 O 4
Wheeler Peak (NV, U.S.A.)
   76 D 4
Wheeling 77 K 3
Whently 7 D 2
Whipsnade 7 D 2
Whitbeck 5 D 2
Whitby 5 E 2
Whitchurch 5 D 3
Whitchurch 7 D 2
White Bay 75 Q 5
White Bear Lake 77 H 2
White Butte 76 F 2
White Cliffs 49 G 5
White Escarpment 66 B 4–5
White Island 73 UV 2
White, Lake 48 D 3
White Mountain (AK, U.S.A.)
   72 E 3
White Mountain Peak 76 C 4
White Mountains 72 H 2
White Nile 60 E 6
White Nile Dam → Khazzān Jabal
   al Awliyā' 60 E 5–6
White Pass 72 L 4
White River (AR, U.S.A.)
   77 H 4–5
White River (IN, U.S.A.) 77 J 4
White River (N.W.T., Can.) 72 J 3
White River (Ontario, Can.) 74 L 6
White River (S.D., U.S.A.) 76 F 3
White Russia 17 J 5
White Sea 24 HJ 2
White Sulphur Springs 76 D 2
White Volta 62 D 3–4
Whitecourt 73 O 5
Whitefish Bay 77 K 2
Whitefish Point 77 J 2
Whitehaven 5 D 2
Whitehead 4 C 2
Whitehorse 72 L 3
Whitehouse 3 B 4
Whiteman Range 51 F 3
Whitemark 50 L 9
Whitewater Bay 77 K 6
Whitewood 49 G 3
Whithorn 4 C 2
Whitley Bay 5 E 2
Whitmore 7 C 1
Whitmore Mountains 91
Whitney 75 M 6
Whitney, Mount 76 C 4
Whitney-on-Wye 6 C 1
Whitstable 7 E 2
Whitsunday Island 49 H 3
Whittier 72 H 3
Whittlesea 49 GH 6
Whittlesey 7 D 1
Whittonstall 5 E 2
Wholdaia Lake 73 QR 3
Whyalla 49 F 5
Wiawso 62 D 4
Wiay 2 A 3
Wibaux 76 F 2
Wichita 76 G 4
Wichita Falls 76 G 5
Wick 2 C 2
Wick (Airport) 2 C 2
Wickenburg 76 D 5
Wickepin 48 B 5
Wickham 48 B 3
Wickham, Cape 50 K 8
Wickham Market 7 E 1
Wicklow 4 B 3
Wicklow Mountains 4 B 3
Widdrington 5 E 2
Widgiemooltha 48 C 5
Widnes 5 D 3
Wielkopolska 15 G 4
Wien 19 G 2
Wiener Becken 19 G 2
Wiener Neustadt 19 G 2
Wienerwald 19 G 2
Wieprz 15 H 4
Wiesbaden 15 E 4
Wiezyca 15 G 4
Wigan 5 D 3
Wigston 7 D 1
Wigton 5 D 2
Wigtown 4 C 2
Wigtown Bay 4 C 2
Wil 19 E 2
Wilbur 76 C 2
Wilcannia 49 G 5

Wilhelm, Mount 50 D 3
Wilhelmina Gebergte 85 G 3
Wilhelm-Pieck-Stadt Guben
   15 FG 4
Wilhelmshaven 15 E 4
Wilkes Land 91
Wilkes-Barre 77 L 3
Wilkhaven 2 C 3
Willamette River 76 B 3
Willapa Bay 76 B 2
Willard 76 E 5
Willcox 76 E 5
Willemstad 84 E 1
Willeroo 48 E 2
William Lake (Man., Can.) 73 R 5
Williambury 48 B 3
Williams (AZ, U.S.A.) 76 D 4
Williams Lake 73 N 5
Williamsburg (KY, U.S.A.) 77 K 4
Williamsburg (VA, U.S.A.) 77 L 4
Williamsport 77 L 3
Willington 5 E 2
Willis Group 49 J 2
Williston (South Africa) 66 C 6
Williston (U.S.A.) 76 F 2
Williston Lake 73 N 4
Willow 72 G 3
Willow Bunch 73 Q 6
Willow Lake 73 O 3
Willow Springs 77 H 4
Willows 76 B 4
Wills Creek 49 F 3
Wills, Lake 48 D 3
Wilmington (DE, U.S.A.) 77 L 4
Wilmington (N.C., U.S.A.) 77 L 5
Wilmslow 5 D 3
Wilson 77 L 4
Wilson Bluff 48 D 5
Wilson, Cape 73 VW 2
Wilson, Isla 84 B 6
Wilson, Mount 76 E 4
Wilson River 49 G 4
Wilson's Promontory 49 H 6
Wilson's Promontory National
   Park 49 H 6
Wilton 7 D 2
Wilton River 48 E 1
Wiltshire 7 CD 2
Wiltz 14 E 5
Wiluna 48 C 4
Wimborne Minster 7 C 2
Winam Gulf 64 E 5
Winbin 49 GH 4
Winburg 66 D 5
Wincanton 6 C 2
Winchcombe 7 D 2
Winchelsea 7 E 2
Winchester (KY, U.S.A.) 77 K 4
Winchester (U.K.) 7 D 2
Wind River 76 E 3
Wind River Range 76 E 3
Windermere 5 D 2
Windhoek 66 B 4
Windischgarsten 19 F 2
Windorah 49 G 4
Windsor (MI, U.S.A.) 74 L 7
Windsor (Nova Scotia, Can.)
   75 P 7
Windsor (Ontario, Can.) 77 K 3
Windsor (U.K.) 7 D 2
Windsor Forest 77 K 5
Windsor Locks 77 M 3
Windward Islands (French
   Polynesia) 53 F 4
Windward Islands (Lesser
   Antilles) 79 L 4–5
Winfield (AL, U.S.A.) 77 J 5
Winfield (KS, U.S.A.) 77 G 4
Wingen 49 J 5
Wingham 7 E 2
Winisk 74 K 4
Winisk 74 K 5
Winisk Lake 74 K 5
Winneba 62 D 4
Winnebago, Lake 77 J 3
Winnemucca 76 C 3
Winnfield 77 H 5
Winning 48 A 3
Winnipeg 73 S 6
Winnipeg 74 J 5
Winnipeg, Lake 73 S 5
Winnipegosis 73 R 5
Winnipegosis, Lake 73 RS 5
Winnipesaukee, Lake 77 M 3
Winona 77 H 3
Winsford 5 D 3
Winslow 7 D 2
Winslow 76 D 4
Winslow (Kiribati) 52 D 3
Winston-Salem 77 K 4
Winter Park 77 K 6
Winterbourne Abbas 6 C 3
Winterthur 19 E 2
Wintinna 48 E 4

Winton (New Zealand) 50 P 10
Winton (Queensland, Austr.)
   49 G 3
Wirksworth 7 D 1
Wisbech 7 E 1
Wisconsin 77 HJ 2
Wiseman 72 H 2
Wishaw 3 C 4
Wisła 15 G 4
Wismar 15 F 4
Wissembourg 19 E 2
Witbank 66 D 5
Witchcliff 48 A 5
Witham 7 E 2
Witham, River 7 D 1
Withernsea 5 F 3
Witney 7 D 2
Witpütz 66 B 5
Wittenberg 15 F 4
Wittenberge 15 F 4
Wittenoom 48 B 3
Witti Range 42 E 3
Witu 65 G 5
Witu Islands 50 E 2
Witvlei 66 B 4
Witwatersrand 66 D 5
Wiveliscombe 6 C 3
Wivenhoe 7 E 2
Wkra 15 H 4
Władys Lawowo 15 G 4
Włocławek 15 G 4
Woburn 7 D 2
Wodonga 49 H 6
Wogr Sheikh 65 H 3
Wokam, Pulau 43 H 5
Woking 7 D 2
Wokingham 7 D 2
Woleai 52 A 2
Wolf 77 J 3
Wolf Creek 76 D 2
Wolf, Isla 84 B 6
Wolf Point 76 E 2
Wolf, Volcán 84 B 6
Wolfratshausen 15 F 5
Wolfsberg 19 F 2
Wolfsburg 15 F 4
Wolgast 15 F 4
Wolin 15 F 4
Wollaston, Islas 89 C 10
Wollaston Lake 73 R 4
Wollaston Peninsula 73 OP 2
Wollastone Lake 73 R 4
Wollongong 49 J 5
Wolmaransstad 66 D 5
Wologosi Mountains 62 BC 4
Wołomin 15 H 4
Wołow 15 G 4
Wolseley 73 R 5
Wolstenholme, Cap 75 M 3
Wolverhampton 7 C 1
Wombfield 7 D 1
Wonarah 49 F 2
Wondo 65 F 3
Wondoola 49 G 2
Wonga Wongué, Parc National de
   63 F 6
Wonju 39 J 3
Wonotobo Falls 85 G 3
Wŏnsan 39 J 3
Wonthaggi 49 H 6
Woocalla 49 F 5
Wood Buffalo National Park
   73 OP 4
Wood River Lakes 72 F 4
Woodall Mountain 77 J 5
Woodbridge 7 E 1
Woodburn 49 J 4
Wooden Bridge 4 B 3
Woodhall Spa 7 D 1
Woodland 76 B 4
Woodlark 51 F 3
Woodroffe, Mount 48 E 4
Woods, Lake of the 74 H 6
Woodstock (New Brunswick,
   Can.) 75 O 6
Woodstock (Queensland, Austr.)
   49 G 2
Woodstock (U.K.) 7 D 2
Woodstock (VT, U.S.A.) 77 M 3
Woodville 77 H 5
Woodward 76 G 4
Woofferton 6 C 1
Wooi 43 J 4
Woolacombe 6 B 2
Wooler 3 C 4
Wooler 5 D 2
Woolgar 49 G 2
Woomera 49 F 5
Wooramel 48 A 4
Wooramel River 48 A 4
Wooton Bassett 7 D 2
Worcester (MA, U.S.A.) 77 M 3
Worcester (South Africa) 66 BC 6
Worcester (U.K.) 7 C 1
Workington 5 D 2
Worksop 5 E 3

Workworth 51 Q 8
Worland 76 E 3
World's View → Rhodes Grave
   66 D 4
Wormit 3 C 3
Worms 15 E 5
Worms Head 6 B 2
Wörther See 19 F 2
Worthing 7 D 2
Worthington 77 G 3
Wosi 43 G 4
Wotho 52 C 2
Wotje 52 C 2
Wour 63 H 1
Wowenda 43 H 5
Wowoni, Pulau 43 F 4
Wragby 7 D 1
Wrangel Island 90
Wrangel 72 L 4
Wrangell Mountains 72 J 3
Wrangell-Saint Elias National Park
   and Preserve 72 J 3
Wreck Reef 49 K 3
Wrentham 7 E 1
Wrexham 6 C 1
Wright Patman Lake 77 H 5
Wrightson, Mount 76 D 5
Wrigley 73 N 3
Wrocław 15 G 4
Wrottesley, Cape 73 N 1
Wroughton 7 D 2
Wroxham 7 E 1
Września 15 G 4
Wu Jiang 38 E 5
Wu Shan 38 F 4
Wu Xian 39 H 4
Wuchale 65 F 2
Wuchang 38 F 4
Wuchang 39 J 2
Wuchuan 38 E 5
Wuchuan 38 E 4
Wuchuan 38 F 6
Wuda 38 E 3
Wudang Shan 38 F 4
Wudaoliang 38 B 3
Wudi 39 G 3
Wuding 38 D 5
Wudu 38 D 4
Wufeng 38 F 4
Wugang 38 F 5
Wugong 38 E 4
Wuhai 38 E 3
Wuhan 38 F 4
Wuhe 39 G 4
Wuhu 39 G 4
Wuhua 38 G 6
Wüjang 40 D 1
Wuji 39 G 3
Wukari 63 F 4
Wuliang Shan 38 D 6
Wuling 38 E 5
Wuling Shan 38 EF 5
Wulong 38 E 5
Wum 65 F 3
Wumeng Shan 38 D 5
Wun Rog 64 D 3
Wun Shwai 64 D 3
Wunnummin Lake 74 K 5
Wuntho 41 G 3
Wuppertal 15 E 4
Wuqi 38 E 3
Wuqia 35 K 3
Wuqiang 39 G 3
Wuqing 39 G 3
Wurno 63 F 3
Wurung 49 G 2
Würzburg 15 F 5
Wurzen 15 F 4
Wushan 38 D 4
Wusheng 38 E 4
Wushi 35 K 2
Wusuli Jiang 39 K 1
Wutai Shan 38 F 3
Wutunghliao 38 D 5
Wuvulu 50 D 2
Wuwei 38 D 3
Wuwei 39 G 4
Wuxi 38 E 4
Wuxi 39 H 4
Wuxing 39 H 4
Wuxuan 38 E 6
Wuyang 38 F 3
Wuyi Shan 38–39 G 5
Wuyiling 37 N 6
Wuyuan 38 G 3
Wuzhai 38 F 3
Wuzhi Shan 38 E 7
Wuzhong 38 E 3
Wuzhou 38 F 6
Wye, River 6 C 1–2
Wymondham 7 E 1
Wynbring 48 E 5
Wyndham 48 D 2
Wynniatt Bay 73 P 1
Wynyard 73 R 5
Wyoming (MI, U.S.A.) 77 J 3
Wyoming (U.S.A.) 76 E 3

Wyoming Peak 76 DE 3
Wyperfeld National Park 49 G 6
Wysoczyzna Ciechanowska
   15 GH 4
Wyszków 15 H 4
Wyzyna Lubelska 15 H 4

X

Xabyaisamba 38 C 4
Xailongmoin 40 E 2
Xainza 40 E 1
Xai-Xai 67 E 5
Xalapa → Jalapa Enríquez 78 C 4
Xambioá 85 J 5
Xá-Muteba 66 B 1
Xangongo 66 AB 3
Xánthi 20 C 2
Xanthos 20 C 3
Xanxerê 88 F 4
Xapecó 88 F 4
Xapuri 86 C 3
Xar Moron 38 F 2
Xar Moron He 39 G 2
Xarag 38 C 3
Xarba La 40 D 2
Xau, Lake 66 C 4
Xauen → Chechaouen 58 D 1
Xaundo 66 B 1
Xavantes, Reprêsa de 87 FG 5
Xavantes, Serra dos 87 G 3
Xavantina 87 F 5
Xayar 35 L 2
Xenia 77 K 4
Xi He 38 D 3
Xi Jiang 38 F 6
Xi Taijnar Hu 38 B 3
Xi Ujimqin Qi 39 G 2
Xi Xian 38 F 3
Xiachuan Dao 38 F 6
Xiaguan 38 D 5
Xiahe 38 D 3
Xiajin 38 G 3
Xiamen 39 G 6
Xi'an 38 E 4
Xianfeng 38 E 5
Xiang Jiang 38 F 5
Xiangcheng 38 C 5
Xiangfan 38 F 4
Xianghua Ling 38 F 5
Xianghuang 38 F 2
Xiangride 38 C 3
Xiangshan 39 H 5
Xiangtan 38 F 5
Xiangyin 38 F 5
Xianju 39 H 5
Xianning 38 F 5
Xianyang 38 E 4
Xiao Hinggan Ling 37 N 5–6
Xiao'ergou 37 M 6
Xiaogan 38 F 4
Xiaojin 38 D 4
Xiaowutai Shan 38 G 3
Xiaoyi 38 F 3
Xiapu 39 H 5
Xichang 38 D 5
Xichou 38 D 6
Xicoténcatl 78 C 3
Xieng Khouang 41 H 4
Xifeng 39 H 2
Xifengzhen 38 E 3
Xigazê 40 E 2
Xiji 38 E 3
Xijir Ulan Hu 38 B 3
Xikouzi 36 M 5
Xiliao He 39 H 2
Xilin 38 E 6
Xilókastron 20 B 3
Ximeng 38 C 6
Ximiao 38 D 2
Xin Barag Youqi 36 L 6
Xin Barag Zuoqi 36 L 6
Xin Xian 38 F 3
Xin'anjiang Shuiku 39 G 5
Xincai 38 F 4
Xincheng 38 D 3
Xincheng 38 E 6
Xincheng 38 G 3
Xindu 38 D 4
Xinfeng 38 F 6
Xinfengjiang Shuiku 38 F 6
Xing Xian 38 F 3
Xing'an 38 F 5
Xingcheng 39 GH 2
Xingdi 38 A 2
Xingguo 38 G 5
Xinghai 38 C 3
Xinghe 38 F 2
Xinglong 39 G 2
Xingning 38 G 6
Xingren 38 E 5
Xingshan 38 F 4
Xingtai 38 F 3
Xingu 85 H 4
Xingu 87 F 3

Xingu 87 F 3
Xingxingxia 38 C 2
Xingyi 38 D 5
Xinhe 35 L 2
Xinhe 38 G 3
Xining 38 D 3
Xinjiang Uygur Zizhiqu 35 L 2
Xinjin 38 D 4
Xinjin 39 H 3
Xinle 38 F 3
Xinlitun 37 N 5
Xinlong 38 D 4
Xinping 38 D 6
Xinqing 37 N 6
Xintai 39 G 3
Xintian 38 F 5
Xinwen 39 G 3
Xinxian 38 F 3
Xinxiang 38 F 3
Xinxing 38 F 6
Xinyang 38 F 4
Xinyi 38 F 6
Xinyi 39 G 4
Xinyuan 35 L 2
Xinzheng 38 F 4
Xiong Xian 39 G 3
Xiqing Shan 38 D 4
Xique-Xique 87 H 3
Xishui 38 G 4
Xiushui 38 F 5
Xiuwu 38 F 3
Xiuyan 39 H 2
Xiwu 38 C 4
Xixabangma Feng 40 E 2
Xixiang 38 E 4
Xiyang 38 F 3
Xizang Zizhigu 40 DE 1
Xorkol 38 B 3
Xpuhil 78 E 4
Xuan'en 38 E 4
Xuanhan 38 E 4
Xuanhua 38 F 2
Xuanwei 38 D 5
Xuchang 38 F 4
Xue Shan 38 CD 5
Xuguit Qi 36 M 6
Xümatang 38 C 4
Xun He 37 N 6
Xundian 38 D 5
Xungru 40 D 2
Xunke 37 N 6
Xunwu 38 G 6
Xupu 38 F 5
Xur 38 C 3
Xuwen 38 F 6
Xuyi 39 G 4
Xuyong 38 DE 5
Xuzhou 39 G 4

Y

Ya Xian 38 E 7
Ya'an 38 D 4
Yabassi 63 G 5
Yabelo 65 F 4
Yablochnyy 37 Q 6
Yablon 37 V 2
Yablonitse, Pereval 20 B 1
Yablonovo 36 K 5
Yablonovyy Khrebet 36 JL 5
Yablonovyy Range 36 L 4–5
Yabrai Yanchang 38 D 3
Yabrei Shan 38 D 3
Yabrīn 61 H 4
Yabrūd (Syria) 22 B 2
Yabuli 39 J 2
Yacuiba 86 D 5
Yacurai 84 E 3
Yadé, Massif du 64 B 3
Yadgir 40 C 4
Yadong 40 E 2
Yaeyama-rettō 39 H 6
Yagodnaya Polyana 24 J 5
Yagodnoye 37 R 3
Yagoua 63 GH 3
Yagradagze Shan 38 C 3
Yagtali, Plato 36 G 2
Yahila 64 C 4
Yahisuli 64 C 5
Yahuma 64 C 4
Yahyalı 21 E 3
Yajiang 38 D 4
Yakacık 21 E 3
Yakima 76 B 2
Yakmach 35 G 5
Yako 62 D 3
Yakoma 64 C 4
Yakovlevka 36 D 1
Yakrik 35 L 2
Yakumo 39 LM 2
Yaku-shima 39 K 4
Yakutat 72 K 4
Yakutat Bay 72 J 4
Yakutsk 37 N 3
Yakuttork 37 U 2

Yakuty 25 R 2
Yala (Sri Lanka) 40 D 6
Yala (Thailand) 41 H 6
Yalakköy 21 E 3
Yale Point 76 E 4
Yalgoo 48 B 4
Yali 64 C 5
Yalinga 64 C 3
Yalleroi 49 H 3
Yallourn 49 H 6
Yaloké 64 B 3
Yalong Jiang 38 D 5
Yalova 20 C 2
Yalpukh, Ozero 20 C 1
Yalta 21 D 2
Yalta 21 E 1
Yalu Jiang 39 HJ 2
Yalutorovsk 25 N 4
Yalvaç 20 D 3
Yalym 25 N 5
Yam Kinneret (Israel) 22 B 2
Yamagata 39 LM 3
Yamaguchi 39 K 4
Yamal Peninsula 25 NO 1
Yamal, Poluostrov 25 NO 1
Yam-Alin', Khrebet 37 OP 5
Yamantau, Gora 25 L 5
Yamarovka 36 K 5
Yamba 64 F 3
Yambering 62 B 3
Yambio 64 D 4
Yambol 20 C 2
Yamburg 25 P 2
Yambuto, Ozero 25 PQ 1
Yambuya 64 CD 4
Yamdena, Pulau 43 H 5
Yamethin 41 G 3
Yamia 63 G 3
Yaminbot 50 D 2
Yamm 17 J 4
Yamma Yamma, Lake 49 G 4
Yamoussoukro 62 CD 4
Yampol' (Ukraine, U.S.S.R.)
  20 C 1
Yamsk 37 S 4
Yamuna 40 D 2
Yamunanagar 40 C 1
Yamzho Yumco 41 F 2
Yan Dağ 20 CD 3
Yan Shan 39 G 2
Yana 37 P 1
Yanam 40 D 4
Yan'an 38 E 3
Yanaoca 86 B 3
Yanartaş Dağları 20 D 3
Yanbian 38 D 5
Yanbu' (Saudi Arabia) 22 BC 4
Yanchang 38 EF 3
Yancheng 39 H 4
Yanchi 38 E 3
Yandang Shan 39 H 5
Yandja 64 B 5
Yandrakinot 72 C 3
Yanfolia 62 C 3
Yang Xian 38 E 4
Yangalia 64 C 3
Yangambi 64 CD 4
Yangarey 25 M 2
Yangbajain 41 F 1
Yangbi 38 C 5
Yangchun 38 F 6
Yanggao 38 F 2
Yanggu 38 G 3
Yangi Emām (Iran) 23 F 2
Yangikishlak 35 H 2
Yangiyul' 35 H 2
Yangjiang 38 F 6
Yangquan 38 F 3
Yangshan 38 F 6
Yangshuo 38 F 6
Yangtze Kiang 38 F 4
Yangxiu 38 G 5
Yangzhou 39 G 4
Yanhe 38 E 5
Yanhuqu 40 D 1
Yanis'yarvi, Ozero 16 K 3
Yanji 39 J 2
Yanjin 38 D 5
Yankan, Khrebet 36 L 4
Yanking 39 G 2
Yankton 76 G 3
Yanqi Huizu Zizhixian 35 LM 2
Yanshan 38 D 6
Yanshan 39 G 3
Yanshi 38 F 4
Yanshiping 38 B 4
Yanshou 39 J 1
Yanskiy 37 O 2
Yanskiy Zaliv 37 OP 1
Yantai 39 H 3
Yanting 38 E 4
Yanwa 38 C 5

Yany-Kurgan 35 H 2
Yanyuan 38 D 5
Yanzhou 39 G 3
Yao 63 H 3
Yaoundé 63 G 5
Yapei 62 D 4
Yapen, Pulau 43 J 4
Yapen, Selat 43 J 4
Yapura 84 D 4
Yaqui, Rio 76 D 6
Yar Sale 25 O 2
Yaraka 49 G 3
Yaraligöz 21 D 2
Yaransk 24 J 4
Yarcombe 6 C 3
Yarda 63 H 2
Yare, River 7 E 1
Yaremcha 20 B 1
Yarensk 24 J 3
Yari 84 D 3
Yarīm 61 G 6
Yarishev 20 C 1
Yaritagua 84 E 1
Yarkant 35 K 3
Yarkant → Shache 35 K 3
Yarkant He 35 K 3
Yarkino 36 G 4
Yarlung Zangbo Jiang 38 B 5
Yarmouth 75 O 7
Yarmouth (U.K.) 7 D 2
Yarongo 25 N 2
Yaroslavl' 24 G 4
Yarra Yarra Lakes 48 B 4
Yarraloola 48 B 3
Yarram 49 H 6
Yarrie 48 C 3
Yarroto 25 O 2
Yarrow 3 C 4
Yartsevo 24 F 4
Yartsevo 25 S 3
Yarumal 84 C 2
Yarwa 38 C 4
Yasawa Group 52 C 4
Yasel'da 17 J 5
Yashalta 21 F 1
Yashi 63 F 3
Yashkino 37 P 5
Yashkul' 21 G 1
Yasin 35 J 3
Yasinovataya 21 E 1
Yasinya 20 B 1
Yasnyy 37 N 5
Yass 49 H 5
Yassachnaya 37 S 3
Yāsūj (Iran) 23 F 3
Yasun Burnu 21 E 2
Yata 86 C 3
Yata 86 C 3
Yatağan 20 C 3
Yatakala 62 DE 3
Yaté-Village 51 J 6
Yathkyed Lake 73 S 3
Yatina 86 CD 5
Yatolema 64 C 4
Yatsushiro 39 JK 4
Yatta Plateau 65 F 5
Yatton 49 H 3
Yauca 86 B 4
Yauna Moloca 84 D 4
Yauyos 86 A 3
Yavarí 84 D 4
Yavatmal 40 C 3
Yavi, Cerro 84 E 2
Yavita 84 E 3
Yawatahama 39 K 4
Yawng-hwe 41 G 3
Yaxchilán 78 D 4
Yay Gölü 21 E 3
Yaya 25 R 4
Yayladağı 21 E 3
Yayva 24 L 4
Yazd 34 E 4
Yazd (Iran) 23 G 3
Yazdān 35 G 4
Yazd-e Khvāst (Iran) 23 F 3
Yazılıkaya 20 D 3
Yazılıkaya 21 D 2
Yazoo 77 HJ 5
Yazoo City 77 H 5
Ybbs an der Donau 19 G 2
Yding Skovhöj 17 E 4
Ydre 17 G 4
Ydzhid Parma 25 L 3
Ye 41 G 4
Ye'almpton 6 C 3
Yebawmi 41 G 2
Yebbi Bou 63 H 1
Yebe-Khay, Gora 36 KL 1
Yecheng 35 K 3
Yecla 18 C 4
Yedarma 36 H 4
Yedinka 37 P 6
Yedintsy 20 C 1
Yedoma 24 H 3

Yedseram 63 G 3
Yeeda River 48 C 2
Yefira 20 B 2
Yefremov 24 G 5
Yeggueba 63 G 2
Yegorlyk 21 F 1
Yegorlykskaya 21 F 1
Yegor'yevsk 24 GH 4
Yegros 88 E 4
Yeha 65 F 2
Yei 64 E 4
Yeji 62 D 4
Yekepa 62 C 4
Yekhegnadzor 21 G 3
Yékiasahal 63 H 2
Yelabuga 24 K 4
Yelan' 24 H 5
Yelanets 20 D 1
Yelantsy 36 J 5
Yele 62 B 4
Yelets 24 G 5
Yelizarovo 25 N 3
Yelizavetinka 25 L 5
Yelizavety, Mys 37 Q 5
Yelizovo 37 T 5
Yel'nya 24 F 5
Yeloguy 25 R 3
Yelovka 37 U 4
Yel'sk 17 J 5
Yelua 58 B 4
Yelvertoft 49 F 3
Yelwa 63 EF 3
Yemanzhelinsk 25 M 5
Yematan 38 C 3
Yematan 38 C 2
Yemen 61 GH 5
Yemet 37 V 3
Yen 63 G 5
Yen Bai 41 H 3
Yena 16 K 2
Yenagoa 63 F 5
Yenakiyevo 21 E 1
Yenanma 41 F 4
Yenashimski Pol'kan, Gora
  36 F 3–4
Yendi 62 DE 4
Yendondin 36 K 5
Yengisar 35 K 3
Yengo 63 H 5
Yengue 63 F 5
Yenice 21 D 2
Yenice 21 D 3
Yenice (Turkey) 21 E 3
Yenice (Turkey) 21 E 3
Yenice (Turkey) 22 B 1
Yenişehir 20 C 2
Yenisey 25 R 2
Yenisey 36 F 4
Yenisey, Bol'shoy 36 G 5
Yenisey, Malyy 36 FG 5
Yeniseysk 36 F 4
Yeniseyskiy Kryazh 36 F 3–4
Yeniseyskiy Zaliv 36 D 1
Yenotayevka 21 G 1
Yeo, Lake 48 C 4
Yeovil 6 C 2
Yepoko 25 OP 2
Yeppoon 49 J 3
Yeraliyevo 34 E 2
Yerbogachen 36 J 3
Yercha 37 R 2
Yerema 36 J 3
Yerema, Bol'shaya 36 J 3
Yerementau, Gory 25 O 5
Yerevan 21 FG 2
Yergeni 21 F 1
Yerka Inadeypur 25 P 3
Yerköy 21 D 3
Yermak 25 P 5
Yermakovo 25 O 3
Yermakovo 25 R 2
Yermakovskoye 36 F 5
Yermentau 25 O 5
Yermitsa 24 K 2
Yermo 78 B 2
Yerofey-Pavlovich 37 M 5
Yeroham (Israel) 22 B 3
Yeropol 37 V 2
Yershov 24 J 5
Yertom 24 J 3
Yertsevo 24 H 3
Yerupajá, Nevado 86 A 3

Yerushalayim 22 B 3
Yesa, Embalse de 18 C 3
Yesil 25 N 5
Yeşilhisar 21 D 3
Yeşilırmak 21 E 2
Yeşilköy 20 C 2
Yessentuki 21 F 2
Yessey 36 H 2
Yessey, Ozero 36 H 2
Yët-Kyuyel' 36 M 3
Yetman 49 J 4
Yetminster 6 C 3
Yetti 58 D 3
Yeu 41 G 3
Yeu, Ile d' 18 C 2
Yevlakh 34 D 2
Yevpatoriya 21 D 1
Yevsyavan' 25 M 2
Yeya 21 E 1
Yeysk 21 E 1
Yeyskoye Ukrepleniye 21 E 1
Yezd (Iran) 23 G 3
Yezhikha 24 J 4
Ygyatta 36 L 3
Yi He 39 G 3
Yi Xian 39 H 2
Yialousa 21 D 3
Yialousa (Cyprus) 22 AB 2
Yi'an 37 N 6
Yiannitsá 20 B 2
Yibin 38 D 5
Yibug Caka 40 E 1
Yichang 38 F 4
Yichuan 38 F 3
Yichuan 38 F 4
Yichun 37 N 6
Yichun 38 F 5
Yidu 38 F 4
Yidu 39 G 3
Yidun 38 C 4
Yifeng 38 F 5
Yifran 59 H 2
Yilan 39 J 1
Yıldız Dağı 21 E 2
Yıldızeli 21 E 3
Yilehuli Shan 37 M 5
Yiliang 38 D 6
Yin Shan 38 E 2
Yinchuan 38 E 3
Yingde 38 F 6
Yingjiang 38 C 6
Yingkou 39 H 2
Yingshan 38 G 4
Yingtan 39 G 5
Yining 35 L 2
Yi'ong Zangbo 38 B 4
Yirga Alem 65 F 3
Yirol 64 E 3
Yirshi 36 L 6
Yishui 39 G 3
Yithion 20 B 3
Yitong 39 HJ 2
Yitulihe 37 M 5
Yiwu 38 B 2
Yiyang 38 F 5
Yiyang 39 G 5
Yizhang 38 F 5
Ylas-Yuryakh 36 J 2
Ylikitka 16 J 2
Yli-Ii 16 J 2
Ylitornio 16 H 2
Ylivieska 16 H 3
Yllästunturi 16 H 2
Ylöjärvi 16 H 3
Yngaren 17 G 4
Ynykchanskiy 37 P 3
Ynysybwl 6 C 3
Yoboki 65 G 2
Yogoum 63 H 2
Yogyakarta 42 CD 5
Yojoa, Lago de 78 E 5
Yokadouma 63 G 5
Yoko 63 G 4
Yokoate-jima 39 J 5
Yokohama 39 LM 3
Yokosuka 39 LM 3–4
Yokote 39 M 3
Yola 63 G 4 a
Yolombo 64 C 5
Yome 43 G 4
Yonago 39 K 3
Yonaguni-jima 39 H 6
Yonezawa 39 M 3
Yong deng 38 D 3
Yong'an 39 G 5
Yŏngan 39 J 2
Yongchang 38 D 3
Yongchuan 38 E 5
Yongchun 39 G 5
Yongde 38 C 6
Yongding 38 G 6
Yonghung 39 J 3
Yongji 39 J 2
Yongjing 38 D 3
Yŏngju 39 J 3
Yongkang 39 H 5

Yongning 38 E 3
Yongping 38 C 5
Yongren 38 D 5
Yongshan 38 D 5
Yongshou 38 E 4
Yongshun 38 E 5
Yongxin 38 F 5
Yongxiu 38 G 5
Yonibana 62 B 4
Yonkers 77 M 3
Yonne 18 D 2
Yopal 84 D 2
Yopurga 35 K 3
York (NE, U.S.A.) 76 G 3
York (PA, U.S.A.) 77 L 4
York (U.K.) 5 E 3
York (Western Australia) 48 B 5
York, Cape 49 G 1
York Factory 74 J 4
York Sound 48 D 1
Yorke Peninsula 49 F 5
Yorkshire Moors 5 E 2
Yorkshire Wolds 5 E 2–3
Yorkton 73 R 5
Yoro 78 E 4
Yoron-jima 39 J 5
Yŏröö 36 J 6
Yorosso 62 CD 3
Yorubaland Plateau 62 E 4
Yosemite National Park 76 C 4
Yoshkar Ola 24 J 4
Yŏsu 39 J 4
Yotala 86 C 4
Yotau 86 D 4
Yotvata (Israel) 22 B 3
You Jiang 38 E 6
Youdunzi 38 B 3
Youghal 14 B 4
Youllemmedene 62 E 2
Young 49 H 5
Youngstown 77 KL 3
Youshashan 38 B 3
Youssoufia 58 D 2
Youyang 38 E 5
Yoxall 7 D 1
Yozgat 21 D 3
Ypaceraí 88 E 4
Ypeihu 86 E 5
Yreka 76 B 3
Ysabel Channel 51 EF 2
Ysgubor-y-coed 6 C 1
Ystad 17 F 4
Ytterhogdal 16 F 3
Ytyk-Kel' 37 O 3
Yu 'Alliq, Jabal (Egypt) 22 A 3
Yu Jiang 38 EF 6
Yu Shan 38 G 5
Yu Xian 38 F 3
Yuan Jiang 38 EF 6
Yuan Jiang 38 F 5
Yuanjiang 38 D 6
Yuanling 38 F 5
Yuanmou 38 D 5
Yuanping 38 F 3
Yuanqu 38 F 3
Yuanshanzi 38 CD 3
Yuanshi 38 F 3
Yuanyang 38 D 6
Yūbari 39 M 2
Yuben' 35 J 3
Yucatán Peninsula 78 E 3–4
Yucheng 39 G 3
Yuci 38 F 3
Yudoma 37 P 4
Yudoma-Krestovskaya 37 P 3
Yudomo Mayskoye Nagor'ye
    37 PQ 3–4
Yudomskiy Khrebet 37 Q 3
Yudu 38 G 5
Yueqing 39 H 5
Yuexi 38 D 5
Yueyang 38 F 5
Yug 24 J 3
Yugan, Bol'shoy 25 O 4
Yugorskiy Poluostrov 25 M 2
Yugorskiy Shar 25 M 2
Yugorskiy Shar, Proliv 25 M 2
Yugoslavia 19 G 3
Yugo-Tala 37 S 2
Yuhang 39 H 4
Yukagirskoye Ploskogor'ye
    37 ST 2
Yukhnov 24 G 5
Yukhta 36 J 4
Yuki 64 B 5
Yukon 72 E 3
Yukon Flats 72 H 2
Yukon Flats National Monument
    72 HJ 2
Yukon, Fort 72 H 2
Yukon Plateau 72 K 3
Yukon Territory 72 KL 3
Yukon-Charley Rivers National
    Preserve 72 J 2–3
Yüksekova 21 F 3

Yuli (China) 35 M 2
Yuli (Nigeria) 63 G 4
Yulin 38 E 3
Yulin 38 F 6
Yulong Kueshan 38 D 5
Yulu Rapids 64 C 4
Yuma (AZ, U.S.A.) 76 D 5
Yuma (CO, U.S.A.) 76 F 3
Yuma (U.S.S.R.) 16 K 2
Yumari, Cerro 84 E 3
Yumbe 64 E 4
Yumbi (Zaire) 64 B 5
Yumbi (Zaire) 64 D 5
Yumbo 84 C 3
Yumen 38 C 3
Yumenzhen 38 C 2
Yumin 35 L 1
Yumurchen 36 K 5
Yumurtalık 21 E 3
Yumurtalık (Turkey) 22 B 1
Yun Xian 38 D 6
Yun Xian 38 F 4
Yunaska 72 C 5
Yuncheng 38 F 3
Yunekit 36 M 3
Yungay 89 B 6
Yunhe 39 G 5
Yunkai Dashan 38 F 6
Yunling Shan 38 C 5
Yunlong 38 C 5
Yunnan 38 D 6
Yuntra 20 C 2
Yunxiao 39 G 6
Yunyang 38 E 4
Yuqing 38 E 5
Yur 37 P 4
Yurga 25 Q 4
Yuribey 25 O 2
Yuriby 25 P 1
Yurimaguas 84 C 5
Yuroma 24 J 2
Yurty 37 U 4
Yurungkax He 35 L 3
Yur'yevka 21 E 1
Yushan (China) 39 G 5
Yushan (Taiwan) 39 H 6
Yushe 38 F 3
Yushkozero 16 K 3
Yushno Muyskiy Khrebet 36 KL 4
Yushu 38 C 4
Yushu 39 J 2
Yusta 21 G 1
Yusufeli 21 F 2
Yuti 86 D 4
Yutian 35 L 3
Yutian 39 G 3
Yuxi 38 D 6
Yuyao 39 H 4
Yuzhno Chuyskiy, Khrebet 25 R 6
Yuzhno-Kamyshovyy Khrebet
    37 Q 6
Yuzhno-Sakhalinsk 37 Q 6
Yuzhnoye 37 Q 6
Yuzhno-Yeniseyskiy 36 F 4
Yuzhnyy 21 F 1
Yuzhnyy Anyuyskiy Khrebet
    37 UV 2
Yuzhnyy Bug 20 D 1
Yuzhnyy, Mys 37 T 4
Yuznoural'sk 25 M 5
Yverdon 19 E 2
Yvetot 18 D 2
Ywamun 41 G 3

Z

Za Qu 38 C 4
Zabarjad (Egypt) 22 B 5
Zabaykal'sk 36 L 6
Zāb-e Kuchek (Iran) 23 D 1
Zabéré 62 D 3
Zabid 61 G 6
Zabok 19 G 2
Zabol 35 G 4
Zāboli 35 G 5
Zabolotov 20 C 1
Zabřeh 15 G 5
Zabrze 15 G 4
Zaburun'ye 34 E 1
Zabzugu 62 E 4
Zacapa 78 E 5
Zacapu 78 B 4
Zacatecas 78 B 3
Zacatepec 78 C 4
Zadar 19 G 3
Zadetkale Kyun 41 G 5
Zadetkyi Kyun 41 G 6
Zadi 41 G 5
Zadoi 38 C 4
Zadran 35 H 4
Za'faranah (Egypt) 22 A 3
Zafīr (United Arab Emirates)
    23 F 5
Zafra 18 B 4

Zag 58 D 3
Żagań 15 G 4
Zaggūt 59 J 3
Zāgh Marz (Iran) 23 F 1
Zaghāwa 60 C 6
Zaghdeh (Iran) 23 G 2
Zāgheh (Iran) 23 E 2
Zāgheh (Iran) 23 F 2
Zāgheh-ye Bālā (Iran) 23 E 2
Zaghwān 59 H 1
Zagora 58 D 2
Zagorsk 24 G 4
Zagreb 19 G 2
Zagros, Kūhhā ye (Iran) 23 EF 2–3
Zagros Mountains (Iran) 23 F 3
Zagros Mountains → Kūhhā ye
    Zagros 34 E 5
Za'gya Zangbo 40 E 1
Zagyva 20 A 1
Zāhedān 35 G 5
Zāhirah (Oman) 23 G 5
Zahlah (Lebanon) 22 B 2
Zaḥrān 61 G 5
Zahrez Rharbi 59 F 2
Zair 34 F 2
Zaire 63 G 7
Zaire 64 CD 5
Zaire (Angola) 66 A 1
Zaječar 20 B 2
Zakak 63 E 2
Zakamensk 36 H 5
Zakataly 34 D 2
Zakharo 20 B 3
Zakharov 37 O 3
Zakharovka 25 O 6
Zakhmet 35 G 3
Zākhū (Iraq) 22 D 1
Zákinthos 20 B 3
Zákinthos 20 B 3
Zakopane 15 G 5
Zakouma 63 H 3
Zakouma, Parc National de
    63 H 3
Zakur'ya 36 J 4
Zalābiyah (Syria) 22 C 2
Zalaegerszeg 20 A 1
Zalāf (Syria) 22 B 2
Zalari 36 H 5
Zălau 20 B 1
Zaleshchiki 20 C 1
Zalesskiy 24 G 4
Zalew Szczecinski 15 F 4
Zalew Wislany 15 G 4
Zalim 61 G 4
Zalingei 60 C 6
Zaliv Akademii 37 P 5
Zaliv Aniva 37 Q 6
Zaliv Chayvo 37 Q 5
Zaliv Kara-Bogaz Gol 34 E 2
Zaliv Korfa 37 V 3–4
Zaliv Kresta 72 B 2
Zaliv Ozernoy 37 U 4
Zaliv Petra Velikogo 39 K 2
Zaliv Pil'tun 37 Q 5
Zaliv Sakhalinskiy 37 Q 5
Zaliv Shelikhova 37 T 3–4
Zaliv Terpeniya 37 Q 6
Zaliv Ushki 37 R 4
Zallah 59 J 3
Zaltan 59 J 3
Zamakh 61 H 5
Zambeze 67 E 3
Zambezi 66 C 2
Zambia 66 D 2
Zamboanga 43 F 2
Zamboanga Peninsula 43 F 2
Zambrów 15 H 4
Zambuè 67 E 3
Zamfara 63 F 3
Zamkowa, Góra 15 H 4
Zamora (Ecuador) 84 C 4
Zamora (Spain) 18 B 3
Zamora de Hidalgo 78 B 4
Zamość 15 H 4
Zamtang 38 D 4
Zanaga 63 G 6
Záncara 18 C 4
Zanda 40 C 1
Zanesville 77 K 4
Zangezurskiy Khrebet (U.S.S.R.)
    34 D 2–3
Zangla 35 K 4
Zanjān (Iran) 23 E 1
Zannone 19 F 3
Zanthus 48 C 5
Zanul'e 24 K 3
Zanzibar 65 F 6
Zanzibar Island 65 F 6
Zaouatallaz 59 G 4
Zaoyang 38 F 4
Zaozernyy 36 F 4
Zaozhuang 39 G 4
Zap 21 F 3
Zapadna Morava 20 B 2
Zapadnaya Dvina 17 J 4
Zapadnaya Dvina 24 F 4

Zapadno-Sakhalinskiy Khrebet
    37 Q 5–6
Zapadno-Sibirskaya Nizmennost'
    25 NQ 3
Zapadnyy Sayan 36 F 5
Zapala 89 B 6
Zapata 76 G 6
Zapolyarnyy 16 K 2
Zaporosh'ye 21 E 1
Zapug 40 D 1
Zara 21 E 3
Zarafshan 35 G 2
Zaragoza (Colombia) 84 CD 2
Zaragoza (Mexico) 78 B 2
Zaragoza (Spain) 18 C 3
Zarand 34 E 3
Zarand (Iran) 23 E 2
Zarand (Iran) 23 F 2
Zarand (Iran) 23 G 3
Zaranj 35 G 4
Zaranou 62 D 4
Zarasai 17 J 4
Zárate 88 E 5
Zarauz 18 C 3
Zaraza 84 E 2
Zard Kūh (Iran) 23 F 2
Zarechensk 16 K 2
Zarghat (Saudi Arabia) 22 C 4
Zarghun 35 H 4
Zarghun Shahr 35 H 4
Zaria 63 F 3
Zarma 62 D 1
Zarqān (Iran) 23 F 3
Zarrīneh (Iran) 23 E 1
Zarrīnshahr (Iran) 23 F 2
Zaruma 84 C 4
Zarumilla 84 B 4
Żary 15 FG 4
Zarya Oktyabrya 34 F 1
Zarzaitine 59 G 3
Zarzal 84 C 3
Zasheyek 16 K 2
Zaskar 35 K 4
Zaskar Mountains 35 K 4
Zaslavl 17 J 5
Zastron 66 D 6
Zaterechnyy 21 G 2
Zatish'ye 37 T 2
Zatishye 20 CD 1
Zatoka Gdańska 15 G 4
Zatoka Pomorska 15 F 4
Zaunguzskiye Karakumy 34 FG 2
Zavetnoye 21 F 1
Zavitinsk 37 N 5
Zavodoukovsk 25 N 4
Zav'yalova, Ostrov 37 RS 4
Zawiercie 15 G 4
Zāwiyat Masūs 59 K 2
Zawiyat Shammās 60 D 2
Zawr, Ra's az (Saudi Arabia)
    23 E 4
Zāyandeh (Iran) 23 F 2
Zayarsk 36 H 4
Zaysan 25 Q 6
Zaysan, Ozero 25 Q 6
Zayt, Ra's (Egypt) 22 A 4
Zayü 38 C 5
Zayü Qu 38 C 5
Zdŭńska Wola 15 G 4
Zdvinsk 25 P 5
Zebak 35 J 3
Zeballos, Monte 89 B 8
Zēbar (Iraq) 22 D 1
Zebediela 66 D 4
Zedness, Mont 58 C 4
Zeehan 50 L 9
Zeehan 52 A 5
Zeeland 14 D 4
Zeerust 66 D 5
Zefat (Israel) 22 B 2
Zegdou 58 E 3
Zeila' 65 G 2
Žēkog 38 D 3
Zelenoborskiy 16 K 2
Zelenodol'sk 24 JK 4
Zelenogorsk 17 J 3
Zelenogradsk 17 H 5
Zelenokumsk 21 F 2
Železnodorožny 17 H 5
Zelfana 59 F 2
Zeline 63 F 2
Zell am See 19 F 2
Žemaičiu Aukštuma 17 H 4
Žemaitiya 17 H 4
Zemgale 17 HJ 4
Zemio 64 D 3
Zémongo 64 C 3
Zenica 19 G 3
Zenza do Itombe 66 A 1
Žepče 19 G 3
Zepu 35 K 3
Zeravshan 35 H 3
Zerav'shanskiy Khrebet 35 H 3
Zerhamra 58 E 3
Zerind 20 B 1
Zermatt 19 E 2

Zernograd 21 F 1
Zestafoni 21 F 2
Zeya 37 N 5
Zeya 37 O 4
Zeya Vodokhranilishche 37 N 5
Zeydābād (Iran) 23 G 3
Zeydār (Iran) 23 G 1
Zeysko-Bureinskaya Ravnina
    37 NO 5
Zêzere 18 B 4
Zgierz 15 G 4
Zgorzelec 15 G 4
Zhag'yab 38 C 4
Zhailma 25 M 5
Zhaksylyk 25 O 6
Zhamanakkal', Ozero 35 G 1
Zhamansor 34 E 1
Zhamshi 25 O 6
Zhanabas 35 H 1
Zhanabek 25 P 6
Zhanang 41 F 2
Zhana-Semey 25 Q 5
Zhanatas 35 HJ 2
Zhangbei 38 FG 2
Zhangguangcai Ling 39 J 1–2
Zhangiz-Tobe 25 Q 6
Zhangjiakou 38 FG 2
Zhangling 37 M 5
Zhangping 39 G 5
Zhangpu 39 G 6
Zhangwu 39 H 2
Zhangye 38 CD 3
Zhangzhou 39 G 6
Zhangzi 38 F 3
Zhanhua 39 G 3
Zhanjiang 38 F 6
Zhantekets 25 Q 6
Zhao'an 38 G 6
Zhaodong 39 J 1
Zhaojue 38 D 5
Zhaoping 38 F 6
Zhaoqing 38 F 6
Zhaosu 35 L 2
Zhaotong 38 D 5
Zhaoyuan 39 J 1
Zhaozhou 39 HJ 3
Zhari Namco 40 E 1
Zharkamys 34 F 1
Zharkova 25 R 4
Zharlykamys 25 P 6
Zharma 25 Q 6
Zharyk 25 O 6
Zhashkov 24 EF 6
Zhatay 37 N 3
Zhaxi Co 40 E 1
Zhaxizê 38 C 4
Zhayma 36 F 5
Zhdanov 21 E 1
Zhecheng 38 G 4
Zhejiang 39 GH 5
Zhelaniya, Cape 90
Zhel'dyadyr 35 H 1
Zhelezinka 25 P 5
Zheleznodorozhnyy 24 K 3
Zheleznodorozhnyy 25 M 2
Zheleznodorozhnyy 36 H 4
Zheleznogorsk 24 F 5
Zheleznogorsk 36 HJ 4
Zhen'an 38 E 4
Zheng'an 38 E 5
Zhengding 38 FG 3
Zhenghe 39 G 5
Zhenglan 38 G 2
Zhengning 38 E 4
Zhengxiangbai 38 FG 2
Zhengyang 38 F 4
Zhengzhou 38 F 4
Zhenjiang 39 GH 4
Zhenkang 38 C 6
Zhenlai 39 H 1
Zhenning 38 E 5
Zhenxiong 38 D 5
Zhenyuan 38 D 6
Zhenyuan 38 E 5
Zherdevka 24 H 5
Zherebtsovo 37 P 5
Zheshart 24 JK 3
Zhetybay 34 E 2
Zhicheng 38 F 4
Zhidan 38 E 3
Zhidoi 38 C 4
Zhigalovo 36 J 5
Zhigansk 37 M 2
Zhigulevsk 24 J 5
Zhijiang 38 E 5
Zhitkovichi 17 J 5
Zhitomir 17 J 5
Zhlatyr 25 P 5
Zhmerinka 24 E 6
Zhob 35 H 4
Zhob 35 H 4
Zhodino 17 J 5
Zholymbet 25 O 5
Zhong Xian 38 E 4
Zhongba 40 D 2
Zhongdian 38 C 5

Zhongning **38** E 3
Zhongshan **38** F 6
Zhongwei **38** DE 3
Zhongxiang **38** F 4
Zhongye Islands **42** D 1
Zhongye Qundao **42** D 1
Zhosaly **25** P 5
Zhou Shan Qundao **39** H 4
Zhoukouzhen **38** FG 4
Zhovnino **24** F 6
Zhovten **20** D 1
Zhovtnevoye **20** D 1
Zhuanghe **39** H 3
Zhuanglang **38** E 3
Zhuantobe **35** H 2
Zhubgyügoin **38** C 4
Zhucheng **39** G 3
Zhugqu **38** D 4
Zhujiang Kou **38** F 6
Zhukovka **24** F 5
Zhumadian **38** F 4
Zhuo Xian **38** G 3
Zhuolu **38** G 2
Zhuozi **38** F 2
Zhupanovo **37** U 5
Zhupanovskiy **37** T 5
Zhuralevka **25** N 5
Zhurban **37** N 5
Zhushan **38** EF 4
Zhuya **36** L 4
Zhuzagashskiy **25** P 6
Zhuzhou **38** F 5
Ziama Mansuria **19** E 4
Zīārān (Iran) **23** F 1

Ziarat **35** H 4
Zibā (Saudi Arabia) **22** B 4
Zibo **39** G 3
Zicavo **19** E 3
Zichang **38** E 3
Zielona Góra **15** G 4
Zigaing **41** F 3
Zīghan, Wāhāt **59** K 3
Zighout Youssef **19** E 4
Zigong **38** DE 5
Zigos Métsevon **20** B 3
Ziguey **63** H 3
Zigui **38** F 4
Ziguinchor **62** A 3
Zihuatanejo **78** B 4
Zilair **25** L 5
Zile **21** E 2
Žilina **15** G 5
Zima **36** H 5
Zimatlán de Alvarez **78** C 4
Zimba **66** D 3
Zimbabwe **66–67** DE 3
Zimbabwe **67** E 4
Zimi **62** B 4
Zimla **58** E 4
Zimnicea **20** C 2
Zimovniki **21** F 1
Zina **63** G 3
Zinave National Park **67** E 4
Zincirli **21** E 3
Zincirli (Turkey) **22** B 1
Zinder **63** F 3
Zinga (Burkina) **64** B 4
Zinga (Tanzania) **65** F 6

Zipaquirá **84** D 2
Ziqudukou **38** C 4
Ziri **58** C 4
Žirje **19** G 3
Ziro **41** F 2
Zistonis, Limni **20** C 2
Zitacuaro **78** BC 4
Zittau **15** F 4
Zitundo **67** E 5
Ziwa Magharibi **64** E 5
Ziyanchurino **24** L 5
Ziyang **38** D 4
Ziyang **38** E 4
Ziz **58** E 2
Zizhong **38** E 5
Zlatarsko Jezero **20** B 2
Zlatibor **20** A 2
Zlatiyata **20** B 2
Zlatni Pyaschatsi **20** C 2
Zlatoust **25** L 4
Zlatoustovsk **37** O 5
Zlītan **59** H 2
Złotów **15** G 4
Zmeinogorsk **25** Q 5
Znamenka **21** D 1
Znamenka **24** F 5
Znamenka **25** P 5
Znamenka **25** P 5
Znamenka **36** H 5
Znamenskoye **25** O 4
Znin **15** G 4
Znojmo **15** G 5
Zobeyri (Iran) **23** E 2
Zobia **64** D 4

Zóbuè **67** E 3
Zoekmekaar **66** D 4
Zoetélé **63** G 5
Zogang **38** C 5
Zogqên **38** C 4
Zohreh (Iran) **23** F 3
Zoigê **38** D 4
Zolotaya Gora **37** N 5
Zolotinka **37** M 4
Zolotitsa **24** H 2
Zolotogorskaya **37** TU 3
Zolotogorskiy **25** R 5
Zomba **67** F 3
Zonga **64** B 4
Zonguldak **21** D 2
Zoo Baba **63** G 2
Zorritos **84** B 4
Zorzor **62** C 4
Zouar **63** H 1
Zoulabot **63** G 5
Zouping **39** G 3
Zourate **58** C 4
Zrenjanin **20** B 1
Zruč **15** G 5
Zuara **59** H 2
Zubets, Gora **37** X 3
Zubova-Polyana **24** H 5
Zudanez **86** D 4
Zuénoula **62** C 4
Zuera **18** C 3
Zufār **61** J 5
Zug **58** C 4
Zug (Switzerland) **19** E 2
Zugdidi **21** F 2

Zugspitze **19** F 2
Zújar **18** B 4
Zuluf (Saudi Arabia) **23** E 3
Zumba **84** C 4
Zumbo **67** E 3
Zungeru **63** F 4
Zunyi **38** E 5
Zuo Jiang **38** E 6
Zuoquan **38** F 3
Zuoyun **38** F 2
Zupanja **19** G 2
Zurbāṭīyah (Iraq) **23** D 2
Zürich **19** E 2
Zürich-See **19** E 2
Zurmat **35** H 4
Zurmi **63** F 3
Zuru **63** F 3
Zuwārah **59** H 2
Zuwaylah **59** J 3
Zuwe **66** C 4
Zvishavane **66** D 4
Zvolen **15** G 5
Zvoron, Ozero **37** P 5
Zwettl **19** G 2
Zwickau **15** F 4
Zwolle **14** E 4
Zyranka **36** D 1
Żyrardów **15** H 4
Zyryanka **37** S 2
Zyryanovo **25** R 3
Zyryanovsk **25** Q 6
Zyryanskoye **25** R 4
Żywiec **15** G 5